D1174134

ATLANTIC STUDIES

Brooklyn College Studies on Society in Change No. 20
Editor-in-Chief Béla K. Király

INFLATION THROUGH THE AGES: ECONOMIC, SOCIAL, PSYCHOLOGICAL AND HISTORICAL ASPECTS

Nathan Schmukler and Edward Marcus
Editors

Social Science Monographs — Brooklyn College Press
Distributed by Columbia University Press
New York 1983

Contents

Part 3 — Policy Issues

Part 4 — Germany

Part 7 — Comparative Studies

Part 8 — Social, Political and Psychological Aspects

Acknowledgments

The Brooklyn College Program on Society in Change conducts research, organizes conferences and publishes scholarly books. The Program has been encouraged and supported by Dr. Robert L. Hess, the President of Brooklyn College. The National Endowment for the Humanities awarded the Program a research grant for the years of 1978–1981, which was renewed for another three year term (1981–1984). Without these substantial and much appreciated sources of support, the Program could not realize its goals, indeed could not exist. Additional financial contributions helped us in completing the research, holding conferences and covering the costs of preparation of the manuscript for publication. Among those institutions that aided our work are the International Research and Exchanges Board, the Joint Committee on Eastern Europe of the American Council of Learned Societies and the Social Science Research Council, the Austrian Institute, and the Center for European Studies (East European Section) Graduate School CUNY.

The copy editing was done by Professor Helene Zahler and Mr. Robert Cambria, the charts are the work of Mrs. Ida Etelka Romann, and the preparation of the manuscript for publication by Mrs. Dorothy Meyerson, Assistant Director, and Mr. Jonathan A. Chanis, Assistant Editor of the Brooklyn College Program on Society in Change.

For all these institutions and personalities, I wish to express my most sincere appreciation and thanks.

Highland Lakes, New Jersey
August 20, 1982

Béla K. Király
Professor of History
Editor-in-Chief

Preface

This book had its origin in a conference on inflation held on March 10, 11, and 12, 1980 sponsored jointly by the Program on Society in Change of the School of Social Science at Brooklyn College and the Center for European Studies, East European Section, of the Graduate School and University Center of the City University of New York. The fifty-four papers which it contains were contributed by scholars from forty-six institutions of higher education in twenty states and ten countries. In accordance with the tradition of this series, the authors include leading scholars with international reputations as well as younger scholars in earlier stages of their academic career.

Although no single volume on a subject such as inflation can be truly comprehensive, the scope of material covered in this book is impressive. There are articles which deal with contemporary problems and others which describe historic cases of inflation in many countries in diverse stages of development. Inflation theory and inflation experience are presented in terms of capitalist, socialist and communist societies. While there is an inevitable emphasis upon economic analysis and historical review, the book as a whole treats inflation from an interdisciplinary, broad social science perspective and includes papers with an orientation drawn from psychology, sociology and political science. No panaceas are to be found on these pages. In fact, the major emphasis of the Society in Change Program has consistently been on study and research rather than on program advocacy or policy formulation. But such an emphasis does not diminish the relevance, or the practical value, of its publications for decision makers. It is not unrealistic to believe that serious scholarly studies will have an impact on resolving the difficult problems of inflation.

No reader of this book will doubt the contribution which it makes to human knowledge. In my mind, the process by which it was created is of equal value. The gathering of scholars from many places, the meetings and discussions, the challenge of ideas, the conflict of minds, the presence and involvement of students at all of the sessions, the mingling of different cultures and different generations engaged in a common search for understanding all served the most fundamental goals of a university. For the City University of New York and for higher education generally, we take pride in what has been accomplished.

Robert J. Kibbee
Chancellor
The City University of New York

Part 1
Theory and Analysis

Inflation:
Monetary and Structural Causes and Cures

JAMES TOBIN

1. YES, INFLATION IS A MONETARY PHENOMENON

Inflation is always and everywhere a *monetary* phenomenon. Milton Friedman says so, and I stipulate my agreement at the beginning in order to avoid misunderstanding. By definition, *inflation* is a decline in the purchasing power of the monetary unit of account. To say that inflation is a monetary phenomenon is not to say that excessive monetary expansion is always its sole or principal cause. There are, I shall argue, several varieties of inflation. The inflations observed at various times and places often differ in their origins, their effects, and their possible remedies. The monetary nature of every inflation does not imply that it is always easy to disinflate by turning off the monetary spigot.

Reconciling the invariable monetary nature of inflation with my thesis that there are various sources and species of inflation is not difficult. There are two points in this reconciliation. First, the velocity of the money stock — however it is defined, whichever of the concepts M_0, M_1, M_1-A or -B, M_2, M_3, is adopted — is variable and elastic. Consequently, some sources of inflation may work by increasing velocity rather than by increasing the stock of money. The second and more important point is *accommodation* by the monetary authorities. The central bank, instead of being the initiator and prime mover of inflationary expansion of money supplies, responds to upward price movements and provides the money to finance them. No central bank does so because it likes inflation. Monetary policy makers accommodate ongoing inflationary trends, usually reluctantly and grudgingly, because the consequences of not accommodating appear to them, rightly or wrongly, as the greater evil.

For example, in the United States in recent years aggregate dollar spending on final goods and services, that is, nominal GNP, was growing at 11 to 12 percent per year. This was financed by an 8 percent per year growth in the *monetary base* — currency outstanding and bank reserve deposits at the Federal Reserve — and by an even smaller rate of growth in M_1, the most common measure of the stock of transactions money. These numbers indicate how fast velocity has been increasing.

The upward trend of velocity is partly rational response to the upward trend of nominal interest rates, which induces economies in cash management. It is partly the result of innovations in financial technology which, however induced, will persist even if and when interest rates fall. Closer examination of the quarter-to-quarter and year-to-year relations between monetary stocks and spending on goods and services would show that velocity and its rate of growth have been highly variable. Their variability is partly random; for example, cash management innovations don't occur smoothly. The variability also reflects systematic responses to short-term variations in interest rates.

In any case, the 11 to 12 percent per annum growth of nominal income obviously exceeds the sustainable growth in real output in the United States economy, which is only about 3 percent. It has also exceeded even the high rates of growth of real output, 5 or 6 percent, typically attained during cyclical recoveries. Such a rate of growth of dollar spending is in that sense obviously inflationary. But it does not follow that the growth in the monetary base or in the transactions money stock that supports such growth in dollar spending is the spontaneous cause of the accompanying inflation. Presumably the monetary authorities could have reduced the growth rate of spending on goods and services whether that was the result of increases in velocity or of increases in monetary stocks. Indeed they have done so this year (1980). They did not do so two years ago because they estimated the costs of nonaccommodation of the existing inflation to be very high.

This brings me to the basic point. Reducing the rate of expansion of money stocks is *necessary* for disinflation but not *sufficient*. Confusion between necessary and sufficient conditions is an endless source of confusion in economics, as in many other aspects of national and personal life. In the long run, if an economy were to experience an era of zero inflation, we would observe a rate of growth of nominal spending on goods and services equal to the rate of growth of real output. In the United States, therefore, we would observe trends in both money spending and real output of about 3 percent per year. That obvious fact, however, does not entitle anyone to believe that a sudden reduction of the rate of monetary spending from 11 percent to 3 percent, engineered by the instruments available to the monetary authorities, would eliminate inflation tomorrow, or this year, or next. Certainly some fraction of the reduction in spending growth would show up in output rather than in prices; I shall argue that output contraction will normally be much the larger share. Neither our Federal Reserve nor any other central bank has any power to channel the effects of its policies into prices and output in the proportions it would like. The institutions of the economy — business enterprises and trade unions — determine those proportions. At this moment, our Federal Reserve has succeeded in contracting sharply the growth of money stocks and of money spending. The result is, as it was in 1974, a sharp recession, a precipitous fall in production and employment. When the authorities choose accommodation, it is because nonaccommodation would result, not in price disinflation, but in substantial and costly reverses in real economic activity.

The main point of this introduction is that those of us who, in examining problems of inflation, look at real events and nonmonetary institutions are not committing a vulgar fallacy. Knowing that inflation is a monetary phenomenon, we carry the analysis one layer deeper when we ask why monetary expansions occur and why they continue.

2. VARIETIES OF INFLATION

I hope therefore that even the monetarists will let me proceed to enumerate three varieties of inflation: (a) excess demand inflation, (b) inertial inflation, (c) conflict inflation.

a. EXCESS DEMAND INFLATION

By *excess demand inflation* I mean the classical scenario, often popularly described as "too much money chasing too few goods." More precisely, it is the inflation that results when aggregate demand at existing prices chronically exceeds the capacity of the economy to produce goods and services. Many episodes of wartime and postwar inflation meet this description. Frequently, but not always, excess demand arises when governments pile their demands for resources into an economy already operating at, or close to, capacity and finance their purchases by printing money or borrowing rather than by taxation. A recent example in the United States was the Vietnam War (1966–69). Orthodox policy prescriptions—restriction of money and credit, increased taxation and reduced public spending (to balance government budgets) are just what the physician orders for excess demand inflation.

b. INERTIAL INFLATION

The second type, which I call *inertial,* is inflation without excess demand. The word coined in the 1970s is "stagflation." Inertial inflation has several characteristics.

First, inertial inflation, as the name implies, is inherited from the past, very often from past excess demand inflation. In the United States, the Vietnam War period left a legacy of inertial inflation that we found in the 1970s very difficult to erase. Second, inertial inflation is perpetuated by contracts and commitments, particularly with respect to wages. In the United States the setting of money wage rates is decentralized. It occurs either in negotiations of employers with trade unions or in unorganized labor markets in periodic administrative decisions by individual employers. The timing of these negotiations and decisions is staggered, not synchronized; every week some contracts are expiring and being renegotiated, and some administered wage settings are being reconsidered. Contracts are long, often for three years; nonunion employers usually change their wage scales annually. In addition to formal contracts and scales, both organized and unorganized workers have implicit assurances and expectations as to the wage treatment that they will receive from their employers. In a modern industrial economy of this kind, wage setting is greatly influenced by workers' concern for their positions relative to other workers. They want above all to keep up with, catch up with, possibly leap ahead of workers with whom they regard themselves as comparable.

Third, the inertia in wages that results from this system supports and is supported by the mark-up pricing conventions of employing firms. Labor and materials costs per unit of normal output are the principal basis for industrial prices; mark-ups vary with demand, but by no means sufficiently to avoid substantial adjustments of output and employment. Together these institutions lead to the sluggishness in wage and price responses in the face of recession and excess supply with which we are all familiar. These inertial wage and price patterns are internally consistent. That is, if each employer follows the going pattern of wage increases, workers will find their relative positions maintained and employers themselves will maintain their competitive positions not only in their labor markets but also in their product markets. If they raise their prices in accordance with the prevailing wage increase they will not lose markets to their rivals. The circle is closed as the price increases feed back into the workers' cost of living, reinforcing the pattern of wage increase itself.

Fourth, the continuation of an entrenched self-consistent pattern of wage and price increase can be described as the establishment and realization of expectations. Expectations are certainly important. It is the employer's expectation that other firms will be following the same pattern that leads him to follow the pattern too. Workers' expectation that prices will rise by the pattern and that other workers will receive similar wage increases leads them to demand and to accept the pattern wage increase. This is true, but the phenomenon is not simply a matter of expectations. Adjustment lags are intrinsic to the contracts, institutions, and conventions of wage and price setting. These provide inertia in the adjustment of wages and prices to economic slack, even when expectations change.

Fifth, inertial inflation has taken a new and particularly troublesome form in the 1970s as a result of price and supply shocks external to the industrial economies of the United States and other developed countries. The principal examples are the two big increases in OPEC prices, first in 1973-74 and then in 1978-79. Our inflation as measured in consumer price indexes is a combination of the built-in core of wage-price inflation and of more volatile elements. These more volatile components are the prices of imports, either from overseas or from the flexible price sectors of our own economies. In recent years the United States has suffered several unpleasant surprises in the prices of food and raw materials and, of course, in the price of oil. These shocks not only increase actual inflation rates while they are being diffused and absorbed; they may also feed into wage demands and settlements and thus accelerate the inertial inflation. Indexation of wages and other prices by the cost of living automatically ratchets the basic inflation rate upward. In the United States, however, this effect has been less severe than in several European economies. Indeed, our wage earners have swallowed significant cuts in their real wages.

Monetarists typically deny that movements in the prices of individual commodities, relative to wages and other prices, can affect overall inflation rates. They stress the dichotomy between specific relative prices, real phenomena, and economy-wide absolute prices, monetary phenomena. The answer, the resolution, is again accommodation and inertia. Relative price shocks would *not*, it is true, affect the economy-wide inflation rate even temporarily if wages and prices were highly flexible. In such an economy we could imagine an increase in the relative price of a particular commodity occurring partly via reduction in the absolute money prices of all other goods and services. We could imagine those prices falling sufficiently that the average price level, the overall consumer price index for example, remains unaffected. In such an economy an OPEC shock like that of 1973–74 or 1979 would not have boosted inflation rates to double digits. The adverse shift in terms of trade would instead have been reflected in reductions of wages and prices in domestic industry. Clearly, we do not live in that kind of economy. In the economy we do live in, the monetary authorities are faced with the unpleasant choice: to accommodate the external price shock or to force a monetary contraction that will result not in immediate disinflation but in recession and unemployment. Hence, the prevalence of unfavorable price shocks in the 1970s has pointed up the difficulties created by inertial inflation.

C. CONFLICT INFLATION

The third type of inflation I wish to distinguish I call *conflict inflation.* Inflation of this type is symptomatic of a fundamental disharmony within the society. There is no consensus on the division of the pie. Neither the mechanisms of the competitive market nor the political process work with sufficient authority to reconcile the several economic interests to the rewards they receive for economic activity, or inactivity. The constituent economic and social groups claim collectively more "pie" than there actually can be. Moreover, each group has the economic or political bargaining power to raise its money income. As the rival interest groups strive in turn to gain larger shares of the pie by claiming higher money incomes, inflation is the outcome.

Of course, this process cannot continue without ratification, accommodation, by the monetary authorities. On the other hand, as long as consensus is lacking, as long as fundamental conflicts continue regarding the distribution of real income and wealth, monetary contraction will not solve the problem. It will not eliminate the inflation, but will simply result in reduction of real economic activity, as in the case of inertial inflation. Hence monetary contraction will just shrink the pie, the total social product over whose division the contestants are fighting. It is not clear that diminishing the size of the rewards in dispute will mitigate the conflict or diminish the inflation symptomatic of the conflict.

Distributional conflict may be exacerbated by losses of real national income, such as payments of "tribute" to OPEC, and by slowdowns of productivity growth, such as we have recently experienced. Even a nation that previously had enjoyed a fairly harmonious consensus about distribution might at least temporarily experience conflict inflation, induced by disagreements about sharing the costs of national reverses in terms of trade and productivity. In this way the relative price shocks of the 1970s may have created conflict inflation.

3. ON THE COSTS AND BENEFITS OF ANTIINFLATIONARY POLICIES

The natural approach of economists to issues of public policy is to balance costs and benefits. In the case of inflation, as in other applications of this approach, it is essential to consider operationally realistic alternatives. That is, we cannot really make a cost-benefit appraisal of "inflation" in the abstract, as if we had a free choice whether to have inflation or not. Disinflation is not a free good. I have given some reasons why it is not, reasons embedded in the institutions of wage and price setting of a modern democratic, capitalist nation like the United States. The supposed costs and discomforts of inflation are not always the same, nor are their distribution among individuals and groups. They vary with the nature and source of the inflation. Most textbook generalizations on these matters are wrong—for example, that inflation always hurts wage earners, always hurts creditors, always benefits debtors, always aids entrepreneurs. We cannot make such generalizations if the inflations that we experience and observe are the results of a variety of causes, different at different times and places. Moreover, the supposed costs of inflation are deeply entangled with the costs of those real economic and political events of which inflation is a joint symptom. Those costs are usually not avoidable; at any rate they are not avoidable by the usual macroeconomic instruments of antiinflationary policy. They are not avoidable even if it were somehow possible to eliminate or suppress the inflationary symptoms of the basic causes.

In recent years, in the United States and elsewhere, "inflation" has become a scapegoat, a universal shorthand explanation for all disappointments and reverses in economic status. When men and women respond in public opinion surveys that inflation is their number one problem and the number one problem of the nation, probably they mean that they are disappointed by losses in their real incomes, losses relative at least to previous trends and expectations. They use the term *inflation* to register those losses and disappointments.

OPEC raised the cost of oil, and the true loss to an importing nation is that it must work harder and longer; we must give up more of our product and our toil to purchase a barrel of oil. That cost in terms of trade would still be there, even if we could have deflated domestic wages and prices enough to avoid the aggregate inflationary impacts of the OPEC shocks. It is muddled thinking, therefore, to attribute to inflation the costs of paying more for imported oil. Those economic statisticians who seek in the record of the 1970s generalizable clues to the national, international, sectoral, and distributional burdens of inflation engage themselves in an inquiry that is doomed from its very conception. When we assess antiinflationary policies, we should recognize that the measures available to our monetary and fiscal policy makers do not include forcing the oil-exporting countries to reduce the price of oil and return us to the happy days before 1973.

The elementary point I am making applies even to classical excess demand inflations. Most of those have occurred historically in connection with wars—for our country in the last half-century, World War II, Korea, Vietnam. Wars inevitably levy large real costs. They consume resources, real resources. We have no right, therefore, to charge the costs of wars to "inflation." The economic approach is to compare inflationary finance with other methods of extracting the resources needed for war. Maybe, even probably, inflation is "the cruelest tax" that could be used for this purpose, but that is not a self-evident conclusion. The gains, if any, from antiinflationary financial policy consist of the differences in social output and consumption and in income and wealth distributions from financing by explicit taxation instead.

Another example is the notorious German hyperinflation of 1923. We have all heard about the serious economic and social costs of that inflation. At the same time, we must remember that the basic burden on the German people was the levy of reparations. Those reparations—like the tax levied by OPEC on foreign consumers of its oil—the German nation had to pay one way or another. Probably the manner in which the Weimar Republic tried to pay the victorious Allies was foolish and socially destructive. But the true comparison is with some other method of taxation, some other mechanism for transfer to the Allies of the real tribute exacted by the treaty.

In short, optimal taxation theory is the proper way to go about examining the desirability of antiinflation policies, as Professor E.S. Phelps has pointed out many times. Even today we may note that a 10 percent inflation in the United States gives the federal government annually $15 billion of equivalent revenue from expanding the monetary base. Taxpayers benefit also from reduction of the real federal debt, since the debt service now is mostly repayment of principal. These effects on federal finance need to be balanced against the costs of other taxes that could and would be used to pay the government's bills.

a. ANTICIPATED INFLATION

In assessing the costs and benefits of antiinflationary policies we need to distinguish between anticipated and unanticipated inflation. By *anticipated* I mean inflation rates to which the private economy has adjusted. What are the costs of anticipated inflation? That is, what are the benefits of reducing it? The main costs that economists have found are the so-called "shoe-leather" costs of economizing holdings of transactions money. These are the costs of making frequent transactions between means of payment on the one hand and interest-bearing assets on the other, in order to avoid the losses of interest incident to large balances of idle cash. Now it is difficult to make shoe-leather costs appear very large and their reduction yield great benefit to the economy. In the United States about $400 billion of transactions balances are used by the nation's households and businesses. If we assume that a 10 point increase in nominal interest rates goes along with a 10 percent inflation, then our 10 percent inflation has meant a shoe-leather cost of $40 billion, which is one-sixtieth of GNP. Moreover, given an elasticity of demand for cash balances with respect to the interest rate of 1/2, a generously large estimate, one more point of the inflation rate would increase the aggregate cost by $2 billion, namely 1/1200 of the GNP.

Martin Feldstein has, it is true, argued that even this small cost on an annual basis has a very large and possibly infinite present value. The reason he advances is that, with the growth of the economy, the shoe-leather costs of inflation and anticipated inflation will grow at the economy's natural rate of growth. He argues further that the revealed discount rate on future consumption by American households is smaller than the growth rate of the economy. Therefore, he finds, the gain from a reduction in shoe-leather costs has an infinite present value.

This argument is not very convincing. If the operational discount rate for the future is really lower than the economy's growth rate, then all kinds of investments, however costly at the outset, will be justified, if they produce gains that grow with the economy. One cannot really make welfare economics arguments with divergent integrals. Specifically, it is necessary to consider the possible stimulus that anticipated inflation gives for capital formation. Anticipated inflation does have the redeeming feature of making investment in real productive assets attractive relative to monetary saving, and this may offset its shoe-leather cost. To put the point another way, a developed capitalist economy may need a real interest rate on safe assets that is close to zero and at times negative; as Keynes pointed out, this is difficult to bring about in the absence of inflation because of the zero floor interest rate on basic money.

The central issue is whether social investment in sufficient unemployment for sufficient time to bring the inflation rate down pays off subsequently in the real advantages of permanently lower inflation. The investment in disinflation reduces current real output and employment, and consequently, it also reduces capital formation. The lost capital formation would have bestowed on the economy an evergrowing benefit, a benefit that is an offset to the evergrowing shoe-leather costs of the inflation. Moreover, the inflation may substitute in public finance for explicit taxation of capital, an investment deterrent Feldstein himself emphasizes in other contexts. We cannot be sure that we have chosen the optimal combination of the inflation tax and income taxation.

Another cost of anticipated inflation often mentioned is the cost of calculation and planning when price changes are more frequent. This, of course, would be a cost of deflation no less than inflation. It is hard to quantify—we don't know how much additional trouble higher inflation rates make for companies that establish price lists or catalogs for the goods they have for sale. We don't know how much confusion between relative and absolute prices arises because prices in general are rising. Remember that relative prices are always changing, even when price indexes are fairly stable. It is not proper to compare an ideal situation of complete certainty and stability of individual prices with a realistic situation in which relative prices vary and attribute the difference solely to inflation. Empirically it has been observed that the variance of inflation rates is greater when the general level of inflation is higher. One reason is that changing price quotations is costly; if prices are changed in discrete jumps on unsynchronized schedules, relative prices do get out of line, the more so the higher the inflation rate. Higher volatility in the movement of prices makes planning and calculation more difficult. But there is a serious problem of identification in the observed correlation of price variances with mean inflation rates. As I have previously observed, a possible source of higher inflation is extraordinary movement in relative prices, of which the OPEC shocks are an example. There the causation runs the other way, given the bias of our institutions toward making relative price adjustments by increases in the one price rather than decreases in the multitude of others. Periods of considerable relative price volatility will be periods of higher inflation and also periods of greater volatility of inflation.

Finally, anticipated inflation is a problem because people think it is a problem. Its social disutility is apparent from people's discontent, even though their distaste for the process may reflect misunderstandings and misperceptions. Their discontent is a fact we must confront.

b. UNANTICIPATED INFLATION

As for unanticipated inflation, the costs are well known. They have to do with the distribution of income and wealth. There are many old clichés about the redistributions resulting from inflation, but they do not apply systematically and regularly. Inflations are not all alike. The redistributions that occur in war-related excess demand inflations are not the same as those that occur in stagflation. We can no longer say with as much truth that inflation hurts older people, retired people, people on so-called fixed money incomes. Social Security is now fully indexed. During inflation of the type we have recently been having, beneficiaries of social insurance are better protected than young workers. There aren't many fixed incomes any more; civil servants, even teachers, no longer fall in that category. Interest rates are adjusting to inflation and compensating those who now save in interest-bearing assets for the inflation. Those of us who invested in common stocks, formerly regarded as the natural hedge against inflation, have suffered more than people who in the recent decade put their funds in short-term interest-bearing dollar claims. Altogether, one can see little change in the size distributions of income and wealth, or in the shares of labor and property. They have remained much the same throughout the postwar period, in both periods of inflation and periods of relatively stable prices.

It is easy to forget that economic life is always risky, always generating capital gains and capital losses, always producing surprising changes in economic welfare both for individual workers and for savers and investors. Fortunes are made and lost mainly by relative prices and relative wages. It is an illusion to believe that a noninflationary environment would be one in which people could feel secure in their careers and their investments. The major losses of recent years are traceable to real causes, not to the process of inflation per se. Consider the owners of gas-guzzling cars, energy-intensive equipment, glass buildings, and ski chalets with electric heat. Consider members of our own academic profession, who as university students choosing careers misread the prospects of supply and demand. Their plight is not really due to inflation.

In weighing unemployment and its costs as against inflation and its costs, we should not forget that unemployment has both global and distributional effects. Many of the losses are concentrated on a small segment of the population. The distributional effects of stagnation and unemployment deserve to be added to the economy-wide losses of production, just as inflation is charged with both social costs and distributional inequity. We should also remember, and remind our students and our lay audiences, that unexpected disinflation would be tough on many people. Consider those who have borrowed long term at high nominal interest rates. It is not just unanticipated inflation that gives rise to unexpected capital gains and losses; surprises come from all unanticipated developments. Remember—at least some of us *can* remember—the redistributions due to deflation in the past, notably in the Great Depression of the 1930s.

In suggesting that we use some perspective in calculating the costs of inflation, in suggesting that we apply our usual apparatus of cost-benefit calculus to the appraisal of antiinflationary policy, I do not want to be misinterpreted. I agree that the deliberate use of inflation for the finance of government is a symptom of social and political failure, failure to reach explicit consensus on how the burden of government activity should be borne. I, too, would deplore the distributional effects of inflationary finance. If it is not the cruelest tax, at least it is an arbitrary and random one, and its consequences are not deliberately debated and assessed by the legislature. At the same time, when our inflation is not the result of deficit finance and excess demand, but the lingering consequence of past events and shocks, or when it is the result of temporary or enduring social conflict, I believe that we must be cautious in recommending the classical cures. As I have suggested, popular discontent with inflation probably reflects disappointment with the progress of real wages and real standards of life. It is ironical that such discontent should be the basis in public opinion of policies that will further reduce incomes and standards of living.

4. POLICY CHOICES TODAY

I turn now to the choices that confront us today. There are really only three choices, hard as it is to face the unpleasant fact. None of the feasible choices is pleasant. Maturity for a nation and its government, as for an individual, consists in willingness to face up to budget constraints.

The three choices are: first, "muddling through" as we were doing, at least until recently; second, severely disinflationary monetary and fiscal policies; third, combining monetary disinflation with an effective incomes policy directly reducing the rate of increase of wages and prices.

a. ORTHODOX MONETARY DISINFLATION

The second course, monetary disinflation alone, is the one in which we have recently embarked. As I suggested earlier, monetary contraction is a necessary, but unfortunately not a sufficient, condition for successful disinflation. Suppose that we do reduce the 11 percent or 12 percent rate of growth of nominal GNP to 4 percent or 5 percent, an amount consistent with 1 percent or 2 percent inflation along with normal sustainable growth of real production. That will not, all of a sudden, bring the desired result. Federal Reserve Chairman Volcker, President Carter or Reagan or Anderson, and the Congress do not control the division of the rate of growth of nominal income as between price inflation and output growth. Past evidence says that the institutions of our economy will divide nominal spending about one-tenth for prices and nine-tenths for output. That is, reducing the rate of increase of nominal spending by 1 point would reduce inflation that year by only one-tenth of a percentage point. Another way to look at it is this. Every additional point of unemployment, maintained for a year, will reduce the built-in core of inertial inflation by at most a half a point. And, when external shocks, OPEC, for example, are working the other way, an extra point-year of unemployment may not do that well. In these circumstances, the prospect ahead of us, if we adopt and maintain a policy of monetary disinflation, is a long period of stagnation, a deep recession with high unemployment, low output, and uncertain success in reducing the core inflation rate.

Some economists say that if the government makes unmistakably clear that it will stick with this draconian remedy, the costs will be less and the cure will be more rapid and less painful. They say that statistical evidence on the past stubbornness of inflation rates in the face of monetary contraction is misleading, because the response was conditioned by the expectation that the government would reverse course quickly and bail out firms and workers hurt by recessions. Wage and price patterns will melt faster, they say, if the government resolutely forswears the compensatory antirecession measures customary in the past. Is a "credible threat" of this kind possible in a democracy? Can our central bank and government say with conviction and truth that come what may they will not accommodate any OPEC shocks, they will not adopt any countercyclical policies—no matter how bad the news of unemployment, production, and profits? Would the remedy, even if adopted and relentlessly maintained, work? I noted before that in our country wage and price decisions are highly decentralized, wage negotiations occur on a staggered schedule, contracts last for as long as three years.

It is hard to be confident that a global macroeconomic threat will have meaning in the local markets, sectoral labor negotiations, and particular enterprises that matter for the course of wages and prices. At these microeconomic levels, employers and employees are concerned with what other unions and other firms have been doing, are doing, and will be doing. They cannot be sure that their rivals and their reference groups will disinflate in response to the threat of unrelenting contractionary macroeconomic policies. If one group obeys the threat while others do not, it will lose relative position. If it does not obey the threat, while others do, it will gain relative position. This is an n+1-person game, n agents and 1 policy maker, and the outcome is not predictable.

In other countries, where labor negotiations follow synchronized annual schedules and are more centralized, there is more coordination between macroeconomic demand policies and the wage and price decisions of management and unions. In Germany, for example, the leaders of the labor federation and the employers' groups meet with representatives of the central bank and the government and discuss the whole macroeconomic picture, including the policies of the central bank and the government for the coming year. It is clear to the firms and to the unions what will be the consequences of a wage and price development inconsistent with the intentions of the monetary authorities. The threat is also a promise—that with moderation in wages and prices, employment and sales will be favorable. Lacking similar mechanisms, we cannot confidently bet that a firmly announced and executed course of restrictive demand management will accelerate the disinflation of wages and prices. But if our policy makers are going to follow that course, they should make it more evident to the whole economy. At the moment it is really difficult for anyone in the private economy to interpret the rather esoteric signals and targets that emerge from statements of the Federal Reserve and discussions of the federal budget between the President and Congress.

b. THE ROLE OF INCOMES POLICY

More important, I think, is the patent need for an incomes policy—yes, for controls of some kind—to supplement any demand management firmly oriented to disinflation. A consistent schedule of declining guideposts for wage and price increases for the next few years would limit the damage which gradual reduction of monetary aggregate demand would otherwise cause. We already have standards for wage and price behavior, but without teeth to make them stick. Indeed, currently our flimsy institutions of incomes policy are relaxing those standards. The core inflation rate will probably increase even while the guns of monetary and fiscal policy take aim at the present inflation. Collision is imminent between contracting monetary demand guided by the Federal Reserve, the President, and the congressional budget makers and the accelerating trend of wages and prices contemplated by unions and managements and accepted by the Council on Wage Price Stability. These two policies must be made consistent if we are serious about accomplishing disinflation without a long period of stagnation.

We should make the standards effective by creating inducements to comply with them. These could be either "carrots" or "sticks," either rewards for employers and employees in economic units that comply with the guideposts or penalties for those that do not. The rewards and penalties would be given in the tax system. There are, of course, costs in any kind of wage and price controls, even of the flexible variety just mentioned. Economists' trained instincts are against controls that alter the relative prices thrown up by the market and interfere with the accompanying allocation of resources. Here again we need to apply the perspective and power of cost-benefit calculus. Against the well-rehearsed costs of controls weigh some benefits. Absent controls, we face very heavy macroeconomic losses, and these too violate optimality and efficiency. Indeed, I think the potential losses from disinflation by demand management alone are larger by orders of magnitude than the allocational distortions that would occur during several years of a transitional program of flexible, tax-based disinflationary guideposts. As I have said on other occasions, it takes a heap of Harberger triangles to fill an Okun gap.

We have only unpleasant choices. Perhaps the choice we are making, consciously or unconsciously, is the first of the three I mentioned, muddling through. Perhaps the society does not have the will to accomplish a disinflation. Perhaps most of the rhetoric against inflation is simply rhetoric and will not lead to any constructive actions. Unfortunately, it can lead to some destructive actions—another deep and long recession, with permanent damage to the future of our economy, permanent damage arising from the losses of physical and human capital resulting from sustained periods of underproduction and underemployment.

It is not easy to detect the nature of the inflations and stagflations that afflict nations today, to tell whether they fall under the rubric of inertia or of conflict. In either case it is doubtful that application of the remedies appropriate to excess demand inflation is a constructive solution. The instincts of the man in the street are correct: there must be more rational solutions than recession and unemployment. An economist can add that there must be less costly ways to save energy than to arrest the economic progress of the globe. The better ways demand social and political consensus, and that in turn depends on leadership that will face squarely the underlying economic realities from which obsession with inflationary symptoms alone diverts attention. To wind down our inertial inflation in an orderly way, we need incomes policies that are supported by the understanding and consent of the major economic interests. To resolve possible conflicts among their claims, we need the same policies, understanding, and consent. It is often said, too often, that the conquest of inflation demands "sacrifices" from us all, but that is only a half truth. Our real incomes and consumption possibilities will not be less if we achieve the consensus that will allow disinflation without stagnation. They will indeed be more. The task is a severe test of democratic institutions, to be sure, but the stakes are high.

Inflation and Inflation Feedback

PAUL BECKERMAN

A. "INFLATION," "INCIPIENT INFLATION," "INFLATIONARY SHOCKS," AND "INFLATION-FEEDBACK"

One reason that recent macroeconomic theory has found it so difficult to deal effectively with the phenomenon of inflation has been a strongly ingrained propensity among economists to employ comparative-static techniques. The trouble, of course, is that inflation is a dynamic problem. Our static models generally suggest that the economy will move toward a general equilibrium, in which, among other system parameters, the purchasing power of money—or, at most, a *steady* rate of change of the purchasing power of money—is determined. Obviously, to the extent that our models yield such an outcome, they fail adequately to represent reality. Inflation is a sustained, continuing deterioration in the purchasing power of money, notoriously characterized by significant variability and unpredictability in its rate. There is clearly an inherent problem in attempting to represent such a process in a comparative-static framework.

Consider the paradigmatic "textbook" model of modern macroeconomic theory, the Hicks IS-LM with an aggregate-supply relation:[1]

$$i(r^*) \hat{=} s(y^*) \cdot t(y^*) - \bar{g} \tag{1}$$
$$\bar{M} \hat{=} p^* l(y^*, r^*), \tag{2}$$
and
$$y^* \hat{=} f(p^*, \bar{K}) \tag{3}$$

where the meanings of these variables are so well known to economists that we may safely relegate them to a footnote.[2] In this model and models like it, $1/p^*$ represents the equilibrium purchasing power of each monetary unit, *given* the stocks of available (outside) wealth assets (such as money, outstanding government securities, physical capital, etc.); the state of expectations maintained by economic agents about the future (such as the expected rate of inflation, the expected real bond rate, the expected real rate of return on capital, or the uncertainty attaching to any of these expectations); and the characteristics of the behavioral functions $i(\ )$, $s(\ )$, $l(\ )$, and $f(\ )$, and others. Models of this kind can easily be made to operate to represent a decrease in $1/p^*$, by having an appropriate change occur in one or more of the "givens," e.g., by having the shift parameter $\bar{M}$ increase. Such a shift may be described as an *inflationary shock*. From the point of view of representing an *inflation*, however, models of this kind possess a characteristic inadequacy: they represent only a once-and-for-all change in the equilibrium value of $1/p^*$, i.e., they yield only an *incipient inflation*. The important question eludes these models: why does the economy fail to settle at p^*? What propagates the decline in the purchasing power of money forward through time?

We consider the matter in purposely general terms. We have a rather clear understanding of how an inflationary shock, e.g., an increase in the money supply, a fall in labor productivity, an increase in petroleum prices, a deterioration in inflationary expectations, an increase in the propensity to consume, etc., can lead to an *incipient* inflation. The essential problem for macroeconomic theory, however, is determining why an incipient inflation should then somehow generate a new inflationary shock—that is, determining why there seems to be an *inflation-feedback mechanism*. This feedback mechanism is the essential inflation problem. *In itself,* an incipient inflation is not so serious a problem: like any other relative-price shift, it may be regarded as an appropriate response to changed circumstances in supply and demand conditions. A properly functioning price system *should* respond in this way. True, the fall in the purchasing power of the monetary unit will induce an effective redistribution of real resources from (inside) creditors to (inside) debtors, and holders of money and other assets will take a capital loss; but then the same could be said of any other significant relative-price shift in a general-equilibrium economic system. The important *inflation* problem is not, therefore, that the purchasing-power value of the monetary unit falls in response to an inflationary shock; rather, it is that the economy fails to settle down in its new equilibrium and, somehow, generates a new inflationary shock out of the incipient inflation.

In mathematical terms, the IS-LM-AS model presents only an *instantaneous* or *momentary* equilibrium for given asset stocks, anticipations, and behavioral-function parameters. Any instantaneous equilibrium outcome is likely to cause changes in the asset stocks, anticipations, and behavioral-function parameters (Branson, 1976). If the changes are inflationary, then an inflation-feedback mechanism is operating. For example, if we allow the asset stocks *alone* to respond (ignoring for the moment the possibility of changes in the anticipations and behavioral parameters) then (following Branson) we might write

$$dM/dt = -[t(y^*) - g]/p^* \qquad (4)$$
and $\quad dK/dt = i(r^*), \qquad\qquad\qquad (5)$

where y^* and r^* are functions of the existing quantities of M and K, solutions of the model (1)–(3) for given M and K:

$$y^* = h^y(M,K) \qquad (6)$$
$$r^* = h^r(M,K) \qquad (7)$$

Equations (4) and (5), with (6) and (7) substituted in, constitute simple differential equations in M, K, and their time derivatives, which may entail a continuing inflationary process, or may converge to a *long-run equilibrium* for which $dM/dt = n$ and $dK/dt = n$, where n is, say, the rate of growth (in efficiency units) of the labor force. It is theoretically *possible*, of course, to have an inflation-feedback process that operates, as we have described, entirely by forcing changes in asset quantities. If we are interested, however, in the way in which the feedback mechanism really works, then we must investigate the possibility that variables other than asset values are affected by changes in p^*; we must consider other possible "channels" for the feedback process. This is the subject of the observations in Section C.

One final point about the definition of inflation that we are using here: We have defined *inflation* as a decline in the purchasing-power value of the monetary unit. By this definition, of course, in words that both Milton Friedman and James Tobin have used (Friedman, 1970; Tobin, in his talk at the present conference) "inflation is always and everywhere a monetary phenomenon." It is important to understand, however, that to say that inflation is a *monetary* phenomenon does not mean that inflation is a "*monetarist*" phenomenon, that is, we may believe that inflations occur for many reasons, not only because of excessive growth in the money supply.

We turn now to the question of why inflation is a social nuisance.

B. INFLATION AND ALLOCATIVE EFFICIENCY

Unanticipated inflation is a social nuisance, first, because it causes unanticipated shifts in the distribution of wealth and income. No less important, inflation is detrimental to allocative efficiency, because it subjects any price or income stream fixed or contracted in nominal terms to uncertainty in terms of purchasing power, and because it subjects relative prices in general to uncertainty, in addition to the uncertainty to which they are subject on account of real prospective demand and production conditions. This causes the allocative mechanism of the price system to malfunction, which leads to inefficiency in production and distribution. The trouble arises from at least four conceptually separable characteristics of the inflation process: the prospect of a capital loss on cash-balance holdings, inflationary "sporadicity," inflationary uncertainty, and inflationary "dispersion" (Jaffee-Kleiman, 1977).

THE PROSPECT OF A "CAPITAL LOSS" ON HOLDINGS OF CASH BALANCES

The expectation that the monetary unit will depreciate in terms of purchasing power discourages economic agents from maintaining cash balances. Presumably, if there were no inflation, the public would maintain some average cash balance appropriate to the level of transactions requirements and the anticipated real rates of return on other assets. Where there is inflation, however, since the expected real rate of return on money is negative, the public should prefer to maintain a smaller average balance. (The real rate of return on money over a given period in terms of purchasing power is given by $-\dot{p}/(100+\dot{p})$ percent, where $\dot{p}$ is the percentage rate of inflation over the period in question. That is, if the price level doubles over a given period, the rate of inflation is 100 percent, but the monetary unit "gains" minus 50 percent of its original purchasing power. This is important because econometric monetary analyses sometimes estimate the effect of inflation on the demand for money incorrectly by using the rate of inflation rather than the real rate of return on money.)

INFLATIONARY "SPORADICITY"

Inflation occurs sporadically and irregularly over time, with the price level now accelerating, now decelerating. The public is therefore continually called upon to change its economic behavior in response to the ever-changing rate of inflation.[3]

INFLATIONARY UNCERTAINTY

The future rate of inflation is always more or less uncertain, and the degree of inflationary uncertainty—apart from the inflationary expectation—inevitably affects the behavior of risk-averse economic agents.[4]

INFLATIONARY "DISPERSION," OR "NONNEUTRALITY"

Inflation typically takes place at different rates over an economy's price array. Put another way, the value of money falls at different rates when measured by its exchange rate with different goods. That is, the inflationary process apparently entails shifts in relative prices that do not derive from changes in demand and production conditions.[5]

Through the last two characteristics—uncertainty and dispersion—inflation causes the worst of the damage to allocative efficiency. Short of a hyperinflation, the first two characteristics are of second-order importance by comparison with the last two. To see why, imagine an inflation that somehow managed to occur without any uncertainty or dispersion—that is, in such a way that the price level at any future moment was known by everyone with certainty, and in such a way that relative prices changed only on account of changes in demand and production conditions. Then, even though the price-level rises occurred sporadically, they would nonetheless be perfectly foreseen, and each economic agent should therefore be able to time his transactions and manage his cash balances accordingly. Furthermore, as long as the price level is perfectly foreseen, inflation should pose no special difficulty for setting the prices in contracts: in setting any price to be paid in the future, the contracting parties could agree on a price in current terms, and then simply multiply this by the ratio of the perfectly foreseen price level at the time of payment to the present price level. People receiving fixed nominal incomes would still suffer a loss of their purchasing power; but it would be relatively simple to calculate an escalating income that would provide a precisely foreseeable quantity of purchasing power, as long as the political will to do so exists. Therefore, although it is true that a "certain and neutral" inflation would still be a nuisance and would entail significant costs in planning and calculation, it would nevertheless be manageable: the effects of the inflation *could* be neutralized through planning and calculation. In contrast, planning and calculation would not suffice to overcome the consequences of uncertainty and dispersion.

Certain economic analyses have taken the effect of a prospective capital loss on cash-balance holding to be the essential negative consequence of inflation. If this capital loss were foreseen with perfect certainty, it would not be so important a problem—again, because economic agents could then plan and calculate around it. In fact, from certain points of view, a negative real rate of return on money can actually be quite favorable to allocative efficiency, because it counteracts whatever tendency an economy has to "liquidity preference"; i.e., it discourages holding money in place of productive assets subject to real risk (Tobin, 1965; Tobin, 1968). Furthermore, from the strictly economic point of view, the "inflation tax" is probably one of the less costly ways for a government to raise revenue. The important objection to the inflation tax is generally not its economic cost, but rather its lack of political authorization (Friedman, 1971).

Inflationary uncertainty and inflationary dispersion are the characteristics of inflation that have the most damaging consequences for allocative efficiency, because economic agents can plan against them, at best, probabilistically. For a given expected rate of inflation, the associated uncertainty may be greater or smaller, and where the public is risk-averse this should imply quantitatively different behavior. For example, as a broad generalization, for a given expected rate of inflation and a given nominal bond rate, we should expect a bond to sell at a higher discount, the larger the "confidence interval" of the public's expectation, that is, the larger the range within which the public expects the future rate of inflation to turn out with, say, 95 percent probability. (For example, consider two situations: in both situations the expected rate of inflation is 15 percent and the nominal bond rate is 20 percent; but in the first situation the public believes that the rate of inflation could turn out anywhere between 14 and 16 percent, whereas in the second situation the public believes that the rate of inflation could turn out anywhere between 10 and 20 percent. We should expect the discount on such bonds to be higher in the second situation.)[6]

Similarly, for any given rate of inflation, the associated dispersion may be of any magnitude: money prices in general may move rather closely with the price level, or they may move at greatly differing rates. For a given rate of inflation, we should suppose that there would be less dispersion in an economy that is competitive, flexible, and well-integrated, and there should be more dispersion in an economy that is oligopolized, unresponsive, and segmented. Speculative activity in particular markets may serve either to mitigate dispersion by moving relative prices more swiftly to their appropriate values, or to aggravate the dispersion by causing "unnecessary" price swings. Dispersion will be greater, to the extent that some prices but not others are regulated in nominal terms by law or custom, to the extent that some prices can be adjusted only at relatively infrequent intervals, and to the extent that prices are fixed by old negotiations that cannot be reopened.

Taken together, inflationary uncertainty and dispersion constitute the essence of the inflation problem for allocative efficiency. Dispersion per se means that real prices, as well as the real incomes derived from them, diverge from their appropriate relative scarcity values; this causes resource misallocation.[7] Uncertainty and dispersion in combination mean that not only future real prices, but real revenues, cash flows, and profits are made more uncertain than market conditions alone would make them.

We can offer some broad generalizations—in fact, testable hypotheses— regarding the relationship between the magnitude of inflationary uncertainty, the magnitude of inflationary dispersion, and the rate of inflation (Jaffee-Kleiman, 1977; Glejser, 1965; Parks, 1978; Cukierman-Wachtel, 1979; Vining-Elwertowski, 1976; Logue-Willet, 1976). First, uncertainty and dispersion are probably both characterized by a kind of heteroskedasticity: the higher the current rate of inflation, the wider will be the public's confidence interval regarding the future rate of inflation; also, the higher the rate of inflation, the wider, the scope for particular nominal price changes, and hence the greater will be the dispersion. In theory, of course, the degrees of uncertainty and dispersion could perfectly well be independent of the rate of inflation. Intuition and experience suggest, however, that the levels of uncertainty and dispersion are both rather higher when the rate of inflation is around, say, 100 percent per year than when it is only around 5 percent.

Second, the degrees of uncertainty and dispersion should bear some relation to the time horizon under consideration. The longer the time horizon, the higher the uncertainty should be, on the common-sense ground that any anticipated economic variable should be more uncertain the farther into the future it is. The relation of the time horizon and the degree of dispersion is more complicated. If the rate of inflation is "moderate," then dispersion would probably be lower for longer time horizons, on the ground that the forces driving relative prices toward their appropriate scarcity values ought to operate more reliably the longer the time horizon in question. On the other hand, in a severe inflation the malfunctioning of the price system would be extremely high even for longer time horizons.

Dispersion is not merely an unfortunate characteristic of inflation; it is the *purpose* of inflation. A neutral inflation would be of no use to anyone. The object of the short-run behavior of individuals, firms, and government that sustains an inflation is always to reap a windfall gain or to restore a recent windfall loss. There are two general ways to accomplish this: by procuring credit—means of payment—and spending it on particular goods and services before prices in general rise to the level appropriate to the new aggregate quantity of means of payment; or by raising a price at the right moment and in the right proportion, given other relevant prices and expectations, so as to maintain or to increase real income. This process clearly entails uneven price adjustments, at least in the short run, and these uneven price adjustments generate new demand for credit, which, if met, sustains the inflation. We shall say more about this sustaining process in the next section.

To summarize this section, inflation diminishes allocative efficiency mainly because it is uncertain and because it is not neutral, and these characteristics require economic agents to take account of uncertainty in determining their behavior. True, there could still be plenty of real uncertainty even in an economy that had no inflation problem; but inflation imposes additional dimensions of uncertainty. Inflation also affects allocative efficiency by discouraging cash-balance holdings and by its "sporadicity," though we have argued that these are problems of second-order importance by comparison with inflationary uncertainty and inflationary dispersion.

C. THE "INFLATION-FEEDBACK" MECHANISM

Given that inflation is a social and economic nuisance, it would stand doubly condemned if it could be shown that "inflation begets more inflation." In this section, we try to explain broadly why inflation over, say, one month will give rise to inflationary pressure in subsequent months. For policy evaluation, it is important to distinguish the "inflation-feedback" mechanism operating in a macroeconomy from the original causes of the inflation. As a generalization, the object of short- and medium-term policy should always be to break into the feedback mechanism. The object of long-term policy should be to weaken the feedback mechanism. There will always be inflationary shocks to macroeconomics, and economic systems and institutions must be developed so as to absorb such shocks without propagating them into sustained inflation.

We can describe at least four interrelated but conceptually separable ways in which an "incipient" inflation occurring over a given period will generate a new inflationary shock in subsequent periods:

1. An incipient inflation may induce an *expectation* of further inflation, and this expectation may induce inflationary behavior, as we shall describe. (Inflationary expectations have been the subject of considerable

research over the past decade, and many theoretical expectations-forma-
tion mechanisms have been described, although the actual mechanisms of
their formation and their consequences remain elusive.)

2. An incipient inflation may induce inflationary *uncertainty*, and this
uncertainty may induce inflationary behavior, again, as will be described.

3. An incipient inflation reduces the outstanding quantity of real money
balances. We refer to this as *inflationary illiquidity*. Given transactions
and precautionary requirements, *and given preexisting contractual obligations*, the reduced quantity of real money balances may "require" the
creation of new real money balances, whether by the monetary authority
or by "inside" financial institutions.

4. An incipient inflation may be accompanied by inflationary *dispersion*,
and this dispersion may "require" further inflation: for reasons that remain less than completely understood, it seems to be easier to allow lagging relative prices to rise in nominal terms rather than to have leading
relative prices fall in nominal terms.

We briefly examine how inflationary expectations, uncertainty, illiquidity, and dispersion operate to sustain inflation. We will identify several
"channels" through which the inflation feedback "flows."

1. The "savings" channel. All other things being equal, any reduction in
the (*ex ante*) aggregate savings rate will be inflationary. Any increase in
the expected rate of inflation, particularly if it is accompanied by increased
inflationary uncertainty and dispersion, should tend to cause such a reduction in the savings rate, for at least the following reasons: first, because a consumer would prefer to purchase durable goods sooner rather
than later when their real prices might rise; second, because the expected
real rates of return on savings media denominated in the monetary unit
(such as savings accounts, government bonds, and money itself) are not
only reduced, but are made more uncertain as well. Furthermore, dispersion—hence relative-price uncertainty—discourages savings in the form
of productive assets. (These effects on the savings rate would be offset,
first, to the degree that interest rates on savings media rise to take account
of expected inflation;[8] second, to the degree that some people actually
respond to increased inflationary uncertainty by saving more, in hope of
building up their wealth for precautionary purposes; third, if the initial
real rates of return on savings media are high on a backward-bending
"savings-supply" curve.)

2. The "investment" channel. All other things being equal, any increase in
the aggregate investment rate would be inflationary in the short run. (A
longer-run increase in the aggregate investment rate would be antiinflationary, because the capital formation would serve to increase aggregate
supply.) An increase in the expected rate of inflation accompanied by an
increase in inflationary uncertainty should serve to decrease firms' per-

ceived cost of capital, and thus encourage investment, because an increase in the expected rate of inflation should decrease the expected real rate of interest, which would entail both a reduction in the expected real cost of borrowed funds and a relative increase in the real valuation of equity. (These effects should be offset to the extent that the increased inflationary uncertainty and dispersion turn the prospective real profits on investment more uncertain.)

3. The "government-budget" channel. The nominal level of the government's expenditures is determined in large measure by the *current* wage and price level. The government's revenues, however, are largely based on the levels of wages, incomes, and prices during an earlier period. For example, suppose that the government's principal source of revenue is an income tax. All other things being equal, to the extent that this year's price level exceeds that of the previous year, the current government budget will tend toward deficit. This will be a source of inflationary pressure, especially if the gap is largely covered by credit from the central bank. Of course, the gap will be more likely to be covered by central bank credit if a higher and more uncertain rate of inflation is anticipated, because in that case government obligations will become harder to sell.

The tax system itself may be a cause of inflation-feedback pressure, although this depends on the precise characteristics of the tax system and on its role in the economy. In a tax system without index-linking, for example, inflation of incomes pushes taxpayers into higher tax brackets, and this increases the real tax take. This may be stabilizing, if its effect is mainly to decrease aggregate demand, but its effect will be inflationary if its negative effect on aggregate supply predominates (Blinder, 1973; Katseli-Papaefstratiou, 1979; Smyth, 1980).

4. The "aggregate-supply" channel. All other things being equal—in particular, the level of aggregate demand—any reduction in aggregate supply will cause upward pressure on the price level. Taken together, an increase in inflationary uncertainty and dispersion will cause a reduction in aggregate supply by impairing the operation of the price system: dispersion causes relative prices, in particular, factor prices, to take on inappropriate values and turns the future paths of relative prices uncertain; uncertainty and dispersion in combination turn the future real values of prices governed by existing or prospective nominal contracts more uncertain. Inflationary uncertainty and dispersion will therefore generate further inflationary pressure through this channel. (To the extent that wages and input prices are governed by preexisting nominal contracts, an increase in inflationary expectations may actually have a positive, antiinflationary effect on aggregate supply, because anticipated real costs under contracts will be reduced, at least until the next round of contract negotiations.)

5. The "demand-for-money" channel. An increase in the level of inflationary expectations and uncertainty would diminish the demand for money.

Ceteris paribus this would be inflationary, because the expected real rates of return on assets competing with money as forms in which to hold wealth—with the exception of financial instruments denominated in the monetary unit—will now become more attractive by comparison with the expected real rate of return on money. In addition, the real rate of return on money will now be more uncertain. The "demand-for-money" channel is one of the most important elements of any true inflationary process. It may operate as a vicious cycle, in which anticipations of capital losses on cash-balance holdings discourage the demand for money, and the consequent diminished valuation of money in terms of commodities then fulfills the anticipations. This cycle may be described as a *"bear market in money."*

6. The "supply-of-money" channel. An increase in inflationary expectations, uncertainty, illiquidity, and dispersion all together is likely to increase the pressure to increase the money supply, through its effects on the commercial banking system's assets and liabilities. (Or, to put it differently, after an incipient inflation, the quantity of contractionary monetary policy that would be required to prevent any inflation in the subsequent period would be much *smaller,* if the price rise were neutral and if the public confidently expected the price rise not to recur.)

The pressure on the commercial banking system develops in the following way: First, the increase in inflationary expectations and uncertainty leads the public to attempt to reduce the real quantity of its demand deposits—that is, to the extent possible, the public will increase its demand deposits at slower rate than the price level. Instead of demand deposits, the public will attempt to hold its wealth in the form of inflation-resistant assets, such as capital assets, inventories, real estate, jewelry, foreign exchange, and so on. At the same time, however, there is likely to be an increase in the real demand for commercial-bank credit, mainly because dispersion changes the relative prices paid and received by firms. This affects their current and prospective cash flows and profits, and some firms are likely to require credit to maintain their position or even to avert insolvency. Hence, the immediate consequence of an incipient inflation is quite likely to be, rather ironically, a state of illiquidity in the commercial banking system.

This places the monetary authority in a dilemma: should it attempt to confront the liquidity crisis or the incipient inflation? Obviously, the authority might try to confront the inflation by tightening credit, or by allowing the liquidity crisis "to run its course": It is likely, however, that this will provoke some bankruptcies and perhaps an incipient recession. It will then seem irrational and unfair to permit bankruptcies and unemployment to result from a temporary relative-price shift or from a temporary cash-flow problem. The authority may even become alarmed; its hand may be forced politically. It will then permit bank-credit expansion, which entails an inflationary increase in the money supply.

This stop-go cycle of tight and easy credit is familiar to observers of developing nations, particularly in Latin America. If the monetary authority did not try to relieve the liquidity crisis, the result would be a recession, similar in essence to the "down" phase of the bank-mediated business cycle described by Irving Fisher and Knut Wicksell (Fisher, 1911; Wicksell, 1936). The cycle as we have described it is especially likely to operate in nations in which commercial bank credit is extremely important to enterprises not only as working capital but for longer-term needs as well; where there are frequent and brusque shifts in relative prices; and where the monetary authority lacks institutional power to carry out its policy.

The feedback effect of inflationary illiquidity remains one of the most poorly understood aspects of the feedback process. It has a peculiar importance in advanced economic systems with complex relationships of debt contracts, particularly where those contracts have been negotiated on the assumption of continued inflation. (On this point, see Minsky's contributions.) In effect, a certain quantity of real liquidity may be necessary for a given economy's financial structure to honor its liabilities, both "inside and outside." The layering and linkage of these liabilities in an economy may mean that a monetary authority, facing a sudden burst of inflation, must nevertheless allow the money supply to grow or accept a chain reaction of bankruptcies.

7. The "foreign" channel(s). The foreign sector affords a variety of possible inflation-feedback channels, depending on such things as the exchange-rate regime, the degree of international financial capital mobility, the reaction functions of foreign economic authorities, and so on. In the "classical" adjustment mechanism of David Hume, with a pure gold standard, the foreign sector operates to deflate and to restore equilibrium following an incipient inflation: since foreign prices become lower than domestic prices following an inflation, exports decline and imports increase, so that some of the nation's money stock is vented. Modern circumstances, of course, are more complicated than those of Hume's day, and in many instances the foreign sector may in fact function as part of the inflation-feedback mechanism. To discuss this in detail would take us beyond the scope of the present work, but there are some obvious examples. Each fall in the domestic purchasing power of the United States dollar leads to pressure for it to be devalued vis-à-vis foreign currencies. The devaluation itself has at least temporary inflationary effects, partly by increasing the United States dollar prices of imports; partly by reducing the vent of money through the foreign sector that the inflation would have caused if exchange rates were fixed; partly by inducing speculative pressure against the dollar. In the specific case of the present-day United States, the decline in the value of the dollar induces oil producers, who hold reserves in dollars, to increase their price. Inflationary illiquidity (as described by some variants of the monetary approach to the balance of

payments) may actually cause the balance of payments to operate in the reverse of the Hume mechanism: demanders of money may *import* money through the balance of payments, with destabilizing consequences (Johnson, 1978).

Let us summarize the argument of this section. An "incipient inflation" is likely to be accompanied by an increase in inflationary expectation, uncertainty illiquidity, and dispersion. These, in turn, are likely to generate renewed inflationary pressure by reducing aggregate savings, by increasing aggregate investment, by pressuring the government budget toward deficit, by reducing aggregate supply, by diminishing the demand for money, and by pressuring the money supply to increase. All these taken together constitute the "inflation-feedback" mechanism. The stronger the mechanism, and the larger the inflation feeding into it, the more determination the authority will require in order to resist, and the harder it will go on business and employment conditions.

CONCLUSION

This essay has argued, in purposely broad and general terms, that the essence of the inflation problem is the feedback mechanism. An incipient inflation, *in itself*, is a problem of much less importance; indeed, an incipient inflation may be a "legitimate and appropriate" response by a macroeconomy (i.e., a move in the direction of general equilibrium) to a change of circumstances, in the same sense that any shift in a relative price may be a "legitimate and appropriate" response to a change in conditions of relative scarcity. The consequent activation of the feedback mechanism, on the other hand, is a much more serious matter: once inflation is anticipated (and uncertain, nonneutral, and sporadic), it has a caustic effect on allocative efficiency. The challenge for economic analysis and for public policy is determining the ways in which the feedback mechanism can be weakened, so that any incipient inflation remains, as nearly as possible, a once-and-for-all static shift with no further dynamic consequences. At all events, a "gradualist" stabilization program that concentrates on weakening the feedback mechanism is likely to achieve a more durable stabilization, even if it takes a relatively longer time, than a "shock-treatment" program that simply amounts to responding to an inflationary shock with a deflationary shock.

Notes

1. Branson (1972) provides an excellent exposition of this model.
2. The variables r^*, y^*, and p^* represent the equilibrium values of the interest rate, the real rate of national income, and the price level; $\bar{g}$ represents the (given) real rate of government expenditures, $\bar{M}$ the (given) outstanding money supply,

and $\bar{K}$ the (given) capital stock; and $i(\ )$, $s(\ )$, $t(\ )$, $l(\ )$, and $f(\ )$ represent the investment, savings, tax money-demand and aggregate-supply functions respectively. The symbol "$\hat{=}$" should be read, "is equal in equilibrium to."

3. The sporadicity of the rate of inflation over a given period may be measured simply by calculating the variance of the monthly rates of inflation over the period.

4. The degree of inflationary uncertainty at a given moment is difficult to measure, for obvious reasons. As in the case of inflationary expectations, we must employ assumptions of various kinds and quality. For example, suppose that we have determined, by some means, a time series of expected rates of inflation for each coming month, x_t. The degree of inflationary uncertainty at time t, σ_t, might then be assumed to be estimated by a distributed lag of the mean squared errors,

$$\sigma_t = \gamma \sum_\tau (1-\gamma)^\tau (x_{t-\tau} - \pi_{t-\tau})^2,$$

where π_t is the actual rate of inflation over time t. Another possibility is to measure the uncertainty attaching to the expected rate of inflation from the reduced form of an econometric model of the economy: if the reduced form is given by

$$\pi_t = \sum_i c_i \alpha_{it} + u_t$$

where the c_i are estimated coefficients, α_{it} are the predetermined variables of the model, and u_t is the error term, then the uncertainty attaching to π_t might be taken to be the estimate of the variance of the error term.

5. The degree of inflationary dispersion is also difficult to measure. It is possible to calculate an "index of relative-price change" between times t and $t=1$, as follows. Let P_{it} represent the price of good i at time t, let $\bar{P}_t$ represent the price index, and let W_i represent the weight of good i in the price index. An index of relative-price change over the period is δ_t, where

$$\delta_t = \sum_i W_i \{ [P_{i(t+1)}/\bar{P}_{(t+1)}/P_{it}/\bar{P}_t)] - 1 \}^2,$$

that is, a weighted average of the squares of the relative-price changes in the economy. Not all of the relative-price change that occurs during a given period can be attributed to inflation, of course. It is a testable hypothesis that δ_t will tend to be greater, the higher is π_t.

6. This may not always be the case, however. The subjective probability distribution of the future rate of inflation maintained by the public might be characterized by positive or negative covariance with the future rates of return on other assets, and such covariance may lead to counterintuitive outcomes. For example, if the public perceives the real rates of return on bonds and equities to be negatively covariant, an increase in the perceived uncertainty attaching to bonds might actually lead to increased demand for bonds. That is, the public might form hedged portfolios in equities and bonds. (On this point see Fischer, 1975.)

7. Professor Arnold Harberger has argued that inflation is likely to inhibit economic growth on essentially similar grounds:

> In this paragraph I set out what I believe to be the principal argument against inflation as the promoter of economic growth. This argument is not really an argument against inflation itself, but rather an argument against the way inflations appear to have worked in practice. It is possible to imagine an inflation which went on steadily at, say 30 per cent per year, and

which was completely and accurately anticipated by everybody, and in which the separate prices of all the different commodities and services in the economy rose steadily at the same pace. This "ideal" type of inflation is not what we have observed in the real world. The inflations of the real world are, by and large not all accurately anticipated, and in them there occurs substantial disparity in the rates of rise of the prices of different types of goods and services. The failure to anticipate accurately and, in particular, the disparity in the pace of adjustment of particular prices blur, so to speak, the vision of the people who are responsible for economic organization. In a country which has a stable general price level it is possible for entrepreneurs to make a judgment that a new process will save, say, two cents in the dollar of production costs, and it is likely that within a stable environment such a new process would in fact be adopted with alacrity. If, however, the economy is undergoing an inflation of, say, 20–30 per cent per annum it will be difficult for entrepreneurs to act on this kind of improvement. They will not know whether the saving of two cents in the dollar of costs will be erased by a rise in wages or in prices of materials in the very near future. During any big inflation all absolute prices are constantly adjusted. They adjust at different rates, and in a pattern which is not at all precisely predictable. I would venture to guess that where in a stable environment entrepreneurs would be happy to make alterations in their method of production on the basis of information which appeared to suggest a saving of two costs in the dollar of costs, in an inflationary environment entrepreneurs might require information suggesting that they might save ten cents in the dollar of costs before they would be willing to undertake a substantial overhaul of their methods of production. This obviously means that fewer growth-producing innovations will take place in an inflationary setting than in a more stable environment (Harberger, 1964, pp. 320–21).

8. Note that nominal interest rates would have to rise by more than any increase in the expected rate of inflation to compensate for increased inflationary uncertainty as well.

References

Beckerman, Paul. "Index-linked Financial Assets and the Brazilian 'Inflation-Feedback' Mechanism," presented at this conference. (Published in Portuguese as "Ativos Financeiros Indexados e o Mecanismo de Realimentacao Inflacionaria no Brasil," *Pesquisa e Planejamento Economico* 9, 1979 [Rio de Janeiro, Brazil]).

Beckerman, Paul. "The Trouble with Index-linking: Reflections on the Recent Brazilian Experience," in P. Beckerman and W. Baer (Eds.), *World Development* (forthcoming); also forthcoming in Portuguese in a collection of essays on index-linking to be published in Rio de Janeiro, Claudio Contador, editor.

Blinder, Alan. "Can Income Tax Increases be Inflationary? An Expository Note," *National Tax Journal*, June 1973.

Branson, William. "The Dual Roles of the Government Budget and the Balance of

Payments in the Movement from Short-Run to Long-Run Equilibrium," *Quarterly Journal of Economics,* August 1976.

Branson, William. *Macroeconomic Theory and Policy* (New York, 1972).

Cagan, Philip. "The Monetary Dynamics of Hyperinflation," in M. Freedman (Ed.), *Studies in the Quantity Theory of Money* (Chicago, 1956).

Cukierman, A., and Wachtel, P. "Differential Inflationary Expectation and the Variability of the Rate of Inflation," *American Economic Review,* September 1979.

Ellis, Howard. "Corrective Inflation in Brazil, 1964–1966," in H. Ellis (Ed.), *The Economy of Brazil* (Berkeley, 1969).

Feige, E.I., and Parkin, M. "The Optimal Quantity of Money, Bonds, Commodity Inventories, and Capital," *American Economic Review,* June 1971.

Fischer, Stanley. "The Demand for Index Bonds," *Journal of Political Economy,* June 1975, pp. 509–534.

Fisher, Irving. *The Purchasing Power of Money* (New York, 1911).

Friedman, Milton. "The Counter-Revolution in Monetary Theory," IEA *Occasional Paper,* No. 33 (London: Institute of Economic Affairs, 1970).

Friedman, Milton. "Government Revenue from Inflation," *Journal of Political Economy,* July/August 1971, pp. 846–56.

Glejser, Herbert. "Inflation, Productivity, and Relative Prices: A Statistical Study," *Review of Economics and Statistics,* February 1965.

Harberger, Arnold. "Some Notes on Inflation," in W. Baer and I. Kerstenetzky (Eds.), *Inflation and Growth in Latin America* (Homewood, Ill., 1964).

Jaffee, D., and Kleiman, E. "The Welfare Implications of Uneven Inflation," in E. Lundberg (Ed.), *Inflation Theory and Anti-Inflation Policy* (London, 1977), pp. 285–307.

Johnson, Harry. "Money, Balance-of-Payments Theory, and the International Monetary Problem" (International Finance Section, Princeton, Essay, 1978).

Katseli-Papaefstratiou, Louka T. "Nominal Tax Rates and the Effectiveness of Fiscal Policy," *National Tax Journal,* March 1979.

Logue, D., and Willett, T.D. "A Note on the Relation Between the Rate and Variability of Inflation," *Economica,* May 1976.

Minsky, Hyman. "Financial Instability, the Current Dilemma and the Structure of Banking and Finance, *Compendium on Major Issues in Bank Regulation,* United States Senate, Committee on Banking, Housing, and Urban Affairs, 94th Cong. 1st Sess., Washington, D.C.

Minsky, Hyman. "Institutional Roots of American Inflation," presented at this conference (1980).

Parks, Richard. "Inflation and Relative Price Variability," *Journal of Political Economy,* February 1978.

Roll, Richard. "Assets, Money, and Commodity Price Inflation under Uncertainty," *Journal of Money, Credit and Banking,* November 1973, pp. 903–923.

Rothschild, Michael, and Stiglitz, Joseph. "Increasing Risk: A Definition," *Journal of Economic Theory,* September 1971.

Smyth, David. "Taxes and Inflation," presented at this conference (1980).

Tobin, James. "Costs and Benefits of Antiinflation Policies," presented at this conference (1980).

Tobin, James. "An Essay on the Principles of Debt Management," in Commission on Money and Credit, *Fiscal and Debt Management Policies*, 1963, pp. 143–218.

Tobin, James. "Money and Economic Growth," *Econometrica*, October 1965.

Tobin, James. "Notes on Optimal Monetary Growth," *Journal of Political Economy*, July-August 1968.

Vining, D.R., and Elwertowski, T.C. "The Relationship between Relative Prices and the General Price Level," *American Economic Review*, May 1976.

Wicksell, Knut. *Interest and Prices* (London, 1936).

Towards a Real Theory of Inflation

DAVID COLANDER

INTRODUCTION

The problem we economists have had in explaining inflation is one of perspective: our general analytic framework is static; the problem of inflation is dynamic. The problem this presents can be seen by analogy: imagine yourself looking at a speeding train, attempting to describe its motion and figure out ways to stop it. With your feet planted firmly on the ground, all you see is a blur. Even if you take photographs of the train with Super Ektachrome Film, all you see is a train at rest; still pictures provide little insight into the movement of the train or how to stop it.

We economists, attempting to explain inflation, have faced precisely this predicament: inflation is a dynamic problem of the aggregate price level that we have attempted to describe through partial-equilibrium static analysis. Consequently we have had little success either in explaining inflation or in designing measures to stop it. For many, the conclusion of this reasoning is that inflation is not an economic problem: monetarists emphasize the political difficulties that stop governments from instituting the "real" monetary solution; radicals claim that inflation demonstrates the irrelevance of neoclassical economics; noneconomists look on with bewildered amusement.

In this paper I suggest that there is a way to make neoclassical economic theory relevant to understanding, and designing a solution for, inflation. To see the argument consider the example of the speeding train. In it, the solution would be to board another train, running parallel to the speeding train and moving at roughly the same speed. Doing so will allow you to study the movements of the train with the same ease and perhaps even the same tools as you would use to study the train at rest.

My proposal is that economists do precisely that in analyzing inflation: drop their static framework and shift to a dynamic framework. Doing so changes static competition to dynamic competition and monopoly to monopolization, both of which are concepts directly relevant for understanding inflation. Moreover, I suggest that neoclassical economics has been schizophrenic in its analysis of the economy, with one foot on and one foot off the speeding train. This schizophrenia demonstrates itself in a dichotomy between formal analysis and heuristic discussion. In formal analysis, a strict static framework is maintained, while heuristic discussions often jump into dynamic interpretations and examples. This duality underlies the current disagreements about the nature of the inflation process.

In discussing my dynamic approach, I first consider the nature of the competitive process, suggesting that economists have often discussed dynamic competition, even while their models have concerned static competition. Second, I briefly develop the concept of *monopolization*, the dynamic counterpart to monopoly, and explain why there is a continual need for monopolization. I suggest that there are two types of monopolization—buyers' and sellers' monopolization—and that one or the other is likely to predominate in an economy for purely technical reasons. These technical reasons underlie the development of market structures and institutions within which the market operates. The analysis of the real economy must reflect these institutional structures because without them markets have no meaning.

This dynamic analysis suggests that in our economy, because of the technical nature of production and consumption, sellers' monopolization predominates, placing an upward pressure on prices and a dynamic constraint on the aggregate economy which does not allow a static supply and demand equilibrium to be reached. Were the economy to expand to a supply/demand equilibrium, the price level would blow up. Thus, to maintain a constant price level, the economy must operate at less than full resource utilization. The resulting underutilized resources increase dynamic competition, placing a downward pressure on the price level that offsets the upward pressure of sellers' monopolization.

Within this theory, the price level and the inflation are primarily determined in the real economy with monetary and credit controls serving as constraints on the nominal income that prevent the price level from blowing up. I call it a *real theory of inflation* to contrast it with the nominal or monetary theory of inflation, in which the price level is determined in the monetary sector.

Finally, having sketched my real theory of inflation, I explain how that theory leads naturally to an alternative method to control inflation—MAP—the market antiinflation plan. MAP provides a direct offset to monopolization by providing an equitable and efficient offsetting pressure that stabilizes the price level.

THE NATURE OF THE COMPETITIVE PROCESS

In theoretical economics one quickly falls into the habit of equating competition with "perfect" competition, in which all individuals are price takers. Specifically, competition is equated with market relationships in which there are so many buyers and sellers that all act as if their individual actions could not affect the market or trading price. In fact, such a view defines an efficient "state" and provides the benchmark by which economic systems are judged. In this static view of competition, individuals do not really compete with each other. They do not even consider the effect of their actions on others, but merely accept the dictates of the "invisible hand" of the market. Such competition is a state, not a process.

This is a quite different view of competition from that presented by Adam Smith in the *Wealth of Nations*. His view was one of individuals *continually* struggling to escape the market control through whatever means possible. In a famous passage he writes:

> People of the same trade seldom meet together, but the conversation ends in a conspiracy against the public, or in some diversion to raise prices.

Smith's view of competition is fundamentally different from the static concept of competition; its foundations are dynamic and it works through everyone's attempting to monopolize but finding those attempts foiled by competition. Everyone *believes* that his (her) actions *can* affect others but, because of competition, ultimately discover that they cannot.

This classical dynamic view of competition is compelling; the problem faced by neoclassical writers was to formalize it. Early writers, such as Alfred Marshall (1890) and John Bates Clark (1899), saw the development of a static analysis of competition as an introduction to a dynamic analysis. But, somehow, that dynamic development never came and the theoretical analysis remained essentially static.

Despite the static nature of the theory, heuristic discussion of competition emphasizes the dynamic process as it works itself out in an uncertain world. A number of incisive writers have developed this dynamic theme (Schumpeter, 1934; Andrews, 1964; J.M. Clark, 1961; Kirzner, 1978). In each of these theories it is the competitive market process, not the static equilibrium concept of competition that is essential.

The numerous attempts at characterizing the competitive process have failed to gain widespread acceptance and the importance of the dynamic concept of competition has often been forgotten. Instead, essentially static analyses of oligopoly, monopolistic competition, and imperfect competition have led to mazes from which most theorists have not returned. The result could have been predicted: dynamic theories become a blur in a static framework.

The only way one will understand dynamic competition is to shift completely to a dynamic framework and interpretation. In this dynamic framework, equilibrium and the adjustment to equilibrium must be analyzed simultaneously since the adjustment process will determine the nature of the expected equilibrium. This means that the analysis of adjustments to shocks, or the disequilibrium analysis, is interwoven with

|

the equilibrium analysis. Equilibrium has no meaning independent of the adjustment process leading to it.

To move to an analysis of aggregate equilibrium, we must move from a supply/demand analysis which concerns relative prices to an analysis of nominal price levels. In our economy, relative prices are set as nominal prices relative to some expected price level. Thus, in the transitions from relative to nominal, expected price levels become crucial. But these expected price levels reflect past experience and if, on average, relative prices are internally consistent, the inflation rate will remain constant at the expected level. Thus supply/demand equilibrium is consistent with a rising or falling price level as long as that rise or fall is expected. These expectations of a rising price level may either be caused or ratified by an increase in the money supply but they must be accompanied by it.

Aggregate dynamic equilibrium does not necessarily mean any specific market is in equilibrium; it is merely a state in which the dynamic adjustments offset each other and the upward pressures on nominal prices are equal to the downward pressures so that the actual price equals the expected price.

DYNAMIC COMPETITION AND MONOPOLIZATION

To analyze dynamic equilibrium one must have two offsetting dynamic forces. Specifically, for the aggregate economy, where *equilibrium* is defined as the level of resource utilization for which there is no tendency for the price level to change, those two offsetting forces are *dynamic competition* and *monopolization*.

To help understand the argument it is useful to think of the speeding train and the suggestion about how to analyze it. Monopoly is a static concept. Trying to analyze the dynamic or moving process of inflation within that static framework can only leave a blur. Moving to a dynamic framework clears up the dynamic process while blurring the static concept of monopoly. What we can see are individuals' attempts to increase their monopoly, and the gradual erosion of monopoly through a process that can be called *dynamic competition*, the dynamic counterpart to static competition.

Individuals are continually attempting to receive more for the same amount of effort—in other words—attempting to free themselves from the rigors of competition. These attempts are defined as monopolization. If monopolization were costless, it would lead immediately to monopoly. But monopolization is not costless; innumerable resources are spent on the process of monopolization. Thus, monopolization need not lead to monopoly profits, although it may lead to greater rents for individuals who have a lower cost of monopolization than others.

To be credible, the theory of monopolization as an explanation of inflation cannot lead to continued increases in monopoly since our economy has not experienced such an increase (although it is consistent with either increases or decreases in monopoly). Moreover, it must describe a continual or steady-state process. Just as a runner on a treadmill runs and runs, getting nowhere, so too must this monopolizing continuously occur, but never consistently gain or lose ground.

What prevents monopolization from leading to increases in monopoly is dynamic competition, which is defined as the continual process of breaking down monopolies. Thus, if monopolization were not a continual process, competition would soon destroy any monopoly that existed. Only a continual monopolization can maintain a constant level of monopoly in an economy. Thus, monopolization is the dynamic counterpart to dynamic competition, and the two provide offsetting forces necessary to understand macroeconomic equilibrium.

EXAMPLES OF MONOPOLIZATION

Monopolization can be the result of investment; it can occur from random shocks, or it can be a combination of the two. Numerous examples of monopolization exist. Some include:

1. Individuals joining together to avoid "cutthroat competition"
2. Advertising of various forms
3. Investment in new technologies
4. Formations of buyers' cooperatives
5. Lobbying for import controls, regulation of entry, or price controls
6. Creation of nongovernmental barriers to entry.

Much can be said about these various processes, but a normative discussion of monopolization is not my purpose. I will merely state that monopolization is inherently neither "good" nor "bad." Some forms of monopolization serve useful purposes; others not. Regardless of its normative implications, it has effects on the nature of the economy that must be considered.

SELLERS' AND BUYERS' MONOPOLIZATION

The law of supply and demand concerns the disequilibrium adjustment of relative prices. It states that the larger the disequilibrium—the faster the relative price adjustment. This law has no underlying theory and is based upon common sense mixed with a feel for the way the economy works. (Only now has theoretical work begun on examining these laws in what is called an analysis of non-Walrasian adjustment systems.) In its supply/demand analysis of the aggregate economy, neoclassical economics makes a very important implicit assumption about the nature of these dynamic forces. It assumes that the upward and downward adjustment forces directly offset each other, so that in the adjustment to random shocks, there will be no pressure on the nominal price level. This allows neoclassical analysis to separate disequilibrium and equilibrium analysis.

The theory of monopolization provides the underlying rationale for the law of supply and demand. Prices rise whenever $Qd > Qs$ and fall whenever $Qs > Qd$ because the returns to monopolization increase. Thus it is individuals responding to disequilibrium situations attempting to increase their income that underlies the adjustment process.

FROM RELATIVE PRICES TO NOMINAL PRICES

Any individual is concerned primarily with his *relative* price. In our economy which uses an average price level unit of account, relative prices are set by setting a nominal price in reference to an expected price level. The quantity weighted relative prices must always sum to one since there is only 100 percent to go around; however, where inflation is unexpected or where there are institutional constraints on raising nominal prices, a rise in the price level can bring the quantity weighted relative prices into equilibrium by raising the denominator and hence lowering relative prices.

It is reasonable to assume that consistent inflation will become expected and will also lead to a breakdown of the institutional constraints; thus inflation can only temporarily fulfill this role and the upward and downward pressures on relative price must be offsetting. Such an equilibrium is an expectional equilibrium and is consistent with any level of expected inflation.

THE DOMINANCE OF SELLERS' MONOPOLIZATION

There is no inherent reason why sellers' and buyers' monopolization should be equal in intensity, and I suggest that in our economy they are not. In our economy, sellers' monopolization dominates, a phenomenon that needs explanation. My suggested explanation relies on the underlying production and consumption technologies of our economy. Specifically, the cost of monopolization tends to be initially lumpy; consequently average costs of monopolization decrease over a significant range. This decreasing average cost of monopolization implies that the individual's optimal strategy will not be to equate his marginal costs in all areas— rather, it will be to concentrate his monopolization in certain areas, although those specific areas of concentration change from time to time.

For the average or representative individual, we find that the marginal cost of monopolization is lower for factors he sells than it is for factors he buys. Consequently, he devotes more effort toward increasing his real income or his income rate through monopolization of the factors he sells. In other words, sellers' monopolization dominates. The reason is quite simple. An individual buys large numbers of different goods. Since there is a lumpy cost or "toll" associated with attempting to monopolize, he devotes little or no effort toward monopolizing any specific good he buys. Rather, he concentrates his monopolization efforts on the prices he receives—primarily his wage, profit, or rental income.

This asymmetry of monopolization instills a continual upward thrust on the nominal price level, unless it is somehow offset. It makes the aggregate price level like a piece of wood—raising prices is moving with the grain, whereas lowering prices is moving against the grain. The asymmetry manifests itself in many ways. Some include:

1. Growth in real income through rising factor incomes rather than falling prices
2. Initial allocation of productivity gains to sellers rather than buyers
3. Prices set predominantly by sellers.

Obviously this asymmetry does not exist in all markets. There are a variety of markets of varying natures. The argument concerns only the *predominant* dynamic market force in the economy which gives the aggregate price level an upward push from sellers' monopolization.

The product markets set the equilibrium conditions; all other auction and bargaining markets adjust to these markets. As long as firms can easily pass on wage increases (and know that other firms will do the same), they do not worry about those wage increases. Thus, the upward pressure from sellers' product markets overrides the downward pressure exerted by firms on wages.

DISEQUILIBRIUM AS A MEANS OF ACHIEVING EQUILIBRIUM

For the aggregate economy to be in equilibrium, this upward push on the price level means that the effective constraint on the economy is the dynamic constraint on the price level, not the static supply constraint on quantities. In the static supply/demand equilibrium, the price level will be continually accelerating. To maintain equilibrium an offsetting downward pressure must hold the price level down.

Downward pressure can be exerted in numerous ways and the analysis of such downward pressure will be the key to understanding antiinflation policies.

In our society, the method that has most commonly been used is to keep the economy in a constant state of disequilibrium (relative to static equilibrium) by limiting the total amount of nominal income or spending in the economy by control of the money supply or credit. Thus the dynamically constrained supply curve becomes the effective supply curve. Since the upward pressure or sellers' monopolization tends to vary in relation to the amount of excess supply in the market, maintaining an excess supply in most markets can generate a downward pressure on relative prices just sufficient to offset the upward monopolization pressure as in Figure 1.

At price P_1, given by the intersection of the dynamically constrained supply and demand, $Q_s > Q_d$ and thus a downward pressure is exerted. Where this downward pressure equals the upward pressure from monopolization, the market is in "dynamic equilibrium," and the expected rate of price change will be the actual rate.

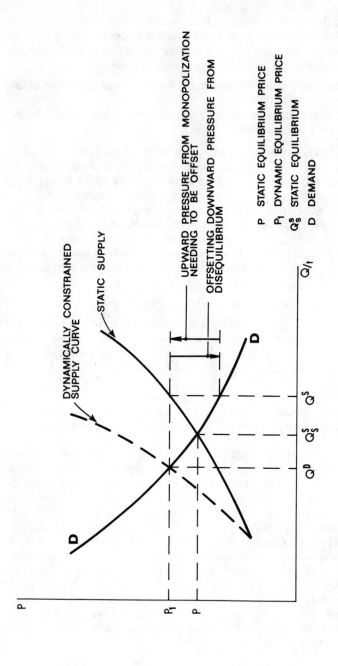

Fig. 1   Market in Dynamic Equilibrium

DYNAMICALLY CONSTRAINED SUPPLY CURVE

STATIC SUPPLY

UPWARD PRESSURE FROM MONOPOLIZATION NEEDING TO BE OFFSET

OFFSETTING DOWNWARD PRESSURE FROM DISEQUILIBRIUM

P   STATIC EQUILIBRIUM PRICE

P_1 DYNAMIC EQUILIBRIUM PRICE

Q_S^S STATIC EQUILIBRIUM

D   DEMAND

Q/t

Q^D Q_S^S Q^S

P

P_1

P

D

D

REINTEGRATING THE ANALYSIS INTO NEOCLASSICAL ANALYSIS

One can better understand the dynamic processes of monopolization and competition by considering the nature of markets more carefully. A market consists of three parts: a buyer, a seller, and a market maker. Static equilibrium analysis reduces these three parts to two, with the market maker disappearing under the "invisible hand" which somehow leads the participants to equilibrium.

In the dynamic view, the adjustment process cannot be treated so cavalierly and becomes an integral part of the analysis. Who precisely carries out the role of market maker and what difference does it make? In answering this question we find that, generally, having a separate auctioneer or market maker is too expensive. Consequently that role is incorporated in the buyer's or the seller's role since their activities in the market require the generation of much the same type of information as that needed by the auctioneer. By incorporating the two roles, total costs can be reduced.

In most product markets, the seller assumes this role. With the assumption, the seller acquires the opportunity to take advantage of any short-run or disequilibrium situation as a normal course of events. Thus, the expected gains from continual random shocks will not be randomly distributed: sellers will have expectations of disequilibrium profits, even when there are no equilibrium profits. The expectations of such disequilibrium profits will encourage entry until the expected equilibrium return is lowered sufficiently to offset the expected disequilibrium profit. This additional entry means that the representative "equilibrium" market is a *buyer's rather than a seller's market,* and the normal state of the market is one in which the seller is demand constrained. Increased sales will increase his profit and an increase in demand will result in an increase in productivity.

Comparing it to a Walrasian or auctioneer market, it is as if the bid price, not the equilibrium price, is always the transaction price. In such markets competition takes quite different forms with sellers' advertising, and interseller competition predominating over the buyer-seller competition. In static analysis, instead of entering into the competitive determination of prices and supplying a direct downward pressure through negotiations or bargaining, buyers supply an indirect downward pressure by searching for alternative sellers.

Because the downward pressure is indirect, initial gains from shocks will go to sellers and only later be diffused throughout the economy. This tendency in our economy can be seen by considering the normal adjustment to a general unexpected productivity gain which expands productive capacity and lowers all suppliers' costs. In an auctioneer market, the selling price should immediately follow the reduction in costs. In markets where the seller determines the trading price, however, the price reduction will be slower, as each seller enjoys the temporary monopoly.

Sooner or later interseller competition will force the price down but not until the sellers have reaped some disequilibrium gains. (Of course, the expectation of these disequilibrium gains will cause the sellers to invest in cost-reducing research which they would not do in an auctioneer market. Thus, we cannot say that the dynamic monopoly is bad—only that it has certain effects which we may or may not like.) The net result of these technological conditions is a continual upward push on the price level as continual random shocks hit the system.

THE ROLE OF INFLATION

The upward and downward pressure is a pressure on relative prices and not on nominal prices. In a monetary economy, relative prices are determined by individuals setting nominal prices with reference to an expected price level. Thus, the pressure is exerted from the effective expected price level, and then only is responsible for increasing and decreasing inflation. Thus, 10 percent expected inflationary equilibrium is as likely as an expected constant price equilibrium. The institutions in our society are designed around money and money prices. This allows some temporary inconsistencies between the upward and downward pressures. Where sellers' monopolization predominates, it can be offset by an upward movement of the price level. Thus, unexpected inflation plays the role of equating inconsistent demands in a monetary economy.

It is also clear, however, that inflation cannot play this role forever. A constant inflationary bias cannot be maintained in the economy. Even the slightest tilt will unbalance the scales and begin an accelerating inflationary process that will ultimately cause the price level to explode.

ALTERNATIVE RELATIONSHIP BETWEEN UNDERUTILIZED RESOURCES
AND MONOPOLIZATION

The nature of the underutilized resources necessary to offset sellers' monopolization depends upon the downward pressure associated with underutilized resources. In the neoclassical theory of supply and demand, there is a direct relationship between the level of underutilized resources and the change in the prices; moreover, it is seen as increasing with the difference between quantity supplied and quantity demanded. If we graph the level of resource utilization (measuring it from right to left so the graph resembles the Phillips Curve) such assumptions would lead to the upward and downward pressures on prices presented in Figure 2. When we add an upward pressure caused by sellers' monopolization, the equilibrium rate of resource utilization compatible with a constant price level decreases to N'. The sole role of the underutilized resources $N-N'$ is preventing inflation.

The existence of underutilized resources does not imply aggregate inoptimality; inoptimality can be judged only by comparing various alter-

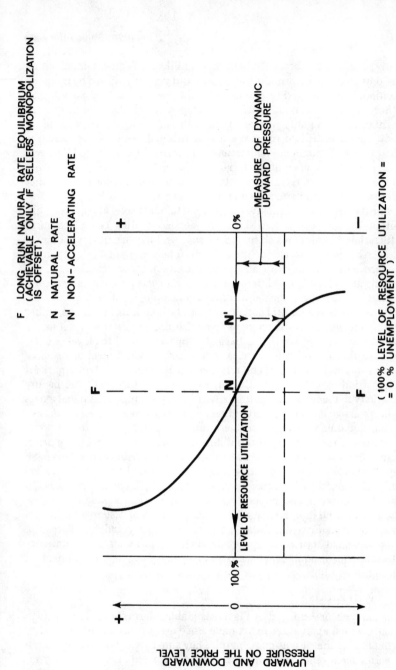

Fig. 2 Neoclassical Dynamic Phillips Curve Relationship

native feasible outcomes. To maintain equilibrium requires an offsetting net downward pressure to offset the upward pressure caused by monopolization. Underutilized resources fulfill the role, and if they do not, then other costly institutions must be developed which do. Judgments concerning the optimality of these underutilized resources will depend on how the underutilized resources are distributed; if distributed equally, their existence might not bother us, but if unequally distributed they will likely violate social equity criteria. Marxian notions of the "reserve army of the unemployed" refer specifically to this phenomenon and tie it together with an underlying ethic of equality.

For the aggregate economy, the only sustainable level of resource utilization will be N', the NAIRU or the nonaccelerating rate of resource utilization. That follows since if all prices rise, such increases will become expected and will accelerate the inflation. Thus, any point other than the nonaccelerating rate will lead to runaway inflation or deflation.

This analysis is quite different from the analysis that normally accompanies discussions of the natural rate of unemployment. In that view the natural rate is the natural outcome of the static equilibrium. Thus, rather than picturing the equilibrium as two offsetting forces, it views it as the result of a real bargain that is basically independent of the level of inflation. In the natural rate there is no tradeoff between level of resource utilization and inflation. (The relationship is given by F-F in Figure 2.) Only if individuals incorrectly perceive future prices will there be any elasticity to the relationship. It follows that any unemployment that exists reflects a social choice of individuals who do not want to work more.

The dynamic view expressed here suggests that, given the institutional structure of the economy, disequilibrium adjustment imposes an *a priori constraint* on the aggregate economy and it never arrives at the Walrasian equilibrium. Thus, it is operating in constant "disequilibrium" with underutilized resources whose sole function it is to hold down the price level. In this dynamic analysis, the society finds itself in a type of prisoner's dilemma in which all individuals might choose a different resource utilization rate, but cannot reach it because whenever they try, inflation flares up!

In technical terms, the aggregate economy faces an additional constraint—the disequilibrium constraint—that prevents achievement of "true full equilibrium."

COST-PUSH INFLATION

The analysis presented above is a reasonable interpretation of cost-push theory which many economists have shied away from, despite an underlying feeling that it was meaningful. They shied away because cost-push theories have relied upon loose heuristic arguments that ultimately reduced to monopoly power. But all neoclassical economists know that *monopoly cannot and does not cause inflation.* Consequently, cost-push theories have been analytically discredited.

As a result, the alternative monetary theory of inflation has been the only show in town. In the monetarist theory a *continual growth* in the money supply causes a *continual increase* in the price level. Both the "cause"—increases in the money supply—and the "effect"—increases in the price level—are dynamic and the theory is at least logically coherent. In my view, this accounts for the power of the monetarist theory.

For many of us, however, it has serious shortcomings—both in its relevance and in its policy prescription. We have therefore continued our attempts to formulate a reasonable cost-push theory of inflation. Most recently Tibor Scitovsky (1978, a, b) has attempted to argue in favor of a relationship between monopoly power and inflation. Despite its common-sense appeal, Scitovsky's, as all previous such attempts, fails because of its underlying static framework in which *monopoly and inflation are not related.* If, however, we move to a dynamic framework, the cost-push argument becomes meaningful and persuasive. There is a connection between *monopolization and inflation,* and it is this connection that cost-push theories of inflation have been attempting to capture. Thus, at full resource utilization there is an upward pressure on the price level from sellers' monopolization.

All one needs to do to arrive at a sociological cost-push theory is to specify a slightly different disequilibrium relationship between prices and resource utilization. Specifically, if one increases the range in which the price level stays constant so that $dP/dQ_D \approx O\,(\nabla N_2 > Q_D > N_1)$ with the normal neoclassical relationships holding on either side of the range the upward pressure/resource utilization relationship would be as presented in Figure 3.

Such a specification of the dynamic relationships would mean that within N_1-N_2 range of resource utilization, the level of aggregate demand or resource utilization is not fundamental to determining the price level; rather, sociological factors overwhelm economic factors within this range. Thus, the economy could maintain a "high level" (N_2) or a "low level" (N_1) of full employment.

If, however, the economy is pushed to a high level of resource utilization, such as K, for a sufficiently long time so that the inflation is built into expectations, then the tradeoff will shift up; and only by running a sufficiently deep depression, moving to a low level of resource utilization such as G for an extended period, will the economy escape the expectational cycle.

THE WORSENING INFLATION PICTURE

In summary, the real theory of inflation provides an explanation of why there has been a consistent push toward inflation. The bias need be only slight since expectations will snowball any consistent bias. Only constant monetary vigilance, maintaining sufficient slack in the system will hold the price level down.

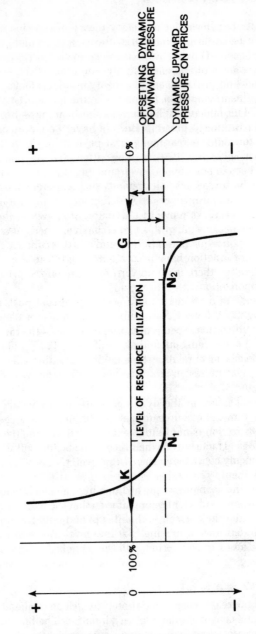

Fig. 3   Cost Push Dynamic Phillips Curve Relationship

N_1 LOW LEVEL OF FULL EMPLOYMENT
N_2 HIGH LEVEL OF FULL EMPLOYMENT

OFFSETTING DYNAMIC DOWNWARD PRESSURE

DYNAMIC UPWARD PRESSURE ON PRICES

0%

G

N_2

LEVEL OF RESOURCE UTILIZATION

N_1

K

100%

UPWARD AND DOWNWARD PRESSURE ON THE PRICE LEVEL

The problem has worsened over the past 40 years for four reasons. First the consumption patterns of individuals have changed toward an increasing variety of goods. Downward pressure decreased as the relative cost of buyers' monopolization increased.

The second and probably most important reason is changing social norms. Society previously accepted the hardship and distress of the unemployed. Once the unemployed were sufficiently hungry, they would be forced to work for less; and as the number of hungry unemployed increased, so too would competition. In the postwar era we have both eliminated depression and reduced the suffering caused by unemployment through a variety of government programs. In doing so, however, we have also reduced the downward pressure on prices exerted by unemployment.

The third reason for the worsening inflation problem is the increase in wealth that has occurred. Security is a luxury, and as incomes have risen, so too has society's expenditure on security. But security frees individuals from the competitive pressures of the market and, hence, reduces competition's effectiveness.

The final reason is the *Law of Diminishing Marginal Control* which states that as any new method of control is used, it will have a diminished effectiveness the next time it is used, until it finally arrives at its "steady-state" effectiveness. As governments have attempted to control inflation by monetary policy, private individuals have developed institutions which provide alternative credit sources in order to avoid the control. Once developed, they reduce the effectiveness of future monetary control.

MAP: AN ALTERNATIVE METHOD OF INSTITUTING A DOWNWARD PRESSURE

Nothing in the preceding analysis suggests that the present method of controlling inflation is either inoptimal or inequitable. That question can be determined only by comparing it to alternative methods. One such method is MAP, the market antiinflation plan, developed jointly by Abba Lerner and me. Under MAP, sellers raising their quantity weighted input prices are required to pay other sellers to lower their quantity weighted input prices by an equal offsetting amount. This means that only relative price changes are allowed; no price level changes can occur (other than technical definitional changes). In this way MAP institutes a direct downward pressure on the price level which offsets the dynamic upward pressure. MAP acts as a *tax on monopolization* and allows the economy to expand to a higher level of resource utilization than would otherwise be possible.

MAP also provides a useful framework within which one can test the competing hypotheses. It is, in a sense, the "shadow price" of raising prices, or a measure of the level of monopolization. Static neoclassical economic theory as embodied in the natural rate hypothesis allows for no monopolization; it would suggest that the price of raising prices—the

MAP credit price—should be zero as long as there is no "excess demand." Any expected excess demand should push the price of MAP credit to its full value. Similarly any excess supply would push the MAP credit price to its full *negative* value.

The dynamic real theory of inflation would predict a quite different behavior of MAP credit prices. Specifically, it would suggest that there will be a positive MAP credit price over a wide range of output levels and that it will vary only slightly with variations in output levels.

Most neoclassical economists expect that MAP credit will have a continually positive price, *even though their formal* underlying theory predicts differently. Perhaps this reflects the dichotomy between their heuristic understanding of the economy, which is dynamic, and their formal modeling, which is static.

CONCLUSION

The issues raised in this paper have not been adequately explored. Innumerable questions remain on the specific formulation of many of the ideas. Yet, it does provide a general framework within which to begin a dynamic analysis and come to grips with inflation.

References

Andrews, P.W.S. *On Competition in Economic Theory* (London, 1964).

Arrow, K. "Toward a Theory of Price Adjustment" in M. Abromovitz (Ed.), *The Allocation of Economic Resources* (Stanford, Calif., 1959).

Bain, J.S. *Barriers to New Competition* (Cambridge, Mass., 1956).

Chamberlin, E.H. *The Theory of Monopolistic Competition* (Cambridge, Mass., 1933).

Clark, J.B. *Distribution of Wealth* (New York, 1899).

Clark, J.M. *Competition as a Dynamic Process* (Washington, D.C., 1961).

Colander, D., and Gigliatti, G. "On Price Flexibility," *Journal of Economics*, 1978.

Colander, D. "Tax and Market Based Incomes Policies: The Interface between Theory and Practice" in M. Claudon (Ed.), *Incomes Policies for the United States: New Approaches* (Boston, 1980).

Galbraith, J.K. *American Capitalism: The Concept of Countervailing Power* (Boston, 1952).

Gordon, D., and Hynes, A. "On the Theory of Price Dynamics" in E. Phelps (Ed.), *Microeconomic Foundations of Employment and Inflation Theory* (New York, 1970).

Kirzner, I.M. *Competition and Entrepreneurship* (Chicago, 1973).

Knight, F.H. *Risk, Uncertainty and Profit* (Boston, 1921).

Lerner, A., and Colander, D. *MAP, A Market Anti-inflation Plan* (New York, 1980).

Marshall, Alfred. *Principles of Economics* (London, 1890).

Phelps, E., and Winter, S. "Optimal Price Policy under Atomistic Competition," in Phelps (Ed.), *Microeconomic Foundations of Employment and Inflation Theory* (New York, 1970).

Robinson, J. "The Impossibility of Competition," in E.H. Chamberlin (Ed.), *Monopoly and Competition and Their Regulation* (New York, 1954).

Schumpeter, J. *The Theory of Economic Development* (Cambridge, Mass., 1934).

Scitovsky, T. "Market Power and Inflation," *Economica*, 1978a.

Scitovsky, T. "Asymmetries in Economics," *Scottish Journal of Political Economy*, 1978b.

A Theory of Institutional Inflation

JANOS HORVATH

INSTITUTIONAL INFLATION ROOTED IN MISAPPLIED GRANTS: A SKETCH

That prices rise when demand exceeds supply is a phenomenon observed through the ages. It is also accurate to say that when supply lags behind demand, prices rise. Now the time has come to restate the interaction between the two actors. This restatement sheds light on the current seemingly paradoxical inflation-unemployment dilemma.

The reason for supply lag could be natural calamity, lack of adequate capacity, or capacity underutilization. Understandably, unmet demand sets off price inflation. Supply lag caused by capacity underutilization leaves some of the factors of production idle; hence underemployment of labor, machines, and land. The very supply drag that causes involuntary unemployment of labor also simultaneously causes the price level to rise. So this train of thought suggests that in the contemporary American economy there is inflation because there is unemployment.

The thickening institutional entanglements of the contemporary American economy have become accompanied by aggravating restraints of performance and production. Paradoxical systemic rearrangements evolved wherein "*implicit grants*" (i.e., subsidies, bounties, tributes, monopoly profits) accrue to strategically situated groups *for the restraint of supply*. The process amounts to reward for nonachievement and reinforcement of *negative* achievement. In more and more sectors of the economy, income shares are kept rigid, sometimes even increase in spite of disservice rendered. This anomaly creeps in and is perpetuated by laws and conventions which stifle dynamic market adjustments, such as cost-cutting technologies and managerial innovations. To make matters worse, the costs of institutionalized inefficiencies are enhanced by the costs of compliance with new vintages of regulation.

The sequence, which runs from restraint of trade to capacity underemployment to product shortages and to higher prices, has a sophisticated microeconomic underpinning and has evolved into a folklore of antitrust. Yet it is crucial to remember that the fashionable scapegoat of antitrust occupies only one place among several protagonists. There are others whose privileged status became institutionalized through laws, regulations, and conventions. They include the beneficiaries of trade protection who retard industrial progress and hold prices above the competitive level; the recipients of subsidies in agriculture who pledge to limit land cultivation; labor unions and professional associations that have power to hold down the supply of skill and service through exclusion of applicants; slum clearance legislation which reduces the supply of cheap housing units, and so on.

Usually, government regulations of business originate from the premise that unfettered production and exchange bring about consequences that conflict with certain societal targets. The visible hand of the regulator is assigned to supersede the invisible hand of the market. One important characteristic of all business regulation is that it also alters the distribution of income and wealth. Therein lies strong motivation for favoring or opposing a particular regulation, or regulatory reform, by special interest groups.

Benefits accruing to gainers and burdens inflicted on losers can be effectively traced and illuminated within the framework of *implicit grants*. Implicit grants result whenever governmental regulations intervene in economic transactions in such a way that prices, or the terms of trade of the contracting parties, are affected.

To advance a particular objective, the lawmaker may bestow privileges or impose constraints by enacting a regulation. The illusion that regulation is virtuous because it is well intended routinely beclouds the costs of eroded efficiency. To compound the irony, benefits and burdens are not readily detectable and they frequently accrue to unintended parties. Instead of remedying market failures, the regulation-induced grants economy is generally imbued with *perverse effects*.

The extra income secured over what it would be under conditions of market competition amounts to that implicit grant which prompts lobbying against market-oriented legislation. Implicit grant flows tend to shrink if the competitive market mechanism solves the task of allocation and distribution. The domain of implicit grants expands if market solutions are replaced by legal-judicial decisions. Redistributional consequences notwithstanding, granting exemptions from the competitive market's discipline tends to reduce the supply of products and thereby fuels price inflation.

This is the clue explaining why in market capitalism the thickening entanglements with regulation have an influential constituency. On principle, the capitalist businessman resents governmental intervention initially, but as time passes, accommodations are found so that regulations are clutched as protective umbrellas. This alliance of government bureaucracy and business management is joined by labor unions. The inflationary impact of the large mass of small regulations is underrated, as if forgetting that little streams make great rivers (21, 37, 50).

The idea of *institutional inflation*[1] *via misapplied grants* sheds new light on the inflation-unemployment paradox. Misguided economic regulations distort the market and give rise to implicit grants which, in turn, reinforce inflationary dynamics. The elimination of such pathological grant flows could remove the motivation for supply drag. The ensuing effective capacity utilization, encouragement to new investments, and subsequent cost reduction—all tempered by the fresh breeze of market competition—could pave the way to inhibiting price increases and occasionally even reverse them.

ON PARTIALLY DEPENDABLE THEORIES

The notion of supply drag helps to put into perspective the conventional inflation theories. Demand pull generates stress mainly because supply lags. Cost push that shifts supply backward stems from rigidities. Last year's experiences generate expectations which stimulate the inflationary cycle. Compliance with certain environmental and safety regulations imposes wastefulness on business. Government deficits grow as public programs complement and replace private activities. Money supplies increase to accommodate transactions in inflated face values. All the prevalent theories have some validity, yet, alas, each remains inadequate in itself because each provides only a partial explanation.

The inflationary recessions of the 1970s have damaged the image of the American economy as well as the reputation of economic science. Comparisons of actual and potential output during the decade estimate a GNP gap of $650–950 billion while sizable proportions of labor, equipment, and land remained idle. Even a fraction of the foregone income could have eased the pressure of such national priority needs as technological progress, energy development, and environmental protection. That chronic slack in resource utilization of this magnitude has been accompanied by persistent inflation causes puzzlement and prompts soul-searching among economists. Apparently, the dominant theories of our time do not adequately abstract contemporary realities. Yet these theories remain at the foundation of national economic policy—a bleak outlook indeed.

Ironically, all the prevalent inflation theories have some validity, yet each remains inadequate in itself because each provides only a partial explanation. Governmental budgetary deficits have become chronic and do exceed the rationale of countercyclical fiscal measures. Instead of countering genuine business cycles, monetary policy also accommodates election cycles. So both policy tools convey demand-pull impulses. Cost-push impulses stem from efforts to catch up with, and gain advances in, setting wages and prices. Demand shift caused by new products creates bottlenecks which lead to wage increases which, in turn, are claimed also in the declining industries. When labor productivity grows more slowly than wage increases, the result is rising prices. Expectation of continuing price hikes in the future triggers a compensatory wage increase in advance. Likewise, present consumer expenditures—particularly for housing and durable goods—tend to become excessive if future price hikes are expected.

It appears that the several agents of inflation form a sort of seamless web of interacting forces. The major unsettled questions concern the details of the transmission mechanism from the creation of demand and supply through inflation. If there is any element of consensus among the contending schools, it is that much more theoretical exploration as well as empirical research is needed before macroeconomic policies become more effective.[2]

While acknowledging each of the prevalent inflation theories, a generalized thesis of this writer is that *the inflationary recession of the 1970s is a phenomenon of institutionally perpetuated disequilibrium between aggregate demand and aggregate supply.* On one hand, aggregate demand increases steadily because of a blend of such primary forces as persistent government deficits, environmental and safety requirements, natural resource depletion, built-in obsolescence, and aggressive marketing. On the other hand, aggregate supply increases only unevenly and generally remains restrained below potential owing to governmental regulations and oligopolistic practices in the product as well as factor markets. Conceivably, from time to time, a leading role will be assumed by one or another of the inflationary actors, such as excessive money, excessive demand, cost push, and expectationary dynamics. These transitory protagonists do not negate that through the longer stretch, the most potent source of inflationary unemployment is capacity underutilization rooted in institutional restraints. Under the umbrella of the institutional inflation hypothesis it will become feasible to trace the synergistic collaboration of all actors.

The institutionalized underemployment that has reached onerous proportions by the 1970s can be traced to three general causes as these evolved historically: (1) monopolistic practices, (2) old economic regulations, and (3) new societal regulations. First, that restraint of trade causes higher prices is a phenomenon long known. This was the rationale for the Sherman Act back in 1890. In the same vein, attention turned to labor unions and also professional associations which have acquired degrees of legalized power to hold down the supply of skill and service through exclusion of applicants. Second, the older economic regulations—i.e., ICC, CAB, acreage control, and scores of others—have major impact by setting rates, licensing routes, adjusting investments, fixing profit, determining quotas, and numerous other interventions. Widely diffused and even when hardly detectable, their role in stagflation is very significant. Third, the societal regulations of the immediate past ten years—mainly environmental protection and occupational safety—have accentuated inflationary pressures because of the redirection of sizable resources.

To complicate the situation, the major protagonists are accompanied by auxiliary actors on the scene: the beneficiary of trade protection who retards industrial progress and holds prices above competitive level; the slum clearance legislation which reduces the supply of low-priced housing units; the governmentally fostered merchant marine industry; the wastefulness imposed on business by compliance with regulatory paperwork; conflicting and inept regulations that discourage technological advance and entrepreneurial innovation, and so on.

The leitmotif of my thesis is that institutionalized obstacles obstruct performance. The institutions of the society have become increasingly geared to the idea of *protecting* privileges which entitle organized groups to secure their particular slice in the national pie, once attained. Fading are the voices which advocate that the rules of the game, not secured privileges, are worthy of protection. For almost half a century, the list lengthened to include all those to whom the society has granted a privilege of one sort or another. The *visible hands* of special interests hold down the *invisible hands* of free enterprise competition, with the resultant underperformance of the national economy. The competitor preempts competition, and ironically, the regulated capitalist businessman advocates continued regulation.[3]

Critics of the institutional inflation hypothesis may argue that the rigidities described have been present in the American economy for longer than the last decade, therefore these could not make the difference between the high inflation during the 1970s vis-à-vis the mild inflation during the earlier decades. The criticism only helps to put into focus the dynamics of institutional inflation.

In fact, the many seemingly minute changes evolving inside the American economy during the past half century have by now reached a threshold where they alter systemic relationships. The cumulative institutionalization has been evolving somewhat similarly to the accumulation of toxins in the human body, a process which goes unnoticed or causes little concern, until the toxins begin to act as carcinogenic agents. The inflation-unemployment phenomena of recent years baffle conventional analysis because their underlying causes have been creeping up gradually. Little wonder that the conventional concepts of economic theory do not fully suffice, even though they could diagnose the earlier past satisfactorily. Today, the dismissal of hosts of institutional rigidities as scratches on the surface actually means neglecting the many *self-inflicted* wounds,[4] each of which does contribute to distress (54, 33, 34).

SUPPLY DRAG EMANATES FROM CAPACITY RESTRAINT

Upon recognizing the crucial role of institutional restraints, the conventional tools of both microeconomics and macroeconomics lend themselves to reconcile the inflation-unemployment contrariety. In the sphere of microeconomics, the trend has been toward increasingly inelastic supply functions. Such supply rigidities result either from old-fashioned monopolistic practices, or from labor union power, or more manifestly from pro-liferating governmental regulations. Clearly, all institutional rearrange-ments and public policies that lead to some unbending of inelastic supply functions—in the product market as well as the factor market—could reduce inflation.

In the sphere of macroeconomics there are more complexities. A great deal of the discourse is conducted around the Phillips Curve concept. The earlier Phillips Curve notions dominant during the 1960s—negative slope offering trade-off options between inflation and unemployment—have been impaired during the 1970s when tradeoffs became either blurred or outright nonexistent. By now a revised view gains in acceptance, accord-ing to which the Phillips Curve has negative slope only in the short run, but in the long run it is vertical at the natural rate of unemployment. Countercyclical monetary and fiscal policies can reduce unemployment below the natural rate only temporarily and even then, at the cost of acquiescence to accelerating inflation rates (64).

That economics is a *dismal* science has become manifest anew, as policy makers find themselves no longer free to choose between two evils or some mixture of them. Rather, both inflation and unemployment must be endured with aggravating discomfort. Countercyclical monetary and fis-cal policy measures do not work as they used to. Expansionary monetary and fiscal policies tend to fuel inflation with or without stimulating out-put. Conversely, contractionary monetary and fiscal policies tend to re-strain output while curbing or boosting price levels. Such challenge to, or disproof of, the neoclassical paradigm generates much controversy in contemporary political economy.

A resolution of this controversy may be assisted by shifting the locus of analysis from comparing inflation and unemployment rates to comparing inflation and capacity utilization rates. Table 1 brings together data that trace through 10 years, 1968–77, rates of capacity utilization representing total manufacturing, as reported in the Federal Reserve Board series. For the same 10 years inflation is reported through the Consumer Price Index. It seems appropriate to scrutinize this particular decade because it is the period when thickening institutional rigidities have reached the threshold of altering systemic and structural relationships within the national econ-omy.

It is noteworthy that the higher rates of inflation do not occur when capacity utilization is highest. For example, 1975 saw the lowest rate of capacity utilization, i.e., 73.6 percent, while the inflation rate was the second highest, i.e., 9.1 percent; the lowest rates of inflation do not coin-cide with the lowest rates of capacity utilization. The association is almost in reverse. For example, 1968 was one of the lowest inflation years, 4.2 percent, coinciding with the second highest capacity utilization rate, 87.0 percent.

Shifting the focus of observation from absolute numbers to trends, certain relationships appear contrary to conventional expectations. For example, from 1973 to 1974, while the capacity utilization rate declined from

Table 1. Rates of Capacity Utilization and Inflation, 1968–1977

Year	Capacity Utilization FRB*	Δ	Inflation CPI	Δ	Direction
1968	87.0		4.2		
1969	86.2	-0.8	5.4	1.2	Opposite
1970	79.2	-7.0	5.9	0.5	Opposite
1971	78.0	-1.2	4.3	-1.6	Parallel
1972	83.1	5.1	3.3	-1.0	Opposite
1973	87.5	4.4	6.2	2.9	Parallel
1974	84.2	-3.3	11.0	4.8	Opposite
1975	73.6	-10.6	9.1	-1.9	Parallel
1976	80.2	6.6	5.8	-3.3	Opposite
1977	82.4	2.2	6.5	0.7	Parallel

NOTE: *Total manufacturing in Federal Reserve Board series.
Source: Economic Report of the President, 1977.

87.5 percent to 84.2 percent (-3.3 percent) the inflation rate increased from 6.2 to 11.0 percent (+4.8 percent). The direction of change went opposite. Similar patterns prevailed when business conditions changed. From 1975 to 1976, capacity utilization increased from 73.6 percent to 80.2 percent (+6.6 percent) while the inflation rate declined from 9.1 percent to 5.8 percent (-3.3 percent).

If the focus of analysis were shifted from annual figures and changes to the observation of time lags, the capacity utilization vs. price inflation data still would not resurrect the Phillips Curve as a viable policy tool. The lag adjustments may reflect fixed price contracts, union wage settlements, or the formation of inflationary expectations. In any case, the literature by now offers quite firm theoretical foundations as well as convincing empirical proofs that the Phillips Curve becomes even less valid for the long run than in the short run.

Without further scrutinizing the capacity utilization vs. inflation relationship, it is clear that the conventional widom is due for some rethinking. The Phillips Curve might have—beyond negative slope on the short run and vertical slope on the long run—periods of positive slope. Indeed, the positively sloped Phillips Curve is deftly dramatized by the *discomfort index,* which is the arithmetic sum of unemployment rate plus inflation rate.[5] This could be regarded as another signaling mechanism offering corroborative evidence that supply drag deserves attention.

The problem is greater than a limping policy tool; the whole Keynesian-cum-neoclassical paradigm has been weakened. Repeatedly, increasing rates of unemployment failed to bring about price deflation. When recessionary aggregate demand—which in the neoclassical framework predicates a *deflationary gap*—continued to coexist with inflation, there emerged a melancholy pronouncement, that *the rules of economics do not work as they used to.*

It was not the rules of economics that failed. Somehow, half of them have temporarily slipped under the embellishment of a Keynesian-cum-neoclassical paradigm. If the neglected half of macroeconomic activity, namely, aggregate supply, is considered in conjunction with aggregate demand, then some of the disjointed members of the economic body fall into place. It is a pivotal Keynesian idea that aggregate demand shifts determine the level of national economic activities. The shifting aggregate demand is posed against a potential full employment output which serves as the benchmark for aggregate supply. So at the full employment level an overheated or underemployed state of affairs could be revealed through an *inflationary gap* or a *deflationary gap*, respectively. But the model breaks down under the weight of stagflation. The failure results from the unbalanced attention given in the Keynesian framework to aggregate supply, which is assumed to follow aggregate demand.

Keynes described the 1930s adequately, but his paradigm is inadequate for the 1970s. Unlike the Great Depression, nowadays aggregate supply chronically lags behind aggregate demand. Increasingly the impact of regulations, coupled with the special interest of operators, does result in capacity restraint. In aggravating the situation, not only capacity utilization lags, but investment (the building of new capacity) also lags behind what it could be under the fresher breeze of a more competitive environment. What really matters is that purchasers are trying to obtain more than is actually being produced and they thereby are inflating the price level. Conceptually, whether the underlying reason is natural calamity, lack of adequate capacity, or simply restraint of production, supply lags behind demand.

STAGNATION SUSTAINS INFLATION: GRAPHICAL EXPOSITIONS

Figure 1 illuminates the pertinent macroeconomic relationships. If aggregate demand is $(C+I+G)_1$ while the full productive capacity is at Y_1, the level of national economic activities will be OY_1 and stable prices prevail. But if owners, operators, or regulators restrain capacity, the actual performance may stay below potential. The subpotential level may be at Y_2. Consequently, aggregate supply tends to fall short of aggregate demand and there emerges b-d, an "active inflationary gap" (33, 747).

Someone might dispute this approach by arguing that instead of Y_1 the restrained level Y_2 should be regarded as full employment capacity which in turn would set in motion dynamic equilibrating processes to lower aggregate demand to $(C+I+G)_2$. If so, point b should eventually prevail as

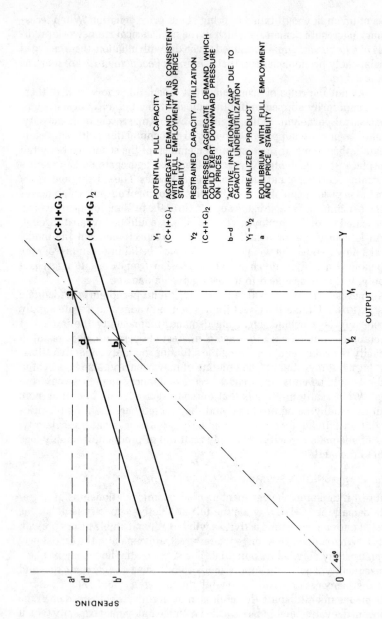

Fig. 1   Graphical Exposition of Inflationary Recession

Y_1 POTENTIAL FULL CAPACITY

$(C+I+G)_1$ AGGREGATE DEMAND THAT IS CONSISTENT WITH FULL EMPLOYMENT AND PRICE STABILITY

Y_2 RESTRAINED CAPACITY UTILIZATION

$(C+I+G)_2$ DEPRESSED AGGREGATE DEMAND WHICH COULD EXERT DOWNWARD PRESSURE ON PRICES

$b-d$ "ACTIVE INFLATIONARY GAP" DUE TO CAPACITY UNDERUTILIZATION

Y_1-Y_2 UNREALIZED PRODUCT

a EQUILIBRIUM WITH FULL EMPLOYMENT AND PRICE STABILITY

full employment equilibrium with stable prices. The objection, however, overlooks the obvious reality that there exist factors of production (labor, land, capital) which claim rewards even when idle. For example, just because some equipment is left outside the production function, the corporation does not cease to pay interest on the bonds which financed that particular investment outlay initially. The idle capacity also drains such fixed costs as property tax, insurance premium, night watchman's wage, etc. A variety of fixed costs must be met for the full capacity Y_1, and not just the restricted capacity, Y_2. In the broader macroeconomic context, several other items belong to this category, such as support to unemployed labor, featherbedding, agricultural subsidies to restrain acreage, and so on.

The label "active inflationary gap" is quite consistent with the nomenclature of macroeconomics. True, under the neo-Keynesian conventional nomenclature only a deflationary gap could exist during recession, not an inflationary gap. Nevertheless, here the adjectives "inflationary" and "deflationary" are perceived as functional and dynamic descriptions rather than taxonomical and static terms. What really matters is that purchasers are trying to buy more than is actually being produced. The inflationary pressure evolves whether the cause be crop failure, devastating earthquake, institutional rigidity, or any sort of supply drag.

It follows from this reasoning that in Figure 1 even some relatively higher amount of spending, such as $O\text{-}a'$, need not cause inflation if full capacity Y_1 is allowed to produce. But with the curbed capacity Y_2 even the lower spending level $O\text{-}d'$ becomes inflationary. Only spending as low as $O\text{-}b'$ could promise stable prices. Since the situation results *not* from absence of employable capacity but institutional restraints, the label "active inflationary gap" does describe the phenomenon aptly.

Upon acknowledging that institutional restraints are at the roots of the problems, it becomes evident that inflation and unemployment are mutually reinforcing forces. The distance between potential full capacity and the restrained capacity, $Y_1\text{-}Y_2$, is an expression of underemployment. A comparison of the distances between the two levels of expenditure, $O\text{-}b'$ and $O\text{-}d'$ approximates the intensity of inflation. It illustrates that the reduced bundle of national products $Y_1\text{-}Y_2$ will be purchased with an inflated amount of expenditures. Now, if in this situation the vertical distance $O\text{-}d'$ is viewed as the expression of aggregate demand and the horizontal distance $O\text{-}Y_2$ as aggregate supply, then it is visible that a disequilibrium exists $(O\text{-}d' > O\text{-}Y_2$, i.e., AD $>$ AS). This disequilibrium causes the active inflationary gap $b\text{-}d$.

The recent economic history of the United States receives some illumination in the framework described here. The substantial increase in government expenditures beginning in 1966, without a concomitant reduction in consumption and investment spending, caused aggregate demand to shift upward as depicted in Graph 2 by schedule $(C+I+G)_3$. If the nation's

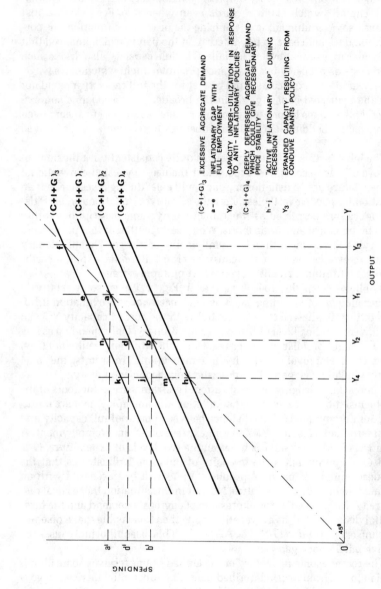

Fig. 2 Inflation Intensified Through Supply Restraint

SPENDING

$(C+I+G)_3$
$(C+I+G)_1$
$(C+I+G)_2$
$(C+I+G)_4$

$(C+I+G)_3$ EXCESSIVE AGGREGATE DEMAND

a – e   INFLATIONARY GAP WITH FULL EMPLOYMENT

Y_4 CAPACITY UNDER-UTILIZATION IN RESPONSE TO ANTI-INFLATIONARY POLICIES

$(C+I+G)_4$ DEEPLY DEPRESSED AGGREGATE DEMAND WHICH COULD GIVE RECESSIONARY PRICE STABILITY

h – j   "ACTIVE INFLATIONARY GAP" DURING RECESSION

Y_3 EXPANDED CAPACITY RESULTING FROM CONDUIVE GRANTS POLICY

OUTPUT

45°

Y_3 Y_1 Y_2 Y_4

Y

productive capacity utilization remained near the previous underemploy-ment level, Y_1, then inflationary gap a-e would represent the intensity of pressure. More likely, capacity utilization remained near the previous underemployment level, Y_2, and the active inflationary gap became larger, b-n. Belatedly, policies were imposed to combat demand-pull inflation, but no significant demand reduction followed because of inflationary ex-pectations, namely, fear of shortages and runaway prices, that prompted people to spend more (39, 17). At the same time, some businessmen, expecting a decline in demand in response to restrictive policies, actually reduced production and supply. Also, supply functions shifted backward as higher rates of taxation and interest were added to the costs of produc-tion, maintenance, and replacement.

Because of such a blend of "rational" and "psychological" behavior on the part of the consumer and the producer, in certain industries aggregate supply might have fallen more than aggregate demand. On Figure 2, level of national economic activities Y_4 is the capacity underutilization in re-sponse to antiinflationary policies; schedule $(C+I+G)_4$ shows that imagi-nary deeply depressed aggregate demand which could give recessionary price stability. The active inflationary gap grew to h-j. Of course, distance h-j is valid on the assumption that monetary and fiscal policies could succeed in depressing aggregate demand to $(C+I+G)_1$. Since this goal could be achieved only partially, the active inflationary gap grew wider; a dis-tance from point h to another point somewhere between j and k: the worst being h-k. Here is a stylized exposition of events as double-digit inflation joins with high rate of unemployment.

Having sketched the argument within the framework of macroeconom-ics, the application of microeconomic concepts may further illuminate the same problem. Figure 3 depicts an industry or the whole national econ-omy. With demand function DD and supply function SS, the price level is OP and the product turnover is OQ. The peculiarity of the situation is reflected by the flabellate supply function. Curve SS is the amount of aggregate output that firms would, in the absence of institutionalized (i.e., restrictive) pricing, want to supply at each price level. Curve SS' repre-sents the reduced supply of aggregate output under institutionalized pric-ing. Capacity underutilization results in the higher price level OP' and the reduced output OQ'. Similarly, on the factor market, curve SS" depicts the supply of strategically positioned agents of production which receive higher factor earnings reflecting higher costs, as shown by price level OP".

In essence, owing to institutionalized constraints and privileges, supply declines and the price level rises. This output readjustment is depicted by the distance E'F and labeled "inflationary gap in the product market." In a similar fashion, the reduction of factor supply is shown by the distance E"H, labeled "inflationary gap in the factor market."

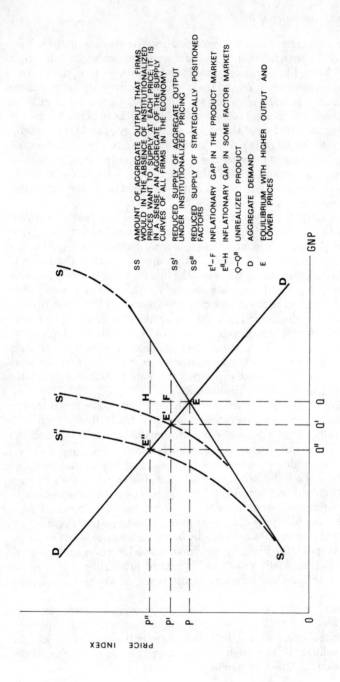

SS — AMOUNT OF AGGREGATE OUTPUT THAT FIRMS WOULD IN THE ABSENCE OF INSTITUTIONALIZED PRICES WANT TO SUPPLY AT EACH PRICE. IT IS IN A SENSE AN AGGREGATE OF THE SUPPLY CURVES OF ALL FIRMS IN THE ECONOMY

SS' — REDUCED SUPPLY OF AGGREGATE OUTPUT UNDER INSTITUTIONALIZED PRICING

SS'' — REDUCED SUPPLY OF STRATEGICALLY POSITIONED FACTORS

E'–F — INFLATIONARY GAP IN THE PRODUCT MARKET

E''–H — INFLATIONARY GAP IN SOME FACTOR MARKETS

Q–Q'' — UNREALIZED PRODUCT

D — AGGREGATE DEMAND

E — EQUILIBRIUM WITH HIGHER OUTPUT AND LOWER PRICES

Fig.3 Market Inflationary Gaps

The above diagrammatic innovations, which display how unrealized product leads to inflation, can shed some light on the inflationary recession vigorously unfolding during 1980. A stylized representation of the main factors is in Figure 4, "Unrealized Output Intensifies Inflation." As institutional rigidities cause supply functions to become increasingly inelastic, the potential aggregate supply (AS_p) shifts to restrained aggregate supply (AS_l). By estimating potential GNP at $2500 billion while restrained GNP is at $2300 billion, there appears a GNP gap of $200 billion. This unrealized product, given a static aggregate demand function, causes the price level to rise, say, by 9 percent.

Quite likely the approximated 9 percent inflation rate could go even higher: (1) if aggregate demand does not shift backward due to expectations and CPI adjusted pay checks; (2) if higher interest rates shift average and marginal costs upward, causing supply functions to shift backward. Even if contradictory economic policies succeeded in creating a recession and reduced demand, the cost functions remain high enough to perpetuate inflation further. So the bitter medicine could cause more pain than cure. Clearly, given the recent ailment of the American economy—i.e., institutional rigidities—there will be no thoroughgoing cure until the diagnostic competence better comprehends the supply side impairment.

ON THE ROAD OF RIGIDITIES

In the 1930s Keynes showed governments how, by manipulating the level of demand, they could promote full employment. The relative success with which the policy tools have been used has created conditions for another problem, rising prices, against which the tools are less effective. Even a most circumspect control of demand does not by itself do the trick. A reduced demand can still be excessive and will force prices upward if supply declines by greater proportions.

The specter of Ricardo's conquest over Malthus may haunt us in reverse fashion. For a century Say's Law, "supply creates its own demand," was upheld as an article of faith in spite of recurrent business cycles. Eventually, Keynes challenged forcefully the doctrine's tenableness. Attention turned to demand. Somehow, the pendulum has swung with such momentum that a generation of Keynesians seems to think that—to paraphrase an inverted Say's Law—demand creates its own supply. The current failure of demand management to conduce simultaneous compliance on the supply side makes one wonder how long it will take before that Keynesian orthodoxy loosens.[6]

Whether from the vantage point of analytical reformulation or the perplexities of the state of the art, the issue at hand is an "underemployment inflation." Aggregate supply lags behind aggregate demand. There exists a strong element of causation that runs from underemployment to product shortages and to higher prices.

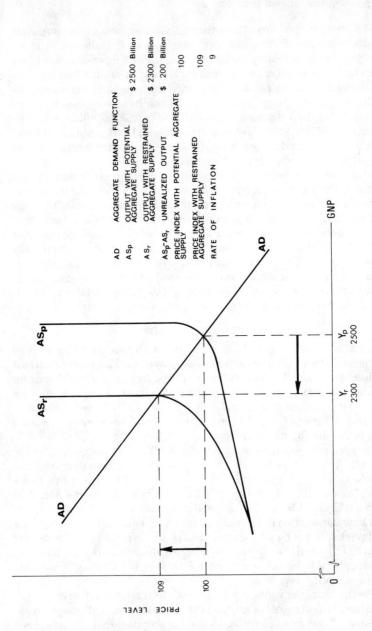

AD	AGGREGATE DEMAND FUNCTION	
AS_p	OUTPUT WITH POTENTIAL AGGREGATE SUPPLY	$ 2500 Billion
AS_r	OUTPUT WITH RESTRAINED AGGREGATE SUPPLY	$ 2300 Billion
AS_p-AS_r	UNREALIZED OUTPUT	$ 200 Billion
	PRICE INDEX WITH POTENTIAL AGGREGATE SUPPLY	100
	PRICE INDEX WITH RESTRAINED AGGREGATE SUPPLY	109
	RATE OF INFLATION	9

Fig.-4   Unrealized Output Intensifies Inflation

The rigidities of the market system are often magnified by ill-advised governmental regulations. After two to three decades of recognition gap, the phenomenon has by now begun to capture attention. Pondering achievable employment policy goals, William Fellner points out that "institutional rigidities exist largely because the bulk of the public misunderstands their consequences and has not been made aware of the harm they do" (18, 138). Eckstein and Girola observe: "Structural changes in the economy's markets have made the economy somewhat more inflation-prone. . . . An exceptionally unfavorable combination of unemployment and inflation can be seen to originate in these independent elements, which are then amplified by the endogenous wage-price-unemployment mechanisms" (15, 332–33). Wachter and Williamson conclude "additional efforts to examine institutional infrastructure . . . will serve further to illustrate the mechanism of inflation" (71, 569).

Empirical evidence abounds. A deft eye opener is John R. Meyer's assessment of transportation regulation:

> Whatever its early historical justification, or even possible successes, government regulation of transportation in the United States is today undeniably a failure. It does not serve anyone's interests well. For consumers and shippers, regulation creates important inefficiencies in transportation services. For many carriers, particularly railroads and airlines, regulation results in return on equity that is lower than that of almost any other major private sector of the U.S. economy. . . . Low returns on capital have driven investment out of the industry, even where it is seemingly still justified by identifiable demand (49, 44). Transportation regulation represents a large departure from the standard American norm of using the marketplace to indicate when, where, and how economic activity should occur. In lieu of the marketplace, a legal-judicial process is used instead, a process that looks backward to precedent rather than forward to evolving technology and demand patterns (49, 44). Technological progress tends to undermine the status quo and to provide alternative means of meeting various transport needs, thus complicating the life of the regulator. It is not uncommon, therefore, to see regulators adopt a very skeptical attitude toward new technology regardless of whether the change could potentially produce lower rates and costs. The classic recent example of regulatory obstruction of technological innovation was the ICC's refusal for many years to allow the Southern Railway to use larger hopper cars, so-called "Big Johns," for moving grain (49, 45–46).

Browsing among public policies toward business provides numerous odd cases. Here are two stories in The Wall Street Journal. One headline reads: "In Pennsylvania a Man Can Be a Lawbreaker for Selling Milk

Cheap" (72). From the story one learns that the United Dairy Farmer Cooperative Association in Pittsburgh has been declared illegal by state authorities and a federal court. Unless the Supreme Court agrees to rule on the case, the manager is bound for jail because in defiance of price-fixing regulations, he sells a gallon of milk 18 cents cheaper and pays slightly more to farmers than other dairies do. The other ill-advised regulation illustrates the complexities of a situation when benefit to some enterprising producers and the mass of consumers, which would result from lower costs and prices, can be prevented by a much smaller group's already established narrow vested interests. "Several railroads want to cut rates for soybean meal sold by Midwestern processors to Southeastern chicken farmers. But their case has been mired by regulatory and other rate-setting proceedings for three years. Southeastern soybean and cottonseed processors are blocking the rate cut by *protesting the potential competition*" (73). (Italics added.) Amazingly enough, time and again the regulatory bureaucracy condones the encroachment of narrow special interests over broad public interests, while ignoring the competitive free enterprise philosophy of the country.

Examples from the market of goods and services can be complemented by cases from the market of productive factors. At least one illustration from the labor market seems to be in order, as abstracted by Nicholas Kaldor. In an economy dominated by large corporations, price competition is not so prompt or effective as to compel firms which experience exceptional reductions in new processes (or a fast increase in selling volume, or both) to pass on the full benefit to the consumer in the form of lower prices *pari passu* with the reduction of costs. The very existence of this situation leads to wage increases that are, in a sense, unnecessarily large—i.e., they are governed by what the employer can *afford* to pay (without compromising his competitive position), not by what he *needs* to pay, in order to obtain the necessary work force (38, 708).

The ill-health of the national economy, as it appears to a seasoned diagnostician, is dramatized by Arthur M. Okun:

> The year of 1977 was marked by a host of self-inflicted wounds in the form of government policies that directly raised costs and prices. . . . Any inflationary force feeds into wages and back into prices in our economy, and hence there is no such animal as one-shot inflation. . . . The problem can be seen in perspective only if the spotlight is focused on the totality of these actions. We need a systematic public monitoring and scoring of all the microeconomic measures taken by government that raise or lower the level of costs and prices . . . [to design] measures that reduce costs through lower indirect taxes, less costly regulatory procedures, and pro-competitive institutional changes. If the public, and the policy-makers themselves,

are adequately informed, perhaps we can stop the self-inflicted wounds (54, 33-34).

Yet governmental regulations have been difficult to reform or abandon, even when recognized as counterproductive, because elements of regulation frequently tend to satisfy certain special interests, real or imaginary.[7] Historically, some business enterprises have sought to avoid competition and have sometimes been aided in doing so by regulation. Some rules and procedures create vested interests and capital values which reform would endanger (6, 146, 1977). It is not at all simple to measure the burden of governmental regulations, but some estimates exist. According to Murray L. Weidenbaum, the annual cost to the consumer of excessive federal government regulation came to over $60 billion during the early 1970s (41, 79). For a more recent year, the cost rose to $102 billion, as estimated by Secretary of Commerce Juanita M. Kreps (43). Studying truck transportation, John R. Felton concluded that entry control, rate regulation, and limitations on the operation have reduced efficiency and added to social costs at least $5.3 billion (20, 12). No doubt there are beneficiaries of the system who act rationally when advocating the perpetuation of the status quo, yet unquestionably, the gainers gain less than the losers lose.

ON THE DYNAMICS OF REGULATION: A GRANTS ECONOMICS VIEW

Whenever in the name of certain societal targets and priorities the invisible hand of the market is superseded by the visible hand of the regulator, the distribution of income and wealth is altered. The actual size and the normative impact of such redistributions can be well analyzed in the framework of grants economics.

Grants economics proposes to update the prevailing neoclassical paradigm by recognizing that some existing views about the nature of our capitalist market economy are outdated at best, and quite misleading at worst. As Martin and Anita B. Pfaff have observed in a systemic study:

> These images reflect what we have learned about our society as being a capitalist market society: economic relationships between households, firms, non-profit institutions, and the government supposedly are based largely on exchange, whereby party A gives something to party B only in exchange for a corresponding return flow of equal value. An examination of the real world will reveal, however, a vast network of nonmarket flows of exchangeables which has become so significant that it tends, by design or accident, to *distort* the prevailing exchange flows. This system of unilateral or one-way flow is termed the *grants economy* (56, 120).

A transaction, if it is not an exchange of equal values, contains a grant element. The usefulness of this framework may be grasped by applying it to familiar policy issues. The grant elements embodied in trade protection, for example, can be sorted out by contrasting the world market price with the domestic price after the imposition of a tariff. The incidence of implicit grants can be traced, as they accrue to the domestic producer and government, at the expense of the domestic consumer and foreign producer. Likewise, grant impact statements could be calculated about government policies aimed at agricultural marketing, regulation Q in banking, environmental protection, the stipulation of routes cum fares for trucks, railroads, and shipping. Other cases abound.[8]

The label *grant* is a generic term for the unmatched transaction of exchangeables when, in an accounting sense, the net worth of the grantor diminishes while the net worth of the grantee increases. This simple definition provides a compass to rectify some deeply ingrained delusions about the functioning of contemporary economic organizations (7). The conventionally held view is that goods, services, and factors of production move from one party to another at a price that generally reflects the values involved. Even though it is recognized that there exists a broad assortment of bounties (donations, subsidies) in one direction and a broad assortment of tributes (extortions, dispossessions) in the other direction, the conventional view is that these transactions occur only on the fringes. So these transactions are routinely kept outside the domain of economic inquiries. In other words, the conventional wisdom holds that quid pro quo (i.e., the exchange of equal values) is the rule and departure from it, the exception. Unfortunately, this conventional attitude unnecessarily narrows the scope and relevance of economic policy analysis (55).

Indeed, an implicit grant structure emerges whenever any regulation, concession, stipulation, or restraint does de facto alter the system of relative prices. More specifically, implicit grants result whenever governmental regulations intervene in economic transactions in such a way that prices, or the terms of trade of the contracting parties, are affected. There might be some measurement problems when the beneficiary of certain unearned gains would prefer to erase the grantee label by calling it an earning. An illustration is agricultural price support rationalized under the rubric of parity (33). Nevertheless, *as a network of policy instruments, the grants economy represents the heart of the political economy, because routinely it is by pulling the levers of positive and negative subventions (i.e., unmatched transfers) that the political system intervenes in the economic system.*

Grants economics, as it complements exchange economics, provides a framework for analyzing all aspects of transactions.[9] Conventional exchange economics deliberately ignores or downgrades many important production and distribution processes which do not fit the Procrustean bed of the neoclassical paradigm. Consequently, a case that does not fit the neat abstraction of prevalent theories is relegated to *grey areas* and the analysis continues *ceteris paribus*. But now grants cum exchange economics can overcome those inhibiting barriers that had confined analysis to rigidly defined production and distribution patterns. Such an integrative economic science—while sharpening the images of production and exchange—is capable of dealing with a largely enhanced sphere of human, social, and political interactions (63, 320–45; 55).

To pursue a policy, the lawmaker may choose to extend benefits or to impose burdens through a regulatory structure. It is a political irony that benefits or burdens may accrue to unintended parties,[10] thereby causing harm to the society at large (7, 53; 33, 744). It is a fact of life that, far from acting as an unconditioned remedy for market failures, the grants economy often is characterized by *perverse effects* (7, 55). An inventory of grant elements stemming from economic regulations tends to find more pathological grants than curative grants. Ultimately, it may become a unique contribution of grants economics to regulatory reform to diagnose and remove pathological implicit grants. Undoubtedly, such measures could reduce the absolute size yet enhance the effectiveness of the regulatory bureaucracy.[11]

IMPLICIT GRANTS AS POLICY INSTRUMENTS AGAINST INFLATION

The main theme of this essay is that institutionalized fetters on the vitality of the national economy throttle full capacity production. The implicit grants—which result from protecting privileges, from accommodating with the regulator, and from perpetuating market power—provide feedback and reinforcement to prevent reforms.[12] The disheartening trend continues as the list of those grows to whom the society has "granted" the privileges to draw gain from the restraint of performance. The paradox of misguided grants reveals itself most painfully in the inherent dynamics of a situation where those high-principled individuals who would refuse the collection of tributes are penalized as long as others ignore their own scruples. The case fits quite well the stereotype fallacy of composition.

Powerful economic and political forces which make for constancy in relative earnings in different trades and occupations and groups often prevent reform toward optimum solutions. As Kenneth Boulding explains:

It is one of the great contentions of economics that the relative price structure is important. It profoundly affects the allocation of resources, the distribution of income, and the direction of technology. There is a great deal of wisdom lying around in economics as to what an optimum price structure might be, especially when modified by a grant economy, that is, a system of one-way transfers. . . . Indeed, we have run into an impasse on macroeconomic policy precisely because we have so completely neglected the relative structure of prices and wages [by interfering with its processes and solutions] (6, 12–13).

Ultimately we are saddled with the predicament that an institutional

structure circumscribes the market forces which in response to technological change and organizational evolution would press for continuous
redistribution of factor earnings. Institutional rigidities are the prime
variable explaining why more historical downward shift of supply functions do not materialize in spite of huge social investment in infrastructure, such as interstate highways, R&D programs, mass education, and so
on.

Those who succeed in capturing disproportionate shares of the society's
progress want to make permanent the arrangements. The extra income
share secured over and above what it would be under conditions of
market competition amounts to that implicit grant which will motivate
campaigns and lobbies against market-oriented reform legislation. Notwithstanding redistributional consequences, granting such privileges reduces the supply of products and thereby inevitably stimulates price
inflation. Of course, no one of these actions can be easily excoriated as
making a critical difference in the battle against stagflation. By a national
standard, each of the sums is small; yet to people striving for benefits to
particular interest groups, the returns are very high (54, 34).

The idea of institutional inflation, as reinforced by misplaced grants,
provides an understanding of the problems at hand, and thus, brings into
sharper focus policy proposals which originate from a variety of sources.
Effective reforms, which would reduce privileges as well as burdens by
rearranging (mostly eliminating) grant flows, require prudent assessment.
The inevitable necessity of such an overhaul has been foreseen by many.
James Tobin wrote years ago: "Someday we must start on the difficult
structural reforms needed to dissolve the cruel unemployment-inflation
dilemma" (67, 107). Gottfried Haberler observed that *to the extent to
which it is possible by antitrust policy or otherwise to introduce more
competition, such policy would have antiinflationary effect* (28, 75). In
1977, Lawrence Klein in his presidential address to the American Economic Association concluded that *the Keynesian policy carried the situation only so far, and undoubtedly underestimated inflation potentials,
leaving us now at the point where new systems of thought, drawing more
on the supply side, are needed* . . . (41, 4–6).

Explicitly or implicitly, all these institutional reform ideas allow for, or
rather insist on, less restrictions in both the product and the factor markets. By pursuing the ideas outlined in this study, there will evolve ways
and means out of the maladjustments where one-fifth of manufacturing
capacity, one-fourth of land, and around 6 percent of the labor force remains perennially idle. Under a rearranged system of national priorities,
grants—implicit and explicit—would flow to those operators who, instead of practicing restraint, excel in capacity utilization and capacity
building.[13] The main thrust is toward the enhancement of supply. Alternatively, sole reliance on countercyclical policy measures, even reinforced

by curbs on wages and prices, would mean settlement for unnecessarily grave pains and still could make only limited contributions. Without impetus to supply-enhancement, the price level will continue to rise and unemployment be prone to stay high.

If there is need for some kind of breakthrough, it is not to undo evil spells, but rather to remove the roadblocks brought about by institutional ironies and intellectual inertia.

SUMMARY AND RECOMMENDATIONS

Misguided economic regulations and excessive market power give rise to pathological implicit grants which, in turn, reinforce inflationary dynamics in consort with supply restraint. Elimination of such pathological grant flows would remove the motivation for supply restraint. The resulting effective capacity utilization, cost reduction, and the breeze of market competition would work toward inhibiting price increases and occasionally even reverse them.

To prepare the stage for curing the American economy from the ailments of institutional inflation, Congress could set certain targets and specify pertinent procedures. A feasible beginning could be to require the Joint Economic Committee, in an Annual Report on Stagflation—in addition to other relevant data and analysis—to do the following:

1. inventory implicit grant elements that stem from institutional rigidities;
2. monitor all governmental regulations that raise or lower specific costs and prices, then calculate the pertaining *grant impact statement*;
3. estimate the cost-increasing vs. cost-reducing effects of environmental, health, and safety regulations so that their net effect on price levels could be gauged;
4. monitor supply restraint by business organizations and calculate *a grant impact statement* which reveals the subsidy-bounty-tribute content of each measure;
5. trace the incidence of implicit grant elements by identifying gainers, losers, and deadweight loss;
6. estimate the leverage of these grant elements on supply functions;
7. describe ongoing efforts and potential actions toward noncompetitive institutional changes for removing pathological grants that curb supply;
8. recommend alternative measures toward unbending rigidly inelastic supply functions by redirecting pathological grants toward curative roles;
9. estimate savings to the taxpayer and consumer by pruning the implicit grants economy;
10. estimate the impact of specific tax increases as well as reductions on costs and prices.

Notes

1. The notion of institutional inflation has been anticipated by several authors. Brunner and Meltzer (10) published the papers of the 1974 Carnegie-Rochester Conference under the title *Institutional Arrangements and the Inflation Problem.* William Fellner underscores that "institutional rigidities" and their consequences are misunderstood (18, 138). Wachter and Williams (71) recommend the examination of the "institutional infrastructure." Eckstein and Girola deplore the "structural changes" that have made the economy inflation-prone (15, 332). William Bryan conjectures that "the world has passed yet another watershed and it may be that a return to reasonable price stability is not attainable within the existing institutions" (11). The author of this paper discussed "Institutional Inflation Via Misapplied Grants" at the 1971 meetings of the American Economic Association (32).

2. Observing pensively that "the economy has inadequate capacity to generate the 'right' prices," Robert Solow underscores that "the basic question is *why* are wages and prices sticky? The persistence of disequilibrium prices and interest rates means that there are Pareto-improvements available that are not being exhausted. Somewhere there are simple or complicated bargains that could be struck from which all participants would gain. Why do those transactions fail to occur?" Labeling the phenomenon a serious intellectual problem Solow recommends the diversion of some research resources in this direction (65, 11, 16).

3. In the words of Alfred Kahn: "Inflation has become a chronic problem . . . because we have experienced a decreasing willingness to rely upon and expose ourselves to the functioning of an uncontrolled market. The fact is that most people in this country don't like the way a truly competitive economy operates, and have found ways of protecting themselves from it" (37).

4. An expression coined by Arthur Okun (54).

5. Okun's "discomfort index" is used by Thomas Dernburg in a recent JEC compendium on stagflation (13).

6. Although countercyclical monetary and fiscal policies geared to aggregate demand continue as the official major policy tools, recently suggestions for alternative measures have begun to surface. For example, Irwin L. Kellner writes in the Summer 1979 *Business Report* of the Manufacturers Hanover Trust Company: "The time has come to pay greater attention to expanding supplies, and less to increasing demand. For only by enlarging supplies can we make some immediate headway against inflation without the need to resort to controls." Earlier a cognate view was intimated in the 1977 midyear economic outlook report of the Organization for Economic Cooperation and Development. In essence, the OECD said that so much slack in manpower and factory capacity exists that extra growth could itself prove an antiinflationary help. "Somewhat stronger recovery should be beneficial" to employers by holding down unit labor costs (75).

7. The Airline Deregulation Act of 1978 offers a vivid example of misconstrued rigidities. Airline corporate management, in unison with labor unions, campaigned and lobbied against deregulation, predicting dire consequences. One year after deregulation, Frank Borman, chairman and president of Eastern Airlines, comments: "I was totally wrong." The experience with wide-open route and price

competition has been "vibrant and exciting" (77, 16). In fact, instead of chaos and bankruptcies, the consequences have been more travels, more revenues, more profits—while price declined in spite of an inflationary milieu.

8. In this vein an interesting case is intuited and traced by Thomas F. Wilson, who writes: "Explicit recognition of the grants economy elevates the vantage point from which one may observe economic phenomena; this is especially true when one assesses the significance of money in the economy. Money serves as a 'medium for transactions' involving grants as well as exchange, and money today is essentially a product of the grants economy, providing an economic return in the form of 'seigniorage.' Seigniorage is a grant, giving the producer (or 'creator') of money, or those to whom the grant has been transferred, command over resources in the economy" (9, 38). "The profit from money creation is, therefore, a grant from society to those who issue money . . ." (9, 42).

9. That inflation is, de facto, an implicit coerced grant (i.e., tribute) to the government might motivate policy makers to cause, or acquiesce in, rising prices. As described by G. L. Bach: "Inflation is, in effect, also a tax that transfers income and wealth to the government. When the government spends without correspondingly increasing taxes and thereby induces inflation, it obtains resources through its expenditures. Those who can buy less because of the higher prices give up the resources, just as if new taxes had been levied on them. Furthermore, the government's gain as a net debtor is also in effect a tax on creditors who hold money and other government debts" (3, 31). The motives behind inflationary monetary expansion are elaborated by Charlotte Ruebling (9, 59–69).

10. It is common knowledge that agricultural subsidies, initially intended for small family farmers, have, as time passed, accrued mostly to large farmers and to tax shelter schemes (33, 44). A more recent irony is the story about governmental regulations designed to protect consumers but hurting them. Certain electric utility companies use their captive-coal operations to reap profits otherwise denied in the rate-making process, sometimes earning three times more on investment than commercial (unregulated) coal operators. For instance, the Pittsburgh-based Duquesne Light Company was able to save 2.4 percent, or an average of 51 cents a ton, on coal it got from its wholly owned Warwick mine. But in 1977 the company began charging itself 31.8 percent above the going market price for coal and passing most of the increase on to customers. Had Duquesne Light bought all its coal on the open market that year the savings to customers would have totaled about $5 million (76).

11. Henry Ford II of the Ford Motor Company, commenting on the regulatory role of the government, said: "It is not just liberal do-gooders, Democrats, unions, consumerists, and environmentalists who are responsible for [it] . . . It's businessmen who want government contracts. It's bankers and transporters and retailers and manufacturers who want protection from competitors. It's insurance companies that lobby for bumper and air bag regulations that might lower their claim costs. It's catalyst suppliers who lobby for tough emission standards. . ." (21, 12).

12. Richard Posner argues that beyond the conventional rationale, namely "to approximate the results of competition or to protect the regulated firm from competition [there is] another important purpose to regulation: we can call it 'taxation by regulation' . . . Foremost among them is the prevalence of 'internal subsidies,' whereby unremunerative services are provided, sometimes indefinitely, out of the

profits from other services" (60, 22). George Stigler anticipated grant impact statements, writing: "With its power to prohibit or compel, to take or give money, the state can and does selectively help or hurt a vast number of industries. . . . The central tasks of the theory of economic regulation are to explain who will receive the benefits or burdens of regulation" (66, 3).

13. Several years before it became a real life issue, the phenomenon was described hypothetically by William Vickrey, who wrote:

> There is indeed no fundamental reason why inflation cannot be accompanied by generalized unemployment, confronting the framer of economic policy with the dilemma that stimulative measures are called for by the presence of excessive unemployment, while at the same time sedative and restrictive measures are called for to halt the inflation . . . The sources of the difficulty presumably lie in some form of rigidity or resistance in the real economy to the forces that are supposed to be at work in the model economy to prevent such an occurrence . . . The difficulty may perhaps be traced to the lack of effective competitive forces acting on large industrial employers on the one hand and strongly entrenched labor unions on the other in major sectors of the economy. In neither case is the remedy easy. The theoretically indicated solution in the latter case, of breaking up the large industrial and labor units sufficiently to restore competitive pressures on prices and wages may not be feasible either for technological or for political reasons; public ownership or public-utility-type regulation of such industries may be equally unattractive solutions (69, 279).

Now the identification, tracing, and redirection of implicit grant flows may provide a solution to the Vickrey predicament.

References

1. Ackley, Gardner. "The Costs of Inflation," *American Economic Review* 68 (May 1978): 149–54.
2. Association for the Study of the Grants Economy. *Tenth Anniversary Brochure,* Augsburg-Leitershofen, International Institute for Empirical Social Economics, 1978.
3. Bach, G.L. "The Economic Effects of Inflation," *Proceedings of the Academy of Political Science* 31 (1975): 20–33.
4. Ball, R.J., and Burns, T. "The Inflationary Mechanism in the U.K. Economy," *American Economic Review* 66 (1976): 467–84.
5. Bosworth, Barry P. "Testimony Before the Subcommittee on Economic Stabilization of the House Committee on Banking, Finance, and Urban Affairs," Washington, D.C., Council on Wage and Price Stability, (21 June 1978).
6. Boulding, Kenneth E. "Successes and Failures," *Challenge* 21 (March-April 1978): 11–13.
7. Boulding, Kenneth E. *The Economy of Love and Fear: A Preface to Grants Economics* (Belmont, Calif., 1973).
8. Boulding, Kenneth E., Pfaff, Martin, Horvath, Janos. "Grants Economics: A Simple Introduction," *American Economist* XVI (Spring 1972): 19–28.
9. Boulding, Kenneth E., and Wilson, Thomas F. (Eds.) *Redistribution through the*

Financial System: The Grants Economics of Money and Credit (New York, 1978).

10. Brunner, Karl, and Meltzer, Allan H. (Eds.) Institutional Arrangement and the Inflation Problem (Amsterdam, 1976).

11. Bryan, William R. "Economic Performance and Policy: Stagflation Issues," in U.S. Congress Joint Economic Committee, Stagflation: A Compendium, 1980. Forthcoming.

12. Chow, Gregory C., and Medgal, Sharon Bernstein. "An Economic Definition of the Inflation-Unemployment Tradeoff," American Economic Review 68 (June 1978): 446-53.

13. Dernburg, Thomas F., "Stagflation: Causes and Cures," in U.S. Congress Joint Economic Committee, Stagflation: A Compendium, 1981.

14. Dorfman, Nancy S., and Snow, Arthur. "Who Will Pay for Pollution Control?" National Tax Journal 28 (March 1975): 101-116.

15. Eckstein, Otto, and Girola, James A. "Long-term Properties of the Price-Wage Mechanism in the United States, 1891 to 1977," Review of Economics and Statistics LX (August 1978): 323-33.

16. Economic Report of the President, 1977, and 1978 (Washington, D.C., U.S. Government Printing Office).

17. Eichner, Alfred S. "Post-Keynesian Theory: An Introduction," Challenge 21 (May-June 1978): 4-10.

18. Fellner, William. Towards a Reconstruction of Macroeconomics (Washington, D.C., 1976).

19. Fellner, William, et al. Economic Policy and Inflation in the Sixties (Washington, D.C., 1972).

20. Felton, John Richard. "The Costs and Benefits of Motor Truck Regulation," Quarterly Review of Economics and Business 18 (Summer 1978): 7-20.

21. Ford, Henry II. "Notable and Quotable," Wall Street Journal, 8 April 1977, 12.

22. Friedman, Milton. "Nobel Lecture: Inflation and Unemployment," Journal of Political Economy 85 (June 1977): 451-572.

23. Frisch, Helmut. "Inflation Theory 1963-1975: A 'Second Generation' Survey," Journal of Economic Literature XV (December 1977): 1289-1317.

24. Gordon, Robert J. "Can Inflation of the 1970s be Explained?" Brookings Papers on Economic Activity, No. 1, 1977, pp. 253-79.

25. Gordon, Robert J. Macroeconomics (Boston, 1978).

26. Gordon, Robert J. "The Demand for and Supply of Inflation," Journal of Law and Economics 18 (1975): 807-836.

27. Göran-Mäler, Karl. "Macroeconomic Aspects of Environmental Policy," in Economic Analysis of Environmental Problems, pp. 27-56.

28. Haberler, Gottfried. Inflation: Its Causes and Cures (Washington, D.C., 1966).

29. Hendershott, Patric H., and Villani, Kevin E. "Grant Elements in the Operation of Federally Sponsored Credit Agencies in the Home Mortgage Market," in Boulding, Redistribution through the Financial System, pp. 227 43.

30. Hirsch, Fred, and Goldthorpe, John H. The Political Economy of Inflation (Cambridge, Mass., 1978).

31. Holt, Charles C., et al. The Unemployment-Inflation Dilemma: A Manpower Solution (Washington, D.C., 1971).

32. Horvath, Janos. "Institutional Inflation via Misapplied Grants," American Economic Association Annual Convention, New Orleans, 1971.

33. Horvath, Janos. "Rural America and the Grants Economy," *American Journal of Agricultural Economics* 53 (1971): 740–47.
34. Horvath, Janos. "Some Measurement Problems in the Interaction of Grants and Exchange Transactions," in *ASGE Tenth Anniversary Brochure,* 2/9.
35. Hotson, John H. *Stagflation and the Bastard Keynesians* (Waterloo, Ontario, 1976).
36. Kahn, Alfred E. "Market Power Inflation: A Conceptual Overview," in Gardiner C. Means, *The Roots of Inflation,* pp. 239–72.
37. Kahn, Alfred E. "Notable & Quotable," *Wall Street Journal,* 20 July 1979, 12.
38. Kaldor, Nicholas. "Inflation and Recession in the World Economy," *Economic Journal* 86 (1976): 703–714.
39. Katona, George. "Behavioral Economics," *Challenge* 21 (September-October 1978): 14–18.
40. Kenyon, Peter. "Pricing in Post-Keynesian Economics," *Challenge* 21 (July-August 1978): 43–48.
41. Klein, Lawrence R. "The Supply Side," *American Economic Review* 68 (1978): 1–7.
42. Klein, Lawrence R. "Keynes and Leontief: Merging the Models," *Challenge* 21 (1978): 64–65.
43. Kreps, Juanita M. "Tax Policy and the Supply Side," *Challenge* 21 (1978): 54–55.
44. Lerner, Abba P. "Stagflation—Its Cause and Cure," *Challenge* 20 (1977): 14–19.
45. Lundberg, Erik (Ed.) *Inflation Theory and Anti-Inflation Policy* (Boulder, Colo., 1977).
46. McCracken, Paul W. "The Cosmetic War on Inflation," *Wall Street Journal,* 18 August 1978.
47. Means, Gardiner C., et al. *The Roots of Inflation* (New York, 1975).
48. Meiselman, David I., and Laffer, Arthur B. (Ed.) *The Phenomenon of World-wide Inflation* (Washington, D.C., 1975).
49. Meyer, John R. "Transportation Regulation," *Challenge* 19 (1976): 44–46.
50. Miller, James C., III. "The Pros and Cons of Trucking Regulation," American Enterprise Institute Reprint No. 95, March 1979.
51. Mills, Edwin S. (Ed.) *Economic Analysis of Environmental Problems* (New York, 1975).
52. OECD. *Macroeconomic Evaluation of Environmental Programmes* (Paris, 1978).
53. Okun, Arthur M., and Perry, George L. *Curing Chronic Inflation* (Washington, D.C., 1978).
54. Okun, Arthur M. "Stop the Self-Inflicted Wounds," *Challenge* 21 (1978): 33–34.
55. Pfaff, Martin (Ed.) *Grants and Exchange* (Amsterdam, 1976).
56. Pfaff, Martin, and Pfaff, Anita B. "The Grants Economy as a Regulator of the Exchange Economy," in U.S. Congress Joint Economic Committee, *The Economics of Federal Subsidy Programs,* Part 1: General Study Papers, 8 May 1972, 120–55.
57. Phelps, Edmund S. "Inflation Planning Reconsidered," *Economica* 45 (1978): 109–123.
58. Phelps, Edmund S., et al. *Microeconomic Foundation of Employment and Inflationary Theory* (New York, 1970).

59. Portney, Paul H., ed. *Current Issues in U.S. Environmental Policy* (Baltimore, Md., 1978).
60. Posner, Richard A. "Taxation by Regulation," *Bell Journal of Economics and Management Science* 2 (1971): 22-50.
61. Ruebling, Charlotte E. "Motives behind Inflationary Monetary Expansion," in Boulding, *Redistribution Through the Financial System*, pp. 59-69.
62. Rutledge, John. *A Monetarist Model of Inflationary Expectations* (Lexington, Mass., 1974).
63. Samuels, Warren J. "Grants and the Theory of Power," *Public Finance Quarterly* 3 (1975): 320-45.
64. Santomero, Anthony M., and Seater, John J. "The Inflation-Unemployment Trade-off: A Critique of the Literature," *Journal of Economic Literature* XVI (1978): 499-544.
65. Solow, Robert M. "Alternative Approaches to Macroeconomic Theory: A Partial View," Queen's University Institute for Economic Research, *Discussion Paper* No. 335, 1979.
66. Stigler, George J. "The Theory of Economic Regulation," *Bell Journal of Economics and Management Science* 2 (1971): 3-21.
67. Tobin, James. "Unemployment and Inflation: The Cruel Dilemma," in A. Phillips and O.E. Williamson (Ed.), *Prices: Issues in Theory, Practice, and Public Policy* (Philadelphia, 1967), pp. 101-107.
68. Van Tassel, Alfred J. (Ed.) *The Environmental Price of Energy* (Lexington, Ma., 1975).
69. Vickrey, William S. *Metastatics and Macroeconomics* (New York, 1974): 278-780.
70. Wachtel, Howard M. and Adelsheim, Peter D. "How Recession Feeds Inflation: Price Markups in a Concentrated Economy," *Challenge* 20 (September-October 1977): 6-13.
71. Wachter, Michael L. and Williamson, Oliver E. "Obligational Markets and the Mechanics of Inflation," *Bell Journal of Economics* (Autumn 1978): 549-71.
72. *Wall Street Journal.* "In Pennsylvania a Man Can Be a Lawbreaker for Selling Milk Cheap," 24 May 1971.
73. *Wall Street Journal.* "Relaxing Regulation," 2 August 1971.
74. *Wall Street Journal.* "Business, Labor Reviews of Carter's Anti-Inflation Proposals are Mixed," 26 October 1978.
75. *Wall Street Journal.* "Many Western Nations Can Spur Growth Without Worsening Inflation, OECD Says," 21 July 1979.
76. *Wall Street Journal.* "Captive Customers: Utility Ownership of Coal Mines, Meant to Assure Fuel, Often Lift Power Cost," 10 May 1979.
77. *Wall Street Journal.* "Relaxing Rules: Federal Agencies Ease, Lift Some Regulations that Burden Business," 4 September 1979.
78. Wallich, Henry C. "Stabilization Goals: Balancing Inflation and Unemployment," *American Economic Review* 68 (May 1978): 159-64.
79. Weidenbaum, Murray L. "A Free Market Approach to Economic Policy," *Challenge* 21 (March-April 1978): 40-41.
80. Weidenbaum, Murray L. *Government-Mandated Price Increases* (Washington, D.C. 1975).
81. White, Ron D. "The Anatomy of Nonmarket Failure: An Examination of

Environmental Policies," *American Economic Review* (May 1976): 454–58.

Institutional Change as a Source of Excessive Monetary Expansion

THOMAS F. WILSON

Institutional arrangements underlie the determination of the monetary base and the money supply built on that base. Institutional changes alter the appropriate composition and the behavior of those monetary aggregates, and they modify the relationships between the aggregates and GNP or the general level of prices. During the 1970s, a breakdown of institutional constraints contributed to excessive monetary expansion. A proliferation of money-issuing powers among private institutions and, concomitantly, a reduction in effective reserve ratios are a manifestation of these changes. Should growth in the monetary base be taken as the measure for assessing policy, the money supply, according to its conventional, M1 definition, understated the rate of expansion in money by about 4 percentage points; the monetary base itself underestimated growth in the money supply by nearly 2 percentage points. The revised definitions of the money supply introduced recently by the Federal Reserve attempt to incorporate the impact of the new institutional setting.[1] This study examines historically the nature and significance of such institutional changes. The conclusion is essentially that the price level in the long run depends largely on the monetary base, and the short-run stability of the financial system depends on the capacity for building money on the monetary base.

The historical evidence presented in this study suggests that a stable price level in the long run rests on a slow, steady rate of change in the monetary base. The institutional transmission of growth in the monetary base into growth in the money supply in general has not permitted an enduring departure in those rates, and concomitantly, in that for the level of prices. In a cyclical setting, in contrast, the institutional structure may, indeed, allow considerable variance in those growth rates, as the volume of money built on the monetary base is subject to sizable fluctuations, and the monetary base may vary cyclically as well. Institutional arrangements govern these rates of change, and they are subject to a competing mixture of government controls and market forces.

INSTITUTIONAL DETERMINANTS OF THE MONEY SUPPLY

The money supply depends upon the behavior of market forces and institutional constraints imposed by laws and regulations. United States monetary history is marked by periods when market forces were dominant and periods when government controls were energetically exercised. Under the gold standard, market forces largely determined the monetary base and the money supply. Under the Federal Reserve System, government controls have assumed the major role in determining the monetary aggregates. Market forces and government controls constitute competing elements in the supply of money, however, and one presents limitations on the other, as markets often override controls and controls typically inhibit market behavior. Colonial America best represents this interaction, but there are numerous examples of this phenomenon in United States monetary history. Over the past several years, regulation of deposit rate ceilings and other regulations have been accompanied by market adjustments (and market-induced regulatory adjustments) to high, inflation-related interest rates, which have created new forms of money. Such adjustments alter the relationship between the monetary base and the money supply, but there should be a tendency toward long-run stabilization in that relationship as institutions adapt to the new environment. Thus, a new form of money may be introduced by government or private innovation, thereby disrupting the association of the money supply with the base, but growth in the money supply will eventually be aligned with that for the monetary base as the new money form is incorporated into the financial system.

Monetary history may, indeed, be a history of currency debasement, but that description sweeps across vastly different experiences. During the first century under the Constitution, the secular trend in prices was basically flat, with the price level in 1889 (and in 1861) essentially the same as that which prevailed in 1789, despite severe fluctuations in prices during war-related suspensions of specie convertibility of paper money. The federal government defined the monetary standard, i.e., it "regulated" the value of coins, but until the Civil War, the monetary base (specie) was composed of foreign and private coins along with United States government coins. After the Civil War, when the federal government gained control over the issuance of the monetary base, there was adherence at least until 1914 to the discipline of the gold standard, and the price of gold was fixed at $20.67 per ounce. The lesson is not that this' nation should resurrect the gold standard, even though that might be the eventual market adjustment to inflation, as some speculators suppose. The lesson is, instead, the dependence of long-run price stability on moderate, fairly steady growth in the monetary base.

Market forces largely determined the monetary base prior to the advent of the Federal Reserve System and there was, perhaps fortuitously, long-run stability in the price level. Discretionary control of the monetary base by the Federal Reserve since 1914, in contrast, has been accompanied by chronic inflation, and over the past twenty-five years, the rate of inflation has exhibited a distinct accelerating trend. Under the gold standard, market-oriented determination of the money supply contributed to short-run financial instability, as the money supply fluctuated widely. The Federal Reserve System was established to prevent financial panics, which, of course, it failed to do, as the banking system collapsed in the early 1930s. Moderate, steady growth in the monetary base has been consistent with stable prices in the long run, but it does not necessarily translate into short-run stability in the money supply, the economy, or prices. In other words, short-run economic stability relates more closely to the stability of the money supply, not the monetary base, unless the two are tightly linked, which certainly was not the case in the short run into the 1930s.

The stability of the banking system since the 1930s, though that quality is being severely tested, probably reflects more than deposit insurance in checking the susceptibility of fractional reserve banking to financial panics. The dismantling of the gold standard, begun in 1933, when private holdings of monetary gold were nationalized, and completed in 1971, when gold convertibility of the dollar for foreign official institutions was suspended, has eliminated impediments to expansive policies. Demand management policies have sustained a reasonably high level of economic activity, despite periodic credit crunches, perhaps because they have been inflationary. Overly expansive policies, coupled with rescue efforts for faltering corporations, may not be sufficient to insure stability of the financial system, especially with the institutional diffusion of money-issuing authority. Limited control of the money supply could, therefore, involve a reversion to the cyclical instability so prominent before World War II.

The money supply is governed by the monetary base and the extent to which the financial system issues money upon that base. The monetary base is now the noninterest-bearing fiat money issued by the federal government, consisting of currency in circulation and reserves held by commercial banks with the Federal Reserve banks. Alternatively, the monetary base can be defined as member bank reserves and currency held by nonmember banks and the nonbank public. Currency held by the nonbank public is included in the money supply, and the reserves component of the monetary base underlies deposits and nondeposit items issued by the private sector, which are included in various concepts of the money supply.

The Federal Reserve System can determine with reasonably close pre-cision the size of the monetary base, thereby exercising a measure of indirect control over the money supply. The tightness of this linkage (through the money "multiplier") determines the effectiveness of control of the money supply. This linkage depends on legal reserve ratios, excess reserves, and preferences for various types of transaction balances and for currency, over which control rests with financial institutions and the general public. Chiefly in response to high interest rates, recent institutional changes have weakened this linkage. Reserve ratios are lower, and new forms of transaction balances have been introduced, such as negotiable orders of withdrawal (NOW) accounts, checking accounts at mutual savings banks, credit union share drafts, automatic transfer services, repurchase agreements, Eurodollar deposits, and money market mutual funds. Thus, a given rate of expansion in the monetary base and the narrow concept of the money supply can sustain a faster growth in GNP, and higher inflation, than before. In addition, ceilings on lending rates are being lifted, thus requiring higher interest rates to restrain aggregate demand. Beyond that, the extent to which the Federal Reserve seeks to stabilize interest rates rather than the monetary base or the money supply, the inflationary undercurrent is strengthened.

The Federal Reserve has clearly accommodated inflationary credit demands. At the same time, the growing capacity for the issuance of private money has limited control of the money supply, and this capacity may have partially disguised the expansiveness of monetary policy. Moreover, diminished growth in productivity translates into higher inflation for a given rate of increase in the monetary base. Beyond flattening the growth path for the monetary base, this study suggests higher, uniform reserve requirements, with interest paid on reserve balances, and a sharper distinction to be drawn between money and money substitutes.

HISTORICAL PERSPECTIVE ON MONEY AND INFLATION

Experience in Colonial American suggests that governments do not necessarily debase the currency. Between 1720 and 1775, wholesale prices rose at an annual rate of merely 0.5 percent.[2] The colonial monetary system can be roughly described as parallel monies, with full-bodied coins mostly of international origin circulating alongside inconvertible, legal tender paper money ("bills of credit"). Although the Spanish dollar was a primary component of the money supply, other foreign coins and coins and tokens issued under government authority and as private business ventures were represented in the money supply as well.[3] No commercial banks were established until 1781. Private, note-issuing "land banks" were formed earlier, but Parliament in 1741, with support of the colonial governments, required immediate redemption of those notes. Massachusetts in 1690 emitted the first paper money, and by 1755, all the colonies had such bills of credit in circulation.[4] At the beginning of the Revolutionary War, paper money constituted 60 percent of the silver value of currency in circulation.[5]

The record on the issuance of colonial bills of credit on balance is favorable, though the performance among colonies is mixed and the quantitative evidence is fragmentary. In New York, New Jersey, Pennsylvania, Maryland, and Virginia the rate of depreciation was moderate, and at times, the purchasing power of paper money remained steady. In New England, in contrast, where the colonial governments competed with each other in the issuance of bills of credit, paper money depreciated at a brisk rate. In Massachusetts, creditors inserted purchasing power maintenance provisions in contracts by stipulating payment in specie.[6]

The Continental Congress relied chiefly on bills of credit to finance the Revolutionary War, and that paper money suffered, as might be expected, horrendous depreciation. From the estimated $242 million of "continentals" issued by the Congress, the loss to the public has been calculated at $197 million.[7] The states issued $209 million of their own paper money, which experienced a similar fate. The Articles of Confederation, ratified in 1781, granted Congress the authority to issue paper money and coins, and state coinage was subject to regulation by Congress. Private entrepreneurs issued coins without official sanction, though private issues were generally required to meet specified legal standards.[8] The first commercial bank was chartered by Congress; the second operated without a charter under the common law tradition that private banking was a business; the third was a state-chartered institution. Private bank notes with specie convertibility were placed into circulation. The states continued to issue bills of credit, and they depreciated dramatically. By the time of the Constitutional Convention, there was a broad consensus to terminate government authority to emit bills of credit.[9]

The Constitution delegated specific monetary authority to the federal government and removed the direct monetary powers of the states:

> The Congress shall have power ... To coin money, regulate the value thereof, and of foreign coin, ... (Article I, Section 8). No state shall ... coin money; emit bills of credit; make any thing but gold and silver a tender in payment of debts; ... (Article I, Section 10).

Thus, the power to coin money was granted to the federal government and withdrawn from the states. The authority to issue paper money was withheld from the federal government and prohibited to the states. Only gold and silver could be assigned legal tender standing; foreign coins (and presumably private coins) were subject to regulation as they had been for many years. Private banking was implicitly sanctioned. It was apparently the intention of the framers of the Constitution that the federal government coin money and preside over a bimetallic standard by regulating the quality of circulating media.

The monetary system formed in the 1790s under the Constitution was basically that which prevailed until the Civil War. Congress in 1792 established a mint and set forth regulations pertaining in part to the "denominations, values, and descriptions" of coins. In 1793, Congress granted legal tender status to certain foreign coins—the legal tender standing of the Spanish milled dollar was not rescinded until 1857. Privately issued tokens and gold coins were also placed into circulation. The Mint Act provided for a bimetallic standard under which the dollar price of gold was $19.39 per ounce, but the United States went on the gold standard de facto in 1834 when the dollar was devalued in terms of gold, making the price of gold $20.69—a slight modification in 1837 set the price at $20.67 an ounce.[10]

A substantial proportion of the nation's currency was supplied by state-chartered banks—other businesses and individuals also issued paper money. State regulations and operations of the Bank of the United States until the 1830s did exert a certain discipline in note issues, but specie convertibility and the market provided the enforcement mechanism. The average ratio of paper money to gold reserves was apparently around 2½.[11] Legal restrictions limited the volume of notes issued by small, country banks, but the supply of notes overall was held in check by their presentation for redemption, which reflected the operations of dealers in paper money.[12] Nonetheless, the money supply fluctuated widely, and financial panics caused suspensions of specie payments in 1814–15, 1837, 1857, and 1861. Specie, then, was hoarded by banks and individuals, and notes were exchanged at varying rates among themselves and with specie. The United States government also issued Treasury notes with money characteristics in 1812–15, 1837–43, 1846–47, 1857, and 1861.[13]

The period from 1789 and 1861 was marked by long-run price stability. As suggested in Table 1, the wholesale price index was the same in both years. Economic growth proceeded at a relatively high rate. During the shorter interval, 1840–61, for which data on world monetary gold are available, the monetary base (gold) expanded at a 4.0 percent rate, and the price level edged downward. As subsequent data reveal, there was, however, considerable short-run variability in money and prices during the era of state bank notes.

The Civil War brought a major transformation in the United States monetary system. The Legal Tender Act of 1862 provided for the issuance of "greenbacks," the first legal tender paper money after ratification of the Constitution. The National Bank Act of 1863 created the national banking system with note issues based on government securities. In 1865, a prohibitive, 10 percent tax was imposed on state bank notes. The federal government, therefore, gained control of the issuance of currency— private tokens and paper money were issued in significant quantities only during financial panics, with the last issues appearing during the Great Depression.[14] Between 1862 and 1879, the United States was on a fiduciary standard, with greenbacks trading at varying rates with gold. The inflation associated with the Civil War was subsequently offset by deflation. Major structural changes in the money supply mechanism had no lasting impact on the price level. The United States was firmly on the gold standard in 1879, and the price of gold was still set at $20.67 an ounce. State banks, of course, survived as deposit-issuing institutions, and they were governed by state-administered regulations. National banks were primarily deposit-issuing institutions as well, and they were subject to a pyramiding set of reserve requirements.[15] The wholesale price index, as shown in Table 1, was essentially the same in 1889 as in 1861. Moderate growth in the monetary base (defined here as United States monetary gold) was accompanied closely by growth in the money supply. Real GNP overall grew at a respectable 4.3 percent rate.

Table 1. Gross National Product, Money, and Prices, 1789–1979

	Annual Percentage Rates of Change						
	1789–1840	1840–1861	1861–1889	1889–1914	1914–1960	1960–1979	1969–1979
Current-dollar GNP	4.5	4.3	4.0	4.4	5.9	8.0	9.7
Constant-dollar GNP	4.4	4.0	4.3	3.6	3.2	3.4	2.9
Wholesale Price Index	0.0	-0.3	-0.3	0.8	2.2	4.9	8.3
Monetary Base	—	4.0	3.4	4.0	5.9	6.2	8.0
Money Supply	5.3	4.7	3.8	6.3	5.7	4.8	6.0

Sources: For GNP, Thomas Senior Berry, *Revised Annual Estimates of American Gross National Product* (Richmond, Va.: Bostwick Press, 1978), pp. 38, 41; U.S., Department of Commerce, *Survey of Current Business*, Vol. 60, No. 1 (January 1980), pp. 36, 38. For the wholesale price index, George F. Warren and Frank A. Pearson, *Gold and Prices* (New York: Wiley, 1935), pp. 12–14, U.S., Department of Commerce, *Statistical Abstract of the United States* (1979), p. 477, *Survey of Current Business* (January 1980), p. S-7. For the monetary base, Warren and Pearson, *Gold and Prices*, pp. 92, 151. Milton Friedman and Anna Jacobson Schwartz, *A Monetary History of the United States: 1867–1960* (Princeton, N.J.: Princeton University Press, 1963), pp. 799–808, and Federal Reserve Bank of St. Louis. For the money supply, Warren and Pearson, *Gold and Prices*, p. 140, Friedman and Schwartz, *A Monetary History*, pp. 705–22, and Federal Reserve Bank of St. Louis.

The subsequent period, 1889–1914, shows an upward drift in the price level, along with a slower rate of economic growth, 3.6 percent. The monetary base, consisting of national bank notes, as indirect obligations of the Treasury, and Treasury currency (including gold), i.e., currency held by the nonbank public and vault cash, expanded at a 4.0 percent rate, but the money supply grew somewhat faster, at a 6.3 percent pace.[16] The expansion in deposit banking contributed to increases in the ratio of bank deposits to bank reserves from 5.46 in 1889 to 8.69 in 1914 and in the ratio of deposits to currency from 3.33 to 7.59.[17] Deposit banking left the financial system nearly as unstable as before, as witness the panic of 1907, which led to formation of the Federal Reserve System.

Soon after the Federal Reserve System commenced operations in 1914 the inflationary surge associated with World War I was launched. The postwar deflation failed to offset fully that inflation, and the Great Depression came too soon to allow one to assess properly the long-run effects of policy. The deposit-reserve ratio, however, climbed to 13.01 in 1929, and the deposit-currency ratio reached 11.22 in 1930, before falling as the banking system collapsed in the early 1930s. The banking system was clearly overextended on its reserve base, even if it is supposed that the Federal Reserve took steps to encourage a one-third contraction in the money supply.[18] The monetary base actually increased from 1929 to 1933,[19] which coincides with the earlier experience that changes in its size corresponded little to cyclical variability in the money supply, and in GNP as well.

The Great Depression brought steps to eliminate the gold standard. President Franklin D. Roosevelt in 1933 issued an executive order forbidding the holding of monetary gold and requiring banks to turn in their gold. Congress, then, passed a joint resolution abrogating gold clauses in all contracts. Devaluation of the dollar was authorized by the Thomas Amendment to the Agricultural Adjustment Act of 1933 and the Gold Reserve Act of 1934. In 1934, the dollar was formally devalued. The price of gold was set at $35 per ounce. The removal of gold from circulation was followed by successive steps to reduce its restrictive role in the conduct of expansive monetary policy, as gold requirements behind Federal Reserve notes and deposits were cut and, then, removed entirely. The dollar was formally devalued again in 1971, with the price of gold raised to $38 an ounce, and dollar convertibility into gold by foreign official institutions was suspended. In 1973, the official price was boosted to $42.22 per ounce, and since the breakdown of the Bretton Woods system of fixed exchange rates, the dollar has fluctuated in foreign exchange value under a system of "managed" float.[20]

The Federal Reserve System, in contrast to the immediately preceding market-oriented monetary regime, has carried out policies consistent with long-run inflation. Between 1914 and 1960, the monetary base (now including Federal Reserve notes and deposits as well as Treasury currency) expanded at a 5.9 percent rate, as shown in Table 1. The money supply (M2) grew at about the same rate, 5.7 percent (5.6 percent for M1). The ratios of deposits to reserves and to currency in 1960 were close to the levels in 1914. After rising to those highs in 1929 and 1930, these ratios fell to 3.24 (1940) and to 4.02 (1945), respectively, before commencing a steady rise after World War II. Compared with earlier periods, faster monetary expansion was accompanied by inflation, with the wholesale price index climbing at a 2.2 percent pace, and modest economic growth, with real GNP rising at a 3.2 percent rate.

The Federal Reserve System from 1960 to 1979 conducted policies compatible with substantially higher inflation. As reported in Table 1, the monetary base expanded at a 6.2 percent rate. While real GNP grew at a 3.4 percent rate, the wholesale price index advanced at a 4.9 percent pace (4.5 percent for the GNP deflator). For the 1969–79 subperiod, the Federal Reserve presided over an 8.0 percent rate of expansion in the monetary base; real GNP grew at a 2.9 percent rate and wholesale prices rose at a swift 8.3 percent clip (6.7 percent for the GNP deflator).

Nominal GNP expanded at a distinctly (though not enormously) higher rate from 1960 to 1979 than the monetary base. In previous periods, the growth rates were comparable. In addition, the money supply (M1) grew at a rate considerably below that which is consistent with nominal GNP. These differentials in growth rates reflect the institutional changes alluded to earlier. Over a longer period, GNP should be expected to be aligned with the monetary base. The same outcome would not be expected for M1. The impact of institutional changes appears in velocity. The "velocity" for the monetary base increased at a 1.8 percent rate over the 1960–79 period (and 1.7 percent for the subperiod), and it jumped to 2.9 percent for the past four years—short-run variations of GNP on the monetary base are the historical norm. The "velocity" for M1 rose at a 3.2 percent rate (and 3.5 percent for the subperiod), and it was 4.9 percent in the last four years. This behavior, of course, reflects the advent of new forms of money with lower (or essentially no) reserve requirements. When money is defined as "total liquid assets," monetary growth is aligned with GNP growth—this holds roughly for other broad concepts of money as well.[21] Thus, institutional changes contributed to almost a 2-percentage-point increment in the transmission of growth in the monetary base to GNP (attributable to lower reserve requirements), and about a 4-percentage-point understatement of monetary growth when measured by M1. Institutional changes imply revision of the appropriate concept of money. Moreover, the substantial expansion of money on the monetary base appears in the deposit-reserve and deposit-currency ratios. When viewing only commercial banks, the deposit-reserve ratio was a lofty 19.84 in November 1979, and the deposit-currency ratio was 8.81.[22]

This analysis lends support to the notion that over extended periods of time growth in nominal GNP tends to approximate growth in the monetary base, as the "appropriate" measure of the money supply adjustments to that base. The rate of inflation ultimately depends on the monetary base, but growth in real GNP does not appear to be so related. Institutional arrangements can at times allow for significant departures in growth rates for the monetary base and nominal GNP, but they are not likely to be sizable or enduring. Extended periods of high inflation are chiefly related to excessive expansion in the monetary base. Short-run variability in the money supply and GNP are not necessarily connected with the behavior of the monetary base, a subject to which closer attention is now given.

SHORT-RUN RELATIONSHIPS FOR MONEY AND THE MONETARY BASE

Short-run variability in the money supply depends upon the monetary base and the competitive operations of financial institutions under regulatory constraints. Three periods have been selected for closer examination of these relationships: 1840–61, 1889–1914, and 1960–79 (and the 1969–79 subperiod). These periods represent considerably different monetary systems. During the state bank note era, market behavior largely governed the financial system under loosely administered regulations. The money supply was subject to federal regulation during the 1889–1914 period, but that was the zenith of the international gold standard. The most recent decades reflect monetary control by the Federal Reserve System with continuing, close regulation of financial institutions. Each period was affected by a war.

A comparison in performance of money, output, and prices is presented in Table 2. The long-run growth rates (G), as shown in Table 1, appear here as well. This section focuses on short-run variability and correlation of monetary aggregates with GNP. As a measure of variability, the standard deviation (S) of annual rates of change was employed. The two earlier periods exhibited considerable similarity in variability, and noticeably greater variability overall than was experienced for 1960–79. When compared with 1960–79, current-dollar GNP fluctuated much more in year-to-year growth in 1840–61 and 1889–1914. The variability of real GNP for the 1840–61 period may not accurately represent performance. Ignoring that figure, moderation in the amplitude of year-to-year changes in real GNP is indicated as well. Variability in the wholesale price index was surprisingly close, however. Increases and decreases in the price level during the two earlier periods were nearly offsetting, of course, whereas in the 1960–79 period most of dispersion appears in the rate of increase—inflation is accompanied by significant relative ("real") price flexibility.

Variations in the monetary base under the gold standard exceeded decidedly those experienced under the Federal Reserve System. For those earlier periods, the money supply and the monetary base were not significantly correlated, however. During the 1960–79 period, the monetary base fluctuated a moderate 1.9 percentage points (and 1.1 percentage points for the 1969–79 subperiod), but year-to-year variations in the two monetary aggregates were relatively highly correlated, with the correlation coefficients at 0.81 on a current basis and 0.73 when the monetary base was assigned a one year lag—the corresponding coefficients for 1969–79 were markedly lower, however, at 0.52 and 0.19. These correlations suggest fairly tight linkage of the monetary base and the money supply (M1) for the full 1960–79 period, and a weakening in that linkage with the advent of other money forms.

Table 2. Money, Output, and Prices: A Comparison of 1840–1861, 1889–1914, and 1960–1979

	1840–1861[a]			1889–1914			1960–1979			1969–1979		
	G	S	$\bar{R}^2$	G	S	$\bar{R}^2$	G	S	$\bar{R}^2$	G	S	$\bar{R}^2$
Current-dollar GNP	4.3	6.7		4.4	6.8		8.0	2.5		9.7	2.3	
Constant-dollar GNP	4.0	1.2		3.6	6.0		3.4	2.4		2.9	3.0	
Wholesale Price Index	−0.3	7.2		0.8	4.9		4.9	5.2		8.3	5.1	
Monetary Base	4.0	3.2	0.13	4.0	4.2	0.10	6.2	1.9	0.68	8.0	1.1	0.66
Money Supply	4.7	9.0	0.50	6.3	5.7	0.52	4.8	1.8	0.57	6.0	1.3	0.50

[a]Definitions of symbols: G is the annual growth rate over the period indicated, S represents the standard deviation of annual percentage changes, and $\bar{R}^2$ is the coefficient of multiple determination, adjusted for degrees of freedom, found by regressing the annual percentage change in current-dollar GNP on the annual percentage changes in the monetary base and the money supply separately for the current year and for the preceding year.

Source: See Table 1.

The state bank note era, as expected, produced substantial variability in the money supply. Fluctuations in the money supply were markedly less from 1889 to 1914. Under accelerating inflation, the Federal Reserve has conducted policies compatible with reasonably steady growth in the money supply since 1960. The behavior of total liquid assets was relatively steady as well, with a standard deviation of 2.3 percentage points (and 1.8 percentage points for the subperiod). Nonetheless, a clear procyclical pattern is evident, with a lead of roughly a year at cyclical peaks, for both the money supply and the monetary base—both, of course, supported steepening inflation.

The "causal" linkage between the money supply and the monetary base and current-dollar GNP was appraised by regressing year-to-year percentage changes in GNP on the year-to-year percentage changes in the monetary aggregates separately, with the latter variables represented on a current basis and lagged one year. The resulting adjusted coefficients of multiple determination ($\bar{R}^2$) are presented in Table 2. Although positive, no significant correlation was found in the two earlier periods between GNP and the monetary base. Variations in the monetary base were sufficiently irregular that they were not transmitted to GNP on a year-to-year basis. The monetary base has not fluctuated so much in recent years, but variations correlate closely with GNP, with the $\bar{R}^2$ at 0.68 for 1960–79 (and 0.66 for 1969–79). These results agree with the observed procyclical pattern for the monetary base, and the contention that discretionary powers exercised in the management of the monetary base have been employed in part in an effort to contain cyclical swings in interest rates. Perfectly stable growth in the monetary base would not be correlated with year-to-year changes in GNP.

The most striking statistical results appear from regressing GNP on the money supply. As shown in Table 2, the $\bar{R}^2$s are nearly the same for each priod. They were nearly the same for very different reasons, however. The banking system must have accommodated expanding demand for credit and, thereby, enhanced the cyclical amplitude of economic activity during both the 1840–61 and 1889–1914 periods. For the 1960–79 period, in contrast, the banking system, or even more broadly the private financial system, and the Federal Reserve, given the correlation of the money supply and the monetary base, jointly accommodated and enhanced cyclical fluctuations in economic activity.

These statistical results emerge from a continuing series of analyses stemming from the monetarist model designed by the Federal Reserve Bank of St. Louis. The latest version of the St. Louis model regresses quarterly percentage changes in nominal GNP on quarterly percentage changes in the money supply (M1) and high-employment (federal) expenditures for the current period and for the immediately preceding four quarters. Covering the period from 1953-I to 1976-IV, the $\bar{R}^2$ is 0.40, compared with 0.53 for the period ending in 1969-IV. The model shows no lasting fiscal policy impact.[23] A Federal Reserve Board study used very similar equations to assess the effect of proposed monetary aggregates, which parallel those adopted recently. The equations were estimated for 1960-IV to 1978-III and for 1960-IV to 1974-II. The $\bar{R}^2$s for M1 were 0.47 and 0.42, respectively. The $\bar{R}^2$s for their proposed M1, which corresponds to the adopted M1-B, were 0.49 and 0.43, respectively. The experiement covered other, broader monetary aggregates as well, and the $\bar{R}^2$s are somewhat lower for both the old definitions and the proposed definitions of money. In contrast with the St. Louis results, a significant impact was found for fiscal policy, which was measured as the change in the high-employment federal deficit.[24]

Richard G. Davis regressed the quarterly percentage change in GNP on quarterly percentage changes for the money supply (M1 and M2) and the monetary base (as defined by the Federal Reserve Board), on a current basis and lagged four quarters. No fiscal variable was employed. For the 1961-I to 1978-IV period, the $\bar{R}^2$s were 0.31 for M1, 0.25 for M2, and 0.08 for the monetary base. If any effect, a fiscal variable apparently does not lower the correlation. Davis also estimated the equations for two subperiods, 1961-I to 1969-IV and 1970-I to 1978-IV. For the earlier subperiod, the $\bar{R}^2$s were 0.23, 0.27, and 0.01, respectively. For the later subperiod, the $\bar{R}^2$s were 0.19, 0.08, and -0.06, respectively.[25] The $\bar{R}^2$s were generally lower for the shorter subperiods than for the full period, and they were lower for the 1970s.

The statistical results reported in Table 2 use annual (year-to-year) percentage changes because only annual data are available for most years. Annual data also deemphasize the erratic component, which is particularly strong in a shorter period, such as the 1970s, and they may be more meaningful from a policy standpoint. The alleged failure of the St. Louis equation in the 1970s rests on a weakening in the correlation with quarterly data. The annual data suggest no significant loosening of the linkage on a correlation basis between GNP and the monetary aggregates. These results do not conflict with the reality of institutional change, however. The partial regression coefficients indicate that each 1 percentage point change in the money supply (M1), and in the monetary base, supported a larger percentage point change in GNP than earlier. The Federal Reserve in the 1970s may have tied policy too close to narrow concepts of money, such that they were deceived by the behavior of those aggregates. The Federal Reserve, however, should have realized the implications of the structural changes taking place, since it was responsible for making regulatory changes that expanded the money-creating powers of private institutions. Moreover, data on broad aggregates were available, and the monetary base was consciously expanded at a highly inflationary pace.

CONCLUSION

This study examines historically institutional change as a source of excessive monetary expansion. The historical record suggests that inflation in the long-run depends largely on the monetary base. The establishment of the Federal Reserve System altered the mechanism for determining the monetary base from one resting largely on market behavior under the gold standard to one subject to discretionary management. The Federal Reserve has presided over chronic inflation. A market-oriented system for determination of the money supply, in contrast, translated into economic instability, as the banking system accommodated and enhanced cyclical swings in economic activity. The exercise of monetary powers by the Federal Reserve in recent decades has reduced the variability in the money supply, but monetary policy is still contributing to, rather than moderating, cyclical fluctuations. Institutional changes over the past few years have caused a proliferation in the power to issue money, and this development raises the specter of financial panics so prominent before World War II.

The policy implications of this study include, as an essential step in calming inflation, moderation in the growth of the monetary base. In order to tighten the linkage between the monetary base and the money supply, it is recommended that high, uniform (equal) reserve requirements be placed on all privately issued money. The Federal Reserve has, instead, used reserve requirements as an instrument to redistribute profits within the financial community and to redistribute income and wealth within the nation. This fiscal (implicit tax/subsidy) power should be further curtailed by the payment of interest on reserve balances.[26] It is also suggested that the broadening private authority to issue money be checked by regulation and that a sharp distinction be drawn between money and money substitutes.

Notes

1. The old definitions of money were: M1 (currency and demand deposits held by the nonbank public); M2 (M1 plus savings and time deposits at commercial banks, excluding large CDs); M3 (M2 plus savings deposits at thrift institutions); M4 (M2 plus large CDs); M5 (M3 plus large CDs). The new definitions of money are: M1-A (M1 less deposits of foreign banks and official institutions); M1-B (M1-A plus NOW, ATS, and credit union share draft balances and demand deposits at thrift institutions); M2 (M1-B plus certain repurchase agreements, certain Eurodollar deposits, money market fund shares, and savings and small time deposits at depositary institutions); M3 (M2 plus large CDs and certain other repurchase agreements); L (M3 plus certain other Eurodollar deposits, bankers acceptances, commercial paper, savings bonds, and liquid Treasury obligations). Thomas D. Simpson, "The Redefined Monetary Aggregates," *Federal Reserve Bulletin* 66 (February 1980):98.

2. George F. Warren and Frank A. Pearson, *Gold and Prices* (New York, 1935), pp. 11–12.

3. Sylvester S. Crosby, *The Early Coins of America; and the Laws of Governing their Issue* (Boston, 1875; reprinted by the Token and Medal Society, 1965), pp. 32–33, 90–115, 117–18, 139–68, 324–27, 345–47; Robert A. Vlack, *Early American Coins* (Johnson City: Windsor Research Publications, 1965), pp. 8–32.

4. Eric P. Newman, *The Early Paper Money of America* (Racine, Wisc., 1967).

5. Arthur Nussbaum, *A History of the Dollar* (New York, 1957), p. 26.

6. Richard A. Lester, *Monetary Experiments: Early American and Recent Scandinavian* (Princeton, 1939), pp. 24, 85, 114, 138; Leslie V. Brock, *The Currency of the American Colonies* (New York, 1975), pp. 29–30, 345–46, 386–87, 402–403, 476–77, 542–43, 594–95.

7. "Alexander Hamilton's Estimate of the Revolutionary War Expenditures, 1790," in Herman E. Krooss (Ed.), *Documentary History of Banking and Currency in the United States* (New York, 1969), pp. 157–61.

8. Vlack, pp. 42–105; Crosby, pp. 170–224, 239–96.

9. Bray Hammond, *Banks and Politics in America: From the Revolution to the Civil War* (Princeton, 1957), pp. 65–66, 105.

10. Krooss, pp. 201–206, 209–210, 1040–44; R. S. Yeoman, *A Guide Book of United States Coins,* 33d edition (Racine, Wisc., 1979), pp. 9–10, 219–39; Davis R. Dewey, *State Banking Before the Civil War* (Washington, D.C., 1910), pp. 150–51; American Numismatic Association, *Selections from the Numismatist: United States Paper Money, Tokens, Medals, and Miscellaneous* (Racine, Wisc., 1960).

11. Krooss, pp. 1050–52.

12. Dewey, pp. 58, 62; William H. Dilliston, *Bank Note Reporters and Counterfeit Detectors, 1826–1866* (New York, 1949), pp. 1–9, 41–58, 74–82.

13. D. C. Wismer, "Early Bank Notes Issued in the United States," in *Selections from the Numismatist*, p. 181; S. P. Breckinridge, *Legal Tender: A Study in English and American Monetary History* (Chicago, 1903), pp. 101–114.

14. Yeoman, pp. 238–41; American Numismatic Association, *Selections from the Numismatist*; Ralph A. Mitchell and Charles V. Kappen, "Depression Scrip in the U.S.," *Calcoin News* (March 1958): 31–36.

15. Harold Barger, *Money, Banking, and Public Policy*, 2d ed. (Chicago, 1968), pp. 148–49.

16. Milton Friedman and Anna Jacobson Schwartz, *A Monetary History of the United States, 1867–1960* (Princeton, N.J., 1963), pp. 780–81.

17. These ratios, as reported here and below, are taken from Friedman and Schwartz, pp. 799–808.

18. *Ibid.*, pp. 712–14.

19. *Ibid.*, pp. 803–804.

20. Henry G. Manne and Roger Leroy Miller (eds.), *Gold, Money and the Law* (Chicago, 1975), p. 23.

21. *Total liquid assets* consist of currency, demand deposits, time deposits at commercial banks and nonbank thrift institutions, savings bonds, negotiable certificates of deposit, short-term marketable United States securities, open market paper, federal funds, repurchase agreements, and money market fund shares. U.S. Department of Commerce, *Handbook of Cyclical Indicators* (Washington, D.C., 1977), p. 41.

These data are reported in the following: U.S. Department of Commerce, *Business Conditions Digest*, March 1979, p. 101; December 1979, p. 71; February 1980, p. 71.

The Federal Reserve Board reported for the various concepts of money the growth rates for 1960–79 and 1970–79 (in parentheses): old M1 (4.9, 6.1), old M2 (7.6, 8.9), old M3 (8.5, 9.9), new M1-A (4.9, 6.0), new M1-B (5.1, 6.4), new M2 (8.3, 9.6), new M3 (9.0, 10.8), and estimated new L (8.9, 10.9). These figures are averages of annual rates of growth rather than annual rates over the period, as given in Table 1. Simpson, "Redefined Monetary Aggregates," pp. 103, 114.

22. Board of Governors of the Federal Reserve System, *Federal Reserve Bulletin* 66 (January 1980): A14–A15.

23. Keith M. Carlson, "Does the St. Louis Equation Now Believe in Fiscal Policy?" *Review* (Federal Reserve Bank of St. Louis) 60 (February 1978): 17. For further analysis and critique of the St. Louis equation, see Benjamin M. Friedman, "Even the St. Louis Model Now Believes in Fiscal Policy," *Journal of Money, Credit, and Banking* IX (May 1977): 365–67; John Vrooman, "Does the St. Louis Equation Even Believe in Itself?" *Journal of Money, Credit, and Banking* XI (February 1979): 111–17.

24. Stephen H. Axilrod, et al., "A Proposal for Redefining the Monetary Aggregates," *Federal Reserve Bulletin* 65 (January 1979): 17, 28–29.

25. Richard G. Davis, "The Monetary Base as an Intermediate Target for Monetary Policy," *Quarterly Review* (Federal Reserve Bank of New York) 4 (Winter 1979– 80): 5.

26. Thomas F. Wilson, "Identification and Measurement of Grant Elements in Monetary Policy," in *Redistribution Through the Financial System: The Grants Economics of Money and Credit*, edited by Kenneth E. Boulding and Thomas F. Wilson (New York, 1978), pp. 38–56.

Sources of Inflation: Old and New

Y. S. BRENNER

Two decades ago writing about the inflation of prices in sixteenth-century England I wrote that intense structural social and economic changes had been accompanied by a remarkable rise in prices.[1] Today, speaking of the twentieth-century, I am tempted to repeat myself. Since the middle of our century intense structural social and economic changes are taking place which are again accompanied by remarkably rising prices.[2] Of course, other periods were tainted by inflation between the sixteenth century and ours, but they were different. Ignoring short price oscillations, the conventional trade cycles, and the relatively modest swells traced by Kondratieff, prices were on the whole fairly stable. The most notable inflations close to and during the French Revolution and Napoleonic wars, the American Civil War, the Franco-German War, and World War I, were all followed by corresponding falls in prices. In all, price increases never exceeded 20 percent and were in one way or another associated with the destruction of productive capacity and massive expansion of the money supply by governments. Even the major inflation caused by World War I was followed by a sharp fall in prices before and during the Great Depression of the 1930s. So was the hyperinflation that occurred in Central and Eastern Europe after World War I. The complete loss of confidence in the currency which was the result of the destruction of the vanquished countries' productive capacities, and their governments' resort to the printing presses to finance rehabilitation and reparation payments, led to astronomical price increases, but as soon as the paper currency was repudiated confidence was restored and deflation followed. Nothing of this sort happened after the currency devaluations in the wake of World War II. Prices continued climbing; first modestly in the 1950s but gaining in momentum as the 1970s drew closer.

Only twice before had so sharp and lasting a rise in prices been recorded since the Middle Ages. In the thirteenth century when the first spate of late medieval urbanization and population increase evolved, and in the sixteenth century when renewed urbanization and commercialization of economic activities coincided with strong population accretion, and when the influx of American treasure into some European countries concurred with currency debasements in several others.

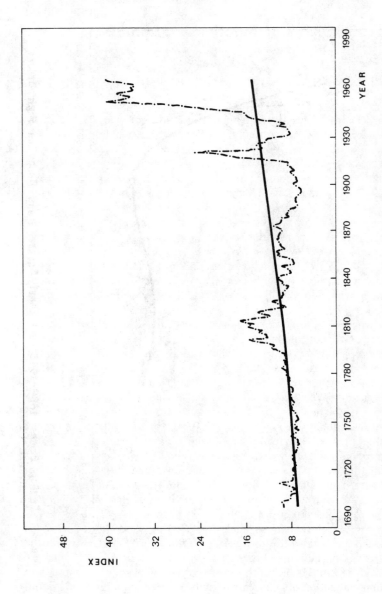

Fig. 1   English Prices 1696-1965 and Least Square Trend. (1913 = 100)³

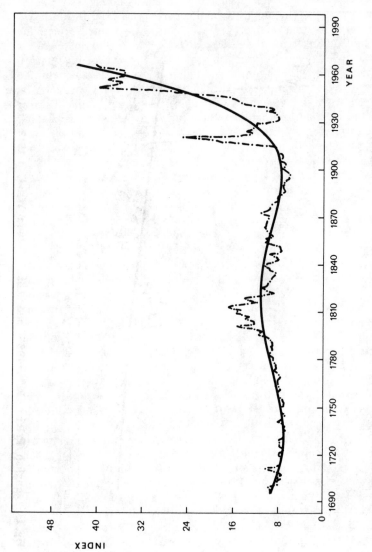

Fig. 2 English Prices 1696-1965 and Least Square Trend Based on High Order Polynomial. (1913=100).[4]

Each of the price increases mentioned roughly coincided with either an augmentation to the stock of precious metals or the expansion of the money supply by governments making use of the banking system or the printing presses. The modestly high general price level from 1850 to 1890 and again from 1896 to 1914, also more or less coincided with the gold finds in California and Australia and in Alaska and South Africa. It was therefore not unreasonable to assume a causal relationship between them. The assumption was that relative prices are determined by "real" forces of supply and demand and the absolute price level by the quantity of money and its velocity of circulation. Implicit in this were the suppositions that the money supply depends on the banking system's reserve base and that on the whole people do not maintain idle cash balances. These suppositions were again not unreasonable for the era before the relaxation of full currency convertibility and the decline of the classical type of manager-owned business organization. The growing complexity of the banking system, and the spread of shareholding joint stock businesses which, as the nineteenth century progressed and turned into the twentieth, also relaxed some of the immediate relationship between profits and investments, led to a more sophisticated formulation of the monetarist explanation of the level of prices. In its new form it maintained that the supply of money is related to the reserve base by a multiplier which is determined by the reserve ratio observed by the banking system, and the ratio between currency and deposits held by the public.[5] The old quantity of money theory explanation for price inflation still remained intact, but it embraced additional elements which made it less exogenously determined. In the 1920s when the business community felt increasingly restrained by the rigidity of the metallic system, it was initially modified (1925) and eventually generally abandoned (1931), except for the settlement of international debts, by Britain and the Scandinavian countries. The severing of the link between gold and money did not produce a rise in prices; they remained depressed until the war.

The dawning recognition that man's actions also exert an influence upon the level of prices and that it is not entirely exogenously determined was, in fact, only one aspect of a much wider development in society's perception of man's relationship with his natural environment. For ages mankind had perceived nature as given, absolute and orderly. Since the Renaissance the world at rest of the Middle Ages became a world in motion but no less orderly and harmonious. Johannes Kepler (1571–1630) even discovered that its regularity was better presented in mathematical terms when in motion than at rest — the orbit of each planet is an ellipse of which the sun's center is one focus, the radius vector of each planet (the line joining its center with that of the sun) moves over equal areas in equal times, and the square of the period of each planet's revolution around the sun is proportional to the cube of its mean distance from the sun. Isaac Newton (1642–1727) was delighted by the unity of nature expressed in the likeness between the apple falling from its tree and the rotation of the moon in its orbit round the earth; by the harmonious motion produced by the gravitational pulls between masses which attracted one another but were held together in their places or orbits in universal harmony because they were postulated each in its right position in relation to all others.

Adam Smith (1723–90) was convinced of the existence of a "divinely ordained harmony by which nature itself converts private quest for gain to the public good," because the rich "in spite of their natural selfishness and rapacity . . . are led by an invisible hand to make nearly the same distribution of the necessaries of life, which would have been made had the earth been divided into equal portions among all its inhabitants." So, economic thought developed in the shadow of a perception of Natural Order or even of a God-willed order governed by a single mechanism. Newton's gravitation was Smith's and his followers' "invisible hand." Newton believed that time and space are absolute and Smith believed in the economic system's eternal search for equilibrium. For Newton reality was a continuum held in balance by gravity, for Smith the economy was a continuum held together by the movement of prices. Newton and Smith believed in a separation of a *fact* from its *observer*; the scientists of the approaching era, early in the twentieth century, insisted on the linking of both. The old approach left man at the mercy of forces outside himself, the new made him part of these forces.

What Einstein, Planck, Heisenberg, and von Neumann destroyed was the belief that nature is governed by a mechanism of cause and effect which is a sequence of before and after, and that there is a universal now and not only a here and now for each observer.[6] They exorcized from nature the ghost of generalization — of the universal workings of causes and effects. From the search for universal rules they confined science to the limited purpose of describing the world in a manner that should enable man to look ahead, to forecast how the world would react to several courses of action between which man is free to choose. The old science described nature with the purpose of explaining it and to take this explanation as a guide to human action. The objective of the new approach was (and continues to be) more limited and direct. It describes nature just to imitate — to recreate it. In fact, scientists and technologists are producing new substances synthetically which are capable of serving our needs and satisfying our wants far better and more reliably than nature's gifts had ever done. The new kinetic theories gave man an understanding of matter which made it eventually possible to split the atom and gain control over sources of energy incomparably more powerful and less spatially restricted than wind, water, and animals. Genetical, biological, and biochemical theories gave rise to man's understanding of life and made it possible for him to interfere with the natural growth mechanisms to obtain predictable results and to reap more, better, and greater varieties of crops than earlier generations could ever have imagined. The formulation of theories about the composition of substances, and their effects upon one another — the study of chemistry — taught man to synthesize, to form compounds and recreate nature, and make materials and substances more suitable for his purpose than those nature had provided. From understanding our environment, scientific efforts were gravitating toward ways to dominate it. In economics this tendency was reflected in the Keynesian Revolution.

Although it seems obvious that scientific discovery influences the direction of social and economic change, or at least its rate, it is even more true that social and economic world views must permeate science.[7] As long as God still ruled the world or "Natural Order" reigned supreme and kept harmony on earth through Adam Smith's "invisible hand," inflation and mass unemployment of workers could be regarded as exogenously determined visitations. The debasement of the currency or the inordinate supply of money by governments provided a plausible explanation for the one and the sinful sexual immoderation of the poor for the other. Once the supply of money has increased, prices will rise and once the supply of labor has exceeded its demand, unemployment and misery must follow and there is little that can be done about it. As Malthus wrote: "the rich do not in reality possess the power of finding employment and maintenance for the poor," and the poor can therefore have no real right to demand it from them.[8]

But with the accelerating progress of industrialization and the development of democratic government and the rise of organized labor which accompanied it such views were becoming less and less politically practicable. In the second quarter of the twentieth century politicians were simply left with no alternative in the democratic free enterprise countries but to seek ways to solve the unemployment problem. For to be nonchalant about it and advise the unemployed to persevere in their misery until sometime in the future when the "automatic" mechanism restored prosperity was certainly no recipe for holding or gaining the public's confidence and vote. So, grudgingly, a society governed by the principle of individual advancement was beginning to make concessions to the collective demands of organized labor and political pressure groups. Full or near full employment became an explicit economic policy objective which justified willed interference with the other assumedly self-regulating mechanisms. The pursuit of the new objective seemed before long to come into conflict with another — namely the maintenance of a stable price level.

But early neoclassical economics was even less equipped than classical economics to deal with these problems. It was the product of an era of competitive individualism. Its orientation was microeconomic not macroeconomic — fitting the solution of the maximization problems of the firm — and not to meet the challenges of the collective problems of the state. Its very methodology excluded change, for it studied economics in "close analogy to statical mechanics . . . treating the laws of exchange as the laws of the equilibrium of the lever."[9] Neoclassical thought was in fact the bourgeoisie's philosophy of consolidation. Having successfully dislodged the old order the bourgeoisie was not disposed to let the revolution go on further. As it could hardly reconstitute the static hereditary society, it put in its place a system of dynamic stability. "Change and social mobility were still accepted as characteristic of society but as the running-in-place rather than an overture of the existing order." Liberal democracy had a vested interest in maintaining the world social order but allowed individuals, on the basis of relative competitive ability, to find their own places in the social structure.[10]

Keynesian economics provided the politically necessary compromise. It revived the link between micro- and macro-economic theory, and it was concerned with the determinants of the level of national income and therefore of employment. By introducing the distinction between planned and actual (*ex ante* and *ex post*) magnitudes, Keynes made inflation the result of the "gap" between planned aggregate demand and supply. If people are willing to buy more goods at the prevailing price level than producers are willing to supply, the gap between the economy's spending power and its ability to provide the necessary goods results in rising prices. The volume of goods which can be bought with the given purchasing power is reduced and the balance between aggregate demand and supply is restored.[11]

Of much greater and more general importance for the adjustment of economic thought to the changing societal reality was the new role Keynes allocated to the state in the economy. When Malthus wrote that "the rich do not in reality possess the power of finding employment and maintenance for the poor," his words were nearer to the truth than they may seem to be today. In his time most people were still engaged in farming and their fortunes were collectively determined by the weather and other forces beyond, or not yet under, human control.[12] When Keynes wrote, in the 1930s, most people in the economically advanced countries were engaged in industry and their fortunes lay in human hands. Profitability had become the arbiter of "employment and maintenance for the poor" and the quest for profit is a *human* trait. The worker experienced this because his employment opportunities were hinging upon his labor's profitability for other persons — the employers; and the employer experienced this because the rewards for his efforts were dependent on other people's — the consumers' — will and ability to procure his goods. The progress of science and technology had overcome the niggardliness of nature — the objective cause of destitution, but society had not yet learned to adjust to the new potentiality. It persevered in its manmade system — allowing poverty within plenty.

The dawning of the realization that man, not God or nature, may well be master of our economic plight was reflected in Keynes's idea that governments may take a direct hand in the direction of the economic mechanisms — that the state must boost demand by expanding its expenditure or by lowering taxation. Incorporating in his work Richard Kahn's[13] concept of the *multiplier,* he showed how increased government spending can create a chain reaction of new receivers and spenders of incomes and the expansion of employment.[14] The idea itself was not entirely new but its impact on policy decisions owed much to Keynes's manner of presenting it and timing. After all, even in the United States Socialists polled close to a million votes in 1932, and their influence then went far beyond their strength in numbers. The Keynesian approach was a departure from the accepted view about the role of government in economic matters, a departure from *laissez faire,* not a break with the bourgeois conception of society. The pursuit of profit continued to be the motive power behind man's economic efforts, and competition — the principle of "to each according to his ability," the pivot on which the system was turning. What Keynes provided was, or seemed to be, an answer to the immediate problem of mass unemployment, an answer which implied a concession to the newly emerging social and political reality. It was not an attack on the existing social order and the hegemony of the bourgeoisie. In the hands of Keynes's successors it was to become, perhaps unconsciously, precisely that.

Studying the business cycle and economic growth post-Keynesian economists soon learned that there was more than just the one-way traffic relating investment to employment. They saw that changes in any of the major aggregates are transmitted to the other and influence the level of activity as a whole. They showed how investment decisions are related to changes in income — how the multiplier effect on investment not only influences the level of employment but is itself determined by it; that as enterpreneurs aim to have the desired stock of real capital to meet the required output the rate of addition to this stock, i.e., new investment, must be a function of the rate of increase of the national income.[15] Searching for "the rate of growth of national income which the maintenance of full employment requires," economists in the post-Keynesian era also tried instead of making employment a function of income to make the labor force employed a function of the ratio between national income and productive capacity, where productive capacity meant the total output of the economy at what is usually called *full employment* (with factors like tastes, the price-wage structure, etc., taken as given). The conclusion thus arrived at was that only a growing income can solve the unemployment problem.

For if increased investment is leading to increased incomes, by way of the multiplier, and at the same time results in a surplus of unused capacity (due to technological progress — i.e., higher productivity), then only an even higher rate of increasing income can prevent unemployment by filling the gap between capacity and demand.[16] So step by step the old view, which sometimes gave the impression that it was man's destiny to serve the needs of the economy rather than the economy to satisfy man's wants, was abandoned. The realization that even small alterations in the rate of change in people's marginal propensity to consume cast a long shadow upon the general level of employment brought to light the enormous growth of the share of producer goods in the economy and the complexity of interaction between capital and labor in the industrial society. It showed the close interdependence between workers and owners, or controllers, of means of production; it reflected the demise of labor's traditional unquestioning acceptance of capital's hegemony, and helped to transform the claim for an equitable distribution of the fruits of production from a pious hope into a matter of economic expediency. It provided legitimization for the rising expectations of working people to share in the economic advantages resulting from rapid technological advancement. By studying the system as it *is* in order to make it work more effectively, positive economics discovered and gave cognizance to the new social reality and indicated the direction in which it *ought* to move if it were to survive. The addition of the pursuit of equity to the older objectives of economic policy became unavoidable.

The great era of fear and desolation which accompanied the rise of industrial society was waning. Before the coming of early industrialization feudal and quasi-feudal affiliations, together with time-honored customs afforded people some sense of social security. Early industrial society deprived the people affected by it of these safeguards. Even the habitual stand-by of the poor, root-gathering and poaching on the masters' land, was lost, and so was the comfort afforded by extended family ties and the village community. In their place came the desolate contest of everyone against everyone in the dire struggle for work and survival and the cold fear of starvation.[17] Competition among workers for employment lowered wages and assured industrial labor discipline and submissive social resignation. But it also made possible the accumulation and concentration of capital without which industrialization would have ground to a halt. It precipitated the inequitable distribution of the fruits of production which restricted workers' consumption and expanded employers' resources for investment and hence industrial progress.

Only belatedly and very gradually in the wake of technological advancement did labor raise effectively its claim to a greater share in what the new mode of production had to offer. Until almost the last decades of the nineteenth century, it was mainly the accretion and urban concentration of population, the ascent of the middle class and the expansion of world markets, which at one time or another, separately or together, kept demand abreast of the increasing output industry was able to supply.[18] Only then did labor become sufficiently organized and conscious of its power to effect a dramatic change in living standards. Only then was industry sufficiently advanced technologically to make this change practicable without drastically reducing growth-promoting investment.

The old growth-producing mechanisms continued to be at work. Employers were still hard pressed to innovate and rationalize by the competitive struggle of one with the other for their relative market shares, but organized labor was increasingly adding another kind of competition to the old, namely that between capital and labor for their relative shares in the fruits of production. The first kind of competition tended to keep prices in line, the second to push them up; together they accelerated even more than before the inexorable search for cost-reducing technological innovations and hastened the process of industrial concentration.

Essentially the rise of the labor movement, in all its forms, was the working-class's reaction to the social and economic evils which attended this progress of industrialization by way of relentless competition. It was the manifestation of opposition to a system which forced workers to choose between working for the going wage rate or to starve, and employers to choose between cutting their workers' wages as much as possible or facing economic ruin for lack of investment funds to keep pace with their competitors. Its attraction lay in the opposition it offered to exploitation, alienation, insecurity, and poverty; its weakness lay in its objective inability to offer a credible general alternative to the prevailing order, at least not before industrialization reached a level of productive efficiency capable of securing a "bourgeois" living standard for everyone. For, as long as capitalism did not accomplish what Marx had called its historical task, namely the creation of a colossal massive productive capacity,[19] labor's alternative could only imply a more equitable distribution but not plenty for all. It offered the reduction of poverty at the one end of society at the cost of less affluence at the other end — not plenty but justice. It left too many people, rightly or wrongly, feeling that they stood more to lose than to gain by overthrowing the system whose cultural hegemony though blemished had not yet seriously been challenged.[20]

In fact, until the middle of the present century, the "cake" was simply not yet big enough to satisfy most if not all who felt entitled to an adequate share of it. And so many nourished the illusion, and a few reckoned correctly, that by the joining the system they had individually a better chance to get a bigger slice than by engaging in a collective effort to abolish it. Consequently the labor movement in most industrial countries became more corrective and reformist than revolutionary. Demands for higher wages, improved working conditions, and greater social security within the system rather than for its abolition became its main *raison d'être*.

The success of labor's efforts in the highly industrialized countries to obtain higher wages, improved working conditions and greater social security cannot be denied, certainly not since the end of World War II. Between 1955 and 1975 average real wages more than doubled, working conditions became considerably better, and almost all workers came to enjoy some kind of social security arrangements, such as unemployment pay, pension funds, health insurance, etc. Few, if any, of these achievements were obtained at the expense of profits. They were the product of even greater increases in productivity.[21] Wherever and whenever wages rose they did so in line with productivity. Whether the labor unions pressing for higher wages were predominantly neoclassical, as in the United States, moderately socialist, as in the Netherlands, or under Communist influence, as in France, made little difference. The outcome was more or less the same everywhere.

Even in the welfare states in Western Europe, where governments take a big hand in running the economy and the provision of social services, and where the burden of taxes on employers is heaviest,[22] little can be seen of a redistribution of the shares of capital and labor in the fruits of production. It seems as if there were two growing "funds," one out of which labor's incomes came, and another for employers' profits. The relative shares of both in the overall growth remain constant over time. Where governments try to alter this, say, by high profit taxes, the old relationship was soon restored by the way the revenue was spent. For example, in many countries where profit taxes are high, government expenditure on "Research & Development" is also high; and where profit taxes are low, "Research & Development" is to a much greater extent promoted by the private sector. But if the rise in wages did not exceed the savings from technological improvements, and the distribution of the relative shares of the growing product between capital and labor remained constant, then, if competition among employers for their shares in the market had remained as it used to be, prices would have had to fall in line with technological advancement, not rise. For under stringent market competition among producers, labor's demands for higher wages would have either had to remain unanswered or would have caused a change in the relative shares of capital and labor in the national product.

It follows that much of the *macro-economic* controversy about whether prices pull up wages or wages push prices is irrelevant. It is the rise of oligopoly that prevents prices from falling commensurably with technologically attainable cost reductions. If several important firms no longer fully react to competitive market pressures, their prices affect the costs of many others and penetrate the system as a whole so that a fall in the general price level is prevented. Of course wage increases raise costs and prices, but they also tend to lead to technological labor-saving innovation, and so with brisk competition, sooner or later the old prices are more or less restored. But with part of the market under oligopoly its share in total production and the importance of its contribution to the general production mix will determine the degree to which wage increases influence the national price level.

The shift from price competition to other matters, such as the provision of extra consumer services, attractive packaging, and advertising, which is characteristic of oligopoly, will make the price hikes irreversible. By making "full employment" and upward wage adjustments politically and economically unavoidable, organized labor hastened the process of capitalistic concentration where price competition lessened. Businesses lacking the necessary capital to innovate in pace with rising labor costs were, in more and more sectors of the economy, either eliminated or taken over by, or amalgamated with, businesses which did not suffer capital constraints. So, price competition diminished while rising wages kept production efficiency on the ascent; labor's purchasing power increased more or less in line with labor's unaltered share in the fruits of technologically conditioned cost reductions but with rising prices.

A crucial development that not unnaturally accompanied labor's rising affluence and greater social security was a relaxation of customers' price consciousness. The attractive display and the often untrue advertising claims of suppliers that their goods are of superior quality or that they convey some kind of social advantage which their competitors' goods do not have more and more tended to tempt customers to pay prices which bear little relation to actual differences in the goods' production costs. Fashion changes hastened by clever advertising increase the obsolescence of products and stimulate waste of resources and the velocity of transactions, and often add to real production costs because of retooling requirements. Easily obtainable credit, like the "continu kredet" offered by banks in the Netherlands, or by "hire-purchase" financiers in England, adds further to consumers' temptation to buy and thus raises the real cost of goods by the measure of interest charges. In fact, increased unemployment and reduced wage rises since the midseventies have not led to an appreciable decline in consumer demand, at least not in the Netherlands. They were, however, accompanied by an expansion of consumer credit.[23] Demand remained brisk because the young generation which grew up in the era of prosperity and full employment is no longer as sensitive to the future dangers the economy may hold as their elders who lived all their lives under the prewar threat of destitution. People did not reduce their habitual expenditure. Its level was sustained partly from social security and unemployment pay and partly, where, for example, only one member of a family lost his job, from borrowed funds, i.e., from loans often contracted in the belief that inflation will cancel the interest charges and that full employment will be restored.

Together with the continuing concentration of capital, the decline in price competition, and the relaxation of consumers' price consciousness, went several new business practices which added fuel to the ongoing price inflation. More and more producers and suppliers, expecting prices to have risen by the time their wares reach the market, and expecting labor, energy, and other costs to have done the same, tend to mark up prices in advance to assure themselves against these probabilities. In fact, they promote a kind of self-fulfilling prophecy. No more than a decade ago, suppliers offered special price reductions to customers paying cash on delivery; they now frequently add punitive interest charges even for short delays in payment. Where price competition remained a significant factor, for example, between certain multinationals vying for their shares in international trade, the pressure is often relieved by "tied" services. If a Peugeot car must be sold at internationally competitive prices, this is far less necessary for Peugeot spare parts. They can be sold far above their cost because the "captive" car owner has simply no alternative but to pay as charged if his vehicle breaks down. Most manufacturers of photographic equipment sell cameras at competitive prices but make sure that the various attachments the owners of the cameras may wish to buy later will fit only if bought from the same make. Similarly it is not uncommon for large manufacturing firms to establish their own sales organizations, or to acquire control of strategically located chain stores and supermarkets, with the sole objective of excluding their competitors' goods from the region or even country in order to keep up prices. You simply cannot buy Shell petrol at an Exxon station. But all these oligopolistic pricing devices are only one aspect of a much wider social and economic development which accompanied the concentration of capital — namely, the rise of *industrial feudalism*, the demise of the cost and price restraining mechanisms, and the gradual legitimization of corruption.

The rise of *industrial feudalism* is reflected in the rise of the managerial "class" which replaced that of the old owner-managers. As more and more firms engaged in different stages of production of the same commodity, and more and more firms engaged in the same stage of production of the same commodity amalgamate — as the vertical and horizontal integration of business increases to achieve greater economic power and higher profits, business becomes less and less manageable by a single person or a single managerial board. And so, as the amalgamations become syndicates, trusts, and holding companies, management is delegated along hierarchical patterns to "submanagers," heads of branches, departments, sections, etc.[24] Eventually, the organizations become so powerful that their top managers, the men who replace the old-style owner-manager capitalist, find that their decisions are far less influenced by market forces than market forces by their decisions. They discover that their share in consumers' expenditure is so large that, subject only to the limitations imposed upon demand by the magnitude of the year-to-year changes in the country's GNP, their decisions have a greater impact on markets and prices than markets and prices on their decisions.[25]

In the Netherlands five big conglomerates directly employ 18 percent of all the working population, and indirectly many more, and these five virtually control, but for foreign competition, the whole field of electronics, metallurgy, food processing, chemicals, and oil. In Germany, some 2,000 businesses employ 50 percent of the total labor force, as against 200,000 businesses which employ the rest. In the United States some 2,000 corporations control about 80 percent of all resources used in manufacturing.[26] Even the most confirmed free enterprise economists cannot deny the price-fixing powers of the large conglomerates. They are states within the states, and their top managers plan just like the top planning officials in government service, only with this difference: They plan for maximization of profits, and the government planners, where they exist, for stability, equity, and growth. Also, not unlike the government officials at the top, they develop "class" characteristics which distinguish them from both the rest of the people "below" them and from the old style capitalist-owner class entrepreneurs. They are united with the top bureaucracy not only by their position but also by their lifestyle and training.

David Noble discovered that the chief executives of the five largest corporations in the United States had all been classmates at MIT.[27] What Eton and Harrow had been for the managers of one empire, the

Ivy League and the engineering department and business school of MIT have become for the managers of another. Only that for those privileged to take part in the games on the "playing fields of Eton" fair play was on an equal footing with winning; on the playing fields of the new elite only victory counts. Unlike the old-style capitalist who belonged to a civilization in which status though connected with control over people was not entirely based on it, the new members of the managerial "class" have only one criterion for attainment, namely, the position a man holds in the organizational hierarchy. To be sure, like the capitalist of old the new manager in industry, government, and international organizations, is also caught up in the relentless race of all against all, only that the race for property — ownership of capital, has become a race for position — rank in the organization. The rules of the race have not changed; halt and you are soon overtaken by others, and being overtaken you fall back until you reach the bottom of the hierarchy. But without the fetters of things "done and not done" of the Western heritage, the race has become much nastier. Is it more than half a century ago that a soccer player who made a foul would admit it freely and be applauded for admitting it by the supporters of his team? The point is that the "race" has become free from the unwritten rules that traditional education had imposed on old-style capitalism — now only *positive* law counts. All is right that the law does not forbid.

Unlike the old-style capitalists, the new managers operate not with their own but with other people's money. Consequently they are prepared to take much greater financial risks to promote their personal advancement than old-style capitalists would have dared to take, and they are also far less restrained in charging personal expenses to the business's account. What matters to them is not whether their expenses are really necessary but whether they can be correctly booked. What matters is not whether they had to go around half the world to meet a business associate whom they might reach by phone but whether they have sufficient receipts to satisfy the accountants that they actually spent the money they claim to have spent on the trip. Losses and unnecessary expenses become production costs and are shifted to consumers' prices.

Another "business cost" which is pushed on to consumers' prices are bribes. Not that traditional capitalism did not indulge in this practice, but no self-respecting capitalist would ever have publicly admitted it. This is no longer so. To quote the ex-Gulf chief Dorsey: "Ethics, morals, customs, values, principles . . . are all nonsense . . . we have to adjust." [28] Dorsey is not alone. When the United States agency Business International questioned the managers of fifty-five multinationals about their experiences with bribery it was told that with the exception of the People's Republic of China the practice of bribery is universal. In several countries, so the inquiry showed, established firms exist specializing in the sale of forged bills and receipts to assist the multinationals and other large companies in this practice.[29] In the Netherlands the Chairman of the Liberal (VVD) fraction in the Upper House, also thinks that under certain circumstances bribery is quite respectable.[30] Bribes are deductable from taxes in Germany, in Japan, in France, and in Italy, practically in all the industrial countries. When a study group on this subject was organized by the United Nations Social and Economic Council, and the American delegation suggested that all payments to persons involved in the arrangement of contracts should be public to avoid corrupt practices, it met with the strongest opposition.[31]

What then is the reason for the great spread and qualitative changes in, corruption? One reason is the increasing business contact with countries where the giving and receiving of "gifts" is part of an accepted way of life. Another, that much of the business with such countries goes via state officials who do not deal with their own but with public funds, and yet another, that much of the business in such countries is done with *unearned* funds, i.e., with foreign aid and long-term loans. The first reason creates the necessary climate; the second provides the strata of society which has the opportunity to benefit from such practices without much financial and personal risk; the third, supplies the material basis, the actual funds which can be appropriated without causing immediate visible loss to the people who are cheated. The donors in the rich countries have no direct interest in the manner in which the funds are utilized abroad because they do not expect a calculable return, and the assumed beneficiaries in the poor countries cannot feel deprived of something they never had.

If in the past, the social climate did not favor such malpractices in the industrial countries and powerful material forces of self-interest tended to limit them, they have in the last decades gradually eroded under the influence of the rise of managerial and regulated capitalism. In the past the people who bought in bulk were owner-capitalists, i.e., people directly interested in making the best possible bargain, for the money they spent was their own. Now, the rise of the large corporations in which the owners have only indirect control over expenditures and of non-profit-making sectors, over whose expenditure the public has only a "bookkeeping" but no real supervision, has created a category of people who control other people's money and have the same opportunities for corruption as their equals in the poorer parts of the world. In addition the great secrecy shrouding expenditure for public goods, such as military equipment, space technology and research, energy, etc., provides almost optimal conditions for financial irregularities. The funds used for these purposes are "unearned," from the point of view of those who disburse them, and their utilization cannot be subjected to the price-mechanism tests of strict cost-benefit analyses. Only the input can be measured, not the output.

The built-in protecting mechanism of manager-owners' self-interest-dominated capitalism, is waning quickly; waste, theft, bribery, etc., all are added to the cost of production and the consumers' bill. The "feudal" ranking of people within each organization, with increasingly more privileges (expense accounts, official cars, etc.) attached to each rank as it comes closer to the top positions, is a well-established practice in government service and the larger business organizations. And as the share of these organizations in total employment increases, more and more people are sucked into this hierarchical system. In fact, close to half of all working people in the industrial countries have already been sucked into it, and with the spreading of services this tendency is bound to continue.

As services are fairly insensitive to the normal functioning of the *price mechanism*, the test for an employee's efficiency becomes less dependent on cost effectiveness than on the hitchless operation of his office. Not the office equipment which provides best value for money is purchased but the one likely to give least trouble though its cost may be exorbitant — who cares? Promotion in the business organization becomes less and less a function of performance and more and more of the personal relationship between inferiors and superiors. The personal "nexus" — whom one knows and whom one serves — becomes the overriding element in one's advancement. In this way a new vertical relationship is forged by which the whole hierarchy within an organization or office is held together. The lower layers protect the ones above them for their position depends upon their status, and the higher layers protect the ones below, for any mistakes they may be responsible for will eventually be put at their door should they be detected.

As each member of the hierarchy has nothing to gain personally, but much to lose in chances for promotion by challenging the quality of the organization's goods and services and by informing the outside world of malpractices, the organization frequently develops a self-sustained ethos — a belief that what it does is right. Its members accept that what *is* is right. They become accustomed to the idea that manual workers and clerks are entitled by virtue of their *position* in the organization — not by virtue of their contribution to, say, production — to good wages and salaries (where *good* means in comparison with other employees of the same categories in other enterprises); that specially qualified personnel receive higher incomes, again by virtue of position; and that administrative staff at managerial level gain access to greater income, again by virtue of position, and additional tax-free advantages in the form of expense accounts, interest-free company loans, the use of company vehicles, etc., fringe benefits which sometimes exceed their salaries.[32] All this is then added to "production costs" and to the prices which consumers pay. And so, while technological innovation reduces the number of workers directly employed in production and raises the value of their labor, false claims are made that it is their wage increases that cause prices to rise. The real cost-inflating expenses, which do not appear in the wage statistics, are conveniently ignored. In the end it is the kind of people who belong to the new "class" which gains most from the "expense account" economy, who do not need to worry about their inflated hotel bills since they never pay them out of their own pocket (but who set the price for all others who have to pay themselves) who also advise "Prices and Incomes Policies" to contain inflation.

Next to the hereto enumerated social causes for the postwar price inflation there is, however, also a "hard" economic cause which prevents the protracted rise in prices from leveling off before the whole structure of the economic system is adjusted to it. This is the accelerating change in the patterns of employment: the dramatic decline of employment in agriculture, the diminishing labor requirements in industry, and the rise in service occupations. The share of employment in the primary sector declined throughout the whole period 1850–1975; the share of employment in the secondary sector increased on the whole until the nineteen sixties but then began falling (for example in West Germany) from 49 percent to 43 percent; and the share of the services rose steadily from 20 percent in the mid-nineteenth century, to 27 percent in the early twentieth century, 43 percent in the sixties, and 53 percent and still rising in 1975.[33] In the United States the share of services rose during the last three decades from 55 percent to 67 percent in terms of employment, and from 31 percent to 41 percent in terms of contribution to GNP.[34]

The decline in labor requirements in agriculture and industry was accompanied by a very considerable rise in the volume of output in these sectors due to a sharp rise in productivity. For example, in the Netherlands productivity in all sectors rose on average 4.16 percent annually between 1960 and 1970 and 3.25 percent between 1960 and 1975, and in industry alone between 1955 and 1974 by approximately 6.5 percent annually.[35] This sharp rise in productivity in agriculture and industry was not matched in the services. Many tasks in this sector do not easily lend themselves to labor-saving mechanization. They often require direct contact between "producers" and "consumers." Services cannot be "stored," are unsuitable for transportation and transference, lack homogeniety, are highly income elastic to demand. But above all it is the first reason — the *Kundenpräsenz*, the necessity for doctors and patients, teachers and pupils, waiters and diners, to be together in the performance of the service, which gives it its special time dimension and influences its quality. This time dimension describes a positive relationship; on the whole, the longer the time allowed for the performance of the service, the better will be its quality. And so, while incomes rise, and the demand for quality increases, wage rates set in the technologically most improving industries will spread to the service occupations, and inflation will penetrate all sectors of the economic system. Thus in the final analysis price movements are determined by the relative shares in total demand of goods and of services. And as the demand for goods is coming closer to saturation, and productivity in the goods-producing sector is improving, labor shifts to the expanding service sector and prices rise until a new equilibrium between the sectors is established. Then they will stabilize but at a higher level than before.

Naturally, neither the increase in the volume of transactions nor the rise in prices could have proceeded without a corresponding expansion of the money supply. The spreading of the credit system and the proliferation of new payment facilities which followed the abolition of the gold standard and several other restrictive reserve requirements accomplished precisely this. After all, bank profits flow from their extension of credit and not from its restriction and they tend therefore, in one way or another, to adjust their facilities to an economy's increasing requirements. So, in contrast to earlier periods when prices rose as a result of monetary expansion, for example, during wars or when the printing presses were operated in Germany and Eastern Europe after World War I, the expansion of the money supply in recent decades is the result of the mounting volume of transactions and of rising prices. With the spreading of oligopoly, and the increasing number of large enterprises with internal sources of finance, it appears that monetary stringency, i.e., rising interest rates, must tend to raise prices rather than constrain them in the expected manner of restricting investment and employment. The higher costs are simply shifted on to consumer prices, which in turn are followed by wage adjustments. In the remaining competitive sectors the concentration of capital at the same time continues with added strength. More and more enterprises fall prey to the few financially powerful enough to ignore the higher interest rates or whose profits are sufficiently high to continue operating at their customary level because of a relative technological or other superiority over their competitors in the same line of business. With the state often coming to the assistance of weaker firms in order to maintain the necessary level of employment, and with social security arrangements preventing a drastic fall in purchasing power even if, in spite of its efforts, unemployment takes its toll, consumer prices will hardly be set on a downward trend for long when interest rates rise. Moreover, with prices on an upward trend for years, people will tend to contract loans to purchase durable and semi-durable goods in the anticipation that much of their interest will in time be "cancelled" by inflation.

In conclusion it appears that there are two different types of price inflation. One is reversible; the other continues until the dramatic and fundamental social and economic developments which give rise to it have fully matured. The former is caused by changes in the money supply, for example when governments work the printing presses, or by disequilibria between supply and effective demand as occurs in times of war or at the height of the business cycle, or by coincidental shortages of some essential resources, such as energy since the oil crisis. The other type of inflation is caused by fundamental changes in the whole social and economic structure of society and in its cultural framework; for example, when the competitive mechanisms making for technological innovation and assuring labor discipline wane, when the basic employment and production structure shifts, when mass unemployment of workers becomes politically untenable, and when expedience replaces truth in the hierarchy of social values. The first type of inflation can be contained and may be reversible because when governments recall inflated currencies, or when economies readjust after wars, or business cycles pass their peaks, or resource shortages are eventually alleviated by the development of substitutes, prices will either fall or stop rising. The second type of inflation will continue until the social and economic transformation is completed and the new structure is established. Something like this happened in the sixteenth century; it is happening again in ours.

Notes

1. "The Inflation of Prices in Early Sixteenth Century England," *Economic History Review* XIV (1961).
2. In seven industrial countries taken together (France, Germany, Italy, Japan, Sweden, the United Kingdom, and the United States) the rate of change of consumer prices compared annually from calendar years was: 2.8 percent for 1956–60, 3.7 percent for 1961–65, 4.1 percent for 1966–70, 9.3 percent for 1971–75. M. Friedman, "Nobel Lecture: Inflation and Unemployment," *Journal of Political Economy* 85 (1977): 461.
3. Jan Reynders, "Het Raadsel van de Lange Golven" (unpublished paper). Annual rate of rise of exponential trend over the whole period is 0.286 percent.
4. *Ibid.*, p. 17.
5. For a concise summary of the early quantity theory of money, see H. G. Johnson, *Essays in Monetary Economics*, 2d ed. (London, 1969), chap. 1.
6. For a fuller discussion of this issue in its social and economic context, Y. S. Brenner, *Looking into the Seeds of Time* (Assen, 1979), chap. 9.

7. For a discussion of this proposition, see R. C. Lewontin, "Evolution" in the *International Encyclopedia of Social Science* (1968) V: 208–209.

8. R. T. Malthus, *Essay on the Principle of Population*, bk. IV, chap. V.

9. Quotation from W. S. Jevons, *Theory of Political Economy*, 3d ed. (London, 1888), pp. vi–vii.

10. Lewontin, p. 208.

11. J. M. Keynes, *How to Pay for the War* and *The General Theory of Employment, Interest and Money* (1936) and also S. Weintraub, "The Keynesian Theory of Inflation: the Two Faces of Janus?" *International Economic Review* 1 (1960): 143–55.

12. The proportion of population engaged in agriculture was in the US, 72.3 percent in 1820 and 38.2 percent in 1900; in England and Wales, 22.8 percent in 1841 and 8.6 percent in 1901; in France 63 percent in 1827 and 33.1 percent, 1901. Data taken from William Ashworth, *The International Economy Since 1850*, 2d ed. (London, 1962), p. 106.

13. "The Relation of Home Investment to Unemployment," *Economic Journal*, June 1931.

14. For a lucid explanation of the *Multiplier*, see R. C. O. Matthews, *The Trade Cycle* (Cambridge), pp. 8–12.

15. P. A. Samuelson, "Interaction between the *Multiplier* Analysis and the Principle of *Acceleration*," *Review of Economic Statistics*, 1939.

16. E. D. Domar, "Expansion and Employment," *American Economic Review* XXXVII, 1947.

17. As Thomas Hobbes (1588–1679) succinctly said: "The condition of man . . is a condition of war of everyone against everyone," *Leviathan* (pt. i, chap. 4).

18. This process was discussed in some detail in my *Short History of Economic Progress* (London, 1969).

19. Karl Marx and Friedrich Engels, *The Communist Manifesto* (1848, p. 5).

20. I discussed this issue at some length in chap. 9 and 10 in *Looking into the Seeds of Time.*

21. For example in the Netherlands, real income from work in industry rose between 1955 and 1975 by 101 percent, and productivity in industry by 174 percent, and in all sectors together by 121 percent, *Centraal Economisch Plan.* C.P.B. s'-Gravenhage 1974 and 1976.

22. For example in the Netherlands the nominal income from work rose between 1955 and 1975 by 416.8 percent but the cost of a worker to the employer by 616.3 percent (social insurance contributions, etc.), *Centraal Economisch Plan.*

23. The Netherlands are mentioned here because the data were easily obtainable, but the situation seems to be similar elsewhere, at least in the welfare states.

24. A. D. Chandler, Jr., *The Visible Hand: The Managerial Revolution in American Business* (Cambridge, Mass., 1977).

25. For examples of how this works, see Brenner, pp. 324–25.

26. J. K. Galbraith, *The New Industrial State* (New York, 1967), chap. 7.

27. D. F. Noble, *America by Design. Science, Technology, and the Rise of Corporate Capitalism* (New York, 1977).

28. Quoted from *Der Spiegel* 9/1976.

29. *Ibid.*, 27/12/1976.

30. Quoted from report on VVD Congress in *de Volkskrant*, 15/3/1976.

31. For a long list of examples selected from the press, see Brenner, pp. 327–30.

32. For a wider discussion of the New Industrial Feudalism, see Brenner, chap. 11.

33. Jean Fourastie, *Die grosse Hoffnung des zwanzigsten Jahrhunderts* (Köln, 1969); W. Dettling, *Die neue soziale Frage* (München, 1977).

34. Eli Ginzberg, *Scientific American*, December 1976, p. 28, November 1977, p. 47.

35. A. Spithoven (unpublished paper), December 1978; F. Neumann, *Daten zu Wirtschaft, Gesellschaft, Politik, Kultur* (Baden-Baden, 1976).

Inflation, the Terms of Trade, and National Income Estimates

EDWARD MARCUS

Real gross national product — real GNP — has been the most common yardstick for measuring changes in a country's real output and well-being, since it purports to correct for price changes, thus giving an indication of an economy's actual growth in goods and services, with the price/inflation element removed from the statistics. Under most conditions this concept is adequate for the purpose, but in times of marked price changes, such as the past decade, it often gives a misleading picture. In particular, it can actually point in the wrong direction if a country's imports change in price markedly differ from the movement in its export prices.[1] In more technical language, the change in foreign trade price relationships — the country's terms of trade — distorts the story that the real GNP figures are telling. For the 1970s this leads to the incongruity that the oil price inflation will improve the real GNP and real foreign trade position of those countries heavily dependent on oil imports, while reducing the real GNP and worsening the real foreign trade balance of the major oil exporters!

To understand the nature of the alleged distortion, a few words about the compilation of real GNP are in order. Essentially, what the national income economists do is to start with money GNP — the country's goods and services turned out during the period, valued at the actual prices prevailing. To arrive at real GNP — output corrected for price changes, to remove the impact of inflation — the money GNP series is deflated — in practice, divided by — a price series that reflects the change in prices since some year selected as the base for measurement.[2] In this way we obtain a fairly good approximation of the change in the volume of goods and services turned out. In practice, the national income and output calculations employ several price series to take into account the complex composition of output characteristic of modern economies. Thus, there might be one series to deflate consumer durables, another for capital goods, a third for services, and still others for exports and imports. In this way the different important sectors are corrected by price series appropriate to their particular composition.

That such a correction is necessary can be seen from data for the United States national accounts. In 1972, for example, our gross national product — money GNP — was \$1171.1 billion. In 1973, it rose to \$1306.6 billion, or an increase of approximately 11.6 percent in money GNP. But during the same period prices on the average had risen by some 5.8 percent. By applying the appropriate deflators to the various components the resultant real GNP — the actual amount of goods and services produced — had risen only 5.5 percent, or less than half the percentage increase recorded by money GNP.

There are serious distortions in this approach, particularly when prices affecting a country's foreign trade shift sharply, as they did in 1973. If the country's terms of trade change appreciably — if export prices over the period move in a way markedly different from import prices — then calculating real GNP the traditional way could lead to some odd results. But first we must see how the foreign sector is integrated with the remainder of the economy in order to arrive at the end GNP number.

Essentially, one adds domestic consumption, investment, inventory changes, the spending by government, etc. To this is then added exports of goods and services and from this we subtract imports of goods and services.[3] Under normal conditions this is a plausible adjustment. More exports mean more output, which, in turn, means more income, and so a rise in exports would lead to a rise in GNP. Analogously, more imports mean less is spent on domestically produced goods and services, and so a rise in imports tends to be correlated with a lower GNP. And since we are measuring real GNP, both exports and imports are deflated by the appropriate price indices, as was done for the other GNP components.

But along come the 1970s when the price of imported oil — as well as that of many other commodities — zooms sky high, with crude petroleum up on the average of more than ten times the price in 1972. This jump in prices induces consumers throughout the world to try to economize on their use of petroleum products, and so the physical volume of oil imports declines somewhat. Assuming that there have been no other changes in the foreign sector, we would have an unchanged export volume and a somewhat smaller import volume. In real terms our real GNP would rise, since we are now subtracting a smaller volume of imports from our total of GNP spending. In fact, not only would real GNP rise as a result of this drop in the volume of imports, but in addition the country's foreign position would show an improvement — in real terms — since it is importing less than before while maintaining the same volume of exports.

But this, as we all know, is completely false for recent years. The sharp jump in oil prices has not made us better off, as the rise in real GNP implies. Nor has our foreign balance improved. For every oil importer, the small drop in import volume has been more than offset by

the enormous rise in the price of the oil that continues to be imported — so much so that the amount of money being spent for foreign
oil has risen appreciably. Virtually every important oil-importing
country now faces a tremendous balance of trade problem.

To illustrate the differences resulting from these calculations, let us
look at American national income data, using 1973–74, the start of the
oil price inflation.

In 1973, we had in money terms a net excess of exports of goods and
services, amounting to $7.1 billion. In 1974, this declined by $1.1
billion, to $6 billion. But when adjusted for price changes for real GNP,
the net export excess *rose* $8.3 billion. In other words, in money terms,
this country's balance on goods and services had deteriorated, whereas
in real terms it had improved appreciably. Dollar imports in 1974 cost
$37.5 billion more than in 1973, but *dropped* $2.8 billion in real terms,
reflecting the smaller volume.

The major oil producers' real position will be equally misleading.
Presumably the steep oil price rise cut world consumption somewhat,
thus leading to a small decline in the volume of oil exports. As we
already explained, a decline in export volume shows up as a drop in
real GNP. The oil producers, in other words, are apparently worse off
now than in 1972, at least in real terms. But is this so? Are the additional billions that they are earning really depressing their GNP? Hardly!
As we all know, the OPEC countries are swimming in surpluses of hard
currencies.

Clearly, there is a problem. We do want to know what the change in
available goods and services really is, abstracting from the inflationary
elements. Yet we do not want to remove so much inflation that we end
up with a false picture, as might be the case if we arrive at real GNP
along conventional lines. In short, money GNP must be corrected for
price inflation to arrive at real GNP. But then real GNP must be corrected to arrive at a final number that also includes an adjustment
factor for the foreign sector.

One possibility would be to adjust for the change in money terms as a
result of the shifts in both export and import prices.[4] For example, in
1974, United States export prices averaged 27.0 percent above 1973.
Applying this number to 1974 exports implies that inflation boosted
export income by $10.8 billion. But over the same period average
import prices had risen 50.3 percent. Presumably, because of inflation
1974 imports cost us $33.1 billion more. Net inflation had worsened
our position by $22.3 billion ($33.1 billion minus $10.8 billion). This
added net cost equalled about 1.6 percent of the GNP. Therefore, we
should treat it as a cost, and deduct it from our real GNP figures. Thus,
1974 money GNP showed an 8.1 percent rise over 1973. When adjusted
conventionally, we get a 1.4 percent drop in real GNP. Adjusted fur-

ther, we would get a final real GNP figure showing a 3 percent drop, or double that reported.

What would be accomplished by the additional correction suggested here is an adjustment of real GNP for the shift in the country's external payments position, especially if this shift arose from a strong adverse turn in import costs.[5] It would alert analysts to the story told by the two sets of real GNP — one, the conventional measure — indicating the flow of goods and services within the economy; the other — the correction suggested — would point a warning finger at the worsening of the country's external payments position, which the conventional real GNP had obscured.

Similarly for the major oil exporters. Their real GNP would not show much of an increase when measured conventionally. But the oil price rise is giving them enormously greater income, much of which is being channeled into foreign investment — savings, so to speak. To conclude that they have not benefited much because so much of their earnings went into the acquisition of foreign assets would indeed be folly. And, roughly, this addition to their foreign assets would be equal to the net addition to earnings arising from the much greater increase in oil export prices than in their import costs. By making this additional correction of the real GNP data we would then obtain a truer picture of the oil countries' improved economic position.

Notes

1. E. E. Hagen and E. C. Budd, "The Product Side: Some Theoretical Aspects" in National Bureau of Economic Research, *Conference on Research in Income and Wealth* 22 (1958): 245.
2. Cf. P. Høst-Madsen, *Macroeconomic Accounts*, International Monetary Fund pamphlet series no. 29 (Washington, 1979), pp. 28–31.
3. Cf. I. B. Kravis, A. W. Heston, and R. Summers, "Real GDP Per Capita for More Than One Hundred Countries," *Economic Journal*, June 1978, p. 229.
4. Cf. J. W. Kendrick, "Measurement of Real Product" in *Conference on Research in Income and Wealth* 22 (1958): 415.
5. Cf. Y. Kurabayashi, "The Impact of Changes in Terms of Trade on a System of National Accounts: an Attempted Synthesis," *Review of Income and Wealth*, September 1971, pp. 287ff.

A Theoretical Analysis of the
Exchange Process and Inflation

PATRICIA F. BOWERS

INTRODUCTION

Since the late 1960s economic models often have not seemed able to answer the questions that economists, businessmen, and government policy makers ask of them. This resulted in a serious questioning of the traditional assumptions underlying economic theory and provides the foundation for what I think will be a revolution in economic thinking, comparable to the one initiated by Keynes and the neoclassicists in the 30s, 40s, and 50s. It is my present purpose to show the implications of these theoretical advances for an understanding of the problem of inflation.

For a consistent model to shed light on real world problems, such as that of inflation, the choice maximization process of individual trans-actors should proceed under the strategic assumptions of game theory, as well as the nonstatic assumptions of disequilibrium analysis, rather than the static, nonstrategic, cooperative assumptions used in most current theoretical analysis. My special interest concentrates on incorporating the former approach into the analysis of the demand for money. This procedure reflects the interchange between micro- and macroeconomics occurring in theoretical economic modeling generally; it also points up some important policy issues facing us as consumers, producers, and citizens. Such a framework highlights that the use of money as a medium of exchange both solves problems and creates problems, and that the more society solves the problems which money as a medium of exchange creates, the more it reintroduces some of the problems money was introduced to solve.

DECENTRALIZED, SEQUENCE ECONOMIES

In order to understand how money aids in the exchange process and how it creates problems that underlie the current inflationary dilemma, it is necessary to work with a decentralized, sequence framework. This utilizes the mathematical structure of the game theoretical approach, as do all modern treatments of the process of general equilibrium theory. In a decentralized economy there is no explicit mechanism, like an auctioneer, for coordinating trades. This means that no particular institutional arrangement is assumed to exist at the outset. Certain rules of behavior, however, are specified. In decentralized, sequence economies, traders may seek one another out on an individual basis, dealing with one agent at a time on a bilateral and sequential basis. Alternatively, they may congregate at a trading post or market for a specific good, again visiting them in sequence. Either of these trading rules yields comparable outcomes. In such an economy, the order and date of transactions affects the opportunities open to an agent. Since transactions are specifically dated, the agent may not face a present value budget constraint, as in the Arrow-Debreau general equilibrium world, but may have to balance his books on every transaction.

Two alternative behavioral rules regarding transactors' response to prices are considered in the literature on decentralized, sequence economies. Under one rule, transactors' quantity adjustments to relative prices result in a sequence economy with flexible prices (Hahn, 1973; Starett, 1973; Kurz, 1974). A second behavioral rule results in a fixed price sequence model. This approach is followed by the authors upon whose work I am building. In the Hicks fixed-price method (Hicks, 1965) it is assumed that prices are fixed, in some unspecified way, for the whole of the trading process and transactors accept these fixed prices. Thus, quantities adjust infinitely faster than prices. The Hicks fixed price method is the opposite case of the Walrasian tatonnement. Hicks fixed price models are disequilibrium models, unless by happenstance (or by assumption) the established prices happen to be the equilibrium price set.

The institutional arrangement that gives each agent perfect information regarding the financial honesty of every other agent; that is, the information that assures the availability of quid pro quo information and no default, as assumed in Arrow-Debreau and called an *assurance game* in game theory, is not guaranteed in all decentralized, sequence market structures. The implication of the existence or lack of this information is part of the problem addressed here.

When individual traders seek one another out in sequence to trade bilaterally in a fixed price model, it is usual for individual excess demands not to be equal (Ostroy, 1973; and Ostroy and Starr, 1974); or when many traders come to a particular market (Benassy, 1975a,b), it is usual for the aggregate of notional excess demands; that is, demands as represented in the utility function, not to sum to zero. Since actual transactions of each agent must sum to zero, and there is no auctioneer to coordinate trades in a decentralized world, a rationing scheme is necessary to go from notional demands to actual transactions.

Many rationing schemes are possible to get around the disequilibrium situation between notional and actual demands; for example, rationing tickets, queuing, priority systems, proportional rationing, odd-even licence plate numbers. The final outcome of the trading process depends, a priori, on the institutional arrangement chosen for the rationing scheme. This means that there are many equilibria in a decentralized, sequence model. The rationing system then determines how shortages are distributed among agents.

Voluntary exchange is the rationing scheme usually assumed in a decentralized, sequence economy (Ostroy, 1973; Ostroy and Starr, 1974; Benassy, 1975a,b). *Voluntary exchange* means that no trader is forced to accept in exchange a good he does not want to hold. Voluntary exchange in disequilibrium implies that traders on the short side of the market, suppliers in the case of notional excess demand (these were the gasoline distributors during the summer gasoline crisis), and demanders, when there is excess supply, realize their notional (and actual) demands (Benassy, 1975a,b). At the same time individuals on the long side cannot be forced to exchange more than they want to. This means each agent has a set of trade-perceived constraints, which depends on the information available to him. Consequently, there were particularly long lines at the gasoline stations on the New Jersey Turnpike during the summer gas shortage, since motorists were assured of being able to make minimum $5 purchases at all hours. Similar results are obtained in models using uniform rationing (Dreze, 1975; Laroque, 1978a,b), in which it is assumed that agents are entitled to the same-sized trades on all markets.

MONETARY EXCHANGE MORE COST EFFICIENT THAN BARTER

The major theoretical contribution to the understanding of the importance of money in the exchange process and the distinction between the exchange process in a world of barter and in a monetized world was made by Ostroy (1973) and Ostroy and Starr (1974). Ostroy and Starr show that a decentralized trading process with barter requires many rounds of trade to attain an Arrow-Debreau equilibrium. Money as the medium of exchange allows the full execution of trade in one round, with the use of a decentralized trading process. This occurs because money reduces the communication necessary for trade, in that one need know only whether one's trading partner will accept the medium of exchange. In essence, one unique exchange plan exists in a monetary economy. The choice problem facing a transactor reduces to the single one of choosing the final transaction vector, as occurs in the Arrow-Debreau model. The question of how to trade is predecided; one uses money as the medium of exchange. But, which commodity (or medium) serves this function must be institutionally imposed from outside the model. In addition, there is a time saving, because there are fewer markets to visit. In an n good world there are only $(n - 1)$ markets to visit sequentially, rather than the $n(n - 1)/2$ markets of a barter economy, since each good trades only against the exchange medium and not against any of the other n goods.

Money inventories break the period-by-period budget constraint that occurs in a world without an auctioneer to coordinate trades between periods. Barter at its best solves only the problem of within-period trade coordination. Decentralized between-period trade requires inventories. This occurs because money inventories provide slack in a sequence economy modeled in stock terms, comparable to the slack provided by commodity inventories, but at an inventory cost saving. With commodity inventories the slack is in quantity terms; with money inventories the slack is in value terms. In this sense money is asymmetrical to other commodities that enter a trader's utility function (Ostroy and Starr, 1974).

In order to attain an Arrow-Debreau competitive equilibrium, it is necessary that the value of each trader's holdings of money be greater than or equal in value to his planned purchases of all other commodities, just as there must be sufficient quantities of nonmonetary commodities for commodity inventories to provide the slack required for attaining equilibrium in one round. If there is too little money in value terms (assuming velocity is constant), trading may stop, where some notional excess demands or excess supplies are not fulfilled. This is the game theoretic concept of equilibrium, since some markets are not cleared.

If trading stops before all notional excess demands are met, two problems arise. First, money may fail to satisfy the quid pro quo behavioral requirement. At the end of the exchange process some traders may be forced to accept (hold) commodities that they desire to sell, but are unable to get rid of, because they are unable to turn them into money, so that they then can fill their notional excess demands. Additionally, less than full information about desired trades has been disseminated. Only information about trades of a particular good for money has been made available; that is, only information regarding either the buy or sell side of trade and only information in the $(n - 1)$ markets, not the full $n (n - 1)/2$ market set found in a barter economy.

Money, thus, serves as an additional constraint, and, if it is binding, it narrows the set of permissible exchanges compared to its barter counterpart (Ostroy and Starr, 1974). Money serves as a constraint, since my desire to trade my labor services as an economic consultant for a fur coat must go through the labor exchange for money market and then through the money exchange for fur coat market, before the final goods exchange is realized.

THE MONETARY EXCHANGE PROCESS AND DISEQUILIBRIA

When the adjustment to disequilibrium prices is through quantity adjustments, as in a Hicks fixed-price model, rather than through price adjustments, as in the Arrow-Debreau model, the adjustment process itself sets up disequilibrating effects. This is the classic Keynesian problem, formulated in a disequilibrium, but nonstrategic framework. Mulbauer and Portes (1978), have diagrammed the Walrasian (Arrow-Debreau) and four disequilibrating, nonmarket clearing regimes (including the Keynesian case) in consumption-labor space.[1] The distinction between the Walrasian market clearing case and the inflation regime with buyers rationed in both the labor and output markets is diagrammed below. The point W in Figure 1A indicates an equilibrium, where all markets clear. The point R in Figure 1B indicates an equilibrium under inflationary conditions, where consumer notional demand by households exceeds consumer goods supply by firms, though actualized consumer demand and supply are equal, and where notional labor demand by firms exceeds actualized labor supply by households in quantity terms. Again actualized labor supply and demand are equal.

Though the work of Ostroy and Ostroy and Starr is formulated within the mathematical structure of game theory, it, like Keynes, also, is nonstrategic. Their development of the choice problem facing a trader in a decentralized, sequence economy sets the stage for the introduction of strategic considerations. Benassy (1975a,b) moves toward a strategic decentralized, sequence model in that his individual traders have information about the demands expressed by all other agents in the economy. This information underlies the set of trade-perceived constraints of each agent in his model. An agent is constrained not just because of his own quantity and budget constraints, but because of his perception of the constraints of others. In other words in Figure 1B, households have some perception of the constraints facing firms (and similarly, have some perception of the constraints households face), as well as the usual Keynesian-type assumption regarding their perception of their own constraints in markets other than the one in which they are trading.

The perceived constraints operate as constraints on the flow of exchanges (as in the commodity and labor markets in a Keynesian model), or on the prices of stocks (as in the money and bond markets in a Keynesian model). They set up a multiplier process that results in a circular transmission of disturbances affecting the level of transactions in each market. The multiplier process occurs because notional demands perceived as being unfulfilled in one market spill over into other markets, with the spillover effects for an individual agent having the same sign for all markets in the chain. Dreze (1975), in a model with uniform rationing, proves that all agents, for which the perceived constraint is binding, will have notional excess demands or all will have notional excess supplies. Laroque (1978b) derives an aggregated

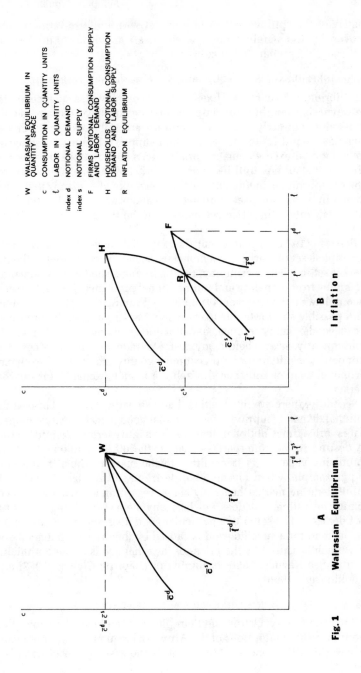

Fig. 1   Walrasian   Equilibrium

matrix of the spillover effect in a model with uniform rationing and proves that the marginal spillover effects are analogous to the Keynesian marginal propensity to consume.

INEFFICIENCIES OF EQUILIBRIUM IN MONETARY ECONOMIES

Equilibrium in a monetary, fixed price, decentralized, sequence model, or Keynesian equilibrium, implies that agents have anticipated the constraints correctly and that quantities are stabilized, even though there is disequilibrium in demand and supply. All constrained agents have notional excess demands or all agents have notional excess supplies, so that all possibilities of trade, market by market, are exhausted. The equilibrium is inefficient, since some notional demands that could be met in the existing set of operating markets are not met at the given price set, unless the price set happens to be the general equilibrium one.

Benassy (1975b) stresses that these inefficiencies exist because the incomplete set of markets in a monetary economy, compared to the full market set in a barter economy, results in unsatisfied excess demands, stemming from signaling and informational problems. Firstly, the set of incomplete markets prevents transactors from realizing trades that are both possible and profitable to everyone. Markets exist only for each of the n goods against money, and not for goods against other goods. Consequently, as said before, my desire to trade my labor services as an economic consultant for a fur coat must go through the labor exchange for money market and then through the money exchange for fur coat market.

Secondly, there are informational and signaling failures because the notional demand (supply) for a particular good is made against money; that is, price times notional demand in quantity terms. No information on desired real counterparts — that is, the other components of the optimizing vector — is transmitted to the market. Thus, in the foregoing example, when my notional desire to sell my labor services is unfulfilled, the market hears my signal regarding my wish to do economic consulting, but does not hear any signal pertaining to my fur coat demand. The seller of a particular good does not know how much the demand for a specific good is caused by the price of that good and how much is caused by the prices of the other goods in the optimizing vector. (See Keynes, 1936, beginning of chap. 16; Clower, 1967; and Leijonhufrud, 1968).

INEFFICIENCIES AND STRATEGY

The work of Ostroy, Ostroy and Starr, Benassy, and Laroque shows that two important assumptions of the Arrow-Debreau model are not viable in a world with monetary trade. One is the assumption of complete information about notional demand and supplies being available to a market coordinator or being transferred through the pricing mechanism. The second is the assumption that agents' maximizing decisions are unaffected by the decisions of others.

Given the incomplete information and the response of agents to the decisions of others in a decentralized, sequence, monetary economy, Laroque (1978b) argues that there is strong reason to study the dynamic behavior of the economy in game theoretic terms, so that the strategic options open to economic agents can be adequately incorporated into the model. Laroque (1978a,b) considers whether market forces will push a monetary economy to the equilibrium price set, since all excess demands (supplies) that can be fulfilled in the existing market structure will be met at the equilibrium price set. Laroque (1978a) shows that, when the actual price is close to the equilibrium price, the agents on the short side of the market always prefer the allocation at equilibrium prices, called a *Walrasian equilibrium*, to the one at disequilibrium prices, whereas the agents on the long side of the market do not. Thus, there is no reason, a priori, to believe that market trading in a dynamic decentralized, sequence economy will ever settle at the equilibrium price set.

Laroque (1978b) carries the problem forward in a model incorporating strategic interdependence, in which the payoff to any agent in a given situation is not dependent upon how that individual acts regarding fixed parameters, as much as upon the choices made by the other agents acting in the same situation. He shows that in a fixed price economy, the choice of price has a collective impact on the transactors, since it completely determines the allocation of output among economic agents. Laroque formulates the Ostroy-Keynesian problems into a decentralized, sequential, strategic monetary model, where the price system is the outcome of a collective bargaining process. Agents know that their allocation varies with prices and act in their best interests. If one starts at a competitive equilibrium, where all resources are fully employed, and then changes the prices slightly, there are virtually no possibilities for substitution among goods. Consequently, the essential phenomenon is one of income redistribution. An increase in the price of a particular commodity is profitable to the sellers of that product, whose gain at the margin exactly equals the loss of the buyers. Thus the interests of buyers and sellers are opposed and the final outcome will be influenced by the strategic skills of the opponents.

For example, in a situation of excess demand (at prices close to the equilibrium price set), the suppliers are on the short side of the market and prefer a Walrasian equilibrium because it means an increase in the price at which they sell. Remember that agents on the short side of the market are unconstrained and can meet the total of their notional demands (supplies). The demanders on the long side of the market, with unmet demands, prefer a price below that at the Walrasian equilibrium. True, they are constrained at a price below the equilibrium price, but to push for a price increase that chokes off this unfilled demand means a loss of real income. In such a model the revelation of true notional demands is not warranted. Both buyers and sellers are induced to lie. This is a further reason why perfect information is not available in a decentralized, sequence model.

Since agents on the long side of the market are aware that their actions affect the constraints of others and that the actions of others affect their market constraints, they face the problem of whether they are better off to act independently or form a cartel. If the longs, in a period of excess demand, act independently and push for a higher price through the expression of their unfulfilled demand, they must accept the loss of real income that the higher price engenders as the cost for reducing their notional demand to zero. This latter cost increases the closer the disequilibrium price is to the equilibrium price. If they collude with the other demanders to hold the price below the Walrasian equilibrium one and then reallocate the real income gain among themselves in such a way as to assure the cooperation of all members of the cartel, they may be better off than if they had acted independently. Consequently, the relative size and cohesion of buyers and sellers plays an important role in determining the final outcome in a decentralized, fixed price, monetary model.

The point being developed by Laroque can be seen by reference to his diagram (Laroque, 1978a, fig. I, p. 140) in price space. The four non-market clearing regimes under fixed-price assumptions as considered by Mulbauer-Portes are presented in consumption-labor price space, rather than consumption-labor quantity space. If we start at a price position close to the Walrasian equilibrium, Laroque shows that if the marginal propensity to consume and the marginal propensity for leisure are both less than one, each of the four regimes will settle at a fixed price Walrasian equilibrium, W, as long as strategic interrelationships are ignored. Once strategic interrelationships are introduced, the outcome becomes indeterminate and depends upon the relative collective bargaining strength of the market participants.

In a period of inflation, the participants are in the SW quadrant. The workers will want to go to the Walrasian equilibrium in the labor market since they are on the short side of the labor market. Labor will, however, wish to stay at the prevailing disequilibrium price set in output markets where it is long. The income gains from low commodity prices compensate workers for bearing the commodity market shortages. If they were to have their way totally, they would move the economy into the classical unemployment regimes, with rising real

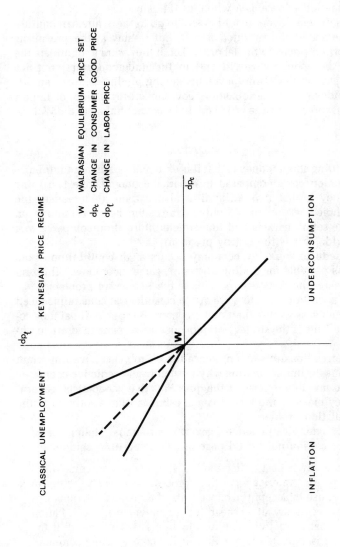

Fig. 2 Walrasian Equilibrium and Disequilibrium in Consumption – Labor Price Set

wages, for those still employed. If the latter were to distribute some of these real wage gains through unemployment and other social security benefits, the labor force as a whole could gain.

Conversely, employers would desire to go to the Walrasian equilibrium price set in the product market, but to stay at the prevailing disequilibrium prices in the labor market. If they were to dominate the outcome, the economy would end in the underconsumption price regime. Again through side payments among producers, for example, through industrywide cartelization, government regulation, or import restrictions, producers as a group could be better off than at the Walrasian price.

CONCLUSION

The good thing about money is that it is extremely efficient in minimizing transaction costs compared to a barter economy. The bad thing about money is that it is an additional constraint that reduces the feasible choice set for an individual transactor, because there is an incomplete set of markets and incomplete information compared to a barter world. This is the Ostroy problem.

When trade in a money economy occurs at disequilibrium, fixed prices, it is possible for trading to stop. A game theoretic equilibrium with uncleared markets occurs. This is the Keynesian problem.

In such a world transactors are apt to consider the constraints faced by other agents, as well as their own in determining an optimal transaction vector. This is the strategy or noncooperative game theoretic problem.

The interrelationships among these three problems have important implications for understanding why most current predictive economic models are not able to answer the questions that economists, government policy makers, and businessmen ask regarding a solution to the present inflation problem.

J. B. Burnham, vice-president, government affairs, Mellon Bank, in the *Wall Street Journal* Op Ed page of 3 October 1979, said:

> Inflation today is best understood as simply an economic consequence of the American political process. If enough groups in society refuse to accept the constraints of monetary relationships (with the economy at or near full employment), the inflation ratchet is set in motion. The explanation is fairly simple: If the price level is expected to remain roughly constant, any commodity or service, whose price rises, implies a lower price for at least one other commodity. In other words, the average price level remains unchanged. But a lower price for that other commodity generally implies lower incomes for its producers. Because our present political system — which encompasses the Federal Re-

serve — tends to operate on the basis of avoiding income losses for any significant bloc of voters . . . , powerful efforts are made to ensure that price increases in one commodity are not allowed to be offset by price declines in one or more other commodities. As a result, there is a rise in the average price level with the rate of advance heavily influenced by the various stages of the business cycle. . . . Solutions for breaking the ratchet appear quite limited: either give up the goal of full employment (and let the struggle for income shares take place below the point at which such struggles generate inflation), or strip government of some of its power to alter the distribution of income.

I am not sure about Burnham's views regarding the solutions of inflation, but I am sure that he is touching upon an important point regarding monetary constraints and the conflicts between buyers and sellers that these constraints impose. Monetary constraints impose quid pro quo conditions and protect transactors from the uncertainty of default, when the honesty of agents with which one is dealing cannot be assumed. Monetary constraints impose period-by-period budget constraints. A welfare state breaks the monetary period-by-period budget constraint and allows individuals to buy insurance against state of the world (exogenous) uncertainty. It minimizes the risk of state of the world induced or exogenous default. However, a welfare state is not able to insure against transactions uncertainty or to control against agent behavior uncertainty. The specter of default (where default is nothing more than a form of income redistribution) reasserts itself in the guise of the conflict between buyers and sellers over the determination of the institutionally determined price level, the fixed price of the decentralized, sequence model. Predictive models that ignore these strategic interrelationships are bound to be useless in a world which abounds with buyer-seller conflicts, as occurs in an inflationary environment.

Notes

1. See Mulbauer and Portes (1978) for the explanation of the shift from the usual Keynesian income-expenditure space to consumption-labor space and a full discussion of the derivation of the four nonmarket clearing regimes.

References

Benassy, J. P. "Disequilibrium Exchange in Barter and Monetary Economics," Economic Inquiry 13 (1975a): 131–56.

Benassy, J. P. "Neokeynesian Disequilibrium Theory in a Monetary Economy," *Review of Economic Studies* 42 (1975b): 503–24.

Clower, R. "A Reconsideration of the Micro-foundations of Monetary Theory," *Western Economic Journal* 6 (1967): 1–8.

Dreze, J. "Existence of an Exchange Equilibrium under Price Rigidities," *International Economic Review* 16 (1975): 301–20.

Foley, D. K., and Hellwig, M. F. "Asset Management with Trading Uncertainty," *Review of Economic Studies* 42 (1975): 327–46.

Hahn, F. H. "On Transaction Costs, Inessential Sequence Economies, and Money," *Review of Economic Studies* 40 (1973): 449–62.

Hicks, J. R. *Capital and Growth* (Oxford, 1965).

Keynes, J. M. *The General Theory of Employment, Interest, and Money* (New York, 1936).

Kurz, M. "Equilibrium with Transaction Cost and Money in a Single Market Exchange Economy," *Journal of Economic Theory* 7 (1974): 418–52.

Laroque, G. "The Fixed Price Equilibria: Some Results in Local Comparative Statics," *Econometrica* 46 (1978a): 1127–54.

Laroque, G. "On the Dynamics of Disequilibrium: A Simple Remark," *Review of Economic Studies* 45 (1978b): 273–78.

Leijonhufrud, A. *On Keynesian Economics and the Economics of Keynes* (Oxford, 1968).

Mulbauer, John, and Portes, Richard. "Macroeconomic Models with Quantity Rationing," *Economic Journal* 88 (1978): 788–821.

Ostroy, J. M. "The Informational Efficiency of Monetary Exchange," *American Economic Review* 63 (1973): 597–610.

Ostroy, J. M., and Starr, R. M. "Money and the Decentralization of Exchange," *Econometrica* 42 (1974): 1093–1113.

Scitovsky, L. *Money and the Balance of Payments* (Chicago, 1969).

Starrett, D. A. "Inefficiency and the Demand for Money in a Sequence Economy," *Review of Economic Studies* 40 (1973): 437–48.

A Marxist Critique of
Natural Unemployment Rate Theories

ROBERT CHERRY

There has always been a conflict between Keynesian and neoclassical economic theory. Keynesians have always claimed that it was impossible to rely on labor market adjustments to generate full employment.[1] They contend that labor markets could never function as auctionlike markets and developed various institutionally determined contract models.[2] Many of these labor models discount the short-run effects of real wage changes on employment and/or the effects of aggregate spending fluctuations on real wage rates. Thus, declines in aggregate spending are not likely to have a significant effect on real wage rates, and even if they did, it is unlikely that changes in real wage rates would influence employment significantly.[3]

With the seeming inability of Keynesian policies to work during the post-Vietnam War era there has been a strong revival of neoclassical labor market models.[4] This revival is reflected by the general acceptance among mainstream economists, even "Keynesians," of the concept of the natural rate of unemployment. The *natural rate* exists when the number of job seekers just equals the number of job vacancies. At this point, the aggregate supply of labor just equals aggregate labor demand. Unemployment still exists because, as a result of a lack of complete information, jobs and workers do not instantaneously match. This lack of information induces individuals to spend more time looking for jobs. Thus, the existence of unemployment reflects voluntary decisions on the part of workers rather than a lack of effective demand (Keynesian unemployment) or even a mismatch of jobs (structural unemployment). Since most neoclassical models imply that the natural rate equals 6–7 percent, they are as interested in explaining why unemployment rates are sometimes too low as the usual (Keynesian) concern as to show why unemployment rates are sometimes too high.

All natural rate models contend that deviations of unemployment rates from the natural rate are due to unanticipated price changes. These models contend that unanticipated price increases induce production and employment to expand and unanticipated price decreases induce production and employment to contract. But once these price changes are fully anticipated, economic agents adjust their decisions so that unemployment returns to its natural rate.

These models indicate that only in the short run is it possible for higher rates of inflation to induce lower rates of unemployment. In the long run, regardless of the rate of inflation, once anticipated, unemployment would be at its natural rate. Thus, all natural rate models posit a short-run downward-sloping but a long-run vertical Phillips Curve.

The major distinction among natural rate models is between those which incorporate some of the institutional constraints associated with Keynesian models and those which assume auction-like labor markets. These two approaches differ on the reasons that unanticipated price changes influence output and the speed at which economic agents are able to adjust their decisions once they more accurately anticipate price changes. According to the institutional approach, identified with the Brookings Institute (Poole, 1974; Gordon, 1976, 1978), contractual obligations constrain labor's ability to adjust money wage rates. Contracts also force labor to commit itself before actual price changes are known. Thus, unanticipated price increases result in a decline in the real wage rate during the length of contracts and induce firms to expand production and employment. Since contracts (formal and informal) may be quite long and catchups may only be partial, the period in which unemployment rates deviate from their natural rate may be quite lengthy.

The other approach identified with rational expectations (Lucas, 1973; Barro, 1976; Sargent and Wallace, 1974) contends that the short-run Phillips Curve results from the differential speed at which economic agents learn about specific price changes. Once they obtain full information, they quickly adjust so that deviations from the natural rate are short. Moreover, these models are capable of demonstrating that under certain circumstances, all government actions, if known in advance, will be fully offset by the actions of rational economic agents. In this case, it would be impossible for the government, using known policy rules, to reduce effectively the size of deviations of unemployment from its natural rate even in the short run.

This paper will critiquely evaluate the theoretical foundations of each of these groups of natural rate models. It will demonstrate that the rational expectations models have not formulated a rigorous explanation for the short-run Phillips Curve.[5] At best, they are able to show that in a world of simple commodity production (each worker owns the complete means of production and is self-employed) output fluctuations would be minor. This, of course, is not a startling conclusion. Marx long ago noted the ability of a laissez-faire economy typified by simple commodity production to quickly offset deviations of supply from demand in the aggregate (Say's Law). Marx also claimed that capitalism was a system in which production was for profits (M-C-M'), whereas in a world of simple commodity production it was for consumption (C-M-C'). This change in the purpose of production is the root cause of economic fluctuations, and it is this change which the more rigorous rational expectations model fail to include.

The Brookings natural rate models are seemingly more credible. They correctly posit the crucial role of contracts in the labor process and that these contracts are not simply a matter of individuals negotiating employment and/or wage stability in the face of risk.[6] These models will be criticized for distorting the meaning of natural unemployment. According to Marxists, what is "natural" under capitalism is to have a minimum necessary size of the industrial reserve army.[7] Marxists contend that circumstances other than unanticipated price increases can explain short-run declines in unemployment below the natural rate. Thus, Marxists agree that there is a rate of unemployment below which a capitalist economy cannot be sustained but differ from natural rate advocates as to the reasons for (1) its existence, (2) deviations of unemployment from this rate, (3) the process by which unemployment rates return to the natural rate.

RATIONAL EXPECTATIONS (RATEX) MODELS

RATEX models have two sets of behavioral equations. The first explains the short-run actions of decision makers. These equations are used to demonstrate that the short-run Phillips Curve results from unanticipated price changes. The second set explains how future price expectations are formed, indicating the process by which the economy moves from the short-run to the long-run Phillips Curve. In most RATEX models this second set of equations implies that government activism is completely ineffective even in the short run. There are two somewhat separate groups of RATEX models reflecting these two different aspects. One group, reflecting the first set of equations, attempts to develop microfoundations for the short-run as well as the long-run Phillips Curve. The other group, reflecting the second set of equations, attempts to counter contentions that government activism can be effective in the short run.[8]

During the mid-1970s a narrowly formed consensus developed within the economics profession which suggested that the only legitimate "Keynesian" position was the advocacy of a fixed monetary rule with an activist feedback mechanism. RATEX advocates, such as Sargent and Wallace, were concerned that even this constrained level of activism was unwarranted. RATEX models were developed in order to demonstrate that when expectations are rationally formed, government activism which follows a fixed monetary rule, would be ineffective in the short run.[9] RATEX models which were directed at this policy issue were not concerned about the reasons for the short-run Phillips Curve and so did not rigorously describe how utility-maximizing individuals would act. Instead, these RATEX models relied upon ad hoc rationales to explain the short-run Phillips Curve.

The first of the ad hoc rationales was offered by Friedman (1968) when he reasoned that workers received information more slowly than capitalists. Thus, an unanticipated price change would be perceived more quickly by capitalists who would be able to "fool" workers into accepting a real wage cut. As a result, output and employment would expand. Since there was no acceptable reason for this asymmetry between workers and capitalists, Friedman (1975) eventually developed another rationale. Sargent and Wallace described this new rationale as follows:

> Unexpected increases in the price level boost aggregate supply, the reason being that suppliers of labor and goods mistakenly interpret surprise increases in the aggregate price level as increases in the relative prices of the goods and labor that they are supplying. This happens because suppliers receive information about the prices of their own goods faster than they receive information about the general price level. (p. 243)

No longer is there asymmetry between workers and capitalists. Both receive information on the goods which they supply at the same time. Now the asymmetry is between information on goods and labor which they supply and goods and labor which they demand. What is the rationale for this asymmetry? One possible explanation is that there could be a spatial difference in the location of markets and individuals receive information on local markets sooner than global markets. In this case, if individuals supply goods and labor in local markets but purchase goods and labor from global markets the information asymmetry is plausible.

For households, it is reasonable to assume that the labor which they supply is to local markets and the goods which they purchase are from global markets. It is not very reasonable to assume that firms supply goods to local markets and purchase inputs, particularly labor, from global markets. Indeed, the reverse is as least as plausible.

If firms received information on their input (labor) costs before their output prices then an unanticipated price increase (in which all prices, including that for labor, rose by the same rate) would be perceived as a rise in the real wage rate. This would induce firms to lower their demand for labor. Moreover, if we assume that production takes time, firms would place more emphasis on current labor costs than on current output prices. In this case, even if firms simultaneously observe an equivalent unanticipated increase in both their labor costs and output price they would reduce current labor demand.

If an unanticipated price increase raises both the demand for and supply of labor, then it is reasonable to assume that output and employment would also increase. In this case, we would have an explanation for the short-run Phillips Curve. But, if labor supply increases but labor demand decreases, the effect on equilibrium employment is not certain. In this case, the shape of the short-run Phillips Curve would be indeterminant. Thus, the asymmetry specified by Friedman cannot be accepted a priori as an explanation for the *downward*-sloping short-run Phillips Curve.

In these policy-oriented models the determination of output changes requires a comparison of changes in money wage rates to perceived price level changes. The second group of RATEX models, most identified with Barro and Lucas, avoids having to make this comparison by substituting simple commodity production for capitalist production. All production is done by self-employed workers who own the necessary means of production. Moreover, in these models there are usually no inventories so that one can discuss labor supply and demand interchangeably with output supply and demand.

In these models there are no variable inputs purchased. Only the individual producer's own labor is required; the goods produced can be assumed to be sold in local markets. Now suppose that each individual producer receives an unanticipated price increase for the specific good being supplied. This would be perceived as a rise in the relative price of that good and, therefore, an increase in the real rate of return to labor. This would induce each producer to increase output by substituting additional labor for leisure. On the demand side, since it is assumed that the unanticipated price increase results from a monetary expansion, there would be a perceived increase in real wealth and this would induce a rise in the demand for goods.[10] Thus, the unanticipated rise in the price level induces an increase in the demand for goods (labor) and the supply of goods (labor).

Barro has noted that the foregoing analysis, reflective of Lucas's model, is incomplete since there should also be a wealth effect on the supply side and a substitution effect on the demand side. On the supply side, if households perceive an unanticipated rise in their real wealth then, independent of relative prices, they would choose to purchase some leisure at the expense of labor income and, hence, reduce their current labor supply. On the demand side, the perceived relative increase in the price of the good which they are supplying should induce households, as consumers, to shift away from current production of that good, thereby lowering its demand. Thus, according to these two responses, with an unanticipated price increase households would reduce their labor supply as well as their demand for goods. Only if the previous responses, specified in the Lucas model, are stronger, for which there is no a priori rationale, would there be a positive correlation between unanticipated price changes and short-run output changes.

Barro and Lucas consider the assumption that production is supplied by self-employed workers to be a mere simplification, but it has been shown that this assumption avoids a problem which plagued the other group of RATEX models. Thus, their analysis cannot be generalized to a capitalist society. Moreover, accumulation, which Marxists consider to be central to the capitalist production process, cannot be incorporated in a meaningful way into these RATEX models. Blinder and Fischer found that when inventories are included accumulation (growth of inventories) is a response to wealth effects, which they admit makes no sense in a capitalist society. Finally, Barro indicates that only if demand-side income affects and supply-side substitution affects are stronger than demand-side substitution affects and supply-side income affects would his model produce a downward-sloping short-run Phillips Curve.

THE NATURAL RATE THESIS

RATEX models are only one set of explanations for the short-run and long-run Phillips Curve. Another set of explanations, identified with the Brookings Institute, emphasizes institutional factors, such as labor contracts. These models have a certain realism and, unlike RATEX models, are internally consistent, but they, too, are flawed. Marxists contend that the most important defect of all natural rate models is their incorrect understanding of the reasons for a minimum level of unemployment in a market economy.[11] Thus, before specifically evaluating these institutional models let us begin by evaluating the natural rate concept itself.

Marxists, like mainstream economists, contend that unemployment rates below some minimum cannot be sustained, regardless of the willingness of the economy to accept high inflation rates. According to Marxists, however, this minimum necessary unemployment rate is dictated by the requirements of a capitalist system rather than any "natural" laws. They contend that the minimum necessary unemployment rate is based on political and economic considerations. Capitalism in its parliamentary democracy form requires that labor "voluntarily" enter into hierarchical exploitative relationships with its employers. Thus, an industrial reserve army is required to maintain the voluntary stability of such exploitative relationships. According to the class struggle thesis, popularized by Boddy and Crotty, when the industrial reserve army is too low, profits are squeezed, bankruptcies occur, capital investment is halted, and an economic contraction begins.

Therefore, owing to the specific requirements of capitalism, there is some barrier below which unemployment rates cannot fall.

Some Marxists (Kalecki) claim that political factors are the most important determinant of the minimum necessary size of the industrial reserve army. They suggest that the "success" of the fascist economies during the 1930s in maintaining full employment was due to their ability to substitute legal requirements for voluntary arrangements in determining labor market outcomes. I have argued elsewhere that after World War II Western democracies were able to sustain historically lower unemployment rates owing to social contracts negotiated between organized labor and the dominant section of big capital. Organized labor leaders agreed to maintain labor discipline and refrain from actions which would threaten profitability. Capital agreed to maintain economic growth and low rates of unemployment in the organized labor sectors. Unemployment rates rose during the 1970s because of the breakdown of the social contracts. Organized labor was unable to fulfill its part of the contract since its influence in the overall labor market was declining. Capital was unable to fulfill its part of the contract due to the intensification of foreign competition, which forced it to slow down real wage growth rates.

The growth in influence of previously disenfranchised groups of workers and capitalists hastened the breakdown of social contracts. Since the 1950s, women and black workers have demanded a greater share of the United States economic pie, while Sun Belt capitalists have begun to compete for a greater share of economic and political power. Therefore, even if organized labor and Eastern capitalists could agree to maintain the social contracts, disenfranchised workers and Sun Belt capitalists could hinder its implementation.[12]

Not only do Marxists differ with mainstream economists as to the reasons for the minimum unemployment rate but they differ as to the reasons for fluctuations of actual unemployment rates. According to the Brookings natural rate models only when workers underestimate future price increases can unemployment decline below its natural rate. In particular, an unanticipated price increase, because labor has contracted at too low a money wage rate, reduces the real wage rate. With a decline in the real wage rate, production expands, profits rise, and unemployment declines below its natural rate.

The Marxist theory of the industrial reserve army offers a dramatically different adjustment process. Marxists contend that, during the latter phase of expansions, rising employment results in lower profits as firms experience the full employment profit squeeze. Thus, in contrast to natural rate theories, Marxist suggest that during the latter phase of expansions when the unemployment rate is declining below its minimum sustainable rate, profit rates are falling.

Both theories also differ as to the causes of the eventual rise of unemployment back to its minimum sustainable rate. According to the natural rate theory, after a time lag, workers are able to negotiate wage settlements which more accurately reflect the rising inflation rate and their real wage rate rises. The rise in real wage rates no longer allows marginal workers to be profitably hired, inducing a contraction in marginal firms and marginal ventures. However, when the contraction begins average profit rates are above historic norms. Therefore, there is still an overall buoyancy to the economy. Some cutbacks are occurring but the typical firm is still experiencing above normal profits. Eventually when unemployment rises back to its natural rate the typical firm's profit rate declines back toward its historic norm.

The Marxist view is strikingly different. It suggests that when the expansion ends because of the falling rate of profit, bankruptcies and financial instability of firms become widespread.[13] Smaller firms fail; somewhat larger firms, in order to protect themselves, increase their liquidity at the expense of long-term expenditures on capital equipment and new products. Larger firms begin to substitute financial investments, particularly the purchase of struggling corporations, for capital spending. Thus, the erosion of profit rates causes bankruptcies, increases in liquidity, and financial takeovers. For all these reasons, corporate production and capital investment decline and unemployment rises back toward its natural rate. However, rather than a return to normal profit rates, this contraction concludes with the profit rate of the typical firm well below its historic norm.[14]

Mainstream economists, such as Arthur Okun and Robert Solow, reject the class struggle thesis because they claim that capitalists do not utilize the reserve army to lower money wage rates. Marxists contend that recessions and the early phase of expansions enable capitalists to raise prices at a faster rate than money wage increases, to reorganize production in order to increase labor productivity; thus, only in rare situations is a literal decline in money wage rates necessary. Moreover, Marxists contend that, during the 1970s, precisely because the capitalists did not hit the working class hard enough, the crisis for United States capitalism worsened. Now that the liberalism of the 1960s has been completely destroyed, we will see if capitalists maintain the benevolence to workers that Okun and Solow cite.

Whatever the experience in individual labor markets, the income shares and profit rate data are very supportive of the Marxian reserve army thesis. Boddy and Crotty note that the profit-wage ratio fell during the latter phase of each of the post-World War II expansions. This was particularly true of the Viet Nam War boom. Similarly, the profit rate data, developed by the Brookings staff, support the Marxian theory but conflict with the natural rate theory. According to estimates by Gordon (1978), the actual unemployment rate continuously declined below its natural rate from early 1965 through late 1969. According to the mainstream view, this should have been associated with declining real wage rates and rising profit rates.[15] Yet, the profit rate data, developed by Feldstein and Summers, indicated that during that entire period the profit rate continuously declined.

The mainstream view implies that at the end of the growth of employment, the profit rate should begin to decline but still be above its historic norm. But, the profit rate data indicate that by 1969 the average profit rate fell below 9 percent while the historic norm was 12 percent. Moreover, during the 1969–70 recession, the profit rate rose rather than declined. Thus, it would appear that Marxian theory[16] can explain fluctuations in profit rates while mainstream theory cannot.

CONCLUSIONS

This paper has indicated that there are serious problems with mainstream theories of the natural unemployment rate and their explanations for fluctuations of actual unemployment rates in the short run. The RATEX models were found wanting in a number of ways. They eliminated the major features of capitalism — class divisions and accumulation — and had no convincing rationales for the short-run Phillips Curve. The Brookings natural rate models seemed to be contradicted by recent profit rate data. Moreover, it was argued that the Marxian reserve army thesis serves as a superior conceptual foundation for the existence of a minimum necessary unemployment rate.

The general acceptance of the natural rate thesis and the broad circulation of RATEX models suggests a fundamental shift in economic analysis by apologists for the capitalist system. The natural rate, stripped of all its elegance, is the first time that the economics profession has openly stated that full employment in its usual sense is impossible under capitalism — that a reasonable degree of unemployment, especially among disadvantaged groups, will be a permanent feature of capitalism. The natural rate theory reflects an intellectual rationale for an end to the liberal reformism of the post-World War II era. No longer should the government ameliorate in any significant way the problems of unregulated capitalism. Only by studying Marxism, in particular Marxian crisis theory, can one fully understand the reasons for, and ramifications of, this shift.

Notes

1. For a recent formulation of this position see the AEA Presidential Address of R. Solow.
2. For an elaboration see Poole (1976).

3.   For estimates of demand elasticity in support of these contentions see Hamermesh (1976).

4.   See Grossman (1979).

5.   A number of other criticisms are leveled against rational expectations models: (1) the models are logically consistent but are inconsistent with either the general workings of markets (Poole) or empirical observations (Solow); (2) the assumption of rationality is inconsistent with learning models of behavior (Evans); (3) the requirement that individuals have a complete model of the economy is unrealistic (B. Friedman, 1979; Fair, 1978).

6.   For a neoclassical theory of labor contracts see Azariadis (1975).

7.   For a detailed presentation of the industrial reserve army thesis see Cherry (1980).

8.   For this reason, most criticisms of RATEX models have been in response to the second set of equations and ignored the inadequacies of the first set.

9.   Phelps (1976) has given examples of how a RATEX model, when the government does not follow a known rule, is capable of explaining severe economic fluctuations.

10.   According to the Lucas and Barro models, households (and firms) have positive wealth; M. Friedman (1975), referring to Fisher, claims that firms have negative wealth.

11.   For a non-Marxist critique of the natural rate see Piore (1978).

12.   For a discussion of the conflict between Sun Belt and Eastern capitalists see Cherry (1980).

13.   Schumpeter saw the bankruptcy of smaller firms as having a beneficial effect on the economy. He characterized it as the "Process of Creative Destruction." Steindl argued that the bankruptcy of the smaller firms would have no adverse effect on capital spending decisions of other firms.

14.   If the process takes too long, damaging the profitability of major firms and solidifying the wage expectations of workers, then a capitalist crisis could result.

15.   Feldstein and Summers (1977) contend that the fall in profit rates resulted from profit "illusion" created by accounting profits; Nordhaus (1974) contends that it was a result of capitalists no longer fearing a severe recession and thus no longer requiring as large a risk premium; and Bernstein (1978) contends that it resulted from overinvestment by overly optimistic managers. Thus, there are non-Marxian ad hoc explanations for the falling profit rate.

16.   For a discussion of other Marxian theories, such as overinvestment, underconsumption, and changes in the organic composition of capital, see Cherry.

References

Azariadis, C. "Implicit Contracts and Underemployment Equilibrium," *Journal of Political Economy* 83 (1975): 1183–1202.

Barro, R. "Rational Expectations and the Role of Monetary Policy," *Journal of Monetary Economics* 2 (1976): 1–32.

Bernstein, P. "Is the System Still Working?" *Challenge* 21 (1978): 22.

Blinder, A. and Fischer, S. "Inventories, Rational Expectations, and the Business Cycle," unpublished manuscript (Princeton, 1978).

Boddy, R., and Crotty, J. "Class Conflict and Macropolicy: The Political Business Cycle," Review of Radical Political Economy 7 (Spring 1975): 1–19.

Cherry, R. Macroeconomics (Reading, 1980).

Evans, G. "Macroeconomic stability under Adaptive and Rational Expectations," unpublished manuscript (Berkeley, 1978).

Fair, R. "A Criticism of One Class of Macroeconomic Models with Rational Expectations," Journal of Money, Credit, and Banking 10 (1978): 411–17.

Feldstein, M., and Summers, L. "Is There a Falling Rate of Profit?" Brookings Papers, 1977, pp. 211–27.

Fisher, I. "A Statistical Relationship between Unemployment and Price Changes," International Labor Review 13 (1926): 785–92.

Friedman, B. "Optimal Expectations and the Extreme Information Assumptions of 'Rational Expectations' Models," Journal of Monetary Economics 5 (1979): 23–41.

Friedman, M. "The Role of Monetary Policy," American Economic Review 58 (1968): 1–17.

Friedman, M. Unemployment versus inflation? An Evaluation of the Phillips Curve (London, 1975).

Gordon, R. J. "Recent Developments in the Theory of Inflation and Unemployment," Journal of Monetary Economics 2 (1976): 185–219.

Gordon, R. J. Macroeconomics (Boston, 1978).

Grossman, H. "Why Does Aggregate Employment Fluctuate?" American Economic Review 69 (1979): 64–69.

Hamermesh, D. "Econometric Studies of Labor Demand and Their Application to Policy Analysis," Journal of Human Resources 11 (1976): 507–25.

Kalecki, M. Selected Essays on the Dynamics of Capitalist Societies (New York, 1971).

Lucas, R. "Some International Evidence on Output-Inflation Tradeoffs," American Economic Review 63 (1973): 326–34.

Nordhaus, W. "The Falling Rate of Profit," Brookings Papers, 1974, pp. 169–208.

Okun, A. "The Great Stagflation Swamp," Challenge 20 (1977): 8.

Phelps, E. "Discussant," Brookings Papers, 1976, pp. 506–509.

Piore, M. "Unemployment and Inflation: An Alternative View," Challenge 21 (1978): 24–30.

Poole, W. "Rational Expectations and the Macro Model," Brookings Papers, 1976, pp. 463–505.

Sargent, T., and Wallace, N. "'Rational' Expectations, the Optimal Monetary Instrument, and the Optimal Money Supply Rule," Journal of Political Economy 83 (1974): 241–54.

Schumpeter, J. Capitalism, Socialism, and Democracy (New York, 1962).

Solow, R. "On Theories of Unemployment," American Economic Review 70 (1980): 1–11.

Steindl, J. Maturity and Stagnation in American Capitalism (Oxford, 1952).

Part 2
Historical Perspectives

Inflation in the Southern Low Countries, from the Fourteenth to the Seventeenth Century: A Record of Some Significant Periods of High Prices

E. H. G. VAN CAUWENBERGHE

Inflation has been a recurring phenomenon throughout history, and discussions abound on rising trends of prices in different countries and in different periods. Undoubtedly, the sixteenth century will remain one of the most fruitful periods for historical investigation of the subject. Politicians, economists, and even historians are involved in the arguments.

I do not intend here to propose a model for the theory of inflation or for what is called the *Price Revolution*. When interpreting price trends, I shall, however, have to explain some particularities of the evolution of prices in the Low Countries. The historical period I am concerned with covers a time span of about 250 years: from the fourteenth to the seventeenth century.

Between the late thirteenth and the fifteenth century, we meet some unexpected periods of high prices, and as in almost every country of Western Europe, the sixteenth century can be defined only as a secular episode of inflation for the Low Countries.

For the late Middle Ages, however, only fragmentary price quotations are available for the County of Flanders and the Duchy of Brabant. There are indications that prices were higher at the end than at the beginning of the thirteenth century and that agricultural prices were often subject to quite violent fluctuations. For example, at the beginning of the fourteenth century, grain prices were four times what they had been at the end of the twelfth century. Coinage, population, and output all increased during the century.[1] Relevant data, however, are too sporadic and too disparate to explain the rise. Yet the deeper penetration and increase of gold coinage in different European states, which brought about monetary stability for almost all the thirteenth century, can be supposed to have affected the general price level.

After the fourteenth century, European price data are less scanty. International comparisons of monetary and nonmonetary factors are now possible (e.g., between France, England, and Spain) with the publication of the studies of E. H. Phelps Brown, Sheila V. Hopkins, and Earl J. Hamilton.[2] Historians have compiled statistics on the basis of this source material to determine rates of change in prices and money wages.[3] But those computations do not seem to have prevented contradictory statements on the subject.

Although results of inflationary pressures and related causes can be indicated in the fourteenth century, the terminology of inflation can hardly be applied to an era in which depression would soon play such a major role. In an attempt to explain price changes in that early period, attention has been increasingly focused on the monetary systems and monetary history.[4]

Recently, Michael Prestwich analyzed the fluctuations of exchange rates in the years prior to the production of English gold coinage.[5] With respect to the southern Low Countries' monetary history, and for the explanation of early fourteenth-century Flemish price trends, this contribution is of great importance. Together with John Munro's magnificent study, *Wool, Cloth and Gold*, it helps to explain some of the sharp rises in prices that confronted both England and Flanders in the early fourteenth century.[6] Previously, in the absence of authoritative price series, the presence of inflationary pressures had to be deduced from more qualitative evidence (demographic pressures, military conflicts, undeveloped administration, etc.).

Up to a few years ago we could only presume that monetary factors were among the causes of raising prices at this time. Little reliable evidence on the monetary influences at work was available. Since J. H. Munro, Prestwich, and M. Mate have published their findings, we have a reasonably good idea of how the significant increase in the number of coins circulating in the early fourteenth century, together with increases in the supply of goods and the fluctuations of exchange rates, affected the general price levels. Any thesis that denies the validity of a monetary explanation for the rise of prices at this time can no longer be accepted without due reservations.[7]

In close connection with the struggle for bullion and the Anglo-Flemish wool trade, the important mints of the southern Low Countries started counterfeiting English sterling on a large scale from about 1310 on.[8] In the 1320s and the 1330s English coinage output fell to a record low.[9] Consequently, Continental debasement and counterfeiting attracted bullion away from the English Mint with favorable effect upon monetary circulation in Flanders.[10]

During this period, industrial productivity in the Flemish towns as well as urbanization of the region were still on the increase. Despite rising production costs, mainly in the traditional high-quality textile sector, overall demand probably exceeded supply, thus keeping prices high.

From the late 1340s through about 1375, the more violent fluctuations of the price index also suggest inflationary pressure. Thereafter, deflation clearly set in and lasted through the fifteenth century.[11]

Historians have principally concentrated their efforts and debates on this "Great Depression." Demographic factors and, in particular, the long-range social and economic effects of famines and epidemics are the chief subjects of research. But the proponents of the quantitative monetary theory and those of the population hypothesis strongly disagree on the primary causes of this problem.[12] A recent and extremely valuable article by John Day posits monetary stringency as an aggravating factor for the depression from the late fourteenth century onward.[13]

In this particular period, from about the middle of the last decade of the fourteenth century on, the Low Countries underwent a less unfavorable development. This contrasts in more than one way with what was happening in the rest of Europe at the time.[14] The specific evolution in the Low Countries was mainly based upon two pillars of progress in the southern Low Countries: *agriculture* and *urban growth*.

Agrarian development in the Low Countries did not collapse from the high level reached at the beginning of the fourteenth century, but was maintained at a reasonable level during the whole of the depression of the fourteenth and fifteenth centuries.[15] In most of Europe, however, the agricultural depression was severe and led to rampant mortality, a sharp decline of profits, and lower productivity of land.[16]

Particularly in Flanders and in Brabant, stabilization occurred on a high level and the decline began only around 1370.[17] In some parts of Brabant and Limburg, increases of productivity were noteworthy. Incomes from temporary leases in the ducal domains in Brabant reflect a general upward movement of agricultural output and profits with symptoms of stabilization occurring only during the last quarter of the fourteenth and the beginning of the fifteenth century.[18] In the County of Namur, there was a powerful secular increase of grain prices and of rents due from 1365 until 1437.[19]

Urban growth also played a crucial role. Population density in the towns of the Low Countries had increased at a phenomenal level during the preceding centuries because of industrial growth and the expansion of trade. The Black Death and frequent wars did not dampen the dynamics of this favorable development. In Flanders, from the middle of the fourteenth century up to 1380, production for the market and developing commerce and urbanization were particularly important in promoting individual freedom and social advancement, although the intensive debasement policy of the Flemish Count neutralized these social advantages.[20]

The time lag between price increase and wage adaptation affected real wages considerably, and the resulting real improverishment of textile workers reached a point where social tensions made conflict inevitable.[21]

Thus, monetary forces and policies were probably important factors in the collapse of the traditional Flemish textile sector and played a role in the commercial and industrial transformation that occurred in the Low Countries in the fourteenth and fifteenth centuries. As John Munro repeatedly stressed, the extremely frequent debasements together with exceptionally large mint outputs in Flanders must certainly be taken into consideration in order to explain the second phase of expansion of the Flemish cloth industry from the 1350s to the 1370s.[22]

These severe debasements affected prices and purchasing power, altered exchange rates, and increased the incomes of those who took money or metal to the mint. It would not be surprising to find that these factors had inflationary effects.

Yet, the inflationary pressures that can be identified in this crucial period of change in social and economic structures may not be attributed exclusively to metallic factors or monetary forces. They were much more complex. Together with the reduction in bullion stocks, the contraction of the means of payment, and demographic stagnation, from now on, physical factors, never entirely absent, would play a major role in the *depression* of the fifteenth century.[23]

There is no doubt that prices rose continuously during the sixteenth century in most of Europe.[24] Historians and economists have long been fascinated by this persistent inflation. The present state of the debate may be summarized as follows:[25]

The monetary explanation is usually expressed in the form of the well-known quantity theory of money (MV = PT) or is based on some variant of I. Fisher's equation $P = MV/T$.[26] Adherents of this theory argue that the rise in prices from the first half of the sixteenth century onward was due to a combination of increased velocity and volume of currency circulation. Several empirical studies have tried to show that the rate of inflation was closely related to the expansion of money.

Adherents of the alternative hypothesis stress the relatively decreased supply and the intensified tightness of demand for essential foodstuffs.[27] Population pressures and inadequate rises in agricultural productivity have only recently been introduced into the discussion as factors stimulating inflation.[28]

The Keynesian approach, which considers the relation between savings and investment as the prime mover of short-term fluctuations, has been a preoccupation of "retrospective" economists rather than of historians.[29]

Whatever the outcome of the controversy between adherents of the quantitative theory and those of the "real," physical hypothesis, no doubt two chief variables — metallic or monetary production and demography — played an important role in the secular changes in the price level.[30]

I should now like to discuss a number of factors that were specifically related to inflation in the southern Low Countries in the sixteenth century. (I shall rely largely on published studies and statistical series.)

The price term raises the least difficulty since we have well-documented, elaborated series. Several important publications (e.g., by H. Van Der Wee) are available for this period.

The extent to which monetary rather than "real" factors influenced inflation in the sixteenth century in the Low Countries is not easy to define. From the data used in earlier studies, it cannot be concluded that the quantity theory of money fully explains inflation. In some countries, of course, the monetary expansion explains inflation better than in others. Therefore the two different types of explanation are combined in an attempt to designate when which of them played the dominant role.

A comparison between Flemish and other Europen prices shows that the *Price Revolution* in the Low Countries was strongest during the first half of the sixteenth century. Obviously, this was earlier than in most other European countries, where the sharpest price rises occurred a half century later. The movements of a composite price index (Fig. 1), which reflects the behavior of agricultural prices very well, show clearly the situation with which we have to deal.[31]

What caused this early upward movement in the southern Low Countries? The traditional or monetary explanation is not tenable: the net increase of the importation of precious metals from the New World and the extension of monetary circulation were less at that time than during the second half of the sixteenth century. In the 1551–1600 period, mint output was reasonably stable and the level of bullion imports resulted in an augmented European money stock.[32] As far as the Low Countries are concerned, monetary factors seem not to have been the crucial variables and played a more passive role in the first half of the sixteenth century. The first strong movement of price increases can be defined as a typical "demand-pull inflation."[33]

On the other hand, during the 1550s and early 1560s, when there was a huge influx of precious metals and an increased use of money, the Low Countries' *Price Revolution* was abating. This noncoincidence of metallic flows with the intervals of price rises in the sixteenth century is also present in various other European countries. Some authors use this as a major objection to the quantity theory explanation.[34]

Whether the New World's treasure was present in the Low Countries or not, the exact volume of the European monetary stock during the

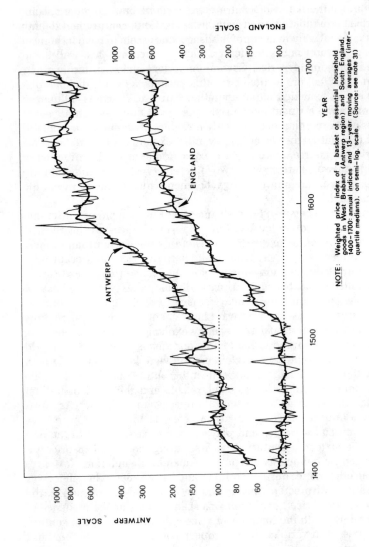

Fig. 1   The Movement of Prices in England and the Low Countries, 1400-1700: annual indices and moving averages (13 year). Base: average of 1451-1475 = 100

NOTE: Weighted price index of a basket of essential household goods in West Brabant (Antwerp region) and South England, 1400-1700: annual indices and 13-year moving averages (inter-quartile medians), on semi-log. scale. (Source: see note 31) sixteenth century is still undetermined — factors other than monetary contributed to relative price differences among countries or disturbed the synchronization of their periods of inflation.

In the southern Low Countries, for instance, the commercial and industrial growth of the first half of the sixteenth century had led to a remarkable expansion of supply. These factors seem to have influenced both price levels and price structures.

During the main period of commercial expansion in the southern Low Countries (1535–64), the combined effects of demographic change — the increase of population had passed its peak — of the persistent favorable situation of agriculture, and of the industrial revival caused a sharp inflationary pressure. The consequences were higher wages in different sectors and a better distribution of income. As H. van Der Wee demonstrated clearly in his magisterial work on Antwerp, these factors were also the basis for the prosperity of the urban middle classes and of a large part of the rural population in the southern Low Countries.[35]

During the difficult years of the revolt in the Low Countries (1565–70), demographic and psychological factors undermined the most vital pillars of the economy: agriculture and commerce. Yet, despite a new wave of high prices in the last third of the sixteenth century, the *Price Revolution* came to an end.

We can conclude this descriptive note by saying that the inflation of the sixteenth century ended as it began, at different times in different places. Most European countries did not reach the peak of their *Price Revolution* until 1620–40, in the southern Low Countries the decrease of prices occurred definitely before 1625. The role played by non-metallic and nonmonetary factors, such as war and political chaos, in breaking the price tension undoubtedly was more significant here than in most other places.

Notes

1   G. Duby, *L'économie rurale et la vie des campagnes dans l'Occident médiéval*, II (Paris, 1962): 563–78.

2.   Earl J. Hamilton, "American Treasure and Andalusian Princes, 1505–1660, A Study in Spanish Price Revolution," *Journal of Economic and Business History* 1 (1928); "American Treasure and the Rise of Capitalism," *Economica* 9 (1929): 338–57; *American Treasure and the Price Revolution in Spain, 1501–1650* (Cambridge, Mass., 1934); "Profit Inflation and the Industrial Revolution, 1751–1800," *Quarterly Journal of Economics* 61 (1942); "Prices and Progress," *Journal of Economic History* 12 (1952): 325–49; E. H. Phelps Brown and Sheila V. Hopkins, "Seven Centuries of the Prices of Consumables, compared with Builders' Wage Rates," *Economica* 92, new ser., 24 (1956); "Wage

Rates and Prices; Evidence for Population Pressure in the Sixteenth Century," *Economica*, new ser., 24 (1957); "Prices and Population: Some Further Evidence," *Economica*, new ser., 26 (1959).

3. Anna J. Schwartz, "Secular Price Change in Historical Perspective," *Journal of Money, Banking and Credit*, Feb. 1973, pp. 247–48.

4. M. Mate, "High Prices in Early Fourteenth-Century England: Causes and Consequences," *Economic History Review*, 2d. ser. 28 (1975): 1–16; M. C. Prestwich, "Edward I's Monetary Policies and Their Falling Prices in the Fourteenth Century," *Economic History Review*, 2d ser. 27 (1974): 1–15; "Currency and the Economy of Early Fourteenth-Century England" in N. J. Mayhew (Ed.) "Edwardian Monetary Affairs (1279–1344)," *British Archaeological Reports* 36 (1977): 45–53; E. Ames, "The Sterling Crisis of 1337–39," *Journal of Economic History* 25 (1965): 496–522.

5. M. Prestwich, "Early Fourteenth-Century Exchange Rates," *Economic History Review*, 2d ser. 32 (1979): 470–82.

6. J. H. Munro, *Wool, Cloth and Gold. The Struggle for Bullion in Anglo-Burgundian Trade, 1340–1478* (Brussels and Toronto, 1973).

7. M. Mate, "High Prices," pp. 1–16; M. M. Postan, *Medieval Economy and Society, An Economic History of Britain, 1100–1500* (Berkeley and Los Angeles, 1972), pp. 238–39.

8. S. E. Rigold, "The Trail of the Sterlings," *British Numismatic Journal*, 3d. ser., 6 (1949–51): 45.

9. J. H. Munro, "Wool-Price Schedules and the Qualities of English Wools in the Later Middle Ages, c. 1270–1499," *Textile History* 9 (1978): 138.

10. See a.o. H. Van Werveke, "Currency Manipulation in the Middle Ages: The Case of Louis de Male, Count of Flanders," *Transactions of the Royal Historical Society*, 4th ser., 31 (1949): 115–27; J. H. Munro, *Wool, Cloth, and Gold*, p. 18; F. and W. P. Blockmans, "Devaluation, Coinage and Seignorage under Louis de Nevers and Louis de Male, Counts of Flanders, 1335–1384" in N. J. Mayhew (Ed.) "Coinage in the Low Countries (880–1500)," *British Archaeological Reports*, intern. ser., 54 (1979): 69–94.

11. H. A. Miskimin, *Money, Prices and Foreign Exchange in Fourteenth-Century France* (New Haven, 1963), pp. 53–71; Earl J. Hamilton, *Money, Prices, and Wages in Valencia, Aragon, and Navarra, 1351–1500* (Cambridge, Mass., 1936); L. Genicot, "Crisis: From the Middle Ages to Modern Times," *Cambridge Economic History*, 2d ed., 1 (1966): 677–94.

12. See, in particular, W. C. Robinson, "Money, Population and Economic Change in Late Medieval Europe," *Economic History Review*, 2d ser., 12 (1959): 53–76; R. S. Lopez and H. A. Miskimin, "The Economic Depression of the Renaissance," *Economic History Review*, 2d ser., 14 (1962): 408–426; N. J. Mayhew, "Numismatic Evidence and Falling Prices in the Fourteenth Century," *Economic History Review*, 2d ser., 27 (1974): 1–15. H. Laurent, "Crise monétaire et difficultés économiques: En Flandre, aux XIVe et XVe siècles," *Annales d'histoire économique et sociale* 5 (1933): 156–60; F. Graus, "La crise monétaire du 14e siècle," *Revue belge de Philologie et d'Histoire* 29 (1951): 445–54; C. M. Cipolla, "Currency Depreciation in Medieval Europe," *Economic Historical Review*, 2d ser., 15 (1963): 413–22; J. V. Nef, "Mining and Metallurgy in Medieval Civilisation," *Cambridge Economic History of Europe*, 2 (1952): 430–93.

13. J. Day, "The Great Bullion Famine of the Fifteenth Century," *Past and Present* 79 (1978): 1–53.

14. H. van der Wee, "The Agricultural Development of the Low Countries as revealed by the Tithe and Rent Statistics, 1250–1800," in H. van der Wee and E. van Cauwenberghe (Eds.) *Productivity of Land and Agricultural Innovation in the Low Countries, 1250–1800* (Leuven, 1978), pp. 3–6.

15. *Ibid.*, p. 2.

16. J. Goy and E. Le Roy Ladurie (Eds.) *Les fluctuations du produit de la dîme* (Paris-The Hague, 1972).

17. H. van der Wee, *The Growth of the Antwerp Market and the European Economy*, II (The Hague, 1963): 7.

18. H. van der Wee and E. van Cauwenberghe, "Histoire agraire et finances publiques en Flandre du XVIᵉ au XVIIᵉ siècle," *Annales, E. S. C.* 28 (1973): 1051–65; E. van Cauwenberghe and H. van der Wee, "Productivité, évolution du prix d'affermage et superficie de l'entreprise agricole aux Pays Bas du 14ᵉ au 18ᵉ siècle," *Workshop on Quantitative Economic History, Discussion Paper* 7602 (Leuven, 1977); E. van Cauwenberghe and H. van der Wee, "Productivity, Evolution of Rents and Farm Size in the Southern Netherlands Agriculture from the Fourteenth to the Seventeenth Century" in H. van der Wee and E. van Cauwenberghe (Eds.), *Productivity of Land* (Leuven, 1978), pp. 125–61.

19. L. Genicot et al., *La crise agricole du Bas Moyen Age dans le Namurois* (Louvain, 1970).

20. M. Jefferson, "A Record of Inflation" in M. Jefferson et al. (Eds.), *Inflation* (London-Dallas, 1978), pp. 24–25.

21. H. van der Wee, *Growth*, 2: 381.

22. J. H. Munro, "Monetary Contraction and Industrial Change in the Late Medieval Low Countries, 1335–1500," *British Archaeological Reports*, intern. ser., 54 (1979): 95–161.

23. J. Day, "The Great Bullion Famine," pp. 46–47.

24. H. A. Miskimin, *The Currency of Later Renaissance Europe, 1460–1600* (London, New York, Melbourne, 1977), pp. 43–46.

25. Several authors have tried to summarize the state of the debate: F. Braudel and F. C. Spooner, "Prices in Europe from 1450 to 1750," *The Cambridge Economic History of Europe*, 4 (Cambridge, 1967), pp. 374–486; Y. S. Brenner, "The Inflation of Prices in Early Sixteenth Century England," *Economic History Review*, 2d ser., 14 (1961): 225–39; "The Inflation of Prices in England, 1551–1650," *Economic History Review*, 2d ser., 15 (1962): 266–84; A. R. E. Chabert, "Encore la Révolution des Prix au XVIᵉ siècle," *Annales, E. S. C.* 12 (1957): 269–74; C. E. Challis, "Spanish Bullion and Monetary Inflation in England in the Later Sixteenth Century," *Journal of European Economic History* 4 (1975): 381–92; C. M. Cipolla, "La prétendue 'révolution des prix': réflections sur l'expérience italienne," *Annales, E. S. C.* 10 (1955): 513–16; D. O. Flynn, "A New Perspective on the Spanish Price Revolution: The Monetary Approach to the Balance of Payments," *Explorations in Economic History* 5 (1978): 388–406; J. D. Gould, "The Price Revolution Reconsidered," *Economic History Reviews*, 2d ser., 17 (1964): 249–66; Ingrid Hammarstrom, "The Price Revolution of the Sixteenth Century: Some Swedish Evidence," *The Scandinavian Economic History Review* 5 (1957): 118–54; H. A. Miskimin, "Population

Growth and the Price Revolution in England," *Journal of European Economic History* 4 (1975): 179–86; J. U. Nef, "The Progress of Technology and the Growth of Large-Scale Industry in Great Britain, 1540–1640," *Economic History Review*, 2d ser. 5 (1934): 3–24; "Prices and Industrial Capitalism in France and England, 1540–1640," *Economic History Review*, 2d ser. 7 (1936): 155–85; R. B. Outhwaite, *Inflation in Tudor and Early Stuart England* (London, Melbourne, Toronto, 1969); P. Ramsey, *The Price Revolution in Sixteenth Century England* (London, 1971); Anna J. Schwartz, "Secular Price Change in Historical Perspective," *Journal of Money, Banking and Credit*, 1973, pp. 243–69; I. Wallerstein, *The Modern World System: Capitalist Agriculture and the Origins of the European World-Economy in the Sixteenth Century* (New York, 1974); V. Zimyani, "A Typology of Central European Inflation in the XVIth and XVIIth Centuries," *Journal of European Economic History* 4 (1975): 399–402.

26. See Wallerstein, *Modern World System*, pp. 67 ff.

27. See Outhwaite, *Inflation in Tudor and Early Stuart England*, pp. 23–36; Hammarstrom, *passim*.

28. Brenner, pp. 225–39; "The Inflation of Prices in England, 1551–1650," pp. 266ff; Gould, *passim*.

29. Gould, p. 259.

30. Miskimin, "Population Growth," p. 185.

31. H. van der Wee, "Prijzen en Lonen als ontwikkelingsvariabelen. Een vergelijkend onderzoek tussen Engeland en de Zuidelijke Nederlanden, 1400–1700," *Album 'Charles Verlinden'* (Gent, 1975), pp. 413–47.

32. Miskimin, "Population Growth," p. 183.

33. J. Fourastie, "Inflation: How We Can Cure It?" in M. Jefferson et al (Eds.) *Inflation* (London, 1978), pp. 169–74.

34. Cipolla, pp. 513–16.

35. H. Van der Wee, *Growth*, II: 434–35.

Sixteenth-Century Inflation
from a Production Point of View

DENNIS O. FLYNN

INTRODUCTION

What caused prices (expressed in terms of silver) to rise by 300 or 400 percent throughout Europe during the sixteenth century?[1] Debate has centered on whether the enormous flow of precious metals from the New World (especially Mexico and Peru) caused prices to rise for a century. The view that the influx of American treasure was responsible for the price revolution is traditionally labeled the *quantity theory of money* interpretation. According to this argument, the influx of treasure augmented the European supply of money and produced price inflation.[2] Recent opposition to this centuries-old view rests largely on evidence of a physical absence of the American metals from countries during their periods of most severe price inflation.

Section I briefly discusses objections based on the physical absence of precious metals during domestic inflationary experiences. These objections are rejected. It is concluded that the production of precious metals can indeed explain the price rise. The body of the paper is contained in Section II which focuses, not on the inflationary effects of the influx of precious metals, but on the *causes* of their increased production. In other words, the flow of precious metals caused prices to rise, but what forces determined the magnitude of the flow itself? This question can be answered only by adopting a production point of view.

I. THE CENTRAL OBJECTION TO
THE QUANTITY-THEORY INTERPRETATION[3]

The flow of treasure into various countries does not appear to have synchronized with their respective periods of pronounced inflation. This has been the most troublesome objection to the quantity-theory interpretation of sixteenth-century price inflation. First to articulate this argument was Carlo M. Cipolla (1955). Cipolla's rejection of the proposition that American metals were responsible for Italian inflation rests on a lack of synchronization in the timing of treasure imports and the Italian price inflation. Inflation seems to have crested in the 1550s, yet the flow of bullion into Italy became significant only after 1570. Jerome Blum (1956, 198) followed suit with a rejection of the monetary explanation of Russia's price rise: "there is no reason to believe that there was a sizeable influx of precious metals into Russia in the sixteenth century. . . ." Next, Ingrid Hammarström (1954, 147, 154) argued that there was also an insufficient influx of American treasure to account for Sweden's price revolution. Nor did significant quantities of New World metals arrive in England until the seventeenth century, according to several authors, so how could these metals account for England's price inflation?[4] Ironically, there were frequent shortages of New World metals in Spain throughout the sixteenth century (Flynn, 1978, 393–96), even though Spain was the direct recipient of the American treasure shipments.

Proper reformulation of the "monetary" point of view eliminates the chronology-based objection just outlined. That is, it is perfectly consistent to accept historical evidence which indicates a lack of synchronization between treasure flows and price inflation in individual countries, while maintaining that the output of precious metals *caused* those countries' prices to rise. *The American mine output resulted in international price inflation. Each country's inflation should not be viewed independently.* Yet there still remains the question of why a particular country did or did not experience an influx of precious metals during its price rise. The latter issue can be resolved by reference to the concept of a national stock demand for money.

The volume of money needed to conduct business is determined by the level of business activity and the level of prices. People have to maintain a larger stock of money when business grows; when business activity falls a smaller stock of money is needed. Likewise, when the level of prices is higher, people need to hold a larger volume of money to accommodate the same number of transactions; lower prices imply a smaller demand for money. If the volume of business activity is determined by producers in the long run, and prices are determined internationally, then the national stock demand for money is already determined irrespective of the policies of those controlling the money supply. Whatever the volume of money demanded nationally, domestic monetary authorities can displace any portion of the country's specie (precious metals) from the country by issuing less valuable substitute monies. A hypothetical example will illustrate the point.

Suppose sixteenth-century Spain's business activity required a 100-million-ducats money stock and that was precisely the amount of money Spaniards desired to hold. Equilibrium existed in the money market; money supply equaled money demanded. If the Spanish government were to have subsequently minted the equivalent of 50 million ducats in base (copper) money, then 50 million ducats in specie would have been driven out of the country. Why? Because people needed only 100 million to transact business and they were suddenly holding 150 millions. If an individual decides to hold a smaller proportion of his (her) assets in the form of money, it is a simple matter — buy something with the excess money balances. But one Spaniard's purchase from another Spaniard leaves the excess money in the domestic economy. Only foreign purchases permit the money stock to shrink.[5] Foreigners did not want to hold Spain's cheap copper money, so it was the full-bodied specie that left the Spanish economy. Excess domestic balances were spent and re-spent until the excess 50 million ducats were forced out of the country.

In reality, the Spanish Crown minted enormous quantities of vellon (copper) money in the sixteenth century. Vellon did push the full-bodied pieces of eight out of the country. The same was true in other countries which lacked bullion and specie — substitutes pushed them out. Thus, for example, England witnessed no significant influx of Spanish treasure in the sixteenth century because the debased issues of the mint precluded importation of Spanish money. Sixteenth-century England's monetary cup had already been filled with debased money.

In sum, the principal criticism of the monetary interpretation is that the flow of treasure to specific countries did not coincide chronologically with inflation in those countries. This criticism is spurious. Prices were determined internationally, not within each country separately. Furthermore, the absence of precious metals from a particular country was determined by whether a national mint issued significant quantities of substitute monies.

The traditional view stands. The output of precious metals caused sixteenth-century price to rise. But what determined that particular quantity of precious metal output? The remainder of this paper focuses on the demand for, and supply of, silver. There are two reasons for the surge in the precious-metal mining in the early modern era: extraordinarily rich mines were discovered and breakthroughs in mining technology lowered the cost of producing silver.

II. A PRODUCTION POINT OF VIEW

Annual United States price increases in the range of 10 percent have become commonplace in recent years. The statement that prices in general can be expected to rise 10 percent next year is exactly the same as the statement that the value of the monetary unit (the dollar) is expected to fall 10 percent during the next twelve months. Since price inflation is the same thing as the falling value of money, it is sometimes useful to investigate the causes of price inflation by focusing on the causes of the falling value of money. In the case of sixteenth-century inflation, the relevant question is this: What caused the value of silver to fall?[6] The answer could not be more straightforward — the supply of silver increased more rapidly than did demand. Supply expanded because of discovery of phenomenally rich silver mines in Mexico and Peru (and Japan) and because of application of cost-saving technology, especially implementation of the mercury-amalgam mining process in the sixteenth century.

It is useful to begin the analysis by considering a series of breakthroughs in mining technology in the middle of the previous century. First, there was a breakthrough in silver mining. In a classic article on the Central European mining boom, J. U. Nef (1941, 576) reported that the year 1451

> marked the Duke of Saxony's grant of the right to use a new invention for separating silver from rich argentiferous copper ores with the help of lead. More than any other invention, this accounts for the great prosperity of mining and metallurgy during the century which followed.

According to Perroy (quoted in Wallerstein, 1974, 41n), other technological improvements soon reduced production costs for all types of mines:

> [There was a] sudden rise of mineral production as of 1460, primarily in Central Europe. In this domain, technology became scientific. The invention of better methods of drilling, drainage and ventilation made possible the exploitation of mines in Saxony, Bohemia, and Hungary as far as 600 feet down; the increased use of hydraulic power increased the strength of the bellows and the drills such that the hearths could have come down from the mountainsides, and be located in the valleys. The building of the first blast furnaces ten feet high tripled the productive capacity of the old hearths. It is not impossible that, between 1460 and 1530, the extraction of mineral quintupled in Central Europe.

Lower production costs rendered handsome profits since the value of silver in international markets remained, for a time, somewhere near its previous level. The demand and supply curves in Figure 1 deserve additional comment. First, it should be pointed out that the demand curve (DD) refers to the demand for silver for all uses, only one of which is for use of money. Second, the supply curve (SS) is almost vertical. The nearly fixed supply of silver reflects the fact that the stock of silver at any point in time is largely determined by past output. Since silver is durable, the quantity of it available depends on perhaps centuries of mine output; therefore, current output would increase the quantity supplied by a small fraction.

Prior to the fifteenth-century technological improvements mentioned by Nef and Perroy, the equilibrium value of silver was relatively

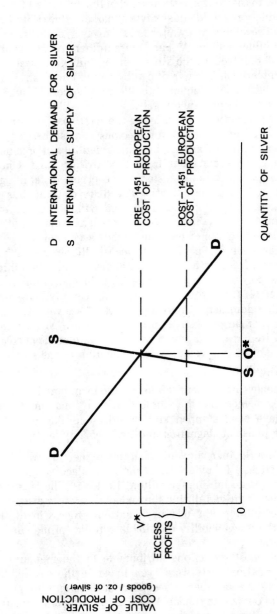

Fig. 1   The International Silver Market

high — this is represented by V* in Figure 1. If we assume that profits were normal in the mining industry at that time, the pre-1451 European cost of production would equal silver's market value. With implementation of the new technology after 1451, however, costs dropped below the market value of silver (V*) and extraordinary profits resulted. "Excess profits" obtained in the silver-mining industry; these profits induced the remarkable boom in fifteenth-century European silver mines. Potential profits also heightened the desire of others to obtain the increasingly valuable precious metals.

The early colonization effort along the west coast of Africa can be partly attributed to the search for precious metals. Iberians used that route to trade with the Far East, but large quantities of precious metals (mostly gold) were extracted from the African coast. Once easily obtainable supplies were exhausted, however, the metal-hungry Europeans turned toward the Atlantic. The diary of Columbus contains some 65 references to the search for gold within two months of his discovery of America (Vilar, 1974, 85–87). The New World soon became the richest source of precious metals ever known.

The initial wave of Spanish-American bullion arriving in Europe resulted largely from confiscation of art objects and gold mining. Prior to the 1530s most treasure, predominantly gold, came from the Antilles (Hamilton, 1934, 43). In the second half of the century, however, mined silver was the dominant American export. There were two principal reasons for this surge of silver production: New World mines were extraordinarily fertile and new technology again reduced costs. Technological innovation involved implementation of the mercury-amalgam mining process.

> It is probable that without the use of the technique based on the properties of mercury, the whole European inflationary process would have been stopped and American mining would have entered a phase of stagnation and decadence (Jara, 1966, p. 37).

Fortunately for Spain, a convenient supply of mercury was discovered at Huancavelica, a Peruvian mine, the only place where the Crown directly engaged in mining (Hamilton, 1934, 15). The Japanese silver mining industry thrived during the sixteenth century also, but it was not possible to adopt the mercury-amalgam process in the Far East because of the unavailability of reliable supplies of mercury (Seiichi Iwao, 1959, 63).

Aside from cost reductions attributable to the mercury-amalgam process, production costs were even lower in the case of the New World mines than for other mines. Marxist historians are particularly quick to point out that the cheap American metals were extracted at the social cost of extermination of a large portion of the indigenous popula-

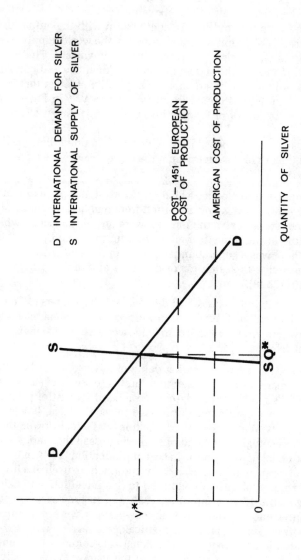

Fig. 2 Differential Production Costs

tion.[7] That is, the cost of replacing existing labor was foregone. Figure 2 represents the cost of producing silver in both Europe and the New World in the second half of the sixteenth century.

American output of bullion, in conjunction with the output of Central European and Japanese mines, increased the world supply of silver sufficiently to slowly drive its market value downward. That is, there was price inflation in the sixteenth century. American and non-American mines produced such an enormous quantity of silver that its market value eventually dropped (from, say, V* to V** in Figure 3) to a level below the cost of producing it in a growing number of European mines.

The prosperous German mines, which had attained their maximum output on the eve of the American mine discoveries, were forced out of business.

> The imports into Spain . . . helped to send the prices of most commodities soaring, and silver fell from one-half to one-third of its former value. Thus, the imports were one of the factors which led to the abandonment of silver mining in all European countries. There was a superabundance of supplies and consequently, little incentive to search for or dig more at home at a high cost (Nef, 1941, 589).

> Silver production at almost all the chief mining centers of Central Europe had fallen off by the beginning of the seventeenth century to anywhere from one-third to one-twentieth of its maximum amount (Nef, *ibid.*, 558).

The steadily decreasing market value of silver did not benefit producers of American silver either; their profits (per unit of silver) shrank as the metal's market value descended toward its cost of production. American mines continued to produce at record pace, however, because the New World cost of production was much lower than the European. Eventually the flood of silver depressed the market value of silver until it fell to the American cost of production (V*** in Figure 4). When that occurred, American mine production itself declined. By 1630 the amount of treasure imported to Spain had fallen to half of its peak rate in the 1590s (Hamilton, 1934, 34). In the early seventeenth century, the once envied Spanish possessions were denounced by contemporary Spaniards as "parasitical colonies" (Vilar, 1974, 23). Their evaluation was correct! The American colonies had generated lucrative profits for a century because the market value of silver exceeded its cost of production. When the difference between market value and cost vanished, excess profits also vanished.[8] There was no longer incentive to produce silver on such a large scale. As a result, the market value of silver stabilized around a technologically determined

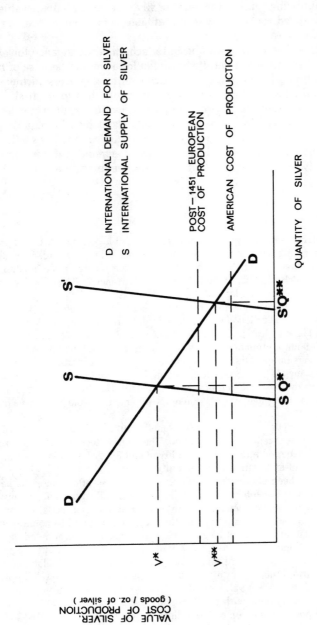

Fig. 3 Curtailment of European Mine Production, 1530's

level of production costs. In other words, prices (expressed in terms of silver) quit rising because the value of silver no longer fell; the value of silver stabilized because it was unprofitable to mine silver at a market value below costs.

The price revolution began because technological advance lowered the cost of producing silver. It continued for a century because of two considerations: (1) the mercury-amalgam mining process further reduced costs, (2) it took a century for new supplies to push silver's market value down to its long-run, cost-equaling equilibrium level. Early modern inflation is easiest to understand by adopting simple supply and demand analysis. In the long run, a commodity's value is determined on the supply side. In this case, the money substance was a commodity — a production point of view is appropriate.

Notes

1.   Actual (i.e., nominal) prices rose by some multiple of this basic rate of price inflation in countries which debased their currencies. Luigi Einaudi estimated, for example, that about half of the sixteenth-century French price inflation of 627 percent is attributable to the influx of precious metals. The other half was due to debasement (Braudel, 1972, 522).
2.   Historians believe that the "quantity theory" interpretation of the price revolution was first articulated by a Spaniard, Martín Azpilcueta de Navarro, in 1556 and later by Jean Bodin in 1568 (Grice-Hutchinson, 1952, 52). The most influential modern proponent of this view is Earl J. Hamilton. Professor Hamilton spent years in Spanish archives in painstaking documentation of the influx of precious metals and Spanish inflation. His prodigious writings on this subject span the past half-century. (See especially Hamilton, 1928, 1934).
3.   For a more complete presentation of the argument outlined in this section, see Flynn (1978).
4.   See Brenner (1961, 228; 1962, 278); Ramsey (1971, 7); Doughty (1975, 187).
5.   This statement requires qualification. The money stock would also shrink if specie were melted into bullion. See Flynn and Roper (1979) for analysis of the melting and exportation of commodity monies.
6.   Silver has been chosen for closer scrutiny because price historians have calculated sixteenth-century prices on the basis of the silver content (or equivalence) of each country's monetary unit. For example, if a certain country debased its currency by removing half the intrinsic content of its coinage, any resulting inflation would not be counted. This procedure was adopted by the International Committee on Price History in order to permit international price comparisons. A side effect of this practice, however, is that calculations suggesting a fourfold increase in prices during the sixteenth century also imply a quartering of the market value of silver. The result, for our purposes, is that inflation is synonymous with a falling market value of silver.
7.   Vilar reports decimation of the indigenous population in the West Indies and on the mainland. In some localities, sixteenth-century Latin America suffered an 80–90 percent population loss.

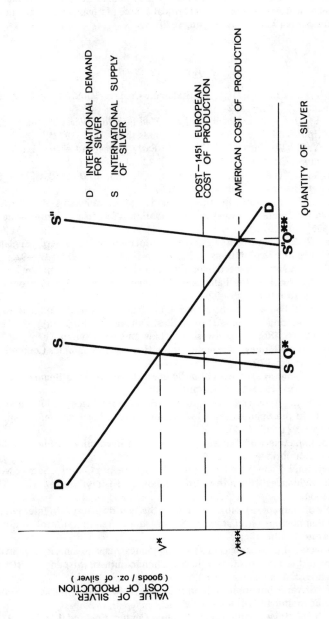

Fig. 4 Curtailment of American Mine Production, Early 1600's

D   INTERNATIONAL DEMAND
    FOR SILVER

S   INTERNATIONAL SUPPLY
    OF SILVER

POST–1451 EUROPEAN
COST OF PRODUCTION

AMERICAN COST OF PRODUCTION

QUANTITY OF SILVER

VALUE OF SILVER,
COST OF PRODUCTION
(goods / oz. of silver)

S"

S

D

S'Q**

S Q*

V*

V***

8. The elimination of excess profits from New World mining had worldwide repercussions. Excess profits had enabled the Spanish Crown to become the dominant world power. Loss of this critical source of revenues resulted in the decay of Spanish hegemony (Flynn, 1979).

References

Blum, J. "Prices in Russia in the Sixteenth Century," *Journal of Economic History* 16 (1956): 182–99.

Braudel, F. *The Mediterranean and the Mediteranian World in the Age of Philip II*, vols. 1, 2, trans. Siân Reynolds (New York, 1972).

Brenner, Y. S. "The Inflation of Prices in Early Sixteenth Century England," *Economic History Review* 14 (1961): 225–39.

Brenner, Y. S. "The Inflation of Prices in England, 1551–1650," *Economic History Review* 15 (1962): 266–84.

Cipolla, C. M. "La prétendu 'révolution des prix': réflexions sur l'expérience italienne," *Annales: Économies, Sociétés, Civilisations* 10 (1965): 513–16.

Doughty, R. A. "Industrial Prices and Inflation in Southern England, 1401–1640," *Explorations in Economic History* 12 (1975): 177–92.

Flynn, D. O. "A New Perspective on the Spanish Price Revolution: The Monetary Approach to the Balance of Payments," *Explorations in Economic History* 15 (1978): 388–406.

Flynn, D. O. "Silver and the Spanish Empire," in J. H. Soltow (Ed.), *Essays in Economic and Business History* (East Lansing, Mich., 1979).

Flynn, D. O., and Roper, D. "Gresham's Law and the Modern Theory of the Demand for Money," Presented at the History of Economics Conference, Urbana, Ill., 1979.

Grice-Hutchinson, M. *The School of Salamanca: Readings in Spanish Monetary Theory 1544–1605* (Oxford, 1952).

Hamilton, E. J. "American Treasure and Andalusian Prices, 1502–1660: A Study in the Spanish Price Revolution," *Journal of Economic Business History* 1 (1920): 1–35.

Hamilton, E. J. *American Treasure and the Price Revolution in Spain, 1501–1650* (Cambridge, Mass., 1934).

Hammarström, I. "The Price Revolution of the Sixteenth Century: Some Swedish Evidence," *Scandinavian Economic History Review* 5 (1957): 118–54.

Iwao, Seiichi. "Japanese Gold and Silver in the World History," in *International Symposium on History of Eastern and Western Cultural Contacts* (Tokyo, 1959).

Jara, A. "Economía minera e historia económica hispâno-americana," in A. Jara (Ed.), *Tres ensayos solore economía minera hispâno-americana* (Santiago, 1966).

Nef, J. U. "Silver Production in Central Europe, 1450–1618," *Journal of Political Economy* 49 (1941): 576–89.

Ramsey, P. *The Price Revolution in Sixteenth-Century England* (London, 1971).

Vilar, P. *Oro y moneda en la historia 1450–1920* (Barcelona, 1974).

Wallerstein, I. *The Modern World-System: Capitalist Agriculture and the Origins of the European World-Economy in the Sixteenth Century* (New York, 1974).

Raising Hell or Raising the Rent:
The Gentry's Response to Inflation in
Sixteenth-Century Holland and Utrecht

SHERRIN MARSHALL WYNTJES

It is generally accepted that the Netherlands was hard hit by inflationary pressure in the second half of the sixteenth century, and that the nobility and the poor were hit hardest.[1] Caught between the monarchy's desire for effective centralization on the one hand and the reality of dwindling incomes and perquisites on the other, this generalization continues, the nobility turned to Calvinism, or at the very least, away from Spain and toward the idea of a revolt, in part to regain their primacy. In 1566, encouraged by the breakdown in the central government during the regency of Margaret of Parma, they seized their chance and fomented a rebellion, which would ultimately lead to the Eighty Years' War and independence for the seven United Provinces in the north.

Like all commonplaces, this one has some truth. Some of the noblemen who joined the Confederation of the Nobility and signed its Compromise — often taken as a starting point for the revolt — do fit this pattern. Still, as the Dutch economic and social historian Enno van Gelder pointed out over forty years ago, great differences in real status can be observed among the noblemen as a group.[2] There were not only differences of character and personal style that one would expect to find in any group of some 300–400 individuals, but differences in social position which were linked to a host of variables: geographic location, family and kin relationships, ties of patronage and clientage, to cite a few.[3]

A comparison of incomes of the lesser nobility (or gentry) of the county of Holland and province of Utrecht in the mid-sixteenth century offers some significant contrasts. The Hollanders had less land, fewer sources of income, and generally less status than their Utrecht counterparts. Contracts in Utrecht are varied, yield considerably more, and, more often than in Holland, are short term.[4]

The relationship between geographical locale and one's social and economic status and behavior thus seems particularly noteworthy in this time of inflation. Clearly, frustration existed over rising prices, particularly when coupled with frustration over one's inability to respond to those rising prices by "raising the rent." When one could not "raise the rent," perhaps it was tempting to go out and "raise hell." Those who were in a position to "raise the rent," we would assume, would be less likely to "raise hell."

The term *raising hell* here signifies dedicated support of the political and/or religious revolt which was detailed and recorded in 1566. The term *raising the rent* is more difficult to define precisely. Rental contracts for some nobles from both areas help us to estimate which incomes were keeping pace with inflation; that is, to determine who had been able to raise the rent and by how much.

Of course, if there was a simple cause-and-effect relationship between the two, *all* the Hollanders would have raised hell. In fact, 53 of some 200 noble families in the county of Holland, or one-fourth, supported the revolt; three-fourth did not. In Utrecht, 10 of 62 noble families, or one-sixth of the total, supported the revolt, five-sixth did not.[5] Thus, the economic factor is one of several that might influence a given individual. It adds one dimension to our understanding of motivating forces behind the revolt.

For evidence, we have some records of contractual incomes confiscated from noblemen who were punished for their role in the revolt.[6] In Utrecht, the only source is the debits of the provincial Rentmaster: a total of 68 contracts on eight individuals.[7] From 1467 to 1540, and in some cases, longer, properties were leased and incomes were collected as usual, in the name, however, of the King of Spain.[8] Although the records from the neighboring county of Holland are more complete, they are still not comprehensive, offering a total of 78 contracts on 14 individuals. Some noblemen that we know were convicted never had incomes listed for confiscation.[9]

Three of the men listed in the debits of the Utrecht rentmaster were related: Gerrit van Renesse, his illegitimate son Willem, and his nephew Johan. Although Gerrit van Renesse was Substitute Stadholder of Utrecht and a member of the provincial Court of Utrecht, his was the side of the family with less real substance. His place in the family by birth was unlucky, to begin with — the fourth son.[10] Thus, he had no *heerlijkheid* or seigniory of his own, and was indebted to others for favors. An early modern "wheeler-dealer," Gerrit exploited his ties as client of William of Nassau, Prince of Orange (for whom he "substituted" as Stadholder when Orange was not in residence in Utrecht) and Floris van Pallandt, Count of Culemborg (from whom he had received his most lucrative longterm income, the lease of Culemborg's peat bogs). Hard-drinking, a womanizer, often intemperate in his words and actions, both politically and religiously, he fits the stereotypical image of the mid-sixteenth-century petty gentleman or nobleman.

What did Gerrit van Renesse's income for 1566 consist of? He received 886 pounds (or gulden) yearly from a total of eight contracts: 6 on land, 1 orchard, 1 tithe.[11] But a more spectacular source of income was yielded by the previously mentioned peat bogs leased from Floris van Pallandt: 700 pounds yearly.[12] That was a fixed rental, based on a contract made at least 25 years before with Culemborg. The fixed rental had redounded to Renesse's advantage, for he subleased those peat bogs which he had so nominally rented for a much larger sum. Culemborg, a Hollander with his own financial pressures, had redeemed the leases in 1566. Renesse's real income decreased drastically as a result. In addition to the Renesse's opportunities as client of Orange and Culemborg, he had also gained for his son a place in the *bande d'ordonnance* of Hendrick van Brederode, Lord of Vianen, and coincidentally the largest landholder in Holland. Brederode, known as the *Grand Gueux* — Big Beggar, the originally derisive name given to the rebels — was one of the most important leaders of the revolt in 1566.[13]

In addition to his legitimate children, Renesse had at least two illegitimate sons, Philip and Willem. Willem had five incomes itemized by the rentmaster, mostly rooms rented in the Inn of the Three Crowns in Utrecht.[14] There was not much of a patrimony for him or Renesse's other illegitimate son, Philip, of whom we know little except that he had a seat on the Town Council of Utrecht, and that he would later be accused, with his half-brother Jan (Gerrit's legitimate first son) of serving in the *bande* of Hendrick van Brederode.[15]

Jan van Renesse was 30 years old in 1566. At the age of nine, he had become prebend of the Dom Church in Utrecht. Although Jan was the second beneficiary of his father's lease of Culemborg's peat bogs, he was regularly short of funds, and had to dip into the principal of annuities held in his name.[16] Future prospects seemed distant when he entered Brederode's service around 1564.[17]

As will be evident from comparison with the Hollanders, Gerrit van Renesse was the recipient of a significant income in 1566. But it was not enough to support his aspirations or alleviate his sense of competition with other branches of the family.

In 1566, the other prominent branch of the family tree that supported the revolt was headed by Johan van Renesse, Lord of Wulven and Wilp.[18] He had the luck that had seemingly eluded his uncle. To begin with, Johan van Renesse was the eldest son of a [surrogate] eldest son. That is, his father, also named Johan, was the third son in a family where the eldest son had died young, and the second son, Adriaen, had become a prominent cleric, deacon of the Dom Church. Johan van Renesse inherited sizable amounts of land and at least ten income-bearing tithes.[19] Additionally, his next brother had died in 1564 at the age of 20, unmarried and childless, so Johan had added that inheritance to his holdings. In 1566, Johan was, at the age of 26, wealthy and secure.[20]

But before we conclude that Johan had no incentive to raise hell, we need to account for other factors in his life. His mother, Aleyd van Bronckhorst en van Batenburg, had been among the early converts to Calvinism. Her husband, Johan's father, had died in 1553 when Johan was only thirteen. Aleyd, a strong-willed member of a fiercely independent family of the neighboring province of Gelderland, brought Calvinist preachers to their manor, and Johan became a convert to the Reformed faith, undoubtedly under his mother's influence.[21] It was to Johan that the Calvinists turned during the crisis of 1566. He led their increasingly belligerent demands for a church of their own; he championed them when rumors of iconoclastic outbursts had infuriated the Utrecht Town Council, but he neither condoned the iconoclasm nor participated in it himself, although his uncle Gerrit did both.[22]

In all accounts and testimony Johan appears as a man who, despite what we might consider ample incentive, did not raise hell. (Because he was a recognized Calvinist, that he did not raise hell was of little consequence — he fled into exile with his family and regained his property with difficulty.) Had he been able to raise the rent? The answer appears to be yes. Only one of 13 contracts in his name seems to be fixed, and that is a hereditary tithe for the insignificant sum of 16 shillings/2 pennies.[23] Possibly, then, we have at least part of the explanation why he did not support the revolt and the demands of the Calvinists more vigorously. (It is also possible, of course, that he was merely deceitful, or at the least, circumspect, but in that case he could not have been as devout a Calvinist as he appears.)

Other members of the Utrecht gentry typify other sources of income. Cornelis van Nyenrode's "vocation" was similar to that of Johan van Renesse's uncle, and Gerrit van Renesse's brother, Adriaen. Nyenrode was a canon of the Dom Church with a "wife or concubine."[24] We know that by 1566 he had already fathered one child because he attempted to arrange for his son to inherit what he had come to regard as "his" property. Included was a commodious house belonging to the Church. By 1566 such behavior — winked at or ignored 30 years before when Adriaen van Renesse did it — was unacceptable.[25] Although Nyenrode was accused of iconoclasm, there is little evidence to support that charge. With his fortunes tied to the Church and unavailable now to his offspring, Nyenrode raised hell — in a quiet way. He sold the house for a tidy 2400 pounds and absconded with wife and children to Germany at the height of the troubles in 1566.[26]

Thus far the emphasis has been on a few Utrecht families, all of whom turned away from the Church in one way or another. Adriaen de Wael, Lord of Vronesteyn, must be viewed somewhat differently. He knew all the troublemakers, and enjoyed a good time himself, but was also regarded as a "good Catholic," albeit one who went infrequently to church. The Church was a repository for superfluous sisters, aunts, and cousins.[27] Adriaen was the eldest son and thus inherited title, lands, and position. His family's nobility was of fairly recent origin, dating to the end of the fifteenth century, but this need not be seen as a hindrance to their advancement.[28] Adriaen's mother was the daughter of the Sheriff and Burgomaster of Utrecht, and he himself married the daughter of a Utrecht magistrate, who brought with her to the marriage not only lands but also *rentes* from the city itself.[29]

Thus, although de Wael was bluff, unlettered, and boisterous — as representative of his estate as Gerrit van Renesse — he had no real desire to raise hell. The iconoclastic outbursts angered him; they seemed an affront to his kin ensconced in convents.[30] After his wife's death in 1560, de Wael was footloose. Perhaps this helps explain his fatal curiosity about the Calvinist hedge preachings. Listening to just one of them provided evidence enough for the Crown to ensnare him and his incomes. Testimony by churchwardens and members of religious orders in his favor was to no avail. But de Wael, in fact, had not raised hell. He had been able to raise the rent through his prosperous middle-class kin connections. (Significantly enough, it was for their *mother's* estate that de Wael's children later petitioned the Crown after their father had been executed on a trumped-up charge of lèse-majesté.)[31]

This brings us to two individuals for whom we are fortunate enough to have several contracts in both provinces. Bernt Uyten Eng was about Jan van Renesse's age, the eldest son of an old and prominent Utrecht family dating back to at least the thirteenth century.[32] But unlike Johan van Renesse, Bernt Uyten Eng raised hell. Why? His total certain income was 455 pounds, from a total of 23 contracts. 105 of those 455 pounds came from three contracts, two of which were one-year contracts on the use of land in Utrecht. The others were incomes shared (with only one exception) with siblings on property which Bernt's mother had left her children in Holland. These rentals, 19 in all (if one excludes the income of 72 pounds which was the only contract in Bernt's name alone) total 26 pounds/10 shillings for Bernt's share, or an average of less than 1½ pounds. That was a trifle, particularly when compared with his Utrecht contracts, which average 35 pounds per contract.[33] As we might suspect by now, Bernt's Holland rentals were very largely long term, seven years or longer, or copyhold rentals.[34] Faced with the prospect of waiting for his father to die to inherit substantial holdings in Utrecht, Bernt joined Brederode's *bande*.[35]

The Hollanders whose contracts are included here present a very different image, but one that is familiar once we can compare them with Bernt Uyten Eng. Dierick Snoy (or Sonoy) was listed with the Hollanders by the Council of Troubles which condemned him, because he lived near the Hague and owned property in Heusden, Asperen, as well as receiving incomes through his wife, a Holland heiress.[36] Accused of joining the Confederation of the Nobility and supporting the Calvinist preachings, Sonoy said in his defense that since he had been born in Cleves he "was no vassal of the King." Nonetheless, his property was confiscated.[37] For all his Holland connections, there was not much to be had; some furniture was sold by the rentmaster and the house in the Hague which he had formerly occupied was now rented to his wife by the rentmaster — an interesting arrangement.[38] Sonoy, it seems, also had a brother, Joost, who lived in Utrecht and this may account for his incomes there. Nine contracts were listed by the rentmaster, seven of which were on the use of land, and totaled 222 pounds. The remaining two were yearly annuities. Five of the land rentals were one-year contracts; the annuities were collected biennially.[39] As was the case with many of the Utrecht contracts, payment had already been made, in every case but one to Sonoy himself. In the ninth contract, payment had been made to Joost Sonoy.[40] Perhaps Sonoy's Utrecht incomes did not provide him with complete ability to raise the rent. Since his affairs were linked to Holland, his Utrecht incomes were, rather, an additional source of income. But that they passed rapidly into his hands, apparently with other Utrecht incomes, too, demonstrates why their structure helped the Utrecht gentry in coping with inflation: they were able to get their hands on the incomes quickly and frequently.

What of the Hollanders whose incomes, as far as we know, came exclusively from properties in Holland itself? Jacob Oom van Wijngaerden, Lord of Wijngaerden, sentenced with his brother Cornelis, forced the abbess of Rijnsburg to open the door of her cloister to the Calvinists.[41] Cornelis informed the nuns at another cloister near the Hague that "they [he and his companions] would turn the cloister into a 'dove-cote.'" What incomes are listed for these two individuals who raised hell? Jacob's accounts brought him a total of 316 pounds. Those on the use of land that include duration specify that they are for either 7 or 9 years.[42] Cornelis received 196 pounds/7 shillings from all of his incomes; as was the case with Bernt Uyten Eng's Holland incomes, several are for insignificant amounts. They included a portion of a rental on less than 1 morgen of land for 12 shillings, a one-third share and a one-sixteenth share of land in the Hague for the sum of 7 shillings/6 pennies. What lands Jacob and Cornelis had were spread throughout the county of Holland, in the new polders which were being created, in the Hague, Gravezande, Wassenaar. Perhaps this made collection of incomes more difficult for them than it was, say, for

Adriaen de Wael, whose incomes were all based on properties near his lands in Jutphas or from the city of Utrecht itself. Even Johan van Renesse (Lord of Wulven and Wilp), seemingly was able to collect incomes from his holdings in Gelderland, a province away, more readily than the Hollanders were able to collect incomes within North and South Holland.[43]

Two more brothers involved with the troubles of 1566 were Ghelyn and Johan van Wassenhoven. Their sentences accused them of supporting the Confederation of the Nobility, associating with others who did so (such as Sonoy), and having stood armed guard during the Calvinist hedge preachings.[44] Nine incomes are listed in Ghelyn's name, and four in his brother's. All the land rentals accruing to Ghelyn van Wassenhoven are on small amounts of land, and total 239 pounds; the two land rentals which his brother Johan received total 62 pounds. On one of those land rentals, which expired in 1568, a new contract was made in 1569. As was often the case in Holland it was for a period of 7 years. The previous contract had specified that each *ghemedt* (a measurement of land of which 2 *meten* = 1 *morgen*) which had previously been used yearly for 3 pounds/9 shillings, would now be used for 5 pounds/ 5 shillings. In this case, the Rentmaster of the County of Holland raised the rent, not the brothers Wassenhoven.[45]

One final example may suffice for the Hollanders. Josua van Alveringen, Lord of Hoffwegen, was not only accused of suppporting the Calvinist hedge preachings but also the military efforts of the Lord of Brederode. With a group that included the Utrechter Jan van Renesse, as well as other Hollanders, he conspired to aid in Brederode's entrance into Utrecht. The group met in October 1566, in Utrecht at a variety of taverns, registering under patently assumed names at each (e.g., Zeger Zegersz., Wessel Wesselsz.) and, through the windows, loudly exhorted others to join them. (One who refused to do so was Adriaen de Wael, who said later that he knew "there was rascalry afoot").[46] Van Alveringen had thus raised hell. His rentals for the use of a mere 22 *morgen* of land amounted to 64 pounds; the remainder of his income of 201 pounds/41 shillings, came from a yearly annuity, a portion of a tithe, and the rental of a pigeon-house or dove-cote for 31 shillings (1 pound/11 shillings) a year.[47] (Obviously Cornelis van Wassenhoven knew what he was talking about when he threatened to turn the convent into a dove-cote!)

In conclusion, of these 78 contracts from the county of Holland, 36 are for the use of land, with or without houses. In every contract where the term of usage is specified, it is at least six years. In one single instance, the rental of a house without contract (*huiercedulle*) is unusual enough to be discussed at some length. The remainder of the incomes are tithes and portions of tithes, yearly *rentes* and portions thereof, and in two cases, inheritances.[48] The largest of the land rentals is for 18 morgen, and a manor house goes with it. More typical are the contracts in the same individual's name for 1 morgen (1 contract) and ½ morgen (2 contracts).[49]

In Utrecht, in the 68 contracts itemized here, the area specified is much greater. Only one of Gerrit van Renesse's six rental contracts was for less than 10 morgen, and the range extends to two rentals of 27 morgen of land. Bernt Uyten Eng held three contracts, of which two are on land rentals, both for 7 morgen.[50] Uyten Eng's property in Holland included one rental of 16 morgen (the largest amount), and several for less than 1 morgen.[51] The Holland gentry was land-poor.

One might argue that the Utrecht gentry had more to begin with, and more begat more. To some extent, this is true. But they also had, as evidenced by the number of contracts for one year or each half-year, far greater flexibility in making new contracts and negotiating new rates than did the Hollanders, locked into their six, seven, nine-year, and hereditary contracts — the last of which I found no evidence for in Utrecht.[52] As we have seen, for some of them (Gerrit van Renesse comes to mind) even this greater economic flexibility was not enough in a time of inflation. But for the others, inflation was a problem with which they were coping — so why raise hell?

Notes

1. For the overall socioeconomic picture, the following are helpful: Jerome Blum, *The End of the Old Order in Rural Europe* (Princeton, N.J., 1978), particularly 11–28, 60–64; Fernand Braudel, *The Mediterranean and the Mediterranean World in the Age of Philip II* (New York, 1972) I: pt. 2, sec. 3, especially 524–36; II: 706–709; H. G. Koenigsberger, *Estates and Revolutions* (Ithaca, N.Y., 1971); Frederic C. Jaher (Ed.), *The Rich, the Well Born, and the Powerful* (Urbana, Ill., 1973); J. W. Smit, "The Netherlands Revolution," in *Preconditions of Revolution in Early Modern Europe*, Robert Forster and Jack P. Greene (Eds.), (Baltimore, 1970).

2. H. A. Enno van Gelder, *Van Beeldenstorm tot Pacificatie* (Amsterdam, 1964); van Gelder, "De Hollandse Adel in de tijd van de opstand," *Tijdschrift voor Geschiedenis* 45 (1930).

3. I have developed this theme extensively in a forthcoming article in *The Sixteenth Century Journal*, "Family Allegiance and Religious Persuasion: The Lesser Nobility and the Revolt of the Netherlands."

4. It is important to note that the conclusions in this paper are based on *all* records of *all* members of the nobility called before the Council of Troubles in the years following 1567. For brevity, I have selected a few examples to illustrate various types of incomes, for example. My conclusions are based on the following sources which will be referred to extensively: for the Holland nobility, Algemeen Rijksarchief the Hague (hereafter cited as ARA the Hague),

Grafelijkheidsrekenkamer van Holland, Rekeningen nos. 4856–4860 (hereafter cited as Rek.); for Utrecht, Rijksarchief Utrecht (hereafter cited as RA Utrecht), Rechterlijk Archief (hereafter cited as Recht. Arch.), no. 365.

5.   For Holland, van Gelder, *op. cit.*, 150; for Utrecht, Sherrin M. Wyntjes, The Lesser Nobility of Utrecht and the Revolt of the Netherlands (unpublished doctoral dissertation, Tufts University, 1972).

6.   In many of these cases, the lands were not confiscated outright, only the incomes. In cases where direct confiscations were made, often furniture and the like were sold. See, for example, the sale of Robbrecht de Cocq van Nerij-nen's furniture, which was all that fell within the jurisdiction of the Holland rentmaster: ARA the Hague, Rek. 4856, fol. IIcXCIX right.

7.   RA Utrecht, Recht. Arch., no. 365, fols. 173 left–178 right; 195 right–202 left; 209 right–211 left; 219 left 219 right; 231 right–234 left; 243 right; 260 right–261 right; 265 right–270 left; 277 right–278 right.

8.   In Utrecht, at least, that resulted in an interesting state of affairs: little was actually collected in dozens of cases for dozens of reasons listed in the rentmas-ter's *Oncosten* or debits. Some reasons were legitimate (having paid the con-demned prior to the "date of Interdiction," in which case the leasor was not obliged to pay again), but others appear spurious, such as repairs to a house involving all but a few pounds of a 200-pound rental. This question will be developed and elaborated elsewhere.

9.   One possible explanation for some of these is that they had properties in other provinces, which were listed by the rentmasters of those provinces. Unfortunately, a search through all provincial archives would not necessarily prove fruitful. In Zeeland, for example, the archive was flooded during World War II and many of the sixteenth-century documents there were destroyed. In Utrecht, the first half of the record book has been lost. In any event, the historian also needs to travel to local archives, where additional documents, the vast majority of them uncatalogued, are to be found. I believe it would be erroneous to conclude that if we do not find records of properties owned in any given province, it indicates the nobility did not have any.

10.   Gerrit van Renesse had no *heerlijkheid* of his own and is thus unlisted in conventional genealogies. The important source for Utrecht is E.B.F.F. Wittert van Hoogland, *Bijdragen tot de geschiedenis van de Utrechtse ridderhofsteden en heerlijkheden*, 2 vols. (The Hague, 1910–12), and Renesse's daughter Agnes is listed there with particulars about her family, II, 234ff. References to Re-nesse's offices can be found in RA Utrecht, Recht. Arch., no. 1866, III, fol. CXIX right. His sentence: J. Marcus, *Sententien en Indagingen van den Hertog van Alba* (Amsterdam, 1735), 106–118.

11.   RA Utrecht, Recht. Arch., 365, fols. 198 right–202 left.

12.   RA Utrecht, Recht. Arch., 361, fols. 9 left–11 left; G. L. F. van Kinschot, *Verbalen van A. van Grijsperre en J. van Lent*, commissarissen in de troubles de annis 1567 en 1568, Codex diplomaticus Historisch Genootschap, 2d series, II, vol. 2 (1853), 101. (Hereafter cited as *Verbalen*.)

13.   See testimony of Jan van Renesse in J. van Vloten (Ed.), *Stukken betrek-kelijk de hervormings-beroerten te Utrecht in 1566 en 1567*, Kroniek Historisch Genootschap XIV, 3d ser., vol. 4 (1858), 246ff., (hereafter cited as Stukken); and also in ARA Brussels, Raad van Beroerten, no. 131, fols. 1–20, 150–59.

14. RA Utrecht, Rechterlijk Archief, no. 365, fols. 277 left–279 left.

15. For the terms of the sentences against them, Marcus, *op. cit.*, and A. L. E. Verheyden, *Le Conseil des Troubles*. Liste des Condamnes, (Brussels, 1961), entries 11,279 (Philip) and 11,280 (Willem).

16. RA Utrecht, Recht. Arch., 361, fol. 11 right; *Verbalen*, 100.

17. *Stukken*, 246–47.

18. van Hoogland, *op. cit.*, II: 47–48; J. van de Water, *Groot Utrecht Placaatboek*, 3 vols. (Utrecht, 1729), I: 282–84.

19. van der Water, II: 211; *Verbalen*, 111, 114–115; RA Utrecht, Recht. Arch., no. 1866, II (1529–1553), fol. XXXIIII right.

20. RA Utrecht, Recht. Arch., no. 1866, III (1554–1571), fol. CLI right.

21. For information on her background, see Sherrin Marshall Wyntjes, "Women in the Reformation Era," in Renate Bridenthal and Claudia Koonz (Eds.), *Becoming Visible* (Boston, 1977), 180; van Gelder, "Bailleul, Bronkhorst, Brederode," in *Van Beeldenstorm* . . . , 49–50, 63, 65.

22. *Stukken*, 274; Marcus, 55; Wyntjes, "The Lesser Nobility . . . ," 45–46; ARA Brussels, Raad van Beroerten, no. 131, fol. 56 left–right; Pieter Bor, *Oorspronk, begin en vervolgh der Nederlandsche Oorlogen* (Amsterdam, 1659), 91.

23. RA Utrecht, Recht. Arch., no. 365, fols. 177 left and right.

24. *Verbalen*, 103.

25. van Hoogland, II: 47.

26. *Verbalen*, 93–94.

27. van Hoogland, I: 294–96; J. Kleijntjens, genealogy of de Wael family, in *De Navorscher*, v. 71 (1922): 206; RA Utrecht, Recht. Arch., 1866, II, fol. XLVI right; J. W. C. van Campan and J. C. J. Kleijntjens, "Bescheiden betreffende den Beeldenstorm van 1566 in de Stad Utrecht," *Bijdragen en Mededelingen van het Historisch Genootschap*, LIII (1932): 74-75.

28. van Campan and Kleijntjens.

29. van Hoogland.

30. *Ibid.*, 101, 107, 109, 110.

31. ARA the Hague, Archief Heereman van Zuydtwyck, no. 2611; RA Utrecht, Recht. Arch., no. 1866, IV, fol. 42 left; Wittert van Hoogland, I: 378.

32. van Hoogland, I: 378.

33. ARA the Hague, Rek., 4859, fols. XIIIcLIII–XIIIcIII right.

34. *Ibid.*; see also charts accompanying this paper.

35. *Verbalen*, 137ff.; Marcus, 111.

36. J. W. te Water, *Historie van het verbond en de smeekschriften der Nederlandsche edelen* . . . 4 vols. (Middelburg, 1779–96), III: 298ff.

37. *Ibid.*

38. ARA the Hague, Rek. 4856, fol. LIIII left–LV right.

39. RA Utrecht, Recht. Arch., 365, fols. 215 left–217 right.

40. *Ibid.*, fol. 215 right.

41. te Water, III: 387ff.; Marcus, 48.

42. For Cornelis, see te Water, III: 385–387; Marcus, 51; for Jacob's contracts: ARA the Hague, Rek. 4859, XIIcXLII right–XIIcLIX right.

43. *Ibid.*, Rek. 4859, fols. XXVII right–XXXV right. It helped to have a competent bailiff or receiver, of course. Bernt Uyten Eng (or more likely, his father

Frederick) had such an individual in Simon Geertz. Storm. Johan van Renesse had a bailiff for his Gelderland properties, although none is mentioned for his Utrecht lands, so possibly he collected these incomes himself.

44. Marcus, 36–37 (Ghelyn) and 30 (Johan).

45. ARA the Hague, Rek. 4859, fols. XIIcLX left–XIIcLXXI right (Ghelyn); fols. XIIcLXXI right–XIIcLXXX right (Johan).

46. *Verbalen*, 253–54; van Campan and Kleijntjens, 129–31; A. van Hulzen, *Utrecht in 1566 en 1567* (Groningen-Batavia, 1932), 67.

47. ARA the Hague, Rek. 4856, fols. LXXXIX right–CII left.

48. This was a house rental in the name of Adriaen van Zwyeten (or Swieten), Lord of Swieten; Rek. 4859, fol. XIIIXI left and right.

49. These contracts were in the name of Lodewijk van der Binchorst, and the manor house (Rodenrijs) was held as a fief van Henrick van Brederode; Rek. 4859, fol. XL right; for other properties, fols. XLIII left–LIII l.

50. For G. van Renesse, Recht. Arch. 365, fols. 199 r–202 l; Uyten Eng, fols. 219 left–219 right.

51. ARA the Hague, Rek. 4859, fols. XIIIcLIIII left–XIIIIcIII right.

52. No effort has been made in this paper to discuss *why* such different patterns developed, only to deal with the results of those different developments. The usual explanation is that the nobility in the north and west of the Netherlands never had as much power as the nobility to the east and south, but I do not find that satisfactory.

Land Measurement

12 lantvoeten	= 1 landtroeden
100 roeden	= 1 line
3 lijnen	= 1 met
2 met	= 1 morgen (or morghen)
6 hondt	= 1 morgen

In modern terminology

1 morgen	= approximately two acres
1 roed	either ¼ acre in area, or 6–8 yards in length

RENESSE (I)

Johan v. Renesse/Lord = Aleyd Freys v.
Amelisweerd, Wulven   Cuynre (d. 1550)
(1470–1535)

1. Jan v. Renesse
   "the younger," Lord Wulven
2. Adriaen v. Renesse, Deacon
   of Dom Church, "married or
   had as mistress" Anna v.
   Abcoude v. Meerten
3. Jan v. Renesse, Lord
   Amelisweerd, see below
4. Lord Gerrit van Renesse
   (see Renesse [II])

5. Maria v. Renesse, m. Johan v. Holtzwyler,
   High Sheriff of Hattem (Gelderland)
6. Hadewich v. Renesse, m. Johan v.
   Drakenburch, Lord Drakenburch, Oudaen
7. Margaretha v. Renesse, M. Ernst v.
   Nyenrode, Lord Zuylensteyn
8. Clara v. Renesse, m. Hendrik v.
   Raaphorst
9. Alyt v. Renesse, Nun, St. Servaescloister,
   Utrecht
10. Cornelis v. Renesse, ditto

Johan v. Renesse, Lord Wulven, = Aleydt v. Bronkhorst en Batenburg
   Wilp, Amelisweerd   Batenburg

1. Johan v. Renesse, Lord Amelisweerd, see below
2. Fredrik v. Renesse, 1544–1564
3. Jan Baptist v. Renesse, m. Anna v. Twickelo
4. Dirk v. Renesse, m. Elisabeth v. Noyelles

Johan v. Renesse, Lord of Wulven, = Margaretha v. Renesse
   Wilp, Amelisweerd   1558   v. Elderen
   (after 1565)   (d. 1574, Leiden)

RENESSE (II)

Gerrit van Renesse v. = Geertruyd van der Haer
   Wulven   (d. 1565)
   (1509–1568)

1. Jan v. Renesse v. Wulven, Canon of
   Domchurch, d. unmarried 1568,
   aged 30
2. Bernt v. Renesse
3. Joriaen v. Renesse
4. Agnes v. Renesse v. Wulven, m. (1551)
   Adriaan v. Renesse van der AA, Lord
   Woudenburg, Ter Aa

illegitimate

1. Philip v. Renesse
2. Willem v. Renesse

De WAEL VAN VRONESTEYN

Lubbert de Wael, Lord = Marie v. Raephorst,
   Vronesteyn   1520   daughter of Johan v.
                           Raephorst, Sheriff
                           Burgomaster of Utrecht

1. Adriaen de Wael, Lord Vronesteyn, see
   below (1520–1568)
2. Wolphard de Wael v. Vronesteyn, Canon
   of St. Pieter, Utrecht

3. Johan de Wael v. Vronesteyn, Page of
   Prince of Orange
4. Margriet, m. Eustachius v. Brakel, Lord
   Killenstein
5. Willem de Wael v. Vronesteyn, m. (1)
   Cornelia v. Renesse v. Moermont
6. Hedwig de Wael v. Vronesteyn, Nun in
   St. Sevaescloister, Utrecht
7. Elisabeth de Wael v. Vronesteyn, Nun,
   ditto

Adriaen de Wael, Lord   =   Beatrix de Vocht v.
   Vronesteyn   1545   Rijneveld, daughter
                             of Fred. de Vocht v.
                             Rijneveld, Lord
                             Blickenburg, Magistrar
                             of Utrecht

1. Frederick de Wael v. Vronesteyn, Lord
   Vronesteyn
2. Lubbert de Wael v. Vronesteyn (Captain in
   the service of Spain!)
3. Frederica, m. Johan v. Winssen, Lord Hoencoop
4. Agatha de Wael v. Vronesteyn, Nun,
   St. Servaescloister, Utrecht

The Myth of Continuous Inflation:
United States Experience, 1700–1980

WALTER W. HAINES*

We have just come through the trauma of a year when consumer prices rose 13 percent, a decade in which they have doubled, and a century during which they have climbed to ten times their 1879 level. If we accept what one might assume to be an optimistic projection by President Carter, we can look forward to only a slight reduction of current inflation rates to 6 percent in 1985.[1]

In my youth my mind was programmed to think of the price of hamburger as 19 cents a pound. My files show an advertisement from a 1933 issue of *Popular Science* offering Plymouths for $495, with an optional automatic clutch for $8 more. Looking at the 1902 Sears, Roebuck catalogue, I can drool over a solid oak dining table for $3.90 or a "Stradivarius model" violin for $2.45.

It is little wonder that people think of inflation as a way of life, as one of the inevitable facts of existence, like death and taxes, a continuous process from which there is no respite or remission.

Yet it is not so. Not in the long run. True, wholesale prices have been rising for most of the period since 1932, but it is also true that they were exactly the same in 1932 as they had been in 1832 and lower than they were in 1782 or for most of the period in between. Indeed as recently as 1957–64 the United States went through a period of remarkable price stability. Have we forgotten? Or did it pass unnoticed?

This paper examines the data for the past 280 years in order to provide historical perspective on our present predicament. The exercise will not lead to proposed solutions to the inflationary problem, but it will point out some of the similarities and differences of price movements over the long sweep of the centuries and thus help us look in the right directions for the causes of the present crisis.

It may be significant to note in passing that the most feverish interest in the history of prices in this country occurred in the thirties, when the great concern was with the grinding deflation that had occurred since World War I and which seemed at that time to be continuing. The bulk of the statistics in this paper come from research projects whose results were published from 1932 to 1938. As prices turned upward, we have lost sight of these materials and with them our sense of historical perspective.

But before I present *any* statistics, a word of caution. A statistician is a person who states an uncertainty with precision. Even today we argue over the methods of collecting, interpreting, and combining the data that go into the Bureau of Labor Statistics (BLS) measurements of current price movements. Such problems are multiplied manyfold as we try to go back and pick up the historical pieces that are necessary for computing a price index in retrospect, and the further back we go, the more formidable the obstacles. The nineteenth century is bad enough; the eighteenth is a nightmare.

We can forget about consumer prices, for in the early period only wholesale prices are available in sufficient quantity. Naturally one would expect a weighted index, but information on quantities sold is so sketchy that we are forced back to unweighted averages. Instead of a national index, we must rely on figures for one or a few cities. These we find difficult to combine because, among other things, in the colonial period each colony had its own currency, so that even the theoretical rationale for a national index is called into question.

It is hard in this period to identify the quality of goods for which price quotations are given, and so we run the risk of comparing prices for what might be substantially different products. And finally, as we push back in time, the information almost totally evaporates. Mention of prices for even a few commodities is so sporadic as to make a continuous series of any kind impossible.

In the face of all these difficulties I have had the temerity to push the frontier back to 1700, 20 years earlier than any published index I know of. The materials for this exercise in building a numerical house out of one and a half bricks come from Anne Bezanson. She did an extraordinary job of ferreting out the raw data, but her professional judgment would not let her attempt to summarize them statistically.

With these red flags signaling the unreliability of the early indexes, let us plunge ahead. Figure 1, then, shows the movement of wholesale prices in the United States from 1700 to 1985.

METHODOLOGY

1. Only annual figures are shown. The original sources give monthly data, which, of course, convey more precise information. Here, however, the purpose is not to examine in detail the proposition that "prices never remain stable for significant periods of time,"[2] nor to show the timing of turning points in cyclical movements (both of which are examined in the original sources), but rather to give an

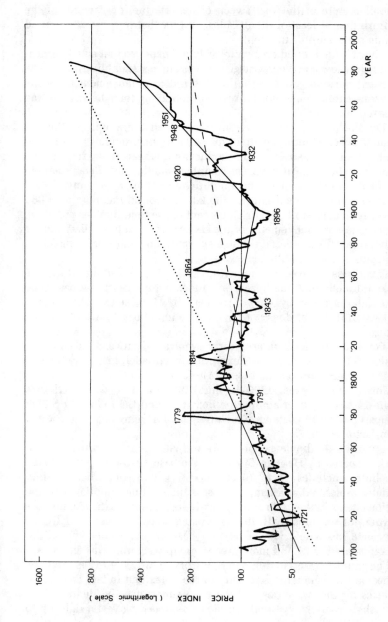

Fig. 1 Wholesale Price Index, 1700-1985. (1910-1914 = 100)

overall picture of the vast sweep of history, the long swings of the centuries, or at least of the decades, and for that purpose 286 plotted points seem amply sufficient.

2. The chart is plotted on semilogarithmic paper so that equal vertical distances show equal percentage changes and a straight line indicates a constant *percentage* rise or fall of the index. A movement from one horizontal line to another represents a doubling (or a halving) of the index.

3. For the period 1700–19 I have computed the simple arithmetic mean of six commodity relatives for Philadelphia from raw data assembled by Anne Bezanson.[3] The products are wheat, flour, rum, sugar, molasses, and salt. Although the sample is small, "these data pertain to six of the most important commodities in colonial economy."[4] And although the data are scant (for the 20-year period there are only 863 monthly figures available, or 60 percent of the total number possible), nevertheless the movements of the six are remarkably similar, and for only 12 months (scattered through six years) are figures missing for all six commodities simultaneously.

This series is based on the period 1741–45 = 100 so that it may be linked directly to Anne Bezanson's index, which is on that base. The two indexes differ by only .7 percent in 1720, suggesting that the linkage in that year does not do violence to the basic level of the two series.

4. For 1720–48 the data are yearly averages of unweighted monthly arithmetic indexes for 20 commodities in Philadelphia, as published by Anne Bezanson on the base 1741–45 = 100.[5]

These two indexes, 1700–19 and 1720–48, were converted to a 1910–14 base by overlapping the Bezanson and the following Stoker indexes for the 26 years for which they both have figures. The conversion factor is .5817.

5. For 1749–96 the data represent a weighted index of prices at New York prepared by Herman Stoker on the base 1910–14.[6] For 1749–87 the index includes 11 to 19 commodities with somewhat arbitrary variable weights that attempt to assess the shifting importance of the various items in the trade of the period (the decrease in the significance of rum, for instance, with its place being taken, at least partially, by chocolate and coffee). For the next 14 years the number of commodities was increased to 71 and more precise group weighting was employed.

The shift from Philadelphia to New York from 1748 to 1749 might be expected to create a discontinuity in the index, but in fact the annual indexes for the two cities in 1749 were almost exactly identical, and they show remarkably similar trends in succeeding years, right up to the Civil War.[7]

This series by Stoker has been published by the BLS as an extension backward of its Wholesale Price Index.[8] It should be noted, however, that although the BLS may give the impression in tabular presentation that this is a national average, and although Warren and Pearson include it with their later data as "wholesale prices in the United States,"[9] the data for the colonial period are strictly from New York.

Stoker has five years for which he gives no figures. For these years I have interpolated, computing annual averages from Anne Bezanson's data for Philadelphia,[10] and assuming that the year-to-year percentage changes for New York (Stoker's series) within each gap were the same as those for Philadelphia. The three-year gap, 1782–84, is preceded by the extraordinary confusion of the Revolutionary War, and so I have used the more normal year of 1774 as the "preceding" year for interpolation, at least partly on the ground that in 1774 the Bezanson and Stoker indexes bear almost exactly the same relation to each other as they do in 1785, the year following the gap.

6. For 1797–1890 the indexes were prepared by Warren and Pearson, whose primary objective was to start with the official Wholesale Price Index and extend it back as far as possible. They included from 110 to slightly more than 140 different items in 11 commodity groups with a sliding weighted average calculated to match up with the BLS index in 1890.[11] Their base period was 1910–14 = 100. This series is probably the most widely used indication of prices in the nineteenth century, but its original data were also obtained (at least up to the Civil War) primarily from New York sources.

7. For 1890–1979 the figures are those of the BLS Wholesale Price Index (currently renamed Producer Price Index). The index was begun in 1902 and extended back to 1890, using about 250 items and weights proportionate to quantities marketed in 1909. The base period, the number of items, and the weights used have been constantly revised. The current index is based on 1967 = 100 and includes over 2700 items. The figures I have used are official BLS data on the 1967 base,[13] converted to a 1910–14 base by overlapping with Warren and Pearson's series from 1890 to 1932. The conversion factor is 2.8318.

8. To project (precariously) into the future I have added the estimates for 1980–85 from President Carter's 1980 Economic Report.[14] His projections are for consumer prices rather than wholesale, but the difference between the two series is likely to be less than the errors in prediction. No one expects prices to fall, or even to moderate their rise substantially, within the next few years, so that it seems reasonable to anticipate some such movement as is here represented.

The series shown in Figure 1, then, despite its flaws, is at least a reasonable picture of the long-term movement of wholesale prices over 286 years, certainly close to the best that we can do with the data now available to us. It is the longest consistent series of prices in this country that I know of. It is supported, for the most part, by other published series, particularly for the nineteenth century, a point to which I shall return later.

RESULTS

What, then, do we see?

1. *Wars.* The most prominent features of the landscape are the mountainous peaks formed by wartime inflation. For early wars the peaks came during the hostilities (1779, 1814, 1864), and the declines tended to be quite precipitous. Wartime controls during World War I delayed the peak until 1920, and the decline to prewar levels occurred in two stages, separated by the jagged plateau of the twenties. For World War II the peak occurred in 1948 after the removal of price controls, and no decline of any substance followed. It is precisely this failure of prices to conform to past experience that produces the current feeling of perpetual inflation. Historically, however, the present situation is unique.

It may be instructive to note that, although inflation has certainly occurred in peacetime, in this as in other countries, there has never been a significant war fought at any period that has not resulted in inflation.

2. *Cyclical swings.* Once our eyes come down from the hills to the valleys below, we are still struck by the unevenness of the terrain even for annual data (for monthly fluctuations the variations are even more jagged, particularly in the first two centuries).[15] Stability is *not* a characteristic of price levels. The lack of stability, however, is definitely in both directions; it is fluctuating, not steeply upward. Part of the fluctuation is cyclical (an aspect of the record that I am not going to pursue here). Part looks remarkably like Kondratieff 50-year long swings.

These swings are accented by the wartime peaks, but even in the interwar periods the U shape of price movements seems clear. Thus, from 1814 prices continued to slide to a low in 1843, from which they entered on a slow rise of 20 years to the Civil War. Similarly, they took 32 years after that peak to reach bottom in 1895, from which the rise to 1920 began. Again, the war peaks of 1920 and 1948 are separated by the deep chasm of 1932.

Even if we were to ignore the war pinnacles, the nature of these U-shaped valleys is fairly clear — except, of course, for the period following World War II, where the wartime peak was exceeded as early as 1951, and which, from the heights of 1980, looks more like a part of the valley itself.

The periodicity of the lows is interesting: 1721–44, 1791, 1843, 1896, 1932. Is this mere coincidence? Is it the long-run effect of the periodicity of wars? (Is the periodicity of wars a coincidence?) Or is there a good economic reason for this kind of swing? I do not propose to answer these questions here, but they certainly merit consideration.

And in passing, one might note that according to this historical periodicity we should be close to a period of deflation. But fortunately (unfortunately?) this historical periodicity has already been totally destroyed by the failure of prices to fall following the last war. So extrapolation of the long cycles in prices is an exercise in futility.

3. *Trends.* Mentally blocking out the wartime highs and the oscillations in between, what is the historical sweep of the last three centuries as a whole? As the eye travels forward from the relative lows of the early 1700s to today's extraordinary levels, it is pulled inevitably upward, and the visual impression is of a long-term upward trend. Yet no long-term trend really fits. Interestingly enough, an extrapolation of the second half of the eighteenth century (shown by the dotted line on Figure 1) would bring us to almost exactly where President Carter expects us to be in 1895, but the extrapolation is based on only 70 years and completely misses 175 years in between as well as the early 1700s.

A trend that comes closer to averaging the whole period (shown by the dashed line) also misses a great deal of the data. Particularly since 1945 we have been wildly above it.

Suppose, however, that we consider a century a long enough period to establish a trend. There are convenient turning points near both of the century years. The light solid line on the chart shows the trends for the three periods separately.

Looking first at the twentieth century, we find our inflationary suspicion confirmed and even strengthened. Though we are high above the trend at the present moment, the rapid rise throughout the century has been interrupted only briefly by the reaction to World War I highs.

Skipping back to the eighteenth century, the picture is somewhat difficult to orient. Ignoring the Revolutionary War, the century appears as a great U, with prices falling to 1721 and rising thereafter. Indeed 1721 is the low point of the whole graph. It would be extremely interesting to know when the previous low point had been, and at what level, but that information is completely lacking. From 1745 to 1775 the rise is 50 percent, and by 1800 the index is twice what it was in the forties. But the drop from 1702 to 1721 cut the index in half, so that the later upward movement is not much more than regaining lost ground. For the century as a whole, however, the trend is certainly upward, though no single line fits the data very well.

When we look at the intervening nineteenth century, the picture is quite different. The 50-year troughs — 1791, 1843, 1896 — march downward. Each nonwar peak — 1801, 1805, 1837, 1857, 1882 — is lower than the last. The trend line falls by about one-third over the hundred years. The nineteenth century was a long sustained period of declining wholesale prices, interrupted only by a minor and a major war.

To take one spectacular, if not wholly representative, example: the price peak of 1796 was never exceeded, except during the exigencies of armed conflict, until after World War II. We came close in 1925, but passed it only in 1943, when the war was well under way.

To repeat, for more than a hundred years, centering on the nineteenth century, the trend of prices in this country was down. There was no continuous inflation. Deflation was not continuous either, but on each occasion when it was interrupted by a rise, the subsequent decline reached lower than the last. Deflation was the dominant tendency.

OTHER INDEXES

Concentrating, for the moment, on this extraordinary performance (extraordinary from the point of view of the continuous-inflation myth) of the Warren and Pearson wholesale price index in the nineteenth century, we need to ask whether perhaps there is something peculiar about the index itself; whether it accurately portrays real facts; whether the decline was not actual, but a peculiarity of some statistical quick.

Although we must remember that any index is subject to a multitude of questions as to its accuracy and representative character, nevertheless a host of other indexes as well as a good deal of raw data show the same general tendencies as the chart we have been looking at.

To save time I concentrate primarily on the nineteenth century: (a) data for the eighteenth are so sparse; (b) the nineteenth seems, from hindsight, to be so peculiar; (c) the record of the twentieth we all know, at least in its broad sweep. For this purpose the data already shown for the nineteenth century in Figure 1 are repeated at larger scale as the heavy line in Figure 2 and compared with other indexes.

BLS. The Bureau of Labor Statistics has extended its current wholesale price index backward to 1801 by linking it up with indexes prepared by Alvin Hansen (1801–1840) and the Senate Committee on Finance (1841–89).[16] This is the light solid line of Figure 2. It shows considerable similarity in general outline, but there are some differences: a higher peak during the War of 1812, a later peak for the Civil War, and a faster drop after that conflict, as well as a lower level in the 1850s. But its primary difference lies in a generally higher level of wholesale prices in the *early* years of the century, with the result that the trend line for the hundred years would be even more steeply downward than the one I have already drawn.

Cole. A similar picture is shown by the wholesale price indexes for individual cities[17] collected for the International Scientific Committee on Price History and summarized in Cole's *Wholesale Commodity*

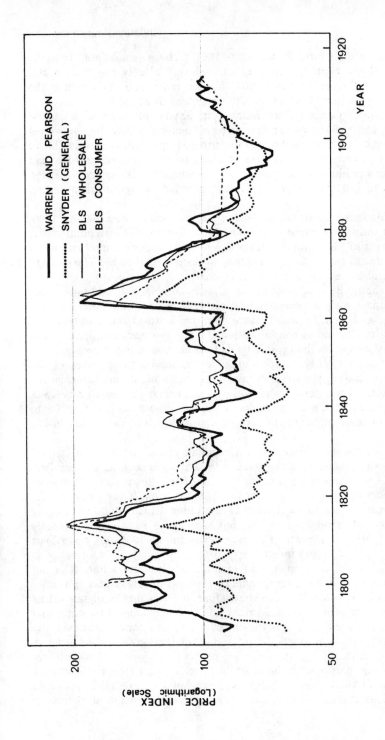

Fig. 2 Price Indexes, 1790–1914. (1910–14 = 100)

WARREN AND PEARSON
SNYDER (GENERAL)
BLS WHOLESALE
BLS CONSUMER

PRICE INDEX
(Logarithmic Scale)

200

100

50

YEAR

1800   1820   1840   1860   1880   1900   1920

Prices in the United States, 1700–1861.[18] These data do not run to the end of the century, but they parallel very closely the Warren and Pearson figures for the period they do cover and confirm that the movement from 1800 to the Civil War was downward.[19]

Snyder's General Price Index. Carl Snyder has devised a general price index designed to measure the influence of a changing price level on bank debits, and although this purpose is quite different from that of other price indexes, the idea of a general price index, broader than either a producer or consumer index, is appealing. His index, as carried back to 1791 by Rufus Tucker,[20] is included in Figure 2 as a dashed line.

This index shows almost a sidewise movement from 1800 to 1900, with only the faintest downward trend. Indeed the low point of the index is in 1843, and this suggests splitting the period into two trends: downward from 1800 to 1843, and upward from then on. The slope of each of these trends, however, is small.

It should be noted that Snyder's index combines several series with arbitrarily assigned weights: wholesale prices, consumer prices, wages, rents, and security prices. Since one would expect wages to rise with productivity and as one indication of a higher standard of living, their heavy weight on the up side tends to counteract the downward movement of the other components. The wholesale price series of the general index, prepared by averaging some eight indexes covering portions of the period, shows the same general pattern already seen, dropping from a decade average of 142.8 in 1800–1809 (1913 = 100) to 73.1 in 1890–99. Meanwhile wages rose, on the same basis, from 26.4 to 67.7.

BLS Consumer Price Index. Consumer prices cannot be measured with any precision in the eighteenth century because of lack of data. How great the precision of such an index is in the nineteenth may be open to question, but at least the BLS has tried. It has extended the Consumer Price Index (Cost-of-Living Index) back to 1800 by splicing Indexes of Prices Paid by Vermont Farmers for Family Living (1800–1851), Ethel D. Hoover's Consumer Price Index (1851–90), and Albert Rees' Cost of Living Index (1890–1912).[21]

The results are depicted in Figure 2 by the dotted line. It is not surprising that the correspondence between producer and consumer prices is not exact. We have known for some time that wholesale prices are more volatile than retail prices, and so all movements are somewhat quieter. But again, the story is one of general downward drift, with the century ending at exactly 50 percent of the level at which it started. A 50 percent drop in consumer prices over 100 years! That certainly contrasts sharply with the ninefold increase since 1900 or the sixfold rise since 1933. Whatever else may be said of the current inflation, even in terms of consumer prices, it is not a mere extension of history.

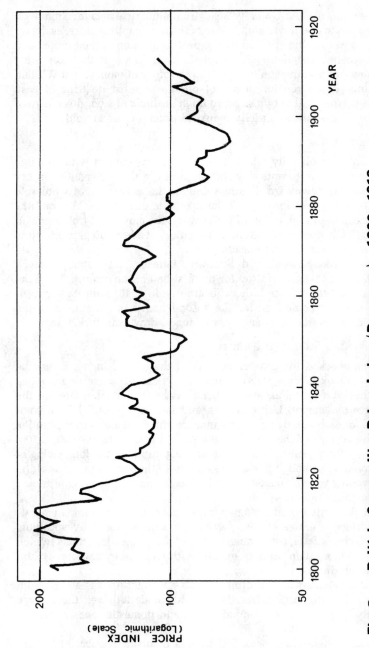

Fig. 3   **British Commodity Price Index (Rousseau), 1800–1913.**
(Average of 1865 and 1885 = 100)

The Cross of Gold. To move away from numerical data for a moment, we may note that it was at the close of the nineteenth century, as debtor farmers were being crushed by the declining value of their crops, and in the belief that the cause of all this suffering was the restraining influence of a limited gold supply on the stock of money, that William Jennings Bryan ran for president on the populist doctrine of easy money: "You shall not press down upon the brow of labor this crown of thorns. You shall not crucify mankind upon a cross of gold."[22]

BRITISH PRICES

It is only peripherally relevant to this inquiry, but not without some passing interest, to note that British prices in the nineteenth century also moved downward. Figure 3 depicts the movement of wholesale and import prices for Great Britain, 1800 to 1913.[23] The War of 1812 produced their high point for the century; the movement from there on is erratically downward, ending the century at a level 50 percent below the average for the first decade.

The Gayer, Rostow, and Schwartz indexes (1790–1850) show a greater than 50 percent drop for the first half of the century,[24] and the Sauerbeck-*Statist* Price Indices (beginning in 1846) indicate a continued, but slower decline for the second half.[25] In Britain, as in the United States, the last century was one of downward price drift.

DIFFERENCES AMONG COMMODITIES

Having checked the general validity of the overall index, it may be useful to look at some of its components. Prices, of course, do not move together, and variations among them may be of as much interest as the average movement. Using Warren and Pearson's data,[26] I have computed for each group of products included in the overall series an index for the average of the decade 1890–99 on the base 1800–1809 = 100, showing the general performance of the group over the long swing of the century. Although this process omits all the twists and turns of the intervening years, it makes it possible to compare all of the groups on a single graph (Figure 4).

The disparity is wide, ranging from a fall of 80 percent for chemicals and drugs to a rise of 200 percent for spirits. Generally speaking, manufactures fell most — chemicals and drugs, metal products (which dropped more than primary metals, with which they are joined), and textile products.

A large element in the drop in fuels and lighting was a shift from imported to domestic coal. Although all foods followed the average closely, imported foods tended to fall and domestic foods to rise in price.

Farm products in general fell by less than the average; hides and

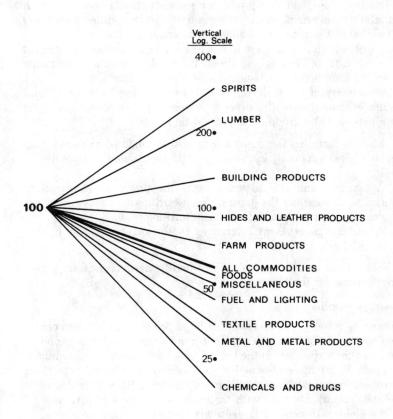

Fig. 4   Wholesale Prices in 1890 – 99 on Base 1800 = 100

leather products hardly fell at all. Building products showed a pronounced rise, primarily due to the remarkably rapid increase in lumber prices, one of its important subgroups. Indeed, looking at a slightly longer time span, we find that lumber prices doubled from 1800 to 1855 and doubled again by 1912.

Lumber, hides, and farm products represent natural resources, which apparently were rising against the trend of all commodities, suggesting a parallel to the present oil and natural resource crisis.

Spirits, which had the highest rise of any group,[27] showed no trend at all prior to 1860. They gained almost the whole of their upward thrust from the high taxes first levied during the Civil War.

A summary of the main observations noted even in this brief and rough examination of the diverse movements of separate groups of products would include three general impressions:

1. Manufactures led the trend downward, as might be expected from technological progress, increased capital inputs, and economies of scale.

2. Agriculture and raw materials were the products whose prices tended to rise against the general downward trend, a movement that conforms to our understanding of diminishing returns.

3. When the government intervenes in the market, it can have a substantial effect on price.

Each of these conclusions, while hardly new, carries important implications for the future.

SHORTER TRENDS

Returning, however, to an examination of prices over the three centuries, we have noted in Figure 1 that trend lines covering a period as long as a century do not fit the United States data as well as they might. A much better fit is obtained if each century is divided into three (unequal) parts, as shown in Figure 5. The trend lines there drawn fit the data remarkably well with the exception of the war periods.

The eighteenth century is definitely U-shaped:

>   1700–1721, falling rapidly
>   1721–1745, level
>   1745–1800, rising moderately

The nineteenth century does not have a recognizable period of stable prices:

>   1800–1843, falling moderately
>   1843–1872, rising moderately
>   1872–1896, falling rapidly

The twentieth century also has three periods, but of opposite sequence:

>   1896–1925, rising rapidly

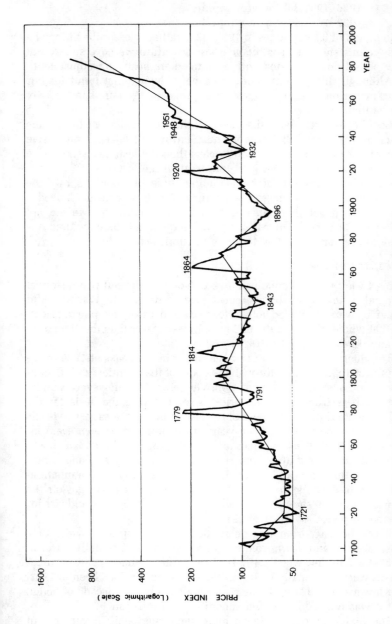

Fig.5 Wholesale Price Index, 1700-1985. (1910-1914 = 100)

1925–1932, falling very rapidly

1932–1985, rising very rapidly

The period of falling prices in 1925–32 is rather brief for the fitting of a long-term trend, but it is the sharpest downturn we have suffered in any period not associated with an immediate postwar readjustment.

Although this pattern produces a very steep rising trend for our current period, it again suggests that prices in 1980 are substantially above their trend.

Looking in particular at the last six of these segments, one finds some fascinating (ominous?) developments. Starting in 1800 each successive deflation has been steeper (and briefer) than the last. Each successive inflation has been steeper (and longer) than the last.

I have no intention of extrapolating these observations into the future, or in any way suggesting that the past will be repeated. Indeed, a basic purpose of this paper is to show that currently we are *not* following historical patterns. Even within the trends here pictured it is easy to see variations that follow no historical precedent.

STABILITY IN THE TWENTIETH CENTURY

What I want to do in conclusion is, in fact, to point out two historical anomalies in the relatively recent past. True, World War I, as did previous wars, produced both a steep rise and a steep decline in prices, so that wholesale levels in 1932 were indeed lower than they had been at any time from 1793 to 1829.

The Roaring Twenties. But in passing from the peaks of 1920 to the depths of 1932 we went through the boom of the twenties, an inflationary period of substantial reputation. The reputation, however, is undeserved. It is true that stock prices soared, laying the basis for the subsequent crash. At the close of the period interest rates rose to levels that had not been seen for ten years and would not be seen again for another forty. Real estate prices took off, leading the Florida land boom into legend. Profits also were rising as productivity exceeded wage increases. But while an increase in the money supply fed the inflationary fires in speculative assets, the prices of goods never got off the ground. Figure 6 shows both producer and consumer price indexes for the boom period of the twenties.[28]

It can be seen from this chart that wholesale prices, while they fluctuated up and down from month to month, were actually lower in 1928–29 than they were in 1922 or in any intermediate year. Consumer prices were fractionally higher in 1928–29 than they had been in 1922, but lower than 1921 or 1925–27. It may have been a decade of boom, but it was not a decade of commodity price inflation.

The Stable Sixties. An even more stable period is of very recent history. And it is illuminating in more ways than one, particularly

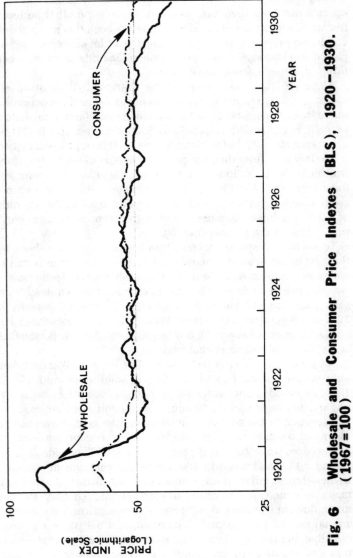

Fig. 6 **Wholesale and Consumer Price Indexes (BLS), 1920–1930. (1967 = 100)**

since it occurred during the height of popularity of the so-called Phillips Curve.

The price facts are shown in Figure 7, along with data for unemployment and industrial production.[29] It can be seen that from December 1959 to December 1964 wholesale prices rose only 0.9 percent. Throughout the whole period they did not vary by as much as 1 percent up or down from their average level. There is no other period in the history of the United States when there has been this much stability in wholesale prices for as long as a single year, let alone for a seven-year period. Yet this idyllic interlude came in the midst of an era most of us think of as persistently inflationary.

Although I have not cluttered the chart with the consumer price index, it is only fair to say that it was not as flat as the wholesale. Yet it too represented a break from the immediate past (and immediate future as well), rising, on the average, only 1.4 percent per year in this period. That is not stability, but it is much closer to it than prices usually come.

To stray a bit from the pure price orientation of my topic, I think it is fruitful at this point to look at what was happening to unemployment during this lull. The Phillips Curve analysis, which some economists seem to hold in reverence and awe, purports to tell us that the only way of achieving lower unemployment is to accept some degree of inflation.[30] This is the famous tradeoff.

To anyone accepting that tradition it must come as a shock to look the facts in the face and discover that in the United States from 1961 (as we recovered from recession) to 1965, while the wholesale price index was absolutely stable and the consumer index rose at a steady and very slow pace, unemployment fell continuously from 6.9 percent in July 1961 to 5.0 percent in December 1964. This is the economist's heaven: stable prices as we approach full employment. Yet few persons seem to savor the satisfactions of that period.

But good things do not last forever. The Vietnam War destroyed not only people, materials, and morale, but stability as well. Starting in 1965, unemployment continued its decline, but prices began to edge up, and we were back to the Phillips tradeoff — an approach to full employment at the cost of inflation. Over the next three years unemployment reached an acceptable low of 3.3 percent, while wholesale prices edged up at the rate of 2 percent per year. This tradeoff, however, turned into a nightmare in 1969, when unemployment started rising again although inflation was speeding up. Stagflation, the worst of both major economic ills at once, accelerated through May 1975, when unemployment peaked at 9.2 percent while prices were rising at an annual rate of 11.7 percent (wholesale) and 9.5 percent (retail). Not only that, but industrial production dropped by 8.9 percent, adding the injury of a falling national standard of living to the insult of declining job opportunities and increasing prices.

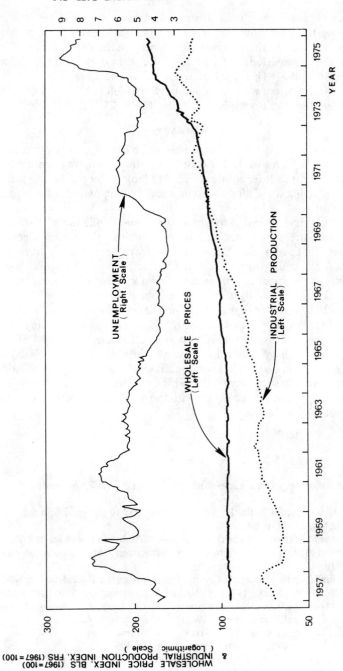

Fig. 7 Wholesale Prices, Unemployment and Industrial Production, 1957 – 1975

Since my main objective is historical perspective, I will not attempt to analyze this period further or to carry the data forward to today, but I would like to underline the lack of congruity in the data. From 1957 to 1975 there were periods in which (a) prices were stable and unemployment rose (1959–61); (b) prices were stable and unemployment fell (1962–64); (c) prices rose and unemployment fell (1965–69, 1971–73); (d) prices rose and unemployment rose (1969–71, 1973–75).

SUMMARY

Contrary to popular belief, inflation is not a continuous phenomenon in the United States (or in Great Britain). The record, fragmentary and subject to error as it is, points strongly to long periods of falling prices as well as rising ones, along with moderately long periods of comparative stability.

The historical record shows that the present inflationary thrust is most unusual; it is not normal; it is not something that we must accept because "that's the way things have always been." They have not always (or usually) been this way. Starting from that historical background, the pertinent questions are: Why not? What is different in this period? What has *changed* to produce our present dilemma?

It would be possible to draw up a long list of changes, but at least that is the place where we must begin. Much, of course, has already been done, but on occasion misleading generalizations like the Phillips Curve analysis have gotten in the way, while the general public and many politicians seem to fall back on a fatalistic acceptance of inflation as inevitable. These last two red herrings, at least, should be thoroughly disposed of so that we can get on with the real business of attacking the root causes of inflation.

Notes

*   The author expresses appreciation to Mary Lou Peck who prepared the graphics.
1.   *Economic Report of the President, Transmitted to Congress January 1980* (Washington, 1980), p. 94.
2.   George F. Warren and Frank A. Pearson, "Wholesale Prices for 213 Years, 1720 to 1932," *Cornell Agricultural Experiment Station Memoir 142* (1932): 10.
3.   Arthur H. Cole, *Wholesale Commodity Prices in the United States, 1700–1861* (Cambridge, Mass., 1938), *Statistical Supplement*, pp. 1–6; data for the base 1741–45 are from Anne Bezanson, Robert D. Grey, and Miriam Hussey, *Prices in Colonial Pennsylvania* (Philadelphia, 1935), p. 422.
4.   Cole, *Wholesale Commodity Prices*, text volume, p. 30.
5.   Bezanson, p. 433; see also Cole, text, pp. 25–49.
6.   Herman M. Stoker, "Wholesale Prices at New York City," in Warren and

Pearson, pp. 201–222; see also Cole, text, pp. 9–24; the actual numbers on which the figure is based are taken from Warren and Pearson, pp. 7–8.

7.   Cole, text, charts 50–52, facing p. 108.

8.   U.S. Bureau of Labor Statistics, "Wholesale Price Index, All Commodities — Yearly Averages (1947–49 = 100), 1749–1926" (mimeographed).

9.   Warren and Pearson, p. 6.

10.   Anne Bezanson, *Prices and Inflation during the American Revolution: Pennsylvania, 1770–1790* (Philadelphia, 1951), p. 344, "Weighted Arithmetic Averages of Price Relatives of Fifteen Commodities, 1770–1790" (base 1771–73 = 100); Cole, text, p. 141, "Unweighted 20-Commodity Geometric Index of Wholesale Prices at Philadelphia, monthly, 1731–1861" (base 1821–25 = 100).

11.   Warren and Pearson, pp. 8–10.

12.   Cole, text, p. 16.

13.   U.S. Bureau of Labor Statistics, "Handbook of Labor Statistics, 1978," *Bulletin* 2000 (Washington, 1979), pp. 437, 454; current figures from U.S. Bureau of Labor Statistics, *Producer Prices and Price Indexes*.

14.   *Economic Report of the President, 1980*, p. 94.

15.   For a good visual picture of the monthly data from 1720 to 1861 see Cole, charts 50–52, facing p. 108.

16.   U.S. Bureau of Labor Statistics, *Handbook of Labor Statistics, 1941* (Washington, 1941) 1: 715. The original sources are Alvin H. Hansen, "Wholesale Prices for the United States, 1801–1840," *Quarterly Publications of the American Statistical Association*, new ser., vol. 14, no. 112 (December 1915): 804–812; *Wholesale Prices, Wages, and Transportation (Aldrich Report)*, Senate Report no. 1394, 52nd Cong., 1893, part 1, p. 9.

17.   Philadelphia, Charleston, New Orleans, and Cincinnati, in addition to New York.

18.   See charts 52 and 53, facing p. 108.

19.   For Philadelphia see also Bezanson, Grey, and Hussey, *Wholesale Prices in Philadelphia, 1784–1861*, 2 vols. (Philadelphia, 1936, 1937), especially chart XIII, facing p. 300.

20.   Rufus S. Tucker, "Gold and the General Price Level," *The Review of Economic Statistics* 16 (January 15, 1934): 8–16; 16 (February 15, 1934): 25–27.

21.   U.S. Bureau of Labor Statistics, *Handbook of Labor Statistics, 1978*, p. 397.

22.   Speech at the National Democratic Convention, Chicago, 1896.

23.   P. Rousseaux, *Les movements de fond de l'economie anglaise, 1800–1913* (Brussels, 1938), as reproduced in B. R. Mitchell, *Abstract of British Historical Statistics* (Cambridge, 1971), pp. 471–73.

24.   A. D. Gayer, W. W. Rostow, and A. J. Schwartz, *The Growth and Fluctuation of the British Economy, 1790–1850* (London, 1953) 1: 468–70 (as reproduced in Mitchell, *Abstract*, p. 470).

25.   Mitchell, *Abstract*, pp. 474–75.

26.   Warren and Pearson, *Prices* (New York, 1933), pp. 25–27; Idem, *Wholesale Prices for 213 Years*, pp. 117–19.

27.   The series for spirits ends in 1889, and my index was computed for that year, which is the lowest of the decade of the 1880s and substantially higher than the index for lumber in the same year.

28.   U.S. Bureau of Labor Statistics, "PPI, All Commodities, Base 1967 = 100" (microfiche); "Consumer Price Index, All Urban Consumers, U.S. City Average, All Items (1967 = 100)" (duplicated).

29.   Prices: *Idem*, "PPI"; Unemployment: *Idem*, "Unemployment Rate All Civilian Workers" (duplicated); Production: U.S. Board of Governors of the Federal Reserve System, *Industrial Production, 1976 Revision* (Washington, 1977), table S-27.

30.   Phillips himself, of course, never said this. Indeed his description of British historical data did not even speak of price levels, but rather of wage levels; see A. W. Phillips, "The Relationship between Unemployment and the Rate of Change in Money Wage Rates in the United Kingdom, 1861–1957," *Economica*, new ser., no. 25 (November, 1958), pp. 283–99.

Monetary Policy and Inflation in the United States, 1912–1978 Evidence from Monthly Data

RONALD L. TRACY
PAUL B. TRESCOTT*

INTRODUCTION

Explanations for inflation tend to fall into two broad categories. On the one hand, there is the view that inflation is purely a monetary phenomenon. If true, it should be possible to show that a relatively simple model would be capable of explaining variations in price level behavior in widely differing locations and at widely differing times in history. In contrast, there is the view that the causes of inflation are numerous and complex, and that each inflationary experience is sufficiently unique that ad hoc explanations must always be sought, particularly in the behavior of individual sectors of the economy. By implication, these views are mutually exclusive. The second largely implies that the monetary explanation alone cannot be adequate.

The monetary interpretation of inflation is associated traditionally with the quantity theory of money. Behind this, however, lies a theory about the real microeconomy, a theory most carefully articulated by Leon Walras more than a century ago. In this view, economic decisions to produce and consume, buy and sell, work, save, and invest, are made on the basis of real quantities and relative prices. There is a relatively unique and invariant equilibrium position for the real quantities produced and consumed, and for their relative prices, independently of the quantity of money. In this view money is neutral; it is a veil.

To be sure, monetary disturbances may initially affect output and employment, and some prices will respond more rapidly than others. In the long run, however, variations in the quantity of money will lead to proportional variations in the price level. This does not rule out other influences that may operate on prices at the same time. The quantity theory of money hypothesized that the partial elasticity of prices with respect to monetary change would be unity.

One difficulty in providing empirical tests of the monetary view is finding an appropriate monetary measure. All measures of the public's holdings of currency and deposits suffer from the common condition that they are not literally determined by monetary policy. For this study, we concentrate our attention on the stock of *high-powered money* (HPM), defined as the sum of currency and bank reserves with the Federal Reserve banks. The total value of HPM is identically equal to the total of the monetary base, which lists the chief assets and nonmonetary liabilities of the monetary authorities. For time series analysis, we adjusted the HPM series for the dollar equivalent of changes in legal reserve requirements. This measure, (HPMA), originally developed by Brunner and Meltzer (1964) provides a relatively comprehensive and unbiased indicator of monetary policy.

Figure 1 illustrates the relationship between the long-run growth rates of HPMA and the consumer price index for the period 1914–1979. Data plotted are the ten-year rates of change of the variables, entered for the final date. (To illustrate, the entry for 1979 is determined by taking the logarithm of HPMA for 1969, subtracting it from 1n HPMA for 1979, and dividing the difference by 10.) From the diagram, it is apparent that the major swings in the inflation rate have been associated with major swings in the growth rate of HPMA. It is also evident, however, that the historical pattern is not a simple uniform relationship. In the remainder of the paper, we have attempted to identify more clearly the similarities and differences in the relation of monetary policy to prices since the formation of the Federal Reserve System.

THE REDUCED FORM MODEL

The simple demand for money function,

$$1n \ Md/P = B_0 + B_1 \ 1n \ Q - B_2 \ 1n \ R + u \tag{1}$$

is used as the basis for our study, where Q represents real output, R interest rates, P the price level, and u the unobserved disturbance term. Assuming that the price level adjusts to equate money demanded with money supplied, we solve for P to obtain

$$1n \ P = \delta_0 - \delta_1 \ 1n \ Q + \delta_2 \ 1n \ R + \delta_3 \ 1n \ M + v. \tag{2}$$

Because of the strong time component in real output, the price level and nominal money balances (Laidler, 1971), it is more appropriate to specify model (2) in terms of first differences, resulting in the model,[1]

$$1n \ P_t - 1n \ P_{t-1} = \delta_4 - \delta_1 \ (1n \ Q_t - 1n \ Q_{t-1}) + \delta_2 \ (1n \ R_t - 1_n R_{t-1}) + \delta_3 \ (1n \ M_t - 1n \ M_{t-1}) + W_t. \tag{3}$$

In the structural model which underlies this work, none of these righthand variables is truly exogenous. To minimize the problem of monetary endogeneity, we use adjusted high-powered money. Since many authors have shown that monetary policy has an impact on prices for many years, the monetary variable will be represented by a

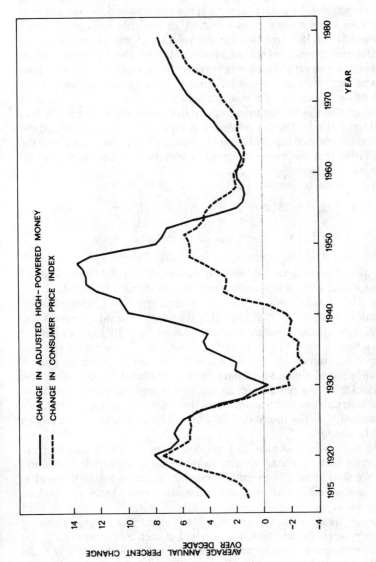

Fig. 1 **Ten-Year Rates of Change in Adjusted High-Powered Money and in Consumer Prices in the United States, 1914-1979**

distributed lag structure. Because of the endogeneity of real output, measures of working-age population (POP) and worker productivity (PROD) are used in its place. In the structural model, interest-rate variations arise mainly from a variety of possible influences which might shift the IS curve or alter the velocity of money. A rise in the interest rate would reflect an upward shift in the IS curve and an increase in velocity which might result from expansionary fiscal actions or from the influence of inflationary expectations or other factors tending to increase incentives to spend.

In regression estimates using annual data, we used the corporate Aaa bond interest rate. For the estimates using monthly data, we added the interest rate on 4–6 month commercial paper. This was done to test the possibility that the two rates contained different information about price expectations.

Model 3 can be rewritten as[2]

$$
\begin{aligned}
\Delta \ln \text{CPI}_t = {} & \gamma_0 - \gamma_1 \, \Delta \ln \text{POP}_t - \gamma_2 \, \Delta \ln \text{PROD}_t + \gamma_3 \, \Delta \ln \text{Aaa}_t \\
& (+ \gamma_{3a} \, \Delta \ln \text{CPR}_t) + \gamma_4 \, \Delta \ln \text{HPMA}_t + \gamma_5 \, \Delta \ln \\
& \text{HPMA}_{t-1} \ldots + \gamma_{4t+s} \, \Delta \ln \text{HPMA}_{t-s} + w_t, \\
& t = 1, \ldots, n
\end{aligned}
\tag{4}
$$

The disturbance terms w_t will be assumed to satisfy the classical assumptions, although some of these assumptions will be tested.

Equation 4 was used as the basis for regression estimates using annual data for 1912–77 and monthly data for 1913 through June 1978. Of the data utilized, monthly data were directly available for adjusted high-powered money, prices, and interest rates. For productivity, we interpolated annual estimates, 1913–46, and quarterly estimates thereafter. For population, annual data were interpolated. Since the supply-side variables are not subject to sharp short-run exogenous changes, these interpolations should not bias the results significantly. Because of seasonality in the monthly data, binary intercept (dummy) variables were included.

The use of both annual and monthly data can be justified in the following manner: because inflation is primarily a long-run phenomenon, we should be able to capture much of its quantitative dimension with annual data. The use of annual data may, however, lead to estimates of lag length which are biased upward, compared with estimates using data for shorter time units. The estimates using monthly data provide a test for the extent of such bias. Fortunately, the correspondence of results between annual and monthly data is quite high, particularly in regard to the monetary influence.

Although Figure 1 makes it pretty clear that the relationship between monetary policy and inflation would not display a single homogenous pattern over the entire period studied, we tested formally the hypothesis that a regression in the form of Equation 4 estimated for the entire period 1912–77 would be stable. A variety of stability tests, notably those developed by Brown, Durbin, and Evans (1975) rejected the hypothesis of stability.[3] (Details are in Tracy and Trescott, 1980).

SUBPERIODS OF STABILITY

We then proceeded to try to identify subperiods of relative stability within the 66-year period under examination, using a three-stage strategy with the annual observations. First, Quandt's Likelihood Ratio Statistic (Quandt, 1958, 1960) was examined for large negative values. Second, an examination of the plot of the CUSUM SQ residuals normalized at successive time periods was made. In analyzing this plot, periods where a slope change occurs were noted. After tentatively identifying subperiods of stability with these two stages, the third stage involved an analysis of the endpoint residuals derived from regression estimates for each subperiod.

Using this strategy, subperiods of *relative* stability are identified as 1912–30, 1930–35, 1936–58, 1957–77. The period 1931–35 was omitted from further analysis. Since HPMA was rising in 1930–33 while prices were falling, the hypothesized model is clearly inappropriate for the period.

Table 1A. Error Sum of Squares Using a Second-degree Polynomial Distributed Lag, Annual Data

Lagged HPMA Terms (years)	Period		
	1912–30	1936–58	1957–77
3	.0092		.0014
4	.0095	.0105	.0013
5	.0091*	.0104	.0012
6	.0092	.0107	.0012
7	.0114	.0103	.0012
8	.0125	.0089*	.0011*
9		.0095	.0012

*Minimizes ESS.

To analyze each of the three subperiods (containing 19, 23, 21 annual observations respectively) with models involving a variety of different length lags would severely curtail degrees of freedom. To solve this dilemma, a second degree polynomial (Almon) distributed lag in high-powered money is used to represent the HPMA term in model 4.[4] In order to determine the proper length of the lag, each period is analyzed using a second degree polynomial with lags ranging between 3 and 9 years. The minimum squared error criterion was then used to choose the statistically appropriate model (Maddala, 1977, 359). With relatively weak assumptions this procedure is equivalent to maximum likelihood estimation (see Tracy and Trescott, 1980). Table 1A compares the error sum of squares of each model and period. Asterisks indicate the number of lagged HPMA terms which minimized the error sum of squares in each subperiod: five, for 1912–30, and eight for both 1936–58 and 1957–77.

Replicating the process using monthly data produced results which are amazingly similar (see Table 1B). Asterisks again indicate the number of lagged HPMA terms which minimized the error sum of squares in each subperiod: 60 (five years), for 1913–30,[5] 108 (nine years), for 1936–58, and 96 (eight years) for 1957–78 (6).[6] Estimates for both these monthly and yearly models (and closely related ones for comparison) are reported in the following section.

Table 1B. Error Sum of Squares Using Second-degree Polynomial Distributed Lag, Monthly Data

Lagged HPMA Terms (months)	Period		
	1913–30	1936–58	1957–78(6)
36	.0157		
48	.0157		
60	.0156*		.00104
72			.00104
84		.0093	.001012
96		.0089	.001010*
108		.0087*	
120		.0088	

1912–30

Estimates of model 4 for 1912–30 using annual data are presented in Table IIA. Equation 2 contains five lagged HPMA terms, the number which minimized the error sum of squares. Since Equation 2 implies significant HPMA impact back only to t-2, an estimate containing only three lagged HPMA terms is also shown (Equation 3). The stability test applied to both models does not reject Equation 2, but rejects Equation 3 at the 10 percent level (CUSUM SQ., forward). However, the lags are amazingly similar with 85 percent of the effect captured by period t-1, and 95 percent by period t-2 in both cases. In addition, in both models the total impact of the monetary variable is similar (1.243 as compared with 1.276) with both values being insignificantly different from unity.

Table 2A. Results of Estimating Model 4, 1912–30, Annual Data

variable (change in log)	Equation 2 5-year lag		Equation 3 3-year lag	
Const	−.0285	(−1.1609)	−.0281	(−1.1497)
$PROD_t$	−.2795	(−1.6424)	−.2447	(−1.4358)
Aaa_t	.1780	(1.1376)	.1663	(1.0629)
POP_t	.6580	(.5602)	.7179	(.6105)
$HPMA_t$	.7136	(6.0487)	.7553	(5.2422)
$HPMA_{t-1}$	.3689	(6.4799)	.3201	(3.4788)
$HPMA_{t-2}$	.1325	(2.5766)	.0931	(1.0973)
$HPMA_{t-3}$	.0042	(.0847)	.0744	(.6281)
$HPMA_{t-4}$	−.0158	(−.3664)		
$HPMA_{t-5}$	.0724	(.7798)		
Sum of HPMA Coef.				
$\Sigma \hat{\gamma}_{t-i}$	1.2758	(5.5135)	1.2429	(6.2580)
R^2, $\bar{R}^2$	.9104	.8656	.9102	.8653
$\hat{\sigma}$, F	.0276	20.327	1.0277	20.2683
DW, N, K	1.7064	19 7	1.6310	19 7
CUSUM Backward	.5321		.5733	
CUSUM SQ. Backward	.2014		.3186	
CUSUM Forward	.4579		.5562	
CUSUM SQ. Forward	.2084		.3773	

(t values in parenthesis)

Both equations fit extremely well for first difference estimates, with adjusted R^2 values around 0.87. This is a period which includes the substantial wartime inflation, a drastic price decline in 1921–22, and comparative price stability in the remainder of the 1920s. Estimated and actual values for ΔCPI are shown in Figure 2. Almost all the explanatory power derives from the monetary variable, as the parameter estimates for population, productivity, and the interest rate are all statistically insignificant. This is clearly shown by Equation A-1 in the appendix, estimated using the monetary variable alone; it has $R^2 = .877$. The Durbin-Watson statistic falls in the upper region of the inconclusive range and thus the hypothesis of no first-order autoregressivity cannot be rejected.

The results of estimating the same model with monthly data are given in Table 2B. These are estimates explaining the month-to-month change in prices. The results are similar to those obtained with annual data, with one interesting exception. The monthly estimates fit much better, with adjusted R^2 values around 0.99. It is clear that the long-term interest rate is responsible for this superior fit. As it is not significant in the annual estimates, we infer it must convey important information about the intrayearly pattern of price changes. We do not find this result in the later periods. The sums of the coefficients of the HPMA terms are now almost exactly equal to one.

Table 2B. Results of Estimating Model 4, 1913–30, Monthly Data

variable (change in log)	Eq. 2' 60-month lag	Eq. 3' 36-month lag
CONST	−.003 (−1.20)	−.003 (−1.16)
PROD$_t$	−.834 (−4.50)	−.791 (−4.33)
Aaa$_t$	.39 (132.4)	.390 (130.)
POP$_t$	−.202 (−.168)	−.081 (−.068)
CPR$_t$	.017 (1.62)	.016 (1.50)
Sum of HPMA coefficients		
$\Sigma\gamma_{t-i}$	1.043 (5.43)	.9451 (6.34)
R^2, $\bar{R}^2$	.990, .989	.990, .989
$\hat{\sigma}$, F	.0089, 1055.	.0089, 1049.
DW, N, K	1.547, 216, 19	1.533, 216, 19
Aaa$_t$ + CPR$_t$	.407 (38.98)	.406 (38.58)

(t values in parenthesis)

The commercial-paper interest rate is not significant. If the two interest rate coefficients are added together one finds that the significance of the interest rate term drops considerably but remains high. Population continues to be insignificant, but productivity becomes highly significant with the correct negative sign.

In the annual estimates, we found significant lagged influence from high-powered money extending back only as far as year t-2. This is substantiated in the monthly regressions, with the earliest significant HPMA term always falling in year t-2, varying from month t-16 to month t-23. Thus, the monthly data appear consistent with the lag pattern indicated by the annual data. Finally, using a cubic polynomial lag with monthly data did not alter the results.

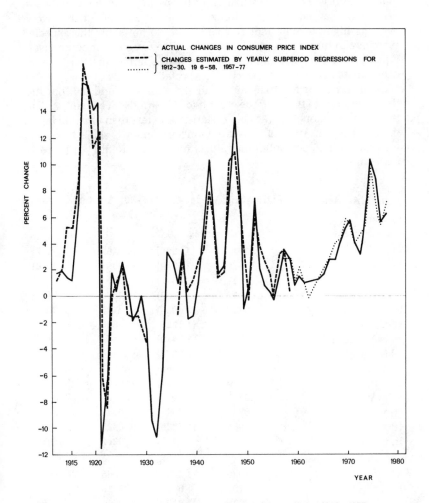

Fig. 2   Year-to-Year Changes in Consumer Price Index in U. S., 1912-1977

1936–58

Table 3A presents yearly estimates for the period 1936–58. Equation 4, using eight lagged terms, minimized the error sum of squares. However, its high-powered money coefficients do not show the expected tendency to turn down as they become more remote. For comparison, Equation 5 shows the results when nine lagged terms are used; here the coefficients behave more nearly as expected.

Goodness of fit for 1936–58 is fair, $\bar{R}^2$ values around 0.6, but distinctly inferior to those for the other two subperiods (See Figure 2). The impact of the monetary variable is statistically less than unity, being on the order of 0.5. And the impact of monetary policy is subject to a very long lag with 95 percent of the impact not captured until period t-7 in both cases.

Table 3A. Results of Estimating Model 4, 1936–58, Annual Data

variable	Eq. 4		Eq. 5	
(change in log)	8-year lag		9-year lag	
CONST$_t$	.0077	(.2226)	.0199	(.5617)
PROD$_t$	−.7979	(−3.7779)	−.8392	(−3.8206)
Aaa$_t$	.2519	(2.8581)	.2661	(2.9448)
POP$_t$	.6013	(.1933)	−.4599	(−.1464)
HPMA$_t$	.0297	(.6090)	.0143	(.2916)
HPMA$_{t-1}$	.0319	(1.1728)	.0323	(1.1350)
HPMA$_{t-2}$	.0358	(1.7419)	.0462	(2.4474)
HPMA$_{t-3}$	.0413	(1.7272)	.0560	(2.7228)
HPMA$_{t-4}$	.0483	(1.8468)	.0617	(2.5411)
HPMA$_{t-5}$	.0570	(2.3082)	.0633	(2.5069)
HPMA$_{t-6}$	.0673	(2.9028)	.0608	(2.5915)
HPMA$_{t-7}$	.0793	(2.4990)	.0542	(2.3916)
HPMA$_{t-8}$	.0928	(1.7236)	.0435	(1.4385)
HPMA$_{t-9}$			.0287	(.5929)
Sum of HPMA Coef.				
$\Sigma\hat{\gamma}_{t-i}$	.4835	(3.7869)	.4608	(3.2629)
R^2, $\bar{R}^2$	.7405	.6432	.7213	.6168
ô, F,	.0236	7.6105	.0244	6.9008
DW, N, K	1.8965	23 7	1.9543	23 7
CUSUM Backward	.5584			.6841
CUSUM SQ. Backward	.1654			.3218
CUSUM Forward	.3797			.5594
CUSUM SQ. Forward	.0877			.07447

(t values in parenthesis)

In contrast with the estimates for 1912–30, Equation 4 and 5 show a significant positive influence for the interest rate. The productivity variable is also highly significant with the expected negative sign. The Durbin-Watson statistic does not reject the hypothesis of no autocorrelation and the stability tests cannot reject a homogeneous time period.

Table 3B summarizes the monthly results for the 1936–58 time period. These results reaffirm the annual results. Very long lags are again indicated with the sum of the high-powered money coefficients falling between 0.4 and 0.5. Goodness of fit is quite poor for the monthly estimates, with the best values for $\bar{R}^2$ being about .2. The Aaa bond interest rate has less influence in the monthly data, than in the annual figures. The total interest rate effect is significant. Population is again insignificant, and productivity is significant with the expected negative sign. As with the yearly data, a significant monetary influence extends to the last period. The commercial-paper rate yields very small coefficients and is statistically insignificant. Cubic polynomial estimation did not alter any of the results substantially.

Table 3B. Results of Estimating Model 4, 1936–58, Monthly Data

variable (change in log)	Eq. 4' 96-month lag	Eq. 5' 108-month lag
CONST	−.00002 (−.393)	−.00005 (−.393)
$PROD_t$	−.495 (−4.48)	−.491 (−4.50)
Aaa_t	.049 (2.02)	.046 (1.93)
POP_t	−.004 (−.032)	−.814 (−.103)
CPR_t	.0078 (1.11)	.0069 (.998)
Sum of HPMA coefficients		
$\Sigma\gamma_{t-i}$	.406 (4.46)	.488 (5.41)
R^2, $\bar{R}^2$	.243, .190	.261, .210
$\hat{\sigma}$, F	.0059, 4.59	.0058, 5.05
DW, N, K	1.376, 276, 19	1.407, 276, 19
$Aaa_t + CPR_t$	.056 (2.61)	.053 (2.47)

(t values in parenthesis)

1957–77

For 1957–77, yearly estimation is presented in Table 4A using eight lagged HPMA terms (Equation 6), which is the number which minimized the error sum of squares. Since the last three HPMA terms are not significant, Equation 7, using only six lagged values, is shown for comparison. Both imply a very similar lag pattern, with 95 percent of the HPMA impact captured before period t-6, and with significant HPMA impact beginning after one year and extending back through period t-5. The average lag is greater than for the 1912–30 period but less than for the 1936–58 period.

Goodness of fit for 1957–77 is again very good; the $\bar{R}^2$ values are very similar to those of 1912–30, being in the neighborhood of 0.89 (see Figure 2). Also, as in the 1912–30 period, the total monetary impact does not differ from unity to a statistically significant degree. The productivity variable is highly significant and negative, but the interest rate and population are not significant. The Durbin-Watson statistic cannot reject the null hypothesis of no first-order autocorrelation.

Table 4A. Results of Estimating Model 4, 1957–77, Annual Data

variable (change in log)	Eq. 6 8-year lag		Eq. 7 6-year lag	
Const	.0438	(2.4320)	.0402	(2.2454)
$PROD_t$	−.7736	(−4.4958)	−.7252	(−4.3103)
Aaa_t	.0053	(.1508)	.0080	(.2338)
POP_t	−1.3122	(−1.3469)	−1.2572	(−1.2829)
$HPMA_t$	.0474	(.4876)	.0400	(.2438)
$HPMA_{t-1}$	.1189	(2.4053)	.1081	(2.2170)
$HPMA_{t-2}$	.1645	(5.3775)	.1526	(2.1644)
$HPMA_{t-3}$	.1842	(4.5970)	.1736	(1.7997)
$HPMA_{t-4}$	.1779	(3.6418)	.1709	(2.1540)
$HPMA_{t-5}$	.1457	(2.9290)	.1446	(2.5555)
$HPMA_{t-6}$	.0876	(1.8160)	.0947	(.6165)
$HPMA_{t-7}$	.0036	(.0590)		
$HPMA_{t-8}$	−.1064	(−1.0943)		
Sum of HPMA Coef.				
$\Sigma\gamma_{t-i}$	.8236	(5.4578)	.8845	(6.2300)
R^2, $\bar{R}^2$	.9215	.8879	.9152	.8789
$\hat{\sigma}$, F	.0088	27.393	.0092	25.1971
DW, N, K	1.5218	21 7	1.5265	21 7
CUSUM Backward	.67725		.3663	
CUSUM SQ. Backward	.3011		.1046	
CUSUM Forward	.5429		.3185	
CUSUM SQ. Forward	.4607		.4155	

(t values in parenthesis)

Table 4B shows the monthly analysis covering 1957–78 (6). In view of our concern for bias in lag length, it is important to note that the monthly data suggest that, if anything, the lags are even longer than those yielded by the annual estimates. HPMA during the current year does not exert a significant influence, but from that point, significant influence is indicated as far back as the t-84 month (year t-6).

Table 4B. Results of Estimating Model 4, 1957–78, Monthly Data

variable (change in log)	Eq. 6' 96-month lag	Eq. 7' 72-month lag
CONST	.0002 (.136)	.0010 (.813)
$PROD_t$	−.214 (−4.67)	−.223 (−4.79)
Aaa_t	.035 (3.57)	.033 (3.32)
POP_t	−.494 (−.590)	−1.06 (−1.32)
CPR_t	−.004 (−1.65)	−.004 (−1.53)
Sum of HPMA coefficients		
$\Sigma\gamma_{t-i}$	1.034 (11.89)	.9375 (12.18)
R^2, $\bar{R}^2$	.551, .515	.535, .503
$\hat{\sigma}$, F	.0021, 15.45	.0021, 14.75
DW, N, K	1.732, 246, 19	1.696, 246, 19
$Aaa_t + CPR_t$	.031 (3.49)	.029 (3.27)

(t values in parenthesis)

In 1957–78, as in 1913–30, the sum of the monthly HPMA coefficients is almost exactly unity. The Aaa bond interest rate has a modest positive influence (very similar to 1936–58). The commercial-paper rate is insignificant, but the total interest rate influence is significant. Population is not significant; productivity is quite significant with the expected negative sign. As before, estimating the monthly model with a cubic polynomial lag structure did not alter the results appreciably.

For month-to-month price changes, the 1957–78 regressions showed adjusted R^2 of about 0.5. This is a respectable showing for monthly changes, but comparison with the year-to-year estimates, with R^2 on the order of 0.9, confirms the view that the accuracy of the monetary model improves when the time unit of measurement is increased.

In analyzing the stability of the yearly data, however, no time period following 1957 could be found that passed all the stability tests. As a result Equations 6, 7, 6' and 7' do not appear to represent a stable relationship over the entire period.

Because of this lack of stability, we undertook a number of exploratory estimations employing yearly data; however, the results were inconclusive (see Tracy and Trescott, 1980). It is hoped that with judicious use of the monthly data we now have more of these questions can now be answered. But it may be unrealistic to assume that there is a model with an invariant lag structure under the conditions of the 1960s and 1970s. Perhaps a model incorporating a variable lag structure should instead be used (see Tanner, 1979).

SOME INTERPRETATIONS

Each of the three subperiods emphasized here contains a major inflationary episode as well as a number of years of relative price stability. For each subperiod, the regression results are consistent with a monetary interpretation of inflationary and noninflationary episodes as well.

The impact of interest rates on price change appears somewhat different in the monthly as contrasted with the annual estimates. With monthly data, one finds a significant positive influence from the corporate Aaa bond interest rate in each period, but the size of that influence is small except in the first period. In contrast, the annual data depict a substantial interest rate influence in 1936–57 but not in the earlier or subsequent period. Had there been some systematic nonmonetary influence at work on prices through aggregate demand, we would expect it to appear in a larger and more consistent interest-rate influence than appears in these estimates.

The influence of variables underlying the aggregate supply of real output is consistent across the regression equations. Productivity is generally highly significant and with a negative sign, as expected. Working-age population is not significant in any regression.

Our first-difference estimates enable us to test for the presence of a significant time trend in inflation which is not directly explained by the variables in the regressions. Such a time trend would appear as a statistically significant positive constant term in the regressions. Of the regressions reported here, none of those for 1912/13–30 or 1936–57 has significant constant terms. Our regression estimates using annual data for 1957–77 do have significant and positive constant terms. This result, however, is not found if the annual first differences are estimated using HPMA alone. And we do not find significant constant terms in the regressions using monthly data, whether those are estimated with or without the monthly dummy variables. Thus the regressions do not give strong support for existence of an independent price trend.

The following are some factors which help explain the variations in timing and and magnitude of monetary response in the three subperiods:

1912–30 Domestic monetary and financial conditions were significantly influenced by international forces, especially during World War I (see Meltzer, 1977). In 1914–18, European demand for United States goods was financed in part by gold flows and in part by liquidating investments and borrowing. These influences tended simultaneously to raise HPMA, prices, and interest rates in the United States. Federal Reserve policy, however, was clearly responsible for the sharp expansion and contraction of HPMA in 1919–21, and for its very slow growth in the 1920s. The timing of the interest-rate decline after 1920 suggests that the Fisher effect was operating.

1936–58. This period was marked by conditions of disequilibrium in the monetary system, in the labor market, and in the capital market.
a. Disequilibrium in the monetary system was marked by the abnormal build-up and subsequent decline in currency and excess reserves, which served as a reservoir for much of the increase in HPMA after 1930. The monetary system after 1933 was also plagued by the existence of thousands of banks undergoing liquidation, with disturbing influence on credit markets in general.
b. Labor market disequilibrium was the most conspicuous malaise of the 1930s. Excess labor supply made the supply schedule of output highly elastic. The rise of aggregate demand after 1933 operated largely to increase output and employment rather than prices. The excess supply of labor was eliminated by the end of 1942.
c. Capital-market disequilibrium to an extreme degree prevailed in the 1930s and 1940s. It helps explain the economy's response to expansion of HPMA in the 1930s and 1940s, and particularly helps us to understand why interest rates fell so markedly in the Depression with so little apparent stimulation to investment.

The fall of output from 1929 to 1933 created a large volume of excess capacity which lasted through the 1930s. Deterioration of asset values raised debt burdens and caused balance sheets to deteriorate. Willingness and ability to borrow were thereby impaired for business firms, homeowners, and farmers. Persistent risk aversion by lenders resulted in severe credit rationing, so that the low interest rates which prevailed on low-risk assets were not reflected in ready availability of loan funds to prospective borrowers.

The catastrophic experiences of the 1930s created expectations concerning demand, prices, and profits which were overpessimistic. This helps explain why the substantial inflation of the 1940s did not generate the kind of behavior we associate with inflationary expectations. Under wartime controls, the stock of physical capital failed to keep pace with expanded output.

Capital market disequilibrium was reflected in the decline in the corporate Aaa bond interest rate from 5.01 percent in 1932 to 2.53 percent in 1946. The low rates reached in the 1940s were not consistent with the true value of the potential productivity and profitability of capital goods, particularly after wartime conditions had eliminated the excess capacity. In the 1950s, the economy moved to eliminate capital-market disequilibrium through a process which involved simultaneous increase in interest rates, stock prices, and the ratio of capital goods to output. This process created a buoyant economy in which prices crept upward in spite of an extremely low rate of increase in HPMA. The end of the period of capital-market disequilibrium can be identified with the tendency for the Aaa-bond interest rate to stabilize around 4.5 percent in 1959–65.

1957–78(6). This period is relatively unique in that its substantial rate of inflation apparently came to be fully anticipated, as reflected in behavior in capital and labor markets. A gradual increase in the monetary growth rate in the 1960s initially raised output and employment, but also generated accelerating inflation and inflationary expectations. The learning process by which these expectations were formed probably accounts for the gradual shortening of the lag and increase in the total impact of monetary policy on prices.

Noting the similarity in the total impact of monetary policy in the periods 1912–30 and 1957–78(6) it is clear that the period 1936–58 is the anomaly historically; yet it has played a disproportionately influential role in shaping our image of the inflation process and methods for dealing with it. It is the period in which the Keynesian analysis took hold. Evidence of the 1930s and 1940s appeared to show that monetary expansion could lower equilibrium interest rates and raise equilibrium output and employment. The link between money and prices appeared to be very loose, so the feasibility of government price controls was not seriously questioned. Actual inflation did not generate inflationary expectations operating on capital markets and interest rates. Thus, the bond-price support program of the Federal Reserve in 1942–51 did not lead to explosive results.

CONCLUSIONS

This study presents evidence of the degree to which a simple monetary model of price-level behavior can account for the three major episodes of sustained inflation in recent United States history, and for the noninflationary periods as well. For 1912–30 and 1957–78, the models perform well with both annual and monthly first differences. Further, in both these periods, the sum of coefficients for high-powered money is approximately unity, consistent with the prediction of the traditional quantity theory of money. In contrast, the model does not perform as well for the period 1936–58, which is not surprising in view of the pervasive disequilibrium conditions affecting the monetary system and the markets for labor and capital in that period. Unfortunately, the experience of the 1930s and 1940s has exerted a disproportionate influence on professional thinking about the relation of monetary policy to inflation.

The time lag from monetary policy to price-level change has also shown wide variation over time. The lag was very short in 1912–30, very long in 1936–58, and still surprisingly long in the most recent period. For 1957–78, significant monetary influence is found extending for as long as five or six years. This has several important implications. Since there is little connection between current monetary policy and current price behavior, any move toward monetary restraint may appear initially ineffective. Second, at the present time we have considerably more inflation "in the pipeline" than we have yet experienced, simply on the basis of monetary growth which has already occurred. Third, there is no reason to expect the lag from monetary policy to prices to remain constant. Cagan's hyperinflation study [1956] suggested the lag tends to become shorter as the inflation rate speeds up. Such a speedup may be going on at the present time.

Appendix

Table A-1. First Difference Regressions, HPMA only, Almon lag, Annual Data

(change in log)	Eq. A-1 1912–30	Eq. A-2 1936–58	Eq. A-3 1957–77
$HPMA_t$	.803	.009	−.059
	(6.32)	(.14)	(−.42)
$HPMA_{t-1}$	.330	.014	.075
	(3.57)	(.42)	(1.07)
$HPMA_{t-2}$	.097	.022	.172
	(1.33)	(.87)	(3.75)
$HPMA_{t-3}$	.021	.032	.231
	(.29)	(.99)	(3.66)
$HPMA_{t-4}$	.017	.045	.252
	(.18)	(1.21)	(3.34)
$HPMA_{t-5}$	.002	.060	.236
	(.01)	(1.75)	(3.20)
$HPMA_{t-6}$		.077	.182
		(2.79)	(2.79)
$HPMA_{t-7}$		.097	.090
		(2.90)	(1.13)
$HPMA_{t-8}$		.120	−.039
		(1.92)	(−.29)
constant	−.022	−.005	−.005
R^2	.877	.373	.746
DW	2.07	1.34	1.33
s.e.	.030	.034	.014
ΣHPMA	1.270	.476	1.139

(t values in parenthesis)

Notes

* The authors wish to express appreciation to David Sivan for extensive assistance.
1. Note that this is equivalent to adding a time trend to model 2 where δ4 is the coefficient of the time trend. Estimates using the levels of the data appear in Tracy and Trescott (1980).

2. Note that the term $\gamma_{3a} \Delta \ln CPR_t$ is included only in the monthly model. The intercept term γ_0 represents the overall intercept and the binary intercept in the monthly model.

3. The first and most straightforward test uses the "homogeneity statistic," which is a generalization of the well known "Chow test" (Chow, [1960]). The remaining two tests were developed by Brown, Durbin, and Evans (1975) and use recursive residuals. These residuals are obtained by estimating the model with the first K (number of exogenous variables in the model) observations and then reestimating the model after adding one additional observation. The string of residuals associated with each additional observation is the recursive residuals. The first statistic involves the cumulative sum of the recursive residuals (hereafter CUSUM); the second statistic involves the cumulative sum of the squared recursive residuals (hereafter CUSUM SQ). Because there are only $N - K$ recursive residuals, it is imperative that both tests be undertaken using a forward and backward ordering of the observations. Since the null hypothesis of a stable relationship over the entire time period implies that a backward ordering is as appropriate, although not as intuitively appealing, as a forward ordering, this presents no problem. For an actual evaluation of the power of these tests see Garbade (1977) and Farley, Hinich, and McGuire (1975).

The idea that the money-price relationship has passed through several different phases is also advanced by Meltzer (1977), but his choice of time periods is not supported by stability tests.

4. This procedure uses only three degrees of freedom regardless of the number of lagged terms used. No end-point restrictions are imposed. Thus the study is not subject to the criticisms levied on the studies that impose such restrictions (Dhrymes, 1971; Schmidt and Waud, 1973).

5. Note that the first monthly observation is January 1913, while the first yearly is 1912. Monthly data for CPI are first available in January 1913.

6. Note that the last monthly observation is June 1978, not 1977 as with the yearly data.

References

Brown, R. L., Durbin, J., and Evans, J. M., *Techniques for Testing the Constancy of Regression Relationships over Time*, Royal Statistical Society, 1975.

Brunner, Karl, and Meltzer, Allan A., "Some Further Investigations of Demand and Supply Functions for Money," *Journal of Finance*, May 1964.

Cagan, Phillip, "The Monetary Dynamics of Hyperinflation," in Milton Friedman (Ed.), *Studies in the Quantity Theory of Money* (Chicago, 1956).

Chow, G. C. "Tests for Equality between Two Sets of Coefficients in Two Linear Regressions," *Econometrica* 28 (1960): 591–605.

Dhrymes, P. *Distributed Lags: Problems of Estimation and Formation* (1971).

Farley, John U., Hinich, Melvin, and McGuire, Timothy, "Some Comparisons of Tests on a Shift in the Slopes of a Multivariate Linear Time Series Model," *Journal of Econometrics* 3 (1975): 297–318.

Garbade, Kenneth, "Two Methods for Examining the Stability of Regression

Coefficient," *Journal of the American Statistical Association* 72 (1977): 54–63.

Laidler, David, "A Survey of Some Current Problems," in G. Clayton, J. C. Gilbert, and Sedgewik, (Eds.), *Monetary Theory and Monetary Policy in the 1970s* (Oxford, 1971).

Maddala, G. S., *Econometrics* (New York, 1977).

Meltzer, Allan H., "Anticipated Inflation and Unanticipated Price Change: A Test of the Price-Specie Flow Theory and the Phillips Curve," *Journal of Money, Credit, and Banking* 9 (1977): 182–205.

Quandt, Richard, "The Estimation of the Parameters of a Linear Regression System Obeying Two Separate Regimes," *Journal of the American Statistical Society* 53 (1958): 873–79.

Quandt, Richard, "Tests of the Hypothesis that a Linear Regression System Obeys Two Separate Regimes," *Journal of the American Statistical Society* 68 (1960): 11–19.

Tanner, J. Ernest, "Are the Lags in the Effect of Monetary Policy Variable?," *Journal of Monetary Economics* 5 (1979): 105–121.

Tracy, R. L., and Trescott, Paul B., "Monetary Policy and Inflation in the United States, 1912–1977," *Monetary Policy: Goals and Conduct for the 1980s*, Hearings before the Subcommittee on Domestic Monetary Policy . . . of the Commmittee on Banking, Finance, and Urban Affairs, U. S. House of Representatives, 1980, pp. 246–75.

Data Sources:

For annual data, see Tracy and Trescott (1980).

CPI: Consumer price index: worksheet data from Federal Reserve Bank of St. Louis.

HPMA: High-powered money adjusted for changes in legal reserve requirements. Milton Friedman and Anna J. Schwartz, *A Monetary History of the United States, 1867–1960* (NBER, 1963), pp. 799–808; worksheets and current publications of the Federal Reserve Bank of St. Louis. Dollar equivalents of reserve requirement changes prior to 1947 were estimated by Professor Trescott from data in *Banking and Monetary Statistics*, Federal Reserve Board, 1943, pp. 340, 396, and current issues of *Federal Reserve Bulletin*.

PROD: Output per hour, private business sector. Quarterly data 1947–78 from worksheets of Bureau of Labor Statistics. For earlier years, annual estimates from U. S. Dept. of Commerce, *Long Term Economic Growth, 1860–1970* (1973), pp. 208–209.

POP: Population aged 14–64, *Long Term Economic Growth*, pp. 200–203, Bureau of the Census, "Estimates of the Population of the United States by Age, Sex, and Race, 1970–1977," (1978), pp. 9–16; *Economic Report of the President*, 1979, p. 213.

AAA: Interest rate on corporate Aaa bonds, *Banking and Monetary Statistics*, 1943, pp. 468–71, 478; *Banking and Monetary Statistics 1941–1970*,

(1976), pp. 720–27; *Annual Statistical Digest, 1971–1975*, p. 126; *Ibid.*, 1973–1977 (1978), pp. 94–99; *Federal Reserve Bulletin.* Values for 1912–1919 were estimated by a regression on railroad bond yields.

CPR: Interest rate on 4–6 month commercial paper. *Banking and Monetary Statistics*, (1943), pp. 449–51; *Banking and Monetary Statistics, 1941–1970*, pp. 674–76; *Annual Statistical Digest, 1971–75*, p. 121; *Annual Statistical Digest, 1973–1977*, pp. 94–99; *Federal Reserve Bulletin.*

Georges Valois and the Franc-Or: A Right-Wing Reaction to Inflation

ALLEN DOUGLAS

The period between the First and Second World wars in European history was strongly marked by two groups of historical events: a series of monetary crises, especially inflation, and the rise of European Fascism.[1] These two developments are usually linked through the following causal structure: postwar inflation contributed to the impoverishment of the middle classes and, thus, to the rise of Fascism, especially German National Socialism. Even in this interpretation, however, the Great Depression plays a more crucial role.[2]

These two trends, Fascism and inflation, were also linked in another, more singular, way. The only organized political movement or party in interwar Europe to give a central place to monetary problems and policy was the movement which gave birth to the Faisceau, France's first Fascist party. Another way to state the same proposition would be to note that the Faisceau, easily the most economically self-conscious of European Fascist movements, saw monetary issues as the crucial links in the political, economic, and social problems of the day.[3] The causes and circumstances of this historical symbiosis are the subject of this study.

The circumstances themselves can be viewed both biographically and chronologically. Biographically, because the history of the Faisceau and its monetary doctrines were bound up with the life of Georges Valois, the Faisceau's founder and chief economist.[4] Valois himself was at once a political chameleon and a jack-of-all-trades. Besides being an economic and monetary theorist and a politician, he was also a journalist, publisher, and corporative organizer. Politically, Valois spent his youth as an anarchist. In his late twenties, he converted to Catholicism and royalism, joining the Action Française which he served for almost twenty years as economic expert and ambassador to the world of labor. After World War I, though he stayed within the royalist Ligue, Valois conducted his own series of political and corporative campaigns. These led directly to the creation of the Faisceau which was founded in November 1925, shortly after Valois's own break with the royalists.

Although some of these campaigns were carried out under the aegis of the Action Française and some under that of the Faisceau, all had an essential organizational and intellectual continuity. Probably the single most important theme connecting these campaigns was the centrality of France's monetary difficulties to the political, economic, and social problems facing that nation.

Chronologically, these campaigns were possible because the period 1919–28 was one of general monetary instability. An almost constant inflation from 1919 to 1927 was marked by two sharp exchange crises, the first in 1924; the second in 1926 when it was accompanied by a financial and political crisis. Though exchange stability was restored in 1927, monetary debate was not closed until the franc was reattached to the gold standard in 1928 by Poincaré, consecrating the loss of four-fifths of its prewar value.[5]

The end of the financial and monetary crisis dealt a serious blow to Valois's political fortunes. Interestingly enough in this context, however, the decline of the Faisceau was accompanied by a sharp move leftward on the part of its founder. By 1928, Valois, having ceased to be a Fascist, either ideologically or politically, officially dissolved the Faisceau. During the rest of his career, which Valois spent on the left as an independent syndicalist, he never gave monetary issues more than passing notice. Thus, Valois' monetary ideas and campaigns can be seen essentially as a right-wing reaction to inflation.

Though Valois did not give any systematic attention to monetary problems or formulate any monetary, or even strictly economic, ideas until after World War I,[6] he did make occasional references to currency-related issues. These references (only two) in effect, constitute the intellectual prehistory of his ideas, showing the original bent of his mind before it had come into contact with the monetary problems of the postwar world. Both references were embedded in polemics with revolutionary syndicalists in which he sought to show the dangers of social revolution. Valois presented two scenarios. In the first, after the success of the revolution, the bourgeois flee taking their gold with them. The workers, who control the factories, demand gold as payment for goods and services. The Jews, possessed of both gold and revolutionary contacts, take over French production. The second scenario was based on a suggestion by Jaurès in l'Humanité. Jaurès proposed that proprietors be indemnified with interest-bearing bonds. Valois explained, however, that these bonds would soon be victims of speculation. As their prices were reduced by a well-organized panic, the Jews would buy them up, once again controlling the French economy.[7] Though these examples most clearly manifest a paranoid anti-semitism, typical of Valois' thought at this time, they also show a thorough distrust of any money or credit not based on gold, allied with the suspicion that monetary problems or speculation would serve as the occasion for the theft of the national wealth.

Valois' postwar reactions to inflation can be divided into several aspects which, though they developed with an unequal tempo, did so in a dialectical relationship with one another. The first aspect would be his analyses of the causes of inflation, both the immediate financial or monetary causes and the ultimate, final, generally political causes. The second aspect would be the problem of the dangers posed by inflation; the third, obviously related to the first two, would be the remedies, from palliatives to complete solutions.

Valois' first tangle with inflation came in 1919 when he attempted to explain the recent dramatic rise in prices that followed the end of the financial solidarity of the Allies and which was popularly known as "la vie chère."[8] Life was dear, he argued, because the French had been impoverished by the war. Production during, and shortly after, the war was hampered by scarcities of raw materials and labor and the disorganization of transportation, all of which raised costs. In addition, through indirect taxes, consumers were also paying some of the costs of the war itself.[9]

As prices continued to rise, Valois changed his analysis. By the beginning of 1920, he recognized that price rises were not being caused by increases in the real costs of production, now stable or in some cases in decline, but by an absolute decline in the value of money, that is, by inflation. The principal cause, he insisted at this time, was what is now called *cost-push inflation*. Higher salaries, caused by what he termed the unilaterally syndicalized economy,[10] unmatched by increases in productivity, led to higher prices and a deflated currency. In passing, he noted that the Bank of France, by increasing the amount of paper in circulation, permitted the process to continue.[11]

In July 1920, Valois added the explanation which would soon dominate all the others: the rise in prices was caused by fiduciary inflation. The Bank of France had reduced the value of the franc by printing too much money, money that had no backing. Money, for Valois, was not a sign or convention but merchandise (generally gold) whose value was its value as merchandise but whose form had been adapted for ease of exchange. Paper money (in France, notes of the Bank of France) was merely a receipt for merchandise pledged or deposited. Bank notes should be issued only upon the receipt of properly endorsed and discounted commercial paper. Advances to the state must be fully covered by the bank's gold reserves. Any other money was false money which diminished, proportionally, the value of all the paper money in circulation. Valois was not against any increase in the money supply. If production increased, an increase would be necessary and would be

produced automatically by an increase in the value of the commercial
paper brought to the bank for discount.

This explanation brought Valois close to the quantity theory of
money and in fact he tended to calculate as if this were operative,
excluding the consideration of velocity. The quantity of money as such
was not a cause for Valois since he did not believe that money or prices
responded to supply and demand, which he considered a false economic principle. Equally absurd for him, was any explanation based on
the balance of trade. The loss in the value of money was caused directly
by its absence of backing and international exchange rates were merely
the recognition of this change. Valois, thus, made no distinction between the internal and external value of the franc.[12]

Ultimately, thus, inflation was caused by the state, though Valois did
not develop this level of causation at this time.[13] What concerned him
more were the immediate dangers posed by inflation. The first and
most obvious was to the *rentiers* for whom inflation was a partial
confiscation. Besides the question of simple justice, the dispossession
of the *rentiers* would discourage others from saving, and the spirit of
saving was one of the pillars of civilization.[14] More serious for Valois
was the damage done to production. Inflation made long-term accounting or contracts impossible. In an arresting image, he compared the
effects of a changing monetary unit to the situation in which a builder
would be placed if his plans had been drawn up according to official
measures but his supplies and pieces were being measured with a
yardstick which kept changing in length: a measuring stick made of
rubber. Similarly, inflation distorted business practices, creating paper
profits and leading workers to seek and receive higher and higher
wages. Seeing the ease with which these were accorded, workers
concluded that up to then they had been robbed and hence became
revolutionary.[15]

The most serious problem caused by inflation, however, was not
disorganization of the economy. Inflation brought about a real transfer
of value into the hands of foreigners and plutocrats, these last being
most easily understood as those who abused the economic system for
their own benefit.[16] Valois explained this transfer through an idea
which, though original, bore some relation to the argument of the "loss
of substance" raised in a few, relatively unsophisticated, French journalistic circles. According to this argument, foreigners, purchasing
French goods at absurdly low prices due to the favorable exchange,
were bleeding the country of its substance.[17] Valois' argument was a bit
more sophisticated: in the first place, foreign debtors could pay their
debts, or the service on their debts, at a fraction of their value (this of
course did not apply to reparations which were figured in gold).

Meanwhile, French debts, due in a stable foreign currency, would be paid at their true value. The same process took place on a smaller scale in commercial transactions. A French firm, buying goods in a foreign market and paying in a month, would pay full value; a foreigner purchasing in France would gain at the end of the month.[18]

The implications of these arguments can best be seen when they are compared with Valois' reaction to the rapid deflation which set in near the end of 1920. The deflation, and any move towards the prewar, gold value of the franc, was a good sign, yet it brought about as many problems as the inflation. Besides disorganizing the economy through paper losses and hoarding, deflation still permitted the theft of the national wealth. Now foreign creditors who benefited; foreign merchants could still turn things to their advantage by stipulating payment in francs, whose value was on the rise. In effect, for Valois, no matter which way it moved, a franc cut off from the gold standard, and to him this was synonymous with an unstable franc, was susceptible to manipulation by plutocratic forces and permitted foreign businessmen, possessing a stable currency, to rob their French counterparts. Hence the real problem was not just inflation, but monetary instability generally.[19]

For the structural problems of economic disorganization and the international commercial danger of systematic losses Valois had a simple, and essentially original solution: the *franc-or*. This was a money of account. Valois did not propose a speedy return to the prewar gold standard, a legal devaluation or the circulation of gold or gold certificates. Amounts due and accounts were to be recorded in *francs-or*, i.e., the gold value of the 1914 franc. At the moment of payment the number of paper francs would be due which equalled, in gold value, the amount previously agreed upon in *francs-or*. This could be done for all payments: salaries, loans, deposits, national and international commerce. The effect would be the complete indexation of all monetary agreements, though the indexation would be based on gold rather than on the internal price level. If this system of calculation were used by the government, the *rentiers* would be protected (or the government in case of deflation). If not, at least Frenchmen could protect themselves in their dealings with one another and with foreigners. This system, which Valois continued to advocate until 1928, recommended itself to him both because of its simplicity and its honesty.[20]

The *franc-or* would, in reality, have solved the twin problems of honesty posed by any attempt to repay the *rentiers* fairly. Those who had lent to the state before the war could be repaid at the gold rate; those who lent after the inflation began would not be overpaid, which they would in the case of a full revaluation of the franc. On the other hand, since the *franc-or* was tied to the international exchange rate, it would have made it impossible for fluctuating exchange rates to change relative French prices to adjust the balance of payments.[21]

Thus, by 1920 Valois had "discovered" the cause of inflation, analyzed its dangers, and proposed a plan to prevent the damage. Imposing his panacea, however, would be a good deal more difficult. One financier, Georges Bonnet of the Conseil d'Etat, caught Valois' eye when he proposed a similar system for international postal exchanges, but for the most part Valois's contacts, both in the Action Française and the book industry, turned a deaf ear to his projects. But Valois, as a publisher, could still print what he liked. Accordingly, when the war veteran and industrialist Jacques Arthuys came to him with an unpublishable manuscript, *Le Problème de la monnaie*, Valois had it printed in his Nouvelle Librairie Nationale. Though Arthuys's economic analyses were a bit more sophisticated than Valois's, both writers agreed on all the major points: the definition of money and its value, and the role of fiduciary inflation as the cause of rising prices. Arthuys was also aware of the problems of deflation and was casting about for some way of putting a stable currency into circulation alongside the legal one. Valois now had a collaborator. The two men were soon joined by a third, Eugène Peschier, a consultant in foreign commerce who proposed payments in "merchandise francs."[22]

To promote his program, Valois used the organizations he had been building as part of his campaign to organize French industry along syndicalo-corporatist lines. The main instrument in this campaign was the Semaine, a device borrowed from the Catholic social movement, which really meant a series of meetings (generally for a week) by representatives of a given industry designed to create rapid agreement for the good of the industry as a whole. At the first Semaine, the Semaine du Livre, Valois succeeded in persuading his counterparts in the book industry to demand the adoption of the *franc-or* and to call for a Semaine de la Monnaie.[23]

In his campaign for a Semaine de la Monnaie Valois was helped by other people he met in the course of his corporative ventures. Eugène Mathon, a leading textile manufacturer from Roubaix-Tourcoing and the head of the powerful Comité de la Laine, backed Valois and organized a Semaine for foreign commerce, whose executive committee also called for the monetary meeting. Valois also received the support of Bonnet and Lucien Romier, editor-in-chief of the influential *Journée industrielle*. Most important, he also received official support. François-Marsal, the banker and finance minister, who had stabilized the advances from the Bank of France and signed a convention for their gradual repayment, thus provoking deflation and an economic crisis, agreed to write the final report. Finally, the Bank of France, hostile to further advances, showed its backing when Jules

Décamps, head of the economic studies department at the bank, joined the organizing committee. The bank also discreetly aided Valois's corporative projects in the book industry.[24]

At the Semaine itself in June 1922, representatives of most of France's largest economic groups and a few economic experts discussed the mechanism of inflation, determined it to be fiduciary inflation, and debated the alternative policies of stabilization: a return to the gold standard or deflation vs. conversion to a different parity or devaluation, which Arthuys defended. As part of a section on technical palliatives, Valois defended the *franc-or* with the assistance of the royalist lawyer Marie de Roux. What the Semaine really accomplished was to stigmatize inflation as the debasement of the currency, and ask the state to repay the advances from the bank by reducing expenses.[25]

Valois did not, however, expect the resolutions of the Semaine to stop inflation in France. For, by 1922, he had decided that the Republic was not likely to solve its financial and monetary problems. This decision was based on two factors: an appreciation of the objective difficulties of the government's financial position and a more developed, political and institutional explanation of inflation. The situation of the government was simply stated: the state was spending over 40 billion francs a year (the most conservative figure) and taking in about 20 billion. The rest was covered by borrowing. Not only was the long-term debt so large that its service was threatening to devour the state's income, but the short-term debt was so large that if, through a crisis of confidence, treasury notes were not almost completely renewed, the treasury would be forced to suspend payment. Nor would reparations cover this debt, even if they were paid, which neither Valois nor Arthuys expected. Large-scale cash payments would depend on heavy German exports; payments in kind had been blocked by French interests who wanted to preserve the profits of reconstruction for themselves.[26]

These objective difficulties were at once created and aggravated by the institutional structure of the parliamentary republic. The major weakness of the parliament, Valois argued, in Maurrasian fashion, was that it combined sovereignty and representation in one body. As representatives, the deputies sought the greatest advantages for their electors and also opposed new taxes. But since they were sovereign, they were free to impose the contradictory desires of their electors; hence the tendency to vote expenses without corresponding revenues, and, hence, inflation.[27]

Valois did not conclude that the size of the debt necessitated inflation to reduce its relative weight. Instead, with the backing of the Action Française and the economic groups involved in the Semaines, he organized a movement for the convocation of the États-Généraux.

The États would be made up of economic and regional groups and could act as a representative body independent of parliament which would continue to be sovereign. Publicly, the États-Généraux was to force the solution of the financial and monetary muddle, but privately, Valois expected it to lead to a constitutional crisis and a national revolution along reactionary corporative lines. In either case, French society would be freed from the ravages of inflation.[28]

In 1923 and 1924, the Committee for the Convocation of the États-Généraux called a series of meetings to which businessmen and other local notables were invited. Though the movement developed some momentum in late 1923 and early 1924, the government never called the États into being, nor was Valois able to impose it on the country. By late 1924, the idea had to be abandoned.[29]

The États-Généraux campaign coincided with the French occupation of the Ruhr and the exchange crisis which followed it. New monetary fluctuations during this period, however, caused Valois to change his analysis of inflation once again. During 1922, after the Semaine, Valois continued to oppose any further inflation caused by increased advances from the bank to the state; this was related to his conclusion that the graph of the price of the dollar (the major currency on the gold standard) followed that of the level of advances from the bank. By the end of 1922, he added a new, psychological, element to his analysis. Since the franc was a paper currency and not exchangeable for gold, its value was not based solely on the amount of gold or merchandise covering the francs in circulation but also, partially, on the credit of the state. This meant, primarily, the probability that the state would repay the bank's advances. Valois, thus, had seen that speculation involved estimations of future economic and financial events. In practice, this meant that it was necessary to continue the repayment of the advances in order to maintain the state's credit. Thus, because of the psychological pressures toward a lowering of the exchange rate (which Valois now argued could provoke inflation), it would be necessary, through the regular reduction of the level of advances, to pursue a gradual deflation. On this basis, Valois considered the decision (at the end of 1922) to reduce the repayment to 1 billion francs, as well as any suggestion that the advances should not be repaid, to be inflationary.[30]

In effect, by leaving aside quantitative considerations and adding a psychological dimension, Valois was opening the causes of inflation to new sets of phenomena, including international politics. The credit of the state, for example, was also based on its chances of collecting reparations. Hence the price of the franc was affected by the invasion of the Ruhr in January 1923. Such firmness, Valois argued, accounted for the temporary rise in the franc. Yet, the trend throughout 1923 was downward, though the level of advances was stable. Shifting the locus of causation, Valois now declared that the primary cause of the franc's decline was the activities of a politico-financial coalition of British and German interests, international finance, and the French left. The British and Germans, by trying to force the evacuation of the Ruhr, were serving their national interests; the speculators profited directly from the inflation thus provoked. The left, perhaps unwittingly, made things worse when it publicly opposed the Ruhr venture.[31]

Valois hesitated between the two levels of responsibility, the French state and outside forces. If the primary cause lay outside, the state bore the onus of leaving its money unprotected. The franc could best be defended by resolute action in the Ruhr, repayment, the institution of gold prices for international commerce (in effect, the *franc-or*) and police actions (including executions) against agents in France of the anti-Ruhr campaign. During the exchange crisis which developed at the end of 1923, Valois shifted his emphasis back to the government and parliament. Finance Minister Charles de Lasteyrie had provoked the current wave of speculation by reneging on repayment and talking about using the funds for the treasury. Since de Lasteyrie was being forced into this policy by the deputies, the monetary crisis was ultimately a crisis of the regime. In January 1924, Valois even went so far as to blame both de Lasteyrie and Prime Minister Poincaré for keeping the fact that speculation was *not* the cause of the exchange crisis from the French public.[32]

Valois's attacks on the government did not help him impose his solutions. On the contrary, in February, while trying to push through the new taxes designed to end the exchange crisis, de Lasteyrie introduced a bill to outlaw the *franc-or* in any of its forms. To Valois this was tyranny since it prevented honesty in dealings between Frenchmen and was clearly designed as a cover for further inflation. To add punch to his denunciations of this monetary evil, Valois explained two new dangers. Financiers and bankers were the only gainers in inflation because they had the power to buy other currencies to keep their assets from declining in real terms; depositors, repaid nominal value, lost. But Valois imputed another, more sophisticated, strategem to the bankers, one which would subsequently prove important in his analyses. During a period of inflation, businessmen, because of everincreasing replacement costs, needed ever larger advances of circulating capital. The banks, after granting such advances, would finally insist on participation in the enterprise. Their participation, though small in real value, would soon become a majority of the nominal capital and the bank would control the enterprise.[33]

Though de Lasteyrie and Poincaré, through new taxes, a loan from the Morgan Bank, and astute maneuvering on the exchanges, suc-

ceeded in beating the speculators and reviving the franc, Valois was far
from confident that France would be free from inflation. In fact, following the elections of May 1924 which brought the Cartel des Gauches to
power, Valois was even more confident that the French government
would founder amid a political crisis and catastrophic inflation. Not
only was the objective position of the government not really improved
but the reputation of the new leftist government would promote further
speculation against the franc. Finally, if the structural and political
problems were not enough, Valois was aware, as many Frenchmen
were not, that a large packet of long-term bonds (about 30 billion
francs' worth) would be falling due in 1925 and 1926, posing severe
treasury problems if they were not all renewed.[34]

The financial problems facing the Cartel governments were not the
whole story for Valois, however. In a sense they were mere mechanisms. On one level, of course, the inflation was being caused by the
financial policies of the governments of the Republic, especially failure
to repay the advances. On another level, the nature of the parliamentary system made it impossible for the deputies to vote appropriate
fiscal measures. The real cause, however, the one which acted through
the other two, Valois now concluded, was a deliberate, secret campaign
by a group of plutocrats to promote inflation and thus take over the
French productive apparatus. These plutocrats through their power
over the press and politicians, as well as the exchanges, manipulated
the political system and acted to prevent the truths Valois had been
enunciating from spreading. Valois was also now in a position to put a
name on this phenomenon: Horace Finaly. The Hungarian-Jewish
financier, a naturalized citizen, was the director of the Banque de Paris
et des Pays-Bas, one of the nation's most important commercial banks.
For Valois, Finaly was the most powerful financier in France. He was
using his bank to gain control over the French press and book industry
and eventually to control French production, favoring the interests of
American capitalism in general, and Standard Oil in particular.

According to Valois, Finaly combined economic with political
power. He had promoted inflation in France since 1919 and had
pushed de Lasteyrie, first into inflation and then into an attack on the
franc-or, only to drop the hapless minister and throw his support to the
Cartel. The organizer and backer of the Cartel, Finaly was the power
behind the scenes in the Herriot government and the ministry of
finances. The Jewish banker's techniques in swallowing up French
savings were the twin devices Valois had identified earlier. The first,
speculation on the exchanges, was all the easier for a banker who,
knowing the secrets of the government, could predict when unusual
demands would be made on the treasury and consequently when more
inflation would be produced. The second technique, that of successive

participations in the capital, could, in a period of catastrophic inflation, lead to the wholesale confiscation of French industry.[35]

But, Valois claimed, Finaly was not without allies. These were the
Communists and other revolutionaries. International financiers, like
Finaly, and the Communists had a common interest in inflation. Rapid
fluctuations in the value of money created ideal conditions for social
unrest. Conversely, the threat of a social revolution helped to lower the
value of the franc. This was a dangerous coalition, though Valois did
not commit himself as to which group was leading the other.[36]

This last explanation of inflation brought Valois's evolving analyses
into a coherent system. The dangers of inflation were also its causes
and the gravest to France was the possibility that those promoting
inflation would succeed in their ultimate goals.

The remedy, in practical terms, was the *franc-or* but this, clearly,
would need to be imposed by a national revolution. Moreover, the
imminent financial crisis would make this revolution both urgently
necessary and, at the same time, possible. Valois accordingly set in
motion a plan for a mass movement which should be ready to take
power by the middle of 1926, at the height of the crisis. This was the
movement that became the Faisceau.[37]

The Faisceau venture was intimately linked to inflation. In the first
place, the Fascist timetable was bound to the fall of the franc: impatient
members were told that D-Day would be the day when the franc stood
at zero. In the second place, the campaign for the *franc-or* helped the
movement itself in two ways. Most obviously, it formed part of the
package being sold to converts, hence it was to help in recruiting
members. Any successes in actually setting up the *franc-or*, however,
would also serve to bring the Fascists to their goal. Money, Valois
argued, was an essential element of sovereignty. Therefore, by utilizing
and popularizing the *franc-or*, Frenchmen would be denying the sovereignty of the republican government and beginning the formation of a
parallel government and economic system which stood ready to replace the legal government (and currency) when this crumbled.[38]

The dangers of inflation and the need for the *franc-or* were, thus,
constant propaganda themes. Certain events, however, led Valois to
particular campaigns around monetary issues. Two such campaigns
were launched in the summer of 1925, during the transitional period
just before the birth of the Faisceau, when Valois was still in the Action
Française. In July, Valois became embroiled in a journalistic campaign against Joseph Caillaux, then Minister of Finances. One point of
interest, for Valois, was Caillaux's project for a "National Liberation"
loan which would have a low interest rate but payments tied to the rate
of exchange. In addition, the loans, whose purpose was to renew
national defense bonds, would be reserved to the holders of these

bonds. Though Valois paid homage to the principle, so close to his own *emprunt-or* (the *franc-or* for bonds), he noted that Caillaux's loan was tied to the pound sterling which, while fairly stable, was not bound to gold. More important, Valois argued, the measure was unjust unless extended to all bondholders. He then went on publicly to demand, as a measure of urgent social justice, the *franc-or* not just for businessmen and bondholders but also for workers. Indexed wages were called the *salaire-or*. For the computation of wages and prices, Valois proposed a quarterly *franc-or* to be based on the average exchange rate of the previous quarter. This would smooth out any sudden fluctuations in the exchange rates and counteract the observed delay between changes in the exchange and changes in the purchasing power of the franc. The *salaire-or* was to take the place of the sliding wage scale (*échelle mobile*), demanded by the Socialists and Communists, which was tied to the cost of living. Like all proponents of automatic (as opposed to managed) adjustment systems, Valois did not trust the managers of a more complex system to calculate it fairly. Besides, a system based on the cost of living would be behind actual price rises. There is, in fact, evidence that the calculation of cost of living indexes at this time, raised severe statistical and political problems.[39]

The *salaire-or* was designed for workers and Valois had an opportunity to sell it to a special group of these, the bank workers, when they went out on strike in the end of July. Banking workers were particularly interesting for Valois since he hoped that they might, if properly organized, be able to influence the policies of their establishments. In addition, these white-collar workers, who often belonged to Catholic unions, were more open to right-wing influence. Despite reservations, Valois backed the strike and asked members of his own corporative group to practice solidarity with the banking workers. By doing so, Valois hoped that he and his followers could persuade the strikers to ask for the *salaire-or*. Instead they demanded the *échelle mobile* and when the strike was effectively broken some weeks later, the Fascists could only express their regrets.[40]

Backing a strike was an unusual move for the Fascists, one which they did not repeat. Much more characteristic was a campaign Valois organized in the spring of 1926. In the end of April 1926, the suggestion was bruited about in the press, and in some governmental circles, that the gold reserves of the Bank of France be used to fight speculation against the franc. The Bank of France was hostile to the idea and so was Valois. For him, since the gold reserve was the last guarantee of the franc, the plan represented an attempt to strip France's currency of all backing: to reduce it to nothing. Valois' response was to call a mass meeting (attended by 3500) and cover the walls of Paris with a poster which began: "Alert! The Last Guarantee of the Franc Is in Danger."

The issue was a popular one with the Fascists but as the idea was dropped, Valois halted his campaign.[41]

Valois was thus not able to impose the *franc-or* on the French economy. He did, however, use it to pay the salaried staff of the Faisceau and the *Nouveau Siècle*, the Fascist daily newspaper, a move which added considerably to his costs during this time of rapid exchange decline.[42] Though Valois succeeded in building an organization with over 60,000 members, from a monetary and financial point of view he was obliged to wait for the crisis he had predicted to materialize.

When, in late July, Poincaré succeeded in mastering the combined political and financial crises, Valois was caught unprepared. Once the franc was on the rise, though not legally stabilized, the nature of the monetary issues changed. The question now became whether to stabilize the franc, and at what level (i.e., how far to pursue the revaluation taking place on the exchanges) or whether to leave room open for an eventually, gradual full revaluation of the franc.

Accordingly, in the late fall of 1926, Valois began a new monetary campaign, in favor of stabilization and against revaluation. The main argument in favor of stabilization (and the one being used by the economic experts at the Bank of France) was that revaluation past a certain point, unless it was accompanied by lower prices and wages (politically unlikely), would ruin France's export trade. Though Valois was aware of this problem, he preferred to rely on more characteristic arguments. First of all, he revived his earlier arguments against deflation, which would create paper losses for businessmen. More to the point, for Valois, however, the campaign for revalorization, like the earlier inflation, was being promoted by the plutocrats who once again would benefit from manipulation of the exchanges. Finaly, having speculated on inflation, was now prepared to speculate on deflation.[43]

Though the most significant part of Valois's campaign was his attack on revalorization, he tried to combine this with an attempt to impose his old panacea, the *franc-or*. Disingenuously, he argued that the use of a money of account would have the advantage of permitting either stabilization or gradual revalorization, since in either case businessmen would be protected from fluctuations in the value of the franc. France could be given two currencies, one for producers, the *franc-or*, and one for *rentiers*, paper francs. In this way, by setting the franc at different levels, the government could give more or less to the bondholders without affecting production.[44]

Reviving an earlier idea, Valois, in February 1927, called for a second Semaine de la Monnaie, this time to examine the problems of stabilization and revaluation. The Semaine was set for May and Valois found a president in the person of Octave Homberg, a colonial financier who was also a leader of the campaign against the the ratification of the Washington debt accords. Though Valois received the backing of a few deputies and professors, drawn largely from the law faculties, the Bank of France did not lend its patronage, nor did François-Marsal or any member of the government. The Semaine concluded unanimously in favor of stabilization and a strong majority voted to permit reckoning and contracts in a gold-based money of account.[45]

In June 1928, Poincaré legally stabilized the franc by returning it to the gold standard, thus ending France's period of monetary instability and Valois's campaigns around these issues, as well. Yet, as has been noted, by mid-1928, Valois had also ceased to consider himself a Fascist and had disbanded his organization. Monetary issues, however, were not completely divorced from his gradual estrangement from Italian Fascism. One of the major points Valois held against the Italians in 1927 was their decision to revalue the *lira*. He recognized that this would jeopardize Italian industry and concluded that the campaign was caused by the plutocrats who had taken control over the Italian government.[46]

When Valois's evolving monetary ideas and campaigns are considered together, a number of points emerge. First, in every phase he was on the same side as the Bank of France. From 1920 to 1926, Valois joined with the bank in attacking further advances to the state and asking that those already granted be repaid. In late 1926 and 1927, both the bank (i.e., the director, not all the regents) and Valois were in favor of stabilization, not revaluation.

Valois's two positions, first against inflation and then against revaluation (like his earlier misgivings about deflation), show another element in his monetary thought: a primary hostility to monetary change as such. When Valois was criticizing inflation in the early 1920s and yearning for the stability of the gold standard, he was expressing conservative economic and monetary dogma, as well as reflecting a general desire to return to the prewar franc. In 1927, however, he departed from most of the French right which backed revaluation.[47] For Valois, stability was more important than justice, and despite his constant references to justice for bondholders, their interests were really secondary, since he was willing to sacrifice them to monetary stability.

This fixation on stability was related to the dangers of inflation, almost all of which were derived from monetary change (the one apparent exception would be the idea of participation by banks in the capital of enterprises) and would operate in reverse with deflation. The appeal of the *franc-or* was based on its supposed ability, not to solve France's financial problems, but to neutralize monetary change. When Valois spoke of honesty, he was not only concerned with giving members of French society their due: honesty included an honest language for all economic dealings, one in which a franc was really a franc. At the same time, the dangers of inflation were not fortuitous but were deliberately caused so that remedying those dangers, through the *franc-or*, would in a sense remove its causes in that the plutocrats would be defeated. Seen another way, the defeat of the causes (the plutocrats) would be necessary in order to impose the remedies for the dangers.

Valois's concern with inflation, thus, was related to a distrust of monetary instability and a suspicion that certain interests might be manipulating the economy to defraud honest, hard-working French producers; and this distrust and suspicion can even be found in germ in Valois's prewar writings. Are these concerns merely biographical in significance or do they bear some special relationship to radical right-wing thought, and especially radical right-wing economic thought? Unlike conservatives, true radical rightists (and this includes Fascists) believe that there are fundamental problems in their economic and social systems as they operate in practice. Most would agree that liberal capitalism is the occasion for social injustice. Unlike Marxist socialists who are willing to locate the source of this injustice in property relations and beneficiaries in the capitalists, right-wing thinkers cannot attack property as such and wish to see the beneficiaries for the most part as not being members of the nation. Hence, the frequent references to international finance, vagabond wealth (the Jews), or the plutocrats. Another possibility would be to attack interest as the fundamental unearned, and hence, stolen income.[48] Valois was himself, however, close to business circles and he understood the role of interest in the distribution of capital. In addition, with his concern with economics and practical details, he was unwilling to accept vague explanations of economic phenomena. Thus, monetary instability as the agency for theft was the perfect solution. It provided an exploitation apparently outside of the productive system, whose beneficiaries had no important role in that system. In fact, Valois's "discovery" that the 1920s witnessed a major plutocratic attempt to rob France filled an important gap in the evolution of his own thought. In Valois's economic thought as elaborated in 1919 and 1920, he explained that the plutocrats were those who unjustly manipulated the economic system for their own benefit. At this time, however, he was able to offer no systematic economic mechanism for this manipulation. Similarly, before, and shortly after, the war, Valois had always had the conviction that French politics and the French economy were secretly controlled by plutocrats. His fight against inflation, he felt, had enabled him to look the plutocrats in the eye and single one of them by name: Finaly.[49]

But the issue of inflation and radical right-wing thought may also be linked in another, more subtle, way. One of Valois's recurring themes was the dangers of a monetary unit, that is, an economic measure, that was itself not fixed: a measuring stick made of rubber. It was imperative that an unchanging measure be put in its place. Could it not be said that a money which was inherently unstable, which did not represent the certainties it used to, and still pretended to, represent, acted as a convenient symbol for a type of social change? Could not inflation stand for the deterioration of other institutions and other values? Was the search for monetary stability a cover for a wider search for a stable, ordered society? Or, to invoke Nolte's terminology, did not inflation represent those atomizing, anonymous aspects of transcendence against which Fascists rebeled?

In a modern industrial society, like the France of the 1920s, or perhaps our own, inflation may come to represent more than a purely monetary and economic problem and its effects may be greater than the economic changes or income readjustments which it directly causes. If it is not understood or controlled, it may become the focus of a generalized distrust of the economic system and of a search for scapegoats. The damage it does to a society can be more than economic, it can also be social, weakening general confidence in the system and reducing the sense of communal solidarity.

Notes

1. Nolte has suggested that Fascism was "characteristic" of this era. So, it could be said, were monetary problems. Ernst Nolte, *Three Faces of Fascism* (New York, 1965), pp. 17–25.
2. See, for example, A.J.P. Taylor, *From Sarajevo to Potsdam* (New York, 1970), p. 130.
3. The economic and monetary ideas of Valois and the Faisceau have received little attention (for bibliography on Valois and the Faisceau, see note 4). Despite its title, Georges Mazières, *L'Oeuvre economique de Georges Valois* (Castelnaudary, 1937), is concerned for the most part with Valois's social ideas and gives limited discussion to strictly economic and monetary points. Marguerite Perrot, in her very interesting *La Monnaie et l'opinion publique en France et en Angleterre de 1924 à 1926* (Paris, 1955), has barely mentioned Valois's campaigns, pp. 131, 165. Typically, those who mention the far right, or particularly the royalists, ignore Valois and mistakenly quote Daudet as representative of royalist economic positions. See, for example, Stephen A. Schuker, *The End of French Predominance in Europe* (Chapel Hill, 1976), p. 80. Discussions of Valois's economic and monetary doctrines can be found in Allen Douglas, Georges Valois and the French Right: A Study in the Genesis of Fascism (unpublished doctoral dissertation, Los Angeles, 1979).
4. On Valois and the Faisceau, see Yves Guchet, *Georges Valois, l'Action Française le Faisceau, La République Syndicale* (Paris, 1975), pp. 7–201; Jules Levey, "The Sorelian Syndicalists," Ph.D Thesis, New York, 1967, pp. 96–160, and by the same author, "Georges Valois and the Faisceau: The

Making and Breaking of a Fascist," *French Historical Studies* VII (1973): 279–304; Zeev Sternhell, "Anatomie d'un mouvement fasciste en France: la Faisceau de Georges Valois," *Revue française de science politique* XXVI (1976): 5–40; Douglas, "Georges Valois."

5.   The best economic survey of the period is Alfred Sauvy, *Histoire économique de la France entre les deux guerres, I (1918–1931)* (Paris, 1965). For a good analysis of the relationships between political and financial problems up to 1924, see Schuker, *French Predominance*; for an excellent view of inside financial and political maneuverings from the viewpoint of one of the most important regents of the Bank of France, see Jean-Noël Jeanneney, *François de Wendel en République* (Paris, 1976), pp. 111–354.

6.   Valois's first systematic exposition of economic doctrine was his *L'Economie nouvelle* (Paris, 1920).

7.   Georges Valois, *La Monarchie et la classe ouvrière* (Paris, 1914), pp. 34–43, 320–323. For Valois's social ideas at the time and particularly his prewar antisemitism, see Douglas, "Georges Valois," pp. 72–84.

8.   On the effects of the end of allied solidarity, see Sauvy, *Histoire*, p. 41.

9.   Valois, *L'État, les finances et la monnaie, Ouevre economique* II (Paris, 1925), pp. 15–22. This volume constitutes a republication of Valois's shorter economic studies from the period, including his regular column in the *Action Française économique et sociale*, a Sunday supplement. They are arranged in chronological order.

10.   By this Valois meant an economy in which everyone was organized for sale but not for purchase. Hence workers would bid up wages and employers, unable to hold down wages, were free to raise prices, Valois, *L'Economie nouvelle*, pp. 184–85.

11.   Valois, *L'État, les finances*, pp. 27–34.

12.   Valois, *L'État, les finances*, pp. 40–43, 118–21. Valois did not believe that the law of supply and demand really existed in the economy, see Valois, *L'Economie nouvelle*, pp. 78–82, and "La valeur et la loi de l'offre et de la demande," in *L'Economie nouvelle, Oeuvre economique* I (Paris, 1924), pp. 5–76. See also, Douglas, pp. 123–25.

13.   This level of causation would subsequently receive increasing attention.

14.   Valois, *L'État, les finances*, pp. 161–64.

15.   Valois, *L'État, les finances*, pp. 4, 43, 46, 123–25, 176–77. Paper profits were caused by the fact that when businessmen sold a product they did so in a climate of higher prices than when they bought the materials for that product.

16.   Valois, *L'Economie nouvelle*, pp. 8–9, 52–53, 55, 229–34; Georges Coquelle and Georges Valois, *Intelligence et production* (Paris, 1920), p. 14. See also, Douglas, pp. 129–33.

17.   Sauvy, *Histoire*, . 159.

18.   Valois, *L'État, les finances*, pp. 36, 75–76.

19.   Valois, *L'État, les finances*, pp. 44–50, 78, 80–81, 83–85.

20.   Valois, *L'État, les finances*, pp. x, 37, 50–52, 54–55, 84–87.

21.   For the problems of "honesty" in the repayment of bondholders involved with revaluation, see Sauvy, *Histoire*, pp. 90–91.

22.   Valois, *L'homme contre l'argent, Souvenirs de dix ans* (Paris, 1928), pp. 39–40, 48–50; Valois, "Considérations sur l'inventeur à propos de l'in-

vention de Jacques Arthuys le 'Solart,'" *Cahiers bleus*, No. 113, July 25–August 1, 1931, p. 23; Valois, *L'État, les finances*, p. x, p. 88; Jacques Arthuys, *Le Problème de la Monnaie* (Paris, 1921), entire, and especially pp. 39–60, 177–89.

23. Valois, "Les Semaines Economiques, préface des États," *Cahiers des États-Généraux* (henceforth *CEG*), No. 4, July 1923, pp. 307–309; Valois, *L'homme contre*, p. 51.

24. Valois, *L'homme contre*, pp. 36, 50–52, 88; "Le Comité Central de la Laine," *CEG*, No. 8, December 1923–January 1924, pp. 330–34; "La Semaine de la Monnaie," *CEG*, No. 8, p. 368; "Qui-es-tu?" *CEG*, No. 11, June 1924, pp. 626–28, 631; "La Bataille culturelle," *Cahiers bleus*, No. 119, May 23, 1932, pp. 14–15. For the importance of the *Journée industrielle*, see Claude Bellanger, et al., *Histoire générale de la presse française*, III (Paris, 1972): 494.

25. Valois, *L'homme contre*, pp. 52–53; "La Semaine de la Monnaie," *CEG*, No. 8, pp. 368–74; Valois and Marie de Roux in *L'État, les finances*, pp. 169–84.

26. Jacques Arthuys, *Comment éviter la Hideuse Banqueroute* (Paris, 1922), pp. 35–63, 211–12, 261–75; Valois, *L'État, les finances*, pp. 195–99, 266–67; Valois, *L'État syndical et la représentation corporative*, Oeuvre economique III (Paris, 1927), pp. 115–25. Sauvy explained the unreasonableness of the debt burden when he noted that with constant francs the service of the postwar debt would demand ten times the sacrifice in revenue as had been consented for the prewar debt, with double the productivity, five times the sacrifice, Sauvy, *Histoire*, pp. 80–81.

27. "Déclaration de la direction," *CEG*, No. 1, April 1923, pp. 2–3; "La Réforme de la représentation," *CEG*, No. 1, pp. 10–12.

28. "Déclaration de la direction," *CEG*, No. 1, pp. 2–3; "La Réforme de la représentation," *CEG*, No. 1, pp. 10–12; Valois, "Réponse au 'Provincial' et à quelques critiques de Paris et de Province," *CEG*, No. 2, May 1923, p. 149; Valois, *L'État syndical*, pp. 155–58; Valois, *L'homme contre*, pp. 57–59.

29. For the history of the États-Généraux movement, see the *CEG* published from 1923 to 1925 and Valois, *L'homme contre*, pp. 57–98. See also, Douglas, pp. 165–96.

30. Valois, *L'État, les finances*, pp. 211–20. Cf. Schuker, *French Predominance*, pp. 35–36.

31. Valois, *L'État, les finances*, pp. 269–72, 277–91, 333–40; Valois, "La Mystère de la rue de Rivoli," *CEG*, No. 5, September 1923, pp. 414–32.

32. Valois, *L'État, les finances*, pp. 325–40, 358–408; Valois, *L'homme contre*, p. 90.

33. Valois, *L'État, les finances*, pp. 409–416, 425–32. Schuker's analysis, interestingly, fails to account for this law, Schuker, *French Predominance*, pp. 55–56.

34. Jacques Arthuys, "La Crise financière," *CEG*, No. 9, February-March 1924, p. 394. This packet of bonds, "the largest volume of long-term government obligations since the end of the war," amounted to approximately 30 billion francs, as large as the annual budget, Schuker, *French Predominance*, pp. 134–35, 151.

35. Valois, *L'État, les finances*, pp. xxv, xxvii, 518–19, 566–67, 570, 627.

36. Valois, *L'État, les finances*, pp. 519, 654–56, 571. Though Valois clearly overshot the mark in his claims regarding Finaly, he was aiming in the right direction. Finaly was mentioned in documents assembled for the ministry of interior as the "financial grey eminence of the Cartel," and he did have an office at his disposal in the finance ministry during the Herriot government. See, in AN F⁷ 12953: A–684, 24 October 1925; A–9.253, 11 November 1925. In AN F⁷ 12954: A.734, 27 January 1926; A.–1.060, 27 May 1926; 2.018, 23 June 1926; A/2.020, 24 June 1926; A.–6.488, 21 July 1926; A–2.079, 27 July 1926; A–7.770, 13 September 1926. See also, Roger Menevée, "M. Horace Finaly," *Les Documents politiques, diplomatiques et financiers*, 18ᵉ année, No. 9, September 1937, p. 416 and Jeanneney, *de Wendel*, p. 308 n. 32, 33 where he reports: "Les noms de Finaly et d'Homberg restent aujourd'hui encore associés, dans le souvenir des vieux 'boursiers,' comme les deux grands 'animateurs' de la corbeille dans ces années vingt." Schuker, *French Predominance*, who does not mention Finaly, describes Herriot as completely lacking sympathetic contacts in the banking world, p. 128.

37. Valois, *L'homme contre*, pp. 118–24.

38. Valois, *L'État, les finances*, pp. x–xii; AN F⁷ 13208, Paris, 18 July 1926; In AN F⁷ 13210: 8 April 1926; Commissaire Spécial, Le Havre, 30 May 1926; 9 October 1926.

39. In AN F⁷ 13208: 20 July 1925; 21 July 1925 and attached copy of poster. Jacques Arthuys, "La Petite épargne" *Le Nouveau Siècle* (henceforth *NS*), No. 22, 23 July 1925, pp. 1–2; Valois, "Le Salaire-Or," *NS*, No. 22 23 July 1925, p. 1. See also, Sauvy, *Histoire*, pp. 319–23.

40. In AN F⁷ 12953: 24 September 1925; A–684, 23 October 1925; "La Grève des employés de banque et le salaire en francs-or," *NS*, No. 24, 6 August 1925, p. 1; Lusignac, "Ce qu'il fallait dire à Painlevé," *NS*, No. 26, 20 August 1925, p. 5; "La Grève et l'emprunt," *NS*, No. 27, 27 August 1925, p. 5; L.(usignac), "Fin de mois," *NS*, No. 28, 3 September 1925, p. 5; L.(usignac), "Fin de grève," *NS*, No. 30, 17 September 1925, p. 5.

41. Valois, *L'homme contre*, pp. 240–41. In AN F⁷ 13210: 21 May 1926; 22 May 1926; 25 May 1926.

42. AN F⁷ 13210, VL./, Paris, 23 October 1926; APP 344, 2.649, "Le Nouveau siècle," 18 February 1927.

43. Valois, "Le Prestige et l'illusion," *NS*, No. 388, 4 December 1926, p. 1; Valois, "L'attitude du Faisceau," *NS*, No. 7, 13 February 1927, p. 5. Inside the Bank of France, Charles Rist reported that a group was forming to speculate on the rise of the franc, Émile Moreau, *Souvenirs d'un gouverneur de la Banque de France* (Paris, 1954), p. 148.

44. Valois, "Pour défendre le franc . . ." *NS*, No. 6, 6 February 1927, p. 2; Valois, "L'attitude du Faisceau," *NS*, No. 7, 13 February 1927, p. 5.

45. Valois, *L'homme contre*, p. 318; Valois, "Vers la Deuxième Semaine de la Monnaie," *NS*, No. 9, 27 February 1927, p. 1; "Les Animateurs — Octave Homberg," *NS*, No. 6, 6 February 1927, p. 1; De la Porte, "Préface," in De la Porte (Ed.), *L'Avenir de la République* (Paris, 1927), p. 24; "IIᵉ Semaine de la Monnaie," brochure in AN F⁷ 13212.

46. Valois, *L'homme contre*, pp. 265–66, 278. For some contemporary — and similar — judgments of Italian monetary policy, see Moreau, *Souvenirs*,

pp. 140–59 and J. M. Keynes, *Essays in Persuasion* (New York, 1963), pp. 190–93.

47. See, for example, Jeanneney, *De Wendel*, pp. 316–54.

48. Valois, *L'Economie nouvelle*, pp. 114, 164–65. This was, for example, the solution of Gottfried Feder with his notion of interest slavery. See, for example, Nolte, *Three Faces*, pp. 411–12. La Tour du Pin, an earlier economic and corporative theorist for the royalists, had also condemned interest, La Tour du Pin Chambly de la Charce, *Vers un ordre social chrétien* (Paris, 1929), pp. 72–82.

49. Valois, *L'homme contre*, p. 353.

Economic Problems and Proposed Solutions in the Mid-Nineteenth Century: Marx's Analysis and Critique

ROSLYN WALLACH BOLOGH

The past decade has seen Marx's influence inspire much literature and contribute to the development of new theoretical perspectives in most if not all substantive areas of sociology, including the development of at least one new area: sociology of the economy. This influence together with that of the phenomenological concern for the foundations of social phenomena, the methods for producing the social phenomena of everyday life (e.g., Garfinkel, 1967; Berger, 1966) have combined to produce a growing interest in Marx's method among some philosophers and social scientists, particularly sociologists (e.g., Bologh, 1979; Sayer, 1979; Applebaum, 1978; Gould, 1978; Nicolaus, 1968; Althusser, 1970, 1969).

The present work shares this interest. It attempts to compare the analysis of, and solutions to, particular economic problems by economists of Marx's day with the analysis and critique of those economists' works by Marx. Not only is such a comparison instructive for understanding the difference between non-Marxist economic methods of analysis and Marx's sociological method (i.e., treating economic phenomena in terms of their foundation in social relations), it also has implications for understanding the economic problems of our day (inflation and recession) from the critical sociopolitical-economic perspective of Marx.

Marx implies that economic crises are an integral feature of capitalism and that no economic solution, however radical, will be able to solve the problem of recurring economic crises. Marx grounds economic crisis in the capitalist mode of production. Bourgeois economists, unlike Marx and the classical political economists who inquire into the foundations of economic phenomena, treat those foundations as unproblematic. Their concern is with solutions, policy recommendations, that leave the foundations unexamined. Unlike the economists of his time, Marx showed how economic crises must be understood as an inevitable feature of capitalism. Even where modern economists do recognize this in their conception of the business cycle, we still find a crucial difference between them and Marx. They accept the periodic recurrence of recessions, for example, as inevitable, but they show a curious lack of outrage, a matter-of-fact acceptance, that contrasts markedly with Marx's outlook. Although one can argue that this difference is attributable to difference in personality, difference in moral outlook, difference in personal sympathies and concerns as well as in class alliances, I would argue that there is a dialectical relationship between these differences and their modes of analysis.

That is, by being an agent of capital, as Marx would put it, a bourgeois economist would not inquire into the grounds of capital, the social relations that make capital possible, but would simply treat the existence of capital as natural and unproblematic. Therefore, if the business cycle and recessions are a necessary feature of capitalist production, there is no more reason for moral outrage than there is for any natural catastrophe. One might sympathize with the victims of the catastrophe, but sympathy and moral outrage are not the same. Treating capital not as a natural thing but as grounded in social relations, on the other hand, leads to, and presupposes, the awareness that those social relations could be otherwise. Economic crises, then, would be seen as no more natural than capital. Abolishing the essential social relations that make capital possible would also entail abolishing those economic problems that are intrinsic to capitalism. Seeing economic crises as grounded in social relations that could be otherwise makes moral outrage possible. Seeing economic crises as natural and unavoidable makes moral outrage impossible. Hence we can have the complacency of economists like Martin Feldstein who argue for increasing unemployment as necessary for eliminating inflation.

It is not that unemployment or recession could be and should be avoided in dealing with inflation. The bourgeois economist and Marx might agree that unemployment or recession is inevitable under certain circumstances. The bourgeois economist would treat those circumstances as natural, whereas Marx would treat them as socially produced and socially alterable although requiring a social revolution in the mode of production, an elimination of capital. Hence an economist such as Feldstein can counsel increasing the unemployment rate as a solution to the problem of inflation without feeling or expressing any moral outrage at the necessity of such a solution. Marx, on the other hand, would analyze the social conditions that make inflation possible, to show that a radical change in those social conditions is necessary for eliminating the possibility of inflation. Marx, therefore, would be outraged not at the economist or his solution, but at the social conditions that produce the possibility of the problem and hence of the economist's solution.

In order to understand better the difference between a concrete economic approach to economic problems and Marx's analytic approach which inquires into the presuppositions or foundations of the problem, let us examine the analysis and "radical" proposals of an influential French economist of the time, Alfred Darimon, and then Marx's critique. Darimon's analysis is particularly interesting because of its resemblance to contemporary monetaristic theorizing.

Darimon explained the economic crisis of the time as due to the flow of gold out of the country and the Bank of France's need to maintain reserves by discouraging borrowing precisely when the "public" most needed to borrow (p. 119). Darimon attributed the gold drain to the crop failures and the subsequent need to import grain from foreign nations who required payment in gold. In addition he referred to the numerous expensive but unproductive undertakings associated with the industrial exhibition in Paris. Marx further cites the failure of the silk harvest and the consequent purchase of silk in vast quantities from China. (Marx's mentioning of the silk points out the irony of capitalist production where a crisis in the production of silk, a luxury item not needed by workers, can result in a crisis affecting those workers; they become dependent on producing superfluous or unnecessary goods.) Darimon also "forgets" the speculations and ventures launched abroad plus the unproductive expenditures of the Crimean War, including borrowings of 750 million francs.

Marx mentions that the loss of capital is due not solely to the failure of domestic production because "the losses in domestic production, in any case, were not an equivalent for the employment of French capital abroad (p. 121)." In other words, even if there had been no crop failure, there would have been a crisis because more capital had been lost (through unsuccessful foreign investment or speculation) than would have been produced had the crops been successfully harvested. The crisis therefore was a result of the loss incurred through capitalist speculation abroad and the financing of the Crimean War as well as the grain and silk failures.

Darimon analyzes the economic crisis as due to the bank's need to maintain its reserves of gold in order to back the currency at a time when there is a great demand for that gold. Given this analysis, his solution reduces to the need for France to go off the gold or metal standard. In this way, the bank would not need to maintain its reserves of gold, and instead of discouraging borrowing, it could make loans available to the "public" and the crisis could be averted.

Marx inquires whether the "philanthropic" grain merchants who represent the "public" in relation to the bank do what Darimon asks of the bank. Do they let the people have the grain on easier terms because the people at that time had the greatest need of it? "Or did they not rather rush to the bank in order to exploit the increase of grain prices, the misery of the public and the disproportion between its supply and its demand?" Marx ends with the ironic statement, "And the bank should be made an exception to the general economic laws? (p. 120)." Thus, according to Marx, the bank's policy of increasing the price of its loans complies with the law of supply and demand, the same "agreeable custom of life" that the borrowers, the grain merchants, follow, and which makes them eager to borrow in the first place. In other words, the borrowers who would be helped by Darimon's solution, want to borrow in order to exploit the misery or need of the French public by buying grain in order to then sell it at an even higher price at a time when there is great demand due to decreased supply.

But Marx does not simply point out the inconsistency in Darimon's analysis of the bank's practices as compared to the grain merchants' practices. He goes on to take Darimon's solution and carry it out to its logical end, showing its inability to solve the problem. He does this by showing that the bank would still have to raise the terms of its discounting even if it did not have to maintain reserves due to the elimination of the gold standard. With the elimination of the metal standard, the bank would no longer have to keep a certain amount of gold on hand in order to back the currency. Instead of the precious metals backing the money, the nation's stock of products and its labor force would back it. But due to the situation cited earlier, that wealth had diminished. Therefore, the price of the products would increase anyway as the supply decreased.

Marx distinguishes between money as medium of exchange or circulation and capital or productive money that represents the actual exchangeable wealth:

> In order to balance the decrease of domestic production by means of imports, on the one side, and the increase of industrial undertakings abroad, on the other side, what would have been required were not symbols of circulation which facilitate the exchange of equivalents, but these equivalents themselves; not money but capital (p. 121).

Without a metallic base, the bank would have been equally forced to raise the terms of its discounting, i.e., raise the price of credit. Making more money available by using the printing press and eliminating the gold basis does not produce more capital, more exchangeable wealth. According to Marx's analysis, the exchangeable wealth of the nation had been absolutely diminished.

> The notes with which it discounts the bills of exchange are at present nothing more than drafts on gold and silver. In our

hypothetical case, they would be drafts on the nation's stock of products and on its directly employable labor force: the former is limited, the latter can be increased only within very positive limits and in certain amounts of time. The printing press, on the other hand, is inexhaustible and works like a stroke of magic (p. 121).

In addition to grain and silk failures, Marx explains that the foreign railway and mining enterprises freeze exchangeable wealth in a form which creates no direct equivalent and, therefore, uses it up for the moment without replacement. Thus the directly exchangeable wealth of the nation is diminished even further. There is also an "unlimited increase in bank drafts. Direct consequence: increase in the price of products, raw materials and labour. On the other side, decrease in price of bank drafts (p. 121)." In order to compensate, the bank would have to raise the price of credit or directly devalue its paper to reflect the decreased value of money relative to commodities (i.e., commodities cost more). Thus the bank's actions, contrary to Darimon's criticism, are perfectly reasonable. With the increase in the price of credit, production would decline.

The bank would not have increased the wealth of the nation through a stroke of magic, (the printing press), but would merely have undertaken a very ordinary operation to devalue its own paper (p. 122).

But with this devaluation would come a "sudden paralysis of production." Therefore, even without the gold standard, even if other countries accepted French currency, simply increasing the money supply would not make available the needed capital; it would only have the effect of a devaluation. This is not to say that eliminating the metal basis might not have a desirable effect, but it would not eliminate the economic crisis. Ultimately, the sourse of crisis is the dependency of production on exchange value. Instead of communal production for direct communal consumption, production is mediated and determined by capital, and capital is dependent on the law of supply and demand.

Against Darimon's analysis, Marx argues that the crisis would be present even if there were no gold standard. The crisis is due not to the drain or outflow of gold or money, but to the loss of capital. In order to understand better the importance of Marx's concept of capital as distinct from money, let us consider the relationship between an important crop failure and an economic crisis of capital without introducing the role of money.

Suppose that the entire English wheat crop were 1 quarter and that this 1 quarter fetched the same price as 30 million quarters previously. . . . If we postulate that the working day necessary to produce 1 quarter = A, then the nation would exchange A × 30 million working days (cost of production) for 1 × A working days (product); the productive force of its capital would have diminished by millions; . . . every working day would have depreciated by a factor of 30 million. Every unit of capital would then represent only 1/30,000,000 of its earlier value, of its equivalent in production costs. . . . The increase in the wheat price by a factor of A × 30 million would be the expression of an equivalent depreciation of all other products. . . . (p. 128).

Thus a grain failure means that every working day has produced less than it had previously. The price of grain, then, represented by the working day (labor time) increases relative to the price of all other commodities.

The rise in the grain price = to the fall in the price of all other commodities. The increased cost of production (represented by the price) at which the quarter of wheat is obtained is = to the decreased productivity of capital in all other forms. The surplus used to purchase grain must correspond to a deficit in their prices (p. 128).

The nation, therefore, would find itself in a crisis not confined to grain but extending to all other branches of production in part because their productivity would have diminished and their price depreciated as compared to their value (which is determined by the normal cost of production) and in part because all contracts, obligations, etc., are based on the average price of products.

For example, x bushels of grain have to be supplied to service the state's indebtedness, but the cost of producing these x bushels has increased by a given factor. Quite apart from the role of money the nation would thus find itself in a general crisis. If we abstract not only from money but from exchange value as well, then products would have depreciated and the nation's productivity diminished while all its economic relations are based on the average productivity of its labor (p. 129).

With the crop failure, each working day produces a fraction of its previous production. The nation's actual capital has diminished. The increase in the price of grain would be the expression of an equivalent depreciation of all other products. The sum which must be expended in purchasing grain is a direct subtraction from its capital, its disposable means. Even if the imported grain were as cheap as the domestically produced grain, the nation would still be poorer to the amount of capital not reproduced by the farmers. But the increased demand for imports presupposes a rise in their prices. The rise in grain price means that the surplus used to purchase grain must correspond to a deficit in the purchase of all other products and hence their depreciation.

> The depreciation of most commodities (labor included) and the resultant crisis, in the case of an important crop mishap, cannot therefore be crudely ascribed to the export of gold, because depreciation and crisis would equally take place if no gold whatever were exported and no grain imported. The crisis reduces itself simply to the law of supply and demand, which, as is known, acts far more sharply and energetically within the sphere of primary needs — seen on a national scale — than in all other spheres. Exports of gold are not the cause of the grain crisis, but the grain crisis is the cause of gold exports (p.130).

Marx does recognize that gold and silver (money) can intervene in the crisis and aggravate its symptoms. His basic claim, however, is that economic crisis results from the capitalist framework based on the law of supply and demand, and that only revolutionizing that framework could eliminate the economic crises that are its consequences.

> Darimon and consorts see only the one aspect which surfaces during crises: the appreciation of gold and silver in relation to nearly all other commodities; they do not see the other side, the depreciation of gold and silver or of money in relation to all other commodities . . . in periods of so-called prosperity. . . . Since this depreciation of metallic money (and of all kinds of money which rest on it) always precedes its appreciation, they ought to have formulated the problem the other way round: how to prevent the periodic depreciation of money . . . the problem would have reduced itself to: how to overcome the rise and fall of prices. The way to do this: abolish prices. And how? By doing away with exchange value. But this problem arises: exchange corresponds to the bourgeois organization of society. Hence one last problem: to revolutionize society economically (p. 134).

Marx reasons that the appreciation of gold and silver is preceded by their depreciation which corresponds to periods of "so-called" prosperity and that the problem reduces to the rise and fall of prices which must be abolished to abolish economic crises. There was another solution proposed to eliminate the effects of the rise and fall of prices and the fluctuations in the value of money. This was the proposed time chit solution put forth by socialists concerned about the declining value of the worker's wage. Time chits were a new form of money.

Time chits were to be pieces of paper representing a certain number of hours of labor. If the hour of labor becomes more productive, then the chit of paper which represents it would rise in purchasing power, and vice versa. Given the general economic law that the costs of production constantly decline, that living labor becomes more productive, that the labor time objectified in products constantly depreciates, paper labor money would enjoy a constant appreciation. "The worker would reap the joys of the rising productivity of his labour, instead of creating proportionately more alien wealth and devaluing himself as at present (pp. 135–36)."

Marx's analysis of this proposal provides a key to his understanding of how capital operates and how so-called prosperity does not necessarily result in propserity for the worker. In the first place, he explains, if we have money, even in the form of time chits, then we have the accumulation of money, as well as contracts, obligations, etc., which are entered into in the form of this money. "The accumulated chits would constantly appreciate together with the newly issued ones (p. 136)." Those able to accumulate chits would benefit. Those who can accumulate are those who do not need the chits to purchase necessaries and who, therefore, can lend their chits. Because the time chits appreciate, the chits that are paid back are worth more than the chits that were lent. The lender benefits. Assuming that the borrower is a worker, he must still work the same number of hours as before to earn the time chits, but those time chits can now purchase more. The worker-borrower, however, does not realize the value of the appreciated chits. The advantage of increased productivity would go to the lender and not to the worker-borrower.

Even aside from this consequence, Marx points out a basic flaw in the reasoning behind the advocacy of time chits. That is the idea that price can be equated with real value, i.e., cost of production. Marx explains that the value of commodities as determined by labor time is only their average value. If one capitalist can lower his price on a commodity due to increased productivity, other capitalists will have to follow suit or have their share of the market taken over by the more productive capital. Prices keep changing, moving above or below the cost of production, as capitalists try to increase profit by selling above their cost of production when productivity has increased above that of their competitors, as capitalists try to maintain their share of the market by selling below their cost of production in order to compete with the more productive capital, etc. Prices keep changing, then, because of changes in productivity, changes in supply and in demand. Changes in the cost of production influence changes in supply and demand; changes in supply and demand influence changes in price. The price of a commodity, therefore, tends to be moving either above or below the value of the commodity (based on costs of production).

The aim of replacing metal money or paper money denominated in metal money with labor money denominated in labor time is to equate the real value of commodities (the cost of producing them compared to the cost of producing other commodities) with their price or money value. This is impossible, however, as the value of commodities is only their average value considered over a period of time. "The time-chit representing *average labour time*, would never correspond to or be convertible into *actual labour time* (p. 139)." This is attributable to changes in productivity of labor. Because the time chit representing average labor time is not equivalent to actual labor time, the time chit would achieve a separate existence of its own corresponding to the nonequivalence. It would take on the same functions and entail the same problems as any other money form, such as gold and silver, and would make for additional problems as well.

Because supply and demand affect the price of commodities, the price of commodities can never be the same as their value. Similarly, because the value of a commodity (cost of production) represents average labor time, the time chit (standing for value) could never be convertible into actual labor time as actual labor time always differs from the average. In order for the price of commodities to equal their value, there would have to be a balance of supply and demand, of production and consumption, which would mean an elimination of the market as such (Bologh, 1979, 225). For the time-chit solution to work, the bank that would issue the time chit in exchange for the product would have to be the general buyer and seller. As general buyer and seller, the bank

1. Would need the power to calculate and establish the exchange value of all commodities, the labor time materialized in them in an authentic manner.
2. Would have to determine the labor time in which commodities could be produced with the average means of production available in a given industry, i.e., the time in which they would have to be produced.
3. Would have to determine not only the time in which certain quantities of products were to be produced, and place the producers in conditions which made their labor equally productive — (i.e., would have to balance and arrange the distribution of the means of labor) — but also the amount of labor time to be employed in the different branches of production in order that the needs of the partners in exchange were always satisfied — supply equalling demand, production equalling consumption (Bologh, 1979, 225).

In this situation, workers would not be selling their labor for wages but would receive the value for the product of their labor. Thus the bank would be not only general buyer and seller, but also general producer. Marx says of such a bank:

In fact either it would be a despotic ruler of production and trustee of distribution or it would indeed be nothing more than a board which keeps the books and accounts for a society producing in common (pp. 155–56).

In order for the time-chit solution to work, the bank would have to wrest power from capital and become a despotic ruler of production, as it is capital, in and through the market, that now determines the three foregoing conditions. Or the rest of society would have to wrest power from capital in order to be able, then, to produce communally. If the bank were not a despotic ruler of production but simply a bookkeeping organ for "a society producing in common" (as opposed to a capitalistic society producing on the basis of individual producers who exchange), then time chits would no longer be an issue, for there would be no discrepancy between price and value. Thus, in order for the time-chit solution to work, the problem which it solves would already have had to be eliminated (Bologh, 226).

RELEVANCE FOR CONTEMPORARY PROBLEMS OF INFLATION AND RECESSION

By way of conclusion, let us try to relate Marx's analysis as just presented to the problems of inflation and recession. Although the totality of Marx's analysis is a great deal more complex than the material presented, that does not preclude the possibility of making inferences from this material. Marx's analysis of the proposed solutions to the economic problems of the 1850s suggests that there are two analytically distinct types of inflation. The first is the type that accompanies periods of so-called prosperity; the other is the type that occurs as a result of a decline in relative productivity.

Prosperity, defined as an increase in productivity, means that it costs less to produce and hence to purchase necessities as the decrease in cost takes the form of lower prices within competitive capitalism. The surplus capital is now available for additional investment that can produce more wealth. The worker's dollar now buys more; the surplus purchasing power can either go into savings, in which case it helps to make more credit available for business, or it can be used for consumption, to purchase more items, with the money again going to business where it provides the incentive and capital for increased production.

If the workers' dollar is paying off past debts, however, they do not realize the increased value of that dollar; they give it up to the lender. The lender benefits from the situation. Money, therefore, is made available for lending, making possible increased capital investment and production. Even if there are no past debts, contracts can be made whereby monopolistic suppliers of desired goods can demand more money, i.e., raise prices and thereby command surplus value (increasing purchasing power) that has been produced through increased productivity. Thus rents can be raised, prices of monopoly-controlled goods raised, and labor would then be unable to realize that increased purchasing power; instead the monopoly capitalist would realize it. Workers might not lose anything compared to the past, except perhaps some jobs as increased productivity might result in the unemployment of some workers! But they would not have gained anything either at a time when their labor had produced more wealth. During prosperity, then, labor would be in a worse position compared to monopoly capital than before.

On the other hand, given the existence of organized labor (which corresponds with the development of monopoly capital), workers can take advantage of this period of so-called prosperity by trying to make contracts favorable to themselves in order to increase their share of the increased wealth produced to pay for the inflated prices of monopoly goods and to realize some of the surplus as well. We then have a situation of competition over the surplus with monopoly capitalists increasing their prices to realize more of the surplus produced, and labor increasing their price (wage demands) in order that they may realize more of the surplus produced. Needless to say, workers as a total class (including the unemployed, the unorganized, etc.) do not come out as victors in this competitive struggle with capital over the surplus, although for some, wages may rise to keep pace with, and in some instances outpace, rises in prices, perhaps even keeping pace with increases in productivity. Analytically, the inflation identified with increased prices during a period of increased productivity does not hurt the economy as a whole, as compared to the type of inflation to be considered next, but it does hurt different sectors. It does not hurt the economy as a whole in the sense that it does not result in a reduction of capital available for reinvestment; i.e., it does not result immediately in cutbacks in production or a recession.

There is another type of inflation which does negatively affect reinvestment and production; inflation due to decreased productivity or increased costs, i.e., when there is an important crop failure, a decline in productivity relative to costs, an increase in the price of some necessary imported commodity that is not matched by increased domestic productivity. In this situation, the increased costs and increased prices cannot be paid for out of increased productivity, increased surplus value. Capitalists and workers compete with, and among, each other to pass the increased costs on to somebody else rather than competing over the appropriation of a surplus. Because of the increased costs, there is less surplus produced and realized, hence less capital available for reinvestment and production. Contributing to this also is the effect on lenders who find that the dollar paid back is now worth less. Hence there is less incentive for lending and less capital available for lending resulting in higher interest rates. The decline in total value produced compared to cost means that there is a relative decrease in total capital. Inflation is the first attempt to avoid the consequences of this decrease by passing the increased cost on to somebody else. But the decline in capital must lead inevitably to a decrease in capital investment and a decline in production, i.e., a recession.

Thus there are two types of inflation, one due to costs of production having decreased (increased productivity) — and the resultant competition over the surplus creating higher prices — the other due to costs of production having increased — and the attempt to pass on these increased costs through higher prices. The former type of inflation does not involve an immediate recession because there is an increase in total capital which can be used for reinvestment and increased production. Eventually, however, increased production leads to the possibility of "overproduction" requiring an eventual cutback and hence recession. Or the increase in prices may exceed the increase in total capital (surplus value) which means those increased prices will have to be paid for by a decline in the sales and/or prices of all other commodities, resulting in some type of recession. The second type of inflation does involve a more immediate recession as a response to the decrease in capital available for reinvestment. This means a decline in production and employment.

We could expect Marx to conclude, if he were writing about inflation, that changes in value of total capital (which he distinguishes from money) as well as changes in its distribution affect prices and supply and demand. These changes regulate the movement of the economy. Change in total capital corresponds to change in productivity, change in the relation between total value produced and total cost. Hence change in productivity, change in value of total capital, ultimately determines the movement of the economy as a whole. The economy can be conceived as always moving because the relationship between demand and supply keeps changing and the relationship between value and price keeps changing. These changes take the form of inflation and recession.

Marx's analysis of productivity and economic crisis is related to his theory of the declining rate of profit (Carlo, 1979), a theory which others (e.g., Applebaum, 1978; Bologh, 1979; Cogoy, 1973; Hodgson, 1974; Sweezey, 1968, 1974; Wright, 1975; Sayer, 1979; Yaffe, 1973) have already discussed and debated. Some social scientists have attempted to derive and evaluate a general theory of social change from Marx's work (e.g., Schneider, 1971; Van den Berghe, 1963), but as Applebaum (1978) points out, these works generally have neglected to examine Marx's theory of social change in relation to his technical and historically specific analysis of the movement of capital; rather they have tended to take elements from his theory in order to arrive at transhistorical abstract propositions about social change.

Applebaum provides a persuasive critique of this "formalistic" approach to understanding Marx's theory of social change. The present work tries to remedy this problem by focusing on Marx's analysis of particular economic problems. But this paper has neither the intention nor the scope to consider Marx's overall theory of the crises of capitalist production but to consider Marx's analysis and critique of the economic problems and proposed solutions of his day in order to show better their relevance for understanding the likely effects of periods of "so-called" prosperity, inflation, and economic crisis or recession, their relation to the movement of capital and to the situation of labor, i.e., their relation to the capitalist class and to the working class.

With respect to the crisis of recession, which we can expect to follow inflation, particularly inflation of the second kind — that reflecting a decrease in capital due, for example, to increased costs or loss from speculation, crop failure, decrease in productivity relative to foreign competitors, etc., for which capitalists try to compensate by raising prices — Marx explains the resulting devaluation of capital as follows:

> Thus, in a crisis — a general depreciation of prices — there occurs up to a certain moment a general devaluation or destruction of capital . . . the destruction of value and capital which takes place in a crisis coincides with — or means the same thing as — a general growth of the *productive* forces, which, however, takes place not by means of a real increase of the productive force of labor . . . , but by means of a decrease of the existing value of raw materials, machines, labor capacity (p. 446).

Let us substitute the more familiar term, *productivity,* for that of *productive force* and consider the import of the preceding excerpt. Productivity is the relationship between cost per worker/hour and value produced per worker/hour. If cost remains the same and value produced increases, productivity is said to rise. If cost declines and value produced remains the same, productivity is again said to rise. If the value produced cannot be realized (i.e., if the commodity cannot be sold or cannot be sold at its value), then the value produced can be said to decrease. Thus, if costs remain the same, but the value produced decreases (product cannot be sold for its value) then productivity can be said to decline — even if there is no change in the quantity or quality of goods produced per worker/hour. Consider this telling line from the *Wall Street Journal,* 20 May 1980, that appeared in a column headlined "Productivity Fell 0.6% Annual Rate in First Quarter," ". . . the productivity report could be read to indicate that employers were slow to lay off workers during the first quarter even as recession was looming . . ."

We may interpret this to mean that productivity declines when employers are slow to lay off workers when a recession looms, i.e., when it is unlikely that the product will be able to sell at its value. If the amount of value produced (and realized through sale) declines while the cost of labor remains the same or fails to decline proportionately, i.e., employers are slow to lay off workers, then we have a decline in productivity. The decline in productivity in this case does not mean that the quantity or quality of work had declined but that the relationship of demand to supply had declined (hence a decrease in value of the total product) without a corresponding change in the cost of production.

Now that we understand better the economic concept of productivity, let us return to explicating Marx's analysis of crisis in the excerpt cited. The first line equates crisis with general depreciation of prices. This means that the product cannot be sold at its value. Either portions of the total product do not get sold at all, bringing down the price realized for the total product, or the total product does get sold but only at a reduced price. The second line states that in a crisis, there is a general devaluation or destruction of capital. In other words, some machinery, factories, labor cease being employed as production declines. Hence they become momentarily worthless or their value decreases. For example, bankrupt factories, nonoperating machinery, unemployed labor may be sold at reduced prices devaluing the total capital.

Continuing with Marx's statement, we find the somewhat confusing assertion that the destruction of capital means the same thing as a general growth of the productive forces, a growth that takes place by means of a decrease of the existing value of raw materials, machines, labor capacity. If, as we have indicated, productivity is the relationship between cost per worker/hour and value produced per worker/hour, then reducing cost without altering the value produced has the effect of increasing productivity. The destruction or devaluation of capital means the same thing as a decrease in the cost of production which has the effect of producing an increase in productivity, with, as Marx indicates, no real increase in the productive force of labor.

Thus, we may understand the consequences of a decrease in real capital (the situation with which we began) as follows: Although capitalists may initially attempt to avoid the loss of capital by raising prices (inflation of the second type — passing the loss on to others), ultimately the loss of capital or decrease in productivity must have the effect of a general devaluation and destruction of capital as a means of raising productivity through decreasing the cost of production, i.e., through a recession or economic crisis.

SUMMARY

This work draws the following implications and conclusions from Marx's analysis:

1. Marx's work differs from most economists' in that the latter treat the foundations of capital as unproblematic whereas Marx's method consists of inquiring into those foundations.
2. The difference between treating the foundations of capital as a taken for granted given and treating capital as founded on social relations that could be otherwise results in the difference between the moral neutrality of most economists with respect to their attitude toward the devastating effects on labor of fluctuations in the economy and the moral outrage of Marx.
3. Prosperity does not necessarily benefit labor, but it does benefit capital.
4. There are two types of inflation: one that accompanies so-called prosperity (an increase in productivity) and one that is an attempt to compensate for a decrease in total value produced. The first type, stemming from the competition among capitalists and between capital and organized labor for the increased value produced, does not result immediately in crisis (decline in production), but the second type, stemming from the attempt by capital to pass on increased costs, does lead directly to recession (decline in production because of decrease in capital).
5. Productivity is not necessarily a measure of the labor process but a ratio of cost to value produced. Therefore, if total exchange value produced decreases due to change in demand, while costs remain the same, then productivity and value of capital decline even if the total items produced remain the same. If total exchange value produced remains the same, but costs of materials needed for production increase, then productivity and value of capital declines in this case as well.
6. In order to compensate for declining productivity (decreasing value of capital), costs must be reduced, hence workers must be laid off. In other words, labor must sacrifice in order to raise the value of capital.
7. Ultimately changes in the relation of supply to demand, and changes in the relation of cost to total value realized (which reflect and affect changes in prices), determine the movement and value of capital: its appreciation and depreciation. This movement creates the economic problems of inflation and recession as well as the situation of so-called prosperity.

8. Because production is determined by capital, and the value of capital changes with changes in productivity and changes in supply and demand, crises of production (e.g., recessions) will continue to recur until production ceases to be determined by capital.

Notes

1. All page numbers in parentheses after quotations refer to Karl Marx, *Grundrisse*, trans. Martin Nicolaus (New York, 1973).

References

Althusser, Louis. *For Marx*. trans. Ben Brewster (New York, 1969).

Althusser, Louis, and Balibar, E. *Reading Capital*, trans. Ben Brewster (New York, 1970).

Appelbaum, Richard. "Marx's Theory of the Falling Rate of Profit," *American Sociological Review* 43 (1978): 67–80.

Berger, Peter, and Luckmann, Thomas. *The Social Construction of Reality* (New York, 1966).

Bologh, Roslyn Wallach. *Dialectical Phenomenology: Marx's Method* (London, 1979).

Carlo, Antonio. "Inflation," *Theory and Society* 7 (1979): 397–415.

Cogo, Mario. "The Fall of the Rate of Profit and the Theory of Accumulation: A Reply to Paul Sweezy," *Bulletin of the Conference of Socialist Economists*, 1973, 52–67.

Feldstein, Martin. "Inflation and Supply Side Economics," *Wall Street Journal*, 20 May 1980, p. 22.

Garfinkel, Harold. *Studies in Ethnomethodology* (Englewood Cliffs, N.J., 1967).

Gould, Carol. *Marx's Social Ontology* (Cambridge, Mass., 1978).

Hodgson, Geoff. "The Theory of the Falling Rate of Profit," *New Left Review* 84 (1974): 55–82.

Marx, Karl. *Grundrisse: Introduction to the Critique of Political Economy*, trans. Martin Nicolaus (1857; New York, 1973).

Nicolaus, Martin. "The Unknown Marx," *New Left Review* 48, 1968; reprinted in R. Blackburn, (Ed.) *Ideology in Social Sciences* (New York, 1973).

Sayer, Derek. *Marx's Method: Ideology, Science and Critique in Capital*.(N.J., 1979).

Schneider, Louis. "Dialectic in Sociology," *American Sociological Review* 36 (1971): 667–78.

Staff Reporter. "Productivity Fell 0.6% Annual Rate in First Quarter," *Wall Street Journal*, 29 May 1980, p. 2.

Sweezy, Paul. *The Theory of Capitalist Development* (New York, 1968).

Sweezy, Paul, "Some Problems in the Theory of Capitalist Accumulation," *Monthly Review* 26 (1968): 1.

Van den Berghe, Pierre. "Dialectic and Functionalism: Toward a Theoretical Synthesis," *American Sociological Review* 28 (1963): 695–705.

Wright, Erik Olin. "Alternative Perspectives in the Marxist Theory of Accumulation and Crisis," *The Insurgent Sociologist* 6 (1975): 5–39.

Yaffe, David S. "The Marxian Theory of Crisis, Capital, and the State," *Economy and Society* 2 (1973): 186–232.

Part 3
Policy Issues

Institutional Roots of American Inflation

HYMAN P. MINSKY

Inflation is a movement of prices through historical time such that representative averages of prices increase. It always takes place in a specific evolving institutional setting. The acute and disturbing inflation that began in the United States in the middle of the 1960s is taking place in a capitalist economy with an institutional framework that, in large part, is a legacy of the first Roosevelt administration. Today's institutional set-up therefore reflects perceptions of the "economic problem" of some fifty years ago.

The reforms of 1933–36 were a response to the great contraction that began in 1929 and culminated in the thorough breakdown of the financial structure and the economy in the winter of 1933.[1] The institutional reforms of 1933–36 aimed to create an economic environment in which a huge decline in employment and a collapse of prices and asset values could not happen again. The record of income, employment, output prices, and asset values since 1936 shows that 1929–33 has not been repeated. There has not been a depression or serious price deflation since 1936. Furthermore acute inflation, in the absence of war, has become a problem for the United States only since the mid-1960s.[2]

It is necessary to examine the relations between the institutional environment and the performance of the economy to determine why there has not been a great depression with prolonged unemployment and serious declines in prices and asset values since World War II and why inflation became a problem only after the mid-1960s.

A large part of the institutional reforms of the 1930s was a response to a contemporary view that the Great Depression was a result of uncontrolled price deflation that made an already large burden of debt intolerable. Two monumental studies under the auspices of the Twentieth Century Fund —*The Internal Debts of the United States* (edited by Evans Clark; 1933) and *Debts and Recovery 1929 to 1937* (written by A. G. Hart) — lay out an overindebtedness view of the origins of the great contraction and a burden-of-debt explanation of the Depression's depth and duration.[3]

The proposition that the combination of price deflation and an excessive debt burden was responsible for the severity and duration of the Great Depression is the guide to the reforms of the 1930s. The reforms were carried through in the absence of a theory of aggregate demand. Keynes's *The General Theory of Employment Interest and Money*, which sets out the theory of aggregate demand that still underlies much of the analysis of the performance of the economy as a whole, was published in 1936 (the preface is dated December 1935).[4] Keynes's ideas and analysis did not filter through to the collective mind of the discipline until several years passed and it took several decades for policy makers consciously to apply the ideas. Furthermore, Keynes's revolution became part of the intellectual baggage of advisers and policy makers in a corrupt Hicks-Hansen form.[5] Several generations of economists dealing with economic theory ignored those parts of Keynes's *General Theory* which dealt with "The City" and financing relations, i.e., the specific institutional framework within which Keynes's theory was relevant. As a result of these intellectual blinders, policy makers ignored banking and financing interrelations when they acted on the precepts of simplified (if not vulgarized) Keynesianism. Keynes's critique of capitalism because of the instability due to capitalist financial relations was ignored as Keynes was transformed into the simpleminded and banal prescriptions for fiscal policy that passes for "Keynesian" economics.[6]

The core of *The General Theory* is an analysis of the relations between investment, capital-asset ownership, and financing. Banks finance business. The liabilities of banks, including money in the form of currency and demand deposits, are created as banks engage in financing. Both investment and the liability structures of the owners and users of capital-assets are related to money. In particular, the finance available from banks and other institutions affects the price level of capital-assets. Such financing creates *liabilities* to banks and financial institutions which are commitments to pay money on a schedule determined by outstanding contracts. Thus Keynes's integration of money and the pricing of capital-assets provides a theoretical foundation for a burden-of-debt analysis of the cyclical behavior of capitalism. Both the monetarist and the standard Keynesian version of today's standard theory ignore the relations between system performance, which generates the cash flows that are available to meet payment commitments, and the payment commitments in the debt structure.

During the first days of the New Deal, an attempt was made to use the quantity theory of money to raise prices. The policy instrument was the price of gold; by raising the price of gold in dollars the value of that which many then and many now think of as "really" money increased. This program was deemed a failure; it did not produce quick enough results for the "crisis" atmosphere. Once the the policy of increasing the money supply was deemed a failure and in the absence of a theory of aggregate demand, policy turned to preventing price declines and inducing price increases by intervening in particular markets.

Agricultural price supports, oil-pumping allotments, regulation of trucking, power, and communication, and doctrines of "fair" competition (NRA) and fair "labor standards" became the backbone of policy. In particular a view that market power was benign, for it made for price stability and "fair" wages, undermined the "in principle" commitment to competitive markets. The acceptance of corporations big enough to have market power as economically desirable was a keystone of the first (NRA) New Deal.

Only briefly, in the stillborn third New Deal of 1938, was the proposition advanced that market power, and thus the bigness that leads to market power, is responsible for price increases that can retard expansion. The *administered-price theory* of Gardner Means, to the effect that market power leads to an absorption of a stimulus to aggregate demand by price increases, is readily transformed into a theory that the exercise of market power leads to inflationary pressures in an economy with stabilized or growing aggregate demand.[7] A combination of a realistic view that market power if available will be used and a sophisticated view of the banking process, which makes the supply of financing responsive to the demand for financing, will go far toward a theory of inflation that rests upon the structure of industry.

A second aspect of the Roosevelt reforms dealt with the debt structure and financial institutions. Because the widespread bankruptcies and declines of financial values made many "insecure" for their old age, the development of Social Security can be interpreted as a financial reform. More explicit financial reforms include deposit insurance, the Securities and Exchange Commission, the fully amortized and government guaranteed home mortgage, the outlawing of interest on demand deposits, and the attempts to simplify financial structures.

A third aspect of the institutional changes that date from Roosevelt is the huge increase in the relative size of the federal government as a purchaser of goods and services, source of transfer payments, regulator, and taxer.

During World War II, the government ran a huge deficit. As a result, by the end of the war an enormous government debt existed. Government debt was the major asset in the portfolio of banks. In addition, because of the profitability of wartime business and the limited private investment opportunities in a regime of wartime controls, at the end of World War II business debt was much reduced and business was a large-scale owner of government debt. The simple liability structure and simple set of financial institutions that had been advocated in the 1930s by reformers like Henry Simons had been inadvertently achieved.[8] A financial structure such as ruled in 1946 is robust in that significant increases in interest rates will not raise the carrying costs of assets for business (business being largely debt free) and the failure of a particular large financial organization will not trigger a wave of failures.

Even though there was a great potential for lending in the banking system and even though business was so liquid that it could finance capital-asset acquisitions out of accumulated cash and near cash, no sustained inflation by the standards of the 1970s took place in the late 40s and 50s. Instead of a quick rush to using the liquidity derived from the war, there was, after World War II, a 20-year period of on the whole tranquil progress. These 20 years between 1946 and 1966 constitute a "golden age" of capitalism in the United States and in the other advanced capitalist economies.

Our current inflation dates from the mid-1960s. The transition from the generally tranquil progress of 1946–66 to the turbulent cyclical inflation *cum* quasi stagnation of 1967 to date needs to be explained. No obvious, legislated institutional change occurred that explains the change in behavior. Of course, a great deal in history can be used for a special-circumstances explanation of the changes: divine wrath for the assassinations of the 1960s, deserved punishment for electing Nixon, the war in Vietnam, and the hubris of Johnson's Great Society are all candidates for special-circumstances "explanations." These explanations neither explain the persistence of instability into the 80s nor offer any handles by which we can do better in the future.

Although there were no striking legislated changes in the middle 1960s, over the postwar period there were cumulative changes in the portfolios of households, businesses, and banks which changed the relations between the payment commitments on debts and the income and cash in hand of these various groupings. Over the years 1950–67 a marked transformation in the financial structure took place. The investment boom of the mid-1960s and the conglomerate movement among corporations of the same period affected the liability structure of business. By the mid-1960s the financial structure of the United States was "ready" for a financial crisis. In the past, financial crises had ushered in deep depressions.[9]

The Federal Reserve "fights" bursts of inflation by attempting to constrain the rate of growth of bank deposit liabilities. Banks make their profits by acquiring earning assets, and they finance their position in earning assets by a variety of liabilities. Ever since the late 50s and early 60s, when the excess ability to finance stored in government bonds during the war years was pretty much used up, banks have reacted to Federal Reserve constraints on their reserve base by innovating and developing liabilities which economize on reserves. In addition, even as banks "avoid" Federal Reserve constraints, innovations by nonbank financial institutions and the emergence of various types of open market paper in response to perceived profit opportunities make the supply of finance responsive to the demand for finance.[10]

One way the institutional change in finance can be measured is by examining the change in the way banks have made positions over the post-World War II era. In the immediate post-World War II era banks were mainly holders of Treasury debt. If operations led to a cash shortage or cash surplus the organization would buy or sell short-term Treasury bills. For giant banks by the middle 1950s, if the shortage or surplus of cash was deemed to be transitory, the bank would lend or withdraw a loan from the dealers in Treasury debt. Furthermore, by the late 1950s the large banks were lending and borrowing federal funds: the federal funds market was the position-making instrument for the giant banks even as the smaller banks still used Treasury bills to make positions.[11]

With the introduction of the marketable certificate of deposit in 1960, the flexibility of bank position-making activity increased. A bank that was short of funds could now raise funds by placing such negotiable certificates. In the first years after 1960, access to the certificate-of-deposit market was pretty much restricted to the very largest banks. As the market grew and matured, almost all banks gained access to the negotiable "CD" market.

The crunch of 1966 saw large banks making positions by borrowing from their overseas affiliates. The growth of the Eurodollar market and its validation by the Federal Reserve in the Franklin National crisis in 1974–75 has led to an increase in the integration of the international banking system. Access to the Eurodollar market has not, however, been generalized to all banks; it still is limited to larger banks.

The evolution has been toward complexity; the bank executive responsible for position making has many more options in 1980 than in earlier years. Position making can take the form of selling off excess Treasury debt, borrowing federal funds, marketing certificates of deposit, issuing commercial paper, borrowing in the Eurodollar market, and executing repurchase agreements using virtually any asset in the portfolio as the instrument first sold and then bought back. The change has been characterized as a shift to "liability management," although in truth banks have always "managed" both sides of their balance sheet.

In a system of complex banks, the link between the "reserves" made available by the central bank and the "credit" accommodations made available by the banking system is much attenuated. There is a schizophrenic aspect to monetary policy, insofar as policy is made on the basis of simple linear relations between reserves and money even as policy makers recognize the complex system of bank and nonbank channels through which the supply of credit responds to changing demands for credit. The complex structure makes the relation between the reserves and credit available a variable that is affected by the ongoing institutional change.

Monetary constraint was effective in 1966, 1969–70, 1974–75, and 1980 in reducing the rate of inflation. In each case, the slowdown in the rate of inflation was accompanied by a significant rise in unemployment. Because of the earlier increases in expenditures on the war in Vietnam there was no "official" recession in 1966. The three other inflations were ended with an official recession.

Each slowdown or recession since the mid-1960s was preceded by a sharp run-up of interest rates and a sharp increase in short-term borrowing. The rise in interest rates and the greater proportion of short-term borrowing increased payment commitments on debts relative to the profits of business and the income from long-term financial assets in portfolios.

A decision to order investment output depends upon the calculation of future profits, which each enterprise does in its own way. Existing capital-assets, which are a legacy of the past and which will be bestowed on the future, are the visible aspects of the productive capacity of an economy. They have a price derived from their expected profits. Newly ordered investment goods will have to yield at least as much in proportion to their cost as the existing capital-assets are earning in proportion to their price. The prices of capital-assets relative to those of investment output along with financing terms yield the demand for investment goods.

A *financial contract* is an exchange of money now for money later. The costs to "borrowers" of financial contracts are the stream of money-later payments. As the streams of money-later payments have an infinite variety of possible time shapes, the various patterns are most readily compared by using the common measure of an interest or discount rate to equate the money-now and the money-later parts of the exchange. The use of an interest rate as a shorthand description of the terms on a financial contract must never obscure the basic relation in a financial contract, which is the exchange of money now for more or less assured money in the future.

The financial system "finances" both production and the carrying of assets. When production is financed the interest payments are costs, just like those of labor and materials, which need to be recovered in output prices. The supply price of outputs rises when interest rates rise. The size of the supply price effect varies with the "gestation" period of the output being produced: it is trivial for quickly produced outputs like most consumer goods and it is very important for outputs with long gestation periods, like nuclear power plants or other investment outputs.

Capital-asset ownership needs to be financed; the debt financing of capital-asset ownership allocates part of the quasi rents that capital-assets are expected to yield to the money-later commitments on debts. When financing costs rise so that more money later must be "promised" for a given amount of money now, the current price of all existing, inherited money-later for money-now contracts falls. But the stock of capital-assets now being used in production is a legacy of past money-now–money-later exchanges that took the form of paying for the production of particular capital-assets. Such capital-assets have current values only as they are expected to yield profits. When the financing costs for holding capital-assets rise, the current value of these inherited capital-assets falls; capital-asset prices fall when interest rates rise.

In principle, an investment decision involves a choice between ordering the production of a new item or purchasing an item from the stock of capital-assets. A rise in interest rates lowers the price of items in the stock of capital-assets even as it raises the supply price of investment output. A rise in interest rates therefore tends to decrease investment unless it is accompanied by a rise in the expected quasi rents that offset the effect of the rise in interest rates. The rise in expected quasi rents can come from two sources: one, substitution of a "permanent prosperity" expectation for a cyclical expectation; two, expected inflation.

Investment in process generates an inelastic demand for financing that "shifts" outward with rising costs of the inputs to producing investment goods and a rising volume of investment in the "pipeline." If the rate of increase of available financing falls short of the rate of increase of the demand for financing due to the increased volume and costs of investment in the pipeline, an explosive increase in interest rates can occur.

Debts not only finance investment output and inputs in the production pipeline, they also finance positions in capital-assets and financial assets. Debt financing of positions in financial assets by individuals is exemplified by margin financing of securities; savings banks, life insurance companies, etc., are institutions that debt finance positions in financial instruments. Any rise in interest rates increases the carrying costs of debts even as it lowers the market value of assets that are in position.

The greater the proportion of debt financing of investment and the greater the proportion of debt financing of positions in capital-assets and financial assets, the more vulnerable the economy is to a rise in interest rates, because a rise in interest rates, by lowering the value of assets and increasing the payment commitments on debts, decreases the margins of safety in asset values and cash flows that makes debt financing viable. The evolution of financial institutions and usages during the on the whole tranquil expansion of 1946–66 transformed the financial structure so that its vulnerability to increases in interest rates increased, even as the institutional arrangements and the structural changes in payment relations, by increasing the likelihood that a shortfall of the rate of increase of available finance relative to the rate of increase of the demand for finance would take place, increased the volatility of interest rates. By the middle 60s the situation was ripe for sharper changes in interest rates, investment and income than hitherto in the postwar period.

Economic policy labors under the handicap that the economic theory that guides policy ignores financing relations. The simple-minded proposition of standard theory is that if the rise in the price level is too great, then the Federal Reserve must decrease the rate of growth of the money supply. This proposition considers the impact of this prescription on payment commitments on debts, the supply prices of output, and the market valuation of capital-assets as irrelevant in determining system behavior. Once the financial system is convoluted and complex, however, the prescribed behavior of the Federal Reserve will lead to a spate of threatened and realized bankruptcies of financial institutions, a collapse of value of debt-financed assets, and a rapid decline in investment. These developments in turn trigger a rush to liquidity which takes the form of a sharp liquidation of inventories.

Thus whether monetary policy actions "pinch off" an expansion or lead to a sharp decline in asset values and investment that threatens an interactive debt deflation depends upon the complexity of institutional arrangements and the structure of liabilities of households, firms, and financial institutions. The evolution of financial institutions and structures from the simple set-up of 1946 to today can be divided into two parts. During the first part, from the war's end until the early 60s, the dominant developments were related to running off and absorbing the extremely liquid position inherited from the war; during the second part, which can be dated from the credit crunch of 1966, new instruments and new institutions dominated in the evolution of financial practices. In both periods, the rate of increase in financing available to business through banks exceeded that made available by central bank policy actions affecting reserves. The first phase, which saw the working off of wartime liquidity was mainly a period of financial market tranquility. During the second period, the new instruments and institutions increased the articulation of receipts, commitments, and refinancing needed for contract fulfillment; financial markets showed ever-increasing volatility in both interest rates and portfolio structures. The increased volatility in financial markets led to increased volatility of output.

The evolution of financial institutions and practices after World War II has taken place in the context of a federal government that is a much bigger proportion of the economy than was true in earlier epochs. There now are a variety of government agencies and a Federal Reserve system that react strongly to a decline in employment or a threat of financial instability. The size of government, active government policy and Federal Reserve lender-of-last-resort interventions have combined to prevent a deep depression in the years since World War II, and most particularly in the years since 1966, when threats of financial instability became regularly recurring phenomena. But the way "big government" and "lender-of-last-resort interventions" combine to brake a threatened deep recession and then to generate a recovery imparts a strong inflationary bias to the economy.

The financial structure rests upon two pillars: one, the flow of income to business firms and households; the other, the price level of assets. In our modern society these pillars have been reinforced by government. The flow of income to business firms and households is now supported by the stabilization of profits that results from big government. The prices of assets are stabilized when the Federal Reserve, acting as the lender of last resort, exchanges its own liabilities for assets, either by outright purchasing or by accepting assets as collateral.

In a capitalist economy, the most important income flows for the fulfillment of the private commitments of the debt structure are gross profits after taxes (what Keynes, following Marshall, called *quasi rents*). If we abstract from details, business profits equals investment plus the government deficit.[12] A big government that is contracyclically active by a combination of automatic fiscal reactions and apt discretionary fiscal initiatives will generate a large enough deficit when investment (and therefore employment) declines so that profits in the aggregate are maintained.

Employment is offered by business as business believes it will make profits from using labor. Government deficits by preventing a free fall of business profits, such as took place after 1929, assure that private employment will be stabilized. Part of the debt structure consists of household debts. With employment "essentially stabilized" because profits are stabilized and with transfer payments sustaining household incomes even as employment falls, the ability of households to "carry" their part of the private debt structure is stabilized during recessions.

In a complex convoluted financial structure, where banks are "managing" their liabilities and there are a wide variety of extra-bank financing channels, an attempt to bring inflation under control by constraining the rate of growth of the reserve base in the face of strong demand for financing from investment in process and holders of assets expected to appreciate at a high rate, will result in a sharp run-up of "interest rates." Interest rates, like a temperture, will "spike." Such a spike leads to a sharp break in investment and places a premium on being liquid to take advantage of the high interest rates on short-term money instruments. One way to become liquid is to sell out positions in assets which are being held for appreciation; a second is by selling off inventories.

As long as the expected price appreciation of inventories and other assets (common stocks, gold, silver, houses, and so on) exceeds the short-term rate of interest by a good margin, holding inventories and assets are "good" bets. Once the short-term rates of interest spikes so that interest rates approach or exceed the expected rate of price appreciation, then liquidity, in the form of short-term interest-earning assets, becomes a "better" bet.

The spiked interest rates lead to a desire to liquidate inventories and positions in assets: a 25 percent cost of money "concentrates the mind" of those who borrow to finance asset holdings of whatever kind, especially assets that yield no cash flow. The spending side of big government, especially the income maintenance programs, and the maintenance of aggregate profits through the deficit which prevents a free fall of unemployment, make it possible to liquidate inventories. Inventory liquidation means that a sharp fall in output and employment takes place, but this of course brings the government's automatic and, with a lag, discretionary fiscal stabilizers into play.

The attempt to liquidate positions in assets leads to a sharp fall in the value of assets that were being held for appreciation. This may be sufficient to compromise the solvency of the units that own the assets and the units that financed the speculation. In the real estate investment trust crisis of 1974–75 and the Hunt/Bache crisis of 1980, the Federal Reserve as a lender of last resort seems to have intervened to assure the solvency of threatened financial institutions.

The government's deficit sustains and even increases gross profits (as in 1975) as output falls. Higher total profits with a smaller output implies that the mark-up per unit of output increases. Not even the most "optimistic" believer in the efficacy of unemployment as a device to halt wage increases or bring about declines in wages holds that the reaction is immediate, i.e., that a tiny rise in unemployment for a very short interval will bring about a large decline in either money wages or the rate of increase in money wages. Therefore a rise in mark-ups will take place even as the money wage out-of-pocket costs do not fall, i.e., supply prices rise. Inflation will continue even as unemployment increases as long as profits are sustained. Sustained profits constrain the rise in unemployment, which means that wages do not fall and scheduled increases take place. As sustained profits are translated into higher mark-ups on unit costs that do not fall, prices continue to increase.

Ever since the credit crunch of 1966 a downturn in income and employment has been ushered in by a financial disturbance. In each case — the credit crunch of 1966, the Penn Central-Chrysler liquidity squeeze of 1969–70, the Franklin National-REIT debacles of 1974–75, and the Hunt/Bache/Chrysler/First of Pennsylvania fiascoes of 1980 — the Federal Reserve and cooperating private and public financial organizations intervened to prevent a "local" embarrassement from becoming a generalized financial crisis.

Each "financial crisis" centered upon a "run" or a "refinancing problem" for some financial institution or usage. In 1966 the use of certificates of deposits by commercial banks, in 1969–70 open market commercial paper, in 1974–75 the Eurodollar market and the short-term financing of REITs, and in 1979–80 the financing of investment bankers by commercial banks were the focal points of the crisis. In each case the Federal Reserve, other government bodies, and private financial institutions intervened to refinance the particular market or institution that stood on the threshold of bankruptcy. This lender-of-last-resort intervention legitimized the instruments and institutions on the brink of default or bankruptcy. As a result of the protection extended to the instrument or institution threatened in the crisis, the instrument or institution survived and was available to finance activity or asset holdings in the subsequent expansion. Therefore each expansion started with a more complex financial structure than the preceding expansions, and during the expansion new complexities were added. Thus a progression of increasing fragility in the financial structure takes place. This progression is associated with higher rates of inflation.

During the sharp downturn of the (successful) inventory liquidation that follows a crisis, the federal government runs a large deficit. This deficit increases the supply of government debt to financial markets. The inventory liquidation decreases bank borrowing by business. Furthermore, the drop in long-term interest rates increases the floating of long-term securities by business, the proceeds of which are used to pay off short-term bank and open market debt. Under these circumstances the commercial banks, whose aggregate ability to hold assets is continuously enhanced by the Federal Reserve's actions, acquire government debt, both newly issued and from the market, at a rapid rate. This change, in which banks increase the proportion of government debt in their portfolios, means that banks store financing which will be available for use during the subsequent expansions.

Once the downturn of income is halted by the combined effects of central bank intervention and the government deficit, the sustained profit of the low-income phase, along with the availability of financing from the "liquid" banking systems and newly legitimized financial markets, leads to a recovery and expansion. At first the recovery may be sufficiently unsatisfactory so that it is labeled a *stagflation,* but quite soon the inflationary boom returns. Beginning with the "credit crunch or financial crisis" as the "peak" we have had three complete cycles of this type: 1966–1969/70, 1969/70–1974/75 and 1974/75–1980.

Thus our inflation has its roots in the institutional structure that has succeeded in preventing a debt deflation. However, much of the detailed intervention into particular markets and the soft policies with respect to market power, mainly corporate but also trade union, that were accepted as part of a structure to prevent deep depressions in the 1930s are quite irrelevant to the way in which deep depressions are in fact prevented in a big-government capitalism. As long as government will run deficits large enough to sustain profits whenever the economy sinks into a recession, a deep depression, such as took place between 1929 and 1933 cannot occur. In the context of present institutions, however, especially the permissive and supportive posture of the authorities with respect to financial innovations that facilitate external financing, successful antidepression intervention leads, with a lag, to inflation such as has plagued our economy since the mid-60s.

The inflation problem cannot be resolved by adjusting the management of monetary and fiscal policy. Technical progress, within a competitive market structure in which money wages are fixed, brings downward pressure on individual prices. A full-employment economy, where full employment is guaranteed by government employment programs for both youth and adults, in the context of competitive markets and stable money wages, is a possible offset to the inflationary pressures which follow from the way threats of a deep depression are offset. If in addition the financial structure and the tax laws are reformed to tilt the economy toward simple equity-based liability structures, the threat of financial crises can be decreased. Under these circumstances, an economy with a government big enough to stabilize profits will not be as "inflation prone" as at present, for the financial complexity that forces lender-of-last-resort interventions will be diminished. A necessary condition for the reestablishment of the tranquil progress that characterized 1946–65 is the reestablishment of a robust financial structure. The open question is "How can this be accomplished?"

Notes

1. Milton Friedman and Anna Jacobson Schwartz, *The Great Contraction 1929–1933* (Princeton, N.J., 1965), gives a view of the collapse that puts too much weight on a simplistic monetary explanation of the collapse. Lester C. Chandler, *America's Greatest Depression 1925–1941* (New York, 1970), is a more balanced view of the Great Depression. John Kenneth Galbraith, *The Great Crash 1929* (Cambridge, Mass., Boston, 1961), is an entertaining view of financial excesses that is not tied down to any precise analytical framework. R. A. Gordon, *Economic Instability and Growth: The American Record* (New York, 1974), is a balanced presentation of the cyclical experience of the era under consideration.

2. With 1967 = 100, the consumer price index was 80.2 in 1955 and 217.4 in 1979. In the 12 years 1955–67 consumer price rose 24.7 percent (1.86 percent per year compounded). In the 12 years 1967–79, consumer prices rose 117.4 percent (6.68 percent per year compounded).

3. Evans Clark, *The Internal Debts of the United States* (New York, 1933); Albert Gailand Hart, *Debts and Recovery* (New York, 1938).

4. John Maynard Keynes, *The General Theory of Employment, Interest, and Money* (New York, 1936).

5. J. R. Hicks, "Mr. Keynes and the Classics: A Suggested Interpretation," *Econometrica* 5 (1937): 147–59. Alvin Hansen, *Monetary Theory and Fiscal Policy* (New York, 1949).

6. Hyman P. Minsky, *John Maynard Keynes* (New York, 1975).

7. Gardner C. Means, *Industrial Prices and Their Relative Inflexibility*, Senate Document No. 13, 74th Cong., 1st sess. (January 1935).

8. Henry C. Simons, *Economic Policy for a Free Society* (Chicago, 1948).

9. No data are presented in this paper. For supporting data see H. P. Minsky, "Financial Resources in a Fragile Financial Environment," *Challenge* 18 (July-August 1975): 6–13; "The Federal Reserve 'Between a Rock and a Hard Place,'" *Challenge* 23 (May-June 1980): 30–36; "Finance and Profits: The Changing Nature of American Business Cycles: Joint Economic Committee of the United States, Compendium," *Business Cycle and Public Policy 1929–79*, forthcoming. Henry Kaufman, James MacKean, and Daniel Foster, *Restoring Corporate Balance Sheets: An Urgent Challenge* (New York, Salomon Brothers, Bond Market Research, July 21, 1980).

10. H. P. Minsky, "Central Banking and Money Market Changes," *Quarterly Journal of Economics* 71 (1957): 171–82.

11. *Ibid.*

12. M. Kalecki, *Selected Essays on the Dynamics of the Capitalist Economy 1933–70* (Cambridge, 1971).

Policy Failure, Growth Failure, and Inflation

PETER S. ALBIN*

This paper presents a structural and political interpretation of the present American inflation. Its compound thesis is that the characteristic structure of the United States economy has remained stable since World War II; that particular features in the postwar structure had been relatively accommodating to conventional growth-oriented policy; but that these same features intensified inflationary tendencies in periods of stagnation and continue to do so. These features, industrial dualism and aberrant growth patterns resulting from firm strategic autonomy, are, by and large, unrecognized in policy determinations although they are well documented in several dissident critical literatures. If the critical view of structure is correct, many policies of the last decade have been misdirected — aimed, in effect, at adjustment of variables in a model with a structure and pattern of reactions significantly different from that of the system which actually exists. As a result of fighting inflation on the wrong battlefield with the wrong weapons, the ability of the actual economy to generate technical advance and real growth has been undermined and is continuing to deteriorate. This means both intensified inflation (above that associated with trends in energy and resource prices) in future years and increasing austerity unless present policy patterns can be checked. Although there has been some recent recognition of the "productivity problem" that underlies the "inflation problem"; the "supply side," "efficiency," and "reindustrialization" strategies now in the air are equally out of touch with the structural realities and offer equally unpleasant prospects.

The argument presented here is complicated since it involves simultaneous consideration of: (1) *structure*, the way parts of the economy fit together to make a whole; (2) *structural perception*, the way economists or authorities specify the parts and their interactions in designing policy; (3a) *policy fit* concerning the effects of policy where structure is misperceived; (3b) *objectives*, concerning the identification of goals and the value of tradeoffs; (3c) *pragmatic politics*, in which displaced objectives, structural misperceptions, and misjudged policies can be willfully or wishfully obscured. The separate sections of this paper (corresponding to the foregoing organization) will attempt to disentangle these much-interwined elements of the policy setting.

STRUCTURE: DUALISM AND CORPORATE STRATEGIC BEHAVIOR

Dualism and *segmented labor markets* refer to a hypothesized chronic condition in which a sector of modern industrial activities, sophisticated services, and a labor force of educated and skilled personnel coexists with a sector of stagnant technologies, incomplete development, and nonexistent or substandard work opportunities for an untrained work force making up some tens of millions of the urban (and ethnic) poor.[1] In Harrington's words the poor are "left behind by technology" and cannot, by bootstrap effort, lift themselves to the educational and skill level required for mainstream economic activities — or otherwise break through discriminatory barriers. They remain in the lower segments of the labor market relatively unaffected by trends and developments initiated by major enterprises in the modern component.

Dualism has been likened to the division between modern and backward sectors in the archetypical LDC — although of course, with sectoral weights reversed. Dualism theorists find it more accurate to describe the United States economy through its developmental compartments than through the standard disaggregations. Specifically, a dollar of demand channeled into the sector labeled *modern, primary, mainstream* or *progressive* would be judged as likely to remain in that sector and have negligible effect on employment, economic activity, or social transformation in the sector variously labeled *peripheral, secondary* or *stagnant*. In this light, dualism appears to be a postwar phenomenon — an aberration in structure resulting in (or associated with) cessation (or narrowed incidence) of the historical modernization process, which over many preceeding decades had transformed an agricultural economy and assimilated massive waves of internal and external migrants into advanced industry and commerce. Although dualistic structure is usually viewed as the exemplar of failure in United States economic development or as the underlying basis for social problems, it can also be regarded as a significant source of inflationary pressure.

On the supply side of the inflationary equation, what employment there is within the secondary component associates with activities of low intrinsic productivity and negligible prospects for productivity increase; on the demand side, transfers can only be a drain on incomes generated within the active sector. At the moment, control over the dollar drain has become a target of policy (the failure of transfer incomes to keep pace with the consumer price index is itself an indication of the extent of suppressed inflation), but interventions to eliminate the developmental anomaly seem forgotten, as are questions concerning the failure of industry to modernize opportunities for the entire society. It is curious that poverty programs are so often categorized as inflationary transfers rather than as antiinflationary structural interventions with immediate and long-term positive impacts on the supply side.

CORPORATE STRATEGIC BEHAVIOR

The second imperfectly recognized structural feature is the prevalence within the modern sector of firms capable of discretionary behavior which can differ qualitatively from that of the mythic profit-maximizing or wealth-maximizing enterprise. The modern firm (according to Marris, Baumol Williamson, and Galbraith) can (and may, under appropriate circumstances) alter its strategic behavior to favor particular styles of technological advance, market development or exploitation, and growth (whether internal, external, or multinational). Since the multinational firm is also the originator, innovator, or critical market for new technology, its strategic choices are also principal determinants of the rate of technical progress, the rate of innovation, the rate of capital accumulation, and the labor-saving bias of technique. Thus, an explanation of the prevailing corporate strategic mode is, in very large part, an explanation of the critical dynamic determinants of general welfare, selective employment, and distribution.[2] Indeed it can be shown that with appropriate macroeconomic stimulus a dominant mode of strategic behavior is likely to emerge and with it a consistent pattern of growth[3] (for details, see Appendix A).

On this view, the postwar history of the mainstream economy can be recounted as a sequence of shifts in the prevailing strategic mode. With respect to inflation, the decade of high sustained real growth from 1959 through 1968 can be associated with the subordination of aggressive pricing for short-term profit in favor of stable pricing to develop markets systematically. The balance shifted away from favoring the growth strategy with withdrawal of macroeconomic stimulus in 1969–70 (and with pressures on productivity-generating mechanisms at this stage of the war). Planning horizons shortened and the apparent emphasis given to aggressive pricing for short-term market exploitation increased through the 1970s. Aside from the implied worsening of the Phillips Curve tradeoff, the critical dynamic effects of the shift in strategic mode could be read in the fall of such indicators as the full-capacity rate, R & D levels, patent rates, indices of accumulation rates and the like. Deteriorated growth, of course, validated the pessimistic consensus strategy — and led to further inflation pressure as the productivity offset to money wage increases dropped to nil. Finally, as Professor Katona has shown elsewhere in this book, discretionary behavior has shifted towards anticipatory pricing and speculation on inflation itself — an equally self-validating stance.

THE STRUCTURAL ASPECT

What specifically is "structural" about these patterns, and to what degree do these patterns result in structural inflation? In the dualist, incomplete-development model, the structural components are the lack of employment responsiveness across labor-market segments, the requirement for human capital investment and social intervention to break down barriers between the components, an apparent propensity of major firms to choose technology so that expansion occurs without broadening employment, and a commitment by government to be the employer of last resort or income guarantor as social pressures rise. Policy is the final structural element; where, as suggested, the policy propensity is to restrict social programs, aggregate demand, and monetary growth in line with the static stabilization model. Although such policy is reasonable for any one period, it leads to reinforcement of the dualistic divisions when replicated period after period — and, accordingly, a dynamic prospect in which there is no upgrading of technically weak activities and no amelioration of social demands. In short, inflationary pressure is made dynamically structural by the repetitive application of short-term "antiinflationary" policy. Now bringing in strategic corporate behaviors, we see intensification of dynamic inflationary pressure; since incentives for growth behaviors are inhibited and the expectational environment is retailored to favor oligopolistic patterns, administered pricing, and new forms of anticipatory pricing.

STRUCTURAL PERCEPTIONS WITHIN THE DISCIPLINE

If the interpretation of structural features just given is at all accurate, the question naturally arises as to why there has recently been near silence on these matters within the literatures closest to policy determination. Such silence was not always the case.

STRUCTURAL AND NONSTRUCTURAL VIEWS OF POVERTY

With regard to dualism, after the "discovery" of the *Other America* in the early 1960s and with declaration of the War on Poverty in the mid–1960s, structural views received considerable attention within the discipline. Although one can cite no single definite controversy within the mainstream literature,[4] the opposition of views within more or less liberal groups could be characterized as *structural*, stressing the poverty syndrome and systematic divisions and emphasizing massive selective policy interventions; or *macroeconomic*, stressing past redistributional and growth successes and emphasizing the "inevitable trickling down" to the problem population of growth gains within the general economy. Advocates on both sides recognized poverty as a special problem (it was not so viewed by others) and measures initiated in the War on Poverty were considered variously (and without necessary contradiction) as structure-changing interventions; redistributional measures taken in relief of case poverty; measures in response to a new pattern of racial politics; or policy to expedite the trickle-down.

With Vietnam concerns and with the political reorientation of the Nixon administration, attention was deflected from the qualitative issue: the dismantling of the Office of Economic Opportunity eliminated a natural forum; FAP, the antipoverty proposal under active consideration, was predicated on the existence of a fully functioning unsegmented labor market. In other words, the issue of structural poverty was never resolved intellectually although it was rendered inoperative by conventional politics.[5] If dualistic structure existed in 1970, it is unlikely that a dozen years of stagnation in real growth per capita could have relieved the condition. The most prominent feature of structural maps drawn in 1964–68, one might think, should have been sketched into operational descriptions of the contemporary economy. If, as has been argued, the dualism phenomenon also accounts for a significant component of inflation, the silence on the matter says a lot about whether analysis leads or follows policy.

CORPORATE MACRODYNAMICS

The silence is only slightly less deafening on matters concerning the inflationary implications of the modern firm in its discretionary behavior and in its strategic role in endogenous determination of growth properties.[6] The supply side and productivity determination are, by now, recognized components of the inflationary syndrome; and individual proposals to repair flagging innovation, R & D, and capital accumulation can, taken as a whole, be interpreted as a call for resurrecting the growth impulse. My personal feeling, however, is that these calls fall short of specifying a structural program or integrated plan to reestablish the growth mode along lines suggested by the discretionary-behavior hypothesis. Why this is so can be a matter only of bald conjecture.

The picture of distinct macrodynamic states corresponding to prevailing corporate strategies bears a close resemblance to Keynes's picture of shifting states of long-term expectations. This critical component of the *General Theory* has never been entirely agreeable to American tastes — its implication being the impotency of monetary policy in the face of depressed expectations and the resultant necessity for socializing the investment function. The policy implications of "shifting corporate strategic behavior" are similar. Where conditions deteriorate, and firms adopt the speculative mode or strategies leading to cost, wage, or profit push, the appropriate remedies could only be controls. Similarly, if there is to be social control over the technical properties of growth, a degree of planning is called for; if there is to be control over dynamic distribution, there is an implied call for incomes policy, manpower policy of Tinbergen type, or some form of codetermination. Fear of the cure might have influenced the diagnosis. There is anomalous consistency in the lack of recognition given to firm strategic autonomy as a macroeconomic determinant. The period of intense United States growth in the 1960s was in effect the joint success (albeit within dualistic structure) of active stabilization policy and explicit pursuit of the growth objective by firms. The special character of firm behavior was ignored then, as well; and the constellation of policies that had enabled such growth were largely unrecognized for this contribution.

POLICY

We conclude by considering three aspects of policy: the implications of policy where structure is misjudged, implied trade-offs under these conditions, and the role of practical politics.

Policy Fit. According to the dualism perspective, antipoverty policy of the manpower, human-capital, structure-changing type should be a major component of supply side, antiinflationary policy. The proximate objective of such policy would be to expand the size of the work force eligible for progressive-sector employment — the policy to be validated by public and private employment programs that would amount to encouraging the expanded scale of modern activities and the private sector rate of growth.[7] Clearly, none of these proximate objectives has been aided by the policy mix of the last decade which features reduced aid to education at all levels, a misdirected public-sector jobs effort, reduced aid to nonmilitary R & D, low capital-formation incentives, and negligible skill-development incentives. At one time or another, each of these noninstruments has been justified as antiinflationary (in the Phillips Curve demand sense) but there has been little attention given to the system-wide impact of a decade of virtually continous restrictions. Obviously, the problem continues. It should be stressed that, absent the structural argument, every individual program or incentive can be presumed to have inflationary impact (relative to the opportunity of reducing overall expenditures).

Objectives. The failure to endorse (even to some small degree) policies implied by the structural view is suggestive as to tacit objectives and social evaluations in policy making, assuming now that the structural explanation is encountered at some time in the process. Although appearing as single-dimensioned absolutes in policy pronouncements, inflation and unemployment are de facto multidimensioned goals —

that how one attains a Phillips Curve position is as important as the position itself. This is manifest in the opprobrium attached to explicit wage/price controls; but the extent to which other instruments have been deemed unacceptable has largely gone unremarked. It is one thing to stipulate an acceptable list of instruments for short-run stabilization; it is quite another to hold to that list for a "short term" that has lasted for more than a decade — the current epoch of demand constraint to restrict inflation.

Practical Politics. Ultimately we must ask how such a situation can persist within the system of electoral and interest-group politics. There are a number of nearly satisfactory answers on this unsatisfactory state of affairs, but two seem apposite. First, it seems quite possible to cultivate and sustain public misperceptions of inflationary processes, their causes and cures. As has been noted often enough, the issue of inflation is a natural for inflated treatment in sloganeering politics. The incidence and apparent burden of inflation is broad, even though its real burden is small and narrowly distributed. Furthermore, the burden of conventional antiinflationary policy (particularly that which undercuts growth and development) is less palpable — even though it is probably an order of magnitude larger in welfare effect than the burden of inflation itself. Second, one must contemplate the possibility that willful misdirection is part of politics. The textbook model of politically directed tradeoffs does not include the possibility of *sub optime*, intentionally chosen. Yet recent history, and not only that of the Nixon administration,[8] suggest that the prevailing pattern may very well be that of obscuring the real tradeoff and cultivating public misperception of the choice. Why structural intervention is perceived to be a political risk and why the path of misdirection is taken are matters for deeper conjecture.

Notes

* Research supported in part by the National Science Foundation.
1. Gordon describes dualism theory as it evolved during the late 1960s and provides abundant bibliography. (For additional bibliography, policy analysis and policy proposals see Shepard et al.)
2. Albin explores the macrodynamics of growth in a dualistic structure. The corporate behaviors sketched here and effects on the parameters of growth are described in some detail.
3. Shifts of an economy from high-growth to low-growth stable equilibria consistent with altered strategic choice are explained in Albin and Alcaly and in Appendix A. A growth strategy is associated with a particular selection of investment prospects by the firm. Typically the "growth portfolio" of projects will emphasize R & D, expansion, high technology, and long planning horizons

as compared to a portfolio of projects associated with ordinary wealth maximization. Both portfolios provide payoffs in the profit and expected-growth-rate dimensions, however; and with variant portfolios a full opportunity set is generated. Higher expected macroeconomic growth (propelled by policy stimulus and/or the supply side-effects of firm growth strategies) can shift the growth/profit opportunity tradeoff in a way that can attract even the most conservative management toward ostensible growth. On reasonable capital-theoretic assumptions the economy can have multiple, locally stable equilibrium growth rates, each corresponding to a different macroeconomic stimulus.
4.   The debate between Aaron and Gallaway comes very close to the implied standard.
5.   Interest in the dualism phenomenon has been sustained by Gordon and M. Reich whose cumulative work is forthcoming. In fact, evidence on black-white wage differentials, urban poverty, and youth unemployment suggests that the dualism pattern is still strong. If there has been any closing of the gap between the compartments of the economy it has been more a matter of the deterioration of the "modern" sector than improved opportunities for the poor.
6.   For reviews of the literature on managerial behavior see Wildsmith and Albin and Alcaly. Hession surveys discussions of Galbraith's system. See also the Solow, Galbraith, Solow exchange in the *Public Interest.*
7.   For one developmental scheme to reactivate the corporate growth impulse see Albin.
8.   The Nixonian political counter to Pareto optimality is explored by Shell. Otherwise, examine the current rhetorical obfuscation surrounding the balancing of the federal budget.

References

Albin, P. S. *Progress Without Poverty* (New York, 1978).

Albin, P. S., and Alcaly, R. "Corporate Objectives and the Economy: Systematic Shifts Between Growth and Profit Goals," *Journal of Economic Issues* 10, June 1976.

Aaron, H., "The Foundations of the 'War on Poverty' Re-examined," *American Economic Review* 57, December 1967.

Baumol, W. *Business Behavior Value and Growth* (New York, 1967).

Galbraith, J. K. "A Review of a Review," *The Public Interest*, No. 9, Fall, 1967.

Galbraith, J. K. *The New Industrial State* (Boston, 1969).

Gallaway, L. "Foundations of the War on Poverty," *American Economic Review* 55, March 1965.

Gordon, D. M. *Theories of Poverty and Underemployment* (Lexington, Mass., 1972).

Gordon, D., and Reich, M. Work in progress.

Harrington, M. *The Other America* (New York, 1962).

Hession, C. H. *John Kenneth Galbraith and His Critics* (New York, 1972).

Katona, G. "Psychology of Inflation" (Part 8).

Keynes, J. M. *The General Theory of Employment, Interest, and Money* (New York, 1964).

Marris, R. *The Economic Theory of Managerial Capitalism* (Glencoe, Ill., 1964

Shell, J. *The Time of Illusion* (New York, 1976).

Sheppard, H. C., Harrison, B., and Spring, W. J. *The Political Economy of Public Service Employment* (Lexington, Mass., 1972).

Solow, R. M. "The New Industrial State or Son of Affluence," *The Public Interest*, No. 9, Fall 1967.

Solow, R. M. "A Rejoinder," *The Public Interest*, No. 9, Fall 1967.

Wildsmith, M. *Managerial Theories of the Firm* (New York, 1974).

Williamson, O. E. *The Economics of Discretionary Behavior* (Englewood Cliffs, N.J., 1964).

Appendix A
Shifting Corporate Strategic Objectives and Realized Growth

Consider the following compound premise.

1. Firms of any economic significance have the ability to choose between neoclassical optimization (profit or wealth maximization) and other objectives (e.g., growth maximization).

2. The parameters determining their choices vary significantly over time, and this variation is dependent upon both exogenous conditions and the political policy settings.

3. Firms' reactions to such parameter variations are systematic, so that particular optimization styles will prevail during particular historical epochs.

4. Compositional problems and recursive conjectures abound, so that an inclination to deviate from the prevailing style of optimization will be heavily penalized by "competitive" considerations.

During the postwar era until the late 1960s it seemed reasonable to link microeconomic behavior to the macroenvironment according to the Galbraith-Maris-Baumol-Williamson description of firms engaged in aggressive pursuit of growth. Individual strategic choices embraced long horizons and long-term plans, aggressive market development, research and development in high-technology industries, and a predisposition toward the use of high-level management and technical personnel. Activities in this style contributed to realized macroeconomic growth and productivity gains, which in turn validated the implicit and explicit expectations embodied in the growth-oriented mode of corporate behavior. Firms were encouraged toward the aggressive mode by their peers, by consultants, and by the preferences of the sources of finance.

The orientation toward growth of a single firm could be the outcome of strategic choice as depicted in Figure 1 where π is a measure of rate of profit and g is the rate of growth of a target variable such as total assets, sales, or profits. The line arbitrarily splits opportunities into those oriented toward growth, "gamma policies," and those oriented toward profits. Position A denotes a selection of investment opportunities described as a choice of *gamma* policy; B is a *nongamma* selection. The opportunity set is drawn for a particular set of anticipations as to G, the proportion of firms that are following a *gamma* policy, and g, the macroeconomic growth rate.

Assume further that firms have a stable structure of preferences as regards *gamma* or *nongamma* policies. This preference structure could be described as *an internal utility function* or as a *bureaucratic procedure*. It is sufficient for our purposes that the firm's final strategic choice should move in the *gamma* direction in reaction to one or more of the following: improved *gamma* opportunities (e.g., increases in the relative growth payoff within the set of available investment opportu-

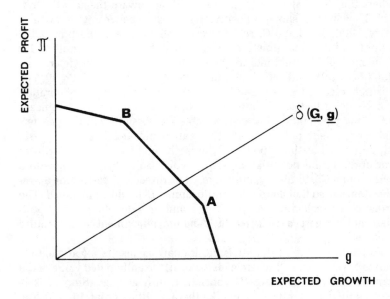

Fig. 1   The Choice Setting

nities, as represented by a shift in the opportunity locus); increased G (denoting relative growth orientation of competitors along with pressure on market share); or increased g (the higher expected aggregate growth rate presumably increases payoffs and reduces project risks for both *gamma* and *nongamma* selections but favors the former). The last effect is illustrated in Figure 2. The broken curves are preference functions, the vertical and horizontal axes represent increments to profit and growth rates, respectively. The straight-line segments represent segments of the growth-profitability opportunity set for expected growth rates $g_1 \ldots, g_4$. The tradeoff moves in favor of *gamma* strategy and at some point the specific firm will shift from choices in the B sequence to the A sequence. The proportion of firms making the shift is, again, the variable G.

SYSTEM BEHAVIORS

Assume further that g^p the growth rate in potential GNP, is itself a function of G, meaning that the projects chosen by *gamma*-oriented firms make a positive contribution to supply-side growth. A plausible form for this relationship is given by the curve g^p in Figure 3. The double inflection suggests that above some threshold value of G there are strong positive effects (e.g., externalities) favoring collective growth; and that there is a natural upper bound to system growth even where the vast majority of firms have shifted toward the growth strategy. The curve g^y shows a positive relationship between g^y, growth in aggregate demand and G. At E corresponding to the proportion G, the output and demand growth rates are equal, a necessary condition for dynamic equilibrium (note we have not yet considered the determination of G which is itself a function of the anticipated growth rate). The position pictured at G_1 shows $g^y_1 > g^p_1$. This arbitrary configuration can be described as an out-of-equilibrium position with significant inflationary potential. However, we note the possibility (through external government policy directed at enhancing technical change via support to education, sponsored research programs, and so forth) of transforming the potential growth schedule so as to give a potential equilibrium E''. Similarly, policy might be directed at restricting aggregate demand so that a growth equilibrium at E' could be obtained. The transformed schedules $g^{p'}$, $g^{p''}$, $g^{y'}$ and $g^{y''}$ denote variant policies and suggest a rich set of dynamic adjustment and stability problems.

Full equilibrium in this dynamic framework occurs for a value g^*, where $g^p = g^y = g^*$, and where g^* is, in turn, the anticipated value of the growth rate that generates G consistent with $g^P = g^y$. Since this is essentially an ad hoc framework, there is little point in detailing equilibrium and stability conditions for the many plausible configura-

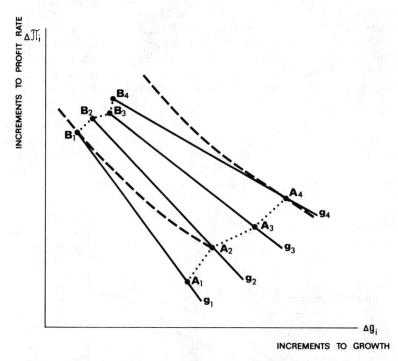

Fig. 2   **Shifts in Expected Returns for Different Values of the Macroeconomic Growth Rate g**

tions of these dynamic terms. Let it suffice that if there is a tendency for firms to cluster around "consensus strategies," the system may be prone to "multiple stable equilibria." Thus the 1946–64 era might be categorized as a relative high-growth equilibrium sustained by corporate growth-oriented policies manifested in high rates of technical change, high R & D budgets, high rates of utilization of educated manpower, high rates of product and process innovation, etc.; and enabled by a complex of government support programs in education and other human-capital developments, R & D technical support, etc. On the other hand, the current position might be categorized as a low-level growth equilibrium associated with non-*gamma* strategic choices by firms and a complex of government policies that seem to be directed at validating depressed anticipations and opening the door to anticipatory pricing and new forms of position taking appropriate to permanent inflationary expectations.

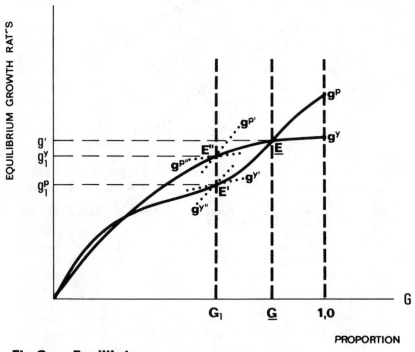

Fig.3   Equilibria

Problems of Current Inflation
in the United States

PAUL JONAS

I

The question of our time is how to get the monetary system back to the right road. Then, how to adjust the signals to avoid malfunctioning, queueing, slow or speedy traffic. The difficulty (or one of the difficulties) seems to be that public confidence is eroded after tons of conflicting statements. In our profession we have Keynesians, monetarists, liberals, supply siders, conservatives, Marxists, other harder-to-classify economists and naturally those who are just watching all arguments and debates with a detached amusement.

True, the economists are always ready to give their evaluation of current inflation and they are not hesitant to propose cures. Recently twenty economists were interviewed by the *New York Times* about the problems of current inflation, and to paraphrase an old witticism, they gave 25 solutions. Almost everybody was there, the famous economists as well as the average teachers, and most of them launched an I-told-you-so attack that stressed the advocacy of their pet ideas, such as monetary restraint, wage and price controls, taxation of luxury spending, 10 percent surcharge on income tax, tax cut to help supply and production, community control, the solution of bioeconomic questions, getting government off our backs, the construction of a socialist economy (Mermelstein, 1979).

Robert Solomon, for many years the Federal Reserve's top international economist in an authoritative, shrewd account analyzing the world economic system tells us: "Like traffic lights in a city the international monetary system is taken for granted until it begins to malfunction and disrupt people's daily lives" (Solomon, 1977).

One could elaborate this simile and extend it. Interestingly the inflation in the international monetary system does not change the signs randomly but rather in a pattern which can be predicted *ex ante*. As the annual cost of living increases, monetary flows are discouraged to enter into roads called "Savings and Investments" or "Research and Development." With double-digit inflation the traffic lights are redirecting the flows to passages called "Loans and Consumptions." Then, after a while, the road becomes dangerous, and warnings such as "Rock Fall Ahead" increase.

The question which will remain the focus of mankind's attention for the coming decade is: "How can we repair our system of signals to lead the national and the international economies along a safe road to greener pastures?"

Surely no one expected consensus. But the question in the mind of an average reader arises: "Can economists *qua* economists arrive at some pragmatic consensus how to solve inflation?" I suggest that our theoretical differences, at least in the so-called leading schools, are not so great as it is often claimed. We learned recently that Keynes, after all, cannot be considered a fiscalist or a neo-Keynesian since he expressed concern and awareness about "crowding out," which seems to be the major difference between fiscalists and monetarists.[1]

Looking at our confronting propositions based on "schools," i.e., ideology, one can predict what one leading economist will say. It is, therefore, rather boring to hear our economists with their policy propositions; they may provide some elegant details, some witty remarks, but their general tune is well known *ex ante* by every graduate student. Under this condition one wonders if a historic approach, i.e., to analyze past economic disturbances, such as inflations, and try to derive conclusions from the economic history of the United States or other nations, is not more fruitful. Indeed the organizers of the Brooklyn College conference, I believe, may suggest this solution by calling our meetings *Inflation through the Ages*. The title suggests that one ought to discover some similarities in the inflations of the world, just as one can find common denominators among epidemics. It is supposed, if I am not mistaken, that the illness of inflation in every place starts with the same infection and, therefore, the same cure could be applied. Indeed, could we not learn from Professor Walter Haines, who, as I understand, will lecture here about the inflations of the United States, 1700–1980? The study of Professor Paul Trescott, who deals with the relationship of monetary policy and inflation, 1912–78, should be also helpful. Some runaway inflations, such as the German post-World War I, could be also very instructive for analysis and the conference devotes a whole plenary session to this topic. (Why was the Hungarian post-World War II inflation not included, which was several time more devastating?)

Sure, this approach can be helpful, it filters ideological biases, and it has been used several times. Cagan's study, *e.g.*, deals with a recent inflation in the United States and describes how a double-digit rate of price increase in 1973–74 was subdued to an annual rate of 5–6 percent in 1976.[2]

Indeed a 5 percent cost of living increase (in fact the actual rate of increase of the GNP deflator as only 4.7 percent in 1976) can be looked at as an ideal price stability for most parts of the current world.

I cannot refrain from mentioning that it is rather unfortunate that Cagan casts his analysis in the familiar Phillips-Curve framework. It is my strong conviction that the Phillips Curve just confuses the basic problems of inflation and stabilization, since it is almost always presented as an analytical tool to understand the *choice* between unemployment and inflation. This interpretation of the Phillips Curve is totally false; there is no *choice*. Cagan, and all of us know very well that rising inflation causes rising unemployment in the long-run, even if one opts for just inflation.

I am writing these rather unstructured lines in Dakar, in an Institute for Leprosy Research, the only place where an economist can find a quiet corner. I am told here that the injection used to cure leprosy causes a temporary dizziness. Should the physician give a leper the option to choose between the injection (which cures leprosy but causes a temporary dizziness) and no injection (which causes an aggravated leprosy but no temporary dizziness)? Is this choice moral if we know that, with an aggravated leprosy, the dizziness will permanently return? Offering such an option would be criminal.

So is the approach of some economic adviser who "explains" to a policy maker his "choice." Usually a technician shows a convex Phillips Curve, selects a point on the hyperbola, and makes the following little speech: "You see we are approximately here. So, as you want to move from this point to a lower inflationary rate this will be accompanied by a successive increase in unemployment. Now I am just a humble economist, an adviser. The decision is yours." What can an economist expect from a pragmatic policy maker who should take into consideration the public concern about unemployment which manifests itself in many different ways and is spelled out in the Employment Act of 1946?

In fact there is no choice. Inflation *cum* high unemployment will be the the outcome of accommodating higher levels of dollar expenditures (through monetary expansion) to keep up a relatively low rate of unemployment.

Now we ought to return to the problem that we left unanswered: "Is a historical approach helpful to find the roots of inflation, i.e., every inflation? Can we expect some findings, by analyzing economic phenomena through the ages, which could provide cures for our present ills?" Sure, one can expect some similarities. I am, however, afraid that a historical approach, in general, would be counterproductive. One reason for this proposition is that conditioning factors change in a dramatic way, and the river into which we are stepping is now totally different from the stream of yesteryear. In the last decades conditioning factors changed in a dramatic way, serious historical shifts occurred between different periods and the *ceteris* are certainly not *paribus*. A decade ago, the economic and financial regime of the world was dominated by the dollar. The world, in our time, became a multipolar system in which the United States is just one nation, interdependent with the others. Turning points in these days often do not occur as economists predict them, by using their old methods of analysis. Therefore, "unexpected" economic phenomena are often evaluated as "events beyond control." We are in a new playground where the rules are more complicated than they used to be. We still did not go through enough of a psychological shock to realize that economic events in this country are no longer a simple function of the good, bad, or neutral decisions of Washington, but depend more and more on policies formulated in Riyadh, Tokyo, Bonn, and other economic centers of the world. The period of arguing for a national economic policy, which will solely shape the United States' economic future, is over.

We live in a period in which international financial movements, some of them speculative, are increasing rapidly. The international economy is linked together with more and more legal and illegal channels. Economists used to be overly worried about such flows. Keynes suggested that England and the United States should establish tight control of international capital movements, and he proposed that for its administration "postal censorship" might be acceptable.[3] Now the speculative flows are with us. They can be tempered only by removing the reasons for the speculations.

The *interdependence* is becoming more and more important in the world economy for all nations. It is usually measured as some ratio of economic activities involving foreign nations related to total economic transactions. In practice, for an approximation, exports and imports are divided by the GNP. These ratios are already high for small or medium-sized nations, but are also rapidly increasing for large countries, such as the Soviet Union or the United States, which, in the past, could afford to be nearly autarkic. The change of the interdependence ratio (I_t) and its forecast for the United States is given below:

Table 1[4]

Change in the Interdependence Ratio

1950	4.5%
1960	5.9
1970	7.9
1980	10.4
1990	13.8
2000	18.2

Interdependence (I_t) increases at an increasing rate for every nation, proving Kenneth Boulding's position, that we live on "Spaceship Earth," in a shrinking world, with nations pushed together more and more. The starting point of this new phase was probably the final collapse of the Bretton Woods era (1945–71), i.e., the American-dominated monetary system of international exchange rates. Shortly after that in 1973 or 1974, with the quadrupling of oil prices by the Middle-East-led oil cartel, the American political and economic hegemony ended.

A historical analysis could pinpoint tricks which worked out successfully, say, a decade ago, but because of changed conditioning factors their application would now be a flop. Walter Heller, adviser to presidents, constantly argues for some policies simply because they succeeded in some previous administration. The scene is not the same, we cannot repeat victorious battles won two decades ago.

The once mighty American economy is now subject to the discipline of the international marketplace.

II

Having established a theoretical proposition that the world is not the same as it used to be, we can further explore the evidence with respect to this tentative striking hypothesis.[5]

What are the main characteristics of this new era outside of an increased interdependence ratio, demonstrated earlier? Just to list a few: the petroleum crisis; the problems of petrodollar recycling; and the corresponding vast, baffling money market which resists any regulation. Is it possible that the current world-wide inflationary trend is related *indirectly*[6] to these phenomena which are still undigested chunks in the stomach of the world's economy?

To jump to the middle of the problem, we learn from an investigative journalist L. J. Davis (1980), who displays an incredible ability to gather information about some vitally sensitive issues. He tells us that the Euromarket contains around a trillion dollars. As it seems, nobody, including the Federal Reserve, knows how this money was accumulated. The Euromarket witnessed a 500 percent increase in the years 1972–79 and a concomitant increase in its uncontrollable velocity. Is it just a coincidence that these years have also been the years of double-digit inflation in the West? The growth in the Euromarket after 1974 was mainly supplied by OPEC oil money coming from the so-called "capital surplus oil exporters": Saudi Arabia, Libya, Kuwait, and the United Arab Emirates. This accumulation, if we correctly understand Henry C. Wallich's statement made in the name of the Board of Governors of the Federal Reserve, will continue in the future: "In the face of increased OPEC surpluses and corresponding deficits of oil-importing countries, the scale of international financial flows may well increase relative to purely domestic flows" (Wallich, 1980).

The Euromarket swells and the concern of many central banks as well as regulatory agencies increases, since it enjoys its blissful freedom, in its trillion-dollar dimension, from the meddling of bureaucrats. The banking system is free, but it could play only a limited role in the recycling process for productive purposes. True, the surplus is high but the canons of banking prevent the financial institutions from lending money for risky investment. The demand for productive investments comes, in its lion's share, from the Less Developed Countries (LDCs) and the East European centrally planned economies (EE-CPEs). The LDCs as well as the EE-CPEs are already characterized by an alarming debt/GNP ratio and many times the borrowing is intended to pay the interest of previous loans. The international monetary system is most afraid of a bank panic when depositors begin calling home their deposits, which could happen if some serious default is committed by some of the large borrowers.

The Euromarket appears on the surface to be more soundly based, but it feeds speculative operations conducted by reputable businesses which established their creditworthiness. The OPEC nations were expected to assume responsibility for recycling the OPEC surplus by providing aid and direct financing of development projects of the LDCs — but they will not. Who can blame them? They use their money on the basis of conservative financial principles. Therefore, a considerable amount of the world's available money supply is floating around loose, used up occasionally for gold, silver, art objects, commodity futures. What, then, is the solution?

A proposal comes from Jacques Chirac.[7]

Chirac, to my knowledge, outlined his plan for the first time at a press conference in February 1980 at *l'Hotel de Ville* in Paris but expanded it and gave a detailed explanation about the "trilogue" a few days later in Sénégal.[8]

The main elements of the Chirac Plan follow. They are compiled from newspaper accounts and also from his several oral statements dealing with this issue during his February 1980 visit in Sénégal, including his briefing given in Saint Louis for the meeting of the Francophone mayors.

The world, he suggests, can be classified into three interrelated groups which could respond to a plan which may well directly benefit all the participants involved.

a. *The oil producing nations* receive for their product in an average year an estimated $300 billion. From this amount they will use 200 billion for various investment projects in their countries, therefore,

$100 billion will wind up in the coffers of the bankers. They will lend it, in our current world situation, for speculative purposes. These operations are known for quick turnover, and the velocity of the money circulation is expected to increase. This, in turn, will create an additional increase in the price level. Since the OPEC countries are talking about indexation, an additional augmentation in the cost of living will force them to increase the price of petroleum. Therefore, we should expect to live in a constant, never-ending spiral, which can be termed *the vicious circle of the inferno.*

b. *The developed industrial nations'* current ills, when the OECD predicted for this once mighty group a zero rate of growth for 1980, are well known. These countries operate way under their capacity. Unemployment in this group is not the exception but the rule, and new heights are expected. The industrial nations badly need orders to see their idle industries move, to get engaged in research and development, and to generate with technological innovations a healthy and easier growth. Prosperous industrial nations are prerequisite for a healthy world economy. If the expectation for the current year is zero growth, this means that nothing from the increment can be distributed to the needy. (The economic problems of the world should never be discussed in the framework of confrontation, so much in vogue these days, but rather in the framework of cooperation.)

c. *The less developed nations'* problems are also well known. These countries need capital in order to finance their development projects since their savings, due to their low incomes, are marginal or nonexistent. This group should also import more than they export, and a constant balance-of-payment gap is the rule of underdevelopment. Capital is there, waiting for investment projects. The private capital in the Euromarket, however, will never be available for most of the less developed countries. We ought to understand that. A banker should never be blamed for avoiding unjustified risks.

Cooperation should be set up between various members of these three groups. One advantage of the proposed plan is that no complicated administrative framework is needed, a tripartite agreement can be started right now if we have cooperating members from these three groups. Would this *ménage à trois* work? An OPEC nation is looked at as the potential banker, the industrial nation as the producer, and the LDC the consumer. A fruitful agreement for the long run should always be based on common interests, which prerequisite can cement together various nations with different ideological or political aims. One could work out a cooperative agreement in the following manner:

An industrial nation and a LDC work out a rational, meaningful economic project utilizing the many locational, natural opportunities the underdeveloped world can offer. The plans should be analyzed carefully; feasibility studies ought to be conducted with respect to costs and benefits; local conditions should be taken into account which would also include weights for expected political stability, disruptive natural forces, and related factors. To demonstrate the advantage for the LDC the multiplier effects must also be calculated. When a suitable project is found, then the LDC requests a long-term loan from a capital surplus oil-producing country. The loan will now be granted, since the LDC will be able to provide a guarantor, banks in the industrialized country, as partners. This OECD nation will pay, from its foreign aid fund, the commercial interest rate or part of it, splitting the rest with the LDC, and will take up the responsibility for any default. The LDC, in return, will contract the project(s) with its guarantor nation.

With this tripartite agreement: (a) a capital surplus oil-producing nation is able to place its unused capital (or part of it) with normal commercial interest rates, in a low-risk, long-run investment; (b) an industrial nation could get orders from an LDC which could create employment, resource mobilization, technological innovations; (c) the LDC would have productive economic investments, enabling its economic development by creating various "poles," forward and backward linkages.

If such tripartite agreements are worked out in several combinations and they multiply, they can affect beneficially the world economy, increase universal welfare, and reduce inflationary pressures.

III

The long-awaited recession is here. It has hit the economy hard; forecasters are predicting dramatic falls in production and spectacular increase in the rate of unemployment.

This rate of inflation is decreasing but it is still too high to compensate average wage earners for all the past losses in the general welfare. We might quibble over details of the new policy actions by the Federal Reserve, but they definitely are in the right direction. The most encouraging aspect is the evidence that Washington is of the urgent need to correct inflation and to stabilize the dollar.

But the game is not over. In the future years expansive official policies, "to get the nation moving again," finally will begin to make a substantial dent in unemployment as the economy shakes off its earlier elements of sluggishness and surges forward across a broad front. This change in the trend of business conditions will be reflected almost immediately in a heightening credit demand by the private sector. The banks' general loans will swell, say, at a rate equivalent to more than 30 percent a year. At the same time, finance companies and nonfinancial corporations will begin to step up their issuance of money market paper, and there will be a substantial strengthening of demand for mortgages. Borrowing in the bond market, however, will remain relatively light.

This will be the time for the Federal Reserve to show whether the lessons of the current inflation were learned. If a strong stand is not taken, early enough, to achieve some deceleration in the growth of bank credit, not by some "fine tuning policies," but by simply increasing money supply by a constant annual rate related to the growth of the national economy, we will be back to our present headaches.

But a sane national financial policy is just the antechamber to stability. One can expect swings from international differentials in interest rates, various trends outside of the country which will generate shock effects. The lessened expansiveness of earlier credit policies could not counteract or moderate the impact of a complex and interdependent world. What to do?

The United States, in the first stage, should think seriously about the possibility of starting tripartite agreements of the sort outlined here, and later to think, even if this looks utopian now, of establishing, in stages, an economic union, first with Canada and later with the European Economic Community in the form of an Atlantic Union.

It may be a dream, but we should start to speak about it. We do not have any other long-term choice.

Notes

1. Shlomo Maital, "Inflation Expectation in the Monetarist Black Box," *American Economic Review*, June 1979.
2. Phillip Cagan, "The Reduction of Inflation and the Magnitude of Unemployment," in William Fellner (Ed.), *Contemporary Economic Problems in 1977* (Washington, D.C., 1977).
3. Herbert G. Grubel (Ed.), *World Monetary Reform Plans and Issues* (Stanford, Calif., 1963), pp. 72–73.
4. The Interdependence Ratio is defined as

$$I_t = \frac{(\text{Exports} + \text{Imports})}{\text{GNP}_t}$$

The estimates were received by fitting past trend to a logarithmic formula and receiving

$$I_t = 0.045 \ e^{0.028t}$$

See also Marina v. N. Whitman, "Economic Openness and International Financial Flows," *Journal of Money and Credit*, November 1969, pp.727–41.
5. A card-carrying economist must establish a theoretical framework not to violate a stern warning: "Every empirical study should rest on a theoretical framework, on a set of tentative hypotheses that the evidence is designed to test

or to adumbrate." Milton Friedman, "A Theoretical Framework for Monetary Analysis," *Occasional Paper*, Number 112, National Bureau of Economic Research, 1971.

6.   Serious monetarists should not worry, the lesson is well learned: "There is no such a thing as cost-push inflation, a rise in costs can cause inflation only in roundabout way of people clamoring for more money to pay higher prices and government giving into this." Frederich Hayek, in the *International Herald Tribune*, 10 March 1980.

7.   Jacques Chirac, French politician, b. 1932, Paris, prime minister, 1974–76, mayor of Paris from 1977. Chirac frequently used adjective is "nationalist" and his critics accuse him of chauvinism. Be that as it may, one should still consider seriously his "Une nouvelle alliance pour le développement" (A New Alliance for Development) which relates to a tripartite cooperation in the world, in order to recycle petrodollars to productive uses.

8.   "Chirac parle," *Le Monde*, Paris (15 février 1980); "Jacques Chirac à Bara Diouf, 'Une nouvelle alliance pour le développement'" (18 février 1980), *Le Soleil*, Dakar; "Un entretien avec Jean Cauet Chirac, "La France est malade de langueur," *Paris Match* (22 février 1980).

References

Solomon, Robert. *Le système monetaire international* (Paris, 1978), p. 1. Original version published as *International Monetary System* (New York, 1977).

Mermelstein, David. "The Threatening Economy," *The New York Times Magazine*, 30 December 1979. pp. 12–15, 33–35.

Davis, L. J. "Bankers' Casino," *Harper's*, February 1980, pp. 43–57.

Statement by Henry C. Wallich, member, Board of Governors of the Federal Reserve System, before the Subcommittee on International Trade, Investment and Monetary Policy of the Committee on Banking, Finance and Urban Affairs, U.S. House of Representatives, 1 April 1980. *Federal Reserve Bulletin*, April 1980.

The Monetary Implications of a
Fixed Exchange Rate System

MILDRED RENDL MARCUS

The recent unsettling actions associated with floating rates indicate a good possibility that another resort to fixed exchange rates will occur. If so, the effects on the United States would differ significantly from today's float, perhaps resulting in even more inflation.

In contrast to orthodox textbook analysis, a United States payments deficit with a fixed exchange rate might not be deflationary, but instead induce added monetary expansion, particularly because of the Euro-currency market. The end result of our deficit could well be an impetus to expansion both within the United States economy and in those economies with whom we have a deficit. This could arise as a result of the normal operations of financing such imbalances, as well as if there is resort to inter-central bank "swap" arrangements.

In the usual textbook discussion of international surpluses and deficits, payment is made through the transfer of gold, the deficit country's central and commercial banks thus losing reserves while the surplus country's central and commercial banks gain reserves. The former's money supply is under deflationary pressure, the latter's money supply is in an expansionary phase. But this orthodox description does not necessarily hold today, especially for a "key currency" country like the United States.[1] The various arrangements evolved since World War II, such as through the International Monetary Fund, have introduced many alternatives, with varying impact — not necessarily symmetrical — on the money supply in the creditor and debtor country.

I. GOLD FLOWS

A brief summary of the conventional transfer pattern will serve as a yardstick. If the country's international balance is in deficit, its residents owe more, as a group, than foreigners owe them. The supply of the country's currency — and thus the demand for foreign currencies — exceeds the demand for the currency in question (and thus the supply of foreign currencies is less than the demand). The price of the currency under examination declines, and if this does not stimulate the demand for it sufficiently, then the currency declines to the minimum support price.[2] At this point the excess supply of the currency is sold to the deficit country's monetary authorities for the desired foreign currency; this adds to the total availability of foreign currencies and closes the supply-demand gap.[3]

The sale of the currency to the monetary authorities usually means that the money is destroyed. Since the authorities have given up an asset — international reserves — they also wipe out a corresponding liability — the money redeemed. This money would probably be either cash drawn from the banks by the sellers, or else a check drawn on their accounts. Thus, both the money supply and commercial bank reserves are decreased by the same amount. We thus have an equal amount decline in (a) commercial bank assets — their reserves; (b) commercial bank liabilities — deposits used by the people owing money to foreigners; (c) central bank assets — gold or other international reserves; and (d) central bank liabilities — the money destroyed when cashed in for the reserves in (c).

Since there has been a one-to-one decline in commercial bank reserves and deposit liabilities, then, given the fractional reserve system, the reserve ratio declines. If it drops below the legal or customary minimum levels, a further contraction of deposits, and thus the money supply, is necessary, unless the central bank supplies sufficient reserves, e.g., through advances or open market purchases.

In any event, the money supply drops. This contracts spending, including spending on imported goods and services, which reduces payments, thus reducing the supply of the country's currency on the foreign exchange market. Since it was an excess supply that triggered the ensuing deflation, the adverse balance is now being reduced, and when eliminated, a new payments balance emerges.

Meanwhile, in the surplus country, monetary reserves are rising — received from the deficit country — and the money supply is increasing. Its residents are receiving more from abroad than they are paying out. Analogously, but opposite to the scenario in the deficit country, an expansionary sequence is set in motion. Spending rises, including spending on imported goods and services. This increases payments to foreigners. Since the expansion was initiated by an excess demand for the surplus country's currency, the rise in payments reduces the surplus, which when eliminated, results in a new balance. In the orthodox explanation, the deficit and surplus countries move in virtually symmetrical — through opposite — paths, something that will not necessarily hold in the subsequent discussion.

II. INTERNATIONAL BANK BALANCES

Probably the most obvious modification of the payments mechanism outlined in the previous section is the maintenance of reserve balances with key currency countries. Most countries now count as part of their international reserves liquid balances in dollars or other major foreign currencies owned by the central bank. Of course, this makes the country in which the balance is located a short-term debtor.

Since these balances can be held in various forms, only the major possibilities will be discussed to illustrate the monetary repercussions. For simplicity, it will first be assumed that the balances arise as a result of a United States deficit — as in section I. This, however, need not be so. For example, if Germany has a deficit with Italy, settlement could be through a transfer of German-owned dollar balances to the Italian central bank. Or, a foreign central bank could sell an acceptable foreign currency to the United States monetary authorities in exchange for a dollar balance.

Initially, it is assumed that, net, Americans must make payments to foreigners in excess of foreign payments due to Americans. Normally, the Americans would buy the necessary foreign currencies from their banks, giving up dollars — demand deposits — in exchange. But, because of the excess offerings of dollars, the banks raise the price of the foreign currencies in demand. Foreign commercial banks might now step in to supply their currency[4] and accept in exchange the excess of dollars. These dollars are then held in some form — to be discussed — rather than resold. The excess supply of dollars has thus been absorbed; simultaneously, the excess demand for foreign currencies has been satisfied. (The excess dollars might have been paid to foreign nonbanking creditors, but then they would probably sell them to their banks, since they would be unlikely to retain dollars except for their own dollar requirements — e.g., for purchases in the United States. This last possibility would have been included in the aggregate foreign demand for dollars, so that the excess supply discussed here is the true — net — excess.)

The addition to foreign-owned dollar balances is initially in the form of foreign commercial bank ownership of demand deposits at United States banks. The United States money supply is unchanged, but it is possible that its velocity will drop. Deposit ownership has passed from more active hands — the Americans who bought foreign exchange —to less active hands — the foreign bank. Since originally there had been an insufficient demand for dollars, it may be assumed that the foreign banks have no immediate need for the dollars, and thus the lower velocity. The deficit has some — mild — deflationary impact.

Inasmuch as demand deposits are nonincome-earning assets, the foreign banks might decide to switch them to time deposits (including the possibility of acquiring newly issued certificates of deposit). This change from high reserve to low reserve deposits would have numerous possible repercussions familiar to students of money and banking. The net result would probably be a decline in demand deposits to some extent, since some reserves must be kept against the new time deposits. The absolute size of the demand deposit decline, however, would be less than the rise in time deposits, thus aggregate deposits rise. In addition, inactive demand deposits held by foreign banks have been replaced by active demand deposits created on the basis of the freed reserves resulting from this deposit shift. The effect of the shift is to reduce the money supply (narrowly defined), but to raise velocity. The net impact on spending would depend on the arithmetic result of the two components. Also, the rise in total deposits would raise total bank assets, affecting market yields of loans and securities, depending upon the form the asset increase took.

Instead of moving into time deposits, the foreign bank could have bought a short-term security in the open market — e.g., a United States Treasury bill. The demand deposit would then pass to the seller, and further analysis would then have to deal with the alternatives at this stage.

Note, however, the contrasting effect of the possibilities discussed here as compared with the textbook case. In the latter, a deficit led to a loss of international reserves followed by deflation in home spending. Here the spending decline was only that associated with the shift in the holding of demand deposits — by the foreign bank — and the resulting decline in velocity. This drop is obviously less than would arise from the decline in the money supply discussed in section I. Moreover, if the foreign bank held its balances as a time deposit or Treasury bill even this velocity decline would be minimized if not offset. In fact, the decline may not occur. The purchase of a Treasury bill would leave the money supply unchanged, the demand deposit being restored to an "active" owner. The switch to a time deposit reduces the aggregate volume of demand deposits, but expanded total bank assets — i.e., combined deflationary with expansionary action. It can, therefore, be concluded that the possibility of a deficit being bridged by a foreign-owned bank balance is much less deflationary than a movement of international reserves.

The impact on the foreign — surplus — country must also be considered. Since it had a surplus, its residents, net, have received payments from Americans, the foreign money supply has expanded and thus spending can be expected to rise. If the foreign commercial bank acquiring the dollar balance can count it as part of its reserve — given the fractional reserve practice — foreign commercial banks could expand deposits by a multiple of this dollar balance. These expansionary tendencies would parallel those concerning the inflow of international reserves. Thus, for the surplus country, the acquisition of dollar balances has the same effect, but the symmetry has gone. In the textbook case, the debtor and surplus countries followed similar but opposite paths whereas with dollar balances the two paths are quite different.

If the United States had a surplus with a dollar balance country, the foregoing discussion would be reversed. Foreign commercial bank reserves and thus the money supply would decline, triggering deflationary repercussions. (If the dollar balances were held by the central bank this drop would be matched by an equal drop in liabilities to the central bank.) In brief, the effects abroad would be similar to a reserve flow to the United States.

In the United States, however, dollar liabilities to foreigners decline. If these are demand deposits, the money supply would remain the same, the demand deposits owned by the foreign banks being transferred to the Americans being paid, and velocity would probably rise. If the balances were in the form of time deposits there would be pressure on United States bank reserves as time deposits were switched back to demand deposits — the reverse of the switch to time deposits discussed previously. If the reserves were Treasury bills the analysis would involve the impact of the sale by the foreign bank, i.e., the effect of the American buyer giving up money for bills. (If a foreigner bought the bills, then there would be a transfer of his balance to the American creditor — similar in effect to a transfer direct from the debtor.) Obviously, this paragraph would be symmetrical with the discussion of a United States deficit. In summary, a United States surplus with a dollar balance country would have much less expansionary influence on the United States economy than would a reserve inflow.

III. EURODOLLARS

In section II, a United States deficit initially placed United States based dollars in foreign hands. These could have been left as a dollar balance in the United States, but, especially since 1958, a new outlet has emerged — the Eurodollar market. *Eurodollars* are dollar balances transferred abroad — mainly to London banks — wherein the receiving bank takes title to the dollar balance and simultaneously owes dollars to the person or corporation transferring the funds. Dollar liabilities of the United States remain the same although the creditor has changed; the liability is to the Eurodollar bank. It is possible that the Eurodollar bank might change the form in which the balance is held, e.g., from a time deposit to a Treasury bill, but this complexity may be ignored. The effects on the United States are the same as in section II — the deficit has increased foreign-owned dollar balances, but the balance is now owed to a Eurodollar bank, rather than to a foreign commercial or central bank.[5]

The dollars, when first paid to a foreigner, may have been to a nonbanking corporation, but unlike previously, the holder may retain them for transfer to the Eurodollar market. In this event there would be little repercussion in the United States or abroad. The United States money supply would remain unchanged although its velocity may be less since active United States owners have given up dollars via a foreign corporation to a Eurodollar bank. The foreign nonbanking corporation has more money — the Eurodollar deposit — and the velocity reaction would depend on the nonbanking corporation's use of the Eurodollar deposit, and the Eurodollar bank's use of the dollar balance acquired from the corporation.

The Eurobank may use the acquired dollar balances as a reserve for a multiple expansion of Eurodollar loans and deposits — just as any bank utilizes excess reserves.[6] As a group, Eurobanks thus expand their loans and deposits. But unlike the expansions discussed in sections I and II, the locale is less certain. That is, a United States deficit with France means that the French economy receives the initial expansionary stimulus, but Eurodollars may be spent anywhere. It is even possible for most Eurodollars to result in increased spending for United States goods and services. This would indeed be a paradoxical result — a United States deficit feeding funds to the Eurodollar market which then produces a multiple flow of funds rebounding as stepped-up demand for United States goods. Here the United States deficit could stimulate the United States economy!

If the United States deficit placed dollar balances in the hands of foreign commercial banks and they transferred the funds to the Eurodollar market, the same repercussions would occur. In addition, however, if the foreign banks include their Eurodollar deposits as reserves they too could expand domestically — just as they did with a dollar balance. The United States deficit could then fuel two expansions — one by the Eurobanks, based on their acquired United States balances, and one by the foreign banks based on their Eurodollar deposit. Incidentally, the United States economy could be getting two sets of stimuli — from the spending of created Eurodollars and the spillover from expansion within the surplus country. Since the volume of Eurodollars is larger than the money supply of any country except the United States,[7] their potency can easily be visualized.

Without repeating all the details, it is evident that a United States surplus financed by foreigners drawing on Eurodollars could be deflationary both in the deficit economy abroad and perhaps in the United States. If foreigners owe Americans, their banks might draw dollars from the Eurodollar market, thus reducing their reserves and setting in motion domestic deflationary pressures. And, by reducing the Eurobanks' reserves they cause a deflation of Eurodollars. Conceivably, therefore, a United States surplus could be deflationary for the United States — the flow of orders could be cut twice — from reduced Eurodollar spending and deflation in the deficit country.

United States deficits and surpluses settled through the movement into, or out of, Eurodollars can create magnified expansion and contractions as compared with reserve flows, and may even react in ways opposite to those of the reserve flow. Since the volume of Eurodollars is so large, this is a significant consideration in payments analysis.

IV. FOREIGN EXCHANGE

A large United States deficit could lead to so large a sale of dollars as to compel the monetary authorities to support the dollar — buying the excess at the support price. The dollars could be bought with any of the acceptable foreign currencies held by the authorities — say, pounds, francs, and marks. A deficit with Germany indicates that Americans are selling dollars to buy marks. At the support point the United States monetary authorities could buy the dollars for marks, if they have them, satisfying the demand for marks directly. (If the United States does not have marks we could get them either from the International Monetary Fund — see section V — or via swap agreements — see Section VI.) In effect the United States would use mark balances as, in Section II, foreigners used dollar balances.[8] In this possibility, the emergence of a United States payment deficit would reduce United States commercial and central bank reserves, creating deflationary tendencies, while the disposition of mark holdings would have a relatively small impact on the German economy. Similarly, a United States surplus with Germany might produce added United States owned mark balances, expanding the United States economy but leaving the German economy little affected.

If, however, the United States had a deficit with Italy and we did not have a lira balance, we could use gold, or, if the Italian banks were willing to accept marks, we would give up our mark balances and the repercussions of the deficit with Italy would be the same as above for the United States. Similarly, if we had a surplus with Italy and obtained mark balances in payment, the repercussions on the United States economy would be the same as though the surplus were with Germany. In Germany the United States-Italian transfers merely change the name of the creditor and should not affect the German economy. In Italy, the gain (loss) of mark balances should be expansionary (deflationary) just as a gain (loss) of dollars balances.

V. INTERNATIONAL MONETARY FUND (IMF)

Since 1945 the international payments mechanism has included the addition of the International Monetary Fund (IMF). Although there are many ways in which the IMF facility can be used, one generalization will illustrate its bearing on the payments repercussions. Assume the United States is in balance with every country except Germany with which it has a large deficit. There is thus an excess demand for marks. The United States could draw marks from the IMF — the latter gaining dollars — and thus bridge the payments gap with Germany. The United States money supply could contract as Americans pay dollars for marks, and the German money supply could expand as marks move from the IMF to German creditors; the results are analogous to the effects of a flow of international reserves.

If the United States were in the gold or supergold tranche its international reserves decline, but if it moves into the credit tranche there is no loss of official reserves. Similarly, if the Germans were in the gold or supergold tranche their reserves rise; if in the credit tranche official reserves are unchanged. Yet, these reserve changes at the central banks are unlikely to affect economic policy since the connection between central bank reserves and monetary policy is now quite feeble. Only if reserves were to dive to alarmingly low levels would the drop trigger policy action. Thus the interposition of the IMF simply parallels those payments reactions which, in its absence, would have occurred with the reserve flow mechanism.

The latest addition to international reserves, the Special Drawing Rights (SDRs), are in effect a new reserve currency for use among official monetary authorities. They are backed by a composite of the currencies of the individual member countries — virtually indentical with IMF membership. Since their backing is limited to paper currencies, the SDRs are also called *paper gold*. Within stipulated limits[9] deficit countries can use them to obtain convertible currencies. Thus they will be giving up reserves — the SDR component — as if they had made an IMF drawing within the gold or supergold tranche, thus reducing reserves. Therefore, the impact on the deficit and surplus countries would be analogous; the surplus country receiving SDRs adds to reserves similar to a situation wherein the deficit country drew the surplus country's currency from the IMF, adding to the latter's gold or supergold tranche.

VI. SWAP AGREEMENTS

In recent years swap agreements have been created to handle short-term payments imbalances at the initiative of the Federal Reserve. For example, if the Bank of England needs dollars, it activates its swap agreement with the Federal Reserve — drawing dollars and paying the equivalent amount of pounds. The Federal Reserve thus owes pounds equal to the dollars owed by the Bank of England; the latter, however, has probably disbursed the dollars to meet its needs whereas the Federal Reserve simply holds the pounds as an asset. Later if the tide turns and the Bank of England gains dollars, they can be repaid to the Federal Reserve in exchange for pounds. If the United States is a deficit country in need of pounds, the same procedure is followed, except that the Federal Reserve would have disbursed the pounds and the Bank of England held the dollars as an asset.

Dollars acquired by the Bank of England need not be restricted to payment to American creditors, nor need any pounds acquired by the Federal Reserve be limited to payment to the British. Both currencies are used to finance transactions all over the world, but to keep the analysis manageable it is assumed that the British deficit is with the United States and the United States deficit with the British. Hence, a British need for dollars is for payment to Americans; an American need for pounds is for payment to British creditors.

There are here four possibilities:

1. The United States has a surplus — the British have a deficit — and the British activate the swap agreement to get dollars.
2. The United States has a surplus — the British have a deficit — and the United States uses the surplus to liquidate a prior swap drawing.
3. The United States has a deficit — the British have a surplus — and the United States activates the swap agreement to get pounds.
4. The United States has a deficit — the British have a surplus — and the British use the surplus to liquidate a prior swap drawing.

1. The United States pays dollars to the Bank of England which turns them over to the American creditors. The United States money supply is thus increased. In effect, the Federal Reserve has engaged in open market purchases, only it has acquired pounds instead of securities. This action is thus expansionary. In Great Britain the money supply is down as the British debtor gives up pounds to acquire the dollars needed to pay his American creditor. This leads to deflation in Great Britain, as would occur with the loss of international reserves.

2. In this instance there is an excess supply of pounds and an excess demand for dollars. Again the Federal Reserve aquires pounds by giving up dollars — expanding the United States money supply —only now the pounds are to be turned back to the Bank of England for the dollars it has been holding — acquired when the United States first activated the swap agreement. The British money supply thus drops by the amount of pounds turned over by the Federal Reserve. As in point 1 the United States surplus is expansionary and the British deficit is deflationary.

Points 3 and 4 are the reverse of 1 and 2, respectively. Both would raise the British money supply and be expansionary for the British economy; both would contract the United States money supply and be deflationary for the United States economy. These results would parallel the impact of reserve flows described in section I.

The use of swap agreements assumes that drawings arising from a deficit will be for only a short period of time; a reverse swing into surplus, it is hoped, would enable the country to liquidate the drawing. Since the United States has had a persistent deficit, this hope could not always be realized for the dollar. To liquidate swap drawings where the surplus does not materialize, the United States has resorted to direct issues of bonds to foreign creditor governments — the so-called "Roosa" bond, named for its originator. In effect, the bond is given to the foreign central bank in exchange for the dollars it is holding. The use the Treasury then makes of these returning dollars would determine their impact on the money supply. If, for example, they were spent to finance ordinary government operations, the money supply would rise and be an expansionary influence. Alternatively, if they were destroyed there would be no further influence. Incidentally, these bonds can always be converted to short-term securities and then be "cashed in" if the creditor country needs the funds.[10]

VII. SUMMARY AND CONCLUSIONS

The settlement of international payments imbalances is no longer the unique sequence associated with gold flows, and different possibilities yield different types of repercussions. In fact, it is possible for a deficit to be not only nondeflationary, but actually expansionary for the United States. Similarly, it is possible for a surplus to be deflationary. These paradoxical possibilities, as noted, are associated, especially, with the use of Eurodollars.

Numerous payments paths make quantitative analysis much more difficult. The data in most cases are not precise enough to isolate the various strands. Most probably payments are being effected through several, if not all, the methods discussed. Since, in practice, the actual surplus or deficit is not identifiable when viewing day-to-day transactions, summary statistics must be employed, and these aggregates then may foreclose the refinement necessary to pursue the investigatory suggestions indicated.

Notes

1.   For a more detailed explanation, cf. E. Marcus and M. R. Marcus, *International Trade and Finance* (New York, 1965), chap. 9. Since the text discusses the theoretical adjustment mechanism, it ignores the United States suspension of convertibility in August 1971.

2.   Before the establishment of the International Monetary Fund, the gold export point was the price at which it paid to export gold in payment of a foreign obligation, rather than sell one's currency at a discount. The support point is the price at which the central bank must buy its currency, delivering gold or acceptable foreign currencies. Under International Monetary Fund rules this support point had to be within 1 percent of par, although since December 1971 the margin was widened to 2¼ percent. Note that either alternative signals the loss of international reserves.

3.   If gold is delivered by the monetary authorities, it can be sold for the

desired foreign currency in short supply, e.g., to the (surplus) foreign currency-issuing authority.

4. For simplicity it is assumed that the banks that intervene have the currencies in excess demand. That is, if there is an excess demand for Dutch guilders it is the Dutch banks that step in.

5. The Eurodollar bank might also be a (domestic) commercial bank, but the difference is the currency it is dealing in. As a (domestic) commercial bank — in the context of section II — it is using its own country's currency — francs for a French bank, marks for a German bank, etc. As a Eurodollar bank its dealings are in dollars. The same bank could have the two separate types of operation.

6. Cf. F. Machlup, "Euro-Dollars, Once Again," Banca Nazionale del Lavoro, *Quarterly Review*, June 1972; A. W. Throop, "Eurobanking and World Inflation," Federal Reserve Bank of Dallas, *Voice*, August 1979; E. J. Frydl, "The Debate Over Regulating the Eurocurrency Markets," Federal Reserve Bank of New York, *Quarterly Review*, Winter 1979–80.

7. Cf. Frydl, p. 19.

8. In practice the foreign central bank might act for the United States if the support point were hit in the foreign currency's market; however, this would not change the analysis in the text.

9. Cf. the International Monetary Fund, *Annual Report 1979* (appendices IIB–IIF).

10. Changes in "Roosa Bonds" and other foreign currency-denominated United States obligations are reported regularly in the Treasury *Bulletin* and periodic article on "Treasury and Federal Reserve Foreign Exchange Operations" in the *Federal Reserve Bulletin*.

The Economic Impact of Inflation on Urban Areas

INTRODUCTION

An amazing paucity of data exists from which one can draw inferences about inflation and its effects on different segments of American society. Investigation of the area of interregional economics has been particularly and continuously hampered by the lack of reliable data. Yet the amount of theorizing on the impact of inflation on different regions of the American economy appears to be inversely proportional to the amount of data available. Perhaps this is how it should be, since many more hypotheses can be generated in the absence of facts.

Economists from David Hume to Milton Friedman have offered theories about inflationary effects on various regions. Some of these theories can actually be tested by a variety of data that are collected in the United States by both the Bureau of Labor Statistics and the Department of Commerce. This paper presents the results of an analytical investigation of these series.

Before we examine any data, let me make the usual disclaimer about economic information. I refer you to the findings so brilliantly expounded in Osker Morgenstern's *The Accuracy of Economic Observations*.[1] My disclaimer intends more than "lip service" to Morgenstern's caveats; I contend that analysis of the series examined in this study can prove valuable as a valid basis for decision making.

A DATA BASE

During the decade of the seventies the Bureau of Labor Statistics reported the Consumer Price Index (CPI) for American cities of various sizes. In the first step in this analysis, the CPI for American cities with populations of 3.5 million or more, (henceforth called lc for large cities),[2] was compared to cities with population sizes of 2500 or less, (called sc for small cities).[3] The data for 1971–79 are presented in Figure 1. An unexpected and unusual pattern is evident. Between 1971 and 1976, the inflation measured by the CPI in the lc exceeds the inflation or CPI of the sc. Beginning with 1977, however, and continuing through 1979 the data reverse themselves and the CPI for sc exceeds the CPI for lc. The CPI for sc was subtracted from the CPI for lc and the resultant series is plotted in Figure 2. The trend displayed in Figure 2

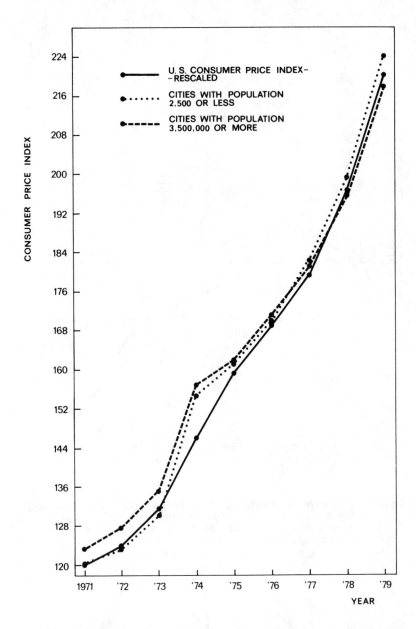

Fig. 1   Consumer Price Index for Very Large, Very Small and All U. S. Cities, 1971 - 79. *Source: Monthly Labor Review Bureau of Labor Statistics*

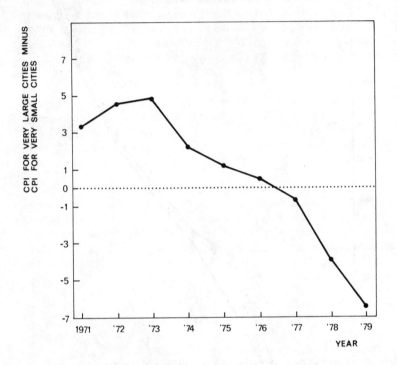

Fig. 2   **Consumer Price Index for Very Large Cities (3,500,000 pop.) Minus Consumer Price Index for Very Small Cities (pop. under 2,500), 1971-79.** *Source: Monthly Labor Review Bureau of Labor Statistics*

was examined by means of a "runs test." By chance such a trend is likely to occur only 1.5 times per 1000 observations.[4] There is a good reason, therefore, to infer that whatever effect operating is not random but systematic.

Also plotted on Figure 1 are CPI data for the United States, for 1971–79, which was rescaled to permit comparison with lc and sc.

When the United States CPI data are compared to the lc and sc, it will be noted that the United States data lie between the lc and sc series in 1971–73 and 1978–79; they lie below lc and sc points between 1974–77. When the "Friedman test" is applied to these trends the probability of obtaining this occurrence by chance is found to be .0001.[5]

STATEMENT OF THE PROBLEM

This paper will explore the possible causes of these trends in order to better understand the impact of inflation on urban and on rural areas. Two questions will be discussed (1) What caused urban areas to be more significantly affected by inflation than rural areas, 1971–76? (2) What caused the reverse to occur, 1977–79?

INFLATION THEORIES

The pursuit of an answer to these questions is guided by the taxonomy of economic theories of inflation which contain two general categories: "monetary/expenditure" theories and "structural/social" theories. Purely monetary theories range from simple notions like "too much money chasing too few goods" to more complex ideas of disequilibrium in the economy which arise out of the relationship between economic stocks and flows or between flows and flows. The large number of stock and flow variables has led to numerous disequilibrium theories each of which emphasizes a particular set of mechanisms. Monetary/expenditure analysis has been expressed in the quantity theory as well as in Keynesian economics. Whether the two approaches are treated separately or whether a synthesis between the two is developed, a common appropriate remedy for inflation results. This remedy advocates manipulation of either monetary measures or fiscal mechanisms or both.

"Structural/social" theories of inflation posit that basic structural pressures start an inflation and that social mechanisms keep inflation going. For example, Marxists have long argued that inflation is brought about by intergroup conflict over the distribution of the social product and is kept going by the social pressures that groups can exert on the political process. Explanations of inflation of this type often use a cumulative circular causation mechanism of the kind described by Myrdal[6] and introduce concepts like wage-price spirals to describe the process.

On occasion, a mechanism that employs elements of both types of theories emerge. The Phillips Curve which postulates a long-term relationship between changes in wages and unemployment can be a useful component of both monetary/expenditure theories and of structural/social ideas. Another such mechanism is the "expectations hypothesis" which postulates that social and economic groups try to anticipate the protracted experience of inflation by strategic acquisition policies and that this behavior will, in turn, worsen inflation.

THE GOVERNMENT AND INFLATION

Whatever the theory of inflation to which one subscribes, one thing is apparent; a primary *cause* of inflation is the behavior of government. No inflation can continue in the long run without government support. This conference has pointed out time and time again that the historic role of government-caused inflation probably goes back to antiquity and is strongly identified in the black money policies of "the prince" in medieval times. Although modern inflation does not bring the same benefits that debased precious metals brought to "the prince," modern governments benefit from inflation in a variety of ways.

Recently, one of the most significant benefits inflation has brought to the government is that both the absolute and relative levels of tax revenues have been raised without the necessity of increasing taxation. This mechanism is simple and is clearly understood. The progressive income tax will always take a larger bite from personal income when wages have been inflated, by putting the taxpayer in a higher tax bracket. Hence, without any legislative activity, politicians can be indirect beneficiaries of increased government revenues. This mechanism has been called the inflation bonus to government. Larger expenditure programs can be enacted from the increased revenue to benefit one or another pressure group.

A second benefit of inflation has its roots in the Phillips Curve. Controlling inflation by reducing aggregate demand through fiscal, monetary, or structural approaches has the effect of increasing the rate of unemployment. Unemployment is always a political liability to a government in power. One way in which inflation can be caused by aggregate demand increases is the absence of increase in productivity to match increased consumer disposable income. Other demand-pull inflationary possibilities include scenarios that might induce unemployment if these are not curtailed rapidly. Moreover, there are supply-induced inflations as well.

As an example, many economists feel that OPEC's control of the crude oil market has resulted in unjustified price increases since crude oil has rather an inelastic demand and supply in the relatively short run. If existing levels of output are maintained, the increase in costs for crude oil to fuel manufacturers results in increases in price. Aggregate supply curves shift upward and equilibrium, given inelastic demand, is shifted to lower levels of output. What happens to employment in the long run, therefore, will depend mainly on the effect the scarcity of oil has on the marginal product of labor. During the 1970s, the supply shocks caused by OPEC policies had a profound effect on the economy of the United States. One effect of OPEC policies was to increase our understanding of how inflation can cause a redistribution of income that is also beneficial to the government. Windfall profits led to windfall governmental revenues. Profit distribution went to economic classes that, in the short run, tended to save and/or invest a higher proportion of income, which leads to economic growth.

Yet another benefit some in government can envision from inflation is the redistribution of wealth from creditors to debtors. An examination of who were creditors and who were debtors in the 1970s is extremely interesting. Households were heavily net creditors. Federal, state, and local governments were large debtors, with net outstanding debts of $326 billion. This debt was approximately equal to the total debt of all business in the United States. Here again, the government might not have benefited if tax reduction rather than expenditure increases had become national policy.

Inflation can also be regarded by some in government as desirable because of the effect it has on foreign trade. During the post-World War II period, and continuing until the mid-sixties, the United States ran a surplus in its balance of trade account. Foreign trade has not been a major component of the United States economy, but it does account for more than 5 percent of GNP. Nonetheless, the United States ran a balance of payments deficit because of capital movements to other nations. Economists agree that the attractiveness of United States capital decreases with inflation. Large-scale capital flows responsible for the balance of payments problems could be curtailed if the balance of trade account could remain in surplus and United States goods could compete on world markets. Therefore, inflation could be envisioned as disciplining United States capital flows without requiring of distasteful legislation.

This view on the impact of inflation allows us to see clearly that a reasonable process exists which endows inflation with several benefits to the government. This in turn creates a governmental investment in inflation. On the other hand, it is also true that governments face rather large costs which are imposed by inflation. For example, the benefits of inflation to the government in international trade which can mean a reduction in capital flows out of the country will, in the long run, turn into a massive cost, inasmuch as the probabilities are extremely high that the balance of trade account will be in a chronically deficit state.

As in all economic decisions it is the ratio of costs to benefits that must be considered in determining an appropriate policy choice.

SOME ASSERTIONS ABOUT THE BEHAVIOR OF CITIES

The previous discussion of policy choice was constructed in order to develop a conjecture that is useful in examining the questions raised at the beginning of this study. Assume for a moment the following propositions for the decade of the seventies:

1. Large cities experienced larger unemployment rates than the nation at large.
2. There was a shift in income and wealth to rural areas and sc.
3. So long as lending markets were available to lc they chose to borrow rather than cut services.
4. Small cities and rural areas were trapped by Wagner's Law because they experienced real increases in income and chose to raise tax revenues or to borrow rather than cut government services.
5. Small cities and rural areas were not shut out of the lending markets.
6. After New York City's financial debacle, lc feared being shut out of the money market. They chose to cut deficits rather than risk exclusion from money lender markets.

SUPPORT OF THESE PROPOSITIONS

Each of the aforementioned propositions will be examined in detail to determine their validity.

Proposition 1: Figure 3 presents unemployment data for 1971–79 for both lc and the entire nation. In every year, the unemployment rate of lc exceeded the unemployment rate of the country. On average, the difference in unemployment rates was .913 percent. In many cases this is translated into a higher rate of public expenditure for poor relief in the lc. State expenditures for public welfare have generally been steadily growing in the United States. In the lc, matching welfare grants are sometimes required. The result of a higher unemployment rate has been larger expenditures on poor relief. In lc it might have been desirable to decrease expenditures in other categories to compensate for required increases in welfare spending. Expenditure patterns in lc, however, show few decreases in any expenditure category. Unfortunately, we cannot measure the precise effect of increased unemployment on expenditures by local governments.

Proposition 2. There was a shift in income and wealth to the sc and rural areas. The market for foodstuffs and feedstuffs are inelastic on both the supply and the demand side. As a consequence, supply reductions have led to large price increases. Eckstein has estimated that

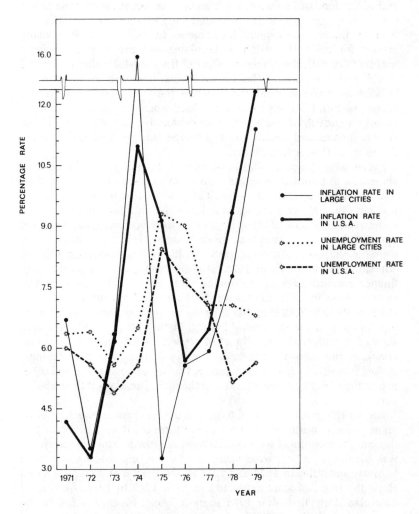

Fig. 3   Unemployment and Inflation Rates for Large Cities and the U. S. A., 1971 - 79

the result of the world shortfall in foodstuffs has been a 4 percent price increase in the overall United States CPI.[7] Farmers, and the industrial end of the foodstuffs sector, are known to be larger savers than urban dwellers. It can also be demonstrated such savings are primarily utilized to finance subsequent investments in their farms. In a rising market for food, the value of farmland and property appreciated rapidly.[8] Overall, the aggregate effect of the foodstuffs shortage in the world, and the trade of the United States, has been to increase the balance on trade account and dampen the OPEC oil shocks of the seventies. But, the price increases of food worsened the terms of trade of largely industrialized and service-centered urban areas so that the shift in income and wealth was, to a degree, interregional in the United States as well as international.

Faced with the redistributional effects caused by worldwide food shortages, lc found themselves with incomes rising less rapidly than those of sc and rural areas. A result of this was that incomes in lc rose less rapidly, and tax revenues in lc lagged behind those of other areas.

Between 1970 and 1973 the large cities were borrowing an average of over $70 billion to cover their annual budget deficits.[9] In 1974 the lc were the recipients of most of the $1.5 billion of impounded health and education funds for fiscal 1973. This released pressures on the lc to finance expenditures by borrowing and resulted in a large overall surplus. New York City led the way with a $1.2 billion surplus. In many cases, as in New York City, the expense budget was decreased by shifts of expense items to the capital budget. In 1974 all lc but Philadelphia showed a budget surplus. In 1974 New York City had come under attack in the money markets and opportunities to borrow to meet budget imbalances had closed, raising fear in the governments of other lc that they might also be attacked in the money markets if they tried to borrow.

Until 1975 lc show a trend to increasing local government employment and expenditures.[10] In the expenditures of all state governments, the pattern was one of exponential rates of growth. The one exception was highways, which were hampered by the impounding of federal highway subsidies in 1974 and 1975 by the President. Figures 4 and 5 show the trend of state expenditures from 1969 to 1978. Additional data also show that after 1975 some lc began to show a fall in the number of full-time equivalent positions in local governments.

Proposition 4. The rural governments and sc were somewhat trapped by Wagner's Law. *Wagner's Law* postulates that the increase in real incomes in an area will cause the demand for public goods to increase in proportions greater than those of nonpublic goods. Increase in incomes in the sc and rural areas was a result of the rise in prices of foodstuffs and feedstuffs and the concommitant rise in value of agricul-

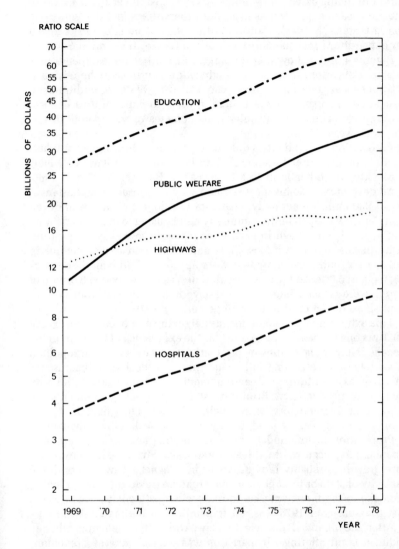

Fig. 4   Trends in State General Expenditure for Selected Functions, 1969-78.   *Source : Impact of Federal Budget on Cities op. cit. pages 90, 91*

tural producing assets. No statistical series exist to verify the extent of the increase in expenditures in sc, but expenditures in states with no lc (i.e., Montana, Nebraska, Iowa, South Dakota, among others) showed an expenditure increase in excess of the CPI for the United States.

Figures 4 and 5 show that the largest increase in state expenditures was for education. In most states education is primarily the responsibility of local government or a school district. State expenditures on education are usually on a matching basis to expenditures of local government. Thus, we can infer that increases in sc expenditures in this area were higher.

Proposition 5. Small cities did not get shut out of the money markets in 1975 or thereafter in spite of the difficulties experienced by New York City and other lc in this time period. Between 1975 and 1980, rural development loans for water and waste disposal were constant at about $600 million annually. Loans for business and industrial development were at $350 million annually and housing loan programs were initiated.[11] Even though interest rates rose, the sc had no major difficulty in floating bond issues. State and local bond issue elections in 1970, 1972, and 1974 show that voter approval of all bond issues was 63, 64, and 62 percent. During the decade as a whole over $70 billion of bonds were issued. State and local governments moved from a 7 percent share of the GNP to over 16 percent by 1979.

This extraordinary demand for capital on the part of cities during the 1970s is one of the leading reasons for the experience of inflation in the decade. Numerous studies of productivity in cities and metropolitan areas have indicated that although cities and local governments can increase expenditures and employment, they have great difficulty increasing productivity. Primarily, state and local governments are labor intensive and service producing. These sectors have had great difficulty in increasing productivity with the scale of employment.

Proposition 6. Inflationary pressure of state and local government financing has occurred in at least three ways. First, the large expenditure growth, (probably brought about by Wagner's Law). Second, the inability of state or local governments to increase productivity. Finally, recourse to the money market to finance budget deficits. Much of the last pressure after 1975 was not transmitted to the market by lc.

After the financial debacle in New York City financing, other lc reduced bond offerings. In part this was due to increased revenues, decreased spending, and a lack of deficits. Average surpluses are reported to be running around $100 million.

SOME INFERENCES ON LARGE CITIES FINANCING

Since much of the expenditure of lc is to local vendors and employees, cutbacks diminished both the stimulus and the inflationary pressures

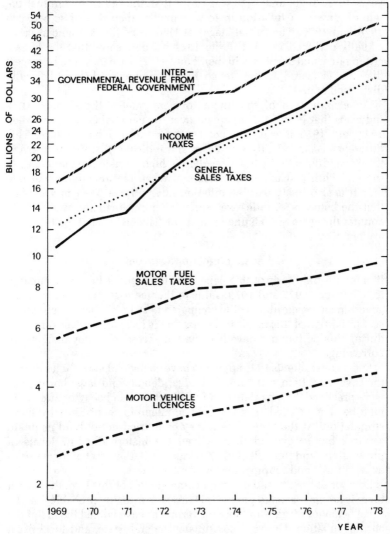

RATIO SCALE

BILLIONS OF DOLLARS

INTER−
GOVERNMENTAL REVENUE FROM
FEDERAL GOVERNMENT

INCOME
TAXES

GENERAL
SALES TAXES

MOTOR FUEL
SALES TAXES

MOTOR VEHICLE
LICENCES

1969   '70   '71   '72   '73   '74   '75   '76   '77   '78

YEAR

Fig. 5   Trends in State General Revenue from Selected Major Sources, 1969-78. *Source: Impact of Federal Budget on Cities, op. cit. pages 90, 91*

of these expenditures. It is clear from the data that the CPI in lc in the years 1977, 1978, and 1979 was lower than the CPI in sc and that the rate of growth of inflation in lc was smaller than that of sc between 1976 and 1979. The initial stages of New York City's financial crisis actually occurred in 1974. From 1974 on, data show that the lc as a group ran actual surpluses in their budgets. These data strongly suggest that the lc feared having to go to the money market in a fiscally distressed state.

An examination of the unemployment rate in the lc after 1977 indicates that it was 1.084 percent over the national average, between 1971 and 1976 it was .828 percent over the national average. This difference is statistically significant and indicates that the decrease in local spending rates by the lc resulted in higher unemployment rates in the lc.[12] Phillips Curves indicates that when the unemployment rate falls it is also likely that the inflation rate will rise. We can speculate that the behavior of cities was such that local financing was used to counter the cycle of high unemployment. This in turn fed the inflationary spiral.

SOME CONCLUDING NOTES

It is the central thesis of this paper that the higher CPI in sc compared to lc between 1977 and 1979 is due to the decrease in the rate of local government expenditures of lc compared to a constant and high rate in sc. Supportive of this thesis is the fact that lc have run budget surpluses during this period and have had limited access to money markets for borrowing.

Local governments in lc appear to have changed their policies during the seventies. Before 1975, high budget deficits and large borrowings were practiced. The explanation for this change in behavior after 1975 may be that lc tried to offset higher unemployment rates by fiscal stimulation. At the same time it may be lc tried not only to maintain services but to expand them. Given the historically low levels of productivity and the inflexibility to increase it, the effect of increases in expenditures and employment was inflationary.

Data for sc are unavailable for a complete test of this hypothesis, but there is ample reason to pursue this thesis. It is highly probable that the fiscal behavior of state and local government have fanned the fire of the current inflation. Unless a coordinated federal, state, and local fiscal policy can be developed along with a consistent monetary policy, inflation is likely to be here for some time. Inflation may then become a mechanism to bring the economy into equilibrium in the terms of trade between the lc and sc and rural areas. It is, however, quite likely that, without curtailment of current inflation, expectations will result in structural/social mechanisms that will act to aggravate the price jumps and make long-term inflation a self-perpetuating condition.

Notes

1. O. Morgenstern, *The Accuracy of Economic Observations*, 2d ed. (Princeton, 1963), *passim*.

2. The cities in the lc category are Chicago, Detroit, Los Angeles, New York, and Philadelphia.

3. The cities in the sc category are a random sample of over 400 cases that vary from year to year.

4. $p < .0015$ for $z = 2.97$.

5. Chi square $= 20.668$ with 2 degrees of freedom had a likelihood of occurrence of $p < .0001$.

6. G. Myrdal, *Rich Lands and Poor; The Road to World Prosperity* (New York, 1958), *passim*.

7. O. Eckstein, *The Great Recession* (Amsterdam, 1978), chap. 8.

8. John A. Schnittker, "The 1972–73 Food Price Spiral," *Brookings Papers on Economic Activity* 2 (1973): 498–506.

9. U.S. Department of Commerce, *State and Government Finances*, 1970–1973.

10. House Banking and Finance Committee and Urban Affairs Committee, *Impact of Federal Budget on Cities*, 1978 ASI index no. 21248.34, p. 83.

11. National League of Cities, *NLC Washington Report*, Vol. IV, no. 4, p. 109.

12. $t = 3.182$ which is significant at the .05 level with 6 degrees of freedom.

Taxes and Inflation

DAVID J. SMYTH

INTRODUCTION

The traditional macroeconomic analysis of the relationship between income taxes, output, and the price level is straightforward but incorrect. It concentrates on the impact of income taxes and changes in tax rates on aggregate demand. But income taxes also have supply-side effects and we neglect these at our peril. The present paper shows that stagflation can be accounted for by these supply-side effects. The standard analysis concludes that money supply or government expenditure increases and tax rate cuts will all be inflationary, causing the price level to rise and output either to rise or remain unchanged. The present analysis shows that when supply-side effects are properly accounted for, the aggregate supply schedule will be downward sloping.[1] Increases in the money stock or government expenditure will simultaneously raise the price level and lower the level of output. A tax rate cut will raise the level of output; its effect on the price level is uncertain.

There are two key elements to the present analysis. First, tax rates are set in nominal terms and are progressive; thus when money wage rates rise, the effective tax rate rises even though real wages may not have risen. This effect should be well known to most of us taxpayers. Secondly, workers are concerned about the post-tax real wage rates that they receive, not the pre-tax real wage rates. We shall show that these two influences cause the aggregate demand and supply schedules to be interdependent and the aggregate supply schedule to be downward sloping.

The aggregate supply effects of income tax changes have not been ignored entirely. Consideration of the supply side effects was initiated in a challenging article by Colin Clark (1945). Clark argued that high tax rates had political and economic effects that were inflationary and that inflationary pressures became acute once taxes exceeded 25 percent of national income. A popular version of Clark's article appeared in *Harper's* (Clark, 1950), and this attracted widespread attention.[2] Within mathematically formulated models, Brownlee (1954) and Hall and Tobin (1955) concluded that an increase in the income tax rate might lead to an increase in the price level. After a lapse of over a decade, interest in the supply-side effects of a tax rate increase was rekindled by President Johnson's 10 percent tax surcharge, but the resulting analyses ignored the earlier work which they failed to advance to any substantial degree.[3]

On the side of aggregate demand, it is rightly assumed that households make their consumption decisions on the basis of their income after tax. On the supply side, the conventional assumption is that workers make their labor supply decisions on the basis of real wages gross of tax. The latter implies that if the real wage rate after tax changes because the pre-tax wage rate changes, then labor supply will change; but if the post-tax wage change is brought about by tax changes with the pre-tax real wage rate unchanged, then there will be no effect on the labor supply. This asymmetric treatment of taxes is clearly inconsistent with a decision-making model of households in which the work-leisure-consumption-saving decisions are interdependent.

The assumption made in this paper that the supply of labor depends on the real post-tax wage rate is to be preferred to the usual assumption on theoretical grounds. In addition, there are various pieces of empirical evidence supporting the assumption. The first type of evidence is anecdotal — workers say that they look at the size of the post-tax wage packet. Secondly, the last Labour government in the United Kingdom and the current Carter administration both believe in the assumption. The Labour government told the trade unions that it would reduce taxes if wage demands were kept down. And the Carter administration devised a scheme by which those workers who agreed to keep wage increases below a certain limit would be recompensated by tax refunds if inflation exceeded that limit. And, finally, there is econometric evidence for the United Kingdom in Johnson and Timbrell (1973).[4]

AGGREGATE SUPPLY

The supply side of our model is given by the following:

$$Y = Y(E, Y_0) \qquad Y_E > 0, \ Y_{EE} = 0 \tag{1}$$
$$W = PY_E \tag{2}$$
$$K = K(W, T^*) \qquad K_W < 0, \ K_{T^*} < 0 \tag{3}$$
$$N = N(X) \qquad N_X > 0 \tag{4}$$
$$X = KW/P \tag{5}$$
$$N = E \tag{6}$$

where the notation is as follows:

Y = gross national product in real terms;
E = demand for labor;
P = price level;
W = nominal wage rate before tax payments;
W/P = real wage rate before tax payments;

K = proportion of the nominal wage rate remaining after payment of taxes (equal to one minus the average tax rate on wages);

T^* = tax schedule such that a rise in T^* represents an increase in tax rates;

N = supply of labor;

X = real wage rate after tax payments.

Throughout shift parameters are indicated by zero subscripts and partial derivatives by the appropriate subscripts — for instance, $Y_E = \delta Y/\delta E$.

Equation (1) is the production function; to keep the analysis as simple as possible, we are assuming constant returns to labor.[5] Profit maximization is ensured in (2) by equality between the real wage rate and the marginal product of labor. In Equation (3) progressive taxation is introduced, the effective average tax rate rising with the nominal wage rate and with increases in the tax schedule; the proportion of the wage rate remaining after taxes, K, falls with both W and T^*.[6] In (4) it is assumed that the supply of labor increases with the real wage rate net of tax, X, which is defined in Equation (5). Equation (6) is the labor market clearing condition.

Totally differentiating Equations (1) to (6) yields, respectively:

$$dY = Y_E dE + dY_0 \tag{7}$$
$$dW = Y_E dP \tag{8}$$
$$dK = K_W dW + K_{T^*} dT^* \tag{9}$$
$$dN = N_X dX \tag{10}$$
$$P dX + X dP = K dW + W dK \tag{11}$$
$$dN + dE \tag{12}$$

Combining (7) to (12) gives the aggregate supply schedule:

$$dY = N_X Y_E^2 (Y_E K_W dP + K_{T^*} dT^*) + dY_0 \tag{13}$$

The slope of the aggregate supply schedule is given by:

$$\frac{dY}{dP|_S} = N_X Y_E^3 K_W < 0 \tag{14}$$

The slope is negative. An increase in tax rates will shift the aggregate supply schedule to the left as:

$$\frac{dY}{dT^*|_S} = N_X Y_E^2 K_{T^*} < 0 \tag{15}$$

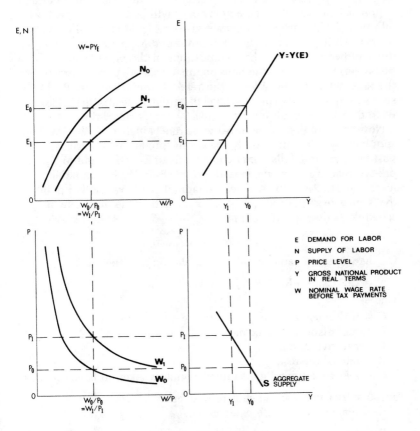

Fig. 1   Derivation of the Aggregate Supply Schedule

Figure 1 illustrates the derivation of the aggregate supply schedule. We take T^* to be given. The northwest quadrant plots the labor demand and supply schedules. The labor supply schedule shifts as the nominal wage shifts because with T^* given, the effective tax rate changes. We start with the labor supply schedule N_0 corresponding to a nominal wage W_0. The labor market is cleared where the labor demand and supply schedules intersect; employment will be E_0 and the real wage rate W_0/P_0. The northeast quadrant gives the production function and we read off the level of output Y_0 corresponding to employment E_0. In the southwest quadrant the combinations of the price levels and the real wage rates that give the same nominal wage are plotted. Drawing in the nominal wage line W_0 we can read off the price level P_0. In the southeast quadrant we plot the level of output Y_0 against the price level P_0 to obtain one point on the aggregate supply schedule.

Now suppose that the nominal wage rate is higher, at W_1. The labor supply schedule shifts to N_1 as, at any pre-tax real wage rate, the post-tax real wage falls. Employment falls to E_1 and output to Y_1. The pre-tax real wage is unchanged, so $W_1/P_1 = W_0/P_0$, and the price level rises, to P_1. In the southeast quadrant, we have another point on the aggregate supply schedule. It is clear that the aggregate supply schedule is downward sloping.

AGGREGATE DEMAND

On the aggregate demand side, we write the IS schedule as

$$Y = C(D,C_0) + I(R,I_0) + G_0 \quad 0 < C_D < 1, \ I_R < 0 \qquad (16)$$

where

C = real consumption;
D = real disposable income;
I = real investment;
R = rate of interest;
G = real government expenditure which is taken to be exogenous;

and 0 subscripts indicate shift parameters.

Real disposable income is given by

$$D = KY \qquad (17)$$

Substituting for D from (17) into (16) and differentiating totally gives

$$(1-C_D)dY = dC_0 + dI_0 + dG_0 + C_D Y dK + I_R dR \qquad (18)$$

The LM schedule is

$$L(Y,R,L_0) = M_0/P \qquad (19)$$

and differentiating totally yields

$$L_R dR = ((dM_0/P) - dL_0) - L_Y dY - (M_0/P^2)dP \qquad (20)$$

Combining (18) and (20) yields the aggregate demand schedule

$$\left(1 - C_D K + \frac{I_R L_Y}{L_R}\right) dY = dC_0 + dI_0 + dG_0 + \frac{I_R}{L_R}\left(\frac{dM_0}{P} - dL_0\right)$$
$$+ C_D Y dK - \frac{I_R M_0}{L_R P^2} dP \tag{21}$$

It is apparent that the aggregate demand schedule is not independent of the aggregate supply schedule for (21) includes dK which, from (9), depends not only on the exogenous dT^*, but also on dW. Thus, the aggregate demand schedule will shift as the money wage rate changes. The easiest way to handle this is to make use of Equations (8) to (12) to eliminate dW and replace it with dP. We obtain

$$dK = K_{T^*} dT^* + Y_E K_W dP \tag{22}$$

and substituting in (22) yields

$$\left(1 - C_D K + \frac{I_R L_Y}{L_R}\right) dY = dC_0 + dI_0 + dG_0 + \frac{I_R}{L_R}\left(\frac{dM_0}{P} - dL_0\right)$$
$$+ C_D Y K_{T^*} dT^* + \left(C_D Y K_W Y_E - \frac{I_R M_0}{L_R P^2}\right) dP \tag{23}$$

The slope of the aggregate demand schedule is

$$\frac{\delta Y}{\delta P}\bigg|_D = \frac{1 - C_D K + \dfrac{I_R L_Y}{L_R}}{C_D Y K_W Y_E - \dfrac{I_R M_0}{L_R P^2}} < 0 \tag{24}$$

The aggregate demand schedule slopes downward for two reasons. First, the usual effect that the value of the real money stock declines as the price level rises. Secondly, because when the price level rises, the nominal wage rate rises and thus the effective tax rate rises.

THE COMPLETE MODEL

The complete model may be written in matrix form as

$$
\begin{bmatrix}
1 - C_D K + \dfrac{I_R L_Y}{L_R} & \dfrac{I_R M_0}{L_R P^2} - C_D Y K_W Y_E \\[3mm]
1 & -N_X Y_E^3 K_W
\end{bmatrix}
\begin{bmatrix}
dY \\[3mm]
dP
\end{bmatrix}
=
$$

$$
\begin{bmatrix}
dC_0 + dI_0 + dG_0 + \dfrac{I_R}{L_R}\left(\dfrac{dM_0}{P} - dL_0\right) + C_D Y K_{T^*} dT^* \\[4mm]
dY_0 + N_X Y_E^2 K_{T^*} dT^*
\end{bmatrix}
\tag{25}
$$

The Jacobian, Δ, is

$$
\Delta = \left(1 - C_D K + \frac{I_R L_Y}{L_R}\right)\left(\frac{\delta Y}{\delta P}\Big|_D - \frac{\delta Y}{\delta P}\Big|_S\right)
\tag{26}
$$

As the first term in (26) is positive, the sign of Δ is given by

$$
\Delta \gtreqless 0 \quad \text{as} \quad \frac{\delta Y}{\delta P}\Big|_D - \frac{\delta Y}{\delta P}\Big|_S \lesseqgtr 0
\tag{27}
$$

We shall assume that the aggregate supply schedule is steeper than the aggregate demand schedule, and hence that Δ is negative. This is the most plausible assumption for two reasons: First, on conventional dynamic assumptions the equilibrium is stable (whereas equilibrium with the aggregate demand schedule flatter than the aggregate supply schedule is unstable). Second, the tax effect that has been introduced rotates a vertical aggregate supply schedule in a counterclockwise direction, and given the aggregate demand schedule, a more substantial tax effect is necessary for the aggregate supply schedule to be the flatter schedule than for it to be the steeper.[7]

Equation (25) may be solved by Cramer's Rule to yield any results of interest. For instance, the output and price multipliers for a change in government expenditure are

$$\delta Y/\delta G_0 = -N_X Y_E^3 K_W / \Delta < 0 \tag{28}$$

$$\delta P/\delta G_0 = -1/\Delta > 0 \tag{29}$$

The money multipliers are

$$\frac{\delta Y}{\delta M_0} = \frac{-N_X Y_E^3 K_W I_R}{P L_R} / \Delta < 0 \tag{30}$$

$$\frac{\delta P}{\delta M_0} = \frac{-I_R}{P L_R} / \Delta > 0 \tag{31}$$

These results are illustrated in Figure 2, where the aggregate demand curve shifts to the right (from D_0 to D_1) causing a fall in output from Y_0 to Y_1 and a rise in the price level from P_0 to P_1.

A tax rate increase means an increase in T^*. We have

$$\frac{\delta Y}{\delta T^*} = -N_X Y_E^2 K_{T^*} \cdot \frac{I_R M_0}{L_R P} / \Delta < 0 \tag{32}$$

$$\frac{\delta P}{\delta T^*} = K_{T^*} \left[N_X Y_E^2 \left(1 - C_D K + \frac{I_R L_Y}{L_R} \right) - C_D Y \right] / \Delta \tag{33}$$

The result of a tax rate increase is a reduction in the level of output. The effect on the price level is ambiguous. The aggregate demand schedule and the aggregate supply schedule both shift to the left and the price level may rise, remain unchanged or fall, depending on the relative magnitude of the shifts and the slopes of the curves. We have

$$\frac{\delta P}{\delta T^*} \gtrless 0 \quad \text{as} \quad N_X Y_E^2 \left(1 - C_D K + \frac{I_R L_Y}{L_R} \right) - C_D Y \gtrless 0 \tag{34}$$

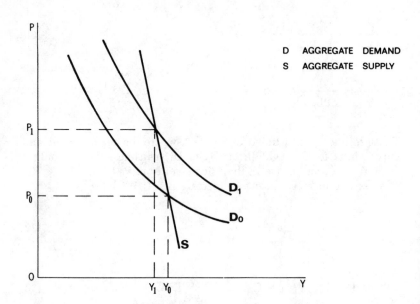

Fig. 2   Effect of an Increase in Aggregate Demand

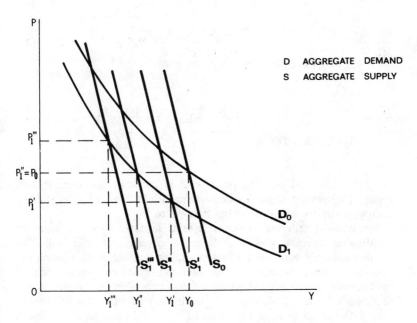

Fig. 3   Effect of a Tax Rate Increase

The possibilities are illustrated in Figure 3, where the aggregate demand schedule shifts from D_0 to D_1, and the aggregate supply schedule shifts from S_0 to S_1', S_1'', or S_1'''.

Finally, we may consider the effect of simultaneously raising government expenditure and tax rates to keep aggregate demand unchanged. This involves setting

$$dT^* = (-dG_0)/(C_D Y K_{T^*}) \tag{35}$$

We obtain

$$\left. \frac{\delta Y}{\delta G_0} \right|_{dG_0 + C_D Y K_T \cdot dT^* = 0} = \left[\frac{N_X Y_E^2 I_R M_0}{C_D L_R Y P^2} - N_X K_W Y_E^3 \right] \Delta < 0 \tag{36}$$

$$\left. \frac{\delta P}{\delta G_0} \right|_{dG_0 + C_D Y K_T \cdot dT^* = 0} = \frac{-N_X Y_E^2}{C_D Y}\left(1 - C_D K + \frac{I_R L_Y}{L_R}\right)\!/ \Delta > 0 \tag{37}$$

Output is lowered and the price level is increased as illustrated in Figure 4 where the aggregate demand schedule does not shift and the aggregate supply schedule shifts from S_0 to S_1.

It may be of interest to sketch a brief scenario here. Consider an administration that wishes to increase government spending. The administration's economic advisers, being familiar with elementary economic theory, recommend that such expenditures be accompanied by tax rate increases just sufficient to keep aggregate demand unchanged so that inflation may be avoided. According to the present model, the effect of such a policy will be a fall in output and a rise in prices. If the administration then attempts to counter the resulting increase in unemployment by further increasing government expenditures or by monetary expansion, it will only make matters worse; there will be a further fall in output and a further increase in prices.

What should we do about stagflation then? If the present model is correct, the remedy is quite straightforward. We should cut government expenditure and impose monetary restraint as these will both expand output and lower the price level. We can achieve the same results by cutting tax rates and holding aggregate demand constant by monetary and other fiscal measures.

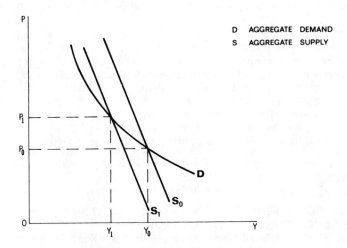

Fig. 4   Effect of Simultaneously Raising Government Expenditure and Tax Rates to Keep Aggregate Demand Unchanged

Notes

1. Earlier studies that used the tax effects to obtain a downward-sloping aggregate supply schedule are Smyth (1975, 1976, 1978) and Katseli-Papaefstratiou (1979). Campbell and Dorenfeld (1979) and Smith (1980) also obtained a downward-sloping aggregate supply schedule for other reasons.
2. For instance, Pechman and Mayer (1952) and Smith (1952).
3. Hotson (1967, 1971a, 1971b), Eisner (1969, 1971a, 1971b), Hansen (1971), Smyth (1973), and Blinder (1973).
4. For a more detailed survey of the evidence, see Smyth (1976, 1978).
5. Thus, $Y_{EE} = 0$, $Y = Y_E E$ and profits are zero. Once we relax the assumption of constant returns to labor, we have to allow for taxes on profits as well as on wages.
6. Note that it is necessary to specify the model so that effective tax rates are progressively related to nominal wage rates not to nominal national income. For the individual worker, what is relevant in his labor supply decision is the effective tax rate on his wages, given the progressive tax structure that he faces, not how aggregate taxes respond to changes in nominal national income for whatever reason. Smyth (1975) and Katseli-Papaefstratiou (1979) both make the specification error of introducing progressivity with respect to national income instead of with respect to the nominal wage rate.
7. If $\Delta > 0$, then the signs of the multipliers given below are reversed.

References

Blinder, Alan S. "Can Income Tax Increases be Inflationary? An Expository Note," *National Tax Journal* 26 (June 1973): 295–301.

Brownlee, O. H. "Taxation and the Price Level in the Short Run," *Journal of Political Economy* 62 (February 1954): 26–33.

Campbell, Harry F. and Dorenfeld, David L. "Money Disillusion and Stagflation," *Journal of Macroeconomics* 1 (Winter 1979): 131–39.

Clark, Colin. "Public Finance and Changes in the Value of Money," *Economic Journal* 55 (December 1945): 371–89.

Clark, Colin. "The Danger Point in Taxes," *Harper's Magazine*, December 1950, 67–69.

Eisner, Robert. "Fiscal and Monetary Policy Reconsidered," *American Economic Review*, December 1969, 59, 897–905.

Eisner, Robert. "What Went Wrong?," *Journal of Political Economy* 79 (May/June 1971): 629–41.

Eisner, Robert. "Fiscal and Monetary Policy Reconsidered: Reply," *American Economic Review* 61 (June 1971): 458–61.

Hall, Challis A., Jr., and Tobin, James. "Income Taxation, Output and Prices," *Economia Internazionale* 8 (August 1955): 522–42; 8 (November 1955): 742–61; 9 (February 1956): 1–8. Reprinted in James Tobin, *Essays in Economics*, vol. 1, *Macroeconomics* (Amsterdam, 1971), pp. 47–82.

Hansen, Bent. "Fiscal and Monetary Policy Reconsidered: Comment," *American Economic Review* 61 (June 1971): 444–47.

Hotson, John H. "Neo-Orthodox Keynesianism and the 45° Heresy," *Nebraska Journal of Economics and Business* 6 (Autumn 1967): 34–39.

Hotson, John H. "Fiscal and Monetary Policy Reconsidered: Comment," *American Economic Review* 61 (June 1971): 448–51.

Hotson, John H. "Changes in Sectoral Income Shares: Some Neglected Factors in Inflation," *Nebraska Journal of Economics and Business* 10 (Winter 1971): 3–13.

Johnston, J. and Timbrell, M. "Empirical Tests of a Bargaining Theory of Wage Determination," *Manchester School of Economics and Social Studies* 41 (June 1973): 141–67.

Katseli-Papaefstratiou, Louaka T. "Nominal Tax Rates and the Effectiveness of Fiscal Policy," *National Tax Journal* 32 (March 1979): 77–82.

Pechman, Joseph A. and Mayer, Thomas. "Mr. Colin Clark on the Limits of Taxation," *Review of Economics and Statistics* 34 (August 1952): 232–42.

Smith, Dan T. "Note on Inflationary Consequences of High Taxation," *Review of Economics and Statistics* 34 (August 1952): 243–47.

Smith, Paul E. "Supply, Wealth Effects, Negative Multipliers and Stability," *Journal of Macroeconomics* 2 (Winter 1980): 41–62.

Smyth, David J. "A Macroeconomic Model for Problems of Resource Allocation Between the Private and Public Sectors," O.E.C.D., Paris, August 1973. (Mimeographed.)

Smyth, David J. "Income Taxes, Labor Supply, Output and the Price Level," *Claremont Economic Papers*, May 1975, 138.

Smyth, David J. "The Macroeconomics of a Declining Economy: Britain," paper presented at the Southern Economic Association annual meeting, November 1976.

Smyth, David J. "Income Taxes, Labor Supply, Output and the Price Level," *Wayne Economic Papers*, No. 52, October 1978.

Inflation and the International Monetary Order

MIKLOS SZABO PELSOCZI

I. INTRODUCTION

Economists are good at splitting hairs. Their record for pulling the different strands of society together and thus creating the preconditions for sustained noninflationary growth has been less brilliant, certainly during the last fifteen years.

One of the meaningless controversies of the hairsplitting type is between monetarism and fundamentalism. The monetarist approach holds that in a closed system, like the world economy, the price level with fixed exchange rates depends exclusively on the money stock, and the velocity of money in circulation. In contrast, the fundamentalists assert that the root cause of price-level, money stock and velocity changes are exogenous to the monetary system. They originate in the political realm and their instruments are wars, the financing of wars, both hot and cold, reparations and war debts, the political preferences of governments with respect to social services or the lack of them, structural differences between countries in peacetime and even more before and after wars, and changes in structural differences due to demographic, technological, and ideological transformation.

Frankly, I do not detect any incompatibility between these two approaches. Money is universal and has been from the dawn of history. So it is with social change. More often than not social change results in monetary change, and the change in the monetary order results in the transformation of the social environment. Instead of being worlds apart, monetarism and fundamentalism are closely interrelated. None of the phenomena described by one could be understood without comprehending the set of facts and relationships described by the other. Some people might prefer to chew their food with either their upper or their lower jaw. I need both.

Having said this, you will not be surprised if I describe the inflation of the 1970s as both monetary and fundamental in origin, in its effects to date and in its probable future course. The inflation of the 1970s was created as much by the destruction of the international monetary order, prevailing for a quarter century following World War II, as the breakdown itself was preceded by political errors and misjudgments. The sorry monetary mess succeeding it, once described as the greatest monetary achievement of mankind, although fortunately not characterized as better or worse, itself opened up ways for social change which reshaped the economic and political structure of the world in ways which would have been impossible otherwise. This social change brought with it more inflation, the erosion of real values and created a maelstrom which, although some of its clouds have a silver lining, is still far from under control.

I will aim in this paper to present a necessarily sketchy outline of both the monetary and the fundamental causes of the inflation of the 1970s and its consequences, present and future, for the international political order in general and for the international monetary order in particular.

II. THE BRETTON WOODS SYSTEM

The first twenty years after the war were relatively clear sailing. Between 1947 and 1966 United States inflation, as measured by the GNP deflator averaged about 1.5 percent, and real GNP growth 4.5 percent. International reserves of central banks, as proxy for world liquidity, were steadily increasing more or less parallel with the annual rate of world trade expansion.[1] Total world reserves of central banks including gold, foreign exchange and later SDR's were $44 billion at the end of 1949, increasing to $55 billion by the end of 1958, and to $134 billion at the end of 1971.

This relative stability, and I do not want to exaggerate its merits, rested on an international monetary system, embedded in the Bretton Woods Agreement of 1944. Exchange rates under this system were fixed, or nearly so. Currencies were convertible into each other, but only the dollar was convertible into gold. World monetary gold remained roughly unchanged, as yearly production of gold and its industrial consumption almost offset each other. The increase of world reserves was almost exclusively due to the holding of dollar reserves by central banks. These reserves increased from $11 billion at the end of 1949 to $17 billion at the end of 1958, and to roughly $70 billion by the end of 1971.

It is clear that an expanding world economy needed liquidity, and that this liquidity under the Bretton Woods Agreement, could have come from nowhere else but United States balance of payments deficits. At the beginning of this process United States balance of payment deficits were modest. Between 1948 and 1959 net losses in United States official reserves were only $10.7 billion or only $1 billion per year. During the next seven years the rate of the worsening reserve position nearly doubled from $1 billion per year to $1.7 billion. The real decline in our reserve position occurred during the 1967–1972 period when the yearly decline in our position amounted to $8 billion per year. The worst years were 1970–1972, averaging $16 billion per year, and up to that date, the worst of all was 1971 when the decline amounted to $30 billion.[2]

Table 1. United States Balance of Payments Deficits 1948–1972
($ billion)

1948–59	$10.7
1960–66	11.9
1967–72	56.0
Total	78.6
Financed by Gold	15.0
Dollar Liabilities	63.6

United States reserve losses were financed partly from the conversion of dollars into gold, partly from the increase of dollar liabilities held abroad. In 1948 the United States held about 700 million ounces of gold, corresponding to about 70 percent of world gold reserves. By the end of 1971 our share of world gold reserves dropped to 28 percent represented by about 280 million ounces. Since 1971 our gold reserves fell further. They amounted to 267 million ounces at the end of 1979. Those who bemoan the (to my mind) completely useless loss of 13 million ounces during the last eight years should think of the 420 million ounces we squandered between 1948 and 1971. The value of the 420 million ounces at the then prevailing official rate of $35 per ounce amounted to $15 billion. The balance, or $62 billion, of our cumulative balance of payment deficit was financed through our increasing indebtedness abroad. The rapid loss of gold led to the closing of the gold window in August 1971. In effect, the United States unilaterally abdicated its contractual obligation to maintain a sound international monetary system.

Were the rise and fall of the Bretton Woods Agreement monetary or fundamental? They were both. The creation of the charter itself was a political act. The international monetary chaos which eventually led to World War II convinced policy makers of the epoch that an international monetary system was needed. Thus the charter was conceived and became essentially responsible for the relatively smooth functioning of the world economy for over two decades. This was a monetary phenomenon. However, American policy insisted at Bretton Woods that the international reserve currency unit should be the dollar and not the SDR or its equivalent. This was an exogenous factor, supposedly in the national interest. There is some form of primitive notion still loose in the country that it is good for the dollar to be a reserve currency. In a recent article a well-known scholar complained that "if the United States would no longer accept responsibility for monetary stability . . . the days of the dollar as the reserve currency might soon come to an end."[3] Of course we must bring our balance of payments into equilibrium, but not for the purpose of regaining the unfair and shortlived advantages, together with the long-lasting, fair, but painful retributions of being a reserve-currency country.

The trouble with being a reserve-currency country is that you must try to accomplish two basically incompatible goals: to provide the world with liquidity and to maintain a balance of payments equilibrium. This is impossible in the long run. You can provide liquidity only through balance of payment deficits. The more liquidity you provide the more your currency loses its value and the less it will be accepted as a reserve currency. On the other hand, if you bring the foreign sector into balance, the world would become illiquid and a world depression would ensue.

Unfortunately, in 1944 United States policy makers saw only the short-term advantages of being a reserve currency. Their ill-understood national interest prevailed. That is why the Bretton-Woods system broke down, and that is why we are in a mess.

My next task is to describe this chaos.

III. THE CURRENT MONETARY CHAOS

Everybody would like to print his or her own money. To some extent we do this through bank overdrafts and the use of credit cards. Nevertheless, the loan collector catches up with normal humans fairly soon. Sovereign states are more free. But in both cases the motive force is the same, namely that the urge to spend is much greater, almost in all cases, than the capacity to produce. In the Middle Ages one pound sterling used to be one pound of silver. Today with $40 per ounce of silver and $2 per BP, 1 lb. of silver is worth 340 pounds. Most of the depreciation of the currency is pre-Keynesian, so let us not blame everything on the Squire of Bloomsbury.

The purpose of an international monetary system, or for that matter of any banking system, is to keep production and spending in reasonable balance. It was this discipline which was imposed by Bretton Woods on most of the world community and subsequently dissolved not in a burst of sorrow but rather of self-congratulation. There is a strand of economic thinking in this country and elsewhere which considers the existence of the IMF as an intolerable burden on the freedom of enterprise. This persuasion worked for a generation not on strengthening the International Monetary Fund (IMF) through the early introduction of the SDR and through its taking over from the dollar the role of an international reserve currency, but on its emasculation.

When the Vietnam tragedy accomplished this, they proclaimed the millenium. From then on there would be no striped pants international bureaucrats telling individual countries what to do, but free market forces would express the real relative purchasing power of each currency. As it was thought that the purchasing power parity is a long-term structural phenomenon not exposed to short-term arbitrary fluctuations, it followed that exchange rates would remain stable on their own, without any government intervention. It was also maintained that this new interpretation of economic freedom would do away with all future danger of inflation since national governments, jealously watching their foreign sector, would not dare to run budgetary deficits and would enthusiastically stamp out the last vestiges of Keynesian thinking.

Unfortunately, the theory, when applied to real life, failed abysmally. The IMF became powerless, all right. But international liquidity creation shifted from international striped pants not to the ubiquitous free market, but to national bureaucrats in burnooses, plain pants, or loin cloths. Why the idea was advanced in the first place, that national bureaucracies would exercise more discipline than international bureaucracies remain a mystery to me. In any case, with international discipline gone, national governments became more exposed to national pressure groups than they were before. The urge to spend more than produced was translated into well-organized national or international lobbies and their power soon found expression in the accelerated activity of printing presses the world over. As a consequence, international liquidity exploded.

Table 2. International Liquidity (billions of SDR)

	Gold	Foreign Exchange	SDR	Total	% Growth per Annum (simple av.)
1949	34	11	—	45	—
1959	40	16	1	57	2.7
1969	41	33	5	79	3.9
1979 without gold valuation:					
	40	237	24	301	28.1
1979 with gold valuation:					
	500	237	24	761	86.0

Source: Robert Triffin, "The Future of the International Monetary System," Conference of the Global Independence Center, Philadelphia, October 1979 + IMF.

Please look at the last two figures in the last column of Table 2. They are not misprints. During the 1950s and 1960s international liquidity grew at a 3 to 4 percent annual rate, during the 1970s the rate increased to almost 30 percent, if central bank gold reserves are calculated at the completely meaningless SDR 35 per ounce IMF bookkeeping price, and 86 percent if gold is valued at approximate market prices. While not every country declared an official revaluation of its gold reserves, it is my view that for all practical purposes central bank gold stocks function as a reserve, which if used will always change hands at market prices unless an official price is once more reimposed by international agreement.

But this is not all. During the 1970s a new form of financing developed in Europe. I am speaking of the Eurocurrency markets. These consist of loans made abroad — thereby essentially escaping the home country's jurisdiction. By the middle of 1979 external assets in foreign currencies of the 10 European reporting members of the Bank of International Settlements (BIS) amounted to $500 billion of which about 70 percent were U.S. dollars, the balance mainly German marks and Swiss francs. At the beginning of the 1970s Eurofinancing did not exceed $100 billion; the $400 billion increment must be added to the already swollen figure of central banks' liquidity. According to some sources the gross figure is closer to U.S. $1.6 trillion. Taking these figures into account it is safe to say that international liquidity during the 1970s increased at an average annual rate of no less than 100 percent with gold valued at market prices and at least 50 percent per year if gold was valued at the unrealistic accounting rate of SDR 35 per ounce.

Not long ago I asked a well-respected Washington financial analyst to explain the reasons for inflation. He very frankly said that he just did not know the causes. It took me a while to understand that my good friend truly did not know because he did not want to know. He was a believer in floating rates, therefore, floating rates could not have been the culprit. He honestly believed that oil consumers should be compensated for their lost purchasing power through budgetary deficits, therefore compensation could not be a major cause. He also thought that gold should not be counted at market rates, because that would be too speculative. He also believed that Eurodollars have nothing to do with it because, as he put it, every dollar asset, whether at home or abroad, has a counterpart liability and therefore is noninflationary. Well, if you eliminate, for doctrinaire reasons, all plausible common-sense explanations, then of course you must fall back to a completely unprofessional "Don't know, therefore, I don't care" attitude.

In contrast, I would suggest that the reasons for the inflation of the 1970s are perfectly clear. First came the breakdown of Bretton Woods, a monetary reason. In the new situation governments had to follow more or less accommodating monetary policies which really meant a free for all. Well, not completely, and not equally free for all. The greatest beneficiaries of an open international monetary order are those with the greatest bargaining or monopoly power. Due to the drought in 1972 and 1973 these were the grain producers. Then the OPEC countries discovered that they could get away with a 400 percent price hike, and they did. Since then, oil prices have tripled again. Organized labor had to play catchup with everybody else, so the inflationary spiral started. Gold prices were bid up of excess liquidity in the system. Gold, because of its role in the central banking system, then became a source of added liquidity. High farm prices caused farmland to appreciate. Therefore food costs went up some more and so on ad infinitum.

Are these changes monetary or fundamental? They are both. Is this inflation of the cost-push or the demand-pull type? It is both. Cost push or demand pull are in any case usually the consecutive waves of the same inflation. If liquidity is strictly controlled, the depth of the waves is shallow and one wave is easily discerned from another. When liquidity is high, the waves are bunched together and a cost-push inflation of the morning can easily become a demand-pull inflation by nightfall.

Yet, there is one unifying feature of the inflation of the 1970s and this is the absence of a positive, legal, international, well-structured monetary order. We should keep this in mind when we now turn to our last question, namely, how this inflation, engendered in the first place by the lack of an international monetary order, will affect the eventual creation of a new monetary order.

IV. RECONSTRUCTING THE INTERNATIONAL MONETARY ORDER

Yet every cloud has its silver lining. If the elimination of Bretton Woods had the purpose of increasing capital transfers to the developing oil-producing countries, this goal was more than admirably fulfilled. Do you still remember the First and Second Development Decades of the sixties and seventies when developed countries were asked to contribute 1 percent of their GNP to the development of the Third World and they could never do more than a fraction of this amount? OPEC exports of oil to the United States are around 8 million barrels per day, which, at $40 per barrel is $320 million per day, or roughly $120 billion per year. This represents about 4 percent of our GNP. A similar, less than voluntary contribution to international development is made by the other industrialized countries as a group. The breakdown of the monetary order is therefore good for OPEC, representing some 300 million people across the globe from Venezuela to Indonesia, not to mention local energy industries elsewhere. It is not so good for developing nonoil-exporting countries because they must pay higher prices for oil imports. However, even in these countries the picture is not entirely bleak. On the one hand, they expect to benefit from the situation, as OPEC countries are wise enough to pass on some of their "windfall profits" to the Third World, thereby holding their allegiance and remaining the cutting edge of the worldwide grass roots, peasant and nomadic revolution which will characterize the last decades of the twentieth century. On the other hand, the financing of the oil-importing less-developed countries' oil imports is being picked up by the world's large commercial banking systems, which found unexpected opportunities in the recycling of petrodollars. If the architects of the open-ended monetary arrangements wanted to help forward-looking democratic countries, like the Union of South Africa and the Soviet Union, they admirably succeeded. Assuming that the world's yearly gold production is roughly 60 million ounces and that these two countries produce 40 million ounces of the total, the increase in gold prices by a factor of 20 from $35 per ounce to $700 per ounce increased their yearly gold revenues from $1.4 billion to $28 billion, an additional modest contribution to world development by the Western industrial world. Interestingly, some of the increased gold revenues, de facto, trickle down to the mining workers, thereby improving their social status. The elimination of international monetary discipline contributed to the breakdown of social values, and the spread of terrorism and violence in our own country, in Europe and elsewhere. It led to sudden shifts in social power structures in countries like Iran which then led to the increase of international tensions as exemplified by Afghanistan. In summary, the elimination of fixed exchange rates gravely weakened the balance of power existing among various groups of countries, thereby undermining the foundations of world peace. This result is dramatically opposed to the intentions of those who celebrated the return to floating rates a decade ago. There is a searing black humor in all this. But it should lead us neither to cynicism nor to vindictiveness. We need, all good men and women, to rebuild a new world order of noninflationary growth upon the ravaged landscape left behind after only one decade of international monetary disorder and world inflation.

The task will not be easy. It actually grows more difficult by the day. Not so long ago economic policy makers were chattering about the convergence of inflation rates, interest rates, productivity measurements, and so on, as a precondition to a return to a more structured exchange rate system. But they missed realizing that in an unstructured situation the centrifugal forces are much greater than the centripetal aspirations. There are vested interests growing up around the current and worsening situation. The flexibility of the economic system is being increasingly reduced.

A good measure of the governability of the economic aggregates is the

GNP elasticity for the price level. Briefly, the price elasticity is infinity if production could be increased infinitely, without any change in the general price level. Both classical and Keynesian economics are built on that assumption. In reality, I know of no historic situation in which this was the case. During the twenty years, following World War II, the United States economy could be characterized by a GNP price elasticity of 3, a relatively high positive figure, where the average annual increase of the CPI was 4.5 percent, and the average annual increase of GNP was 1.5 percent. In simplified form: $E = $ delta GNP/ delta $P = 4.5/1.5 = 3$. Since 1971 this measurement has fallen continuously as inflation, due to the breakdown of the monetary system and the hardening of supply constraints, reduced the flexibility of the economy toward zero or even into the negative sector.. In 1980 with, say, 1 percent growth and 15 percent inflation, the elasticity of the United States economy will be 1/15, 45 times less than it was during the relatively good years of the 1950s and 1960s.

However, the difficulties cannot deter us. Actually our choice is only between paying a smaller price for establishing the preconditions of noninflationary steady growth now, or paying an infinitely greater price, and facing the possibility of much less success later.

In my view it is imperative that we stop inflation now and that we return to a structured international monetary order. The President should declare a national economic emergency, a quiet emergency, with the following remedies:

1. An intelligent national works program which would remove unemployment as a concern for economic policymaking.
2. A one-year price-wage freeze through individual and corporate pledges, rather than regulations. It would amount to a one-year "stop the clock" arrangement.
3. Import quotas on oil, gasoline rationing, with a white market for coupons through the banking system, oil price decontrol, production quotas for energy producers.
4. A presidential request of the world at large, to cooperate in the quiet emergency and to call jointly, with appropriate United Nations agencies, for a world economic conference and for a new economic order.
5. Reestablish a more structured international monetary order.
6. Negotiate workable international commodity and energy agreements.
7. Create a kind of Marshall Plan for the Third World.
8. Continue liberal trade policies under GATT.[5]

The administration's current measues are inadequate. They might succeed in slowing down inflation for a while at a high cost to employment, productivity, and investment, but unless the fundamentals are cured, as I suggested two years ago in the framework of the cited eight points, inflation will soon flare up once more. Foreign exchange rates can be stabilized from time to time through central bank interventions, as the history of the last 16 months shows. But interventions are only emergency measures, and ad hoc consultations are no substitute for a global economic policy. Controlling the unlimited expansion of the Eurocurrency market might help temporarily, but again it is no substitute for a limited, regular international liquidity creation through the IMF. The substitution account is a good idea, but it would be really effective only in the overall framework of my quiet emergency program.

I am not optimistic that any of this program will be adopted. It would bring the desired result, but it has no political constituency, neither here nor abroad.

It is a pity. After the lessons learned during the last decade from the destruction of a meaningful international monetary order and the ensuing world inflation we could still make our way back, or rather ahead, toward an SDR-based, reasonably structured new IMF. If we do not, we can slow down our slide toward damnation using superficial, temporary, measures. At the end of that slide are 50,000 atomic bombs. Hitler's horrible gas ovens killed 6 million. The 50,000 bombs could kill 6 billion.

The past, the present and the future of world inflation and of the international monetary order must be viewed in this perspective so that they may be properly understood. After all, we are not passive onlookers at a mildly interesting but otherwise harmless experiment. We are the world's intellectual and political leaders and we cannot passively watch the world go up in flames through forces we generated ourselves or could have, but failed to, stop.

Inflation is not an "it," the international monetary order is not an "it," and the world economy is not an "it." They are "us," you and I. Let us, as fast as possible, recognize past errors, put them behind us and build a new international monetary order permitting, in spite of the all too obvious difficulties, a new period of noninflationary growth.

Notes

1. Robert Triffin, *Gold and the Dollar Crisis* (New Haven, 1960), p. 72.
2. "Systems of International Payments: Dollar and Gold," Conti Commodity Services, 10 August 1973.
3. Robert W. Tucker, "The Conduct of American Foreign Policy," *Foreign Affairs* 58, no. 3 (1980).
4. For a more detailed account see: M. Szabo-Pelsoczi, "A Brief Note on the GNP Price Elasticity," *Global View* I, no. 2, 15 February 1978.
5. For a more detailed discussion, see: M. Szabo-Pelsoczi, "The Quiet Emergency," *Global View* I, no. 4, 5, 6, 31 March, 19 April, 10 May, 1978.

Part 4
Germany

Repressed Inflation and Uncertainty in Postwar Germany

NICHOLAS W. BALABKINS

Since President Carter took office in January 1977, consumer prices have gone up at an average annual rate of more than 9 percent. That is, in the past three years, our dollar has lost almost one-third of its purchasing power. During these years President Carter has also presided over three fiscal years involving at least $130 billion in deficits. It is expected that by 1981 federal taxes will consume almost 22 percent of our Gross National Product, almost as much as the all-time record of 22 percent in 1944 during the height of World War II. Needless to say, persistent open inflation also caused headaches for Presidents Ford, Nixon, and Johnson. As compared with the 1945 dollar, when the United States emerged as a victor of World War II, today's dollar has only 25 cents of purchasing power left. In other words, during the past 35 years of peace, the dollar has lost 75 percent of its purchasing power. It is not exactly an achievement we can be proud of.

During the past three decades the United States has pursued a full employment policy at almost any cost, but today there is a loud chorus throughout the country clamoring for the government to do something about inflation, preferably to outlaw it by price and wage controls. It was President Nixon who in 1971 instituted the first peacetime wage-price freeze in our history.[1] This step was taken in accordance with the recommendations of a majority of economists and with the repeated urging of the Joint Economic Committee. We know today how ineffective those controls were! Yet today, ten years later, one presidential candidate is calling for such mandatory controls. The White House has repeatedly denied that such a course of action is contemplated, but the stronger the denials, the stronger the suspicions in the American business community and among the unions. And the process of preemptive price and wage increases has already begun![2]

For the past 35 years the majority of American economists firmly believed that a "little bit of inflation" was not too bad, and they concentrated their efforts on policies designed to generate full employment. They talked endlessly and glowingly about balanced budget theorems, "fine tuning" of the economy, and "spend-yourselves-rich schemes." The country's politicians eagerly followed the macroeconomists' advice and freely spent the taxpayers' money. Huge budgetary deficits did not disturb people, because deficits were part of the new creed. Spending taxpayers' money freely also maximized the staying power of our elected officials in Washington, state capitals, cities, and towns. But a decade of almost two-digit inflation proved a bit too much, and today people are screaming about the consequences. Many insist on wage and price controls, and it is possible that our capricious politicians may institute such controls again. In this context the experience of repressed inflation in the occupied zones of Germany 1945–1948 may be of some value for American economic policy makers. But before we can talk about price and wage controls and how they could influence our persistent open inflation, a short sketch of the nature and function of direct or physical controls is in order.

I. PHYSICAL CONTROLS DURING ALL-OUT WARS

In recent history, direct controls have been used primarily either for economic mobilization during major wars or for purposes of "forced draft" industrialization (in Communist countries). The Nazis used various combinations of direct controls for economic exploitation of the occupied countries in Europe. But whatever the objective, imposition of direct controls partially or entirely suppressed the operations of market forces. Price, wage, and rent controls, rationing of consumer goods, direct allocation of floor space (housing), manpower, raw materials, and capital goods replaced the free market mechanism and became the main pillars of the new economic structure.

Since wars are collective efforts, governments have always assumed responsibility for their direction. In this century armed conflicts have often escalated to total wars — wars which ended in victory, annihilation, or unconditional surrender. To fight such wars, a huge administrative effort by the government is indispensable. Mobilization of the existing manufacturing capacity must take place quickly and totally and cannot be entrusted to slow-working market forces. Consequently, the government must take over and partially or totally suspend the market mechanism by subjecting the economy to direct controls.[3]

In wartime, manpower and the available productive capacity are fully utilized. With an urgent and virtually limitless government demand for resources, aggregate demand, at constant prices, exceeds aggregate supply. This excess is known as the *inflationary gap*, and its control constitutes the very crux of wartime inflation.[4] In the absence of direct controls, there would be practically no limit to the rise in wages and prices. The government as a bidder with unlimited resources would attempt to obtain all the resources needed fo the conduct of war regardless of prices. Scarcity of consumer goods would be reflected in high prices, and most likely in high profits for the producers of such goods. The wealthier classes would then make consumer goods scarce, whereas poorer and weaker bidders would go empty-handed. In such circumstances, the production of consumer goods would tend to be particularly lucrative, and prospective high profits would make producers of goods unessential to war generous bidders for manpower and resources. Such continuous bidding would send prices and wages upward. The "real" income of wage earners and those with fixed nominal incomes, including millions of servicemen's families, would decline, whereas incomes of profit takers would tend to rise sharply. Declining real wages would surely promote labor unrest, because war profiteering has always been the object of particular resentment. Continuously rising prices would tend to distort the distributive justice of scarce goods among the civilian population and would likely diminish the motivation for an all-out war. This declining will to fight, in turn, might jeopardize the entire war effort. Apart from the social effects of a continuous wartime price-wage spiral, unrestrained price advances would greatly increase the costs of war, and would probably degenerate into a hyperinflation.[5]

All hyperinflations lead inevitably to substitution of goods for currency. Such substitution merely reflects the repudiation of the existing monetary unit by the society. Absence of an effective unit of account makes a monetary economy impossible, and a clumsy barter system replaces it. The breakdown of the monetary economy has disastrous effects on total output because barter is incompatible with the division of labor and industrial specialization.[6] No modern war economy can be sustained on a barter basis, and avoidance of such a calamity is one of the most important tasks of wartime administration. The surest way to escape monetary chaos, with all its consequences, is by checking the excess wartime aggregate demand by direct controls. Imposition of such controls would prevent income receivers from spending their earnings and might extract sufficient real savings to match the wartime government expenditure.

II. THE OTHER SIDE OF DIRECT CONTROLS: REPRESSED INFLATION

Subjecting the war economy to direct controls is designed to keep the tidal wave of demand in check. Freezing prices and wages is designed to forestall the inevitable consequences of excess demand from materializing in the form of higher prices and wages. Under such a system, physical controls become of primary importance, whereas the monetary factor is reduced to secondary importance. Direct controls do not eliminate excessive monetary demand, but merely prevent it from influencing prices of consumer goods and factors of production. Rationing consumer goods directly affects society's propensity to consume, whereas direct allocations of manpower, raw materials, and capital goods check the propensity to invest. Such a system of physical controls, together with legal price, wage, and rent fixing, is known as *repressed inflation*, or, to use Galbraith's term, the *disequilibrium system*.[7]

Under repressed inflation, earning a monetary income does not automatically entitle its recipient to claim goods and services. Goods can be bought only if currency is accompanied by rationing coupons, special purchase permits, or points. Monetary income, however, as far as it can be spent on legal purchases and rations, retains stable purchasing power. Those portions deprived of legal purchasing power because of a lack of coupons or points must be saved, spent in the noncontrolled sector if it exists, or used for black market operations. Thus, under a system of repressed inflation, two kinds of monetary incomes exist: first, incomes endowed with legal purchasing power where the consumer's dollar bill jointly with rationing coupons will buy foodstuffs and consumer goods; second, monetary incomes rendered powerless for legal purchases because of the lack of rationing points or coupons. This excess income may, of course, be used for payment of taxes, fees, or for accumulating savings. The difference between those portions of money incomes with legal purchasing power and those without it, constitutes the *monetary overhang*, or waiting purchasing power in an economy subject to direct controls.[8] With a given after-tax income, the "waiting purchasing power" would be large or small, depending on the degree of repression or the comprehensiveness of direct controls. The more universal the direct controls, the larger the amount of the "waiting purchasing power," and the stronger the tendency for the marginal value of incomes earned beyond legal expenditure to fall to zero. The utility of marginal increments to savings would tend to fall, and the substitution of leisure for work would take place in a variety of forms, with all the inevitable consequences of declining productivity and falling GNP. On the other hand, if only part of the economy was subject to direct controls and the other was not, incomes beyond legal expenditures in the controlled market could be used for purchases of goods and services in the uncontrolled sector at prevailing market prices. Of course, the greater the free market, the greater the utility of additional income and the greater the incentive to work.[9] Although rationing of consumer goods and allocation of manpower and raw materials physically limits total aggregate civilian demand, taxation, direct and indirect, is an indispensable part of direct controls. Taxation is used to absorb additional purchasing power, thus further to curtail the civilian demand and to release additional resources for war-essential industries. Taxation for such purposes must, however, be used with circumspection. To be sure, taxation would diminish purchasing power, but if taxes took away too large a portion of incomes earned, incentives to work and to produce would be blunted. For instance, if wartime income taxes reduced the marginal dollar for overtime to less than the standard hourly rate of pay, workers would prefer leisure to overtime work. If, due to sharp increases in personal taxes, such shifts in workers' attitudes toward work occurred on a considerable scale, then the entire war production could be jeopardized. Since the size of GNP is primarily determined by the size of the labor force and its productivity, falling average productivity of labor, loss of overtime work, and the rising rate of absenteeism could result in greatly reduced overall output of goods and services. No belligerent could afford this, therefore wartime taxation must be handled cautiously.

To avert such a possibility during wartime, Keynes devised an ingenious scheme of deferred pay.[10] Although Keynes was aware of the shortcomings of wartime taxation, he wanted to tax, as well as to preserve, incentives. The "deferred pay" plan was his answer to this dual problem. Keynes's plan proposed to idle a portion of current incomes, which were to be put into special accounts and released only after the war. Keynes's effort aimed at killing two birds with one stone: first, "freezing" a part of wartime incomes, in contrast to direct taxation, would preserve incentives to earn money incomes, and preservation of incentives would also prevent the withdrawal of labor from the labor market; second, the "deferred pay" plan would bring about a further cut in civilian demand and thus release additional resources for the war effort. Even though his plan was only partially implemented, it still dramatized the role taxation can play in the overall scheme of direct controls.

III. INDUSTRIAL DISARMAMENT POLICY IN THE AMERICAN ZONE OF OCCUPATION

When the United States Army took over its zone of occupation in Germany, the widespread feeling among Americans at home and in the military government was that Germany should be reconstructed on an agricultural basis, with industry drastically curtailed.[11] Economic policy for the American occupation zone was clearly spelled out in a directive of the Joint Chiefs of Staff (JCS 1067) in April 1945.[12] This directive, which remained nominal law for American military government officials for two years, was aimed at keeping Germany down and making sure that it could never wage another war. This normative orientation of the American occupation policy rested on the assumption that the "incurably" bellicose Germans could not be trusted and that Germany must be made "so impotent that she can not forge the tools of war."[13] Further, destruction of German industry was initially regarded as a potential blessing to the rest of the European economy.

Thus, in the early stages of occupation, the Americans gave moral reasons among other rationalizations for the pleas to engage in *large-scale deindustrialization of Germany*. The specific objectives of the American occupation were given as industrial disarmament, demilitarization, denazification, and administrative decentralization.[14]

To implement the industrial program, which had priority over reparations, paragraph 32 of the directive of the Joint Chiefs of Staff permitted only minimum industrial production of iron and steel, nonferrous metals, machine tools, radio and electrical equipment, automotive vehicles, heavy machinery, and their related parts.

Furthermore, to debilitate German potential in physics, chemistry, and engineering, the framers of JCS/1067 spelled out in detail techniques of "technological disarmament." Paragraph 31 prohibited virtually all research activities and required abandonment of all laboratories, research facilities, and similar technical establishments except those considered necessary for protection of public health. In addition, paragraph 8 prescribed arrest categories for security reasons on the basis of position held, and "not the particular culpability of the individual occupying the position."[15] Many German businessmen and government officials were taken into custody for this reason. According to Robert Murphy, when the United States forces moved into their zone of occupation, JCS/1067 had supposedly "prescribed thirty-three automatic arrest categories, mostly on account of membership, high or low, in a Nazi organization. . . ."[16] Those who remained free were subjected to the removal-from-office program that virtually denuded the German economy and government of skilled and trained manpower.

The directive was such a strange document that General Clay's advisers, William H. Draper and Lewis W. Douglas, "were shocked by the detailed prohibitions . . ." and Douglas supposedly exclaimed that JCS/1067 "was assembled by economic idiots."[17]

No matter how brutal the initial American occupation policy was, the Germans took it comparatively well because they were fully aware of how fortunate they were in having Americans for their conquerors instead of Russians. The initial, stringent form of JCS/1067 determined the overall policy in the American zone only in the fall of 1945; from then on, a drift in policy eventually led to formal repudiation of the directive in July 1947. As long as JCS/1067 was not formally revoked and the lower administrative echelons in Germany and the various policy-making agencies in Washington were staffed by adherents of Morgenthau's implacable policy, its provisions were enforced. For this reason, United States Military Government officials were quite reluctant to take responsibility for allowing German plants to resume production or even to repair war damages. The British were considerably more circumspect in their zones; they wanted no part of the American-inspired program of making Germany an industrially impotent nation.[18]

IV. DIRECT CONTROL AFTER THE UNCONDITIONAL SURRENDER

After the unconditional surrender of the German armed forces to the Allies, the four Allied military governments retained virtually the entire body of Nazi economic legislation, and carried the previous existing system of direct controls into the postwar period.[19] Although with the defeat of the Third Reich the goals of the Nazi economic policy evaporated, the policy of repressed inflation continued. All consumer goods and foodstuffs remained rationed, with the exception of certain low-utility items and low-calorie foodstuffs. Labor was subject to general labor conscription and capital goods were subject to allocation controls. Rents remained frozen and floorspace controls were strictly enforced. But in view of the inability of the Allied Control Council to agree on a currency reform in the immediate post-surrender period, it was generally expected that Reichsmark savings eventually would become only a fraction of their nominal value. Such an expectation was responsible for the hoarding of goods by producers in industry, crafts, and farms and for various forms of withdrawal of effort by the labor force.

To understand the existing inflationary threat it is important to keep in mind that from 1936 to the end of the war, the Reich debt grew from about RM 30 to RM 400 billion, excluding war-induced claims which came to another RM 400 billion. During the same period, currency in circulation increased from RM 5 to RM 50 billion, and bank deposits expanded from RM 30 to RM 150 billion. In contrast to the spectacular increase in the monetary sector, German real wealth, in terms of 1939 prices, had shrunk from about RM 500–600 billion in 1939 to RM 300 billion in 1946.[20]

Analytically speaking, three ways were open to handle the inflationary potential:

1. Removing all controls on prices and wages and allowing the price mechanism to reestablish the monetary equilibrium.
2. Reducing wartime monetary wealth by currency reform.
3. Retaining the existing direct controls and gradually working off the excess demand by increasing the supply of goods and services.

The first was unacceptable to the Allied powers for two reasons: open inflation always implies forced savings which may be used for capital formation in the form of plant and equipment. During the German hyperinflation after World War I, the flight out of the mark into real values was particularly heavy, and the expansion of basic German industries continued unabated until the stabilization of the mark. At the end of the hyperinflation, Germany possessed greater capacity in heavy industries than in 1913.[21] Some American wartime economic planning experts felt that the German monetary chaos after World War I was the work of the government of the Weimar Republic, the major industrialists, and the underground German General Staff.[22] By pleading poverty and creating a monetary jungle, the German government could claim inability to pay reparations, whereas in fact, German industrialists were building greater and better industrial empires than they ever had before. To prevent the repetition of such experiences after World War II, the Allies used direct controls. The envisaged industrial disarmament program of Germany called for an across-the-board reduction of German industry: it was imperative to prevent the Germans from rebuilding industry through open inflation. But in addition, the Allies wanted to prevent open inflation for social reasons. The social consequences of hyperinflation after World War I were disastrous because it broke the backbone of the German middle class. The economic base of the former German middle and ruling classes disappeared in galloping inflation. The officers corps, public servants, intellectuals, and white-collar workers were impoverished and threatened with the loss of social status, and the economic uprooting of the German middle class was one of the most important factors in the emergence of the Nazi movement. The process of the "proletarization" of the German middle class during the early 1920s supposedly contributed greatly to the rise of Nazism.[23] The Allies feared that another period of hyperinflation might promote the emergence of a new totalitarian doctrine which would "strike at the heart of Allied hopes for a democratic Germany."[24] To nip the inflationary potential in the bud, the Potsdam Agreement, the JCS/1067 directive, and the various legislative measures of the Allied Control Council called for the preservation of the entire gamut of direct controls. The two specific objectives were, first, to facilitate the industrial disarmament of Germany; second, to avoid the social effects of open inflation.

By contrast, a sweeping currency reform was the most logical and promising method of coping with the existing inflationary potential. In fact, during the first two postwar years, the four Allies negotiated without success for a currency reform for Germany as a whole.[25] Since the four occupation powers could not agree either on the question of German economic unity or on a currency reform, the monetary and financial policies of the four zones of occupation were determined by the respective directives of the Allied Military Governments. For instance, in the United States zone of occupation, paragraph 44 of JCS/1067 forbade the United States Military Governor "to take any steps designed to strengthen German financial structure." Under these circumstances, a separate currency reform for the United States zone was ruled out, and the existing inflationary potential had to be checked by direct controls. During the war, earnings were high and business profits good. Existing direct controls severely restricted the propensity to consume and the ability to invest, and substantial savings came into being. The patriotic appeal during the war was strong, and the Nazi government's promise fully to convert wartime savings into goods after victory was taken seriously by the general public. Almost throughout the war, the Reichsmark remained the store of value, and no perceptible flight into goods took place. Of course, the unconditional surrender of the Nazi armies destroyed all hopes for full convertibility of wartime savings into goods. The protracted negotiations on the pending quadripartite currency reform in the Allied Control Council destroyed the Reichsmark as a store of value. Rumor had it that up to 90 percent of the existing money supply would be destroyed during the monetary conversion. Widespread fear by the public and business community that the forthcoming currency reform would drastically scale down the existing monetary claims resulted in the flight from the Reichsmark into material values.[26] Individuals and German business establishments rushed into goods, and at the beginning of 1946, hoarding goods became an accepted feature of the economic landscape of the Bizonal Area of Germany. Month after month, the United States military governor reported that firms kept unusually large inventories of raw materials and finished products because of the uncertain currency situation.[27] Various German Chambers of Industry and Trade also reported that the widely expected currency reform was the principal reason for hoarding. To preserve the working capital of the firm, everybody kept as much in the form of goods as possible, and the reluctance to sell at existing prices was widespread.[28] As the discussions on the quadripartite currency reform in the Allied Control Council led nowhere, and as the attitude of the principal Western Allies toward Germany turned from a punitive to a constructive policy, anticipations of a separate currency reform for the Western zones of occupation grew. Under the unsettled currency situation, the German business community pleaded forcefully and eloquently that hoards of consumer goods were indispensable for the successful launching of any future currency reform. Many high German administrators, including the future Chancellor of West Germany, Ludwig Erhard, openly encouraged the hoarding of goods. It is difficult to quantify precisely the extent of hoarding out of current production during 1947 and the first half of 1948, but it is safe to say that 50 percent of the output was either hoarded or used for compensation. The other 50 percent was sold to special, high-priority customers, such as coal miners and the employees of the German Railways, who were entitled to "incentive" goods, leaving nothing for "normal" consumers. In 1947, for example, the Bizonal output of textiles and leather goods fluctuated around one-third of 1936 volume, but since the normal consumer was not entitled to "incentive goods," he could buy almost no consumer goods, and from his point of view, the production of practically all useful goods was zero.[29] In addition to the hoarding of goods, expectation of a currency reform gave rise to widespread hoarding of coins. It was rumored that coins would be converted into new coins at better terms than note currency and bank deposits, and there was a mad rush into coins. It was reported, for instance, that one streetcar conductor in Stuttgart had a greater hoard of coins "than that in the possession of any single Stuttgart bank."[30] In general, all material values were preferred to monetary values, and the cigarette-currency emerged next to the existing Reichsmark currency. Cigarettes, easily divisible and at that time internationally acceptable, frequently bought goods which the Reichsmark did not. Although the cigarette was, of course, never declared to be legal tender, in practice it became the accepted form of currency.[31] The widespread apprehension that the Reichsmark would lose most of its value during the forthcoming currency reform induced people to prefer cigarettes to Reichsmarks. The cigarette became "good money," while the Reichsmark was treated as "bad money." This preference, *per se,* reversed Gresham's principle, and the so-called good money, the cigarette, to some extent, drove out the bad. The history of past monetary upheavals refers to this phenomenon time and again.[32] In the early 1920s German hyperinflation resulted in a continuous depreciation of the mark. In the last stages of monetary chaos, the mark was repudiated as a store of value, as a unit of account, and as a medium of exchange. By way of contrast, direct controls after World War II repressed inflationary potential. The Reichsmark retained a stable purchasing power in so far as it was required for the legal food ration, and to pay rent, gas, electricity, taxes, and fares. *The Reichsmark remained a unit of account and a medium of exchange, although it bought virtually nothing more than the highly inadequate food ration.* Distrust in the future value of the Reichsmark, especially during the last half of the year prior to currency reform, led to flagrant hoarding.[33]

The third policy listed entailed retention of the existing direct controls and working off the inflationary potential by a gradual increase of the aggregate supply. Indeed, Allied Control Council Law No. 1 retained the Nazi legislation of direct controls, but by such retention the Allies did not subscribe to the aims of the third alternative. Norway after the end of World War II, for instance, kept the system of price controls, rationing, wage controls, allocations, import controls, and even direct allocation of labor in an attempt to speed up its economic recovery.[34] To accelerate capital formation, private consumption was to remain somewhat below the 1939 level for the first five postwar years. Existing inflationary pressures were to be worked off not through a drastic currency reform but by increased production and considerable *import* surpluses. Thus the Norwegian government used direct controls deliberately and systematically to bring about the eventual disappearance of inflationary pressures at a higher level of real output. The postwar British Laborite government kept wartime direct controls in existence for similar reasons.

But in occupied Germany the situation was different. Because industrial disarmament was one of the main objectives of the occupation, it was out of the question that direct controls would be used to step up industrial output, to raise productivity, and to expand productive capacity, and thus gradually work off the inflationary pressures. Such a policy, resembling the Norwegian and British policies, would have worked at cross purposes with the aims of industrial disarmament. In operational terms, the industrial disarmament of Germany implied a considerable reduction of German heavy industries. Outright destruction of industrial facilities, imposition of production ceilings, and delivery of machinery as reparations to the victors or Allied nations, necessarily involved a reduction in future German output of all goods and services. Hence, eventual disappearance of inflationary pressures at a higher level of real output was not contemplated. The victors were merely interested in keeping wages and prices stable in order to prevent open inflation, and a severe repression of demand was one way to stem the tide of the inflationary potential. But since the policy of industrial disarmament actually throttled German industrial activity, inflationary pressures mounted. Without higher levels of real output, wartime monetary wealth could not be worked off merely by freezing prices and wages. Scaling down swollen bank deposits and currency in circulation was indispensable for the restoration of some balance between the permitted level of industrial activity and the aggregate demand.

In the Soviet zone of occupation, all bank deposits were blocked by the Soviet Military Government immediately after the onset of occupation in 1945, while the currency in circulation remained untouched. This measure eliminated a considerable portion of the existing monetary wealth in the Soviet zone, and with one stroke of the pen it flattened the monetary "overhang." No comparable steps were taken in the American and British zones of occupation, and it became obvious that sooner or later monetary reform would be necessary. This possibility haunted all Germans and the expectation of such a reform generated a set of attitudes which greatly aggravated the overall operations of the German economy.

The general distrust of the Reichsmark by the German business community during this period gave rise to another unique institution, the compensation trade. Compensation deals generally involved the barter of goods at fixed prices. The main purpose of compensation activity was to obtain raw materials, semifabricated and finished goods which were not legally obtainable. To make such transactions look legal and acceptable to the tax authorities, they were booked as regular sales at fixed prices.[35] To demonstrate: a shoe manufacturer in northern Germany needs bricks for the repair of his bombed-out plant, and his request for an allocation of bricks at the local economics office has been turned down presumably because no bricks were available for distribution. At this point, the manager of the firm turns to self-help: he knows that the manager of the local brickmaking firm has bricks, but he needs typewriters and electrical switches and cannot get them through legal channels. A number of requests by the brickmaking firm for the purchase permits for typewriters and switches have also been turned down by the economics office. The two producers meet and agree on a barter deal. The shoe producer knows that electrical switches can easily be obtained from a firm in southern Germany in exchange for shoes, and he dispatches a "compensator" for that very purpose at once. Another "compensator" would go to Erfurt, in the Soviet zone, where typewriters could be exchanged for shoes. After the return of the two "compensators" with typewriters and electrical switches, the compensation deal would be consummated. The shoe manufacturer would get bricks, and the brickmaker would obtain typewriters and electrical switches. The entire transaction would then be legalized by the accounting department. It would be recorded as a regular sale at fixed prices.

The amount of time and effort spent for such transactions was almost unbelievable. To keep the industrial wheels turning at all, and at the same time to prevent the dissipation of raw material stocks and inventories, the German business community had to resort to such measures. Widespread fear of currency reform eliminated the Reichsmark as a store of value, and inventories of finished and semifabricated goods and raw materials were generally preferred to bank accounts. The spreading compensation trade resulted in a considerable "primitivization" of economic activity, since barter is incompatible with the specialization and cooperation of an industrial community. All highly developed economies are based on specialization, or the industrial division of labor and its roundabout method of industrial production depends on the existence of a functioning monetary economy. When this broke down, barter spread, and although more people did more work, output remained low.

Despite the massive bombing raids of the Allied air fleets, the greatest portion of German manufacturing capacity survived the war intact.

Industrial pipelines were also reasonably well filled, and German industry had ample stocks of raw materials and semifabricated items on hand.[36] But because the Allies imposed an import embargo on raw materials, German industry had to live off wartime stocks. For over two years, firms produced and sold from wartime stocks without replenishing them. With the approach of the currency reform, considerable amounts of the available raw materials and semifabricated goods were unquestionably hoarded. The official allocations of raw materials, in 1946 and in 1947, amounted to 20 percent of the required supplies, but in most cases even less was actually distributed.[37] The virtual impossibility of legally obtaining raw materials, fuels, and industrial supplies, drove German business into compensation trade as a source of needed supplies.[38] Through such makeshift arrangements, German producers were able to operate on a limited basis and to keep their working capital intact as well. It was estimated that in 1947 as much as 50 percent of the entire output of the bizonal economy was traded in compensation deals.[39]

With the deterioration of economic conditions, violations and disregard of existing economic legislation were rife. German officials pleaded repeatedly with American and British administrators that only by making "economic misbehavior" subject to the death penalty, would it be possible to cope with the situation. For example, Mr. Schlange-Schöningen, the director of the Bizonal Food and Agricultural Administration argued that the worst aspect of the gray market, i.e., compensation trade, would be severely checked if a few people were hanged.[40] The Western powers, however, did not heed Schlange-Schöningen's plea, because in Anglo-American law "economic misbehavior," as a general rule, is not punishable by death. On this very question the London *Economist* commented that during the Nazi period Germans obeyed the control regulations because there was a state to worship and gallows to fear. Now there is no state, but a despised occupation authority which "Does Not, and Should Not, make HITLER'S use of the gallows."[41] Without the gallows, however, nothing could stop the spreading barter which, like a cancer, slowly but steadily was destroying the entire system of postwar economic control.

In November 1947, Bavaria, for instance, again introduced industrial quotas for compensation purposes. Out of fear of the higher authorities, the new compensation directive was oral, not written. From then on, the United States and the United Kingdom occupation officials tolerated officially approved barter as a sine qua non for the maintenance of minimum operations of German industry. Needless to say, the system of controlled barter led to flagrant abuses, and many firms exploited the situation. Officially, only 10 percent of a firm's output could be used for legally unobtainable supplies, the other 90 percent of the output could be sold at legal prices. But in reality, often as much as 90 percent of all goods produced went either into rapidly growing inventories or into compensation.[42] This figure may be too high, but it cannot be denied that the hoarding spree of the German industrial community took place at the expense of the wage earners. For about three years, the "normal" consumer could buy practically nothing, except the inadequate food ration, although hoards of consumer goods were quite substantial.

The existence of the barter trade, the black market, and the legal trading activity at fixed prices, split the postwar German economy into legal and illegal sectors. In the legal sphere, goods were bought and sold at legal prices either against rationing coupons or purchase permits. In the illegal sector, goods were obtained in two ways: either in the black market by paying prices as high as 100 times the fixed, legal prices, or through the channels of compensation trade. Thus the postwar German economic system was split into three separate flows; the legal, the black market, and the barter. Due to the absence of a store of value, an increasing portion of output circulated in the two illegal sectors, mostly in the compensation sector. As currency reform drew closer, an ever-growing proportion of the German industrial output entered "bartering channels," leaving little for the legal market.

The Reichsmark remained a unit of account and a medium of exchange, although it bought virtually nothing more than the highly inadequate food ration. Distrust of its future value led, especially during the last half of the year before the currency reform, to flagrant hoarding of goods.[43] Under the prevailing administrative chaos, the interests of the business community ran counter to the wishes of the consuming public, and in the absence of a strong hand it was impossible to cope with the hoarding spree. The Allied-imposed price freeze contributed to the German economic standstill. The zonal split, shortages of fuel and power, low productivity caused by malnutrition, lower output per machine caused by obsolescence and lack of repairs, the damage to industrial plants, and the overall stagnation of West German industry combined to produce sharply raised production costs. With legal prices often much lower than the costs of production, losses were inevitable.

For the time being, however, the Allies were unwilling to revise prices upward; hence the only way for a firm to avoid financial ruin was to circumvent the outdated price freeze by manufacturing "new," formerly unknown goods. During the three years from the surrender until currency reform, more than 5000 price increases were granted, mostly for the production of "new" goods.[44] Ash trays, fancy lamps, dolls, chandeliers, and other low-utility items poured forth while the production of cups, pails, pots, knives, forks, plates, needles, shoe-laces, and other daily necessities stagnated.[45] The price freeze made the incentive to produce directly inverse to the social utility of the product. The more useless a proposed new product, the greater the probability that it had not been available before the war and thus the easier it was to convince the authorities to agree to a profitable price. As a result, the Western zones of occupation before currency reform had what one Swiss economist called a "hair-oil, ash-tray, herb-tea economy."[46] The German economy was at the end of its rope. In the view The Economist, the first three postwar years were "utter economic hell."[47]

V. THE RELEVANCE OF THE FOREGOING EXPERIENCE FOR THE AMERICAN ECONOMY IN THE 1980s AND THE 1990s

Could the experience just described have any relevance for the future of the United States of American in the 1980s and 1990s? Such a question may appear absurd. After all, barring a major conventional war or a nuclear holocaust, peacetime America could not possibly approach the kind of repressed inflation that confronted the defeated Western remnants of the Third Reich. Yet despite the mind-boggling possibility of such a repressed inflation in peacetime America, it is nevertheless true that Dr. Pick's Silver and Gold Report has for years warned that eventually our current dollar will be replaced by a new dollar. When and why this debacle of the dollar will come to pass, nobody seems to know, but these ominous clouds are just over the horizon these days.

Over the past 35 years, the majority of Americans have enjoyed almost unprecedented prosperity and continuous high levels of em-ployment. The price for this material bliss has been continuous and rising rates of inflation. When the rate of inflation reached 18 percent, per annum, in early 1980, it "hit" the average American hard, and he screamed. Inflation at that clip was intolerable and the interest rate of 20 percent was an outrage! As long as the inflation rate was below 10 percent the mass of American wage earners did not seem to mind. They were the effective political majority, and they lived with it and had their jobs! They knew how to cope with it and they were not particularly interested in risking the painful cures of an open inflation they could not comprehend. They believed in the soundness of the adage "better the devil you know!" For the average American open inflation was not perceived as a great danger. Most Americans have grown up with the lore of the Great Depression, its breadlines, hope-lessness, poverty, hardship, and mass unemployment, firmly in mem-ory. Americans are instinctively afraid of the words "depression" and "mass unemployment"; this fear that persuaded Congress to pass the Full Employment Act of 1946. During the Carter administration, the rate of inflation accelerated, and Americans developed what might be called the *endless inflation syndrome,* or plainly "inflationitis." As recently and graphically detailed by Martin Baron of the Los Angeles Times, people's attitudes are being shaped by the gut feeling, "It pays to be a debtor."[48] It manifested itself daily in the popular approach: "Buy it today, even though you do not have the money. You can charge it! Do your Christmas shopping in July because by December you will have to pay more." In this connection it may be worth noting that absolute power corrupts absolutely, and it seems that the utter infatuation of American consumers with the "charge it" mentality has utterly blinded them to the devastating social and economic consequences of an accelerating open inflation.

Was all this the unintended consequence of the full employment policies of the past thirty-five years? The late Jacob Viner once feared that such a policy actually amounted to "full employment at whatever cost."[49] In March 1980, President Carter announced his intention to balance the budget in fiscal year 1981. He also asked Congress to trim the so-called fat from the federal budget, but Congress was not too eager to follow the President in an election year. President Carter was also running for a second term, and the problem of budget cutting and reducing the rate of inflation had to be carefully weighed so as not to lose the election. The President was aware of the dilemma; the business community considered his suggested budgetary cuts "too late and too little," and the American masses did not believe that either the federal government or Congress was serious about cutting the budget appreciably or reducing the rate of inflation. No one knows at this time what the outcome of this budget-cutting exercise will be. But on the basis of our 35-year experience, one can guess, and hopefully be wrong, that for the next two decades our inflation rate is likely to remain double digit. Reducing the rate of inflation is like a withdrawal from a drug; it is painful, and all plans to fight it involve unpleasant choices.[50]

Open inflation has not only economic, political, and social consequences, but a psychological dimension as well. In this connection, it is useful to note that in contrast to American Depression-related folklore, German folklore is heavily colored by inflation-induced experiences of the 1920s and 1940s. For instance, a German grandfather tells his grandchildren how he took their grandmother to dinner in 1923, at the time of hyperinflation when prices were rising hourly, and had to pay for the dinner before they ate it. If he had waited until they had finished the dinner, he would have had no money left to pay for it. Such a story leaves an indelible imprint on a youngster. Middle-aged Germans, on the other hand, would tell their children the story of the post-World War II situation when prices, wages, and rents were frozen at wartime levels, and yet their wages bought, at constant prices, nothing but the 1500 calorie food ration and paid the rent. Since all Germans knew that the wartime Reichsmark would be replaced by a new mark, the business community and the rest of society fled out of the Reichsmark into real values. This flight out of the Reichsmark was almost universal but since no one quite knew what the exchange rate for the new currency unit would be, they hoarded real goods and disposed of their marks as quickly as possible. In Germany the collective folk-memory about inflation is real, and Germans fear and dread open as well as repressed inflation, whereas in America the real fear is mass unemployment. After all, American went through hyperinflation ages ago, in the 1780s, and most Americans do not even know it!

I suspect that during the next two decades America will try to curb the persistent inflation by some populist political price control tsar. Congress will attempt to impose wage and price guidelines, if not strict wage and price controls. I also believe that they will be violated on a mass scale by the general public, labor unions, and the business community. I am also concerned that our legal system will not be able to cope with this massive evasion of such controls and that open inflation will proceed unchecked. After each collapse, a new set of wage-price guidelines — something more comprehensive — will be tried only to fail and keep the price-wage spiral going.

In this country, the concept of economic misbehavior is not well known and our judiciary system will need to learn to cope with it. Even if it does, what will happen when there is mass violation of federal wage and price guidelines? We cannot fill all the jails, nor can we fine everyone. Under such circumstances, wages and prices will continue their upward spiral. Eventually a currency reform will be decreed. But at what cost? How many old United States dollars will be exchanged for new ones? This *uncertainty*, in my opinion, will induce the flight out of dollars into real values, a phenomenon which negatively affects the level of specialization and brings about a sharp decline in the level of GNP. Will the specter of mass unemployment, so abhorrent to the American people and so far-reaching in its social consequences, rise out of economic policies of full employment at whatever cost?

Notes

1. U.S. Congress, Joint Economic Committee, *The President's New Economic Program*, Hearings, 92nd Cong., 1st Sess., Part I, August 19, 20, 23, 1971 (Washington, D.C., 1971), p. 3.
2. "Covering Bets? Fear of Price Controls Leads Some Companies to Consider Rises Now," *The Wall Street Journal*, 29 Feb., 1980, pp. 1, 31.
3. J. K. Galbraith, *A Theory of Price Control* (Cambridge, Mass., 1952).
4. R. Turvey, "The Inflationary Gap," *Ekonomisk Tidskrift*, 1948, pp. 10–17.

See also Turvey, "A Further Note on the Inflationary Gap," *Ibid.*, 1948, pp. 92–72.

5. A. C. Pigou, *The Political Economy of War* (New York, 1941), p. 118.

6. For the mechanics of hyperinflation, see C. Bresciani-Turroni, *The Economics of Inflation* (London, 1953), p. 222.

7. J. K. Galbraith, "The Disequilibrium System," *American Economic Review* 37, no. 3 (1947): 287–302.

8. W. Röpke, "Offene and zurückgestaute Inflation," *Kyklos* 1 (1947): 57–71.

9. For various types of repressed inflation, see H. K. Charlesworth, *The Economics of Repressed Inflation* (London, 1956), pp. 35–48.

10. J. M. Keynes, *How to Pay for the War* (New York, 1940), p. 59.

11. H. Zink, *The United States in Germany, 1944–1955* (Princeton, N. J., 1957), p. 252.

12. U.S. Department of State, *Germany, 1947–1949: The Story in Documents* (Washington, 1950), pp. 22–23.

13. J. M. Blum, *From the Morgenthau Diaries, Years of War, 1941–1945* (Boston, 1967), p. 356.

14. G. Moltmann, "Zur Formulierung der Amerikanischen Besatzungspolitik in Deutschland am Endes des Zweiten Weltkrieges," *Vierteljahresheft für Zeitgeschichte* 15 (1967): 299–322.

15. E. Plischke, "Denazification Law and Procedure," *The American Journal of International Law* 41 (1947): 812.

16. R. Murphy, *Diplomat Among Warriors* (New York, 1964), p. 294. The idea that industrial managers should be treated as war criminals was first advocated by Emil Ludwig, *How to Treat the Germans* (1943). He demanded that the German industrial captains should not escape unpunished. Louis Nizer, in his book, *What to Do with Germans*, charged that all German big industry conspired against world peace, and thus should be treated as "war criminals."

17. Murphy, p. 251.

18. D. C. Watt, *Britain Looks to Germany* (London, 1965), p. 53.

19. W. Abelshauser, *Wirtschaft in Westdeutschland, 1945–1948* (Stuttgart, 1974).

20. H. Möller, *Zur Vorgeschichte der DM* (Basel, 1961), p. 216.

21. For the best treatment of the German industrial concentration during the hyperinflation of the early 1920s, see C. Bresciani-Turroni, pp. 107–207.

22. U.S. Congress, Senate, Committee on War Mobilization, *A Program for German Economic and Industrial Disarmament* (Washington, 1946), pp. 578–79.

23. F. Lütge, "An Explanation of the Economic Conditions which Contributed to the Victory of National-Socialism," *The Third Reich* (London, 1955), pp. 420–24.

24. U.S. Office of Military Government, *A Year of Potsdam, The German Economy since the Surrender, 1946*, p. 149.

25. For a detailed account of the negotiations, see M. Gottlieb, "Failure of Quadripartite Monetary Reform 1945–1947," *Finanzarchiv*, NF, 17 (1957): 398–417.

26. H. Sauermann, "The Consequences of the Currency Reform in Western Germany," *The Review of Politics* 12 (1950): 178–79.

27. For some typical examples, see, U.S. Office of Military Government,

Monthly Report No. 8, March 1946, p. 44; *Ibid.*, No. 31, January 1948, p. 16.

28. Köln Industrie- und Handelskammer, *Bericht für das Jahr 1947*, p. 5; Ludwigsburg, Industrie- und Handelskammer, *Denkschrift, Grundsätzliche und aktuelle Probleme unserer wirtschaftspolitischen Aufgabe*, 1947, p. 20.

29. F. A. Burchardt and K. Martin, "Western Germany and Reconstruction," *Bulletin of the Oxford University Institute of Statistics* 9 (1947): 405. See also Wirtschaftsrat des Vereinigten Wirtschaftsgebietes, Amerikanisches und Britisches Besatzungsgebiet in Deutschland, *Wörtlicher Bericht über die Vollversammlung*, no. 7, 29/30 Oct., 1947, p. 229.

30. U.S. Office of Military Government, *Monthly Report*, No. 27, Sept. 1947, p. 19.

31. G. Stolper, *German Realities* (New York, 1947), p. 99.

32. C. Bresciani-Turroni, p. 174.

33. T. Balogh, *Germany: An Experiment in "Planning" by the "Free" Price Mechanism* (Oxford, 1950), p. 12.

34. A. Bourneuf, *Norway: Planned Revival* (Cambridge, Mass., 1958), pp. 14–15; see also M. W. Leiserson, *Wages and Economic Control in Norway, 1945–1957* (Cambridge, Mass., 1959), pp. 21–40.

35. U.S. Office of Military Government, *Monthly Report, Trade and Commerce*, No. 21, Feb./March 1947, p. 19.

36. The yearly reports of the various German Chambers of Trade and Commerce are particularly revealing on the general state of German industry after the end of hostilities; see, for instance, a/Reutlingen. Industrie- und Handelskammer, *Wohin fürt der Weg? Eine-sehr nüchterne Betrachtung zur Wirtschaftslage anlässlich der Jahreswende*, 1947, p. 5; b/Bremen, Industrie- und Handelskammer, *Nachkriegsbericht der Handelskammer Bremen über Jahre 1945–1947*, 1947, p. 5.

37. For instance, the steel industry never obtained more than 20 percent of the requested amounts of needed supplies. See Verwaltung für Stahl und Eisen, *Bericht über die Tätigkeit des Verwaltungsamtes für Stahl und Eisen*, 1946, p. 5.

38. H. Mendershausen, "Prices, Money and the Distribution of Goods in Postwar Germany," *American Economic Review* 39 (1949): 655.

39. F. H. Klopstock, "Monetary Reform in Western Germany," *The Journal of Political Economy* 57 (1949): 279.

40. For his testimony, see Wirtschaftsrat des Vereinigten Wirtschaftsgebietes, Amerikanisches und Britisches Besatzungsbiet in Deutschland, *Wörtlicher Bericht über die Vollversammlung*, no. 8, 21 Nov., 1947, p. 209.

41. *The Economist* 153 (1947): 707. On the same point, see also Stolper, p. 100.

42. For a somewhat biased description of the entire complex of the compensation trade, see *Gewerkschaftszeitung* (Munich), vol. 2, 1947, no. 10, p. 13.

43. Balogh, p. 12.

44. U.S. Office of Military Government, Manpower Division, *Unemployment and Underemployment in the Bizonal Area of Germany* (1949), p. 18. (Mimeo.)

45. W. Eucken and F. W. Mayer, "The Economic Situation in Germany," *The Annals of the American Academy of Political and Social Science* 260 (1948): 59.

46. W. Röpke, "Das Deutsche Wirtschaftsexperiment: Beispiel und Lehre," in

A. Hunold, (Ed.), *Vollbeschäftigung, Inflation und Planwirtschaft* (Zurich, 1953), p. 271.

47. "The German Lesson," *The Economist* 221 (1956): 6425, viii.

48. M. Baron, "Many Benefit as Inflation Goes Higher," *The New York Times*, 3 April, 1980.

49. J. Viner, "Full Employment at Whatever Cost," *The Long View and the Short* (Glencoe, Ill., 1958), p. 155.

50. S. Lohr, "Scholars Theorize on Inflation," *The New York Times*, 12 March, 1980.

Inflation and Electoral Politics in Germany 1919–29

THOMAS CHILDERS

The failure of democratic government in Germany following World War I remains the subject of a vast and constantly growing scholarly literature. With the rise of Hitler's National Socialist party as its dominant theme, much, indeed most, of this imposing literature has quite naturally focused on the economic depression and the growth of political radicalism. Employing a variety of methodological strategies, these studies have probed the disintegration of the democratic party system and the concomitant emergence of a broad fascist constituency after 1928.[1] The erosion of the Weimar party system, however, did not begin with the onset of the Great Depression but earlier, in the protracted era of inflation 1919–24. During this period a critical realignment of electoral sympathies took place which destabilized the social foundations of democracy in Germany. Although most treatments of socio-political interaction in the Weimar Republic acknowledge the importance of the inflation in these early political dislocations, the critical electoral shifts of this period and their relationship to economic developments have not been subjected to rigorous empirical analysis. Thus, the impact of the Great Depression, and particularly unemployment, on voting behavior and the rise of fascism have been investigated, but the very serious social and political ramifications of inflation have not.

Even a cursory glance at the aggregate returns from the elections of the predepression period reveals that a substantial segment of the voting public, particularly those strata which had traditionally formed the constituencies of the liberal parties, had become dissatisfied with the traditional alternatives of bourgeois politics (Table 1). Much of this disaffection may be reflected in defections to the conservative party (DNVP), yet the predepression era also witnessed a phenomenal growth of special-interest parties which flourished under the republic's system of proportional representation. In the elections of 1919 and 1920, the first national elections of the postwar era, these small parties accounted for only 3 percent of the vote. By May 1924, however, they represented over 10 percent of the German electorate.[2]

Table 1. Results of the Reichstag Elections of the Weimer Republic
(percentages)

	1919	1920	1924a	1924b	1928	1930	1932a	1932b
NSDAP	—	—	6.5	3.0	2.6	18.3	37.3	33.1
DNVP	10.3	14.9	19.5	20.5	14.2	7.0	5.9	8.5
DVP	4.4	13.9	9.2	10.1	8.7	4.9	1.2	1.8
Zentrum	19.7	18.1	16.6	17.3	15.2	14.8	15.7	15.0
DDP	18.6	8.3	5.7	6.3	4.8	3.5	1.0	1.0
SPD	37.9	21.6	20.5	26.0	29.8	24.5	21.6	20.4
KPD	—	2.1	12.6	9.0	10.6	13.1	14.3	16.9
Other	1.5	3.3	10.3	7.7	13.7	14.4	3.2	4.7

Significantly, that percentage did not decline during the period of relative economic recovery and political stability in the mid-twenties. In the 1928 elections, ballots for these marginal splinter parties constituted 14 percent of the vote, while both the liberal (DVP and DDP) and conservative parties suffered a symptomatic decline in popular support. In short, voter identification with the traditional parties of the center and right had begun a process of decay well before the effects of the depression were felt in Central Europe. Both contemporary observers and subsequent scholarly analysts have emphasized the economic, social, and psychological trauma associated with the hyperinflation of 1923 as a major catalyst in dissolving the traditional compounds of bourgeois politics. Yet, although economic and social investigations of the inflation have made significant progress in identifying its principal victims, little empirical research has been undertaken to establish the response of voters to the twin crises of inflation and stabilization.[3]

Because of the thematic limitations of the traditional historical literature, a number of very critical questions concerning the political ramifications of inflation remain largely unanswered. It is, for example, quite clear that important social groups within the middle class were hard hit by the inflation and the subsequent stabilization. But what were the political consequences of these economic developments for small shopkeepers, white-collar employees, civil servants, and pensioners? The inflation and stabilization crises, it is often asserted, served to radicalize elements of the middle-class electorate, thus destabilizing the Weimar party system and paving the way for the ultimate triumph of fascism. If this is so, which groups were driven from their political moorings and at what point? Did the inflation contribute to a fundamental electoral reorientation of these groups or were the political effects of inflation simply crisis-related and therefore transitory?

Finally, the existing historical scholarship on the inflation has focused almost exclusively on the fate of the *Mittelstand*, ignoring the ramifications of the twin crises on working-class politics.

Treatment of each of these issues is clearly beyond the scope of this essay. Nevertheless, a brief examination of one of these groups and the efforts of the parties to tap its resentment springing from the inflation can shed some light on the interaction between economics and politics in the Weimar Republic. Several factors facilitate this task. As contemporary and subsequent sociologists have noted, status formalization, based largely on occupation, was sharply pronounced in Weimar Germany.[4] As a result, campaign literature tended to be addressed explicitly to farmers, white-collar employees, civil servants, etc. — occupational terms which were not abstract classifications developed by the Statistisches Reichsamt but terms which enjoyed widespread public currency and conveyed obvious social content to German voters. A content analysis of campaign literature from the period 1923–29[5] reveals that the parties dealt generally with inflation in addressing a wide range of these socio-occupational groups, but emphasis on inflation-related issues was most salient in appeals directed to pensioners, disabled veterans, rentiers, and others living on fixed incomes. In 1925 these groups were subsumed under the census category *Berufslos* (without occupation). This classification, therefore, contains a number of groups traditionally considered to be among the principal victims of the inflation and stabilization crises and can serve as an important and useful social variable in a statistical (regression) analysis of electoral developments between 1919 and 1929.

Some property owners undoubtedly benefited from the nullification of debts; some high-income entrepreneurs profited from inflation speculation, but the dramatic depreciation of the currency reduced many creditors, holders of fixed interest securities, and recipients of insurance payments from private companies to virtual poverty. As savings evaporated, retirement funds dwindled, and government bonds were drained of value, a groundswell of discontent mounted among small investors, the disabled, the elderly, and other pensioners suddenly deprived of their economic security.[7]

Among the most drastically affected by the inflation were the millions of small investors who had regularly set aside a significant portion of their income in private savings, government and municipal bonds, or other capital assets. With the disintegration of the currency in 1922–23, these investments, often representing the assiduous saving of a lifetime, were reduced to a mere fraction of their anticipated value. As the situation deteriorated, a number of pressure groups were organized to prevent complete financial ruin and to bring pressure on government to protect the interests of these small investors. By the close of 1922 these regionally organized groups had formed a national organization, the Protective Association of Mortgages and Savers (*Hypotheken-Glaübiger- und Sparer-Schutzverband für das Deutsche Reich*, later the *Sparerbund*), to prevent continued repayment of loans and mortgages in devalued currency and to achieve a revalorization of those debts already liquidated in worthless paper marks.[8]

The Reich government, however, continued to insist that "a mark equals a mark," denying any distinction between the gold mark of prewar transactions and the inflated paper mark employed to liquidate current financial obligations. In November 1923 the German Supreme Court rejected this interpretation, arguing that the government's policy was in conflict with the principles of "Trust and Good Faith" found in the German Civil Code. This decision forced the government's hand. Hoping to avoid massive legal proceedings which would have delayed economic recovery, the government of Wilhelm Marx began consideration of a law to effect a revaluation settlement. The bill which emerged from these deliberations limited revalorization of private paper mark debts to 15 percent of their original gold mark value and exempted all government obligations from any revaluation until after the reparations issue had been resolved. Under this plan, those debts already settled were not affected, and settlement of outstanding obligations was postponed until January 1932. Realizing that this scheme would encounter considerable opposition, the Marx government presented the bill to the public in the Third Emergency Tax Decree of 24 February 1924. By incorporating it in this emergency decree, the Reich government insured that the revalorization settlement went into effect under the Enabling Act of 8 December 1923, which allowed its implementation without approval by the Reichstag.[9]

Predictably, the Third Emergency Tax Decree outraged the small investment interests which had been organizing for over a year, and the plight of the small investor, pensioner, and disabled veteran became a major issue in the campaign to elect a new Reichstag in the spring of 1924. Each of the parties addressed this problem during the campaign, but among the major nonsocialist parties, only the conservative DNVP and the fascist DVFB (*Deutsch-Völkische Freiheitsbewegung*) were not compromised by participation in the unpopular Marx government. Not surprisingly, both parties mounted highly aggressive campaigns to exploit pensioner disenchantment with the coalition parties. The DNVP, in particular, focused much of its campaign propaganda on the problems of the pensioner, small investor, and disabled veteran, while placing prominent leaders of the revalorization movement on its national ticket. Though never committing itself to a definite figure, the DNVP vigorously championed a higher rate of revaluation. Hergt, the party's national chairman, was even widely reported to have promised that "within twenty-four hours after their entrance into the cabinet, the Nationalists will bring about a revaluation of one hundred percent."[10] The DNVP repeatedly charged that the Reich government had failed to recognize the material and psychological needs of the inflation's middle-class victims. The ruling coalition, Hergt typically declared:

> ... has irresponsibly neglected the moral obligations owed to owners of gilt-edged securities, supposedly guaranteed by the state, to holders of war bonds ... the truest of the true in the hardest of times ... to all those who sacrificed body and health in the war and to the middle class, so severely weakened by economic developments.[11]

The DNVP, therefore, demanded that the government eliminate this alleged inequitable treatment and ensure that "the *Mittelstand* alone" was not forced "to bear the costs of the war."[12]

Although among the major parties the DNVP was most assiduous in its efforts to cultivate a constituency among the *Berufslosen*, the National Socialists (DVFB), participating in their first Reichstag campaign, offered a serious challenge to the conservatives. While remaining characteristically vague on specifics, the Nazis demanded "a just revalorization of medium and small savings accounts" as well as the immediate revocation of the Third Emergency Tax Decree.[13] This "shameful law," the Nazis asserted, had "robbed the entire middle class, workers, and civil servants of all their savings," while bringing "indescribable misery to millions of aging people." The Third Tax Decree, the Nazis claimed, had reduced the elderly to "hunger, despair, and death." The inflation had been a form of "finance Bolshevism," amounting to "the most shamelessly and ruthlessly executed expropriation" of all times, and the government's revalorization policy had given this crime "the official stamp of approval." It meant the "breach of public promises" and "annuled private obligations to creditors," thus "unjustly dumping billions upon billions into the lap of debtors."[14]

Nazi opposition to the government's revalorization program also overlapped with the party's assault on the Republic's treatment of the elderly, disabled veterans, and the dependents of those lost in the Great War. Indeed, the first two demands of the party's social platform in 1924 called for "a generous extension of government assistance for the elderly" and, as a second point, pledged that the "highest duty of the *völkisch* state" would be to provide for the "security of the war's victims, specifically welfare for disabled veterans and surviving dependents of the war dead."[15] Disabled veterans, the party claimed, belonged to the "poorest of the poor," and had been abused by the Republic's government. "What has happened to us disabled veterans?"

one widely distributed Nazi pamphlet asked. "Instead of support and understanding," the disabled veteran received nothing but "scorn and ridicule." The Nazis conceded that pensions had been provided for in the Reich Welfare Law of May 1920 but maintained that when payments at last started flowing, they came in worthless, inflated currency. "Anyone not wishing to starve had to go begging. To the disgrace and shame of revolutionary Germany, disabled veterans had to sit on the street and display their mutilated limbs like billboards in order to get a few beggar's pennies tossed at them by the parasites of the revolution."[16]

Other pensioners had suffered greatly under the impact of the inflation, and the Reich government's emergency decrees had only exacerbated the situation, the Nazis asserted. The coalition parties had reduced the pensions of public employees and civil servants, while other persons living on fixed incomes, the Nazis scornfully noted, were receiving "only a fraction" of their expected benefits.[17]

To the pensioners, veterans, and small investors wounded by inflation and enraged by the government's stabilization measures, the Nazis consistently maintained that they alone had been steadfast and forceful in representing their interests. The DVP, DDP, and Zentrum, the Nazis described as "notorious government parties," declaring that they could, therefore, never "offer serious opposition" to the revalorization policy which they had helped formulate. The National Socialist movement, on the other hand, was pictured as entering the campaign in inner agreement with the program of the Protective Association of Mortgagees and Savers and had, as Nazi pamphlet literature pointed out, named an influential member of that organization as a special adviser to its Reichstag delegation and placed his name on a secure place in the party's national electoral list.[18]

In this highly charged atmosphere, the two liberal parties proved unable to develop a credible approach to the victims of the inflation. Assailed by the political right and the representatives of the revalorization movement, the DVP and DDP adopted a defensive posture during the campaign of 1924 from which they were never to escape. The DVP weakly condemned the Conservative and Nazi promises to pensioners and small investors as "vague" and "irresponsible" and, in the summer of 1924, even endorsed an increased rate of revaluation, indicating that 25 percent might be acceptable.[19] Still, Stresemann, speaking for his party and the government, bitterly complained that the DVP "cannot satisfy utopian hopes."[20]

The DDP also pointed out that the Third Tax Decree need not be the last word on the revalorization issue. Yet, at the same time, the party appealed to pensioners and small investors to keep the revalorization question in perspective.

It is fundamentally wrong for an impoverished *Rentner* to orient his voting behavior according to whether the (party) list contains men whose mouths are crammed with promises of revaluation. . . . The decisive consideration must be the position on the great questions of domestic and foreign policy and not on a single issue, no matter how painfully it touches one's personal life. You must decide if the listed candidates are for the Republic and peaceful development or for monarchy and new disorder, if they are for accommodation with the outside world or for a new war. After all, the fate of revalorization depends on these things . . .[21]

These arguments, however, failed to impress the leaders of the emerging revaluation movement and the constituencies which they represented. Tensions between the liberal parties and the revalorization forces were heightened during the fall when representatives of the Protective Association of Mortgagees and Savers (*Sparerbund*) approached the leadership of the nonsocialist parties in an effort to secure support for their demands. While the DNVP, NSFB (National Socialists), and Zentrum accepted the association's recommendations, the liberals balked. As a result, the *Sparerbund* pointedly refused to endorse either the DVP or DDP in the December elections.[22]

A regression analysis of voting in a sample of approximately 200 geographically distributed and socially diverse communities ranging in size from 15,000 to over 1 million inhabitants reveals that in 1920 the *Berufslose* variable had been a solid predictor of both the liberal and conservative electoral performance.[23] Four years later, however, the disintegration of this liberal-conservative cleavage had begun, with the liberal coefficients slipping precipitously (Table 2). The figures suggest that the National Socialists had succeeded in winning a marginal constituency in this politically important element of the electorate, but

Table 2. Party Vote and % Berufslose
Partial R^2
Controlling Percentage Catholic
(N = 135)†

	1920	1924a	1924b	1928	1930	1932a	1932b
NSDAP	—	+.50	+.31	+.15*	+.60	+.80	+.68
DNVP	+.99	+1.12	+1.14	+.92	+.56	+.38	+.60
DVP	+.75	+.13*	+.11*	+.09*	+.05*	+.09	+.07*
DDP	+.32	+.06*	+.02*	+.03*	+.04*	+.02*	+.04*

*indicates that coefficient is less than two times the standard error.
†The figures in this table are drawn from communities with a predominantly Protestant population. The same trends were evident in the smaller Catholic subsample, when controlling for percentage Protestant.

the primary beneficiary of the inflation and stabilization crises appeared to be the conservative DNVP. The coefficients also indicate that the failure of the liberal parties to maintain their previous appeal was not simply a temporary setback. For the pronounced rightward shift of political sympathies within that section of the middle class dominated by small investors, pensioners, creditors, and others susceptible to the pressures of inflation clearly dates from the "inflation election" of May 1924. Thereafter, despite improving economic conditions, this segment of the voting public refused to return from the right-wing or special-interest fringes of German electoral politics.

Do these figures then support the traditional view that the inflation and stabilization crises radicalized a significant portion of the middle class electorate and prepared it for fascism? Certainly the liberal parties seem to have been unable to reassert their appeal to the groups examined here, even after the return of economic stability. In the Landtag elections held between 1924 and 1928, both the DDP and DVP stumbled at the polls, and the Reichstag election of May 1928, in which the liberal vote slipped from its 1924 level of 16.4 percent to 13.5 percent, confirmed that the declining popularity of liberalism was not simply a regional phenomenon.

Yet, although the political stock of German liberalism slumped in the relatively prosperous mid-twenties, the DNVP was unable to take advantage of that decline. Indeed, the DNVP's position also deteriorated strikingly in the period of stabilization. Upon entering the cabinet in 1925, the party came under increasingly heavy pressure from influential agricultural and industrial interests to modify its position on the issue of revalorization. Torn between these organized interests close to the party and its electoral constituency, the DNVP settled for an increase of the rate from 15 to 25 percent. The leaders of the revalorization movement were predictably outraged at this solution, and in the aftermath of this conservative shift, the various wings of the movement began serious negotiations in hope of establishing a strong national party to represent creditor interests. Two parties devoted to this task had been founded in November 1924, the German Revalorization and Construction Party (*Die Deutsche Aufwertungs- und Aufbaupartei*) and the Revalorization and Reconstruction Party (*Die Aufwertungs- und Wiederaufbaupartei*), and in 1926 the Reich Party for People's Justice and Revalorization (*Reichspartei für Volksrecht und Aufwertung*) joined them.[24] Although none of these parties succeeded in becoming the effective instrument of creditor interests on the national level that their founders intended, they clearly detracted from the conservative electoral performance after 1924.[25]

Confronted by this challenge, the DNVP consistently warned pensioners, creditors, and small investors that these splinter parties would only have a "destructive effect on the bourgeois camp and contribute in the most tragic way to the strengthening of *vaterlandsfeindliche* elements."[26] The *Rentner* could be saved, the DNVP contended, only by "a strong organization, encompassing millions, a party which understands you and your desires, which has always stood up for you and will be able to fight for you in the future."[27]

These Nationalist appeals, however, proved increasingly less effective. Between 1924 and 1928 the DNVP, like the liberals, suffered disquieting setbacks in the state elections, and in 1928 faltered badly in the national campaign. In December 1924 the party had received 20.5 percent of the national vote, in May 1928 only 14.2 percent. Certainly the other parties, and particularly the NSDAP, reminded pensioners and other creditors of the DNVP's failure to fulfill its electoral promises concerning revalorization,[28] and regression analysis of the 1928 returns indicates that support for the DNVP among the *Berufslosen* showed the first signs of an erosion which would continue into the Great Depression. But unlike the elections after the onset of the World Economic Crisis in 1929–30, this conservative decline was not matched by a rise in the National Socialist figures. In the years between the hyperinflation and the Great Depression, the NSDAP, which in 1928 won less than 3 percent of the national vote, wandered on the fringes of German electoral politics, unable to capitalize on the fading fortunes of the DNVP.

On the eve of the Great Depression, German voters, even those who had suffered from the inflation and stabilization crises, hardly seemed radicalized. Support for the traditional conservative right appeared to be eroding, and the National Socialists represented merely one of a number of small splinter parties jostling to inherit that support. Yet, while the 1928 elections represented a defeat for the radical right and resulted in the formation of a Great Coalition headed by a Social Democrat and extending to Stresemann's DVP, signs of the nascent destabilization of the Weimar party system were also discernible.

In the Landtag elections of the mid-twenties, German voters were turning away from the traditional alternatives of bourgeois politics, liberalism and conservatism, toward a plethora of special-interest parties, of which the revalorization parties were in many ways typical. In Saxony, Thuringia, Brunswick, and the Mecklenburgs, these special interest parties had attracted between 12.2 percent and 18.5 percent of the vote in elections held between June 1926 and January 1928, while both the liberal and conservative parties slipped steadily.[29] Moreover, the DDP, DVP, and DNVP lost votes in the Reichstag election of 1928, but these special-interest parties maintained and even extended their constituencies. Together they outpolled the two liberal parties and almost matched the conservative totals. Rather than an endorsement of the Republic, the election of 1928 reflects a fundamental breakdown of voter identification with the traditional parties of the bourgeois center and right. The Nazis, of course, did not profit immediately from this fragmentation, but without the destabilization of traditional voting patterns within the middle-class electorate, the spectacular rise of National Socialist electoral fortunes after 1928 is hardly conceivable. Indeed, the dramatic Nazi breakthrough in the Reichstag election of September 1930 came primarily among those social groups which had been hard hit by the inflation and stabilization crises 6 years earlier.[30] The *Berufslose* variable, for example, becomes a stronger predictor of the Nazi than of the Nationalist vote in 1930 and remains so in the final elections of the Weimar era in 1932.

Still, the process of electoral change was more complex than the traditional analyses of the depression period have assumed. Although more research, especially dealing with regional elections between 1919 and 1929, is necessary before the exact stages of this electoral transformation can be ascertained with confidence, it is clear that the disintegration of the traditional bourgeois party system, reflecting a fundamental shift within the middle-class electorate, was already far advanced before the bankruptcies and unemployment lines of the depression became harsh realities of German economic and political life. Regional and special-interest parties had existed in the Wilhelmian Reich, but the symptomatic surge in the popularity of such parties clearly dates from the troubled period of inflation and stabilization. Although these parties represented different sets of interests and concerns within the highly fragmented *Mittelstand*, they nonetheless spoke for a sizable element of the bourgeois electorate which was alienated by the traumatic developments of 1922–25 and which thereafter was lost to the traditional liberal and conservative parties. If the complex relationship between economic developments and political change in the Weimar Republic is to be analyzed fruitfully, that analysis must, therefore, begin not with the depression of the early thirties but with the impact of the inflation and stabilization on the German party system.

Notes

1. See, for example, James K. Pollock, "An Areal Study of the German Electorate 1930–1933," *American Political Science Review* 38 (February 1944): 89–95; Samuel A. Pratt, "The Social Bases of Nazism and Communism in Urban Germany. A Correlation Study of the July 31, 1932 Reichstag Election in Germany," (M.A. Thesis, Michigan State University, 1948); Karl O'Lessker, "Who Voted for Hitler? A New Look at the Class Basis of Nazism," *American Journal of Sociology* 74 (July 1968): 63–69.

2. For results of the 1920 and 1924 elections see Statistik des Deutschen Reichs, vol. 291, 315.

3. See, for example, Werner Kaltefleiter, Wirtschaft und Politik in Deutschland. Konjunktur als Bestimmungsfaktor des Parteiensystems (Cologne, 1968); Heinrich Bennecke, Wirtschaftliche Depression und politischer Radikalismus 1918–1938 (Munich-Vienna, 1970).

4. Talcott Parsons, "Democracy and Social Structure in Pre-Nazi Germany," T. Parsons, Essays in Sociological Theory (New York, 1964), p. 112.

5. This analysis is based on a systematic examination of the official partisan press as well as electoral pamphlet literature found in the collections of the Bundesarchiv, Koblenz; Zentrales Staatsarchiv, Potsdam; Geheimes Staatsarchiv Preussischer Kulturbesitz, West Berlin; Landesarchiv, West Berlin.

6. Statistik des Deutschen Reichs, 408: 23. Category G of the census, "persons without occupation (ohne Beruf und Berufsaufgabe) was comprised of a variety of groups, including inmates of prisons, students not residing at home, and patients in mental institutions. Over three-quarters of those classified as Berufslose, or berufslose Selbständige, were persons living on accumulated assets, investments, rents, and pensions. More than half (53 percent) were over 60 years old; and 78 percent were women, the majority of whom were either widowed or divorced. Together with their dependents, these Berufslose represented approximately 10 percent of the German population. This category did not include unemployed persons.

7. Constantin Bresciani-Turroni, The Economics of Inflation. A Study of Currency Depreciation in Post-War Germany 1914–1933 (London, 1953), pp. 315–20; Karsten Laursen and Jorgen Pedersen, The German Inflation 1918–1923 (Amsterdam, 1964), pp. 118–20; Franz Eulenburg, "Die sozialen Wirkungen der Währungsverhältnisse," Jahrbücher für Nationalökonomie und Statistik 122 (1924): 757–58.

8. Werner Fritzsch, "Sparerbund für das Deutsche Reich 1922–1939," Die bürgerlichen Parteien in Deutschland. Handbuch der Geschichte der bürgerlichen Parteien und anderer bürgerlicher Interessenorganisationen vom Vormärz bis zum Jahre 1945, II (Berlin, 1974): 648–53.

9. Claus-Dieter Krohn, Stabilisierung und ökonomische Interessen. Die Finanzpolitik des Deutschen Reichs 1923–1927 (Düsseldorf, 1974), pp. 22–53; Karl-Bernhard Netzband and Hans Peter Widmaier, Währungs- und Finanzpolitik der Ära Luther 1923–25 (Basel and Tübingen, 1964), pp. 168–223. See also Peter-Christian Witt, "Finanzpolitik und sozialer Wandel in Krieg und Inflation 1918–1924," in Hans Mommsen, Dietmar Petzina, Bernd Weisbrod (Eds.), Industrielles System und politische Entwicklung in der Weimarer Republik (Düsseldorf, 1974), pp. 395–426; Charles S. Maier, Recasting Bourgeois Europe. Stabilization in France, Germany, and Italy in the Decade after World War I, pp. 441–58.

10. These promises were never incorporated into official Nationalist platforms in 1924, though the party's rhetoric on the revalorization issue was certainly intended to foster extravagant hopes in creditor and pensioner circles. See Werner Liebe, Die Deutschnationale Volkspartei 1918–1924 (Düsseldorf, 1956), p. 180. See also "Die Aufwertungsansprüche des Hypothekengläubigers und ihre praktische Durchführung," Flugschriften des 'Tag,' Berlin, 1924.

11. *Kreuzzeitung,* 4 April 1924.

12. *Der Tag,* 2 December 1924.

13. "Wahlaufruf der Nationalsozialistischen Freiheitspartei," *Reichstags-Handbuch* (Berlin, 1924), p. 155.

14. National Socialist pamphlet, "Deutsche Sparer! Deutsche Kleinrentner! Deutsche Hypothekengläubiger! Fort mit der 3. Steuerverordnung!" Geheime Staatsarchiv Preussicher Kulturbesitz, Hauptabteilung XII (Zeitgeschichtliche Sammlung) IV, Flugblätter und Pakete (cited hereafter as GStA).

15. National Socialist pamphlet, "Deutschvölkische Freiheitspartei (Allgemeine grundsätzliche Richtlinien)," GSTA, HA XII, IV, Nr. 211.

16. National Socialist pamphlet, "Der Dank des Vaterlandes ist Euch gewiss," NSDAP Hauptarchiv, Reel 42, Frame 843.

17. National Socialist pamphlet, "Beamte! Beamtinnen! Angestellte! Pensionäre! der Reichs-, Staats- und Kommunalverwaltungen!" GStA, HA XII, IV, Nr. 211.

18. National Socialist pamphlet, "Deutsche Sparer! . . . , GStA, HA IV, Nr. 212.

19. German People's Party pamphlet, "Der Parteitag der DVP für Aufwertung," GStA, HA XII, IV, Nr. 166.

20. *Neue Tägliche Rundschau,* 1 Dec. 1924.

21. German Democratic Party pamphlet, *Für Vaterland und Freiheit. Wahlzeitung der DDP,* Nr. 4, 1924, "Aufwertung," Bundesarchiv, Koblenz, Zeitgeschichtliche Sammlung 1, Nr. 17/19(4), DDP, 1924.

22. Larry Eugene Jones, "Inflation, Revaluation, and the Crisis of Middle-Class Politics: A Study of the Dissolution of the German Party System, 1923–28," *Central European History* 12 (June 1979): 155–56.

23. The figures in the table are partial regression coefficients. Simply stated, these coefficients indicate the amount of change to be expected in the dependent variable for every unit of change in the independent variable when the effects of a third variable are statistically controlled. Thus, the Conservative vote in 1924a (May) increased 1.12 percent for every 1 percent increase in the number of *Berufslose* in a community, controlling for the effects of the Catholic population. The literature on ecological analysis is quite extensive. Among the most useful treatments of its strengths and weaknesses are Allan J. Lichtman, "Correlation Regression, and the Ecological Fallacy: A Critique," *Journal of Interdisciplinary History* 4 (Winter 1974): 417–34; J. Morgan Kousser, "Ecological Regression and the Analysis of Past Politics," *Ibid.,* 4 (Autumn 1973): 237–62.

24. Jones, pp. 162–64.

25. In Saxony, for example, the revaluation parties received only 20,000 votes in December 1924; in October 1926, however, they polled just over 98,000, or 4.2 percent of the vote. In Hessen, the revaluation parties, which in 1924 had won less than 1 percent of the vote, claimed a full 5 percent in the Landtag elections of November 1927. The DNVP, on the other hand, fell from 20.5 percent to 14.5 percent, in Saxony and 7 percent to 5 percent in Hessen. The results of the Landtag elections are found in *Wirtschaft und Statistik* 6 (1926): 783; 7 (1927): 998.

26. German National People's Party pamphlet, "Die Aufwertung und die DNVP," GStA, HA XII, Nr. 189.

27. German National People's Party pamphlet, "Rentner! Ihr seid bestohlen und betrogen!" GStA, HA, XII, IV, Nr. 192.

28. See, for example, Wilhelm Frick, "Die Nationalsozialisten im Reichstag 1924–1928," Nationalsozialistische Bibliothek, Heft 4, 1928, 45; and the DDP pamphlet, "Hilfe für die Kleinrentner muss die Reichstagswahl bringen," GStA, HA XII, IV, Nr. 192.

29. For the election results in these states see *Wirtschaft und Statistik* 6: 783; 7: 156, 568; 8: 148.

30. Childers, 17–42.

The Historian and the German Inflation

GERALD D. FELDMAN

In surveying the state of research on the German inflation and the tasks facing historians in this field in 1976 at the Berlin symposium on Historical Processes of the German Inflation 1914–1924, I attempted to explore why it was that the great German inflation, presumably one of the most extraordinary traumas ever to affect an advanced industrial society and one of the major underlying causes of the triumph of Nazism in Germany, should have been the subject of so little historical research and to have remained the virtual monopoly of economists and non-German economists at that.[1] In my attempt at a reply, I argued that this neglect was no simple function of some alleged more general neglect of German social and economic history since, quite aside from the fact that plenty of work was being done in these fields now, the relative proportion of work done on the inflation was strikingly minimal. I might have added that political historians had done precious little to explain the political legacy of the inflation either. In the last analysis, the professional historical image of the inflation remained remarkably close to the popular image with its emphasis upon the hyperinflation of 1922–23 and vague allusions to inflation profiteers like Hugo Stinnes, the supposed ruin of the middle class, and the Beer Hall Putsch. The historical confrontation with the German inflation, not only the sensational final phase of hyperinflation but rather the full 10-year period of inflation that began in 1914 and ended in late 1923, had not yet taken place.

I sought to explain historians' shyness in approaching the inflation in terms of the vast methodological difficulties study of the inflation presented and quoted a passage from Knut Borchardt's essay on the structural effects of the inflationary process which deals with problems of contemporary inflation but which has relevance to the historical study of the German inflation as well:

> Precisely because the manifold distributive effects of inflation are so diffuse and unexplained, inflation can go on for so long a time without becoming an acute scandal. The effects do not suddenly become evident to everyone in a visible manner, as is the case with unemployment, where no scientific investigation is necessary to determine who is unemployed. The unemployed can be

named and located. Because of this asymmetry in the social effects of unemployment and inflation one can probably explain why full employment has until now indisputably been the higher aim of economic policy.[2]

These difficulties in identifying and evaluating the effects of inflation as they occur in the course of an inflationary process do constitute at one and the same time an enticing but also discouraging hurdle to inflation research. For the general historian, these methodological problems are further compounded by economists having dominated the field. Historians would find some compensation for the technical inaccessibility of some of the economists' arguments if the latter could agree, that economists are often in such sharp disagreement about the causes and consequences of the inflation exacerbates the anxieties already entertained by historians in seeking to deal with the German inflation. Ultimately, however, I argued in Berlin and would argue now, historians must come to grips with the German inflation because of its intrinsic importance and because, once they confront the issues and arguments raised by economists and economic historians — to whom we must be grateful for making a sophisticated discussion of the German inflation that takes us beyond traditional clichés possible — historians can add considerably even to their discussions by raising neglected issues, uncovering facts, and compelling a consideration of the so-called exogenous factors.

Since the 1976 symposium in Berlin, some of my colleagues on this panel and others have joined in an international, multidisciplinary project supported by the Volkswagen Foundation on Inflation and Reconstruction in Germany and Europe, 1914–1924. We have done so in the belief that this topic lends itself to a broadly based cooperative scholarly effort, and that such an experiment, uncommon among historians, may point the way to more appropriate modes of attacking the complex problems of historical investigation into modern industrial societies than the highly individualistic, frequently unidimensional, and almost invariably isolated manner in which historical research is generally conducted. Obviously, this project is too young to permit the presentation of extensive findings, but discussion of research strategies entailed in the construction of the project and some of the research already carried out by myself and my colleagues in the project have helped us to a more clearly defined sense of the ways in which the historian can best deal with the German inflation, and it is to this that I wish to address myself here.[3]

To begin with, the historical investigation of the German inflation cannot easily be separated from the problems of reconstruction or from a consideration of the alternative types of reconstruction pursued by the various nations after World War I. It would be a mistake to attribute solely to inflation developments which were in fact largely or partially the product of the war economy and the reconstruction process and which, one might add, must in any case be viewed from the perspective of longer-term trends in the socioeconomic development of advanced industrial societies.[4] The issue is always the role played by inflation in accelerating, retarding, and modifying these developments in either a positive or negative sense. The disproportionate redevelopment of the older heavy industrial sector of the economy during and after the war, for example, certainly was encouraged and assisted by inflation, but the overcapacities experienced after the inflation were no less attributable to reconstruction policies that would have been pursued to a greater or lesser extent even under less inflationary conditions because of energy crises and immediate postwar demands and, from a long-run perspective, were reflective of basic structural problems that still trouble us today.[5] In any case, the German inflation must be considered within the context of the more general problem of postwar reconstruction, and this not only nationally but also internationally.

It must be borne in mind that different nations experienced different forms of monetary reconstruction after the war. One may identify three such types of reconstruction: The first, of which Germany was the most prominent representative, ultimately succumbed to hyperinflation and was compelled to stabilize on the basis of a new currency. Austria, Hungary, Poland, and Russia also took this route. The second group, composed of France, Italy, Belgium, and Czechoslovakia, experienced moderate inflation, stabilizing with a devaluation of their currencies as over against prewar rates. Finally, there were nations — Great Britain and the United States being the most prominent, but also including Holland, Spain, and the Scandinavian states — which pursued a deflationary course and sooner or later restored the prewar relationship of their currencies to gold.[6] The identification of these groups should be an incitement to comparative study within and among them, but it also reminds us that nations chose alternative strategies of reconstruction and that the degree of decision making and the kinds of decision making processes involved are of the utmost significance for historians because of their very important consequences for the nations concerned and for the international economic and political order.

To return to the German case, there is by now a consensus among historians and economists that the German inflationary reconstruction enabled Germany to revive its economic life both in terms of domestic productivity and foreign trade at a pace far faster than would have been possible had it pursued a deflationary policy and that the German inflationary reconstruction permitted it to enjoy increasing productivity and high employment while countries pursuing a deflationary policy succumbed to a severe depression in 1920–21. Indeed, Professor

Holtfrerich recently has gone so far as to argue that Germany's high level of economic activity during the world depression of 1920–21 played a crucial role in bringing about the relatively quick recovery of America and England from the depression, an advantage they did not enjoy in the Great Depression of the next decade.[7]

Do these findings then lead to a "rehabilitation" of the German inflation? Certainly this would be a very delicate matter in an American environment where inflation has officially been raised to the rank of the nation's Number One Enemy and, worse yet, with respect to a nation whose contemporary economic policies are persistently influenced by the bitter memories of the Great Inflation. Yet, the contemporary distaste for inflation — more often a matter of words than of deeds anyway — should not stand in the way of a realistic recognition of the functional advantages Germany enjoyed through her inflation. Such a positive assessment certainly is not new to economists, since both the older work of Frank Graham (1931) and the more recent Keynesian analysis of the Scandinavians Karsten Laursen and Jørgen Pedersen (1964) have emphasized the importance of the inflation to Germany's postwar reconstruction.[8]

It is important, however, to avoid unhistorical perspectives, to refrain from a confusion of consequences with motives, and not to read into the inflationary practices of the Germans intentions which were not there or which were there in a form that had precious little to do with the kind of consciously pursued economic policies and doctrines of a much later period.[9] One of the chief tasks of the historian of the inflation, therefore, is to distinguish carefully between instances of active decision making and instances of passive drift and to understand the motives for both.

Such distinctions must be made within carefully defined time frameworks that conform to the various stages of the inflation.[10] One cannot emphasize enough that this was a 10-year period of inflation that began in August 1914 and ended in the fall of 1923, not just the famous hyperinflation that began in the summer of 1922. Little need be said about the wartime inflation, which was a universal phenomenon, although certainly exacerbated in Germany by the huge drain of the Hindenburg program after 1916, the persistent effort to maintain productivity and social peace by allowed price/wage tradeoffs, and the failure to develop an adequate system of taxation.

With the end of the war, I think that it is possible to identify four periods of development useful for our purposes here. The first period encompassed the Revolution, the signature of the Treaty of Versailles, and the Kapp Putsch. This was a period of significant mark depreciation largely induced by domestic factors, particularly the government's efforts to maintain social peace through work creation programs, high unemployment supports, and benevolence toward price and wage increases. It can be argued that the influence of the Versailles Treaty and reparations deliveries in kind during this period played a secondary role. The second period, from the spring of 1920 to the spring of 1921, is one of relative stability, politically and economically. It is a period in which the mark remains depreciated enough for Germany to enjoy relatively high employment and strong export advantages in comparison to the victor nations, which are undergoing a severe depression induced by their deflationary policies, but in which the process of mark depreciation has slowed down sufficiently for there to be some hope that a stabilization would be possible. At this time, as recent research has shown, Americans are privately investing millions of dollars in short-term credits repayable in marks on the theory that the mark was bound to rise in value.[11] A third period of severe depreciation begins in the spring of 1921 in response to the setting of the reparations bill by acceptance of the London Ultimatum of May 1921 and the various domestic and international crises which follow fast and furious upon this event: the murder of Erzberger in August 1921 and the successive failures of the Wirth governments to find a satisfactory domestic foundation for their fulfillment policies. A similar combination of circumstances, failures in Germany's international negotiations coupled with the murder of Rathenau in June 1922, triggers the final phase of hyperinflation, a hyperinflation whose chief motor until the Ruhr occupation, was the Reichsbank's decision to discount commercial bills as an answer to the growing credit crisis arising from the fact that fewer and fewer foreigners were willing to speculate on an increase in the value of the mark. To keep the economy going, the Reichsbank gave enormous amounts of credit to industry with full knowledge that it was a desperate measure bound to increase the mark's depreciation.[12] Thus, financing the passive resistance to the French in 1923 by the printing press merely completed a process already begun months before the occupation.

The inflation taken as a totality rested upon what might justifiably be termed a broad *inflation consensus*[13] with respect to its functional utility, although appreciation of the various benefits of the inflation and their significance varied over time and among different groups. The inflation served three basic functions which were viewed positively, albeit often with severe reservations, by the dominant groups in German society. The first was social pacification, a matter of particular importance during the war and in the revolutionary phase which followed it. Efforts to prevent or reduce revolutionary unrest by providing public works and other contracts, by reducing working hours, controlling food prices and rents while granting regular wage increases and by introducing measures of social legislation were of particular importance in 1918–20, but continued to be employed throughout the inflation whenever the sociopolitical situation seemed to require them. Insofar as labor and industry were able to engage in formal cooperation through the so-called Working Community Policy (*Arbeitsgemeinschaftspolitik*),[14] these policies were based on a high degree of consensus, but insofar as industry in particular resisted labor pressures at certain times, the government itself sought to maintain social peace through an elaborate system of binding arbitration and met with relatively little employer resistance because the latter were able to pass the costs on to consumers or taxpayers through higher prices. A good argument can be made that the survival of the Weimar Republic during the initial phase of its existence depended on these inflationary trade-offs, while the subsequent survival of the Republic depended upon the skillful use of the system of binding arbitration created during the inflation to shore up the shaky social compromise upon which the Republic continued to rest.[15]

The second positive aspect of the German inflation lay in its function as an instrument of economic recovery. While the aforementioned policies kept employment high and encouraged productivity, control of prices for basic necessities combined with the payment of low real wages gave Germany a competitive edge in world markets. The export "boom" and high export profits of 1919–20 were maintained during the period of relative stabilization in 1920–21 through an elaborate system of export controls. The foreign exchange profits from these exports, when combined with the substantial amounts of speculative short-term foreign capital which poured into Germany at this time on the assumption that the mark would recover and thus permit speculators to make a "killing," served to promote further industrial expansion.[16]

Last but not least, the inflation served as a remarkably useful weapon of economic and political warfare against the victors of World War I in the effort to force them to moderate their demands on Germany. If there was consensus about anything in Germany during this troubled period it was over the impossibility of fulfilling the London Ultimatum and various other provisions of the Versailles Treaty and on the need for a moderating of these demands and for large-scale foreign assistance before Germany could get its own house in order. Whatever their tactical disagreements with respect to the so-called Policy of Fulfillment, trade union leaders and employers shared the desire to use Germany's inflationary advantages and export boom to promote unemployment abroad and thus compel Germany's oppressors to see the light. A fatalistic attitude toward the inflation could thus be legitimized on the highest patriotic grounds.[17]

Today it is easy enough for the historian to establish and demonstrate this broad inflation consensus. Furthermore, the documents abound with evidence of a high degree of conscious decision making on both the public and the private levels with respect to the three components of the inflation consensus just described. Even acts of desperation, such as the Reichsbank decision to discount commercial bills in the late summer of 1922, one of the major triggers of the hyperinflation, turn out not to have been the fanatical application of dubious economic theories historians have previously supposed. Professor Holtfrerich has shown that Reichsbank President Havenstein and his colleagues were not blind devotees of the balance-of-payments theory of inflation and knew full well that they were courting hyperinflation; my own research on this subject emphasizes that the entire business and banking community was pressing for the discounting of commercial bills as the one means of keeping the economy going in the face of a mounting credit crisis.[18] This action would appear symptomatic of the entire inflation, namely, a persistent choice of the least unsatisfactory alternatives facing Germany to enable it to survive until a situation developed both externally and internally that made stabilization seem more attractive and possible.

It must be borne in mind that a consensus is necessary not only to sustain inflation but also to end it, and in Germany, the stabilization consensus encompassed the twin beliefs that Germany could only stabilize on the one hand, by reducing real wages, increasing working hours, and enduring substantial unemployment and, on the other hand, by receiving relief in the area of reparations and large infusions of foreign capital. It would be impossible to demonstrate this point within the time allowed here; I would simply like to emphasize that even organized labor participated in this stabilization consensus to a remarkable degree and that its bitter conflicts with industry in 1922–23 were not over the medicine itself but rather over the dosage and the manner of its administration. Fundamentally, labor wished a voice in the deflationary policy which it, too, considered unavoidable and inevitable. The grimmer aspects of this stabilization consensus were made tolerable by the fantasy of a return to normality defined in terms of the prewar world in which a long deflationary century had been accompanied by rather spectacular economic growth.[19]

If the two consensuses and the bundles of decisions connected with each of them are considered together, then perhaps we can move some steps forward in identifying the next sets of problems confronting the historian of the German inflation. The "rehabilitation" of the German inflation as a series of least unsatisfactory solutions to a variety of intractable problems may satisfy the historicist but it is hardly the most satisfactory form of historiography. How is it to be measured against the substantial economic, social, political, and moral damage the inflation left in its wake — the indubitable, if as yet unmeasured, economic distortions it fostered; the expropriation of the savings, pensions, and investments of an entire class of persons; placing a large portion of the social costs of the stabilization on the backs of the workers; robbing creditors on an unheard-of scale; the impetus it gave to the further fragmentation of German political life through a truly grotesque exfoliation in the realm of interest-group politics; and the general sense of unpredictability and injustice felt throughout German society that could only serve to undermine respect for the Republic? The paradox that the anti-reevaluation forces could argue with considerable cogency in 1924–25 that the good credit of the German Government depended upon its capacity to sustain the elimination of its debt to its citizens who had loyally bought war bonds and that the creditworthiness of the economy as a whole depended upon a similar treatment of private creditors is a good illustration of why the inflation was identified with the grossest forms of moral turpitude.[20]

We will not get very far, however, by trying to measure the gains against losses in this manner, because at the point of final analysis, i.e., from the perspective of 1924, the costs of the inflation were simply the obverse side of its benefits as both had been worked out over time and then hammered into their historical legacy in the hyperinflation. The more interesting question, at least from a heuristic point of view, is whether these costs could have been reduced or modified prior to that fateful descent into hyperinflation in 1922 when all the benefits of inflation from the standpoint of social pacification and foreign trade disintegrated because everybody began calculating in foreign currencies, German domestic prices rose to world market levels, and the industrialists, especially the heavy industrialists, emerged as the only group in German society with the strength and credit to define the basic terms on which the inflation was to culminate.[21] Here, it seems to me, Professor Witt has been and is making a particularly valuable contribution with his emphasis upon the dynamic, experimental, and more innovative than previously imagined policies of the Weimar governments between 1918 and 1922.[22]

Historians have been so hypnotized by the debate over why the Revolution of 1918–19 failed that they have neglected the degree to which it succeeded in very important ways. These include not only the creation of a parliamentary government in Germany but also in laying the foundation for a degree of socioeconomic experimentation and innovation that was unique for its time. The ministerial offices and halls in Berlin abounded with interesting plans and programs that did address themselves to real issues in promising ways and even managed to enjoy a measure of practical application. The planned economy programs of the economics ministry under Rudolf Wissell and Wichard von Moellendorff, the efforts of their successors Robert Schmidt and

Julius Hirsch to develop an effective *Konjunkturpolitik* so as to maintain stable levels of industrial activity and employment, the desire to create a balance between producer and consumer interests by giving the latter some form of institutionalized voice in dealing with organized producer interests, the redistributive intentions of the Erzberger Finance reform, and the attempts by the labor ministry to use its arbitration powers to link wages and productivity through what we today would call an *incomes policy* that would temper managerial arbitrariness and prevent disruptive labor conflict — all these were no less significant and remarkable for their time just because of their very limited success or failure.[23] The inability to steer a path toward some other more economically and sociopolitically satisfactory transition from inflation to stabilization is the as yet unwritten history of the domestic politics of the early Weimar Republic that one hopes is now in the process of development.

It must be understood, however, that these governmental efforts suffered from the inherent defect that inflation may not only encourage and make possible social experimentation, but it may also make it unrespectable and undermine the authority of those who would pursue it. There is nothing like inflation when it comes to producing an exaggerated respect for the traditional virtues since they are persistently being verbally honored while being actually breached, and even many of those who are profiting the most are troubled by the sense that they are living in sin.[24] Inflation cannot be studied only from the perspective of decision makers at the top but must also be studied from the perspective of the total society and, so to speak, from the bottom up as well. The social and political consequences of the German inflation were not only determined by decisions made by governmental and powerful interest group leaders acting upon a passive society below them. Rather, they were also determined by the differential adaptations of various institutions and social groups whose interaction with one another and with the authorities produced those consequences.[25] Those who benefited most from the inflation were those who were in a position to learn most quickly how to adapt to it, were economically and politically positioned to use their knowledge, and by dint of these attributes, were able to prevent or at least minimize interference with their activities. Without such differential learning and adaptation and strategic advantages, it would have been impossible for the inflation to have persisted, as was clearly demonstrated in late 1922 when nearly everyone seemed to have learned how to calculate in foreign currencies and the inflation consensus was being rapidly replaced by the stabilization consensus.

In this context, some traditionally powerful groups were not powerful enough, and this played a major role in determining the redistributive effects of the inflation. Hence, the great need for sectoral and branch analyses, differentiated analyses within social groups, and regional analyses if we are to understand the modes of adaptation to the inflation and their consequences. The banking sector, for example, was understandably hyperactive in the course of the inflation, but its position vis-à-vis industry was severely weakened not only by the deterioration of its real capital resources but also by industry's increasing direct access to capital.[26] The commercial sector appears to have been another relative loser and chafed under foreign trade controls which aided certain export industries at its expense. Homeowners may have benefited as they paid off their mortgages, but they suffered from rent controls. The agrarian sector is traditionally portrayed as a winner in the inflation, but this can now be shown to be vastly exaggerated and, at best, is applicable to the large East Elbian landowners and even then only in a limited sense. The ability of the peasantry to pay off their mortgages in debased currency did not spare them the irritations and disadvantages of food price controls however much they violated them and it did not provide them with the resources they needed to meet the agrarian structural crisis of the later 1920s.[27] Similarly, whether rightly or wrongly, the small retailers felt themselves particularly victimized by the ungainly and confusing antiprofiteering laws that exposed them to unfamiliar and humiliating contacts with the police, on the one hand, and episodes of consumer violence against their shops and persons, on the other.

One may venture the hypothesis that distaste for economic controls, already nurtured by the war economy, was intensified by the inflation and united producers against consumers. At the same time, the capacity of certain producers to profit from these controls or circumvent them, while others were too inadequately organized to do either served to give new life to those preindustrial, anticapitalist sentiments so important in German history and in the prehistory of fascism.[28] Needless to say, these various discontents served also to undermine governmental efforts at economic and social management during the inflation.

It is not sufficient to consider the social and political history of the inflation only from the perspective of interclass and intersectoral rivalries and alliances, however. Intraclass divisions and intergenerational conflicts were nurtured by the inflation as well. There is good reason to believe that traditional blue-collar–white-collar tensions, while initially reduced during the war, were intensified again in the course of the inflation when the white-collar trend to the left and unionization failed to prevent a continued loss of real earning power and status. Blue-collar trade unions also proved highly critical of civil service militance during this period and often expressly used the allegedly easy working conditions of the civil service and their pay increases to increase their own demands and claims.

Within the ranks of blue-collar labor itself, reduction of age, skill, and sex differentials, now regarded as a standard inflation phenomenon, created significant conflicts within the working class. There is considerable evidence of generational conflict induced by the efforts to introduce the so-called social wage, i.e., wages that took family status and number of dependents into account. The attitude of older trade union organized workers toward their younger, allegedly disproportionately affluent and frequently radical colleagues was often extremely harsh. Indeed, it would be interesting to explore the hypothesis that the inflation encouraged more severe generational conflicts in the working class, where many young workers turned Communist and were subjected to ruthless trade union purges, than in the middle class, where youthful right-wing radicalism received the sympathy of an older generation whose material and status frustrations caused them to identify with the frustrations and rage of the youthful members of their class.[29]

Such hypotheses and speculations do not exhaust the problems encompassed by a social history of the German inflation that would have as its goal understanding how German society as a totality experienced the inflation and what the social and political consequences of this experience actually were. If nothing has been said here about the arts, the sciences, and cultural institutions, it is because so little has been done. One way, however, the areas covered will suffice to suggest the scope of the task and point in directions that will prove fruitful for historical investigation.

Notes

1. Gerald D. Feldman, "Gegenwärtiger Forschungsstand und künftige Forschungsprobleme der deutschen Inflation," in Otto Büsch and Gerald D. Feldman (Eds.), *Historische Prozesse der deutschen Inflation 1914 bis 1924. Ein Tagungsbericht*, Einzelveröffentlichungen der Historischen Kommission zu Berlin, Bd. 21 (Berlin, 1978), pp. 3–21.
2. Knut Borchardt, *Strukturwirkungen des Inflationsprozesses*, Schriftenreihe des Ifo-Instituts für Wirtschaftsforschung, Nr. 50 (Berlin and Munich, 1972), pp. 15f.
3. The project, which involves the active participation of about 40 persons from various European and American universities, was formally launched in the winter of 1979. A steering committee composed of Professors Gerald D. Feldman, Carl-Ludwig Holtfrerich, Gerhard A. Ritter, and Peter-Christian Witt is responsible for its overall direction, and it benefits from the regular collaboration of Professor Otto Büsch, Director of the Historische Kommission zu Berlin, where the project is centered. This paper leans in part on the general project proposal (*Rahmenantrag*) submitted to the Volkswagen Foundation.
4. Here, I have come to agree with Werner Abelshauser, "Inflation und Stabilisierung. Zum Problem ihrer makroökonomischen Auswirkungen auf die

Rekonstruktion der deutschen Wirtschaft nach dem Ersten Weltkrieg," in Büsch and Feldman, pp. 161–74. Abelshauser convincingly deflated my presentation of the inflation as a paradigm "for the total complex of socioeconomic and political conditions which characterizes the development of advanced industrial societies." See Büsch and Feldman, p. 18.

5. See Gerald D. Feldman, Iron and Steel in the German Inflation, 1916–1924 (Princeton, N. J., 1977), pp. 13ff., 445ff. for a discussion of German heavy industry in these various perspectives.

6. R. Nurske, The Course and Control of Inflation. A Review of Monetary Experience in Europe after World War I (Geneva, 1946), pp. 23ff., and Derek H. Aldcroft, From Versailles to Wall Street 1919–1929 (London, 1977), pp. 66ff., 131ff.

7. Carl L. Holtfrerich, "The Role of the German Inflation in Overcoming the 1920–21 U.S. and World Depression," paper given at the annual meeting of the American Historical Association, New York City, December 1979. More generally, see Abelshauser.

8. Frank D. Graham, Exchange, Prices and Production in Hyper-Inflation: Germany 1920–1923 (Princeton, N.J., 1930), pp. 317–20; Karsten Laursen and Jørgen Pedersen, The German Inflation 1918–1923 (Amsterdam, 1964), pp. 123–27.

9. See my criticisms of Laursen and Pedersen on this score in Feldman, Iron and Steel, pp. 280ff.

10. For this periodization, see Constantino Bresciani-Turroni, The Economics of Inflation. A Study of Currency Depreciation in Post-War Germany, 1914–1923 (London, 1923) and Friedrich Hesse, Die deutsche Wirtschaftslage von 1914 bis 1923 (Jena, 1938). Both works generally employ this periodization, as does the essay by Professor Holtfrerich in this book.

11. See Carl-Ludwig Holtfrerich, "Amerikanischer Kapitalexport und Wiederaufbau der deutschen Wirtschaft 1919–23 im Vergleich zu 1924–29," Vierteljahrschrift für Sozial- und Wirtschaftsgeschichte 64 (1977): 497–529.

12. Holtfrerich, "Reichsbankpolitik 1918–1923 zwischen Zahlungsbilanz- und Quantitätstheorie," Zeitschrift für Wirtschafts- und Sozialwissenschaften 13 (1977): 193–214 and Feldman, Iron and Steel, pp. 312ff. As Professor Witt's paper in this book will show, the massive tax evasion made possible by the tax assessment system provided another important cause of hyperinflation at precisely this time.

13. The felicitous term was provided by Professor Gerhard A. Ritter in Büsch and Feldman, p. 59.

14. On the Arbeitsgemeinschaftspolitik and demobilization policies, see Gerald D. Feldman, "German Business between War and Revolution: The Origins of the Stinnes-Legien Agreement," in Gerhard A. Ritter (Ed.), Entstehung und Wandel der modernen Gesellschaft. Festschrift für Hans Rosenberg zum 65. Geburtstag (Berlin, 1970), pp. 312–41; "Economic and Social Problems of the German Demobilization 1918–19," Journal of Modern History 47, no. 1 (March 1975): 1–47; "Die Freien Gewerkschaften und die Zentralarbeitsgemeinschaft 1918–1924," Heinz O. Vetter (Ed.), Vom Sozialistengesetz zur Mitbestimmung. Zum 100. Geburtstag von Hans Böckler (Cologne, 1975), pp. 229–52.

15. On social policy, see Ludwig Preller, *Sozialpolitik in der Weimarer Republik* (Stuttgart, 1949); on the sytem of arbitration, see Hans-Hermann Hartwich, *Arbeitsmarkt, Vebände und Staat 1918–1933. Die öffentliche Bindung unternehmerischer Funktionen in der Weimarer Republik* (Berlin, 1967).

16. For a discussion of the export policies and their effects in general and with specific reference to two major industrial sectors, heavy industry and machine construction, see Gerald D. Feldman, *Iron and Steel*, pp. 81ff., 130ff., 187ff. Whether the term *boom* is appropriate, considered either in terms of prewar exports or even in terms of absolute value during the years in question remains to be investigated, although there can be no question that it was so perceived or interpreted by influential contemporaries. In any case, the German government, as the unpublished papers of Undersecretary of Economics, Julius Hirsch, show, consciously manipulated the value of the mark during the period of relative stabilization so as to maintain Germany's export advantage. This is discussed in some detail in my unpublished paper, "Employment, Price and Wage Policies in Germany during the 1920–21 World Depression" delivered at the December 1979 American Historical Association meetings in New York City.

17. See Stephen A. Schuker, "Finance and Foreign Policy in the Era of the German Inflation: British, French and German Strategies for Economic Reconstruction after the First World War," in Büsch and Feldman, pp. 343–61.

18. See note 12.

19. See Feldman, *Iron and Steel*, pp. 319ff.; and Vetter, pp. 250–52.

20. A brief survey of the social consequences of the inflation is provided by Bresciani-Turroni, pp. 286ff. See also, Franz Eulenberg, "Die sozialen Wirkungen der Währungsverhältnisse," *Jahrbücher für Nationalökonomie und Statistik* III (1924): 748–94; Peter-Christian Witt, "Finanzpolitik und sozialer und Wandel in Krieg und Inflation 1918–1924," in Hans Mommsen et al. (Eds.), *Industrielles System und politische Entwicklung in der Weimarer Republik: Verhandlungen des Internationalen Symposiums in Bochum vom 12.–17. Juni 1973* (Düsseldorf, 1974), pp. 394–425. A dissertation on the treatment of creditors and the reevaluation controversy is being completed by Michael Hughes at the University of California, Berkeley. An imposing program for research on the social and political history of the inflation is provided by Jens Flemming, Claus-Dieter Krohn, and Peter-Christian Witt, "Sozialverhalten und politische Reaktionen von Gruppen und Institutionen im Inflationsprozess. Anmerkungen zum Forschungsstand," in Büsch and Feldman, pp. 239–63.

21. Feldman, *Iron and Steel*, pp. 302ff.

22. Peter-Christian Witt, "Capitalist Constraints upon Government Economic Policy Formation in the Inflation," paper given at the meeting of the American Historical Association, New York City, December 1979. This theme will be developed in Witt's study of economic and financial policy in the inflation now being completed.

23. There are a few studies of economic policy in the early Weimar Republic: Hans Schieck, "Der Kampf um die deutsche Wirtschaftspolitik nach dem Novemberumsturz 1918" (unpublished doctoral dissertation, Heidelberg, 1958); Michael Honhart, "The Incomplete Revolution. The Social Democrats' Failure to Transform the Germany Economy, 1918–1920," Ph.D. diss. (Duke

University, 1972); David E. Barclay, "Rudolf Wissell, *Planwirtschaft* and the Free Trade Unions, 1919 to 1923. Some Tentative Observations," in Büsch and Feldman, pp. 295–309; David E. Barclay, "A Prussian Socialism? Wichard von Moellendorff and the Dilemmas of Economic Planning in Germany, 1918–19," *Central European History* XI (March 1978): 50–82. Systematic study of the papers of the Reichswirtschaftsministerium, Reichsarbeitsministerium, and Reichswirtschaftsrat will provide the basis for the forthcoming longer studies by Professors Witt and me.

24. For a discussion of this psychology, see Feldman, *Iron and Steel*, pp. 283–84.

25. I have tried to analyze this differential learning process in *Iron and Steel*, but it needs to be done, and can be done, clear across the social spectrum.

26. Manfred Pohl, "Die Situation der Banken in der Inflationszeit," in Büsch and Feldman, pp. 83–95.

27. See Martin Schumacher's comments in Büsch and Feldman, pp. 215–17 and his fine book, *Land und Politik: Eine Untersuchung über politische Parteien und agrarische Interessen, 1914–1923*, Beiträge zur Geschichte des Parlamentarismus und der Politischen Parteien, No. 65 (Düsseldorf, 1978). Robert Moeller's dissertation on the Westphalian peasantry now being completed at the University of California, Berkeley, should prove particularly illuminating on these problems.

28. In my own research, I have gathered considerable amounts of material to support these comments in the Hamburg State Archives and in the papers of the Prussian Ministry of Trade and Commerce (Bestand R 120) at the archives in Merseburg. See also the very illuminating article by Larry Eugene Jones, "Inflation, Revaluation, and the Crisis of Middle-Class Politics: A Study in the Dissolution of the German Party System, 1923–28," *Central European History* XII (June 1979): 143–68.

29. Illustrations of some of these tensions are provided in my article, "Arbeitskonflikte im Ruhrbergbau 1919–1922. Zur Politik vom Zechenverband und Gewerkschaften in der Überschichtenfrage," *Vierteljahrshefte für Zeitgeschichte* 28 (April 1980): 1–56. On the white-collar workers, see Jürgen Kocka, "Zur Problematik der deutschen Angestellten 1914–1933," in Mommsen et al., pp. 792–811. A dissertation now being completed by Andreas Kunz at the University of California, Berkeley, will illuminate the development of the civil service unions in the Weimar Republic.

Political Factors of the German Inflation 1914–23

CARL L. HOLTFRERICH

I

To structure my discussion of political factors of the German inflation 1914–23, Irving Fisher's equation of exchange can serve as a point of departure:

$$M \cdot V = T \cdot P \text{ or } P = M \cdot V/T$$

or expressed in growth rates:

$$\dot{P} = \dot{M} + \dot{V} - \dot{T}$$

where M stands for the quantity of money in circulation, V for the velocity of circulation, T signifies the transaction volume determined mainly by the level of domestic production and by foreign trade, and P expresses the price level. The equation contains a tautology, which offers the advantage that everybody can agree on it. By definition then, a variation in P is connected with a variation in one or all of the other items. When we are looking for political factors which affected the upward movement of P, we might just as well search for those that affected the other three components of the preceding equation.

Older versions of the quantity theory of money were usually based on the assumption that V and T were relatively constant or changed little, at least in the short run, and that therefore variation in M was the decisive factor for movements in the level of P.[1] The neo-quantity theory of money à la Friedman also allows for variation in V as a result of changes in the demand for money but assumes a constant and thus predictable function between the demand for money and changes in permanent income, interest rates, and prices, which again makes M the decisive factor for movements in the level of P.[2] Theorists of neo-Keynesian background allow for some instability of the demand for money connected with the inherent instability of expectations.[3] This leaves room for regarding V as an independent factor of variations in the movement of P. Finally, it does not need much explanation that in times of war, revolution, unusual strike activities, and disturbances in international trade, which characterized the period 1914–23 in Germany, there were autonomous movements in the level of T independent of the other items in the equation of exchange.

II

So I start with a discussion of political factors that contributed to the increase in German money circulation 1914–23, which is evidenced by Diagram 1. In the absence of more comprehensive data, it shows the expansion of central bank money. It includes banknotes, treasury notes, loan bureau notes, coins in circulation, plus deposits with the Reichsbank. There are roughly three periods of different growth trends discernible:

1. The outbreak of the war in 1914 to the summer of 1916
2. The autumn of 1916 to the middle of 1922 and
3. The summer of 1922 to the final stages of the inflation.

The growth of money circulation in the first two periods is almost exclusively a reflection of the deficit financing of war and postwar expenses of the Reich; the third period is also characterized by private access to the printing press, i.e., the discounting by the Reichsbank of private bills of exchange in addition to treasury bills.[4]

At the start of the war, legislative measures were taken in Germany to loosen the barriers which had been erected at the time of the creation of the Reichsbank in 1875 to prevent the government from direct access to the Reichsbank credit. The main measures taken in August 1914 were:[5]

1. The gold convertibility of Reichsbank notes (and of a small limited amount of treasury notes) was removed.
2. Loan bureaus were created under the supervision of the Reichsbank to meet the private demand for credit on collateral outside of the Reichsbank. These institutions issued loan bureau notes which could be used as circulating medium directly or could be exchanged for notes from the Reichsbank.
3. The cover regulations for the Reichsbank notes, which before the war had essentially consisted of one-third in gold as primary cover and two-thirds in private bills of exchange as secondary cover, were changed: one-third of the banknote issue had to be covered in gold *and* loan bureau notes; the secondary cover of the remaining two-thirds could consist not only of private bills of exchange, but also of treasury bills.

These measures did not yet mean the total removal of all barriers to government access to the printing press, since the amount of treasury bills discountable at the Reichsbank was still limited by the requirement of a one-third cover of the Reichsbank note circulation in gold and loan bureau notes. The amount of the latter reflected mainly the demand for credit by private business and, after 1916, by state and communal governments.[6] The 1914 measures opened the floodgate for inflation to only a limited degree, but all barriers were finally taken away in May 1921, when the one-third cover requirement was dropped altogether.[7]

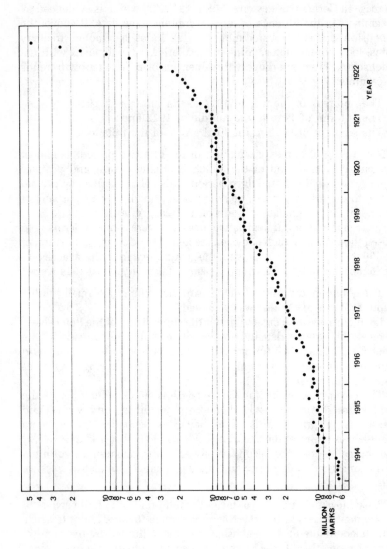

Fig. 1   Monetary Base, 1914-1922 (monthly, end of month).   Sourc :   Itfrerich, p. 50-52.

During the period 1914–1918, governments in all the belligerent countries had recourse to deficit financing through the printing press in order to finance war expenditure. Yet the extent was different: According to different estimates Great Britain raised 20–30 percent of war expenditure in taxes, and the rest in short-term and long-term loans; Germany covered only 0–6 percent by taxes and the remaining 94–100 percent in government debt.[8] Even in the second half of the war, when the short-term debt of the Reich with the Reichsbank could no longer be totally funded by the sale of government bonds, the German government raised taxes only to cover additional interest payments on the increasing government debt.[9] The financial option chosen by the German govenment was determined by:

1. Reasons of domestic politics, mainly the weak constitutional position of the Reich vis-à-vis the *Länder* (federal states) in financial matters. The *Länder* kept direct taxation as their source of income; the Reich had access only to the indirect tax sources. Since imports and private consumption, the basis of indirect taxation, shrank during the war, it was difficult to increase total tax income by raising indirect tax rates then. Furthermore, the tightening of the tax screw during World War I was disliked by the German politicians, because it threatened the *Burgfrieden* among the political parties agreed upon at the start of the war. This political truce was necessary for reinforcing the German war effort. It was endangered, when with substantially increased taxation the question would have had to be answered, which social groups and classes would eventually have to shoulder the burden of financing the war.[10]

2. Reasons of international, namely, reparation, politics. This is evidenced by the famous statement of Germany's secretary of finance Helfferich before the Reichstag in August 1915 that the Allies were to blame for the war and they, not the German taxpayer, would have to pay for it after Germany's victory. "May they carry the leaden billions through the decades, not we."[11] At the outcome of the war, the international situation was exactly the reverse.

When the war had ended, Germany like the Allied countries found itself confronted with the task of restructuring the economy from wartime to peacetime needs. A return to the status quo ante 1914, however, was beyond Germany's reach. On the international level, restructured European markets, trade impediments abroad, and burdens imposed by the Treaty of Versailles excluded this possibility. At home, the necessities of the war had greatly strengthened labor's position.[12] Also — in one competent observer's opinion — it had produced "the greatest wave towards democracy which has ever swept over peoples."[13] The revolution against the monarchy and its aristocratic power structure in November 1918 left those political groups that predominantly fought for labor's interest, primarily the Social Democratic Party and the labor unions — for the first time in Germany's history — with government responsibility and key positions in controlling economic life.

The labor unions could win formal recognition by employers who cooperated with them closely throughout the inflation years in the so-called Central Working Community of the German Commercial and Industrial Employers and Employees. The eight-hour day was agreed upon at the close of the war. Employers met ensuing strike activities and wage demands, partly for political reasons, by adjusting nominal wage rates upward fairly generously to ease the political tensions of the year 1919 and to win the labor unions as an ally in their fight against even more Socialist or Communist demands, for instance for the nationalization of German industry and banks. They were able to finance their concessions largely by covering cost increases through price increases.[14]

The monetary margin for the inflationary spiral was provided for by the ongoing deficit financing of the Reich's budget. With the new pace in price rises shortly before and after the end of the war, the real tax income of the government diminished. Even more diminished was the government income from borrowing: a loan offering in 1919, the only one after the war, turned out to be a failure, since for lack of confidence the bonds could not be sold.[15] On the expenditure side of the Reich's budget, we find war expenditure of the period up to 1919 replaced by other expenses, namely "very heavy burdens imposed by the conditions of the armistice, by the expenses of demobilization, by the disorder of all life, political, economic, and social, after the revolution of November 1918, by the maintenance of the unemployed, by the purchase of provisions for the people, and by the extravagances of those who were raised to new authority by the revolution."[16] The result was an ongoing increase in the unfunded debt of the Reich, of which a changing proportion — reflecting the liquidity situation of the private banking system — was kept by the Reichsbank and thus increased the money supply.[17] Erzberger's fiscal reform in 1920, which made the Reich's income independent of the individual states' cooperation and established a federal income tax and numerous other tax sources in favor of the Reich, did not succeed in changing the general course of deficit financing. The growth of expenditure outpaced the growth of tax income, which lost value in real terms from the time of assessment to the time of actual payment. Even during the period of relative stability of prices (and exchange rates) from early 1920 to the middle of 1921 (Diagram 2), the deficit kept growing.

This might well be intepreted as a reflection of the high priority

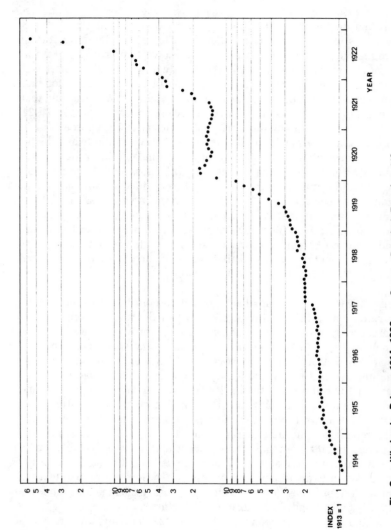

Fig. 2   Wholesale Prices, 1914 - 1923.   *Source : Bresciani - Turroni, p. 442.*

economists and politicians in Germany had placed on the establishment and maintenance of full employment and high growth. In 1919 the economist F. Bendixen had already warned against an economic policy primarily aiming at the price or exchange rate stability and had advised the government: "Not a certain predetermined price or wage level fits in with the needs of the hour, but rather the most intense productivity of the entire economy, and any price or wage level that brings about or works towards such a situation should be most welcome. . . . Unemployment and the shortage of goods are much too high a price for the restoration of the currency's value."[18] W. Rathenau, then a consultant to the German government, remarked in January 1921, when outside Germany the world economic crisis was approaching its climax, that he was not afraid of inflation. To avoid an infection by the depression which had already swept over England, he recommended intensifying the working of the printing press and to finance big construction projects with the money thus produced "so that we may stem the tide of the crisis through these employment measures." It was not correct to say that the printing press was making Germany *kaputt*, he argued.[17] In fact, Germany's postwar inflation produced low unemployment rates which contrasted sharply with the 20 percent or so unemployment rate of Great Britain or the United States in the summer of 1921.[18]

Until 1921, the Reichsbank had opposed the continuous recourse of the government to the printing press and had demanded more rigorous measures to balance the budget. It was, however, unable to stop financing the deficit, since it was not autonomous and could be subjected to instructions of the government. But after the London Ultimatum of May 1921, which finally fixed Germany's reparation bill at a total of 132 billion gold marks, it gave up even verbal opposition and now argued that balancing the budget and stopping the printing press could be achieved only after the reparation debt had been reduced.[19] The reparation question from now on dominated discussions on the national and international political scene and was seen as the origin of the inflation in Germany: the French argued that Germany was using the inflation to avoid paying reparations; the Germans argued that the reparation bill was destabilizing the mark exchange rate and the Reich's budget and thus caused the inflation.

At the Cannes conference in early 1922, Germany was granted a moratorium from cash payments due under the London schedule of payments, subject to the condition, first, that effective measures to balance the budget were taken and, second, that the Reichsbank was granted autonomy. As to the first obligation, a financial compromise was reached in March 1922 — reducing expenditure, raising tax income, and imposing a forced loan on capital owners — but since the paper mark was kept as the basis for the assessment of taxes and for payments to the government, the result was poor; with money depreciation the real yield of taxation kept on diminishing.[22]

As to the second obligation, the Reichsbank was granted autonomy in May 1922. It did not stop discounting treasury bills thereafter, as might have been hoped in Allied countries when demanding its autonomy. Instead, beginning in July 1922, it resumed discounting private bills of exchange on a large scale to ease credit shortages the private sector of the economy had complained about in the first half of 1922. The result was a marked increase in the growth rate of money circulation characteristic of the third period mentioned earlier and usually referred to as the *period of hyperinflation*, which lasted until stabilization in November 1923. It might be worth mentioning that, on two occasions, when the Reichsbank used part of its gold and foreign exchange reserves to stabilize the mark exchange rate — in June 1922 and during the Ruhr occupation from January to April 1923 — it continued increasing the money supply by discounting treasury bills or private bills of exchange.

Here, I have described institutional factors that had contributed to triggering the last stage of the inflation. I shall come back to some political factors later on. Meanwhile let me sum up the dominant political reasons for the continuous increase in money supply and budget deficits in postwar Germany:

1. The priority of satisfying labor's demands for higher wages, better working conditions, and especially full employment to ward off the revolutionary threat to the private enterprise system, on the one hand, and to the parliamentary system, on the other, which hung over the early stages of the Weimar Republic.

2. The actual burden of the peace treaty obligations, with which weak governments in the young republic were unable to cope through effective tax measures, while large, powerful groups in society were unwilling to shoulder them and to cooperate with the parties in power accordingly.

Until the London Ultimatum of May 1921, labor and employment policies seem to have predominated; after that date the reparation issue came to the foreground.[23]

III

Next, I would like to discuss some political factors which affected the amount of goods available to meet the monetary demand. The outbreak of the war in 1914 produced two consequences relevant in this connection:

1. Industrial production showed a continuous decrease throughout the war years (Diagram 3) resulting from problems with the raw material supply, the labor supply, and wear and tear on the existing plant and machinery, while reinvestment was lagging.[24]

2. The war produced a blockade of German foreign trade, which made it not only difficult to export, but also to provide for the raw material and food imports which were necessary to keep the industrial machinery running and to avoid a food crisis. The blockade lasted longer than the war and was lifted only after Germany had signed the Treaty of Versailles in the summer of 1919. Since exports were reduced more than imports throughout this period, a massive import surplus of about 15 billion gold marks during the war — and maybe one-third of that during the year 1919 — accumulated. The foreign sector of the economy thus contributed to an increase of goods available for sale to meet monetary demand at home. But the structural problems arising out of the disruption of world trade and out of the reorientation of production capacities toward the wartime and then peacetime needs resulted in a fall of domestic output much greater than the swing in the balance of trade toward an import surplus.

Immediately after the war, German industrial production fell to a record low in the year 1919. This was partly the effect of the ongoing blockade of German foreign trade until mid-1919. It also reflected the loss of German territory stipulated in the Treaty of Versailles, which reduced industrial production capacities by a rough 10 percent and disturbed the smooth functioning of the rest. Transport bottlenecks resulted from Germany's obligation to hand over to the Allies almost its total merchant fleet and about 20 percent of railway rolling stock. Low industrial production in 1919 was also the consequence of production disturbances caused by strike activities of an unprecedented dimension and civil disturbances that reflected the ongoing struggle between different factions among the supporters of the Revolution of November 1918 and between them and right-wing groups.[25] After the domestic scene had settled in early 1920, industrial production picked up and quickly rose to a peak in 1922. In 1923 again, domestic production fell to a new low for politial reasons, namely, the Ruhr occupation, to which the French had driven the struggle over reparations and to which the Germans reacted with passive resistance. Production in the Ruhr, the industrial heart of Germany, came almost to a halt, resulting in production disturbances in other German regions as well. The lack of goods greatly contributed to the final collapse of the mark in the course of the year 1912, just as it had aggravated inflationary problems in 1919.

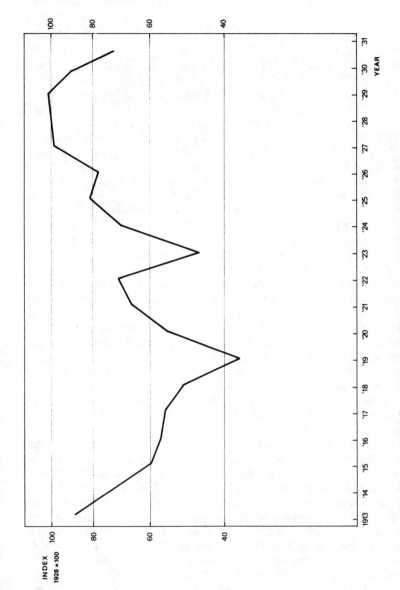

Fig. 3 German Industrial Production, 1913-31. Source : Wegenführ, pp. 22, 28, 56.

IV

Finally, I come to the discussion of political factors that provoked changes in the velocity of money circulation V, which in more modern versions of monetary theory, Keynesian or Friedmanite or even younger approaches, are formulated as changes in the demand for money. Ph. Cagan[26] in support of Friedman's neo-quantity theory tried to prove that a stable function of the demand for money existed even in situations of extreme hyperinflation like the German one.[27] He interpreted the demand for money under such circumstances as a function of past price changes assuming adaptive expectations of individual holders of money. Regressing the time series for M/P (= real cash balances, supply = demand) on a variable for past price changes, he obtained very high regression coefficients. In my view, this is partly the result of regressing trends, namely, the diminishing real cash balances and the increasing pace of price increases, which by definition belong to an inflationary process that culminates in a hyperinflation. It has also been pointed out that Cagan's model is not correctly specified, because it "expresses one dependent variable, the logarithm of real money balances, as a function of another dependent variable, the rate of change of prices." Therefore, "the impressive empirical results are illusory."[28]

A visual comparison of the development during the German inflation of money circulation, on the one hand, and of prices or price changes, on the other hand (cf. Diagrams 1 and 2), will immediately lead to the conclusion that, at least in the short run, other factors than the money supply were at work in determining price changes. The money supply was growing fairly continuously between 1918 and 1922, but price developments show several phases with different growth trends and a long period of relative stability from early 1920 to mid-1921. The resultant is the development of real cash balances M/P which is shown in Diagram 4.

Monetary theory sees variation in the demand for money (real cash balances) in hyperinflationary processes as being determined mainly by changes in expectations about the rate of return on holding money as opposed to other forms of holding wealth.[29] In times of rapid price variations, changing expectations as to the future value of money, in other words price expectations, are seen as the main determinant for changes in the demand for money. Cagan assumed that expectations were formed by past price developments (adaptive expectations).[30] This would make them predictable and the demand for money stable in its development. But Diagram 4 shows turning points in the development of the demand for real cash balances during Germany's post-World War I inflation, which leads to the conclusion that expectations were at least partly determined by events which are unpredictable by past developments; current political and/or economic incidents, which

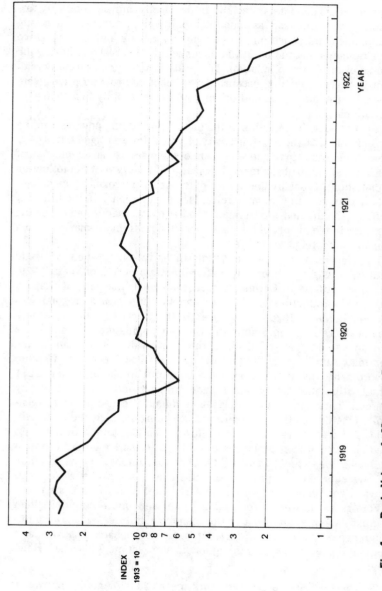

Fig. 4   Real Value of Monetary Base, 1919 - 1922 (monthly).   Source : Holtfrerich, p. 185.

induce money holders to change expectations independently of past experiences. Therefore, especially in politically and economically turbulent years, one can assume that political events exert a strong independent influence on the demand for money and thus on price developments. Let me point to a few such political factors during the course of the German inflation. The postwar years are especially relevant in this connection, because government controls on prices were lifted, for the most part, and prices could react rapidly to a change in conditions.

A very heavy depreciation of the mark's purchasing power set in the second half of 1919, after the Treaty of Versailles was signed. It is even more pronounced in the development of the mark exchange rate than of the internal value of the mark. Bresciani-Turroni gave it the following explanation: "Probably the signing of the treaty provoked a psychological crisis in certain German circles, lack of confidence in the future of Germany dominated the German mind and was manifested — for the first time in the history of the mark — in a flight from the mark, i.e., in a demand for foreign exchange."[31]

The depreciation came to a halt in early 1920, when domestic political struggles calmed down after the Kapp putsch of March 1920; living conditions in Germany eased somewhat, the pace of German industrial production accelerated, and Erzberger's tax program was adopted in March 1920.[32] ". . . it seemed that a certain faith in the mark was again established among the German population."[33] Confidence and favorable expectations about the future value of German money dominated until, in fulfillment of the Versailles Treaty, the German government was forced to sign the London Ultimatum of May 1921 which stipulated Germany's reparation debt and annuities to pay thereon. These, in view of Germany's financial capacities, were generally regarded by German politicians as being too high and unacceptable, and were presented as such to the German public in the mass media.[34] Attempts at procuring a billion gold marks worth of foreign exchange due to the Allies until October 1921 under the new schedule of payments led to a precipitous fall in the mark exchange rate and dragged confidence in future monetary stability down in Germany.

Foreigners, however, for a long time were more confident than Germans themselves in Germany's financial future.[35] They accumulated paper marks in the form of bank notes, bank deposits, and German bonds. To explain this phenomenon, let me quote R. G. Hawtrey:

> To practical men a German mark meant 23.82 cents [= prewar parity, C.L.H.]. If for the time being the market quoted it at 6 or 4 or 3 cents, they attributed the fall to an adverse balance of trade.

Once Germany's urgent needs for imports were satisfied, surely, they argued, the mark would recover, perhaps not to its old parity (for loss of credit through defeat in war might prevent that), but at least to the 12 or 15 cents quoted after defeat had occurred and before the imports has begun. Rather than sell their marks at ruinous sacrifice, many of them held on.[36]

The foreign exchange earned by Germany through the sale of paper marks abroad allowed it to finance import surpluses, especially the import of much needed raw material and food supplies in the immediate postwar years in spite of the absence of long-term credit sources for Germany abroad.[37] "In a certain sense, therefore, it can be admitted that the increase of the paper-money issues aided Germany in surmounting the post-war crisis,"[38] especially since these holdings of marks abroad were totally depreciated later on and the original sale of foreign exchange to Germany thus turned into a free gift.

As I have shown elsewhere,[39] foreigners finally lost confidence in Germany's future monetary stability and tried to change their mark positions from bull to bear in 1922. Poincaré, who stood for confrontation instead of compromise in the struggle over reparations, succeeded the Briand government in January 1922 in France. This made international financiers more hesitant to place funds in German marks. But the refusal of the Reparation Commission's bankers committee under the leadership of J. P. Morgan on 10 June 1922 to recommend loans to Germany before the reparation debt was scaled down, shattered foreigners' hope for a recovery of the German currency's value on the exchange markets. The murder of Rathenau, who on the German side stood for cooperation and compromise with the Allies in reparation questions, on 22 June 1922, shook confidence in the future domestic political stability of Germany and aggravated the situation. The "flight from the mark" of foreigners in addition to that of German citizens and firms triggered the final hyperinflationary stage beginning in June 1922, which culminated in the total collapse of the mark in autumn 1923.

V

In conclusion, there can be no doubt that the increase in money circulation in Germany 1914–23 — mainly due to the deficit financing of the government budget — was "an essential condition without which the general rise in prices could not have gone far."[40] The political factors which caused this deficit, therefore, carry the main responsibility for price developments in the long run. In the shorter run, however, fluctuations in the volume of production and trade as well as changes in the demand for money dominated the course of the German inflation. Among these, the demand for money reflecting the state of expectations about the future value of money — in other words, the state of confidence — seems to have been the most volatile element in determining the inflationary course. Especially during the postwar inflationary period, when government controls on the economy were reduced or lifted, political events influenced price movements almost instantaneously via expectations and the money demand variable.

Notes

1. Joseph A. Schumpeter, *History of Economic Analysis* (New York, 1954), pp. 1095–1105.
2. Milton Friedman, "The Quantity Theory of Money — A Restatement," in M. Friedman (Ed.), *Studies in the Quantity Theory of Money* (Chicago, 1956), pp. 3–21.
3. David E. W. Laidler, *The Demand for Money. Theories and Evidence* (Scranton, Pa., 1969).
4. Quantitative and explanatory information is contained in the three standard studies of the German inflation: Frank D. Graham, *Exchange, Prices, and Production in Hyper-Inflation: Germany, 1920–23* [New York (1930) 1967]. Constantino Bresciani-Turroni, *The Economics of Inflation. A Study of Currency Depreciation in Post-War Germany* [London (1931), 1968]. Karsten Laursen and Jørgen Pedersen, *The German Inflation 1918–1923* (Amsterdam, 1964). Also in Friedrich Hesse, *Die deutsche Wirtschaftslage von 1914 bis 1923. Krieg, Geldblähe und Wechsellagen* (Jena, 1938). Carl-Ludwig Holtfrerich, *Die deutsche Inflation 1914–1923. Ursachen und Folgen in internationaler Perspektive* (Berlin-New York, 1980).
5. *Die Reichsbank 1901–1925* (Berlin, 1925), pp. 39–40.
6. Data in Rudolf Will, *Die schwebenden Schulden der europäischen Großstaaten* (Tübingen, 1921), p. 104.
7. *Die Reichsbank*, pp. 99–100.
8. Robert Knauss, *Die deutsche, englische und französische Kriegsfinanzierung* (Leipzig, 1923), p. 175. His estimate for Germany is 6 percent, for Great Britain, 20 percent, compared to 0 percent for Germany and 28 percent for Great Britain in Will, pp. 28, 109. For further international comparisons on this subject, see Ludlow Bogart, *War Costs and Their Financing. A Study of the Financing of the War and After-War Problems of Debt and Taxation* (New York-London, 1921). Gerhard Colm, "War Finance," in *Encyclopedia of the Social Sciences* 15 (New York, 1935): 347–352. Gerd Hardach, *The First World War 1914–1918* (London, 1977).
9. Konrad Roesler, *Die Finanzpolitik des Deutschen Reiches im Ersten Weltkrieg* (Berlin, 1967), pp. 105–106. Heinz Haller, "Die Rolle der Staatsfinanzen für den Inflationsprozeß," in Deutsche Bundesbank (Ed.), *Währung und Wirtschaft in Deutschland 1876–1975* (Frankfurt/M., 1976), p. 128.
10. Karl Helfferich, *Der Weltkrieg*, Vol. II: *Vom Kriegsausbruch bis zum uneingeschränkten U-Bootkrieg* (Berlin, 1919), p. 156. Georg Solmssen, "Das deutsche Finanzwesen nach Beendigung des Weltkrieges," in G. Solmssen,

"Das deutsche Finanzwesen nach Beendigung des Weltkrieges," in Solmssen, *Beiträge zur deutschen Politik und Wirtschaft 1900–1933. Gesammelte Aufsätze und Vorträge,* Vol. 1 (Munich, 1935), p. 124.

11. Quoted in Will, p. 110 and in Peter Czada "Ursachen und Folgen der großen Inflation" in H. Winkel (Ed.), *Finanz- und wirtschaftspolitische Fragen der Zwischenkriegszeit* (Berlin, 1973), p. 18.

12. Gerald D. Feldman, *Army, Industry, and Labor in Germany 1914–1918* (Princeton, 1966). Karl-Ludwig Ay, *Die Entstehung einer Revolution. Die Volksstimmung in Bayern während des Ersten Weltkrieges* (Berlin, 1968). Jürgen Kocka, *Klassengesellschaft im Krieg. Deutsche Sozialgeschichte 1914–1918* [Göttingen (1973) 1978²]. G. D. Feldman, E. Kolb, R. Rürup, "Die Massenbewegungen der Arbeiterschaft in Deutschland am Ende des Ersten Weltkrieges," in *Politische Vierteljahrschrift* 13 (1972).

13. My translation from Wilhelm Groener, *Lebenserinnerungen. Jugend, Generalstab, Weltkrieg* (Ed.) F. v. Gaertringen (Göttingen, 1957), p. 360. Since 1916, General Groener was the head of the German government's war department.

14. On these questions see the important recent studies of Gerald D. Feldman, *Iron and Steel in the German Inflation 1916–1923* (Princeton, N.J. 1977), and Charles S. Maier, *Recasting Bourgeois Europe. Stabilization in France, Germany, and Italy in the Decade After World War I* (Princeton, N.J., 1975), pp. 19–87.

15. Hesse, p. 137.

16. Bresciani-Turroni, p. 51.

17. Data in *Germany's Economy, Currency, and Finance* (Berlin, 1924), p. 63.

18. Friedrich Bendixen, *Kriegsanleihen und Finanznot. Zwei finanzpolitische Vorschläge* (Jena, 1919), pp. 12–13.

19. Bundesarchiv Koblenz R 2/3216. Protocol of a meeting in the German foreign ministry, 24 January 1921.

20. Derek H. Aldcroft, *From Versailles to Wall Street 1919–1929* (London, 1977).

21. Carl-Ludwig Holtfrerich, "Reichsbankpolitik 1918–1923 zwischen Zahlungsbilanz- und Quantitätstheorie," *Zeitschrift für Wirtschafts- und Sozialwissenschaften* (1977): 193–214.

22. Bresciani-Turroni, pp. 59–61.

23. Stephen Schuker has documented that German politicians and industrialists saw the inflation after May 1921 as a political tool to force a revision of the London schedule of payments. Stephen A. Schuker, "Finance and Foreign Policy in the Era of the German Inflation: British, French, and German Strategies of Economic Reconstruction after the First World War," in O. Büsch and G. D. Feldman (Eds.), *Historische Prozesse der deutschen Inflation 1914 bis 1924* (Berlin, 1978), pp. 343–63.

24. Rolf Wagenführ, "Die Industriewirtschaft, Entwicklungstendenzen der deutschen und internationalen Industrieproduktion 1860–1932," *Vierteljahreshefte zur Konjunkturforschung* 31 (Berlin, 1933), pp. 22–28. Statistisches Bundesamt, *Bevölkerung und Wirtschaft 1872–1972* (Stuttgart, 1972), p. 176.

25. Erich Eyck, *A History of the Weimar Republic,* Vol. 1 (Cambridge, 1962). Wolfgang Mommsen, "Die deutsche Revolution 1918–1920. Politische Revolu-

tion und soziale Protestbewegung," *Geschichte und Gesellschaft* 4 (1978): 362–91.

26. Phillip Cagan, "The Monetary Dynamics of Hyperinflation" in M. Friedman (Ed.), *Studies in the Quantity Theory of Money* (Chicago, 1956), pp. 25–117.

27. By looking for the stability of the money demand function, Cagan as well as Friedman tried to reassert the overwhelming importance of the supply of money for price developments against the more Keynesian view which attributed relatively little importance to the quantity of money for prices.

28. Rodney L. Jacobs, "A Difficulty with Monetarist Models of Hyperinflation," *Economic Inquiry* 13 (1975): 357.

29. Cagan, p. 31.

30. *Ibid.*, p. 37.

31. Bresciani-Turroni, p. 54.

32. Also in March 1920 the so-called hole in the West was closed, i.e., the open trade frontier between France and Germany through which uncontrolled French exports penetrated into Germany in exchange for scarce foreign exchange. This was regarded by German politicians as one factor in the mark's rapid depreciation in 1919.

33. Bresciani-Turroni, p. 57.

34. This opinion, however, was not restricted to Germany. See in Great Britain, John M. Keynes, *A Revision of the Treaty being a Sequel to The Economic Consequences of the Peace* (London, 1922), and in the United States, Harold G. Moulton and Constantine E. McGuire, *Germany's Capacity to Pay. A Study of the Reparation Problem* (New York, 1923).

35. Hesse, p. 354, described this two-tier phenomenon as follows: "The speculative expectations are ambiguous. From the side of Germany, they undoubtedly reckon on a depreciation of the mark, from abroad, however, on an appreciation." (My translation, C.-L. H.).

36. Ralph G. Hawtrey, *Currency and Credit* (London, 1923), p. 375.

37. Holtfrerich, "Amerikanischer Kapitalexport und Wiederaufbau der deutschen Wirtschaft 1919–23 im Vergleich zu 1924–29," *Vierteljahrschrift für Sozial- und Wirtschaftsgeschichte* 64 (1977): 497–529.

38. Bresciani-Turroni, p. 52.

39. Holtfrerich, "Internationale Verteilungsfolgen der deutschen Inflation 1918–1923," *Kyklos* 30 (1977): 271–92.

40. League of Nations (R. Nurkse), *The Course and Control of Inflation. A Review of Monetary Experience in Europe after World War I* (Geneva, 1946), p. 17.

John H. Williams on the German Inflation: The International Amplification of Monetary Disturbances

BERNARD MALAMUD[1]

INTRODUCTION

This paper is about the vicious-circle economics of John Henry Williams. It concentrates on the instabilities that Williams saw in the international economy and on the inflationary consequences that he believed they had on Germany after World War I. The balance-of-payments theory that Williams and others advanced to explain the German inflation as it unfolded is reviewed here. The themes of inflation and cumulative causation that Williams addressed in his studies of the German situation are traced in his later works. These are largely concerned with ways to stabilize international economic relations against volatile capital flows.

In presenting the balance-of-payments view for serious consideration, I necessarily enter the old debate between its adherents and those of the purchasing power parity doctrine . . . and join it on Williams's side. He posited a causal chain in the German inflation running from a payments deficit owing to reparation payments to price inflation and then to money inflation. Purchasing power parity theory, in strict adherence to the quantity theory of money, *insists* on exactly the reverse chain of causation. It therefore holds Williams's balance-of-payments view to be in error and unworthy of consideration.

Williams agreed that an increase in its supply reduces both the internal and the external purchasing power of a currency. Multiple disturbances could result in price inflation, according to him. In the German instance, Williams argued, exchange rate, price, and money stock experience showed that international payments shocks dominated money creation in propelling the inflation through 1922.

Williams's relevance in these present times of distressing inflation is twofold. His writings on the German inflation point out a process that is likely to be exacerbating American inflation, namely, the payments deficit — exchange depreciation — price inflation causal chain. Inasmuch as this process is similar to the Keynesian wage-price spiral, it does receive considerable attention in economic discussions. More importantly, Williams's works recommend nondoctrinaire analyses of economic disturbances. He examined and applied competing theories without regard to their ideological lineage, seeking better understanding of, and control over, the economic system.

John H. Williams has led a distinguished career as an academic and a government economist. He received his Ph.D from Harvard in 1919 and joined its faculty in 1922. In 1933, he was named Nathaniel Ropes Professor of Political Economy at Harvard and from 1937 to 1947, he served as the first dean of Harvard's Graduate School of Public Administration. He also had a long association with the Federal Reserve Bank of New York, serving as a vice-president of the bank from 1936 to 1947. Williams was president of the American Economic Association in 1951.

In a 1951 volume of contributed essays, Williams was cited as

One to never attach himself to any particular school of thought or to seek to impose fixed ideas upon others. What his friends and students most admire about him is his detached and freely inquiring attitude, his extraordinary intuition for the special nature of each problem, his willingness to sacrifice the comfortable assurance of dogmatic conclusions in favor of continued flexibility of thought, and his readiness, in consequence, to accept the occasional burden of a minority position (17, v).

This statement is not entirely correct. Williams did accept Adam Smith's inductive doctrine of progress through the division of labor without reservation. His most enduring contribution to economic literature, "The Theory of International Trade Reconsidered" (47), highlights the cumulative effects of market expansion and factor flows on the international economy. Williams's frequent rejection of conclusions drawn from Ricardian equilibrium models and his criticism of the static Keynesian model of unemployment equilibrium stem from his grounding in Smith's doctrine. An economics of cumulative causation, of "virtuous circles" building on increasing returns and of "vicious circles" fueled by protective responses to adversity, follows naturally from the Smithian premise.

RESPONSES TO INTERNATIONAL SHOCKS

Williams's dissertation concerned balance-of-payments adjustment under flexible exchange rates. His teacher, Frank W. Taussig, had theoretically described a mechanism for payments equilibration in 1917 (22). Williams studied the mechanism's operation in late nineteenth-century Argentina (28).

Under flexible rates, a payments deficit causes exchange rate depreciation. According to Taussig, this depreciation affords a bounty for exports that works to eliminate the deficit. The process depends on prices of traded goods rising immediately with a currency's depreciation while prices of nontraded goods and costs of production lag behind. Wage lag is critical to successful operation of the Taussig mechanism. Resources in the deficit country are shifted from production for domestic use to production for export. Imports are reduced as well because of their higher prices. With quantity of money held constant, the general price level in the country rises, in conformity with the orthodox quantity theory. Fewer goods are chased by the same quantity of money as before. The mechanism is interesting in that price movements are opposite those experienced under the gold standard in response to payments pressure and that a balance-of-payments disturbance, not a money stock change, initiates price inflation.

In the Argentine case studied by Williams, the peso depreciated sharply in 1890 and 1891 when foreign capital inflows on which its balance of payments had largely depended abruptly ceased. This turnaround in international capital flows culminated in the Baring Panic. Williams found that within Argentina, adjustment proceeded as predicted by Taussig. Export prices rose while wages lagged (28, p. 193); a trade surplus replaced foreign borrowings in Argentina's accounts. Williams judged the exchange rate to follow the payments balance closely during this period and to have little association with money stock movements (28, pp. 145–46). The balance of payments dominated exchange rate, price, and trade developments during this "transition period" from trade deficit to trade surplus for the Argentine economy, Williams concluded.

In his thesis, Williams scrupulously avoided connecting money creation and the price increases caused by exchange depreciation. As Letiche points out, the Taussig adjustment mechanism assumes fixed money supplies and circulation velocities; any change in money is an independent matter (16, pp. 121–22). Williams did not dispute the importance of money supply in affecting prices. In a spirit characteristic of his later work, he argued that the balance of payments "deserves to be classed as a main determinant, coordinately with the quantity of paper issued," of the value of paper money (23, p. 9). Williams readily admitted multiple factors and channels of causation.

Taussig and Williams soon applied this reasoning to the major international economic issue of their day, namely, German reparation payments after World War I. In a paper presented at the December 1919 American Economic Association meetings, Taussig cited the balance-of-payments mechanism as the means by which German reparations could and would be transferred in goods (21). He pointed out that the bounty for German exports that the process entailed would discomfort the victorious Allies as German products flooded their domestic and traditional foreign markets, but he saw no technical impediment to the mechanism's operation.

Williams, in a discussion of Taussig's paper, was less sanguine about the ability of the payments mechanism to secure an equilibrium of international payments and trade under the burden of massive reparation flows (40). In two brief paragraphs of his comments, he suggested a circularity and indeterminateness of economic responses in the absence of fixed exchange rates. To quote Williams,

> an inconvertible paper situation is by its very nature one of instability. Every change in the balance of payments effects a change in the value of the paper currency and every change in the value of the currency in turn sets in motion forces which react upon the trade balance; and this process is unceasing so long as paper . . . is not freely convertible into gold at a fixed rate of exchange. . . . In an inconvertible paper money situation a state of equilibrium is an impossibility. . . . In applying the Ricardian mode of thought to so complex a situation as that which will arise (in Germany) . . . one needs to be keenly aware of its limitations, above all its extremely artificial simplicity and preciseness (40, pp. 51–52).

Williams did not elaborate on the disequilibrating feedbacks from trade balances to payments balance that he foresaw for Germany. He did speak of the difficulties of reviving German export trade, so he may have expected mark depreciation to worsen rather than improve Germany's trade balance. Characterization of Williams as an elasticity pessimist is discussed later. Williams did not predict explosive inflation for Germany in his discussion, though it logically follows from unceasing operation of the balance of payments "adjustment" process. His remarks well reflect his skepticism of unqualified predictions derived from economic theory, even a theory with which he himself was closely identified.

In a later 1920 comment on the German situation, Williams allowed that currency depreciation might not even provide a bounty for exports (35, p. 201). He nonetheless restated the Taussig adjustment mechanism, reiterated its dependence on a lag of wages behind prices — export prices, in particular — and here expressed the opinion that it would operate dependably in the German case.

The mechanism did, in fact, operate as expected throughout 1920 and into 1921, based on data and arguments presented by Williams in a late 1922 study (26, pp. 10–13); also (38, p. 486). Mark depreciation did stimulate German exports and inhibit German imports. This last fact is particularly impressive, since Germany's traditional exports of finished goods normally required prior imports of raw materials, a factor contributing to inelasticity in the German balance of trade (39, p. 488), (3, p. 232).

The Taussig equilibrating mechanism broke down, however, with the sharp depreciation of the mark in the summer and fall of 1921. This followed the May 1921 London Ultimatum, which set the amount and schedule of reparation payments, and the entry of the German government into foreign exchange markets to acquire currencies with which to make payments. Despite the depreciation, German imports increased and exports decreased. Williams's suspicions, expressed in his 1919 discussion, were validated, though not for any reason that he had anticipated at the time. In a number of pieces published in 1922, Williams attributed the trade reversal to importer and exporter confusion and, most significantly, to a German "buyer's panic" triggered by observation of the depreciation itself (39), (38, pp. 498–99), (26, pp. 17–18).

Events had led Williams to develop a theory of hyperinflation. In it, a payment deficit causes exchange depreciation, leading to higher prices but also to increased demand in correct anticipation of yet higher prices. The trade and payments deficits do not improve because of the increase in demand, and also because of what Williams termed "correct" policies of export control to prevent denudation of the economy by foreigners buying at bargain basement prices. Events progress in a vicious circle until the depreciated currency becomes irrelevant. "Under such conditions," Williams wrote, "trade tends to be financed, as is coming to be the case in Germany today, not in terms of the worthless native currency, but in foreign currencies.... Germany appears also to have obtained her imports in part by barter, or methods approaching barter" (26, pp. 18, 22).

Williams saw money creation as a by-product of balance-of-payments-led price inflation. "The Reichsbank has not inflated for its own amusement," he observed. Rising prices lead to increased credit demands by government and by the private sector. The government meets its credit needs, reflecting a budget forced into deficit by price inflation, by issuing treasury bills. Banks acquire these bills, but then discount them at the Reichsbank to meet the credit demands of their customers. The Reichsbank has no choice but to emit banknotes when treasury bills are presented to it, Williams argued (26, pp. 24–25); (38, p. 502).

To Williams's thinking, the resultant increase in money supply exacerbated the price inflation initiated by a payments deficit. As noted before, Williams did not reject the quantity theory of money. For the particular situation, however, he argued that only a lifting of the reparation burden from Germany's balance of payments could stop the hyperinflation process. Strictly interpreted, the process that he described would continue even without the creation of new money, albeit at a slower pace.

THE LOGIC OF WILLIAMS'S ASSUMPTIONS

Williams's arguments can be challenged at three points: (1) Could the government truly not have balanced its budget, e.g., by indexing taxes. (2) Could the Reichsbank truly not have limited the quantity of money in circulation, e.g., by refusing to discount treasury bills as freely as it did. (3) Would not either of these strong policy measures have reversed expectations from destabilizing (buyer's panic) to stabilizing and allowed the balance of payments equilibrating mechanism to operate smoothly?

Williams believed that real government expenditures were rather inflexible. Coal needed by the nationalized railroads had to be purchased at market prices; reparation payments were fixed in real, gold terms. Writing in 1922, before the billionfold price inflation of 1923, Williams did not conceive of taxes levied in real terms rather than in nominal terms against prior period incomes. The assassinations of Matthias Erzberger and Walter Rathenau, two German politicians identified with attempts at credible taxation and reparation fulfillment, may have influenced his views on the practicality of valorizing taxes. In Argentina, Williams had observed another situation where system responses to a balance-of-payments deficit automatically led to a budget deficit. There, revenues had been largely tied to import duties and these declined with the correction of the payments deficit (28, p. 96). In any case, given his assumptions about government expenditures and the system of taxation, budget deficits do follow mechanically from price inflation.

Williams's views on the passivity of the German budget find powerful support in Keynes's *A Revision of the Treaty*, which appeared in early 1922 (15, pp. 52–53). Williams referred extensively to this work in his own 1922 publications. Concerning the political practicality of balancing the German budget, Keynes wrote,

> Once this issue is faced, . . . the struggle will be bitter and violent, for it will present itself to each of the contending interests as an affair of life and death. The most powerful influences and motives of self-interest and self-preservation will be engaged. Conflicting conceptions of the end and the nature of society will be ranged in conflict. A government which makes a serious attempt to cover its liabilities will inevitably fall from power (15, p. 55).

As to the second point, concerning the Reichsbank's refusal to issue banknotes, Williams accepted the real bills doctrine. He expected the monetary authority to accommodate the needs of trade.[2] Throughout his career, Williams was skeptical of the power of monetary policy to effect desired ends. He was among those, for example, who saw Federal Reserve policy during the Great Depression as being rather loose (37, p. 190).

Williams, of course, said nothing about the feasibility of curbing the German buyers' panic by means of budgetary or monetary discipline. In his schema, expectations turned on the state of the exchanges and were logically independent of the budget and the money supply. He was aware of the formiable magnitude of the Reichsbank's gold stock in comparison with the real value of Germany's money stock (26, p. 24), yet he never examined the possibility that gold be used to support the mark's exchange value and thus reverse expectations.

In the final analysis, Williams recognized the disruptive consequences of reining in demand, even frenzied demand, by exchange rate, monetary, or whatever policy. He saw inflation as the lesser evil in comparison with "the slowing down of industry, with its attendant unemployment, which has been experienced by the United States, Britain . . . (and other) high exchange countries" (39, p. 608). Here, but only here among his 1922 publications in which most other points (and many sentences) are repeated, did Williams hint at German policy tradeoffs. These were eloquently stated the same year by Keynes:

If the present exchange depreciation persists and the internal price level becomes adjusted to it, the resulting redistribution of wealth between classes will amount to a social catastrophe. If, on the other hand, there is a recovery in the exchange, the cessation of the existing artificial stimulus to industry . . . based on the depreciating mark may lead to a financial catastrophe" (15, p. 67).

The need to devise politically tolerable as well as technically correct economic policies was a recurrent theme in Williams's later works.

THE LITERATURE: REPETITIONS AND ELABORATIONS

The causal chain advanced by Williams to explain the German inflation was observed and commented on by others at the time. Even Keynes, who generally adhered to the quantity theory of money and its derivative purchasing power parity theory of exchange rates in his writings on the German inflation, recognized the temporal lead of depreciation in the process, as the foregoing quotation shows. German economists, many of whom served as advisers to, and spokesmen for, the German government, were the foremost proponents of the balance-of-payments view.[3] This view, it is recalled, places responsibility for the German inflation on the reparation burden and exonerates Reichsbank emission of banknotes.

Karl Helfferich, German Finance Minister during the war and the principal economic adviser to the Reichsbank after the war, stated the chain of causation more succinctly than Williams had:

> The depreciation of the mark . . . caused by the excessive burdens thrust on Germany and by the policy of violence adopted by France; . . . the increase of prices of all imported goods; . . . the general increase of internal prices and of wages, . . . increased need for means of circulation, . . . and the increase of the paper mark issues . . ." (12).

Helfferich was also explicit in his belief that Reichsbank refusal to accommodate monetary demand would result in an intolerable collapse of wages, prices, and economic activity (12, pp. 597–98).

Moritz Bonn, another German contributor to the balance-of-payments literature, cited inelasticity in the German trade pattern — the need to import raw materials before finished goods could be exported, etc. — to justify treating trade adjustment as inoperative in the German case (2). Bonn also admitted destabilizing speculation into his discussion of balance-of-payments-led inflation. Mark depreciation initiated by reparation payments fueled a flight from the mark to foreign currencies, worsening the payments deficit and the depreciation, in his view.

By and large, German writers of the balance-of-payments school described the German economy as helpless, with few if any active elements through which events might be influenced. It responded passively to "French violence," i.e., the reparation burden on the German balance of payments. Holtfrerich presents evidence that, prior to May 1921, this was argued by Reichsbank spokesmen for public consumption only (13). The Germans knew that monetary policy could stem inflation. So long as there was a change of a favorable reparation settlement, however, they emphasized the importance of the payments balance, hoping thus to engender stabilizing expectations regarding the mark. After the London Ultimatum, they, like Williams, fully accepted budgetary and monetary policy as passive. In this, they shared a common ancestry in the British banking school of the early nineteenth-century bullion controversy.

Historically, the German inflation proceeded in stages. Before the May 1921 London Ultimatum, expectations were generally stabilizing. The mark recovered some of the internal and external purchasing power it had lost in the aftermath of the war. From May 1921 through the end of 1922, the period of destabilizing expectations with which Williams was concerned, there was a more than hundredfold depreciation of the mark and about a sixtyfold increase in consumer prices. Following the French-Belgian invasion of the Ruhr in January 1923, depreciation and price inflation were on the billionfold order of magnitude. German passive resistance in the Ruhr was financed with newly created government money.

Some contemporary observers, like Thelwall and Kavanagh, switched from a balance-of-payments explanation of the German inflation in their pre-1923 commentaries to a monetary explanation of the entire inflation in their post-1923 commentaries (23, p. 99), (23, p. 3). In 1938, Joan Robinson put forward a Keynesian wage-price spiral model of the inflation that accommodated both balance-of-payments and monetary — or, at least, budgetary — views as special cases (19). High effective demand, particularly consumption demand following passively from money wage income, fueled price inflation in Robinson's model. For the period treated by Williams, Robinson concurred that mark depreciation caused by a payments deficit was the initiating disturbance. She saw wage increases, spurred by increased living costs stemming from depreciation, however, as necessary for vicious-circle inflation to take hold. Given increases in money wages, demand for imports remained high and the payments deficit did not close, according to Robinson. Her story is essentially the same as Williams's, except that increased money income rather than buyers' panic explains the persistence of a payments deficit. Inflationary expectations entered her process nonetheless, reinforcing the inflation. They heightened demands for goods out of any income. They also reduced the demand for money, causing a reduction in interest rates and hence an increase in investment spending, in accordance with the *General Theory* paradigm. Robinson, however, did not believe that the latter effect was very important in the German inflation.

Robinson saw the budget deficit, stemming from German government support of passive resistance, as triggering the explosive inflation in 1923. She insisted that the deficit's impact on effective demand and not on money supply was of crucial importance and that spiraling inflation required that money wages successfully chase prices. At one point, Robinson allowed that a halt to money creation would have contained the inflation. The resulting high interest rate would have reduced investment and the propensity to consume, caused unemployment, and hence braked money wage increases. But she quickly cited "the various official and unofficial supplementary currencies which were improvised to meet the demand for money" (19, p. 75). Thus, like Williams and the German balance-of-payments school, Robinson accepted monetary policy as impotent, in a practical sense, to bring inflation under control in post-World War I Germany.

THE LITERATURE: CHALLENGE AND RESPONSE

The debate over economic causes of the German inflation centers on the admissibility of multiple causes. Few economists deny the influence of money creation on the progress of inflation. The issue is, then, does only money matter? At the time of the German inflation, adherents of the quantity theory did take this position. Gustav Cassel was at the forefront of those who insisted that money inflation causes price inflation and price inflation causes exchange depreciation — not and never the other way around (6). This was the purchasing power parity doctrine that Cassel championed.

Williams reacted heatedly to Cassel's "untenable" assertion. "There is ample evidence that the balance of international payments can affect exchange rates fundamentally. . . . It is a mistake to maintain that any one factor is responsible for depreciated exchange" (26, pp. 6–8); also (36). In argumentation uncharacteristic of Williams's body of work, he complained that Cassel's doctrine did not contribute anything beyond the bullion controversy of 1810, that "as a guide to financial policy it is dangerous," and that speculator disappointment by the mark's failure to recover its purchasing power parity on exchange markets in 1921 and 1922 was "striking recent proof" of his point.

Many students of the German inflation confirmed Williams in the temporal precedence of exchange depreciation over price inflation over money inflation prior to 1923. These included Angell (1, p. 195), Bresciani-Turroni (3, pp. 80ff), Ellis (8, p. 291), Graham (10, pp. 76–77, pp. 172–73), and Young (49). Of these authors, however, only Ellis agreed that the data confirmed the balance-of-payments explanation of the German inflation. Angell emphasized psychological factors, i.e., destabilizing speculation (1, pp. 195, 446). The others argued that budgetary and monetary excesses lay at the heart of the process nonetheless.

Bresciani-Turroni insisted that "German experiences show us the fundamental importance in the determination of the level of internal prices and of the currency's external value, of the quantity of money issued by the Government." The Reichsbank could limit the quantity of money and when it did, he argued, control was exercised over the exchange rate as well; German industrialists and merchants were forced to sell their foreign exchange to obtain marks (3, p. 398).

The spirit of Bresciani-Turroni's conclusion, laying the cause of the German inflation to budgetary and monetary policy, pervades later monetarist studies of the German inflation. In a seminal paper, Cagan calibrated money demand functions for the German and other hyperinflations (4). He found public demand for real money balances to be a stable function of expected price inflation, even in chaotic times. The German inflation, according to Cagan, was not self-inflammatory, to use an earlier phrase of Graham's. The public did not reduce its holdings of real balances in response to experienced price inflation so violently as to cause explosive feedbacks upon prices and real balances. Price explosion, then, resulted from persistent government deficits and money issues, not from buyers' panic or flights from the currency.

Cagan assumed that the public formed its price expectations adaptively, i.e., expected price inflation depended on past price inflation. Jacobs argued that in regressing real balances on past price inflation, Cagan biased his results in favor of his hypothesized money demand function (14). A rapid price increase automatically reduced *real balances* since these are money holdings deflated by the price index that has risen. Jacobs reestimated real balance demand as a function of past money creation, the force driving price inflation in the monetarist paradigm and properly in the view of a rational public as well. Cagan's results were absurd; a stable, money demand function could not be found.

In their response to Jacobs, Cagan and Kincaid insisted that the demand for real balances depends on expected price changes, whether caused by money creation or by export pressures and exchange depreciation, by speculation, or by fiscal influence (5). They thus admitted alternative explanations of the German inflation, including a balance-of-payments explanation.

Cagan had initially dismissed this view as getting the direction of causation all wrong (4, pp. 90ff). He had repeated an argument (to be discussed), that the temporal lead of exchange depreciation over prices reflected public anticipation. He had disparaged Robinson's thesis of a cost-price spiral initiated by worsened terms of trade. Yet he accommodated himself to these alternative views rather than concede a basic monetarist premise, namely, that money demand is stable.

Benjamin Friedman has shown, however, that the conditions for demand stability in Cagan's model are more stringent than Cagan himself had supposed (9). According to Friedman, Cagan's results suggest money demand instability in the German inflation and in most other hyperinflations. Buyers' panic in periods of extreme political and economic instability is sufficient to explain occurences of hyperinflation.

Another problem with the Cagan model identified by later writers concerns its assumption of adaptive expectations. During hyperinflation, the public's expectations, based on prior inflation, irrationally lag behind the inflation that actually occurs. Sargent and Wallace showed, however, that adaptive expectations are quite rational, given some plausible assumptions about the money supply process and the public's correct perception of that process (20).

In Cagan's model, Sargent and Wallace demonstrated, the actual rate of price inflation depends on current and *expected* future rates of money creation. Cagan, like Bresciani-Turroni and the quantity theorists before him, had argued that hyperinflation results from government efforts to command resources through inflationary finance. A rational public would expect the government to emit new money at rates sufficient to maintain the real proceeds of its inflation tax in the face of rapidly rising prices. Sargent and Wallace showed that when rates of money creation depend on past rates of price inflation (the government's model for predicting inflation?), the resulting price inflation itself depends on these past rates of inflation. An adaptive expectations scheme turns out to be the best predictor of inflation after all.

This rational expectations formulation of the monetarist model takes the money supply process to be endogenous in hyperinflation. Rising prices put pressure on the government budget, as Williams had argued, and the monetary authority passively accommodates the government's deficits, as Williams had argued. Sargent and Wallace also presented partial econometric validation of Williams's position. They found that prices indeed did cause money, in a statistical sense, and that money did not cause prices in the German inflation. The issue of whether the government and the Reichsbank *had* to act passively during the hyperinflation is not addressed and, of course, not resolved by this literature.

Arguments similar to Sargent and Wallace's were advanced earlier by Young (49). He placed anticipation and speculation at the center of the hyperinflation process. The temporal lead of exchange depreciation, for example, reflected public expectations that the budget would not be balanced and that inflation would spiral along. Given these expectations, it did. To Young, the process was driven by public psychology keyed to the present and expected future states of the national budget. "This construction," Ellis objected, "seems to me somewhat specious. It really quite abandons quantity of money as an objective magnitude and substitutes for it a purely subjective thing, an estimate, a surmise, a vague feeling . . ." (8, p. 294).

The material discussed generally confirms Williams in his description of the German inflation. It demonstrates, however, that there is ample opportunity for disagreement over a prime and singular cause of a vicious-circle process.

LATER WORKS. . . . PRIOR THEMES

In his later works, Williams rarely referred to his writings on the German inflation. When he did, it was to his remarks at the 1919 American Economic Association meeting, pregnant with allusions to instability and indeterminateness in the international economy (43, p. 30). To Williams, the international economy presented a latent source of destabilizing shocks and an environment of undependable equilibrating mechanisms. At times, these could run in reverse and amplify rather than attenuate economic disturbances of domestic or of foreign origin.

Williams viewed capital flows as the active element in international economic relations to which trade flows must adapt themselves. Sometimes the adaptation succeeded, as in the Argentine situation that he studied. Sometimes it did not, as in the German situation. Failure of trade to restore balance to international payments upset by a capital account impulse, or by an extraordinary item like reparation payments, could send the economic system into a vicious circle terminated only by collapse. Best not to take chances on the elasticity of internal and external economic relationships, Williams counseled.

He generally advised policy intervention to offset payments imbalance that threatened instability, thus buffering the real sector from the full impact of an exogenous disturbance. In this spirit, he argued for reduction and deferral of the reparation burden on Germany after World War I and for Marshall Plan reconstruction aid to Europe after World War II. He also supported controls on speculative capital flows after World War II (31, p. 653); (45).

Williams distilled his economic principles inductively. His inclination to buffer trade from capital shocks, for example, stemmed from his reading of the gold standard system's long success: payments adjustments were normally effected by stabilizing capital flows responding to the Bank of England's discount rate rather than by the Humian mechanism of inflation and deflation (29, p. 175); (30). Characteristically, however, he described an instance where the gold standard could foster a vicious circle. This, when capital inflows cause price inflation, leading to higher profits and heightened capital inflows to the inflating country (29, p. 194); (23, p. 154). He also recognized potential destabilizing consequences of actions that initially dampen instability. Here he cited United States capital exports to Germany after 1923, associated with the Dawes Plan. As the flow became increasingly short-term in nature, according to Williams, the stage was set for the flight of short-term capital from Europe in 1931 and the collapse of the international monetary system (32, p. 76).

Williams might be casually classified and quickly dismissed as an elasticity pessimist. He was aware, for example, that his analysis of the German inflation rested on assumed response rigidities and frictions in international markets (43, p. 255). The small importance that he attached to the technics of stability conditions in economic models is reflected in a 1937 article. There, he relegated to a footnote the various factors that can result in vicious circles, ". . . such as the magnitude and speed of change, the relative restrictions on trade and capital movements, comparative sensitivity to interest rates and prices, the relative response to security price changes and goods price changes, panic, fear and uncertainty, elasticities of demand-supply, price rigidities, speculation, etc." (25, p. 154n).

Williams's whole body of work suggests that stability depends on these and on other factors that economists are not even aware of. Elasticity pessimism is not a casual matter, as evidenced to Williams by the German inflation of the 1920s and by the vicious circle of competitive devaluation of the 1930s (29, p. 195). He advised the emplacement of a flexible system of international controls, administered with flexible habits of mind, to be deployed against threats to stability as they arose.

His conception of a key currency system for international monetary relations called for maintenance of a stable dollar-pound exchange rate through coordination of United States–United Kingdom internal economic policies (26; 30; 31; 44). Williams expected the currencies and economies of other countries, dependent on conditions in the major trading countries, to fall into place on their own. Stability in the major economies would assure world-wide stability, according to Williams. He drew an analogy between the post-World War II burden of foreign military commitments on the British economy and the post-World War I burden of reparations on the German economy, insisting that British retrenchment was necessary for stabilization. Although there is no trace of Williams's key-currency plan in the formal structure of Bretton Woods, de Cecco argues that the system's de facto operation adhered to the plan's outlines once the pound was stabilized by dramatic devaluation in 1949 (7, p. 56).

Williams remained skeptical about the potency of monetary policy throughout his career. He believed that the post-World War II national debt, largely held by commercial banks, effectively prevented the Federal Reserve from pursuing an independent policy. "The public and the Treasury, as well as the banks, develop a strong vested interest in the stability of (low interest) rates," Williams observed (36, pp. 217ff.). He also pointed with concern to the inflationary potential of Keynesian monetary policies "designed to saturate liquidity preference" (27, p. 60). Williams believed that the best hope for economic stability lay with encouraging private investment and fostering a Smithian virtuous circle of productivity and output increases (33, pp. 5–6; 46).

SUMMARY AND CONCLUSIONS

A number of John H. Williams's professional contributions have been reviewed here, particularly those relating to international instability and to the German inflation. Williams articulated perceptive explanations of evolving economic processes. Since these were keyed to the events themselves, they are difficult to refute. This is demonstrated by the extensive literature on the German inflation, which provides ample support for his arguments.

The consistent message in Williams's work is that the economic world is a dangerous place in which all manner of unstable processes can break loose. Policy makers must remain alert to developing instabilities and be willing to counter them. Their responses should not be shackled by dogmas. In this changing environment, Williams argued, "it is a close matter whether it is worse to be lost in the woods (without a theory) than in one's theory, pursuing its internal consistency to the point where contact with reality is lost" (33, p. 28).

In his appraisal of Keynesian economics, Williams approvingly cited Bagehot and Cliffe Leslie in their objections to generalizations. His evaluation of them perhaps was intended for himself as well:

> The weakness of such men, from the standpoint of the impression they have made on later generations of economists and on their own was that they set up no rival system. By the nature of their objections they could not, and had no interest in trying (27, p. 44).

Notes

1. Professor of Economics, University of Nevada, Las Vegas. I benefited from discussions with Professors Howard S. Ellis, Gerald Feldman, and John Letiche in preparing this paper. All errors, of course, are my own. The research was done while on sabbatical leave from UNLV.
2. Williams's acceptance of Bankers' School doctrine is reflected in his interpretation of a comment by Keynes in the *Manchester Guardian*, later to appear in Keynes's *A Tract on Monetary Reform*. Keynes remarked on the small magnitude of the German money stock in real (British pound) terms. Williams read this as indicating the divergence between the internal and external purchasing power of the mark. Because internal prices were low(er), the money supply need not be all that large when translated into high-valued pounds. An alternative interpretation, of course, is that Germans did not wish to hold much money, given its record of depreciation.
3. See Ellis (8) for a complete survey of the balance-of-payments literature.

References

1. Angell, James W. *The Theory of International Prices* (New York, 1965; first published, 1926).
2. Bonn, Moritz J. *Stabilization of the Mark*, First National Bank of Chicago, April 1922.
3. Bresciani-Turroni, Costantino. *The Economics of Inflation*, trans. Millicent E. Sayers (London, 1937; first published in Italian, 1931).
4. Cagan, Phillip. "The Monetary Dynamics of Hyperinflation," in *Studies in The Quantity Theory of Money*, ed. Milton Friedman (Chicago, 1956), pp. 3–21.
5. Cagan, P., and Kincaid, George. "Jacobs' Estimate of the Hyperinflation Model: Comment," *Economic Inquiry* 14 (1977): 111–18.

6. Cassel, Gustav. "Some Leading Propositions for an International Discussion of the World's Monetary Problem," *Annals of the American Academy* 89–90 (May 1920): 258–67.

7. de Cecco, Marcello. "Origins of the Post-War Payments System," *Cambridge Journal of Economics* 3 (1979): 49–61.

8. Ellis, Howard S. *German Monetary Theory, 1905–1933,* Harvard Economic Studies, vol. 44 (Cambridge, Mass., 1934).

9. Friedman, Benjamin M. "Stability and Rationality in Models of Hyperinflation," *International Economic Review* 19 (1978): 45–64.

10. Graham, Frank D. *Exchange, Prices, and Production in Hyperinflation, Germany, 1920–1923* (Princeton, N.J., 1930).

11. Graham, F. D. "International Trade Under Depreciated Paper: The Case of the United States, 1862–1879," *Quarterly Journal of Economics* 36 (1922).

12. Helfferich, Karl. *Money,* trans. Louis Infield (New York, 1969; first English edition, 1927).

13. Holtfrerich, Carl-Ludwig. "Reichsbankpolitik, 1918–1923," *Zeitschrift für Wirtschafts- und Sozialwissenschaften* 3 (1977): 193–214.

14. Jacobs, Rodney L. "A Difficulty With Monetarist Models of Hyperinflation," *Economic Inquiry* 13 (1975): 337–60.

15. Keynes, John Maynard. *A Revision of the Treaty,* vol. III, *Collected Writings of John Maynard Keynes* (London, 1971; first published, 1922).

16. Letiche, John M. *Balance of Payments and Economic Growth* (New York; first published, 1958).

17. *Money, Trade, and Economic Growth,* in Honor of John H. Williams (New York, 1951).

18. Ohlin, Bertil. *Interregional and International Trade,* rev. ed., Harvard Economic Studies, vol. 39 (Cambridge, Mass., 1967; first published, 1933).

19. Robinson, Joan. "Review of *The Economics of Inflation* by C. Bresciani-Turroni," *Economic Journal,* Sept. 1938; reprinted as "The Economics of Hyper-Inflation," in *Collected Economic Papers,* vol. 1 (New York, 1951), pp. 69–77.

20. Sargent, Thomas J., and Wallace, Neil. "Rational Expectations and the Dynamics of Hyperinflation," *International Economic Review* 14 (1973): 328–50.

21. Taussig, Frank W. "Germany's Reparation Payments," *Proceedings of the American Economic Association,* vol. 10, Supplement (1920): 33–49.

22. Taussig, F. W. "International Trade Under Depreciated Paper. A Contribution to Theory," *Quarterly Journal of Economics* 31 (1916–17): 380–402.

23. Thelwall, J. W. T., assisted by Kavanagh, C. J. *Report on the Economic and Financial Condition in Germany to March 1922,* rev. to March 1923, rev. to April 1924, Department of Overseas Trade, London, 1922, 1923, 1924.

24. Viner, Jacob. *Canada's Balance of International Indebtedness, 1900–1913,* Harvard Economic Studies, vol. 26 (Cambridge, Mass., 1924).

25. Williams, John H. "The Adequacy of Existing Currency Mechanisms Under Varying Circumstances," *Proceedings of the American Economic Association* 27 (March 1937): 151–68.

26. Williams, J. H. *America and World Finance,* a study prepared for the Economic Policy Commission of the American Bankers Association, 1922.
27. Williams, J. H. "An Appraisal of Keynesian Economics," *Proceedings of the American Economic Association* 38 (May 1948); reprinted in *Economic Stability in a Changing World* (Oxford, 1953), pp. 43–63.
28. Williams, J. H. *Argentine International Trade Under Inconvertible Paper Money, 1880–1900,* Harvard Economic Studies, vol. 22 (Cambridge, Mass., 1920).
29. Williams, J. H. "The Crisis of the Gold Standard," *Foreign Affairs* 10 (Jan. 1932): 173–87.
30. Williams, J. H. "Currency Stabilization: American and British Attitudes," *Foreign Affairs* 22 (Jan. 1944): 233–47.
31. Williams, J. H. "Currency Stabilization: The Keynes and White Plans," *Foreign Affairs* 21 (July 1943): 645–58.
32. Williams, J. H. "Economic Lessons of Two World Wars," *Foreign Affairs* 26 (Oct. 1947), reprinted in *Economic Stability in a Changing World* (Oxford, 1953), pp. 67–88.
33. Williams, J. H. "An Economist's Confessions," *American Economic Review* 42 (March 1952), reprinted in *Ibid.,* pp. 3–28.
34. Williams, J. H. "Europe After 1952 — The Long-Term Recovery Problem," *Foreign Affairs* 27 (April 1949), reprinted in *Ibid.,* pp. 106–28.
35. Williams, J. H. "Foreign Exchange, Prices, and the Course of International Trade," *Annals of the American Academy* 84 (May 1920): 197–210.
36. Williams, J. H. "Foreign Exchange Under Depreciated Paper," *Journal of the American Bankers Association* 14 (Jan. 1922): 492–94.
37. Williams, J. H. "Free Enterprise and Full Employment," in *Financing American Prosperity,* a symposium by six economists (New York, 1945; reprinted in *Economic Stability in a Changing World,* pp. 187–224.
38. Williams, J. H. "German Foreign Trade and the Reparation Payments," *Quarterly Journal of Economics* 36 (1922): 482–503.
39. Williams, J. H. "German Trade and the Reparation Payment," *Journal of the American Bankers Association* 14 (March 1922): 605–609.
40. Williams, J. H. "Germany's Reparation Payments — Discussion," *Proceedings of the American Economic Association* 10 (March 1920): 50–56.
41. Williams, J. H. "International Monetary Plans: After Bretton Woods," *Foreign Affairs* 23 (1945): 38–56.
42. Williams, J. H. "International Trade Theory and Policy, Some Current Issues," *Proceedings of the American Economic Association* 41 (May 1951), reprinted in *Economic Stability in a Changing World,* pp. 29–42.
43. Williams, J. H. "The Monetary Doctrines of John Maynard Keynes," *Quarterly Journal of Economics,* August 1931; reprinted in *Ibid.,* pp. 225–255.
44. Williams, J. H. "Post-war Monetary Plans," *Proceedings of the American Economic Association* 34 (March 1944).
45. Williams, J. H. "The Task of Economic Recovery," *Foreign Affairs,* July 1948, reprinted in *Economic Stability in a Changing World,* pp. 89–105.
46. Williams, J. H. "Testimony before H. R. Committee on Foreign Affairs in Post-War Recovery Program," 1948, reprinted in *Ibid.,* pp. 257–68.

47. Williams, J. H. "The Theory of International Trade Reconsidered," *Economics Journal* 39 (1929): 195–209.
48. Williams, J. H. "The World's Monetary Dilemma — Internal vs. External Stability," *Proceedings of the American Academy*, April 1934, reprinted in *Post-war Monetary Plans and Other Essays* (New York, 1944), pp. 191–98.
49. Young, Allyn A. "War Debts, External and Internal," *Foreign Affairs* 3 (March 1924): 397–409.

Money Demand and Expectations in the German Hyperinflation: A Survey of the Models

The German hyperinflation has attracted two waves of inquiry by economists. The first wave asked a wide range of questions that reflected their concern with avoiding hyperinflations in the future and understanding the real economic impact of Germany's hyperinflation (Williams, 1922; Helfferich, 1923; Schacht, 1927; Graham, 1930; Bresciani-Turroni, 1931; Laursen and Pedersen, 1964). These economists asked what caused the hyperinflation, how did it affect aggregate output; how did it alter the distribution of income and wealth, etc. They used a wide range of empirical evidence, but their analytical procedures were unsophisticated and especially inadequate with regard to the question of causality. The recent wave of inquiry by historians has similarities in style and emphasis with the first wave of economists' studies (Born, 1977; Büsch and Feldman, 1978; Feldman, 1977; Holtfrerich, 1977a, 1977b).

The second wave of economists has used more sophisticated statistical procedures on a narrower range of data to answer a narrower range of questions. Some looked only at the German case (Frenkel, 1977, 1979; Abel, et al., 1979; Holtfrerich, 1980), but many examined most of the hyperinflations of this century: Austria in 1921–22, China in 1946–48, Greece in 1943–44, Hungary in 1923–24 and 1945–46, Soviet Union in 1921–22, and Poland in 1923–24 (Cagan, 1956; Allais, 1966; Barro, 1970; Sargent and Wallace, 1973; Jacobs, 1975, 1977; Khan, 1975, 1977; Friedman, 1978). They have used data series on the aggregate money supply, aggregate price level, and the forward premium on foreign exchange to test hypotheses about the demand and supply of money functions and about the formation of price expectations. The second wave of inquiry has reached an impasse where many similar but subtly different hypotheses are on the table, all of which are largely consistent with the data used to test them. The chief reason for the impasse is that the full models, which hypothesize about interactions between half a dozen to a dozen variables, are compressed into reduced-form equations, which can be estimated with two or three data series.

There has been little coordination between the two waves of inquiry because of the differences in their methods of analysis. Because their strength and weaknesses are complementary, both approaches would benefit from more cross-fertilization.[1] Toward this end the following survey aims to indicate opportunities for opening up the monetarist models of the hyperinflation to a wider range of empirical evidence.

CAGAN'S MODEL

The second wave of economists' inquiry into the hyperinflation derives from Cagan's seminal article (1956) and explores mainly the agenda of issues he raised. The general model from which Cagan starts posits a demand for real money balances (the money supply divided by the price index) that depends positively on real wealth and income and negatively on the opportunity cost of holding cash, namely the available yields on securities (stocks, bonds, etc.) and the rate of increase of prices of nonperishable commodities. He assumes that a fall or rise in demand for real balances pushes prices up or down; so the supply of real balances always equals demand, no matter what the supply of nominal balances as determined by the Reichsbank. To simplify the real balance demand function, Cagan notes that real wealth and income, and even interest rates, were stable relative to the large fluctuations in real balances. "The only cost of holding balances that seems to fluctuate widely enough to account for the drastic changes in real cash balances during hyperinflation is the rate of depreciation in the value of money or, equivalently, the rate of change of prices. This observation suggests the hypothesis that changes in real cash balances in hyperinflation result from variations in the expected rate of change in prices" (Cagan, 1956, 31–33). Formally, the natural logarithm of the demand and supply of real money balances is a linear and negative function of the inflation rate that people expect in the immediate future:

$$\ln (M/P) = -\alpha E - \gamma, \tag{1}$$

where M is an index of the quantity of money in circulation, P is an index of the price level, α (necessarily positive) and γ are constants, and E is the expected rate of change in prices (Cagan, 1956, 27–35). An essentially equivalent way to express this relationship is that the current inflation rate equals the growth rate of the money supply plus some constant times the amount by which people expect the inflation rate to change in the near future.

Since no record of price expectations is available, Cagan hypothesizes that the expected rate of change of prices depends on actual rates of change in the past. Specifically, "the expected rate of change in prices is revised per period of time in [constant] proportion to the difference between the actual rate of change in prices and the rate of change that was expected." This assumption is expressed by

$$(dE/dt)_t = \beta(C_t - E_t),$$

(2)

where C is the actual rate of change of prices $(\ln P_t - \ln P_{t-1})$ and β is a positive constant, "which can be described as a 'coefficient of expectation,' since its magnitude determines the rapidity with which expected rates of change in prices adjust to actual rates. The smaller is β, the slower is the adjustment" (Cagan, 1956, 37). This means that the expected inflation rate in any period (E_t) is an exponentially weighted average of the actual inflation rates in past periods, with the weights $(e^{\beta X})$ becoming smaller for periods more distant in the past:

$$E_t = \frac{(1 - e^{-\beta})}{e^{\beta t}} \sum_{X = -T}^{t} C_X e^{\beta X}.$$

(3)

Expectations of this sort are called *adaptive*. If the average rate of inflation went up or down, adaptive expectations would gradually adjust and eventually equal the actual average rate, if it continued forever. If the rate of inflation is accelerating, people with adaptive expectations (and β less than 1) will consistently underpredict inflation.

Cagan combines his theories about the demand for real balances and the formation of expectations and arrives at the following testable hypothesis: the natural logarithm of the demand and supply of real balances is a negative, linear function of a weighted average of past rates of inflation with the coefficients α, β and γ:[2]

$$\ln (M_t/P_t) = -\alpha \left[\frac{(1 - e^{-\beta})}{e^{\beta t}} \sum_{X = -T}^{t} (\ln P_X - \ln P_{X-1}) e^{\beta X} \right] - \gamma.$$

(4)

Cagan uses the wholesale price index as both the deflator of the money stock and the basis of inflationary expectations. His data for Germany are monthly from September 1920 to July 1923. The equation as a whole and the estimates of the individual coefficients are highly statistically significant. His model could explain 99 percent of the variation in real cash balances. His estimate of the coefficient of expectations (β) was .20, implying that it would take a year for expectations to make 90 percent of their adjustment in response to an increase in the rate of inflation.

Subsequent studies have modified Cagan's model in various ways. Some of these are econometric refinements which fall outside the scope of this survey (e.g., Sargent, 1977; Khan, 1975). The other modifications and criticisms imply reinterpretations of the economic behavior in the hyperinflations and often require testing with different empirical evidence. These reformulations focus on 4 overlapping areas: (1) the form of the money demand function, (2) the choice of data series, (3) the conditions of stability and instability, (4) the formation of expectations.

FUNCTIONAL FORM OF THE MONEY DEMAND

Although his early model of hyperinflation was equivalent to Cagan's, Allais's (1966) later hereditary-relativistic-logistic formulation of the demand for money differed substantially. He built his model around the concept of a psychological time scale. The rate of psychological expansion (Z) and the rate of forgetfulness (χ'), analogous to Cagan's inflationary expectations (E) and coefficient of adaptation to expectations (β), were assumed constant in terms of psychological time. When reconstructed in "physical" time, the ratio of the velocity of circulation in a base period of constant prices (v_0) to the current desired velocity of circulation is a function ψ of Z, which varies in terms of physical time. Allais assumes that the supply and demand for money are always very nearly equal. Since velocity by definition equals the real output (assumed constant for hyperinflation) times the price level divided by the nominal money supply, real balances would equal a constant times $\psi(Z)$ divided by the velocity in the base period: in terms of logarithms

$$\ln (M/P) = q + \ln [\psi(Z)] - \ln (v_0). \tag{5}$$

The rate of forgetfulness during the constant-price base period (χ_0) divided by the current rate of forgetfulness (χ), both in terms of physical time, is also assumed to equal $\psi(Z)$, where

$$\psi(Z) = \frac{(1 + b)}{(1 + b\,e^{aZ})} \tag{6}$$

The demand for real money balances in Allais's model is thus a logistic function of E, expected inflation. Allais's adjustment mechanism for Z is also more complex than Cagan's:

$$(dZ/dt)_t = C_t - \frac{\chi_0}{\psi(Z_t)} Z_t \tag{7}$$

Allais's model becomes more elegant when he introduces constraints on the three constants a, b, and χ_0. Allais assumes that the inverse of the velocity is much less than 1, which implies that a equals 1. He assumes that in the neighborhood of stability $(Z = 0)$ people's behavior is symmetrical for economic expansions and contractions, which implies that b equals 1. He assumes further that people forget the past at the same rate at which they discount the future, which implies that χ equals the riskless interest rate. In the United States from 1880 to 1956, which Allais considers a suitably stable base period, the interest rate averaged 5 percent per annum, so he constrains χ_0 to be .004 per month (= .05 per annum). The coefficients to be estimated are the initial values Z_1 and v_0.[3] This he does by minimizing the average squared error in estimating nominal balances with Equation 5. With the constrained model Allais gets very good fits (average R-square = .99) not only for seven hyperinflations including Germany's but also for various peacetime periods in France, Britain, and the United States. This empirical proof of its predictive power is the chief point in favor of Allais's model. Despite the elaborate symmetry of its logic, it contains no story about profit-maximizing behavior.

Barro (1970) modified Cagan's money demand relationship by specifying explicitly two mechanisms by which real money balances could decline while aggregate real income and the volume of transactions remained constant. First, firms could pay their employees more frequently. Second, people could conduct a larger proportion of their transactions with some medium other than paper marks. Barro's model included fixed real costs of making each adjustment in the payments period or in the use of currency substitutes, so the speed of adjustment as well as the desired ratio of income to money balances would increase as the expected rate of inflation increased.[4] Barro showed econometrically that the price level and the money supply behaved in ways consistent with his hypotheses about currency substitution and the payments period. Although many accounts verify the existence of these phenomena in the German and other hyperinflations, Barro did not present any direct evidence on whether they occurred at the rate which his model predicted.

Several studies take the log of price expectations or other opportunity-cost term as well as of real balances (Barro, 1970; Frenkel, 1977, 1979). For instance,

$$\ln (M/P) = -\alpha' \ln(E) - \gamma. \qquad (8)$$

This implies that the percentage change in desired real balances has a constant proportionality to the *percentage* change in the expected rate of opportunity cost, instead of the absolute change. This functional form has the advantage that it corresponds to several standard money demand functions derived from specific stories about how people choose the size of their money balances. In the models of Tobin, Baumol, and Barro, people or firms balance the advantages of keeping larger average balances in interest-earning accounts and therefore less cash against the cost of more frequent trips to the bank or payments to employees. The demand for cash is then inversely proportional to the square root of the interest rate or E, the expected opportunity cost of keeping cash (Baumol, 1952; Tobin, 1956; Barro, 1970). In other words, α' is Equation 8 should be 0.5. In the Miller-Orr-Whalen models, the transaction and precautionary demand for cash is inversely proportional to the cube root of the rate of opportunity cost of holding cash, i.e., α' should be 0.33 (Miller and Orr, 1966; Whalen, 1966). When estimating the double log equation, therefore, one has some standards by which to judge the reasonableness of the point estimates of α' (Frenkel, 1977). Or, from an alternative viewpoint, one can test the validity of the theoretical models.

CHOICE OF DATA SERIES

Several studies use the cost of living index in place of the wholesale price index, which Cagan uses (Frenkel, 1977, 1979; Barro, 1970; Abel et al., 1979). In discussing the choice of price series, it is important to recognize that what is appropriate for the left side of Equation 4 is not necessarily most appropriate for the right side. On the left side, the price index deflating money balances should reflect the transactions needs of those holding the money balances. For businesses this would probably be the wholesale price index, for households, the cost of living index. For the whole economy it should be the average of the price indexes, weighted by the share of money balances held by the groups to whom the index was most relevant. Frenkel (1977) estimates the share weights for wholesale prices (Θ) and consumer prices ($1-\Theta$). Θ was less than one-half and not significantly different from zero, so he concluded that, if a choice has to be made, the cost of living is the more appropriate deflator. In other words, most of the money seems to have been held by households, whose major transactions were in consumer goods and services. By estimating a constant Θ throughout the hyperinflation, Frenkel assumes that the sectoral distribution of cash balances remained constant. If firms adjust to inflation faster than households, as other results of Frenkel's suggest (1977), then as inflation accelerated, households would end with a growing share of the cash balances.

The inflationary expectations term, estimated on the right side of Equation 4, should reflect the opportunity cost of not investing in some bundle of commodities instead of holding cash. Use of the cost of living index for this purpose by Barro (1970) and Abel et al. (1979) seems inappropriate, since the cost of living includes services like housing and utilities, which one could not stockpile and whose prices rose much more slowly than average. In terms of the composition of the commodity bundle, the inflation of the wholesale price index provides a superior measurement of the opportunity cost of holding cash. As inflation accelerated, people probably stockpiled a wider range of commodities, since it would become profitable to stockpile an item when the rate of inflation exceeded its rate of physical depreciation and storage cost.

As Cagan (1956) noted, expected price inflation is not the only opportunity cost of holding cash. Frenkel (1977) tried the rate of interest on short-term loans, the most volatile of the interest rates, but the coefficient on this independent variable did not differ significantly from zero. None of the studies looked at the return from investment in common stocks as an alternative to holding money. The forward exchange discount is the most promising addition to the opportunity-cost variables on the right hand side.

Fluctuating exchange rates after World War I, which forced all major currencies except the dollar off the gold standard, led to the development of markets for future contracts to exchange currencies. The exchange rate in a futures contract would differ from the current or "spot" rate to the extent that the people in the market expected the exchange rate in the future to differ from the spot rate. The forward exchange premium is the percentage difference between the exchange rate specified in futures contracts and the spot exchange rate. Since the forward exchange premium is the only direct quantitative indicator we have of expectations about the mark's future value, it seems an important variable to include in the demand for money function. Frenkel (1977, 1979), Abel et al. (1979), and Holtfrerich (1980) do so in various ways.[5]

Obviously the forward premium indicates some kind of opportunity cost, but there is disagreement as to exactly what kind. If the (expected) purchasing power of the mark at home relative to its purchasing power abroad after conversion into foreign currency had remained constant, then the forward exchange premium would reflect the expected inflation of domestic prices. In that case one should omit any other price expectations term in the money demand function, as Frenkel (1977, 1979) does. If people did not expect constant purchasing power ratios, then the forward exchange premium should appear in the money demand function in addition to the domestic price expectations terms, as in Abel et al. (1979) and Holtfrerich (1980). Whether or not purchasing power ratios are constant, the forward exchange premium measures the expected opportunity cost of holding marks rather than foreign currency (specifically, British pounds). Both Frenkel and Abel et al. interpret this as the opportunity cost to Germans; Holtfrerich interprets it as the opportunity cost to foreigners holding marks. Both groups would, of course, vary their demand for marks as the forward premium varied. The forward exchange premium used in these calculations is that published weekly in London by the Anglo-Portuguese Colonial and Overseas Bank, Ltd. (reprinted in Einzig, 1937, 449–81). That these rates do not appear in any German newspaper and that laws limited the amount of foreign exchange that Germans could own suggest that, as Holtfrerich argues, the forward rate reflected mainly the perceptions of foreign holders of marks. This was more true at the beginning than at the end of the hyperinflation, when for the most part, only Germans held marks. Another interpretation, not previously on the table, also helps account for the explanatory power of the forward exchange premium. Throughout the hyperinflation, and particularly toward the end when even the government began issuing some certificates based on gold value, loans were made with repayment specified in terms of "gold marks," i.e., dollars (Schacht, 1927, 77–78). If the real interest rate on these loans was constant, then the (opportunity) cost of holding marks would have been the expected rise in value of a gold mark relative to paper marks. The forward exchange premium on dollars relative to marks equalled this expected appreciation of the gold mark and so could affect the domestic demand for marks even if holding actual foreign currency was not an option for Germans.

DYNAMIC STABILITY

Several writers have strongly criticized Cagan's model on the ground that it is not dynamically stable. A model is *dynamically unstable* if a once-and-for-all shock — say, an exogenous increase in prices — could cause a perpetual and generally rising rate of inflation without any further increase in the money supply. The story would be that the rise in prices raises people's expectations about future inflation, which lowers the amount of cash they want to keep, which leads them to try to buy more goods, which bids up prices even more, and so on indefinitely. To have this kind of self-generating inflation in Cagan's model, the sensitivity of money demand to inflationary expectations times the speed with which people adjust their expectations, α times β, must be greater than 1 (Cagan, 1956, 64–69). Since hyperinflations have in fact occurred if and only if there were enormous increases in the money supply, economists justifiably question the validity of any model whose estimated coefficients imply dynamic instability.[6] Cagan's point estimates of $\alpha\beta$ exceeded 1 for Germany's and the Soviet Union's hyperinflations. Although the 90 percent confidence intervals in both cases include values below 1, the confidence intervals for two other cases also include values above 1 (p. 69). When Khan (1975) reestimated Cagan's model with corrections for serial correlation of errors, however, he found $\alpha\beta$'s clearly less than 1 for all seven hyperinflations.

Friedman (1978) proves that, when Cagan's model is translated into discrete time form and estimated with discrete time (e.g., monthly) data, $\alpha\beta$ being less than 1 precludes only monotonic instability. He shows that estimates of $(\alpha + 1)\beta$ greater than 1 imply that there were month-by-month oscillations in desired balances and that these oscilla-tions would have exploded in amplitude if $(\alpha + \frac{1}{2})\beta$ exceeded 1. Both Cagan's (1956) and Khan's (1975) estimates of α and β imply that money demand oscillated, perhaps explosively, in the German and several other cases. Since no one ever observed such oscillations, the estimated models are presumably wrong to some extent. Friedman suggests that more nearly continuous data would improve the results. Although some weekly data exist for the German case, Friedman did not try using them.

Jacobs (1975) raises the stability issue in a different way. He worries that, because the price level appears on both sides of Cagan's estimating Equation 4, a good statistical fit would appear even if the model were fundamentally incorrect, as he contends. The spurious fit would result from errors in the estimate of the price level on the left side of the equation being canceled out by the appearance of the price level on the right side. Jacobs makes similar criticisms of Allais's and Barro's models. The importance of this criticism depends essentially on how large a weight is on the current price level in the supposedly exogenous inflationary expectations term.

The possibility of dynamic instability arises in Cagan's and similar models, where people form expectations adaptively by looking at current and past inflation. If expectations actually formed in different ways and we so modeled them, then there might be less possibility for instability.

RATIONAL EXPECTATIONS

Expectations, particularly about inflation, have taken on increasingly central roles in recent macroeconomic models. Whether people fully anticipate price changes or have (generally inaccurate) adaptive expectations makes a big difference for the effectiveness of monetary policy. Cagan's model of adaptive expectations formation was one of the first and for many years the most popular method for estimating expectations. So attacks on and defenses of adaptive expectations have figured prominently in recent macroeconomic literature.

The, in principle, most radical alternative to adaptive expectations is rational expectations.

> Expectations about a variable are said to be rational if they depend, in the proper way, on the same things that economic theory says actually determine that variable. By contrast, the usual [e.g., Cagan's] method of modeling expectations involves supposing that they are formed by extrapolating past values of the variable being predicted, a scheme that usually, though not always, assumes that the people whose expectations count are ignorant of the forces governing the variable they are trying to predict (Sargent and Wallace, 1973, 328).

Of course, "economic theory" is not unanimous about what determines the level of prices or any other variable, so *rational expectations* are, in practice, expectations constrained to be consistent with (the rest of) whichever model is being used. Against the standard of rational expectations, Walters criticizes Cagan's model for "serious internal inconsistencies" (1971, 273), for indeed his adaptive expectations look more like slow-witted fumbling than rational forecasting.

Sargent and Wallace (1973), major protagonists for rational expectations, come to Cagan's rescue, however, with a model in which adaptive expectations would be rational (consistent with the model's predictions). As Cagan posited (Equation 1), the level of prices depends on the nominal money supply and the expectations of inflation. The rationally expected inflation then must relate directly to the rationally expected change in the money supply. Sargent and Wallace test two alternatives. With one, the money supply and its rate of change are autonomous with respect to the rate of inflation (and the price level), in which case people should look at current and past rates of money creation, not at prices, in order to predict the future money supply and prices. "In this system, money creation influences current and subsequent rates of inflation; but given lagged [past] rates of money creation, past rates of inflation exert no influence on money creation. In such a system, adaptive expectations schemes like those of Cagan are not rational" (Sargent and Wallace, 1973, 337). With the second alternative, the level of prices determines the change in the money supply, because, for instance, the government prints enough new money to finance a given level of real expenditures, no matter what the nominal cost. Cagan's model of adaptive inflationary expectations would be rational for such an economy, because money creation and therefore inflation would be best predicted by extrapolating past rates of inflation.

Statistical tests of the two foregoing propositions show for the German and other hyperinflations "that inflation strongly influences subsequent rates of money creation, but that the influence of money creation on subsequent rates of inflation is much harder to detect" (Sargent and Wallace, 338–39). Using different econometric methods, Frenkel (1977) comes even more strongly to this conclusion that wholesale prices cause money creation and not vice versa. This supports the hypothesis that Cagan's adaptive expectations are rational in the sense of being consistent with a process that might have determined the rates of inflation. Since both Frenkel and Sargent and Wallace compare only two extreme alternatives, they have established beyond doubt neither their model of the money supply nor the rationality of adaptive expectations. Jacobs (1975) also lends left-handed support to the contention that inflationary expectations based on past prices were more rational than expectations based on past rates of money growth. He reformulates Cagan's money demand equation so that the expectations term is a weighted average of past rates of money growth. This equation does not fit as well as Cagan's original and gives illogical, negative estimates for some β's.[7]

Friedman (1978) takes Sargent and Wallace's argument to the logical conclusion that the money supply process for which adaptive expectations are rational would make each period's change in the money supply equal the previous period's change in the money supply plus a random increment whose average value is zero. Friedman tests and rejects the hypothesis that the money supply grew like this in the German or most of the other hyperinflations. His result could mean either that Sargent and Wallace's whole approach is wrong or merely that they need to take into account changes in the underlying real expenditure which the government financed by printing money. The changes in spending demands on, and tax resources of, the German government have center stage in most traditional accounts of the hyperinflation (Bresciani-Turroni, 1931, 1937, 53–64, 91–91; Graham, 1930, 30–48, 75–77; Schacht, 1972, 40, 55–66; Stolper, 1940, 137–51). Jacobs (1977) also shows that the government's real inflationary revenue varied significantly during the German and Austrian hyperinflations.

Although Cagan's adaptive expectations mechanism might be rational, so might many other ways of forming expectations. Frenkel (1975) and Mussa (1975) present in adjacent articles the empirical and theoretical justifications for an expectations formation mechanism with separate components for the long run and the short run. Frenkel reports the common observation that when the rate of monetary expansion increases, the rate of inflation only gradually increases to the new rate of money expansion, resulting at first in an increase of real money balances. In Cagan's basic money demand relationship (Equation 1), the logarithm of real money balances is a negative function of the expected inflation rate. Therefore, the initial increase of real balances indicates that people at first expected a *lower* rate of inflation than before the increase in money growth.

Frenkel's adaptive-regressive model predicts such a pattern of expectations. As in Cagan's model, the demand for real money balances depends negatively on the expectations of inflation in the short run. The difference is in the way that the short-run expectations adjust. The adjustment of short-run expectations (E) depends positively on the difference between the actual inflation rate (C) and the short term rate that was expected. This adaptive component is identical to Cagan's. The adjustment also depends, however, *negatively* and more strongly on the difference between the actual rate and the long-run expected rate of inflation (π), which is the regressive component. So if actual inflation is above the expected long-run average in one period, then people will to some extent (δ) expect inflation in the next period to be below the long-run average, in order for inflation to average out to the expected long-run average. Algebraically,

$$dE/dt = \beta(C-E) - \delta(C-\pi); \quad \delta>\beta>0. \tag{9}$$

The long-run expected inflation also adjusts adaptively, but more slowly than the short-run expectations:

$$d\pi/dt = g(C-\pi); \quad \beta>g>0. \tag{10}$$

An alternative explanation for the initial rise in real money balances when the money supply growth rate increased is that the supply and demand for money were not always equal. A temporary disequilibrium, a lag in the adjustment of prices, reflected by phenomena like price controls and customers lining up at stores, would cause real balances to rise. Simple adaptive expectations with lags in the adjustment of prices would give at least the same qualitative behavior of real balances in response to changed rates of money creation as would the adaptive-regressive expectations with instantaneous price adjustment.

Mussa (1975) shows that adaptive-regressive expectations about prices are rational in the sense defined earlier, if the supply of money has an analogous adaptive-regressive behavior. In other words, the percentage increase of the money supply is a random variable whose expected (mean) value is the sum of (1) the long-run rate of growth of money, a policy variable, (2) a random disturbance, whose average value is zero, and (3) a correction term showing the monetary authority's attempt to compensate for the random disturbance in the previous period. When people see the money supply or price level rise at a more rapid rate than they expected, they think it is most likely just the random disturbance, an error which the monetary authorities will try to offset in the subsequent period. This is the rationale for the strong regressive component in people's expectations. Only if the higher rate of money growth persists will people revise their expectations about the long-run inflation rate. Mussa does not test whether the German Reichsbank or any other central bank actually made its policy in an adaptive-regressive fashion during a hyperinflation.

The effort at modeling rational expectations in hyperinflations has, in short, involved reformulating the functions for generating both inflationary expectations and the money supply, in order to make them mutually consistent.

RETROSPECTIVE

The main empirical issues raised but left unanswered by the monetarist studies of the hyperinflation fall into two categories.

The first group of issues concerns the microeconomic adjustment to the hyperinflation. Did the shortening of the payments period and the use of currency substitutes actually take place at the pace which Barro hypothesized and estimated that they would? What was happening in Germany's financial markets to keep the nominal interest rate so low that it has no explanatory power as the opportunity cost of holding money balances? Which sectors were most active in stockpiling real goods to hedge against inflation, and what range of items did they hoard? How was foreign exchange allocated within the German economy and what role did it play as a substitute asset for paper marks? These questions are important not only for economists wishing to know how economies react to accelerating inflation, but they are also important for understanding the distributional effects of Germany's hyperinflation, which so concern social and political historians.

The second group of issues relates to whether expectations of inflation were rational and whether they made the inflation process self-sustaining (dynamically unstable). Direct observations of expectations, such as the forward exchange premium, offer some limited opportunity for further empirical investigation, but the greater opportunity lies with improving our understanding of the money supply process, for which there are much better data. The two major types of hypotheses about the money supply process are (1) that monetary policy autonomously followed some rule in terms of a target for the rate of money growth or price inflation; (2) that the money supply grew in accordance with politically determined needs to finance real government spending and perhaps private investment. Knowing what determined the money supply is essential to tell whether any particular expectation formation mechanism was rational. This may in turn guide us to an expectations model that is less prone than Cagan's to predicting dynamic instability. Furthermore, knowing what determined the money supply may be a fundamental step toward answering the traditional question of what caused Germany's hyperinflation.

Notes

* The author gratefully acknowledges the helpful comments received on earlier versions of this paper at the Economic History Workshop at the University of Michigan and at the German Inflation Workshop at the Brooklyn College Conference on "Inflation Through the Ages." A Rackham Faculty Research Grant and Fellowship from the University of Michigan supported this research.
1. Holtfrerich has made commendable contributions in this direction.
2. Actually price expectations and desired money holdings vary continuously. To use the monthly data series, however, Cagan made discrete time approximations, as in Equations 3 and 4.
3. Note that by letting v_0 take any value to maximize the model's fit, rather than

constraining it to readily observed values, Allais essentially unbinds one of the other constraints.

4. Khan (1977) made a simpler modification to Cagan's model, in which the speed of adjustment, β in Cagan's Equation 2, varies as a linear function of the rate of inflation and the change in that rate. In the German case, Khan found no significant relationship between the speed of adjustment and the rate of inflation, but found a significant positive relationship between the speed of adjustment and the change of the inflation rate.

5. Actually, Holtfrerich combines the forward exchange discount with the (relatively constant) differential in interest rates between London and Berlin to get the "swap rate." In his regressions he enters the cube root of the swap rate.

6. Goldman (1972) shows that $\alpha\beta$ greater than 1 also implies the heresy that increasing the growth of the money supply would slow down inflation.

7. Jacobs would not interpret this as verification of the rationality of Cagan's adaptive expectations.

References

Abel, Andrew, Rudiger, Dornbusch, Huizinga, John, and Marcus, Alan. "Money Demand During Hyperinflation," *Journal of Monetary Economics* 5 (1979): 97–104.

Allais, Maurice. "A Restatement of the Quantity Theory of Money," *American Economic Review* 56 (1966, part 2): 1123–57.

Barro, Robert J. "Inflation, the Payments Period, and the Demand for Money," *Journal of Political Economy* 78 (1970): 1228–63.

Baumol, William J. "The Transactions Demand for Cash: An Inventory Theoretic Approach," *Quarterly Journal of Economics* 66 (1958): 545–56.

Born, Karl E. "The German Inflation after the First World War," *Journal of European Economic History* 6 (1977): 5–48.

Bresciani-Turroni, Constantino, trans. 1937. *The Economics of Inflation: A Study of Currency Depreciation in Post-War Germany, 1914–1923* (New York, 1931).

Büsch, Otto, and Feldman, Gerald D. (Eds.). *Historische Prozesse der deutschen Inflation, 1914 bis 1924: Ein Tagungsbericht* (Berlin, 1978).

Cagan, Phillip. "The Monetary Dynamics of Hyperinflation," in Milton Friedman (Ed.). *Studies in the Quantity Theory of Money* (Chicago, 1956).

Einzig, Paul. *The Theory of Forward Exchange* (London, 1937).

Feldman, Gerald D. *Iron and Steel in the German Inflation, 1916–1923* (Princeton, N.J., 1977).

Frenkel, Jacob A. "Inflation and the Formation of Expectations," *Journal of Monetary Economics* 1 (1975): 403–21.

Frenkel, J. A. "The Forward Exchange Rate, Expectations, and the Demand for Money: The German Hyperinflation," *American Economic Review* 67 (1977): 653–70.

Frenkel, J. A. "Further Evidence on Expectations and the Demand for Money During the German Hyperinflation," *Journal of Monetary Economics* 5 (1979): 81–96.

Friedman, Benjamin M. "Stability and Rationality in Models of Hyperinflation," International Economic Review 19 (1978): 45–64.

Goldman, Stephen M. "Hyperinflation and the Rate of Growth in the Money Supply," Journal of Economic Theory 5 (1972): 250–57.

Graham, Frank D. Exchange, Prices and Production in Hyperinflation: Germany, 1920–1923 (Princeton, N.J., 1930).

Helferrich, Karl. Money, trans. (New York, 1927; originally published, 1923).

Holtfrerich, Carl-Ludwig. "Internationale Verteilungsfolgen der deutschen Inflation 1918–1923," Kyklos 30 (1977): 271–92.

Holtfrerich, C. L. "Amerikanischer Kapitalexport und Wiederaufbau der deutschen Wirtschaft 1919–23 im Vergleich zu 1924–29," Vierteljahrschrift für Sozial- und Wirtschaftsgeschichte 64 (1977): 497–529.

Holtfrerich, C. L. "Domestic and Foreign Expectations and the Demand for Money during the German Inflation, 1920–1923," in Charles P. Kindleberger and Jean-Pierre LaFargue (Ed.), Financial Crises and the Lender of Last Resort (Cambridge, 1930).

Jacobs, Rodney L. "A Difficulty with Monetarist Models of Hyperinflation," Economic Inquiry 13 (1975): 337–60.

Jacobs, R. L. "Hyperinflation and the Supply of Money," Journal of Money, Credit and Banking 9 (1979): 287–303.

Khan, Mohsin S. "The Monetary Dynamics of Hyperinflation: A Note," Journal of Monetary Economics 1 (1975): 355–62.

Khan, M. S. "The Variability of Expectations in Hyperinflations," Journal of Political Economy 85 (1977): 817–24.

Laursen, Karsten, and Pedersen, Jørgen. The German Inflation, 1918–1923 (Amsterdam, 1964).

Miller, M. H. and Orr, D. "A Model of the Demand for Money by Firms," Quarterly Journal of Economics 53 (1966): 413–35.

Mussa, Michael. "Adaptive and Regressive Expectations in a Rational Model of the Inflationary Process," Journal of Monetary Economics 1 (1975): 423–42.

Sargent, Thomas J. "Demand for Money during Hyperinflations under Rational Expectations: I," International Economic Review 18 (1977): 59–82.

Sargent, Thomas J., and Wallace, Neil. "Rational Expectations and the Dynamics of Hyperinflations," International Economic Review 14 (1973): 328–50.

Schacht, Hjalmar. The Stabilization of the Mark (New York, 1927).

Stolper, Gustav. The German Economy, 1870–1940 (New York: 1940).

Tobin, James. "The Interest Elasticity of Transactions Demand for Cash," Review of Economics and Statistics 80 (1956): 314–24.

Walters, A. A. "Consistent Expectations, Distributed Lags, and the Quantity Theory," Economic Journal 81 (1971): 273–81.

Whalen, E. L. "A Rationalization of the Precautionary Demand for Cash," Quarterly Journal of Economics 80 (1966): 314–24.

Williams, John H. "German Foreign Trade and the Reparations Payments," Quarterly Journal of Economics 36 (1922): 482–503.

Tax Policies, Tax Assessment and Inflation: Toward a Sociology of Public Finances in the German Inflation 1914–1923*

PETER-CHRISTIAN WITT

I

It was no accident that during the First World War the study of public finance was stimulated in a new direction by Rudolf Goldscheid and Joseph A. Schumpeter. The uncontested view held until this time was that the study of finance was the "theory of the state budget."[1] This, however, was shown to be too purely formal an approach in light of the finance policies practiced by Germany and Austria during the war to cover the enormous war costs and the political and social problems which arose from them. It was shown to be an approach unsuitable not only for identifying the problem, but also for developing solutions to the problems. In any case, the science of public finance, Rudolf Goldscheid believed, eventually must make the focus of its research interests the "conditioning by society of the state budget and the latter's reciprocal function as a conditioner of social development."[2] In this way it would become theoretically adequate to deal with not only the economic aspects of finance, but also its political aspects. This would enable it to develop strategies for shaping of public finance during, and still more importantly, after the war.

Joseph A. Schumpeter took up Goldscheid's idea and generalized it with his inimitable intellectual clarity:

> Finances are [according to his apodictically formulated view] one of the best points of attack for researching the social mechanism and particularly, although not exclusively, the political mechanism. The fruitfulness of this approach is especially demonstrated when applied at a point of transition or, better said, period of transition, in which the existing financial techniques are dying out and giving way to new ones and there are continual financial crises under the old techniques. This is equally the case with respect to causal factors, in so far as developments in the realm of state finances are an important causal element in every other sort

of change, as it is with respect to symptomatic factors, insofar as everything which occurs impinges upon the realm of finances.[3]

The point of Schumpeter and Goldscheid is that with the formulation of a new, future-oriented, and (in contrast to the existing traditional scale), decidedly expanded set of problems for the study of finance, a much more promising beginning for the investigation of the past was also being offered. In particular, a means was presented to investigate the most recent past starting from the beginning of the industrial age in which an ever-larger portion of the social product in whatever form was involved in state-regulated taxation and distribution policy. In the the study of finance, however, some research problems, despite very promising beginnings,[4] were not pursued in sufficient measure; namely, analyzing the state budget from the point of view of its "conditioning by society . . . and its reciprocal function as a conditioner of social development" and using this as a scale of measurement for the "political and social condition of the state," and how this reciprocal conditioning process functioned as a means of inducing as well as hindering the process of social and political change.[5] On the whole in the discipline of history the analysis of state finances has been almost entirely neglected.[6]

The investigation of public finances is a very promising point of departure particularly for the analysis of the sources and consequences of hyperinflation; particularly as all hyperinflations of the twentieth century are causally bound with the state's taxation and distribution policies during both war and the confusion of revolution. Certainly an analysis of the state budget cannot be satisfied with previously widely held naive assumptions such as those recently expressed by Heinz Haller in his study on "The Role of State Finances for the Inflationary Process."[7] In this he says that Germany was pulled into inflation through the war and that the post-war inflation was "finally the unavoidable result of the lost war." Furthermore, Germany did not find itself as Great Britain did in the "fortunate situation to have disposal over a system of taxation which could be immediately harnessed for war financing." And in the postwar period, had Germany had "a government which would have immediately put rigorous tax measures into effect" it would have had "as good as no chance for survival." Put more emphatically, it was precisely the renunciation of rigorous taxation and the conscious acceptance of inflation which "secured the parliamentary system for the period of the Weimar Republic."

The last assertion might easily be viewed ironically — the parliamentary system of the Weimar Republic, to whose security the "great inflation" apparently contributed so decisively, did not last all that long as a functioning entity, but was already finished as such by 1930.

And, although it could be pertinently argued following Haller's reasoning that if avoiding a higher tax burden in the postwar period was at all a goal of the administration (which according to this argument first gave it a chance of survival) then attention should be given at this point to an important fact in Haller's presentation of evidence: he concedes without reservation — completely in agreement with the results already produced by contemporaries — that the public finance policy of Germany in and after the First World War was a decisive causal factor in the German inflation of 1914–23. But his interest ends with the merest assertion of this phenomenon; in reality it must be the point of departure for further inquiry. Taxation policies are not the result of fate or coincidence. The real task, therefore, lies in the analysis of the social and political power constellations behind the formulation of finance policy or governmental financial systems which determine the capability of governments to react to altered situations with altered methods.

If it is correct therefore that the public finance policies of Germany represent the essential source of inflation, so with reference to Rudolf Goldscheid's dictum for the analysis of the conditioning by society of inflation and the reciprocal function of inflation's conditioning of social development, a structural investigation of public finances in war and the postwar period becomes theoretically a particularly promising point of departure. Within the limits of this essay this objective is not realizable. Therefore, after a short analysis of wartime financial policy as an expression of the distribution of power in the German Empire, and an equally short sketch of the conceptions of financial and tax policy held by the postwar governments — which, above all, stresses the novel quality of the financial policies developed by them — we turn to the social conditioning of inflation and its reciprocal function as a conditioner of social development with help from an analysis of the causal relationship between tax assessment and inflation. The shift of the question to be investigated from the connection between tax *policy* and inflation to the connection between tax *assessment* and inflation can be easily justified theoretically and is meaningful in that only by being so formulated can it lead to satisfactory answers.[8] In practical application this procedure necessitates dropping into the quagmire of "everyday" policy making and of even more "everyday" actual administrative practice (probably a contributing reason why the theoretical insight into the importance of this question has not been complemented by practical research in this area).

II

There are few differences of opinion among researchers on the actual results of German wartime financial policies; namely, the incapacity to finance a significant portion of the additional expenditures for the war from current or additional tax income[9] resulted in rapidly rising long-term indebtedness. And since the end of 1916, as the consolidation of intermediary financing through treasury note credits was no longer successful, the result was a rapidly accelerating increase in the quantity of money. Of particular significance from the standpoint of the distribution of burdens in all this, was that the payment of interest and amortization of the Reich debt required the entire tax income of the Reich. The situation in the federal states looked somewhat better as a whole owing principally to the Reich's assuming many of their mandatory expenditures.[11] For the communal finances, on the other hand, which were particularly affected by social expenditures, there are only a few reliable accounts and absolutely no general balance. Certainly one can assume, with a high probability of correctness, an increased imbalance between income and expenditure, since communities, too, were allowed to practice large-scale financing of their expenditures through new indebtedness.[12] All three administrative bodies of the Reich during World War I therefore gave up all claim to finance by taxation either the increased direct or indirect burdens of the public sector which developed as a result of the war. Nor did they even try to undertake such financing through long-term loans. On the contrary, they financed an essential portion, about half, through floating short-term loans.

This very comparison of the financial policy of all three types of territorial bodies in the Reich during the First World War shows that an interpretation of Germany's wartime financing that primarily emphasizes the weak constitutional position of the Reich in financial matters falls short of the mark. It could, to be sure, explain why the Reich could or wished to employ direct taxes upon income and property only toward the end of the war, and then very hesitatingly, but it would help little in explaining the failure of the federal states and the communities to increase these taxes drastically — a possibility which fell within their provenance under the dominant constitutional interpretation.[13] Of equally little explanatory value is referring to the "seduction" of responsible statesmen and public opinion by the idea of being able to place the "lead weight" of war costs on the enemy.[14] The interpretation which argues that the political truce introduced at the beginning of the war drastically reduced the freedom of action of responsible leaders and made impossible practically any alteration in financial jurisdiction as between the central government and the federal states as well as any redistribution of the relative burdens among the various social strata is also caught up in a concentration on superficial phenomena.

This interpretation can, however, be the point of departure for an analysis of the causes. This has to apply first to the distribution of expenditures and income among the federal government, states, and communities. Without going into minute details, the distribution of expenditures was as follows: the central government had to bear, besides the financially practically insignificant functions, such as the establishment of legal uniformity and representing the nation abroad, only the defense or war burdens as really cost-intensive functions. In contrast, the states and communities divided among themselves all the remaining expenditures; in particular they took care of almost all the welfare functions. To meet these expenditures, indirect (consumption) taxes and excises stood at the central government's disposal; at the states' and communities' disposal, next to their extensive productive property in agriculture, transport, and industrial enterprises, stood the taxes on personal income and property as well as inheritance. Such a system of division of expenditures and finance sources between superior and subordinate territorial bodies was and is not unusual in federal states. The actual problem developed in Germany because the political representation — the chances for individual social groups and political parties to achieve their goals, or even the possibility of sharing in the political decision-making process at the different levels of nation, states and communities — was deeply divided. At the national level, at least in principle, if not in fact, democratic suffrage was in effect. Almost all the federal states and communities, in contrast, had unequal, chiefly plutocratic suffrage.[15]

This division was the actual source of the inflexibility in the distribution of the sources of revenue between the federal government on one side and the states and communities on the other and was already evident before World War I. It also blocked all attempts for a new organization during the war although the expenditures of the central government had increased drastically while those of the states and communities were relatively reduced. The slogan which the conservatives expressed before the war with remarkable frankness was that direct taxes could not be allowed "in the hands of a parliamentary body elected on equal suffrage."[16] This opinion, to be sure, was no longer articulated with the same kind of brutal openness. Instead, reference was made as legitimization to the historical nature of the system which had developed.[17] In practice, however, the ruling conservatives in the Prussian parliament shortsightedly clung to this goal and through the Prussian state ministry which was dependent upon it, succeeded in blocking all attempts toward a stronger exploitation of direct taxation by the federal government.[18] Blocking of this transfer of direct taxation to the Reich did not, however, hinder the federal states from at least tapping these sources of revenue themselves. But with the exception of smaller and financially weaker states which saw themselves compelled to make a considerable increase in the tax rate, the states declared themselves satisfied with minimal corrections.[19] Beyond that they even undermined the efforts, undertaken too late in any case, to unify or at least make similar the tax schedules among the federal states.[20]

Perhaps more politically and financially significant — in any case more burdensome to future tax policies than the unsuccessful extension of direct taxes — was the dominating conservatives' successful opposition in Prussia, to the creation of a specialized technical tax administration. Furthermore, as a kind of old estate prerogative, they kept for themselves the privilege that the assessment of all direct taxes was to be subject only to a vote of officials, the Landräte, chosen from their own social class.[21] Thus it was made certain, as one of those involved put it, that "the Prussian Junker had and held so much that his ancestral estate was maintained and that he was able to send his sons into the service of the king as soldiers and officials."[22] In other words, the ruling class added to its position of strong political privilege through the Prussian voting system and strong social privilege through the selection of officials during the war[23] the additional means of tax power "to heighten their own prosperity and to strengthen their economic position."[24] In such questions of social and political division of power, not in constitutional abstractions, is to be found the causes which determined the war financing of the German Reich and which laid a massive foundation for the inflation of the postwar years.

III

The political revolution of November 1918 swept away the existing barriers preventing a rational disposition of finances, severe taxation of income, property, and inheritance and an effective tax administration. The representatives of the previously privileged strata also[25] understood this and in the first months of the revolution, the so-called Erzberger finance program, which laid the basis of reform was conceived.[26] More important, the revolutionary government put together a series of resolutions affecting expenditure which added a debt of approximately 20.6 billion marks[27] for the rest of the projected budget year 1918 and the budget year 1919. The financial means of covering this debt (besides the issuance of treasury notes) existed neither theoretically nor practically because the legal diversity inherited from the empire meant that building up the new system of German taxation would necessarily take a long time.[28] Apparently the practice which had originated in the empire simply repeated itself. The ruling social class — and this was the workers during the relevant period discussed here (November 1918 to spring 1919) — essentially used their control over government expenditures "to increase their own prosperity."

Incontestably, almost all these additional expenditures brought the broad mass of the population some form of social benefit and were explicitly directed toward winning greater justice in distribution. To emphasize this aspect alone, however, would not satisfactorily characterize the goals which were pursued at that time. For in reality the finance policy was imbedded in a well-considered concept of an integrated economic, social, and financial policy intended to overcome the evident economic difficulties after the war's end. This would be achieved by means of a cyclical policy (*Konjunkturpolitik*) financed with deficit spending which would simultaneously guarantee economic growth, social security, and political democracy.[29] Financing the additional expenditures was authorized through short-term indebtedness and their inflation-stimulating tendencies were consciously taken into account — by all the socially relevant interest groups, because at first such a policy appeared to improve the lot of everyone without hurting anyone. Certainly the government had foreseen deficit financing only for the period of the "transition economy" (*Übergangswirtschaft*). Thereafter it promised on the basis of the comprehensive finance program developed at the same time, to be able not only to cover current expenditures, but also to create a surplus of debt amortization.[30]

The particulars of this finance program cannot be gone into here; its essential legal characteristics were as follows: (1) exclusive competence of the Reich; the central government assumed legal jurisdiction and administrative sovereignty over all taxes and levies; (2) the central government was required to establish a legal framework for the entire tax law and for the management of public income and expenditures; (3) the central government claimed all taxes falling on income, property, and inheritance, all consumption taxes and excises, and permitted the states and communities a certain freedom to negotiate only on taxes on real property. That meant that the subordinate administrative units would depend for much of their income on grants from the national taxes.

Materially the finance program contained, on the one hand, increase of existing excises and consumption taxes as well as an essential increase in the general sales tax which had already been introduced during the war. On the other hand, the program received a bundle of completely newly conceived direct taxes, of which the most important were the inheritance tax (legacy, inheritance yields, and gift tax), property tax (capital levy, tax on war profits), and finally, the income tax (income tax on natural persons, capital gains tax as a base tax, corporation tax). The yield relationship between indirect and direct taxes in their final state should have been 35 to 65 percent. This program was pushed through the law-making machinery of the Reich between August 1919 and March 1920 with relatively few changes in the government's proposals. Measured against the time taken to pass the prewar finance program which spent much less, this was a very short period. The leading politicians and particularly Erzberger objected repeatedly to the haste: there was not enough time to explore all the legal ramifications and it would make continous amendments necessary to improve it. But measured against the financial necessities of the government, the time taken was already a fatal delay in the attempt to stop the sources of inflation in the national budget. The central government had to raise its floating debt yet another 53 billion marks to a total of 130 billion marks between August 1919 and August 1920, the period of the first income flow from the new tax program.[31] To be sure, much was to be said for the fact that after the successful passage of single laws at the end of 1919, the mere existence of the reform program exercised a positive influence against depreciation of the mark, and the final passage of all the laws of the program at the end of March 1920 essentially contributed to the relative stabilization of the mark which followed.[32]

IV

The result of the great tax reform of Mattias Erzberger never fulfilled the expectations placed on it. In the budget year 1920 the taxes brought exactly 36 percent, in 1921 barely 45 percent, in budget year 1922 about 35 percent, and in the rump budget 1923 (March–December) exactly 11 percent of the income necessary to cover expenditures.[33] Exceptional increases in expenditures did not play a decisive role in this reduced proportionate coverage of expenditures from taxation. On the contrary, in the budget years 1920–1922, public expenditures of all territorial entities continuously diminished. Only in budget year 1923 did they greatly increase, and only as a reuslt of the Ruhr occupation.[34] An analysis of the sources of this failure could only be conditionally explained by the appended alterations to the final group of tax laws which had the effect of somewhat reducing the direct taxes.[35] Although these later laws reflected the symptomatic agitation against the alleged "unbearable tax burdens" carried out by interest groups from industry, commerce, the middle class, and agriculture, the alterations in the tax law which actually came into effect were too insignificant to explain the meager net result.[36]

In this context other factors were much more important. To begin with, the German tax system operated, with respect to indirect (consumption) taxes and tariffs, generally speaking, on taxation schedules based on quantity; that is, a tax levy of a set amount in marks on a legally established quantity of a product. In this system, the price of the product was of no interest to the taxing authorities. Only in a few cases was it foreseen in the tax or customs regulations that the tax contribution by quantity did not always remain the same, but that with increased quality and price the tax also increased. In these cases too, however, no attempt was made to make some link between price of the product and level of the tax in the form of a percentage tax payment which varied with price. A phenomenon accompanying this system was that, with increasing currency depreciation, the real percentage tax per quantity of a product continuously went down — in other words, this system of tax rates exhibited little responsiveness to inflation. If the originally intended tax burden was to be restored, legal measures would have been required which would have entailed tedious political conflicts. Only in three cases did the German system deviate from the general principles of organization: namely, in the general sales tax and in the coal tax, established during the First World War, which taxed a fixed percent of sales, i.e., the sales price determined the tax burden, and in a series of tariffs which in 1919 managed at least partially to encompass the actual import price beyond the so-called gold excise premium. The higher responsiveness to inflation of the last-named taxes and excises ensured, however, that the relative significance of the indirect taxes and excises for the entire tax intake, with the exception of the year 1920, lay continuously above Erzberger's intended 35 percent quota in the finance program.[37]

The same problem was exhibited in the tax rates of the so-called direct taxes, i.e., income, capital gains, corporation, inheritance, legacy, and gift taxes as well as the one-time tax conceived of as a tax on wealth in the form of a capital levy (*Reichsnotopfer*). The applied graduated rate used for tax assessment made necessary relatively high tax rates for large incomes and great wealth or large inheritances in order to secure the desired tax yields. To be sure, not only the politicians and officials responsible for setting the tax rates, but also those really affected by the high progressive assessment at the top rate levels, were aware that the average tax burden was very much less oppressive than it gave the appearance of being.[38] It was, however, maintained, not only for the usual narrow practical reasons or because this system had a tradition in Germany, but because in two respects it permitted the exercise of first-rate demagoguery. To the enemy demanding reparations, it was possible to maintain that oppressive taxes were being imposed, but unfortunately reparation payments could still not be met.[39] In internal political conflicts, the same argument could be used with all groups demanding that a heavier burden fall upon "business" or the "rich." Note that this system, which became a vehicle of political demogoguery, was not originally created by opponents of effective progressive taxation of large incomes and wealth, but by Social Democratic tax policy makers who, in the individual federal states after the revolution, had set, for example, the income tax schedules for 1919 for especially high incomes in the last tax bracket at over 100 percent of the income liable to taxation. At the same time they carefully made sure that in their tax districts there were no taxpayers who received such incomes and who would be obligated to pay such a tax.[40]

The existing tax rate system negatively influenced the tax yield only in the case of most of the indirect taxes and excises — though the door was opened wide to political demogoguery with respect to direct taxes — but the system of tax assessment proved to be a financial catastrophe. At the same time it became important that the fragmented bureaucratic authorities had laboriously to create a unified finance administration when the new taxes were introduced.[41] This fact played an important, but not a decisive role. More important were the factors imminent in every assessment system: first, after the legally stipulated period there followed a declaration of the taxpayer to the tax offices of the relevant tax particulars. Only then was the tax office in a position to determine the amount of tax and demand payment. This tedious process, depending on the kind of tax being assessed, could require from a very few months up to two or three years between fixing and paying the tax because of the very complicated data usually involved. Once this system was in operation, it would cease to be problematic since, after the first regular assessment it would be possible to collect by means of prepayment at least approximately correct tax yields from each current tax year. The critical moment was the first assessment since there would be no flow of income for a certain period.

The situation would have been even more critical when nothing resembling stable monetary conditions obtained, but rather open inflation, because then the deficit in the state budget grows as a consequence of the missing tax yields, thereby heating inflation and serving as an incentive to the taxpayer to delay at each separate step of assessment: making a tax declaration, getting the tax amount, and paying it. This delay was accomplished by using all the legal devices in all the tax laws which necessarily provide for the protection of the taxpayer.

In Germany, generally speaking, even for the most indirect taxes, a post facto assessment system was in effect in the case where the person owing the tax and the actual taxpayer were not the same person. For example, for the sales tax a quarter year was foreseen as the tax period after which the taxpayer had to send in a record of his sales. A month after expiry of this tax period, a tax declaration had to be submitted and after the subsequent determination of the tax indebtedness by the tax office, payment had to be made within 14 days.[42] In practice this meant that even during periods of stable money values, the person owing the tax had an interest-free operating credit for several months. Under inflationary conditions, this meant not only that in real terms the treasury received only a portion of the outstanding amount owed while the taxpayer profited from the interest, but also — as he quickly recognized — the difference between the real value of the taxes when they were being created and when they were paid. In principle the consumer bore the full intended tax burden.[43] As consumption taxes through the assessment system revealed themselves under inflationary conditions as a system of redistribution among private persons, so did the assessment system of the direct taxes lead not only to a radical reduction of the intended tax debt, but also a radical reversal in the planned distribution of the tax burden among the taxpayers. This was true for the direct taxes in so far as there was no provision, as in the case with the straight capital gains tax, of a 10 percent tax at the source and only later payment was foreseen on the assessment of income. This will be illustrated here by the center piece of the Erzberger tax reform, the income tax.[44]

In the financial planning for 1919 it was projected that the income tax should bring in approximately one-third of the national tax income; by the same token, it should realize from the estimated 25 million taxpayers on small and medium incomes from up to 14,000 marks per year (at the time the law was introduced in the Reichstag this corresponded to approximately 2600 marks in 1913 prices) should provide about 30 percent of receipts, whereas the approximately 5 million taxpayers with higher incomes would provide about 70 percent. The tax rate schedule and the progression of tax brackets were arranged with this objective in mind.[45]

But actually, except for 1922, the receipts from income tax never reached that which had been planned, and the distribution of the tax burden on small and medium incomes on the one hand and on larger incomes on the other turned out dramatically differently from that which the creators of the income tax law had anticipated. If one searches for the causes of this development, one is compelled to consider the problem of assessment. Because of the very different legal arrangements among the old state income taxes and as a result of the Reich's using the states' assessments for convenience, the first year of the national income tax produced differing tax burdens for persons with the same income although the tax law had foreseen a complete revision of the assessment system. After the expiration of the tax for fiscal year 1920, the first assessment according to the new law was made in order to create, so to speak, the same conditions for all taxpayers.[46] On the other side it was naturally seen by the officials creating the law that the initial assessment involving more than 30 million taxpayers would inevitably lead to a complete breakdown of the tax administration. Furthermore for the many millions of taxpayers, who received income only from wages or salaries, a post facto application of taxes would be accompanied by considerable practical difficulties — this, in any case, was the experience with older federal state incomes taxes. Therefore they had in principle an ingenious idea: to burden all wage and salary earners with a straight tax rate of 10 percent and oblige the respective employers to deduct this tax from the wage or salary payments at the source (pay as you earn system, PAYE). With this method, two birds would be killed with one stone: first, the tax offices would be freed of an immense workload; at the same time, they would be assured that the tax on wage and salary earners would actually be applied. To be sure, a post facto assessment was also projected for them, but, because the tax rate was chosen in such a way that a great majority of the wage and salary earners actually had paid their taxes by a wage deduction, this post facto assessment was not relevant financially and also could be omitted if need be. Through these technical tax regulations developed in principle three classes of income taxpayers: (1) Those who paid only wage taxes. (2) Those whose wage or salary income was not sufficiently taxed through the 10 percent base deduction and/or had other sources of income. (3) Those who possessed income from property owning, industry, or capital investment, or self-employment and lay exclusively under post facto assessment.

Tables 1–3 show the financial results of the income tax for 1920–22.[47] An important fact becomes quite clear from Table 2, namely, the relative significance of the income tax within the total tax income, even if the projections were never fulfilled. The other important fact is that in fiscal year 1920 only the wage tax was paid in and, with the exception of just a few months in the first half-year 1922, the wage tax continuously provided a far higher portion of tax yields than the assessed income tax; in only a single month, February 1922, did the relationship between the wage tax and the assessed income tax stand at 30 percent to 70 percent somewhat as the drafters of the law had conceived (compare Table 1). The relatively high ability of the wage tax to respond to inflation as a base tax made this result just about impossible to avoid, although one should note that real tax income out of the wage tax could have been very much higher had employers not increasingly delayed in paying the deducted wage tax and thus created for themselves at the cost of the employee and the state treasury an interest-free operating credit whose real repayment value declined with the increasing acceleration of the inflation.[48] In Table 3 an attempt is made to compare the theoretical assessment results and the real yields of the wage and income tax. Here it is shown that the assessment results which, it might be noted, were continuously used in political propaganda internally and externally,[49] were as good as worthless. According to the assessment, those taxpayers who should have paid only on their wages (57–67 percent of all taxpayers) should contribute only about 28 percent in 1920, about 18 percent in 1921, and about

14 percent in 1922. They actually paid for 1920, some 52 percent, for 1921, about 53 percent, and for 1922, about 37 percent of the assessed tax balance. For they continuously paid 100 percent of their tax in real terms, while the other taxpayers paid in real terms only about 36 percent (1920), 19 percent (1921), and 27 percent (1922).

Table 1. Yield of Income Tax (million marks)

1	Total 2	PAYE 3	% col. 2 4	Assessed Income Tax 5	% col. 2 6
1920 April	—	—	—	—	—
May	—	—	—	—	—
June	44.3	44.3	100	—	—
July	394.3	394.3	100	—	—
Aug.	553.9	553.9	100	—	—
Sept.	769.6	769.6	100	—	—
Oct.	1080.7	1080.7	100	—	—
Nov.	1403.4	1403.4	100	—	—
Dec.	1458.1	1458.1	100	—	—
1921 Jan.	1321.6	1321.6	100	—	—
Feb.	1239.7	1239.7	100	—	—
March	1975.4	1975.4	100	—	—
Budget Year 1920/21	10241.0	10241.0	100	—	—
1921 April	1040	968	93	72	7
May	1103	957	87	146	13
June	1163	963	83	200	17
July	1367	879	64	488	36
Aug.	1409	764	54	645	46
Sept.	1276	653	51	623	49
Oct.	1791	980	55	811	45
Nov.	2064	1026	50	1038	50
Dec.	2763	1584	57	1179	43
1922 Jan.	3489	2264	65	1225	35
Feb.	4431	1349	30	3082	70
March	7816	3390	43	4426	57
Budget Year 1921/22	29712	15777	53	13935	47
1922 April	4299	2192	51	2107	49
May	5746	2871	50	2875	50
June	5812	3397	58	2415	42

July	7687	4773	62	2914	38
Aug.	9933	5675	57	4258	43
Sept.	13851	8079	58	5772	42
Oct.	21895	15757	72	6138	28
Nov.	29119	22071	75	7048	25
Dec.	48053	39506	82	8547	18
1923 Jan.–					
March	387046	336580	87	50466	13
Budget Year					
1922/23	533441	440901	83	92540	17

Note: The total yield of the income tax as well as the yield of PAYE and assessed income tax are shown in marks (current value); by this the figures for the budgets 1920 to 1922 are fairly meaningless, only the monthly figures show the relative importance of PAYE and assessed income tax, respectively. Nevertheless the figures for the budgets are important in the respect that they were used in the political maneuvers of political parties and economic interest groups.

Source: ZSTA Potsdam, RFM Nr. 1100–1120 (Files on the assessment and date of payment of the income tax — "pay as you earn" — system and assessed income tax.)

Why this evident disproportionality was tolerated cannot be explained without knowledge of the actual process of assessment. Although severe political conflicts had taken place at the actual introduction of the wage tax and the payers of this tax had opposed deductions with strikes,[50] all the political and social groups finally agreed that the utilization of the wage tax was unavoidable for administrative and financial reasons. And they all recognized, at least verbally, that the wage tax regulation demanded as a necessary compensation a speedy assessment of those taxpayers subject only to an assessed income tax and a similarly speedy collection of the tax burden established for these persons for 1920 as well as the resulting prepayments for 1921 and correspondingly for 1922 thereby established.

The sharply worded instructions to the tax authorities which were issued by Finance Minister Wirth emphasized this point constantly: it was absolutely necessary to get on with the work of assessment with the greatest of speed, so that "the complaints of the wage and salary earners about their priority in being burdened in contrast to the other taxpayers would finally lose its basis."[51] At first these warnings remained without result; only in the last quarter of 1921 were the tax offices able to send out the tax bills for 1920 and thereby also demand realistic prepayments for 1921, and finally in the months between May and July 1922 the tax bills for those with particularly large incomes were sent out in substantial numbers.[52] For the first time in the taxation of incomes the assessed taxpayers appeared to be required to make

Table 2. Income of the Central Government (million marks deflated by cost of living index, yield of government borrowing and taxes shown as % of total)

1	Total	Treas. Bills	Taxes Total	Income PAYE	Tax assess.	Capital Levy	Estate, etc. Duties	Sales Tax	Alcohol, Tobacco	Import Duties	Export Duties	Coal Tax	Misc. Taxes
	2	3	4	5	6	7	8	9	10	11	12	13	14
1920 April	419.6	80.48	16.87	—	—	0.02	3.47	2.54	3.64	2.92	—	3.16	1.12
May	700.7	83.77	14.64	—	—	0.51	3.25	1.09	2.99	1.90	—	3.95	0.95
June	1244.3	85.73	13.37	0.33	—	1.33	2.23	0.67	2.08	1.53	—	3.32	1.88
July	1133.1	79.08	19.95	3.28	—	1.12	2.42	0.59	2.48	1.29	—	3.67	5.10
Aug.	880.8	73.95	23.98	6.11	—	0.69	3.23	0.97	2.62	0.93	—	4.22	5.21
Sept.	1111.6	77.37	21.64	6.85	—	0.99	2.54	0.98	0.95	1.04	1.95	3.67	2.67
Oct.	527.4	41.05	56.84	19.15	—	5.14	6.62	2.16	4.99	3.15	3.05	6.22	6.36
Nov.	1032.5	60.39	38.32	12.12	—	4.96	3.68	1.48	2.87	1.81	2.71	3.65	5.04
Dec.	1083.8	42.01	56.97	11.60	—	20.23	7.48	1.34	2.81	1.73	1.17	3.91	6.70
1921 Jan.	805.0	27.78	70.84	13.89	—	23.41	4.53	7.99	3.63	2.41	2.75	3.66	8.57
Feb.	1145.5	47.89	51.14	9.41	—	11.81	4.61	9.86	2.98	1.95	1.66	3.06	5.80
March	1181.6	48.15	50.91	10.04	—	12.36	3.91	8.50	4.13	1.62	1.07	3.87	5.41
Budget 1920/21	1265.6	62.51	36.31	7.65	—	7.26	3.90	3.30	2.86	1.72	1.18	3.77	4.67
1921 April	1040.7	53.76	45.43	8.23	0.61	13.38	4.42	8.26	2.58	2.18	1.05	1.35	5.95
May	911.6	39.26	59.82	9.37	1.43	14.67	9.30	10.21	3.29	2.33	0.58	3.51	5.13
June	1223.0	58.78	40.53	6.73	1.40	8.74	5.22	5.54	2.93	2.06	4.60	2.80	0.51
July	905.2	49.88	49.19	7.77	4.31	7.88	7.21	6.25	3.41	3.68	0.62	3.42	4.64
Aug.	1302.3	69.72	29.64	4.41	3.72	3.39	4.04	3.72	2.29	2.06	0.47	2.57	2.97
Sept.	921.1	60.31	38.78	5.18	4.95	3.16	4.99	3.94	4.78	3.35	0.74	4.33	3.36
Oct.	913.1	54.04	45.04	7.15	5.92	3.43	7.39	5.17	3.15	5.33	1.02	4.03	2.45
Nov.	892.4	54.59	44.46	6.50	6.57	4.52	6.22	5.49	3.27	3.93	1.52	3.42	3.02
Dec.	1484.5	71.43	28.00	5.53	4.12	1.64	4.42	3.19	2.25	1.60	1.57	2.03	3.29
1922 Jan.	868.7	49.38	49.65	12.78	6.91	1.80	7.25	6.07	2.68	2.99	2.76	4.58	1.83
Feb.	692.7	42.08	56.71	7.95	18.16	1.33	6.89	6.16	3.64	3.44	2.74	4.76	1.64
March	808.6	38.92	60.04	11.46	15.19	1.06	6.85	8.21	3.69	4.34	3.38	4.63	1.23

Budget 1921/22	11963.6	55.40	44.52	7.47	5.44	5.46	5.96	5.80	3.07	2.95	1.73	3.28	3.36
1922 April	650.2	40.28	59.06	9.80	9.42	1.11	7.66	11.32	7.81	3.23	3.97	4.06	0.68
May	686.4	31.83	67.54	11.01	11.02	2.13	8.99	16.74	3.89	3.28	3.74	6.09	0.65
June	573.2	24.48	74.77	14.28	10.15	1.26	10.22	10.15	6.23	5.72	3.95	12.30	0.51
July	640.3	36.92	62.41	13.83	8.44	0.77	6.15	11.48	3.31	5.22	4.58	7.93	0.70
Aug.	712.4	42.55	56.88	10.27	7.70	1.19	4.79	16.66	3.86	3.40	3.79	5.67	0.29
Sept.	1139.9	78.75	20.87	5.32	3.80	0.21	2.03	1.99	1.54	1.72	2.67	1.51	0.08
Oct.	923.9	74.92	24.61	7.73	3.01	0.23	2.01	3.60	1.16	2.13	3.19	1.47	0.08
Nov.	892.4	69.03	30.41	6.47	2.07	0.18	2.07	5.08	2.29	1.90	8.07	2.21	0.07
Dec.	1155.5	82.87	16.75	4.99	1.08	0.06	1.42	1.25	1.05	1.17	3.20	2.51	0.02
1923 Jan.	779.7	67.18	32.27	9.42	1.40	0.09	2.20	4.95	1.50	2.20	2.80	7.70	0.01
Feb.	702.1	81.19	18.20	4.87	0.73	0.01	1.61	4.47	1.37	1.13	3.10	1.45	0.83
March	1237.4	85.32	14.34	4.65	0.69	0.01	2.09	1.18	0.82	0.71	1.33	2.82	0.04
Budget 1922/23	9965.0	64.07	35.41	7.90	4.29	0.50	3.73	6.35	2.52	2.36	3.46	4.13	0.17

Note: The figures are adjusted according to the original accounts of the Reichshauptkasse.
Source: Übersicht der Einnahmen des Reiches, Reichsministerialblatt 1920–1923; Übersicht über die Bewegungen der Reichshauptkasse 1920–1923, BA Koblenz, R 43 I Nr. 2356 ff. ZSTA Potsdam, RFM Nr. 859; ZSTA Potsdam, RFM Nr. 1100–1120.

Table 3. Income Tax (number of taxpayers, yield of tax assessment, real value of income tax paid)

Currency totals, million marks	Budget 1920/21 April 1920– March 1921	Tax Year 1921 April–Dec.	Tax Year 1922 Jan.–Dec.
1. Total number of taxpayers (million)	30.5	29.8	29.7
2. Taxpayers subject only to PAYE (mill.)	17.4	16.8	20.1
3. %	57.1	56.4	67.7
4. Taxpayers subject to PAYE and assessed income tax (mill.)	7.9	7.9	4.7
5. %	25.9	26.5	15.8
6. Taxpayers subject only to ass. income tax (mill.)	5.2	5.1	5.0
7. %	17.0	17.1	16.5
8. Total yield of income tax (mill. marks)	28297	42316	490000
9. Yield of income tax by taxpayers subject only to PAYE	7900	7545	68000
10. Yield of income tax of taxpayers subject to PAYE and ass. income tax	20397	34771	422000
11. Real value of yield of income tax, deflated by cost-of-living index: total	2586	3030	3258
12. Real value of PAYE (cf. col. 9)	722	540	452
13. Real value of PAYE & ass. income tax (cf. col. 10)	1864	2490	2806
14. Real value of PAYE paid by taxpayers subject only to PAYE	722	540	452
15. Real value of PAYE by taxpayers subject to PAYE & ass. inc. tax	140	94	426

16. Real value of ass. income tax paid by taxpayers	528	388	331
17. Col. 15 and col. 16 as % of col. 13	35.8	19.4	27.0
18. Yield of income tax collected by the Reichshauptkasse	862	977	1592

realistic payments. This progress was destroyed through an explosive increase in the prices indexes, and real income from the assessed income tax began once again to sink continuously until in nearly 1923 at the end of the budget year 1922, it still contributed monthly only a few million gold marks (deflated against the cost of living index). The multiplier which was finally introduced in March 1923 for the prepayments and the income tax debt of 1921 in principle changed nothing, as they were introduced too late and with much too small a factor.[53]

The temporal sequence of events, which becomes evident from the assessment documents, suggests the interpretation that beyond other factors, such as the willingness of the Reichsbank to discount commercial bills, the murder of Rathenau in June 1922, and the resultant growing doubts about the political stability and the economic promise of Germany, the system of tax assessment, particularly the income tax, contributed to the German inflation's finally turning into a hyperinflation in June/July 1922. At this time, the first assessed income tax as well as the corporation tax,[54] appeared to become noticeable burdens. This led to a perceptibly higher opposition to the taxes by the possessors of larger incomes as well as by juridical persons,[55] and also certainly encouraged the inclination to avoid the tax burden with the help of inflation.

Notes

* The author wishes to thank Anne MacLachlan for this translation from the German.

1. Cf. Wilhelm Gerloff, "Grundlegung der Finanzwissenschaft," in *Handbuch der Finanzwissenschaft* I (Tübingen, 1926): 1ff.

2. Rudolf Goldscheid, "Staat, öffentlicher Haushalt und Gesellschaft. Wesen und Bedeutung der Finanzsoziologie," *ibid.*, I: 147; Goldscheid, *Staatssozialismus oder Staatskapitalismus* (Jena, 1917).

3. Joseph A. Schumpeter, "Die Krise des Steuerstaates," in *Aufsätze zur Soziologie* (Tübingen, 1953; originally published 1918), pp. 5ff.

4. The most important works on this are by Fritz Karl Mann, "Finanzsoziolo-

gie, Grundsätzliche Bemerkungen," *Kölner Vierteljahreshefte zur Soziologie* 12 (1933): 1–20; "Beiträge zur Steuersoziologie," *Finanzarchiv, Neue
Folge* (1934): 281–314; "Zur Soziologie der finanzpolitischen Entscheidungen," *Schmollers Jahrbuch* 57 (1933): 705–730; "The Sociology of Taxation," *Review of Politics* 5 (1943): 225–35; "The Fiscal Component of Revolution," *ibid.*, 9 (1947): 331–49; "Die Finanzkomponente der politischen Revolutionen," *Kölner Zeitschrift für Soziologie* 4 (1951/52): 1–18; *Steuerpolitische
Ideale. Vergleichende Studien zur Geschichte der politischen und ökonomischen Ideen und ihres Wirkens in der öffentlichen Meinung 1600–1935* (Jena,
1935); in the new textbooks, such as in Günter Schmölders, *Finanzpolitik*, 3d
rev. ed. (Berlin-Heidelberg-New York, 1970), the concepts of finance sociology,
tax sociology, etc., are not even mentioned.

5. Peter-Christian Witt, "Finanzpolitik und sozialer Wandel," in H.-U. Wehler
(Ed.), *Sozialgeschichte Heute. Festschrift für Hans Rosenberg zum 70. Geburtstag* (Göttingen, 1974), pp. 565ff.

6. Among the most recent work on German finance history in which reference
is made to sociological considerations of finance, only my book *Die Finanzpolitik des Deutsches Reichen 1903–1913. Eine Studie zur Innenpolitik des Wilhelminischen Deutschland* (Lübeck-Hamburg, 1970) and several of my articles
in periodicals and collections can be mentioned.

7. *Währung und Wirtschaft in Deutschland 1876–1975*, Deutschen Bundesbank (Ed.), (Frankfurt, 1976), pp. 115–55, at p. 150.

8. Compare, for example, recent studies, such as J. Daviter, J. Könke, O. Graf
Schwerin, *Steuernorm und Steuerwirklichkeit*, vol. 1, *Steuertechnik und
Steuerpraxis in Frankreich, Grossbritannien, Italien und Deutschland* (Köln-
Opladen, 1969); B. Beichelt, B. Biervert, J. Daviter, G. Schmölders, B. Strümpel, *Steuernorm und Steuerwirklichkeit*, vol. 2, *Steuermentalität und Steuermoral in Grossbritannien, Frankreich, Italien und Spanien* (Köln-Opladen,
1969). Among older studies are the excellent works by Franz Meisel, "Wahrheit
und Fiskalismus bei der Veranlagung der modernen Einkommensteuer,"
Finanzarchiv 31, 2 (1914): 144–68 and *Britische und deutsche Einkommensteuer, ihre Moral und Technik* (Jena, 1925). The collection of essays by Fritz
Karl Mann, *Finanztheorie und Finanzsoziologie* (Göttingen, 1959), is particularly stimulating for the central question.

9. The estimates in the literature vary between 0 and 13 percent for the amount
of war expenditures financed by taxes. Cf. Robert Knauss, *Die deutsche,
englische und französische Kriegsfinanzierung* (Leipzig, 1923), p. 175; Rudolf
Will, *Die schwebenden Schulden der europäischen Grossstaaten* (Tübingen,
1921), p. 28; Walther Lotz, *Die deutsche Staatsfinanzwirtschaft im Kriege*
(Stuttgart-Berlin-Leipzig, 1927), pp. 105ff. My conclusion (based on the published material, augmented by unpublished material from the federal treasury,
in which the total army and navy costs were assigned to the war costs after the
close of the war), is that up to 97.7 percent of the expenses authorized during
the war, including servicing the debt, was covered by loans to the extent of
approximately 156 billion marks. (Cf. Peter-Christian Witt, "Die Finanz- und
Wirtschaftspolitik des Deutschen Reiches 1918–1924," unpublished, 1980,
table 4a, 4b, pp. 14ff.). Of the total expenditures of both the Reich and the
federal states in fiscal years 1914–18 amounting to 211.6 billion marks, about

81.8 percent was covered through loans, 11.1 percent through taxes, and about 7.1 percent through surpluses/profit from public enterprises.
10. Cf. Carl-Ludwig Holtfrerich, Political Factors of the German Inflation (1979), pp. 2ff.
11. In the fiscal years 1914–18, the Reich received a total of 17.4 billion marks in tax yields, from which debt service required some 17.6 billion marks. In the federal states, 6.1 billion marks were received from taxes, 3.5 billion of which went to servicing their debts. (Cf. note 9.)
12. See in addition the petitions of the mayor of Essen (17/10/1918) and German Cities Conference (24/4/1919) to the Prussian finance minister, Zentralstaats Archiv (hereafter ZStA) Merseburg, Rep. 151 II Nr. 823.
13. See on this complex question Peter-Christian Witt, Die Finanzpolitik des Deutschen Reiches, pp. 17ff.
14. Karl Helfferich (then secretary of the treasury) on 20/8/1915 in the Reichstag, Stenographische Berichte über die Verhandlungen des Reichstags 306:225.
15. See on this section, Peter-Christian Witt, "Finanzpolitik und sozialer Wandel in Krieg und Inflation," in H. Mommsen, et al. (Eds.), Industrielles System und politische Entwicklung in der Weimarer Republik (Düsseldorf, 1979), pp. 404ff., as well as Witt, "Reichsfinanzminister und Reichsfinanzverwaltung," in Vierteljahrschrift für Zeitgeschichte (hereafter VJZG) 23 (1975): 4ff.
16. The leader of the conservatives Ernst v. Heydebrand and the Lasa (10/7/1909) in the Reichstag, Stenographische Berichte über die Verhandlungen des Reichstags, 237:9322.
17. Octavio Frhr. v. Zedlitz-Neukirch, Neuaufbau der Finanzen nach dem Krieg und qualitative Sparsamkeit (Stuttgart, 1917), p. 7.
18. See on these maneuvers, documents ZStA Merseburg, Rep. 151 HB Nr. 1444 and ZStA Potsdam, Reichskanzelei (hereafter Rkz) Nr. 219. The statements by Roesler in Die Finanzpolitik des Deutschen Reiches im Ersten Weltkrieg (Berlin, 1967), pp. 103ff., limit themselves to a very superficial reference to the tax programs.
19. For particulars, see Johannes Popitz, "Einkommensteuer," Handwörterbuch der Staatswissenschaften, 4th ed., vol. 3 (Jena, 1926), pp. 400–91, esp. pp. 439–45.
20. Cf. the protocol on the results of the meeting with the federal states' finance minister (23–24/9/1918) in General Landes Archiv Karlsruhe, 237/31922, Aufz. Wagner (26/9/1918); Staats Archiv Hamburg, Senatskommission für die Reichs- und Auswärtigen Angelegenheiten II, II A I fasc. 3 Bd. 1, Aufz. Schaefer (25/9/1918).
21. Cf. Peter-Christian Witt, "Der preussischen Landrat als Steuerbeamter 1891–1918," in I. Geiss and B. J. Wendt (Eds.), Deutschland in der Weltpolitik des 19. und 20. Jahrhunderts (Düsseldorf, 1973), pp. 205–219.
22. ZStA Potsdam, Rkz Nr. 951, v. Klitzing to Bethmann Hollweg (3/5/1912).
23. Cf. in addition the report of 5/11/1918 by the general director of direct taxes in the Prussian finance ministry, ZStA Merseburg, Rep. 151 II Nr. 117.
24. Fritz Karl Mann, Finanztheorie und Finanzsoziologie (Göttingen, 1959), p. 117.

25. Cf. in addition the memoranda by conservative Otto Hoetzsch (5/11/1918), published with an introduction by the author in *VJZG* 21 (1973): 337ff.
26. Cf. in addition particularly the protocol of the Finance Ministers Conference of 29–30 January 1919, ZStA Merseburg, Rep. 151 HB Nr. 1444, maschinenschriftliches Protokoll, p. 146.
27. Peter-Christian Witt, *Die Finanz- und Wirtschaftspolitik des Deutschen Reiches*, table 12, p. 94.
28. In anticipation of a federal regulation of the tax rate, the federal states raised the income tax sharply (from the 1913 average 4.6 percent of taxable income; the 1919 average 13.1 percent of taxable income, including communal surcharges on the state income tax) without, however — insofar as this judgment is possible given the deplorable condition of the finance statistics — bringing about an essential increase in income. See "Die deutsche Einkommenbesteuerung vor und nach dem Kriege," *Statistik des Deutschen Reiches*, vol. 312 (Berlin, 1925): 24ff. (Steuertarife): 46ff. (assessment results); *Vierteljahreshefte zur Statistik des Deutschen Reiches IV* (1922): 71–113 (for the actual results of the tax assessment).
29. Cf. here Peter-Christian Witt, "Bemerkungen zur Wirtschaftspolitik in der 'Übergangswirtschaft 1918/19," in D. Stegmann et al. (Eds.), *Industrielle Gesellschaft und politisches System* (Bonn, 1978), pp. 79–96; Witt, "Capitalist Constraints upon Government Economic Policy Formation in the German Inflation, 1918–1923," paper delivered at the AHA meeting, New York, 1979.
30. *Der künftige finanzielle Bedarf des Reichs und seine Deckung. Denkschrift des Reichsfinanzministers* (5/8/1919), *Stenographische Berichte über die Verhandlungen des Reichstags*, vol. 337: 601–614. For the origins of the program see Klaus Epstein, *Matthias Erzberger und das Dilemma der deutschen Demokratie* (Berlin, 1962), pp. 369ff. as well as my own study (note 9).
31. Cf. *Deutschlands Wirtschaft, Währung und Finanzen* (Berlin, 1924), p. 62.
32. Constantino Bresciani-Turroni, *The Economics of Inflation* (London, 1937), pp. 54ff.; with respect to this, see in addition, my essay, "Finanzpolitik und sozialer Wandel," in H. Mommsen et al. (Eds.), *Industrielles System*, pp. 395–426, at p. 418. I do not want to exclude the opposite effects of the proclamatory nature of the tax program. Possibly, in the unexplained tax transference problem, the announced tax increase shifted the problem onto the consumer through the previously denied price increase.
33. Cf. *Deutschlands Wirtschaft, Währung und Finanzen* (Berlin, 1924), p. 30, table IIu.
34. Cf. Witt, "Finanzpolitik und sozialer Wandel," in Mommsen et al (Eds.), *Industrielles System*, p. 424, table I.
35. *Ibid.*, pp. 417f.
36. Cf. in addition the documents in ZStA Potsdam, RFM Nr. 915–931 and 941; the flood of the interest group organizations' own publications, the petitions to the Reichstag, and the other publicity sources cannot be listed here separately.
37. 1920, about 35 percent; 1921, approximately 38 percent; 1922, circa 53 percent; 1923 (until November), about 48 percent, *Deutschlands Wirtschaft, Währung und Finanzen*, p. 34; see table II.
38. Cf. in addition, the discussion on the income tax, Berichte über die

1–5. Sitzung der Finanzkommission (15/5–27/6/1919), General Landes Archiv Karlsruhe, 237/13318; Bericht der Unterkommission für die Einkommensteuer (18/6/1919), ZStA Potsdam, RFM Nr. 915.

39. In the Reich's finance ministry ongoing calculations were produced on the alleged tax distribution for the purposes of propaganda which — as all those involved knew perfectly well — had nothing to do with reality. See as example ZStA Potsdam, RFM Nr. 775.

40. Cf. *Die deutsche Einkommenbesteuerung vor und nach dem Kriege; Statistik des Deutschen Reiches* 312: 36ff. In Mecklenburg-Strelitz, to give an example, the tax rate for the 5 million mark excessive incomes was set at over 100 percent: this cost nothing since, according to the statistics on income tax, in this state there had never been a taxpayer whose income exceeded 1 million marks.

41. Cf. article cited in note 15.

42. Cf. sections 35ff. of the sales tax law of 26/12/1919, as well as the implementation regulations and decrees of the Reich finance ministry, ZStA Potsdam, RFM Nr. 1630.

43. This statement turns all the lovely calculations about the distribution of the tax burden among the population which the Reich finance ministry put together on the basis of paying in the tax yield into the treasury in so-called goldmarks (deflated against the cost of living index) to scrap paper.

44. Owing to the shortage of space I omit discussion of the corporation tax as an income tax on juridical persons, the capital levy, or inheritance taxes. It must be emphasized, however, that the assessment system had quite similar effects for them too.

45. Cf. Johannes Popitz, "Einkommensteuer," pp. 446ff.

46. See in this context especially Bericht der Unterkommission für die Einkommensteuer (18/6/1919), ZStA Potsdam, RFM Nr. 915.

47. The following exposition is based on a series of documents, RFM Nr. 915–931, 1100–1122 and 1197–1199, ZStA Potsdam; reference to single documents will be omitted.

48. See as exemplary the report of the president of the Hanover state finance office, 4/9/1922 (ZStA Potsdam RFM Nr. 1107), in which it is indicated that next to employers' reluctance to make wage tax deductions, there were also an increasing number of cases where the deducted wage taxes never, or only in part, reached the Reich treasury.

49. It is, by the way, by a special perfidy that Johannes Popitz, in his article on the income tax in the *Handwörterbuch der Staatswissenschaften* (see note 45) reproduced the distribution of the income tax according to tax levels for the year 1920, which would suggest to the unbiased reader that the approximately 27.3 million income taxpayers with incomes up to 14,000 marks had paid only around 27 percent of the tax while the remaining 3.2 million with higher incomes had paid 73 percent. As director of the tax section of the Reich finance ministry, Popitz naturally knew well that the taxes assessed and actually paid were divergent in the extreme.

50. Cf. the document Bundes Archiv Koblenz, R 43 I Nr. 2414; for the strike in Württemberg *Vorwärts* Nr. 429, 435, and 444 (28/8/–1/9; 7/9/1920).

51. ZStA Potsdam, RFM Nr. 1100. On 16/9/1921 there were further similar

decrees to all presidents of the state finance offices which came out every two or three months regularly and set in motion the assessment process.
52. ZStA Potsdam, RFM Nr. 1100–1120, Compilation on the State Assessment, the tax instructions sent out and the resultant tax debts for the tax years 1920/1921/1922. These compilations show significant regional differences which cannot be expanded on further due to lack of room.
53. Cf. Peter-Christian Witt, "Reichsfinanzminister und Reichsfinanzverwaltung," *VJZG* 23 (1975): 58ff.
54. Cf. ZStA Potsdam, RFM Nr. 1625, Zusammenstellungen über die Veranlagung und das Ergebnis der Körperschaftssteuer.
55. Cf. the rapidly increasing number of claims against the tax instructions (from the compilation in ZStA Potsdam, RFM Nr. 1100–1120) as well as the complaints before the finance courts (see the unpublished decisions of the Reich finance court in ZStA Potsdam, RFM Nr. 1256–1259; and the collection of decisions and recommendations of the Reich finance court, vols. 1–17, Munich 1920–25).

Part 5
East Central Europe

Inflation in Post-World War I East Central Europe

GYÖRGY RÁNKI

The circumstances that led to inflation were many and various. Nevertheless, it is not difficult to find some common roots and causes of this phenomenon in Eastern Europe. The East European inflation, therefore, may be discussed as belonging to two types: namely, hyperinflation — such as Austria-Hungary and Poland experienced — and a milder inflationary trend, experienced by the Balkan countries, Rumania, Yugoslavia, and Bulgaria. It would be relatively easy to argue that the differences in inflation originated in political differences among these countries. The states that lost the war had, in fact, experienced hyperinflation; the victorious countries had been able to overcome their economic difficulties through a milder inflationary trend. Although one cannot deny an apparent causal relationship here, this is by no means a simple matter. Bulgaria and Poland prove the point; Bulgaria was on the wrong side in the war, yet it was able to avoid hyperinflation; Poland, despite being one of the "victorious" powers, could not do so.

After the war, economic, social, and political conditions in the East Central European region were in such a deplorable state that a speedy return to prewar economic processes was impossible. In this region, all the economic indicators that point to an inflationary process were present. In Poland the physical destruction of fixed capital was probably the most significant; here, war damage was up to $2 billion in 1913 value. In the previously Russian-occupied part of the country, industrial enterprises suffered a loss of nearly 60 percent.

Serbia, after having become a battlefield, experienced an equally grave economic decline, more in agriculture than in industry. In other countries, such as Austria, where physical destruction of fixed capital did not occur, the depreciation of industrial equipment, the lack of raw materials and fuel, and the shortage of manpower resulted in the decline of agricultural and industrial production to around 50 percent of the prewar level. In Hungary, the Rumanian army which had helped to overthrow the Hungarian Republic of Councils dismantled and carried off a considerable quantity of machinery and rolling stock.

Industrial stocks had generally been exhausted, industrial production — except in a few branches of industry — had already shown a considerable decrease during the war years as a result of wear and tear on existing plant machinery and the difficulty of securing necessary raw material.

In Serbia, where industry was less significant, roughly one-half of all hogs and sheep were lost; losses of horses and cattle came to more than one-third of the entire stock. In Rumania, the wartime occupying powers confiscated 30 percent of existing agricultural equipment and the larger part of the livestock.

But one should also remember the special conditions emerging from the great upheavals that characterized this region after the war. Revolutions occurring in some of these countries, introducing programs and ideas to cure the ailing economic systems, to speed up economic growth, contributed, in the short run, as much to the inflationary process as did counterrevolution.

Looking for the causes of inflation, however, one must first remember the effects of the total reorganization of this part of the world. The breakup of the central force of this region — the Austro-Hungarian empire — and the creation of the so-called independent nation-states were certainly among the major reasons — at least for the short run — for the economic difficulties which all the newly created states experienced. Weak governments and bad administrations could not have effected a quick stabilization and rapidly established a taxation system creating a budget equilibrium, even if they had inherited a sane, working economic system. This, however, was certainly not the case.

The new states had to reconstruct their economies; in this situation, physical capital was expected to accumulate more rapidly than in a peaceful era. But this certainly was not a normal, peaceful period; it was complicated partly by the war, and partly by the struggle for territory, as well as by the necessity to consolidate the newly acquired lands. In most cases, taxation did not even ensure a sufficient budget income for the respective states, and expenditures were usually increased well above peacetime levels; this was the result partly of enormous continued military spending and partly of the economic cost of unifying railroad systems, as was the case in Poland, Czechoslovakia, and Yugoslavia.

On the one hand, in the cases of Austria and Hungary, reconstruction was complicated by the need to adapt the economic system to their reduced size. On the other hand, different problems were created in the case of Poland, where three segments of the state, formerly belonging to different economic entities, had to be integrated. To some extent the situation was similar in Yugoslavia. Rumania's problem, too, was complicated by its need to cope with the enormous increase of its territory.

The political implications of the changed situation in East Central

Europe contributed to the financial difficulties of the region. For the defeated countries, reparations seemed a very important issue, even before they started paying them. The prospect of having to pay reparations increased already existing uncertainties, made it almost impossible to balance the budget of the respective states, and to obtain foreign financial help to curb the inflation.

The East Central European states had been unable to ensure their needed capital for their growing economies even before the war. Foreign financial help in the form of capital was badly needed even then; it seemed even more necessary to obtain such help now. But foreign help was simply inadequate. The so-called relief deliveries were mainly in the form of short-term loans for food, but those hardly enabled these countries even to feed their populations. The various taxation systems were mostly inefficient. It is difficult to determine the major cause of this latter situation: in some cases, the tax system was badly organized; in others, the countries were just as poor as their state treasuries. In either case, the state was deprived of income that, under normal circumstances, taxpayers might contribute to its balancing the budget. I would, however, be reluctant to pursue this line of reasoning, since I am not willing to accept the view that the main cause of inflation was a budget deficit.

There is little doubt that nineteenth-century orthodox fiscal policy focused on the need for a balanced state budget and regarded the process of the money supply only as a function of monetary policy. Such a view, in fact, disregarded the connections between monetary factors and economic factors, not to mention the role of noneconomic elements.

The increase in the money supply when the supply of goods was well below peacetime averages was a consequence of the general situation, not just a process created by the governments that were actually responsible for the increase and the inflation itself. Actually, regarding inflation as a potential contributor to the financial needs of reconstruction by deliberately restricting consumption was an idea that had not yet occurred to contemporary economists. Inflation even in its moderate phase was considered to be deplorable, something that ought to be overcome. Inflation was certainly created by the governments, but not as part of general economic policies, only as an answer to financial needs. Everybody was convinced that inflation was very harmful for the economic process. Generally economists and statesmen both believed that whenever the state's budget was balanced, the economy in question was on its way to recovery, and that nothing more need be worried about. Misunderstanding of the inflationary process led to some attempts — which, of course, were bound to fail — to stop inflation by raising taxes as well as by other methods, even though, obviously, the measures employed proved much more harmful for the economy than the sickness which they tried to cure.

Nevertheless, inflation must be regarded as a cumulative process. After a certain period it lost even its former capital-forming effect. When the countries entered into the phase of runaway inflation, the velocity of money speeded up and caused a shortening of the payment period. In such a situation, inflation caused much faster price increases and this negated methods of financing the economy by an increasingly worthless currency. In this phase of hyperinflation, price increases occurred so rapidly that they destroyed all the economic processes; for instance, collecting taxes cost more than the funds that the collections brought into the state treasuries.

In the following part of my discussion, I would like to touch upon three issues:

1. The inflation of the 1920s.
2. The problem of whether inflation was the result of deliberate state policy, or did it come about on account of objective circumstances?
3. What was the role of inflation in the economic development of the countries involved?

In the following session of this conference you are going to hear four papers discussing the inflation in various countries. These papers will discuss the causes and effects of inflation. There is no way I could repeat or anticipate what will be said in these discussions.

But the history of inflation had shown that Austria entered the second phase relatively early, Hungary and Poland somewhat later, and other countries did not encounter the runaway phase at all. Was the Austrian economic system ruined more than that of the others? I can hardly believe that. The territory of the Austrian state was spared entirely by military events and economic assets had never been confiscated. The blockade imposed by the Entente that so severely contributed to the breakdown of the Austrian economy during the war had been suspended relatively early. Although the collapse of the empire was followed by the complete collapse of the economic system (and this we must not forget), we may say that noneconomic factors significantly contributed to Austrian inflation.

One of the most important causes of the inflationary process was that Austria, shorn of large tracts of territory and left with a population of only 6 million, was forced to increase government spending to help overcome the effects of the influx of former officials from the lost regions of the empire.

We may ask as well if military expenditures which were increased by 33 percent in Poland's budget had nothing to do with the Polish inflation? Bulgaria's state deficits were caused, according to Berov, mostly by the extraordinary expenditures induced by the Neuilly Treaty and the requisitions.

The previous arguments are all based on the supposition that inflation was caused by the budget deficits and not the other way around. Such an argument, however, excludes two other factors which may have been very important in contributing to the inflationary process: the movement of foreign exchange rates and the balance of payments.

All these lead directly to the second issue. Immediately after World War I, the financial theories that originated in the nineteenth century were still being followed, and they suggested that inflation was the No. 1 enemy of a rational economic system; hence, it would be hard to argue that the inflation process was deliberately utilized for any direct economic purpose.

Let us assume for the moment that this argument is correct. Let us accept the view that prevailed at the first international economic conference at Brussels in September 1920; the participants argued that budget reform was the prerequisite of any successful stabilization efforts. This basic principle of financial orthodoxy might have survived in the minds of economic experts or professors of economics. But statesmen and politicians in charge of actual government policies might have been easily convinced by facts belying orthodox theories; this provided incentives for them to permit the growth of inflation, even if for a limited time. (We know quite well that German foreign policies directed against reparations, intending to lighten their burden, contributed to the inflation in that country directly as well as indirectly.) There can be little doubt that in a certain phase of its history, the Austrian and Hungarian inflation was related not only to the deplorable economic situation in these states, but also to manipulations on behalf of the governments using inflation either for political purposes or in order to obtain foreign financial help.

The question has been raised before in the literature on German inflation, whether more draconic measures taken by the German government against the inflationary process would have caused much more serious effects in terms of raising unemployment, etc., and would not have led to the total collapse of the German economy. The same question could be raised in the case of Austria, but not as far as the other countries were concerned.

There is simply no evidence whatsoever for the argument that, in spite of prevailing economic orthodoxy, fostering inflation was a conscious economic policy for the purpose of either avoiding social collapse or speeding economic recovery. But I must say that during the inflationary process the governments which regarded the rapidly increasing money supply as harmful to the economy slowly became convinced that inflation might prove some sort of a blessing in disguise and could be utilized for governmental purposes. But this depended upon two conditions.

1. One, that inflation remain under control so that it would not reach the phase when price quotations rose far in advance of the actual increase of the money supply.

2. Second, that the foreign exchange depreciation — that is, its external value — should not move too much ahead of internal depreciation and that speculation be restricted and not become the dominant factor in the economy. When speculation prevailed, instead of the flight to capital goods (*Flucht zum Sachwerke*), the flight of capital became the underlying mood, and the normal functions of the economic processes were hampered, interestingly enough, by shortage of money.

We must keep in mind that even in the moderate phase of the inflationary process, the budget deficit and the depreciation of the external value were acting in a complementary way.

In all East European countries the devastation of the economy, the breakdown of production (agricultural production was down to about 50 percent in 1920, and industrial production was even lower) and the exhaustion of raw material resources, were reflected not only in budget deficits, but in increased imports without compensating export opportunities. Even if the Brussels conference rejected any direct assistance which these states needed for long-term capital investment, working capital was certainly available for them.

In the "victorious" Western countries, there emerged a tremendous greed for buying assets cheaply, due to the inflation, and selling goods due to internal economic difficulties. These trends could have had a short-term antiinflationary effect. Foreign-bought assets and notes were withdrawn from circulation and a great many goods — capital goods among them — came into the East European countries. The supply of goods was increased and had a counterinflationary effect. By the sale of capital interests and real estate foreign means became available for further foreign requirements. Where capital inflows occurred, the economy soon came into temporary equilibrium. There was a short period of recovery everywhere in Eastern Europe, inflation slowed down, the supply of goods increased, production volume and productivity also increased. Circulating capital and savings bank deposits almost disappeared; on the other hand, a great deal of former debt had also been liquidated. Investment once again became profitable because the cost of production became cheaper through the reduction of expenses. For instance, real wages were reduced. But inflation gave a new impetus to enterprises not only by making investments more profitable but by creating an economic situation where investment became almost the only way to preserve wealth and capital.

Even while the short reconstruction period — started by a tremendous increase of imported goods — lasted, its real meaning became quite apparent; cheap money gave a greater impetus to exports and functioned as a special barrier to imports. This peculiar kind of recovery that accelerated the replacement of losses caused by the war occurred everywhere. For example, in Austria, unemployment in May 1919 reached roughly 200,000; by the end of 1921, this was reduced to an insignificant 10,000. Production in some branches of the economy almost reached prewar levels; replacement of industrial equipment in general surpassed that level. Similar data may be cited in the case of the other East European states. In Hungary, the production of the iron industry almost doubled, 1921–22; that of the engineering industry rose by 25 percent. The number of employees in these branches of industry reached the prewar levels, and the production volume was about 75 percent of prewar volumes. While imports increased between 1920–21 by 25 percent, between 1921 and 1922, the increase slowed down to only 3 percent; between 1922 and 1923, imports declined to 20 percent (all in real terms).

In Poland, industrial employment increased by 135 percent during 1920–22, reaching 82 percent of the 1913 level. Unemployment was almost completely eliminated; it fell from 318,000 in July 1919 to 52,000 in October 1923. In all three countries, however, inflation soon increased to uncontrollable levels, and this led to hyperinflation. The reasons for this process are ambiguous. It is almost impossible to locate the turning point in this process or the extent to which it was influenced by political factors (such as, for instance, the possibility of an independent Austria's surviving, the reparations problem in Hungary, etc.).

Foreign factors also may have been important, if not decisive. In the period of moderate inflation, many foreigners bought large amounts of depreciated money in hope that an eventual consolidation of its value would bring them large profits. Later, hopes for the consolidation of external value lessened, foreign assets were withdrawn, even domestic funds started to move out because more and more gold and foreign currencies became the standards of value. This process further speeded the depreciation of the currency. The inflationary process thus moved from an equilibrium to imbalance. At this phase of the runaway or hyperinflation, the decline of currency values became the leading factor in the mechanism of inflation, and budget deficits lost their immediate effect on the depreciation of the currencies in question, and on the working of the paper presses. The flight of capital was impoverishing exactly those countries in which capital imports were badly needed. A reversed Graham's Law prevailed, namely, the domestic currencies were less and less functional as a means of payment, and their role was being taken over by "better money," namely, gold and good foreign currencies.

The exchange depreciation worked through the balance of trade and the balance of current payments. Gradually, the whole economy grew more and more dependent on the foreign quotations of the local currency; domestic wage rates and cost prices became directly related to the quotations. All this may leave one with the impression that weakness in the balance of payments and capital outflow were responsible for the depreciation of the exchange rates. This process had as its consequence the rise of internal prices, whether the price of imported goods and services, or those available for export, or potentially competitive with imports. By this process the propensity to save vanished entirely. There was a flight from real investment to money, and this very sharp inflationary stimulus may have produced another kind of crisis, leading directly to hyperinflation. As usually happens during the starting phase of hyperinflation, the depreciation of currency was faster than the volume of currency accumulation. It is therefore justifiable to maintain that, in the second phase of inflation, problems in the balance of trade and payments became almost as important factors of currency depreciation as budgetary difficulties.

But, trade balance difficulties were decisive even in the cases of nations that escaped hyperinflation. For instance, in Yugoslavia, the balance of trade was entirely negative between 1919 and 1922. This was exactly the period when exchange depreciated violently, and the circulation of currency increased. The first measures leading to stabilization were introduced in 1923; these were intended to check imports and raise exports. Inflation itself was being alleviated by the introduction of this entirely administrative method. One could find a very similar phenomenon both in timing and degree in Rumania. To the end of 1921 and the beginning of 1922, imports increased tremendously, and the depreciation of the foreign value of Rumanian currency was rapid. By 1922, import control was introduced, and measures concerning this control were sharpened by 1923. Between 1923 and 1925, the value of the leu was fairly stable, and the currency began to depreciate only in 1925, clearly as a consequence of serious balance of trade problems. Between 1919 and 1921 Bulgaria, too, suffered a heavy trade deficit. True, the trend had been stopped in 1922, and further to impede the depreciation of money, a foreign currency monopoly was given to the National Bank. When the Bulgarian leva became de facto stable in 1924, the country's budgetary and trade positions were almost in equilibrium.

I would like to come now to the third point of my discussion, namely, whether inflation was a help or an obstruction to the reconstruction process. According to Professor Aldcroft, the four important channels through which inflationary conditions might be beneficial to an economy are the following:

1. Forced savings that enable governments and businesses to achieve goals that would have been difficult to achieve under different circumstances.
2. Depreciation of the currency which automatically checks imports and stimulates exports.
3. An export boom that encourages investments in new capacity and government support with nonvalorized credits (in Poland, 20 percent of the money issued supported the investment boom).
4. Wages tend to lag behind prices, thus profit margins increase.

Permit me to cite some examples:

In Yugoslavia, the inflation-induced boom inspired feverish entrepreneurial activity. During the period of inflation, the total growth of the volume of investment increased by 25 percent; manpower in industry increased by 38 percent. Between 1918 and 1922, more than 500 new factories were established. In Hungary, the number of workers employed in the steel and metal industries increased by one-third, those in the machine industry by 25 percent. Coal production reached the prewar level, and total industrial production, after the 35 percent increase in the manpower employed, reached about 75 percent of prewar level. In the Austrian case we could quote similar figures.

In spite of the investment boom, which seems to be the most important benefit of the inflation, the level of production in general in the countries discussed nowhere reached prewar levels. Nevertheless, it is my opinion that inflation was an important instrument of economic recovery in East Central Europe. It goes without saying that inflation did not solve the grave problems produced in the region by the lack of capital, by the insufficient accumulation of domestic capital, and by the interruption of connections with foreign capital that happened after the war. But it certainly helped to overcome economic difficulties for a short time.

The same view has been taken by Professor Landau in his paper to be presented here. According to him, "inflation had a generally positive impact on the rate of reconstruction and the starting of the domestic industry." He sees the contribution of inflation to the recovery in four sectors:

1. The diminishing cost of credit, namely, the difference between actual value and the value at the time of repayment of credit.

2. The diminishing tax burden.

3. Decreasing transportation costs.

4. The decreasing share of labor costs in the total cost of production.

Mutatis mutandis, the same argument and the same sort of evidence may be presented for the other East European countries. Furthermore, attempts to curb inflation in its early period, efforts that failed, may also be regarded as a common feature of the economies of these countries.

In Hungary, such attempts had been made by Minister of Finance Lóránt Hegedüs, and in Poland, at almost the same time, by Treasury Minister Michalski. These attempts had failed not only because they overestimated the possibility of halting inflation without any significant foreign help, by improving taxation, introducing a capital levy, and shifting the burden of stabilization to the wealthy classes of the population, but because experience had shown very rapidly that the consequence of the abrupt halt in the issuance of banknotes was harmful for the economy. As a consequence, production declined and unemployment grew, imports increased while exports decreased; very soon, therefore, the business communities in question began to protest this sort of monetary policy.

To this point, issuing banknotes was more or less a compulsory task of the government; after this failure, the approach of the governments in question changed; the monetary benefits were appreciated, and inflation was consciously used to stimulate an industrial boom. We must emphasize, however, that the quality and productivity of such investments was extremely dubious, and in some ways the direction of the investments was distorted. Bresciani-Turroni in his book on German inflation rightly remarked, "in the acutest phase of the inflation Germany offered the grotesque and sometimes tragic spectacle of a people which rather than produce food, clothes and shoes and milk for its own babies, was exhausting its energies in the manufacture of machines or the building of factories."

Perhaps it would be worthwhile to emphasize that Bresciani's position is an exaggeration, consciously overestimating the economic value of the investment boom both for the short and the long run. In fact, during the hyperinflationary period, real inflationary incentives became weaker, and their effects more and more negative. The inflation or the depreciation of the currency diverted capital from productive purposes and directed it into speculative activities; thus, the economic processes became completely distorted and could no longer function effectively. Some argued that the bad effects of inflation were more important than its benefits. But there can be little doubt that various social groups went through the inflationary period in different ways.

The inflationary process is always a sort of redistribution of the national income. It is obvious that entrepreneurs profiting from nonvalorized credit, landowners whose debts were wiped out, and even some artisans whose needs for starting capital were lowered, not to mention speculators, banks as middlemen of the banknote credit business, were partly or even mostly on the gaining side; all benefited from inflation. A new study completed in Hungary based on examination of the secret balances of a few Hungarian banks and large industrial enterprises has shown that, to a great extent, the published balances that had shown a loss of their former wealth were falsified.

It is also well known that employees and wage earners were in an entirely different position. The distribution of income became more unequal during the inflation. Wages lagged greatly behind prices, and this remained the case almost during the entire inflationary period. True, in the peak period of the inflationary investment boom, even the depreciation of real wages was slowed down if not totally halted. If we take into account the increase in employment, then we may consider the proposition that the situation of the working class may have also improved, but only for the short run. It continued to lag behind a prewar level that was not really impressive in any case. According to Professor Landau, real wages in Poland were 63 percent of the prewar level in 1921 and 49 percent in 1923. He was wondering whether it would not have been better to have higher real wages and large-scale unemployment than lower wages and less unemployment. He would opt for the latter solution because, as he put it, this case would have a larger multiplying effect for the economy and less propensity to savings. The real wages of the Hungarian working class were also about 50 percent of the prewar level during the inflation.

The economic losses of the lower middle class and those with fixed incomes and small savings are too well known; their social and political effects certainly included the rise of right radical movements; this is something that we do not intend to discuss here in detail.

Aldcroft refers in his work on the economy of the 1920s to the long-term repercussions of the inflationary episode. He maintains that years of turmoil, poverty, starvation, and sociopolitical tensions hardly contributed to the health of society. Indeed, he is correct; he was also correct in pointing out that after the end of the inflation, a deflationary period and budget and monetary policies hampered normal economic activities for almost two years. Furthermore, economic policy even during the 1929–32 depression was still conditioned by the disastrous effects of the inflation.

There can be little doubt that these remarks are valid for East Central Europe as well. The issue that must be discussed and which is still open, is whether he is right to say, "it is difficult to believe that the German position would have been any worse under a more orthodox financial policy." The weakest point in this argument is that it assumes that inflation was entirely dependent upon governmental fiscal policies. I can hardly believe that this was really the case in Germany, and I am certainly convinced that it was not so in the East Central European countries. As I tried to show, inherent economic and political factors were to be blamed for the inflation, and when in one phase inflation was characterized by private access to the printing press, through discounting private bills or by nonvalorized credits, one would be hard put to say that there existed a real choice.

Inflation had its far-reaching results in the deflationary years in all the countries involved, and there can be little doubt that its memory made a less rigid fiscal policy more difficult during the Great Depression. Nevertheless, these difficulties cannot all be blamed on the inflation itself. The political and social changes in this area, the new trends developing in the world economy, and the long-lasting economic changes in Europe, had a great deal more influence on all the difficulties of East European economic developments. These structural changes were connected with the altered position of Europe in the world economy and were the consequences of the imbalance of the division of labor between Eastern and Western Europe, the imbalance between market and credits, the new role of food and raw material supplies, and the new lines of production. With foreign capital needed more than ever but more expensive than before the war, in a situation when exports were needed more than ever but markets were less available than before, it was impossible to balance the economic system. In a situation where cooperation was ever more necessary, but economic policies were based on a more narrow-minded nationalist economic policy; when the replacement of imports by homegrown industry was made necessary by overpopulation and by political and economic reasons, but such a policy was not backed up by a developing agricultural system, mostly because of unfavorable international circumstances — there were few chances for the East European countries to overcome economic difficulties and their underdevelopment. Inflation, therefore, was not the sole reason for these difficulties.

References

The data are in T. I. Berend and Gy. Ránki, Közép-Kelet Európa gazdasági fejlödése a 19–20. században (Budapest, 1976), pp. 252–92.
Works on the postwar inflation in East Central European countries: G. Gratz and R. Schüller, Der wirtschaftliche Zusammenbruch Österreich-

Ungarns (Wien, 1930); K. Rothschild, *Austria's Economic Development* (London, 1946); W. T. Layton and Ch. Rist, *The Economic Situation of Austria*, Report presented to the Council of the League of Nations, Geneva, 1925; J. Faltus, *Povojnová hospodárska kriza v rokoch 1921– 1923 v Československu* (Bratislava, 1966); K. S. Patton, *Kingdom of Serbs, Croats and Slovenes* (Washington, 1928); M. Mirković, *Ekonomska Historija Jugoslavije* (Zagreb, 1958); H. Prost, *La Bulgarie de 1912 à 1930* (Paris, 1931); Th. Alton, *Polish Postwar Economy* (New York, 1956); J. Taylor, *Economic Development of Poland. 1919–1950* (New York, 1952); S. Strakosch, *Der Selbstmord eines Volke* (Wien, 1922); Berend and Gy. Ránki, *Magyarország gazdasága az első világháboru után 1919–1929* (Budapest, 1966).

Inflation and Deflation Policy in Bulgaria during the Period between World War I and World War II

LJUBEN BEROV

Bulgarian economic thought first came up against the problem of inflation during and after World War I. The press occasionally touched on the considerable rise in the cost of living as early as 1909–1912 but inflation was never mentioned. This is also true of the attitude of bourgeois economic thought toward the rise in the cost of living during the Balkan War (1912–13) and the ensuing short peaceful period in late 1913, 1914, and early 1915. (After maintaining a short-lived formal neutrality Bulgaria openly joined World War I on 1 October 1915, Julian calendar.) Prices did not shoot up during the Balkan War (1912–13) as the war was comparatively short and the quantity of taxes and comandeered livestock was not substantial. War expenditure was not substantial either, compared to 1915–18. For those reasons, no serious disorder occurred in the country's economy and the term *inflation* was not used by the press. The first hints in this respect date to World War I when, despite attempted state regulation of production and supply, there was general economic disorder and a sharp rise in prices. Still, the rise in prices before 1919 was not so steep because it was held back to some extent by the existing coupon system and fixed prices for staple commodities.

Following World War I inflation raged on a wide scale, progressively advancing until mid-1923. The rates of development during this first stage until 1923 are shown in Table 1.

Most bourgeois economists in Bulgaria during the first postwar years considered the reason for the inflationary rise in prices in this country to be due only to the great number of new banknotes being put into circulation in connection with budget deficits and the increase of paper circulation while maintaining the same or even decreased quantity of monetary gold at the Bulgarian National Bank (the country's national bank of circulation). They failed to link this phenomenon with other economic indexes on a national scale. In this respect, some authors try to relate the inflationary rise in prices to the increase of the treasury's debt to the Bulgarian National Bank. The narrow views of the then bourgeois economists should be accounted for by the gaps in the statistical information in Bulgaria in the early 1920s, explained further on.

Bulgarian Marxist economic thought treated the issue of the direct causes for inflation in an essentially similar way, occasionally allowing for budget deficits to be regarded as an unavoidable chronic ailment of the capitalist system during the general crisis of capitalism. In the first postwar years, a discussion was started among Marxist economists in Bulgaria on the causes and nature of the inflationary high cost of living, without, however, arriving at a more thorough elucidation of the problem. It ended with the dispute on whether capitalism, under the new conditions following the October Socialist Revolution, would be in a position to curb inflation processes and balance paper circulation. Under the conditions of the rapid growth of the scope of influence and activity on the part of the revolutionary working-class movement in Bulgaria during the first postwar years (until the defeat of the national uprising in September 1923), Marxist economic thought in Bulgaria could not possibly assign more of its adherents to a further investigation of the causes and nature of postwar inflation.

In this period some petty-bourgeois and Marxist authors were trying to link the sharp increase of prices with the currency speculation of the big private banks in the country, as well as with the speculative activities of merchants operating to inflate prices under the conditions of a sustained shortage of foodstuffs and industrial goods on the internal market. This, however, did not lead to an analysis of the direct objective factors causing inflation in the country. There is hardly need to prove that the merchants or banks could give a correct or wrong interpretation to the situation at the moment, but in their overall activity they could not turn into willful, unrestrained dictators of prices in the country — in the long run their speculation was limited by the objective parameters of the country's economy. Later there appeared a number of more detailed investigations on the history of money circulation and prices in Bulgaria for the period between World War I and World War II. These made no further contribution to the problem, as attention there was primarily focused on the qualitative, technical, and formal juridical aspect of the issue.

Detailed investigation of inflation factors in Bulgaria during the first phase in its development (World War I until the middle of 1923) is made more difficult by certain gaps in Bulgarian statistics. Although bourgeois Bulgaria stood out among the capitalist countries for having rather well-organized economic statistics, it has to be noted that the development of statistics covering the banking system in the country lagged behind. Data on the basic indexes for the activities of private banks started being officially published in statistical annuals only in 1929. For the 1911–1928 period, a similar statistical surveillance was carried out by the department of finance studies and the Bulgarian National Bank, publication of the data being restricted. For similar reasons, more detailed data on Bulgaria's balance of payment until 1924 are also lacking; there is available, though limited, information on the investigation of Bulgaria's national income by A. Chakalov for the period after 1924.

During the 1920s more detailed annual statistics for the basic indexes of the country's industrial output are also lacking, except for the 1921 data covering industrial enterprises. Official annual publication of statistical data in the field of industry in specialized statistical works and in the general statistical annuals started in 1929. Until that year the annuals contained irregular and limited information about some branches of industrial production under the fiscal supervision of the state, such as the production of sugar, salt, and tobacco products. Indeed, at that time all large industrial enterprises employing more than 10 workers regularly submitted annual statistical reports to the ministry of trade, industry and labor, but those reports were statistically summarized only with respect to a number of general indexes and referred exclusively to the 1911–12 and 1923–29 periods. This marks the beginning of detailed annual industrial statistics.

Up to World War I there were no statistical data on the development of stockbreeding output in the country — there is only incomplete information on cattle slaughtered at the slaughterhouses and a single representative inquiry into the 1933–34 agrarian output. There is no statistical information on the country's national income up to 1923. No statistics are available on unemployment up to 1935. Even after 1935 the existing statistical information provides data only about the number of people seeking jobs through specially established employment offices and the number of those employed without covering the total number of the unemployed in the country and their percentage of the whole working class. The inadequate coverage is due to the existence of a great number of semiproletarian poor farmers or younger members of their families who, without completely joining the working class, were constantly migrating between urban and rural areas in accordance with fluctuations in employment; if unemployed in the town, they temporarily went back to the village. There are no statistical data about money circulation velocity; inferences are possible only about the period 1924–39.

Nevertheless, a careful analysis of the statistical data available, certain gaps being supplied by evaluation, makes it possible to draw concrete conclusions as to the factors determining the parameters of the inflation process in Bulgaria after World War I. From this point on, the devaluation of the national monetary unit (the Bulgarian lev) on the home market is taken to denote the basic index for measuring inflation.

The devaluation is estimated on the basis of the official common index for retail prices in the towns. (Separate wholesale price data have been gathered in Bulgaria since 1926.) The contemporary rate of exchange of the Bulgarian lev against other sound foreign currencies (such as the Swiss franc) is not taken as the basic inflation index because, beginning in December 1918 Bulgaria established a regime of state control (later also a state monopoly) over foreign currency operations; under those circumstances the rate of exchange of the Bulgarian paper lev was artificially maintained at a higher level. For this reason, the rate of devaluation of the lev according to its rate of exchange against the Swiss franc in 1939–39 was lower than the devaluation resulting from the retail prices on the home market, as is clearly shown in Columns 2 and 3, Table 1.

Data analysis of the debt of the treasury to the Bulgarian National Bank for each year until 1923, as given in Table 1 shows no strict interrelation between this index and variations in the common price iindex. Budget deficits have not always been formulated as an officially declared debt of the state to the Bulgarian National Bank. Deficits have often been partially covered by funds belonging to other public institutions or hidden behind other balance accounts of the state bank of circulation. Hence, a direct statistical connection between the increas-

Table 1. Rate of Inflation and Some Indexes of Money Circulation in Bulgaria, 1912–23

Year	Index of market prices 1912 = 100	Rate of exchange for the Swiss franc (leva for 100 francs, yearly averages)	Unconsolidated debt of the state treasury to Bulgarian National Bank, million leva by 1 January	Amount of money in circulation, million leva, yearly averages	Index of the amount of money in circulation 1912 = 100
1912	100	100	—	132	100
1913	110	—	7	188	142
1914	112	—	146	195	148
1915	125	107	134	269	204
1916	201	136	146	569	433
1917	360	173	260	1148	873
1918	697	166	612	1884	1433
1919	1315	433	839	2509	1911
1920	2460	1054	1742	3266	2480
1921	2272	1958	2891	3301	2502
1922	2756	2846	3667	3789	2881
1923	3045	2281	4600	3863	2928

ing amount of the state debt to the Bulgarian National Bank and the increasing amount of paper circulation in the country for the period under consideration cannot be expected.

Comparing the average annual amount of paper circulation and the increase of the common price index for each year in Table 1 shows that those two indexes are parallel to a much higher degree (as compared with the case of the amount of the state debt to the Bulgarian National Bank), but this could hardly be estimated as the only causal relationship. For example, in 1917 the common price index, on a 1912 basis, rose 3.6 times; the volume of paper circulation increased 8.7 times for the same period. Taking 1912 as the basis, the rise in those two indexes in 1919 is 13.1 against 19.1; in 1920, 24.6 against 24.8; in 1921, 22.7 against 25.0; in 1922, 27.5 against 28.8; in 1923, 30.4 against 29.2. The rather lower rate of increase of the official common price index as compared to the rate of increasing paper circulation during World War I can be explained by the existing system of rations coupon supply at artificially maintained low prices fixed by the state. (Official statistics do not include "black market" sales at considerably higher prices.) By the end of 1919, however, coupon supply and the policy of fixed prices were almost completely abolished; nevertheless, even under the conditions of a liberalized state economic policy, the difference between the two indexes for 1919 and 1921 remains considerable; only in the period 1922–23 does it significantly diminish and change direction.

The presence of insufficiently solid parallel relationship between the movements of the common price index and that of the average annual volume of money circulation shows that inflation parameters depended on other factors as well. The most important of them is the significance of the amount of deposits with credit institutions (private joint-stock banks, some state banks, popular cooperative banks and agricultural credit cooperations). The amount of those deposits, together with the funds in possession of the public (the amount of money in circulation) gives the overall amount of the potential purchasing capacity of the people and capitalist enterprises at a given moment. Its movement does not always run completely parallel to the amount of money circulation itself, as far as individuals and capitalist enterprises could, to a different degree, spend or save their current incomes. (They could, also to a varying degree, keep the remaining part of the income saved in ready money or deposit it with banks.) Table 2 makes an attempt, despite the shortage of statistical information mentioned, to provide a general picture of deposit movement in Bulgaria during the first stage of inflation after World War I until 1923.

In this connection, however, one should bear in mind that inflation parameters also depended a great deal on the changes in the volume of material goods and services on the home market, running counter to

Table 2. Bank Deposits and General Amount of the Potential Purchasing Power of the Population in Bulgaria, 1912–23

Bank deposits (million leva) in:

Year	Private banks	Bulgarian agricultural bank and Bulg. central cooperative bank	Postal savings bank	Credit coopera- tives and "popular banks"	Potential purchasing power of the population (bank deposits and money in circulation), million leva	The same, index 1921 = 100
1912	63.4	75.1	—	4.7	275.2	100
1913	. . .	217	127	. . .	. . .	. . .
1918	547	283	141	20	2875	1047
1919	839	291	110	40	3789	1380
1920	1072	400	98	200	5036	1833
1921	1384	601	97	400	5783	2105
1922	1287	885	96	600	6657	2423
1923	1550	1290	79	831	7613	2775

the existing purchasing capacity of the population and the capitalist, cooperative, and other enterprises in the country. Clearly, it is possible for a country not to have an inflationary increase of prices even after a considerable rise in the volume of money circulation when it is accompanied by an adequate or greater increase of production for the same period. For this reason, an attempt has been made in Table 3 to present an overall evaluation of the changes in the output of agricultural, stockbreeding, and industrial output in the country. (The changes in other branches, such as craftsmanship, construction, transport, etc., are taken to have changed approximately along the same lines.) This can be provisionally accepted as an approximate index for the growth of the aggregate social product in the sphere of material production at constant prices.

When considering the alterations in the volume of the commodity fund as opposed to the potential purchasing capacity of the population, account should be taken of the flow of goods from the country, due to the passive or active trade balance. In reality, however, it could not lead to more accurate results since Bulgarian foreign trade statistics in the period between the two world wars did not cover actual export prices for some significant export items (tobacco, for instance) or exports being realized by firms working on foreign capital. It is not certain how completely they recorded on their customs declarations at the Bulgarian border the real selling prices for the tobacco exported. The matter is further complicated because occasionally (especially in the early 1920s) the export or import of certain lots was registered by Bulgarian statistics later on, so that the commodity in question would

Table 3. Gross National Product, Bulgaria 1912–23

Year	Index of amount of agricultural production 1912 = 100	Index of amount of stockbreeding production 1910 = 100[a]	Index of volume of industrial production 1911 = 100[b]	General index of gross product in main branches of material production 1911–12 = 100[c]	Index of potential purchasing power divided into index of gross national product
1912	100	...	101	100	100
1919	81	90	80	83	1662
1920	75	102	100	83	2215
1921	78	104	123	88	2393
1922	77	107	138	90	2696
1923	85	110	153	97	2860

[a]Estimation from data about cattle stock in 1910 and 1920.
[c]Estimated from archive data about individual enterprises and industrial branches.
[c]Mean proportional after the relative weight of main branches of the material production (industrial production 8.8 percent, agricultural production 55 percent, cattlebreeding production 19 percent).

not be included in the statistical data covering the actual year of export but would figure in next year's data. Due to those factors the active or passive balance of trade is not taken into consideration. An additional reason for statistical uncertainty is that the degree to which the inflow of foreign goods during a passive trade balance was due to goods imported on consignment or against long- or short-term trade credits in foreign currencies has not been established.

Division of the aggregate index movement of the potential purchasing capacity on the home market (Table 2) by the aggregate social product movement in material production (Table 3) results in a combined index reflecting the activity of the basic inflation factors. Comparing the alterations in that index (last column, Table 3) and those in the common price index on Table 1 shows a higher degree of parallelism than that obtained when tracing the amount of money circulation only. The amount of the deviations between the quantities of the price index for a given year and the combined index as shown on Table 3 for the period 1919–23 is 12 percent less than that obtained by comparing the price index with money circulation index.

As shown, the process of inflation in Bulgaria during the first postwar years before 1923 was due to a considerable increase of money circulation and deposits against a diminished goods and services fund (compared to prewar levels) during the postwar crisis going on in Bulgaria until 1923. The increase of money circulation was largely due to state budget deficits continuing after the end of the war mainly because of extraordinary expenditures made to comply with the Neuilly-sur-Seine Peace Treaty and the payments for commandeered livestock, vehicles, grain, etc., the latter having started in 1919. For the fiscal year 1919–20, the deficit amounted to 469 million levs and 1,043 levs for 1921–22; for the remaining years of the decade, the deficit is smaller. The increase of money in circulation, however, is also linked with the activity of the Bulgarian National Bank as the central institution imposing a state monopoly over foreign currency trade, as well as carrying out a number of undertakings in support of Bulgarian private banks in this country.

It was only from 1924 that the bourgeois state managed to end the further increase of the volume of money in circulation and keep prices from shooting up, without, however, being able to avoid another two weak, transient waves of additional rises in the cost of living (1925, 1928–29; see Table 4). The statistical data available do not point to a similar scale for the two price-rise waves. In the former (up to 1932), "market price statistics" (the actual statistics covering retail prices in urban areas) prices in 1925 rose 7 percent over 1924; in 1929, they rose 9.5 percent over 1926. According to new parallel statistics (begun in 1926) on retail prices covering an expanded range of commodities, the cost of living in 1929 rose 8 percent over 1926. (These results are considered more reliable.) Apart from those differences, it becomes clear that the temporary forcing up of prices during the late 1920s does not match the parameters of inflationary development during the first part of the decade.

Thus 1924–fall, 1929 marked a new stage in the inflationary postwar development of Bulgaria, characterized by a slight and unsteady further increase of the price level without any really pressing attempts at partial deflation policy to reduce the volume of money in circulation through external state loans. There were budget deficits again at the beginning of the period. For fiscal 1923–24, the deficit amounted to 116 million levs; in 1925–26, it soared to 1,112 million levs. It did not, however, lead to an increase of the average annual amount of money in circulation as a clearing house was set up in 1925, registering and partially or completely compensating for mutual payments between the banks, insurance companies and some other enterprises, thus speeding up money circulation. Another factor helping the reduction of money in circulation in the ensuing years was the utilization of a part of the funds from the "stabilization" state loan, contracted with West European and American banks in 1928, to meet a portion of the treasury debt to the Bulgarian National Bank. Owing to this loan the state budget for the fiscal 1928–29 ended with a surplus of 502 million levs, thus influencing money in circulation.

The aforementioned policy of restricting the state budget was more distinctly pursued in the period 1926–29, when the amount of state expenditures was fixed at about 6.2–6.4 billion levs per annum, bringing about a balance in the state budget. This policy was backed up by the obligation (supported by proper fiscal control) — assumed by the Bulgarian government by virtue of the agreements concluded under the wardship of the financial committee with the League of Nations for two substantial foreign loans in 1926 and 1928 — that the treasury should effect payment only within the framework of its own current receipts from taxes and revenues without recourse to credits granted by the Bulgarian National Bank and correspondingly increasing the state debt to the same bank. The importance of this policy should not, however, be exaggerated, as in spite of the control mentioned, infringements sometimes occurred. In 1926–27 a small deficit was allowed, only 3 percent of state expenditure. A similar deficit exists also in the following fiscal year, amounting however to less than 1 percent of expenditure.

The data in Table 4 show that the deposit amount during the second

Table 4. Main Indexes of Money Supply in Bulgaria, 1924–39

Year	General index of prices 1935 = 100		Money in circulation, million leva yearly averages	Bank deposits, million leva by 31 December	General amount of the potential purchasing power of the population, million leva
	Retail prices[a]	Wholesale prices			
1924	... (175)	...	4220	5959	10179
1925	... (187)	...	4215	7263	11478
1926	176 (176)	164	3677	7764	11441
1927	171 (170)	164	3796	9281	13077
1928	188 (174)	177	4128	12435	16563
1929	190 (193)	182	4116	14027	18143
1930	149 (159)	148	3595	13759	17354
1931	119 (130)	122	3553	12646	16199
1932	104 (109)	107	3495	12394	15889
1933	93	95	3556	11420	14976
1934	99	99	3630	12026	15656
1935	100	100	3423	12791	16214
1936	99	102	3586	13555	17141
1937	108	115	3876	14685	18561
1938	116	119	3886	16298	20184
1939	116	121	4813	17567	22380

[a] In brackets data of the former "statistics of market prices" (recalculated from the original basis 1908–1912 = 100 to basis 1935 = 100 and by the presumption that in 1926 this index amounted to 176).

half of the 1920s, during the favorable situation of an upsurge in the economy, went up abruptly without leading to a permanent rise in prices due to the substantial increase of agricultural and industrial production in the meantime. The scale of the increase is evident from the yearly data in Table 5, showing the amount of "primary" national income (in constant 1939 prices); the "secondary" incomes of employees and other social strata due to the redistribution of the national income have not been included. These figures are from the study by A. Chakalov which, with reservation, can be considered as an indication of the rate of growth of the aggregate social product in material output.

The juxtaposition of the price index movement to the average annual amount of money circulation for each year, 1924–29, shown in Table 4 reveals the lack of logical connection between those two indexes. The same applies to the phase of the 30s. This leads one to the conclusion that the scale of money in circulation, at least since the mid-30s, had stopped playing a decisive role in the movement of prices in Bulgaria. The data analysis in the last column of Table 5, as compared to the movement of the price index on Table 4 for the period 1924–29, clearly shows that inflation and deflation in Bulgaria depended precisely on the alterations in the aggregate index of the potential purchasing capacity of the population (capitalist enterprises included) in combination with the index of the volume of the aggregate social product in material production.

The same conclusion can be drawn from analysis of the corresponding data for the 30s (Table 4, 5) concerning the next stage of development. It is characterized by frequent, though not substantial, state budget deficits that had not been overcome before 1936–39. Those deficits, however, fail to influence the direction of increase of money in circulation during the first half of the 30s, largely due to the abrupt drop in commodity prices following the great economic crisis of 1929–33. The 30s are also characterized by a distinctly moderate rate of growth of deposits without its leading to a significant rise in prices as the result of the almost uninterrupted growth of the country's agricultural and economic production. For this reason the price level toward the end of the 30s remained approximately 33–37 percent lower than that of 1929. Thus the period of the 30s stands out as one of partially and gradually overcoming the consequences of postwar inflation in Bulgaria dating back to the 20s.

Thus outlined, the features of the process of inflation in Bulgaria during the period between the two world wars can be considered as generally characteristic of the south European countries at that moment. Analysis of the available information on Romania points to a definite analogy. Romanian development for the same period runs

Table 5. Correlation between the Changes in the Price Level and the Aggregate Index of Inflation Factors in Bulgaria, 1924–39

Year	Index of the national material product[a] 1924 = 100	Index of potential purchasing power from table 4	Index of national material product divided into the index of potential purchasing power	Correspondence (x) or lack of correspondence (–) between the aggregate index and the index of prices in table 4
1924	100	100	100	...
1925	105	113	107	x
1926	131	112	85	x
1927	141	118	84	x
1928	140	162	115	x
1929	135	179	133	x
1930	145	170	117	x
1931	166	159	95	x–
1932	162	156		x
1933	164	147	96	x
1934	151	154	89	x
1935	146	159	102	–
1936	180	168	109	–
1937	195	182[b]	93	x
1938	201	198[b]	93	x
1939	202	220[b]	98	
			109	

[a] Recalculated after data about the sum of "primary" national income in stable prices.
[b] The increase of the annual amount of paper money in circulation in 1937–39 was due to the preponderance of Bulgarian exports to Germany over the import of German goods. According to the Bulgarian-German clearing agreement from 1932 the central state bank in Bulgaria (Bulgarian National Bank) had to pay in leva to Bulgarian exporters all goods exported to Germany no matter how far the Bulgarian export for Germany was compensated with import of German goods in Bulgaria. This was a new factor of inflation in Bulgaria. Its influence sharply increased in the war years. The same occurred in Romania.

parallel to that of Bulgaria, but unfortunately, space limitations on this paper do not allow a more detailed treatment of this problem. The only essential difference between Bulgaria and Romania at that time lies in the more substantial parameters of inflation in Romania. By 1929 prices in Bulgaria went up 30 times over prewar (1914) against 54 times in Romania. But the role of the factors determining inflationary development of prices in Romania is highly analogous to that in Bulgaria, particularly after the second half of the 20s, the only exception being that in Romania the national bank held more assets in gold and sound foreign currencies than did the Bulgarian National Bank. The absolute and relative quantity of those assets was smaller in Bulgaria as a result of a smaller relative amount of money in circulation (in 1930, recalculated in Swiss francs, the amount of money in circulation per capita in Bulgaria was 22 francs against 36 francs in Romania; in 1939, 46 against 99 francs).

Inflation in Romania during the Post-World War I Period

MUGUR ISARESCU

ROMANIAN ECONOMY AFTER THE FIRST WORLD WAR: GENERAL TRENDS

The period between the two world wars was perhaps the most challenging period in the development of capitalism in Romania. Against the background of a contradictory and cyclical economic development, during these two decades important shifts on the economic and social scene occurred in a context of strong political and ideological confrontations.

The year 1918 marked the historical moment of completing the establishment of the Romanian national unitary state when Transylvania joined Romania. Romania came out of the First World War as a united country, but one challenged by a host of difficulties long needing to be tackled: the slow pace of industrial development; the feudal relics still existing in agriculture; the unfavorable impact of control of the national economy by foreign capital; the disorder in the monetary system, and many others. In spite of progress in its economic, social, and cultural development, between the wars Romania continued to face unsolved difficulties, above all the lack of a strong national industry. A major feature of the economic development of Romania in the interwar period was that the country continued to remain underdeveloped, with a low living standard and an economy dominated by agriculture.

One can distinguish four different periods in the interwar history of Romanian economic development, each of them characterized by specific problems and specific behavior of economic magnitudes.

During the early years after World War I, the main problem was the recovery of economic potential throughout the territory of reunited Romania. Only in 1924 were the prewar levels of production in the main branches of industry attained. This delay was due to the social unrest following the war as well as other difficulties among which a crucial role was played by the monetary disorder. Intensifying all these problems was the urgent question of solving the whole set of difficulties raised by the backwardness of Romanian agriculture. In 1921 a major agrarian reform was implemented as a consequence of the pressing demands and the struggle of the masses. This produced important shifts on the land as well as in the social pattern of the rural population.

A process of accelerating industrial development took place after 1924. That period was characterized by speeding up the concentration and centralization of capital and production, by strengthening the national bourgeoisie's opposition to foreign investment, by developing and consolidating those theories of pragmatic approaches to economic development called *do it yourself* that were carried out by the liberal party of the Romanian bourgeoisie.

As happened all over the world, economic development and life in Romania was seriously affected by the world economic depression of 1929–33. The suggested remedies and plans were numerous, but their common denominator was shifting the burden of the economic difficulties of the depression to the popular masses, by drastically cutting wages (putting in practice the so-called sacrifice curbs). Promoters of "do it yourself" gave up in face of the "open gates" doctrine supported by the national rural party. The new rulers of Romania put this doctrine into practice — with a direct consequence on accelerated penetration of foreign capital into the Romanian economy.

For the Romanian economy, foreign capital became an important instrument of draining the national wealth rather than a factor stimulating economic development. (We could cite the oil industry especially in this respect.)

Failure of the economic policy of "opening the gates" to foreign capital brought back the theory of "do it yourself"; that gained momentum, starting a period of strengthening measures protecting the national industry. Gradually, in 1934, the Romanian economy started to drag out of depression. In the years to come industrial and agricultural production grew continuously, in 1938 reaching the highest level ever attained by the capitalist economy in Romania. The process of concentration and centralization of capital and production brought about the emergence of monopolistic groups which began to dominate the country's economic and political life.

The history of inflation in Romania between the two world wars recorded specific developments in the four periods mentioned earlier.

Up to 1924 a strong inflationary process developed in Romania, characteristic — as a matter of fact — of all the countries which had taken part in the war. The attempts at monetary stabilization made in 1924–29 substantially slowed but could not completely eliminate the inflationary pressures. During the depression, between 1929 and 1934, the tendencies reversed, with a severe deflation of prices and wages taking place.

From 1935 to 1939, inflation accelerated in parallel with the development of economic recovery and was due especially to the increase in military expenditures and to war preparations.

THE EXTENT OF INFLATION DURING THE 1918–29 PERIOD

After two years of neutrality Romania joined the Allied Powers, declaring war on the Central Powers on August 14/27, 1916. Financing military expenditures during the war through new currency issues unleashed the first severe wave of inflation in the modern history of Romania.

Skyrocketing prices surpassed any known historical records and brought about a massive deterioration of the purchasing power of Romanian currency (leu). At the end of 1918 flour was sold at 14 leu per kg as against 0.80 leu at the beginning of the war; meat, 12 leu per kg as against 0.80 leu; milk, 12 leu per liter as against 0.50 leu; sugar, 25 leu per kg as against 1.3 leu; cotton fabric, 30–60 leu per meter as against 1.25 leu; linen, 100 leu per meter as against 4–7 leu; woolen cloth, 250–300 leu per meter as against 40 leu; footwear, 300–400 leu per pair as against 40–60 leu.[1] By 1918 flour was 17 times dearer than in 1916, meat 15 times dearer, milk 24 times, linen 40 times, and so on. (The data listed are based on prices influenced by the black market especially in the immediate postwar period.) Average prices for consumer goods were nine times higher in 1919 than in 1914.[2]

As a result of the more rapid increase of prices than nominal wages, a substantial decrease of real wages took place. Consumer goods prices increased by the rates cited, but nominal wages hardly doubled by 1918; in 1919 they were only 2.8–3.5 times higher than in the prewar years. In 1919 the real wage index of the railway, oil, and metallurgical workers was only 23–38 percent of the prewar years. The real wage index made up of 16 different branches was only about 43 percent of the prewar level.[3]

Increases in prices, although at more moderate rates, continued even after the final cessation of hostilities; still they were high for times of peace. Thus, starting with 1921 (the first year for which we have official statistical data for the whole territory of Romania) until 1924 the retail price index increased more than 200 percent. In 1923 especially speculative tendencies brought about by excessive currency issues and by the scarcity of goods led to an accelerating increase in retail prices (Table 1).

The inflationary depreciation of the Romanian currency was reflected by the decrease in the value of the leu on the exchange markets. In 1919 the leu lost half its value as against the Swiss franc, the exchange rate being 51 Swiss francs for 100 leu. After a continuous and steep depreciation, by the end of 1920, the exchange rate of leu reached

Table 1. Retail Prices Trend 1921–29
  (1929 = 100)

Year	1921	1922	1923	1924	1925	1926	1927	1928	1929
Retail prices index	31.1	39.6	62.4	75.0	83.5	94.2	100.2	99.9	100.0

Source: *Enciclopedia României*, vol. IV, *Economia Naţională* (Bucharest, 1943): 929.

the point of 8.1 Swiss francs per 100 leu; by 1923–24, 3–5 francs per 100 leu.[4] The same trend was visible as to the exchange rate of the leu against the dollar, which was quoted in Bucharest at 136 leu in 1922 and 250 leu in 1925.[5]

The increase of almost 20 times in exchange rate of the Swiss franc against the leu (compared with prewar levels) suggests that the depreciation of the leu on the exchange markets exceeded the rate of inflation on the domestic market. This disparity between the domestic depreciation of the Romanian currency and the drop of its exchange rate on the exchange markets was relied upon as a main argument for the policy of revaluating the leu. It was considered that the real measure of the depreciation of the Romanian currency was its domestic purchasing power.

In fact the situation developed in the opposite direction. The low value of Romanian currency on the exchange markets caused the acceleration of the rise of domestic prices. The Romanian government attempted to control galloping domestic prices by introducing export taxes and quotas. These measures led to the worsening of other problems confronting the national economy, among them, for example, the increasing deficit of the trade balance. As a consequence the government had to give up the policy of keeping domestic prices under world prices.

INFLATION DURING 1918–29

The inflation in Romania during the post-World War I period was a typical war inflation, fueled mainly by monetary developments. The causes of this inflation are wholly connected with the war and its consequences:

1. Excessive issues of currency to finance military spending during the war.
2. Economic pillage by the enemy in the occupied territories during the war, including illegal issues of Romanian currency by the Germans.
3. Scarcity of goods and services as a result of war damages.
4. Additional issues of money to finance the postwar reorganization of the state and the monetary unification of the country after the war.

A brief analysis of all these causes also reveals other features of the inflationary process in Romania during this period.

Financing the War Effort. The rapid increase of the monetary base started from the period of neutrality as a result of the credits granted to the government by the National Bank of Romania. Thus, the value of the banknotes in circulation increased from 529 million leu in 1914 to over 1,005 million leu in 1916, on the eve of Romania's entry into the war.[6] The coverage in gold of the banknotes issued (the gold reserves of the National Bank and the stock of gold drafts) was a very good one during this period as a result of a substantial surplus in the balance of payments: 50 percent in 1914; 57.1 percent, June 1916. Under these circumstances the doubling of the money supply between 1914–16 cannot in itself be considered as an inflationary factor.

Between 1916–18 when war was waged on the territory of Romania, the value of the monetary issues recorded a more rapid increase, about 150 percent, from 1,005 million leu to 2,613 million leu. This was almost an exclusive consequence of the credits obtained by the government from the National Bank. The debt of the government increased during this period by 1,000 percent from 138 million to 1,596 million leu. In 1916, government debts amounted to 15 percent of the monetary issue; in 1918, such debts stood at 60 percent.

One cannot omit mentioning that the new issues of banknotes were meant to cover the needs of only part of the national territory, the largest part of Romania being occupied by German troops. This point is necessary in order to assess the degree of the inflationary pressures produced by the volume of the money supply at the end of the war. Moreover, even within this diminished part of the country's territory, the supply of goods and services was much smaller than in peacetime. Thus, the increase of 1.5 times in the money supply during 1916–18 was even larger compared with the real need of currency.

The new currency issues emitted with the gold reserves at the same level led to the decrease of the percentage of gold coverage of banknotes in circulation, from 57.1 percent in 1916 to 35.1 percent in 1917 and 32.2 percent in 1918. The monetary law valid at that time stipulated as a minimum level of coverage 34 percent. This could lead us to conclude that, from this point of view, the situation was still relatively bearable. A brief analysis of the reserves covering the banknotes in circulation at the end of the war shows that these reserves underwent important structural changes. If at the outset of the war (1916) the reserves stood at a percentage of 86 percent gold (and the rest gold drafts), at the end of the war they had no more than 58 percent gold (the rest consisted especially of high-risk gold drafts). We must also have in mind that the gold reserves of the National Bank of 500 million lei were widely spread, being kept in three countries (Russia, Germany, and

England), and only the part kept in England remained entirely at the disposal of the Romanian government.

It is also important to mention that the whole financial effort of the Romanian state was financed by means of this system to get "war special credits" from the National Bank. Neither a rise in taxes increasing the fiscal burden, nor loans floated on the domestic and foreign capital markets were utilized by Romania during this period.

Even during the neutrality period, the Romanian National Bank stopped the export of gold. In 1916 the bank suspended convertibility of banknotes into gold. All these measures were needed to meet the financial needs of the government. In this way, the gold standard introduced in Romania in 1890 was abolished de facto. The banknotes issued by the National Bank became fiat money. The way to monetary inflation by uncontrolled issue of banknotes, beyond the economic necessities, was largely opened.

Economic Pillage in the Occupied Romanian Territories, including Illegal Issue of Romanian Currency by the Germans, as the Second Major Cause of the Inflation in Romania after the First World War. Even before the German troops entered the Romanian territory the general headquarters of the invading German army had already given precise orders for systematically organizing the pillage. Among the main directions followed by the Germans to this end were:

Maximization of production, by using if necessary the compulsory labor of the Romanian population, so that Romania would have to become the Central Powers' main supplier of grain and other products and raw materials.

Putting under control and commandeering the whole Romanian production and forbidding trade of such products.

Control of the distribution of products. The greater part of the output had to be used for the supply of the occupying army and to be exported to the Central Powers; the Romanian population was to receive quantities reduced as much as possible, strictly rationed, sufficient only for survival.

The necessary means for financing this plan for economic exploitation was obtained using many channels. As soon as the German troops entered Bucharest, the German high command ordered the seizure of all cash deposited in the government pay offices. Besides that, the German invaders imposed many collective fines on numerous towns and villages. At the same time, the Romanian population in the occupied territory was obliged to pay two "war participations": one up to the amount of 250 million leu in May 1917 and another one up to 400 million leu in 1918.[7]

But the main way the Germans got funds was by their own issue of

"war money," also called leu. (We note that the Germans used the
German mark on a large scale in occupied Belgium and Poland and that
contributed to aggravating the inflationary depreciation of the German
currency.)

The "war-leu" issued by the occupying Germans cost them nothing
except paper and printing; they had no coverage either in gold or in
commercial drafts. Their only cover was the conquerers' position. The
"war-leu" was issued on 29 January 1917 by order of General Macken-
sen, High Commander of the German troops. The order stipulated that
all inhabitants of the occupied territory recognize as legal tender the
"war-leu" at its full nominal value. Drastic penalties were stipulated
against citizens who refused this paper money.

On the whole until 10 November 1918 when the German army was
obliged to withdraw from Bucharest, the Germans dumped into the
monetary channels more than 2,114 million war-leu, of which they
used 45.44 percent to pay for grain, oil producing, and other products,
42.60 percent for the maintenance of their troops, 12.26 percent for the
German administration in the occupied territory, and 1.7 percent for
other operations.

In other words, in only two years the Germans issued an amount of
war-leu equalling the whole money supply issued in Romania in
1890–1918. That illustrates the contribution of this factor to aggravating the inflationary pressures in postwar Romania.

On the other hand, a large quantity of goods was taken out of
Romania. According to figures published in German records, between
1 December 1916 and 30 December 1918 the following quantities of
goods were shipped out of Romania: 2,161,905 tons of grain and other
food products; 1,140,809 tons of oil products; 422,434 tons of raw
materials. As far as livestock was concerned, at the end of the war one
could count on no more than approximately 10 percent of that existing
in the prewar period.

*The Third Important Cause of Inflation Was the Severe Limitation of
the Supply of Goods Following the War Devastation.* At the end of the
war, the Romanian economy was confronted with difficult problems.
The great majority of the factories in the occupied territories had been
dismantled by the Germans; the heavy machinery, the tools, the inventories had been sent to Germany, Austria-Hungary, Bulgaria, and Tur-
key. The losses suffered by large industries alone were valued at
roughly 700 million gold leu. The oil industry was reduced to almost
nothing. At the request of the British government, Romania had destroyed all the oil installations to prevent the enemy from getting the
supplies of oil products they so badly needed; 1,500 oil wells were
closed, the majority of the refineries had been put out of commission,

and approximately 800,000 tons of oil products had been burned. To a large extent, transport and communications systems were wrecked.

In 1919 for a railway network measuring roughly 3,500 km, in old Romania, there were only about 198 locomotives in use. Whereas before the war Romania used to sell abroad approximately 3 million tons of grain yearly, in 1919 she had to import grain from the United States and Australia. The trade balance which in 1911 had shown a surplus of approximately 121 million lei, in 1919 recorded a deficit of over 3,500 million lei. During the Peace Conference in Paris, the Romanian delegation put forth a list of the damages caused to the state, the districts, and private citizens which amounted just for old Romania to an aggregate sum of 31,099 million gold French francs. Romania obtained but a very small part of the war damages she was entitled to from Germany and that very late. For example, the German debts resulting from the issue of the "war-leu" as well as from the gold deposited with the Reichsbank representing the cost of grain sold during the neutrality period were solved only in 1928, the Romanian government finally accepting a lump sum of 75 million gold marks.

All these considerable losses which determined a severe reduction of the availability of goods must be related to the increase of the money supply. At the end of the war on the old territory of the country paper money of the National Bank and "war-leu" issued by the Germans amounted to an aggregate sum of over 4,600 million lei compared to 500 million lei in August 1914. Thus, in the four years of war the quantity of money in circulation increased nine times.

The Supplementary Issue of Paper Money between 1919–1921 Meant to Supply the Necessary Funds for the Post-war Reorganization of the State and the Monetary Unification of the Country. That was the last but not the least important factor which fueled the inflation in Romania after the First World War.

Until 1921–22, the state finances could not be reorganized, so that the government expenses had to be met the same way: obtaining credits from the National Bank which had to be based on the inflationary issue of paper money. Consequently, between 1919 and 1922, the state had to borrow to the amount of 5,208 million lei, that is three times more than it had done during the whole period of the war.

In addition, completion of the unification of the national Romanian state raised with great urgency the problem of monetary unification. In 1920, on Romanian territory four currencies were in circulation:

1. The leu, issued under the law by the National Bank.
2. The Austro-Hungarian crown.
3. The Russian ruble.
4. The "war-leu" issued by Germany.

Such a situation undoubtedly posed a great danger for the national economy.

The convention of 1 June 1920 between the government and the National Bank agreed on the means by which the Austro-Hungarian crowns, the Russian rubles, and the war-leu were to be withdrawn from circulation and the Romanian monetary system unified. Exchange of the Austro-Hungarian crowns, the Russian rubles, and the "war-leu" forced the government to borrow again from the National Bank, to the amount of 7,066 million leu. It is estimated that delay in the exchange operations, 1920–21, and the monetary unification placed an additional burden of approximately 3,500 million leu on the state budget, because a large quantity of rubles and crowns had been illegally brought into the country to benefit from the exchange.

As a consequence of all these operations, at the beginning of 1922 the money issue of the National Bank amounted to 14,345 million leu out of which 12,355 million leu (i.e., 90 percent) represented the state debt. Comparison of the figures reached by the circulation of banknotes in 1922 speaks for itself about the dimensions of monetary inflation in Romania after the First World War.

THE POLICY OF UNIFICATION

With the monetary unification of 1921, the epoch of monetary chaos in the economic life of the country was concluded. Starting with 1922, the government went decisively for a policy of financing budgetary expenses from its own income, ending inflationary loans contracted with the National Bank. Notwithstanding, following the still powerful inflationary potential created by the previous monetary issue, the inflationary pressures continued taking the form of everincreasing domestic prices and the depreciation of the leu on the exchange markets.

By 1924, the Romanian government started stabilizing the leu. It rested basically on the recipe of monetary stabilization fashionable at that time which advocated — in one form or another — a return to the gold standard.

In 1925, through two conventions concluded between the finance department and the National Bank, a revaluation of the leu (by increasing its purchasing power) was attempted through deflation: a gradual reduction of the volume of the money in circulation, particularly by repaying the state debt to the National Bank. Due to the combined action of a multitude of factors, the attempt at revaluing the leu resulted, as in the case of other countries, in an almost complete failure. The increase in domestic prices continued until 1929.

After the unsuccessful attempts to bring the leu back to what it had been before the First World War, a new, more realistic policy was adopted. It rested on the official recognition of the leu's depreciation and simultaneously taking measures "to consolidate the existing situation." The complex of measures, commonly known under the name of *monetary stabilization* was adopted 9 February 1929. Unfortunately, soon afterward, the whole structure meant to stabilize the leu collapsed under the pressures of the economic crisis of 1929–33. Thus, the monetary reform of 1929 did nothing else but validate the strong inflationary depreciation of the leu generated during the First World War and in the following years.

Notes

1. G. O. Creangă, *Politica financiară a României* [Financial Policy of Romania] (Bucureşti, 1927), p. 49; Costin C. Kiriţescu, *Sistemul bănesc al leului* [Monetary System of "Leu"] (Bucureşti, 1967), vol. II: 130.

2. D. Pop, *Scumpetea, cîteva constatări* [Points of View Regarding Cost of Living] (Bucureşti, 1919), p. 11.

3. *Studii privind istoria economică a României* [Studies on the Economic History of Romania], vol. I (Bucureşti, 1961), p. 173.

4. N. C. Angelescu, "Politica monetară" [Monetary Policy], *Enciclopedia României*, vol. IV, = *Economia naţională* (Bucureşti, 1943), p. 688.

5. Virgil Madgearu, *Evoluţia economiei româneşti*, Biblioteca econonomia.

6. Kiriţescu (Bucureşti, 1967), chap. XI, XIII, XIV.

7. *Ibid.*, II: 115.

Inflation in Poland after World War I

ZBIGNIEW LANDAU

1. REASONS FOR INFLATION

The Polish inflation of 1918–23 was a direct consequence of war damage and the necessity to create the Polish state apparatus after more than a century of partition by Russia, Prussia, and Austria. The basic reason was the war damage, whose value in industry alone was estimated at about 10 billion gold francs.[1] As a result, in fall 1918, that is, after Poland regained independence, industry in the previously Russian sector could employ only 14 percent of the workers employed in 1913.[2] Similar losses were born by other branches of the national economy like agriculture, then the major line of Polish production. Crop production fell and livestock diminished.

Under these circumstances, the financial needs of the Polish state were much higher than usual because of the needs of reconstruction, creation of the state apparatus, organization of administration, army, police, judicature, education system, border and customs guards, etc. All these required budgetary expenditures. On the other hand revenues were much lower than those derived from the Polish territories by the partitioning powers before 1914. This again was connected with the war's destruction and postwar confusion. Under these conditions a budgetary deficit was inevitable. Meeting it was the problem.

At first the Polish state tried to raise extraordinary revenues by floating an internal loan. The sums obtained, however, were too small to meet the needs in the long run. A radical rise of tax rates was impossible, as any increase of taxation would diminish the interest of businessmen in reconstructing destroyed factories. This was incompatible with the policy of the state which fought huge unemployment in the towns. Remember, too, that unemployment was not only a social or economic problem but first of all a political issue. The unemployed were susceptible to Communist slogans, therefore any increase of their number might lead to a social revolution in Poland. At the same time, increased taxation of workers or peasants was impossible in view of their very low incomes whose further decrease could also raise the revolutionary tension.

The years 1918–23 saw numerous attempts to obtain foreign loans to cover budgetary deficits, but all of them failed in view of the geopolitical, economic, and political situation of the new state organism.

Under these circumstances, succeeding governments resorted to the relatively easiest method for covering budgetary deficits — to printing banknotes. This policy was facilitated because the central issuing bank — Polska Krajowa Kasa Pożyczkowa — was state-owned and by the readiness of the Polish Seym — whose authority included control of emission of the contemporary currency, the Polish mark — to accept increases of note circulation.

Budgetary deficits were the initial reason for Poland's inflation policy. In the years 1918–21 the inflationary spiral grew rather slowly. As compared with the end of 1918, the note circulation in 1919 was 70 percent higher; in 1921, it grew by 365 percent. This was a result of the inflationary spiral and the lack of counteraction on the part of the government. In the second half of 1923, inflation in Poland turned into hyperinflation. The note circulation grew by 3,415 percent over the last six months of 1923. More details concerning the course of inflation in Poland are presented in Table 1.

Close interrelations between budgetary deficits and banknote issues may be proved by data presented in Table 2.

These data show that increments of emission were closely connected with excess of budgetary expenditures over revenues. It is, however, noteworthy that, except for 1919–20, increments of emission were higher than deficits (in 1921, 11 percent; in 1922, 20 percent; 1923, 10 percent). This means there were other reasons for the growth of note circulation besides budgetary deficits. These include first nonvalorized credits granted by the Polska Krajowa Kasa Pożyczkowa to private business.

Table 1. Development of Inflation in Poland in 1918–1923

Date	Circulation (million Polish marks)	Increase of circulation (%)	U.S. $ in Polish marks	Increase of the exchange rate U.S. $: Polish mark
Nov. 11, 1918	8,000	100	8	100
Dec. 31, 1918	9,000	113	9	113
Dec. 31, 1919	15,300	191	110	1,375
Dec. 31, 1920	49,362	617	590	7,375
Dec. 31, 1921	229,537	2,869	2,923	36,537
Dec. 31, 1922	793,438	9,911	17,800	225,000
Dec. 31, 1923	125,371,955	1,567,149	6,375,000	7,968,750

Source: E. Taylor, *Inflacja polska* (Poznań, 1926), pp. 22–23; J. Zdziechowski, *Finanse Polski w latach 1924 i 1925* (Warsaw, 1925), pp. 13–15.

Table 2. Comparison of Budgetary Deficits and Banknote Issues, 1919–23 (billion Polish marks)

Year	Deficit	Increase of Issue	Year	Deficit	Increase of Issue
1919	8.9	6.3	1922	470.1	563.9
1920	58.5	34.1	1923	113,704.0	125,578.5
1921	162.7	180.2			

Source: Z. Landau, J. Tomaszewski, *W dobie inflacji 1918–1923* (Warsaw, 1967), p. 280.

In the first years of independent Poland, the role of credits given by the PKKP was rather insignificant — in 1919 they accounted for only 2 percent of the note circulation; in 1923 their share grew to 33 percent.[3] According to calculations by an outstanding Polish economist, E. Taylor, in 1922–23, PKKP loans absorbed about 20 percent of emission.[4] Altogether it was estimated that private business and communal unions obtained from the state as unreturnable subsidies due to non-valorized loans $80–194 million (US).[5] Excessive credits, not based on banking deposits and owned funds but covered by succeeding emissions of banknotes, were a serious mistake. Especially after 1921, the situation of Polish industry was so good that there were real conditions for further reconstruction and development on the grounds of normal private capital formation. Banknote issues due to budgetary needs and granting credits to private entrepreneurs had to increase more rapidly than they would once they were subject to only one of these factors. Joint influence of both factors accelerated inflationary processes.

So far it has not been explained why the rate of fall of the Polish mark against the dollar was higher than that of the note circulation increase. Simplifying the whole thing a little, there were three basic reasons for this phenomenon. The first one was psychological. Making economic decisions, people, who had observed a gradual decrease of value of the Polish mark for a certain time, forecast its further fall and tried to protect themselves against the losses involved. In other words, they fixed sales prices adding corrections for anticipated depreciation of the Polish mark. Fearing losses, they calculated the corrections so that they exceeded actual depreciation of currency. Under the Polish postwar conditions, where the market supply was insufficient and flight from the national currency was common, price rises did not cause sales drops. Thus the psychological factor led to price increases, further currency depreciation, and an accelerated inflationary spiral.

The second reason was foreign trade. After World War I, in view of huge damage and economic confusion, Poland imported much more than it could export. This led to a large deficit in its trade balance. Partially it was covered by foreign loans, but even then its major part could be balanced only by purchasing foreign currencies in Poland or by transfers of Polish marks abroad. The keen demand for foreign currencies made their rate in relation to the Polish mark rise much more rapidly than the note circulation increased (cf. Table 1). The extremely low demand for Polish marks abroad made foreign businessmen accept Polish marks at a lower rate of exchange than current quotations indicated.

Finally, the third reason was hoarding of foreign currencies by Poles. Mistrust of Polish marks made people put savings and deposits almost exclusively in gold, jewels, and foreign currencies. Thus they were in great demand. Hoarding purchases influenced the Polish mark rate in a way similar to purchases of foreign exchange to cover import expenditures.

Inflation due to banknote issues to cover budgetary deficits and for credit purposes was therefore accelerated by other factors of which three have been discussed. Those, however, were not stable and their role grew the more rapidly the inflationary processes developed. Inflation increased spontaneously and even a temporary check on issues of Polish marks could not slow it.

2. IMPACT OF INFLATION ON THE NATIONAL ECONOMY

Inflation had a very strong influence on economic life in Poland in 1918–23. Yet evaluation of this impact on the national economy and the standard of living of various social groups is very difficult, as it cannot be shown in monetary terms. Most Polish economic historians thought inflationary processes played a rather negative role. Before World War II they were mainly considered from the point of view of their influence on the development of savings and, after 1945, from the point of view of real wages. It seems these criteria are not sufficient to evaluate the influence of inflation on the Polish economy and may thus lead to false conclusions.

In my opinion, moderate inflation, before it reached the stage of hyperinflation, had a generally positive impact on the rate of reconstruction and beginning domestic industry. This phenomenon has been recorded not only in Poland but also in other countries. Inflation simply changed proportions in the distribution of national income and stimulated growth of production.

After World War I, and particularly in the years 1919–22, inflation in Poland considerably extended markets and decreased basic costs of industrial production. A parallel increase of demand and decrease of production costs made business profits increase and influenced further expansion of production.

Constant depreciation of domestic currency discouraged people from placing savings in Polish marks. Thus most of workers' cash incomes was spent on consumption. Increase in domestic market sales applied above all to goods manufactured in Poland. Imported goods were less competitive in view of their relatively higher price. A. Wierzbicki, Director General of the Polish Association of Industry, Trade, and Finance, said: "The inflationary barrier for imported goods has strengthened the position of domestic industry on the Polish market."[6] At the same time inflation helped Polish exports. It caused the so-called inflationary export bounty. The influence of inflation on industrial activity may be illustrated by the fact that when, at the end of 1921 Polish Minister of Treasury J. Michalski temporarily checked banknote issuing, production immediately fell and unemployment grew.[7] The same was recorded in 1924, when W. Grabski successfully carried out the Polish currency and budgetary reform.

The impact of inflation on the decrease of costs of production had many directions. As a rule it consisted in a shift of some costs from producer to consumer.

First, costs of credits in Polish currency diminished. The moment a credit was given its real value was much higher than when it was returned in depreciated currency. The difference went for the benefit of the debtor and — when he was an industrial entrepreneur — decreased his costs of production.

Second, the tax burden diminished. Taxes were usually collected some time after the production of goods. During inflation, entrepreneurs included taxes in selling prices but delayed paying them, which brought about benefits due to a fall in their real value. Knowing this mechanism, entrepreneurs consciously delayed tax payments.

Third, real railway transportation costs decreased. Freight tariffs of the state-owned railway company grew more slowly than selling prices.

Fourth, the share of labor costs in the total costs of production fell. The rate of increase of nominal wages from mid-1921 on was lower than that of the inflationary process. Producers paid wages with delay relative to the time of production. Thus after mid-1921 they paid their workers a lower share of real value than if real wages were stable.

These factors decreased costs of manufacturing and, given the seller's market, raised profits. Inflation encouraged entrepreneurs to expand. As a result industrial employment increased by 135 percent, 1920–22, reaching 82 percent of the 1913 level.[8]

Of course, it is not possible to state to what extent this development was due to inflation or to other factors. There are simply no measures to find it out. But undoubtedly the years of inflation saw a rapid reconstruction of the Polish national economy and the beginnings of a very difficult process of unification. Until 1913, each sector of the partitioned country developed separately, in a close connection with the economy and interests of the partitioning power. Economic links between the various Polish territories incorporated in Russia, Prussia, and Austria were very weak and were reflected in a limited turnover among them.

Transition from a creeping to a runaway inflation in 1923 brought about a slowdown of business activity. The propensity to save vanished. Entrepreneurs, used to high inflationary profits, decreased investments or exported their capital. Hyperinflation destroyed floating assets and credit. The real value of note circulation fell. In November 1918 it was equal to $110 million; in December 1923 it amounted to only $20 million.[9] In the course of hyperinflation, all costs calculations in Polish marks were abandoned. Gold and foreign currencies became the only standard of value. It appeared that manufacturing in Poland was more expensive than abroad, a result of the out-of-date technical equipment of Polish factories. The inflationary export bounty disappeared and the Polish market was opened to imports. Imported goods became more and more competitive with domestic production.

3. INFLATION AND THE STANDARD OF LIVING OF VARIOUS SOCIAL GROUPS

Positively evaluating the influence of the creeping inflation on the Polish economy after World War I, it is necessary to remember that various social groups felt inflation in different ways. We have already noticed that banknote issues were aimed at covering budgetary deficits and granting credits for reconstruction of the national economy. But printing money does not produce new values. It is clear that thanks to inflation the state could cover its expenditures but only through an increased participation in distribution of the national income. Thus the share of other social groups in the national income had to fall.

An excessive emission of Polish marks led to the so-called inflationary tax which fed the treasury. The inflationary tax consisted in the fact that all users of the Polish mark who did not spend it at once were gradually losing some of its previous purchasing power. The difference between the value of goods one could buy the moment one received money and the value of goods actually bought was collected by the state. A Polish economist W. Fabierkiewicz explained this process as follows: "Collection (of the inflationary tax) consists in withdrawal of utility values (labor or goods) from circulation at old prices by means of a new purchasing capacity in the shape of a new banknote issue."[10]

The inflationary tax was therefore paid by all owners of Polish paper currency. The greater the role of Polish marks in the economic life of a group, the greater its share in financing state expenditures.

All estimates of the value of the inflationary tax are very difficult. There were a few attempts to calculate it in Poland. According to the method adopted, the result varied between $533 million and $809 million.[11] The highest estimate is most popular and is included in our considerations. In order to realize the amount collected by the treasury in the inflationary tax, it is worth comparing it with other budgetary revenues (Table 3).

Table 3 shows that the inflationary tax accounted for 64 percent. There are, however, estimates indicating it amounted to as much as 78 percent.[12] All these data show how large the state revenues due to inflation were. By spending the budgetary funds the state redistributed the national income. Most of the profits therefrom were derived by business. In 1919–21 the government financed private producers by giving them outright subsidies or advances on account of future deliveries. These advances were depreciated in the course of inflation and so most frequently became unreturnable subsidies. These budgetary expenditures were actually profits of entrepreneurs. Obviously workers, peasants, or salaried people were not given depreciating advances or subsidies and could not get richer thereby. Nevertheless, they also participated to a certain degree in the budgetary expenditures through unemployment relief, public works, or government aid to reconstruct the rural economy. Despite a lack of reliable statistical evidence, economists and historians are unanimous that benefits derived from the inflationary redistribution of the national income by the "world of business" were higher than these of other social groups.

This is why the second largest beneficiary of inflation was the propertied classes, mainly industrial producers and, to a lesser degree, landowners. They derived great profits from credits granted by the state or its banks and participated in the secondary distribution of the national income through the state budget. They also benefited from depreciating taxes. Moreover, inflation released the propertied classes from a large part of credit charges, except for credits in foreign currency terms, brought about profits due to a decrease in the real value of freight tariffs and customs duties, created the export bounty, made imports noncompetitive, and thus stimulated sales of goods manufactured in Poland.[12] Thanks to inflation, the propertied classes managed to shift a major part of the cost of maintaining the state. If budgetary expendi-

Table 3. Structure of Budgetary Revenues, 1918–23 (million U.S. $)

Revenues	1918	1919	1920	1921	1922	1923	Total
Taxes and state			29	38	57	49	214
monopolies	6	35	30	25	55	59	236
Other revenues	6	61					
Inflationary tax		276	230	108	71	124	809

Source: T. Szturm de Sztrem, *Żywiołowość w opodatkowaniu: podatek inflacyjny* (Warsaw, 1924), p. 49.

tures were not covered by banknote issues, the government would have had to increase taxes, to float compulsory loans, or introduce other measures taxing the most well-to-do social groups.

While inflation was bringing the state and the private business circles direct profits, some other sector was losing or limiting current consumption.

Inflation was a great drain on all the owners of the Polish mark, that is on all wage earners, workers, clerks, and professionals. Entrepreneurs, rentiers, and small-scale producers could to a large extent protect their incomes against the inflationary tax — some due to depositing their resources in foreign currencies which were not depreciated — others (like craftsmen or peasants) due to selling only when they had to buy necessary goods. Both groups usually kept Polish marks for only a very short time between transactions. This protected them against the inflationary tax or limited its burden.

Wage earners were in a different position. In order to protect their incomes against depreciation they could not spend all the earned money at once. It was not possible to buy necessary foodstuffs for a whole week or a month. Wages had to be spent gradually and thus became the basic source of the inflationary tax.

The inflationary tax burden borne by various users of the Polish mark was subject to the rate of inflation and to the time the money was kept. The longer the money was kept and the more rapidly inflation grew, the higher the inflationary tax burden on wage earners. The first factor could be somehow moderated by the Polish mark users, but the second left them completely helpless. At first, the burden of inflation was more or less evenly distributed among various social groups. As the inflation developed, it hit wage earners more and more. The propertied classes could improve methods of avoiding the inflationary tax and shifted it onto the social groups that could not resist it. A Polish economist, T. Szturm de Sztrem, estimated that in the first quarter of 1922 the Polish proletariat paid 0.8 percent of inflationary tax; in the fourth quarter of 1923, 39.9 percent.[13]

This explains the changes in the purchasing power of workers' wages. In the first half of 1921, real wages amounted to 98 percent of the 1914 level (in 1919 they had accounted for only about 30 percent); afterward, they rapidly fell from 85 percent in the first half of 1922 to 71 percent in the first half of 1923. In the second half of 1923 they were a mere 57 percent of the 1914 level.[14] As a result of hyperinflation the real wages of workers were only about 27 percent higher than the hunger level of 1919.

At the same time, however, the inflationary prosperity liquidated unemployment. For instance, in July 1919 the number of registered unemployed amount to 318,000 (actually it was much higher); in

October 1923 it was only 52,000.[15] Despite growing employment, the real wages of all Polish workers had seriously fallen over the years 1921–23. In 1921 they amounted to 63 percent of the 1913 level (due to employment being lower than before the war); in 1923, they fell to 49,[16] mainly due to a rapid fall of real wages. Altogether, the total real wages of workers in Poland perceptibly diminished, although mass unemployment was eliminated. It is an open question whether, the working class as a whole would be better off if stable real wages were accompanied by growing unemployment or full employment was accompanied by a reduction of real wages. In my opinion, the second solution is better not only for wage earners but also for the whole national economy. In this case the multiplier effects are much stronger than in the other one. Underemployment and relatively high wages make the propensity to save higher than in the case of a higher employment and lower average wages. Thus the real market demand is higher in the latter case.

Salary earners did not feel inflation any less than workers. It was perhaps even more painful for them, because inflation did not bring about an increase in employment similar to that of workers. In view of a considerable deficit of brain workers connected with the organization of a new state apparatus, unemployment did not affect the intelligentsia. Thus they could not feel improvement of their situation due to increase of employment.

Evaluating the influence of inflation on the situation of peasants, accounting for about 70 percent of population in Poland, is not an easy task. On the one hand inflation brought a decrease of the tax burden[17] and diminished indebtedness of farmers, as they repaid debts in depreciating Polish marks. On the other hand inflation almost destroyed their savings, except those deposited in foreign currencies, and deteriorated the terms of trade, worsening the ratio between prices for goods sold by peasants and those purchased by them. However, a balance of benefits and losses of peasants can hardly be carried out in measurable quantities. Thus the general evaluations found in the Polish literature of the subject include both negative and positive conclusions as regards the influence of inflation on the financial standing of Polish peasants.

4. WAY OUT OF HYPERINFLATION

Transition from a creeping inflation to a hyperinflation brought about serious economic perturbations which affected the propertied classes. At the same time, workers' dissatisfaction increased and led to the revolutionary wave of fall 1923. Strikes and armed demonstrations of the urban proletariat took place in many industrial centers in Poland. Further development of hyperinflation would mean not only economic difficulties but also political upheavals. Thus combating hyperinflation became of vital interest for the state and the propertied classes at the end of 1923. Previous governments tried to counteract inflation but their policies were inconsistent because inflation was the basic source of budgetary revenues. Business was also interested in maintaining moderate inflation. This is why the government attempt to combat inflation could not produce results. The situation changed in fall 1923.

On 19 December 1923, Władysław Grabski was made premier and minister for treasury, a post he had held twice before. The basic task of the Grabski government was to carry out a budgetary and monetary reform, putting off the solution of other problems. The reform was to go in two directions — substitution of a new currency unit for the Polish mark and liquidation of the budgetary deficit, the essential reason for inflation. In spite of contemporary principles of economic policy, Grabski decided to solve both problems at once, as he thought it wrong to postpone the monetary reform until a permanently balanced budget could be achieved. Under Polish conditions a total mistrust in the Polish mark made all counterinflationary policies very difficult.[18]

In all the Central European countries affected by inflation (e.g., Austria, Hungary, Germany), monetary reforms were based on large foreign loans connected with international control by creditor organizations. The Polish government feared to enter this road, as it might have led to limitation of the country's sovereignty. At the end of 1923, major loans could be obtained only in Great Britain or through the Financial Committee of the League of Nations which was also connected with British financial circles. Great Britain, like the United States some time later, was concerned for the reconstruction of Germany. Therefore Grabski was afraid foreign loans could be used to subordinate the Polish economy to the economic and political interests of the neighboring Weimar Republic. This is why he finally chose a variant aimed at overcoming inflation by use of the country's own resources. Foreign loans were to play a minor role, and Grabski made a point of avoiding their connection with unfavorable economic or political conditions for Poland. He preferred to accept even more unfavorable financial terms. This is why some loans cost 24–30 percent per annum, costs of special privileges for creditors included.[19]

The essential problem however was to balance the budget. The government planned to achieve it through reduction of expenditures, valorization of taxes, increase in tax rates, and even more important, through application of the August 1923 bill concerning a special levy paid by all owners of real assets. Within three years, this levy was to give the treasury an equivalent of 1 billion francs, sufficient to cover the 1924–26 deficits. It was thought after these three years the Polish economy would be strong enough to produce normal budgetary revenues capable of covering the state expenditures.

The Grabski program was ambitious but hard to fulfil. The major burden would be put on the propertied classes which would have to pay the levy and suffer from valorization of taxes. Grabski realized however that only this social group could give the necessary funds. Peasants and workers were too poor.

The prime minister decided to liquidate the previous state bank of issue — Polska Krajowa Kasa Pożyczkowa — and to establish instead a new joint-stock bank majority of private shareholders — the Bank Polski. The new bank was to issue a new monetary unit, the złoty, with a 30 percent gold cover. The złoty gold parity was equal to the Swiss franc (1/31 g of gold = 1 złoty; 1 dollar = 5.18 złotys).[20] Apart from banknotes issued by the Bank Polski, fractional money and silver coins were allowed to circulate but in precisely limited quantities. The złoty was put in circulation 28 April 1924; the Polish mark was gradually withdrawn at the exchange rate of 1.8 million Polish marks per złoty. The gold and foreign exchange reserves accumulated in the Bank Polski provided for an 87 percent coverage of the złoty circulation (given the statutory reserve of 30 percent) in 1924.[21]

5. COIN INFLATION

In 1924 the government succeeded in fulfiling its programs: the budget was balanced and the Polish mark was replaced by złotys. In 1925, however, the situation got worse for several reasons. The economic depression which started in fall 1923 (called a *postinflation* crisis), the outbreak of a tariff war with Germany which badly hurt Polish exports, delay in the payments levied on the propertied classes — all these brought back budgetary deficits. The Grabski government had to cover them with additional issues of coins. In the first quarter of 1925, coin circulation had grown by 66 million złotys; in the second, by 54 million; in the third quarter, by 99 million złotys more.[22] On 31 December 1924, the total circulation of 676 million złotys included 81.5 percent of banknotes and 18.2 percent of coins; at the end of 1925, the circulation of 815 million złotys included only 46.8 percent banknotes.[23] Another inflation was approaching causing a doubling of circulation. Banknotes issued by the Bank Polski and covered with gold were accompanied by increased issuance of coins. The Bank Polski feared losing its reserves and refused to exchange coins for banknotes and foreign currencies. Thus złoty coins and banknotes had different rates of exchange.

Even more serious than this doubling of circulation was the rebirth of the inflationary trend. In the course of the postinflation depression the industrial output of 1925 fell by 14 percent as compared with that of 1923,[24] while the circulation of coins and banknotes increased by 51 percent from June 1924 to September 1925.[25] It meant that money circulation grew more rapidly than market needs.

Polish society, with hyperinflation memories still fresh in mind, nervously reacted to the revival of the inflationary trend. The złotys were got rid of, which increased the gold and foreign exchange outflow from the Bank Polski. On 23 July 1925, the general management of the Bank Polski limited the exchange of złotys and made Polish importers cover their payments abroad in złotys. The excessive supply of Polish złotys in foreign monetary markets and their incomplete exchangeability made the exchange rate of the złoty against the dollar increase to 5.8–6 złotys at the end of July 1925, whereas the parity rate of exchange was 5.18 złotys per dollar.[26] The exchange intervention of the Bank Polski pegged the Polish złoty but when it was stopped in November 1925, in view of the limited reserves of the Bank Polski, the exchange rate of Polish currency fell again to 6.2–6.9 złotys per dollar.[27] In this situation, Grabski, who was for pegging the exchange rate of the złoty through interventionist purchases, resigned along with his ministers.

A new government was formed by Aleksander Skrzyński and the treasury went to Jerzy Zdziechowski. The latter thought a drop of the exchange rate of the złoty would help Polish exports. Therefore he paid special attention to the budgetary situation seeing a key to the monetary problems there. He intended to overcome the budgetary deficits by means of indirect taxes charged consumers and a radical cut of expenditures, not like Grabski, by means of charging the well-off people with a levy. Successful fulfilment of Zdziechowski's plans was, however, mainly due to recovery in the market from February 1926 on, which brought about an increase of tax revenues and state monopoly profits. By April 1926 the monthly budgetary deficit was very small. Złoty quotations improved; in December 1925 the exchange rate was 9.1; by March 1926 it improved to 7.8 złotys per dollar.[28]

The May coup d'état of Józef Piłsudski did not change monetary and financial policy. It was continued by J. Zdziechowski's successor in the ministry of treasury — Gabriel Czechowicz.

Further improvement of the market situation and attainment of a favorable balance of trade (due among other things to the 1926 strike of British miners which made possible an increase in Polish coal exports) thus led in the second half of 1926 to both a balanced budget and złoty stabilization at 8.91 złotys per dollar. On 13 October 1927, it was confirmed by a bill. The złoty was devalued by 42 percent as compared with the gold parity fixed in 1924. 5,924.44 złotys were now equal to 1 kg of gold, compared with 3,100.00 złotys previously. The Polish currency unit was to be converted into gold and foreign exchange without limitations, except for gold, which could be bought in quantities not less than 20,000 złotys. The minimum cover in the Bank Polski was raised from 30 percent to 40 percent.[29]

Both the first (1924) and the second (1927) stabilization were based on the country's own resources. In both cases foreign aid played only a minor role. The stabilization loan contracted by the Polish government in October 1927 was rather aimed at entering foreign financial markets and not at strengthening stability of the Polish złoty. The government hoped the loan would attract the interest of foreign business in investing in Poland. These hopes failed.

Stabilization of currency and balancing the budget on the grounds of domestic resources was something really new in the European monetary reforms of the mid-1920s. In other countries affected by hyperinflation, stabilization was carried out in cooperation with, and thanks to, the financial aid from the Financial Committee of the League of Nations (Austria, Hungary) or great powers (Germany). Under Polish conditions, stabilization based on foreign aid might have led to subordination of Poland to the then hostile international financial centers. Such plans were considered mainly in London, New York, and Berlin. It was expected monetary difficulties would make Poland search for credits and the conditions imposed in this connection would help the German Reich master the Polish economy.[30] Thus Germany would obtain a favorable market for industrial goods and thereby be able to pay war damages and return credits received under the Dawes Plan. Germany always hoped that economic subordination of Poland would further revision of the Versailles Treaty frontiers. This danger was successfully avoided.

Notes

1. W. Grabski, *Wyjaśnienia do ratyfikacji Traktatu Pokojowego z Niemcami i umowa Wielkich Mocarstw z Polską przez delegata pełnomocnego Polski na Kongresie Pokojowym.* Paryż 1919, p. 22. (Top secret, printed as a manuscript.)

2. F. Zweig, "Stosunki gospodarcze" in *Wielka Encyklopedia Powszechna,* XIII: 75.

3. E. Taylor, *Inflacja polska* (Poznań, 1926), p. 189.

4. *Ibid.,* p. 188.

5. T. Szturm de Sztrem, *Żywiołowość w opodatkowaniu: podatek inflacyjny* (Warszawa, 1923), p. 52; Taylor, p. 255; S. Starzyński, "Myśl państwowa w życiu gospodarczym" in *Na froncie gospodarczym 1918–1928* (Warszawa, n.d.), p. 10.

6. A. Wierzbicki, "Ogólny pogląd na rozwój przemysłu polskiego" in *Bilans gospodarczy dziesięciolecia Polski Odrodzonej.* Vol. I: 301.

7. For details, Z. Landau, "Jerzy Michalski (1870–1956)," *Finanse,* No. 2 (1974), pp. 56–67.

8. Z. Landau, J. Tomaszewski, *W dobie inflacji 1918–1923* (Warszawa, 1967), p. 93.

9. J. Zdziechowski, *Finanse Polski w latach 1924 i 1925* (Warszawa, 1925), pp. 13–15.

10. W. Fabierkiewicz, "Jakie warstwy społeczne i w jakiej wysokości opłacają podatek emisyjny" in *Skarb Rzeczypospolitej* (Warszawa, n.d.), p. 46.

11. Landau, Tomaszewski, p. 288.

12. S. Starzyński, p. 9.

13. T. Szturm de Sztrem, p. 48.

14. J. Derengowski, "Płace realne w Polsce w latach 1918–1928" in *Bilans . . .*, II: 354; S. Rychliński, *Płace i zarobki robotników przemysłowych w dziesięcioleciu 1918–1928* (Warszawa, 1929), p. 10.

15. J. Drecki, "Bezrobocie w Polsce niepodległej" in *Bilans . . .*, II: 379.

16. Z. Landau, J. Tomaszewski, *Robotnicy przemysłowi w Polsce. Materialne warunki bytu 1918–1939* (Warszawa, 1971), p. 199.

17. K. Philip, *Podatek gruntowy i budynkowy na terenie byłego Królestwa Kongresowego w okresie inflacji [1919–1924]* (Warszawa, 1931), p. 77. (Typescript in the SGPiS Library, Warsaw).

18. On W. Grabski's program and activity, J. Tomaszewski, *Stabilizacja waluty w Polsce* (Warszawa, 1961).

19. Z. Landau, *Polskie zagraniczne pożyczki państwowe 1918–1926* (Warszawa, 1961), pp. 232, 276.

20. Dziennik Ustaw R.P. 1924, No. 7, item 75.

21. *Statystyka obiegu pieniężnego w 1924 r.* "Przemysł i Handel," 1925, pp. 359–61.

22. *Rocznik Statystyki R.P.* 1927, p. 269.

23. Ibid.

24. *Materiały do badań nad gospodarką Polski. Part 1 — 1918–1939* (Warszawa, 1956), p. 269.

25. *Rocznik Statystyki R.P.* 1927, p. 269.

26. *Sprawozdanie Banku Polskiego za r. 1925* (Warszawa, 1926), p. 17.

27. A. Krzyżanowski, *Dwa programy finansowe [jesień 1925 i wiosna 1927]* (Kraków, 1927), p. 28.

28. *Annuaire statistique du Ministère des Finances* (Varsovie, 1931), p. 388.

29. Dziennik Ustaw R.P. 1927, No. 88, item 790; No. 97, item 855–856.

30. Cf., e.g., documents published by B. Ratyńska, *Niemcy wobec stabilizacji waluty polskiej w latach 1925–1926.* "Sprawy Międzynarodowe," 1960, No. 9.

Inflation in Hungary

GYÖRGY RÁNKI

Hungary faced an entirely different economic position after the war than before. Territorial changes, not to be discussed here, were far too large, and the disturbances occurred in an already critical economic situation stemming from wartime exhaustion which had largely contributed to the disorganization of production, thus accelerating the currency depreciation which had been started by the war.

Agricultural production declined by roughly 50 percent; industry probably produced still less. In the summer of 1919, the crown stood at 15 percent of its prewar value; by February 1920, it had fallen to one-eighth of its value of the previous summer.[1]

In the summer of 1921, 17.326 billion crowns were in circulation. A year later, this sum had trebled. By the summer of 1923, it had reached 44.00 billion crowns; by the spring of 1924, the height of inflation, 2.5 trillion. As a result of the mounting issue of banknotes the value of the currency dropped precipitously. In August 1919, one gold crown was worth 9.9 paper crowns; in June 1921 it fetched 50.7 paper crowns.[2]

The history of the Hungarian inflation was complicated by the problem of the privilege of issuing banknotes. Until the end of the war, this privilege was in the possession of the Austro-Hungarian Bank. After the breakup of the empire, it became necessary to arrange financial independence for Hungary as well. For the time being, the notes of the former Austro-Hungarian Bank were regarded as valid, although they had gradually been losing their value. During the revolution in Hungary, the government was cut off from its former money supply and issued its own banknotes without withdrawing from circulation the banknotes previously issued. After the collapse of the revolution, the new counterrevolutionary government, more for political than economic reasons, proclaimed that the face value of the banknotes issued by the Bolshevik government was to be cut by 50 percent.[3] The counterrevolutionary government's need to maintain a large army and to finance a great many civil servants who had fled from Hungary's lost territories increased state expenses greatly, while revenues remained on a very low level. Finally, the government decided to borrow a large amount from the former Austro-Hungarian Bank. Needless to say, this contributed to the inflationary process.

In the early 1920s, Hungary was obliged by the peace treaty to complete the separation of its currency from that of Austria. All the banknotes in circulation had to be sealed, and half of them were to be taken away from their owners as a forced loan. The purpose of this forced loan was partly to meet the needs of the state budget; to eliminate or to diminish the deficit, and at the same time, to slow down the depreciation of the currency. The effect of this was very limited. The external value of the Hungarian crown between February and July 1920 rose from 1.9 Swiss centimes to 3.4 centimes. After that it started to decline again, and at the end of the year it was down to 1.15 centimes.[4] In any case one could hardly regard this measure as a serious attempt to stop inflation. First, with no important changes in the level of production and inventories and with the prevailing shortages of goods any serious attempt to maintain the value of the currency was doomed to failure. Second, the government failed to carry out its plan for a forced loan. Pressure groups were able to change the original conception. Thus, current accounts and saving accounts in the banks were exempted from the capital levy, due to this modification and to some other successful maneuvers. For instance, one of Hungary's largest banks, the Commercial Bank, which was originally supposed to deliver 155 million crowns to the treasury succeeded in reducing the amount to 60 million crowns.[5]

A more serious attempt to stop inflation was made in the first half of 1921 by Lóránt Hegedüs, the new minister of finance. Coming from the former nobility, he made a successful career in business. For a while, he was director of the Hungarian Association of Manufacturers, then managing director of the Commercial Bank and the president of the Association of Hungarian Banks and Savings Banks. He was a true representative of the alliance between the traditional Hungarian ruling class and the new business elite.[6] After the difficulties of revolution and counterrevolution whose economic policies — if those could be called economic policies at all — were harmful to business interests, Hegedüs was regarded as the man who would carry out an economic policy promoting economic restoration and stabilization. His first measure was to stop working the currency press. He was smart enough at the beginning not only to stop the inflow of new banknotes but even to decrease their circulation by 10 percent. By his measures he created a shortage of money because the value of the money in circulation actually was far below 50 percent of its prewar level. The shortage of money led to the rise of interest rates and lured money to the banks instead of into speculation in gold or foreign currency. Hegedüs declared that in order to raise confidence in the Hungarian crown he was even willing to pay the interest on former Hungarian loans if interest rates were decreased from 5 percent to 4 percent.[7]

Initially, his economic and fiscal policy seemed to be very successful. On the foreign stock exchanges speculation on the improvement of
the Hungarian crown seemed to be a promising business and due to
this expectation, a lot of Hungarian banknotes were bought by foreigners. The external value of the crown increased from 1.15 to 2.62
centimes at the Zurich stock exchange. The dollar in Budapest went
down from 572 to 240 crowns.[8]

The idea of stabilization was based on a balanced budget. The
minister of finance was really very imaginative in finding new forms of
taxation. But, his main idea for balancing the budget was based on a
relatively large capital levy. According to his plans, wealthy individuals, merchants, financiers, and industrialists had to give 10 to 20 percent of their fortunes to the state budget. Landowners would have to
pay 5 percent of the value of their lands in either cash or land. In
addition Hegedüs tried to connect these taxes with a moderate land
reform.[9]

To collect this capital levy was difficult. Even in purely financial
terms, the idea had inherent contradictions: namely, the levy to be
collected in cash might, under the given circumstances, have lost its
value very quickly; and there was only a small probability that stabilization could be based upon it. But, the possessing classes — particularly the landowners — were strongly opposed to the levy. The amount
coming in to the treasury was, thus, far below expectations.

Yet this difficulty might have been overcome. Probably the most
serious weakness of Hegedüs's monetary policy and his stabilization
attempts was his one-sided financial approach to the issue and his
disregard of the short-run effect on the economy of this monetary
policy. The few favorable economic effects that had occurred because
of the halt in issuing new banknotes slowly disappeared. With the
shortage of money, the investment boom stopped and the incentives to
export provided by the decreasing value of the currency disappeared.
Imports increased and the balance of trade deteriorated.

Businessmen and landowners turned more and more against Hegedüs's deflationary monetary policy, seeing it as devastating for the
Hungarian economy. The interests of financial recovery and industrial
recovery seemed to be separated.

During the summer of 1921 it became clear that Hegedüs could not
eliminate the budget deficit. Confidence in the improvement in the
value of the crown quickly disappeared, and foreign owners of crowns
tried to sell their stock quickly. From the high of 2.62 centimes, the
crown fell in Zurich to 1.97 centimes in July and to 1.14 in September.[10]
The attempt at stabilization failed. In his speech to the Hungarian
parliament, Hegedüs admitted his failure. He blamed the whole nation
because it was not willing to bear the necessary sacrifices for stabiliza-

tion.[11] He resigned and his successor based his monetary policy on the banknotes press.[12]

Hegedüs had certainly been right to blame the possessing classes for his failure. But if we try to view his attempt in historical perspective, we must admit that his policy was based on old-fashioned conservative monetary policy. This fiscal policy was elaborated in the works of Heinrich Rau and later by Adolf Wagner and Lorenz Stein and in the nineteenth century it was certainly regarded as the dominant approach to public finance.[13] Supposing a harmonious balance in the economy, as was usual among classical economists, all imbalances were regarded as extremely harmful. The sole role of the state was seen as dealing with the budget. Any other connections between the state's activity, the budget, and economic life were overlooked. We may say in this occasion that large contradictions existed between the needs and the illnesses of the economy on the one hand and the cure the doctors offered on the other.

After publication of the budget and the resignation of Hegedüs, inflation rapidly accelerated. A new institution for issuing banknotes was established and this became an almost unlimited source of credit for the state and the business community. Inflation became more and more a means of promoting business interests. An ever larger fraction of the issue of new banknotes took the form of credit to private business. Three months' bills of exchange for 6 or 8 percent interest were given by the state bank to industry and trade; this was an important support for entrepreneurs in livening up economic activity by nonvalorized credits.[14] Even though interest rates on those credits had been gradually raised, they remained well behind the rate of inflation. In 1921 only 10 percent of the new banknotes came into circulation in the form of state credits to large-scale business; by the latter part of 1922 this figure had risen to 50 percent; in 1923 it was 65 percent.[15]

Inflation served to cut production costs markedly by reducing real wages. Between the middle of 1914 and the beginning of 1924 prices increased 8000 times but wages rose only 3500 times.[16] Thus, inflation permitted real wages to be cut to less than half of the prewar level. The advantages of inflation benefited every stratum of the property-owning classes. The great landowners in particular took advantage of the inflation to rid themselves of their former debts. During the preceding decades of economic development, landlords had accumulated substantial indebtedness. Now they were able to repay their obligations, totaling 3 billion dollars in 1913 value, in inflated currency, in nearly worthless paper money.[17]

The value of these enormous loans was not fixed in terms of gold or any other standard. They were made in rapidly depreciating paper money, so that when they were repaid at face value it was in a currency which had meanwhile shrunk to a fraction of its former worth. True, interest rates on these loans were raised gradually from 8 percent to 12 and later to 18 percent but at this stage, a usurious interest rate already prevailed, above 18 percent even on short-term loans.[18]

The government tried some counteraction to slow down the runaway inflation. The most important among these measures was the introduction of exchange control in 1922. Without the exchange control the crown might well have lost its value even before 1924 and have ceased to exist as a currency much earlier. But in spite of these measures the depreciation of the crown continued to accelerate:[19]

	Value of the Crown (Swiss francs)	Gold Crowns per paper crown
1921 Dec.	0.76	137.84
1922 June	0.56	190.33
1922 Dec.	0.23	466.06
1923 June	0.08	1,820
1923 Dec.	0.03	6,442
1924 May	0.0065	17,866

Before the stabilization in June 1924, the value of the crown went down to 18,000–19,000.

In the worst phase of runaway inflation, stabilization became unavoidable for economic, social, and political reasons. Due to many factors, Hungarian stabilization became an international issue. Control of inflation with external help appeared to be a reasonable solution not only because of the failure of 1921 but because the Hungarian government wanted to connect stabilization with the unsettled question of reparations.[20] Exploratory discussions with English financiers made it clear that the London money market was willing to support a Hungarian loan, provided that it would be executed under the political auspices of the League of Nations, and as security, the income of the state revenues sequestered for reparation payments were to be freed for the purposes of the loan.

To cut a long story short, the Hungarian government asked for the help of the League. But only after a long diplomatic skirmish, overcoming French and Little Entente hostility, was it able to arrive at concrete negotiation.[21] A delegation went to Hungary to examine the financial situation and after this, a project was elaborated for a $50 million loan for a two-and-a-half-year reconstruction program. The League of Nations committee made certain economic recommendations according to good old orthodox economic theory concerning the use of the loan, the currency to be set up, and the economic policies to be pursued.[22]

Preparations for stabilization started in the spring of 1924. First of all, the flow of nonvalorized credit ceased. Even former credits were supposed to be repaid at a certain rate of valorization. But, in spite of this, inflation was still in full swing. Stabilization started in July by fixing the ratio of the gold crown to the paper crown at 1 to 17,000; the Hungarian National Bank was created as a corporation, formally independent of the state with a monopoly on currency issue. The Bank reserves of gold and foreign exchange were bolstered by a loan of £4 million by the Bank of England.[23] Thus, the Hungarian currency was connected to the pound sterling and the gold standard.

The first part of the loan started to come in July. Half of the loan was subscribed in England; the other half in six other countries, chiefly the United States and Italy. Terms were extremely unfavorable. Interest was high and the rate of issue was low.[24]

After half a year it became quite obvious that the money was not so badly needed by the Hungarian government as had been supposed. Roughly 25 percent of the loan was sufficient to cover the budget deficit in the first half of the period. The deficit disappeared in 1925, two years sooner than had been anticipated.[25] With a not too burdensome capital levy, the deficit might have been overcome by use of internal resources without the restrictions on Hungarian sovereignty imposed by the League of Nations. One should not, however, approach this question only in terms of the stabilization process. The loan had a very important political aspect, namely, English protection against French and Little Entente political pressures.[26] And it had a further financial and economic consequence by opening the gate for a further infusion of Western credits. How these credits were used, to what extent they were able to contribute to strengthening the Hungarian economy, and their role in the financial collapse of 1931, is beyond the scope of this paper.

Notes

1. T. I. Berend and Gy. Ránki, *Magyarország gazdasága az I. világháború után* [Hungarian Economy after the First World War] (Budapest, 1966), p. 70.
2. Imre Borcza, comp., *Valuta- és ártáblázatok* [Currency and Price Tables] (Budapest), pp. 38–40.
3. *Az 1920 évi nemzetgyűlés irományai* [Records of the 1920 National Assembly], I: 99.
4. Tibor Rácz, *Valutaügyünk története a Magyar Nemzeti Bank alapításáig* [The History of Our Currency Situation until the Foundation of the Hungarian National Bank] (Budapest, 1934), p. 12.
5. Országos Levéltár [National Archives], Kereskedelmi Bank [Commercial Bank], 19 August 1920, 5971.

6. Berend and Ránki, *Magyarország gazdasága*, p. 71.

7. *Az 1920 évi nemzetgyűlés . . . Napló* [Protocol of the National Assembly, 1920], 29 December 1920.

8. *Statisztikai évkönyv 1919–1922* [Hungarian Statistical Yearbook, 1919–1922], p. 123 and Gyula Domány, *A magyar szanálás* [Hungarian Stabilization] (Budapest, 1927), p. 17.

9. Országos Levéltár, Pénzügyminisztérium, Szabóky iratok [National Archives, Finance Ministry, Szabóky Papers], X3. (1–11)

10. *Statisztikai évkönyv, 1919–1922* [Statistical Yearbook, 1919–1922], p. 123.

11. *Nemzetgyűlési Napló*, 22 September 1921.

12. Országos Levéltár, Állami Jegyintézet [National Archives, National Note Issuing Institute], 19 October 1921.

13. Farkas Heller, *Pénzügytan* [Theory of Finance] (Budapest, 1943).

14. Berend and Ránki, *Magyarország gazdasága*, p. 81.

15. G. Heidelberg, *Die Wirkung der Inflation und Sanierung auf dem ungarischen Geld- und Kapitalmarkt* (Budapest, 1927), pp. 70, 105; Béla Imreh, *Az inflációs évek hitelpolitikája* [Credit Policy during the Years of Inflation] (Budapest, 1926), p. 8.

16. Berend and Ránki, *Magyarország gazdasága*, p. 89.

17. Ernő György, *Az infláció mérlege* [Inflation Reconsidered] (Budapest, 1932), p. 23.

18. Berend and Ránki, *Magyarország gazdasága*, p. 81.

19. *Statisztikai évkönyv 1919–1922* [Statistical Yearbook, 1919–1922], p. 123; 1923–1925, p. 174.

20. Mária Ormos, *Az 1924 évi magyar államkölcsön megszerzése* [The Acquisition of the Hungarian State Loan in 1924] (Budapest, 1963).

21. *Ibid.*

22. Országos Levéltár, Pénzügyminisztérium, Szabóky iratok, 2/3. cs.

23. Országos Levéltár, Nemzeti Bank [National Bank], 30 August 1924.

24. Országos Levéltár, Pénzügyminisztérium, Szabóky iratok.

25. Országos Levéltár, Miniszterelnökség [Office of the Prime Minister], 158 cs.

26. Berend and Ránki, *Magyarország gazdasága*, p. 155.

A Comparative View of the Inflation of the 1920s in Austria and Czechoslovakia*

ALICE TEICHOVA

I

"Clearly it is the duty of the present generation to do its utmost to arrive at a clear analysis of what has happened to the world's currencies. . . ." In these words, Gustav Cassel exhorted his listeners to examine what he called the "revolution in all monetary conditions . . . connected with the World War" of 1914–1918 when he presented his Columbia University lectures in 1928. He thought that "in all future times people . . . will be astonished at all the mistakes of monetary policy in this period, and take the highest interest in the consequences of these mistakes. . . ."[1]

Yet, a thorough study and analysis of the postwar inflation has not been made. Only relatively recently have economic historians begun to turn their attention to the inflations of the 1920s in Europe.[2] The causes and impact, as well as the consequences of the hyperinflation in Weimar Germany, form a vital part of this interest, but a great void still exists in our knowledge of the inflations of the East-Central European successor states. Inflations in the successor states reached immense proportions in the wake of the disintegration of the Habsburg empire and in the process of transition from a war to a peace economy. The study of similarities and dissimilarities of causes, durations, magnitudes, and effects of them provide a virtual laboratory for the economic historian.

This does not imply that precise guidelines to solve contemporary problems of inflation can be found in the lessons of the monetary upheavals of the 1920s, but a more informed knowledge of both the quantitative and qualitative aspects of the processes of the most intense and widespread inflationary experience in the first half of the twentieth century may contribute to distinguishing identical and different phenomena in the second half of our century.

Among the wealth of possibilities which offer themselves for comparison the immediate postwar development of the two successor economies, Austria and Czechoslovakia, provide a unique case for a comparative study of the history of inflation. Starting out from a common basis given by the Austro-Hungarian monarchy they inherited, besides a similar economic structure, a common currency problem, a similar dependence on what became their foreign trade, and similar immediate needs for massive state intervention in the economy. They applied from the onset both similar and divergent policies and achieved opposite effects. One could almost say that here is a case where there is no need for counterfactual speculative methods, since historical reality allows us an insight into two relatively small, similarly structured industrial economies, one of a defeated and one of a victorious successor state, with all the consequences which this important difference implies.

The present state of research, or rather lack of research, permits me to give, at the most, an outline of the possibilities for applying comparative economic history.

II

Before the largely autarchic economic unit of the Austro-Hungarian empire disintegrated into several national markets, its most industrialized parts were situated in Cisleithania on the territory of postwar Czechoslovakia and Austria where the relatively greatest share of the national wealth was generated. Table I shows that the later Czechoslovakia contributed almost 45 percent and the later Austria just under 30 percent to the total income of the Austrian half of the monarchy.[3] Austrian, and in Czechoslovakia, Bohemian and Moravian industries had by 1913 reached a level of industrialization generally comparable with the advanced economies of Western Europe. Within the new frontiers, Austria comprised about one-eighth of the total territory and

Table 1. National Income (Austrian part of Habsburg Monarchy) (average, 1911–13)

Region	Domestically produced National Income (Mio. K)	Percentage Shares	
		National Income	Population
Austrian half	15,024.6	100	100
Successor states			
Austria	4,466.0	29.7	22.3
Czechoslovakia	6,710.3	44.7	34.3
Poland	2,267.7	15.1	29.3
Italy (portion)	780.7	5.2	5.4
Yugoslavia	536.8	3.6	5.9
Romania (portion)	236.1	1.7	2.8

Source: Norbert Schausberger, *Der Griff nach Österreich* (Vienna, Munich, 1978), p. 82.

population and one-third of the industry of the former monarchy, and Czechoslovakia retained one-fifth of the territory, one-fourth of the population and far more than half (up to 70 percent has been estimated) of the total industrial capacity of the former Habsburg empire.[4] After 1918, they were each faced with an immensely diminished home market and their Austro-Hungarian structure emphasized the problem of foreign trade for both countries, as they had to export between 30 to 50 percent of their total output in order to survive. The problems of disproportion between the industrial and agricultural sectors and between the individual branches of industry of each new state were among the greatest affecting their economic reconstruction. The most pressing need was changing industrial production from supplying a protected domestic market to producing for exports. Extraordinary difficulties arose, at the same time, because of the uneven level of economic development within the borders of the two successor states. With respect to Austria, the most striking differences existed between the excessive size and industrial, commercial, and administrative concentration in Vienna and the rest of the country. Czechoslovakia, again, inherited the west-east gradient of economic development of the empire, since its territory consisted of two regions at substantially different levels of industrialization (industrially advanced Bohemia and Moravia, formerly part of Cisleithania in the west, and relatively backward Slovakia, formerly incorporated into Transleithania in the east).

In spite of the great disproportions which they inherited, Austria's and Czechoslovakia's initial positions were based on similarly favorable assets when they established themselves as formally politically independent republics in October 1918. Unlike other less fortunate parts of the former Danubian monarchy, Austrian and Czechoslovak industry escaped the physical destruction of war — which provided their economies with greater potentialities for recovery. The example of other small European states whose industrial capacity was far greater than their home market (e.g., Switzerland and Denmark) seemed to suggest that these difficulties need not be insurmountable.

At the end of the war, however, the heritage of the two industrialized countries consisted of productive capacity but not of actual production, for that had been disrupted. Plant and equipment were severely run down, desperate shortages of essential raw materials, particularly coal, reduced output drastically and brought whole branches of industry to a virtual halt. Rail and river transport was disorganized not only through destruction in war, but through dispersal of rolling stock as well as ships which were allocated to the individual successor states only by 1920. Thus in Czechoslovakia there was a shortfall of 40,000 wagons which were urgently needed for the transport of coal during

1919;[5] in Austria, the dire need for coal led to shutdowns in industry and cuts of supplies to the public.[6] Productivity fell to an all time low in 1918–19 as the workers were exhausted by long hours of work and undernourishment. Production was further disrupted because of stoppages caused by strikes. At the end of the war, food was so scarce that the working population, especially of Austria, suffered from starvation. Estimates vary but in comparison with 1913, total production in Czechoslovakia fell to less than half and in Austria to about 25 to 30 percent by 1918,[7] and continued to decline in 1919.

Since the bulk of the Dual Monarchy's working class was concentrated in the two new republics — 44 percent of the total labor force in Czechoslovakia[8] and 35.6 percent in Austria[9] — food riots, strikes, and revolutionary uprisings which, in the last year of the war, had in increasing number and violence been directed against the collapsing Habsburg regime continued into the early years of the existence of Austria and Czechoslovakia against the background of the economic plight inherited from the war. As soldiers returning from the war to their homes in Austria could neither find jobs nor a decent place in civilian life, unemployment soared to 355,000 in 1919 — the greatest number experienced up to that time in the history of that region of the former monarchy and highest level in the first decade of Austria's independent existence (Table 5).[10] The provinces of Bohemia and Moravia in Czechoslovakia could more readily absorb demobilized soldiers into industrial employment as recovery was stimulated more speedily there than in Austria. Although wages in Czechoslovak industry were far below the prewar level as prices had risen much faster than wages — indeed, this constituted a factor conducive to recovery — social unrest was tempered by national pride and thus less intense than in Austria. Immediately after the war, however, workers and soldiers in both countries, whether employed or unemployed, were demoralized and influenced by the Bolshevik Revolution in Russia. In their uprisings and strikes they demanded greater social justice and the socialization of large industrial enterprises and banks; they expected the representatives of the Social Democratic Party leaders in government office to meet these demands. Table 6 shows the rising strike movement which reached its peak in Czechoslovakia in the General Strike of December 1920 and in Austria during the hyperinflation of 1921 and 1922. Industrial strife intensified in tune with rising prices which for the strongly organized Austrian trade unions resulted in agreements on index-linked wages. Even so, wages invariably lagged behind the cost-of-living index (cf. Table 2 for Austria, Table 3 for Czechoslovakia).

Violent confrontations, particularly in 1919, did not occur merely because of the gap between wages and prices. Economic grievances

Table 2. Indexes: Retail Prices, Cost of the Prewar Diet, Nominal Weekly Wages according to Collective Agreements 1914–23 — Austria (1914 = 1)

End of Year	Retail Prices (food, clothing, heating, & lighting)	Cost of Prewar Diet	Nominal Minimum Weekly Wages		
			(a) Skilled workers (average of 12 trades)*	(b) Unskilled workers ment	woment
1914	1	1	1	1	1
1918		15.60	3	5	—
1919	July 31.02	30.09	10	11	11
1920	Oct. 69.60	61.84	31	39	40
1921	661	704	416	499	524
1922	11737	13327	8319	9276	10303
1923	13948	15565	11909	14100	13062

*Masons, engineers, joiners, tanners, tailors, dressmakers, shoemakers, bookbinders, bakers, bricklayers, carpenters, decorators, and painters.
†Unskilled masons, engineers, carpenters, building laborers, decorators.
‡Unskilled female labor in the following trades: engineering, joining, and building.
Source: *Statistisches Handbuch für die Republik Österreich* (1924–25).

Table 3. Indexes: Retail Prices, Nominal and Real Wages in Czechoslovakia, 1913–21

Year	Retail Prices	Index of Average Wage of Insured Workers			
		Daily		Yearly	
		Nominal	Real	Nominal	Real
1913	100	100.0	100.0	100.0	100.0
1914	112	104.6	93.4	94.2	84.1
1915	172	111.2	57.9	104.0	54.2
1916	248	124.0	50.0	122.8	49.5
1917	389	161.2	41.4	154.9	39.8
1918	660	218.4	33.1	199.2	30.2
1919	990	370.7	37.4	342.0	34.5
1920	1750	634.5	36.2	601.1	34.3
1921	1914	1018.8	53.2	950.9	49.7

Source: Olšovský et al., p. 141.

were linked with political demands and threatened to destroy the capitalist system which the post-1918 governments tried to reconstruct in both successor states. During the social upheavals of 1919 the Austrian government appointed a Socialization Commission to meet, at least formally, the urgent demand for the nationalization of large private concerns; while through the back door of the Ministry of Finance it tried covertly to reprivatize state-owned enterprises or sell them to foreigners to reduce its budget deficits.[11] No such moves seemed necessary in Czechoslovakia where similar demands were voiced, but where the threat of nationalization was averted by identifying it with Czechoslovakization (or repatriation) of property.

There is ample evidence that the unstable social and political conditions both in Austria and Czechoslovakia, and especially the fear of socialization, undermined business confidence at home and abroad and prevented speedy stabilization.[12] Only great concessions, such as the eight-hour day and far-reaching social reforms by Social Democratic parties in power, were able to restore government control.[13] This policy of pacification required large state expenditure in addition to the urgent necessity to subsidize food supplies for the population. Inevitably, inherited budget deficits grew and the presses printing money were put to work at a greater pace. The increase in money supply to cover budget deficits combined with the drastic lack of goods engendered price rises and kept the inflationary spiral going. The monetary phenomenon was, thus, the result of economic disruption, the inability of production to satisfy consumption, and deep political conflicts in society and cannot be understood without taking account of these factors.

III

Inflationary conditions were inherited by all successor states, including those like the Czechoslovak Republic which belonged as an Associated Power to the victorious camp of the Entente. As one of its bequests, the monarchy left the successor states with the most depreciated currency of immediate postwar Europe (outside Russia). Between July 1914 and December 1918 banknote circulation in the Austro-Hungarian monarchy had risen 14 times; and in the new state banknotes continued to be issued at an increasing rate in Vienna until by December 1923 Austria's banknote circulation had increased 14.251 times.[14] After the peace treaties had been signed the Austro-Hungarian crown (K) emerged with the lowest gold cover of 0.6 percent (23 September 1919) in comparison with 58.1 percent at the outbreak of the war in 1914 (see Table 4A for comparison with other countries), and its value had fallen to one-third of its gold parity on the foreign exchange market, only to keep on falling until the end of 1922 in Austria where

Table 4A. Effective Gold Cover of Selected Note Issuing Banks before and after World War I

Bank	Date	Cover (%)
Austro-Hungarian Bank	22/7/1914	58.1
	23/9/1919*	0.6
Deutsche Reichsbank	23/7/1914	71.8
	15/9/1919	3.9
Bank of Italy	22/7/1914	66.6
	20/7/1919	8.3
Bank of France	22/7/1914	69.4
	24/9/1919	10
Bank of England	22/7/1914	137.0
	24/9/1919	108.1

*Date as near as possible after the Austro-Hungarian Bank went into liquidation on 11 September 1919.
Source: *Compass*, Deutschösterreich, Österreich-Ungarn (Liquidation), I (1923): 100.

the K steadied at 1/14.400 of its gold parity.[15] Czechoslovakia managed to protect its currency from tumbling into hyperinflation.

In spite of the disintegration of the monarchy into separate political units, economic ties persisted; therefore, initially, currency unity was retained while inflation spread, especially from Vienna where the Austro-Hungarian Bank was strongly influenced by the Austrian government.[16] The influx of paper money from neighboring successor states into each other's economies exacerbated difficulties of controlling the money supply within the individual states at a time when the gap between demand and supply of any goods whatsoever was so enormous that anything that could be produced was easily sold without regard to prices, which kept on soaring. Because the purchasing power of the Austro-Hungarian crown on Czechoslovak territory and its rate of exchange in Swiss francs (Frc) quoted in Prague was higher than in other parts of the former Austria-Hungary, notes and coins were transferred across the borders into Czechoslovakia. By March 1919 it was estimated that whereas one-fifth of the total Austro-Hungarian note circulation was within Austria, almost a third of total Austro-Hungarian notes circulated in the territory of Czechoslovakia (cf. Table 4B). At this juncture, in March 1919, the Czechoslovak government took the first significant steps toward extricating its economy from the old Austro-Hungarian unit through currency separation.

Thus the obvious cut-off point for quantifying the divergent inflationary development in the two countries is midnight, 25 February 1919 when the Currency Separation Act came into force and the

Table 4B. Estimate of the Distribution of Austro-Hungarian Notes in the Different Territories in March 1919 (in million £s)

Czech countries	500
German Austria	333
Hungary	292
Yugoslavia	187
Transylvania	83
Austrian Poland	42
Russian Poland and Ukraine	42
Trentino and Istria	21
Foreign markets	104
	£1604*

*Banknote circulation in the Austro-Hungarian Monarchy July 1914, 2,405,350,660 K; December 1918, 34,888,999,890 K.

Source: *Statements of Currency Expansion, Price Movements, and Production in Certain Countries* (No. Cmd. 734), cited in J. van Walré de Bordes, *The Austrian Crown* (London, 1924), pp. 42, 46–47.

Czechoslovak Republic closed its frontiers to transport of goods, persons, and money transmissions. During the first week of March 1919 followed the stamping of banknotes to 1 percent of their nominal value.[17] At the same time, 50 percent of privately held banknotes as well as of bank and savings accounts were withdrawn and converted into a 1 percent compulsory public loan. Payments from these blocked securities and accounts could be released for tax arrears and for the impending property levy designed to tax war profits or drawn upon in urgent cases only if special permission was obtained. Gradually much of this money seeped back into circulation, although at the time it was estimated that as a result of the monetary reform total money in circulation on the territory of Czechoslovakia diminished by about one-quarter.[18] No critical shortages of money occurred, as production had reached its lowest ebb and the dearth of goods on the market was at its greatest; on the contrary money had flooded into the banks whose interest rates had fallen to less than 1 percent and some even refused to accept deposits.

Further, administration of the national currency was completely separated from the Austro-Hungarian Bank and taken over by the bank office of the ministry of finance (Bankovní úřad ministerstva financí — BÚMF) established on 6 March 1919. As the forerunner of the National Bank of the Czechoslovak Republic the BÚMF was entrusted with the monopoly of issuing money and the regulation of the currency within the national economy.

A new monetary law on 10 April 1919 launched the Czechoslovak crown (Kč) on its independent career at home and on foreign ex-

Table 5. Comparative Statistics — Austria (A) and Czechoslovakia (ČS) 1919–25

Unemployment in Austria and Czechoslovakia

Year	Total Number Unemployed (monthly average)		Rate of Unemployment (% of total labor force)		Unemployed Receiving Benefit (% of total unemployment)	
	A	ČS	A	ČS	A	ČS
1919	355.0	—	18.4	—	44	—
1920	79.0	—	4.2	—	41	—
1921	28.0	90.6	1.4	—	42	37
1922	103.0	195.1	4.8	22.3	48	60
1923	212.0	268.9	9.1	—	53	55
1924	188.0	113.2	8.4	8.7	48	—
1925	220.0		9.9	3.2	68	—

Source: For Austria, Dieter Stiefel, *Arbeitslosigkeit. Soziale, politische und wirtschaftliche Auswirkungen — am Beispiel Österreichs 1918–1938*, Schriften zur Wirtschafts- und Sozialgeschichte, Bd. 31 (Berlin, 1979), p. 29.
For Czechoslovakia, *Statistická příručka Republiky československé*, II (1925): 457 (no data for 1918–20 are available); *Zprávy Státního úřadu statistického* (1925), p. 784.

Table 6. Strikes in Austria (A) and Czechoslovakia (ČS)

		1919	1920	1921	1922	1923	1924
No. Strikes	ČS	242	590*	424	263	225	
	A	151	329†	435	381	268	401
No. Enterprises	ČS	744	4,080	1693	7894	1078	
Involved	A	1627	10,032	7739	5846	1793	6960
No. Strikers	ČS	177.4	491.8	183.7	437.7	181.3	
(000s)	A	69.7	179.4	207.9	211.4	116.7	268.7
Lost Shifts	ČS	574.5	2148.3	1846.8	3679.8	4468.3	
(000s)	A	220.8	927.4	1762.9	1635.4	1074.4	2295.5
Average No. of	ČS	3.2	4.4	10.0	8.4	24.6	
Shifts lost per Strike	A	3.5	5.2	8.5	7.7	9.2	8.5

*General strike in December 1920 in Czechoslovakia.
†In addition 5 sympathy strikes and 10 political strikes.
Source: R. Olšovský et al., *Přehled hospodářského vývoje Československa v letech 1918–1945* (Prague, 1963), p. 171; *Statistisches Handbuch für die Republik Österreich* (1921–1925).

Table 7. The Austrian and the Czechoslovak Crown, Zurich
Quotations 1919–23 (Frs/100 Kč, /100 Ö.Kr.)

Date	Prague Frs./ 100 Kč	ČS Retail price level (July 1914 =100)	Vienna Frs./ 100 Ö.Kr.	A Retail price level (July 1914 =1)	A* Index of Cost of Prewar Diet (July 1914=1)
1919					
21 Feb.	26.00		23.50		
31 Mar.	26.00		20.10		
30 Apr.	31.30		19.15		
17–24 May	34.00		22.00		
31 May	31.50		19.50		
30 July	25.90		12.25	31.02	30.09
30 Aug.	19.75		10.75		
10 Sept.	14.50		8.50		
30 Sept.	21.65		8.50		
31 Oct.	13.00		5.50		
21 Nov.	8.80		3.85		
29 Nov.	10.95		3.775		
19 Dec.	9.30	884	3.10		
1920					
31 Jan.	5.60		1.85	49.22	45.87
5 Feb.	5.00		1.675		
28 Feb.	6.225		2.40		
31 Mar.	7.40		2.65		
30 Apr.	8.80		2.65		
29 May	12.40		4.21		
30 June	12.70		3.82		
31 July	11.70		3.45		
31 Aug.	10.10		2.80		
30 Sept.	8.125		2.65		
30 Oct.	7.15		1.975	69.60	61.84
30 Nov.	7.70		1.975		
30 Dec.	7.40	1562	1.55		
1921					
31 Jan.	8.55		1.85	92.18	97.88
28 Feb.	7.50		1.30		
31 Mar.	7.55		1.55		
30 Apr.	7.55		1.50		
31 May	8.35		1.35		
30 June	8.00		1.00		

19 July	7.65		0.87		
30 July	7.65		0.67		
31 Aug.	6.90		0.70		
30 Sept.	6.05		0.37		
31 Oct.	5.10		0.25		
30 Nov.	5.60		0.15		
31 Dec.	7.60	(I) 1550	0.19	661	704
		(II) 2402			
1922					
31 Jan.	9.90		0.19	830	902
28 Feb.	9.10		0.10		
31 Mar.	9.60		0.60		
29 Apr.	9.95		0.06		
31 May	10.05		0.04		
30 June	10.10		0.02		
31 July	12.15		0.01		
31 Aug.	17.30		0.00		
30 Sept.	16.60		0.00		
10 Oct.	19.20		0.0062		
31 Oct.	17.45		0.0073		
30 Nov.	16.90		0.0075		
19 Dec.	15.05		0.0074		
30 Dec.	16.40	(I) 1289	0.0074	11737	13327
		(II) 1618			
1923					
31 Jan.	15.32		0.00475	11836	13497
28 Feb.	15.80		0.007475		
29 Mar.	16.075		0.0076		
30 Apr.	16.357		0.007725		
31 May	16.555		0.007825	14285	16333
30 June	16.90		0.007987		
31 July	16.575		0.007887		
31 Aug.	16.3125		0.0078		
29 Sept.	16.80		0.007875		
31 Oct.	16.475		0.007925		
30 Nov.	16.625		0.008075		
31 Dec.	16.675	(I) 918	0.008075	13948	15565
		(II) 1023			

*Index of cost of prewar diet in Austria calculated from average quantities of essential food products consumed by a Viennese workman's family in a four week period (flour, bread, sugar, potatoes, meat, fat, milk, eggs, pulse, vegetables, beer, wine) cf. Walré de Bordes, p. 94.
Group I food, fuel, kerosene, and soap.
Group II textiles and shoes.
Source: Olšovský, p. 706.

changes as the legal tender of the new republic. The monetary reform, undoubtedly, produced an immediate stabilizing effect, especially abroad, and lessened the impact of imported inflation.[19] From the separation of the currencies carried through in Czechoslovakia and also in Yugoslavia, the value of the Austrian crown fell more rapidly than before. Austria had to follow suit in stamping her notes in order to give those circulating within her new borders the mark of legal tender. It was estimated that, at the end of the stamping requirement on 24 March 1919, the notes bearing the stamp "Deutschösterreich" amounted to 4804 million; but in addition the "old crown" or the "unstamped crown" became a separate "liquidation currency" and continued to be quoted on foreign exchanges. As the successor of the monarchy, Austria stuck to the illusion that 1 crown equals 1 crown and until 1921 the Austro-Hungarian Bank continued to issue unstamped notes on "old accounts" as a kind of Austro-Hungarian liquidation banknote.[20] The amount of money in circulation continued to increase inexorably week by week.[21] Before the currency separation the rate of circulation had been greater than the fall in the value of the Austrian crown (K); after it, the crown depreciated faster than the rate of circulation. Table 7 confirms the strengthening of the Kč on foreign exchanges in the first few months after currency separation while the Austrian K continued on its downward path. Soon, however, the value of the Kč began to decline, although to a lesser extent, in rhythm with the depreciation of the Austrian K.[22] Also, prices pursued an upward trend in both countries; again, the climb was much steeper in Austria (cf. Table 7). Thus the Czechoslovak monetary reform did not stop inflation at home.

The aim of Czechoslovakia's currency separation and monetary reform was not primarily deflationary. In fact, Czechoslovak Finance Minister, Alois Rašín's, original plan to withdraw 80 percent of the banknotes in circulation was defeated because of fears that a drastic deflationary incision would inevitably cause economic hardships, followed by social turmoil, which in the prevailing politically unstable conditions, could get out of hand.[23] The main purpose of the whole currency reform package was to sever direct financial ties with the other successor states, especially with Vienna and Budapest, to create a national monetary and banking system, and to provide a monetary framework for an independent national economy. The main thrust of the monetary reform was thus directed against former Austrian economic dominance.

Currency separation had been part of the plans for independence drawn up by the Czechoslovak National Committee (the "men of the 28th October") before the breakup of the empire.[24] But because of the closely knit web of financial and business links inside the Austro-

Hungarian economy, this could not be realized at the very origin of the republic. Nevertheless, preparatory moves were made immediately by the newly established Czechoslovak authorities to prevent being drawn into the whirlwind of the Habsburg monarchy's inflation. Uppermost, Czechoslovak statesmen and entrepreneurs were conscious of the economic potential of the republic and of the instrument of power they wielded to consolidate their position in relation to the rest of Austria-Hungary. They did not want to be identified with the losers and wished to distance themselves and their country clearly from the war and, therefore, from its burdensome aftermath. To cut ties with Vienna, the financial center of the former empire, and to reduce the money supply at home were for Czechoslovakia two sides of the same coin.

One of the first moves of the Czechoslovak National Committee (2 November 1918) was to forbid the branches of the Austro-Hungarian Bank on the territory of Czechoslovakia to accept war loan securities. At the same time permission to pay war taxes with war bonds was canceled. Therefore, masses of these securities flooded into Vienna to be presented there, which added fuel to the inflation in Austria. Later, on 14 November 1918, the Czechoslovak branches of the Austro-Hungarian Bank were not allowed to pay banks out of their current accounts except for funds they needed for wages and salaries. This constituted an attempt to curb the volume of currency put into circulation by the Austro-Hungarian Bank but, at the same time, to loosen the links of banks in Czechoslovakia with the former monarchy's central bank in Vienna by inserting the Czechoslovak state's authority between them. Similarly, the establishment of the Czechoslovak Post Office Savings Bank as a giro center and the founding of the Prague Stock Exchange (in November–December 1918) served to facilitate the eventual independent control of the state's means of payment.

Once complete currency separation was put into effect, it became impossible for the great Viennese joint-stock banks to finance their own numerous and most valuable subsidiaries in industry, commerce, and banking on the territory of Czechoslovakia directly from Vienna. This meant losses for the financial centers in Vienna while opportunities arose for Czech banks, particularly the Živnostenská banka, to gain influence in these enterprises.[25] Czechoslovak relative advantages were enhanced during 1919 by legislation of the government in Prague in furtherance of its nationalization program[26] and by the movement of the Austrian inflation into hyperinflation, when Czechoslovak banks and enterprises could acquire Austrian-owned shares on very favorable terms.

In their endeavor to establish an independent state with a clearly defined national economy and its own distinctive currency, the Czechoslovak political leadership could appeal for, and count on, popular support. For in the first exhilarating experience of having achieved independent nationhood the great majority of Czechs and Slovaks had confidence in their new state and its ability to build a viable, more equitable, and democratic economic and social system. Confirmation of these expectations came within a few days of the existence of the Czechoslovak Republic with the splendid popular response to the National Committee's issue on 5 November 1918 of the one-milliard-crown "loan of national liberation" to help meet public expenditure but also intended to skim off excessive currency in circulation. A similar purpose was pursued by the Czechoslovak government with the requirement that Czechoslovak citizens register their wealth as part of the monetary reform of March 1919 which was to provide the basic information for a progressive property levy. Patriotic fervor, however, did not stand that test as well as the "loan of national liberation," for procrastination in giving and gathering information, avoidance and evasion of the tax, and appeals against tax assessments in connection with the levy resulted in long delays in collecting the property levy. In the end, the levy yielded only about half of the expected revenue of 12 milliard Kč and did not contribute substantially to reducing recurring budget deficits. Certain parts of the large state expenses for national defense, food subsidies, and social services were covered from foreign loans and relief credits but the main coverage of budget deficits came through government borrowing from domestic banks and from public subscriptions to internal loans.[27] The Czech strategy could not be applied in Austria where pessimism ruled out the raising of an internal loan.

Government proved more successful in raising tax revenue in Czechoslovakia than in Austria in the inflationary period. No important changes were made in the system of taxation compared with that obtaining before the war in either of the two successor states. In Czechoslovakia, however, tax receipts were consistently higher than government estimates anticipated.[28] To raise its income and to hive off spending power the Czechoslovak government took recourse to increased indirect taxation on consumption, to imposing a turnover tax, and a most debatable tax of 30 percent on the wholesale price of coal. The latter tax slowed down reconstruction at a time of severe coal shortages, but brought the greatest share of revenue from indirect taxes. In Austria, at the same time, the tax system yielded progressively less, only inflation levied its "perverse taxation"[29] on the majority of the Austrian population.

The general optimistic outlook in Czechoslovakia, above all of her entrepreneurs, contrasted sharply with the misery, desperation, and gloom in neighboring Austria. Currency separation signified the differing attitudes and the parting of the ways of monetary and fiscal policies. Its implementation makes it possible to measure the comparative pace and periodization of the inflation in both countries (as illustrated in Table 7). From the beginning of the currency separation in March 1919 the Austrian K depreciated continuously while prices increased first steadily and, in the hyperinflation, from the end of 1921, by leaps and bounds, until in the *Kronensturz* of August 1922, the exchange value of the K hit rock bottom. Its value picked up slightly, aided by the stabilization loan of the League of Nations, and was arrested at the very low level of 14,000 paper crowns to 1 gold crown (or 0.008075 Swiss frc. to 100 Austrian K) where it stayed until the introduction of the schilling in 1924. Prices continued to rise in Austria after the exchange rate had ceased falling and steadied around 15,500 times the prewar retail price level (cf. Table 7).

In comparison, the case of Czechoslovakia shows (Table 7) that the highest quotation of Kč in Swiss francs. (34 Kč = 100 Frc.) was reached in May 1919, followed by a declining trend which hit the lowest point (5.1 Frc. = 100 Kč) in October 1921. The depreciating Kč was accompanied by a price inflation, but hyperinflation was avoided. Between November 1921 and the summer of 1922, Czechoslovak prices fell and the value of the Kč stabilized first at 17.3 Frc. and then at 16.6 Frc. to 100 Kč in August–September 1922 when the Austrian K was at the height of inflation. November–December 1921 marked the beginning of the divergent movement of exchange rates and prices in the two countries (cf. Table 7). From November 1921 to August–September 1922 diametrically opposite policies decided the different method and manner of stabilization of the currencies in Czechoslovakia and Austria.

IV

A powerful factor which deeply influenced the quantifiable divergencies in the inflationary development but which itself is quite unquantifiable is the difference in the economic and sociopolitical climate of the two countries under discussion. From this aspect, the true point of departure is not the currency separation, but 28 October 1918 when the new Czechoslovakia ranked with the victorious states and Austria with the defeated. Policy makers in Austria either by necessity or affected by psychological influences continued to think on an empire basis and, for a long time, could not accept or believe in the "economic viability" of Austria in its post-1918 borders. Their attitudes and pessimistic expectations largely determined their conviction that Austria would have to seek a way out of her dilemma either by an *Anschluss* with Germany[30] or to demonstrate that the residual state (that is, little Austria) would be unable to exist without substantial foreign aid. Austria could not emulate Czechoslovakia and launch an internal loan for no one would

Table 8

Postwar Public Debt of the Czechoslovak Republic — 1920–21 (million Kč)		Postwar Public Debt of the Austrian Republic — Dec. 1920 (million K)	
A. Internal Debts		**A. Internal Debts**	
(a) 4% Liberty Loan	1,000	(a) German Austrian	
(b) 4% Treasury Bills	1,048	State Loan	573.4
(c) 4½% State		(b) 2½% State	
Premium Loan	540.8	Treasury bonds	35,106.8
(d) 5% Treasury Bills	952.8	(c) 4% Austrian Lottery	
(e) Treasury Bonds		Loan	1,200
(3 months)	1,536.2	(d) 6% State Treasury	
(f) 4th Government		bonds	1,550.4
Loan	1,500	(e) Debt owing to the	
(g) 6% Treasury Bills	677.3	Immobiliarbank	13.8
(h) 5½% bonds for			
most urgent military		Total	38,444.4
requirements	322		
(i) 2% Premium Loan	25		
(j) 3½% Currency Loan	250		
(k) 6% Productive			
Loan for railways,			
telegraphs, and			
telephone	470		
Total	8,322.1		

B. External Debts		**B. External Debts**	
(a) Credit from French		(a) Mark Loan against	
govt. for military		Treasury bills M200	
authorities	7.47	million	412.4
(b) Mark credit for		(b) Treasury bills in	
productive expendi-		Dutch currency	
ture on wagons M125		Fl. 3,842,810.59	247.2
(c) M100 million		(c) Treasury bills in	
— paid back		Norwegian currency	
(d) Credit from British		Crs. 1,500,000	67.9
govt. £2 million		(d) Treasury bills in	
	780	Swiss currency	
Total		Fcs. 6,806.264.25	240.7
	787.47	(e) Currency	
		Fcs. 369.675.05	11.1

(f) Dutch Government Credit Dutch Fl. 4,000,000	564.9
(g) Allied Credit American Credit $48 million	33,600
American 200,000 tons wheat credit $24,066.799	16,846.7
Total	51,990.9

Total Internal Debt	8,322.1	Total Internal Debt	38,444.4
Total External Debt	787.47	Total External Debt	51,990.9
Total Public Debt	9,109.57	Total Public Debt·	90,435.3

Source: A. Rašín, *Financial Policy of Czechoslovakia during the First Year of its History* (Oxford, 1923), pp. 119–20.

Source: *Report on the Industrial and Commercial Situation in Austria*, Department of Overseas Trade (HMSO, London, 1921), app. IV.

subscribe to it without a foreign guarantee as confidence in the new state was far too low. Due to want of confidence of the Austrian population in themselves and, even more so, in their government, an almost unquestioning reliance on foreign help, even foreign control, developed. Indeed, after the height of inflation had been reached, and with it the practical collapse of the K on foreign exchanges in summer 1922, the mere promise of the League of Nations loan led to the return of public confidence toward the end of 1922.[31] No assessment of the Austrian inflation can ignore this psychological factor: the strong inclination toward nonexistence, nonviability, and insecurity.

Problems of insecurity were heightened in Austria by uncertainties about the nature of the conditions of the peace in the period between the armistice and the signing of the Treaty of St. Germain. Czechoslovakia, as part of the victorious camp, could be certain that it would not be involved in payments of war debts nor be held responsible for war damages; on the contrary, it had hopes of participating in receiving reparations. Very soon, however, hope was dashed when a "liberation payment" was imposed on the governments of Czechoslovakia, Yugoslavia, Romania, and Poland the greatest share (50 percent) of which was allocated to Czechoslovakia because of the relative strength of its economy and its capacity to pay. Also the prewar debts of the Habsburg monarchy were divided among the successor states. Responsibility for honoring war debts was placed on Austria. On the other hand, Czechoslovakia could expect to be reimbursed for war bonds. Also, as the relatively most solvent successor state its internal indebtedness exceeded its external debt, whereas its Austrian neighbor's foreign debts were greater than domestic debts (cf. Table 8).

Austria, on the contrary, found that the conditions of the Treaty of St. Germain imposed on it were, against expectations, essentially identical with those imposed on Germany. The only mitigating circumstance concerned trade preferences between her and the successor states for the first three years after signing the treaty.[32] Under pressure from the Allies, Czechoslovakia guaranteed coal deliveries to Austria, since Austria could supply at the most about 12.45 percent of her total requirements, but at the end of the war and during 1919 this had, in the case of hard coal, fallen to about 0.6 percent.[33] The general climate of insecurity continued even after the Peace of St. Germain had been signed, for the deliberations of the Reparation Commission lasted until 1921. Until then the exact extent of reparations was not known, but the commission's receivers were at work assessing Austria's state finances. Among other uncertainties, the Austrian government did not know whether the Austro-Hungarian Bank was only in liquidation or whether it was bankrupt, as it was for the liquidators of the Reparation Commission to pronounce a verdict.[34] In the meantime ever-increasing public expenditure and the widening gap between expenses and income in the budget and in the balance of payments could not be closed by the Austro-Hungarian Bank's repeatedly rising note issues.

The Austrian government continued to try and pay its way in this manner, taking the path of least resistance, because it could not restrict the growth of expenditure or increase taxation sufficiently as long as a large part of the population was living on the brink of starvation.

Indeed, among the largest items of state expenditure since 1919 was the provision of cheap food for the population (in April 1921 estimated to cost 2700 million K per month, one-third of total expenditure in the budget of 1920–21). This was discontinued in December 1921 only to cause food riots and plundering.[35] Strikes multiplied (cf. Table 6), adding elements of sharpening social conflict to the spiraling inflation. In the second place, the state had to pay the salaries and pensions of an army of officials who had, until 1918, served an empire; these sums were calculated at 39,000 million K per annum. Taking state employees and their families into account, over 10 percent of the Austrian population were living on public funds; if the provincial bureaucracy and municipal employees are added, every sixth family was maintained out of public funds.[36] These outlays could not be met out of income; revenue from taxation was negligible, even the cost of collecting income tax was by 1921 higher than its yield. Thus the authorities made little effort to bring it in. In addition, all state undertakings except the saccharine monopoly were run at losses.[37] Therefore, the printing presses were kept going, fueling inflation further. Austria was maintained by foreign relief credits in 1919 and 1920, by charities which effectively prevented the starvation of children, and by consuming its own capital. While the Austrian Republic was accumulating new debts, its prewar and war debts had more than halved owing to depreciation of the currency; when stabilization came, those debts were virtually wiped out. At the same time Austria's new foreign indebtedness was mounting (cf. Table 8) and it appealed consistently for more assistance. For 18 months, until spring 1922, despite numerous appeals, the creditor powers left Austria to its own resources. Failure to secure foreign credits engendered repeated panics connected with a headlong flight from the Austrian crown. Businessmen hastened to cover their requirements in foreign exchange and the general public purchased foreign money in anticipation of further inflation. During that time Austria turned the corner into hyperinflation.

Quite apart from the reluctance of lenders to take the risks connected with loans to the East Central European area, the Austrian government had nothing that could be pledged for new credits. According to Article 197 of the Treaty of St. Germain, all Allied states had first charge on all possessions and revenues of the Austrian state to meet their claims arising from costs of occupation and reparations; in addition, another charge had been given to the states which had provided Austria with relief credits. Thus, before any further foreign credits could be negotiated, the creditor powers would have had to raise the liens on Austrian assets. When the British government promised Austria an advance of £2 million in February 1922, in anticipation of an eventual League of Nations stabilization plan, the Austrian government pledged the state Gobelins as security.[38] Loans were, moreover, withheld for political reasons. Negotiations about a substantial credit to support the Austrian currency between Britain and Austria dragged on through 1921 and 1922 and were not concluded until the Bank of England and the Foreign Office received convincing assurances that the Austrian government had definitely dropped *Anschluss* plans and that the Versailles Agreement would be fully implemented. This included promises to aim at balancing the budget and to establish a National Bank of Austria (actually founded 1 January 1923) according to the concept of the Governor of the Bank of England, Montague Norman, by which general European stabilization was to be achieved. On the basis of these conditions the British credit was offered as an interim loan until the League of Nations scheme should be adopted and the Austrian economy put under international supervision.[39]

Until November 1922 it was absolutely impossible for the Austrian government to issue a successful internal loan. With the prospects of

international financial aid and control Austrian businessmen subscribed 30 million gold crowns for the capital of the National Bank of
Austria and 50 million gold crowns for unguaranteed internal loans
between November 1922 and mid-January 1923.[40] The economic climate changed as business confidence spread in spite of the hardships
to be expected from the reforms necessary for balancing the budget
which the League Commissioner was to put into effect.

V

The Treaty of St. Germain as part of the Versailles system of 1919
codified the changes in the balance of power which had arisen as a
result of the outcome of the war. Its financial and economic clauses
created favorable conditions for the expansion of business from the
victorious to the defeated economies.[41] Among other advantages, the
Allies and Associated Powers enjoyed unilateral most-favored-nation
treatment on the territory of the Central Powers for the first five years
after signing the peace treaty.[42] Accordingly, although Austria received
certain concessions concerning her trade with the other successor
states, she became vis-à-vis the Entente powers a free trade area. The
effect of this unilateral most-favored-nation clause on Austrian foreign
trade in terms of limitations imposed on exchange control and export
policies of the government has not yet been assessed. Austria, like
Czechoslovakia, experienced an inflation-led export-based boom; but
even though her exports grew as her currency depreciated, her balance
of trade deficit did not disappear (see Figure 1). One of the main
reasons can be found in the failure of Austrian industry to produce the
required quantities of goods, mainly because of the high import content
of Austrian exports. But also its position under the treaty conditions
put Austria at a disadvantage in international trade which undoubtedly
contributed to outweighing the advantages gained through inflation.

The depreciation in its exchange rates also gave Czechoslovakia an
initial advantage in world markets. As an Associated Power the
Czechoslovak state was able to protect its domestic industries by
introducing a transitional protective control economy which, in terms
of scope, was one of the most extensive in contemporary Europe.[43]
From the end of 1919 Czechoslovakia continuously enjoyed a favorable
balance of trade surplus (see Figure 2). Although these influences
cannot as yet be quantified, there can be no doubt that the changes
consequent upon the peace treaty and the impact of inflation affected
the redirection and reconstruction of the foreign trade of post-1918
Austria and Czechoslovakia, when the firm cords among the successor
states and between them and Germany were beginning to break.

Among the economic advantages accruing to the victorious camp
from the Versailles treaties was the protection of the property rights of

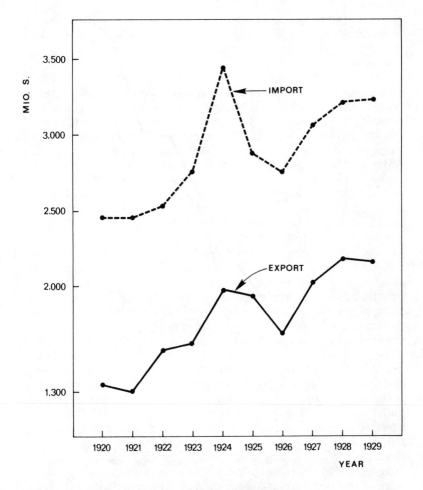

Fig. 1   Austrian Foreign Trade,   1920-1929.
Source : Peter Berger, op. cit. p. 193.

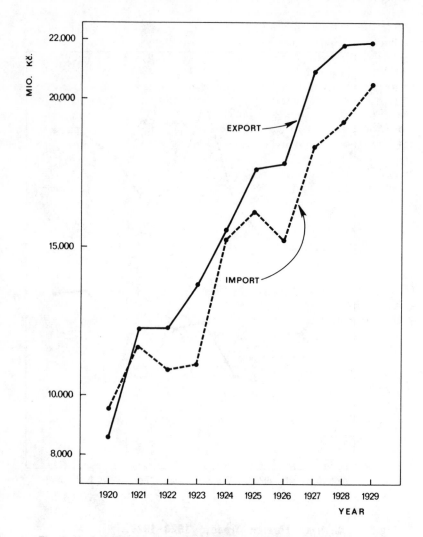

Fig. 2   **Czechoslovak Foreign Trade, 1920-1929.**
*Source: Československá statistika, 67/II, Zahraniční obchod
v r. 1929, p. 21; in Peter Berger, op. cit. p. 216.*

Entente nationals, companies, and associations in the economies of the defeated countries for a period of five years.[44] In addition, the position of creditors from the Entente Powers was greatly strengthened in relation to debtors from the Central Powers by the treaty provision that each of the Allied and Associated states could dispose of enemy assets within its jurisdiction.[45]

These conditions facilitated the aims of the policy makers at the Quai d'Orsay and at the British Foreign Office to eliminate Germany as a serious rival in international trade. They sought to penetrate into former German markets and thus prevent a renewal of Germany's prewar economic, financial, and diplomatic position. Austria-Hungary had been a gateway for German expansion to southeast Europe, therefore Austria and Czechoslovakia were not only of economic but also of political interest to the Allies as a barrier against renewed German *Mitteleuropa* aspirations.[46] Business circles of France, Britain, and other Western European states, such as Belgium, Holland, Switzerland, were encouraged by their governments and assisted by their diplomatic representatives in Vienna, Budapest, and Prague to participate directly in the successor states' economies. France sought to secure influence in Central Europe through decisive long-term participation of her leading companies in key enterprises in the area. She was most successful in Czechoslovak heavy and armament industry. Britain pursued the expansion of her trading interests through purchases of shares in banks and transport and shipping companies in belief that Vienna would regain its role as a financial and trading center in the Danubian region and an intermediary between Western and Eastern Europe.[47] Also the *Nostrifikation* of Austrian shares in Czechoslovakia needs to be assessed in this light, and not only as an expression of Czech nationalism; because treaty provisions encouraged the replacement of German and Austro-Hungarian economic links by American, British, French, or other Allied and Associated nations' interests.

Obviously, businessmen of the leading Allied states with relatively stable currencies were in a favorable position to purchase shares in reputable banks and industrial enterprises much below their true value in East Central European countries, above all in Austria, whose currencies were inflated out of all proportion. Yet, because of the truly desperate shortages of capital, raw materials, and foodstuffs, and under the pressure of inflation a "grand sale of East Central European assets" did take place between 1919 and 1921–22, as bankers, industrialists, and leading politicians of the successor states, most intensively the Austrians, competed for loans and investments mainly from Britain and France. Indigenous entrepreneurs offered shares of their firms in payment for deliveries of raw materials and machinery to keep their production going. By their action, they exacerbated the urgent demand for capital for, in order to procure capital, they encouraged prospective investors to take advantage of the inflationary situation in their own country. At the same time a virtual stream of foreign businessmen from the Entente and neutral countries descended, mainly upon Vienna, with the intention of buying up valuables or shares at bargain prices. The Austrian government supported this influx of Western capital, even at substantial losses. It hoped to cover rising budget deficits, to prop up the currency, but also to persuade foreign, particularly British, investors to assist the Austrian government in negotiations for foreign credits and to intervene on Austria's behalf at the Reparation Commission for the release of Austrian assets before a definitive verdict on indemnities should be announced.

The Czechoslovak government also tried to attract foreign equity investments and loans from the West in order to consolidate the economy, provide foreign exchange, and replace Austro-German capital. At the same time Czechoslovak capital, aligned with Western European business groups operating in the country, acquired investments in the other successor states.

The extent of the inflow of foreign capital into Austria and Czechoslovakia during the inflation is as yet not known. It is, therefore, difficult to judge the effect of this capital import, partly induced by inflation. But by 1921 all the great Viennese banks were internationalized and two of them — the *Österreichische Länderbank* and the *Anglo-Österreichische Bank* — had become fully foreign-owned Paris- and London-based institutions.[48] Foreign business groups, mainly French and British, by 1923 had majority holdings in the largest industrial enterprises in Czechoslovakia[49] and in Austria. Although in the latter country, the most valuable prize went to the German Stinnes group when they acquired the majority share in the Alpine Montangesellschaft after the Italian buyers were unable to hold on to it.[50]

The crucial period of this shift of property relations coincides with the inflationary years when capital was in catastrophically short supply. It was a process which accelerated inflation and, concurrently, by which inflation speeded up the closer integration of the East Central European area into the international economy centered on London, New York, and Paris.

VI

The buoyant industrial development during the inflations of the 1920s in Austria and Czechoslovakia created the illusion that the problems of postwar economic reconstruction were being solved. Manufacturers produced for a home market where demand so far outstripped supply that the public feverishly purchased anything in sight. This led to wasteful deployment of scarce resources as many industrial enterprises emerged or haphazardly expanded only to disappear into oblivion when indiscriminate buying subsided. At the same time production could more easily be directed to the export market where the depreciating Austrian and Czechoslovak currencies gave goods from these countries a price advantage.

This reality might have had a favorable effect upon the rate of economic reconstruction had the advantageous opportunities been fully used to implement a rational investment strategy. Only a careful analysis of changes in the branch structure and output of industry caused by inflation would permit us to test the assumption that inflation, in the East Central European area, played a positive role in economic growth.[51] Such detailed data are not available as yet. In the meantime judgments have to be based on aggregate figures of industrial production, although their accuracy has been the subject of scholarly debate for many years.[52] Discussions mostly concern the precise magnitude of estimates; there is a large area of agreement about the upward and downward trends in the individual years to which the indexes of production apply. It is the increase or decrease in the index points of production in relation to the movement of wholesale and retail prices with which the comparison between Austria and Czechoslovakia in Table 9 is concerned.

If the index of industrial production is compared to the price index (cf. Table 9), it appears that inflationary price increases tended to stimulate output in both countries between 1919 and 1921, but that

Table 9. Comparative Statistics of Movements in Prices and Industrial Production in Austria and Czechoslovakia (1920–1923)

Year	Point increase (+), decrease (−) (index of production)		Wholesale prices (July 1914 = 100)	Retail Price Index	
	Austria	ČSR	ČSR	(1914 = 100) ČSR	(1914 = 1) Austria
1920	+ 7	+25		1562	70
1921	+13	+11	1670	1550	661
1922	+11	− 8	980	1289	11737
1923	+ 4	+ 4	900	918	13948

Source: Calculated from Index of industrial production of the State Statistical Office of the ČSR published in Vlastislav Lacina, "K dynamice hospodářského vývoje v předmnichovské ČSR," *Sborník historický* 23 (1975): 144; Wholesale price index from Faltus, p. 67; Retail price index for Austria and ČSR cf. Table 7; index of production for Austria from Wagenführ statistics cited by D. Stiefel, *Konjunkturelle Entwicklung*, p. 37.

hyperinflationary price rises in Austria in 1922 and 1923 coincided with relatively falling output, and an absolute decrease in industrial production followed upon falling wholesale and retail prices in Czechoslovakia during 1922. In 1923 industrial ouput in ČSR recovered slightly, although prices continued to fall.

In Austria's case the favorable effect of inflation on the rate of reconstruction must be seriously doubted. As Table 9 shows, increasing prices certainly induced a considerable transitional rise in industrial production, also unemployment substantially decreased in 1920 and virtually disappeared in 1921 but rose again steeply during hyperinflation from 1922 (cf. Table 5). Certain advantages accrued to industry, as wages did not catch up with prices; but wages were kept lower than they otherwise would have been by government food subsidies, which represented an indirect state subsidy to manufacturers.

Businesses expanded, new companies shot out of the ground like mushrooms in these favorable conditions of low labor costs, high prices, and insatiable consumer demand. The number of joint-stock and limited companies in Austria trebled between 1918 and 1923 and their total capital rose astronomically as they had recourse to repeated capital issues at a time when the banks were not able to meet the needs of industry. Within a year of stabilization, however, more than a third of existing companies failed, either going bankrupt or into liquidation (cf. Table 10). This can be seen as a wholesome shrinking process, but

Table 10. Total Number and Paid-up Capital of Joint-stock Companies (A.G.) in Austria 1918–25

Year	No. 31 Dec.	Paid-up Capital (1000 K) 1 Jan.	31 Dec.	Change (i.e., increase)
			(1000 K)	
1918	459*	3,506,616	3,964,273	457,657
1919	488*		4,500,331	536,058
			(Mio K)	
1920	509		7,122	
1921	596		16,136	
1922	843		197,538	181,402
1923	1066	197,029	506,061	309,032
			(1000 S)	
1924	1230	51,636	85,058	9,740
1925	1207†	85,426	106,803	21,377

*132 companies with production mainly outside Austrian territory (1918).
 130 companies with production mainly outside Austrian territory (1919).
†65 liquidations and bankruptcies.

Total Number and Capital of Limited Companies (G.m.b.H.) in Austria 1918–25

Year	No.	Nominal Capital (1000 K)	Paid-up Capital
1918	2102	682,389	600,412
1919	2745	932,084	813,091
1920	3897	1,582,832	1,413,060
1921	5011	2,823,820	2,639,241
1922	5820	7,879,045	7,519,991
		(Schilling)	
1922	5813	787,904	751,999
1923	6176	3,195,303	3,070,357
1924	5957	11,576,795	10,301,976
1925	4552	17,157,244	15,516,134

Changes in Numbers of Austrian A.G.s and G.m.b.H.s 1918–1925

Year	Increase A.G.	Increase G.m.b.H.	Decrease A.G.	Decrease G.m.b.H.	Change A.G.	Change G.m.b.H.
1918	22	338		65	22	273
1919	29	748		105	29	679
1920						
1921		1386		272		1114
1922	267	1193	20	384	247	809
1923	247	871	24	509	223	362
1924	148	449	21	668	127	−219*
1925	41	112	65	1517	−24	−1405*

*In 1924 460 GmbH's were liquidated, 26 went into bankruptcy, and 126 cancelled their registration as against 429 new registrations; in 1925 1082 GmbH's were liquidated, 84 went into bankruptcy, and 344 cancelled their registration as against 109 new registrations.

Source: *Statistisches Handbuch für die Republik Österreich* (1921–25).

the question remains which was more harmful to the Austrian economy: the inflation or its stabilization? In spite of increasing prices, low wages, little unemployment, greater business activity, the gap between production and consumption was not closed during the inflationary boom. The persistent lack of coal, raw material, and above all, capital remained unsolved in the Austrian economy; indeed, the hyperinflation exacerbated these problems.

Even the apparently positive features of the Austrian export boom which was stimulated by the depreciating currency need to be critically examined. The shortfall of production to cover demand for exports has been mentioned. In addition, when goods were sent out of the country, the community paid foreign buyers a bonus in the form of subsidized wages, as the Austrian state supplied the population with relief food. A further bonus accrued through the difference in exchange rates between the receipt of goods and payment of the invoice. Austrian manufacturers, especially small ones who had not learned to balance their accounts in a stable currency, were thus consuming their real capital, although they thought that they were making large profits in crown transactions. Those who borrowed working capital from the banks were able to shift the losses onto them, or rather their depositors. However one looks at this inflation-induced export, a large part of it — such as jewelery, works of art, heirlooms, but also ordinary goods at lower prices than their real costs of production — partook of the nature of capital expenditure at a time of severe shortages of working capital and long-term investments. In spite of a booming export trade, Austrian imports greatly exceeded exports (cf. Figure 1) and the unfavorable balance of trade made the sale of securities and assets necessary to reduce the deficit in Austria's balance of payments.

The Austrian government did reap certain advantages by using inflationary economic policies which stimulated industry, alleviated unemployment, and avoided violent social confrontations, but the structural problems of the Austrian economy had not begun to be solved. Whether hyperinflation was brought on by deliberate policies of the Austrian government is debatable; however, its destructive effects contributed to proving the inability of the Austrian state to meet its international commitments. Austria's public finances had so deteriorated by August 1922 that her government appealed to Britain and to the Supreme Council of the Allies for immediate aid emphasizing that "neither the present nor any other Government is in a position to continue to administer the State."[53] Within two months the Geneva Protocols were drawn up under the auspices of the League of Nations and aid was promised, subject to conditions of strict League of Nations control of Austrian finances.[54]

Only hyperinflation and the threat of violent social revolution in summer 1922 led to the realization of the League of Nation's stabilization loan and the appointment of a League Commissioner who was to hold the purse strings in Vienna. The international credit furnished through the League imposed great and long-term financial burdens upon the Austrian economy, since it was used mainly unproductively to pay off previous debts, support the currency, and balance the budget rather than employed for investment to restructure Austrian industry and adapt it to the post-Versailles realities.

In Austria's case, stabilization came entirely from outside and was immediately generally accepted. A stabilization consensus was estab-

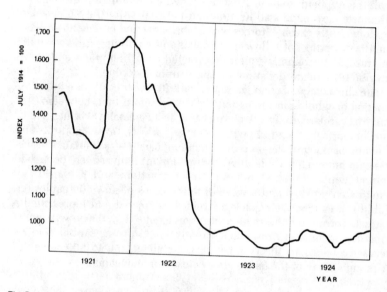

Fig. 3 Index of Wholesale Prices in Czechoslovakia, 1921-1924.
Source: Jozef Faltus, Povojnová hospodárská kríza v rokoch 1921-1923 v Československu (Bratislava, 1966), p. 67 (calculated from relevant Zprávy Státniho úřadu statistického)

lished surprisingly swiftly and led to a quick recovery which amazed the experts of the League of Nations Commission. This development confirms the view that there existed more viable forces of reconstruction in the Austrian economy than the inflationary experience seemed to suggest. In the event, the currency was stabilized but the economy was not.

Czechoslovakia, on the contrary, wished to convince Allies and potential business partners and creditors of its solvency, of the people's readiness to help themselves, and thus its ability to pay. Stabilization took the opposite path to Austria's when a combination of objective circumstances made stabilization and revaluation of the Kč possible, predominantly through forces within the economy. In Czechoslovakia, stabilization did not follow upon deflationary policies, as is generally believed, but economic conditions created by falling prices and recession in 1921 made deflationary intervention possible.

The chronology of stabilization starts with the break in the inflationary rise of wholesale prices (cf. Figure 3). Before that, between 1919 and 1921, relatively moderate inflation in Czechoslovakia had facilitated exports (cf. Figure 2) which — together with import controls and a strong backlog of demand on the home market — stimulated industrial production (cf. Table 9). At the same time an investment boom had started which initiated renewal, reconstruction, and expansion of existing enterprises and a wave of foundations of new companies (cf. Table 11). Productive capacities were thus created and represented a source of growth in the 1920s which was greater than the growth rate of most European countries. Concurrently, the number, capital, and reserves of banks in the country grew by about 250 to 300 percent.[55] Although many of the banks either closed or amalgamated with bigger

Table 11. Total Number and Capital of Joint-stock and Limited Companies in Czechoslovakia: 1919–25

Year	Total Number		Total Nominal Capital (million Kč)	
	Joint-stock Companies	Limited Companies	Joint-stock Companies	Limited Companies
1919	605	1543	2533	447
1920	757	2123	3157	658
1921	952	2324	4337	848
1922	1089	2329	5064	917
1923	1193	2227	5824	928
1924	1241	2158	6743	941
1925	1265	2095	7005	889

Source: *Statistická ročenka Republiky československé*, relevant volumes.

institutions by 1923–24, the large Czechoslovak banks changed from provincial to national and international financial centers.[56]

Czechoslovakia had initially better chances for fundamentally restructuring its economy, but during the inflationary boom the inherited disproportions were not sufficiently removed. Signs of the negative effects of the inflationary period became visible by 1921 when companies began to fail (cf. Figure 4).

These were mainly new and expanded enterprises which had not been integrated into production and the market, but had benefited from protective tariffs, import restrictions, and shortages on the home market. As extraordinary postwar conditions of shortages were overcome, demand on the domestic market was satisfied, and the market relatively oversupplied, controls were lifted. Also foreign exchange controls were loosened. The relatively steep fall in prices was a reflection of crisis conditions brought about by need to adjust production to the new demand structure and influenced further by the postwar economic recession in the world.

Under these circumstances deflationary measures followed during 1922 when deflation became official Czechoslovak government policy. It succeeded because political stability had been achieved, production exceeded consumption, favorable trade balances had been reached and maintained from 1920, and the Czechoslovak bank of issue, the BÚMF, engaged in a series of speculative maneuvers on the international money market to raise the value of the Kč abroad. In purely monetary terms, the operation succeeded in increasing demand for the Kč on foreign exchanges, as it was aided substantially by the first installment of the British credit to Czechoslovakia in 1922,[57] and also, inadvertantly, by the flight from the mark into foreign currencies, including the Kč, during Germany's hyperinflation. This policy, however, disregarded the reality of the economic situation of 1922–23 at home and abroad, and resulted in a relative overvaluation of Czechoslovak currency (cf. Table 7), which erased the price advantages of Czechoslovakia's exports. Thus Alois Rašín's monetarism negatively influenced output and employment at a time when the Czechoslovak economy suffered from depression[58] (cf. Table 9, 5). Ironically, just as the flight from the mark had enhanced the value of the Kč, the French occupation of the Ruhr and Germany's need for imports as well as her inability to export alleviated the harsh consequences of the Czechoslovak government's deflationary policy, as Germany's competitors, including the industry of Czechoslovakia, stepped into the breach and fulfilled German orders. Full recovery came to the Czechoslovak economy only with the reimposition of controls and with the general upswing in the world economy from 1924, in which both countries — Austria and Czechoslovakia — participated.

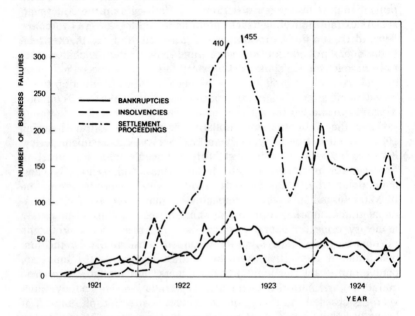

Fig. 4 **Bankruptcies, Insolvencies and Settlement Proceedings in Czechoslovakia, 1921-1924.** *Source : Jozef Faltus, op. cit., p. 71 (calculated from Měsíční úvěrové zprávy Bankovního úřadu Ministerstva financí)*

In general, neither Czechoslovak government economic policy nor the investment strategy of Czechoslovakia's entrepreneurs utilized fully the relatively favorable conditions created by the inflation of the early 1920s and no conscious effort was initiated, in order to adapt the industrial structure to the new economic and political reality. The only solution was seen, not in fundamental economic reconstruction, but in an all-out export drive supported by a protectionist tariff system and government subsidies, which perpetuated the structural weaknesses of the economy.[59] During the continuing upswing of exports, investments flowed into protected industries and doubtlessly contributed to the remarkable growth of aggregate production until 1929.[60] At the same time, the increasing Gross Domestic Product (GDP) from 1923 to 1929 concealed structural weaknesses during the first decade of the existence of the Czechoslovak Republic.

VII

This paper aimed at showing the cumulative process of the inflation in the two most industrialized successor states of the former Habsburg monarchy. It discussed the similarities and differences in the course inflation and stabilization took in the immediate postwar years in Austria and Czechoslovakia. At the same time it sought to convey the coincidence of different types of inflation which intertwined in complex relationships in both economies: from inherited and excess-demand inflation to conflict inflation, to anticipated and self-propelled inflation, to hyperinflation.

Monetary phenomena provided a measure of the pace, periodization, and duration of the inflations, but it was shown that the monetary component was decisively influenced by production, consumption, and social and political factors. In Austria as well as in Czechoslovakia — although in very different ways — the inflation-induced economic boom and the setback through stabilization contributed to the failure of both countries to adapt their economic structure to the changed conditions of the postwar world. The full extent of missed opportunities was revealed during the economic crisis of 1929 to 1933 from which neither Austria nor Czechoslovakia could recover sufficiently before the outbreak of the Second World War.

Notes

* The author wishes to thank the Social Science Research Council, United Kingdom, for financial support for her Research Project on "Multinational Companies in East Central Europe" (certain material gathered during the project was used in the paper). She also wants to thank Dr. Philip Cottrell for

reading the paper. His comments and the stimulating discussions at the conference were helpful in the preparation of the final draft of this paper. Thanks are also due to Dr. Peter Berger for providing statistical data from Austrian sources.

1. Gustav Cassel, *Post-war Monetary Stabilization* (New York, 1928), p. 1.

2. Cf. Otto Büsch and Gerald Feldman (Eds.), *Historische Prozesse der deutschen Inflation 1914 bis 1924* (Berlin, 1978).

3. Norbert Schausberger, *Der Griff nach Österreich* (Vienna, 1978), pp. 82–83.

4. For Austria cf. Dieter Stiefel, *Konjunkturelle Entwicklung und struktureller Wandel der österreichischen Wirtschaft in der Zwischenkriegszeit*, Forschungsbericht Nr. 135 (Institut für höhere Studien, Vienna, November 1978), p. 11; for Czechoslovakia, cf. Rudolf Olšovský et al., *Přehled hospodárského vývoje Československa v letech 1918–1945* (Prague, 1963), pp. 19–24.

5. Jozef Faltus, *Povojnová hospodárska kríza v rokoch 1921–1923 v Československu* (Bratislava, 1966), pp. 22, 30.

6. Cf. Karl Bachinger and Herbert Matis, "Strukturwandel und Entwicklungstendenzen der Montanwirtschaft 1918–1938" in Michael Mitterauer (Ed.), *Österreichisches Montanwesen* (Vienna, 1974), pp. 114–15.

7. Cf. for Czechoslovakia, Alice Teichova, "Industry" in M. C. Kaser and E. A. Radice (Eds.), *The Economic History of Eastern Europe since 1919*, vol. I (Oxford, 1982), chapt. 5; for Austria, Iván T. Berend and György Ránki, *Economic Development in East-Central Europe in the 19th and 20th Centuries* (New York, London, 1974), p. 175.

8. Zora P. Pryor, "Czechoslovak Economic Development between the Two Wars," *Papers in East European Economics* 11 (Oxford, 1972): 2.

9. Peter R. Berger, "Der Donauraum im wirtschaftlichen Umbruch nach dem ersten Weltkrieg" (Doctoral dissertation, Wirtschaftsuniversität, Vienna, 1980), p. 131.

10. Relatively high unemployment remained a structural feature of the Austrian economy arising out of the "shrinking process" which it underwent. Cf. Dieter Stiefel, *Arbeitslosigkeit. Soziale, politische und wirtschaftliche Auswirkungen-am Beispiel Österreichs 1918–1938* (Berlin, 1979), pp. 19–20.

11. Finanzarchiv, Vienna — Dept. 17/Frieden — Elaborat Sozialisierungskommission 1919, and a great amount of evidence about efforts to sell state-owned shares in industrial enterprises, such as Alpine Montan-Aktien, Sprengstoffwerke Blumau, Wöllersdorf, Süddeutsche Donaudampfschiffahrtsgesellschaft.

12. Alois Rašín's first sentence in the Preface to his book begins thus: "The present book was written in December 1921, at a time when we had, in consequence of the progress achieved, already overcome the influences of Russian Bolshevism . . ." *Financial Policy of Czechoslovakia during the First Year of Its History* (Oxford, 1923), p. xi; J. van Walré de Bordes wrote ". . . a certain liberality in State expenditure had been advisable in view of the menace of Bolshevism." *The Austrian Crown Its Depreciation and Stabilization* (London, 1924), p. 17.

13. Cf. van Walré de Bordes, p. 12.

14. Calculated from *Compass Deutschösterreich Österreich-Ungarn* (Liquidation) (1923); for Austria, cf. van Walré de Bordes, pp. 48–50.

15. *Statistische Nachrichten* 1 (1924).

16. van Walré de Bordes, p. 44.

17. 10,000 K banknotes were not recognized, as they were issued by the Austro-Hungarian Bank after 27 October 1918 without the consent of the Czechoslovak authority. For the legal measures of the monetary reform see *Compass Tschechoslowakei, Jugoslawien,* vol. II (1922), pp. 5–10.

18. R. Olšovský, p. 114.

19. This ignores smuggling of notes and counterfeit money, the impact of which was not negligible and has yet to be assessed.

20. Since currency separation about 1500 million of these unstamped notes were issued. From 4 October 1920 they had to bear the date of issue and from 1921 the Receivers of the Reparation Commission at the Austro-Hungarian Bank forbade such issues. Cf. *Compass Deutschösterreich Österreich-Ungarn* (Liquidation) (1923), pp. 114–15.

21. *Ibid.*, pp. 101–102.

22. The trends in depreciation tally also with the falling value of the German mark, because not only were the two countries, i.e., Austria and Czechoslovakia, each other's second largest trading partners but Germany was the largest trading partner of both.

23. Rašín, pp. 24–25.

24. Cf. Věra Olivová, Robert Kvaček, *Dějiny Československa IV* (Prague, 1967): 8–14.

25. Cf. A. Pimper, *České obchodní banky za války a po válce* (Prague, 1929), p. 138.

26. The nationalization program of 1919 included the Currency Separation Act, the Bank Acts, and the *Nostrifikation* Act. Cf. Alice Teichova, "Structural and Institutional Changes in the Czechoslovak Economy 1918–1938," *Papers in East European Economics* 6 (Oxford, 1972): 10.

27. Cf. Rašín, Part II, *National Finance,* pp. 87–129.

28. *Ibid.*, p. 112.

29. John Maynard Keynes, *A Tract on Monetary Reform* (London, 1923), p. 37.

30. Negotiations in preparation of customs and currency union had progressed very far, and details had been worked out by the finance ministries of Austria and Germany. Finanzarchiv, Vienna, Urk. 1919.

31. Report on the Industrial and Commercial Situation of Austria, Department of Overseas Trade (August 1923), p. 7.

32. Cf. N. Almond and R. H. Lutz (Eds.), *The Treaty of St. Germain* (London, 1935).

33. K. Bachinger and H. Matis, pp. 112–115; also Elaborat über die Kohlenfrage des Subkomitees für Produktion, Rohstoffe und Kredit 27 November 1919, Finanzarchiv, Vienna, A.P. 1919.

34. *Compass Deutsch-Österreich Österreich-Ungarn* (Liquidation) (1921), pp. 85–87.

35. Report on the Industrial and Commercial Situation in Austria, Department of Overseas Trade (HMSO, London, 1921), p. 24. For data on the 1920–21 budget cf. Stiefel, p. 20, note 33.

36. Report on Austria, Department of Overseas Trade (July, 1922), p. 8.

37. Budgets of Austrian State in *Compass Deutschösterreich* (1920–24).

38. Report on Austria (July 1922), p. 6.

39. Haus-, Hof- und Staatsarchiv, Vienna, London Berichte, 1921, 1922–24.
40. van Walré de Bordes, p. 32.
41. Almond and Lutz, Parts IX and X.
42. *Ibid.*, Art. 217–220.
43. Autonomous tariffs were introduced on 20 February 1919 to protect domestic industries which were adapted to inflation by additional sums for certain product groups. Differentiated tariffs were imposed from 1 June 1921 and these were raised on 1 January 1922 in order to protect Czechoslovakia against the influx of goods from countries whose currencies were heavily depreciated as a result of hyperinflation.
44. Almond and Lutz, Art. 228, 229.
45. *Ibid.*, Art. 201.
46. For a detailed analysis, cf. Alice Teichova, *An Economic Background to Munich International Business and Czechoslovakia 1918–1938* (Cambridge, 1974).
47. These statements and the later part of this section are more specifically examined in Teichova, "Der Kapitalexport in die österreich-ungarischen Nachfolgestaaten zu Beginn der 1920er Jahre," *Südosteuropa im Spannungsfeld der Grossmächte 1919–1939* (Mainz; forthcoming).
48. Teichova, "Versailles and the Expansion of the Bank of England into Central Europe" in Norbert Horn and Jürgen Kocka (Eds.), *Recht und Entwicklung der Grossunternehmen im 19. und 20. Jahrhundert* (Göttingen, 1979); Philip L. Cottrell, "Aspects of Western Equity Investment in the Banking System of East Central Europe" in A. Teichova and P. L. Cottrell (Eds.), *International Business and Central Europe 1919–1939* (Leicester; forthcoming).
49. Teichova, *Economic Background.*
50. Finanzarchiv, Vienna, Dept. II, Dept. 15, 1919–23.
51. Cf. the recent reappraisal of the inflation in Germany in the 1920s, by Büsch and Feldman (Eds.) and its review by Karl Häuser, "Ansichten zur Inflation," *Zeitschrift für die gesamte Staatswissenschaft* 135 (1979): 4; cf. also the contributions of György Ránki and Zbyněk Landau to this book.
52. Polemics have been concerned mainly with Czechoslovak interwar development of industrial production, cf. in Czech publications, e.g., Václav Průcha, "Polemika vstoupila do hospodářské historiografie," *Československý časopis historický* (1969), pp. 905–911; most recently Vlastislav Lacina, "K dynamice hospodářského vývoje v předmnichovské ČSR," *Sborník historický* 23 (1975): 119–66. In Western publications cf. Frederic L. Pryor, Zora P. Pryor, Miloš Stádník, and George J. Staller, "Czechoslovak Aggregate Production in the Interwar Period," *The Review of Income and Wealth* 17 (1971): 35–59, contains new calculations and a critical view of previously published statistics.
53. Public Records Office, London — FO 371–38833, C12770: Problems of the Austrian Economy, p. 42.
54. Currency stabilization and the origin of the schilling (also its fate until the 1970s) is traced by Karl Bachinger and Herbert Matis, *Der österreichische Schilling Geschichte einer Währung* (Graz, Vienna, Cologne, 1974), pp. 50–85.
55. Olšovský, pp. 86–88.

56. The international links of the large Czechoslovak joint-stock banks are discussed in Teichova, *Economic Background*, pp. 336–67.

57. *Ibid.*, pp. 367–71 on international loans to ČSR; on the diplomatic and economic prelude to the British loan to Czechoslovakia of 1922 cf. Teichova, "Versailles and the Expansion of the Bank of England," p. 383.

58. Jozef Faltus, *op. cit.*, substantiates the postwar economic crisis in industry and banking in Czechoslovakia by a detailed empirical analysis proving that recession occurred before, and concurrently with, deflationary measures. Although F. L. Pryor et al., pp. 44–45, maintain that the Czechoslovak economy completely avoided the world crisis of 1920–21, they agree that Rašín's revaluation of the Czechoslovak currency was ill-timed.

59. Contemporary economists and economic commentators were aware of the danger of these policies for longer-term development, cf. the series of lectures published by the Národohospodářská společnost československá (Czechoslovak economic society); discussions were revived between Czechoslovak economists and historians on the economic profile of the pre-Munich Republic, cf. references to the relevant publications in Lacina, *op. cit.*

60. cf. Pryor, p. 45.

Part 6
Other National Experiences

Index-Linked Financial Assets and the Brazilian Inflation-Feedback Mechanism*

PAUL BECKERMAN

INTRODUCTION

After nearly a decade of declining rates of price increase, the Brazilian economy suffered an inflationary relapse following the 1973 oil crisis. Unlike the relatively brief "oil inflations" of many other nations, Brazil's inflation persisted and remains a serious problem at this writing. Brazil's inflation problems have been compounded by severe disarray in the short-term financial markets. By now, of course, it is clear that the Brazilian inflation is much more than an "oil" inflation. Analysts of the Brazilian economy have vigorously debated the causes of persisting inflation and financial turbulence, without reaching broad agreement. There is a widespread suspicion, however, that one of the important causes of Brazil's macroeconomic stabilization problems is the availability of index-linked financial assets. The purpose of the present essay is to examine this possibility. We shall argue that even if the availability of index-linked assets cannot set off inflation, it can serve to propagate inflation forward through time. Moreover, we shall argue that the Brazilian data suggest that this has indeed happened. (We shall also argue, however, that the "inflation-feedback" process operates through several channels; since the introduction of financial index-linking effectively opens some and suppresses others, we cannot be absolutely certain that the Brazilian inflation-feedback mechanism would be less robust if index-linking had never been introduced.)

This essay is organized in three sections. The first provides a brief review of Brazil's experiment with financial index-linking. The second discusses the macroeconomic theory of the "inflation-feedback" mechanism and notes the conditions under which the availability of index-linked financial assets might mitigate or aggravate that mechanism. The final section describes the operation of the inflation-feedback mechanism in Brazil after 1973.

The Brazilian experience is revealing and disturbing in a number of ways. First, we shall see that the introduction of financial index-linking cannot neutralize the effects of inflationary uncertainty on the economy. In effect, index-linking only shifts the channels through which inflationary uncertainty operates on the economy, roughly speaking, from the IS to the LM. Second, contrary to the view that financial index-linking enables closer monetary control, the recent Brazilian experience seems to have been that index-linking made monetary control more difficult. Given that the Brazilian military regime could not risk financial panic or industrial unemployment, the rate of growth of its money supply effectively became endogenous — the monetary authority found itself forced to maintain the *real* money supply. A third theme that emerges from our discussion is that the introduction of index-linking amounted to the introduction of a parallel unit of account, creating a situation rather like one in which pounds and dollars circulated together in the same economy with a fluctuating exchange rate.[1] This had two further consequences. (1) Since few private firms would risk placing themselves in a position in which they were backing index-linked obligations with assets or anticipated revenues denominated in the monetary unit, the government *cum* monetary authority had to place itself in this position if there were to be any index-linked financial assets. Only the government *cum* monetary authority is exempt from the threat of domestic bankruptcy, so that if what it owed on its index-linked obligations exceeded what it anticipated it could always create the money to pay it. (2) Any deterioration in the prospects of inflation amounts to a diminution of the real rate of return on money relative to that on index-linked assets. Consequently, any increase in anticipated inflation *may* lead to a larger shift out of money, and hence to a greater reduction in the real value of money — i.e., a greater increase in the price level — than there would be in the absence of index-linked assets.

I. THE BRAZILIAN EXPERIMENT WITH FINANCIAL INDEX-LINKING[2]

Index-linked financial assets have been available in Brazil since 1964, when a military government assumed power. The military government inherited a large budget deficit of some years' standing, as well as the consequent inflation (which reached an annual rate of 100 percent in early 1964). On the advice of its civilian economic ministers, the new government introduced index-linked government bonds as a means of financing the deficit with a minimum of money creation. They reasoned that Brazilian financial investors would never purchase nominal government obligations while the future rate of inflation remained high and unpredictable.[3] Since the government felt that it could not bring the budget under control immediately, and since it preferred to control the inflation gradually in order to avoid bankruptcies and perhaps depression, it seemed inevitable that the inflation would persist at high rates for some time. The index-linked bonds were intended as a temporary means of mitigating the inflationary effect of

Table 1. Measures of Brazilian Inflation, Output Growth, and Money-supply Growth, 1961–76 (percentage changes, December/December)

	1961	1962	1963	1964	1965	1966	1967	1968	1969	1970	1971	1972	1973	1974	1975	1976
(1) General price index	47.7	51.3	81.3	91.9	34.5	38.8	24.3	25.4	20.2	19.2	19.8	15.5	15.7	34.5	29.2	46.4
(2) Wholesale price index	53.2	45.5	83.2	84.5	31.4	42.1	21.1	24.8	18.7	18.7	21.3	16.1	15.6	35.2	29.4	44.9
(3) Cost of living in Rio de Janeiro	42.9	55.8	80.2	86.6	45.5	41.2	24.1	24.5	24.3	20.9	18.1	14.0	13.7	33.7	31.2	44.8
(4) Money supply	52.5	64.1	64.6	81.6	79.5	13.8	45.7	39.0	32.5	25.8	32.3	38.3	47.0	34.0	42.8	37.2
(5) Monetary base	61.8	62.1	69.9	86.2	66.6	26.4	25.2	46.5	29.9	19.4	34.2	25.6	42.7	32.9	36.4	49.8
(6) Real gross domestic product	10.3	5.3	1.5	2.9	2.7	5.1	4.8	9.3	9.0	9.5	11.1	10.4	11.4	9.5	4.2*	8.8*
(7) Implicit deflator	33.3	54.8	78.0	87.8	55.4	38.8	27.1	27.8	22.3	19.8	20.4	17.0	15.5	34.0		

*Provisional data. The 1975 figure is given by *The Economist*, 13 March 1976, p. 77. The 1976 figure is the preliminary estimate of the Fundacao Getulio Vargas announced in February 1977.
Source: *Conjuntura Econômica*, April 1977; A. Lemgruber, "Inflation in Brazil," in L. B. Krause and W. S. Salant, *Worldwide Inflation*, pp. 395–448 (Tables 1, 2, pp. 400–401).

Table 2. Nominal Value of Index-linked Government Bonds, in *cruzeiros*
(After 1966, these were the values of the Standard Accounting Unit, or UPC, of the SFH.)

	1964	1965	1966	1967	1968	1969	1970	1971	1972	1973	1974	1975	1976
January		11.30	16.60	23.23	28.48	35.62	42.35	50.51	61.52	70.87	80.62	106.76	133.34
February		11.30	17.05	23.78	28.98	36.27	43.30	51.44	62.26	71.57	81.47	108.38	135.90
March		11.30	17.30	24.28	29.40	36.91	44.17	52.12	63.09	72.32	82.69	110.18	138.94
April		13.40	17.60	24.64	29.83	37.43	44.67	52.64	63.81	73.19	83.73	112.25	142.24
May		13.40	18.28	25.01	30.39	38.01	45.08	53.25	64.66	74.03	85.10	114.49	145.83
June		13.40	19.09	25.46	31.20	38.48	45.50	54.01	65.75	74.97	86.91	117.13	150.17
July	10.00	15.20	19.87	26.18	32.09	39.00	46.20	55.08	66.93	75.80	89.80	119.27	154.60
August	10.00	15.20	20.43	26.84	32.81	39.27	46.61	56.18	67.89	76.48	93.75	121.31	158.55
September	10.00	15.70	21.01	27.25	33.41	39.56	47.05	57.36	68.46	77.12	98.22	123.20	162.97
October	10.00	15.90	21.61	27.38	33.88	39.92	47.61	58.61	68.95	77.87	101.90	125.70	168.33
November	10.00	16.05	22.18	27.57	34.39	40.57	48.51	59.79	69.61	78.40	104.10	128.43	174.40
December	10.00	16.30	22.69	27.96	34.95	41.42	49.54	60.77	70.07	79.07	105.41	130.93	179.68

the government deficit while the inflation persisted. In the event, the rate of inflation fell even more gradually than the government had hoped: financial index-linking ceased to be a stop-gap expedient and became an institutionalized means of "living with inflation."

Since their introduction the goverment bonds have been readjusted every three months according to the Brazilian wholesale price index lagged by several months. The precise formula for the readjustment has been altered several times (see the explanatory note to Table 3). At least until 1975 and 1976, when fundamental changes were made in the readjustment formula, the government bonds have been as close to perfect inflation hedges as was technically feasible in Brazil. This is shown by Tables 2 and 3, which present the nominal and deflated values of the government-bond principals since 1964. After 1964 the bonds were clearly successful as a means of financing the government deficit. (See Tables 4 and 5.)[4]

The government subsequently extended the index-linking principle to other areas of the economy, particularly to the important national Housing Finance System, which was set up between 1964 and 1966 in an attempt to resolve Brazil's desperate housing shortage.[5] The various private and public agencies of the Housing Finance System capture savings through index-linked "housing bonds" and passbook savings accounts. The principal social-security fund is applied in index-linked accounts to the National Housing Bank, which is the central financial and coordinating agency of the Housing Finance System. In the late 1960s the National Housing System came to account for virtually all of Brazil's index-linked savings stock. Since then the government has also established several other index-linked "forced savings" funds. Certain state-owned enterprises (notably the national electrical-infrastructure company, Eletrobrás) have issued index-linked debentures; and several state and municipal governments have issued index-linked obligations.

Despite efforts of the government to encourage them, however, private corporations and financial institutions have proved reluctant to issue index-linked obligations. The reasons for this reluctance are disputed by economists. The view of this writer is that such enterprises have been unwilling to take on index-linked obligations backed by current assets that cannot, by their nature, be proof against inflation with certainty.[6] For private commercial banks, finance companies, investment banks, and the government's development banks (which remain to this day the only domestic source of long-term industrial finance), the government has allowed the use of what it calls "pre-fixed" index-linking, through which the securities and loans of such institutions carry a government estimate of the percentage increase in the price level over the term of the contract, in addition to the legal

Table 3. Value of Government Index-linked Bonds (deflated by the wholesale price index and the general price index*)

Deflated by Wholesale price index / General price index

		1964	1965	1966	1967	1968	1969	1970	1971	1972	1973	1974	1975	1976
January	WPI		8.31	9.29	9.15	9.25	9.27	9.28	9.33	9.38	9.30	9.15	8.97	8.65
	GPI		8.39	9.17	9.25	9.12	9.10	9.00	9.00	9.16	9.13	8.98	8.84	8.54
February	WPI		7.92	8.75	9.05	9.08	9.28	9.35	9.34	9.30	9.23	9.02	8.92	8.59
	GPI		8.00	8.78	9.06	8.96	9.11	9.07	9.40	9.11	9.06	8.83	8.77	8.44
March	WPI		7.78	8.71	9.10	8.96	9.33	9.41	9.32	9.24	9.22	8.91	8.85	8.47
	GPI		7.77	8.67	9.10	8.90	9.11	9.12	9.00	9.05	9.06	8.72	8.73	8.29
April	WPI		8.85	8.71	8.99	8.91	9.57	9.33	9.19	9.22	9.20	8.63	8.92	8.36
	GPI		8.70	8.60	9.00	8.85	9.19	9.06	8.88	9.04	9.04	8.45	8.75	8.18
May	WPI		8.68	8.59	8.98	8.96	9.61	9.46	9.11	9.25	9.20	8.29	8.95	8.28
	GPI		8.51	8.53	8.92	8.78	9.23	9.10	8.85	9.04	9.01	8.16	8.77	8.09
June	WPI		8.54	8.71	9.14	9.13	9.62	9.42	9.07	9.38	9.24	8.14	8.99	8.28
	GPI		8.38	8.69	8.93	8.90	9.24	9.06	8.81	9.11	9.03	8.05	8.79	8.05
July	WPI	10.00	9.57	8.90	9.32	9.15	9.48	9.35	9.01	9.46	9.24	8.27	8.92	8.34
	GPI	10.00	9.38	8.90	9.11	8.92	9.17	9.00	8.79	9.19	9.03	8.17	8.76	8.07
August	WPI	9.41	9.34	8.83	9.26	9.24	8.86	9.26	9.06	9.44	9.22	8.57	8.89	8.20
	GPI	9.41	9.14	8.85	9.13	9.01	9.10	8.92	8.84	9.21	9.04	8.42	8.72	7.97
September	WPI	9.12	9.51	8.82	9.33	9.29	9.17	9.14	9.18	9.40	9.20	8.87	8.79	8.04
	GPI	9.13	9.33	8.93	9.19	9.06	8.92	8.81	8.93	9.14	9.02	8.72	8.62	7.87
October	WPI	8.74	9.41	8.90	9.23	9.19	9.06	9.05	9.22	9.35	9.19	9.05	8.74	8.02

November	8.79	9.21	8.93	9.10	9.02	8.82	8.73	9.00	9.10	9.01	8.88	8.59	7.87
	8.35	9.34	8.89	9.16	9.16	8.98	9.11	9.30	9.33	9.11	9.08	8.70	8.13
December	8.42	9.15	8.99	9.03	8.94	8.75	8.75	9.08	9.11	9.42	8.95	8.59	7.96
	7.71	9.34	9.02	9.15	9.15	9.04	9.22	9.33	9.28	9.09	9.06	8.68	8.24
	7.87	9.17	9.12	9.02	8.98	8.80	8.90	9.14	9.08	8.92	8.93	8.56	8.05

*The interpretation of Table 3: The value of the index-linked bonds has been determined each month by adjusting the previous month's value according to the wholesale price index lagged several months, using the following formula:

$$V_t = V_{t-1} \cdot \frac{I_{t-4} + I_{t-5} + I_{t-6}}{I_{t-5} + I_{t-6} + I_{t-7}},$$

where V_t is the value of the bond at time t and I_t is the wholesale price index. (Originally the index-linked bonds were adjusted every three months, according to the formula:

$$V_t = V_{t-1} \cdot \frac{I_{t-4} + I_{t-5} + I_{t-6}}{I_{t-7} + I_{t-8} + I_{t-9}}.)$$

The principal changes made in the calculation of the bond values were these: in 1969 a new wholesale price index was used, removing the wholesale prices of goods for export. In 1972 and 1973 a complicated formula was employed, weighting the formula just given by 60 percent and making the formula remaining 40 percent of the formula depend on the government's target for inflation over the coming period. During 1974 the previous formula was adopted again. In August 1975 the wholesale price index was "purged" (of price increases deemed to have been the consequence of the agricultural failures that occurred around that time) for purposes of calculating the bond readjustment. After April 1976 the adjustment formula became (approximately):

$$V_t = 0.8 V_{t-1} \cdot \frac{I_{t-2} + I_{t-3} + I_{t-4}}{I_{t-3} + I_{t-4} + I_{t-5}} + 0.2 V_{t-1} (1.15)^{1/12}.$$

If the bonds were perfect hedges against inflation, the correction formula would be:

$$V_t = V_{t-1} \cdot \frac{I_{t-1}}{I_{t-2}}. \quad (\S)$$

The first figure given for each month in Table 6b is the value:

$$\hat{V}_t = V_t \cdot \frac{I_{\text{June 1964}}}{I_{t-1}} .$$

If the formula ($) had actually been used to adjust the bonds beginning in August 1964, this first figure would be 10.00. To the extent that our calculated figure falls short from 10.00, therefore, the bonds have failed to incorporate the full inflation (measured by the wholesale price index) that occurred since July 1964. To determine the real rate of return (net of interest) on a bond held between times t_0 and t_1, calculate

$$\frac{\hat{V}_{t_1} - \hat{V}_{t_0}}{\hat{V}_{t_0}} .$$

At least between 1965 and 1974, our table shows that index-linked bonds have pretty much retained their value. Between any given dates, however, the bonds do clearly have real gains or losses. The second figure given for each month shows the value

$$\bar{\bar{V}}_t = V_t \cdot \frac{I_{\text{June 1964}}}{G_{t-1}} ,$$

where G_t is the general price index.

Table 4. Internal Debt in Government Securities, 1964–76
(millions of new *cruzeiros*)

	Government Obligations Outstanding			Net Sales of Government Obligations			Average maturity of Outstanding Obligations		Gross Domestic Product	(3) ÷ (9) Percentage	"Nonidentified" Holdings of Government Bonds	(11) ÷ (1)
	Index-linked Bonds	Treasury Bills	Total	Index-linked Bonds	Treasury Bills	Total						
	-1-	-2-	-3-	-4-	-5-	-6-	-7-	-8-	-9-	-10-	-11-	-12-
1964	41		41	40		40	59m21d		23056	0.0	30	0.73
1965	430		430	337		337	47m 9d		36818	0.1	314	0.73
1966	1401		1401	629		629	24m12d		53724	2.6	822	0.59
1967	2482		2482	448		448	24m21d		71486	3.5	894	0.36
1968	3491		3491	93		93	24m12d		99879	3.5	1625	0.47
1969	5881		5881	797		797	20m 9d		155695	3.8	2169	0.37
1970	9412	700	10112	1624	658	2282	17m11d	20d	206565	4.9	3859	0.41
1971	11565	3880	15445	290	2697	2987	16m11d	1m13d	274267	5.6	4364	0.38
1972	15975	10204	26179	1792	5094	6886	21m23d	2m20d	359133	7.3	3493	0.22
1973	20944	17400	38344	1156	4601	5757	27m22d	3m21d	477163	8.0	3824	0.18
1974	32969	14800	47801	2539	-5166	-2595	31m 2d	3m 4d	676617	7.1	8412	0.26
1975	60112	37400	97548	15311	16388	31649	37m29d	3m14d	897194	10.9	12342	0.20
1976	84397	69404	153889	-2467	13236	10814	31m28d	3m19d	1397829	11.0	15949	0.19

Source: Banco Central do Brasil: *Relatório Annual*: 1972, pp. 131–33; 1976, pp. 163–65; 1977, pp. 135–37.

Table 5. The Brazilian Federal Deficit and Its Finance (millions of *new cruzeiros*)

	-1-	-2-	-3-	-4-	-5-	-6-	-7-	-8-	-9-	-10-	-11-	-12-
	Revenues	Expenditures	Surplus or Deficit (1)–(2)	Gross Domestic Product	(2)÷(4)	(3)÷(2)	(3)÷(4)	Financed by Monetary Authorities	−[(8)÷(3)]	Financed by Public Borrowing	−[(10)÷(3)]	(9)+(11)
1966	5910	6496	−586	53724	0.12	−0.09	−0.01	−190	−0.32	606	1.03	0.71
1967	6814	8039	−1225	71486	0.11	−0.15	−0.02	716	0.58	509	0.42	1.00
1968	10275	11502	−1227	99879	0.12	−0.11	−0.01	1089	−0.88	138	0.11	0.99
1969	13953	14709	−756	155695	0.09	−0.05	−0.00	−733	−0.97	1489	1.97	1.00
1970	19194	58872	−738	206565	0.29	−0.01	−0.00	−839	−1.14	1577	2.13	0.99
1971	26980	27652	−672	274267	0.10	−0.02	−0.00	−2022	−1.87	2694	4.00	2.13
1972	37738	38254	−516	359133	0.11	−0.01	−0.00	−7685	−14.89	8201	15.89	1.00
1973	52863	52568	295	477163	0.11	0.01	0.00	−6499	22.03	6204	−21.03	1.00
1974	76810	72928	3882	676617	0.11	0.05	0.01	−8790	2.26	4908	−1.26	1.00
1975	95446	95373	73	897194	0.11	0.00	0.00	−16356	224.05	16283	−223.05	1.00
1976	166220	165797	423	1397829	0.12	0.00	0.00	−18594	43.96	19955	−47.17	−3.21

Source: *Boletim do Banco Central do Brasil.*

maximum interest rate of 12 percent per year. (The usury law limiting interest to 12 percent per year remains in force, although it is now defined for legal purposes as *net* of the rate of inflation.) The government has generally tried to control nominal interest rates. Consequently, since the government had discretionary power to set the estimate of the future rate of inflation, the "pre-fixed" index-linking procedure has functioned essentially as a means of controlling nominal rates.[7]

Given the persistent if declining inflation of 1964–73, it is difficult to deny that financial index-linking permitted Brazil certain important economic achievements. The government deficit, which persisted until 1973, was financed in an essentially noninflationary form. The housing sector accumulated a massive volume of savings, which has been applied not only to housing but to municipal infrastructure and has generated considerable employment in the construction industry. Financial investors and household savers have had inflation-resistant assets in which to hold their wealth, and there is no question that the forced-savings schemes would have been inconceivable without their being protected against erosion of their real value.

Nevertheless, the Brazilian public has never been very happy about the experiment with index-linking. For one thing, understandably enough, Brazilians have never liked to take on inflation-proofed debt, and this has been the major reason why private financial institutions outside the Housing Finance System have been unable to use index-linking. Even the Housing Finance System was forced to compromise the index-linking principle for its mortgages: mortgages are now readjusted through a complicated scheme under which the monthly payments of amortization and interest calculated when the mortgage is signed are adjusted annually according to the government's annual *wage* guidelines.[8] (The Brazilian government has generally maintained a tight wage policy since 1965.) Brazilian consumers are persuaded that any index-linked debt would mushroom unreasonably, if not turn perpetual; Brazilian businessmen fear that the prices of their own products would fail to maintain pace with the price index. Thus, whereas Brazilians are pleased to be able to hold index-linked assets, they remain quite unwilling to hold index-linked debt.

The most widespread misgiving about index-linking among Brazilians has been the conviction that it somehow strengthens what is called the *inflation-feedback* mechanism. The general argument is that current inflation is caused only in part by current demand-pull and cost-push factors: it is caused also by the inflation that occurred in the recent past. The earlier inflation is said to "feed back" through the formation of expectations and the force of previous commitments to generate inflationary pressure in the current period. Now such a feedback mechanism undoubtedly exists in any economy. Brazilians, however, have come to believe, as a virtual truism, that index-linking has made their feedback mechanism particularly robust. Some of the most enthusiastic Brazilian proponents of index-linking have admitted that they accept this view.[9] Nevertheless, there has been little theoretical analysis to substantiate the view that financial index-linking strengthens the feedback mechanism. There is even some empirical evidence in a recent paper by Cláudio Contador that seems to suggest that index-linking has had no such effect in Brazil[10] (although we will argue in footnote 23 that Contador's results must be interpreted carefully).

We turn, therefore, to examine the theoretical bases of the inflation-feedback mechanism.

II. CHANNELS OF THE INFLATION-FEEDBACK PROCESS

The macroeconomic inflation-feedback mechanism which we describe here operates through the formation of inflationary expectations and uncertainty. We take it to be generally true that an increase in the rate of price increase leads to increases in inflationary expectations and uncertainty;[11] these increases set off the feedback process. For brevity, allow us to refer henceforth to an increase (for *whatever* cause) in the rate of inflation that causes increases (1) in the expected rate of inflation and (2) in the uncertainty attaching to this expectation as *an inflationary deterioration*. First, we briefly review the reasons that an inflationary deterioration would be likely to have inflationary effects on the rates of saving and investment and on the demand for and supply of money. Then we ask whether the introduction of financial index-linking would be likely to diminish or to augment these inflationary effects.

Suppose first that no index-linked assets are available in the economy. An inflationary deterioration would tend to decrease *the rate of savings*, which would be inflationary, for the following reasons: first, because consumers would prefer to purchase durable goods sooner rather than later when their prices (might) rise; second, because the expected real interest rate on savings is reduced; third, because the uncertainty attaching to this real rate is increased. (These effects on the savings rate would be offset, if the initial real interest rate is high on a backward-bending savings-supply curve, and to the extent that the public responds to an increase in inflationary uncertainty by saving more rather than less, in an attempt to maintain its real savings stock for precautionary purposes.)

An inflationary deterioration would probably increase *the rate of investment*, which would also be inflationary. This would happen, first, because of the decrease in the expected real rate of interest, which entails both a reduction in the expected real cost of borrowed funds and an increase in the valuation of equity, and hence a reduction in the cost of capital perceived by firms; and second, because of the increased uncertainty attaching to the expected real rates of return on money, which would probably generate an increase in the valuation of equity. (These effects on the investment rate would be offset to the extent that the increased inflationary uncertainty turns the prospective cash flow on possible investment projects more unpredictable.)

Next, an inflationary deterioration would surely decrease *the demand for money*, which would be inflationary. This is because the expected real rates of return on assets competing with money — *with the exception of nominal bonds and nominal savings instruments* — would now be higher relative to the expected real rate of return on money. In addition, the uncertainty attaching to the expected real rate of return on money would be increased, and in general this should also serve to decrease the demand for money.[12]

Finally, an inflationary deterioration is quite likely to force an increase in *the money supply*, through its effects on the composition of the banking system's assets and liabilities. This happens in the following way: One likely consequence of an inflationary deterioration would be an attempt by the public to run its demand deposits as low as possible, and to move its wealth out of money and into inflation-resistant assets — capital goods, real estate, jewelry, foreign exchange, and so on. At the same time, however, there would probably be a sharp increase in the demand for bank credit, first, because as part of the inflationary process the real prices paid and received by firms would be altered considerably; and second, because the inflation was not anticipated when contracts currently in force were originally signed. Both these effects tend to create situations in which firms are compelled to ask for bank credit. Hence the immediate consequence of an inflationary deterioration is quite likely to be, ironically, a liquidity crisis in the commercial banking system. This places the monetary authority in a dilemma: Should it attempt to confront the inflation or the liquidity crisis? Obviously, the authority will be subject to political pressure on both sides. At first the authority may try to confront the inflation by tightening credit, or by at least allowing the liquidity crisis to "run its course." But this is likely to provoke some bankruptcies, and perhaps a recession. This would alarm the authority and probably force its hand politically. It would then permit bank-credit expansion, which almost inevitably entails an inflationary increase in the money supply.

This cycle of tight and easy credit is familiar to observers of developing nations, particularly in Latin America. The cycle is especially likely to appear in nations where commercial bank credit is important, where commercial banks and their creditors are politically powerful, where there are frequent and brusque shifts in anticipations and aggregate-supply conditions, and where the monetary authority lacks institutional power.[13]

Now let us suppose that index-linked financial assets become available in the economy. How would this change the inflation-feedback mechanisms that we have described?

First, consider the savings and investment functions. If the savings media are index-linked, then an inflationary deterioration should have no effect on the expected real rate of interest on savings: an index-linked fixed-return asset is, virtually by definition, an asset with a *certain, fixed* real rate of return. Hence there should be relatively little reason for savings to decrease following an inflationary deterioration. If investment-finance instruments are index-linked, capital investors should reason that, to the extent that higher future returns anticipated on a given investment project are part of an anticipated inflationary trend, these returns would go to pay the cost of the finance. Moreover, if index-linked assets compete with equities in the financial markets, increases in inflationary expectations and uncertainty should have a smaller positive effect on the valuation of equity. Consequently, an inflationary deterioration should have a *smaller* inflationary effect on savings and investment in a regime with index-linking than in a regime without index-linking. (For future reference, note that the bulk of Brazil's investment instruments are *not* index-linked, although medium-term government bonds and some savings instruments are index-linked.)

On the other hand, an inflationary deterioration should have a *greater* inflationary effect on the demand for and supply of money in a regime with index-linking. The reason for this is as follows: In a regime without index-linking, only equities and real assets are available as a hedge against inflation, and these assets are uncertain hedges at best. The discount on nominal bonds may be increased to take account of an increase in the expected rate of inflation, but the bonds are still subject to the same degree of inflationary uncertainty as money. Where index-linked bonds are available, in contrast, wealth holders can protect their real wealth with certainty by acquiring such bonds. An inflationary deterioration would therefore generate a greater decrease in the demand for money where index-linked assets are available than where they are not. Moreover, an inflationary deterioration would probably place the commercial banking system under more acute pressure where index-linked assets are available, because the effective flow of real resources out of the banking system should be far more efficient. For where index-linked assets are not available, there are considerable transactions costs to obtaining even uncertain protection of wealth from inflation: some real estate must be found, dollars must be purchased on the black market, and so on. Index-linked securities, on the other hand, would be liquid, legal, readily available in any denomination, and virtually perfect hedges against inflation. Money holdings can be converted all too easily into index-linked assets. Consequently, the real value of each new injection of money into the banking system would be decreased, through increases in the price level, far more rapidly as people move their wealth out of money and into index-linked assets.

To summarize, the introduction of financial index-linking *diminishes* the inflationary consequences of an inflationary deterioration on savings and investment (i.e., on the IS), but *augments* the inflationary consequence of an inflationary deterioration on the demand for and supply of money (i.e., on the LM). Without additional information, however, we cannot say whether the effect on the IS of introducing financial index-linking would be more important than the effect on the LM.[14] Therefore, we cannot say for sure whether index-linking renders the inflation-feedback mechanism more or less robust.

III. THE INFLATION-FEEDBACK MECHANISM IN RECENT BRAZILIAN EXPERIENCE

In this section we consider the facts of the recent Brazilian inflationary experience. We begin by describing the inflationary deterioration that set off the resurgence of inflation in 1974. We then describe the evidence from Brazilian financial statistics that the demand-for-money function was shifted back by the inflationary deterioration. Next, we provide evidence that the Brazilian banking system went into a liquidity crisis at the end of 1974, and that the increase in the money supply during 1975 was a response to this crisis.

A. THE INFLATIONARY DETERIORATION OF 1974

A number of inflationary shocks occurred during 1973 and 1974 in the Brazilian economy. All of them probably contributed to the 1974 resurgence of inflation, although their relative importance is open to question. (1) The first inflationary shock was the world oil-price increase in October 1973: since Brazil is heavily dependent on oil imports (about 80 percent of Brazil's oil consumption must be imported), the heavy increase in world oil prices inevitably had a cost-inflationary effect.[15] (2) In April 1974 there was a major bank failure: one of the nation's largest banking houses, the Halles Group, was placed under "intervention" by the monetary authority, and a large quantity of credit expansion had to be permitted in order to prevent the Halles failure from generating a wider financial panic.

Several actions of the new government that took office in March 1974 probably also had inflationary consequences. (3) Beginning with the annual minimum-wage adjustment of May 1974, the government began

Table 6. The National Housing Bank, 1966–76
(millions of new *cruzeiros*; percentage of total assets)

	1966	1967	1968	1969	1970	1971	1972	1973	1974	1975	1976
Assets											
1. Liquid assets	31	43	39	41	30	24	60	133	737	380	254
	0.20	0.05	0.02	0.01	0.01	0.01	0.01	0.01	0.02	0.01	0.00
2. Refinancings	89	451	1873	3582	6231	9927	14205	19839	34062	53250	92836
	0.57	0.48	0.79	0.81	0.84	0.84	0.77	0.75	0.74	0.76	0.79
a. State housing companies	50	171	438	783	1412	1883	2374	2958	4142	5632	9366
	0.32	0.18	0.18	0.18	0.19	0.16	0.13	0.11	0.09	0.08	0.08
b. Caixas Econômicas (state and federal)	16	121	461	662	690	825	754	709	1486	2600	6582
	0.10	0.13	0.19	0.15	0.09	0.07	0.04	0.03	0.03	0.03	0.05
c. Housing cooperatives	14	68	224	601	1147	1981	2876	3462	3727	3431	2917
	0.09	0.07	0.09	0.14	0.15	0.17	0.16	0.13	0.08	0.05	0.02
d. Real estate credit societies	1	13	148	286	482	951	3377	5344	8190	13155	20933
	0.01	0.01	0.06	0.07	0.06	0.08	0.18	0.20	0.18	0.19	0.18
e. Savings and loan associations			17	117	224	340	960	1550	2812	5430	9650
			0.01	0.02	0.03	0.03	0.05	0.06	0.06	0.08	0.08
f. Commercial banks							2047	3927	8925	15333	31535
							0.11	0.15	0.19	0.22	0.27
g. Investment banks							783	1369	2487	3041	2978
							0.04	0.05	0.05	0.04	0.03
h. State development banks							317	351	876	1892	3574
							0.02	0.01	0.02	0.03	0.03
3. Security holdings	27	416	425	688	1047	1697	3702	4951	8715	11485	13604
	0.17	0.45	0.18	0.16	0.14	0.14	0.20	0.19	0.19	0.16	0.12
4. Total assets	155	934	2371	4389	7431	11888	18397	26384	46180	70394	117657

Liabilities											
5. Own resources	110	185	310	526	942	1553	2527	4354	9228	13558	20007
	0.71	0.20	0.13	0.12	0.13	0.13	0.14	0.17	0.20	0.19	0.17
6. Social-security program accounts		629	1902	3611	6040	9813	14788	20982	32897	48413	79011
		0.67	0.80	0.82	0.81	0.83	0.80	0.80	0.71	0.69	0.67

Table 7. Loans by the Housing-Finance-System to Final Borrowers, 1965–76 (millions of new *cruzeiros*)

December	1965	1966	1967	1968	1969	1970	1971	1972	1973	1974	1975	1976
1. Housing Bank (total loans)	19	89	451	1873	3582	6231	9927	14295	20620	34062	53250	92836
		+368.4	+406.7	+315.3	+91.2	+74.0	+59.3	+44.0	+44.2	+65.2	+56.3	+74.3
2. Housing Bank (loans to final borrowers)	19	72	303	993	2006	3762	5808	6057	7370	9286	11799	17584
		+278.9	+320.8	+227.7	+102.0	+87.5	+54.4	+4.3	+21.7	+26.0	+27.1	+49.0
3. Loans by Housing-Finance-System agencies:		38	408	1771	3465	5839	10038	18386	30982	55552	89794	173424
			+973.7	+334.1	+97.7	+68.5	+71.9	+83.2	+68.5	+79.3	+61.6	+93.2
a. Federal Savings Bank		23	133	484	958	1736	2752	3942	5725	10375	21122	45201
			+478.3	+263.9	+97.9	+81.2	+58.5	+43.2	+45.9	+80.4	+103.6	+114.0
b. Savings Banks of states		11	65	238	456	401	757	1237	2426	4725	7802	19326
			+490.9	+266.2	+91.6	−12.0	+88.8	+63.4	+96.1	+94.8	+65.1	+147.7
c. Real estate credit societies		4	196	763	1362	2284	3958	8624	14535	23330	32728	55126
			+4800.0	+289.3	+78.5	+67.7	+73.3	+117.9	+68.5	+60.5	+40.3	+68.4
d. Savings and loan associations				32	178	345	568	1436	2649	4834	7876	15684
					+456.3	+93.8	+64.6	+152.8	+84.5	+82.5	+62.9	+99.1
4. Total loans by the Housing-Finance-System	19	110	711	2764	5471	9601	15846	24443	38352	64838	101593	191008
		+478.9	+546.4	+288.7	+97.3	+75.5	+65.0	+54.3	+56.9	+69.1	+56.7	+88.0
5. Total loans by the Housing-Finance-System deflated (general price index)	19	81.8	381.1	1191.7	1881.6	2746.4	3715.4	4896.8	6652.9	7224.5	8760.6	11252.5
6. Gross domestic product	36818	53724	71486	99879	155695	206565	274267	359133	477163	676617	897194	1397829
7. Deflated (gen. p. index)	36818	38920.3	40378.4	45416.7	58628.9	64933.2	71586.7	80139.9	92490.3	101915.4	105819.1	116701.0
8. Δ real loans (real g.d.p.) Δ(5)÷(7)		0.00	0.01	0.02	0.01	0.01	0.01	0.01	0.02	0.01	0.01	0.02

*Includes loans made by the Housing Finance System through commercial banks, developments banks, and investment banks.

Table 8. Index-linked Passbook Savings Accounts in the Housing-Finance System, 1970–76

December:	Number of accounts (thousands)				Average balance (new cruzeiros)				Total (millions of new cruzeiros)				Nominal return, previous 12 months			
	Savings Banks	Real estate credit societies	Savings and loan assoc.	Total*	Savings Banks	Real estate credit societies	Savings and loan assoc.	Total*	Savings Banks	Real estate credit societies	Savings and loan assoc.	Total*	Savings Banks	Real estate credit societies	Savings and loan assoc.	General price index
									261	49	20	330				
									752	81	60	893				
1970	998	188	163	1349	1801	851	822	1550	1797	160	134	2091	26.3	28.7	28.4	19.2
1971	1529	376	334	2239	2131	814	650	1689	3258	306	217	3781	30.3	32.7	32.4	19.8
1972	1900	771	563	3234	3366	1067	888	2387	6395	823	500	7718	25.6	26.9	26.7	15.5
1973	2490	1515	832	4837	4201	1789	1138	2919	10640	2710	947	14118	19.7	22.0	21.7	15.7
1974	3239	2414	1153	6806	6520	2501	1534	4250	21118	6037	1769	28924	38.4	40.9	40.4	34.5
1975	4442	3840	1656	9938	8950	3186	1958	5558	39756	12234	3242	55233	30.5	32.3	32.7	29.2
1976	5602	5733	2338	14142	13313	4590	3078	7915	74579	26314	7169	111934	41.4	41.4	43.7	46.4

* Includes other Housing-Finance-System agencies.
Source: Boletim do Banco do Brasil, April 1977.

to set rather higher guidelines for collective wage contracts, in an attempt to increase real wages. The government did this, both on the view that since 1964 labor had not received a fair share of the nation's economic expansion and in the hope that increased wages would generate greater consumer demand. (4) In August 1974 the government published its "Second National Development Plan," through which it hoped, first, to decentralize Brazil's industrial growth away from the congested Rio de Janeiro–São Paulo–Belo Horizonte growth poles, and more important, to promote the nation's basic-inputs industries, whose growth had lagged dangerously behind that of Brazil's consumer durables industries. One of the aims of the new five-year plan was to forestall the inflationary pressure that the structural imbalance seemed to be generating. Ironically, however, the very announcement of the Second National Development Plan probably itself constituted an inflationary shock. The plan was not only extremely ambitious; it assigned the key role to new investments by enterprises owned by the government, to be financed by funds captured by the government's development banks. Accordingly, it generated widespread fears in Brazil's already hard-pressed private sector that its demand for credit would be crowded out. (In the event the plan proved too ambitious to carry out and by 1975 it was largely allowed to lapse.) (5) Yet another event that was probably a kind of inflationary shock came in November 1974: in spite of the opposition of a good part of military and business opinion, the government carried out the first relatively free nationwide elections for congress since 1965. The opposition political party made important gains throughout the nation, and Brazilian business passed through a period of considerable uncertainty, concerned that the changed political equation might have unfavorable consequences.[16]

The situation was complicated by the growing problems in Brazil's international economic sphere. Since 1968 Brazil had maintained real output growth above 9 percent per year, led in large part by expansion of exports. Brazil managed to maintain its ouput growth through most of 1974 — for the year as a whole its real national product grew 9.5 percent. But the OECD nations, Brazil's main customers, reported a reduction of 0.2 percent in their incomes and moreover had to direct a larger share of their import expenditure to oil. Brazil's nonoil imports continued to increase, and at first the government took no steps to contain this increase because it thought that it could still maintain export growth. Hence (6) on top of the credit expansion the government permitted to relieve the confidence crisis caused by the Halles collapse, it allowed credit to agricultural and industrial exporters to expand, in part to tide them over while foreign demand remained in recession, in part to stimulate export production. In the event Brazil had a current-account deficit of almost US $7 billion in 1974, compared with a deficit under US $2 billion the previous year; and the nation's total foreign debt rose drom US $12.6 billion to US $17.2 billion.[17]

The relative importance of the changes that we have noted in setting off Brazil's inflationary resurgence is open to debate. (It is worth noting however, that for once in Latin-American inflationary experience a government budget deficit cannot be held to blame for an inflation: beginning in 1973 Brazil's annual federal budget has actually been in surplus.) But there can be little doubt about their consequences: in 1974 and 1975 Brazil's general price index rose by 34.5 percent and 29.2 percent respectively, whereas the rates of increase for 1970, 1971, 1972 and 1973 had been 19.2, 19.8, 15.5, and 15.7 percent respectively. Furthermore, the rate of inflation worsened in 1976: for that year the general price level rose 46.4 percent, and only with great difficulty the government managed to reduce the rate of price increase to 29.2 percent in 1977. Now in view of the inflationary shocks of 1973 and 1974 it was quite understandable that Brazil's rate of inflation rose sharply in 1974. But how are we to explain the sustained inflation after 1974? Our argument is that during 1974 and 1975 the inflation-feedback mechanism propagated the inflationary shocks of 1973 and 1974 forward through time. Since index-linked financial assets were available in Brazil, we claim that the inflation-feedback mechanism operated largely through the demand for money and the supply of money. Let us examine each of these in turn.

B. THE BRAZILIAN DEMAND-FOR-MONEY FUNCTION IN 1974

The basic data for the analysis of the Brazilian demand for money are presented in Tables 9–13. As inflation, inflationary expectations, and inflationary uncertainty rose during 1974, following years of declining rates of inflation, the Brazilian public evidently responded by shifting its wealth out of monetary and other nominal assets and into index-linked assets. The magnitude of the shift can be seen in Tables 9 and 10. In Table 9, we can observe that in 1972 and 1973 roughly 24 percent of gross domestic savings was carried out in the form of nominal nonmonetary assets (i.e., nominal time deposits, with pre-fixed index-linking; exchange acceptances; and government bills); in 1974, only 9 percent of gross domestic financial savings was carried out in this form. The same table shows that while in 1972 and 1973, 12 percent and 10 percent of gross domestic financial savings were carried out in the form of index-linked assets, in 1974, 19 percent of gross domestic financial savings were carried out in this form. Table 10 provides evidence for a related point: during 1974 the nominal stock of passbook-savings accounts in the Housing Finance System increased by 104.8 percent, the nominal stock of private holdings of index-linked government bonds increased by 58.3 percent, and the nominal stock of

Table 9. Gross National Financial Savings, 1972–76 (millions of new *cruzeiros*)

Yearly flows	1972	1973	1974	1975	1976
1. Monetary assets	17564	30006	31350	54160	69000
2. Time deposits*	7530	8794	7660	21097	18564
3. Exchange acceptances	6580	13847	7788	13201	12583
4. Government bills	6300	7196	−2599	22599	32004
5. Nominal fixed-yield assets: (2) + (3) + (4)*	20410	29837	12849	56897	63151
6. Savings deposits	3929	6409	14803	26309	52305
7. Housing bonds	1885	1502	1770	650	842
8a. Government bonds	4410	4969	12159	27149	24285
8b. State & municipal bonds	231	1511	2185	8417	9396
9. Index-linked assets: (6) + (7) + (8)	10455	14391	30917	62525	86828
10. Forced savings programs	7419	10968	21593	30720	57658
11. Insurance companies' technical reserves	316	280	1490	832	1724
12. Variable-yield securities	28282	42857	53362	83498	101278
13. Gross domestic financial savings	84470	128339	151458	288631	379691
14. Gross foreign financial savings	17636	17151	36350	36216	49270
15. Gross financial savings	102106	145490	187808	324827	428961
16. Gross domestic product	359133	477163	676617	897194	1397829
Percentages:					
17. (5)/(13)	24.2	23.2	8.5	19.7	16.6
18. (5)/(15)	20.0	20.5	6.8	17.5	14.7
19. (5)/(16)	5.7	6.3	1.9	6.3	4.5
20. (9)/(13)	12.4	11.2	20.4	21.7	22.9
21. (9)/(15)	10.2	9.9	16.5	19.2	20.2
22. (9)/(16)	2.9	3.0	4.6	7.0	6.2
23. (13)/(15)	23.5	26.9	22.4	32.2	27.2
24. (15)/(16)	28.4	30.5	27.8	36.2	30.7

*Certain time deposits at investment banks yield ex post index-linking. These are small in quantity, less than 5 percent of the total. They are included with nominal time deposits.

Source: Boletim do Banco Central do Brasil.

private holdings of index-linked state and municipal bonds increased by 67.6 percent. At the same time, the nominal stock of nominal time deposits increased only 29.7 percent; the nominal stock of exchange acceptances incrased by 22.4 percent; and the nominal stock of government bills held by the public increased by 14.2 percent. Since the general price level rose by 34.5 percent over 1974, it is clear that in real terms the stock of each category of index-linked assets rose considerably, while the stock of each category of nonmonetary nominal assets declined.

Most interesting for our purposes, the inflationary deterioration clearly affected the demand for real money balances adversely. In real terms the money supply (M–1) actually fell by 0.8 percent over 1974, even though the nominal money supply increased by 33.5 percent. For comparison, during 1972 and 1973 the real money supply had increased by 19.7 and 27.0 percent, respectively. (See Table 12.) Private commercial banks were particularly hard-pressed: over 1974, their total real deposits fell by 3.5 percent in real terms, whereas in 1971, 1972 and 1973 their total real deposits had increased by 17.8, 23.2, and 20.7 percent, respectively. (See Table 11.) Real deposits in the Banco do Brasil, the government's commercial bank, increased by 5.1 percent over 1974 (see Table 12) compared with increases of 7.2 and 32.2 percent in 1972 and 1973; virtually all the 1974 increase took place during the first three months of the year. During 1974 the Brazilian public was allowing its real money balances to fall slightly, despite an increase in real gross national product of 9.5 percent, just as it was allowing its real holdings of nonmonetary nominal assets to fall. This was the natural effect on the demand for money of the inflationary deterioration in an economy in which index-linked assets were available.

This interpretation of the shift in Brazilian asset-holding patterns begs a number of interesting questions. Before discussing the consequences of the inflationary deterioration on the supply of money, let us digress to consider these.

First, why could not the rates offered on nominal assets simply rise to meet the competition of index-linked assets? It is clear that the nominal rates on time deposits with pre-fixed index-linking were barely permitted to rise at all during 1974, and the effective prohibition on paying interest on commercial bank demand deposits was maintained as before. For want of data, it is not possible to determine the precise response of the discount on such short-term nominal securities as exchange acceptances and certificates of deposit during 1974; although it apparently rose slightly, it could not rise sufficiently to stem the shift of investors away from holding these assets. In part, the problem was that controls were retained throughout the year on the loans financed by these securities. (See Table 13.)

Table 10. Selected Financial Assets, 1972–76
(millions of new *cruzeiros*; percentage change over the preceding period)

	December 1972	December 1973	March 1974	June 1974	September 1974	December 1974	March 1975	June 1975	September 1975	December 1975	March 1976	June 1976	September 1976	December 1976
1. Monetary assets	63829	93835	97521	105032	107993	125185	121139	138419	149957	179337	174709	204105	207744	248345
		+47.0	+3.9	+7.7	+2.8	+15.9	−3.2	+14.3	+8.3	+19.6	−2.6	+16.8	+1.8	+19.5
(December/December)						+33.4				+43.3				+38.5
2. Index-linked savings accounts in the SFH	7713	14122	16030	18480	22421	28925	34303	40201	47807	55234	64721	76834	91677	107539
		+83.1	+13.5	+15.3	+21.3	+29.0	+18.6	+17.1	+18.9	+15.5	+17.1	+18.7	+19.3	+17.3
(December/December)						+104.8				+91.0				+94.7
3. Time deposits*	17017	25811	27725	28635	30978	33471	35858	42472	50191	54568	56727	66053	68656	73132
		+51.7	+7.4	+3.3	+8.2	+8.0	+7.1	+18.4	+18.1	+8.7	+4.0	+20.4	+3.9	+6.5
(December/December)						+29.7				+63.0				+34.0
4. Index-linked housing bonds	5015	6517	6772	6945	7645	8287	8550	8212	8686	8937	9031	9448	9574	9779
		+30.0	+3.9	+2.6	+10.1	+8.4	+3.2	−4.0	+5.8	+2.9	+1.1	+4.6	+1.3	+2.1
(December/December)						+27.2				+7.8				+9.4
5. Index-linked state and municipal bonds	1721	3232	3272	3752	4607	5417	5856	6875	8537	13834	14644	15661	18593	23230
		+87.8	+1.2	+14.7	+22.8	+17.6	+8.1	+17.4	+24.2	+62.0	+5.9	+6.9	+18.7	+24.9
(December/December)						+67.6				+155.4				+67.9
6. Government bonds held by the public	15893	20804	22300	25373	29843	32937	35119	42489	49727	57690	62677	66890	76197	80857
		+30.9	+7.2	+13.8	+17.6	+10.4	+6.6	+21.0	+17.0	+16.0	+8.6	+6.7	+13.9	+6.1
(December/December)						+58.3				+75.2				+40.2

7. Government bills held by the public (December/December)	8054	12612 +56.6	13598 +7.8	13149 −3.3	11486 −12.6	14405 +25.4 +14.2	17439 +21.0	21071 +20.8	24619 +16.8	22136 −10.1 +53.7	34034 +53.7	49347 +45.0	55335 +12.1	64750 +17.0 +192.5
8. Exchange acceptances (December/December)	20973	34820 +66.3	38442 +10.4	38761 +0.8	40275 +3.9	42608 +5.8 +22.4	44034 +3.3	46586 +5.8	50508 +8.5	55809 +10.5 +31.0	58530 +4.9	61965 +5.9	64680 +4.4	68392 +5.7 +22.5
9. Total principal financial assets (excepting equities)	142448	216681	227871	246851	260081	291695	307377	352038	399881	465267	479334	561395	608260	684306
10. General price index (December/December)	343	397 +15.7	438 +10.3	486 +11.0	507 +4.3	534 +5.3 +34.5	567 +6.2	602 +6.2	647 +7.5	690 +6.6 +29.2	769 +11.4	847 +10.1	946 +11.7	1010 +6.8 +46.4

*Most of the time deposits in Brazilian commercial banks — probably more than 90 percent — carried ex ante, not ex post, index-linking, and should therefore be regarded as nominal assets.

Table 11. Private Commercial Banks Operating in Brazil, 1970–76 (millions of new cruzeiros; proportion of total assets)

	December 1970	December 1971	December 1972	December 1973	March 1974	June 1974	September 1974	December 1974	March 1975	June 1975	September 1975	December 1975	March 1976	June 1976	September 1976	December 1976
Assets																
1. Required reserves	3645	4909	6562	10118	10773	10753	10783	10830	8771	10461	11831	13690	14192	18202	24208	29258
	0.13	0.12	0.11	0.12	0.12	0.11	0.10	0.09	0.08	0.08	0.08	0.08	0.08	0.09	0.11	0.11
2. Total reserves	5505	7864	11164	16967	15476	16208	15982	19319	15694	18902	18841	23995	22646	30484	35459	48863
	0.20	0.19	0.18	0.20	0.17	0.16	0.15	0.17	0.14	0.14	0.13	0.15	0.13	0.15	0.16	0.19
3. Total loans	16573	25099	36697	56984	54974	59014	64495	71877	73423	84085	93548	106055	115365	131694	141486	157328
	0.59	0.61	0.59	0.60	0.61	0.60	0.62	0.62	0.63	0.63	0.66	0.65	0.68	0.62	0.64	0.62
4. Securities holdings	576	1041	1655	2361	3454	4042	4221	4764	4664	6002	5633	8803	7578	11489	10916	15149
	0.02	0.03	0.03	0.03	0.04	0.04	0.04	0.04	0.04	0.04	0.04	0.05	0.04	0.06	0.05	0.06
5. Total assets	27978	41112	61679	85011	89849	98585	104301	116148	116192	134017	142597	162351	170684	202369	219438	254850
Liabilities																
6. Total deposits	18646	26296	38037	52283	53124	55672	57344	67857	65645	75882	81337	97918	94567	110682	113008	136530
	0.67	0.64	0.62	0.62	0.59	0.55	0.55	0.58	0.56	0.57	0.57	0.60	0.55	0.55	0.51	0.54
7. Debt to monetary authority	1511	2243	3020	3782	4561	6106	8234	6136	9032	11704	13769	12931	17918	19497	20138	18718
	0.05	0.05	0.05	0.04	0.05	0.06	0.08	0.05	0.08	0.09	0.10	0.08	0.10	0.10	0.09	0.07
8. Debt to government financial institutions	649	1004	1482	1750	1945	2096	2392	2927	3189	3384	3585	3957	4154	4735	5462	6249
	0.02	0.03	0.02	0.02	0.02	0.02	0.02	0.03	0.03	0.03	0.03	0.02	0.02	0.02	0.02	0.02

9. Foreign exchange liabilities	2702	4823	9606	13902	17006	20186	20979	20596	19924	21526	21136	21962	27038	34422	41734	51546
	0.10	0.12	0.16	0.16	0.19	0.20	0.20	0.18	0.17	0.16	0.15	0.14	0.16	0.17	0.19	0.20
10. Liabilities for collection	875	1593	2656	3740	3551	3532	4724	6117	5395	6227	7342	8029	8605	10131	11404	12865
	0.03	0.04	0.04	0.04	0.04	0.04	0.05	0.05	0.05	0.05	0.05	0.05	0.05	0.05	0.05	0.03
11. (1) ÷ (2)	0.66	0.62	0.59	0.60	0.70	0.66	0.67	0.56	0.56	0.55	0.63	0.57	0.63	0.60	0.68	0.59
12. (3) ÷ (6)	0.89	0.95	0.96	0.98	1.03	1.06	1.12	1.16	1.12	1.11	1.15	1.08	1.22	1.14	1.25	1.15
13. (6) deflated by the general price index	18646	21958	27052	32660	30079	28409	28050	31514	28712	31260	31177	35194	30498	32407	29626	33524
percentage change (December/December)		+17.8	−23.2	+20.7	−7.9	−5.6	−1.3	+12.3	−8.9	+8.9	−0.3	+12.9	−13.3	−7.9	−8.6	+13.2
								−3.5				+11.5				−4.7
14. Index: cleared checks + demand deposits (1966 = 100)	128	172	183	199	192	185	210	239	256	330	380	350	361	413	391	446

Table 12. The Brazilian Monetary Authorities, 1971–76, i.e., the consolidated balance of the Banco Central do Brasil and the Banco do Brasil (millions of new *cruzeiros*; percent change from period to period)

Assets	December 1971	December 1972	December 1973	March 1974	June 1974	September 1974	December 1974	March 1975	June 1975	September 1975	December 1975	March 1976	June 1976	September 1976	December 1976
1. Credit to commercial banks (December/December)	3799	5711 +50.3	9015 +57.9	10243 +13.6	12644 +23.4	17061 +34.9	18169 +6.5 +101.5	22078 +21.5	27721 +25.5	30969 +11.7	32541 +5.1 +79.1	39136 +20.3	45503 +16.3	51900 +14.1	47627 −8.2 +46.4
2. Credit to development banks (December/December)	1155	2156 +86.7	3595 +66.7	4418 +22.9	5301 +20.0	6936 +30.8	10329 +49.8 +187.3	11603 +11.6	13424 +15.7	15846 +18.0	19349 +22.1 +87.3	21062 +8.9	26146 +24.1	30122 +15.2	34616 +14.9 +78.9
3. Credit to other financial institutions* (December/December)	354	635 +79.3	779 +22.7	856 +9.9	2305 +169.3	3803 +65.0	5222 +37.3 +570.3	6674 +27.8	7535 +12.9	8060 +7.0	8950 +11.0 +71.4	9330 +4.2	11913 +27.7	13832 +16.1	22381 +61.8 +150.0
4. Credit of the Banco do Brasil to private sector (December/December)	22469	30277 +34.8	45422 +50.0	48969 +7.8	56958 +16.3	64634 +13.5	80643 +24.8 +77.5	88274 +9.5	107079 +21.3	117448 +9.7	132727 +13.0 +64.6	141365 +6.5	171608 +21.4	186725 +8.8	214115 +14.7 +61.3
5. Foreign-exchange assets	15800	33133	48811	52294	54239	51239	51280	47621	44039	45592	51432	52098	56195	69779	104236

Liabilities	December 1971	December 1972	December 1973	March 1974	June 1974	September 1974	December 1974	March 1975	June 1975	September 1975	December 1975	March 1976	June 1976	September 1976	December 1976
6. Liabilities on account of the National Treasury (December/December)	−4549	1954 (−143.0)	6786 +247.3	12008	14190	14738	17587 +159.2	22626	30004	35403	30107 +71.2	41956	47815	54935	52449 +74.2
7. Resources of Banco Central finance programs (December/December)	16081	21332 +32.7	28825 +35.1	30406	32337	33922	36894 +28.0	38435	41296	45215	54828 +48.6	59724	67293	75066	90620 +65.3
8. Resources of Banco do Brasil	292	1453	4788	5952	7807	9617	11298	14025	17249	20951	22994	26973	30402	35903	39197

	1	2	3	4	5	6	7	8	9	10	11	12	13	14	15
finance programs (December/December)	+397.6	+229.5					+136.0				+103.5				+70.5
9. Foreign-exchange liabilities	4409	6248	7583	8280	9086	10673	12263	15180	15117	16503	16799	19485	20535	23083	31806
(December/December)	41.7	+21.4					+61.7				+37.0				+89.3
10. Deposits in the Banco do Brasil	7735	9574	14631	17051	18910	19993	20681	21304	23248	26246	27475	27236	33412	34673	36879
(December/December)	+23.8	+52.6	+16.5	+10.9	+5.7	+3.4	+32.9 +41.5 +3.0	+9.1	+12.9	+4.7 +32.9	-0.9	+22.7	+3.8 +34.2	+6.3 +34.2	
11. Monetary base	23392	27724	40776	42564	46232	46288	54202	50686	55039	59901	73934	67001	83641	89403	110752
(December/December)	+18.5 +47.1	+4.4	+8.6	+0.1	+17.0 +32.9	-6.5	+8.6	+8.3	+23.4 +23.4	-9.4	+20.6 +36.4	+10.6	+23.9 +49.8		
12. Total assets of the monetary authorities	56464	86181	127642	138527	156962	168435	195453	207770	236817	258838	300812	325601	377795	419991	496925
13. Money supply	44514	61550	90490	93857	100885	103574	120788	116573	133144	143819	172433	165953	192791	196521	236502
(December/December)	+38.3	+47.0	+3.7	+7.5	+2.7	+16.6 +33.5	-3.5	+14.2	+8.0 +42.8	+19.9	-3.8 +37.2	+16.2	+1.9	+20.3	
14. Money multiplier (13)÷(11)	1.9	2.2	2.2	2.2	2.2	2.2	2.2	2.3	2.4	2.4	2.3	2.5	2.4	2.2	2.1
15. (10) deflated by the general price index	6459	6922	9140	9654	9649	9780	9605	9318	9577	10060	9875	8784	9783	9090	9055
(December/December)	+7.2	+32.0	+5.6	-0.1	+1.4	-1.8 +5.1	-3.0	+2.8	+5.0 +2.8	-1.8	-11.0 -8.3	+11.4	-7.1	-0.4	
16. (4)÷(10)	2.9	3.2	3.1	2.9	3.0	3.2	3.9	4.1	4.6	4.5	4.8	5.2	5.1	5.4	5.8
17. (13) deflated by the general price index	44514	53295	67698	63643	61652	60674	67180	61062	65687	66019	74221	64094	67602	61698	69546
(December/December)	+19.7	+27.0	-6.0	-8.9	-1.6	+10.7 -0.8	-9.1	+7.6	+0.5 +10.5	+12.4	-13.6 -6.3	+5.5	-8.7	+12.7	

*Includes investment banks, finance companies, savings banks of the federal and state governments, and cooperatives.

Source: Boletim Banco Central do Brasil.

Table 13. 12 Months' Yield of Selected Securities: Nominal Return over the 12 Months to the Date Given, 1973–76 (percent per year)

	March 1973	June 1973	September 1973	December 1973	March 1974	June 1974	September 1974	December 1974	March 1975	June 1975	September 1975	December 1975	March 1976	June 1976	September 1976	December 1976
Interbank overnight	14.0	12.9	12.4	13.3	13.9	15.1	15.5	14.7	14.8	13.9	14.0	16.7	18.9	23.2	27.5	
Government bills: 91 days — secondary mkt.	20.0	19.2	18.2	17.6	17.0	17.2	17.7	19.4	20.7	22.1	22.4	22.6	25.5	31.0	38.1	45.6
Government bills: 365 days — primary mkt.					15.8	15.0	15.0	15.4	15.9	17.4	21.0	20.7	22.6	18.6	21.8	20.6
Index linked government bonds	18.9	18.3	16.9	17.1	19.9	21.5	28.4	39.5	39.4	39.8	30.2	28.9	30.9	33.0	37.2	
Passbook savings — Savings Banks	22.0	21.5	20.0	19.7	20.5	21.2	25.4	38.4	40.4	41.7	40.4	30.5	32.1	33.9	36.9	41.4
Comm. banks' time deposits: with CD	24.0	24.0	24.0	24.0	21.0	21.0	21.0	21.0	21.0	24.0	26.0	26.0	26.0	26.3	26.0	31.2
without CD	24.0	24.0	24.0	24.0	21.0	21.0	21.0	21.0	21.0	24.0	27.0	27.0	27.0	26.3	26.0	31.2
Investment banks' time dep. with CD	24.0	24.0	24.0	24.0	21.0	21.0	21.0	21.0	21.0	25.0	27.0	27.0	27.0	26.3	26.0	29.8
without CD	24.0	24.0	24.0	24.0	21.0	21.0	21.0	21.0	21.0	25.0	28.0	28.0	28.0	26.3	26.0	29.8
Investment banks' time dep. index linked, with CD	23.6	23.0	21.6	21.8	23.3	24.9	36.4	42.3	42.2	42.8	33.4	32.2	34.1	36.2	40.2	
index linked, without CD	23.6	23.0	21.6	21.8	23.3	24.9	36.4	42.3	42.2	42.8	33.4	32.2	34.1	36.2	40.2	

Exchange acceptances:																
Primary market	25.8	25.3	24.3	24.2	22.3	22.1	22.1	22.0	23.6	25.2	26.8	27.0	26.7	26.7	26.8	26.5
Secondary mkt., 30 days									24.5	25.4	26.3	27.4	28.3	31.0	33.9	
Secondary mkt., 360 days									25.8	28.2	25.4	27.6	28.8	28.8	28.6	
Rio de Janeiro stock exch. index	−48.9	−5.6	−3.5	−12.7	35.6	−23.8	−14.9	40.5	9.1	66.5	81.9	34.9	56.1			
Stock mutual funds:																
Regular — 10 largest	−29.5	− 5.1	12.0	2.0	20.4	−10.8	−23.3	0	−18.6	45.4	56.4	38.0	69.8	37.5		
Decree Law 157 — 4 largest	−25.2	−12.9	−1.7	−6.5	5.8	−11.1	−18.8	0	−15.4	37.5	38.9	25.0	54.8	31.8		
General price index	14.7	15.2	14.0	15.7	22.3	31.0	32.7	34.5	29.5	23.9	27.6	29.2	35.6	40.7	46.2	46.4
Foreign exchange correction	8.0	7.4	6.5	4.7	2.0	6.3	9.8	12.0	17.9	18.8	13.4	14.3	16.1	24.3	30.7	

There are some fundamental reasons why the rates on nominal assets could not rise to meet the competition of index-linked assets.[18] Consider the situation of commercial banks. The deposit rate in Brazilian commercial banks was limited, by regulation, to zero; but in any case these banks had little incentive to raise their deposit rates in response to increase inflation. Their lending rates were subject to official controls through the mechanism of pre-fixed index-linking (although to some extent the banks were able to earn more than the legal limit through such devices as banking commissions and compensating balances, and besides, Brazilian commercial banks have traditionally rationed credit heavily). In these circumstances the banks' profit rates were at least adequate, regardless of the rate of inflation, because whatever increased inflation took from the real rate of interest earned by the banks on their loans it also took from the real rate of interest paid by the banks on their deposits. It makes little difference to a bank if it "earns," say, real interest of minus 10 percent on its loans if it "pays" real interest of minus 40 percent on its deposits — it is still earning a spread of 30 percent. And even if the real deposit rate is very negative, commercial banks will not find themselves entirely without funds, for the public must hold some demand deposits for transactions purposes.

True, a bank might be able to attract more resources if it offered a higher rate of return on its deposits, and these resources could probably be lent out profitably. But a commercial bank that paid a higher deposit rate would have to charge a higher lending rate, and a risk-averse bank would tend to prefer not to: higher lending rates would increase the likelihood that creditors would default, particularly in view of the uncertain circumstances and the real-price "dispersal" that inevitably accompany an increased rate of inflation. Furthermore, a commercial bank would have to change its deposit rate frequently and perhaps very sharply in order for its deposit accounts to compete with index-linked assets. Nominal assets compete disadvantageously with index-linked assets in a period of rising inflation, not only because the expected real rate of interest on nominal assets cannot match the rate offered on index-linked assets, but because the real rate on a nominal asset is uncertain, whereas the real rate on an index-linked asset is not. Thus if commercial banks were to attempt to compete with index-linked assets through the deposit rate, they would have to offer a relatively high nominal rate — some component of which would in effect be a risk premium to the depositor — and they would have to vary the rate frequently. This would turn the banks' operations unacceptably volatile.

Nonbank financial intermediaries are in a somewhat more difficult position, because they do not receive demand deposits. They can still function in an inflationary context with relatively low rates on the instruments that they sell to the public, however, mainly because their largest purchasers are enterprises with fluctuating cash balances. Such enterprises should be willing enough to purchase short-term nominal securities, because they are liquid and because, even if their real rate of return is negative, it will assuredly be higher by their nominal rate than the real rate of return on money. In Brazil the lending rates of the nonbank financial intermediaries are generally controlled by the monetary authority, and the competing bank-loan rates are usually relatively low for the reasons we have given. (On the other hand, the demand for credit from nonbank financial intermediaries is always heavy, particularly because of the banks' rationing practices, and there is usually considerable upward pressure on the lending rates.) Again, as long as they maintain a positive spread between their lending and borrowing rates, nonbank financial intermediaries can maintain themselves well enough even if their borrowing rate is negative. The situation of such financial institutions is more precarious than that of commercial banks, the more so where there is inflation. Marketable paper can carry a discount; thus the real interest rate in this market can vary much more than the real rate on bank deposits. The discount notwithstanding, money-market instruments will be able to compete effectively with index-linked assets only if they are sold for very short terms. For longer terms, the inflationary uncertainty attaching to the real rate on nominal paper becomes too high.

But then, one might ask, why not insitute index-linking more comprehensively — why not require commercial banks and nonbank financial intermediaries to index-link both their lending and deposit rates? For one thing, short-term borrowers would not stand for it. Commercial credit is generally repaid from sales and accounts receivable: by their nature, these cannot be made proof against inflation. But even if commercial bank loans could be index-linked, it must be remembered that a significant part of commercial banks' assets are held in the form of cash — required reserves and vault cash. In order for commercial banks to index-link their demand deposits, their reserves must be index-linked — which is to say, the money supply as a whole must be index-linked. But that would be pointless. If the currency unit were index-linked, the currency unit would be changed: instead of the *cruzeiro*, the monetary unit would effectively become the index-linked *cruzeiro*. Prices would then come to be set in terms of index-linked cruzeiros, and the true measure of inflation would be the index-linked-cruzeiro price index. The ordinary *cruzeiro*-price index would be irrelevant. Whatever previously caused inflation through creation of *cruzeiros* would now cause inflation through creation of index-linked *cruzeiros*, and the economy would be right back where it started before index-linking was introduced. This observation amounts to a description of what *index-linking* really is: index-linking is the institution of a second monetary unit alongside the unit of the circulating medium. The advantages and problems of index-linking both arise because, although this second monetary unit is not subject to inflationary uncertainty, the exchange rate between the two monetary units *is* subject to inflationary uncertainty; moreover, the second monetary unit cannot be used for transactions purposes.

C. THE BRAZILIAN SUPPLY OF MONEY, 1975–1976

The radical shift in asset-holding patterns that took place during 1974 inevitably brought a more institutional inflation-feedback mechanism into play: the monetary authority found itself forced to permit the inflation to continue. There were further inflationary shocks after 1974: for example, in mid-1975 a series of agricultural disasters throughout the country not only caused supply problems but occasioned an inflationary credit expansion. We argue here, however, that the shift in asset-holding patterns in 1974 was, by itself, a significant source of pressure on the monetary authority to inflate: consider, therefore, the developments in Brazil's money supply during 1975 and 1976.

It is clear that by the end of 1974 the government had become painfully aware that the shift out of nominal assets into index-linked assets was causing a liquidity crisis in the banking system and severe problems for the financial system generally.[19] In November 1974 the government took several measures to mitigate the asset shift: the National Housing Bank effectively prohibited anyone but private individuals from maintaining index-linked passbook savings accounts in the Housing Finance System and also reduced the grace period after the start of each month for deposits in passbook savings accounts during which new deposits would be treated as though they had been made on the first of the month.[20] Firms were thus excluded from holding index-linked assets for the very short term. The immediately critical problem, however, was the situation of the commercial banks. The demand for loans that they faced rose considerably throughout the year, undoubtedly by considerably more in nominal terms than the rate of inflation in view of the severe real economic problems, while deposits fell in real terms. The banks clearly tried to meet some of this loan demand. During 1974 their ratio of loans to deposits rose above one, and their real loans increased. (See Table 11.) By the beginning of 1975 their credit tightness had reached severe proportions, and there is clear evidence that after October 1974 the economy suffered an industrial recession that threatened to become very serious.[21]

This situation left the monetary authority little choice. In late February 1975 it began an expansionary monetary policy by reducing required reserve ratios. The magnitude of the expansion was greatly increased during March and April, when a special six-month loan facility was made available to the private commercial banking system. This facility, known as the *Compensatory Refinancing*, was intended to provide temporary relief to the banks without — it was hoped — interfering with the government's longer-run stabilization effort. Altogether an amount equal to approximately 10 percent of the money supply was loaned out under the facility to the commercial banks, who used it to expand their loans. (See Table 11.) The increased liquidity had a stimulating effect on the economy, and although it was, of course, inflationary, the government hoped that it could rein in the money supply again when conditions improved. Unfortunately, the availability of index-linked assets maintained the inflation-feedback mechanism as robust as ever: the stock of index-linked assets grew by almost as much as it had in the previous year (see Table 10), and the real money supply increased very slowly (see Table 12), barely making up the fall in the real money supply during the first part of the year.

A further development complicated the financial situation in 1975. During this year the money market turned hyperactive in Brazil's principal financial centers. The money market's rates and volumes rose heavily, and became highly variable; the maturities of money-market paper shortened drastically. Nonbank financial intermediaries came increasingly to employ a characteristically new mode of operation in their competition for resources with index-linked assets: the repurchase letter. The *repurchase letter* was a document accompanying the sale of a security, such as an exchange acceptance or a certificate of deposit, promising that the seller of the security would repurchase the security after a given number of days at a specified price. In such a transaction the repurchase letter became the true financial instrument, and the security merely collateral. Since the repurchase letters were generally of extremely short maturity, their real rate of return was subject to relatively little inflationary uncertainty. Thus they could compete effectively with index-linked assets. Their drawback, of course, was that they went to finance business and commercial loans of longer terms, while the money-market rates might fluctuate considerably. Funds were thus attracted back into the nominal sector of the economy, particularly since firms could no longer hold funds in passbook savings accounts, and since the public believed, seeing that the government was carrying out an expansionary monetary policy, that it was best to buy such securities now before their real rates of return went down. This money market has come to be known in Brazil as "o Open Market" (the English expression is used), because it employs the same financial infrastructure that is used for transactions in the government's (nominal) bills and (index-linked) bonds.

Severe problems developed toward the end of 1975, however, when the government shifted course and tried to return to a contractionary monetary policy. At the same time the Compensatory Refinancing loan came due; in anticipation of the due date of the huge facility, the banks had gone heavily into government bills. Between, roughly speaking, September and November, a massive amount of paper poured on to the Open Market, as the commercial banks sought to go into cash to pay back the loan and investors sought to dispose of securities that would probably now suffer a capital loss. As the short-term rates rose sharply, many financial institutions found themselves in deep trouble. This event is generally described in Brazil's financial community as the first *open crisis* — further crises were to ensue in 1976 as the monetary authority tried to tighten its policy but sometimes had to loosen credit. The monetary authority had been intervening in some financial institutions and providing emergency loans to others since the Halles collapse in 1974, and during 1975 and 1976 it had to provide increased support: during these two years the monetary authority's credits to nonbank financial institutions increased by 71.4 and 150 percent respectively. These credits alone amounted to 19 and 36 percent of the respective increases in the monetary base in these two years, and therefore must be regarded as a major cause of the 46.4 percent increase in the general price level that occurred over 1976. (The remainder of the 1975 and 1976 growth in the monetary base is accounted for by Central Bank credit to commercial banks, the expansion of demand deposits/credit of the government-owned Banco do Brasil, and — after 1976 — the growth of foreign reserves. Since the Banco do Brasil is not subject to the required-reserve ratio, its deposits are part of the monetary base. And although to avoid complication we have deliberately avoided discussing Brazil's foreign financial relations in this essay, it should be noted that Brazil is very much an open economy where credit is concerned: foreign banks have remained willing to supply credit to Brazil in spite of Brazil's economic difficulties, and so at times when domestic credit became tight, Brazilian enterprises naturally turned to foreign sources.)

To summarize, the role of financial index-linking in forcing increases in the Brazilian money supply must be regarded as critical. Simply put, the availability of index-linked assets placed severe pressure on monetary institutions whenever there was an inflationary deterioration, as the Brazilian public sought to reduce its real money holdings in favor of index-linked assets. The Brazilian monetary authority has been obliged to respond to the flight from real money by replenishing the money supply, and this has served to propagate the inflation forward through time. The Brazilian government has been well aware that index-linked assets have been placing a severe strain on the nation's financial system: in August 1975 it announced that henceforth it reserved the right to edit "accidental" price increases, i.e., price increases resulting from aggregate-supply shocks such as the agricultural disasters of that year, out of the index; and in April 1976 the government made a more drastic change, announcing that henceforth index-linked assets would be corrected according to the formula

$$(.8 \div I + .2 \cdot 15) \text{ percent (in annual terms)},$$

where I is the rate of increase that would previously have been applied to index-linked securities.[22] The stated purpose of these changes was to reduce inflation feedback and to relieve the competitive pressure that financial institutions faced from index-linked assets. It is not clear, however, how much farther the government can go in the direction of making index-linked assets less attractive, since the Housing Finance System, the forced-savings funds, and other institutions have so strong a vested interest in them.

CONCLUSION

We have argued that our evidence from Brazil's recent inflationary experience suggests strongly that the inflation-feedback mechanism has operated there since 1974 through the availability of index-linked assets.[23] Does this conclusion amount to an argument that no nation should ever introduce financial index-linking? It is difficult to say. In the first place, as we observed in Section II, we cannot show that the inflation-feedback mechanism must be more robust where index-linked assets are available than where they are not available. Second, it cannot be emphasized too strongly that as long as the rate of inflation remains short of hyperinflationary levels, financial, index-linking permits accumulation of savings and government borrowing from the public. One must retort, however, that at the same time the competition of index-linked assets places severe stress on the operations of financial enterprises that operate with nominal instruments and forces the economy to operate with two currency units with a variable and uncertain exchange rate — to the inevitable detriment of the transactions-currency unit.

In sum, financial index-linking has its advantages and its drawbacks. On the one hand, it preserves the value of the national savings stock in an inflationary context. On the other hand, it places severe pressure on the currency and the financial system. The real conclusion, perhaps, is that for the long run there can be no simple technocratic substitute for government policy to control inflation. Index-linking may be a sensible temporary expedient for a serious stabilization program, where inflationary expectations and uncertainty are coming down. It is not a magical device for living painlessly with continuing inflation.

Notes

* The research on which this paper is based was supported by a grant from the Social Science Research Council. This research was largely carried out at the Instituto de Pesquisas Economicas of the Universidade de Sao Paulo, Sao Paulo, Brazil. Particular thanks are due to Adroaldo Moura da Silva, Werner Baer, Dwight Jaffee, Alan Blinder, and William Branson for comments and advice. None of these gentlemen is responsible, of course, for any errors of fact or judgment in this essay.

Published in Portuguese in *Pesquisa e Planejamento Economico* (Rio de Janeiro), August 1979 as "Ativos financeiros indexados e o mecanismo de realimentacao inflacionaria no Brasil."

1. I am indebted to Professor Adroaldo Moura da Silva of the Universidade de São Paulo for convincing me of this point.

2. More detailed histories in English of Brazil's introduction of index-linking are provided in Baer and Beckerman (1974); Beckerman ("The Trouble . . . , 1978); and Fishlow (1974). Histories in Portuguese are given in Chacel, Simonsen, and Wald (1970); Ness (1977); and Simonsen (1975).

3. It is important to understand that this was not really because of the Brazilian usury law, which limited the annual interest on the government's bonds to 12 percent. Government bonds could always have been sold at a discount to raise their effective yield above the anticipated rate of inflation. What made government obligations unsalable was the uncertainty associated with the high rate of inflation, which rendered the a priori real rate of return on any fixed-return security unacceptably uncertain to the financial markets. Consequently, it would not have helped much simply to raise the rate of return offered on government obligations. The real rate of return had to be made not only positive, but reasonably certain, and this could be accomplished only by index-linking the securities *ex post facto* — that is, readjusting their principals periodically according to an appropriate price index.

4. A history of the formulas that have been used to readjust index-linked assets is given in "Correcão monetária e realimentacão inflacionária," *Conjuntura Econômica*, June 1976, pp. 88–94.

5. Kampel and Miranda do Valle (1974) describes the Housing Finance System in detail.

6. There is a growing literature on the question of why index-linked assets have not appeared spontaneously in private capital markets. See Siegel (1974), Fischer (1975), and Blinder (1977). See Liviatan and Levhari (1977) for an analysis basically in agreement with the view of this writer. The Brazilian attempt to introduce private index-linked securitiess is described in "A Nova Lei do Mercado de Capitais e a Resolucão No. 21 do Conselho Monetário," *Conjuntura Econômica*, March, 1966, pp. 9–12. See also Syvrud (1972), pp. 124–26.

7. See Syvrud.

8. See "O Plano de equivalência salarial e a correcão monetária," *Conjun-*

tura *Econômica,* March, 1970, pp. 65–68. See also Beckerman ("Adjustment for Inflation . . . ," 1978).
9. Contador (1977).
10. *Ibid.*
11. This is certainly true if inflationary expectations and uncertainty are simply adaptive in character. If inflationary expectations are rational, then there are various possibilities, especially if the rational expectation takes full account of the feedback process. We are assuming simply that, whatever the underlying reason, inflationary expectations are elastic with respect to the rate of inflation.
12. It is theoretically possible, however, that an increase in the uncertainty attaching to the real rate of inflation would *increase* the demand for money. This could happen if the subjective probability distributions of the real rates of return on money and equities were negatively correlated.
13. The argument that the liquidity condition of banks may vary according to the expected rate of inflation is similar in spirit to Irving Fisher's theory of how the business cycle could be propagated through the banking system. See Fisher (1911).
14. This writer has developed a model from which formal conditions can be derived under which the effect on the IS of introducing financial index-linking would be more important than the effect on the LM. See Beckerman ("Index-linked Government Bonds . . .", 1978).
15. One might argue that the increase in international oil prices should not be regarded as inflationary in itself, since for any given nation the increase represented only a shift in relative prices. True enough; but in Brazil and in many other nations the shift in relative prices inevitably occasioned an increase in the demand for bank credit, and this caused an increase in the money supply to the extent that the monetary authorities permitted — or were forced to permit — the banking system to meet this demand.
16. See Beckerman, "The Trouble . . ." (1978) for a slightly more detailed discussion of these developments.
17. See "Brazil counts its debts," *The Economist,* 13 March 1974, pp. 77–78.
18. Ness (1977) argues that the failure of nominal rates to rise sufficiently was a major cause of the problems faced by the Brazilian financial system after 1974.
19. See *Conjuntura Econômica,* October 1974, p. 48.
20. The new ruling provided that index-linking and interest would be paid for a given month only on quantities deposited by the fifth of the month, rather than the fifteenth of the month as under the previous regulation. Under the previous regulation, savers could profitably invest funds in moneymarket securities between the first and the fifteenth before returning the funds to the savings accounts, thus earning from two sources on the funds. (See *Conjuntura Econômica,* November 1974, p. 32.) Enterprises had been using the Housing Finance System savings accounts for their spare cash, a use that made the accounts quite volatile and contrary to their purpose.
21. Figures for the consumption of electrical energy in the Rio de Janeiro-São Paulo-Minas Gerais area suggest that there was indeed such a recession. The figures (in million kilowatt-hours) are

September 1974:	1663	January 1975:	1587
October 1974:	1584	February 1975:	1586
November 1974:	1654	March 1975:	1590
December 1974:	1581	April 1975:	1640

(*Boletim* do Banco Central do Brasil, March 1977, p. 149).

22. See "Correcão monetária e realimentacão inflacionária," *Conjuntura Econômica*, June 1976, pp. 88–94. That is, the adjustment was diluted, with 20 percent of the adjustment now being made as though the annual rate of inflation had been 15 percent.

23. In a recent paper, Cláudio Contador presented a statistical analysis of the relationship between two Brazilian time series, the rate of inflation and the percentage adjustments applied to outstanding index-linked assets. Contador's results may be summarized briefly as follows: (a) quarterly regression analysis using an Almon lag shows a strong positive relationship between the current rate of adjustment and lagged rates of inflation (which stands to reason, since the adjustment of index-linked assets is based on a moving average of the rates of inflation between three and six months before); (b) quarterly regression analysis using an Almon lag shows a weak, statistically not significant relationship between the current rate of inflation and lagged rates of adjustment; (c) spectral analysis finds that the rate of adjustment has no leading effect on the current rate of inflation, either for short- or long-run analysis. Contador concludes that "the empirical tests leave little margin of doubt that index-linking does not feed back into the inflationary process in Brazil." How can we reconcile his results with the analysis that we have given.

Dr. Contador and the present writer are really discussing two different feedback processes. Dr. Contador's empirical analysis establishes that the *adjustment* of index-linked assets does not apparently propagate inflation through time. This stands to reason, especially in view of the way that index-linking has been implemented in Brazil. Since commercial, industrial, and agricultural credit is generally not index-linked, there is little reason for adjustment of index-linked assets to be translated into cost pressure; moreover, the additional income received by savers and financial investors on index-linked assets is generally also saved, and thus adds little to aggregate expenditure.

The argument of the present essay, on the other hand, is that the *availability* of index-linked assets, rather than their adjustment per se, is a key element in the inflation-feedback process: earlier increases in the rate of inflation, operating through formation of inflationary expectations and uncertainty, affect the current rate of inflation by stimulating assetholders to move out of money and into index-linked assets, thereby effectively decreasing the real value of money and forcing the monetary authority to increase the money supply.

APPENDIX

This appendix presents a simple version of the familiar IS-LM model incorporating the expectation of the real rate of return on money and the uncertainty attaching to this expectation as shift parameters. Conditions are then derived under which an increase in inflationary expectations and uncertainty — i.e., "an inflationary shock" — will generate greater inflationary pressure in an economy in which nonmonetary financial assets are index-linked than in an economy in which such assets are nominal.

Suppose first that nonmonetary financial assets are nominal. Define the following symbols:

i = nominal rate of interest,

r = prospective real rate of interest,

$-\pi$ = prospective real rate of return on money,

$\delta = r - (-\pi)$;

π and therefore r ($= i - \pi$) are taken to be stochastic variables distributed according to subjective probability distributions held by all participants in the economy. (If the fractional rate of price-level increase over a given period is $\dot{p}$, the corresponding real rate of return on money held over the same period is given by $-\pi = -\dot{p}/(1+\dot{p})$; e.g., over a period in which the price level increases by 100 percent, money loses 50 percent of its real value.) Let $\bar{\pi}$, $\bar{r}$, and $\bar{\delta}$ represent the expectations of, and $\tilde{\pi}$, $\tilde{r}$, and $\tilde{\delta}$ the uncertainties attaching to, the variables π, r, and δ. Let

y = real rate of national income,

p = price level,

$S(\ )$ = real-rate-of-savings function,

$I(\ )$ = real-rate-of-investment function,

$M(\ )$ = nominal-money-supply function,

and

$L(\ )$ = real-money-demand function.

The principal simplifying assumptions are as follows:

1. The real rates of savings and investment depend, positively and negatively respectively, on the expectation of the real rate of interest and, in some way, on the uncertainty attaching to this real rate. (Regarding uncertainty, see Assumption 4.)

2. The real demand for money is taken to be a negative function of $\bar{\delta}$, the difference between the expectations of the real rate of interest and the real rate of return on money (as would be the case for a Baumol inventory-theoretic demand for money); it is also, in some way, a function of $\tilde{\delta}$, the uncertainty attaching to this difference.

3. The nominal supply of money is taken to be a positive function of δ, for the reasons discussed earlier, that is, a high spread between the real rates of return on nonmonetary financial assets and monetary assets leads to a drain of *real* resources from the banking system, and this obliges the banking system to create additional *nominal* money balances. (If the reader finds this notion too exotic for his taste, he may take $M_\delta = 0$ in the model below.) The nominal supply of money is also in some way, a function of $\bar{\delta}$.

4. Although the discussion in the text suggests that we take savings and investment to be negatively affected by increases in inflationary uncertainty, demand for money to be affected negatively by an increase in δ, and the supply of money to be affected positively by an increase in δ, in the present analysis we will allow for any possibility.

If nonmonetary financial assets are nominal,

$$\delta = (i - \bar{\pi}) - (-\bar{\pi}) = i;$$

since i is not stochastic, no uncertainty attaches to it, so that

$$\bar{\delta} = 0.$$

The simple IS-LM model with nominal nonmonetary assets may then be written as follows:

$$I(\bar{r}, \bar{\bar{r}}) = S(y, \bar{r}, \bar{\bar{r}}), \quad I_{\bar{r}} < 0, \quad S_y, \quad S_{\bar{r}} > 0, \quad I_{\bar{\bar{r}}}, \quad S_{\bar{\bar{r}}} \gtreqless 0; \tag{1--n}$$

$$M(\bar{\delta}, \bar{\bar{\delta}}) = p \cdot L(y, \bar{\delta}, \bar{\bar{\delta}}),$$

$$L_y > 0, \quad L_\delta < 0, \quad M_\delta > 0, \quad L_{\bar{\delta}}, \quad M_\delta \gtreqless 0; \tag{2--n}$$

$$r = i - \bar{\pi}; \tag{3--n}$$

$$\bar{r} = \bar{\pi}; \tag{4--n}$$

$$\bar{\delta} = (i - \bar{\pi}) + \bar{\pi} = i; \tag{5--n}$$

$$\bar{\bar{\delta}} = 0; \tag{6--n}$$

we close the model with an "aggregate-supply" equation,

$$y = F(p), \quad F_p \gtreqqless 0.$$

(The parameters $\bar{\pi}$ and $\bar{\bar{\pi}}$ could be introduced in the aggregate-supply function, but this function should not be changed by the use of index-linked bonds, so for simplicity we leave the function in its present form.)

If nonmonetary assets are index-linked, then the model is changed as follows:

(1) r is now known with certainty, so $\bar{r} = 0$;

(2) $\bar{\delta}$ now equals $r - (-\bar{\pi}) = r + \bar{\pi}$, and $\bar{\bar{\delta}}$ now equals $\bar{\bar{\pi}}$.

We assume for simplicity that the functions S, I, M, and L are not changed by the introduction of index-linked assets. (Beckerman, 1978, "Index-linked Government Bonds . . . ," analyzes the consequences of dropping this assumption.) With index-linked assets the model becomes

$$I(\bar{r}, \tilde{r}) = S(y, \bar{r}, \tilde{r}), \tag{1-i}$$

$$M(\bar{\delta}, \tilde{\delta}) = p \cdot L(y, \bar{\delta}, \tilde{\delta}), \tag{2-i}$$

$$\bar{r} = r, \tag{3-i}$$

$$\tilde{r} = 0, \tag{4-i}$$

$$\bar{\delta} = r + \bar{\pi}, \tag{5-i}$$

$$\tilde{\delta} = \tilde{\pi}, \tag{6-i}$$

$$y = F(p). \tag{7-i}$$

In this model, $\bar{\delta}$ is simply the expected nominal rate of interest.

The question, under which regime would "an inflationary shock" (as we have defined it) have a stronger inflationary impact? may be answered in theory by comparative-statics analyses of the two models, to determine for which model $dp/d\bar{\pi}$ and $dp/d\tilde{\pi}$ is the greater.

For the model $(1-n) - (7-n)$, it turns out that

$$\frac{dp}{d\bar{\pi}}\bigg|_n = [M_{\bar{\delta}}^- - pL_{\bar{\delta}}^-)^{-1}(L + L_y F_p p) + (S_{\bar{r}} - I_{\bar{r}})^{-1} S_y F_p]^{-1}; \tag{8-n}$$

$$\frac{dp}{d\tilde{\pi}}\bigg|_n = \frac{dp}{d\bar{\pi}}\bigg|_n (S_{\bar{r}} - I_r)^{-1}(S_{\tilde{r}} - I_{\tilde{r}}) \tag{9-n}$$

For the model $(1-i)-(7-i)$, it turns out that

$$\frac{dp}{d\bar{\pi}}\bigg|_i = \frac{dp}{d\bar{\pi}}\bigg|_n; \tag{8-i}$$

$$\frac{dp}{d\tilde{\pi}}\bigg|_i = \frac{dp}{d\bar{\pi}}\bigg|_i (M_{\bar{\delta}}^- - pL_{\bar{\delta}}^-)^{-1}(M_{\tilde{\delta}}^- - pL_{\tilde{\delta}}^-). \tag{9-i}$$

Equation (8-i) shows that increased inflationary expectations per se have the same inflationary effect in the two models. This stands to reason, because index-linking makes a difference only for inflationary uncertainty. In a world of perfect certainty there is no difference between the two models, because in such a world there is no reason to choose between nominal and index-linked assets, as long as the nominal return on nominal assets incorporates an adjustment for the expected rate of inflation. Whether an increase in inflationary uncertainty would have a greater inflationary effect where nonmonetary assets are index-linked depends on whether expression (9-i) is greater than expression (9-n). On theoretical grounds there is no reason to believe a priori that this condition either would or would not be fulfilled. Indeed it is not certain a priori that (9-i) is greater than zero, although if

$$\frac{dp}{d\bar{\pi}}\bigg|_i > 0, \ M_{\tilde{\delta}}^-, M_{\bar{\delta}}^- > 0, \ \text{and} \ L_{\bar{\delta}}^- < 0,$$

as "crude intuition" suggests, then (9-i) will in fact be greater than zero. The argument of the text is that the recent Brazilian experience suggests that equation (9-i) is greater than zero for Brazil. Beckerman, 1978, "Index-linked Government Bonds . . ." presents a more sophisticated version of the model described here, incorporating equities and dropping some of the simplifying assumptions.

References

Baer, Werner. *Industrialization and Economic Development in Brazil* (Homewood, Ill., 1965).

Baer, Werner. "The Brazilian Boom 1968–72: An Explanation and an Interpretation," *World Development*, August 1973, pp. 1–15.

Baer, Werner, and Beckerman, Paul. "Indexing in Brazil," *World Development*, October–December 1974, pp. 35–47.

Baer, Werner, Kerstenetzky, Isaac, and Simonsen, Mario H. "Transportation and Inflation: A Study of Irrational Policy-making in Brazil," in *Economic Development and Cultural Change* (January 1965).

Banco Central do Brasil. *Boletim* (monthly).

Banco Central do Brasil. *Relatório* (annually).

Beckerman, Paul. "The Trouble with Index-linking: Notes on the Recent Brazilian Experience," unpublished paper, University of Illinois, 1978.

Beckerman, Paul. "Index-linked Government Bonds and the Efficiency of Monetary Policy," forthcoming, *Journal of Macroeconomics*.

Beckerman, Paul. "Adjustment for Inflation in the Brazilian National Housing-Finance System," unpublished paper, University of Illinois, 1978.

Blinder, Alan. "Indexing the Economy through Financial Intermediation" in K. Brunner and A. Meltzer (Eds.), *Stabilization of the Domestic and International Economy* (Amsterdam, 1977), pp. 69–105.

Branson, William. *Macroeconomic Theory and Policy* (New York, 1972).

Cagan, Philip. "The Monetary Dynamics of Hyperinflation" in M. Friedman (Ed.), *Studies in the Quantity Theory of Money* (Chicago, 1956).

Chacel, Julian, Simonsen, Mario H., Wald, Arnoldo. *Correcão monetária* (Rio de Janeiro, 1970).

Cipollari, Pedro, and Macedo, Roberto. "Indexation of Wages: Some Aspects of the Brazilian Experience," NBER-IPE Seminar on Indexation, São Paulo, Brazil, February 26–28, 1975.

Conjuntura Econômica. "O Sistema Brasileira de Poupanca e Empréstimo," March 1974, pp. 65–70. (Part of an "Estudo Especial" on the Sistema Financeiro da Habitacão, pp. 45–117.)

Conjuntura Econômica. "Inflacao, correcão monetária, e índices de precos," September 1975, pp. 91–94.

Conjuntura Econômica. "Correcão monetária e realimentacão inflacionária," June 1976, pp. 88–94.

Contador, Cláudio. "Correcão mentária, expectativa de inflacão e a demanda por ativos financeiros," *Revista Brasileira de Mercado de Capitais*, January–April 1976, pp. 5–23.

Contador, Cláudio. "O Efeito realimentador da correcão monetária," unpublished paper, Rio de Janeiro, 1977.

The Economist. "How Brazil Showed the Way," 27 April 1974, pp. 82–83.

The Economist. "Brazil Counts its Debts," 13 March 1976, pp. 77–78.

The Economist. "Change in Direction: A Survey of Brazil," 31 July 1976.

Fischer, Stanley. "The Demand for Index Bonds," *Journal of Political Economy,* June 1975, pp. 509–534.

Fisher, Irving. *The Purchasing Power of Money* (New York, 1911).

Fishlow, Albert. "Indexing Brazilian-Style: Inflation Without Tears?" *Brookings Papers on Economic Activity* No. 1 (1974): 261–82.

Friedman, Milton. "Monetary Correction" in Herbert Giersch (Ed.), *Essays on Inflation and Indexation* (Washington, D. C., 1974).

Kafka, Alexandre. "The Brazilian Stabilization Program, 1964–1966," *Journal of Political Economy,* August 1967, pp. 596–634.

Kampel, Luiz Cezar, and Miranda do Valle, Maria Thereza. *Sistema Financeiro da Habitacão* (Rio de Janeiro, 1974).

Kleiman, Ephraim. "Monetary Correction and Indexation: The Brazilian and Israeli Experience," *Explorations in Economic Research* (NBER), Vol. 4, No. 1, Winter 1977.

Jaffee, Dwight, and Kleiman, Ephraim. "The Welfare Implications of Uneven Inflation," IEA Conference on Inflation, Saltsjöbaden, Sweden, August 28, 1975.

Lemgruber, Antônio. "Inflation in Brazil" in L. B. Krause and W. S. Salant (Eds.), *Worldwide Inflation* (Washington, D. C., 1977), pp. 395–448.

Liviatan, Nissan, and Levhari, David. "Risk and the Theory of Indexed Bonds," *American Economic Review,* June 1977, pp. 366–75.

McKinnon, Ronald. *Money and Capital in Economic Development* (Washington, D. C., 1973).

Ness, Walter. *A Influência da correcão monetária no sistema financeiro* (Rio de Janeiro, 1977).

Pastore, Affonso. "A Oferta de moeda no Brasil — 1961/72," *Pesquisa e Planejamento Economico,* December 1973.

Peláez, Carlos Manuel, and Súzigan, Wilson. *História monetária do Brasil* (Rio de Janeiro, 1976).

Siegel, Jeremy. "Indexed versus Nominal Contracting: A Theoretical Examination," unpublished paper, University of Chicago, 1974.

Silva, Adroaldo Moura da. "A Conjuntura econômica brasileira, 1974/1976" *Tibiricá,* January–March 1977, pp. 5–20.

Simonsen, Mario Henrique. *Inflacão: Gradualismo x tratamento de choque* (Rio de Janeiro, 1970).

Simonsen, Mario Henrique. "Correcão monetária — a experiência brasileira," *Conjuntura Econômica,* July 1975, pp. 65–69.

Sprenkle, Case. "Large Economic Units, Banks, and the Transactions Demand for Money," *Quarterly Journal of Economics,* August 1966, pp. 436–42.

Syvrud, Donald. "Estrutura e política de juros no Brasil 1960/70," *Revista Brasileira de Economia,* January–March 1972, pp. 117–40.

Tobin, James. "An Essay on the Principles of Debt Management," in Commission on Money and Credit, *Fiscal and Debt Management Policies,* 1963, pp. 143–218.

The Effect of Inflation on the Rate of Return on Common Stocks in an Inflation Intensive Capital Market: The Israeli Case 1965–79*

MENACHEM BRENNER
DAN GALAI

INTRODUCTION

This paper summarizes previously published results on the relationship between the rate of inflation and the rate of return on common stock and extends the analysis to include evidence up to 1979. The Israeli experience is of interest due to two factors. First, Israel has experienced double-digit inflation since the early 70s, and its annual rate of inflation for 1979 passed the 100 percent mark. The high variability of inflation while potentially harmful economically and socially, provides a good sample from a statistical inference point of view, and may enhance our understanding of the economic effects of inflation. Second, a major investment tool is made available in Israel in the form of bonds linked to the cost-of-living index which offer the investor a riskless real interest rate. It is interesting to analyze the data for the stock market to find whether such an alternative, which neutralizes the effect of inflation, affects the yield on common stock.

The effect of inflation on the value of financial assets has been the topic of much research since the work of Irving Fisher was published at the beginning of the century. The current interest in the subject is a response to the relatively high inflation rates experienced by most of the industrialized countries in the last decade.

The common belief is that stocks of companies should compensate their holders for the increase in the cost of living. The main justification is that the shares represent an ownership of productive real assets and resources. Alchian and Kessel raised the issue of the effect of inflation on the value of the corporation's monetary liabilities as well as assets. Their claim was that if the corporation is a net debtor it should profit from inflation, but if it is a net creditor its value will decrease in real terms.

In principle, in an efficient market, anticipated inflation should be taken fully into consideration and be fully reflected in stock prices. Unanticipated inflation may benefit the company or make it worse off. Firms may profit from inflation through the appreciation of fixed assets and the depreciation of fixed interest liabilities. They may also profit if the inflation is not neutral and their output appreciates by more than their inputs. Capital losses may stem from an excess of fixed interest or nominal assets over equivalent liabilities, and income losses from worsening in the terms of trade of the corporation. Another source of income loss lies in the taxation system which allows for depreciation of investments in terms of the historical values and thus increases the real tax liabilities of corporations.

The empirical studies carried out in the United States — e.g., Bodie (1976), Jaffe and Mandelker (1976), Nelson (1976), Fama and Schwert (1979) — found negative relationships between the rate of inflation, both anticipated and unanticipated, and the rate of return on common stocks. This negative relationship for the United States data seems to be significant; it is quite puzzling, since no satisfactory economic explanation is provided to justify such a relationship. Similar tests applied to English and Australian data — Saunders (1978) and Saunders and Tress (1979), respectively — also yielded significant negative relationships.

The Israeli experience is somewhat different: The variability of stocks' returns during the period 1965 to 1974 cannot be explained, in a statistical sense, by the changes in the rate of inflation. The difference between the return on index-linked bonds and the inflation rate as a proxy for the real rate of interest also fails to yield any significant results in explaining the return on stocks. Over a prolonged period, however, the stocks yielded positive real returns (Brenner and Galai, 1978, 1979).

THE DATA

The sample consists of 60 stocks of firms registered on the Tel Aviv Stock Exchange. The firms are divided among 5 sectors: 19 firms in the "Banking, Insurance and Financial institutions," 15 firms in "Investment Companies Group,"[1] the "Land Development" group includes 9 firms, the "Manufacturing" group, 14 firms: the fifth group contains 5 firms engaged in energy-related areas. For each stock the total rate of return[2] was calculated on a quarterly basis, for 1965–79. All the stocks in the sample were registered for the whole period on the exchange and, with a few exceptions, have 59 quarterly observations. Note that a selection bias may exist, due to the procedure of selecting only surviving firms for the sample.

The Cost of Living Price Index (CPI) was taken from the official publication of the Central Bureau of Statistics. The index is published on a monthly basis on the fifteenth of each month for the month before. In our calculations we used the changes in the index as published on a quarterly basis. In addition, we used another version, where the index was adjusted for the middle of the month price to make it consistent with the data for the stocks.

THE RESULTS

Table 1 contains summary statistics for the CPI, the 5 sectors, and for the market index, R_M. The latter is based on the equally weighted average of the 60 stocks. The average inflation rate for the whole period 1965 to 1979 was 5.4 percent per quarter. It was only 1.3 percent for the first subperiod 1965 to mid-1971 and rose to 8.7 percent for the second subperiod 1971 to 1979. The average inflation rate in the second subperiod was about seven times its size in the first; but the standard deviation SD, grew by only about 4 times, from 1.5 to 5.8 percent per quarter; hence the coefficient of variation was somewhat reduced. By combining the two subperiods, a strong serial correlation of the inflation rate is induced. The first serial correlation is about .3 for each subperiod and .6 for the whole. The second-order serial correlation is rather small for each subperiod. This observation is quite important for the statistical tests that follow.

The average rate of return for the stock market went up from close to zero in the first subperiod to 11.4 percent in 1971–79 and the standard deviation increased by approximately 100 percent. It is interesting to note that for the total period of 15 years the average rate of return of each sector is very close to the average of any other sector, and all averages are between 6.4 and 7.0 percent. This phenomenon is not observed for each subperiod. In the first subperiod the range of the averages is between − .8 and 2.3 percent, and the range for 1971–79 is 10.3 to 13.0 percent. It may be the case that in the long run most rates tend to the same average and this average is above the average rate of inflation. For the whole period the real rate of return[3] on common stocks was about 2.9 percent on an annual basis (see Table 2). This real rate was approximately equal to the promised rate on the index-linked bonds. On an after-tax basis the real rate on stocks was larger than on bonds, due to the absence of a capital gains tax.

The variability of the real rate of return was above the variability of the nominal rate of return for each subperiod and for the whole period. The effect of the inflation, it may therefore be claimed, was to increase the dispersion of the real rates. It did not offset, even partially, the variability of the nominal rates.

Table 1. Summary Statistics of Quarterly Rates of Inflation and Rates of Return on Stocks

Period		I	R_M	Financial	Invest-ment	Land	Manufac-turing	Energy
I/1965–III/1979	MN	.054	.067	.065	.064	.069	.070	.065
	SD	.058	.137	.124	.151	.177	.139	.242
	ϱ_1	.592	.172	.161	.164	.127	.140	.092
	ϱ_2	.436	.342	.255	.307	.307	.229	.209
I/1965–II/1971	MN	.013	.007	.016	−.006	−.008	.023	−.006
	SD	.015	.070	.051	.081	.094	.079	.114
	ϱ_1	.290	−.106	−.150	−.221	−.254	.244	−.115
	ϱ_2	−.010	.090	−.051	.001	.234	.160	.074
III/1971–III/1979	MN	.087	.114	.103	.119	.130	.108	.120
	SD	.058	.159	.149	.110	.202	.164	.299
	ϱ_1	.357	.052	.066	.032	.028	.022	.053
	ϱ_2	.108	.247	.173	.197	.160	.154	.160

R_M — average rate of return for the stock market (with equal weights).
I — average inflation rate.
ϱ_i — serial correlation estimate with lag i.
MN — mean.
SD — standard deviation.

Table 2. Summary Statistics of Quarterly Real Rates of Return on Stocks

Period		I	R_M	Financial	Invest-ment	Land	Manufac-turing	Energy
I/1965–III/1979	MN	.054	.013	.012	.011	.016	.018	.013
	SD	.058	.132	.119	.140	.169	.014	.236
	ϱ_1	.595	.156	.193	.092	.090	.144	.112
	ϱ_2	.436	.249	.207	.217	.227	.142	.177
I/1965–II/1971	MN	.013	−.006	.003	−.019	−.021	.010	−.018
	SD	.015	.072	.052	.082	.099	.083	.116
	ϱ_1	.290	−.057	−.065	−.197	−.232	.254	−.065
	ϱ_2	−.010	.155	.095	.051	.270	.192	.106
III/1971–III/1979	MN	.087	.029	.019	.034	.044	.024	.037
	SD	.058	.165	.153	.170	.206	.171	.298
	ϱ_1	.357	.171	.216	.106	.107	.116	.123
	ϱ_2	.108	.245	.216	.212	.169	.122	.173

A direct test of the relationship between the quarterly rate of return on stocks R_t and the rate of inflation I_t was carried out by running the following linear regression:

$$(1) \quad R_t = \alpha_0 + \alpha_1 I_t + \alpha_2 I_{t-1} + \varepsilon_t$$

where ε_t is the residual term, and α_i $(i = 0, 1, 2)$ is an estimated regression coefficient. The results for each sector and for each period are such that we cannot reject the null hypothesis, that no linear relationship exists. There is no apparent correlation on quarterly basis between the inflation rates and the rates of appreciation of the firms in market value terms in Israel. As an illustration, the estimated regression function for the whole period for the market index is as follows:

$$\hat{R}_{Mt} = .050 + .084 \ I_t + .270 I_{t-1} \qquad \bar{R}^2 = .00$$
$$(1.862) \ (.203) \quad (.580) \qquad\qquad DW = 1.72$$

(The t-statistics are in parentheses.)

For 1971–79, the coefficients of the inflation and lagged inflation variables were negative but not significantly different from zero (at 5 percent significance level). When the regression function of R_t on I_t was estimated for each individual firm for the whole period, for only 7 firms out of 60, the coefficient of the inflation variable came out significantly different from zero (at 5 percent). In all seven cases, the coefficient was positive and not significantly different from 1, which is the expected or hypothesized coefficient in many studies — for example, Fama and Schwert (1977), Bodie (1976), Jaffee and Mandelker (1976), and Nelson (1976).

The inflation rate in the preceding tests was adjusted by means of linear interpolation to middle-of-month terms to coincide with the measurement of the rate of appreciation of stocks. When the original inflation data are used (in terms of end-of-month inflation), the statistical relationship tends to weaken even more. From the foregoing results one may conclude that rates of return on common stocks in the Israeli financial markets are not directly affected by the high rate of inflation. The various tests to explain the real rate of return on stocks by the changes in the inflation rate failed to provide any significant results. In general, the real rate is negatively related to the inflation and lagged inflation variables, but the explanatory variables add very little to the explanation of the changes of the real rate around its mean.

A test of market efficiency was suggested by Fama (1975). He claimed that in an efficient market, lagged rate of return R_{t-1} should contain information about the rate of inflation I_t. He ran a similar regression on the bond market data:

$$(2) \quad I_t = a_0 + a_1 R_{t-1} + a_2 I_{t-1} + \varepsilon_t$$

and expected a_1 to be close to 1 and a_2 close to zero. Table 3 contains the results for a similar test conducted on the data for the stocks on the Tel Aviv Stock Exchange. It is a continuation of the results reported by Brenner and Galai (1979). For 1965–79 the adjusted R^2 is about 41 percent, but most of the explanatory power came from the lagged inflation rate, I_{t-1}, rather than from the lagged rate of return on stocks, R_{t-1}.[4] The coefficient for the latter was not significantly different from zero. For the subperiod with the high inflation rate, 1971–79, the t-statistics for the coefficient of R_{t-1} were very small.

Table 3. Summary Statistics for the Regression
$I_t = a_0 + a_1 R_{t-1} + a_2 I_{t-1} + e_t$

Period	Sector	$\hat{a}_0$	$t(\hat{a}_0)$	$\hat{a}_1$	$t(\hat{a}_1)$	$\hat{a}_2$	$t(\hat{a}_2)$	$\bar{R}^2$	D.W.
I/1965–	Financial	1.646	1.930	.025	.524	.718	6.207	.41	2.10
III/1979	Investment	1.659	2.001	.037	.906	.700	5.953	.41	2.10
	Land	1.663	1.985	.021	.640	.717	6.234	.41	2.09
	Manufacturing	1.425	1.651	.050	1.203	.723	6.408	.42	2.09
	Energy	1.792	2.132	−.006	−.231	.724	6.382	.40	2.09
	All	1.603	1.891	.033	.765	.714	6.202	.41	2.09
	Financial	5.127	2.676	−.016	−.239	.467	2.511	.12	1.86
III/1971–	Investment	4.941	2.620	.000	.001	.470	2.535	.12	1.86
III/1979	Land	5.196	2.657	−.014	−.292	.461	2.458	.12	1.86
	Manufacturing	4.743	2.352	.012	.198	.478	2.516	.12	1.86
	Energy	5.624	3.023	−.032	−.980	.435	2.342	.15	1.89
	All	5.139	2.399	−.013	−.216	.465	2.484	.12	1.86

Again it can be concluded that the return on stocks contained very little information on the future expected inflation rate. This conclusion is robust to various adjustments to the regression model, such as using continuously compounded rates rather than discrete, or using alternative measures for the expected inflation, and more. It is surprising to find in the stock market a very strong cross correlation between every pair of sectors (a correlation of .80 at least), which indicates the existence of a strong market factor, which is unrelated to the high rate of inflation. This is even more surprising since investors have the alternative of investing in index-linked bonds and thus assuring themselves of a fixed real interest rate.

The inflation may affect the firm in two ways. First, the level of inflation affects the value of the firm's assets, liabilities, and future net cash flows. Second, uncertainty about the level of inflation may affect the firm's investment schedule by raising the cost of capital. It may also change the required rate of return of the investors. The latter effect has not yet been modeled in a satisfactory way in the literature. It should be solved in a general equilibrium framework. We tried in various ways to measure empirically the uncertainty concerning the inflation rate and relate it to the rate of return on common stock, to see whether there was any such effect. The measures, their justification, and the results, are now detailed:

(a) If the best predictor of I_t is I_{t-1}, then the difference $I_t - I_{t-1}$ will measure the estimation error. By regressing the quarterly rates of return, R_t, on the difference $I_t - I_{t-1}$ we found in general a negative, though not significant, relationship. Adding $I_{t-1} - I_{t-2}$ to the regression did not improve it at all.

(b) The inflation rate is given on a monthly basis. This additional information was used to calculate the monthly average rate of return and the standard deviation for each year in our sample. The standard deviation will measure the dispersion of the rates during the year rather than unanticipated changes. For each year we thus have one estimate of standard deviation against four quarterly observations on the rates of return. The results of regressing R_t on the estimated standard deviation did not yield significant results. We also regressed R_t on $3\bar{I}_T - I_t$ where $\bar{I}_T$ is the monthly average rate of inflation for year T.[5] In this case $\bar{I}_T$ is assumed to be the expected monthly rate and $3\bar{I}_T - I_t$ is the deviation from expectation.

(c) Following the logic of alternative (a) we also calculated the following measure for each year T:

$$V_T = \sum_{t=1} (I_t - I_{t-1})^2$$

If $I_t - I_{t-1}$ is the estimation error, and assuming that I_{t-1} is an unbiased estimator of I_t and hence the average of the estimation error is equal to zero, the estimate V_T is the variance of the estimation error. The regression of R_t on V_T (where T is the index for the year and t is the index for the quarter in the year), yielded some interesting results. For the first subperiod, the relationship was negative, though generally not significantly different from zero.[6] For the second subperiod the relationship is mostly positive and, again, not significant.

For the total period, however, the coefficient to V_T is positive and significant. To illustrate it, the regression for the market index is given below:

$$R_{Mt} = \underset{(1.272)}{3.068} + \underset{(2.133)}{.847 V_T} + \hat{\varepsilon}_t \qquad \begin{aligned} \bar{R}^2 &= .06 \\ F &= 4.55 \\ DW &= 1.84 \end{aligned}$$

The F-statistics indicate that we can reject the null hypothesis of no linear relationship with the probability of making an error less than 1 percent.

The preceding results should be taken as suggestive rather than conclusive. The relationship between the variability of inflation and the yield to investors in capital assets should be modeled before the statistical results can be fully interpreted. In addition, a more refined measurement of the unanticipated variability of inflation should be devised to get an estimate at each point in time.

SUMMARY AND CONCLUSION

The conclusion of our previous research about the lack of relationship between rates of inflation and rates of return on common stocks remained unchanged. The addition of five years with unprecedented rates of inflation has reconfirmed our previous results on the existence of a strong market factor which does not seem to be affected by the rate of inflation. Also, we have stronger support for the conclusion that, in the long run, rates of return on common stocks *do* compensate for the rate of inflation.

Notes

* We wish to thank A. Rivlin for his computational assistance.
1. The firms in this group invest in other companies which may, or may not, be registered on the Tel Aviv Stock Exchange.
2. The rate of return includes the price change between the middle of the month of either January, April, July, or October and the middle of the month three months later. Cash dividends were assumed to be invested in the shares of the company on the payment day; rights were assumed to be sold on the first day of trading rights and the proceeds immediately reinvested in the firm's shares.
3. The *real rate of return* is defined as one plus the rate of return divided by one plus the rate of inflation.
4. By adding I_{t-2} as an explanatory variable very little was contributed toward explaining $I_t \cdot I_{t-1}$ captured most of the information with respect to I_t.
5. $\hat{I}_T$ is multiplied by 3 to bring it to the quarter basis like the rest of the rates.
6. The exception was the "manufacturing" sector for which V_T explained almost 20 percent of the variability of R_t around its mean.

References

Bodie, Z. "Common Stock as a Hedge Against Inflation," *Journal of Finance* 31 (May 1976): 459–70.

Brenner, M., and Galai, D. "The Empirical Relationship between Inflation and Financial Assets in an Inflation Intensive Capital Market" in M. Sarnat (Ed.), *Inflation and Capital Markets* (Cambridge, Mass., 1978).

Brenner and Galai. "The Effect of Inflation on the Rate of Return on Stocks in Israel: 1965 to 1974," *Bank of Israel's Economic Review*, 1979.

Brenner and Galai. "The Determinants of the Return of Index Bonds," *Journal of Banking and Finance* 2 (1978): 47–64.

Fama, E., and Schwert, G. W. "Asset Returns and Inflation," *Journal of Financial Economies* 5 (1979): 115–46.

Jaffe, J., and Mandelker, G. "The Fisher Effect for Risky Assets: An Empirical Investigation," *Journal of Finance* 31 (May 1976): 447–58.

Nelson, C. "Inflation and Rates of Return on Common Stocks," *Journal of Finance* 31 (May 1976): 471–83.

Saunders, A., and Tress, R. B. "Inflation and Stock Market Returns: Some Australian Evidence," WP No. 173, Salom Brother Center for the Study of Financial Institutions, New York University (June 1979).

Saunders, A., "Expected Inflation, Unexpected Inflation and the Return on U.K. Shares, 1961–1973," *Journal of Business Finance and Accounting* 5 (1978): 309–320.

Inflation, Poverty and the Third World: India's Experience

YOGESH C. HALAN

The Third World countries, over the past 30 years, have experienced an extraordinarily rapid economic growth: per capita income has gone up by almost 3 percent per year, with the annual growth rate accelerating from about 2 percent in the 1950s to 3.4 percent in the 1960s.[1] Moreover, the growth rates compare extremely favorably with the growth rates achieved by the developed countries during their development phase: income per person grew by less than 2 percent in most of the industrialized nations of the West over the 100 years of industrialization beginning in the mid-nineteenth century. Even in Japan, which is considered to be the fastest-growing industrialized economy, long-term annual growth rate was less than 2.5 percent.[2]

A substantial body of scholarly literature on economic development in the developing countries has brought forward another fact: the respectable growth in the Third World countries has not been able to alleviate the incidence of poverty there. In Pakistan, where a sustained 6 percent growth was observed during the 1960s, unemployment increased, real wages in the industrial sector declined by one-third, and concentration of industrial wealth became an explosive economic and political issue. In India, despite a 242 percent increase in real national income between 1950–51 and 1975–76, 40 to 50 percent of the total population was still not much better off than it was in 1950. Brazil achieved a growth rate close to 7 percent but persisting maldistribution of income continues to threaten the very fabric of its society.[3]

Worse, the number of the poor has increased in spite of the rapid economic growth in most developing countries. Two well-known studies, one by V. M. Dandekar and Nilakantha Rath and the other by Pranab Bardhan, have concluded that the proportion of rural people below the poverty line increased during the sixties. The study by Bardhan has shown a definite increase in the rural poor from 38 percent in 1960–61 to 54 percent in 1968–69.[4] Experiences of the other Third World countries are not different.

The fateful and unhappy conclusion is that after three decades of economic development the economic condition of the majority Third

World citizens is still worse. In writing the Foreword to the *World Development Report, 1978*, World Bank President Robert S. McNamara mentions ". . . some 800 million individuals . . . trapped in . . . absolute poverty: a condition of life so characterized by malnutrition, illiteracy, disease, squalid surroundings, high infant mortality, and low life expectancy as to be beneath any reasonable definition of human decency."[5] The actual number of the poor is much more than this hard core of "800 million." According to an estimate of the International Labor Office (ILO) the total number of the poor in the Third World was 1815 million in 1972.[6]

Thus, the situation in the Third World is grim and the outlook for the future even grimmer. Why, even after three decades of development, despite "unprecedented change and progress in the developing world," is absolute poverty still on a massive scale? Why are the benefits of economic growth not reaching the masses who remain malnourished and shelterless? Answers to questions like these are difficult and depend on how you look at these problems. In our opinion, the main factor responsible for the deteriorating condition of the poor is the severe inflation in almost every country of the world. It is devastating to the poor particularly in the Third World. The problem area is vast, but the object of this paper is a limited one. Here we will make an analytical effort to study the process of the inflation in a major Third World country, India. An effort will be made to find out how the inflation is corroding the welfare of the poor. The Indian experience can be a useful point of reference to the other developing countries similarly plagued by inflation.

Without entering into any controversy on the meaning and definition of inflation, we find it necessary to provide historical background on the present inflationary trend in India. Without this background, it would be extremely difficult to analyze the inflationary process or to formulate useful conclusions about the effects of inflation on the poor. The term *inflation* will be used in the formal sense of a rise in the general price level whatever the causes.

India, at the time of independence in 1947, inherited inflation as a legacy of World War II. During the war, prices were persistently rising throughout the world. The price rise in India, however, was much higher than in the other major countries of the world. For example, with 1938 as the base year, the price index in 1943 rose to 167.4 in the United Kingdom, 134.7 in the United States, 140.7 in Australia, and 128.3 in Canada; the price index in India was 218.1[7] During the seven-year period, 1939–45, prices, as shown in Table 1, increased by 144.4 percent — at the compound annual rate of 14.1 percent. The price rise was slow at first but generated momentum as the war advanced. Inflation was particularly disturbing in the food sector where the prices more than doubled, 1940–44. The British government denied the existence of inflation and threatened to prosecute C. N. Vakil, an eminent economist, who made an effort to create public awareness of the inflationary conditions by publishing a book: *The Falling Rupee*.[8] Another reknowned economist, J. C. Kumarappa, was in fact prosecuted and sentenced to two years' imprisonment when he wrote a number of articles on inflation in *Harijan*, a journal devoted to Gandhian ideas.[9] The government did, however, take some antiinflationary measures, particularly price control and rationing, which were not at all effective. The main cause of inflation during the war, as in the other countries of the world, was a fast increase in the money supply. The volume of currency notes in circulation during the war increased from Rs.1.82 billion in 1938–39 to Rs.11.6 billion in 1945–46 — an increase of 600 percent. The bank money rose correspondingly.

Table 1. Wholesale Price Index in India
  (base = 1938)

Year	Price Index	Percentage Change over Previous Period
1939	105.9	5.9
1940	118.1	11.5
1941	129.8	9.9
1942	159.4	22.8
1943	218.1	36.8
1944	241.3	10.6
1945	244.4	1.3

Source: R. J. Venkateshwaran, *The Tragedy of Indian Rupee* (Bombay, India, 1968), p. 9.

The people were given to believe that inflation was a wartime phenomenon and as the situation became normal, the inflation would wither away. The hopes of the people were unfortunately belied and the inflationary spiral continued even after the war. Prices between 1945 and 1951, as shown in Table 2, increased by 213 percentage points. The annual compound rate of price rise was 11.2 percent. The major cause of the steep price rise during the postwar period was the partition of the country in 1947. This historical event severely disrupted the country's economy and affected production in industry and agriculture. The colossal expenditure on the rehabilitation of refugees, the devaluation of the rupee in September 1949, and the Korean War in June 1950, intensified inflation.

The period important for the present study is the planned development era starting in 1950–51. The government of India decided to introduce central planning in 1951. The major objectives of planned economic development were raising real incomes and living standards, reducing unemployment and income disparities, and accelerating the pace of industrial development. The planners presumed that prices would not rise sharply during the following years, for they thought that by controlling allocation of resources the Planning Commission would have complete control over prices. The presumption proved true during the First Five-year Plan (1950–51 — 1955–56) when prices, compared to 1950–51 fell by 17.3 percent. After 1955–56, prices kept on rising continuously.[10]

Table 2. Index Number of Wholesale Prices in India
   (base 1938)

Year	Index	Percentage Change over Previous Period
1946	266.7	9.1
1947	294.8	10.5
1948	367.1	24.5
1949	381.1	3.8
1950	400.7	5.1
1951	457.5	14.2
(April)		

Source: (See Table 1).

The next five-year period of the Second Plan (1955–56 — 1960–61), showed an upward trend in the general price level. Between 1956 and 1961, the general price level rose by 35 percent. The annual compound rate of growth was 6.3 percent. The highest growth of 45.5 percent was shown by industrial raw materials. Food prices rose by 26.7 percent, and manufactured articles prices by 23.2 percent.[11]

The inflationary tendencies remained dominant during the Third Plan (1961–62 — 1965–66). Between 1961–62 and 1965–66, the general level of prices increased by 31.6 percent. The annual compound rate of price increase was 5.8 percent. The prices of manufactured articles showed a modest increase of 17 percent, but the prices of agricultural commodities were up by 41.7 percent. The price of certain essential food articles — cereals (wheat, rice, corn, etc.) and pulses (certain types of lentils) showed an increase of 45 percent and 75 percent, respectively. Compared to 1950–51 (= 100), the general level of prices in 1965–66 was up by 47.2 percent.[12]

The years 1965–66 should be considered as a watershed. Though the economy was growing at a modest rate before those years, growth rate and prices were stable. The performance of industry was at its best as industrial output in large and small units was expanding rapidly. The agricultural output was pushed along a rising trend line due to favorable monsoons, expanding cultivable acreage, and the completion of a number of major irrigation projects. All this ended in 1964. The effects of the Chinese attack were visible on the price level; there were severe droughts during 1965, 1966, and 1972; and India twice had border conflicts with Pakistan, in 1965 and 1971. The political instability after the death of Jawaharlal Nehru, the first prime minister of free India, also affected the price situation.

Following the Third Plan, 1966–67 and 1967–68 were the two years when the economy observed double-digit inflation in a row, 14 percent and 12 percent, respectively. In 1968–69, a bumper harvest caused a 1 percent fall in the price level. This generated a fresh wave of optimism and caused resumption of five-year planning, which had been frozen in 1966. The first year of the Fourth Plan (1969–70) showed a modest increase of 3.7 percent in the general price level. Inflation remained within limits, 5.5 percent and 5.6 percent, during the following two years. During the last two years of the Fourth Plan, 1972–73 and 1973–74, inflation was again in double digits, 10 percent and 20.2 percent respectively. This was the time when, due to fourfold increase in oil prices, inflation crossed the boundaries of India and became a world-wide phenomenon. January 1973–September 1974 was the worst 21-month period for India when prices were increasing at a monthly average rate of 2.7 percent.[13]

The inflationary situation had become sufficiently serious by this time. The zenith, however, was yet to come. It arrived in 1974–75 when the rate of inflation was 25.2 percent during the whole year. It was the highest annual rate of price rise ever recorded in the inflation history of Independent India.[14]

There was a dramatic change on the inflation front in September 1974 when the price index, after attaining the climax, started falling and, except for a few occasions, continued falling up to March 1976. During April 1975 and March 1976, the general level of prices fell by 1.1 percent. That was the end of the falling prices period, and with the beginning of the third week of March 1976, inflation again resumed its trend. The price rise during the following year (1976–77), however, was not much; only 2 percent. The increase took prices to the peak level of September 1974. The price index maintained a reasonable degree of stability after March 1977 and between March 1977 and January 1978, increased by only 0.6 percent. The inflationary trend again became alarming during 1978 and 1979, particularly during the latter year when prices were rising at the rate of about 2 percent per month.[15]

The overall view of the inflation which I have tried to present shows that the Indian economy managed to maintain relatively stable prices during the earlier years of planned economic development. After 1965–66, however, the economy witnessed a period of severe and continued inflation (see Figure 1). In order to comprehend the entire situation better, it would be appropriate to divide the entire 27-year experience into two periods: the first period of fifteen years, 1950–51 to 1965–66, and the second period of eleven years, 1966–67 to 1976–77. In the first period, the general index of wholesale prices increased by about 47 percent. The annual compound rate of inflation was 2.9 percent. If we exclude the first five-year period of the First Plan, during which prices declined by 17.3 percent, the increases in the general price level between 1955–56 and 1965–66 (a 10-year period) comes out to about 78 percent. But in the next eleven years (1966–67 to 1976–77), the wholesale price index increased by 136 percent. The annual compound rate of inflation of 8.7 percent thus became three times that of the earlier period. Even if the exceptionally bad drought years 1965 and 1966 are excluded, the rise in the general index will be about 107 percent in ten years from 1967–68 to 1976–77. The annual compound rate of inflation comes to 7.9 percent which is marginally lower than the 8.7 percent rate during the entire eleven year period.

The foregoing discussion was an effort to show that the general price level in India had been increasing with virtually uninterrupted regularity. In some years it has risen faster than in others, of course, but almost always it has risen. The level of prices in 1951 was more than 4½ times the level of 1939; and in 1977 more than 3½ times the level of 1951. In other words, the purchasing power of the Indian rupee is only about one-eighth what it was about 40 years back. During the past decade alone, the value of the rupee has fallen by about 50 percent. The current rate of inflation in India is about 2 percent per month. Why has it happened? To what extent have the poorer sections of the population been affected by the inflation? These are the two important questions to which we can address ourselves. Detailed analysis cannot be presented here, nevertheless an effort can be made to find a brief answer to both questions.

WHY HAS INFLATION HAPPENED?

Looking at the basic causes of inflation, we can say that most, if not all, of the people would agree with Lord Robbins who looks at the conception of inflation as an excess of actual or anticipated expenditure over supply at constant prices — a process which brings about an adjust-

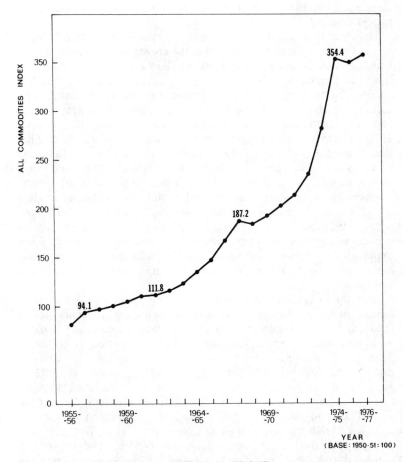

Fig. 1 Derived Price Index 1955-56 to 1976-77. *Source: S. L. Shetty, Structural Retrogression in the Indian Economy since the Mid-Sixties; (Economic and Political Weekly, Bombay, 1978), Table 27, p. 33.*

ment of prices in order to achieve some aggregate equalization.[16] In brief, inflation occurs when aggregate demand exceeds aggregate supply and goods become scarce in stores. Though inflation may emanate from a number of different sources other than excess demand, in the developing countries different sources of inflation ultimately cause excess demand.

The most conventional view about the source of inflation is that a rise in the money supply, in excess of the growth in demand for money balances, will produce excess demand. The view is fully applicable to the Indian economy where the rise in the price level was certainly encouraged by sharply increased monetary expansion. From an average annual rate of 4.2 percent during the 1950s, the money supply in India suddenly started growing at the rate of 15 percent during the 1960s and 1970s. The total money supply with the public in 1950 was Rs.20.2 billion; it went up to Rs.28.7 billion in 1960; Rs.71.4 billion in 1970, and Rs.175.8 billion in 1978. The enormous increase of 770 percent in the money supply has been an important influence on inflation.[17]

Monetary explanation, though valid, is not the basic cause of gross imbalance in the economy. If monetary explanation is not the basic cause of inflation in India, it is perfectly legitimate to ask why inflation became so severe after independence. Here we want to advance a few explanations for the inflationary trend in India. Similar causes may have caused severe and widespread inflation in the other Third World countries.

First, the long-term growth rate in the Indian economy has shown a falling tendency. The compound growth rate during the second period (1966–67 to 1976–77) declined to 3.67 percent per annum as compared with 4.11 percent per annum during the first period (1951–52 to 1964–65). The annual growth rate of national income (at 1960–61 prices) was 3.66 percent during the First-Plan period (1951–52 to 1955–56). It increased to 4.14 percent during the Second Plan (1956–57 to 1960–61) and further to 4.63 percent in the first four years of the Third Plan (1961–62 to 1964–65). There was deceleration in the growth rate after the Third Plan. The growth rate started falling from 3.99 percent per year during the Annual Plans (1966–67 to 1968–69) to 3.50 percent during the Fourth Plan (1969–70 to 1973–74). In the first three years of the Fifth Plan (1974–75 to 1976–77) the trend of falling growth was reversed when the annual growth rate went up slightly to 3.6 percent. However, with 3 to 4 percent negative growth rate during 1978–79, the annual growth rate during 1974–75 to 1978–79 would be much lower than the rate achieved during the Fourth Plan.[18]

A more important aspect than the slowing down of the growth process has been increasing unsteadiness in the annual growth rates during the second period than in the first. An overview of postinde-

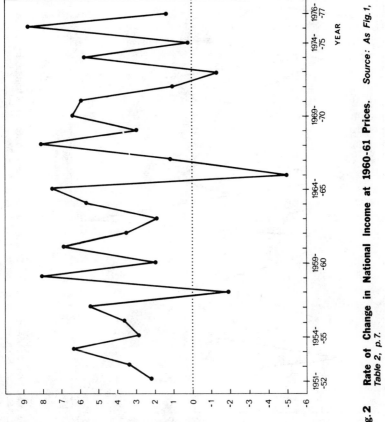

Fig. 2 **Rate of Change in National Income at 1960-61 Prices.** *Source: As Fig.1, Table 2, p.7.*

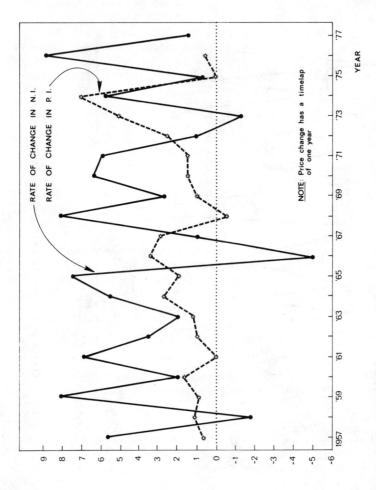

Fig.3 Relation between Rate of Change in N. I. and Rate of Change in Price Index.
Source: Same as Fig. 1, Table 2, p. 7 & Table 27, p. 33.

pendence growth movement is provided by Figure 2 which shows rates of change in national income at 1960–61 prices. The figure shows that up to 1964–65, growth was somewhat stable but after that year there were wide fluctuations. The steadiness of the first period can be seen in a significantly lower coefficient of variation in the growth rates of the first period than for the second period, 0.6375 and 0.8296, respectively. If rates of change in wholesale prices are superimposed on Figure 2, as we have done in Figure 3, we find steadiness in prices up to 1964–65 and wide fluctuations thereafter.

Secondly, imbalances in the production structure have been responsible for an inflationary trend in India. If the whole economy is divided into two broad categories: the commodity sector (primary and secondary sectors which produce goods); and the noncommodity sector (service sector which does not produce goods but provides services), we find output in the noncommodity sector rising at a faster rate than that in the commodity sector. Table 3 shows growth rates in net domestic product originating in commodity and noncommodity sectors. Since independence, the growth rate in the noncommodity sector's GNP has been higher than that in the output of commodity sector. During the entire 25-year period of 1950–51 to 1975–1976, the output in the commodity sector was rising at an annual rate of 4.6 percent but the annual growth rate in the noncommodity sector was 8.5 percent, 85 percent higher than the growth rate in commodity sector. The faster growth of the noncommodity sector injected massive financial liquidity into the economic system and thus imposed excessive pressure on the slowly growing commodity sector. It caused a steady decline in the availability of wage goods. The ratio of noncommodity output to commodity output was 1:2.76 in 1950–51 and 1:1.90 in 1975–76.

Table 3. Growth Rates in Net Domestic Product Originating in Commodity and Noncommodity Sectors at 1960–61 Prices

Year	Total of Commodity Sector (Rs. billions)	Percentage Increase over Previous Period	Total of Noncommodity Sector (Rs. billions)	Percentage Increase over Previous Period
1950–51	66.94	—	24.28	—
1955–56	79.03	18.1	29.67	22.2
1960–61	95.14	20.4	37.49	28.8
1964–65	111.49	17.2	48.79	27.7
1966–67	101.82	−8.7	51.83	6.2
1975-76	144.46	41.9	75.99	46.6

Source: Central Statistical Organization, *National Accounts Statistics: 1960–61 to 1974–75* (New Delhi, 1976); and Government of India, *Economic Survey 1977–78* (New Delhi, 1978).

Within the noncommodity sector, inflation-promoting sectors like public administration and defense and banking and insurance have shown a phenomenal step up in growth rate. During 1965–66 to 1975–76, the annual compound growth rate of incomes from public administration and defense comes to 7.4 percent against 3.5 percent growth in the incomes of the commodity-producing sectors during the same period.

Thirdly, the production of various commodities in the commodity sector has not been in keeping with the masses' demands on the economy. Output of goods needed by the masses increased at a moderate rate, but output of goods needed by the rich increased at an astronomical rate. For example, during 1965–66 to 1976–77, the output of coal, cotton yarn, soap, bicycles, electric fans, sugar, and tea increased at an annual average rate of 4.47 percent, 1.61 percent, 5.45 percent, 6.39 percent, 8.5 percent, 3.16 percent, and 3.46 percent, respectively. Against this, during the same period, the output of motorcycles and scooters, domestic refrigerators, glazed tiles, rayon yarns, and beer was increasing at an annual rate of 42.66 percent, 24.42 percent, 46.59 percent, 6. 16 percent, and 32.57 percent, respectively.[19] The *Draft Five Year Plan 1978–83* admitted that an unduly large share of resources was absorbed in production which related directly or indirectly to maintaining or improving the living standards of the higher-income groups.[20]

The phenomenon was not confined to the manufacturing sector, but was also visible in the agricultural sector where "the composition of foodgrains output has been changing in favour of superior cereals like wheat and rice at the expense of millets and pulses."[21] This is due partly to the technological change which has favored wheat and rice and partly to the price policy which ensured support prices for these two crops. The support price for wheat particularly, became a cause of inflation when, due to political pressures, the government fixed prices much higher than justified by cost data.[22] The Reserve Bank of India accepted that the "procurement prices for kharif cereals for the 1973–74 season were 20 to 31 percent higher than those for the preceding season. Likewise, following an announcement of the new wheat policy for the 1974–75 marketing season, the procurement price for wheat was fixed at Rs 105 per quintal for traders as well as farmers which was about 38 percent higher than in previous year."[23] This policy definitely contributed to the inflation of 1973 and 1974 and the following years.

Fourthly, increasing subsidies from the government have kept prices higher, raised the tax burden on industry and the common man, and cut seriously into development outlays. The total amount of subsidies from the Central Budget increased by 1912 percent during a brief ten-year period of 1965–66 to 1976–77. Subsidies were only Rs.480 million in 1965–66 but steadily rose to Rs. 9660 million in 1976–77. Several studies have shown that the subsidies by the government were disproportionately large and not warranted by the market situation.[24]

Table 4. Percentage Distribution of Net Domestic Product at Factor Cost at 1960–61 Prices

Years	Commodity Sector	Noncommodity Sector Total	Sector Transport, etc.	Banking and Insurance	Public Adm. and Defense
1950–51	73.4	26.6	3.6	0.9	3.6
1955–56	72.7	27.3	3.9	1.1	3.5
1960–61	71.3	28.7	4.3	1.2	4.0
1964–65	69.5	30.5	4.7	1.4	5.0
1966–67	66.3	33.7	5.3	1.4	5.7
1975–76	65.3	34.5	5.5	1.8	7.8

Source: (See Table 3).

Lastly, a continuous increase in indirect taxes has also been responsible for the inflationary trend in India. Imposition of heavy excise duties on most commodities and the high rates of state sales taxes have inflated the prices of almost all commodities. In 1951–52, total revenue from indirect taxes was Rs. 5.3 billion, which was 5.8 percent of GNP. It went up by 1514 percent to Rs. 85.7 billion in 1975–76, 39 percent of the total GNP. Since indirect taxes are mostly levied on the production and the sale of commodities, it might be interesting to note that the tax revenue from indirect taxes was 7.1 percent of the GNP generated in the commodity sector in 1950–51; it became 59.3 percent in 1975–76.[25]

INFLATION AND THE POOR

Thus, the inflation in India, like many other runaway inflations, has been primarily a result of excessive demand created because of a distorted production structure and the budgetary policy of the government. The inflationary spiral has hit every human being hard and the whole population of India, including the highest-paid citizens, has suffered because of inflation. It is rather difficult to find out the effect of inflation on the poor because information on income, assets, and consumption pattern is neither complete nor reliable. Nevertheless, whatever limited evidence we have supports the proposition that during the last 30 years, the effects of inflation were more adversely felt by the poor, defined in any reasonable terms, than the rich. This is brought out by the figures given in Table 5. The table presents a comparative study of the movement of the wholesale price index and the behavior of three types of consumer price index numbers: for working class/industrial workers; for urban nonmanual employees; and for agricultural laborers. The poorest section of Indian society is agricultural labor and the consumer price index for this class of people showed the maximum increase, 268 percent during the period 1960–61 to 1974–75. The next better-off group is the industrial workers, and their consumer price index showed an increase of 217 percent. Urban nonmanual employees constitute the least poor group among the three mentioned here, and their consumer price index increased by only 170 percent. Thus, the poorest group paid 58 percent higher prices than those paid by the least poor group. This is also proved by the fact that the prices of basic consumer goods that have a large weight in the consumption of the poor have shown the largest rises in prices. The major part of the incomes of the poor, 70 to 80 percent, is spent on food, and agricultural wholesale prices during 1950–51 and 1976–77 increased by 237.8 percent, whereas the prices of manufactured products increased by 221.1 percent.[26]

Table 5. The Wholesale Price Index and the Consumer Price Indexes: A Comparison

Year	Wholesale Price Index	Consumer Price Index Working Class/Industrial Workers	Consumer Price Index Urban Nonmanual Employees	Consumer Price Index Agricultural Laborers
	1961–62 = 100	1960 = 100	1960 = 100	1960–61 = 100
1960–61	99.8	100	100	100
1965–66	131.6	137	132	158
1970–71	181.1	186	174	192
1971–72	188.4	192	180	200
1972–73	207.1	207	192	225
1973–74	254.2	250	221	283
1974–75	313.0	317	270	368
1975–76	302.8	313	277	317
1976–77	310.5	301	277	302

Source: Planning Commission, *Basic Statistics Relating to the Indian Economy, 1950–51 to 1965–66* (New Delhi, 1966); and the Reserve Bank of India, *Reports on Currency and Finance 1960–61 to 1976–77* (Bombay).

The effect of inflation on the poor can also be looked at with the help of two other measures. One, finding out how the consumption of the poor has been affected during the last several years. Several studies made during the last ten years have shown a definite decline in the consumption standards of the poor. Dandekar and Rath in their study concluded that the "per capita consumption of the lower middle class and the weaker sections constituting the bottom 40 percent of the urban population declined by as much as 15 and 20 percent. . . . In the rural areas . . . the consumption of the poorest 5 percent actually declined by about one percent."[27] Another study by Indira Rajaraman showed that between 1960–61 and 1970–71, the share of the bottom 20 percent in total consumption declined from 10.4 percent of total consumption to 8.9 percent.[28] Pranab Bardhan also found no signs of rising prosperity among agricultural laborers in the Punjab following the "green revolution." If this is the situation in the most prosperous (and a rapidly growing) region of India, the condition of the poor in other less-prosperous (and slowly growing) areas like Bihar and eastern Uttar Pradesh, can be imagined. In fact, no less than the bottom 40 percent of the rural and urban population has suffered a decline in real living standards.

Another way is to see how the share of the poor in total assets is changing. In this sphere, too, several studies have been made. According to one study by V. V. Divatia, the share of the lowest 30 percent of rural householders in total assets declined from 2.5 percent in 1961–62 to 2 percent in 1971–72. Phatak, Ganapathy, and Sarma (1977) reached a similar conclusion. According to Dandekar and Rath, 40 to 50 percent of the total population has a per capita income below the official poverty line and the per capita income of this group has declined over the last two decades while the average per capita income went up.

The preceding discussion sought to focus attention on two points: Indians have been living in an inflationary economy since 1942–43; the degree and extent of inflation has varied from time to time; the inflation is badly affecting the poor — the poorer the person, the hardest he is hit by inflation. In summing up, it can be emphasized that the high rate of inflation is the consequence of the operation of the Indian economic system in a wrong way. The system is not propelled by the objectives of higher economic growth and the welfare of the poor, but by the drive for profit and wealth accumulation by the vested interests. All the evidence suggests that sluggish industrial growth, falling rate of productivity, and the staggeringly large number of unemployed, which continues to increase year after year, have added fuel to the inflation fire.

Unfortunately, the government of India (and for that matter most governments in the Third World) has not fully realized the gravity of the situation and has not adopted effective policies to check inflation and protect the poor. The monetary, fiscal, and other measures taken by the government to cope with the situation were most ineffective. Main emphasis was given to a public distribution system which remained badly organized and ineffectively run. The outcome was that the effects of persistent inflation were devastating for all sections of the society. The ills of inflation, however, fell most heavily on that large number of people who were below the poverty line.

It is not our purpose to present a solution to the problem because it is beyond the scope of this paper. Yet, it can be briefly mentioned that the most appropriate solution to save the poor from the adverse effects of inflation is to create conditions for full employment, higher wages, and greater productivity. Efforts should be made to create employment opportunities in almost every sector, with particular emphasis on agriculture. Goods which are in fact needed by the poor should be manufactured on a mass scale. The heart of the solution is to shelter the poor from the effects of inflation; it is necessary that they have more purchasing power in their hands and that the market have the goods which they need. In other words, there is a need for a realism in planning and socioeconomic policy, the main purpose of which should be to support the weaker sections of the society.

Is it feasible within the prevailing social, political, and economic order? The answer is no. But can we wait till the day the fundamental social transformation arrives? The answer is "We cannot." Then what can be done? In order to answer this question, we must realize that inflation is not purely an economic problem; it is a political problem with economic consequences. Therefore, it is necessary that, besides inflation-fighting programs, the poor should be able to raise their voice effectively. At the moment, what can be done is to strengthen the poor by organizing them so that they have the capacity to influence the power structure to take decisions in their favor. Researchers and scholars can contribute their mite by conducting more researches into how hard the poor are being hit by the inflation.

Finally, a word of warning: when inflation continues for a long period it becomes increasingly intolerable for greater numbers; like fire it engulfs more and more people within its fold. The fabric of the society is corroded and the human costs become incalculable. We hope the memories of the German inflation of 1923 and the Chinese inflation of 1937–1949 are still fresh in the minds of the older generation. In order to save modern societies, it is essential that the present inflationary trend be checked. If it is not done, the inflationary trend will emit such powerful forces that the prevailing economic and political system will not be able to defend itself. On the debris of this system, what new system would emerge, no one can say for sure.

Notes

1. See World Bank, *World Development Report 1978* (New York, 1978), p. 3; also see International Labor Office (ILO), *Employment, Growth and Basic Needs: A One-World Problem* (New York, 1977), p. 16.

2. World Bank, p. 3.

3. Mahbub ul Hag, *The Poverty Curtain: Choices for the Third World* (New York, 1976), p. 32; for India see *Economic Survey* published each year by the Government of India, normally in the month of February.

4. V. M. Dandekar and Nilakantha Rath, "Poverty in India" (The Ford Foundation, New Delhi, December 1970), p. 37; and Pranab Bardhan, "On Minimum Level of Living of the Rural Poor," *Indian Economic Review* (New Delhi), April 1970.

5. World Bank, p. iii.

6. ILO, pp. 21–22.

7. R. J. Venkateshwaran, *The Tragedy of Indian Rupee* (Bombay, 1968), p. 8.

8. C. N. Vakil, *The Falling Rupee* (Bombay, 1943).

9. C.N. Vakil, *Poverty, Planning and Inflation* (Bombay, 1978), p. 255.

10. See Planning Commission, *First Five Year Plan* (Government of India, New Delhi, 1952); *Second Five Year Plan* (1956).

11. See Reserve Bank of India (RBI), *Report on Currency and Finance* published each year, and *Economic Survey* of relevant years.

12. See *Report on Currency and Finance*, and *Economic Survey*, for relevant years; also see Planning Commission, *Fourth Five Year Plan* (1966) and *Fourth Five Year Plan 1969–74* (1969).

13. Pramit Chaudhuri, *The Indian Economy: Poverty and Development* (New Delhi, 1978), pp. 89–92.

14. *Economic Survey, 1975–76* and *1976–77*.

15. *Ibid.*, 1976–77, 1977–78; also see *Report on Currency and Finance, 1976–77* and *1977–78*.

16. Lord Robbins in Randall Hinshaw (Ed.), *Inflation as a Global Problem* (Baltimore, 1972), p. 130.

17. See *Report on Currency and Finance* for relevant years.

18. See Central Statistical Organization (CSO), *National Accounts Statistics: 1960–61 — 1974–75* (New Delhi, 1976); Uma Datta Roy Choudhury and Pratap Narain, "Current National Income Statistics: What They Tell," *Economic and Political Weekly* (Bombay), 27 September 1975, pp. 1540–52; and *Economic Survey; 1977–78*, p. 57.

19. See *Economic Survey 1967–68* and *1977–78*, pp. 73–74; CSO, *Monthly Abstract of Statistics, August 1977* (New Delhi), pp. 22, 23, 26.

20. See Planning Commission, *The Draft Five Year Plan 1978–83* (New Delhi, 1978).

21. C. H. Hanumantha Rao, "Agricultural Growth and Rural Poverty: Some Lessons From Past Experience," *Economic and Political Weekly*, Special Number, August 1977, p. 1369.

22. See "Cost of Production of Wheat in Punjab During the 1974–75 Crop Season," *Agricultural Situation in India* (New Delhi), October 1976.

23. RBI, Report on Currency and Finance, 1973–74; p. 17.
24. S. L. Shelty, *Structural Retrogression in the Indian Economy since the Mid-Sixties* (Bombay, 1978), pp. 53–54.
25. See *Economic Survey* for various years.
26. Chaudhuri, p. 92.
27. Dandekar and Rath, p. 34.
28. Indira Rajaraman, "Poverty, Inequality and Economic Growth: Rural Punjab, 1960–61 — 1970–71," *Journal of Development Studies*, July 1975.

Alternative Models of Inflation in the United Kingdom under the Assumption of Rational Expectations

PAUL ORMEROD*

INTRODUCTION

In recent years a number of alternative hypotheses have been put forward to explain the rate of inflation in the United Kingdom. The standard model of a wage-price spiral, in which prices are determined by a mark-up on cost and the exchange rate by purchasing power parity, has been the subject of a number of criticisms. The most forceful of these criticisms centers around the fact that monetary factors play no direct role in the determination of inflation in this model. The London Business School — see, for example, Ball, Burns, and Warburton (1979) — has argued that changes in the money supply exert a direct influence on the exchange rate which, in turn, will affect the domestic price level. Minford and Brech (1979) constructed a model which effectively amounts to an assertion of the validity of the long-run quantity theory of money.

The aim of this paper is twofold. First, to construct models which embody the key elements of the different schools of thought in the current debate over inflation in the United Kingdom and to estimate these models consistently over the same sample period, which covers the data since the introduction of a floating exchange rate in 1972. The models are then run in dynamic simulation mode over the complete sample period, which provides a very stringent validation test for each of the models. Second, to use rational expectations in the formation of price expectations in each of the models.

The first section of the paper provides a brief description of the three models to be investigated. The second section discusses the role of rational expectations and, in particular, the consistent estimation of models under the assumption of rational expectations. The third section provides a description of the preferred estimated equations and concludes by comparing the relative performance of the models in long dynamic simulations from fixed initial conditions.

1. THE MODELS

The first two models comprise three equations for prices, wages, and the exchange rate. The third model adds an extra equation which specifies the determination of the domestic money supply. The models are intended to capture the essential elements of the three main alternative views of the determination of inflation current in the United Kingdom.

The first model, Model I, represents the main ingredients of a fairly typical wage-price system in which prices are determined by a mark-up over costs. In the form in which it is specified, any endogenous feedback from demand onto either wage or price behavior is omitted, although United Kingdom evidence suggests that such a feedback is weak, certainly in the price equation. An exogenous demand variable is however included in the wage equation. The exchange rate is assumed to be determined by purchasing power parity. In general notation, Model I is as follows:

$$\dot{p} = a_1 (\dot{p}m/\dot{e}) + a_2\dot{w} + a_3 t$$

$$\dot{w} = b_1\dot{p}^e + b_2D + b_3 (w/p) + b_4t$$

$$\dot{e} = c_1 (\dot{p}w/\dot{p})$$

The variable $\dot{p}m$ in the price equation is the cost of imports in foreign currency; the time trend allows for the net effects of trend movements in profit rates, productivity, and other cost factors, such as overhead costs of labor. The wage equation is a type of expectation-augmented Phillips Curve, in which D is a pressure of demand variables. This form of wage equation has figured frequently in the United Kingdom literature on wage inflation. It is very similar to the equation used by Sargan (1964), Johnston and Timbrell (1973), and Henry and Ormerod (1978). It is frequently represented as a bargaining equation, representing in some way the pressure from the union side for wage increases which are assumed, implicitly, to be met. The exchange rate equation, in which e is the spot exchange rate, is a simple reduced form equation on the assumption that the rate adjusts to clear the foreign exchange market. Flows are assumed to be produced by variations in relative prices (pw/p) on the current account. The capital account is omitted, although this assumption is not implausible as far as the long-run level of the exchange rate is concerned. Changes in relative interest rates, perceived risk and other factors which determine the allocation of a portfolio will lead to adjustments in stocks of asset holdings, which imply limited flow movements. The model compares with the latest version of the Treasury model which has the exchange rate determined by current account factors in the long run, although it allows capital account factors to influence short-run levels of the rate (Spencer, 1979).

Model II retains the same wage and price equations as Model I, but allows the money supply, assumed to be exogenous, a direct impact on the domestic price level via the exchange rate.

$$\dot{p} = a_1 \dot{w} + a_2 (p\dot{m}/\dot{e}) + a_3 t$$
$$\dot{w} = b_1 \dot{p}^e + b_2 D + b_3 (w/p) + b_4 t \tag{2}$$
$$\dot{e} = c_1 (m\dot{w}/\dot{m}) + c_2 \Sigma \, BAL + c_3 (\ln IP/WIP - c_4 t)$$

where m and mw are domestic and world money supplies respectively. The justification for the equation is as follows (see Ball et al.). Setting out the model in terms of a set of long-run relationships, ignoring lags, the starting point is the assumption that the demand for real balances for the domestic economy is determined by real income.

$$M/P = k_o \, Y^{a_1} \tag{3}$$

where M is the domestic demand for nominal money and Y is the domestic level of real income. A similar equation exists for the rest of the world in aggregate.

$$MW/PW = k_1 \, YW^{b_1} \tag{4}$$

Assuming that the law of one price holds for traded goods in the long run

$$P_T = PW_T/E \tag{5}$$

where E is the exchange rate, and assuming that the price level as a whole is equal to the price of traded goods multiplied by the ratio of productivity in the traded goods sector to productivity in the economy as a whole, for both the domestic and world economies

$$P = qP_T \tag{6}$$

$$PW = q_1 \, PW_T$$

a long-run relationship can be derived

$$E \cdot M/MW = K \, (Y^{a_1}/YW^{b_1})(q/q_1) \tag{7}$$

Ball et al. argue that (7) defines an equilibrium exchange rate toward which the system would tend to move in the absence of official intervention in exchange markets. There are, however, special factors at any moment in time which might alter the relationship between the actual and the equilibrium rate. The variable $\Sigma \, BAL$ is one such factor and is the cumulated sum of the current account of the balance of payments, which proxies official intervention in exchange markets.

The variables *IP* and *WIP* are United Kingdom and world industrial production respectively, and the term (ln $IP/WIP - c_4{}^t$) represents the term

$$((Y^{a_1}/YW^{b_1})(q/q_1)) \quad \text{in (7)}$$

The third model which we examine is similar to the one proposed by Minford and Brech, and essentially rests upon the long-run quantity theory of money. The price level is a function of the money supply and the equilibrium level of real output, which is determined in the long run by (exogenous) supply factors; this latter variable is represented in our model by a time trend, although Minford has prices determined by the money supply alone. The wage equation in Model III is identical to the one in Models I and II, although its interpretation in this context is by no means obvious. It is probably best thought of as an equation to determine the distribution of nominal output between labor and capital. The exchange rate is a function of purchasing power parity, and the complete model is

$$\dot{p} = a_1 \, \dot{m} + a_2 \, t$$
$$\dot{w} = b_1 \, \dot{p}^e + b_2 D + b_3 \, (W/P) + b_4 \, t \tag{8}$$
$$\dot{e} = c_1 \, (\dot{p}w/\dot{p})$$
$$\dot{m} = d_1 \, DEF$$

The fourth equation is intended by Minford to add an IS/LM model linking, through the government budget constraint, money supply growth and the public sector budget deficit. The variable *DEF* is a centered moving average of the public sector borrowing requirement as a percentage of money GDP. In the long run, it is asserted that the money supply must grow at a rate determined by the budget deficit. This view has considerable currency in policy debates in the United Kingdom, and is certainly held by government ministers to be a key relationship in the way the economy works. (See, for example, *The Government's Public Expenditure Plans for 1980/81*, Cmnd. 7746, 1979).

2. RATIONAL EXPECTATIONS

Rational expectations were originally defined by Muth as being "essentially the same as the prediction from the relevant economic theory." In other words the rational expectations of the variable X at time t is given by

$$X^e{}_t = E(X/I_{t-1})$$

where X^e is the mathematical expectation of the stochastic variable X, given all the information available at the end of the preceding period, I_{t-1}. This information includes the structure of the relevant model as well as realizations for all exogenous variables entering the system. The potential advantages of such an expectation scheme over mechanistic rules like adaptive expectations is clear. It is required to use all information in an efficient way, and the expectation formation becomes endogenous for the model. Previous attempts to model expectations endogenously in the context of a wage-price system have relied heavily upon adaptive expectations, which have not proved entirely success-ful. Our approach to rational expectations is to regard it as being potentially a powerful tool in applied economics. The key question is whether it is empirically useful in enabling us to construct well-specified and robust models of the wage-price system.

There are, of course, several well-known logical and empirical prob-lems in using rational expectations. One of the most important prob-lems is the "transitional" problem which is concerned with the model-ing of the process of acquiring information by agents, and propositions about their behavior while they are in the process of learning. At one extreme, the agent may be assumed to be rational in the sense of Rawls, using information currently available in an efficient manner. The agent may not know "the model" of the economy in this description. At the other extreme, the agent is rational in the full rational-expectations sense, not only using all information efficiently but knowing the underlying structure of the economy which, by assumption, is error orthogonal and time invariant (see, for example, B. Friedman, 1979). In this full sense, the informational requirements are clearly very strong, which must cast doubt on the relevance of the implications of full rational expectations for policy. As pointed out earlier however, our interest is to see whether rational expectations is useful in empirical analysis. A preliminary study by Henry and Ormerod (1979) suggests that it can be of value in analyzing the United Kingdom wage-price system, in particular outperforming a weakly rational expectations model, and it is in this spirit that we use it.

Wallis (1980) derives an expression for rational expectations in the context of a linear model. For the dynamic linear model

$$B(L) Y_t + AY_t^e + C(L)X_t = U_t \qquad (9)$$

where $B(.)$ and $C(.)$ are matrixpolynominals in the lag operator L of order r and s, respectively, and A is suitably redefined by including columns of zeros, the rational expectation is

$$Y_t^e = -(B_o+A)^{-1} \cdot E\left[(C(L)X_t + B_1Y_{t-1} + \ldots + B_rY_{t-r})/I_{t-1}\right]$$
$$= -(B_o+A)^{-1} (C_o\hat{X}_t + C_1X_{t-1} + \ldots + B_rY_{t-r}) \qquad (10)$$

where $\hat{X}_t$ is the optimal predictor for X_t dictated by the time series realization

$$F(L)X_t = G(L)\, e_t \tag{11}$$

where e_t is white noise.

The expectation thus depends upon the optimal prediction of the exogenous variables, and lagged values of exogenous and endogenous variables, the lag structure being given by the dynamics of the structural model. In estimating (10) we may proceed by either (a) treating $\hat{X}$ as data, that is, first of all fitting (11) and obtaining $\hat{X}_t$ as one-period forecast; from that model. Appropriate estimation of the structural parameters will depend on the presence or otherwise of overidentifying restrictions. Approach (b) is to estimate the structural parameters and the parameters of (11) jointly by substituting (11) into (10) and estimating by a nonlinear system method. This is clearly desirable, but it is very difficult to implement in practice. Lack of availability of a sufficiently nonlinear systems estimation program means that we had to adapt the first approach.

There is a further practical problem in estimating (10), which is discussed by Henry and Ormerod and by Fair (1979). This is the need to ensure that the coefficients used in the reduced form to generate the series for Y^e_t are consistent with the coefficients in the estimates of the structural equation. In other words, to obtain the initial estimates of the structural model (9) in which the rational expectation Y^e_t is embedded, an initial trial data series for Y^e_t needs to be constructed. Having obtained consistent estimates of (9), the Y^e_t series should be revised, being based upon the new fitted values from the estimates of the structural parameters in (9). The model then needs to be reestimated using the new Y^e_t series, and this reestimation leads in turn to a further series for Y^e_t. This iterative procedure should be continued until the estimated structural coefficients in (9) change by an arbitrarily small amount between one iteration and the next. We adopted this procedure in estimating (1), (2), and (8), the convergence criteria used being that none of the structural parameters should change in the third place of decimals between one iteration and the next.

3. THE RESULTS

The endogenous variables used are the consumer price index P, average earnings in the whole economy W, and the IMF exchange rate E. All data are seasonally adjusted on a quarterly basis and are taken from the NIESR data bank. A full description of the definition and sources of these variables is available in National Institute *Discussion Paper*, No. 28 (1979). An important point to note is that the series for W is defined as income from employment divided by employees in employment. It therefore includes elements of employee conpensation, such as overtime payments and payments by results, as well as the basic weekly wage. Other variables used in the models are as follows:

UV: Unemployment minus vacancies, 000s. *Source:* Economic Trends.

PM: The deflator of United Kingdom imports of goods in foreign currency. *Source:* NIESR data bank.

PW: The weighted consumer price index of six major foreign countries, weighted by the weights used in the calculation of the IMF exchange rate. *Source:* Statistical Appendix, National Institute *Economic Review.*

CB: The current balance of payments cumulated from 1970 Q1, £mn, as a percentage of current price expenditure GDP at factor cost. *Source:* Economic Trends.

RIP: Index of United Kingdom industrial production divided by weighted index of industrial production for six major countries, the weights as for MW.

M: Index of M1 plus quasi money in the United Kingdom. *Source:* IMF *Financial Statistics.*

MW: Weighted index of M1 plus quasi money in six major foreign countries, weighted by the weights used in the calculation of the IMF exchange rate. *Source:* as for M.

D: Centered five-period moving average of the public sector borrowing requirement (with sign reversed) divided by current price expenditure GDP at factor cost. *Source:* Economic Trends.

The sample period covers the period of sterling as a floating currency, from 1972 Q3 through 1979 Q1.

The models outlined in (1), (2), and (8) are general sets of equations and in particular, make no assumption about the possible effects of lags in the system. We investigated the question of dynamics in detail, making substantial use of the dynamics specification testing procedures used by Davidson, Hendry et al. (1978), and Hendry (1979). These consist essentially of starting with a specification which is as general as possible, given the need to retain degrees of freedom, and then testing down until a preferred parsimonious specification is obtained.

The initial estimates were carried out using ordinary least squares on the GIVE program written by D. F. Hendry and F. Srba of the London School of Economics. Sequential F-tests were used to obtain the preferred equation. Substantial use was made at this stage of tests of the validity of specification of the equations, which were not available on the simultaneous estimation programs at the disposal of the author. Four such tests were used. The Box-Pierce Q-statistic for a random correlogram of the residuals and also the Lagrange Multiplier test for residual autocorrelation. The Chow F-test was used to test for post-sample parameter stability, and use was also made of a post-sample parameter stability test of the joint null hypothesis that the parameters are stable and that the residual variance is constant in the post-sample period on the assumption that the parameters are known with certainty.

The preferred equations in each model were then estimated by full information maximum likelihood (FIML), and the iterative procedure just described was carried out using FIML in order to ensure that the coefficients used in the reduced form to generate the series on price expectations were consistent with the coefficients in the estimates of the structural equations.

The general equations used were as follows:

Model I:

$$\Delta \ln P = \alpha_{10} + \sum_{i=1}^{2} \beta_{1i} \Delta \ln P_{-i} + \sum_{j=0}^{2} [\gamma_{1j} \Delta \ln PM_{-j} + \delta_{1j} \Delta \ln E_{-j}$$
$$+ \varepsilon_{1j} \Delta \ln W_{-j}] + \theta_{11} \ln(P/W)_{-1} + \theta_{12} \ln(P/PM/E)_{-1}$$
$$+ \theta_{13} \ln W_{-1} + \phi_{11} TIM \qquad (12)$$

$$\Delta \ln W = \alpha_{20} + \beta_{20} \Delta \ln P^{e} + \sum_{i=1}^{3} \gamma_{2i} \Delta \ln W_{-i} + \theta_{21} \ln(P/W)_{-1}$$
$$+ \theta_{22} [\sum_{j=2}^{8} \ln(P/W)_{-j}] + \theta_{23} \ln P_{-1} + \phi_{21} TIM + \phi_{22} \ln UV$$
$$+ \phi_{23} \ln UV_{-1}$$

$$\Delta \ln E = \alpha_{30} + \sum_{i=1}^{2} \beta_{3i} \Delta \ln E_{-1} + \sum_{j=0}^{2} \gamma_{3j} \Delta \ln(PW/P)_{-j}$$
$$+ \theta_{31} \ln(E/PW/P)_{-1} + \theta_{32} \ln(P/PW)_{-1} + \theta_{33} [\sum_{k=2}^{8} \ln(E/PW/P)_{-k}]$$

Model II:

$\Delta \ln P$:   as Model I
$\Delta \ln W$:   as Model I   (13)

$$\Delta \ln E = \alpha_{30} + \sum_{i=1}^{2} \beta_{31} \Delta \ln E_{-i} + \sum_{j=0}^{3} \gamma_{3j}(\Delta \ln M - \Delta \ln MW)_{-j}$$
$$+ \theta_{31} \ln(E/M/MW)_{-1} + \theta_{32} [\sum_{k=2}^{8} \ln(E/M/MW)_{-k}]$$
$$+ \theta_{33} \ln(M/MW)_{-1} + \phi_{31} CB + \phi_{32} CB_{-1}$$
$$+ \phi_{33}(\ln RIP - 0.0062 TIM)$$

Model III:

$$\Delta \ln P = \alpha_{10} + \sum_{i=1}^{3} \beta_{1i} \Delta \ln P_{-1} + \sum_{j=0}^{3} \gamma_{1j} \Delta \ln M_{-j}$$
$$+ \theta_{11} \ln(P/M)_{-1} + \theta_{12} \ln M_{-1} + \theta_{13} \sum_{k=2}^{8} (\ln(P/M)_{-k})$$
$$+ \theta_{14} TIM$$

$\Delta \ln W$: = as Model I
$\Delta \ln E$: = as Model I   (14)

$$\Delta \ln M: = \alpha_{40} + \sum_{i=1}^{3} \beta_{4i} \Delta \ln M_{-i} + \sum_{j=0}^{3} \gamma_{4j} D_{-j}$$

The general specifications for the equations in P, W, and E contain the proportional, derivative, and integral control elements of control theory — the article by Phillips (1957) was an early application of it in economics. Each of these equations has a long-run equilibrium solution in steady-state growth compatible with economic theory.

Model I:

$$P = k_1 W^{\alpha}1(PM/E)^{\beta}1 \, e^{\gamma_1 TIM}$$
$$W = k_2 P^{\alpha}2 UV^{\beta}_{2e}{}^{\gamma_2 TIM}$$
$$E = k_3 (PW/P)^{\alpha}3 \tag{15a}$$

Model II:

P, W as Model I

$$E = k_3 (M/MW)^{\alpha}3 \, CB^{\beta}3 \, (RIP\text{-}0.0062TIM)^{\gamma}3 \tag{15b}$$

Model III:

W, E as Model I

$$P = k_1 M^{\alpha}{}_1 e^{\beta}{}_1{}^{TIM} \tag{15c}$$

where $\beta_1 < 0$

The preferred equations testing down from the general specifications (12), (13), and (14) were as follows:

Model I:

$\Delta lnP =$ $0.349 + 0.264 \, \Delta lnP_{-1} + 0.131 \, \Delta lnPM_{-1} - 0.066 \, \Delta lnPM_{-2}$
      $(0.158) \, (0.157) \quad\quad (0.049) \quad\quad\quad (0.052)$

      $+0.125 \, \Delta lnE_{-2} + 0.145 \, \Delta lnW + 0.144 \, \Delta lnW_{-2}$
      $(0.062) \quad\quad\quad (0.111) \quad\quad (0.112)$

      $+0.168 \, ln(P/W)_{-1} - 0.064 \, ln(P/PM/E)_{-1} - 0.0013 \, TIM$
      $(0.070) \quad\quad\quad (0.032) \quad\quad\quad (0.0004)$

$R^2 =$ 0.849; S.E. $= 0.0069$; $Q(8) = 9.52$; $F(4,13) = 1.76$;
      $PPS(4) = 25.0$ $(16a)$

$\Delta lnW =$ $0.0008 + 0.749 \, \Delta lnP^e + 0.422 \, \Delta lnW_{-1} + 0.404 \, \Delta lnW_{-2}$
      $(0.043) \quad (0.370) \quad\quad (0.170) \quad\quad (0.194)$

      $+0.458 \, ln(P/W)_{-1} + 0.0016 \, TIM - 0.0094 \, ln \, UV$
      $(0.119) \quad\quad\quad (0.0006) \quad\quad (0.0032)$

$R^2 =$ 0.597; S.E. $= 0.0145$; $Q(8) = 7.51$; $LM(4) = 8.55$;
      $F(4,17) = 0.611$; $PPS(4) = 3.50$

$\Delta lnE =$ $1.351 + 0.966 \, \Delta ln \, (PW/P)_{-1} - 0.740 \, \Delta ln \, (PW/P)_{-2}$
      $(0.492) \, (0.586) \quad\quad\quad (0.578)$

      $-0.316 \, ln \, (E/PW/P)_{-1}$
      (0.114)

$R^2 =$ 0.340; S.E. $= 0.029$; $Q(8) = 6.55$; $LM(4) = 3.68$; $F(4,19) =$
      0.69; $PPS(4) = 2.93$

Model II:

P, W as Model I

$$\Delta \ln E = \quad 0.295 + 0.270\ \Delta \ln E_{-1} + 0.369\ \Delta \ln E_{-2}$$
$$(0.181)\ (0.235) \qquad\qquad (0.246) \qquad\qquad\qquad\qquad (16b)$$
$$-0.489\ (\Delta \ln M - \Delta \ln MW)_{-1} - 0.422\ \ln(E/M/MW)_{-1}$$
$$(0.390) \qquad\qquad\qquad\qquad\qquad (0.181)$$
$$+0.050\ \overset{8}{\underset{k=2}{\Sigma}}\ \ln(E/M/MW)_{-k} + 0.302\ (\ln\ RIP\text{-}0.0062TIM)$$
$$(0.023)\ \ ^{k=2} \qquad\qquad\qquad (0.293)$$

$R^2 = \quad$ 0.288; S.E. = 0.032; Q(8) = 2.29; LM(4) = 2.23; F(4,16)
= 0.95; PPS(4) = 4.31

Model III:

$$\Delta \ln P = \quad 0.0663 - 0.528\ \Delta \ln P_{-3} - 0.19\ \Delta \ln M$$
$$(0.0062)\ (0.129) \qquad\qquad (0.086)$$
$$-0.0246\ \ln\ (P/M)_{-1} - 0.0005\ TIM$$
$$(0.0034) \qquad\qquad\qquad (0.0002)$$

$R^2 = \quad$ 0.816; S.E. = 0.0067; Q(8) = 11.93; LM(4) = 6.45; F(4,18)
= 0.715; PPS (4) = 6.13

W, E as Model I   (16c)

$$\Delta \ln M = \quad 0.037 + 0.408\ \Delta \ln M_{-3} - 0.267\ D_{-1}$$
$$(0.014)\quad (0.161) \qquad\qquad (0.149)$$

$R^2 = \quad$ 0.349; S.E. = 0.017; Q(8) = 8.32; LM(4) = 3.07; F(4,20) =
1.05; PPS(4) = 4.51

The figures in brackets are standard errors and S.E. is the standard error of the equation. In the estimation of the variance-covariance matrices of the models, no account was taken of the fact that P^e_t is estimated along with the coefficients. In other words, for the purpose of estimating the matrices, the P^e_t series was treated as if it were known with certainty — see Fair (1979). Q(8) is the Box-Pierce statistic with eight degrees of freedom, a chi-square statistic testing the null hypothesis of a random correlogram of the residuals from one through eight lags. LM(4) is the Lagrange Multiplier test of the null hypothesis of no serial correlation in the residuals from one through four lags. It has a chi-square distribution, in this case with four degrees of freedom. The statistic F(n,k) is the Chow F-test with (n,k) degrees of freedom of the hypothesis of post-sample parameter stability. Each preferred equation was estimated over the period 1972 Q3–1978 Q1, and the test for stability carried out over the period 1978 Q2–1979 Q1. The statistic PPS (4) is an additional test of stability, described above, again over the period 1978 Q2–1979 Q1. It has a chi-square distribution.

All the foregoing equations appear to be well specified, in that the null hypothesis of random residuals was not rejected at the 5 percent level on any of the tests used. Further, in every case except one, the null hypothesis of post-sample stability was not rejected at the 5 percent level. The exception was the PPS test with the price equation in Model I, although the Chow F-test does not reject the null hypothesis of stability in this case. The coefficients are all correctly signed, again with one exception, and the long-run solutions to the equations yield results compatible with economic theory. (The solutions to the rational expectations FIML versions are given below.) The exception was the equation in Model III relating changes in the money supply to the budget deficit. The equation appears to be very well specified, and indeed the coefficient on D_{-1} is almost identical in absolute value to that obtained by Minford over the period 1960 Q1–1975 Q4. Unfortunately it is the wrong sign. Nevertheless, it was retained in case the FIML results yielded the correct sign.

Equations 16 (a), (b) and (c) were then estimated using FIML. These results were broadly similar, except that the terms $\Delta\ln W$ and $\Delta\ln W_{-2}$ in the $\Delta\ln P$ equation in Model II, and the term $\Delta\ln P_{-3}$ in the $\Delta\ln P$ equation in Model III became completely insignificant and were dropped in subsequent estimates. In order to form the rational expectations prediction for P, optimal predictions were required for the current value of the exogenous variables. These were obtained from the time series model.

$$\Delta\ln UV = 0.024 + 0.344\ \Delta\ln UV_{-2} - 0.357\ \Delta\ln UV_{-7}$$
$$\quad\quad (0.046)\ (0.176)\quad\quad\quad (0.173)$$
$$R^2 = \quad 0.261;\ \text{S.E.} = 0.202;\ Q(8) = 8.47;\ LM(4) = 0.24$$

The results for the final FIML version of the models were:

Model I:

$$\Delta\ln P = \quad 0.475 + 0.235\ \Delta\ln P_{-1} + 0.191\ \Delta\ln PM_{-1} - 0.052\ \Delta\ln PM_{-2}$$
$$\quad (0.132)\ (0.134)\quad\quad\quad (0.060)\quad\quad\quad\quad (0.046)$$
$$\quad +0.172\ \Delta\ln E_{-2} - 0.592\ \ln W + 0.378\ \Delta\ln W_{-2}$$
$$\quad (0.054)\quad\quad\quad (0.248)\quad\quad (0.186)$$
$$\quad -0.119\ \ln(P/PW)_{-1} - 0.090\ \ln(P/PM/E)_{-1} - 0.0015 TIM$$
$$\quad (0.086)\quad\quad\quad\quad (0.028)\quad\quad\quad\quad\quad (0.0004)$$

$$\Delta\ln W = \quad -0.015 + 0.574\ \Delta\ln P^e + 0.434\ \Delta\ln W_{-1}$$
$$\quad (0.069)\quad (0.203)\quad\quad\quad (0.148) \quad\quad\quad\quad\quad\quad (18a)$$
$$\quad +0.579\ \Delta\ln W_{-2} + 0.474\ \ln(P/W)_{-1} + 0.0016 TIM -$$
$$\quad (0.069)\quad\quad\quad\quad (0.130)\quad\quad\quad\quad (0.00053)$$
$$\quad 0.00702\ \ln UV$$
$$\quad (0.0053)$$

$$\Delta\ln E = \quad 1.335 + 1.062\ \Delta\ln(PW/P)_{-1} - 0.854\ \Delta\ln(PW/P)_{-2}$$
$$\quad (0.502)\ (0.534)\quad\quad\quad\quad (0.518)$$
$$\quad -0.312\ \ln\ (E/PW/P)_{-1}$$
$$\quad (0.105)$$

Model II:

$$\Delta\ln P = \quad 0.313 + 0.283\ \Delta\ln P_{-1} + 0.107\ \Delta\ln PM_{-1} - 0.064\ \Delta\ln PM_{-2}$$
$$(0.108)\ (0.122) \qquad (0.038) \qquad\qquad (0.042)$$
$$+0.107\ \Delta\ln E_{-2} - 0.228\ \ln(P/W)_{-1} - 0.056\ \ln(P/PM/E)_{-1}$$
$$(0.048) \qquad\qquad (0.050) \qquad\qquad (0.025)$$
$$-0.0013\ TIM$$
$$(0.0003)$$

$$\Delta\ln W = \quad -0.017 + 0.825\ \Delta\ln P^e + 0.295\ \Delta\ln W_{-1} \qquad\qquad (18b)$$
$$(0.085)\quad (0.296) \qquad (0.155)$$
$$+0.510\ \Delta\ln W_{-2} + 0.529\ \ln(P/W)_{-1} + 0.0018 TIM$$
$$(0.153) \qquad\qquad (0.134) \qquad\qquad (0.0005)$$
$$-\ 0.0029\ \ln UV$$
$$(0.0059)$$

$$\Delta\ln E = \quad 0.263 + 0.270\ \Delta\ln E_{-1} + 0.389\ \Delta\ln E_{-2}$$
$$(0.138)\ (0.200) \qquad (0.207)$$
$$-0.581\ (\Delta\ln M - \Delta\ln MW)_{-1} - 0.409\ \ln(E/M/MW)_{-1}$$
$$(0.326) \qquad\qquad\qquad (0.153)$$
$$+0.049\ \overset{8}{\underset{i=2}{\,}}\ \ln(E/M/MW)_{-i} + 0.306\ (\ln RIP - 0.0062 TIM)$$
$$(0.020)\ ^{i=2} \qquad\qquad\qquad (0.246)$$

Model III:

$$\Delta\ln P = \quad 0.059 - 0.622\ \Delta\ln M - 0.087\ \ln (P/M)_{-1} - 0.00041 TIM$$
$$(0.009)\ (0.163) \qquad (0.028) \qquad\qquad (0.00030)$$

$$\Delta\ln W = \quad -0.082 + 1.267\ \Delta\ln P^e + 0.458\ \Delta\ln W_{-1}$$
$$(0.057)\ (0.390) \qquad (0.147)$$
$$+0.456\ \Delta\ln W_{-2} + 0.608\ \ln(P/W)_{-1} + 0.0021 TIM$$
$$(0.155) \qquad\qquad (0.143) \qquad\qquad (0.0006)$$
$$-0.0019\ \ln UV$$
$$(0.0065) \qquad\qquad\qquad\qquad\qquad\qquad (18c)$$

$$\Delta\ln E = \quad 1.089 + 1.007\ \Delta\ln(PW/P)_{-1} - 0.803\ \Delta\ln(PW/P)_{-2} - 0.255$$
$$(0.413)\ (0.506) \qquad\qquad (0.497) \qquad\qquad\qquad (0.098)$$
$$\ln (E/PW/P)_{-1}$$

$$\Delta\ln M = \quad 0.0429 + 0.413\ \Delta\ln M_{-3} - 0.352\ D_{-1}$$
$$(0.0113)\ (0.136) \qquad\quad (0.128)$$

The long-run solutions of the models are as follows:

Model I:

$$P = \quad k_1 W^{0.569}\ (PM/E)^{0.431}\ e^{-0.0071 TIM}$$
$$W = \quad k_2 P \cdot UV^{-0.015}\ e^{0.0034 TIM}$$
$$E = \quad k_3\ (PW/P)$$

Model II:

$$P = k_1 \, W^{0.803} \, (PM/E)^{0.197} \, e^{-0.0046TIM}$$
$$W = k_2 P \cdot UV^{-0.015} e^{\,0.0034TIM}$$
$$E = k_3 \, (M/MW) \, (RIP - 0.0062TIM)^{0.748}$$

Model III:

$$P = k_1 \, M \cdot e^{-0.0047TIM}$$
$$W = k_2 \, P \cdot UV^{-0.003} \cdot e^{\,0.0034TIM}$$
$$E = k_3 \, (PW/P)$$

Judged as a whole, these results are satisfactory. In Models I and II, the sum of the components of cost is in each case equal to unity. In Models I and III, the coefficient on relative prices in the exchange rate equation is unity in the long run. In all the wage equations, the coefficients on *UV* and *TIM* are correctly signed, although (18c) shows that the coefficient on *UV* in Model III is completely insignificant from zero. There is a unit elasticity on money in the price equation in Model III, and the time trend in this equation is correctly signed. The outstanding problem is the coefficient on *D* in the money supply equation in Model III, which remains incorrectly signed.

There are, of course, differences between the models, particularly relating to the size of the coefficient on price expectations in the wage equations. It is clearly difficult to distinguish between the models on the basis of these results, except that Model III has one of its key parameters signed incorrectly. But this does not affect the signs of other parameters in the model and in fact by substituting for *M* in the price equation, Minford's result that increases in the budget deficit lead to increases in the price level still holds (although not very strongly: a sustained rise of 1 percentage point in the budget deficit as a percentage of GDP in each quarter leaves the price level six years later 3.2 percent higher than it would otherwise have been).

Our final step, therefore, was to run the models in dynamic mode, over the complete sample period, after solving the model to give the *levels* of *P*, *W*, *E* and *M* as a dependent variables. Tests of dynamic stability are recognized as very stringent tests of a model as a whole, Klein (1979), for example, commenting that: "Complete system solutions for long dynamic periods from fixed initial conditions provide the most stringent validation test (of models) among those considered." Table 1 gives a comparison of the three models in terms of their summary error statistics for the dynamic simulation.

The results of Model II can only be described as bad. The poor performance is due to the exchange rate equation, which explains the rate as a function of relative money supplies. In the first few periods of simulation, the fitted value of the exchange rate falls much faster than the actual value, so that by 1974 Q3 the rate is underpredicted by 26.1 percent. These errors feed through into the price and wage equations.

Table 1. Dynamic Simulation Error Statistics (%): 1972 Q3–1979 Q1

Model	P			W			E			M		
	$\bar{e}$	$|\bar{e}|$	RMSE	$\bar{e}$	$|\bar{e}|$	RMSE	$\bar{e}$	$|\bar{e}|$	RMSE	$\bar{e}$	$|\bar{e}|$	RMSE
I	0.12	0.92	1.07	0.17	1.08	1.27	−0.38	2.99	4.19		n.a.	
II	−10.43	10.47	12.68	−11.06	11.14	13.37	10.30	10.43	13.73		n.a.	
III	2.12	3.29	4.00	2.65	4.10	4.81	−2.13	4.12	5.62	5.83	5.88	6.52

where $\bar{e} = \frac{1}{n} \sum_{i=1}^{n} e_i$, $|\bar{e}| = \frac{1}{n} \sum_{i=1}^{n} |e_i|$, and RMSE $= \sqrt{(\frac{1}{n} \sum_{i=1}^{n} e_i^2)}$.

Both Models I and III show good results, although Model I has a clearly superior performance for all the variables. None of the equations in these models shows strong tendencies for cumulation of errors away from the historical path, although here again the performance of Model I is superior. The average percentage errors in Model I of P, W, and E for the period 1978 Q2–1979 Q1 in the dynamic simulation beginning 1972 Q3 are 0.01, 0.51, and 1.59, respectively. The relevant figures for Model II are 6.59, 8.31, and 5.73. The exchange rate equation is the least satisfactory in Model I, there being considerable overprediction at the end of 1976, a period of intense speculative activity against sterling. It is possible that the addition of capital account factors could improve its performance, although the behavior of the exchange rate in 1976 Q4 in particular has proved to be extremely difficult to model econometrically.

CONCLUSION

This paper has considered three alternative models of inflation in the United Kingdom. The dynamic specifications have been examined in detail and well-specified single equation results attained. The models were then estimated by full-information maximum likelihood, under the assumption of rational expectations in the generation of price expectations. The results were again satisfactory, except for the equation in the monetarist Model III linking changes in the money supply to the budget deficit. The models were then simulated dynamically over the complete sample period, in a further attempt to discriminate between them. Model I, in which prices are determined by a mark-up on cost and the exchange rate by purchasing power parity, clearly performed the best. Model III, in which the long-run quantity theory of money holds, performed reasonably well. The performance of Model II, in which the exchange rate is determined by United Kingdom money supply relative to world money supply, performed very badly. Overall, both in terms of the consistency of its estimated parameters with the a priori views of economic theory and in terms of its performance in the stringent validation test of dynamic simulation over a long period from fixed initial conditions, Model I emerges as the model best suited to explain inflation in the United Kingdom over the period 1972–79.

Notes

* I am grateful to Brian Henry of the National Institute and to members of the Economics Faculty of Birkbeck College, University of London, for comments on an earlier draft. The work received financial support from the Social Science Research Council.
1. This relationship was obtained from the OLS regression from 1972 Q1 through 1979 Q1: 1nRIP = −0.00062TIM where the figure in brackets is a
$$(0.0003)$$
standard error, $R^2 = 0.57$, S.E. $= 0.032$, DW $= 0.583$.

References

Ball, R. J., Burns, T., and Warburton, P. J. "The London Business School Model of the UK Economy: an Exercise in International Monetarism," in P. A. Ormerod (Ed.), *Economic Modelling* (London, 1979), pp. 86–114.

Davidson, J. E. H., Hendry, D. F., Srba, F., and Yeo, S. "Econometric Modelling of the Aggregate Time Series Relationship between Consumers' Expenditure and Income in the UK," *Economic Journal* 88 (1978): 661–92.

Fair, R. C. "An Analysis of the Accuracy of Four Macroeconometric Models," *Journal of Political Economy* 87 (1979): 701–718.

Friedman, B. "Optimal Expectations and the Extreme Information Assumptions of Rational Expectations in Macro Models," *Journal of Monetary Economics*, 1979.

Hendry, D. F. "Predictive Failure and Econometric Modelling in Macroeconomics: The Transactions Demand for Money," in P. A. Ormerod (Ed.), *Economic Modelling*, pp. 217–42.

Henry, S. G. B., and Ormerod, P. A. "Incomes Policy and Wage Inflation: Empirical Evidence for the UK 1961–1977," *National Institute Economic Review* 85 (1978): 31–39.

The Government's Expenditure Plans 1980–81. Cmnd. 7746, London, 1979.

Henry, S. G. B., and Ormerod, P. A. "Rational Expectations in a Wage-Price Model of the UK," paper presented to the SSRC Conference on Rational Expectations, University of Sussex, 1979.

Johnston, J., and Timbrell, M. "Empirical Tests of a Bargaining Theory of Wage Rate Determination," *Manchester School* 41 (1973): 141–68.

Klein, L. R. "Use of Econometric Models in the Policy Process" in P. A. Ormerod (Ed.), *Economic Modelling*, pp. 309–329.

Minford, A. P. L., and Brech, M. "The Wage Equation and Rational Expectations," SSRC — University of Liverpool Research Project, *Working Paper*, No. 7901, 1979.

Phillips, A. W. "Stabilisation Policy and the Time-Forms of Lagged Responses," *Economic Journal* 67 (1957): 265–77.

Sargan, J. D. "Wages and Prices in the UK," in P. E. Hart (Ed.), *Econometric Analysis for National Economic Planning, Colston Paper*, Vol. 16, 1964.

Spencer, P. D. "Modelling the Exchange Rate," HM Treasury, paper presented to the SSRC Economic Modelling Study Group, 1979 (mimeo).

Wallis, K. F. "Econometric Implications of the Rational Expectations Hypothesis," *Econometrica* 48 (1980): 49–74.

Economic Well-Being in the Soviet Union
Inflation and the Distribution of Resources

WOLFGANG TECKENBERG

THEORETICAL PROPOSITIONS

Sociologists, bearing in mind Soviet surveys on economic well-being or rather poverty, often wonder when economists, specializing in socialist countries, claim a high rate of repressed inflation in the Soviet Union. Whereas inflation prevails in capitalist societies, it is said that socialist countries — perhaps Poland and the USSR more than Hungary or the German Democratic Republic (Laski, 1977; Nove, 1979, p. 188), can be characterized by a money overhang on the side of the consumers created by relatively high wages and low prices or simply by the lack of goods, food, and durables.

How does this fit into the pattern of empirical sociological investigations which show that about two-fifths of the Soviet population has to be considered as "poor" even by official Soviet definitions (on poverty see McAuley, 1979, chap. 4, p. 305).

A further relevant question in a socioeconomic context concerns the assumed dependency of the labor supply on repressed inflation. Motivation to participate in production or increase one's productivity is dependent on the purchasing power of one's income which, even under socialism, is seen as a stimulus for engaging in production.

Some more theoretical issues should also be discussed in this context concerning the clash of interest and role conflict between the interests of workers as producers of goods, trying to increase their wages even if the output produced is of poor quality, and their interest as consumers in a broad range of products at low prices. In fact, there is contradiction in Soviet-type socialism: wealth and the means of production have been formally socialized under the administration and planning systems of the bureaucracy but distribution remains in the still existing "bourgeois" mode. The Soviet government controls only the demand side of the labor market, again, the sphere of production. In an almost "classic" article on inflation in the Soviet Union, Holzman argues that the authorities do not really have effective control over the money supply, which grows by way of wage overexpenditures. The competition between enterprises for labor supply is said to bid wages up (Holzman, 1960). Similarly A. McAuley summarizes parts of his findings:

> Shortages of particular skills, high rates of labor turnover, falling participation rates, and a general unwillingness to exercise initiative would all adversely affect economic performance and plan fulfillment. And . . . there is a degree of autonomy built into the determination of actual earnings, however rigidly the authorities control formal rates. The logic of the planned economy provides an incentive for managers to ignore the state's structure of differentials if this conflicts with the demands of plan fulfillment (1979, p. 315).

Mainly in the context of these quesions, some tentative answers are presented using Soviet sociological surveys. Although these empirical investigations sometimes are locally limited, they do allow some insights into the process of wage attainment and consumption which is more than just "impressionistic." Stress is laid on the elaboration of the first problem: the rather low level of incomes and value differences reflected in different consumption styles under the conditions of a marked shortage of goods. Whether this situation then still can/should be called *repressed inflation* remains open for discussion.

THE SOVIET UNION: A SHORTAGE ECONOMY

The states of present "real" socialism are still far away from the communist ideal of a society abundance. The ideology for this final stage predicts full equality and distribution according to the principle "to each according to his needs"; during socialism the principle "to each acccording to his labor" prevails. In fact, instead of abundance, constantly higher plan targets and investments in sector A (machine construction and heavy industry) have created an extreme shortage of sector B articles (light industry and food). The ninth Five-Year Plan did urge a greater increase in the production of consumer goods (an increase of 50 percent was planned) than the output of the means of production, this target was not met. The actual increase of consumer goods of 37 percent was again surpassed by sector A in 1975 (Hoehmann; Seidenstecher, 1978, p. 19).

Thus the term *shortage economy*, which J. Kornai first applied to Hungary may be even more appropriate in the Soviet case, because the living standard is known to be higher in Hungary (Kornai, 1976; Laski, 1977, p. 23), and repressed inflation seems to be less of a problem. This has led some researchers to believe that the reason that some authors (like Portes) deny the existence of repressed inflation in socialist societies is mainly because their examples are from Hungary (Nove, 1979, p. 191; Laski, personal communication).

A shortage economy is characterized by suction on the market for goods because of excess demand and a high degree of consumer purchasing power. Although some products (more than others) can be substituted, this is not true of food and basic clothing and footwear. The actual amount of "forced substitution" in the final act of purchasing is difficult to assess. Here too, of course, sociological considerations play a role: what may be acceptable for one social group may not pass the stricter group norms of another. Prestige aspects and aspirations for differentiation between individuals play a role which is not "rational" in purely economic terms. In Max Weber's terms it is typical for societies which lack class distinctions — and here one has to think of the Soviet Union which at least formally abolished the class discrepancies — to be stratified along estatist (or status) lines and to be marked by strong value clashes and cleavages. We know, too, and will elaborate further on, that in the Soviet Union a lot of goods are distributed via the organization or enterprise. Here, it is not purchasing power but restricted access that hinders free consumer behavior. This can best be described in Weber's terminology:

> Every society where strata [estates — W.T.] play a prominent part is controlled to a large extent by conventional rules of conduct. It thus creates economically irrational conditions of consumption and hinders the development of free markets by monopolistic appropriation and by restricting free disposal of the individual's own economic ability (Weber, 1947, p. 395).

When goods are as scarce as in the Soviet Union, control of access or control of the information where and when to get these goods may be more important than money, and it is dependent on the occupation or organizational location and milieu of the social groups in question. (For an application of Weber's analysis to the Soviet Union, see Teckenberg, 1980, chap. 1.)

Besides the problem of different standards and consumption patterns and preferences another problem in measuring shortage has been mentioned by Kornai (1976, p. 339) when he points out that the extent of queuing is not a very good indicator of shortages:

> Exactly at times of growing shortages [it is] that people are inclined to join several queues simultaneously. E.g., in Hungary they put down their names for a car, a co-operative flat and foreign exchange for tourist purposes, although they know that if all three of their requirements were fulfilled at the same time, they could not pay for them. In this way a multiplied fictitious demand presents itself, which is not co-ordinated with the actual budget of the buyer.

ON THE POSSIBILITY OF MEASURING REPRESSED INFLATION

We should like to leave a closer examination of inflation in the Soviet Union to economists, but we want to stress that price inflation, indeed, does not have the same importance there as in Western societies. Official data, showing almost nonexisting price increases in the last 20 years may only tell us half the story because price indexes refer to old brands while new brands are distributed at higher prices but with only slight modifications (Schroeder, 1975), yet, price inflation is very low compared to capitalist societies (Nove, 1979, pp. 180–84). When Western researchers constructed an indicator to avoid the flaws of the official Soviet one, a price inflation of only about 1 percent (or 1.3 percent) per year could be found (Schroeder, Severin, 1976, p. 631). Therefore researchers have warned not to overestimate "hidden" price inflation in the Soviet Union (Thieme, 1980, p. 53).

The maintenance of a certain price level is possible only by huge state subsidies. The cost of agriculture is enormous and amounts to one-third of all investments. The subsidy to livestock raising now amounts to 23,000 million rubles per year (Nove, 1980, p. 9).

Now we turn to the assessment of repressed inflation. Lately economists have noted a growing rate of savings in socialist societies. A recent source gave a figure of 8 percent of the total money income of the population in the USSR by the end of 1975 (Fedorenko, Rimashevskaia, 1979, p. 205). This would make Laski's figure of 4.2 percent for 1971–75 a rather conservative estimate and more or less in the same range as the figures given for Poland (Laski, 1977, pp. 22–24). Another sociological investigation tells us that in 1968 money savings were not very popular. Even among the affluent groups of the population only 11.7 percent showed inclinations to save money; it is said that this attitude was changing by 1976 (Zhilina, Sokolov, 1980, p. 54). When all savings on state accounts were taken together and compared with the total sum of earnings, the share of savings was 31 percent in 1971–75 and only 13 percent in 1961. The savings of the population enabled the state to finance 43 percent of the short-term credits in the economy in 1971 and 60 percent in 1976 (Fedorenko, Rimashevskaia, 1979, p. 205). The question remains. Does a rise in savings necessarily indicate repressed inflation. Compared to German data on savings and assets, one can see that in this society with inflationary rather than deflationary tendencies, savings rose from 60,000 German marks per capita in 1953 to 290,000 in 1973 or almost five times. Although these data pertain only to savings recorded for taxation and therefore give hardly any indication of the actual amount of total savings, they may serve to show that an increase in savings may be an indicator of repressed inflation but not sufficient to assess its magnitude (*Gesellschaftliche Daten* — Bundesrepublik Deutschland, 1977, p. 180). In the German Federal Republic savings and assets amounted to 145 billion marks they were only 14.4 billion (Russian milliards) in the Soviet Union in 1978, thus exceeding total retail sales (9.2 billions) by 56 percent (Vogel, 1979, p. 165). The ratio of savings seems to be smaller in socialist societies than in market economies. It cannot tell us very much about inflationary pressures. (Thieme, 1980, p. 57) because it is dependent on cultural values, as could be shown in the comparison of savings rates in the United States and Germany (as presented by Professor Katona in this book).

Another way of grasping the phenomenon of repressed inflation has been seen in the differences between state prices and prices on the "free" market of kolkhoz farmers. The discrepancy between state-fixed and free prices reached an almost 1:2 in 1976 (Nove, 1979, p. 185), but the share of kolkhoz market in total food distribution was only 4.4 percent in 1970 and 4.0 percent in 1971 (Levin, 1973, p. 131).

Other possibilities of deducing repressed inflation (see also Laski, 1977, p. 6) in the Soviet Union are of a more or less impressionistic character. For example, reference is often made to queues in front of shops or waiting lists for goods. For the latter, Kornai's comment on fictitious demand by multiple inscription in these lists must be born in mind; the queues in front of shops could at least partly be explained by other social variables:

1. The aforementioned impressions often refer to cities like Leningrad and Moscow. While these are relatively privileged in supply, and people do queue because they still expect some food, whereas they might not queue in Sverdlovsk because they know there is no food. These cities are also characterized by an immense density of population. The 6 square meters per capita of living space reported as an average for Leningrad and Moscow in 1965 (Trufanov, 1973, p. 130) has led to a dense agglomeration in the city centers. About 1250 people inhabit a square kilometer in German cities, but there are 6000–7000 inhabitants in Moscow's center (Saushkin, 1964, p. 197). With a population density like this, the existing shops must always be crowded even if one does not take into account the high number of commuters coming to the city only to shop.

2. Under conditions of limited information on the quality and prices of goods on the market it is well known in Western sociology concerning consumer behavior that customers often only orient themselves by the size, market share, or, esteem of the supplier although this may say nothing about the quality or pricing of the goods. We should allow for different kinds of "irrational" consumer behavior in the USSR. Given a

very low level of advertising or supplier competition, the customer there is often quite well advised to take the length of a queue as a functional equivalent to advertising. This argument is backed by Soviet studies on the most efficient forms of advertising: in one of these studies it was shown that by far the best effects were obtained by billboards and loudspeaker announcements in the large shops. Customers in the USSR are more ready to react immediately in the shops and not to hitherto unknown spots on radio or television and or to propaganda in newspapers and journals. Often a prestige component is added when something is obtained which everybody knows it is difficult to get. Thus hunting for prestigious restaurants definitely is such a "sport" (for excellent examples see W. Fisher's guide to Moscow restaurants, 1974).

Thus queues indicate shortage but not repressed inflation. And if these indicators sometimes seem impressionistic, why not tell the whole story?

SOME NOTES ON WELL-BEING, POVERTY, AND CONSUMPTION

In discussing models of repressed inflation in various socialist systems, economists sometimes tend to neglect the empirical evidence of the living standards in these societies. A thorough analysis of poverty, welfare, and economic inequality in the Soviet Union was recently presented by the British sociologist Alaistair McAuley (1979). His analysis of mostly aggregate data of the Soviet Central Statistical Office can be supplemented by some of my previous studies (1977; forthcoming in the United States, 1980), based mainly on reanalysis of Soviet sociological surveys. Some new data were also given in a recent Soviet publication (Fedorenko, Rimashevskaia, 1979) and can be compared — showing a high degree of congruence, by the way — to a survey among Soviet emigrants to Israel by G. Ofer and A. Vinokur (1979).

We restrict ourselves in this necessarily short account to workers and employees (state-employed) and do not take into consideration rural living standards, especially of the kolkhoz membership which are usually not included in the same categories in national surveys. When *earnings* or *wages* and *salary* are referred to, we usually, in this paper, have in mind earnings from employment including premiums, not however, income from secondary economic activity, which can be assessed only in the study of Ofer and by some scarce evidence from Soviet surveys (Chansen, 1975).

As a basis for determining purchasing power, it is often better to depart from the total or per capita income of the household. These income figures also include transfer payments like pensions and stipends. Because we are not interested here in a closer examination of regional variation in income we leave these aspects out of the discussion of repressed inflation and well-being.

Because there was only a slight increase in prices, Soviet economists assumed in 1965–67 a minimum budget of per capita income of 50 rubles. That is still in use today although some authors in 1972 claimed a budget of 70–75 rubles to be more realistic as a minimum for material satisfaction (Gordon, Klopov, 1972, p. 36). In the late 1960s, 59 percent of this 50 ruble budget was used for food, drink, and tobacco, 27 percent, for clothing and furniture, and 14 percent for rent and other utilities (McAuley, 1979, p. 17).

In 1965 in the USSR 76.8 percent of the family budget was spent on clothing, food, and beverages; a family in Great Britain then needed only 40 percent of its income to buy these items (Beyme, 1975, p. 201). Comparison of the food consumed also reflects a low level of Soviet nutrition. In the USSR in 1973 twice as much bread and potatoes was consumed as in the United States or Germany while meat consumption was only half of that of the United States or 66 percent of that of Germany (Bush, 1975, p. 57).

This high amount of food expenditure is an indicator in E. Engel's law for groups living at the borderline of physical existence. At this low level this law postulates a steep rise in food expenditures with increasing income, the rise then reaches a limit, and costs for food decline as income grows. This level however evidently is not yet reached in the Soviet Union, because workers earning higher wages still spend increasing amounts of income on food. In a 1974 survey the personal expenditure on food was higher among scientific personnel than among workers with lower wages (Pokrovskaia, 1976, p. 170). Some Western researchers have commented on the high income elasticity for food in the USSR (Nove, 1979, p. 188, especially referring to meat). Even in the emigrant-study of mostly Jewish people who spend much less on liquor, food and beverages amounted to 50 percent of the budget (Ofer, 1979, p. 59).

Given the relatively high number of people living below the poverty line, which even among the urban population is about one-third to two-fifths (McAuley, chap. 4, p. 305), "excess demand" seems too strong a word except for food, especially meat and fruits, which then take up most of their total income. Against the interpretation presented here, one might object that although some are poor, others are very rich and do exert excess demand, or one can point to existing possibilities of secondary earnings not listed in official Soviet income statistics.

Following the first objection, one would have to assume a highly skewed distribution of incomes, with the mode far out on the left side, a relatively flat middle, and a mean much distorted to the right by high upper incomes. This is not the case, however, as will be shown after examining whether subsidiary earnings radically change the pattern of poverty or relatively low well-being.

Some scarce data do in fact identify some secondary earnings, but these are not sufficiently large to alter the picture substantially. Data on the extent of secondary earnings gave figures of about 6–8 percent of all employed in the 1960s. This seems to be more common among the intelligentsia and a necessity in some families with children or other dependents. Only in a survey in Estonia, conducted in 1973, about one-fifth of the employed had a secondary job, either doing a second task within their employing organization or enterprise (*sovmestitel'-stvo*) —9 percent of the employed — or taking up a second job with another employer — as did 5 percent (39 percent of these were working for private people); both alternatives occurred for 4 percent of the cases in this survey. The same survey showed that the intelligentsia preferred a secondary job in their employing organization. They had to work longer for less money (0.8 rubles per hour) than the workers, often doing some kind of repair or craft-type work for private persons where they earned 1.4 rubles an hour. The monthly returns from secondary jobs in the organization were 49 rubles; returns from a second employer were 33 rubles. Of the latter group, however, only 45 percent earned more than 20 rubles a month. In most cases, the situation of the family forced the breadwinner to take up another job, and this kind of secondary employment was much more common among 25–39-year-old men; thus, secondary employment was sought mostly out of material necessity and not really to achieve a state of "luxury" (Chansen, 1975, pp. 120–23).

Ofer's questionnaire of Soviet emigrants to Israel can be used to test the reliability of the Soviet data, although this survey is strongly biased in favor of white-collar employees. Surprisingly, his data are in about the same range, giving a figure of about 18 rubles a month from secondary work (Ofer, 1979, p. 34). Wages from the main place of work constitute the biggest share, with 91 percent of all earnings from this work (*ibid.*, p. 42).

The other objection, referring to wide discrepancies of purchasing power among social groups will be examined now. The argument of excess purchasing power certainly holds for an elite of perhaps half a million people, having more than 400 rubles per capita a month. But McAuley argues after his thorough analysis: "The elite is so small numerically that substantially different assumptions about its income have a barely perceptible impact on average living standards (1979, p. 67). A similar objection to substantial money overhang of the strata above the poverty level can be raised when Soviet income distribution is compared to that of other countries. The degree of inequality, measured in the upper and lower decentile distance was extremely low in the data from 1968, which McAuley mainly uses for his computations (1:2.83; see Fedorenko, Rimashevskaia, 1979, p. 90). It probably increases somewhat more than was conceded in McAuley's further estimate (3.14–3.21, p. 66) to 1:3.46 in 1976 (Fedorenko, Rimashevskaia, 1979, p. 95). In any case it is smaller than the income difference in the United States, which was 1:6.7 in 1968 (Wiles, 1974, p. 48). Having three times more income than the lower third of those 30 percent below the poverty level does not mean that this population group is living in "abundance." Although rents are low and services take up only about 10 percent of income (e.g., transport, community services, cultural activities, see Kocherga, 1979, p. 133), people have to choose their purchases, except food items, carefully.

In a typical Moscow housing area in 1976 440 families were interviewed and classified according to their per capita income. The per capita income was less than 60 rubles in 23.9 percent of all families although Moscow employees are considered to be comparatively well off. Only 18 percent had more than 100 rubles per capita (Yankova, 1976, p. 9). Average earnings of men were 126 rubles, and women 111 rubles a month. More data from other surveys and cities do not alter this picture (Teckenberg, 1980, chap. 2.2). Even the total increase in earnings in the Soviet Union which is often said to be exceptionally high is not so impressive when compared to other countries, although one would have to subtract the amount of income in capitalist societies which is practically eaten up by inflation. Soviet average income rose from 71.8 rubles to 100 rubles between 1955 and 1966 (an increase of 39 percent) and from 122 to 146 between 1970 and 1975 (Narodnoe khoziaistvo, 1976, p. 546), an increase of 19.5 percent. Male workers in Germany, by comparison, experienced a gross wage increase from 430 (1955) to 895 marks in 1965 (108 percent) and between 1970 and 1975 (gross wage average for a male worker, 1868 marks), the wage level was raised by 47 percent (Gesellschaftliche Daten, 1979, p. 171). The increase in employee salaries was of about the same magnitude.

In 1966–70 the Soviet wage level increased faster than planned; it slowed down more quickly than the planned index between 1971 and 1975 (Nove, 1979, p. 185). Soviet authors sometimes criticize wage increases lagging the rising level of productivity (Trufanov, 1973, p. 60). One must point out that lately, however, wages have increased faster than the national income (GNP). These costly tendencies of satisfying state employees' earnings demands by raising the minimum wage to 60 rubles in 1968 and 70 rubles starting in 1970 cannot be maintained at the same pace.

In summarizing this chapter, one can say that on the basis of the income data a macroimbalance — where total demands exceed total supply — seems very unlikely. We probably should interpret queues and similar phenomena not in terms of excess purchasing power but of an extreme shortage of goods per se or of quality goods, when one assumes that a quality-conscious consumer has emerged in the Soviet Union, as might be argued, since many nonfood items are being unmarketable and in stock (12 percent in 1972; Schroeder, 1975, p. 42). Microimbalances, with some goods in excess supply, while others are scarce, seem more likely. Furthermore, some goods are in extremely short supply (like meat) because everybody wants them, but the shortage in some durables is difficult to assess because the prestigious, symbolic effect of these goods is not equally valued by all occupational groups. Particular tastes are something a shortage economy can be glad about but only if it can offer a wide range of different products so that each group can use other articles or symbols of its specific lifestyle and success. This is, however, hardly achievable in mass production.

ESTATIST LIFE STYLES: CONSUMPTION DIFFERENCES IN THE MIDDLE MASS

Some conflicts might arise in the Soviet Union over the distribution of income and wealth, but I should like to assert that these are not so important, given the relatively equal "well-being" of all. They are not as important as conflicts in the sphere of consumption as indications of special life styles, values, and preferences of certain groups. These differences can be conceptualized by Max Weber's term *estates* (later translated as status groups) as indicated earlier.

The limitation of access to goods and the social closure of certain privileged groups finds its clearest expression in the Soviet Union in the existence of closed shops. This, however, is only the most obvious indicator of the functioning of such a system. It operates only slightly differently in cities like Moscow, Leningrad, and Akademgorodok in the form of closed professional circles or associations, the writers' union, the architects' club, the restaurant with its exclusive cinema for people engaged in the film industry.

It would be wrong, however, to restrict the description of a "closed shop" system or of social closure only to the political elite. It is only less visible to observers walking through the shops, because in most cases, the services rendered or goods and information exchanged are distributed via the institution or enterprise where people work. This system functions for the working class as well and is bound to the financial strength or connections (Russ.: "blat") that go along with their institutional affiliation. It then depends very much on the "cleverness" of the administration or the consumption funds of the enterprise to organize the closed distribution for "their" workers, as is suggested in a Soviet study (Pokrovskaia, 1976, p. 171). In fact, this mechanism might bridge the interest gap between the worker's role as a producer and as a consumer; the more or the better the output produced by a worker, the higher the enterprise's profit and the more it can redistribute either in kind or in money. One might add that some researchers — Hensel in Germany; see also Haffner, 1980, p. 13 — argue that central planning would be possible or even better by planning and accounting with values in kind! A closed system of production and consumption might resolve the conflict of interest between consumers and producers but it would lead to greater competition between enterprises for scarce labor, greater effort, and lack of coordination. If the particular interests of each enterprise and its employees were acknowledged, the disparities among them and the living standards of their employees would further increase (Kuczynski, 1978).

Some variations in values and tastes as far as consumption is concerned are visible to everyone traveling through the USSR. The youth culture is trying to acquire Western life-styles; and that which no cultural exchange program could achieve is symbolized by disco and blue jeans. These symbols of certain milieus are often traded; meanwhile, the cultural intelligentsia distributes rare books within their circles, often gaining some additional income by renting books out for a night. The prestige of books, especially fiction and belles-lettres is growing, those dealing with social and political topics went down from 11.8 percent in 1966 to 9.4 in 1978, as a survey among 10,000 readers showed (Chernova, 1980, p. 128): Possessing a book like Bulgakov's *Master and Margerita* which is not "forbidden," just printed in a very small edition, is a symbol of very high prestige among the cultural intelligentsia. Given at least some possibility of choice in purchasing, access to goods — often mediated by connections and friends with a similar value orientation — is a more important privilege than money alone. The existence of different value systems building the base for desire to buy different goods was recently stressed by Soviet sociologist Titma (et. al., 1979, p. 108).

If we look at differences in consumption more closely, we notice that there is still no sign of abundance. Some basic foods are cheap, but eggs, meat, and fruit are twice as often on the table of families whose per capita income exceeds 100 rubles as on that of those with only up to 50 rubles (Komarov, Cherniavskii, 1973, p. 198). In many surveys, food was seen as the most important factor of expenditure, but for durables and services there were great variations according to preferences as can be seen from Table 1.

More variations in preferences between the strata are discernable, as will be shown in further data, yet it is important to note that even in comparable income groups preferences may be markedly different. The following data show the cultural distance between workers and lower white-collar employees. Although the latter often earn less or about the same as workers, their styles can be differentiated by a greater import-

Table 1. **Variation of Consumer Preferences (rank order) in the Research and Production Department of a Large Trust, 1974–75** (Pokrovskaja, 1976, 164)

	Workers	Semiprofessionals, Assistants	Professional Researchers
Food	1	1	1
Furniture, carpets	3	4	8
Tape-recorder,	6	9	4
color TV	4	3	5
Books	7	5	3
Tourism			

ance attached to cultural activities and reading. Workers prefer the cinema; white-collar employees go to the theater more often (Pokrovskaia, 1976, p. 175). Material well-being is demonstrated by workers more by expenditures on carpets (Zhilina, Sokolov, 1980, p. 56), and electric household equipment (Yankova, 1976, p. 52) and they therefore are reluctant to use the public laundry; white-collar employees try to economize on these items and buy books instead. But even in professional circles the differences in lifestyle preferences are quite marked. For example, principals of schools and directors of enterprises had very different free time budgets: school principals spent most of their free time reading (43.3 percent); enterprise directors watched television most of the time (35.6 percent). There was a variation in other interests as well as in going to public entertainments (cinema and theater) which took up about 10 percent of school principals' free time but was of no great importance for the heads of enterprises (Kuchkina, 1976, p. 98). The differential distribution of household equipment was also brought to light in an international time-budget study (Table 2).

In a large survey in the Leningrad machine construction industry in 1965, the industrial personnel were asked about their household equipment and their per capita income. The data are presented in Table 3. The equipment was classified according to the following four indexes:

1. Radio, TV, sewing-machine
2. Camera, washing-machine, scooter, or motorcycle
3. Vacuum cleaner, refrigerator, accordion
4. Tape-recorder, car, piano

The table displays a considerable variation in lifestyle indexes which is not really reflected to such an extent in income. It is noteworthy, that the per capita size of the apartment is larger among unskilled and lower-skilled employees than among workers, although those in pro-

Table 2. Standard of Living Indicators by Occupation; Pskov (P), USSR and Jackson (J), U.S. (Szalai, 1972, 541) — in percent

Occupational Group:	Bathroom Facilities*		Telephone		More than 100 Books		Personal Car		TV	
	P	J	P	J	P	J	P	J	P	J
Professionals	65	99	16	48	21	44	4	98	58	98
Low white-collar technical	49	98	6	59	10	23	3	97	52	99
Skilled worker	33	93	2	61	3	15	1	98	52	99
Unskilled worker	28	92	3	48	1	10	1	83	29	100

*consisting of running water, lavatory, etc.

Table 3. Lifestyle Index, per capita Income, and Apartment Size in the Leningrad Machine Construction Industries (Trufanov, 1973, 131)

	Index in percent of each group				Per capita Housing Space	Income
	1	2	3	4		
1. Unskilled laborers	44.2	41.7	11.8	2.3	6.1	60.9
2. Unskilled nonmanual	43.3	40.6	13.1	3.0	6.6	58.5
3. Operators	43.8	40.6	13.4	2.2	6.0	64.6
4. Skilled workers (craft type)	41.7	40.0	15.5	2.8	6.2	62.3
5. Skilled workers in auto production	40.8	38.9	16.7	3.6	6.4	62.6
6. Qualified semiprofessional	38.2	37.0	19.1	5.7	6.8	67.2
7. Professionals, science	35.9	34.5	22.8	6.8	6.7	72.2
8. Supervisors, directors	37.3	37.3	19.8	5.6	6.8	71.1
mean:	40.7	39.6	15.7	4.0	6.3	63.3

duction have a higher income. This was confirmed in other studies (Vasil'eva, 1973, p. 103). Housing in a survey conducted in a large trust and its research department was better among the semiprofessional assistants and engineers, nevertheless, they expressed less satisfaction, which clearly shows the higher importance attached to private living space (Pokrovskaia, 1976, p. 172).

Even if the disposable income of lower employees is smaller than workers', they try to economize by not buying many of the durables, especially television sets, and prefer spending their money on books, for instance. This is often seen by Soviet researchers in connection with the parental values of stressing self-development and better educational attainment for their children, which then in effect shapes the cultural milieu of the next generation (Vasil'eva, 1973, pp. 19–34).

In discerning a material component of lifestyles and a cultural component due to special estatist beliefs among occupational groups, one can better predict their consumer behavior. It is important to note that differences in consumption patterns may be influenced by education more strongly than by variation in income. (This can be shown by analysis of the actual correlations, as in Table 4.) That is why the Czech sociologists Šafář and Machonin spoke of a cultural differentiation of lifestyles and behavior. Although we do not question this thesis in general, we doubt whether this dimension of differentiation is less pronounced in nonsocialist societies. Given smaller variations in income, however, in socialist societies these symbols of estatist lifestyles, following Weber, can be used to demonstrate:

> A typically effective claim to positive or negative privilege with respect to social prestige so far as it rests on one or more of the following bases: (a) mode of living, (b) formal processes of education which may consist in empirical or rational training and the acquisition of the corresponding modes of life, or (c) on the prestige of birth or of an occupation (Weber, 1947, p. 393).

J. Krejčí points to a similar development for Czech society:

> In the living standard, however, . . . this homogenisation was reflected in the basic material consumption such as food and basic industrial goods rather than in the consumption of cultural goods and services and the style of life connected with this (1972, p. 41).

Table 4 is appropriate as a short summary of this chapter. Income varies more clearly with sociooccupational grouping, where by definition the lower employees are ranked only in the second lowest position; per capita income reflects educational differences, thus presenting the blue-collar–white-collar gap. Income varies quite markedly with age, indicating the seniority principle in Soviet industry. The index of household equipment is greatly determined by cultural status. Possession of books and reading were also determined by education, reflecting estatist preferences more than material distinction.

The Soviet study did not control whether the distribution of per capita income highly covarying with education might be the actual underlying dimension.

Now we can sum up our findings in the light of the three questions listed at the beginning. We do not agree that in the case of the Soviet

Table 4. Correlations between Some Characteristics of Social and Demographical Factors of the Kazan' Population in 1967 (Trufanov, 1973, 82)

	Income	Per Capita Income	Possess Private Plot	Housing Space per capita	Equip- ment Index*	Books Pos- sessed	Reading News
Socio-occupa- tional group†	0.255	0.122	0.054	0.093	0.156	0.188	0.166
Education (years)	0.160	0.122	0.050	0.094	0.165	0.235	0.198
Nationality	0.079	0.039	0.030	0.053	0.076	0.084	0.092
Age	0.161	0.094	0.060	0.088	0.084	0.085	0.060

It is difficult to compare the reported Tschuproff coefficients to any measure used in American studies.

*Index from Table 3.

†The classification from Table 3 is used. Because lower white collars in this grouping are ranked in the second lowest position, but were known to have more housing space and better equipment, more books, etc., this might severely lower the correlations between socioeconomic groups and the other items.

Union one can speak of any excess demand, at least not if a sociological and comparative perspective is chosen. The demand for food and some basic articles of daily use is, for a large part of the population, at a level necessary for subsistence. As far as durables and household equipment are concerned, we may say that people have to economize on these items generally because most of the family budget is spent on food and necessary clothing. Poverty is often connected with having many children or other dependents who are not sufficiently subsidized by the state by transfer payments (McAuley, 1979, p. 298). This situation forces most women into the labor force and/or men to take up a secondary job. This is probably why, at the present level of consumption, one can not really say that the high income attainment and lack of purchasing possibilities will at the present time cause the participation rate in the labor force to go down. There may be an *ex post* correlation between wage level and declining employment rates (Howard, 1976), but this might be caused by other factors. In fact the labor force is still growing although the limits become visible, and more intensive growth a necessity. Capital investment for a further increase of the employment ratio in fact, becomes irrationally high (Hoehmann, Seidenstecher, 1978, p. 53), and with the exceptionally high inclusion of women in the labor force the limits of extensive labor growth become apparent.

The preceding remarks mainly pertained to an absolute shortage of goods and income, but we also know that about two-thirds of the population are living above the poverty level. Although income differences among this "middle mass" are not very marked, their lifestyles and consumption preferences clearly set apart social groups, which reflect mainly differences in milieu and education. In the German Democratic Republic some conclusions have been drawn from this heterogenization and some analysis of consumer behavior has begun in order, it is said, to serve for further planning in the sphere of distribution (Ludz, 1980, pp. 294–98). At the moment, no such approaches are discernable in the Soviet Union. In cases of consumer rebellion or critical demands, the state has often relied on the functioning of a secondary distribution system via services and payments in kind and on the more direct feedback system inside very large enterprises, thus creating enclaves which become more independent of the planning center by developing and taking up not only production but also distributive functions to a considerable degree (Teckenberg, 1980, chap. 1.2.2). This might cease to function, when demands rise and then include, for example, electrical equipment. But demands are increasing, and thus the exploration of consumer behavior might become more important. This is reflected in some articles from the latest issue of the Soviet Sociological Association's journal. In a survey conducted in 1968, it reported, a tape-recorder was considered to be absolutely necessary by only 1 percent of the parents of secondary school graduates. More than 30 percent of the parents and 42 percent of the pupils, however, considered this a necessity in 1978. In connection with these developments, Soviet sociologists warn that the "commercial ideology of youth deforms their personality."

Thus a main problem of socialist societies will emerge more clearly in subsequent years: it is not really the transformation of the property relationships in the sphere of production that is problematic, but rather "rational" and accepted restrictions and redistribution principles in the sphere of distribution that will lead to conflicts. Contrary to earlier expectations, the changes in the sphere of production did not lead automatically to "rational" insights of the *summum bonum* by a new socialist personality.

References

Adam, Jan. *Wage Control and Inflation in the Soviet Bloc Countries* (London, 1979).

Beyme, Klaus von. *Ökonomie und Politik im Sozialismus* (Munich, 1975).

Bondarčik, V. K. *Izmeneniia v bytu i kul'ture gorodskogo naseleniia Belorussii* (Minsk, 1976).

Bush, Keith. "Soviet Living Standards — Some Salient Data," *Economic Aspects of Life in the USSR* (Brussels, 1975), pp. 49–64.

Chansen, Ch. "Prirabotok i ego sotsial'no-ekonomicheskie problemy" in Iu. Iu. Kachk (Ed.), Sotsial'naia struktura, trud, svobodnoe vremia (Talin, 1975), pp. 112–29.

Chernova, N. V. "Izuchenie faktorov opredeliaiushchikh spros na knizhnuiu produktsiiu," Sotsiologicheskie issledovaniia 1 (1980): 127–29.

Fedorenko, N. P., and Rimashevskaia, N. M. Potrebnosti, dokhody i potreblenie (Moscow, 1979).

Fisher, Wesley, and Fisher, Lynn. The Moscow gourmet — Dining Out in the Capital of the USSR (Ann Arbor, Mich., 1974).

Gesellschaftliche Daten Bundesrepublik Deutschland. Presse- und Informationsamt der Bundesregierung (Bonn, 1979).

Gordon, L. A. and Klopov, È. V. Chelovek posle raboty (Moscow, 1978).

Haffner, F. "Erklärungsmomente für nationale und monetäre Disproportionen aus einer Theorie der unvollkommenen Planwirtschaft" in K. E. Schenk (Ed.), Lenkungsprobleme und Inflation (Berlin, 1980).

Hoehmann, H.-H., and Seidenstecher, G. "Sowjetunion" in Hoehmann (Ed.), Die Wirtschaft Osteuropas und der Volksrepublik China 1970–80 (Stuttgart, 1978), pp. 9–58.

Holzman, F. D. "Soviet inflationary pressures, 1928–57. Causes and Cures," Quarterly Journal of Economics 74 (1960): 167–88.

Howard, D. H. "The Disequilibrium Model in a Controlled Economy," American Economic Review 66 (1976): 871–79.

Iankova, Z. A. Mikroraion bol'shogo goroda: Sem'ia i byt (Moscow, 1976).

Ioffe, M. Ia. and Usov, V. V. "Sotsiologicheskie issledovaniia effektivnosti reklamy," Sotsiologicheskie issledovaniia 1 (1980): 122–26.

Kocherga, A. I. Sfera obsluzhivaniia naseleniia (Moscow, 1979).

Komarov, V. E. and Cherniavskii, U. G. Dokhody i potreblenie naseleniia (Moscow, 1973).

Kornai, J. "The Measurement of Shortage," Acta Oeconomica 16 (1976): 321–44.

Krejcí, J. Social Change and Stratification in Postwar Czechoslovakia (London, 1972).

Kuchkina, V. N. "Biuzhet vremeni rukovoditelia shkoly kak sredstvo opisaniia ego obraza zhizni" Sverdlovskii gos. pedagogicheskii institut. Nauchnye trudy 276 (1976): 85–99.

Kuczynski, W. "The State Enterprise under Socialism," Soviet Studies 30 (1978): 313–35.

Laski, K. Inflationsprobleme in den sozialistischen Ländern, Wiener Institut für Wirtschaftsvergleiche, Bericht, No. 38, 1977.

Levin, A. I. Sotsialisticheskii vnutrennii rynok (Moscow, 1973).

Ludz, P. C. Mechanismen der Herrschaftssicherung — Eine sprachpolitische Analyse gesellschaftlichen Wandels in der DDR (Munich, Vienna, 1980).

McAuley, Alastair. Economic Welfare in the Soviet Union: Poverty, Living Standards and Inequality (Madison, Wisc., 1979).

Nove, Alec. Political Economy and Soviet Socialism (London, 1980); "Problems and Prospects of the Soviet Economy," New Left Review, January–February, 1979, pp. 3–19.

Ofer, G. and Vinokur, A. Family Budget Survey of Soviet emigrants in the Soviet Union, Hebrew University Paper No. 32, Jerusalem, 1979.

Pokrovskaia, M. V. "Sotsial'naia differentsiatsiia lichnykh potrebnostei i sover-shenstvovanie planirovaniia ikh razvitiia na predpriiatii" in I. V. Bestu-zhev-Lada (Ed.), *Prognozirovanie sotsial'nykh potrebnostei* (Moscow, 1976), pp. 167–79.

Saushkin, Iu. G. *Moskva — Geograficheskie kharakteristika* (Moscow, 1964).

Schenk, K. E. (Ed.). *Lenkungsprobleme und Inflation in Planwirtschaften* (Berlin, 1980).

Scherhorn, G. "Konsum" in René König (Ed.), *Handbuch der empirischen Sozialforschung* (Stuttgart, 1977), 11:193–265.

Schroeder, G. "Consumer Goods Availability and Repressed Inflation in the Soviet Union" in *Economic Aspects of Life in the USSR* (Brussels, 1975), pp. 37–47.

Severin, B. "Soviet Consumption and Income Policies in Perspective" in *Soviet Economy in a New Perspective*, Joint Economic Committee, United States Congress (Washington, 1976), pp. 620–60.

Szalai, A. (Ed.). *The Use of Time — Daily Activities of Urban and Suburban Populations in 12 Countries* (The Hague, 1972).

Teckenberg, W. *The Social Structure of the Soviet Working Class in International Comparison. Towards an Estatist Society?* (forthcoming as special issue of the *International Journal of Sociology*) In German "Die soziale Struktur der sowjetischen Arbeiterklasse im internationalen Vergleich" (Munich, Vienna, 1977, 1980).

Thieme, J. "Probleme der Definition und Messung von Inflation in Systemen zentraler Planung" in Schenk, pp. 45–70.

Titma, M. Ch. and Sil'dmjae, T. I. "Faktory formirovaniia domashnei predmetnoi sredy" in *Sotsiologicheskie issledovaniia* No. 3 (1979): 108–115.

Trufanov, I. P. *Problemy byta gorodskogo naseleniia SSSR* (Leningrad, 1973).

Vasil'eva, È. K. *Sotsial'no-professional'nyi uroven' gorodskoi molodezhi* (Leningrad, 1973).

Vogel, H. "Konsum und Wirtschaftswachstum in der Sowjetunion" in Bundesinstitut für ostwissenschaftliche und internationale Studien, *Sowjetunion 1978/79* (Munich, 1979), pp. 160–66.

Weber, Max. *The Theory of Social and Economic Organization* (London, 1947).

Wiles, P. *Distribution of Income: East and West* (Amsterdam, 1974).

Zhilina, L. N. and Sokolov, V. M. "Problemy formirovaniia razumykh potrebnostei v material'nykh blagach," *Sotsiologicheskie issledovaniia* 1 (1980): 52–59.

A Contribution to the Study of Inflation in the Interwar Period*

HERMAN VAN DER WEE

The decades immediately preceding World War I are generally considered the high point in the orderly development of the international monetary system. This balanced development is often ascribed to the operation of the gold standard, but in fact, the monetary system operated in a much more complex way both domestically and abroad. There was very little resemblance to the automatism that is the essence of the gold standard according to the manuals.

In this short contribution, I shall sketch the evolution of the money base in Belgium between 1918 and 1940. In particular, I shall indicate the pattern of Belgian money creation between the two world wars, the international events that influenced it in this period, and the precise consequences for the evolution and composition of the total money supply and the policy interventions of the national bank.

The money-creating activity of the national bank must be treated in any study of the money base. The counterpart of the money base is divided into three major components, each of which, in turn, refers to other determinants. The claims of the monetary authorities abroad, or the international reserves, are dominated by developments in the balance of payments; the claims on the government are conditioned by the evolution of the budget; and the claims on the private sector are a reflection of the tightness of the money market and the national bank's own discount policy. Figure 1 traces the evolution of these three major components and the influence of the most important national and international political and monetary events.

The rate of expansion of the money base over the entire period was markedly greater than that of the total money supply because of the downward trend of the money base multiplier after 1929. Unlike other periods of history, strong monetary fluctuations were common during the period between the two world wars.

With respect to the money base, 1914–1940 can be divided into various subperiods. Table 1 gives the fluctuations of the money base for each of these periods and their causes.

The first period ended in July 1919. The enormous expansion of the money base — from 3.3 to 7.2 billion francs (31 October 1918–30 June

1919) — was due almost entirely to money creation by the national bank for the government. Because of the war, the credit granted by the national bank to the government had risen to 6.4 billion francs by mid-1919. This represented no less than 87 percent of the total money base, which indicates the minimal importance of the other two components.

Fluctuations of the Money Base and Their Causes: December 1913–April 1940

Period		Changes (million francs)		
	Money Base	Claims Abroad	Claims on the Private Sector	Claims on the Authorities
Jan. 1914–June 1919	+5,890	−302	−245	+6,288
July 1919–Dec. 1925	+1,222	+74	+1,701	−409
Jan. 1926–Oct. 1926	+2,212	+768	+405	+1,029
Nov. 1926–Dec. 1926	+181	+5,772	−1,509	−4,191
Jan. 1927–Dec. 1931	+9,469	+8,394	+1,241	−34
Jan. 1932–Dec. 1934	−690	−2,780	+1,599	+182
Jan. 1935–June 1935	+9,083	+10,306	−784	−322
July 1935–June 1937	−273	+961	−1,304	+121
July 1937–June 1938	−4,712	−5,960	+724	+733
July 1938–June 1939	+1,041	+1,681	−701	+66
July 1939–Apr. 1940	+7,072	+3,008	−59	+4,218
Jan. 1914–Apr. 1940	+30,495	+21,922	+1,068	+7,681

The second period runs from July 1919 to December 1925. The money base remained quite stable in this period. Despite numerous declarations of intent, the government did not succeed in perceptibly reducing its debt to the national bank with a view of bringing about the desired deflation. The money base even increased somewhat, largely because of an accumulation of credit in the private sector during the business revival of 1923. At this time, Belgium was operating under a floating exchange rate system; hence the gold and currency reserves of the national bank were shielded from international monetary events and had almost no influence on the movements of the money base. At least in principle, this did not have to be the case with floating exchange rates. The bank could, if it wished, influence the expansion or contraction of the exchange market and thereby the rate of the franc. This would also have led to corresponding money creation or money destruction to the same degree. In fact, this only occurred to a certain extent after 1925. The large dollar loan floated by the authorities at the end of 1924 and the middle of 1925, along with the foreign credits that the bank itself received in October and December 1925, provided the necessary currency reserves. With these reserves, the national bank carried out four major support interventions for the state: the first in May 1925, the second in November-December 1925, the third from the middle of January to the middle of March 1926, and the fourth on 12 July 1926. The first three were intended to maintain the exchange rate at 107 Fr per pound sterling, the rate proposed for stabilization. The last was done to "alleviate the panic" when the rate reached 240 Fr per pound.

Since the support interventions of the bank were entered into a separate account, they did not appear in the normal accounting. But there is no doubt that a considerable amount of Belgian francs were thus drained from the economy: between 15 May and 2 June 1925 and between 15 September 1925 and 15 March 1926, the interventions amounted to 276 million and 1900 million francs, respectively. The demand for repayment of treasury bonds, which had such a harmful effect on the stabilization policy of the government, probably ought to be attributed in part to the monetary effect of the support interventions, i.e., to the shrinking of the available money supply.

The third period in this phase of the monetary history of Belgium is formed by the first nine months of 1926, the year of stabilization. In this brief, rather dramatic period, the money base increased by 26 percent, an expansion set in motion by the massive resort to the national bank by the treasury, which was forced to this because the private banks, under the pressure of the great flight of capital, were no longer prepared to renew the floating public debt. Shortly thereafter, the money base received another stimulus when the private banks in their turn were obliged to appeal to the national bank to resolve their liquidity problems. The claims of the national bank on the private sector ultimately became an important source of currency creation during this nine-month period.

The period from October 1926 to May 1935 can be divided into four short evolutionary phases. The first phase was completely dominated by the stabilization of 25 October 1926. As is shown by Figure 1, the structure of the money base was completely changed by this monetary operation. The immediate easing of the money market enabled the banks to liquidate their debts to the national bank. The private component of the money base thus fell rather quickly back to the insignificant level of 1923. Because of the specific modalities of the stabilization, moreover, the government could drastically reduce its debt to the national bank, and the international component of the money base took on such importance that from then on it would almost completely dominate the movements of the money base.

First, the increase of the international reserves was determined by

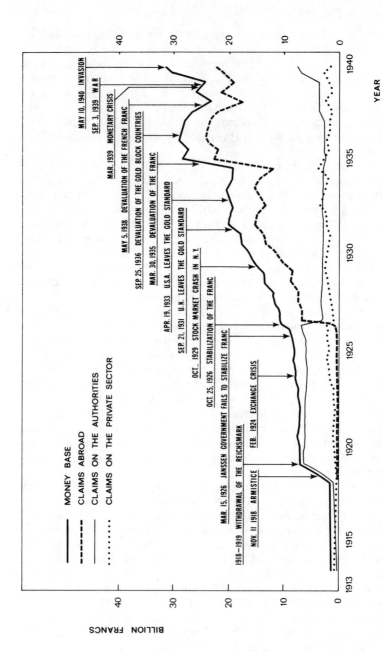

Fig. 1   Determinants of the Money Base : 1913–1940 (in billions of francs)

the foreign stabilization loan of the government, the proceeds of which were transferred to the national bank as repayment of the government's debt. Second, the increase was fed by the profits that flowed from the reevaluation of existing gold holdings. This profit accrued to the treasury, which transferred it to the national bank with the same purpose. Third, the increase was the result of the influence of the repatriation of capital that had already begun in the summer of 1926. According to an estimate of L. H. Dupriez, about 773 million francs were thus repatriated between April and 25 October 1926, and another 599 million francs between 26 October 1926 and 4 November 1926.

During the second phase, from the beginning of 1927 to July 1929, gold and currency reserves increased steadily: in these 30 months, they increased by 23 percent. The improvement in the balance of trade was a contributory factor, but the primary cause was the continuing inflow of capital. Foreign investors became interested in Belgian stocks, and Belgian companies issued their debenture loans abroad because of tax advantages and probably also because of the oligopolistic interest policy of the large Belgian banks.

The monetary authorities, fearing the possible inflationary effects of this behavior, tried to counteract it after 1927 with low discount rates, prohibition of foreign government loans, and a policy of gold sterilization whereby the national bank sold gold to the Postal Account Agency, the Treasury Fund, and some public credit institutions. This gold, supposedly, was to serve as a cover reserve for specific operations of these institutions. In addition, the repayment of a certain number of foreign government loans was accelerated.

The third phase, which extended from the second half of 1929 to September 1931, must be seen against the background of international events. Capital outflows to the United States quickly ceased with the stock market crisis in New York. At the same time, the uneasiness about the economic future of the Anglo-Saxon world led to a capital flight to countries with stronger currencies, among them being Belgium. Accordingly, there was a remarkable acceleration in the growth of Belgian gold and currency reserves. The stability of these capital flows is clearly illustrated by the events of the first half of 1919. In spite of the restrictive discount policy of the Federal Reserve System, the national bank had maintained its discount rate of 4 percent since July 1928. Thus, it became profitable to export short-term capital to the United States and to resort to the national bank to take care of the resulting liquidity shortage. This is clearly manifested in the increase of the private component of the money base in this period. The interest-induced speculative capital outflow was so strong that the money base even decreased in the first half of 1929.

Suspension of the gold standard by Great Britain in September 1931 introduced the fourth phase. Here a contrary evolution can be seen: the gold and currency reserves of the bank showed, for the first time, a serious tendency to decrease. This downward tendency was briefly interrupted by the inflow of flight capital from the United States that occurred between the abandonment of gold parity for the dollar on 19 April 1933 and the stabilization of the dollar in the beginning of 1934. Figure 1 clearly shows that the devaluation in the sterling countries constituted an initial turning point in the confidence in the future of the franc. The stabilization of the dollar was another definitive turning point.

The formation of the gold bloc could not reserve the fundamental and growing distrust in the franc. As a result, capital outflows gradually increased in intensity and took on menacing proportions after October 1934. The formation of the Theunis government, in which Francqui also participated, provided a glimmer of hope, which quickly faded. The gold losses from the national bank reached such a dramatic high point in March 1935 — 280 million francs worth of gold were withdrawn in two hours on 16 March — that devaluation of the franc was inevitable.

The movements of the bank's cover reserve, therefore, played a decisive role in the monetary events during the periods of world boom and depression, and the change in the international component of the money base was the reason for the decision in March 1935 to devaluate.

Figure 1 also shows that, for the entire 1926–35 period, neither the public nor the private component was as important as the international reserves. But it can be noted that the claims on the private sector in these years reflected inversely, as it were, what was happening on the international level: the three peaks in the private component of the money base coincide with low points of the international reserves. In the first half of 1929, it was largely a matter of capital flight caused by the interest policy of the national bank. The peak in 1932 is associated with the deleterious effects on the Belgian economy of the floating pound sterling. The record granting of credit in the beginning of 1935 is accounted for by the contraction of the money market as a consequence of the capital flight that preceded the devaluation. As regards the public component, Figure 1 shows hardly any movement in this period. The repayments of the public debt via the Fund for the Discharge of the Public Debt were, indeed, too small to restrain monetary expansion perceptibly. The claims on the authorities even increased slightly as a result of the sterling losses in 1931.

The devaluation of March 1935 ushers in the last period: 1935–40. During this period, the gold reserves of the bank continued to have a strong effect on the evolution of the money base. The gold supply increased by 82 percent in the first three months after the devaluation, and in July 1935 it represented almost 80 percent of the money base. The reasons for this exceptionally rapid expansion must be sought, first of all, in the repatriation of Belgian flight capital that had been waiting abroad for a devaluation profit. Moreover, the devaluation of the Belgian franc held out the prospect of analogous adjustment of the exchange rates of other currencies in the gold bloc. The national bank, therefore, had to cope with the rush of flight capital from the gold bloc countries and particularly from France. Since this capital was only seeking protection against the danger of devaluation, the banks hesitated to put it into long-term investments, keeping it liquid or investing it only on a short-term basis. The current account of the private sector in the national bank thus went from 927 million francs on 28 March 1935 to 6860 million francs on 13 June 1935.

The banks had judged the situation correctly. After the French devaluation in 1936, which was followed by devaluations in the other gold bloc countries, the capital flowed out again. The decline of the bank's cover reserve once again took on frightening proportions after 1937. Between 1 January 1937 and 30 June 1938, the gold supply declined by more than 26 percent. The persistent weakness of the French franc, to which the future of the Belgian franc was wrongly linked, was a contributory factor. Of no less importance, however, was the increasing danger of war. The *Anschluss* of Austria on 11 March 1938 and the invasion of Czechoslovakia shortly thereafter led to a general capital flight from Europe to America. In May 1938, the crisis reached a high point when the French franc was devalued again. Fear of a devaluation of the Belgian franc was so great that the cover reserve of the national bank declined by 3.9 billion francs between 5 and 19 May 1938.

Thanks to the energetic policy of the bank, the recovery did not have long to wait. Nonetheless, the period was fundamentally uncertain so that new foreign and domestic tensions again led to severe monetary disturbances in the beginning of 1939. Between the beginning of February and the beginning of May 1939, the national bank lost roughly 4.4 billion francs in gold and currency reserves. Curiously enough, the declaration of war in September 1939 was not accompanied by a mass exodus of capital. Instead, the bank's cover reserve held at a satisfactory level and soon began to increase. Undoubtedly, the large balance of payments surplus contributed significantly to this development. Presumably, too, the danger of maritime transport had a favorable effect, along with Belgium's ability to maintain its neutrality until May 1940 while most of the surrounding countries already were at war.

The money base evolution thus again began to increase during the second half of 1939. However significant the influence of the cover reserve might have been in this regard, this upward movement after

1939 was largely determined by the expansion of the advances from the bank to the treasury. It must also be pointed out that the influence of the treasury on the creation of currency in the preceding years was actually larger than appears from Figure 1. This needs to be explained.

Upon the devaluation of March 1935, the profits that resulted from the revaluation of the gold supply were allotted to the government by analogy with what had happened in 1926. The government, however, did not use this devaluation profit to reduce appreciably its debt to the national bank. Instead, it used that profit primarily as its own gold reserve. Thus, the government had a gold supply worth 4801 million francs at its disposal in April 1935. Although the devaluation operation as such had little effect on the volume of currency, the allocation of the devaluation profit to the government gave it an indirect power over the creation of money, for every time the government made use of its own gold reserves, conversion into Belgian francs was necessary. These conversions automatically increased the gold and currency supplies of the bank and, as a consequence, the volume of currency: 21 percent of the increase of the bank's reserve during the first half of 1935 can be ascribed to such conversions.

During the next two years, the government was able to build up its gold supply again, thanks to a favorable movement of the budget. But during the second half of 1937, the needs of the government were again so large that 1854 million francs worth of gold had to be converted, and new sales followed in 1938 and 1939. The interventions of the stabilization fund in the government bond market played an important role in this regard between 1935 and the beginning of 1938.

The movements of the government's gold supply during this entire period except for the first half of 1935 exercised a leveling effect on the development of the bank's cover reserve and of the monetary base. The transfer of 2237 million francs worth of gold by the government to the bank in the first half of 1935 immediately expanded the money base and thus contributed, not insubstantially, to easing the monetary tension. And the massive gold sale by the government to the bank during the restless period from the middle of 1937 to the middle of 1938 undoubtedly was a welcome compensation for the gigantic flight of capital that was then occurring. It is certain that what was involved here was not a reasoned monetary policy on the part of the authorities: the liquidity needs of the government gave rise to the actions. For all of that, the monetary leveling effects were no less real.

By the second half of 1938, the government's gold reserves were virtually exhausted, and tax receipts were much less than had been expected. Initially, the issuing of government loans satisfied defence financing requirements. But after 1939, this source was also jeopardized, and the national bank had to help by directly creating more money. Beginning in September 1939 in particular, the government was granted substantial advances in the context of the new open market policy. The claims on the public authorities, therefore, again became a significant cause in the rise of the amount of currency, thereby announcing the start of wartime inflation.

Finally, as regards the private component of the money base, the same familiar scenario was played out in this last period. The repatriation of flight capital immediately after the devaluation of 1935 led to a surplus of liquidity that lowered the interest rates of the market significantly under the already low discount rate of the national bank, making the credit of this institution unnecessary and unattractive. The monetary crises of 1938 and 1939 and the resulting capital flight led, as before, to compensatory movements of private credit. This illustrates the function of the national bank as the lender of last resort.

By way of conclusion, however, it must be stated that the period between the two world wars can only be fully understood from the monetary point of view when the evolution of bank money is studied together with the fluctuations of the money base. The influence of the money base was undoubtedly of essential importance at the two extremities of this period. In between, the money base retained its importance via the fluctuations of the international reserves of the bank, but bank money also played a very dynamic role in the monetary process both during the phase of expansion and during the subsequent years of contraction. The creation of currency was, at that time, dominated by international capital movements, and the creation of bank money was dominated by the activities of the private banks. The national bank had no control over either. This was the painful paradox: the bank was responsible for the monetary policy, its essential mission, but it was completely impotent in the face of the two principal forces that determined the monetary system from 1918 to 1940.

Notes

* For documentation and sources, see Herman Van der Wee and Karel Tavernier, *La Banque Nationale de Belgique et l'histoire monétaire entre les deux guerres mondiales* (Brussels, 1975), pp. 385–410.

Part 7
Comparative Studies

Fast and Gradual Anti-Inflation Policies: Evidence for Germany, Italy, and the United States

WILLIAM G. DEWALD

INTRODUCTION

Inflation became a world-wide phenomenon in the 1970s even as national policies became prospectively independent with the advent of flexible exchange rates. The 1970s saw not only higher inflation but also an increasing attribution of it to (1) higher monetary growth rates, whether the latter resulted from government budget deficits, creation of international payments reserves, or central bank attempts to keep market interest rates excessively low, (2) market power as exercised by the OPEC oil cartel.

This paper (1) presents a "simple common model" of the inflationary process in three industrial countries, (2) appraises how long it would take to get rid of inflation and at what cost in economic slack, (3) evaluates whether monetary policy ought to be accommodative in the face of import price shocks. The simple common model represents a modification of the Federal Reserve of St. Louis model of the United States economy.[1]

The analysis supports the view that excessive monetary growth is the main source of excess demand and inflation. Reducing monetary growth to eliminate inflation would be effective, but long and costly. The analysis finds that autonomous increases in import prices contribute to both inflation and unemployment in the short run. Within the framework of the simple common model, such autonomous price increases can be accommodated to ease the transition of the economy in response to the associated change in real prices. The analysis finds that a recession generated from reduced monetary growth is different from a recession generated from import price increases, and different dynamic adjustments are entailed. (Figures 1 and 2 show stylized versions of the alternatives.)

In Figure 1 higher import prices are assumed to reduce potential real growth from $\dot{X}F_0$ to $\dot{X}F_1$. For given growth in aggregate demand $\dot{Y}_0$, this raises the equilibrium inflation rate from $\dot{P}_0$ to $\dot{P}_1$. The *dynamics of adjustment* embedded in the estimated simple common model are such that real growth $\dot{X}$ alternately falls below, and rises above, its new

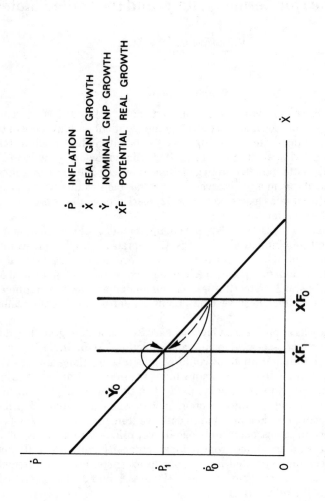

Fig.1 Supply Shock

$\dot{P}$ INFLATION
$\dot{X}$ REAL GNP GROWTH
$\dot{Y}$ NOMINAL GNP GROWTH
$\dot{X}F$ POTENTIAL REAL GROWTH

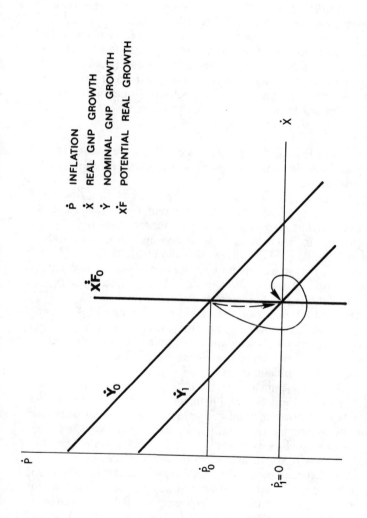

Fig. 2 Demand Shock

$\dot{P}$ INFLATION
$\dot{X}$ REAL GNP GROWTH
$\dot{Y}$ NOMINAL GNP GROWTH
$\dot{X}F$ POTENTIAL REAL GROWTH

potential, and inflation rises above and falls below its new equilibrium until the system comes to rest at $\dot{X}F_1$ and $\dot{P}_1$. Appropriately accommodative monetary policies could avoid excessively slowed real growth by temporarily increasing demand growth, thereby producing a gradual reduction in real growth (the dotted line) to its new lower potential. In Figure 2 inflation rate $\dot{P}_0$ can be brought down to zero by cutting demand growth sufficiently. But because of long lags in the adjustment process, simply curbing demand growth to the value associated with zero long run inflation would cause overshooting of the zero inflation rate, setting up shock waves of alternating deflation and inflation, excess supply and excess demand until the system came to rest at zero inflation. An appropriately targeted monetary growth rate could avoid wasting economic slack on producing too much deceleration of inflation. The targeted monetary growth would be aimed at inflation directly, thereby producing a steady deceleration of inflation (the dotted line) to the desired level.

THE MODEL

The equations of the simple common model appear in Table 1. It is a model of aggregate demand and supply which jointly determine inflation and real growth.

Nominal Demand. Percentage changes in nominal Gross National Product or spending ($\dot{Y}$) are determined not only by percentage monetary growth ($\dot{M}$) but also percentage government spending ($\dot{G}$) and exports ($\dot{E}$) growth. Each variable is in nominal terms and each is considered to be determined autonomously outside the model.[2]

Real Supply. Percentage changes in high employment real output ($\dot{X}F$) are determined outside the model by such factors as capital accumulation and population growth. For the United States, the high employment output series of the President's Council of Economic Advisers was used. For Germany and Italy, high employment output series were similarly constructed from interpolations between cyclical peaks in output. These series were then adjusted down to best fit demand pressure to inflation.

Inflation. Percentage changes in the GNP price deflator are directly affected by expected inflation and demand pressure — the percentage difference between real demand and supply. Real demand is defined operationally as nominal demand (Y) divided by the expected price level (P^a). Factors such as monetary growth that affect nominal demand influence inflation through their effect on demand pressure.

Inflationary Expectations. Inflationary expectations ($\dot{P}^a$) are considered to be based on an estimated relationship between inflation and earlier observations of inflation and import price inflation ($\dot{W}$). In other words, economic units are considered to form expectations of inflation

Table 1. The Model

Estimated Equations

Total Spending (Aggregate nominal demand):

1. $\dot{Y}_t = \text{Constant} + \sum\limits_{i=0} m_i \dot{M}_{t-i} + \sum\limits_{i=0} g_i \dot{G}_{t-i} + \sum\limits_{i=0} e_i \dot{E}_{t-i}.^*$

Equation Used to Calculate Inflationary Expectations $\dot{P}^a_t$:

2. $\dot{P}_t = \sum\limits_{i=1} p_i \dot{P}_{t-1} + \sum\limits_{i=1} w_i \dot{W}_{t-i}; \quad \Sigma p_i = 1; \quad \Sigma w_i = 0.$

Inflation:

3. $\dot{P}_t = \dot{P}^a_t + d_0 D_t.$

Definitions†
Y = Total Spending (GNP)
X = Real GNP
M = Money
G = Government Expenditures
E = Exports
W = Import Price Deflator

Calculated Values

XF = Potential real GNP   Calculated from interpolations between cyclical peaks adjusted downward to maximize fit of Equation 3.

P = GNP deflator = Y/X
P^a = Anticipated P (from Equation 2)
$\dot{X} = \dot{Y} - \dot{P}$ = Real growth
$\hat{Y}/P^a$ = Aggregate real demand
$D = \text{Ln}(\hat{Y}/P^a) - \text{Ln}(XF)$ = Demand pressure

*Dots over variables such as $\dot{Y}_t$ indicate a logarithmic first difference for quarter t which is generally referred to as percentage change in the article. ^ indicates an estimated value. Third-degree polynomial distributions were specified in estimating each of the distributed lag relationships in the spending equations. No end point constraints were imposed.

†Sources:
1. Bank of Italy, *Quarterly Bulletin.*
2. Federal Reserve Bank of St. Louis, *Monetary Trends.*
3. Federal Reserve Bank of St. Louis, *Rates of Change in Economic Data for Ten Industrial Countries.*
4. *Federal Reserve Bulletin.*
5. ISCO, *Conti Economici Trimestrali.*
6. *International Financial Statistics.*
7. U.S. Department of Commerce, *Survey of Current Business.*

Variable	Germany	Italy	United States
Y	3	3	7
X	3	3	7
M	M1:3	M2:1	M1:3
G	Line 82:6	Line 82:6	2
E	Line 70:6	Line 70:6	7
W	Line 75:6	Line 75:5	7
Sample	1962:Q2–1978:Q4	1963:Q1–1978:Q2	1962:Q2–1979:Q3

only on the basis of past price behavior rather than on "rational expectations" of inflation based on the underlying factors that influence it.

Real Growth. Percentage changes in real GNP $(\dot{X})$ are estimated simply by the difference between estimated percentage changes in nominal demand $(\dot{Y})$ and estimated inflation $(\dot{P})$. The model is recursive insofar as percentage changes in nominal demand affect inflation and/or output but not the other way around. As a consequence, transitory increases in inflation from other than factors linked to nominal demand and potential real output in the model have the effect of reducing real growth correspondingly.[3]

In summary, the quarterly model determines spending growth, inflation expectations, demand pressure, inflation, and real growth. The variables are related to such autonomous variables that are not explained by the model as growth rates in the quantity of money, government spending, exports, import prices, and high employment potential output, and the estimated parameters that define and measure the relationships among the variables in the model.

Table 2 records the spending equation estimates. M1 money (Currency and Demand Deposits) was the monetary variable for Germany and the United States, M2 (M1 plus Time and Savings Deposits) for Italy. In every case, monetary growth was the dominant factor explaining spending growth, though growth in exports was estimated to have had a significant effect, at least on impact, in Germany and Italy. Growth in federal government spending was estimated to have had a significant transitory effect in the United States. The estimated monetary growth effects are quite robust whereas the estimated government spending and export effects are quite sensitive to the choice of the sample period.

Table 3 records the estimated equation from which anticipated inflation was calculated. These calculated values would represent anticipations for the period subsequent to the last observation in the sample if individuals evaluate past information as specified. Inflation expectations are specified to be related to past inflation and import price inflation. The estimates are constrained so that the sum of the weights

Table 2. Spending Equation Estimates

$$\hat{Y}_t = \text{Constant} + \sum_{i=0} m_i \dot{M}_{t-i} + \sum_{i=0} g_i \dot{G}_{t-i} + \sum_{i=0} e_i \dot{E}_{t-i}$$

	Germany 1962:Q2–1978:Q4		Italy 1963:Q1–1978:Q2		United States 1962:Q1–1979:Q3	
	Coefficient	(t-value)	Coefficient	(t-value)	Coefficient	(t-value)
Constant	−.004	(−.17)	−.010	(−1.23)	.020	(1.50)
m_0	.031	(.22)	.217	(.91)	.443	(2.64)
m_1	−.014	(−.10)	.075	(.29)	.073	(.38)
m_2	.529	(3.74)	.441	(1.67)	.268	(1.33)
m_3			.237	(.91)	.242	(1.25)
Σm_i	.546	(3.16)	.969	(4.35)	1.026	(4.78)
e_0	.282	(5.78)	.100	(3.48)	.017	(.84)
e_1	.048	(1.21)	.038	(1.28)		
e_2	−.044	(−1.32)	.037	(1.47)		
e_3	−.024	(−.60)	.015	(.51)		
e_4	.081	(1.66)	−.110	(−3.46)		
Σe_i	.344	(2.89)	.082	(.96)	.017	(.84)
g_0	.031	(.22)	.026	(1.81)	.033	(.74)
g_1					.098	(2.19)
g_2					−.073	(−1.63)
g_3					.044	(.94)
Σg_i	.031	(.22)	.026	(1.81)	.102	(1.15)
$\bar{R}^2$	.354		.506		.402	
F	5.514		5.922		4.563	
SE	.046		.015		.029	
DW	2.211		1.973		1.828	

Annual Growth Rates
Mean (standard deviation)

$\dot{Y}$	.0797	(.057)	.124	(.078)	.0838	(.035)
$\dot{M}$	.0827	(.048)	.150	(.046)	.0522	(.025)
$\dot{E}$	.1009	(.133)	.175	(.356)	.1234	(.188)
$\dot{G}$	.0870	(.207)	.169	(.564)	.0884	(.080)

Table 3. Estimated Equation from Which Anticipated Inflation Was Calculated

$$\dot{P}_t = \sum_{t=1} p_i \dot{P}_{t-i} + \sum_{i=1} w_i \dot{W}_{t-i} \cdot \Sigma p_i = 1; \quad \Sigma w_i = 0.$$

	Germany 1962:Q2/1978:Q4		Italy 1963:Q1–1978:Q2		United States 1962:Q1–1979:Q3	
	Coefficient	(t-value)	Coefficient	(t-value)	Coefficient	(t-value)
p_1	.105	(.83)	.496	(3.45)	.412	(3.04)
p_2	.440	(3.84)	−.067	(−.42)	.117	(.81)
p_3	.357	(3.02)	.281	(1.76)	.312	(2.15)
p_4	.098	(—)	.053	(.33)	.055	(.38)
p_5			.128	(.81)	.122	(.82)
p_6			.199	(1.25)	−.076	(−.47)
p_7			.059	(.37)	.061	(.37)
p_8			−.005	(−.03)	−.019	(−.12)
p_9			−.033	(−.18)	−.093	(−.58)
p_{10}			−.111	(—)	.042	(.25)
p_{11}					−.123	(−.74)
p_{12}					.191	(—)
Σp_i	1.000	(—)	1.000	(—)	1.000	(—)
w_1	.055	(1.91)	.033	(1.06)	.058	(2.34)
w_2	.040	(1.23)	.087	(2.42)	.021	(.68)
w_3	.045	(1.41)	.031	(.84)	.002	(.07)
w_4	−.016	(−.50)	−.041	(−1.18)	−.052	(−1.54)
w_5	−.063	(−1.99)	−.077	(−2.29)	.024	(.70)
w_6	−.061	(—)	−.033	(—)	−.032	(−.98)
w_7					−.021	(—)
Σw_i	0	(—)	0	(—)	0	(—)
R^2	.311		.763		.813	
F	13.250		11.915		14.649	
SE	.023		.009		.014	
DW	2.035		2.000		2.000	

Annual Growth Rates
  Mean (standard deviation)

$\dot{P}$	.043	(.028)	.086	(.064)	.049	(.027)
$\dot{W}$	.015	(.101)	.091	(.179)	.070	(.112)

on past inflation equals unity and the sum of the weights on import
price inflation equals zero which ensures that actual inflation is fully
reflected in anticipations in equilibrium. Thus, anticipated inflation is
a weighted sum of past inflation with import price inflation exerting
only a transitory effect. Introducing demand pressure or other autonomous variables than import price inflation into the price anticipations
equation did not yield consistent results across countries nor in general
improve the statistical fit.

In every case, observed inflation over the previous nine months
accounted for about three-fourths of current inflationary expectations.
The remainder was estimated to be distributed in a not very consistent
pattern: only one quarter in Germany but seven and nine quarters in
Italy and the United States respectively. A consistent pattern of the
influence of import price inflation on inflation was estimated for each
country, with a positive influence being built up over two or three
quarters which is then eliminated over the next three or four quarters,
presumably as import price effects get incorporated into the general
price level. Unconstrained regressions yielded much the same qualitative estimates as the constrained ones that appear in Table 3.

Table 4. Inflation Estimates

$$\hat{P}_t = \dot{P}^a_t + d_0 D_t$$

	Germany 1962:Q2–1978:Q4		Italy 1963:Q1–1978:Q2		United States 1962:Q1–1979:Q3	
	Coefficient	(t-value)	Coefficient	(t-value)	Coefficient	(t-value)
d_0	.127	(1.15)	.228	(1.51)	.087	(1.84)
R^2	.404		.764		.818	
SE	.0214		.0312		.0116	
DW	1.961		1.920		2.098	
Mean (standard deviation)						
D	.003	(.023)	.002	(.024)	.024	(.027)

Table 4 shows the inflation equation estimates. Inflation is related to
current anticipated inflation and demand pressure. Demand pressure is
measured as the percentage difference between estimated real demand
and high employment potential ouput. The estimated coefficient of
anticipated inflation is constrained to unity so that when demand
pressure is zero, inflation equals anticipated inflation.

Potential output was calculated in two stages:

1. For the United States, the high employment estimates of the President's Council of Economic Advisers were used; for Germany and Italy,
interpolations between peaks in real output were calculated.

2. Equation 3, Table 1 was estimated with a constant added, thereby adjusting the *level* of potential output to maximize the fit between inflation, anticipated inflation, and demand pressure. The first stage potential output figures were estimated to have overstated the supply of real output by about 2 percent for Italy, 3 percent for Germany, and 4 percent for the United States. To illustrate, actual output and estimated potential output for Germany are shown in Figure 3.

The inflation equation results reported in Table 4 show a small but consistent positive effect of demand pressure on inflation in each country. An increase in demand pressure of 1 percentage point is estimated to increase the contemporaneous inflation rate by roughly .1 of 1 percent in Germany and the United States and .2 of 1 percent in Italy. This does not seem like much of an effect, but, as simulations of the model demonstrate, large and persisting demand pressure (or slack) can have substantial effects in accelerating (or decelerating) inflation.

Table 5. Real Growth Estimates

$$\hat{X}_t \quad \hat{Y}_t - \hat{P}_t$$

	Germany 1962:Q2–1978:Q4 Coefficient		Italy 1963:Q1–1978:Q2 Coefficient		United States 1962:Q1–1979:Q3 Coeffficient	
R^2	.467		.250		.514	
SE	.0414		.0523		.0263	
Mean (standard deviation)						
$\dot{P}$	.0432	(.028)	.0862	(.064)	.0494	(.027)
$\dot{Y}$	.0797	(.057)	.1240	(.078)	.0838	(.035)
$\dot{X}$	.0365	(.057)	.0379	(.060)	.0344	(.038)

Table 5 shows real growth estimates which are obtained in the model by subtracting estimated inflation from estimated spending growth. From one-fourth to just over one-half of the variation in real growth in the countries studied is explained by the simple common model. All told, the model explains a significant part of the movements in spending, the price level, and real output over the 1960s and 1970s and provides a framework for appraising how long it might take these economies to adjust to antiinflationary monetary policies and what impacts on inflation and real output might accompany large increases in import prices.

SIMULATIONS

The models for each country were simulated through 2028 — a period of about 50 years. In the first simulation each of the autonomous

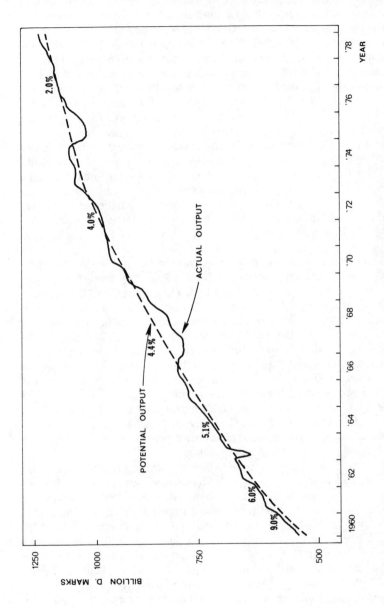

Fig.3   Actual and Potential Real Output in Billions of 1975 Deutsche Marks

variables except monetary growth was set at the assumed growth in potential output: respectively 3 percent, 2.5 percent, and 2 percent in Italy, the United States, and Germany. Monetary growth was set at a rate that eventually would eliminate inflation. In the framework of the models, annual M1 growth in Germany was cut from 9 percent in the year ended 1979: Q2 to 3 percent and kept there. M2 growth in Italy was cut from 22 percent in the year ended 1978: Q2 to 7 percent, and M1 in the United States, from 6 percent in the year ended 1979: Q4 to 0. In the second set of simulations, monetary growth was slowed gradually over 5 years to the rates associated with zero long-run inflation. In the third simulation, the fast antiinflationary monetary impulse was combined with a one-year increase of import prices of 25 percent.[4]

Table 6 shows the results of the fast and gradual antiinflation monetary policies. Germany which had a lower built-in inflation rate than Italy or the United States required a smaller antiinflationary monetary impulse and less economic slack to squeeze inflation out of the economy. Furthermore, there was less overshooting of the zero inflation target.

The pattern of timing of impacts was similar in the three models: cutting the monetary growth rate immediately to the rate that would eliminate inflation in the long run took 3 to 5 years to cut the inflation rate to zero. It took 7 to 8 years in the simulation of a gradual cut in monetary growth. Because demand pressure was estimated to have a comparatively smaller effect on inflation in the United States, the percentage of slack (negative demand pressure) at the predicted trough was much higher for the United States than Germany or Italy. Using an estimated "Okun's Law," -16.5 percent demand pressure in the United States model translates into an increase in the unemployment rate by 6 percent above the high employment-unemployment rate. Demand pressure of -7.3 in Germany and -12.1 in Italy in contrast translates into unemployment rates only 2 percent above the respective high employment-unemployment rates.

It is no surprise that maximum slack was uniformly lower under the gradual antiinflationary policy. But its duration was uniformly longer. In every case of gradual antiinflation monetary impulses, there was *less* overshooting of zero inflation, a result from which one can infer that once sufficient slack is created to decelerate inflation, it would be possible to ease restrictive policies to permit growth in demand to avoid deflation (if that is not desired). As the models are specified, real output would be unaffected in the long run. But a "soft landing" policy could limit instability. Though slack would exist over a longer period, the economy would avoid a roller coaster in real growth that Figure 4 illustrates would otherwise continue for many years. To permit a soft landing, the policy authorities would need to understand inflationary

Table 6. Simulation: Fast and Gradual Antiinflation Monetary Impulses

		Presimulation		Zero Inflation	Trough in Demand Pressure		Recession Duration*	Maximum Deflation Induced by Over-shooting Zero Inflation	
	Period	Annual Inflation	Annual Demand Pressure	Years after Impulses	Years after Impulses	Percent	Years	Years after Impulses	Percent
Germany									
Fast	1978:Q4	3.7	1.8	4.5	4.25	− 7.3	2.75	7.25	− 2.2
Gradual				8.0	6.25	− 3.5	1.5	9.75	− 1.1
Italy									
Fast	1978:Q2	12.2	− 1.4	3.0	2.75	− 12.1	1.5	5.0	− 5.9
Gradual				6.75	6.5	− 8.8	0	8.75	− 4.3
United States									
Fast	1979:Q3	8.9	2.3	4.5	4.25	− 16.5	3.25	8.5	− 4.9
Gradual				7.0	6.75	− 13.2	.75	11.0	− 4.0

* Recession is defined as two or more quarters of negative real growth.

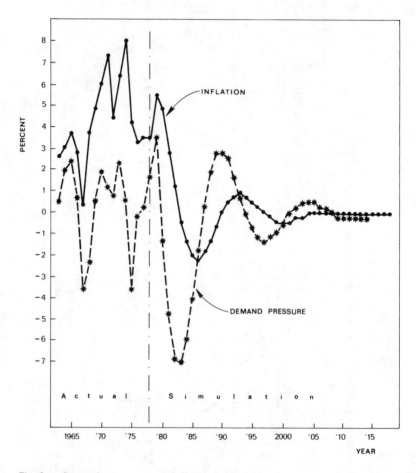

Fig. 4   Demand pressure and Inflation in Germany

forces better than the public, which is a heroic assumption. Even if a well-controlled soft landing is too much to hope for, the apparent sensitivity of the real economy to nominal shocks makes a gradual antiinflation policy attractive. The policy prescription is to persist in maintaining demand pressure *weak enough, to keep inflation falling* until it is eliminated. This is shown in stylized form in Figure 2.

Import price inflation can affect inflation in the short run in the simulation models and, if potential real growth is thereby affected, also long-run inflation. The simulation of a one-year 25 percent increase in import prices focuses on the short term. For the purpose of this comparison look at the fast antiinflation monetary impulse simulations reported in Table 6 and the import price shock impulses coupled with the fast antiinflation simulations in Table 7. In every case such an autonomous increase in inflation (and inflationary expectations) augments the magnitude but shortens the duration of the recession already accountable to antiinflation monetary impulses. The monetary authorities could damp the effects of an import price shock. In the models, this would mean permitting monetary growth to increase demand enough to avoid creating more slack than necessary to stabilize inflation as is shown in stylized form in Figure 1.

CONCLUSION

For the long run, aggregate demand growth must be matched to real growth to eliminate inflation. But how long might that take?

To answer the question a simple common model for Germany, Italy, and the United States was estimated with quarterly data for the 1960s and 1970s. Monetary growth was found to affect demand significantly and quickly. Inflation was specified to depend on expected inflation and demand pressure. Expected inflation depended on observed inflation and import price inflation, the latter exerting only a temporary influence. The estimated contemporaneous effect of demand pressure on inflation was generally small, which, coupled with lags in the formation of expectations, implies that inflation adjusts slowly to changes in demand pressure. This was demonstrated in simulations of major shocks emanating from changes in monetary growth rates and import prices.

Though the models are specified such that long-run real growth is independent of aggregate demand, the simulations show that by reducing monetary growth, inflation could be eliminated in each country and further that monetary growth could be controlled to avoid reverberations in real growth induced by antiinflation monetary impulses or import price shocks. Even such an optimally designed policy could not hide from economic slack — the fundamental mechanism within the models to reduce inflation.

Table 7. Simulation: 25 Percent Increase in Import Prices for One Year and Fast Antiinflation Monetary Impulse

		Presimulation		Simulation							
				Peak Inflation		Trough in Demand Pressure		Recession Duration	Initial Zero Inflation	Maximum Deflation Due to Overshooting Zero Inflation	
	Period	Annual Inflation	Annual Demand Pressure	Years after Impulses	Percent	Years after Impulses	Percent	Years	Years after Impulses	Years after Impulses	Percent
Germany	1978:Q4	3.7	1.8	1.5	9.0	3.0	−9.1	2.5	4.25	6.25	−2.8
Italy	1978:Q2	12.2	−1.5	.75	12.5	2.50	−13.6	1.0	2.75	5.0	−7.1
United States	1979:Q3	8.9	2.3	.75	10.2	4.25	−18.7	3.0	4.25	8.25	−5.5

The results are not optimistic. The simulations show that even a gradual approach to eliminating inflation could result in an extended period of economic slack and high unemployment. These results reflect the estimated models that link inflation to a large extent to inflationary expectations which in turn reflect past experience with inflation. Countering the impact of these expectations would require slack for an extended period where built-in inflation is substantial as in Italy or the United States.

Some economists argue that inflationary expectations could be reduced by imposing wage and price controls coupled with policies to restrict aggregate demand growth. Others contend that inflation expectations could be reduced quickly if the monetary authorities would announce a policy of reducing monetary growth to a noninflationary rate. In either case, if the public believed that the policy would work, inflationary expectations would doubtlessly decrease and inflation could consequently be eliminated faster and with less cost in terms of economic slack than is implied by the simulations reported in this paper. But based on past experience, it is unlikely that the public would believe the pronouncements of policy makers in the absence of firm evidence that not only inflation, but the underlying causes of it were under control. Substantial inflation has never been eliminated without a recession. Building on that experience, the models of Germany, Italy, and the United States discussed in this paper demonstrate that the old-fashioned remedy of reducing aggregate demand growth would produce a recession, but it would succeed in eliminating inflation.

Notes

1. Leonall C. Andersen and Keith M. Carlson, "A Monetarist Model for Economic Stabilization," *Federal Reserve Bank of St. Louis Review*, April 1970, pp. 7–25. Leonall C. Andersen and Jerry L. Jordan, "Monetary and Fiscal Actions: A Test of Their Relative Importance in Economic Stabilization," *ibid.*, November 1968, pp. 11–24. Replication and modification of the St. Louis model was reported in William G. Dewald and Maurice N. Marchon, "A Modified Federal Reserve of St. Louis Spending Equation for Canada, France, Germany, Italy, the United Kingdom, and the United States," *Kredit und Kapital* 11, no. 2 (1978): 194–212, and idem, "A Common Specification of Price, Output, and Unemployment Rate Responses to Demand Pressure and Import Prices in Canada, France, Germany, Italy, the United Kingdom, and the United States," *Weltwirtschaftliches Archiv* 115, no. 1 (1979), pp. 1–19.
2. Similar variables have been used in other studies. For example, for Germany, Manfred J. M. Neumann, "Fiskalisch oder monetär ausgerichtete Stabilisierungspolitik?" in H. Schneider et al. (Eds.), *Stabilisierungspolitik in der Marktwirtschaft* (Berlin, 1975), pp. 971–96; Nikolas K. A. Läfer, "Fiskalpolitik

versus Geldpolitik: zur Frage ihrer relativen Bedeutung: eine empirische Unter-suchung für die BRD," *Kredit und Kapital* 8 (1975): 346–78, and for Italy, Bruno Sitzia, "Monetary and Fiscal Influences on Economic Activity: The Italian Experience," *Ricerche Economiche* 1–4 (1973): 270–81.

3. Charles R. Nelson, "Recursive Structure in U.S. Income, Prices, and Out-put," West Coast Academic/Federal Reserve Economic Research Seminar, 1978, 2–26.

4. Comparable simulations of the U.S. model have been reported in William G. Dewald, "Estimation and Policy Simulation of a Small Model of Output, Inflation, and Unemployment in the United States," Contract #J9K80012, U.S. Department of Labor, Bureau of International Labor Affairs, December 1979, and idem, "Fast vs. Gradual Policies for Controlling Inflation," *Economic Review*, Federal Reserve Bank of Kansas City, January 1980, pp. 16–25. De-tailed results for Germany and Italy appear in William G. Dewald and Wil-

Two Decades of Inflation in Western Industrialized Countries under Fixed and Flexible Exchange Rates

HUGO M. KAUFMANN

INTRODUCTION: MACROECONOMIC GOALS OR THE SQUARING OF THE CIRCLE

Irrespective of the existing exchange rate system and changes in the international institutional monetary and general economic setup (Common Market, Free Trade Association, European Monetary Union, etc.) the macroeconomic goals of most industrialized Western countries (among which Japan is generally included) can be clearly defined for the period since World War II. They consisted of the simultaneous attainment of price stability, reasonable full employment levels, sustainable economic growth rates, and balance of payments equilibria. In some cases, fixity of exchange rates has presented a separate goal, at least implicitly, if not explicitly. This was amply demonstrated by countries' reluctance to revalue or devalue their currencies despite the Bretton Woods System's provision that exchange rates ought not to remain fixed in the face of "fundamental" disequilibria in the balances of payments. Grouping together the first three and the other two goals, one can say that macroeconomic policy was (supposed to be) directed toward the joint achievement of internal and external equilibrium.

The sequence in which the individual policy goals were listed does not imply a ranking of priorities — neither of all countries at any given moment of time, nor of any single country through time. According to their own pronouncements, economic policy makers (e.g., in Germany and Switzerland) concentrated on achieving that goal which happened to be most endangered. In contradistinction to experience in other countries (with the possible exception of Switzerland) Germany generally exhibited greater sensitivity to the price stability goal. Little wonder, then, that it was exposed to frequent criticisms, primarily from abroad, of having neglected the other goals, especially those of full employment and more rapid growth rates. These criticisms became particularly pronounced in the late 1960s and the second half of the 1970s.

In today's international economic environment, one might easily overlook that the price behavior of some countries, including Germany, was not quite as good as that of the United States — until 1966. Only thereafter did the price level rise considerably faster in the United States than in Germany. During the 1950s and 1960s, Germany, trying to achieve price stability, found itself continually frustrated by what it called *imported* inflation, which, at times, combined forces with home-made inflationary developments. Little wonder, then, that in the mid-1970s, Germany could not be easily persuaded to give up her hard-won success and thus resisted the "locomotive argument."

When German and Swiss policy makers were generally concerned more about inflation than about unemployment, it was, in the latter case, because unemployment was nil for the longest time. In the German case, it was not necessarily at the expense of concern over potential or, in more recent years, actual unemployment, as critics often would have it. Rather, it was based on conviction that "full employment at any cost" would produce undesirable price effects, first, and unacceptable ones, later. And this would only aggravate the unemployment problem rather than alleviate it. The most significant exceptions to Germany's general stance, came in the early 1970s, when the federal government's emphasis on unemployment was widely perceived as a full-employment guarantee. Yet, after wildcat strikes had brought with them double-digit wage settlements, and after the renewed wage explosions of 1973–74, the government insisted that the unions, like the other sectors of the economy share in the responsibility for the achievement of price stability.[1]

Most of the other major OECD countries did not take the same position, until the price-wage explosion erupted on an international scale in the mid-1970s. The linking of inflation and unemployment as constituting two sides of the same coin rather than two coins between which policy makers can choose, could until then be found only in those countries which emphasized the price stability goal. This view appeared in the theoretical literature of the late 1960s and the 1970s and found its initial academic pronouncement in Friedman's dictum that "there is no long-run, stable trade-off between inflation and unemployment."[2] I should hasten to add that this view is not shared by all academicians, including James Tobin, according to whom a long-run Phillips Curve is "alive and well."[3]

Whatever may have been the ranking of goals, the most striking economic experiences in the Western industrialized countries during the last two decades have been a major change in their ability to reach those goals and in the international economic framework within which domestic economic policies are being formed. Many observers have been tempted to establish a causal relationship between these two changes, leading from the change in the international monetary setup (from a fixed to a flexible exchange rate system) to higher inflation and unemployment rates and lower economic growth. Others would disagree with the line of causation, considering it a *post hoc propter hoc* fallacy; alternatively, they might even argue that the causation was really the other way around.

INFLATION UNDER THE PEGGED EXCHANGE RATE SYSTEM

During the years when the Western countries were on the Bretton Woods System of essentially pegged exchange rates, some low-inflation countries — particularly Germany — experienced large balance of payments surpluses. Surpluses on current account and — with few exceptions on "unrecorded transactions" — resulted in foreign exchange accumulation at the Deutsche Bundesbank in most years until the late 1970s, since capital exports were either smaller than the current account surpluses or, what proved to be more problematical, Germany's capital account was also positive.[4] Some other countries were able to keep their inflation rates below what they would have been by accumulating balance of payments deficits. The possibility of hiding some of the inflationary pressures behind the façade of balance of payments deficits and financing them by running down foreign exchange reserves or by borrowing from abroad, was tantamount to shifting the inflation burden onto the surplus countries. Many economists and politicians, especially on this side of the Atlantic, liked to argue that the United States, having had a lower inflation and higher unemployment rate than other countries (primarily European countries — it was they who complained about the United States' "exhorbitant privilege") could not have been in a position of "exporting" inflation; you cannot export what you haven't got.[5]

In the world of the Phillips-Lipsey tradeoff between unemployment and inflation, ability to export part of one's own inflation would have permitted the deficit countries to keep employment on a higher plateau than they would have afforded otherwise since a degree of money illusion was preserved. And last but not least, it also was instrumental in the observed lower variance of inflation rates among the major OECD countries, when compared to the variance under the floating exchange rate regime. Expressed differently, the pegged exchange rate system transmitted inflation rates (visible and not so visible) more fully from the higher-inflation to the lower-inflation countries than the floating system. It is a different matter altogether, that the level of inflation rates was lower under the Bretton Woods System than what we have experienced since its collapse.

Balance of payments surpluses in Germany were combined with full employment at home under the pegged rate system, which created the dilemma situation in which the application of one policy tool in pursuit of one goal aggravated one of the other imbalances. Monetary policy, directed at the attainment of price stability, would render the achievement of external equilibrium (i.e., reduction of the surplus) more difficult, whereas concentration on the external goal through easier monetary policy, would inevitably add to inflationary pressures.

During the fifteen years, starting in the late fifties, when the simultaneous attainment of two goals — balance of payments equilibria and price stability — eluded the major industrial countries, and only a multilateral currency realignment could have provided a solution, widespread rejection of this adjustment proposal prompted the search for substitute measures. Tinbergen had stated that the number of instruments had to equal the number of goals, especially when the goals were mutually contradictory, such as a reduction in the balance of payments surplus and slowdown of domestic economic activity.[6]

Mundell, thereafter, elaborated that no less important than the equality of instruments and goals was the proper pairing of specific instruments with specific goals — the "assignment" issue, based on the "effective market classification."[7] Accordingly, monetary policy was to be assigned to achieve external, and fiscal policy was to be directed toward achieving internal equilibrium. Only then could dual equilibrium be approached under a system of fixed exchange rates. Improper pairing, on the other hand, would move the economy further away from equilibrium.[8] The proposed solution seemed neat and rather painless — especially if both deficit-low employment and surplus-high employment countries participated in the adjustment process — yet major problems would remain. First, there remained the inside and outside lags, the former consisting of recognition, decision, and action lags. The *outside lag* refers to the time lag between the initiation of policy action and the time it has the desired effect upon the economic variables at which policy is directed. (Monetary policy is purported to have a shorter inside lag than fiscal policy because the latter must go through the political process.)

I suggest, however, that the dichotomy of the duration of lags along the lines of monetary and fiscal policy is adequate for a closed-economy analysis. Yet, it will not serve us well when the subject matter is an open economy with high capital mobility, when the exchange rates are fixed (or pegged), and when the purpose of monetary policy is to correct external disequilibria according to the effective market classification. Under these conditions, the outside lag of monetary policy can become very short indeed, as deficit countries can raise interest rates to generate capital inflows sufficiently large to reduce external disequilibria.

The inside lag, on the other hand, could be and has been considerably longer — as much as a few years. Central banks of both the deficit and the surplus countries may determine that external disequilibria are transitory rather than fundamental and conclude that corrective measures are not (yet) required, thus lengthening the recognition lag. Once it has been established that disequilibria are "fundamental," one must still decide who is to do the adjusting and how the adjustment "burden" is to be distributed between deficit and surplus countries. But this is as much a political as an economic issue, lengthening the decision and action lags.[9]

What we have come up with is a *reversal* of the respective lengths of inside and outside lags of monetary policy as we shift our analysis from a closed to an open economy where exchange rates are fixed and capital movements are interest elastic. This has important implications for the generation and transmission of inflation.

A second major problem with the assignment of instruments to goals was that no agreement could be found as to what constituted the goals: price stability and full employment combined with balance of payments equilibrium or — was it exchange rate stability? Nor was it resolved whether monetary and fiscal policy was one instrument (Meade) or two (Mundell). Furthermore, the long-run implications of balance of payments adjustment through capital movements would not be as painless in the long run as originally perceived. In particular, financing balance of payments deficits with capital imports would impede internal growth later on, as deficit countries would have to offer ever-higher interest rates to maintain a level of capital inflows. Progressively higher interest rates would be detrimental to long-term investments.

Under conditions where deficit countries were not compelled quickly to curtail domestic absorption to correct their external deficits, the surplus countries continued to accumulate foreign reserves and had their money supply grow at a rate that was not determined by their own central banks.[10] This behavior of deficit and surplus countries has (or should have) substantially diminished the validity of the argument that a system of fixed exchange rates per se is less inflationary because it imposes strict discipline on deficit countries and compels them to engage in adjustment policies. It still remains true, though, that in an ultimate sense an asymmetry in the adjustment process exists in that it is easier for a surplus than for a deficit country to postpone adjustment. Much depends, however, on the willingness of the surplus countries to go on accumulating foreign reserves and maintaining an undervalued currency.

In this environment, the surplus countries imported inflation through various channels: the goods market and the monetary sector. Transmission via the goods market is reflected in the current account surpluses and the so-called goods arbitrage. An undervalued currency makes the domestic currency prices of imports more expensive as other countries experience inflation and exchange rate changes do not compensate for inflation rate differentials. On the other hand, exports are stimulated as the terms of trade move against the low-inflation country. This in turn will add to domestic inflationary pressures.

Moreover, price and income increases in the tradable sector will transmit themselves to the nontradable sector according to the the "Scandinavian" model, according to which world inflation rates transmit themselves fully to the small open economies.[11] With the greater integration of economies, the small open economies model gains greater relevance for the large open economies.

In an important sense, Germany contributed to its problem of imported inflation by refusing to revalue the Deutschmark during the 1960s, as well as before, during the late 1950s. Imported inflation, which was generated through the trade account, was augmented by the influence of capital movements into Germany, which took place in anticipation of revaluations of the Deutschmark and, at times, by interest rate differentials in favor of Germany.

Thus, the monetary channel is added to the goods channel in the transmission process of inflation, as the central bank is forced to augment the domestic money supply in order to maintain the exchange ratios against the other currencies. Capital movements, which bear some of the balance of payments adjustment burden, tend to spread the effect of monetary expansion in one country to others, affecting both traded and nontraded goods.[12] The monetary approach, like the Scandinavian model, demonstrates that, in the long run, both traded and nontraded goods sectors are similarly affected by foreign price behavior.

The transmission of monetary disturbances is faster than that taking place through goods arbitrage. This stems from the high degree of capital market integration which supports high capital mobility. According to one estimate, a "substantial part" of monetary actions of one country is transmitted to other countries within one or two quarters, whereas the full effect of goods arbitrage "should perhaps be measured in years rather than in quarters."[13]

What then remained for surplus countries to do; what was the alternative to accepting imported inflation? The options were flexible exchange rates or outright revaluation. Neither alternative was easy to adopt. Against the former stood the obligations countries had within the Bretton Woods arrangement which made no provision for a flexible exchange rate system. The latter, i.e., revaluation, was not chosen lightly — certainly not the first time in the case of Germany and the Netherlands, which revalued in 1961.[14] An undervalued currency is tantamount to an export subsidy, with the added advantage that it does not violate any international rules (such as GATT's) which prohibit export subsidies.

Economists had warned that this export subsidy would ultimately be lost to inflation if the surplus (deficit) countries refused to revalue (devalue), through the various transmission mechanisms that have been mentioned. More recently, expectations as a channel for transmission of inflation has joined the other transmission mechanisms. According to the expectations argument, people in low-inflation countries will adjust their inflation expectations to the world inflation rate, even though there may be some time lags, and the adjustment might take place only in the longer run. In the short run, the world inflation rate might stay higher than expectations. But in the long run, the adjustment will be complete. This limits the efficacy of domestic monetary and fiscal policy to the short run, which could, however, last quite some time.[15]

It is noteworthy that inflation, which turned out to be an international phenomenon in the late 1960s and during the 1970s, was nevertheless treated on a national basis. Yet, according to the quantity theory, under open-economy conditions, price levels and changes in price levels are determined by the world quantity of money and changes in the world money supply, respectively, irrespective of which country (countries) generates changes in the money supply. The question which country engages in expansionary monetary policy affects merely the level of reserves and the distribution of reserves.[16]

INFLATION UNDER THE FLEXIBLE EXCHANGE RATE REGIME

It was in this economic climate that a system of greater exchange rate flexibility was advocated on both sides of the Atlantic. Under the system of fixed exchange rates, it has been recognized that international economics and the exchange rate system have a double meaning for domestic economic policy: they can become an extension of domestic economic policies under fixed exchange rates, and domestic stabilization policies can be affected and disturbed by the impact of the foreign sector. Since the international inflationary link could not easily be cut under a fixed exchange rate system, it was in the interest of stability-oriented countries to opt first for greater flexibility of the exchange rate system. Since in a fundamental sense, balance of payments disequilibria were seen to be a monetary phenomenon, and since changes in the money supply were seen to have a direct impact on domestic money income and prices, it was the more inflation-prone countries which would determine the "world" inflation rate, as they determine the "world" money supply. Germany first experimented with flexibility of exchange rates in the late sixties before pegging the new exchange rate for the mark at a higher level. It did so again in 1971, as did Switzerland and Austria, before the gold window of the United States was closed in August 1971. With this move, the dollar was set free to float against other currencies. A last attempt to save the Bretton Woods System through the Smithsonian Agreement of December 1971 ultimately failed in 1973, after which the flexible exchange rate system became well entrenched.

In the 1960s, when the international monetary system was exposed to great strains, economists argued that adoption of a flexible exchange rate system would solve many of the (intractable) problems simultaneously. First, under freely flexible exchange rates, balance of payments problems—deficits or surpluses—could not arise since the exchange rate would do the adjusting. Consequently there would no longer be a need for central banks to accumulate (unwanted) reserves, nor for deficit countries to worry about the sufficiency or insufficiency of reserves. Some economists went so far as to suggest that a flexible exchange rate system would eliminate the demand for international reserves, a view which was, however, not shared by all who favored a flexible exchange rate system. In any case, how freely exchange rates were permitted to fluctuate would be visible from the central banks' changes in international reserves.

Secondly, once these very large reserve movements were eliminated, so would be the international transmission of inflation as central banks were again in control of domestic money creation. Whereas under the system of fixed exchange rates demand pressures generated in foreign countries led to pressures within the surplus countries, under flexible exchange rates excess demand would be reflected in a depreciation of the exchange rate and hence upward pressures on the domestic price level of the country in which the demand pressures originated. In other words, inflationary tendencies would be "bottled up" in the countries which engaged in inflationary (expansionary) policies, now that the "shock absorber" of the fixed rate mechanism had been removed.

Thirdly, for believers in the existence of a short-run as well as a long-run Phillips-Lipsey tradeoff between unemployment and inflation, countries would be free to choose that combination of inflation and unemployment which corresponded to their social indifference curves and the political preference schedules between inflation and unemployment.

Furthermore, the policy dilemma situation, which we have discussed earlier, would be resolved elegantly. A country that experienced full employment (underemployment) combined with balance of payments surpluses (deficits) would find its currency appreciate (depreciate) against other countries. Gone would also be the problem connected with possible inside and outside lags which could have made active monetary and/or fiscal policy procyclical rather than, as intended, anticyclical.

Finally, among the advantages of a flexible exchange rate system compared to a pegged one with intermittent adjustments in the exchange rate was the elimination of political wrangling over which country should adjust its exchange rate. This, however, does not mean that no political elements are involved in a floating exchange rate regime, especially when central banks bend the clean-float rule and adopt a "dirty" float mechanism through intervention in the foreign exchange market. One reason for adopting a pegged exchange rate system under the Bretton Woods agreement was fear that countries might otherwise engage in competitive devaluations to stimulate employment. More recently, some suspected that countries might have engaged in or at least attempted exchange rate manipulations to achieve a "competitive revaluation" in the wake of the oil shock, in order to reduce the inflationary impact of rising raw materials imports.

It would be difficult to prove that a country purposefully distorted its exchange rate rather than that it intervened in the foreign exchange market to smooth otherwise excessive exchange rate fluctuations, but an appreciating currency has helped countries in their effort to bring inflation rates down. This aspect has become so important during the high-inflation years of the 1970s, that advantages of flexible exchange rates have been seen in this light rather than in their effect on the balance of payments per se. This emphasis finds its support in the monetary view of the balance of payments, which states that the balance of payments effect of exchange rate changes is static in nature and ignores the long-run effect of exchange rates on money supply and prices. If the elasticities are right and a devaluation improves the trade account in the short run, the increased money supply will restore the devaluing country's price level, measured in foreign currency, to the predevaluation level.[17]

The antiinflation effect of currency appreciation is furthermore aided by a slowdown of capital inflows and with it of domestic money creation that runs counter to central bank antiinflation policy. No longer will the central bank have to absorb any quantity of foreign currency to peg the exchange rate.

The implications of the monetary interpretation of the balance of payments and international transmission of inflation, also labeled *international monetarism*, stands in no conflict with the results we obtain from the Scandinavian model and the purchasing power theory (law of one price). Consequently, one need not be a monetarist to be sceptical about the corrective balance of payments effect of exchange rate changes while seeing the significance of greater exchange rate flexibiliy in domestic (anti-)inflation policy.

The expectations for reducing or eliminating balance of payments disequilibria and international inflation, which have been connected with theorizing about, and adoption of, a system of flexible exchange rates, were very much shattered by the dismal record on both fronts. Under the Bretton Woods System of pegged exchange rates, which lasted till 1971 and with some modifications till 1973, inflation rates of the Western industrialized countries were considerably below those that followed after the transition to a flexible exchange rate regime. On the other hand, the difference in inflation rates between countries was considerably smaller in the earlier period. According to a study by Genberg, the break in the dispersion of the inflation trend among countries came as early as 1967; thereafter the standard deviation has been increasing. The date coincides with the years during which exchange rates have been changed more frequently than before.[18]

Little wonder then that there has been considerable disenchantment with the flexible exchange rate system. It did not bring the relief on the balance of payments front that was expected of the new regime, and inflationary movements have become more pronounced. Before long, the new system itself was being blamed for the failure along both lines. This conclusion may well be unjustified and belong in the category of the *post hoc ergo propter hoc* fallacy. Another possible explanation for the dismal record after the breakdown of the Bretton Woods System presents itself. Inflationary pressures had been building up long before the breakdown, first in connection with the financing of the Vietnam War, then, in 1972–1973, with the synchronized expansion in the major OECD countries, which led to a raw materials boom and concomitant price increases. These factors in turn have strained the system of fixed exchange rates excessively and led to its ultimate demise. A system of fixed or stable exchange rates, however, can function properly only as long as actual and desired growth rates and inflation rates remain similar in those countries which are linked through that exchange rate system. This precondition no longer existed after 1967, and neither did the alleged disciplinary mechanism of the fixed exchange rate system. Countries were able to engage in excessive credit creation, and the United States, a key currency country, made full use of this facility. But as the countries which opted for higher inflation in order to achieve lower unemployment rates in the presumed Phillips-Lipsey tradeoff were able to export some of their own inflation into the countries that had the reverse preferences, the latter group (Germany and Switzerland in particular) exported stability. This aspect is generally overlooked in the literature. This export of stability is another reason for the narrower inflation differentials among the industrial countries during the "fixed" exchange rate system.

One argument in favor of flexible exchange rates was precisely the potential for countries to extricate themselves from the international inflation nexus. The implication is that countries which exhibit less concern about price stability would find their inflation rates rise more than under the old system. This explains the greater variance of inflation rates in the 1970s compared to those of the 1950s and 1960s.

Confidence in the existence in the longer run of what seemed to be a robust tradeoff relationship between unemployment and inflation waned during the 1970s. More in harmony with empirical evidence was that countries' unemployment rates would settle at a level which came to be known as the *natural* rate of unemployment. Any deviations from it would be short-lived; in particular, any reduction below the natural rate would be inflationary without any permanent impact on the unemployment ratio.[19] The argument of the tradeoff was relegated to the short run and to conditions in which money illusion existed. The inflationary experience of the 1970s left little room for money illusion. And in the wake of increased familiarity with the inflationary impact of depreciating currencies — provided that central banks and treasuries did not engage in the needed contractive policies (which they did not) — the exchange rate illusion disappeared as well. Many governments, including the United States, however, continued to operate under a Phillips-Curve illusion; they saw in the system of flexible exchange rates the opportunity to select what they considered to be a desirable rate of expansion of aggregate demand.

The policy of demand expansion became particularly important in some countries after the first oil shock and the ensuing deep recession. Whereas countries with high priority for price stability emphasized the inflationary impact of the oil price hike, the others stressed the deflationary effect of the income transfer to the Organization of Petroleum Exporting Countries (OPEC). Consequently, the former group engaged in contractionary economic policies and did not expect their central banks to validate the inflationary impact of the OPEC quadrupling of the oil price; the latter group, however, hoped to escape the deflationary impact of the worsening of their terms of trade by expansionary domestic economic policies. This move then set those countries on what came to be known as the vicious circle of a depreciating currency, wherein inflation would beget currency depreciation which in turn would raise import prices, adding a new twist to the inflationary spiral with further depreciation of the currency, and so on, until domestic economic policy would change its course. Of course, the opposite, a virtuous circle, would hold true for the first group of countries; they

would be assisted in their antiinflation effort by a continuously appreciating currency.[20]

Another cause of the prolonged reluctance to adopt antiinflationary
measures in countries more worried about recession than inflation, was
that inflationary pressures were ascribed to "special," exogenous conditions, such as the oil price hike, increases in other raw materials
prices, and a rise in agricultural products prices owing to bad harvests.
Since, according to this interpretation, accelerated inflation was caused
by special events, one hoped that these pressures would subside by
themselves in due course. Only after some considerable time lag did
policy makers recognize that those inflationary impulses may be or
have become endogenous in nature.

For all these reasons which we mentioned, countries which were
more successful in fighting inflation were reluctant to play the role of
"locomotive" and stimulate economic activity in order to help others
extricate themselves from the inflation *cum* unemployment quagmire.[21]
Their interpretation of what happened was in line with the monetarist
argument that an unemployment-inflation tradeoff existed, if at all,
only in the short run and that after the short-lived improvement
unemployment would revert to the previous level, with the important
difference that the country ended up at a higher inflation level. Since
the majority of the important countries initially, at least, did not
subscribe to this point of view, the policy options which they perceived as being available to them under the system of flexible exchange
rates intensified existing inflationary pressures.

CONCLUSION

What emerges from the discussion and the historical record is that over
the past two decades inflation has beset the Western economies with
ever greater intensity; furthermore, over the same time span, the international monetary system gradually changed from an intermittently
fixed to a flexible one, with admittedly substantial central bank intervention. That these two developments occurred in tandem does not
prove any causal relationship. Rather, it emerges that the latter system
has given countries greater latitude for dealing with some exogenous
disturbances, but also greater latitude for transforming them into endogenous disequilibrating elements. It could be and has been argued
that the external shocks would not have been inflationary, had monetary policy not validated the price increases (inflation being a monetary
phenomenon). Yet, there were limits to central banks' uncooperative
policy. Countries' professed goals of striving for full employment and
adequate growth rates determined the expectational structure in some
as did emphasis on price stability in others. With the oil tax superimposed upon domestic redistribution attempts, the central banks could

not have eliminated the inflation impact completely without at the same time causing serious social dislocations. Moreover, the monetary authorities had to steer between the Scylla of gradualism and the Charybdis of a "big bang" in applying monetary pressures.

In this complex environment, the flexible exchange rate system — inasmuch as it was permitted to function — was overstrained, in that policy makers wanted it to act as a "super" shock absorber. They expected that no matter what their domestic policies, the external price mechanism would absorb any excesses.

Inflation on an international scale has occurred under the various exchange rate regimes. The main difference was that under fixed exchange rates, inflation was ultimately imported, whereas in the short run it might be homemade. Under flexible exchange rates, the long-run inflation is homemade, whereas in the short run, individual countries cannot completely extricate themselves from the international inflation nexus.[22]

Notes

1. Gerhard Fels, "Inflation in Germany" in L. B. Krause and W. S. Salant (Eds.), *Worldwide Inflation* (Washington, D. C., 1977), p. 594.

2. M. Friedman, "What Price Guideposts?" in G. P. Schultz and R. Z. Aliber (Eds.), *Guidelines: Informed Controls and the Market Place* (Chicago, Ill., 1966), p. 33.

3. J. Tobin, "How Dead is Keynes?" *Economic Inquiry* 15 (October 1977), p. 466.

4. The substantially lower foreign exchange accumulation, measured in Deutschmark, at the Bundesbank after 1974, when compared to the magnitude of foreign exchange accumulation between 1970 and 1973, stems not only from the transition to a system of (dirty) float, but also from the revaluations and appreciations of the Deutschmark.

5. For a recent statement along these lines see J. M. Fleming, "International Aspects of Inflation" in E. Lundberg (Ed.), *Inflation Theory and Anti-Inflation Policy*. Proceedings of a Conference held by the International Economic Association at Saltsjöbaden, Sweden (Boulder, Col., 1977), p. 159.

6. J. Tinbergen, *On the Theory of Economic Policy* (Amsterdam, 1952).

7. R. A. Mundell, "The Monetary Dynamics of International Adjustment under Fixed and Flexible Exchange Rates," *Quarterly Journal of Economics* 74 (1960); reprinted in his *International Economics* (New York, 1968), p. 163.

8. R. A. Mundell, "The Appropriate Use of Monetary and Fiscal Policy under Fixed Exchange Rates," International Monetary Fund, *Staff Papers*, March 1962; reprinted in his *International Economics* (chap. 16).

9. Since there are more decision makers involved on the international scene than the domestic one, the decision and action lags may very well be considerably longer than in the case of fiscal policy on the national level.

10. Complete sterilization of the monetary impact of foreign reserve accumulation was either not feasible, or not possible when the outstanding government debt was too small and the bond market not broad enough.

11. A summary of the Scandinavian model can be found in H. Frisch, "Inflation Theory 1963–1975: A 'Second Generation' Survey," *Journal of Economic Literature* 15 (December 1977): 1305–08.

12. A. K. Swoboda, "Monetary Approaches to Worldwide Inflation" in Krause and Salant (Eds.), *Worldwide Inflation: Theory and Recent Experience*, p. 40.

13. H. Genberg, "Purchasing Power Parity under Fixed and Flexible Exchange Rates," *Journal of International Economics* 8 (May 1978): 261–62.

14. The revaluation debate started as far back as the mid-1950s; see H. M. Kaufmann, "A Debate Over Germany's Revaluation 1961: A Chapter in Political Economy," *Weltwirtschaftliches Archiv* 103 (1969): 181–212.

15. Lars Nyberg, "Imported and Home-made Inflation under Fixed and Floating Exchange Rates" in A. Lindbeck (Ed.), *Inflation and Employment in Open Economies*. Studies in International Economics, vol. 5 (Amsterdam-New York, 1979): 145–50.

16. E.-M. Claassen, "Stabilisierungspolitik in interdependenten Wirtschaften" in H. K. Schneider et al (Eds.), *Stabilisierungspolitik in der Marktwirtschaft*, Schriften des Vereins für Sozial-politik, N.F., vol. 85/II (Berlin, 1975), pp. 776–77.

17. According to a recent study, there were some parity changes (under the system of pegged exchange rates) — Germany's in 1961, Canada's in 1961–62, Spain's of 1959–60, Finland's of 1957–58, and France's of 1957–58 — which had brought about 'permanent' changes in relative export prices. See P. W. Robinson, T. R. Webb and M. A. Townsend, "The Influence of Exchange Rate Changes on Prices: A Study of 18 Industrial Countries," *Economica* 46 (February 1979), p. 44.

18. H. Genberg, "Purchasing Power Parity under Fixed and Flexible Exchange Rates," pp. 252–253.

19. This reasoning is connected with the monetarist view of the Phillips Curve and, consequently, not yet generally accepted.

20. Under the system of flexible exchange rates expectations play an even bigger role than under fixed exchange rates. According to current thinking, price expectations play a more significant role than cost competitiveness in exchange rate determination and fluctuations. Thus, expectations can lead directly to domestic inflationary pressures via the exchange rate mechanism. See J. F. O. Bilson, "The 'Vicious Circle' Hypothesis," International Monetary Fund, *Staff Papers* 26 (1), March 1979, p. 6.

21. For a discussion of this reluctance, see H. M. Kaufmann, "Germany's Option to be a Mini-Locomotive: A Reassessment of 1977," *Economia Internazionale* 31 (3–4), August–November 1978, pp. 196–211, and "From the 'Locomotive Hypothesis' to 'Concerted Action' — The Metamorphosis of an Idea," *Economia Internazionale* 32 (2–3), May–August, 1979, pp. 267–282.

22. See also Nyberg, "Imported and Home-made Inflation," p. 157.

The Inflationary Seventies: Comparisons among Selected High-income Countries

RICHARD T. SELDEN*

This paper has a relatively modest aim: to examine the relationship between monetary growth and inflation during the 1970s. A large amount of evidence linking monetary expansion to recent inflation has already been published, especially for the United States.[1] Indeed, among economists it has become almost axiomatic that a serious inflation cannot take place without roughly commensurate monetary growth. But controversy continues. First, the vast contemporary literature on inflation contains an abundance of discussions that ignore or even repudiate the importance of money, either because the demand for money is regarded as highly flexible or because central banks allegedly can be counted on to expand money sufficiently to accommodate the "real" determinants of inflation. Second, there are conflicting views over the nature of the channels that link monetary growth and inflation. In particular, it is generally understood that inflations spread across national boundaries much like a contagious disease, but it is not clear exactly how these international linkages work. In addition, there is disagreement about important details, such as the length of lags between monetary growth and inflation and the most appropriate statistical measures of money and prices. A further question pertains to the applicability of monetary models of inflation outside the United States.

The distinctive feature of the paper is its analysis of a number of high-income countries within a common format. Eight countries are examined: Belgium, Canada, the Netherlands, Norway, Sweden, Switzerland, the United Kingdom, and the United States. Although all of them have been studied previously, most studies have focused on a single country. In view of the disparate time periods and methodologies employed, cross-country comparisons have been difficult to make. Moreover, none of the earlier studies has incorporated the experience of the late 1970s.

Some readers may wonder why these countries were selected. Aside from the basic requirement of readily available quarterly data, I have sought a group of countries that are both similar and dissimilar to the United States: similar in respect to levels of affluence and social and political framework, dissimilar in respect to the degree of activism in economic policy and dependence on foreign trade.

Section I is devoted to a brief discussion of conceptual and measurement issues. The experiences of the United States and the other seven countries through the end of 1977 are analyzed in Sections II and III. In Section IV, I examine the acceleration of inflation in the United States in 1978–79. Finally, in Section V, I consider the inflation outlook for the first half of the 1980s.

I

Even within the "monetarist camp" a number of alternative models of inflation have been developed. I shall not attempt to compare these competing models here. Rather, I shall work simply with a slightly elaborated version of the exchange identity,

$$M V = P O \tag{1}$$

where M is the average money stock outstanding during some period, V is the velocity of circulation or turnover rate of M, P is a price index of currently produced goods and services, and O is real GNP or a similar measure of aggregate output. We can write Equation 1 in terms of rates of change rather than levels:

$$m + v = p + o \tag{2}$$

or $$p_t = (v_t - o_t) + m_t \tag{3}$$

where time subscripts have been added as reminders that the identity holds only as long as all the rates of change are taken over the same time interval.

By itself, Equation 3 is merely a highly useful device that helps us classify the various events that take place during an inflation. In order to construct a *theory* of inflation we must add assumptions about the real-world behavior of the right-hand variables.

A fully articulated theory of inflation would have to include several additional equations depicting the demand and supply of money, a production function, the labor market, and perhaps other relations. In my judgment, however, the spirit of monetarism is captured by a far simpler model which rests on two critical assumptions: First, that over medium-term periods the relationship between the rates of change in velocity and output does not change much:

$$v_t - o_t = \alpha \tag{4}$$

where α may be taken approximately as a constant. The second monetarist assumption is that monetary growth does not affect the rate of inflation immediately; i.e., there are monetary lags. Further, it is reasonable to suppose that these lagged effects of m on p are not discrete but are distributed over many periods. Hence we can write

$$p_t = \alpha + \sum_{i=0}^{n} w_i m_{t-i} \tag{5}$$

where the w_i are weights attached to a series of current and past monetary growth rates.

Whether these characteristic monetarist assumptions are reasonable can be determined only empirically. It should be noted, however, that both v and o have followed fairly stable trends, and they are highly correlated during ordinary cyclical disturbances. Except for occasional abrupt breaks in trend, the treatment of α as a constant does not appear to be far-fetched. As for lags, they may be analyzed into two components: (1) delayed responses of nominal GNP to monetary changes; (2) a well-established tendency for changes in GNP to take the form initially of output changes, and only later, price changes. The existence of long-term contracts and widespread regulatory constraints suggests that price adjustments are unlikely to take place promptly when either demand or supply conditions change.

Nothing has been said so far about two issues that have appeared prominently in discussion of inflation lately: the role of expectations and the international transmission mechanism. It is reasonable to suppose that the length of the lag between monetary growth and inflation will depend on whether or not the monetary growth has been generally anticipated. Where a monetary acceleration has been widely expected, there is likely to be greater reliance on short-term contracts, escalators, and other devices that lead to prompt price-wage adjustments, so money-price lags should be shorter than in the case of unexpected monetary changes. I have no quarrel with this important theoretical distinction, but I have chosen to ignore it in my basic empirical work — in effect, therefore, assuming stability over time in the public's inflation expectations. Given the huge rises in inflation rates during the 1970s, the wisdom of this procedure will seem questionable to some readers. But in the final analysis this becomes an empirical matter that must be settled by the data.

For the present study, the international transmission issue seems both more important and more complicated than the expectations issue. Insofar as a country's monetary growth rate reflects international impulses, there is no problem. The monetarist model ignores the circumstances responsible for monetary changes; the only thing that matters is the *size* of the change. It is often argued, however, that inflations may be transmitted internationally wholly apart from measurable monetary changes, especially under a regime of floating exchange rates.[2] Or at the very least, it is contended that monetary accommodation is likely in the wake of an internationally transmitted inflation, which would imply quite a different lag structure from the one just suggested.

I have no neat solution for this international transmission problem. The work reported proceeds *as if* all of the countries involved are closed economies, even though they obviously are not. Again, having called attention to the problem, I suggest that judgment be suspended until the empirical findings are presented.

There are three other potential pitfalls for a study such as this. One is the propensity of governments to impose wage-price controls from time to time, thereby destroying the normal relationship between monetary growth and inflation. Except for Switzerland, all the countries included in this study adopted an "incomes policy" at least once during the 1970s. In the case of the Netherlands, controls have been in effect almost continuously for decades. I have dealt with this problem by inserting dummy variables during control (and decontrol) periods. Another disturbance that cannot be ignored is the switch to high-rate value-added taxes in five of the countries studied early in the 1970s: Belgium (1971), the Netherlands (1969), Norway (1970), Sweden (1969, 1971), and the United Kingdom (1973). There is no reason to think that the long-run inflation rate depends on the nature of the tax system, but it is clear that the introduction of VAT had significant one-time impacts on short-run inflation rates in the countries involved. The solution, again, is to introduce dummies at the time of major VAT rate changes.[3] Finally, there is the question of exogenous supply shocks — most notably, the quantum leap in world oil prices during the winter of 1973–74. My own belief, argued later, is that the role of supply shocks in general and of the 1973–74 oil shock in particular has been exaggerated in writing about inflation. Nevertheless, undoubtedly there was a massive and presumably permanent deterioration in the terms of trade, and hence in real incomes, in all eight countries because of the relative increase in oil prices. In terms of Equation 5, this implies an abrupt decline in the variable o during early 1974, and thus a rise in α and in p. Once again, this shift seems best handled by dummy variables.

In addition to these theoretical issues, there are a number of questions to be settled with respect to data, study periods, and specification of lag structures. For all countries except Norway, I have analyzed quarterly data over the period 1958–I to 1977–IV. In the case of Norway, the empirical work covers 1962–I to 1977–IV because of data limitations. In the cases of Belgium, Canada, the Netherlands, Switzerland, and the United States, narrow money was used. I have been guided in this choice partly by data availability, partly by closeness-of-fit considerations.[4] Except for the United States, I have used official consumer price indexes as reported in country sources or in OECD's *Main Economic Indicators*. The GNP deflator was used for the United States. All results have been derived from third-degree Almon-lag equations without end-point restrictions, covering monetary growth in the current and 19 lagged quarters.

Ideally, it would be better to smooth the highly choppy quarterly inflation rates, which are buffeted by all sorts of irrelevant momentary disturbances, including measurement errors. I have experimented with various smoothing techniques but have encountered intractable serial correlation problems.[5] Accordingly, in all the work reported, the dependent variables are quarter-to-quarter percentage changes, expressed as annual rates, even though I strongly suspect that economic models will never be able to account fully for observed movements in these short-term measures of inflation.

II

The United States price explosion of the mid-1970s has had a traumatic impact on inflation theory. Because it coincided quite closely with several supply shocks, most notably the OPEC-administered oil shock, there has been a strong inclination to hold this episode up as a prime example of the inadequacy of monetarist theories of inflation. After all, it is pointed out, the United States experienced double-digit inflation (a peacetime first) for four consecutive quarters, with a rate as high as 12.3 percent in the final quarter of 1974, despite contemporaneous M1 growth ranging from a mere 5.3 percent (1974–II) to less than 1 percent (1975–I). In only one quarter during the entire decade did M1 growth reach double digits — a 10.1 percent rate in 1971–II.

Contrary to such views, however, United States inflation experience in the 1970s is fully compatible with monetarist doctrine as outlined earlier. When the quarterly inflation rate is regressed on current and past M1–B growth rates, as in Equation 1.1 of Table 1, the sum of the coefficients on monetary growth (PCM) turns out to be easily significant at the 1 percent level. Indeed, the regression coefficients in that equation do not differ greatly from those of Equation 1.6, derived from the precontrols period. Both equations indicate that the average lag between M1–B growth and inflation is long, on the order of two years or more. Virtually identical results were obtained from estimations based on growth in M1–A.[6]

It is likely that the regression coefficients in Equation 1.1 are biased because of the impact of the Nixon Administration's price-wage controls, introduced in August 1971, on reported prices. During the initial freeze and the subsequent Phase II, in which controlled increases were

Table 1. Inflation Regressions for the United States

	58-I to 77-IV				58-I to 71-II	
	1.1	1.2	1.3	1.4	1.5	1.6
PCM	1.251	1.332	1.10	1.095	1.051	1.049
	(7.00)*	(8.55)	(6.22)	(10.10)	(7.18)	(10.66)
WPCON		−2.156	−1.755	−1.839	−1.681	
		(2.55)	(2.62)	(2.87)	(2.20)	
DECON			2.676	2.371	2.243	
			(4.10)	(3.39)	(2.47)	
OIL				1.150	.412	
				(1.18)	(.34)	
XR					.004	
					(.06)	
XR_{-1}					−.008	
					(.08)	
XR_{-2}					−.011	
					(.12)	
XR_{-3}					−.010	
					(.12)	
C	−1.020	−1.133	−.408	−.384	2.702	−.323
	(1.26)*	(1.64)	(.86)	(.86)	(.53)	(1.04)
R^2	.762	.780	.808	.812	.811	.725
D.W.	2.14	2.12	2.00	1.98	2.00	2.25
S.E.R.	1.33	1.29	1.21	1.21	1.25	.95
Rho	.515	.443	.197	.142	.211	
Mean Lag	7.4	8.3	10.2	10.5	9.6	9.8
	(3.22)*	(4.27)	(9.52)	(6.69)	(3.52)	(5.95)

*Figures in parentheses are absolute values of t statistics. The dependent variable is the annualized quarter-to-quarter percentage change in the GNP deflator.

See Appendix for a glossary of variables.

permitted, the official price indexes were held well below levels that would be expected on the basis of prior monetary growth. Toward the end of 1972 there were signs that the controls were becoming less effective, which prompted President Nixon — now safely reelected — to initiate a greatly relaxed set of price-wage rules at the beginning of 1973. Prices began to climb rapidly toward levels consistent with prior monetary growth, resulting in momentary double-digit inflation rates.

This "snapback" period of adjustment was exacerbated by the roughly simultaneous "oil shock" which hit the world late in 1973 and early in 1974. By early 1975 these abnormalities had subsided, and actual inflation rates quickly retreated to levels close to the trend rate of monetary growth.

These abnormalities of the early and middle 1970s are analyzed in Equations 1.2, 1.3, and 1.4 by use of dummy variables. WPCON, the controls dummy, enters the regressions during 1971–III to 1972–IV; DECON, the decontrol dummy, enters during 1973–I to 1974–IV, and OIL, the oil-shock dummy, enters during the final quarter of 1973 and the first two quarters of 1974. It can be seen that both WPCON and DECON are significant, whether OIL is included or not. OIL fails to pass conventional significance tests but it does have the expected positive sign.

A recurring theme in inflation literature is that exchange depreciation may contribute importantly to inflation. Since the Federal Reserve's index of the trade-weighted average value of the dollar fell from 121.6 in 1971–I to only 93.9 in 1975–I — a 23 percent depreciation — it seems reasonable to test for the contribution of exchange-rate changes to the inflation explosion of the mid-1970s. Equation 1.5 does this by adding exchange-rate variables for the current and three preceding quarters to Equation 1.4. The results are somewhat surprising. Although the three lagged exchange-rate variables have the expected negative signs, none of them comes close to achieving statistical significance.

For purposes of investigating the post-1977 acceleration in inflation in the United States and making simulations to the mid-1980s, it appears that Equation 1.4 may be the most satisfactory. Equations 1.3 and 1.4, it will be noted, closely resemble the precontrols Equation 1.6 in terms of estimated coefficients and mean lags.

III

I turn now to the results of similar regressions on quarterly data for seven other high-income countries, taken in alphabetic order as listed in Table 2. As was mentioned earlier, in each instance Almon-lag regressions were run with third-degree polynomials without end-point constraints. For all countries, the specifications match exactly those of the United States, the sole exception being the inclusion of dummies for value-added taxes (VAT) in quarters of initial adoption or substantial rate hikes. No such dummy was used for Sweden, since the Swedish consumer price index (CPI) used here is a "net" index that has been adjusted for tax changes. Canada and Switzerland (like the United States) have not employed value-added taxes. VAT dummies were entered for Belgium in 1971–I, for the Netherlands in 1969–I and 1976–IV, and for Norway in 1970–I.

The most striking feature of Table 2 is the similarity between the results reported there and those of Table 1 for the United States. A glance across the top row of the table reveals a strong association — for every country and for every specification — between inflation rates and previous monetary growth rates extending over many quarters into the past. The estimates of mean lags shown on the bottom row are remarkably similar to United States estimates, ranging from a little over two years for Canada to more than three years for Norway, but tending to cluster around 9 or 10 quarters. These findings are especially interesting in view of the sharp differences among countries in degree of openness and in stabilization strategies.

Consider, for example, the contrast between Switzerland and the Netherlands. Both countries are deeply involved in foreign trade and therefore presumably are sensitive to external inflationary impulses. Germany is a next-door neighbor and important trading partner of both countries — which suggests similarities in the *types* of external impulses. Their inflation experiences, on the other hand, have been quite different, reflecting no doubt their radically different approaches to macro-policy. Prices and wages in the Netherlands have been subject to sporadic freezes, to prenotification requirements, and to other policy constraints throughout the period studied. Switzerland, in contrast, has rejected almost totally such interventionist policies, preferring instead to rely on a combination of fiscal orthodoxy and strong monetary policies. The simple correlation coefficient between the Dutch and Swiss quarterly inflation rates for 1962–79 is a mere .26; the mean inflation rate was a relatively high 6 percent for the Netherlands compared with only 4.3 percent for Switzerland, and the standard deviations 4.7 and 3.2, respectively. Nevertheless, mean lags exceed two years in both countries for all specifications, and there can be little doubt that "money matters" as far as the inflation rate is concerned in both countries, with the monetary impact persisting for periods as long as four or five years.

We have space here only to highlight a few of the findings reported in Table 2. It can be seen that the VAT dummies perform strongly in some countries, weakly in others. The lack of significance for VAT in Belgium may reflect the nature of the specific tax substitutions made in that country early in 1971, VAT replacing an earlier turnover tax which probably exerted similar effects on the CPI. The sign of VAT is positive, as expected. VAT did not arrive in the United Kingdom until 1973–II, a period in which a relatively stringent incomes policy was holding prices and wages below equilibrium levels. It is not surprising, therefore, that British regressions show a negative (but nonsignificant)

Table 2. Inflation Regressions for Selected High-income Countries

	Belgium				Britain	
	2.1	2.2	2.3	3.1	3.2	3.3
PCM	1.275	1.263	1.228	.997	1.013	1.001
	(6.91)*	(6.99)	(8.11)	(8.48)	(9.65)	(8.85)
S1				.510	.500	.502
				(.46)	(.45)	(.45)
S2				3.411	3.403	3.402
				(2.88)	(2.93)	(2.92)
S3				−3.835	−3.842	−3.796
				(3.50)	(3.51)	(3.43)
VAT		1.755	1.618			
		(.82)	(.77)			
WPCON		.788			−3.567	−3.512
		(.41)			(2.53)	(2.44)
DECON						
OIL			5.401			.924
			(2.88)			(.32)
C	−3.581	−3.563	−3.406	−.619	−.311	−.251
	(2.84)*	(2.91)	(3.31)		(.27)	(.21)
R^2	.684	.687	.715	.739	.760	.760
D.W.	2.06	2.04	2.03	1.94	1.94	1.94
S.E.R.	2.23	2.25	2.15	3.83	3.70	3.72
Rho	.386	.362	.270	.215	.144	.151
Mean Lag	9.0	8.8	9.2	9.4	8.9	9.0
	(4.68)*	(4.53)	(5.60)	(6.39)	(6.26)	(6.14)

	Canada			The Netherlands		
	4.1	4.2	4.3	5.1	5.2	5.3
PCM	.934	.974	.949	1.069	1.047	1.043
	(12.01)	(9.84)	(9.51)	(6.80)	(6.94)	(6.82)
S1				2.279	2.357	2.279
				(1.91)	(2.07)	(2.05)
S2				3.411	3.831	3.857
				(2.85)	(3.36)	(3.32)
S3				−4.206	−4.032	−3.986
				(3.54)	(3.49)	(3.39)
VAT					7.452	7.501
					(2.81)	(2.80)
WPCON		.672	−.645		−1.360	−1.334
		(.66)	(.64)		(.87)	(.85)
DECON					3.998	3.974
					(1.09)	(1.07)
OIL			2.319			.808
			(1.45)			(.26)
C	−2.103	−2.266	−2.127	−4.285	−4.409	−4.427
	(3.74)	(3.67)	(3.43)	(2.71)	(2.93)	(2.91)
R^2	.686	.688	.697	.574	.629	.630
D.W.	2.08	2.08	2.08	2.36	2.34	2.34
S.E.R.	1.99	2.00	1.98	3.76	3.58	3.60
Rho						
Mean Lag	7.3	7.7	8.1	9.2	9.0	8.9
	(6.83)	(4.37)	(5.40)	(5.24)	(5.20)	(4.87)

| | | Norway | | | Sweden | |
	6.1	6.2	6.3	7.1	7.2	7.3
PCM	.806	.816	.773	1.117	1.096	.880
	(4.82)	(5.01)	(4.70)	(3.42)	(3.46)	(3.58)
S1	5.039	5.428	5.361	1.050	.952	1.359
	(3.70)	(4.04)	(4.02)	(.65)	(.62)	(.97)
S2	1.773	2.159	2.357	−.702	−.726	−.163
	(1.21)	(1.49)	(1.64)	(.69)	(.76)	(.18)
S3	2.071	1.462	2.259	.509	−.018	.366
	(1.38)	(1.44)	(1.55)	(.55)	(.02)	(.42)
VAT	20.325	19.875	20.035			
	(6.08)	(6.08)	(6.19)			
WPCON		−4.337	−4.358		−5.621	−6.141
		(1.88)	(1.90)		(2.11)	(2.64)
DECON					5.300	4.550
					(1.67)	(1.49)
OIL			3.174			8.873
			(1.37)			(3.54)
C	−2.519	−2.838	2.731	−4.081	−3.546	−2.174
	(1.34)	(1.57)	(1.50)	(1.52)	(1.36)	(1.07)
R^2	.654	.679	.692	.447	.521	.587
D.W.	1.99	1.99	1.93	2.16	2.20	2.16
S.E.R.	3.12	3.04	3.01	3.35	3.16	2.96
Rho				.417	.434	.310
Mean Lag	14.6	13.2	12.7	7.4	8.0	9.8
	(3.73)	(3.44)	(3.10)	(3.13)	(3.38)	(4.30)

	Switzerland	
	8.1	8.2
PCM	.558	.589
	(3.93)	(4.41)
S1	−2.557	−2.417
	(2.74)	(2.77)
S2	−1.974	−1.538
	(2.14)	(1.76)
S3	−1.900	−1.414
	(1.97)	(1.55)
VAT		
WPCON		
DECON		
OIL		7.089
		(3.33)
C	1.263	.590
	(1.05)	(.52)
R^2	.444	.519
D.W.	1.55	1.50
S.E.R.	2.76	2.58
Rho		
Mean Lag	13.2	11.9
	(5.45)	(5.49)

*Figures in parentheses are t statistics. The dependent variable is the annualized quarter-to-quarter percentage change in an index of consumer prices.

See Appendix for a glossary of variables.

coefficient for VAT. For this reason I have omitted the VAT regressions from Table 2. The Norwegian and Dutch equations, on the other hand, have highly significant VAT variables with positive coefficients; omission of this variable greatly reduces the significance of monetary growth in Norway, but the significance of Dutch monetary growth is scarcely affected.

There are also differences among countries in the effectiveness of the OIL dummy. In the Belgian, Swedish, and Swiss equations, OIL contributes substantial explanatory power. Britain, Canada, the Netherlands, and Norway, on the other hand, resemble the United States in having nonsignificant OIL coefficients. These results may well reflect policy differences across countries — a hypothesis that I plan to explore in future work.

Finally, it is interesting to note that only in the cases of Britain and Sweden, among the countries included in Table 2, are there statistically significant coefficients on WPCON, the controls dummy. Neither of these countries has a significant coefficient on DECON. This is not surprising since there is no clear distinction between having and not having controls. In practice, countries usually move into — and especially out of — controls in a series of steps; there may be no clean policy switch that can be well represented by a dummy variable. These results suggest that incomes policies have had relatively little impact on the measured rates of inflation of most countries, despite the attention they have received in recent years.

IV

The real test of regression equations such as those of Tables 1 and 2 is their performance outside the sample used to derive them. Table 3 shows actual and predicted inflation rates during 1978 and 1979 for all countries. Once again the results are highly diverse: in Belgium, the Netherlands, Norway, and Switzerland actual inflation was generally less than predicted inflation; the reverse was true in the other countries. The United States equation correctly predicted a rising inflation rate for this period, but it underpredicted inflation by fairly substantial margins in all eight quarters. Monetarists, it should be stated, were not alone in underestimating inflation in the late 1970s. The same could be said of nearly all economists, regardless of forecasting methods employed.

One reason for these underpredictions of United States inflation in the late 1970s was the growing obsolescence of United States monetary statistics. Before publication of the new M1–A and M1–B series in February 1980, inflation analysts had to work with either the old M1 or the old M2. Both of these older time series were closely related to inflation over the period 1958–77, but their value as inflation predictors was seriously impaired toward the end of the 1970s by rapid growth of checkable deposits that were excluded from M1. A particularly important step in this direction was taken 1 November 1978, when commercial banks were empowered to offer "automatic transfer" savings accounts. Many holders of demand deposits switched balances to these interest-bearing "ATS" accounts, thus retarding growth in the old M1 and understating growth in total transactions balances. The importance of this factor can be indicated quite precisely: United States inflation in 1979–IV should have been only 6.42 percent, according to an equation based on old M1, compared with a prediction 7.11 percent based on M1–B, as shown in Table 3. M1–B, of course, includes checkable time deposits.

But even 7.11 percent is well below the actual 1979–IV rate of 8.37 percent, as measured by GNP prices. Three explanations of this large discrepancy have received considerable attention in recent discussions of United States inflation. The first is essentially an extension of the point discussed in the preceding paragraph — namely, that we have underestimated growth in cash balances. Prominent among these types of "uncounted cash" are Eurodollar deposits held by Americans, overnight repurchase agreements held by corporations as interest-earning substitutes for demand deposits, and shares in money market mutual funds. All three were expanding rapidly during the late 1970s, and money market fund shares were being used increasingly for transfers of large balances (subject usually to a $500 minimum) to third parties.

A second hypothesis attributes the underprediction of United States inflation in 1978–79 to depreciation of the dollar against other leading currencies. The magnitude of this depreciation was substantial, amounting to about 16 percent between the beginning of 1977 and late 1978. A careful review of the evidence by Joel L. Prakken found that the cumulative effects of exchange depreciation during 1977 and early 1978 had boosted the rate of inflation in the consumption deflator by 1.4 percentage points in the second half of 1978. A boost of this size would explain most of the discrepancies noted in Table 3. Nevertheless, the failure of regression Equation 1.5 (Table 1) to find significant effects of exchange depreciation on United States inflation during 1958–77 suggests that we should be cautious about accepting this hypothesis for the late 1970s, despite its surface plausibility.

A third hypothesis regards the new round of oil price hikes in 1979 as a major source of accelerating inflation in the United States in the late 1970s. This hypothesis has obvious difficulties explaining inflation developments in 1978, but it does seem relevant to United States developments in 1979. Oil prices rose in the United States in 1979 not only because of OPEC actions but also because domestic price ceilings

Table 3. Actual and Predicted Rates of Inflation, 1978I–1979IV

	1978I	1978II	1978III	1978IV	1979I	1979II	1979III	1979IV
Belgium								
Actual	5.03	1.66	5.94	4.22	3.86	4.14	5.99	6.21
Predicted	9.55	9.10	8.69	8.66	8.42	8.35	8.39	8.37
Britain								
Actual	7.30	11.24	6.02	8.08	12.41	17.16	24.80	10.40
Predicted	9.80	12.59	5.96	9.92	10.97	13.72	7.01	10.98
Canada								
Actual	8.60	10.06	5.70	8.42	11.61	8.61	8.14	9.47
Predicted	7.62	7.40	7.12	6.99	6.80	6.68	6.69	6.82
Netherlands								
Actual	1.36	5.07	8.01	.65	5.88	1.93	7.05	4.09
Predicted	10.34	11.99	4.10	7.38	8.58	10.16	1.47	4.67
Norway								
Actual	19.65	5.10	10.62	1.36	2.17	5.94	4.26	6.05
Predicted	11.19	7.12	7.94	7.96	13.02	10.96	10.92	9.89
Sweden								
Actual	23.03	2.18	5.78	7.12	9.79	6.96	10.26	11.02
Predicted	7.94	5.90	6.06	5.50	7.77	6.11	6.53	6.13
Switzerland								
Actual	.80	1.93	.77	.77	8.05	8.27	2.21	1.83
Predicted	−1.04	.27	.99	3.08	.82	2.91	3.43	5.62
United States								
Actual	6.08	10.34	6.90	8.60	8.93	8.99	8.30	8.37
Predicted	5.46	5.66	5.85	6.06	6.26	6.60	6.91	7.11

Note: Predicted rates of inflation were derived from regression Equations 1.4, 2.3, 3.3, 4.3, 5.3, 6.3, 7.3, and 8.2, using actual monetary growth rates through 1979IV. For Britain, the Netherlands, and Switzerland, monetary growth in 1979IV was assumed to be the same as in 1979III.

were raised. If one adds the 1.15 percent OIL coefficient from regression Equation 1.4 to the predicted inflation rate for 1979–IV of 7.11 percent shown in Table 3, one gets an amended estimate of predicted inflation of 8.26 percent, which is only negligibly below the actual rate of 8.37 percent. Thus it is not unreasonable to interpret the inflationary surge of the late 1970s as reflecting in part the renewed eruption of oil prices, superimposed on a strongly rising trend in M1–B growth.

V

The evidence reported in this study provides strong support for two major conclusions: First, in each of the eight countries examined, a close association exists between the rate of inflation and current and past rates of monetary growth. This is true despite sharp differences across countries in policies, institutions, and degree of international exposure. Second, the impact of changes in monetary growth rates on inflation is distributed over long time spans, with average lags ranging from two to three years.

From these findings it follows that knowledge of current and recent monetary growth can be coupled with central bank announcements of planned monetary growth to form inflation forecasts far into the future. In this final section we shall present inflation forecasts through 1984 under alternative monetary scenarios.

The first three columns of Table 4 show the inflation implications of maintaining M1–B growth through 1984 at the upper end, midpoint, and lower end of the Federal Reserve's target range for 1980. The Fed, of course, has no intention of holding to a fixed target range over a period of years. Chairman Paul A. Volcker and other Fed spokesmen have affirmed a long-run goal of gradual reductions in monetary growth to (unspecified) noninflationary rates. Nevertheless it is useful to consider the consequences of steady monetary growth at the announced rates for 1980.

Steady M1–B growth at the 6.5 percent upper end of the target range for 1980 would result, according to column I of Table 4, in virtually no slackening of inflation before late 1982 — except for an assumed slackening in the second half of 1980 due to the settling down of oil prices. With steady growth in M1–B of 5.25 percent (Column II), inflation would begin to moderate a little sooner and should be running a full percentage point under the rate associated with 6.5 percent growth by the middle of 1983. With an even lower maintained growth rate in M1–B of 4 percent, the United States could expect inflation in GNP prices to sink below 7 percent by the first quarter of 1982.

Columns IV and V of Table 4 present scenarios that are more consistent with the recommendations of most monetarists since they illustrate the inflation implications of gradual reductions in monetary growth. It can be seen in column IV that a relatively slow rate of decrease in M1–B growth — by .25 percent per quarter — would imply consistently higher inflation through 1984 than would an immediate drop to a steady 4 percent level. The 7 percent inflation barrier would not be pierced under such a policy before the final quarter of 1982; the 5 percent barrier only in 1984. The more rapid monetary deceleration that is illustrated in column V — .5 percent per quarter — would probably be considered unacceptably rapid by most economists, but even that scenario would not bring inflation below 7 percent before the second quarter of 1982.

Finally, it is worth noting that inflation in GNP prices in the United

Table 4. Inflation Projections for the United States Based on Regression Equation 1.4, 1980–84

Period	I	II	III	IV	V	VI
80-I	8.46	8.44	8.42	8.46	8.46	8.34
80-II	8.61	8.56	8.51	8.61	8.61	8.35
80-III	8.20	8.12	7.99	8.18	8.15	7.76
80-IV	7.77	7.65	7.52	7.74	7.71	7.13
81-I	7.84	7.67	7.50	7.79	7.73	6.95
81-II	7.88	7.65	7.42	7.79	7.70	6.69
81-III	7.87	7.57	7.27	7.73	7.59	6.32
81-IV	7.78	7.41	7.03	7.58	7.39	5.83
82-I	7.69	7.23	6.77	7.42	7.15	5.30
82-II	7.61	7.06	6.51	7.25	6.89	4.74
82-III	7.50	6.85	6.20	7.03	6.55	4.12
82-IV	7.37	6.62	5.86	6.77	6.16	3.45
83-I	7.25	6.39	5.53	6.49	5.74	2.78
83-II	7.14	6.18	5.21	6.21	5.27	2.13
83-III	7.06	5.99	4.93	5.94	4.83	1.52
83-IV	6.97	5.82	4.66	5.64	4.34	.96
84-I	6.87	5.63	4.39	5.31	3.81	.43
84-II	6.75	5.44	4.14	4.94	3.24	−.04
84-III	6.72	5.37	4.02	4.65	2.76	−.30
84-IV	6.74	5.37	4.00	4.40	2.33	−.38

Column I: Constant PCM = 6.5% per year.
Column II: Constant PCM = 5.25% per year.
Column III: Constant PCM = 4.0% per year.
Column IV: Gradually declining PCM by .25% per quarter until PCM = 0.
Column V: Gradually declining PCM by .5% per quarter until PCM = 0.
Column VI: Constant PCM = 0% per year.
Note: All projections have included the coefficient on OIL at full value for 1980-I and 1980-II and at half value for 1980-III.

States would continue to exceed 5 percent per year through early 1982 even if the Fed were to put an immediate halt to M1–B growth. Because of the long lags embodied in regression Equation 1.4, zero growth in M1–B, initiated early in 1980 and rigidly maintained for the next several years, would not produce a zero inflation rate until 1984. It would, however, probably produce massive unemployment and steep declines in declines in output for several years.

Table 5 presents similar projections for the other seven countries, based on what one hopes is the unrealistic assumption that 1979 rates of monetary growth will be maintained through 1984. These rates are

Table 5. Inflation Projections for Canada and Six European Countries, 1980–1984, Based on Continued Monetary Growth at 1979 Rates

Period	Belgium	Britain	Canada	The Nether-lands	Norway	Sweden	Switzerland
80-I	3.97	11.62	6.86	5.67	15.05	8.17	2.56
80-II	3.56	14.62	6.93	6.56	11.68	6.81	3.61
80-III	3.01	7.47	7.02	−1.62	11.07	7.59	3.85
80-IV	2.67	11.30	7.02	1.99	8.56	6.65	5.27
81-I	2.02	11.80	7.01	4.10	13.68	10.21	2.89
81-II	1.84	14.68	7.09	4.82	10.41	9.19	3.75
81-III	1.23	7.46	7.21	−4.17	9.85	10.05	3.88
81-IV	.76	11.21	7.39	−.89	7.23	9.74	5.26
82-I	.33	11.64	7.63	.83	12.51	11.82	2.88
82-II	−.11	14.47	7.77	2.31	9.62	9.97	3.64
82-III	−.16	7.21	7.87	−5.49	9.51	9.98	3.60
82-IV	−.30	10.96	7.93	−1.60	7.52	9.29	4.73
83-I	−.14	11.45	7.95	.62	13.33	11.24	1.56
83-II	−.43	14.36	7.96	2.01	10.63	9.49	2.37
83-III	−.26	7.18	7.97	−5.71	10.40	9.85	2.36
83-IV	−.07	10.98	7.97	−1.72	8.03	9.38	3.59
84-I	.17	11.49	7.97	.44	13.53	11.75	1.23
84-II	.58	14.38	7.94	1.80	10.41	10.00	2.58
84-III	.34	7.19	7.91	−6.00	10.11	10.26	2.74
84-IV	.36	10.99	7.89	−2.01	7.61	9.98	4.15
Average monetary growth in 1979*	3.09	11.31	10.56	2.33	13.37	13.69	6.03
Long-run noninflationary monetary growth rate	2.77	.25	2.24	4.24	3.53	2.47	−1.00

*For Britain, the Netherlands, and Switzerland, average monetary growth was calculated over the period 1978IV to 1979III. Projections are based on equations 2.3, 3.3, 4.3, 5.3, 6.3, 7.3, and 8.2. Except for seasonal dummies, all dummy variables were assigned values of zero for purposes of making projections.

shown at the bottom of the table, along with the growth rates that would be consistent with zero inflation in long-run equilibrium.

We have already seen (in Table 3) that four countries — Norway, the Netherlands, Belgium, and Switzerland — enjoyed relatively low rates of inflation in 1979. Three other countries — the United States, Canada, and Sweden — had considerably worse records in 1979, in the range of 8 to 10 percent inflation. Britain's mean quarterly inflation rate was far above these levels at more than 16 percent.

It is no surprise that a rough correlation exists between 1979 inflation rates and 1979 monetary growth rates. Norway is the sole exception to this generalization: its monetary growth far exceeded both noninflationary levels and actual rates of inflation. Accordingly, it is likely that Norway will join the ranks of the rapid inflators in 1980 and 1981. Continuation of its 1979 growth rate through 1984 would imply first-quarter inflation rates above 13 percent per year through 1984, compared with an actual rate of only a bit over 2 percent in the first quarter of 1979.

The other three low-inflation countries in 1979 have considerably better prospects. If Belgium were to maintain monetary growth through 1984 at 1979 rates, it would achieve an inflation rate close to zero by early 1982 and would settle into an equilibrium rate of less than .5 percent by 1984. If Dutch policy makers hold to their low 1979 monetary growth rate of 2.33 percent, they will bring inflation to a standstill by late 1981, according to Table 5. Indeed, the trend of the Dutch price level should be downward by 1982. This is because its noninflationary monetary growth rate of 4.24 percent is well above its growth rate for 1979. Switzerland, on the same assumption of a maintained monetary growth rate equal to that of 1979, can expect inflation to stay in the range of 3 to 4 percent per year through 1984. Continuation of monetary growth at rates experienced in 1979 would imply steady inflation in the neighborhood of 8 percent in Canada and the United States, about 10 percent in Sweden, and a depressing 11 percent in Britain.

There is, of course, no inherent reason for expecting the highly inflationary monetary growth of countries such as Britain, Canada, Norway, Sweden, and the United States to continue in the early 1980s. In Belgium, the Netherlands, and Switzerland, policy makers have demonstrated that monetary growth *can* be brought down to noninflationary levels without repercussions on output and employment more severe than those experienced by countries whose inflations have gone unchecked. There is reason to hope that this lesson has now been learned and that the 1980s will see a return to more moderate rates of monetary growth — and hence to more moderate rates of inflation — than those of the inflationary 1970s.

APPENDIX

GLOSSARY OF VARIABLES

C	Constant
DECON	Decontrol dummy (value of 1 in quarters immediately following abrupt terminations of wage-price controls; value of 0 in all other quarters).
OIL	Oil crisis dummy (value of 1 in 4th quarter of 1973 and 1st and 2d quarters of 1974; value of 0 in all other quarters).
PCM	Quarter-to-quarter percentage change in stock of money, expressed as annual rates.
S1, S2, S3	Seasonal dummies for 1st, 2d, and 3d quarters.
VAT	Value-added tax dummy (value of 1 in quarters of adoption or substantial increase in tax rates; value of 0 in all other quarters).
WPCON	Wage-price controls dummy (value of 1 in quarters in which comprehensive controls were in effect; value of 0 in all other quarters).
XR	Average trade-weighted foreign exchange value of United States dollar (index, 1973-I = 100).

Notes

* I wish to acknowledge the support of the University of Virginia's Thomas Jefferson Center for Studies in Political Economy in the early stages of this research. A portion of the work was done while I was a visiting scholar at the Institute for International Economic Studies, University of Stockholm, October–December 1978.

1. For United States evidence, see Berman, Dutton, Selden, and Tatom. Among the many studies that could be cited for other countries are Korteweg (The Netherlands), Myhrman (Sweden), and Vogel (Latin America).

2. Salant has discussed this issue at considerable length. For more recent discussions, see several of the papers in *Managed Exchange-Rate Flexibility: The Recent Experience,* Federal Reserve Bank of Boston Conference Series No. 20, as well as the careful survey of United States empirical studies by Hooper and Lowrey.

3. Korteweg has adopted this procedure in his study of Dutch inflation.

4. The United States regressions reported in Table 1 were run with both M1 and M2 (old definitions), as well as with M1–B (new definitions). Only the latter regressions are reported here. As I have noted in the text (Section II), the differences in results between M1 and M1–B are extremely negligible. Regres-

sions based on M2 result in slightly lower R^2s and considerably longer average lags; in other respects, however, they are highly similar to the results reported in Table 1.

For Canada, the substitution of M2 for M1 has relatively little effect on the relationship between monetary growth and inflation other than to reduce average lags by a couple of quarters.

5. In my 1977 article (and in several earlier papers), I adopted the expedient of converting the variable into three-year or four-year rates of change. Although I still see considerable merit in such an approach, I have abandoned it here in order to avoid the serial correlation problem.

6. These two monetary aggregates were nearly the same until the early 1970s; they did not diverge substantially until late 1978.

References

Berman, Peter I. *Inflation and the Money Supply in the United States, 1956–1977* (New York, 1978).

Dutton, Dean S. "The Economics of Inflation and Output Fluctuations in the United States: 1952–1974" in *The Problem of Inflation*, Carnegie-Rochester Conference Series on Public Policy, vol. 8 (Amsterdam, 1978).

Hooper, Peter, and Lowrey, Barbara R. "Impact of the Dollar Depreciation on the U.S. Price Level: An Analytical Survey of Empirical Estimates," *Staff Studies* No. 103 (Washington, D.C., Board of Governors of the Federal Reserve System, 1979).

Korteweg, Pieter. "The Economics of Inflation and Output Fluctuations in the Netherlands, 1954–1975: A Test of Some Implications of the Dominant Impulse-cum-Rational Expectations Hypothesis" in *The Problem of Inflation*.

Myhrman, Johan. "The Determinants of Inflation and Economic Activity in Sweden" in Assar Lindbeck (Ed.), *Inflation and Employment in Open Economies* (Amsterdam, 1979).

Prakken, Joel L. "The Exchange Rate and Domestic Inflation," *Federal Reserve Bank of New York Quarterly Review*, Summer 1979.

Salant, Walter S. "International Transmission of Inflation" in Lawrence B. Krause and Walter S. Salant (Eds.), *Worldwide Inflation: Theory and Recent Experience* (Washington, 1977).

Selden, Richard T. "Inflation: Are We Winning the Fight?" *Morgan Guaranty Survey*, October 1977.

Tatom, John. "The Link between Money and Prices — 1971–76," *Federal Reserve Bank of St. Louis Review*, June 1976.

Vogel, Robert C. "The Dynamics of Inflation in Latin America, 1950–1969," *American Economic Review*, March 1974.

Part 8
Social, Political and Psychological Aspects

The Psychology of Inflation

GEORGE KATONA

Inflation, a general and enduring increase in prices, has usually been viewed as an economic-financial process in the market place brought about by monetary disturbances. In ancient times debasement of coins, later excessive printing of paper money, large government deficits, or unjustified credit expansion led to more money being available than was needed to absorb the supply of goods. Driving prices up was also acknowledged as a result of cutting down on the supply of goods, as for instance during the siege of Paris by the Prussians in 1871 when inflation was rampant due to a lack of goods. Thus the old adage about "more money chasing fewer goods" appears well justified from experience over several centuries.

Still, obviously, the adage is incomplete. Money hardly does the chasing; it is human beings who use their money to drive prices up. Emperors, dictators, as well as democratic governments, financed their wars and welfare programs by the creation of excess money. Nor is the private sector blameless; entrepreneurs and labor unions may contribute to inflation by unjustified price increases or wage demands.

Whether the human factor is introduced in describing and explaining inflation makes for a great difference. Consideration of the human factor makes it necessary to study changes in people's motives, attitudes, and expectations, i.e., to analyze psychological processes which in most economic-financial studies are disregarded or neglected. The psychology of inflation consists primarily of a study of motives and expectations contributing to bringing about inflation as well as to slowing it down. The substantial role of such psychological phenomena should not, however, imply that psychological changes alone do or can bring about inflation. In all known instances, both market forces and psychological factors have contributed to inflation by reinforcing each other. In this paper, to be sure, relatively little attention will be paid to financial forces; the role of psychological factors will be emphasized.

THE COMMON REACTION TO INFLATION: SAVING MONEY

Since the end of World War II, the Survey Research Center of The University of Michigan and the author of this paper have continuously studied people's attitudes toward inflation and their reactions to price increases. The most conspicuous finding was the practically unanimous opinion of the American people that inflation was an evil. They attributed unfavorable consequences to inflation, both regarding general economic trends and personal finances. When people felt worse off because of price increases and highly uncertain about the future because of price movements, expectations were strongly influenced and general sentiment worsened. Of course, in several inflationary years many Americans enjoyed large increases in wages and salaries. But even these people complained about inflation. It was generally thought that a higher income was an accomplishment of the earner: he did well or advanced in his career and therefore deserved to make more money. Inflation, however, reduced the enjoyment of the well-deserved fruits of one's labor and therefore cheated those who made more money.

The unfavorable connotations of inflation were reinforced by ignorance: people in general were unable to understand inflation and its causes. When asked about the reasons for inflation and given a list of possible contributory factors, the majority of Americans acknowledged the role of each of the factors mentioned — government, business, labor, etc. The acceptance of a variety of causes indicates little understanding of how inflation came about. When asked simply to tell in their own words why we have inflation, in the late 1970s the largest number of people answered "Nobody knows."

Being worse off and being uncertain makes for less spending, especially discretionary spending. Reduced spending often leads to higher saving, which is justified in inflationary times by the notion that because of the price increases more money will be needed later to pay for necessities. Cross-section data indicated in the 1950s and 1960s that at time of heightened inflation people reported saving more than at times of relative price stability. Aggregate data examined over many years by Juster and Wachtel also indicated that in these years inflation was associated with increased saving. Thus during an extensive period of creeping inflation, the widely proclaimed theoretical principle about inflation consisting of and leading to accelerated expenditures was contradicted and increased saving reduced the extent of inflation.

THE DISRUPTIVE RESPONSE TO INFLATION: SPENDING MORE

Economists often search for fundamental and unchanging relationships between various processes — say, between inflation and unemployment; psychologists long ago gave up the notion of the existence of one-to-one relations between stimuli and responses. Intervening variables mediate between information received and people's reactions to it, and these variables may differ from person to person and, as time goes by, for the same person. In other words, psychologists consider man's basic capacity to learn. Therefore it is not to be expected that people would always react to inflation by saving more.

In 1950 in response to news about military defeats in Korea, and again in 1973 in response to news of sharply rising food prices following large grain exports to Russia, in two periods, each lasting several months, American consumers hastened to stock up and hoard goods. In the years beginning with 1978, buying in advance and in excess of needs became more general still, especially with respect to such major purchases as one-family houses and automobiles. By asking survey respondents whether it was a good or bad time to buy houses or cars, the majority of Americans were found to say that it was indeed a good time because prices would be higher later on. They confidently expected prices to go up further and thus to be priced out of the market at a later date. It could be estimated from the frequency of such statements by actual buyers of houses and cars that in 1978–79, not fewer than 40 percent of all purchasers of houses and cars were motivated by the expectation of further price increases rather than immediate need.

Thus we find that at certain times American consumers responded to price increases by stepping up their expenditures, just as economic theory postulated rational men should behave when they expected prices to go up. Under which circumstances did the one, and under which circumstances did the other form of behavior occur? The distinction between anxiety and fear may be appropriate to point to a major difference between the circumstances of the two reactions, increased saving and rush buying. When a general malaise prevails and people are uncertain regarding inflation, they may be apt to add to their savings in order to increase their capacity to resist. On the other hand, fear of a specific confidently expected development — e.g., much higher prices for one-family houses in the near future — may elicit the specific response of rush buying, which in turn contributes to the inflationary spiral.

In the 1950s and 1960s rapid inflation was considered out of the question. The American people on the whole were optimistic and confident and their aspirations for better living standards and more security were largely fulfilled. Toward the beginning of the decade of the 1970s, however, there were fundamental changes that characterized a new economic era.[1] Its main features were distrust of the government and of experts in general, lack of understanding and even confusion about what was going on in the economy, scaling down of aspirations, uncertainty and volatility of attitudes and actions. Trust in the government was most relevant in explaining the difference in people's reactions to inflation. In the 1950s and the early 1960s many people argued that what goes up must come down. When asked why this should happen, a large proportion of survey respondents pointed to probable appropriate action by the government (of course, without being able to specify how the government should act). In the 1970s when trust in the government collapsed — first because of Vietnam, then because of Watergate, and finally because of rapid inflation — people's response to inflation differed greatly.

IS EVERYBODY HURT BY INFLATION?

When asked about the greatest problem confronting them, most people refer to inflation and generally agree that it has graver consequences than unemployment and other domestic problems of the 1970s. Therefore one might have assumed that most Americans were badly hurt by inflation and had every reason to complain about the losses they have suffered because of it. A survey carried out in 1979 did not quite confirm this conjecture. To be sure, the questionnaire and the question sequence had to be carefully prepared because of the widespread stereotyped opinion that inflation is bad. Survey respondents were first asked about various unfavorable consequences of inflation, and then about possible favorable consequences, before the following summary question was raised: "Would you say that on the whole you have been hurt by inflation, you have managed to stay even with inflation, or have you gotten a little bit ahead of inflation?"

Table 1 indicates that many more respondents said they had stayed even with inflation or even got ahead of it than complained about having been hurt by inflation. Among high-income people, in which group substantial income increases were rather frequent, one-fifth said they succeeded in getting ahead of inflation in 1979.

The differences were surprisingly small among age groups, with the majority of those over 65 saying that they had stayed even with inflation. Education does make a small difference; a larger proportion of college graduates than of others said they had stayed even with inflation. The data indicate that inflation has a different impact on different people. Some are hurt badly and some manage to profit from it. These differences represent an important reason for fighting inflation.

It follows further from the data that it would be incorrect to assume that every American has good reason to oppose inflation and especially to make sacrifices in order to slow down inflation. That inflation is viewed as bad, even by people with substantial income increases, is true because inflation hurts continuously. Every shopping trip reveals price increases that are damaging, while increases in wages and salaries occur only occasionally. But the assumption that every American has good reason to fight inflation is not quite justified.

In a special survey conducted with managers of business firms, similar findings were obtained. Although the proportion of business

Table 1. Proportion of Family Units Hurt by Inflation, 1979*

Proportion saying . . .	All (%)	Income under $10,000† (%)	Income over $20,000‡ (%)
Hurt by inflation	37	39	32
Stayed even	48	53	47
Got ahead of inflation	12	5	19
Don't know	3	3	2
Total	100	100	100

*N = 2110
†Approximately one-fourth of all family units.
‡Approximately one-third of all family units.

firms hurt by inflation was somewhat higher than that of households, managers reported financial progress in 1979 more frequently than consumers. Furthermore, when asked to estimate the proportion of American companies benefiting from inflation, many business executives set the proportion rather high.

CONTRIBUTIONS TO INFLATION IN 1978–79

Results in full accord with the preceding discussion were obtained when survey respondents were queried about their ways of coping with inflation. To be sure, complaints about difficulties in passing on increases in wages or other costs were frequent. On the other hand, reports on inventory gains were also obtained and two specific questions about setting prices brought about surprisingly high affirmative answers.

Question	Answers* (%)
Is your company making an effort . . .	
to pass on increases in costs more rapidly?	Yes . . . 55; No . . . 45
to set prices in anticipation of increases in costs?	Yes . . . 39; No . . . 61

*By proportion of business establishments, weighted by number of employees.

It was, of course, expected that many business firms were making an effort to pass on increases in costs more rapidly than before. But anticipatory pricing, i.e., increasing prices in response to expected rather than actual cost increases, was also reported frequently, especially by manufacturing establishments. Anticipatory pricing of course does not prevent the business firm from increasing prices again when costs actually go up.

In 1978 and early 1979 the objective circumstances promoting rapid inflation improved. Money supply did not increase, government deficits became smaller, the dollar improved in foreign markets, and the price and wage guidelines had some beneficial effects. Nevertheless, the rate of price increases accelerated in the course of 1979. This development was widely attributed to an inflationary spiral and to what has been called *inflationary psychology.* Businessmen confidently expecting continuous rapid price increases adapted their policies and developed pricing methods which contributed to inflation. Similarly, defense mechanisms became widespread among consumers. We have already reported that instead of saving more, in 1978–79 very many people decided to buy a wide variety of goods in excess and in advance of immediate needs in order to obtain them at prices lower than would prevail later.

In the summer of 1979 when asked whether people *should* buy houses, cars, appliances, and the like, even before they are really needed, one-fifth of respondents in a representative sample answered in the affirmative. In spite of the widely accepted notion that everything we buy we do need, every fifth respondent, undeterred by the phrase "buy even before they are needed," expressed approval of trying to beat inflation by advance buying. Spending-mindedness contradicted the impact of pessimistic expectations and the anticipation of a recession which therefore was delayed or occurred only on a small scale. The acquisition of manifold highly cherished goods in these years of course likewise made inflation fairly tolerable, and for some people even enjoyable.

Economic trends in 1979 might better be described by the term *stagnation* than *recession.* Personal incomes, the total income earned by all households, rose in that year by 12 percent, i.e., at a similar rate as prices went up. Therefore a very substantial proportion of American families must have gotten increases in their incomes which exceeded the price increases; others suffered loss of income and had to curtail their outlays and reduce their standard of living. Many Americans refused to do so. What went down were amounts saved, rather than amounts spent. In previous years 6 or 8 or even higher percentages of income were saved — in some Western European countries and Japan, saving reached twice that rate — the proportion of income saved in 1979 fell to the low of 4½ percent (in the fourth quarter 1979 even to 3.3 percent). This sharp decline was not simply due to the reduction of the money Americans put in banks. Purchases of houses and cars were financed by credit — mortgage and installment loans — which represent negative saving and are deducted from amounts saved when total savings of a country are determined. Owing to a substantial increase in consumer debt, aggregate saving practically disappeared. Yet saving is important not only because it stimulates capital expenditures promoting growth and productivity, but also because it represents the most important drawback to inflation. Amounts saved, i.e., not spent, cut down the pressure on prices.

The data indicate that during 1979, attempts by American businessmen and consumers to cope with inflation contributed to it. Their behavior, motivated by their expectations, served to accelerate the rate of price increases. No doubt this process continued in 1980. The increase in oil prices by OPEC, of course, also contributed to inflation both directly and by raising the inflationary expectations of the American people.

FIGHTING INFLATION

Inflation must be fought. The main reason lies not in the widely held belief that inflation hurts people, but rather that it is unjust and creates uncertainty, which in turn disrupts orderly economic activities. When two-digit inflation endures for some time and the belief is widespread that nothing can be done to slow it down, many people are preoccupied with trying to "stay even," rather than with doing the best job they are capable of. Productivity suffers, and speculation flourishes.

A decline in average real incomes or in the value of average assets is not an inevitable consequence of inflation. Certain assets, such as bank deposits, lose in value if expressed in terms of their purchasing power; other assets, and especially the largest asset of American families, the owner-occupied house, gain in value at time of inflation. To be sure, for most people it is difficult if not impossible to use the gains in house values. At the same time, young families suffer: Would-be buyers of first houses, who have no house to sell, are finding it harder and harder to achieve their cherished goal.

Clearly, both economic-financial and psychological measures are required to slow down inflation. The former alone, even if they are very restrictive and bring about a recession, may not suffice if businesses and households do not trust them and continue to raise prices and expenditures. Psychological factors alone cannot be effective because confident expectations of slower price increases can arise only on recognition of objective factors which would bring them about.

An increase in interest rates to unprecedented high levels, as initiated in 1979–80, contributes little to the fight against inflation and has very unfavorable psychological consequences in addition to adding to business costs. It contributes to the expectation of further inflation and may even promote additional borrowing because of fear of further increases in interest rates.

The most radical way of stopping price increases is of course to forbid them. General mandatory price and wage controls, however, can succeed only if the people cooperate with them, as well as with rationing which usually must accompany them. Price control may be evaded in many ways and when this is done by very many people, the government is powerless. In 1978–79 the climate required for effective price control did not exist. Whether the international crises in 1980 and the presidential election campaign will restore confidence in the government remains to be seen.[2]

At the same time price and wage guidelines may be of substantial help. They are intended to restrict rather than prohibit action contrary to public interest. They may be flexible and may be useful even if occasionally violated. Guidelines also require cooperation by businesses and consumers and recognition that over the long run it is in the interest of families as well as businesses to put an end to rapid inflation. Thus trust in the government, severely impaired in the 1970s, is a requirement for success in fighting inflation. Guidelines may be reinforced by some highly selective mandatory controls in segments of the economy with few sellers where they are enforceable.

Price and wage guidelines must be supported by a variety of economic-financial measures, among which a reduction of government deficits and of the increase in money supply are important. Yet what is necessary first of all is a revival of inclination to save rather than to spend. Substantial tax advantages granted to savers might be useful in this respect. If the public realizes the need to slow down inflation and believes that the means used will be successful, long-range considerations may override attempts to profit from inflation over the short run.

It is necessary that the new policies catch people's imagination and create an atmosphere of confidence. Only then can they be seen as representing a new start, terminating the era of the 1970s. Only after inflation has slowed down can we expect some real growth in the American economy.[3]

Notes

1. This is the title of a book by George Katona and Burkhard Strumpel (1978) which presents data on differences in attitudes and behavior in the first 25 years following World War II and in the 1970s.

2. This author published a little book shortly after Pearl Harbor entitled *War Without Inflation* (Katona, 1942), in which he argued that World War II could be the first great war in history fought without substantial inflation. Not only was the knowledge of the needed economic and administrative measures available, but the psychological conditions for approval of, and cooperation

with, such measures were also present. Helping the war effort was something done willingly rather than viewed as a sacrifice. The book implied that inflation might come after the end of the war, when patriotic fervor would vanish and measures taken against violators of controls might fail because of widespread evasion. A sharper contrast could hardly be imagined than that between the attitudes prevailing during World War II and in the 1970s.

3. The author wrote on the psychology of inflation in the following earlier books: *The Powerful Consumer* (New York, 1960), chap. 12; *Mass Consumption Society* (New York, 1964), chap. 14; *Psychological Economics* (New York, 1975), chap. 9. *War Without Inflation* was published by Columbia University Press in 1942; George Katona and Burkhard Strumpel, *A New Economic Era* was published by Elsevier (New York, 1978).

See F. Thomas Juster and Paul Wachtel, "Inflation and the Consumer," *Brookings Papers on Economic Activity*, 1972:1.

More information on the inflation survey conducted by the Survey Research Center in 1979 is contained in an article in *Public Opinion*, April 1980.

The Nature and Components of a
Political Theory of Inflation

DAVID J. WEBBER

I. INTRODUCTION

One uninterrupted trend in the past decade's record of inflation is the increasing realization that this economic phenomenon is, in part, a political phenomenon. Economists have increased the attention paid to the political feasibility of economic policy proposals and to effects of government activity on the general price level. Additionally, many citizens and public officials have advocated broad policy changes intended to slow the inflation rate. One example is the current proposal calling for a constitutional convention to consider an amendment to the United States Constitution requiring a balanced national budget.

Despite public concern and economists' effort focused on reducing inflationary pressures in the economy through politically acceptable policy changes, there is no developed theory examining the political aspects of inflation. There has been a drastic increase in the emphasis political scientists placed on policy analysis, but this has not included a political theory of inflation explaining general price rises as a result of political, noneconomic activity. This paper attempts to outline what a political theory of inflation needs to include and identifies select political science and economic literature that can be incorporated into such a theory.

Some preliminary remarks concerning the meaning of *theory* are necessitated by the ambiguous use of the term in political science as well as its rather narrow definition among economists. The notions "economic theory" and "political theory" generally include methodological and substantive interpretations, but the term *theory* here does not refer to a specific type of theory, such as rational choice or optimal behavior theory which together constitute much of the corpus of economic theory. Instead, the objective is a general framework focusing on political and economic events that affect general prices.

Section II discusses the distinction between economic and political aspects of inflation in terms of how each set of factors influences the economic system. Additionally, this section presents an overview of a political theory of inflation that is developed in the remainder of the paper. Sections III, IV, and V deal with the three principal segments of the political theory focusing on institutional arrangements, popular control of, and political response to, rising prices and the behavior of government officials. Political-economic interactions involving several political variables which are viewed as a determined reaction to economic affairs, thus linking the two systems in a dynamic way, are identified in Section VI.

Throughout this paper *inflation* is understood to mean the general rising price level of an identical bundle of commodities. Emphasis on the identity of the commodities is necessitated by the growing popularity of the notion that government regulation causes inflation by increasing the cost of affected products. Although environmental regulations and safety and health standards can normally be expected to increase the cost of a commodity, the modified product should not be considered to be the same product as that produced before the regulations were imposed. Despite the increased cost of automobiles as a result of requirements of the Clean Air Act, the product has been modified; a car which does pollute is not identical with a pollution-free car despite an identity of other more prominent performance characteristics.[1]

No specific economic theory of inflation needs to be adopted, but it should be emphasized that several widely held views as to the causes of general price changes are consistent with the development of a political theory of inflation.[2] The monetary explanation, linking all general price increases to an increase in the money supply, is incomplete in that it does not account for the increase in the money supply; more importantly for inflation policy, it does not posit the conditions under which growth in the money supply will be slowed. Likewise, investment-productivity theories of inflation must incorporate explanations as to why government programs and policies affecting investment were adopted. Weidenbaum's (1975, 1978) analysis of the increasing contribution of "government-mandated price increase" to the current inflation should be supplemented by a corresponding political theory which would account for the political adoption of indirect financing of government programs. Such a political theory would also explain the likelihood of the adoption of inflation remedies.

In no sense is it suggested that inflation is solely a political problem that escapes the explanatory grasp of economic theory. Rather it is argued that economic policy formation is sensitive to political influence and that the development of a political theory of inflation to accompany economic theories of inflation is required fully to understand and correct, general price rises.

II. POLITICAL VS. ECONOMIC FACTORS IN A THEORY OF INFLATION

Standard economic theory focuses on economic variables that are understood to capture the relationships involved in the production and distribution of goods and services. Economic theory generally includes references to various demand and supply functions as reactions to variations in monetary aggregates, wages and prices (including taxes), and changes in the environment of the economic system, such as government and international trade in a closed system, and exogenous shocks often exemplified by crop failure and other natural disasters.

Economic theory does provide for the influence of political events on the economic system, but not as part of the theoretic system explaining economic affairs. Governmental decisions affecting economic stability, such as expanding the money supply or changing various tax rates and provisions, are recognized as important in developing a stabilization theory, but these decisions are considered to be discretionary and outside the realm of economic theory. These political forces are viewed as external factors that do not respond in a systematic fashion to economic events and are not, therefore, systematic, predictable influences themselves on the level of economic activity.

Public finance, the subfield of the economic discipline directed at the analysis of taxation and government expenditures, has a well-developed literature examining the incidence of various tax regimes, the differential multiplier of alternative budget allocations, and the limitations of a market economy which requires the general provision of certain public goods. The starting point for the analysis of these items is usually an assumption that a tax provision or an expenditure is adopted, followed by analysis of the allocation and distributive effects of such action. The adoption process itself is left unexplained as an exogenous influence.

Political scientists, on the other hand, have concentrated on describing and explaining the political process in general without an attempt to incorporate this knowledge of policy formulation into a political theory of inflation. There exists a body of literature analyzing the institutional organization of the policy-making process, the responsiveness of representatives to popular opinion, as well as several significant aspects of the behavior of government officials. This body of research needs to be recast and extended in order to develop a political theory that would contribute to our understanding of the role of political actors in influencing the level of general prices.

Just as economic theory considers political factors to be outside that body of knowledge, the development of a political theory of inflation in this paper will consider traditional economic variables as exogenous. This limitation is required in order to make the scope of this effort more manageable, although several interrelationships between an economic theory of inflation and a political theory of inflation will be identified.

Additionally, the final section explicitly discusses interaction between the economic and political systems.

Several political institutions directly bear on macroeconomic stability. A political theory of inflation must include the relevant aspects of these institutions, discuss their behavior in affecting inflation and allow for the impact of alternative institutional arrangements to be anticipated. To accompany this description of institutional arrangements in a political theory of inflation, an accounting of the behavior of governmental officials in terms of the differential performance of institutional roles needs to be developed. Further, the linkage between public preference and government policy must be included. A highly developed political theory of inflation, in addition to delineating the significant components of the political system that affect economic stabilization, would provide for the dynamic interaction of these components with the appropriate aspects of the economic system.

In light of the foregoing discussion, the framework for a political theory of inflation will be considered in three parts. First, the institutional arrangements constituting the American political system will be outlined. Second, the role of consumer-citizens will be examined in terms of their control of, and response to, rising prices. Third, the behavior of government officials, focusing primarily on the propensity and the ability of officials to manipulate the economy for political benefit, will be addressed.

III. INSTITUTIONAL ARRANGEMENTS AFFECTING INFLATION

The textbook description of Keynesian economic policy prescriptions to promote price stability and full employment are well known. Less known, however, are the facets of the political process that limit the applicability of the Keynesian solution in a rapidly expanding economy. Buchanan and Wagner (1977) argue that the legacy of Keynes is the legitimacy his ideas provide for the already existent tendency of democratic governments toward deficit spending, rapid growth of the government sector, and increased transfer payments and other expenditures which respond to the voters' desire to receive governmentally provided benefits without directly paying for them.

Buchanan and Wagner criticize some of the purely economic aspects of Keynes' general theory, but their most relevant contribution toward a political theory of inflation is the evaluation of Keynes in terms of the political responsibility of his proposals. They submit that Keynes's proposals are a one-sided theory since the political adoption of budget surpluses to dampen excessive demand is inconsistent with the political theory of democracy. While suggesting that Keynes had a more elite system of government as the model on which he formulated his general theory, Buchanan and Wagner suggest that the creation of surpluses should have been viewed as fundamentally different from the creation of budget deficits to achieve economic stability (1977, pp. 78–84).

One specific characteristic of the American political process that is amenable to the irresponsible adoption of Keynesian policy is the structure of the legislative process that separates the adoption of a government program requiring funding from the appropriation of funding itself. Public finance theory, resting on general equilibrium analysis, posits that the marginal valuation of government programs should be equal to that of private goods and that the mix of public goods provided should be at a level where the marginal benefit–marginal cost ratio is equal across the set of governmentally provided goods. The procedure of separating the authorization and appropriation functions of the budgeting process makes these microeconomic conditions all but impossible to achieve.

Despite major revisions in the congressional budget process in 1974, aimed at increasing congressional control over the total level of expenditures, the internal structure of the legislative process remains unchanged, with the numerous committees and subcommittees maintaining a decentralized decision-making process (LeLoup, 1977). This fragmented process continues the conflict between the authorization of legislators' favorite projects and a unified balanced budget or a budget that allocates funding in an efficient way.

The popular criticism of present-day government that regulations and programs are often continued beyond their usefulness touches another weakness in the economic policy-making process. Despite the Carter Administration's initial enthusiasm for "zero-based budgeting," the practice of incremental approval of long-standing programs without regular evaluation continues. Wildavsky (1974) examines this aspect of the budgetary process and presents strategies employed by both bureaucrat and legislator to protect and continue their favorite programs.

The recent appearance of a "taxpayers' revolt," best exemplified by Proposition 13 in California, suggests another flaw in the institutional structure of economic policy making. Federalism consists of multiple levels of governmental jurisdictions, normally geographical, that together contribute to satisfying the demands of citizens for the provision of public goods. Superimposed on the governmental institution aspect of federalism is an electoral system with varying provisions at each level. National electoral participation is limited to voting for candidates for office, whereas many states and localities permit citizen participation through referenda and initiatives. In addition to encouraging more participation of citizens at the state and local levels, this set of electoral arrangements presents an opportunity for the contamination of the policy-making process at one level by attitudes toward the government and policy at another level. Several studies, discussed in Section IV, find support for this electoral contamination in a federal political system.

The implications of this contamination for a political theory of inflation are several. First, the process of translating voter demands to the appropriate government level is imprecise. A voter may prefer to reduce expenditure at the national level, but if the only opportunity for direct expression of one's position on expenditures is at the local level, many voters will vote against their initial preference due to the structure of the electoral procedures. Second, this contamination may lead to distortions or hardships among some sectors of society due to voter action that would otherwise not have occurred.

The fiscal policy-making process has received some research attention probably due to its reliance on the constitutionally defined institutions of government. Pierce (1971) presents a detailed discussion of the fiscal policy process including the function of "Troika" in preparing governmental forecast, the role of the Council of Economic Advisers as well as the congressional involvement in these processes. While much of this effort is descriptive and does not permit formal explanation of fiscal policy politics, it has resulted in contributions to an awareness of how fiscal policy is formulated.

The process of monetary policy formation has gone virtually unnoticed. Since the actual operations of the Board of Governors of the Federal Reserve System are low-key and not carried out in a politically charged environment, the procedure has apparently not captured the attention of institutional scholars. Buchanan and Wagner assume that since the major monetary policy makers are politically appointed, the same political pressures that affect fiscal policy makers influence the monetary authorities (1977, pp. 116–18).

Although political institutions are seldom neutral in their formulation of a policy position, scholars of democratic governments have directed much attention at public demands for, and officeholders' supply of, public policy action. Mass political behavior that could be considered to be demands for policy action is discussed in the following section.

IV. POPULAR CONTROL OF AND POLITICAL RESPONSE TO ECONOMIC POLICY

A political theory of inflation in a democracy is heavily dependent on how far popular preference translates evaluations of the government's economic policy into political action through voting, direct lobbying, and expressions of public opinion. The more responsive and demanding public reaction to economic policy is, the more compact a political theory of inflation will be. This section examines three related areas dealing with political control and response to changing economic policy. First, portions of the literature dealing with the economics of voting are reviewed. This is followed by a discussion of the interrelation of attitudes across the multiple levels of government. Finally, the potential for direct lobbying as a response to economic policy is presented.

ECONOMICS OF VOTING

Kramer (1971) is generally considered by political scientists as responsible for reinitiating interest in the systematic empirical investigation of the importance of economic conditions in the voter's decision making. Downs had provided the theoretical framework for such research in *An Economic Theory of Democracy* (1957) where the traditional spatial model of consumer choice theory was reinterpreted in the context of political decisions. Downs focused mainly on the process and consequences of spatial decision making and did not identify the precise factors which are included in a voter's decision making calculus, but he did suggest that economic factors are of central importance to voters and that their visibility to citizens made them important political variables as well.

Kramer's empirical examination of Downs's theory involved United States congressional elections from 1896 to 1964. Assuming an underlying satisficing model where satisfaction with the incumbent party is reflected by a vote for that party, Kramer tested the hypothesis that an increase in unemployment and prices will reduce the aggregate vote for the congressional incumbents and an increase in income will increase the incumbent vote. Kramer found that real income and increased price levels are important determinants of congressional voting behavior, whereas the unemployment rate is not. Kramer concludes that economic fluctuation can account for about one-half of the variance in the aggregate congressional vote.

Arcelus and Meltzer (1975) attempt to extend the model of voter decision making by providing for two distinct decisions. First, they argue, a decision to vote is made, followed by a decision between the two candidates. Examining House of Representative elections between 1920 and 1970 they find little influence of economic factors and conclude that "with the possible exception of inflation, aggregate economic variables affect neither the participation rate in congressional elections nor the relative strength of the two parties" (p. 1238).

Two sets of authors immediately suggested major revisions to the work of Arcelus and Meltzer. Goodman and Kramer (1975) reexamine and reinterpret the data and find that unemployment, inflation, and real income affect not only participation rates but also the actual vote and conclude that voters punish the party in power according to its economic performance. Bloom and Price (1975) present an alternative theory of voting after finding that a decline in real income decreases the votes for an incumbent president's party. They suggest that a party is punished for poor economic performance but not rewarded for satisfactory handling of economic affairs. Additional research focused on the effects of economic variables on presidential approval ratings and the nature of voters' perception of economic factors. Both Monroe (1978) and Kernell (1978) find that although economic variables are significant influences on presidential popularity, changing prices have a strong consistent impact but the impact of unemployment is not general.

The shortcomings of aggregate data analysis in examining the relationship between economic and political variables resulted in the use of survey data to examine how economic factors influence voting behavior. Fiorina (1978) employs the election surveys of the Center for Political Studies at the University of Michigan for 1956–74. Fiorina concludes that, overall, economic variables are important. He finds that a voter's personal economic condition did affect the presidential vote and the congressional vote in 1956 and 1960, but not since. These findings are consistent with Wides' earlier conclusions (1976) in his examination of the direction of change in personal economic condition. Wides found that voters whose conditions are stable or improving are more likely to support the incumbent than those whose conditions are declining.

Kinder and Kiewiet (1979) examine the importance of the personal dimension of economic conditions and find that voting in congressional elections between 1956 and 1976 was not influenced by personal economic conditions but by judgments regarding trends in general business conditions and by opinions concerning the relative competence of the two major parties to manage national economic problems. This suggests that more general ideological opinions of voters about economic policy may influence the perception of economic conditions and the evaluation of economic policy.

Kuklinski and West (1980) extend the examination of the importance of personal economic conditions to "prospective voting" in both House of Representative and Senate elections. They argue that all aggregate studies and many individual studies rely on indicators of past economic conditions measured by changes in inflation, unemployment, or real income over the previous year. Voting is a forward-looking act, they argue, so rational voters will incorporate expected economic condition into their voting decision. Kuklinski and West find that economic prospective voting is evident in Senate elections, with individuals who expect their personal financial situation to decline more likely to vote Republican (nonincumbent party).

This body of research provides mixed support for the generally held notion of the importance of economic variables. There is not, however, agreement on what are the conditions under which economic factors are important or exactly how they influence political attitudes and behavior. In studies that found economic affairs an important component of the voting decision, inflation was found to be more significant than unemployment among the economic variables considered.

INTERRELATION OF ATTITUDES ACROSS LEVELS OF GOVERNMENT

The influence of economic affairs on political behavior at the local and state level has recently been demonstrated by the "taxpayer revolt of 1978." There is evidence that the results of several referenda were influenced by the history of taxing and spending patterns of the state and that general economic sentiment through attitudes toward different taxes contributed to the revolution.

Mikesell examined the eighteen states that considered either a tax or spending control referendum in 1978 in terms of each state's history of spending and taxing policy. He concluded that there is a consistent and sensible pattern among the affected states. First, eight of the ten property-tax-limiting states have an effective property tax rate on single family houses which is greater than the national median. Second, increases in state and local spending appear to have an impact on the incidence of tax-limiting referenda. Mikesell posits that some voters see taxing and expenditure controls as the only way to slow or prevent additional tax liabilities in an era of inflation where progressive tax systems and property tax reassessment increase the taxation burden without an apparent increase in real income or wealth.

In an effort to explain the 1978 taxpayer revolt, Hebert and Bengham reviewed public opinion poll responses from 1969 to 1978 and found that there was no clear trend indicating that a revolt would occur. For example, when asked if each of four taxes (federal individual income, local property, state sales, and state income) were too high, the average number of affirmative responses across the the four taxes ranged from 56 percent to 60 percent during the 10-year period. Disfavor for the federal individual income tax was highest (average over the 10-year period of 69 percent), followed by local property tax (62 percent), state sales tax (51 percent), and the state income tax (47 percent).

A second example of the absence of evidence of increasing dissatisfaction is found by Hebert and Bingham's investigation of respondents' objections to spending levels in seven different issue areas. They find that the average objection rate does not increase but that instead an increase in support for, say, higher welfare expenditures is offset by a decrease in support for defense expenditures.

The one finding in Hebert and Bingham's analysis that might have predicted the increased saliency of taxes to voters was a slight trend in the following question: "Have you reached a breaking point when it comes to taxes?" which shows an increase in affirmative response from 54 percent in 1969 to 66 percent in 1978, with a reduction of "not sure" responses from 12 percent to 4 percent over the same years.

The analysis of citizen attitudes toward expenditures and tax control referenda suggest that institutional arrangements in which referenda take place might play a large part in the often confusing results. Although dislike for the federal income tax exceeds dislike of the taxes that are the subject of state spending and taxing referenda, an opportunity for a single, direct referendum on federal income tax is not possible. Instead, citizen sentiment must be channeled through electoral behavior and organs of public opinion and by expressing general dissatisfaction wherever any opportunity is available even if it involves another level of government.

The rhetoric of the political environment surrounding the 1978 taxpayer revolt as well as the effort to balance the federal budget often includes arguments as to the growing size of the government sector and the resulting inflation caused by deficit spending. This welding of antiinflation sentiment with antigovernment attitudes contributes to the confusion in determining the role of economic variables in explaining political behavior, such as voting, for the average citizen or the execution of official duties of an elected official. Additionally, an attempt to ascertain the popular preference for government services or tradeoff between stable price and other social preferences is compounded by the intertwining of price changes and the demand for public services.

DIRECT LOBBYING AND ECONOMIC POLICY

Despite the recent concern in American politics over the rise of single-issue interest groups, only a sparse literature in political science attempts to expose this form of political influence on matters of economic policy. Given the importance of government policies in determining the disposable income of both individuals and business firms, one would expect to find a high level of activity intended to influence specific economic policies.

The public finance literature, including Olson's The Logic of Collective Action (1971), suggests that only under certain conditions will special interest groups form to attempt to influence general policy. Given the large organizational costs and the relatively small personal benefit derived from a policy change, many citizens will remain unorganized and inactive despite dissatisfaction with current government policy.

Salamon and Siegfried (1977) empirically examine the impact of economic power on economic policy as a test of the relationship between economic power and political power. They reason that business firms prefer low tax rates and that, through trade organizations and business affiliations, businesses, like many other groups, attempt to influence the policy-making process in order to obtain favorable policy. Salamon and Siegfried also examine the relationship between variations in firm and industry characteristics and the securing of favorable tax policies. The effective federal corporate tax rate in an industry and state gasoline excise taxes are used as examples of public policies of concern to the industries under examination. Salamon and Siegfried conclude that large firms do exhibit more political power in the two policy areas and that Olson's "free rider problem" is supported by the finding that larger industries are less successful in procuring favorable tax rates.

In a different type of study focusing on the relationships between interest groups and federal agencies, Aberbach and Rockman (1978) find that although members of the House of Representatives believe that close bureaucratic-clientele relationships are desirable, they are cautiously aware of the excessive influence of interest groups within the federal agencies. Aberbach and Rockman point out that the institutional fragmentation of Congress encourages and reinforces the development of close ties between interest groups and the federal bureaucracy. (The role of elected representatives in the economic policy-making process is now considered.)

V. THE ROLE OF ELECTED REPRESENTATIVES IN A POLITICAL THEORY OF INFLATION

The traditional model of a democracy is a society in which candidates and political parties make issue positions known and an educated, informed citizenry supports the candidate or party closest to its policy preference. Subsequently, the elected representative performs the official duties of a representative consistent with the positions announced in the campaign. A democratic government, therefore, results in public policy outcomes that reflect citizen preference.

In addition to making stringent assumptions as to the attentiveness of citizens in the society, this model also demands that the elected representative behave in a responsible way, or at least that the official be held accountable by the voters. The existence of a sizable, unelected bureaucracy increases the difficulty of preserving an accountable and responsible government and makes greater demands on the elected representative to oversee and control the administrators.

Recent public sentiment is critical of "bureaucrats" for forcing the growth of government and causing inflation, but Fiorina (1977) argues that, in fact, Congress is "the keystone of the Washington establishment." He contends that the increased professionalization of Congress has reduced the turnover of seats, eliminated competitive districts so that in recent years more than 80 percent of representatives come from "safe districts," and virtually ensured the reelection of incumbents, with 90 percent of veteran representatives returned to their seats. Fiorina submits that this change in the nature of the legislative branch is related to the growth in the activities of the federal government. As a result of voters and representatives following their self-interest, members of Congress have changed their behavior from legislative functions toward an ombudsman role. Instead of remaining primarily concerned with committee work and floor activities, Fiorina posits that casework involving citizens' affairs with regulatory agencies and program administrators is becoming a dominant concern of members of Congress.

Fiorina points to increased staff in the home district, multiple home offices, and the increased involvement of Representatives in specific cases as evidence of their changing role. These nonlegislative functions are noncontroversial in that they do not result in division within the representative's constituency. Thus, the office holder is rewarded by a victory at the polling place. Fiorina suggests that Representatives are willing to accept this redefinition of congressional roles because "it is better to be elected as a messanger boy than not to be elected at all."

This same self-interested behavior of voters and representatives has often been identified in the popularly held notion that elected representatives improve their performance in matters of public policy shortly before the election and the voters, who demand the policy provided, find it difficult not to support that party or representative in the next election. In the context of a political theory of inflation it is expected, then, that there is an observable pattern in the performance of economic policy reflected in macroeconomic indicators.

The conclusions of studies by Nordhaus (1975) and Tufte (1978) provide support for the existence of a political business cycle. Nordhaus found that nine out of ten American presidential elections were marked by a declining unemployment rate in the last half of the preceding presidential terms, following an increasing unemployment rate in the first half of the term. Assuming that these events are independent, the probability of this set of observations occurring by chance is 0.011 and, thus, a political business cycle is suspected.

Tufte's findings support a four-year cycle in unemployment and suggest a two-year cycle in real disposable income. Additionally, Tufte finds that the greater the political stakes, the greater the improvement in real income is likely to be. Specifically, he calculates that in nonelection years, real income averages an increase of 1.5 percent, in presidential election years with no incumbent running, an increase of 2.0 percent is recorded, in congressional mid-term years an increase of

2.8 percent can be expected, and in reelection years, there is a 3.4 percent increase in real income (p. 24). An additional feature of Tufte's support for a political business cycle is the discussion of the "heaping of benefits" at strategically beneficial periods of the electoral cycle. Tufte finds "biennial kyphosis" in the flow of transfer payments in 1962, 1964, 1970, and 1972, suggesting that the timing of some government expenditures is influenced by the election calendar (pp. 39–43).

VI. POLITICAL-ECONOMIC INTERACTIONS IN A THEORY OF INFLATION

As has been shown to this point, the political science and the economic literature both contain efforts that can contribute to a broad theory of inflation, although no comprehensive theory is presented as such. What is demonstrated, however, is that the institutions of the economic policy-making process allow voters and elected representatives to behave in a way that permits an expanding economic policy to be continually adopted and reinforced. What is further required of a political theory of inflation is a model that links political variables with economic policy instruments and shows the process by which political behavior and economic policy are interrelated.

Frey and Schneider (1978) present a sophisticated model of such political-economic interactions. They provide for a popularity function which describes the impact of economic conditions on government (presidential) popularity and a reaction function which posits how the government uses policy instruments to steer the economy. Frey and Schneider support the general findings of Kernell regarding the sensitivity of presidential popularity to economic conditions in each presidential term. Specifically, they find

> a one point increase in the rate of inflation decreases presidential popularity by one half to one percentage point; an increase in unemployment of one percentage point decreases popularity by somewhat more than four percentage points; and a one percentage point increase in the growth rate of nominal consumption increases presidential popularity by about seven-tenths of a percentage point (pp. 177–78).

This model includes three policy instruments (current nondefense expenditures, transfers to private households, and the number of civilian jobs), and three constraints on the president's behavior (an administrative constraint, an economic structure and budget constraint, and a popularity constraint). The popularity constraint is most obvious to traditional political scientists; the other two constraints provide a link to the bureaucratic aspects of inflation and the way that the structure of the economy is incorporated into the voters' utility function. This economic constraint may, for example, indicate that a balanced budget is a policy objective and that, therefore, it is required that tax revenues equal government expenditures.

The reaction function of Frey and Schneider links actual presidential popularity rating and a "target" popularity rating to the selective use of policy instruments. If there is a popularity deficit, the president sees he will not be elected if economic affairs go unchanged so he undertakes expansionary policies. Further, if there is a popularity surplus, the president can pursue ideological goals as reflected in indicators of government expenditures of transfer payments and civilian jobs.

The work of Frey and Schneider brings together the two popular notions of economic-oriented politics: voters vote according to economic conditions, and officeholders perform their function through the strategic use of economic policy so as to receive favorable support from the citizens. By linking voter response to government officials' behavior, it is possible to conceptualize the processes employed by both voters and officials in a political system where the activities of both are broad and unchecked. Elected officeholders, for example, possess incentives to undertake expenditures that are visible to their constituents, are immediate and focused in their impact, and are so presented that the elected representative can claim responsibility while spreading the cost of the expenditure widely in hidden and delayed ways.

A general test of five major explanations often set forth to explain government expansion is provided by Cameron (1978). Using government expenditures for eighteen capitalist countries since 1960, the following explanations are examined:

1. An economic explanation suggested by "Wagner's Law" that citizens' demands for services and their willingness to pay taxes are income elastic.
2. A fiscal explanation based on "fiscal illusion," suggesting that nations with the most rapid increase in reliance on indirect taxes and social insurance contributions will have the largest increase in the government sector.
3. A political explanation linking competitiveness and frequency of elections to an expanding public economy.
4. An institutional explanation focusing on the degree of centralization as well as the existence of multiple levels of independent governments.
5. An international explanation that relates an open economy to growth of the public sector.

Cameron finds that the first four explanations are not strongly related to expansion of the public sector. Based on the comparison of the beta coefficients, the international explanation is overwhelmingly the most important factor, followed by, in order of decreasing importance, the political explanatory variables, the institutional variables, "fiscal illusion," and finally, the economic explanation. Together the five explanatory variables have a coefficient of determination of .75.

Two aspects of Cameron's argument are directly related to a political theory of inflation. The political and institutional explanations were discussed earlier as major components of a theory of price changes. Cameron found that the partisanship of government is important since leftist or liberal parties are strongly linked to expansion, whereas the frequency of electoral competition is negligible when the effect of party is controlled for. Federalism tends to slow the degree of expansion; centralization furthers public sector growth.

Cameron's finding with respect to the importance of an open economy in the international sector includes further reliance on political-institutional forces. He posits that openness of the economy as measured by a relatively large international trade sector is related to a high level of industrial concentration resulting in high unionization and collective bargaining. This encourages strong labor political action and liberal governments which adopt spending for income supplements, thereby expanding the public economy. This linkage between international trade and the public sector rests on an unidentified process of political influence of labor organizations.

As well as demonstrating the type of political-economic interaction that needs to be incorporated into a political theory of inflation, Cameron's work suggests that the Salamon and Siegfried research as to the link between economic power and political power needs to be extended to include labor organization strength as well as the firm and industry strength which they analyzed.

VII. PROSPECTS FOR A POLITICAL THEORY OF INFLATION

The components of a political theory which would explain the operation and the relative importance of political institutions in affecting the level of general prices has been outlined. An attempt has been made to incorporate portions of the relevant literature into the framework for a theory as well as to establish links between a political theory and standard economic theory.

Overall, the rudiments of a political theory of inflation are evident in the literature. The knowledge accumulated by political scientists in describing the workings of economic policy-making institutions has not been viewed from a macroeconomic stability perspective. For example, research showing that the congressional budget procedure is a piecemeal process has not been extended to assess the implications for price level changes, nor has it been related to other political factors involving inflation.

Most importantly for the development of a political theory of inflation is the lack of a step-by-step process that identifies the factors which contribute to inflation as well as the links between these factors. The identification of the overall process can be seen as a first step in this development of a detailed outline identifying and linking the components involved in a political theory of inflation.

Notes

1. Weidenbaum (1975, 1978) presents an analysis of government-mandated price increases and gives the overall impression that the associated governmental regulations are the cause of inflation. He gives passing attention to the conditions under which regulation does not contribute to inflation (1978, p. 18).
2. For a review of economic theories of inflation see J. S. Fleming, "The Economic Explanation of Inflation" in Hirsch and Goldthorpe (1978).

References

Aberbach, Joel D., and Rockman, Bert A. "Bureaucrats and Clientele Groups: A View From Capitol Hill," *American Journal of Political Science* 22 (1978): 818–32.

Arcelus, Francisco, and Meltzer, Allen. "The Effect of Aggregate Economic Variables on Congressional Elections," *American Political Science Review* 69 (1975): 1232–39.

Bloom, Harold, and Price, H. Douglas. "Voter Response to Short-Run Economic Conditions: The Asymmetric Effect of Prosperity and Recession," *American Political Science Review* 69 (1975): 1240–54.

Buchanan, James M., and Wagner, Richard E. *Democracy in Deficit: The Political Legacy of Lord Keynes* (New York, 1977).

Cameron, David R. "The Expansion of the Public Economy: A Comparative Analysis," *American Political Science Review* 72 (1978): 1243–61.

Downs, Anthony. *An Economic Theory of Democracy* (New York, 1957).

Fiorina, Morris P. *Congress: Keystone of the Washington Establishment* (New Haven, Ct., 1977).

Fiorina, M. P. "Economic Retrospective Voting in American National Elections: A Micro-Analysis," *American Journal of Political Science* 22 (1978): 426–43.

Frey, Bruno, and Schneider, Friedrich. "An Empirical Study of Political-Economic Interaction in the United States," *The Review of Economics and Statistics* 60 (1978): 174–83.

Goodman, S., and Kramer, Gerald H. "Comment on Arcelus and Meltzer, The Effect of Aggregate Economic Conditions on Congressional Elections," *American Political Science Review* 69 (1975): 1255–65.

Hebert, F. Ted, and Bingham, Richard D. "Public Opinion, the Taxpayers' Revolt, and Local Governments" in John P. Blair and David Nachmias

(Eds.), *Fiscal Retrenchment and Urban Policy*, vol. 17, Urban Affairs Annual Reviews, (Beverly Hills, Calif., 1979).

Hirsch, Fred, and Goldthorpe John H., (Eds.). *The Political Economy of Inflation* (Cambridge, Mass., 1978).

Kernell, Samuel. "Explaining Presidential Popularity," *American Political Science Review* 72 (1978): 506–522.

Kinder, Donald R., and Kiewiet, D. Roderick. "Economic Discontent and Political Behavior: The Role of Personal Grievances and Collective Economic Judgments in Congressional Voting," *American Journal of Political Science* 23 (1979): 495–527.

Kramer, Gerald H. "Short-Run Fluctuations in U.S. Voting Behavior, 1896–1964," *American Political Science Review* 65 (1971): 131–43.

Kuklinski, James H., and West, Darrell M. "Prospective Economic Voting in House and Senate Elections," paper presented at the Conference on Congressional Elections at the University of Houston, January 1980.

LeLoup, Lance T. *Budgetary Politics: Dollars, Deficits, Decisions* (Brunswick, Ohio, 1977).

Mikesell, John L. "The Season of Tax Revolt" in John P. Blair and David Nachmias (Eds.), *Fiscal Retrenchment and Urban Policy*, vol. 17, Urban Affairs Annual Reviews (Beverly Hills, Calif., 1979).

Monroe, Kristen. "Economic Influences on Presidential Popularity," *Public Opinion Quarterly* 42 (1978): 360–69.

Nordhaus, William D. "The Political Business Cycle," *Review of Economic Studies* 42 (1975): 169–90.

Olson, Mancur, Jr. *The Logic of Collective Action* (Cambridge, Mass., 1971).

Pierce, Lawrence C. *The Politics of Fiscal Policy* (Pacific Palisades, Calif., 1971).

Salamon, Lester M., and Siegfried, John J. "Economic Power and Political Influence: The Impact of Industry Structure on Public Policy," *American Political Science Review* 71 (1977): 1026–43.

Tufte, Edward R. *Political Control of the Economy* (Princeton, N.J., 1978).

Weidenbaum, Murray L. *Government-Mandated Price Increases* (Washington, D.C., 1975).

Weidenbaum, M. L. "The Impacts of Government Regulation." A study prepared for the Joint Economic Committee, U.S. Congress, Working Paper No. 32, Center for the Study of American Business, Washington University, St. Louis, Mo., 1978.

Wides, Jeffery W. "Self-Perceived Economic Change and Political Orientations," *American Politics Quarterly* 4 (1976): 395–411.

Wildavsky, Aaron. *The Politics of the Budgetary Process*, 2d ed. (Boston, 1974).

Social and Political Consequences of Inflation and Declining Abundance

ARTHUR J. VIDICH*

Historically, America has put forth an image of itself as an open society providing the promise and frequently the actuality of opportunity for almost all groups and classes. The cheap land of the American frontier and 150 years of industrialization have supported a continuously expanding economy capable of absorbing generations of immigrants and supporting the mobility aspirations of almost all classes and groups except the Blacks. Now, for the first time in American history there is the prospect for a long-term decline in the rate of economic growth and expansion, and hence, an abrogation of that promise that in the eyes of many constituted the essential character of America. This change is related in part to such long-term trends as

1. The increasing age of our capital base and increasing competition of more efficient producers in other parts of the world.
2. Increasing dependency on monopoly-determined high-cost petroleum imports necessitated in part by overutilization in the past of low-cost domestic petroleum.
3. The rising cost of agricultural land relative to its productivity, caused in part by massive investments in land by international corporations, by holders of cheap dollars in dollar-rich countries, and by Middle Eastern and Latin American investors.
4. Fundamental changes in attitudes toward work resulting in replacement of the older work ethic based on a production mentality with a consumption mentality linked to a desire to achieve a given lifestyle at a chosen level without regard to the value of work and mobility per se.

Seen in long-term perspectives, these trends are part of a world-wide sociocultural process. For the past several hundred years, the New World and especially the United States have been at the center of world civilization. The apex of American power was probably reached between World War II and the beginnings of detente. Now it appears that it is losing some of the initial advantages which accrued to it because its industrialization had the advantage of taking place in a large virgin territory and because its inhabitants brought with them to its shores social and psychological predispositions which released vast stores of human energy into economic activities. These initial advantages are now not so great, as other societies and civilizations move toward a world with a new center or perhaps to a world with no center.

The dependence of the United States on an uncontrolled and perhaps uncontrollable world economy has, for the first time in this century, placed it in the position where it can no longer operate on the assumption of an autonomous national economy, directable without outside constraints. The internationalized world economy, in part created by the United States, now subjects its internal social and economic life to extrinsic processes.

These same trends measured in terms of growth rates point to annual rates of expansion well below 5 percent. The rate of expansion for 1979 was approximately 2 percent and it is expected that the economy in 1980 is likely to contract at an annual rate of 1.5 percent.[1] Moreover, these declines in rates of expansion have been accompanied since the late sixties by increasing rates of inflation *and* levels of unemployment stabilized between 6 and 8 percent; and that has exacerbated the social effects of the contraction by placing a disproportionate share of carrying the burden of rising costs on the poor, the aged, youth, and minorities — all of whom are least able to bear them.

The rate of inflation in 1979 was 11 percent and is expected to be higher in 1980; unemployment for 1980 is expected to average 7.5 percent, up from the 1979 rate of 6 percent. All these trends are expected to coincide with a recession of the American economy during 1980–81.

It is expected that a recession in the United States will lead to an adjustment to lower rates of interest and to an improvement in America's external payments position, but these purely technical considerations — even should they occur — are not likely to benefit all classes and groups in the society. The improvement of our external payments position by slower growth will depend upon maintaining present levels of individual taxes and not lowering interest rates — in short, by spreading the costs of the recession, inequitably to the lower and middle classes.

By maintaining present burdens of maldistribution, the policy of inducing slower economic growth is expected, or hoped, to improve our external payments position, which ran at a deficit of $13.9 billion in 1978, and is hoped to run at a lower deficit in 1979. It is also hoped that this deficit will be converted into a surplus of $6 billion by the end of 1980.[2] Under these policies, the hoped-for reversal of our external payments deficit would place us in a position of pay-as-we-go for oil and other imports.[3] To achieve these goals, most classes and groups in the society will be asked to tighten their belts and work more as inflation cuts into real income and unemployment rises.

The 1979–80 oil crisis has resulted in the attribution of larger and larger percentages of living costs, especially those of housing and transportation, to energy costs. At the same time, vast windfall profits fall into the hands of producers and distributors of domestic crude and refined oil whose prices, independent of governmental fiscal and monetary policies, have an important effect on the distribution of costs and profits to all classes and groups that make up the society. Federal governmental policy has lost its capacity to regulate the direction of the movement of the economy by the fiscal and monetary means available to it.

The decisive fact of economics in the period of the post-sixties is the loss of control over national economics by the state apparatus, accompanied by the increase in the economic independence of international corporate business leaders.

Many observers consider Keynesian economic theory no longer adequate as a basis for the management of public economic policy.[4] In many important respects this is true.

A key aspect of Keynesianism included the willingness of business and labor to accept the mediation of government in setting wage-price guidelines which would be commensurate with regulating rates of inflation at approximately 3–4 percent a year. These agreements born in the Depression of the thirties, when the American business system had faltered, have clearly broken down; government has lost its ability to impose price restraints on business. The oil industry and OPEC countries have appropriated the right to set prices on petroleum and by so doing set the pace for almost all other pricing. By the same token, the rest of the business community has appropriated the right to establish prices within the framework of oil-based inflationary advances.

Seen in these terms, pricing authority has been arrogated by the international oil industry. The idea of the regulation of prices for the public good as in Keynesian economics does not apply to international economics. Before 1973, international Keynesianism rested on international agreements — dominated by the United States and Western Europe — that no one nation would exploit its position at the expense of all others. The rise in OPEC price increases was, in fact, a breakdown of international Keynesianism in which oil companies used their monopoly position to force prices up far in excess of 4 or 5 percent. These international corporate regulators remind one of Weber's idea of "booty" capitalism. United States governmental policy is no longer a sufficient instrument for managing its own and the Western European economy and hence can discipline neither American nor international business.

The international economic order established by the Bretton Woods Agreements in the 1940s began to break down when President Nixon unilaterally abrogated a fixed relationship between the value of the dollar and gold. It was further weakened when OPEC broke ranks and began to set prices on crude oil without regard to the effects of increased prices for inflation in the industrial countries. The vast pool of dollars already floating throughout the world was added to by the huge increases in the costs of petroleum until the point was reached where no productive investment opportunities for these dollars existed. As the dollar decreased in value, additional dollars previously hoarded were added to the float. Increases in the prices of gold and precious metals drew out further supplies of dollars. At this point, a vast number of dollars shuttle back and forth in international paper transactions designed to protect their value relative to other currencies and to inflation. No national or international agency can control these speculative transactions, whose net effect is to exacerbate inflation and reduce the effectiveness of fiscal and monetary methods to control inflation.

Yet the federal government continues to administer the other central elements of Keynesianism, namely, the distribution of wealth and income by means of taxation policies and deficit spending. The size of the federal budget, which is an index of this aspect of Keynesianism, continues to grow and remains a major instrument of social policy. Since the presidency of Richard Nixon, however, the benefits of Keynesianism have largely favored the business classes in the form of government contracts and tax legislation.[5] Thus the elements of Keynesianism associated with taxation and redistribution still exist, but the beneficiaries of this system are no longer the poor and the unemployed. Only by equating the public good with the welfare of the business classes — a turnaround of the ethic which originally inspired the new deal — has Keynesianism survived, i.e., in its present form it mocks its own principle.

The economic trends just described are occurring in the wake of a long period of economic expansion and almost full employment stretching from World War II to the early seventies. During that period the new middle classes, the older ethnic working classes, and some of the newer minority classes learned to hope for and to expect an expanding share in the American dream. Many, in fact, had acquired homes in the suburbs, education for their children, and other material benefits associated with the good life. Others — the later arrivals —had only begun to achieve these benefits but took them over in a kind of anticipatory socialization as their own standards for American living. The expectations, hopes, and standards established in the earlier period are now threatened by inflation, decreasing rates of expansion, and in some cases by unemployment. Because this new climate of scarcity in production, income, consumption, and savings follows a period of great expansion, the psychological adjustment of these rising groups will be made even more difficult than for those during the Great Depression and their responses to their new life situations are apt to be more unpredictable.[6]

Even if looked at from a purely economic point of view, not all individuals and groups are equally effected by inflation, unemployment, and decreases in the rates of expansion. With regard to inflation, some groups have neither cost or income elasticity; others may have both. It is also possible for groups to have income but not cost elasticity, or vice versa, and of course, different groups may have varying degrees of cost and income elasticity.[7] Unemployment and underemployment may effect some age grades, occupations, ethnic groups, or races more than others, depending upon how particular industries or businesses are related to contractions or expansions of different sectors of the economy. Ethnic groups or races typically associated with declining industries may suffer; others associated with expanding markets may benefit. Property-owning classes may experience losses or gains, depending on the profile of their investment portfolios; those with investments in nuclear-energy–related industries may suffer losses; others who own rights in land or shares in oil companies may be beneficiaries of great increases in both demand and prices. It cannot be argued that the effects of inflation, unemployment, or economic contraction will have a unitary effect across the social structure.

Although an analysis of all the market situations of the multiplicity of groups and classes that make up American society should be done, in this essay we can only point to the effects on some groups of the economic trends noted above. Our discussion will examine some sectors of the *upper* and *middle classes* and some *economically marginal groups,* and will focus on the following questions.

1. Which groups and classes are to bear the burden of unemployment, inflation and decreases in the rates of economic expansion?
2. What tensions and conflicts are likely to arise as a result of differential distribution of the economic burden and what kinds of social resentments and hostilities will this engender?
3. What are the long-term prospects for American society of a reversal in its dominant public ideology of maintaining an open society with opportunity for all?

THE UPPER CLASSES

Those portions of the upper classes — for the most part the older upper classes whose original wealth was based on land grants, shipping, railways, and post-Civil War heavy industry — who are now owners of land, resources, and stocks (in heavy industry, utilities, and minerals) and insulated from both the negative effects of inflation and declines in the rate of expansion so long as they can retain the benefits of tax and inheritance laws and interest policies in their own favor. The value of their assets and income moves in phase with inflationary rates and may exceed those rates if the value of real property, minerals, and commodities rises at faster rates than inflation. To the extent that these wealth holders have diversified their portfolios to include fossil fuels and minerals, they are hedged against almost all short- and long-term economic fluctuations. Their economic position is stable in the sense that it can be altered only by a change in the fundamental character of capitalism itself.

The economic stability of this sector of the upper class could be threatened by political instability and social unrest arising out of the dramatic downturn in the life situations of other groups. If economic decline or stagnation erode the social and economic positions of the lower and the middle classes to the breaking point, the result could be large-scale discontent and dissatisfaction among classes which hitherto have always shared a basic commitment to the American economic system. Such erosion of political commitment could be exploited by political parvenus — populist and charismatic figures — promising easy solutions to the economic and status problems of threatened groups. Under such circumstances, the old aristocracy of America and its descendants, who live off unearned income and who have been instrumental in setting the cultural tone of the country, may find it necessary to make bargains with new political brokers who promise to protect their economic privileges. Thus, efforts to maintain their market advantages would be increasingly dependent on precisely those political means which they themselves cannot supply, but can buy only at some cost to themselves; tax, inheritance, and other favorable legislation can be purchased only from lobbyists and legislators who, in their own quest for an economic or political *quid pro quo* are likely to exact a high price. Should this occur, a historic American economic sinecure based on control and ownership of natural resources would be transformed into a precariously protected political privilege. The phenomenon of the politically protected sinecure may arrive in America to create not a class of kept noblemen, as has been the case in Europe for a long time, but rather a nobility of the economically functionless epigoni of those Anglo-Saxon Puritans whose original economic success undermined the ideological foundations of the Puritan character that is today so heavily prized. Of course, if it is politically protected, such a class can sustain itself so long as the economic system is willing to support it in the lifestyle to which it has been accustomed. However, when this class begins to slide, its defensive political responses will reverberate throughout the society.

These older upper classes are to be distinguished from the newer upper classes economically based in mass communications, electronics, government contracts, aircraft, and especially in oil, petroleum products, and petroleum-linked machine tools. An important segment of the newer upper classes are Texas oil millionaires who have partly shoved aside the older upper classes. The new upper classes cannot always be separated from the older upper classes in terms of wealth; they are distinguished from them by having been tied from the beginning to politically determined market privileges in a society where, since the New Deal and the beginnings of Keynesianism, government contracts, franchises, subsidies, and tax write-offs have become a prerequisite for access to market opportunities. From the beginning, therefore, they have been openly and conspicuously identified with politics and have played perhaps the most significant role in influencing the executive and legislative branches; they were, in fact, prompt to rationalize and accredit the arts of lobbying and to organize them as the major "nongovernmental" industry in Washington, D.C.

These business and industrial interests have now come to be associated with the interests of regions, cities, and sometimes occupational groups; what is good for the automotive industry is good for Detroit, and what is good for Detroit is good for the automobile unions. The special interests of business and industry are thus supported by constituencies that see their own interests linked to those of particular segments of the business classes — what might be termed a society-wide bread-and-butter unionism wherein all groups become conscious of where their interests reside and, barring a rare outbreak of altruistic idealism, respond only in terms of those interests. Under this pattern of political economy, self-interest and instrumental rationality guide the actions of all organized groups and groups seek to make political alliances that will be to their mutual benefit. Thus, the political role of the new upper classes is not only conspicuous, it has also been accepted by large parts of the society as a "necessary" part of the system. More important, however, the newer politically active upper classes are tied in an infinite number of ways to the managers, administrators, and employees of industry who, in turn, see their own fate as tied to that of business. These relationships — *people's capitalism,* so termed in the 1950s and 1960s — provide a source of political stability that might otherwise be threatened by advancing inflation and declining abundance. The political-economic administrative apparatus created as part of New Deal Keynesianism in the 1930s is now a foundation for political stability in its own right and serves to mute if not absorb some social resentment.

Those parts of the upper classes whose sources of wealth are based in petroleum are a special case because petroleum is a resource that links the older and the newer upper classes—particularly parts of the Eastern establishment and the newer Texas and Southwestern oil fortunes. Because of the crucial role of petroleum for world industrialization and because of the international nature of the competition for its control, the oil-based upper classes have been obliged to limit and regulate their own domestic competition in order to cooperate for purposes of enhancing their positions on the world competitive market. A common interest in the prices and supplies of world oil thus connects one sector of the newer and older upper classes in the United States, creating a unique group that stands apart from, and above, the rest of the upper class because its ability to influence the production and distribution of crude refined petroleum on a world scale gives it tremendous power above and beyond the level of national governments. Part of the power of this group is based on its contacts and relationships with OPEC countries and monarchs who are themselves newer members of this now transnational class. But because their position is dependent on these foreign contacts and relationships, oil companies and their executives have a highly developed sense of international politics and class identifications which both free them from some domestic political constraints and increase their domestic political power. They may find themselves, willingly or unwillingly, in the role of political brokers between those who control the supply and those who determine its allocation for consumption, a kind of independent political position similar to that described by Lincoln Steffens of the old time political "boss" in the late nineteenth–early twentieth century American cities — highly visible, highly resented, and all-powerful. Theirs is, however, a kind of supra-institutional position which encourages ruthlessness, political experimentation, and above all, the use of extreme measures when necessary in order to protect narrow class interests. The internationalization of the world economic "order" and the destruction of the institutional framework of Keynesianism has opened up a new frontier for capitalism.

In a period of declining rates of expansion, the upper classes are likely to have increasing resort to political means to protect and enhance their market positions. Such efforts are not facilitated by the inability of political leaders to restrict and limit the predatory activity of oil companies and OPEC with respect to prices. In addition, political leaders find it difficult to mobilize public opinion against them because the public is itself made up of a complex mix of groups which perceive their own interests as being partly linked to business and industry. The public hopes that it might partly gain from the overall opportunities made available by the business system; people's capitalism enlarges the size of the predatory group. The result has been that the business managers of the newer upper classes gain a preponderant influence in governmental policy making, especially with regard to energy agencies. Political leaders, unable to organize and manage public resentment against the predatory groups, experience a political paralysis that leaves the field open to economic interests to legislate economic, welfare, and social policy by pricing decisions. The paralysis of government and the high-handed methods of oil interests has led to increasing resentment of the oil companies and of OPEC and to some advocacy for public ownership of oil resources. The more that governance is managed by this method in the face of increasing inflation and unemployment, the more the political economy is likely to disadvantage the poor, economically marginal Blacks, marginal youth, welfare classes, and workers who are not organized to resist either inflation or unemployment.

ECONOMICALLY MARGINAL AND LOW-INCOME GROUPS

By low-income and economically marginal groups, we refer to all those (a) whose income is pegged at or near the minimum wage; (b) whose jobs are outside the organized labor force; (c) whose work is contingent upon day-to-day or week-to-week contracts; (d) whose sole source of income is some form of welfare. Because their absolute income is low, economically marginal groups have the least income and cost elasticity; compared to other groups, a larger percentage of their income is spent on inflation-related necessities such as food, clothing, and shelter and their incomes are least likely to be indexed to inflationary rises. The specific sectors of the population in this category include a mixed racial and ethnic aggregate of impoverished urban and rural immigrants, traditionally poor indigenous Americans, the welfare classes, including some portions of aged Social Security recipients, and those young people who have not found a point of entry into the job market.

These groups are disproportionately penalized by inflation, unemployment, and declines in opportunity resulting from decreasing rates of economic expansion. The wages of unorganized workers do not keep pace with rising costs and parttime and hourly wage workers have fewer opportunities for working extra hours or holding second jobs. Welfare remittances decline in value as inflation and rents increase and the welfare classes find it more difficult to secure financial aid and social services as critics cut back on welfare budgets in periods of urban economic crisis. Both rural and urban poor become increasingly marginal to job and welfare markets and are steadily disenfranchised from society, with the result that the economy comes to produce an ever-enlarging group of internally displaced persons who have no recourse other than some form of social and economic dissent. Yet the lack of militancy on the part of these groups is startling. Youth crime may be an expression of resentment, but it can also be a source of income. Similarly, small-scale white-collar crime may serve similar purposes for other groups who "sublimate" their hostility by finding ways to beat the system.

When social descent occurs among these groups, it is not likely to be supported by the kind of survival cushions that existed during the depression of the nineteen-thirties — return to the family homestead or to relatives on the farm, though there is the possibility of a certain amount of doubling-up in urban apartments and of adult sons and daughters insisting on a prolonged stay in the homes of their more economically comfortable parents. The older ethnic ghetto which in the past was a welfare system in its own right no longer exists. The older political party patronage systems have been displaced by state and federal welfare bureaucracies, and the newer Black and Hispanic ghettoes have not developed internal systems of mutual aid because such cultural traditions of benevolence have been based on family ideology rather than community institutions. Transiency as in the world of the hobo and bum is today less tolerated by urban and state police who are under political pressure to keep the municipal and state public image of "downtown" areas favorable for tourism and industry. As the poverty of some city dwellers increases, its visibility will be less tolerated by those committed to urban renewal of downtown areas and by property owners whose real-estate values are threatened by the presence of the visibly destitute: beggars, prostitutes, scavengers, bag ladies, and others who pollute the visual harmony and aesthetic beauty of the urban landscape. Of course it is understood that the chronic poor do not have high expectations in the first place and that their income and status decline is measured from such a low starting point that it can barely be called a *descent*. This is true, but it must also be remembered that the ascent of other groups relative to them is much greater. The poor may be more aware of their descent when they compare it to the upward mobility of other groups. But again the absence of militancy is remarkable; the militancy of the 1960s seems not only to have been premature, but also may rob this decade's disfavored groups of a chance to repeat that militancy so soon after its prior expression.

Social Security classes — i.e., those whose only source of income is Social Security benefits — are said to be protected by a system of indexed Social Security payments designed to reflect rates of inflation. Such indexing lags behind and does not compensate for rises in rents, taxes, and other inflationary costs, since the discretionary income of those who are wholly dependent on Social Security is marginal in the first place. Even as the economic position of these classes is eroded by inflation, their costs to society are still high; Medicare and Medicaid benefits save the patient and prevent his bankruptcy, but primarily benefit the professional middle classes whose jobs are related to hospitals, nursing homes, and medicine. These classes will be more resented by the salaried middle-income groups whose income taxes increase proportionately to meet the increased costs of indexing and medical care. The salaried middle groups have continued to ask why they should bear the burden of supporting the aged and to inquiry, "Who will pay for my indexed Social Security benefits when I retire?" Congressmen may find it difficult not to listen to their complaints and, should this be the case, Social Security classes may begin to lose some of the political power that up to now has supported indexed Social Security payments.

In modern society the youthful disadvantaged have become older and older. In some cases, youths may not enter the job market until the age of thirty or even later, but at the same time, poorer young people may enter the labor force even before teenage. The class of economically marginal youth embraces a complex, heterogeneous aggregate of the uneducated and unpropertied, a substantial fraction of the population, which in the very nature of the developing occupational and economic system is not able to make an effective occupational claim.

The life chances of any new generation will be partly governed by levels of opportunity and rates of economic expansion prevailing at the time it enters the job market. In periods of rising unemployment and decreasing expansion, penetration of that market becomes more difficult. The newest generation of lower-class youth has for the past 10 years found it increasingly difficult to gain a foothold in that market. During the four-year period of economic growth that ended in early 1979, unemployment rates among Black people between the ages of 15 and 25 ranged between 30 and 50 percent; the rates for other youth have been considerably higher than the national rate of unemployment. CETA programs designed to address this problem have provided only temporary incomes coupled with training for jobs that do not exist. Moreover, at times such CETA opportunities have been appropriated by middle-class youth on the basis of their political connections. Significant numbers of people who have reached maturity in the past decade have either been excluded from the market altogether or have been included only partially and occasionally. If the recession expected in 1980 results in an even greater rise in unemployment, the already dangerously large army of unemployed youth will be joined by both those now coming of age and by those who presently, because they are young and without seniority, will be the first to be laid off. To the extent that youth dropouts of the late sixties have ventured back into the occupational structure, they intensify high levels of existing competition. It is to be expected that youth will bear a disproportionately high share of the burden of unemployment and economic constriction.

The unemployed youth of the present generation are comparable only to the unemployed youth generations of the thirties in the sense that their social and psychological predispositions toward society will remain with them as they pass through the social structure over the course of their life-spans. But in some respects this generation's youth are in a worse situation than that of their predecessors in that unskilled minority youth seem to have become part of a permanent underclass with no hope of being redeemed by rising employment. Unless a major effort is made now to incorporate them into society, they are likely to be a permanently disaffected group who will find it difficult to make ideological and career adjustments. For unskilled minority youth, the situation is even worse since it appears that these people will become part of a permanent underclass with no hope of being redeemed by opportunities for employment. If no legitimate political or economic means are found to solve their job and career problems, they are likely to find their own solutions in marginal and illegal activities or in forms of deviant and self-destructive conduct which will have deleterious effects on the quality of civic life in cities, suburbs, towns, and countryside.

Increasingly the marginal welfare and youth classes will be cut off from the mainstream of society and become a subproletariat based on minimal consumption and segmented social participation. Insofar as they lack skills or motivation there will be no way to incorporate them into the system. Insofar as the earth's land mass is saturated and the world no longer offers opportunities for rewarding adventure, mercenary employment, or promising emigration to overseas territories, they will have to be absorbed internally. They are likely to resent newer immigrant groups as competitors for nonexistent jobs, and they are likely to resent all those — such as the aged with fixed incomes or employed youth — who are secure. They are not likely to be committed to the American social and economic system and its values and will be open to whatever alternative private and political solutions arise. The social control of their resentments will be a continuing and increasing problem for the political managers of the society.

THE MIDDLE GROUPS

The middle groups in the society are numerically dominant and, at present, are the most committed to the system. Their social privileges and rewards in terms of income, position, profession, occupation, leisure, and medical and retirement benefits were secured during the period of economic expansion, 1950–75, but they are by no means a unitary group. They are continuously subdivided into smaller and smaller segments at various skill, occupational, professional, industrial, agricultural, and lifestyle levels which are in turn subdivided even further by ethnic, racial, and regional variations. The middle-class segment can include such diverse categories as skilled workers, teachers, professionals, managers, clerks, and administrators. Their only common characteristic is their commitment to the system which has provided them with their good life.

At another level they can be differentiated with respect to their cost and price elasticity in relation to inflation. For example, professionals and industrial workers whose fees or contracts are tied to inflationary indexes suffer inflation less than those whose incomes are not. Those who own real property, especially their own homes, or income-producing paper, can regard such investments as a hedge against further inflation and the changing rates of interest. Yet large sectors of the middle group live off relatively inelastic sources of income and suffer the depreviation of inflation in varying degrees, depending on family size, ages of children, accrued equity, and the number of family wage earners. Although these middle groups may be variously disadvantaged or advantaged by inflation, they all have in common an awareness that they must adapt and adjust to it in order to try to shield themselves from its most serious consequences. In an effort to cope with inflation, they attempt to enhance their chances to maintain or increase their living standards which were set well in advance of the inflationary spirals of 1974 and 1978–80. A powerful sense of market rationality currently has driven the middle classes into an orgy of speculative activity in real estate, government bonds, precious metals and stones, antiques, and other price-elastic investments. Such economically defensive speculations exacerbate the problem of inflation because their cumulative effect is to increase inflation by increasing prices in transfer goods in the hope of beating the system. Up to a point, such speculative activity succeeds, provided that no depression occurs, but should a depression occur the last purchaser will be left holding the bag. On the other hand, some people in this group attempt to hold their own by taking overtime, second jobs or by pooling the resources of household members. For them, status and economic defensiveness become a dominant practical and psychological orientation to the world.

At a political level, their efforts to defend themselves against inflation are expressed as strident opposition to increases in taxes by support of cutbacks of those social expenditures from which they do not directly benefit, and by an aggressive defense of established gains. At all levels, they are prepared to displace the costs of inflation and unemployment on groups other than their own. The numerical size of special interest groups becomes smaller and smaller as each group takes a more radically self-interested attitude. This middle sector is engaged in a vast competitive struggle within itself as well as with the rest of society to protect its present position from erosion. Those whose market positions within the middle classes are the weakest — i.e., those who are vulnerable to cutbacks in the public payroll or to layoffs in industry — may join the unemployed and suffer economic disaster and social humilitation. As the competitive struggle to protect one's market position increases, the middle classes become less liberal, less able to take a civic or social attitude, and more subject to political appeals that offer easy, often irrational, solutions to personal economic problems.

Three occupational subsegments of the middle classes are worthy of special discussion because their occupations give them a special relationship to the processes and consequences of inflation: (1) business managers and political administrators who deal with pricing policies and labor costs; (2) small- and medium-sized businessmen who attempt to anticipate future prices and costs relative to their own business operations; (3) intellectuals and academicians who either try to understand these social processes or devise policies for dealing with them.

Business managers and political administrators confront directly the consequences of inflation on labor costs, production expenditures, and budgets. In addition they are in a crucial position to influence pricing and investment policies, chart the value of labor, and advise management on overall policy. Their decisions have a direct influence on the distribution of the burden of inflation across the spectrum of society. Of course, managers and administrators must work within the constraints of corporate and organizational and political policy and are not free of pressures from others, including political and labor leaders. They owe their own jobs to corporate owners and politicians and they are indebted to labor leaders who assure them a disciplined labor force. They are obliged to respond favorably to those pressure groups upon which they are most dependent. Consumers of their products (services in the case of government bureaucracies and educational institutions, and commodities in the case of industry) do not constitute an organized group capable of either engaging in boycotts or withdrawing consumption functions. Thus, managers and administrators respond in terms of the requirements of their own immediate situation. And as a result their responses to the pressures of special interests almost always result in price rises or reduction in services to consumers. Because no social instrument exists to coordinate their independent actions, each acts in terms of his own expectations of the responses of his counterparts in other organizations and administrations. As other-directed organization men, they respond solely in terms of their relevant other and each is collectively affirmed in his decisions by the similar responses made by the others. Thus, the managerial and administrative classes, although holding decision-making jobs, do not resist inflationary tendencies because there is neither social nor psychological machinery to coordinate their individual decisions and because deflationary actions would run counter to their own interests.

Small and medium-sized businesses — run by private owners of retail outlets, service establishments, subcontractors, franchise operators, corporate medical groups, and so forth — have become larger and larger because we now measure the size of such businesses in relationship to the giant corporations and not in relationship to their past size. Collectively, such enterprises account for a significant portion of the total volume of business and can make an important contribution to inflation since their own prices can be highly elastic in relation to their costs. Yet, they attempt to move their incomes in phase with, or faster than, rates of inflation. To the extent that they try to adapt rationally to future prices rises, they raise prices and fees in anticipation of actual rises, thus exacerbating inflation by gaining temporary windfall profits. Furthermore, because these businessmen are continuously buying and selling, they are highly attuned to daily fluctuations in the value of the dollar, stocks and bonds, costs, interest rates, prices and fees, and they become aware that their income and profits are as much a result of price fluctuations and on the so-called money market as upon the productive value of their services and the merchandise they sell. As a result their professional and merchandizing activities take on a purely business quality, with the further result that every increase in prices intensifies their sensitivity to additional speculative and price opportunities. Not only does this result in further inflation, but it also leads to growing resentment against them by the groups in society who are dependent upon them for their goods and services and who cannot pass on price increases or escape from them. Whatever hatred of and hostility toward big business that exists is paralleled by an even greater resentment against the small- and medium-sized business classes whose success is immediately visible to all other groups below them. Petit bourgeois success accents the latter groups' helpless inability to defend themselves against their own sufferings from the seemingly inexorable inflation and unemployment spiral. It is understandable that shoplifting and white-collar crime will become more prevalent, and looting and burning in crisis situations should not be unexpected.

Academicians and intellectuals are in some respects a special case. During the period of the late fifties and especially the sixties, they were major beneficiaries of the enormous expansion of the educational industry under the enlarged "welfare" state. From the beginning of

Inflation through the Ages

President Johnson's administration to the middle of President Nixon's second term (1970 — Kent State University), vast resources were invested in university construction, academic research, and federal subsidization of professional salaries and student stipends. Government support of university libraries in turn lent new support to the publishing industry, and other federal programs provided financial aid to the arts, the humanities, and social science research of all kinds. Some professors achieved semiautonomous positions within the universities, and even intellectuals without an institutional foundation could at least survive if not flourish in the open marketplace. In the seventies, the decline of all of these areas of opportunity has coincided with inflation and cutbacks in the university budgets and has led, on the one hand, to the demoralization of part of the professoriat and, on the other, to intensified efforts on the part of university administrators to generate new business by opening up so-called new career opportunities and revitalizing professionally oriented programs. Such activity has increased enrollments in business schools, law schools, and medical and criminal justice programs, but has also further demoralized the discipline-oriented professoriat in the social sciences and humanities as well as political and civic-minded intellectuals.

In the nature of the case, it is to be expected that academicians and political intellectuals would be the first to analyze and verbalize both the social consequences of inflation and the long-term societal implications of declining abundance, but it is a characteristic of the present situation that they have been slow to respond to these problems, if they can be said to have responded to them at all. Instead they have focused their attention on the internal problems of their own professions and universities. No doubt this turn inward is related to the institutional absorption of academic intellectuals into policy-oriented research and state-supported programs which make criticism more difficult, but this explanation does not seem sufficient if one remembers that academic intellectuals during the sixties led the civil rights movements and the antiwar movements at a time when educational institutions were most heavily supported and subsidized by the federal government whose policies they attacked.

The silence of the intellectuals seems to be related to a sense of helplessness as well as to a change in their own career and intellectual situations. For one thing, they are now older by ten to fifteen years and so see life from the perspective of a tenured and entrenched civil service class. This fact alone would tend to narrow their vision of the world and to discourage them from criticism at a time in life where such criticism would be of no advantage to them, and would have the negative effect of exposing them to the charge of antisocial or perhaps even un-American activity, in a period when the country is suffering considerable international losses as well as perplexing and seemingly insoluble domestic crises. "Newer" professors, those still in graduate school ten years ago, must compete for positions and tenure with the established professoriat and, if they hold regular positions, seem to direct much of their intellectual energies to the internal political affairs of the university, or, if they do not hold regular positions, exhaust themselves in commuting from one parttime teaching position to another. But the decline of political activism and of social criticism by the professors is not explained only by their new career situations.

Much more important than these career considerations is the problem of the failure of social science theory to supply an explanation and interpretation of the present condition of American society in its own terms and in its relations with the world. It is now self-evident that the theoretical paradigms of the sixties — especially structural-functionalism and behaviorism in sociology and political science and Keynesianism and monetarism in economics — lack any congruity with social reality, leaving social scientists without the tools and perspectives to orient themselves. Their response to their intellectual disorientation has led them on the one hand to seek concrete solutions to their own economic problems and on the other to seek solutions in ideological tail thrashing: simultaneously, we witness a vast competitive struggle for government grants and for students, intensive efforts to refinance and reorganize universities, and a proliferation of centers of both conservative and radical thought looking to past ideologies and social theories in order to understand the present. Very few have sought to understand the present in its own concrete terms. Academicians and intellectuals have behaved neither like Mannheim's "detached" or Schumpeter's "unemployed" intellectuals. They have responded as a middle class acting in terms of its own occupational and lifestyle interests. Thus, the intellectual stratum has neither articulated the causes of the present condition nor has it offered solutions at the level of societal policy for the problems of youth, the poor, the aged, or those other groups now undergoing the experience of economic disenfranchisement for the first time. Along with their partial economic disenfranchisement, the intellectuals have intellectually disenfranchised themselves.

If inflation continues at its present levels, and if over the next few years unemployment and underemployment increase due to decreasing rates of expansion, more and more groups will be placed on the defensive with respect to maintaining their received or anticipated standards of living. If in this respect the United States should become more economically autarchic, competitive struggles between groups and classes to maintain or increase their economic share will be accompanied only at the expense of each other. Such competitiveness is then likely to be expressed at all institutional levels — in the open marketplace, in legislative struggles over the allocation of state and federal budgets, and in taxation, tariff, monetary, and fiscal policies that influence the distribution of income and wealth. No area of life is likely to be free from such competition, and each group is increasingly likely to be aware of specifically who its direct competitors are. Yet, it is equally likely that there will be an increasingly large number of losers who see their losses as a direct result of the gains of others; this will be all the more the case as levels of political sophistication increase on the part of competing groups, and with it, awareness that political means become economic determinants.

In a society highly fragmented by almost infinite subdivisions of groups based on differences of skill, occupation, class, lifestyle, race, religion, ethnicity, and country of origin, the number of special interests and individual interests is almost too staggering to imagine. Yet as these groups become increasingly aware of their special interests, they may also organize for the purpose of protecting those interests. Each organized group makes its claim on the system in order to protect, preserve, or enhance its own interests, developing such ideologies as are necessary to justify its actions to itself and to others. The management of these interests is the central political problem of the day. Managing such a system is relatively easy, so long as all or most groups receive the shares, or at least the promise of shares, commensurate with their positions. But all political efforts to adjudicate the competing claims face a single dilemma — i.e., how to meet the claims of groups who want more or, at least not less, in a period when it is impossible at an economic level to meet all the demands. When competition for shares increases because of a decline in shares, the competition between these goups and competitive struggle to gain political influence intensifies; political and economic constituencies are likely to split and mix in complex patterns that are not likely to follow class lines. The problem of political management of social resentment, intergroup hostility, hatred of leaders, and disgust with the system as a whole would seem to have no rational solution because it appears to be impossible to make compromises that require some legitimate groups to make sacrifices while others benefit. The demands placed on the system are more than political leaders can satisfy by the economic and administrative means currently available to them.

Under these conditions, one test of political leadership will be its capacity to find noneconomic means for satisfying the competitive claims. Noneconomic means include such methods as discrimination and prejudice, scapegoating, an immoral equivalent to a "war on poverty," xenophobic nationalism, jingoism, red-baiting, antiintellectualism, and other even less palatable methods almost too frightful to contemplate in a highly internationalized world. At times, international events beyond political leaders' direct control may, as in the case of the Ayatollah Khomeini or Russia's invasion of Afghanistan, inadvertently supply us with a unifying scapegoat. Other noneconomic means include the formation of a system of coalition politics under which groups trade their votes for special favors promised in advance of elections. All such political bargaining for economic patronage essentially rests on promises to be delivered after the election. In the nature of the election system in the United States, there is always a preelection inflation of promises which cannot be fulfilled by the successful candidate; with declining shares, more promises will go unfulfilled, and it is likely that groups whose promises are not fulfilled will be less willing to wait the full four-year term of the presidency for their next chance to trade their votes for future promises. It will become more difficult to meet political mortgage obligations when outstanding promissory notes exceed available supplies of capital, though it is always possible that such notes may be renewed at shorter and shorter intervals.

Still another means is to exhort groups on the basis of civic values or Christian ideals to reduce their claims in the interests of the common good, but it is difficult to define a common good for groups whose competition with each other includes different ideas of what is the common good, and which function in a society where Puritan religious values have declined and narcissistic ideologies have captured the imagination of much of its youth.

Even the psychological means available to political leaders to coordinate mass psychology becomes more difficult because the multiplication of audiences makes it difficult to find slogans that can transcend the psychological boundaries of particular constituencies. Political management depends increasingly on the coordination of mass psychology. When political leaders lose their credibility with the masses, the masses are prepared to replace them with new ones.

In some instances, as for example, that of President Nixon during Watergate, political leaders lose their ability to manage mass psychology, and its management passes into the hands of the mass media. Yet the media cannot manage it because they have not yet developed a political line of their own other than to respond in terms of audience responses. Perhaps the media can temporarily absorb resentments and hostilities by playing to the resentment and hostilities of all groups simultaneously and thus render some stability to mass psychology.

Pragmatically, the solution is likely to rest in acceptance by all concerned groups of a slow and gradual decline in consumption standards and living styles. So long as the decline comes in small steps and slow stages, it will not be sufficiently noticeable to precipitate a general crisis, and no major group will feel that it is carrying an excessive burden relative to its immediate competitors. If this is to be the case, much of politics will concern itself with a form of deescalation of economic and social expectations, and each step in the deescalation will be fraught with political dangers stemming from the resentment of those groups which regard themselves as paying too high a price. There is some question whether the American political system can produce a leader who is capable of this type of social and economic orchestration, since the leaders themselves are part of the class and regional competition. But all such seemingly "unresolvable" processes can be rescued by a war, a depression, or by some unexpected form of "good luck," though the latter is hardest to imagine. More likely, the conditions we have attempted to analyze will result in forms of political instability and/or a chronic sense of malaise with which American society has heretofore not had to contend.

None of the internal economic conditions we have discussed is independent of long-term changes in the United States position in world economic and political affairs. The overarching cause of its problems is, thus, the absolute reaching of the marginal utility of national states to regulate and ensure their own society's life conditions. This marginal utility of national economics is the result of significant changes in the international economic order. The great expansion in number and size of multinational corporations which are beyond the controls of federal law, regulation, and perhaps even nationalization has resulted in an international laissez-faire economy reminiscent of that of the United States in the nineteenth century.

Within the framework of such laissez-faire internationalism, the post-colonial world has begun to assert its claim to price and market its own natural resources. The apotheosis of this post-colonial and civilizational (e.g., Islam) "nativistic" assertion finds its economic power in the historical accident of ownership of fossil fuel beds which are vital to the industrial nations, including the United States. Other Third World countries possess primary extractive resources for whose possession industrialized countries increasingly compete. The competition to control and market crucial national resources throughout the world has created new international oligopolies that render much economic theory and practice obsolete, because it rests on the assumption of an international order and on the presumption that the state will be the largest unit for economic management. Neither the internal nor the external economic problems of the United States are manageable within the framework of its own institutions. Like the countries of the old worlds, the United States is now becoming an old country. It remains to be seen how, under these conditions, it will use its power for the future reshaping and reorganizing of a world in which it will suffer frustrations when it cannot prevail on its own terms.

Notes

* I wish to thank Joseph Bensman and Stanford Lyman for the valuable criticisms and suggestions they gave me during the preparation of this paper.
1. As reported by the Organization for Economic Cooperation and Development. See Paul Lewis, "Economic Adjustment Seen in the U.S.," *New York Times,* 14 November 1979, p. D4.
2. *Ibid.*
3. In all these expectations and hopes, economists and policy makers have been notoriously inaccurate in the past and there is no reason to assume greater accuracy in the future.
4. See the following discussion: Abba P. Lerner, "From the Pre-Keynes to Post-Keynes," *Social Research* 44 (1977): 387–415; Edward Nell, J. A. Kregel, and Joseph Halvei, "Comments on Abba Lerner's 'From Pre-Keynes to Post-Keynes'," *Social Research* 46 (1979): 207–254.
5. Joseph Bensman and Arthur J. Vidich, "The Crisis of Contemporary Capitalism and the Failure of Nerve," *Sociological Inquiry* 46 (1976): 207–217.
6. For a discussion of the responses of these groups to the economic effects of the Vietnam War and to President Nixon's economic and social policies, see Bensman and Vidich, *op. cit.*
7. See Joseph Bensman and Arthur J. Vidich, *The New American Society* (New York, 1971), for a discussion of the theoretical relationships between business cycles, long-term secular trends, and class structure.

Toward a Sociology of Inflation

EDWIN HARWOOD

One of my sociology professors at Stanford used to poke fun at a tendency which he claimed had begun to accelerate in sociology as that discipline began its rapid post-1960 growth. He called this tendency *the sociology of* . . . the blank space to be filled in with anything under the sun that could conceivably interest a sociologist. And how prophetic he was! In the manner of the great commercial conglomerates of 15 years ago, sociology has managed an acquisitions program of considerable scope, which now includes such subspecialties as the sociology of sports, literature, gambling, witchcraft, and even animals, among other calcifying deposits that today line and, some would even say, clog our sociological arteries.

In proposing the sociology of inflation as a new subfield of study, I am fully aware that I risk bringing down on my head the mirth of my old professor. But there are advantages to getting to market first with a new conceptual orientation to a problem even when that problem may have been packaged adequately enough under other labels in other disciplinary containers. In any case, with the explosive growth in public concern over inflation, scholars will be rushing to fill the breach with explanations as well as panaceas. And sociologists, who have always cut themselves in on the action in the public issues and social problems market — one need only consider the earlier surfeit of urban crisis and crime-in-the-streets books — will be sure to follow hard on the heels of the current public distress over inflation.

Might I, then, have the honor of lighting the way with conceptual beacons for colleagues in sociology who are certain to follow, and indeed in great numbers if the road turns out to be paved with federal largesse in the form of grants to study the problem?

But now seriously: can a *sociology* of inflation be justified as a new approach to this economic and social demon, or will it merely turn out to be an assembly point for research findings already gathered by others?

First, one must ask whether there are aspects of the inflation problem that other disciplines have not addressed adequately? Many important aspects of inflation are probably well covered by economists and economic historians, but those aspects that relate to the specific cultural, social, and psychological adjustments that societies are making in the present inflationary environment have been analyzed largely by journalists and commentators outside the social science disciplines and in a few instances by pollsters, some of whom are social scientists but without academic portfolios.[1] This is not to say that economists have not considered these adjustments, but rather that when they have considered them, it has tended to be from the standpoint of the range of narrowly *economic* choices open to individuals as investors, workers, consumers, and the like. The aggregative statistics of macroeconomics bring many of these behavioral adjustments into view, as for example, the tendency of people to find cheaper substitutes when inflationary conditions erode their real incomes or to cut gasoline use by 1.5 to 2.0 percent for every 10-cent rise in price. And yet much behavior may be significant and yet remain buried under the macroeconomic topsoil, as when small but growing numbers of individuals develop novel and unanticipated strategies for coping with inflation such as buying more expensive goods with a longer life-span or speeding up their purchases of goods when, on the basis of past experience, it was expected that inflationary pressures would lead them to build up their savings instead.[2] Economist George Katona and his associates at the University of Michigan's Survey Research Center anticipated precisely that change in consumer response in the late 1970s. They were able to do so, and thereby improve on conventional econometric forecasting, by using a conventional sociological method, the questionnaire survey, to probe shifts in consumer optimism. Thus they correctly forecast the severe 1973–75 recession before other economists were able to catch the changing macroeconomic signals. They also observed that whether Americans will tend to respond to inflation by saving, as happened during inflationary bursts in the 1950s and 1960s, or respond instead by a furious burst of new expenditures, as has been happening the past several years, depends very much on the collective state of mind. If people anticipate *continuing* inflation, they will spend and hoard.[3]

Surveys of subgroups of the American public can help to uncover shifts in attitude and behavior which, though initially confined to small segments of the population, may point to significant adjustments among larger numbers in the future. Thus Dorothy Leonard-Barton and Everett Rogers, both researchers at Stanford's Institute for Communication Research, find some evidence of a growing movement toward "voluntary simplicity," whereby individuals curtail material consumption not from dire economic necessity, as in the case of the poor, but from choice. Thus the substitution of biking for auto transport, the recycling of cans, bottles, and paper, the substitution of one's own labor in car and home repairs, and the purchase of clothing at second-hand stores and of major furniture items at garage sales were among the items included in the voluntary simplicity scale (VSS) to arrive at an estimate of the scaling-down of consumption among individuals surveyed in northern California who were assumed to be under no economic pressure to reduce their consumption. Although the motivations for "voluntary simplicity" have emerged, according to Rogers and Leonard-Barton, primarily from environmental and conservationist concerns (the view of resources as being finite) and lifestyle changes (the anticonsumption ethic generated by the countercultural upheaval of the late 1960s), the current pressures of inflation might well broaden the appeal of such adjustments to many more than the 4–5 million people who are roughly estimated to be wholehearted converts to "voluntary simplicity."[4]

Evidence from a number of national surveys finds Americans increasingly pessimistic about their economic future. Over the past decade, the percentage of survey respondents expecting inflation to worsen has nearly doubled (from 30 percent to 52 percent in the Harris poll); the percentage expecting that their incomes would not keep pace with inflation was found by the Survey Research Center to have increased from 35 to 45 percent in just two years (1976–78). Not surprisingly, a large majority of Americans claim that inflation is forcing them to curtail buying of luxuries, and more than half claim that they have been forced to cut back even on necessities.[5]

Surveys indicate that pessimism runs deep on this issue (though it is predictably deeper among older than younger Americans), but how Americans respond in terms of both changed attitudes and behaviors is an important field for research. One might assume that Americans will behave like British or Argentinian trade unionists and simply push wages up in tandem with rising costs, with precious little concern for the relation between their productivity and income on the one hand, or the public good on the other. The anomic and embittered striking by our public sector workers is hardly grounds for optimism on this score. Yet it is also conceivable that many other Americans might react by accepting reductions in their consumption as part of a new ethic along the lines of the "voluntary simplicity" movement. The substitution of bicycle for auto transport by commuting professionals in places like Palo Alto and Cambridge, Massachusetts, may be only the latest variant of environmental chic among upper-middle-class people. On the other hand, it may be symptomatic of a more far-reaching response that, like jogging and other fads, begins in the better-educated professional strata but finally works outward to other income and occupational groups who also finally reach the view that personal thrift and ascetism may be virtues after all and provide psychic "income" commensurate with the prior satisfactions of a socially enforced ethic of consumption. For many families, that earlier ethic may have been as much a "forced march" keeping-in-step-with-the-Joneses as it was a truly voluntary option.[6]

The survey analysts Yankelovich and Lefkowitz find, besides the heightened economic pessimism noted earlier, evidence of conflict in the American psyche over how to respond to the changed economic circumstances. Many feel entitled to the good life, having listened to prophets of postindustrialism who beckoned them to "actualize" and develop their "selves" to the fullest, leaving the drudgery of goods production to the new proletariats of Taiwan, Hong Kong, Brazil, and other industrializing countries. Thus Americans "want more but are willing to give less for it" in the words of Yankelovich and Lefkowitz.[7] Many also engage in wishful thinking, believing that deficit budgets, one of the major sources of inflation, could be reduced merely by eliminating government waste without having to cut back on welfare and social spending.[8]

On the other hand, Americans also appear to favor, by a small majority (55 percent) the view that "doing without something and living a more austere life would be a good thing," and a very substantial majority (79 percent) agree that "teaching people to live with basic essentials" is to be preferred to striving after a higher standard of living.[9] But as the authors note, the expression of virtuous attitudes is one thing, behavior quite another. That Americans vote five-to-one in favor of nonconsumption-oriented experiences over goods in response to a single questionnaire item hardly means that their behavior will conform to the sentiment expressed. Yet it is interesting to note that although the present substantial reductions in gasoline use and driving appear to be motivated largely by the dramatic gasoline price rise, some of the motivation to use less gas also appears to be the result of a kind of "economic patriotism" in which public-spirited virtue and economic self-interest have finally found a common anchorage.[10]

On another level, a sociology of inflation should consider how a society's response to inflation is not merely to the economic logic of choice of the situation but also to the "symbolic environment" that grows up around it and can have potent secondary effects. Let me clarify: if, for example, the price of gasoline rises beyond the increase in a person's income, either he buys as much as he is accustomed to and does without something else or he buys less; or perhaps he buys as much or even more than he is accustomed to and digs into assets or goes into debt. He will optimize his behavior as a consumer according to some schedule of current priorities and some forecast of his future situation.

This is an economic response to inflationary increases.[11] Yet it is quite clear that because people respond to inflation in symbolic terms, their adjustments can be moved and even distorted beyond what economics alone might indicate. Although a sample of "one" is very risky for drawing inferences, let me use my father's response as an example. My father was prodded to take the capital he inherited over 20 years ago out of passive investments vulnerable to inflation and put it instead into real estate, and to a lesser extent, gold and silver, not primarily because of the real inflation he was suffering but because of anxieties that may have been partly induced by his travels in South America and sometime residence in Mexico.[12]

I have chosen to distinguish the "symbolic" from the economic response to inflation because symbolization can amplify the behavioral and attitudinal adjustments to "real" inflation. Not just the exposure given the topic by the mass media, but the apocalyptic content of the hard-money newsletters that my father and people like him subscribe to mightily reinforce the response to "symbolic inflation" (or "inflation-as-a-social-problem") above and beyond their direct economic experience of it. Not surprisingly, the hard-money gold and silver advisory newsletters have increased dramatically from approximately 25,000 to 750,000 in their combined subscriber readership over the past decade. Of course millions of less affluent people are now exposed to "inflation-as-a-social-problem" by the daily television news as well as by the print media.

It would be useful to have cross-cultural data to assess whether the symbolic environment of inflation looms as large in other societies. It is widely believed, for example, that Americans express disproportionately greater alarm than do the citizens of countries like Uruguay, Mexico, or Argentina because continuous peacetime inflation is so radically disjunctive, given both our long enjoyment of a stable monetary unit and our work ethic. Perhaps this is so. But it is also possible that citizens in these other societies have less exposure to public symbolizations of issues because of a less dense media environment and lower educational levels. Thus smaller dosages of inflation may have more far-reaching behavioral effects in the United States partly because of the pervasive focusing of media attention on this issue along with the tendency of a better-educated public to attend to social issues generally. The public response to "crime-in-the-streets" in the late 1960s and early 1970s offers itself as an analogous example. Much of the anxiety urbanites experienced then arose not because they actually had been victimized but because they *feared* that they might be victimized. True, the real probabilities of victimization had increased in many urban places, but there can be little doubt that much of the increased public apprehension was generated by unrelieved and persistent media attention to the problem.[13]

In the quarterly surveys of consumer attitudes conducted by George Katona and his associates at the Michigan Survey Research Center, one of the questions asked of respondents is: "During the last year or two, would you say that your (family) income went up more than prices, went up about the same as prices, or went up less than prices?" By and large, respondents have no difficulty answering this although from 1 to 4 percent either cannot or will not answer the question. The intriguing question is: how do respondents develop a basis for their judgment and hence response? Do they compare a statistic like the Consumer Price Index with their raise in salary for the year? Do they make a rough guess based on the changes in prices of items which are most salient to them, say gasoline or utility costs, for example? In the absence of an objective measuring rod that shows the extent to which their salaries keep pace with inflation, it seems probable that they would be highly susceptible to the "symbolic environment" of inflation in arriving at a judgment.[14]

Let me digress briefly to show how public symbolizations can distort economic fact and reality by looking at past and current interpretations of unemployment. During the Great Depression, many assumed, quite mistakenly, that the unemployed were out of work because of purely local conditions or personal failings. Yet 30 years later, in the prosperous era of the 1960s, many educated people, including most media newscasters, had come to learn finally, thanks to the tutelage of social scientists, that unemployment could only be the result of inadequate job opportunities; and this view became the legitimated symbolic filter applied wherever the unemployed were spotted, as during forays by newscasters into ghetto and Skid Row areas. In consequence, much unemployment that may have been voluntary, as was the case with most youth unemployment then, or the result of personal inadequacy (dereliction, emotional disturbance, etc.) was erroneously attributed to the economy's failure to provide enough jobs.

The symbolic misconstruing of the unemployment rate is now much better understood thanks in part to the work of Harvard economist Martin Feldstein, among others.[15] When we hear, for example, that 7 out of every 100 persons in the labor force are out of work, we are now less apt to have in our mind's eye a view of seven needy breadwinners with families to support. In fact, only one or two may fall into that category. Another may linger on out of work because his unemployment compensation is too competitive with other jobs available to him; one or two may be young adults moving between jobs; another may be a housewife looking for just the right part time job to pay for her child's private school tuition, while yet another has arranged with his employer to get laid off in order to qualify for unemployment so that he can live better as a graduate student when he resumes his studies.[16]

I am not, however, trying to make the point that inflation, like unemployment, has been misinterpreted or exaggerated as a public issue. I merely wish to point out that symbolic reconstructions of the underlying reality of social problems are clearly inevitable and that sometimes they can go widely astray because of a fashionable but erroneous conventional wisdom which continues to hold important publics and opinion makers in its thrall despite a changing social reality.

There is certainly much less ambiguity attaching to measures of inflation than attaches to measures of unemployment. Although the Consumer Price Index, the most widely cited inflation barometer, does involve a number of conceptual problems, as long as one has faith in the sampling techniques employed by the Census Bureau, rises in prices are unambiguous indicators of inflation in a way increases in unemployment are not. And since we all must buy goods, we all have personal experience with inflation.

But as a public symbolization of inflation, the CPI is not completely immune to distortion. Perhaps because television newscasters are inclined to refer to it as a "cost-of-living," measure, the public has come to accept it as a symbolic stand-in for rises in the cost of living. Yet the CPI does not take into account *changes* in the market basket of goods and services consumers may be purchasing. If consumers have been switching from beef to chicken, or are buying less fuel oil and gasoline but more clothing, then their cost of living will not escalate at the rate of CPI-measured inflation, because the march of price increases is not uniform over all goods and services. By adjusting to inflation through expenditure shifts they are avoiding paying the full toll as it were.[18] Paradoxically, people whose wages or welfare payments escalate in tandem with the CPI through cost-of-living adjustment clauses may very well do *better* than just beat inflation if their market basket of goods and services differs from the typical market basket used to weight the various expenditures that comprise the CPI.

Does the CPI as symbolic stand-in distort the perception of inflation upward or downward? This is a difficult question to answer. First, the CPI does not include the cost of income taxes and Social Security levies which, for many families, are rising faster than the general level of price increase. On the other hand, noncash consumption is also missed in the CPI. If individuals are receiving more fringe benefits, e.g., use of a company- or state-owned car, expense-account travel and meals, special compensation for increased mortgage costs when moving, an office WATS line, etc., then inflation is offset for them personally by the enlarged size of the fringe-benefit wedge in their consumption pie.[18] (Perhaps this is one way that organizations help to compensate their work force for inflation since, as substitutes for income, these fringes escape taxation to the individual recipient and thus are relatively inflation-proof.)

The main point I want to stress is that individuals and families who, using the CPI indicator as a symbolic stand-in for inflation, come to feel that they are losing ground by the rate expressed in the CPI (18 percent in January 1980, for example) may indeed be experiencing inflation, but through a symbolic filter. They cannot know their own "individual" rate of inflation without an elaborate and onerous bookkeeping system. Were it within the power of the Office of Prices and Living Conditions to develop an individualized rate for anyone who wanted it, then clearly there would be considerable variation as between households according to the differences in family market baskets. In the cases of households that have experienced significant appreciation in the value of their homes, the rate of inflation could be close to zero or even negative! Yet individuals who experience appreciation in their housing may not be aware that this could be considered a valid offset against rises in their other costs (according to one measure of shelter cost which the CPI lists separately but does not use).[19] They may look at their appreciated home value as a windfall gain in the manner of a stroke of luck at a Las Vegas craps table or as the reward for foresight instead of as an offset against other price increases. Thus they, along with many others, may complain loudly that inflation is victimizing them when, in terms of their enhanced net worth, they are clearly among the gainers rather than losers in this economic saga.

By the same token, the relationship between one's cost of living and one's standard of living involves complexities that are sometimes overlooked. There may well be some net psychological gains for individuals who come to view inflation as a challenge to find cheaper or more healthful substitutes for goods formerly taken for granted. Thus thrifty behavior may give rise to psychic rewards that offset the loss of prior satisfactions obtained from trading in one's car every three years or "burning rubber" in indiscriminate joy-riding through town and country. Studies of the used car market by the Hertz Corporation show a dramatic increase in the number of families (75 percent) whose primary vehicle is no longer a new car but a recent-model used auto.[20] Whether this is motivated by a desire to *save* for other purposes or simply because a brand-new car is not affordable, it is not clear that such a substitution in expenditure patterns should be taken as symptomatic of a decline in living standards. Moreover, when people feel "bad" because of inflation-induced cutbacks in consumption, this may be not so much the result of the direct loss of satisfactions intrinsic to the use of a good as of the social and cultural significance of feeling that one is now among all those who must make do with less and may, because of future uncertainty, have to make yet further sacrifices.[21]

What I have sought to show is that inflation has effects that are symbolically mediated as well as directly economic in terms of the adjustments a population makes. Perhaps this is too obvious a point.

Yet if some countries seem inclined to "underreact" to inflation by our own standards, whereas others, faced with less drastic increases, appear to take the whole business much more seriously, then it would seem to be worthwhile to ask why this is so. A sociology of inflation should investigate this aspect of inflation along with other problems.

On the institutional or macrosociological level, a sociology of inflation has still one or two other services to perform. Economists peer behind the veils of the money supply to track down the institutional and structural forces in the modern postindustrial economy that *create* inflationary pressures. And pollsters are able to gauge the changing climate of public opinion on this matter, which in turn can be seen to mirror changes in American value patterns. Americans may dislike inflation, but it appears they would dislike even more any revocation of the political status quo, of welfare expenditures, and other fiscal policies aimed at economic stabilization, which would eliminate one very important inflationary pressure. Unless the surveys of the past decade are very much in error, which I doubt, it appears that "collective economic security" has been displacing "individual self-reliance and risk-taking" as a central American value at least since the 1930s.

A sociology of inflation would try to account for these shifts in values which have an inflationary bias along with a variety of institutional changes which augment the pressures that surface from political wells in state and federal legislatures. (One thinks, in this connection, of the pressure to expand consumer credit of all kinds although this may now be easing because of recent Federal Reserve actions along with high interest rates.)

And just as a sociology of inflation would explore the attitudinal and cultural soils which nourish inflation, it would also want to consider the political institutional impact of severe and continuing inflation. It has been widely assumed that governments which promote this great paper chase bring collective commotions and turmoil down on their heads, but much more study is certainly needed to assess the *differences* in societal response. Invariably, writers of "hard-money newsletters," such as Howard Ruff and others — along with conservative writers generally — see political chaos as an almost inevitable byproduct. It is certainly foolish to view inflation as anything other than malign in its impact on the polity, yet it is difficult to argue that chaos is its inevitable result. Countries such as Brazil, Israel, and Britain experience the high "South American" rates without falling apart politically. The sociology of inflation should seek to determine what other factors must combine with high inflation before political havoc is wreaked and collapse assured and how it is that some democracies and limited "authoritarian" regimes manage to hold their own despite severe inflationary erosion.

Lastly, although sociologists should do responsible research on both the causes and consequences of inflation as they relate to social institutional trends and attitudinal and behaviorial adjustments, they may also want to add their counsel as citizens to the counsel of others who are apt to have the ears of our policy makers.

As a discipline, we have tended to take sides with the "underdog" groups of society, and this has led us to urge upon our politicians some of the very programs of increased public expenditure and regulation that are now part and parcel of the inflation problem. We have not as a profession tended to worry over the healthy functioning of our capital markets, or the advantages of encouraging savings and investment among our middle and upper classes (which many of us have tended to view only as exploiters of the poor and deprived). We need, in my judgment, to reappraise this ideological one-sidedness in our profession.

As a society, we need — if I may inject a note of advocacy — to become once again savers and builders of capital. And we need to communicate to our lawmakers that we are capable of the sacrifice and deferred gratification that made our way of life possible. They should know that however much they may choose to dispense largesse on themselves and their liegemen in their Versailles-on-the-Potomac, they need not rush forth to us with bottles of fiscal formula everytime they think they hear a cry. If our forefathers had not been able to defer gratification for years, and in many cases for lifetimes, it is not likely that our nation would have expanded much beyond the original 13 colonies in view of the hazards. And had the thrifty and saving among them and among the suppliers of capital for new ventures not been fairly rewarded, it is not probable that we would enjoy the standard of living we still have today despite the ravages of the longest peacetime inflation we have experienced since our nation's founding.

Notes

1. Some of the best accounts of how Latin Americans, for example, have been adjusting to inflation in terms of changes in their daily behavior and attitudes are found in newspaper and magazine accounts. I recommend, in particular, the feature stories that have appeared in *The Wall Street Journal* over the past decade.
2. The current controversy over adaptive vs. rational expectations theory as a framework for econometric projections and policy formation reflects the discontent with the earlier heavy reliance on macroeconomic models that merely extrapolated from past economic series into the future without taking into account the highly complex psychological horizons of individuals whose

future anticipations could lead them to abort and change the economic response policy makers had come to expect.

3. Thus Katona and his associates were hardly surprised to find single-family home sales increasing in 1977 despite large increases in prices and interest rates. Expecting further price increases, consumers had no incentive to defer their purchases. See George Katona, "Behavioral Economics," *Challenge*, September–October, 1978, pp. 16–18.

4. But of course, to the extent others are driven by economic pressure into the arms of this movement, the lifestyle is no longer *voluntary* simplicity. One criticism of the VS survey studies is that there is no way to determine whether some of the reduced consumption behavior is in fact due to inflationary pressures. Although the surveys were administered to San Francisco Bay area homeowners, who might be assumed to be more affluent than the general California population, even the seemingly affluent may feel economic pressure to cut back on consumption. In addition to which, not all homeowners are affluent. See Dorothy Leonard-Barton and Everett M. Rogers, "Voluntary Simplicity in California: Precursor or Fad," paper, delivered at the American Association for the Advancement of Science in San Francisco, January 1980.

5. These and other recent survey findings are reviewed by Daniel Yankelovich and Bernard Lefkowitz in "National Growth: the Question of the '80s," *Public Opinion*, December–January 1980, pp. 46–57.

6. But caution is needed here. It can be fun to save through bargain hunting, goods substitutions, and the like, but it will still remain fun to consume in what my buddies in the Army liked to call "the land of the great PX (Post Exchange)." Americans may be, paradoxically, only saving on "this" in order to spend on "that." See Michael Phillips, "SRI is Wrong about Voluntary Simplicity," *The Co-Evolution Quarterly*, Summer 1977, pp. 32–34.

7. Yankelovich and Lefkowitz, p. 55.

8. *Ibid.*, p. 52.

9. *Ibid.*

10. See the recent front-page story, "Sputtering Along" in the 3 April 1980 *Wall Street Journal* and the companion essay on the efforts that corporations, police departments, and private citizens are making to cut back on gasoline use in a manner reminiscent of the backyard victory gardens of World War II.

11. I assume that inflation is a problem primarily because most of the population eventually experiences a decline in *real* purchasing power. If inflation created no real decline in purchasing power for anyone, then the problem of how people adjust to inflation would be less of an issue for the sociology of inflation. There would be accounting and related problems for firms and banks, just as there might be a real loss in economic efficiency because of the absence of a stable monetary unit. Thus inflation might still be a social problem even if no loss in real purchasing power occurred.

12. Of course, there is a realistic basis for such fears since we currently all experience a very real inflation. My point is not that inflation is merely a perceptual chimera. It is clearly a real and ominous issue. My point is, rather, that the response populations make to a given rate of inflation is mediated by public symbolizations of the problem.

13. Rises in the FBI crime index were cited then in the worried manner of the

Bureau of Labor Statistics Consumer Price Index today. For a discussion of the symbolic environment surrounding the crime issue see John E. Conklin, *The Impact of Crime* (New York, 1975), pp. 15–42.

14. Taken from Table 9, "Surveys of Consumer Attitudes," Institute for Social Research of The Survey Research Center, University of Michigan, February 1980.

15. I found in field work I conducted in the late 1960s that much youth unemployment was not serious. For many males caught between adolescence and adulthood, freedom from family obligations allowed them to take a cavalier attitude toward jobs and work. Many worked as they needed money and balanced off income in the form of freedom and leisure against discipline and work. Edwin Harwood, "Youth Unemployment: A Tale of Two Ghettos," *The Public Interest*, Fall 1969.

16. I am indebted for this last example to my colleague Jack Douglass who knew students who used this ploy in California.

Today there is considerably more sophistication in recognizing the conceptual problems in both measuring and interpreting unemployment rates at the Bureau of Labor Statistics. And this more sophisticated understanding appears now in mass media presentations of the issue.

17. For a discussion of this issue see "The Consumer Price Index: Concepts and Content Over the Years," May 1978, U.S. Bureacu of Labor Statistics, Report No. 517. See also Ronald Alsop, "Containing Costs: Most Families Become Resourceful and Beat Rise in Consumer Index," *The Wall Street Journal*, CXCV, No. 57.

18. Some of this can be considered "quasi consumption," in that business is combined with "pleasure." Or perhaps this depends on your point of view. I tend to look at most of my conference and convention travel as a "quasi vacation," a refreshing break from the tensions of the job even though some work is usually required in preparation.

19. This could happen using the "user-cost" $X-2$ and $X-3$ function to estimate the rise in the homeownership components in the CPI. In fact, however, the overall CPI continues to rely on a flow-of-services measure which counts the investment return on houses as a shelter cost to consumers. Thus all consumers are assumed to be buying shelter each month at the current cost, which of course is not true.

20. See the article by William G. Flanagan in *The Wall Street Journal*, 11 February 1980, p. 38. During 1979, I substituted about 2800 auto miles by using my 10-speed bike. The feeling of virtue (saving gas and money, getting in shape, etc.) greatly outweighed the costs in increased transportation time and occasional soakings when caught by a shower.

21. Of course, there are cases of real material deprivation among the poorest elements of our society in which the erosion of living standards means acute physical discomfort.

Income Level and Inflation in the United States: 1947–1977

WALTER F. ABBOTT
J. W. LEASURE*

Inflation is one mechanism by which the life chances[1] of a person may be affected, either absolutely or relatively, without a change in occupation or other status. Inflation, of course, is not a recent phenomenon; indeed, it is a historical one. The existence of persistent inflation in the United States on an accelerated scale is, however, an unusual occurrence and warrants serious investigation for its possible consequences on the reordering of life chances in the social order. Using official data reported by the United States Bureau of Labor Statistics, this paper attempts to determine whether inflation from 1947 to 1977 in the United States has been differentiated by income level. An analysis of aggregate trends in real income and employment is reported in the first section. The methodology of constructing income-specific consumer price indexes based on official statistics is presented in the second section. The third section reports trends in estimated consumer price indexes by income level from 1947 to 1977. Limitations to the design used in this paper are considered in the concluding section.

AGGREGATE ANALYSIS

Table 1 and Figure 1 report aggregate trends in real income and employment in the United States, 1947–77. The index of real income is the difference between the annual percentage increase in median family income and the Bureau of Labor Statistics's (1979) Consumer Price Index. The income data are reported by the Bureau of Census (1979). The rate of employment is defined as 100 minus the rate of unemployment. The average, time-lagged by one year, is reported for each President from Truman's second term through the Nixon-Ford administration. Three observations may be made of the aggregate historical data.

1. The average increase in income has been greater than the average increase in the CPI from 1947 to 1977 for each administration, except for Nixon's second term. This finding seems generally consistent with studies by Bach and Ando (1957), Cargill (1969), and Livitan and

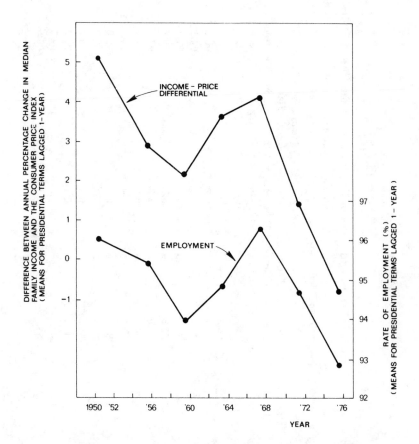

Fig. 1   The Difference between Annual Percentage Change in Median Family Income and the Consumer Price Index and the Rate of Employment : 1950-77

Table 1. Median Family Income, Consumer Prices, and Rates of Employment in the United States: 1947–1977

Year	Median Family Income		Consumer Price Index		Difference Between Annual Income & Price Index		Rate of Employment (%)	
	Current Income (1)	Annual Change (%) (2)	CPI (1967=100) (3)	Annual Change (%) (4)	Difference (2) – (4) (5)	Mean for Presidential Administration (1-yr.lag) (6)	Current Rate (7)	Mean for Presidential Administration (1-yr. lag) (8)
1947	3031	—	66.9	—	—		96.2	—
1948	3187	5.1	72.1	7.8	-2.7		94.1	
1949	3107	-2.5	71.4	-1.0	-1.5		94.7	
1950	3319	6.8	72.1	1.0	5.8		96.7	96.0
1951	3709	11.8	77.8	7.9	3.9	5.1	97.0	
1952	3890	4.9	79.5	2.2	2.7		97.1	
1953	4233	8.8	80.1	0.8	8.0		94.5	
1954	4173	-1.4	80.5	0.5	-1.9		95.6	95.4
1955	4421	5.9	80.2	-0.4	6.4	2.9	95.9	
1956	4783	8.2	81.4	1.5	6.7		95.7	
1957	4971	3.9	84.3	3.6	0.3		93.2	
1958	5087	2.3	86.6	2.7	-0.4		94.5	93.9
1959	5417	6.5	87.3	0.8	5.7	2.1	94.5	
1960	5620	3.7	88.7	1.6	2.1		94.5	

1961	5737	2.1	89.6	1.0	1.1		93.3	
1962	5956	3.8	90.6	1.1	2.7		94.5	
1963	6249	4.9	91.7	1.2	3.7	3.6	94.3	94.8
1964	6569	5.1	92.9	1.3	3.8		94.8	
1965	6957	5.9	94.5	1.7	4.2		95.5	
1966	7500	7.8	97.2	2.9	4.9		96.2	
1967	7933	5.8	100.0	2.9	2.9	4.1	96.2	96.3
1968	8632	8.8	104.2	4.2	4.6		96.4	
1969	9433	9.3	109.8	5.4	3.9		96.5	
1970	9867	4.6	116.3	5.9	−1.3		95.1	
1971	10285	4.2	121.3	4.3	−0.1	1.4	94.1	94.7
1972	11116	8.1	125.3	3.3	4.8		94.4	
1973	12051	8.4	133.1	6.2	2.2		95.1	
1974	12902	7.1	147.7	11.0	−3.9		94.4	
1975	13719	6.3	161.2	9.1	−2.8	−.8	91.5	92.8
1976	14958	9.0	170.5	5.8	3.2		92.3	
1977	16009	7.0	181.5	6.5	0.5		93.0	

Source: U.S. Bureau of Labor Statistics, Handbook of Labor Statistics: 1978, Bulletin 2000, June, 1979; U.S. Bureau of the Census, Current Population Reports, Series P-60, No. 118, 1979.

Taggart (1971) that challenge the proposition that prices rise more rapidly than wages — the wage-lag thesis. The amount has been variable, however, and appears to be on the decline. It is thus of special interest to analyze the post-1977 period as information becomes available to ascertain whether, in fact, the United States is entering a state of long-run decline in real income. A clear trend in this direction is evident. The political and social implications of a secular decline in real income are far-reaching, and include consequences on politics and class relations, the maintenance of an optimistic economic ideology, and the extension of the state into the direct control of production.

2. There is a linkage between the party holding the presidency and the trend in real income and employment. The trend in employment and real income was downward during the three Republican administrations (Eisenhower, Nixon, Ford) and upward under the three Democratic presidents (Truman, Kennedy, Johnson). Is this pattern due to fiscal and monetary policies that are ideologically linked with parties, or is it due to the coincidental emergence of wars under Democratic presidents?

3. The variability in the trends suggest that the analysis of life chances in the United States require temporal data. It is thus the aim of this paper to analyze inflation by income level using a longitudinal design.

The differential effects of changing real median income is an open question. Class-specific data are needed to demonstrate differential effects. In an aggregate analysis of the American economy from 1939 to 1953, for example, Bach and Ando (1957, 1958) found that the labor share increased. They concluded that ascertaining differential effects by income level, occupation, net worth, and age requires "analysis cutting across and through the broad functional income groups to individuals and small groups with clearly lagging incomes." Determining whether real incomes are affected differently by inflation thus requires data showing trends in income and consumer prices differentiated by income level. There are thus two data-collecting phases in such an analysis, both of which must be undertaken with presently inadequate official statistics. The difficulty in collecting data on differential income trends is made complex because of the necessity to consider all sources of compensation. The sources of income also vary by income level. Official data are readily available in the periodic reports of the Census's P-60 series on only direct payments in the form of wages, salaries, gratuities, retirement benefits of various types, interest payments, dividends, profits, capital gains, and public assistance. These, however, do not exhaust all sources of compensation. In addition to direct payments, such indirect payments as supplementary benefits ("fringes") and redistributional payments in the form of Medicare, welfare services, and food stamps must be added to direct payments to derive a measure of total compensation. Since indirect payments are likely to vary by economic class, the analysis of real income differentials is incomplete without taking such indirect payments into consideration in deriving total income.

This paper is restricted to an analysis of *inflation* as this term is strictly defined: changes in prices for a constant quantity of goods and services. The specific problem is to attempt determining whether price changes are patterned in such a way that income classes are affected differently because of varying lifestyles and budgets. A staff report prepared for the Joint Economic Committee (U.S. Congress, 1975, 15) indicates the generalization that is being subjected to test: "It is generally recognized that during most inflationary periods, prices rise by the same amount for all income groups." It is also indicated, however, that price increases were slightly higher for the low-income consumer than the high-income consumer in 1972–74. This paper attempts to provide estimates of price changes by income level for the entire period 1947–77.

INCOME LEVELS, BUDGETS, AND CONSUMER PRICES: METHODOLOGY

The Bureau of Labor Statistics publishes monthly and annual consumer price indexes in nine forms: a general index for all items (the CPI) and indexes for eight major groups of goods and services. The eight groups are food, housing, apparel and upkeep, transportation, medical care, personal care, reading and recreation, and other goods and services. The major task in deriving consumer prices indexes for different income levels is to establish the weights needed to adjust the special indexes to derive a composite index which reflects the cost of a "market basket" for each class. Budgets are thus needed for each income class to derive appropriate weights.

The Bureau of Labor Statistics (1973, 326–28) has published hypothetical budgets for three income levels of families in urban areas and major cities in the United States. The Autumn 1971 budget is used to derive the weights for the indexes. The *family* is defined to consist of an employed husband 38 years old, a wife not employed outside the home, an 8-year-old girl, and a 13-year-old boy. The lower, intermediate and higher levels were defined as annual budgets of $7214, $10,971, and $15,905 respectively in 1971 in current dollars. These budgets represented incomes that were respectively 70.1, 106.7, and 154.6 percent of the median family income for 1971. The lower budget is not officially intended as a poverty-line-level budget. Since the 125 percent poverty threshold for a nonfarm family of four was established in 1971 at $5171 (Bureau of the Census, 1978, 205), this budget is approximately 40 percent above the poverty threshold. The poverty threshold, however, does not include deductions for social security and other items. The figure of 40 percent is thus too high. For present purposes, it is nevertheless unfortunate that at least one substantially higher budget and a clearly poverty-level budget were not also published by BLS.

The expenditures are classified into two categories in Table 2. The first category consists of those items that overlap with the consumer price indexes for the major expenditure groupings. These are identified as "index" items, and include food, housing, transportation, medical care, and clothing and personal care. (The latter is the average of the "apparel and upkeep" and "personal care" indexes.) The remaining components of the budgets appear either to be outside the system of consumer price indexes (such as personal income taxes) or are not clearly definable. The "index" items in the budgets comprise 75.9, 72.4, and 67.9 percent of the three budgets, respectively, indicating the proportions of the budgets covered by the estimated class-specific consumer price indexes.

The food index may be used as an illustration. In the lower-budget family, food comprised 35.9 percent of the index items; in the intermediate and higher levels, 31.9 and 29.6 percent. The price indexes for food for the three class-specific indexes are thus assigned weights of .359, .319, and .296, respectively. The housing, transportation, clothing and personal care, and medical care indexes are weighted on the same basis. The class-specific index is the sum of the weighted indexes. The class-specific indexes are reported in Table 3. The class-specific indexes for 1967 (the base year for current BLS indexes) presented in Table 3 are thus equal to 100.0, but vary for the other years.

INCOME LEVELS, BUDGETS, AND CONSUMER PRICES: FINDINGS

Some indication of the relation between the class-specific price indexes may be gained from examining the distribution of the expenditures in the lower, intermediate, and higher hypothetical budgets in Table 2. The expenditure patterns are quite similar. Expenditures for food, for example, are 27.2, 23.1, and 20.1 percent of the total budgets respectively for the three income classes. The range between the lower and higher budgets is thus only 7.1 percentage points. In the case of housing, the directions are reversed; housing constitutes 21 percent of the lower budget, increasing to 25 percent for the higher budget. The range, however, is only 4 percentage points. Differences in budget expenditures for transportation and clothing and personal care are negligible. In the case of medical care, 8.4 percent of the total budget is expended for this purpose in the lower budget, declining to 4.0 percent in the higher budget. Although the higher-budget family enjoys a substantially higher living in absolute terms (except in the case of medical care), expenditure patterns are very similar. Changes in prices for each expenditure grouping may thus be expected to result in strains on all budgets to maintain lifestyles.

Table 3 reports changes in consumer price indexes and the estimated class-specific indexes from 1947 to 1977.[2] Row 12 in Table 3 indicates annual changes in the all-items CPI. Row 12 is also reported graphically in Figure 2. The peaks and secular trends in Figure 2 are of special interest. The first decade (from 1948 to approximately 1959) appears erratic, with peaks and throughs occuring within short-term intervals. The first peak occurred as the Korean War was well under way (1951), although inflation was apparently under control as the Korean War and the Truman administration were ending. A minor peak (by present standards) also occurred during the Eisenhower administration in 1957. If the peak periods (culminating in 1951 and 1957) are disregarded, the secular trend for the entire period indicates a progressively higher level of consumer prices. The consistency of the progressively inflationary price level was especially apparent under the Kennedy-Johnson administrations. The first Nixon administration was apparently on the way toward controlling inflation, but was ineffectual afterward.

Are these trends consistent by economic class? Rows 9–11 report the annual indexes by economic group. In 1947, for example, the indexes for the lower, intermediate, and higher budgets were 65.4, 65.5, and 65.8 respectively. The series thus begins with very similar values. Rows 13–15 report the annual changes in absolute points in the class-specific indexes from 1948 to 1977. In 1948, for example, the increases were 4.9, 5.0, and 5.0 points for the lower, intermediate, and higher budgets, respectively. In 1977, or the year marking the end of the series, the changes were 12.0, 11.8, and 11.7 points, respectively. Row 16 (the "bottom line") is a summary measure which indicates the differences between the changes in the lower budget index (Row 13) and the higher-budget index (Row 15). (The intermediate budget values fall within the range of values for the lower and higher budgets for all years except 1960 and 1971.) A negative value in Row 16 thus indicates that the lower budget either increased at a lower rate than the higher budget or, if both indexes are negative, decreased at a greater rate. In 16 of the 30 years of change, the lower-level budget either increased at a lower rate than the higher budget, decreased to a greater extent than the higher budget, or was equal to the change in the higher budget. With one exception (1973), however, the differences in changes in either direction did not exceed .3 point. (In 1973, the increase in the lower budget was .7 point greater than the higher budget, which was undoubtedly due to the 17.9-point increase from 123.5 to 141.4 in the food index from 1972 to 1973.) The differences between the changes in the lower and higher budgets for the 30-years sum to 1.5. These find-

Table 2. Derivation of Class-Specific CPI Item Weights: Distribution of Expenditures for Low, Intermediate, and Higher Budgets for Four-Person Family in the United States, Autumn, 1971

	Lower-Level Budget[a]					Intermediate-Level Budget[a]					Higher-Level Budget[a]				
	Annual Budget	Monthly Budget	Percent of Total	Percent of Index	CPI Wt.	Annual Budget	Monthly Budget	Percent of Total	Percent of Index	CPI Wt.	Annual Budget	Monthly Budget	Percent of Total	Percent of Index	CPI Wt.
Total Budget	$7214	$602	100.0	—	—	$10971	$914	100.0	—	—	$15905	$1326	99.9	—	—
"Index" Items															
Food	1964	164	27.2	35.9	.359	2532	211	23.1	31.9	.319	3198	267	20.1	29.6	.296
Housing[b]	1516	126	21.0	27.7	.277	2638	220	24.0	33.2	.332	3980	332	25.0	36.8	.368
Transportation[c]	536	45	7.4	9.8	.098	964	80	8.8	12.1	.121	1250	104	7.9	11.6	.116
Clothing and Personal Care[d]	848	71	11.8	15.5	.155	1196	100	10.9	15.1	.151	1740	145	10.9	16.1	.161
Medical Care[e]	609	51	8.4	11.1	.111	612	51	5.6	7.7	.077	638	53	4.0	5.9	.059
Subtotal	(5473)	(457)	(75.9)	(100.0)	1.000	(7942)	(662)	(72.4)	(100.0)	(1.000)	(10806)	(901)	(67.9)	(100.0)	(1.000)

Other Items															
Other Family															
Consumption	368	31	5.1	—	—	684	57	6.2	—	—	1129	94	7.1	—	—
Other Costs[f]	357	30	4.9	—	—	560	47	5.1	—	—	937	78	5.9	—	—
Social Security and Disability	387	32	5.4	—	—	419	35	3.8	—	—	419	35	2.6	—	—
Personal Income Taxes	629	52	8.7	—	—	1366	114	12.5	—	—	2614	218	16.4	—	—
Subtotal	(1741)	(145)	(24.1)	—	—	(3029)	(252)	(27.6)	—	—	(5099)	(425)	(32.0)	—	—

[a] Family consists of an employed husband, age 38, a wife not employed outside the home, an 8-yr.-old girl, and 13-yr.-old boy.

[b] Housing includes shelter, household operations, and house furnishings. All families with the lower budget are assumed to be renters.

[c] Average budgets for automobile owners and nonowners are weighted using the following proportions of families: Boston, Chicago, New York, and Philadelphia, 50 percent automobile owners and nonowners. All other metropolitan areas: 65 percent automobile owners, 35 percent nonowners. Nonmetropolitan areas: 100 percent automobile owners.

[d] Considered to be equivalent of two groups in Consumer Price Index: "Apparel and Upkeep" and "Personal Care." The mean of the indexes for the two groups is used in the analysis.

[e] In total medical care, average budgets for medical insurance were weighted by the following proportions: 30 percent for families paying for full cost of insurance; 26 percent for families paying half cost; 44 percent for families covered by noncontributory insurance plans (paid by employer).

[f] Allowances for gifts and contributions, life insurance, and occupational expenses.

Source: U.S. Department of Labor (1973, 326–28). Monthly budget derived from annual budget and rounded to nearest dollar.

Table 3. General and Class-Specific Consumer Price Indexes in the United States: 1947–75 (1967 = 100)

Index	1947	1948	1949	1950	1951	1952	1953	1954	1955	1956	1957	1958	1959
I. Consumer Price Indexes													
(01) CPI: All Items	66.9	72.1	71.4	72.1	77.8	79.5	80.1	80.5	80.2	81.4	84.3	86.6	87.3
(02) Food*	70.6	76.6	73.5	74.5	82.8	84.3	83.0	82.8	81.6	82.2	84.9	88.5	87.1
(03) Housing*	65.2	69.8	70.9	72.8	77.2	78.7	80.8	81.7	82.3	83.6	86.2	87.7	88.6
(04) Transportation*	55.5	61.8	66.4	68.2	72.5	77.3	79.5	78.3	77.4	78.8	83.3	86.0	89.6
(05) Apparel and personal care*	72.1	75.9	74.2	73.7	80.4	80.5	80.5	80.6	81.0	83.5	85.7	87.2	88.5
(06) Medical care*	48.1	51.1	52.7	53.7	56.3	59.3	61.4	63.4	64.8	67.2	69.9	73.2	76.4
(07) Reading and recreation	68.7	72.2	74.9	74.4	76.6	76.9	77.7	76.9	76.7	77.8	80.7	83.9	85.3
(08) Other goods and services	63.8	66.8	68.7	69.9	72.8	76.6	78.5	79.8	79.8	81.0	83.3	84.4	86.1
II. Class-specific Consumer Price Indexes													
(09) "Lower budget" CPI	65.4	70.3	69.9	71.0	76.9	78.7	79.3	79.6	79.4	80.8	83.6	86.1	86.8
(10) "Intermediate budget" CPI	65.5	70.5	70.3	71.4	77.3	79.1	79.8	80.1	79.9	81.3	84.1	86.6	87.3
(11) "Higher budget" CPI	65.8	70.8	70.6	71.8	77.6	79.3	80.1	80.4	80.3	81.6	84.5	86.8	87.5
III. Annual Change: CPI and Class-specific Indexes													
(12) All items (CPI)	—	5.2	-0.7	0.7	5.7	1.7	0.6	0.4	-0.3	1.2	2.9	2.3	0.7
(13) "Lower budget" CPI	—	4.9	-0.4	1.1	5.9	1.8	0.6	0.3	-0.2	1.4	2.8	2.5	0.7
(14) "Intermediate budget" CPI	—	5.0	-0.2	1.1	5.9	1.8	0.7	0.3	-0.2	1.4	2.8	2.5	0.7
(15) "Higher budget" CPI	—	5.0	-0.2	1.2	6.0	1.7	0.8	0.3	-0.1	1.3	2.9	2.3	0.7
(16) Difference (lower minus higher-budget CPIs)	—	-0.1	-0.2	-0.1	-0.1	0.1	-0.2	0.0	-0.1	0.1	-0.1	0.2	0.0

	1960	1961	1962	1963	1964	1965	1966	1967	1968	1969	1970	1971	1972	1973	1974	1975	1976	1977	Sum
(01)	88.7	89.6	90.6	91.7	92.9	94.5	97.2	100.0	104.2	109.8	116.3	121.3	125.3	133.1	147.7	161.2	170.5	181.5	—
(02)	88.0	89.1	89.9	91.2	92.4	94.4	99.1	100.0	103.6	108.9	114.9	118.4	123.5	141.4	161.7	175.4	180.8	192.2	—
(03)	90.2	90.9	91.7	92.7	93.8	94.9	97.2	100.0	104.2	110.8	118.9	124.3	129.2	135.0	150.6	166.8	177.2	189.6	—
(04)	89.6	90.6	92.5	93.0	94.3	95.9	97.2	100.0	103.2	107.2	112.7	118.6	119.9	123.8	137.7	150.6	165.5	177.2	—
(05)	89.9	90.5	91.6	92.7	93.6	94.5	96.6	100.0	104.8	110.4	114.7	118.3	121.1	121.1	136.8	146.5	154.1	162.6	—
(06)	79.1	81.4	83.5	85.6	87.3	89.5	93.4	100.0	106.1	113.4	120.6	128.4	132.5	137.7	150.5	168.6	184.7	202.4	—
(07)	87.3	89.3	91.3	92.8	95.0	95.9	97.5	100.0	104.7	108.7	113.4	119.3	122.8	125.9	133.8	144.4	151.2	157.9	—
(08)	87.8	88.5	89.1	90.6	92.0	94.2	97.2	100.0	104.6	109.1	116.0	120.9	125.5	129.0	137.2	147.4	153.3	159.2	—
(09)	88.1	89.1	90.2	91.4	92.6	94.2	97.4	100.0	104.2	110.0	116.4	121.2	125.4	134.4	151.2	165.4	174.6	186.6	—
(10)	88.5	89.5	90.6	91.7	92.9	94.4	97.4	100.0	104.1	109.9	116.4	121.1	125.3	133.8	150.6	164.7	174.0	185.8	—
(11)	88.8	89.7	80.8	91.9	93.0	94.5	97.4	100.0	104.1	109.9	116.4	121.2	125.3	133.6	150.2	164.3	173.6	185.3	—
(12)	1.4	0.9	1.0	1.1	1.2	1.6	2.7	2.8	4.2	5.6	6.5	5.0	4.0	7.8	14.6	13.5	9.3	11.0	—
(13)	1.3	1.0	1.1	1.2	1.2	1.6	3.2	2.6	4.2	5.8	6.4	4.8	4.2	9.0	16.8	14.2	9.2	12.0	—
(14)	1.2	1.0	1.1	1.1	1.2	1.5	3.0	2.6	4.1	5.8	6.5	4.7	4.2	8.5	16.8	14.1	9.3	11.8	—
(15)	1.3	0.9	1.1	1.1	1.1	1.5	2.9	2.6	4.1	5.8	6.5	4.8	4.1	8.3	16.6	14.1	9.3	11.7	—
(16)	0.0	0.1	0.0	0.1	0.1	0.1	0.3	0.0	0.1	0.0	-0.1	0.0	0.1	0.7	0.2	0.1	-0.1	0.3	1.5

*Components of the class-specific indexes: "Apparel and personal care" is an average of the "Apparel and Upkeep" and "Personal care" indexes.

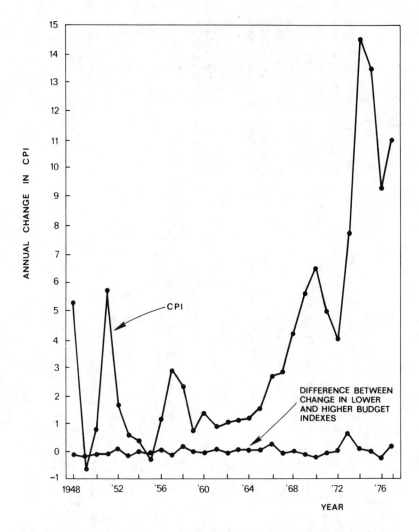

Fig.2   Annual Change in the Consumer Price Index, 1948-1977

ings do not indicate that the lower-budget index changed in a pattern markedly different from the higher-budget index.

If there is a political dimension to these patterns, it would appear that lower-budget families fared most favorably in the Truman, Eisenhower, and first Nixon administrations and least favorably under the Kennedy-Johnson and second Nixon administrations. It is appropriate to compare those results with one of the few research studies directed at this specific problem. In the Joint Economic Committee study (U.S. Congress, 1975, 15), it is reported "During the past three years, . . . prices have increased unevenly with a resulting differential impact on income groups." Their evidence indicates (1975, 15) that the differences between a "Poor Person's Index" and a "Rich Person's Index" from October for 1971–72, 1972–73, and 1974–75 were .5, 2.3, and .5 points, respectively. The year 1973 thus appears to have been a year in which, if a trend were established, a clear differential inflationary pattern could emerge.

The similarity in changes in the class-specific indexes of Table 3 is explained by the similarity in the budgets (as reported in Table 2) and the high intercorrelations between the CPI (all items) and the indexes for class-specific budgets. The correlation (Pearson's r) for 1947–74 between the CPI and each of the three budget indexes is .9998. Changes in the CPI will thus be reflected in the special indexes. Although the conclusion is reached that the effects of inflation have not been differentiated by income groups in the United States from 1947 to 1977, the possibility that differences in prices by class could occur in the future requires that annual movements in prices by income class receive close scrutiny.

CONCLUSION

American society has experienced a progressive inflation in consumer prices since the end of World War II. The purpose of this paper has been an attempt to determine whether the effects of this inflation are differentiated by income level. Class-specific consumer price indexes have been estimated from published BLS price indexes for the major groups of consumer goods and services. The Bureau of Labor Statistics has published budgets on three levels — $7214, $10,971, and $15,905 as of Autumn 1971 — indicating allocations for major classes of consumer goods and services. Three class-specific indexes were estimated through weights for the special consumer price indexes for major expenditure groupings based on the class-specific budgets. Comparisons of the annual changes in the class-specific indexes from 1947 to 1977 indicate that the differences among the indexes are negligible. The conclusion is consequently reached that price changes, as such, have not affected economic classes differently; however, this conclusion must be considered tentative and limited to the restrictions of the study.

Limitations of four types result from difficulties in obtaining class-specific data. The most serious is that a real income index, based on the relation between total income and consumer prices, cannot be developed without information on all sources of income by economic class, as well as budget-specific consumer prices. In addition to direct payments to individuals of all types, any estimate of total income by class must take into account numerous redistributional services likely to vary by income level that are increasingly becoming institutionalized into the American system of distribution. The second limitation is that only a restricted range of income levels has been considered. Upper-income and clearly poverty-level budgets are not analyzed. Other bases for differentiating needs should also be considered. Determining whether life-cycle budgets are differently affected by inflation is another direction in which inflation research should proceed. Thurow (1969), for example, presents convincing evidence that the stage in the life cycle is an especially pertinent basis for differentiating needs. Young families, for example, experience special strains because consumption needs are greater at this age, but income tends to be greater at a later stage in the career cycle. The postretirement stage of the life cycle also needs study. Variation in race and marital status (our data pertain only to families) is an additional direction of investigation. Third, the class-specific consumer indexes have been derived from weights applied to consumer price indexes for the major expenditure groupings (food, housing, etc.). The assumption is thus made that the specific items comprising the expenditure groupings are similar across income classes. It is possible that they are not, and weighting procedures used in this paper to derive the class-specific indexes may not be appropriate. Finally, since lifestyles change, it needs to be determined empirically whether changes in lifestyle are sufficient to affect the weightings used to adjust the special price indexes through time.

Notes

* We should like to acknowledge the bibliographic suggestions of Curtis Harvey and Charles Hultman, both economists, in preparing this paper. Roseanne Hogan assisted in may of the details of research.

1. The use of Weber's concept of "life chances" is to be preferred to the term *economic welfare* because of the difficulty in converting the latter into operational terms. *Life chances* pertains to the objectively defined rewards that may be obtained by persons or groups from the ability to command income (Weber, 1946, 181).

2. A clerical error was made in the April 1974 transportation index, with the result that the published monthly indexes for all items (the CPI) and transportation must be revised downward for April–September 1974. The CPI and transportation index in Table 3 are based on revised data. The sampling procedures for the CPI were revised and the present series are to end in June 1978 (Bureau of Labor Statistics, 1978, 8).

References

Bach, G. *The New Inflation* (Providence, R.I., 1972).

Bach, G., and Ando, G. "The Redistributional Effects of Inflation," *Review of Economics and Statistics* 39 (1957): 1–13.

Cargill, T. "An Empirical Investigation of the Wage-lag Hypothesis," *American Economic Review* 59 (1969): 806–16.

Levitan, S., and Taggart, R. "Has the Blue-collar Worker's Position Worsened?" *Monthly Labor Review* 94 (1971): 23–29.

Thurow, L. "The Optimum Lifetime Distribution of Consumption Expenditures," *American Economic Review* 59 (1969): 324–30.

U.S. Bureau of the Census. *Current Population Reports*, Series P-60, No. 115, 1978.

U.S. Bureau of the Census. *Current Population Reports*, Series P-60, No. 118, 1979.

U.S. Bureau of Labor Statistics. *Consumer Price Index: Detailed Report* (December, 1978).

U.S. Bureau of Labor Statistics. *Handbook of Labor Statistics: 1973* (Washington, D.C., 1973).

U.S. Bureau of Labor Statistics. *Handbook of Labor Statistics: 1978* (Washington, D.C., 1979).

U.S. Congress Joint Economic Committee. "Inflation and the Consumer in 1974." Studies in Price Stability and Economic Growth, Paper No. 1 (Washington, D.C., 1975).

Weber, Max. *Max Weber: Essays in Sociology* (trans. Hans Gerth and C. Wright Mills (New York, 1946).

Inflation and Female Labor Force Participation

BETH T. NIEMI
CYNTHIA B. LLOYD

The rapid rise in women's labor force participation is a familiar phenomenon by now. Although there has been considerable discussion of the implications and social significance of this ongoing trend, there still appears to be disagreement as to whether it represents a fundamental shift in women's attitudes and commitment to market work, or merely a short-run response to a convergent set of economic inducements to women's labor force participation. The most important of these factors are the growth in women's market opportunities, on the one hand, and the erosion by inflation of the real value of actual and expected family income, on the other. Now that slightly more than 50 percent of all women aged 16 and over are in the labor force in any given week, it is important to ask what this level of participation means for the future. Influential economists like Easterlin believe that women's current participation in the labor force is fundamentally temporary and secondary, and therefore, easily reversible if certain expected economic changes, such as a relative growth in real earnings of younger male cohorts, should occur. In fact, he expects a new baby boom — which would be unlikely to develop in the absence of some retreat on the part of women from current levels of participation — to emerge in the late 1980s. Such predictions coexist with a considerable and growing body of evidence that the characterization of women workers as "secondary" is becoming less and less accurate, and that female labor force attachment, however measured, has grown along with participation.

Our objective in this paper is to reassess the determinants of women's labor supply response in the light of recent declines in real wage growth and accelerating rates of inflation. The first section documents the multidimensional nature of women's growing commitment to the labor force. In the second part, we examine the determinants of changing female labor supply, in terms of both long-run trends and shifts in responsiveness. Our findings seem to suggest that, at least in the short run, inflation has had a positive and independent effect on women's labor supply. At the same time, however, the responsiveness of women's labor supply to labor market conditions (especially the real wage) appears to have diminished as women have become more committed labor force participants. The net result appears to be that, even though the recent stagnation in the real wage has not been the major source of discouragement for women that it once would have been, inflation is having an independent positive effect on female labor force participation.

TRENDS AND PATTERNS IN FEMALE LABOR SUPPLY

Not only has the aggregate female labor force participation rate risen by over 12 percentage points, from 37.8 percent to 50.1 percent, between 1960 and 1978, but this growth has been most dramatic among those subgroups who have traditionally had the lowest rates of participation. For example, the labor force participation rate of married women with children under 6 was 39.3 percent in 1977, as compared to 18.6 percent in 1960, an increase of 111 percent. The labor force participation rate of married women with children aged 6–17 increased 43 percent and that of those with no children under 18 increased only 23 percent over the same period.[1] As we have pointed out elsewhere (Lloyd and Niemi, 1979), the juxtaposition of radical change in the level of female labor force participation with virtually no change (or very little) in the earnings, unemployment rates, and occupational distribution of women relative to men is paradoxical. A possible explanation is that the dramatic participation changes we have observed significantly overstate growth in the average market labor supply of women because either (1) the percentage of women working parttime has increased and average hours of work per woman have decreased and/or (2) interlabor force turnover has increased, so that more women are working fewer weeks and/or shorter and less continuous periods. In the extreme, either of these hypotheses could imply that a group's labor supply remained unchanged despite an increase in its labor force participation rate, because of a reduction in average hours per week or per year. Under less extreme assumptions, the effect of increased labor force participation on total labor supply would be weakened by these other changes, but not completely eliminated. Thus the two dimensions of average weekly hours and the continuity of labor force attachment of women must be analyzed before we can speak with complete confidence about trends in female labor supply.

Parttime work is becoming more prevalent among both men and women, but the rate of increase in recent years does not appear to have been more rapid for women than for men, and there is no evidence whatever that the vanishing dip in participation rates at age 25–34, the low point on the traditional two-peaked age-participation profile, is being replaced by a dip in hours of work (Lloyd and Niemi, pp. 55–59).

Differences in timing, for individuals who spend less than 100 percent of their available time in the labor force, can take place not only in hours worked per week, but also in weeks worked per year. Variations in these two dimensions of labor supply are not perfect substitutes for one another. Part-year work allows nonmarket time to be concentrated during certain portions of the year, whereas year-round parttime work allows nonmarket time to be spread evenly throughout the year. Because of child-rearing responsibilities and school vacation schedules, women may be more likely than men to use weeks as a variable in their labor supply decisions. Although it is true that, on the average, women work 4 or 5 fewer weeks per year than men, there is no sign that women's increased labor force participation has been accompanied by a reduction in their average weeks per year. On the contrary, the available evidence (Lloyd and Niemi, table 2.5, p. 60) suggests that, if anything, these have increased. Given the evidence concerning trends in hours per week and weeks per year among women workers, we conclude that the dramatic increases in female labor force participation have not been offset by declines in these other dimensions of labor supply.

The relationship between levels of participation and continuity of attachment among women must now be analyzed. Differences between groups in average weeks per year cannot be interpreted as a complete measure of differences in continuity, although they may well be part of the story. Some jobs, such as teaching, are part-year in their very nature; even if, for example, all teachers worked without interruption from year to year, they would be counted correctly as working less than the maximum number of weeks per year.

The relationship between labor force participation and interlabor force turnover is not a simple one and could conceivably take a variety of forms. Although interlabor force turnover is necessarily low among groups with very high participation rates (i.e., if 90 or 95 percent of a group is always in the labor force, there is simply very little leeway for movement in and out), such turnover may be either high or low among groups (such as women) with participation rates significantly below 100 percent. A group with a labor force participation rate of 50 percent, for example, would be characterized by no interlabor force turnover and continuous labor force attachment on the part of participants in the case of complete heterogeneity and specialization, where the same 50 percent of the group is always in the labor force and the other half of the group never enters the labor force. On the other hand, there would be considerable turnover and discontinuity if such a group were completely homogeneous, so that each member's behavior conformed to the average of spending exactly half of his or her working life in the labor force.

Within the intermediate range (approximately 30 to 50 percent) over which female labor participation rates have been rising during the past 30 years, one can easily visualize higher levels of participation being linked to either increasing or decreasing labor force turnover. The question whether today we have more women working, but for shorter and less continuous periods, or more women entering the labor force and then remaining there longer, is crucial and must be answered if we are to understand dynamic changes in female labor supply.

Evidence concerning actual labor force turnover on an annual basis gives no indication that female labor force turnover has been rising. Interlabor force turnover among women, as measured by the ratio of the labor force experience rate (the percentage of total women working some time during the year) to the annual average labor force participation rate, has decreased as labor force participation has risen over the past 20 years, both in the aggregate and within each age group, and particularly in the prime ages, 35–64 (Niemi, 1977, p. 26). This implies that not only are more women in the labor force, but the average woman worker is more permanently attached.

Recently, there has been an increasing availability of the longitudinal data, most appropriate for analysis relating to continuity and patterns of life-cycle behavior, and this information is being utilized in ways that creatively address these questions. Studies using both the (NLS) National Longitudinal Surveys and the (MID) University of Michigan Panel Study of Income Dynamics clearly confirm that past experience is, in fact, strongly related to current labor force status for women, which appears inconsistent with the hypothesis of a homogeneous female population characterized by high rates of movement in and out of the labor force. The two major explanations for the relationship between previous and current work status are heterogeneity and the investment effect of previous work experience. These are by no means mutually exclusive, and in fact there is considerable evidence that both effects exist (Heckman, 1979; Heckman and Willis, 1977). The assumption of heterogeneity means that unobserved differences among women in tastes and productivities result in different propensities to participate in the labor force. Past experience and present status will be positively correlated; thus a woman's work history will be helpful in predicting the probability that she will be in the labor force. Because of heterogeneity, the labor force participation rate cannot be used as an unbiased estimate of the fraction of her life an individual woman will spend in the labor force.

In addition to this innate heterogeneity, additional heterogeneity is created by differing labor market experience and the fixed costs of labor force entry and exit (Mincer and Ofek, 1979). Very simply, work experience provides women with training that raises their wage rates and thus makes future participation more likely and labor market exit more costly.

Certainly the dynamic human capital model implies that increased labor force participation will eventually (although perhaps with a time lag) result in an increase in accumulated labor market experience. Thus the current alltime high in the participation rate of 20–24-year-old women has long-run implications for higher and more continuous future female labor force participation. All the available evidence appears to imply that recent increases in female labor participation, particularly among women with young children, are the result of a trend toward long-term career commitment rather than an increase in marginal workers with high turnover rates as has sometimes been suggested (cf. for example, the 1973 *Economic Report of the President*, chap. IV, p. 100).

THE DETERMINANTS OF CHANGING FEMALE LABOR SUPPLY

We have documented the important ways in which women's labor supply has increased over the past 20 years. This ongoing change raises further questions about its causes and consequences. What have been the major factors attracting women into the labor market? Has the responsiveness of female labor supply itself been modified in important ways as a consequence of these trends? To answer these questions, we have analyzed annual and quarterly data covering the period 1956–77 on female labor force participation and its important determinants. Of particular interest to us were the effects of the trend in real wages, employment opportunities, and inflation on women's labor force participation, and any changes that have taken place in women's actual responsiveness to these variables.

Although it is well documented in studies based on cross-sectional data that women's labor supply elasticity with respect to their own wages is positive and significant, this has not been extensively tested using time-series data. In fact, only two studies (Fair, 1971; Wachter, 1972) have analyzed the effect of real wages and inflation on labor force participation, using time-series data, and neither study includes the decade of the 1970s. Both these studies confirm the strong positive effect of the real wage and, in addition, show that for most demographic groups (particularly women) inflation has a short-run positive effect on labor supply which can be explained by some form of money illusion.[2] The questions addressed by Fair and by Wachter are of renewed interest in the 1970s because women's labor force participation rates have increased substantially in recent years, despite a significant slowing of the growth in real wages and dramatic acceleration of the rate of inflation.[3] In fact, between 1973 and 1975, real wages fell in two successive years, yet women's labor force participation continued to grow. This suggests the possibility that other factors, affecting either employment opportunities or perceived income needs, may also be important determinants of labor supply.

Although the difficulties involved in time-series analysis are myriad and well known, it is still essential that such analysis be undertaken. Cross-sectional and longitudinal data do provide a wealth of information on personal, family, and economic characteristics which are not similarly available on the aggregate level, and the coefficients derived from cross-sectional studies can yield important insights into the determinants of changes that are taking place over time. But, the application of these coefficients to an explanation of secular change must be seen as complementary to, rather than a substitute for, confrontation of the actual time-series data. Despite autocorrelation problems and the lack of detail implicit in aggregation, the marginal contribution to our knowledge made by direct time-series analysis is both positive and essential.

Our research strategy involves estimating labor supply elasticities with respect to the variables previously mentioned, from both annual and quarterly data. Then, these same elasticities were reestimated for the earlier (1956–66) and later (1967–77) periods separately, so as to test for any behavioral shifts over time. The quarterly data have the advantage of providing more observations and allowing us to enter some of the key independent variables with three-month lags. The annual data, on the other hand, permit the use of age- and sex-specific measures of earnings.

In all the equations estimated, the civilian labor force participation rate is the dependent variable. Therefore, strictly speaking, the elasticity estimates relate, not to total labor supply, but only to labor force participation. Our previous discussion, however, suggests a strong correlation over the past twenty years between trends in labor force participation rates for women and trends in their full labor supply. For this reason, and also to avoid unduly cumbersome language, we refer to our estimated coefficients as *labor supply elasticities*.

LONG-RUN TREND, 1956–77

Regressions were run for all women (16+) and for three broad age groups (16–24, 25–54, and 55+). All equations were run in log linear form, and since autocorrelation was clearly a problem, the Cochrane-Orcutt iterative technique was used. The first equation relates the civilian labor force participation rate for the group in question (LFP) to the unemployment rate (UN), a measure of the real wage (RWAGE or RINC), and a measure of structural shifts in the sex composition of the demand for labor (EMPW).

$$\ln \text{LFP} = a + b_1\text{UN} + b_2 \ln \text{RWAGE} + b_3 \ln \text{EMPW} \tag{1}$$

The second equation replaces the real wage by its two component variables: the money wage (WAGE or INC) and the consumer price index (CPI).[4]

$$\ln \text{LFP} + a' + b'_1\text{UN} + b'_2\ln\text{WAGE} + b'_3\ln\text{EMPW} +$$
$$b'_4\ln\text{CPI} \tag{2}$$

In the equations using quarterly data, the unemployment, wage, and price variables were entered with a three-month lag, and three dummy variables were added to take care of seasonal adjustment.

The unemployment rate used was that of men aged 35–44, which provides the "cleanest" index of cyclical fluctuations in the overall level of the demand for labor. Since $\text{UN} \cong -\ln(1 - \text{UN})$, the coefficient on UN can be interpreted as minus the labor supply elasticity with respect to the *employment* rate. The predicted employment ratio (EMPW) for women in each period was estimated by weighting the total employment for each industry in that period by the average proportion of females in that industry over the entire period, and aggregating this over all 11 industries.[5] Both the overall level of demand and its distribution across industries should affect women participation decisions. The other important dimension of market opportunities is the wage. Ideally, we would like to have a measure of the average hourly wage specific to the sex and age group being considered. However, the only measure that is available on a quarterly basis for the entire 22-year period is "average hourly earnings excluding overtime of production workers on manufacturing payrolls" (WAGE), which is not available by sex. On an annual basis, we do have data on the income of yearround, fulltime workers in each age and sex group (INC), so that we can use each group's fulltime income as an alternative wage measure in these equations.[6]

An examination of the results for Equation 1, presented in Table 1, reveals systematic differences between the yearly and quarterly data sets. In the annual data, both demand variables (UN and EMPW) are consistently significant, and show an encouragement effect for young and prime-age women. Older women, on the other hand, appear to behave as added workers, moving into, or staying in, the labor force when unemployment is high and/or when employment opportunities in traditionally female industries are relatively low.[7] The income variable is also significant and positive for prime-age women. Although the age-specific income measure should be superior to the wage variable, and this appears to be the case among the 25–54 age group, its inclusion does not drastically change the other results, and we thus view our wage and income variables as reasonably close substitutes for one another in practice.

Table 1. Equation 1, 1956–77, Annual and Quarterly Data

Annual Data	UN	RWAGE	RINC	EMPW	R²	Durbin-Watson Statistic
Total, 16 +	−1.59† (−2.51)	.109 (.459)		3.33* (4.75)	0.979	1.68
	−1.065‡ (−1.79)		.269 (1.61)	2.55* (3.43)	0.982	1.57
16–24	−2.74† (2.6)	.008 (.019)		5.105* (4.35)	0.968	1.65
	−3.068* (−3.84)		−.137 (−.635)	5.42* (6.8)	0.969	1.74
25–54	−1.955† (−2.77)	.101 (.382)		4.08* (5.03)	0.981	1.60
	−1.247‡ (−1.88)		.344‡ (1.98)	2.93* (3.25)	0.984	1.21
55 +	1.626‡ (1.87)	.137 (.473)		−2.46† (−1.92)	0.835	1.29
	1.699‡ (2.07)		.142 (.905)	−2.64‡ (−2.09)	0.840	1.31
Quarterly Data						
Total, 16 +	.481‡ (1.8)	.309‡ (1.72)		.575 (1.63)	0.985	2.26
16–24	.726 (1.62)	.618† (2.05)		−.047 (−.08)	0.979	2.29
25–54	.508‡ (1.73)	.276 (1.4)		.701‡ (1.8)	0.987	2.07
55 +	−1.185 (−0.88)	.086 (0.15)		.006 (0.0)	0.330	2.20

Note: The dependent variable in each equation is ln LFP for women in the age group in question. The numbers in parentheses are the *t*-values.
*Significant at 1 percent confidence level.
†Significant at 5 percent confidence level.
‡Significant at 10 percent confidence level.

A comparison of these results with those based on the quarterly data shows that the demand variables tend to be less significant and the wage variable tends to be more significant, a puzzling result, given the cyclical fluctuations in demand and the strong upward trend in real wages. In addition, the coefficient on the unemployment rate is positive, indicating a net added worker effect for women in general and prime-age women in particular, which is the opposite of the expected net discouragement effect. The real wage variable is consistently positive as expected and often significant, and the demand for female workers (EMPW) is positively related to labor force participation for prime age women.

In Equation 2, the money wage and the consumer index are included separately (Table 2). In the annual data set, this change causes a systematic reduction in the significance of the demand variables. For all women and for older women, the money income measure now has a significant coefficient, whereas when the same variable was adjusted for inflation and entered directly as an estimate of the real wage, it did not. The most interesting result, however, is the positive and significant coefficient on the consumer price index for young and prime-age women, which suggest that inflation has an important independent effect on their labor supply behavior, over and above its effect on the real wage. In fact, in the case of prime-age women, the money wage, the real wage, and the consumer price index all affect labor supply positively, though only the last has a significant positive coefficient. On the other hand, for older women, inflation seems to have an independent negative effect on labor supply.

If money wages and the price level each affect labor supply only via their effect on the real wage, then Equations 1 and 2 would be equivalent specifications of the labor supply function, and $b'_4 = -b'_2$ (that is, $b'_2 + b'_4 = 0$) in Equation 2. If this is not the case, workers are said to suffer from either "money illusion" or "price illusion," overreacting to changes in money wages or the price level, respectively, without taking the other determinant of real wages sufficiently into account. The hypothesis that $b'_2 + b'_4 = 0$ was consistently rejected. The t-values for $(b'_2 + b'_4)$, shown in the last column of Table 2, tend to be highly significant.[8] The money wage and the consumer price index do not appear to have equal and opposite effects on labor supply behavior, which strongly suggest that money or price illusion is a determinant of the trend in female labor force participation. Inflation does seem to have been an independent factor luring young and prime-age women, in particular, into the labor market. This result is consistent with the short-run money illusion found in the studies of both Fair and Wachter.

Money illusion appears evident in the quarterly results for all groups

Table 2. Equation 2, 1956–77, Annual and Quarterly Data

	UN	WAGE	INC	CPI	EMPW	R²	D–W	t(b'₂ + b'₄)
Annual Data								
Total, 16+	.675 (−1.5)	.150 (.964)		.102 (.644)	.623 (.914)	0.992	1.81	5.25*
	−.399 (−1.26)		.279* (3.63)	−.036 (−.421)	−.062 (−.166)	0.995	1.79	9.35*
16–24	−1.21 (−1.39)	.066 (.22)		.328 (1.07)	.794 (.605)	0.984	1.66	4.28*
	−1.37‡ (−1.97)		−.002 (−.014)	.394† (2.33)	1.01 (.883)	0.984	1.66	4.18*
25–54	−.136 (−.407)	.041 (.415)		.323* (3.2)	−.455 (−.805)	0.997	2.29	9.73*
	−.162 (−.579)		.174† (2.48)	.180‡ (2.08)	−.283 (−.59)	0.997	1.89	9.83*
55+	1.285 (1.38)	.071 (.263)		−.272 (−.991)	−1.42 (−.906)	0.863	1.51	−1.92‡
	−.549 (−.715)		.352† (2.27)	−.703* (−4.16)	−1.54 (−1.51)	0.847	1.84	−5.12*
Quarterly Data								
Total, 16+	.266 (.97)	.404* (2.79)		−.209 (−1.17)	.422 (1.19)	0.986	2.19	3.7*
16–24	.551 (1.22)	.683* (2.66)		−.357 (−1.12)	−.338 (−.57)	0.981	2.26	3.43*
25–54	−.447‡ (−1.65)	.348* (3.02)		−.035 (−.29)	.218 (.61)	0.989	1.85	12.2*
55+	−.209‡ (−1.78)	−.166 (−.33)		−.24 (−.48)	3.82† (2.41)	0.439	2.04	−4.6*

Note: The dependent variable in each equation is 1n LFP for women in the age group in question. The numbers in parentheses are the *t*-values.
* Significant at 1 percent confidence level.
† Significant at 5 percent confidence level.
‡ Significant at 10 percent confidence level.

except the oldest and in the annual results for the aggregate group. Evidence of some price illusion among older women is present in both the annual and quarterly results. On the other hand, the annual results for the young and prime-age women show a significant *positive* effect of inflation, indicating more primary workers behavior in the context of some price illusion. Overall, female labor force participation is increasing, in response to rising money wages and/or prices, more rapidly than would be predicted simply on the basis of changes in real wages.

CHANGES IN RESPONSIVENESS

The 1970s have been characterized by strong growth in female labor force participation on the one hand and by atypically high levels of both inflation and unemployment on the other. We have estimated the average responsiveness of female labor supply to various dimensions of labor market opportunities, on the implicit assumption that the underlying labor supply function was unchanged over the 22-year period. This may not, however, be the correct assumption; patterns of response may themselves have changed during this period, and the entire labor supply function may have shifted. In this section, we address the question whether the labor supply elasticities differ significantly between two 11-year subperiods (1956–66 and 1967–77). Equations 1 and 2 were estimated for each subperiod separately, and these results are presented in Tables 3 and 4.

A preliminary test for significant shifts in responsiveness to the real wage, the money wage, or inflation between the two periods also involves the estimation of two additional equations covering the entire 22-year period. These equations include among the independent variables a dummy variable for the later subperiod (D = 0 for 1956–66, D = 1 for 1967–77), and interaction terms between this dummy variable and each of the other independent variables.

$$\ln \text{LFP} = \alpha + \beta_1 D + \beta_2 \text{UN} + \beta_3 (D \times \text{UN}) + \beta_4 \ln \text{RWAGE} + \beta_5$$
$$(D \times \ln \text{RWAGE}) + \beta_6 \ln \text{EMPW} + \beta_7 (D \times \ln \text{EMPW}) \qquad (3)$$

$$\ln \text{LFP} = \alpha' + \beta'_1 D + \beta'_2 \text{UN} + \beta'_3 (D \times \text{UN}) + \beta'_4 \ln \text{WAGE} +$$
$$\beta'_5 (D \times \ln \text{WAGE}) + \beta'_6 \ln \text{EMPW} + \beta'_7 (D \times \ln \text{EMPW}) +$$
$$\beta'_8 \ln \text{CPI} + \beta'_9 (D \times \ln \text{CPI}) \qquad (4)$$

Equations 3 and 4 represent this specification including the real wage and the money wage and consumer price index separately, respectively. Significant changes in the elasticities with respect to real wages, money wages, and the price level can be discerned if β_5 (shown in the last column of Table 3), β'_5 and β'_9 (t-values shown in the last two columns of Table 4) are significantly different from zero.[9]

It is interesting that women in general, and young and prime-age women in particular, appear to be behaving more like primary workers

Table 3. Equation 1, 1956–66 and 1967–77

	UN	RWAGE	RINC	EMPW	R²	D–W	DxRWAGE
Annual data							
Total, 16+							
1956–66	1.764‡	−.069		1.54	0.863	1.76	
	(−2.18)	(−.183)		(1.18)			
1967–77	−5.57*	−1.3*		7.15*	0.967	2.29	−0.90
	(−4.14)	(−3.49)		(6.29)			(−1.69)
1956–66	.248		.582‡	−.309	0.924	1.18	
	(.274)		(2.21)	(−.407)			
1967–77	−2.22‡		−.163	4.13*	0.938	1.70	−0.85‡
	(−2.03)		(−.536)	(4.25)			(−2.05)
16–24							
1956–66	−3.54†	−.813		2.90	0.586	1.94	
	(−2.63)	(−1.24)		(1.28)			
1967–77	−6.74†	−1.27		8.89†	0.936	2.13	0.0
	(−2.61)	(−1.63)		(3.39)			(0.0)
1956–66	−3.29‡		−.309	.942	0.539	2.02	
	(−1.95)		(−.814)	(.914)			
1967–77	−3.06†		−.406	5.30*	0.947	2.17	−0.086
	(−2.39)		(−1.85)	(6.68)			(−0.21)
25–54							
1956–66	−1.49‡	0.86		1.58	0.943	1.79	
	(−2.3)	(.303)		(1.62)			
1967–77	−8.13*	−2.05*		10.3*	0.973	2.23	−1.68*
	(−5.56)	(−5.13)		(8.4)			(−3.11)
1956–66	.691		.687*	−.145	0.983	1.74	
	(1.66)		(5.78)	(.411)			
1967–77	−2.59		.073	5.05*	0.944	1.45	−0.725
	(−1.81)		(.179)	(3.51)			(−1.54)

55+

1956–66	−.759 (−.854)	.211 (.579)		1.39 (1.13)	0.895	1.68	
1967–77	4.66* (3.41)	.799 (1.58)		−5.71* (−4.23)	0.926	1.30	0.81 (1.42)
1956–66	−.724 (−.742)		.142 (.598)	1.46 (1.46)	0.895	1.86	
1967–77	2.74† (2.63)		.466† (2.67)	−2.9 (−1.7)	0.940	0.925	0.43 (1.47)

Quarterly data

Total, 16 +

1956–66	.268 (.797)	.730† (2.56)		1.09† (3.09)	0.934	1.89	
1967–77	−.268 (−.94)	−.032 (−.23)		.525 (1.29)	0.984	2.42	−0.18 (−0.63)

16–24

1956–66	.618 (.934)	.971‡ (1.79)		.842 (1.22)	0.929	1.97	
1967–77	−.168 (−.401)	.269 (1.37)		−.365 (−.61)	0.988	2.04	0.28 (0.54)

25–54

1956–66	.229 (.566)	.533† (2.35)		1.01† (2.38)	0.937	2.07	
1967–77	−.412 (−1.37)	−.109 (−.77)		.834‡ (1.95)	0.991	2.17	−0.03 (−0.09)

55 +

1956–66	−.917 (−1.63)	.308 (1.19)		1.09 (1.6)	0.867	1.67	
1967–77	.335 (.13)	−1.52 (−1.63)		−.038 (−.01)	0.406	2.05 (1.5)	−1.57 (−1.5)

Note: The coefficients of (DxRWAGE) are estimated from Equation 3. The dependent variable in each equation is 1n LFP for women in the age group in question. The numbers in parentheses are the *t*-values.

*Significant at 1 percent confidence level.
†Significant at 5 percent confidence level.
‡Significant at 10 percent confidence level.

Table 4. Equation 2, 1956–66 and 1956–66 and 1967–77

	UN	WAGE	INC	CPI	EMPW	R²	D–W	t (b'₂ + b'₄)	t (DwWAGE)	t (DxCPI)
Annual data										
Total, 16 +										
1956–66	.271	−.096		1.09*	−.668	0.985	2.10	6.44*		
	(.708)	(−.781)		(5.16)	(−1.26)					
1967–77	−.204	.132		.154	−.473	0.994	1.87	6.39*	1.2	−3.77*
	(−.304)	(.647)		(.821)	(−.494)					
1956–66	4.82		.026	.932‡	−.883	0.983	2.03	4.42*		
	(1.03)		(.125)	(2.39)	(−1.81)					
1967–77	−.225		.237†	.073	−.594	0.997	2.19	10.7*	−2.3†	0.0
	(−.874)		(3.28)	(1.10)	(−1.36)					
16–24										
1956–66	.332	−.546		2.19*	−1.29	0.879	1.52	3.85†		
	(.329)	(−1.68)		(3.78)	(−.91)					
1967–77	.151	.155		.244	−2.23	0.989	2.57	4.53*	0.0	0.0
	(.152)	(.506)		(.877)	(−1.49)					
1956–66	−.333		−.491‡	2.12*	−1.23	0.900	2.25	4.24*		
	(−.344)		(1.99)	(4.29)	(−1.08)					
1967–77	−.077		.074	.303†	−2.11	0.989	2.39	3.97†	2.12‡	−3.77*
	(−.107)		(.542)	(2.46)	(−1.7)					
25–54										
1956–66	−.732*	−.096		.757*	.422	0.997	2.63	9.62*		
	(−4.17)	(−1.22)		(6.48)	(1.45)					
1967–77	−.673	.056		.309	.082	0.997	1.37	8.17*	−0.26	−1.56
	(−1.13)	(.307)		(1.82)	(.094)					
1956–66	.156		.193†	.439†	−.265	0.998	2.18	5.77*		
	(.984)		(2.68)	(3.09)	(−1.45)					
1967–77	−.758†		.179‡	.219†	.389	0.998	1.10	11.37*	−1.2	−0.2
	(−2.53)		(2.06)	(2.63)	(.779)					
55 +										
1956–66	−.178	.157		.244	.493	0.909	1.79	1.23		
	(−.15)	(.405)		(.381)	(.304)					
1967–77	3.314‡	.529		−.688	−3.026	0.945	1.27	−1.3	0.82	−1.4
	(2.0)	(1.05)		(−1.46)	(−1.25)					
1956–66	−.451		−.009	.450	.925	0.906	1.76	0.53		
	(−.419)		(−.286)	(.548)	(.734)					

						R²	DW			
1967–77	2.66‡		.33	−.47‡	−2.58	0.947	0.99	−1.16		
	(2.3)		(1.25)	(−1.99)	(−1.3)				1.05	−1.27

Quarterly data

Total, 16 +

1956–66	.242	.765†		−.259	.965†	0.938	2.01	1.58		
	(.736)	(2.56)		(−.597)	(2.65)					
1967–77	−.519‡	−.005		.273†	.124	0.989	2.19	10.5*		
	(−1.9)	(−.05)		(2.54)	(.32)				1.13	−1.72‡

16–24

1956–66	.58	1.04‡		−.153	.622	0.933	2.12	0.9		
	(.89)	(1.8)		(−.179)	(.864)					
1967–77	−.287	.366‡		−.007	−.524	0.989	1.96	6.5*		
	(−.66)	(1.93)		(−.03)	(−.84)				−1.09	0.99

25–54

1956–66	−.67†	−.129		.798†	.446	0.954	1.78	4.4*		
	(−2.25)	(−.684)		(2.6)	(1.03)					
1967–77	−.634†	−.067		.432*	.117	0.994	2.10	14.0*		
	(−2.24)	(−.66)		(4.02)	(.30)				−0.47	−1.4

55 +

1956–66	−.733	.769‡		−1.31‡	1.42‡	0.874	1.71	1.4		
	(−1.28)	(1.97)		(−1.83)	(1.99)					
1967–77	−1.96	−1.78‡		1.35	6.12‡	0.468	1.96	2.1		
	(−.75)	(−2.13)		(1.61)	(1.7)				−1.75‡	1.06

Note: The coefficients of (DxWAGE) and (DxCPI) are estimated from Equation 4. The dependent variable in each equation is 1n LFP for women in the age group in question. The numbers in parentheses are the *t*-values.
* Significant at 1 percent confidence level.
† Significant at 5 percent confidence level.
‡ Significant at 10 percent confidence level.

recently; their labor supply elasticity with respect to the real wage has tended to become less positive, and to be essentially zero or even negative (backward-bending) in the second subperiod. The few shifts that are statistically significant are all found in the annual data, and the reliability of these estimates may be somewhat questionable owing to the very small number of degrees of freedom in each subperiod. When money wage and CPI are included as separate variables, it appears that there may have been some shift from money illusion to price illusion, with the rising money value of wages having an independent positive effect on labor supply in the first period, and accelerating inflation having an independent positive effect in the second period. The two periods differ sharply with respect to the average quarterly percentile increase in the CPI: the average increase was .492 in the first period and 2.30 in the second period. This suggests that estimates of labor supply responsiveness to inflation over the 20-year period may give biased estimates of the inflation-labor supply relationship, because of the major change in the rate of inflation between the two periods. Expectation of a "normal" rate of inflation must have been significantly different between the two periods, with larger absolute changes in inflation necessary to induce significant labor supply response in the second period relative to the first.

Notes

1. See *Employment and Training Report of the President* (1978), table B–4, p. 238.
2. Wachter's (1972) study is primarily interested in the effect of the "relative wage" on the labor supply of secondary workers. Although his results are not inconsistent with Fair's, his use of ordinary least squares resulted in autocorrelation problems which reduce the reliability of his estimates. Fair (1971) used the Cochrane-Orcutt technique and distributed lags to measure the effect of the wage and the consumer price index on labor supply. He found that the rapid rise in the labor supply of women aged 20–34 between 1956 and mid-1970 was primarily due to growth in the real wage and the employment ratio; for women over age 35, there was evidence of some short-run money illusion as well.
3. The money wage increased 42.5 percent between 1956 and 1966 and 108 percent between 1967 and 1977. The price level, however, as measured by the CPI, rose less than 23 percent in the earlier period and almost 88 percent in the later period, substantially shrinking the gains in real wages. The successively lower rates of growth of real wages were as follows: 7.5 percent over 1956–60, 7.2 percent over 1961–66, 4.8 percent over 1967–71, and only 3.5 percent over 1972–77.
4. RWAGE = WAGE/CPI
5. EMPW is an estimate of the relative employment demand for women workers based on the assumption that women's share of employment in each of the 11 major industries remains fixed, but the distribution of employment across industries changes over time. It is calculated as

$$\text{EMPW} = \sum_{j=1}^{11} a_j E_{jt} / \sum_{j=1}^{11} E_{jt}$$

where E_{jt} = total employment in industry j in time period t and a_j = the average proportion female employment in industry j over the entire 22-year period.
6. The correlation between the general manufacturing wage measure and the income measures for each age group of women is always over 0.97, which suggests that the former measure is not hopelessly biased as an estimate of this

dimension of women's market opportunities. The BLS data on "usual weekly earnings," which probably come closest to the age- and sex-specific wage measures that we ideally should have, are available only for 1967 and 1969–77, and thus could not be used in estimating either equations covering the entire period or shifts over time.

7. However, the indeterminate values of the Durbin-Watson statistic for the oldest group may imply that the significance of these coefficients is overestimated.

8. The test statistic is

$$\frac{\overline{b'_2 + b'_4}}{\sqrt{\text{Var } b'_2 \text{ Cov } (b'_2 b'_4) + \text{Var } b'_4}}$$

This test is equivalent to an *F*-test, using the weighted residual sum of squares, comparing Equation 2, which allows the coefficients of the money wage and the CPI to differ, and Equation 1, which constrains them to be opposite in sign and equal in absolute value.

9. If ordinary least squares were used to estimate these equations, estimating Equations 3 and 4 would be identical to estimating Equations 1 and 2 separately for the two subperiods. This is not the case for generalized least squares, however. For example, estimating Equation 3 constrains ϱ (the coefficient of serial correlation) to be the same across both subperiods, while estimating Equation 1 for each subperiod allows ϱ to differ from subperiods. To the extent that the true values of ϱ are different, these two estimates will give different results. Further work may be necessary to develop accurate tests for shifts over time. For example, an *F*-test, using the weighted residual sum of squares, that compares Equation 3 to Equation 3', which constrains the coefficient of the real wage to be the same in both subperiods, could be performed.

$$\ln \text{LFP} = A + B_1 D + B_2 \text{UN} + B_3(\text{DxUN}) + B_4 \ln \text{RWAGE} + B_5 \ln \text{EMPW} + B_6(\text{Dx ln EMPW}) \tag{3'}$$

However, this approach also constrains ϱ to be unchanging, and a test of equality or inequality between *b* coefficients in separate equations for the two subperiods would be desirable. Since we cannot assume independence between such pairs of coefficients, but we do not know their covariances, the nature of such a test is far from immediately obvious.

References

Blau, Francine D. "Longitudinal Patterns of Female Labor Force Participation," *Dual Careers* 4:27–55, U.S. Department of Labor, R & D *Monograph* no. 21, 1976.

Fair, Ray C. "Labor Force Participation, Wage Rates and Money Illusion," *Review of Economics and Statistics* 53 (1971): 164–68.

Heckman, James J. "New Evidence on the Dynmics of Female Labor Supply" in Cynthia B. Lloyd, Emily Andrews, and Curtis L. Gilroy (Eds.), *Women in the Labor Market* (New York, 1979).

Heckman, James J., and Willis, Robert. "A Beta-Logistic Model for the Analysis of Sequential Labor Force Participation by Married Women," *Journal of Political Economy* 85 (1977): 27–58.

Lloyd, Cynthia B., and Niemi, Beth T. *The Economics of Sex Differentials* (New York, 1979).

Mallan, Lucy B. "Changes in Female Labor Force Experience 1961–71 and the Effect on Earnings," paper presented at the Annual Meeting of the American Economic Association, San Francisco, 1974.

Mincer, Jacob, and Ofek, Haim. "The Distribution of Lifetime Labor Force Participation of Married Women," *Journal of Political Economy* 87 (1979): 197–201.

Niemi, Beth. "Recent Changes in Differential Unemployment," *Growth and Change* 8 (1977): 22–30.

U.S. Department of Commerce, Bureau of the Census. *1970 Census of Population: Employment Status and Work Experience*. Subject Reports PC (2) 6A (Washington, D.C., 1973).

U.S. Department of Labor, Employment and Training Administration. *Employment and Training Report of the President* (Washington, D.C., 1978).

U.S. President. *Economic Report of the President* (Washington, D.C., 1973).

Wachter, Michael L. "A Labor Supply Model for Secondary Workers," *Review of Economics and Statistics* 54 (1972): 141–50.

The Impact of Inflation upon Homeownership Affordability: Comparisons by Race and Sex for the South

I. INTRODUCTION

The purpose of this paper is to examine the differential impact of inflation upon the affordability of homeownership in the South for households headed by members of different race and sex groups. The impact of inflation upon homeownership affordability is of interest because of the belief that a nation of homeowners is also a nation of citizens who will invest in other forms of wealth and production in society.[1] The area of analysis is limited to the South both because data for female-headed households by race are available only for this region, 1969–77, and because the South as the region of historically greater poverty should be the region in which the financial burden of affordability is most pronounced.

Households headed by minorities and women have historically been deprived of access to homeownership, and hence to wealth accumulation, because of their low incomes and because of discrimination in the credit and search markets for housing. In a study of adjustments made to inflation during the 1974–75 recession, Caplovitz noted that many households used homeownership as a hedge against it.[2] To the extent that many households headed by minorities and women are underrepresented among homeowners, for whatever reasons, these same households lack one of the most commonly used mechanisms to lessen the severity of the impact of inflation. For this reason, issues of race and sex are here explicitly introduced into the discussion of homeownership affordability.

Rather than using the CPI, the customary indicator of the burden of inflation, shelter-income ratios are used to reflect the financial burden of acquiring homeownership. Census Bureau data series provide the income and shelter cost figures underlying these ratios. Critical levels for the shelter-income ratios are defined and the statistics for 1969–77 are compared to these levels. Statistically significant differences are consistently found when shelter-income ratios are compared by race and sex for the population subgroups. Inflation is thus shown to have a substantial and often differential impact upon the affordability of shelter for the different population subgroups.

The rest of this paper is organized in the following manner. In Section II, the methodology employed is discussed in detail. In the third section, findings are presented and analyzed; in the final section, conclusions are stated.

II. METHODOLOGY

As just noted, changes in homeownership affordability will be examined using shelter-income ratios for the households of interest, instead of CPI cost figures.[3] More specifically, price-income and monthly shelter cost-income ratios are calculated for potential owners by race (Blacks, whites) and sex of household head. The value-income ratios found in the *Annual Housing Survey* (AHS) volumes separately for Blacks and all races are also examined.

These price-income and monthly shelter cost-income ratios are compared over time to one another and to the levels determined to indicate financial hardship. In addition, difference of means *t*-tests for matched pairs of the ratios are performed for the households of the selected race and sex subgroups. Conclusions are drawn about the statistical significance of the differences observed. In the following paragraphs, relevant definitions and data sources are discussed in greater detail.

When seeking to construct cost figures for owned units, definitional variations may result from the treatment of any one of the following:[4] the inclusion of opportunity costs in homeowner shelter expenditures, the inclusion of expected capital gains in homeowner shelter costs, and the definition of homeowner costs in light of the income tax benefits. We need suitable definitions for converting owner cash outlays, which reflect both consumption and investment in housing, into expenditures for the flow of housing services derived. In other words, an ideal definition of shelter expenditures would include all of these items:[5]

1. Mortgage payment
2. Property tax
3. Insurance
4. Maintenance and repairs
5. Utilities
6. Opportunity cost of equity
7. Present value of future capital gains
8. Tax savings from homeownership.

The definition of income for homeowners also involves ambiguities. These ambiguities center about the treatment of homeowner imputed rent and the choice between the use of current and permanent income measures.[6]

In the computation of price-income and monthly shelter cost-income ratios in this research, the final three categories of shelter cost are omitted because of a lack of data. None of the shelter cost or price figures are race or sex specific in and of themselves. The race and sex distinctions are made on the income side of the ratios. Though race and sex specific, the homeowner income figures do not include imputed rent, and all data are reported as current income. Thus, the price-income and monthly shelter cost-income ratios reflect the potential, rather than actual, financial burden of homeownership. Ratios from the AHS do, however, reflect the actual financial burden of homeownership.

Data for the price and shelter cost computations are gathered from the following sources. Given appropriate median annual house values, monthly mortgage payments are obtained from amortization tables. Interest rates are taken from the *Federal Home Loan Bank Board Journal*, and payments are calculated under the assumptions of a 75 percent loan-to-value ratio and a mortgage term of 25 years. Data for the other owner shelter cost items are taken from statistics on units sold under HUD's Section 203 program.

Though the stock of owned housing cannot be stratified by specific types (i.e., cooperatives, condominiums, mobile homes, etc.) it is stratified according to whether the owned unit is part of the existing stock, a constant quality unit, or a new but sold unit. Arguments have been made and the affordability issue itself has been examined exclusively in terms of new units. Arguments to support such analysis center about the allegation that trends in new house prices are ultimately reflected in trends in the prices of all housing. But Black owners often acquire units that are not new. Thus, the interest in both existing and new but sold units arises.

Median sales prices for existing single-family houses, 1968–77, by region are available from the National Association of Realtors' series, *Existing Home Sales*. For new single-family houses sold, 1965–77, median sales prices by region are available from various issues of, and tables in, the U.S. Census Bureau, *Construction Reports: New One-Family Homes Sold and For Sale*, Series C-25.

In addition to existing and new but sold units, median sales prices for a constant quality of housing are examined. The examination of the shelter cost-income ratios that result with these prices is to determine whether the cost of a fixed quality or amount of housing has increased, decreased, or remained the same over time. In other words, this data series and the resultant cost-income ratios will allow one to focus upon whether the typical household can currently afford more or less housing than in the past. The median sales prices for this data series are from various issues and tables in the U.S. Census Bureau, *Construction Reports: Price Index of New One-Family Houses Sold*, Series C-27.

Sources of income data also require some explanation. Median income statistics for nonwhites only are available in 1965 and 1966. From 1967 to the present, median income statistics are reported for Blacks alone. Data for whites are available for the entire period of interest. The source of all income figures is the *Current Population Reports: Consumer Income*, Series P-60. For female-headed Black and white households, only mean income statistics in the South are reported for every year 1969–77, and these are available only for households below the poverty level. These facts relevant to the income data for female-headed households of both races limit the regional analysis to the South even though income data for all households by race are available separately for all four regions.[7]

The choice to use current income measures was made in part because of the availability of appropriate data. The decision to do so is, however, buttressed by arguments made by David M. Nelson.[8] Nelson notes that the current income reported by the Census Bureau is akin to permanent income because it omits many types of positive transitory income (such as property sale return, gifts, lump sum inheritance, and insurance payments). In addition, he feels that when reporting income on surveys, households actually state a measure that reflects their mental fix on a permanent earnings stream rather than on actual current income.

The value-income ratios for actual owners taken from the AHS reflect the definition of owner shelter cost adopted for that survey. Statistics for 1970 and for 1973–76 are from the AHS volume *General Housing Characteristics*, Series A. Data are available for all four regions of the United States — Northeast, North Central, South, and West — and for Blacks and all races.

Once the preceding ratios have been calculated to compare homeownership costs and incomes, they are also compared to appropriate standards to reflect the extent of financial burden. In lieu of nice definitive statements, history has provided rules of thumb as standards for an acceptable level of housing expenditure as a fraction of income. In the nineteenth century in company towns in the United States, workers were charged one week's wages for one month's shelter.[9] This practice was enforced by money market operations in the 1920s and then translated into the nearly universal axiom that one should spend only 25 percent of income for shelter.

In a report issued in 1932 by the task force on housing objectives and programs of President Hoover's Committee on Home Building and Homeownership, standards for the rental and purchase of shelter were promulgated.[10] The rental of adequate housing should not exceed 20 percent of income, and the purchase price of a home should not as a rule exceed twice the assured annual income. The rule for affordability of owner-occupied units has been adjusted to reflect housing price increases over time. The owner-household is now commonly considered able to afford a house whose purchase price is 2.5 times its income.

III. ANALYSIS OF FINDINGS

Findings from the analysis of homeownership affordability for potential owner households (Black, white, and female-headed) in the South are presented and discussed. The results underlying this discussion appear in Tables 1–6. This discussion is followed by an examination of the value-income ratios for actual homeowners (Blacks and all races) in all regions of the United States (Tables 7–10 contain these results).

A. POTENTIAL HOMEOWNERS

Data presented in Tables 1–6 are comparable though there are differences in coverage between Tables 1–3 and Tables 4–6. On Tables 1–3, data for Blacks and whites as potential owners of one of the three types of units — existing single-family, constant-quality single-family, and new but sold single-family — are found. Tables 4–6 give data for Black female-headed households and white female-headed households as potential owners of the same types of units.

The comparisons made using these tables are of three general types. Price-income ratios for each year are compared to the standard that at most 2.5 times income should be spent to purchase housing. The monthly shelter cost-income ratios for each year are compared to the standard that only 25 percent of income should be devoted to acquiring shelter. The final comparison is that of median (mean) annual incomes for each year with the annual income needed to afford housing of each of the three types. Difference of means *t*-tests for matched pairs of the price-income ratio series and for matched pairs of the monthly shelter cost-income ratio series are performed.

A difference that is statistically significant at the .001 level of confidence with a 2-tailed *t*-test is found between each of the paired series of price-income and monthly shelter cost-income ratios by race in the South for each type of housing. For example, this allows us to say that observed differences over time in the price-income (or monthly shelter cost-income) ratios for potential Black and white owners of a constant quality unit in the South are meaningful. It is also found that differences between the paired series of price-income ratios for female-headed households and all households of each race and for each housing type in the South are statistically significant at the .001 confidence level, with a 2-tailed *t*-test. Comparable differences for the monthly shelter cost-income ratios are significant at the .05 level.

The final *t*-tests of paired series of price-income and monthly shelter cost-income ratios for statistical significance — that of female-headed

Black households against female-headed white households — also indicate statistical significance for observed differences at the .01 level of confidence with a 2-tailed test. Thus all the differences cited in this text are statistically significant ones.[11]

Comparisons by race alone will be cited first. In the potential acquisition of existing single-family houses (Table 1), the price-income ratios for Blacks exceed 2.5 in all years, whereas the price-income ratios for whites exceed 2.5 only for 1971–77. The shelter-income ratios for Blacks are greater than .25 in all years; the same ratios for whites exceed .25 in the years 1970–77. Median income for Blacks is less than the income needed to afford an existing unit in every year; for whites, this is true for 1970–77.

When the potential acquisition of the 1974 constant quality unit is considered (Table 2), both the price-income and the shelter-income ratios exceeded their standards (2.5 times income and .25 of income) for Blacks and for whites in all years. As for existing houses, in all cases the price-income and shelter-income ratios for Blacks uniformly exceeded those for whites. The median incomes for both Blacks and whites are less than the incomes needed to afford this constant quality unit throughout time.

In the acquisition of new but sold single-family units (Table 3) it was found that price-income ratios for Blacks always exceeded 2.5. The same ratio for whites exceeded 2.5 in all years except 1970–72 when its values were less than or equal to 2.5. The shelter-income ratios of Blacks always exceeded .25, while the same ratios for whites exceeded .25 in all years except 1967 and 1970–72, when they were less than or equal to the standard. The median income for Blacks was less than the income needed to afford new but sold units at all times. The median income of whites was less than the needed income for new but sold units in all years except 1970 and 1971, when it exceeded the needed income level.

The foregoing differentials by race of household can be summarized. Black households are in the chronic position over time of being unable to afford all three unit types by the given standards. White households, however, can be characterized as experiencing an acute condition of being unable to afford the various types of owned units primarily in the 1970s when inflation gets underway in the economy at large. Households of both races are finding it increasingly difficult to afford a fixed quality of housing or new housing.

For female-headed households in poverty (see Tables 4–6), certain trends persist despite differentiation by race or type of unit. The price-income ratios for acquisition of all three unit types greatly exceed 2.5 in all years among both Blacks and whites. Similarly, the monthly shelter cost-income ratios consistently exceed .25 in all years. As well,

Table 1. Owner Housing Cost and Income Comparisons by Race for Existing Single-family Houses in the South, 1968–77

Years	Median Sales Price[1]	Median Monthly Housing Expense[2]	Median Annual Housing Expense	Annual Income Needed to Afford Housing[3]	Blacks			Whites		
					Median Annual Income[4]	Price-income Ratio	Median Monthly Shelter-income Ratio	Median Annual Income[4]	Price-income Ratio	Median Monthly Shelter-income Ratio
1968	19,000	160	1,920	7,680	4,283	4.436	.448	7,963	2.386	.241
1969	20,300	176	2,109	8,437	4,987	4.071	.423	8,764	2.316	.241
1970	22,200	198	2,374	9,495	5,226	4.248	.454	9,240	2.403	.257
1971	24,300	207	2,487	9,949	5,414	4.488	.460	9,706	2.504	.256
1972	26,400	227	2,722	10,887	5,763	4.581	.473	10,465	2.523	.260
1973	29,000	248	2,977	11,907	6,434	4.507	.463	11,508	2.520	.259
1974	32,300	289	3,465	13,860	6,730	4.799	.515	12,050	2.807	.288
1975	34,800	317	3,800	15,201	6,559	5.306	.579	11,479	3.032	.331
1976	36,500	332	3,989	15,956	7,390	4.939	.540	12,413	2.940	.321
1977	39,800	363	4,360	17,442	7,744	5.139	.563	13,474	2.954	.324

[1] From National Association of Realtors, *Existing Home Sales*, June 1979, p. 10.

[2] This includes amortized monthly mortgage payment + taxes, maintenance, repairs, heat, and utilities. Monthly mortgage note is determined using interest rates from *Federal Home Loan Bank Board Journal* under the assumptions of a 75% loan/value ratio and 25 years to repay loan. All other items are from table entitled "Characteristics of 1-Family Home Transactions, Sec. 203," HUD, *Series Data Handbook Covering Section 203b Mortgage Characteristics*, October 1978.

[3] Using the 25% of income rule, these figures are the product of 4 × median annual housing expense.

[4] From *Current Population Reports: Consumer Income*, Series P-60, various issues and tables.

Source: Prepared by the National Urban League Research Department.

Table 2. Owner Housing Cost and Income Comparisons by Race for the 1974 Constant Quality Single-family House in the South, 1965-1977

Years	Median Sales Price[1]	Median Monthly Housing Expense[2]	Median Annual Housing Expense	Annual Income Needed to Afford Housing[3]	Blacks			Whites		
					Median Annual Income[4]	Price-income Ratio	Median Monthly Shelter-income Ratio	Median Annual Income[4]	Price-income Ratio	Median Monthly Shelter-income Ratio
1965	22,700	161	1,929	7,716	2,979	7.620	.648	6,141	3.696	.314
1966	23,700	171	2,051	8,205	3,446	6.878	.596	6,773	3.499	.303
1967	24,200	181	2,168	8,673	3,966	6.102	.546	7,408	3.267	.293
1968	25,200	192	2,304	9,216	4,283	5.884	.538	7,963	3.165	.289
1969	27,000	213	2,553	10,213	4,987	5.414	.511	8,764	3.081	.291
1970	28,000	233	2,794	11,175	5,226	5.358	.534	9,240	3.030	.302
1971	30,100	239	2,871	11,485	5,414	5.560	.531	9,706	3.101	.296
1972	31,900	257	3,082	12,327	5,763	5.535	.535	10,465	3.048	.295
1973	34,100	277	3,325	13,299	6,434	5.300	.517	11,508	2.963	.289
1974	36,800	317	3,801	15,204	6,730	5.468	.565	12,050	3.198	.315
1975	40,200	351	4,208	16,833	6,559	6.129	.641	11,479	3.502	.366
1976	43,000	374	4,493	17,972	7,390	5.819	.608	12,413	3.464	.362
1977	47,200	408	4,900	19,602	7,744	6.095	.633	13,474	3.503	.364

[1] From *Construction Reports: Price Index of New One-Family Houses Sold*, Series C27, selected issues and tables.

[2] This includes amortized monthly mortgage payment + taxes, maintenance, repairs, heat, and utilities. Monthly mortgage note is determined using interest rates from *Federal Home Loan Bank Board Journal* under the assumptions of a 75% loan/value ratio and 25 years to repay loan. All other items are from table entitled "Characteristics of 1-Family Home Transactions, Sec. 203," HUD, *Series Data Handbook Covering Section 203b Mortgage Characteristics*, October 1978.

[3] Using the 25% of income rule, these figures are the product of 4 × median annual housing expense.

[4] From *Current Population Reports: Consumer Income*, Series P-60, various issues and tables. For 1965 and 1966 income data are for nonwhites; for rest of years they reflect Blacks only.

Source: Prepared by the National Urban League Research Department.

Table 3. Owner Housing Cost and Income Comparisons by Race for New Single-family Houses Sold in the South, 1965–77

Years	Median Sales Price[1]	Median Monthly Housing Expense[2]	Median Annual Housing Expense	Annual Income Needed to Afford Housing[3]	Blacks Median Annual Income[4]	Blacks Price-income Ratio	Blacks Median Monthly Shelter-income Ratio	Whites Median Annual Income[4]	Whites Price-income Ratio	Whites Median Monthly Shelter-income Ratio
1965	17,500	137	1,641	6,564	2,979	5.874	.551	6,141	2.850	.267
1966	18,200	145	1,739	6,957	3,446	5.281	.505	6,773	2.687	.257
1967	19,400	156	1,868	7,473	3,966	4.892	.470	7,408	2.619	.252
1968	21,500	173	2,076	8,304	4,283	5.020	.485	7,963	2.700	.261
1969	22,800	190	2,277	9,109	4,987	4.572	.456	8,764	2.602	.260
1970	20,300	187	2,242	8,967	5,226	3.884	.428	9,240	2.197	.243
1971	22,500	196	2,355	9,421	5,414	4.156	.435	9,706	2.318	.243
1972	25,800	222	2,662	10,647	5,763	4.477	.462	10,465	2.465	.254
1973	30,900	258	3,097	12,387	6,434	4.803	.481	11,508	2.685	.269
1974	34,500	301	3,609	14,436	6,730	5.126	.536	12,050	2.863	.300
1975	37,300	333	3,992	15,969	6,559	5.687	.608	11,479	3.249	.348
1976	40,500	358	4,301	17,204	7,390	5.480	.582	12,413	3.263	.347
1977	44,100	389	4,672	18,690	7,744	5.695	.604	13,474	3.273	.347

[1] From Construction Reports: New One-Family Houses Sold and For Sale, Series C25, selected issues and tables.

[2] This includes amortized monthly mortgage payment+taxes, maintenance, repairs, heat and utilities. Monthly mortgage note is determined using interest rates from Federal Home Loan Bank Board Journal under the assumptions of a 75% loan/value ratio and 25 years to repay loan. All other items are from table entitled, "Characteristics of 1-Family Home Transactions, Sec. 203," HUD, Series Data Handbook Covering Section 203b Mortgage Characteristics, October 1978.

[3] Using the 25% of income rule, these figures are the product of 4 × median annual housing expense.

[4] From Current Population Reports: Consumer Income, Series P-60, various issues and tables. For 1965 and 1966 income data are for nonwhites; for rest of years they reflect Blacks only.

Source: Prepared by the National Urban League Research Department.

Table 4. Owner Housing Cost and Income Comparisons by Race and Sex of Household Head for Existing Single-family Houses in the South, 1969–77

Years	Median Sales Price[1]	Median Monthly Housing Expense[2]	Median Annual Housing Expense	Annual Income Needed to Afford Housing[3]	Black Female-headed Households			White Female-headed Households		
					Mean Annual Income[4]	Price-income Ratio	Median Monthly Shelter-income Ratio	Mean Annual Income[4]	Price-income Ratio	Median Monthly Shelter-income Ratio
1969	20,300	176	2,109	8,437	2,070	9.806	1.020	1,767	11.488	1.195
1970	22,200	198	2,374	9,495	2,174	10.212	1.093	1,860	11.935	1.277
1971	24,300	207	2,487	9,949	2,169	11.203	1.145	1,842	13.192	1.349
1972	26,400	227	2,722	10,887	2,387	11.060	1.141	1,855	14.232	1.468
1973	29,000	248	2,977	11,907	2,511	11.549	1.185	2,052	14.133	1.450
1974	32,300	289	3,465	13,860	2,605	12.399	1.331	2,279	14.173	1.522
1975	34,800	317	3,800	15,201	2,896	12.017	1.314	2,457	14.164	1.548
1976	36,500	332	3,989	15,956	3,146	11.602	1.266	2,790	13.082	1.428
1977	39,800	363	4,360	17,442	3,164	12.579	1.377	2,661	14.957	1.637

[1] From National Association of Realtors, *Existing Home Sales*, June 1979, p. 10.

[2] This includes amortized monthly mortgage payment+taxes, maintenance, repairs, heat, and utilities. Monthly mortgage note is determined using interest rates from *Federal Home Loan Bank Board Journal* under the assumptions of a 75% loan/value ratio and 25 years to repay loan. All other items are from table entitled "Characteristics of 1-Family Home Transactions, Sec. 203," HUD, *Series Data Handbook Covering Section 203b Mortgage Characteristics*, October 1978.

[3] Using the 25% of income rule, these figures are the product of 4 × median annual housing expense.

[4] From *Current Population Reports: Consumer Income*, Series P-60, various issues and tables.

Source: Prepared by the National Urban League Research Department.

Table 5. Owner Housing Cost and Income Comparisons by Race and Sex of Household Head for the 1974 Constant Quality Single-family House in the South, 1969–77

Years	Median Sales Price[1]	Median Monthly Housing Expense[2]	Median Annual Housing Expense	Annual Income Needed to Afford Housing[3]	Black Female-headed Households			White Female-headed Households		
					Mean Annual Income[4]	Price-income Ratio	Median Monthly Shelter-income Ratio	Mean Annual Income[4]	Price-income Ratio	Median Monthly Shelter-income Ratio
1969	27,000	213	2,553	10,213	2,070	13.043	1.235	1,767	15.280	1.447
1970	28,000	233	2,794	11,175	2,174	12.879	1.286	1,860	15.054	1.503
1971	30,100	239	2,871	11,485	2,169	13.877	1.322	1,842	16.341	1.557
1972	31,900	257	3,082	12,327	2,387	13.364	1.292	1,855	17.197	1.663
1973	34,100	277	3,325	13,299	2,511	13.580	1.324	2,052	16.618	1.620
1974	36,800	317	3,801	15,204	2,605	14.127	1.460	2,279	16.147	1.669
1975	40,200	351	4,208	16,833	2,896	13.881	1.454	2,457	16.361	1.714
1976	43,000	374	4,493	17,972	3,146	13.668	1.427	2,790	15.412	1.609
1977	47,200	408	4,900	19,602	3,164	14.918	1.547	2,661	17.738	1.840

[1] From Construction Reports: Price Index of New One-Family Houses Sold, Series C27, selected issues and tables.

[2] This includes amortized monthly mortgage payment+taxes, maintenance, repairs, heat, and utilities. Monthly mortgage note is determined using interest rates from Federal Home Loan Bank Board Journal under the assumptions of a 75% loan/value ratio and 25 years to repay loan. All other items are from table entitled, "Characteristics of 1-Family Home Transactions, Sec. 203," HUD, Series Data Handbook Covering Section 203b Mortgage Characteristics, October 1978.

[3] Using the 25% of income rule, these figures are the product of 4 × median annual housing expense.

[4] From Current Population Reports: Consumer Income, Series P-60, various issues and tables.

Source: Prepared by the National Urban League Research Department.

Table 6. Owner Housing Cost and Income Comparisons by Race and Sex of Household Head for New Single-family Houses Sold in the South, 1969–77

Years	Median Sales Price[1]	Median Monthly Housing Expense[2]	Median Annual Housing Expense	Annual Income Needed to Afford Housing[3]	Black Female-headed Households			White Female-headed Households		
					Mean Annual Income[4]	Price-income Ratio	Median Monthly Shelter-income Ratio	Mean Annual Income[4]	Price-income Ratio	Median Monthly Shelter-income Ratio
1969	22,800	190	2,277	9,109	2,070	11.014	1.101	1,767	12.903	1.290
1970	20,300	187	2,242	8,967	2,174	9.338	1.032	1,860	10.914	1.206
1971	22,500	196	2,355	9,421	2,169	10.373	1.084	1,842	12.215	1.277
1972	25,800	222	2,662	10,647	2,387	10.809	1.116	1,855	13.908	1.436
1973	30,900	258	3,097	12,387	2,511	12.306	1.233	2,052	15.058	1.509
1974	34,500	301	3,609	14,436	2,605	13.244	1.387	2,279	15.138	1.585
1975	37,300	333	3,992	15,969	2,896	12.880	1.380	2,457	15.181	1.626
1976	40,500	358	4,301	17,204	3,146	12.873	1.366	2,790	14.516	1.540
1977	44,100	389	4,672	18,690	3,164	13.938	1.475	2,661	16.573	1.754

[1] From Construction Reports: New One-Family Houses Sold and For Sale, Series C25, selected issues and tables.

[2] This includes amortized monthly mortgage payment + taxes, maintenance, repairs, heat, and utilities. Monthly mortgage note is determined using interest rates from Federal Home Loan Bank Board Journal under the assumptions of a 75% loan/value ratio and 25 years to repay loan. All other items are from table entitled, "Characteristics of 1-Family Home Transactions, Sec. 203," HUD, Series Data Handbook Covering Section 203b Mortgage Characteristics, October 1978.

[3] Using the 25% of income rule, these figures are the product of 4 × median annual housing expense.

[4] From Current Population Reports: Consumer Income, Series P-60, various issues and tables.

Source: Prepared by the National Urban League Research Department.

the mean annual incomes of female-headed households in poverty in all years fall far short of the annual income needed to afford each housing type.

When Black (white) female-headed households in poverty are compared to all Black (white) households, the female-headed households are found to remain in a position of disadvantage. The female-headed households have larger price-income ratios and larger monthly shelter cost-income ratios than do all households in the respective race categories.

In the comparison of female-headed households in poverty by race to one another, regarding the potential purchase of all three types of units, an interesting trend emerges. Though excessive in all years and for both races, the price-income and monthly shelter cost-income ratios for Black female-headed households are lower than those for white female-headed households. For mean incomes for poverty-level, Black, female-headed households consistently greater than the mean incomes of poverty-level, white, female-headed households account for this.

As expected, poverty-level female-headed households of both races are clearly priced out of the market for ownership of all types of units in all years. Also, relative to households of the corresponding racial group, female-headed households are at a distinct disadvantage. Though this disadvantage was expected a priori, the monthly shelter cost-income ratios greater than one and the price-income ratios as much as five times greater than the standard are useful to indicate the severity of the financial burden of homeownership for these groups.

The slight advantage of Black female-headed households in poverty over the corresponding white female-headed households as potential owners just mentioned is worthy of further comment. Since family size is not controlled for in available income data series, one cannot determine whether poverty per household member varies by race, i.e., whether Black female household heads have not only higher mean incomes but also larger families to support than do white female household heads. Also, despite this larger mean income, Black female household heads may still encounter more hardships than white female household heads when seeking to purchase housing. These hardships may be due to discrimination on any one of the following grounds: race, sex, or family size. Though of little comfort to white female-headed households in poverty, they are subject to only two of these types of discrimination.

B. ACTUAL HOMEOWNERSHIP

The percentage distributions of Black households and of households of all races according to value-income ratios are presented for 1970 and

1973–76 in Tables 7–10. The distributions are available both across a wide range of categories and for simply those paying "less than 2.5 times income" vs. those paying "2.5 and greater times income." The modal category for the expanded distribution is those paying "less than 1.5 times their incomes" for owned housing. The percentage of Black households in this category is greater than the percentage of households of all races herein for all regions and in all years with two exceptions. The first exception arises in the South in 1970, when the percentage of households of all races in the modal category exceeds the corresponding percentage of Black households. The other exception is in the West, where the percentage of households of all races in the modal category exceeds the percentage of Black households in every year except 1976.

For both all races and Blacks, the percentage paying "less than 1.5 times income" has fluctuated about a declining trend between 1970 and 1976. Over the same time period that the percentage in this modal category has been decreasing, the percentage in each category from "2.0–2.4" up to "4.0 and greater" has been increasing. No single category, however, appears to be the primary locus of the redistribution of households.

The percentages of Black households and of households of all races paying "less than 2.5 times their incomes" are over half of both household groups in all regions and in all years, except for Blacks in the West in 1976. As for the category of "less than 1.5 times income," the overwhelming numerical trend is that larger percentages of Black households than of households of all races are found to spend "less than 2.5 times income" in all regions and in all years.

These results support the use of the critical level of 2.5 for price-income ratios. Clearly, few households of any race or sex are allowed to borrow enough from banks to purchase units costing much more than 2.5 times their incomes. Given the magnitude of some of the incomes reported here, if able to acquire a unit at 2.5 times income, one is often likely to be consuming a very substandard unit.

The preceding analysis of potential affordability reveals that the median (mean) income household in various race and sex subgroups of the population can ill afford homeownership. Actual value-income ratios substantiate this finding. The median (mean) income household and all earning less than this household (and probably some earning more as well) have been effectively precluded from the home purchase market.

IV. CONCLUSIONS

The analysis in the preceding section revealed that homeownership

Table 7. Value-income Ratios by Race in the Northeast, 1970, 1973–76

	Less than 1.5	1.5 to 1.9	(Percentage Distribution) 2.0 to 2.4	2.5 to 2.9	3.0 to 3.9	4.0 and Greater	(Percentage Distribution) Less than 2.5	2.5 and Greater
Blacks								
1970	49.6	15.9	9.8	6.1	6.5	12.2	75.2	24.8
1973	42.7	17.1	10.5	8.0	8.0	13.6	70.4	29.6
1974	43.9	18.0	5.9	8.9	9.8	13.4	67.9	32.1
1975	41.8	16.0	9.9	5.4	11.6	15.3	67.7	32.3
1976	41.1	14.0	14.0	6.9	8.9	15.1	69.1	30.9
All Races								
1970	36.8	20.3	13.9	8.3	8.2	12.5	71.0	29.0
1973	23.7	18.6	15.3	11.1	13.0	18.3	57.6	42.4
1974	24.9	19.6	14.3	12.2	11.6	17.5	58.7	41.3
1975	23.6	18.7	15.7	10.6	13.2	18.1	58.1	41.9
1976	23.3	19.1	16.1	10.9	12.5	18.2	58.4	41.6

Source: Prepared by the National Urban League Research Department from tables in the *Annual Housing Survey, Series A, General Housing Characteristics*, 1973–1976.

Table 8. Value-income Ratios by Race in the North Central, 1970, 1973–76

	Less than 1.5	1.5 to 1.9	(Percentage Distribution) 2.0 to 2.4	2.5 to 2.9	3.0 to 3.9	4.0 and Greater	(Percentage Distribution) Less than 2.5	2.5 and Greater
Blacks								
1970	48.6	17.3	9.9	5.7	6.2	12.4	75.7	24.3
1973	46.1	17.9	12.3	8.0	4.9	10.7	76.4	23.6
1974	49.3	16.1	10.5	5.7	5.0	13.5	75.8	24.2
1975	52.2	14.0	8.9	4.9	7.5	12.4	75.2	24.8
1976	47.6	14.9	10.6	5.0	9.4	12.6	73.0	27.0
All Races								
1970	40.4	20.2	12.6	7.2	7.1	12.6	73.1	26.9
1973	31.2	20.1	14.2	8.9	9.7	15.9	65.5	34.5
1974	31.7	19.8	14.8	9.3	9.5	14.8	66.4	33.6
1975	30.2	20.4	14.8	9.8	9.9	15.0	65.3	34.7
1976	29.0	20.5	14.9	9.5	10.5	15.7	64.3	35.7

Source: Prepared by the National Urban League Research Department from tables in the Annual Housing Survey, Series A, General Housing Characteristics, 1973–1976.

Table 9. Value-income Ratios by Race in the South, 1970, 1973–1976

	Less than 1.5	1.5 to 1.9	2.0 to 2.4	2.5 to 2.9	3.0 to 3.9	4.0 and Greater	Less than 2.5	2.5 and Greater
			(Percentage Distribution)				(Percentage Distribution)	
Blacks								
1970	41.2	14.9	9.5	6.9	8.4	19.1	65.6	34.4
1973	34.0	18.4	11.2	9.5	9.0	18.0	63.5	36.5
1974	35.6	16.6	10.8	8.2	10.0	18.8	63.0	37.0
1975	31.5	18.1	12.1	8.8	8.7	20.9	61.6	38.4
1976	32.8	14.2	11.1	9.1	9.9	22.9	58.1	41.9
All Races								
1970	42.7	18.3	11.2	6.8	7.2	13.8	72.2	27.8
1973	31.2	18.9	12.7	9.6	10.9	16.8	62.7	37.3
1974	31.1	18.4	13.9	9.1	10.7	16.8	63.4	36.6
1975	30.0	18.9	13.5	9.3	10.5	17.8	62.4	37.6
1976	28.3	18.2	14.2	10.2	11.0	18.2	60.6	39.4

Source: Prepared by the National Urban League Research Department from tables in the *Annual Housing Survey, Series A, General Housing Characteristics,* 1973–1976.

Table 10. Value-income Ratios by Race in the West, 1970, 1973–76

(Percentage Distribution)

	Less than 1.5	1.5 to 1.9	2.0 to 2.4	2.5 to 2.9	3.0 to 3.9	4.0 and Greater	Less than 2.5	2.5 and Greater
Blacks								
1970	26.5	19.9	14.4	9.4	10.5	19.3	60.8	39.2
1973	16.0	21.3	16.7	7.6	14.8	23.6	54.0	46.0
1974	21.0	21.0	18.5	7.6	11.6	20.3	60.5	39.5
1975	19.8	19.4	11.7	12.0	11.0	26.1	50.9	49.1
1976	18.5	13.2	14.6	10.1	14.3	29.3	46.3	53.7
All Races								
1970	29.8	21.5	15.2	9.0	9.1	15.4	66.5	33.5
1973	22.9	21.0	17.1	10.5	10.9	17.8	60.8	39.2
1974	23.9	19.9	17.0	11.2	11.4	16.6	60.8	39.2
1975	22.2	19.1	15.6	11.7	12.5	18.9	56.9	43.1
1976	18.2	18.1	16.8	12.6	14.0	20.4	53.0	47.0

Source: Prepared by the National Urban League Research Department from tables in the *Annual Housing Survey, Series A, General Housing Characteristics,* 1973–1976.

has not been affordable for the median income potential Black owner in the South throughout the period 1968–77 for three types of units. This analysis has also revealed that inflation in the 1970s, as reflected by an increase in housing acquisition costs, has begun to make homeownership not affordable for the median income potential white homeowner in the South (see Tables 1–3). Homeownership has never been affordable for Black or white female-headed households in poverty in the South for 1969–77 (Tables 4–6).

The percentage distribution of actual owners by value-income ratios for Blacks and all races during the 1970s (Tables 7–10) reveals that actual purchasers have by and large been restricted to acquiring units which cost less than 2.5 times their incomes. Though the percentages have shifted slightly between categories (i.e., from less than 2.5 to greater than or equal to 2.5) from 1970 to 1976, nearly half of all households still fall in the former. This means that the prospects of homeownership and hence of wealth accumulation for Black and female-headed households are rather slim, given both the affordability standards enforced by banks and the ability of these household to acquire units for the prices they could afford to pay.

Table 11 shows that from 1960 through 1976 in all regions of the United States at least half and often as many as 73 percent of all Black households have rented rather than purchased their units. For whites in all regions over that same period at least 58 percent and as many as 72 percent of all households have owned their houses. In addition, Table 12 indicates that the percentage of all rented units occupied by nonwhites has increased from 13 percent to 19 percent between 1950 and 1974, at the same time that the percentage of rental units out of all units has fallen from 45 percent to 35 percent. Though this shift cannot be directly attributed to inflation, it has bearing on the homeownership affordability situation that is affected by inflation. What options do Black and female-headed households have if unable to afford to buy and if the available rental stock is diminishing? Inflation has begun to make white households address this question as well.

Bernard J. Frieden has suggested four mechanisms for coping with the inflation in housing costs.[12] Households could trade up from their existing housing to more expensive housing and thereby ride the crest of inflation. Households could pool multiple wage earner incomes to be able to afford units, could stretch existing resources, or could improve existing housing. Though Caplovitz cited evidence that many owners weathered the 1974–75 recession/inflation with the aid of their property equity (and Frieden's first suggestion is an example of how to do so), female-headed households and Black households too often lack that initially owned unit with which to trade up. As unemployment continues to rise with the inflation rate, the incidence of two wage

Table 11. Percentage of Occupancy by Tenure

| | Blacks | | Whites | |
	Occupied Units Owned	Occupied Units Rented	Occupied Units Owned	Occupied Units Rented
1960				
Northeast	27.0	73.0	58.1	41.9
North Central	35.8	64.2	69.1	30.9
South	41.6	58.4	66.4	33.6
West	44.6	55.4	62.5	37.5
1970				
Northeast	28.6	71.4	60.4	39.6
North Central	42.0	58.0	70.2	29.8
South	46.9	53.1	68.2	31.8
West	40.1	59.9	60.2	39.8
1973				
Northeast	29.5	70.5	62.2	37.8
North Central	44.1	55.9	71.4	28.6
South	48.5	51.5	70.1	29.9
West	42.8	57.2	62.1	37.9
1974				
Northeast	29.9	70.1	62.6	37.4
North Central	45.0	55.0	71.4	28.6
South	49.5	50.5	70.2	29.8
West	40.8	59.2	62.9	37.1
1975				
Northeast	29.0	71.0	62.9	37.1
North Central	46.9	53.1	71.5	28.5
South	48.7	51.3	70.1	29.9
West	41.2	58.8	63.0	37.0
1976				
Northeast	30.0	70.0	63.1	36.9
North Central	44.9	55.1	71.6	28.4
South	48.6	51.4	70.2	29.8
West	42.0	58.0	63.3	36.7

Source: Prepared by the National Urban League Research Department from data in *The Statistical Abstract of the U.S.*, 1976 and in the *Annual Housing Survey: General Housing Characteristics*.

Table 12. Rental Units as Percentage of Total Stock

Year	No. Rental Units* Blacks + Others	Whites	Total	Rental Units as Percent of All Units	Percent of Rental Units Occupied by Blacks* Others
1900	1,452	7,057	8,509	53.3	17.0
1910	(NA)	(NA)	10,954	54.1	—
1920	1,923	11,315	13,238	54.4	15.0
1930	2,185	13,439	15,624	52.2	14.0
1940	2,516	17,143	19,659	56.4	13.0
1950	2,464	16,803	19,266	45.0	13.0
1960	3,171	17,057	20,227	38.1	16.0
1970	4,014	19,551	23,565	37.1	17.0
1974	4,641	20,405	25,046	35.4	19.0

(NA) not available
*In thousands

Source: Prepared by National Urban League Research Department from data in Table 1271, The Statistical Abstract of the U.S., 1976.

earner Black families has declined.[13] Thus, the ability of Black households to cope with the inflationary impact upon housing costs is again diminished. Likewise, stretching existing resources and improving existing housing have limits which are all too quickly reached by female-headed poverty-level families.

The bottom line of this analysis is that the groups one would expect to be priced out of homeownership — Blacks and female-headed households — are. Because inflation in the 1970s has begun to price out of the homeownership market those who had heretofore used it most effectively as a cushion (i.e., whites), there is every reason to believe that Blacks and female-headed households will continue to remain out of the market. The societal implications of such findings for wealth accumulation, productivity, and economic growth can be serious.

Notes

* The work that provided the basis for this publication was supported by funding under a Grant with the U.S. Department of Housing and Urban Development. The substance and findings of that work are dedicated to the public. The author and publisher are solely responsible for the accuracy of the

statements and interpretations contained in this publication and such interpretations do not necessarily reflect the views of the Government.

1. J. M. Gries and J. Ford (Eds.), *Home Ownership, Income, and Types of Dwelling*, vol. IV, *Report on the President's Conference on Home Building and Home Ownership* (Washington, D.C., 1932), p. 1.

2. David Caplovitz, *Making Ends Meet: How Families Cope with Inflation and Recession* (New York, 1978), p. 70.

3. Clear explanations of the technical reasons for not using CPI housing cost measures are contained in the following: Neil Mayer, *Homeownership: The Changing Relationship of Costs and Incomes, and Possible Federal Roles* (Washington, D.C., 1977), p. 4; Hugh O. Nourse, "The Affordability of House-ownership," paper presented at the American Real Estate and Urban Economics Association's Seventh Annual Mid-Year Meeting, Washington, D.C., May 1979, p. 6.

4. Judith Feins and Carl White, Jr., *The Ratio of Shelter Expenses to Income: Definitional Issues, Typical Patterns and Historical Trends* (Cambridge, Mass., 1977), pp. 46–47.

5. *Ibid.*, p. 51.

6. *Ibid.*, p. 47.

7. The author will make available to interested readers the comparable tables prepared for all households by race in the other regions.

8. David M. Nelson, "The Income Elasticity of the Demand for Housing Service" (doctoral dissertation, University of Oregon, 1975).

9. David W. Budding, *Draft Report on Housing Deprivation Among Enrollees in the Housing Allowance Demand Experiment* (Cambridge, Mass., 1978), p. 52.

10. Gries and Ford, *Housing Objectives and Programs*, vol. XI, *Report on the President's Conference on Home Building and Home Ownership* (Washington, D.C., 1932): 193, 195.

11. The author will make available to interested readers the test statistics calculated for the difference of means, matched pairs *t*-tests.

12. Bernard J. Frieden, "The New Housing-Cost Problem," *The Public Interest* XLIX (Fall 1977): 74–76.

13. The decline in the percentage of two wage-earner Black households is documented in Robert B. Hill, *The Widening Economic Gap* (Washington, D.C., 1979), p. 7.

The Inflation of Housework

BETTINA BERCH

The literature on the economic effects of inflation is filled with pious asides about who is "hurt" by inflation — the usual litany includes creditors, those on fixed income, and those who consume disproportionate amounts of goods that have gone up in price relatively quickly. Inflation is seen only as a price crisis, never as a work crisis. But who is responsible for purchasing these inflating goods? Who in the American economy can tell you the price of flour, meat, or vegetables without consulting the consumer price index? Whose job is it, in fact, to *manage* the declining real income of workers in America? The housewife's major work in the twentiety century is "consumption management,"[1] which in inflationary periods means buying the household's standard of living on a fixed budget in the face of rising prices.[2]

Time spent on consumption management in housework has increased dramatically in the modern period, even while "labor-saving devices" have cut down on time spent on other housework, such as food preparation and clean-up.[3] Rather than assume that the increased time spent in "marketing and record-keeping" or "shopping and managerial tasks" is due to the increased loneliness[4] of the housewife, or to a Parkinson's Law phenomenon,[5] I will argue that inflation increases the real work in housework: it increases the time spent in budgeting, purchasing, and managing consumption, as well as time spent in food preparation, and other antiinflation work.

It is clear to most consumers that since inflation means paying higher prices while living on a falling or steady real income, inflation also means more work. In a 1978 study of consumers, Shama found a majority agreed that stagflation meant "there are more cents-off coupons in newspapers"; they "spend more time (on average) shopping." They agreed that "I must work harder to be able to afford my present way of life."[6]

There are many components in this increased work burden. There is more work spent on budgeting and purchasing of necessities. Shama's sample of consumers overwhelmingly agreed on certain typical responses to stagflation: "Become more of a comparative shopper" (88.9 percent), "shop for 'specials' and bargains more than I used to" (83.0 percent), "look for cheaper products" [e.g., private labels][7] (60.9

percent). In other words, as prices rise fast and unevenly, the consumer has to spend more time comparing goods, gathering information about prices and comparative virtues of known and unknown brands. The budgeting work may become more and more unpleasant in the inflationary crunch; a majority of respondents indicated that they "argue about financial matters."[8] Stretching a tight budget by clipping, saving, and buying with cents-off coupons, although extremely time-consuming, may be effective, although industry is worried that some consumers are not doing their housework properly: they estimate that they lose $100 million per year in fraudulent coupon redemptions.[9]

One particular budgeting strategy effective in inflationary periods is stockpiling goods on "special," or against future expected price increases. This strategy is impossible for the poor — who have neither the extra money for such investment nor the storage facilities in their homes. These difficulties are compounded for inner city residence, with less access to cheap retail outlets.[10]

In addition to increased time spent on budgeting, product comparisons, and coupon-clipping, more time is spent on the shopping itself, as purchase are spread over more stores, in order to "bargain hunt." Some consumers have even shifted toward shopping in the "inconvenient stores," cash-and-carry outlets or food cooperatives. Not that the conventional large supermarket is any time-saver — retail food specialists admit that "the large supermarket . . . cannot be heralded as a time-saver," given their large floor area (30,000 square feet, on the average) and cost-cutting moves by retailers, reducing check-out personnel and baggers.[11] The rich seem to be switching from the supermarkets to the higher-priced "convenience stores";[12] middle-income and poor buyers shop in the time-consuming and expensive supermarkets or the time- and energy-consuming but less expensive warehouse food outlets or cooperatives.[13] One of the most time-saving (and energy efficient) methods of shopping, telephone ordering, is rarely mentioned anymore, perhaps since Hoover's World War I message to housewives to give up telephone marketing in favor of personal marketing, to gain "actual knowledge of prices and abundance or scarcity of foods . . ."[14]

So inflation means more housework, because it means more work in budgeting and shopping for the household's necessities. But the content of the market basket shifts as well, and this spells more *work*. Consumer food expenditures shift in two ways: the proportion of home-prepared meals to meals eaten outside the home increases and the amount of the relatively more expensive "convenience foods" declines in relation to the more time-consuming but cheaper self-made foods. According to recent analyses of consumer expenditures, the proportion of expenditures on food prepared at home had *been* declining through the 1960s until 1973, when rapid food inflation began to cause an increase in the proportion of food prepared at home.[15] Likewise, a recent food industry survey noted the declining sales of fast food restaurants and gourmet-convenience foods for home use, and the increased demand by consumers for less-prepared staples, such as flour, cornmeal, etc.[16]

Given that housework increases as people eat at home more and go out to eat less, the content of their home consumption must be examined. As *Business Week* noted, during the present inflation people are shifting from high-cost prepared "convenience" foods, toward the less-processed foods requiring more work to prepare. As Shama's consumers noted, since stagflation one "became a do-it-yourself person."[17] As the USDA in 1953 noted, ready-to-serve meals took least time to prepare and cost the most, partially prepared foods next in these rankings, and totally home-prepared foods cost least in money and most in time. They also found that the home-prepared meals ranked highest in taste acceptability, followed by the partially prepared meals; the ready-to-serve were least acceptable.[18]

Not all consumption managers can follow this strategy of coping with inflation by preparing more food from basic foodstuffs and avoiding high-priced processed foods. This particular time-money tradeoff is often limited by another strategy used against inflation pressures: returning to the labor force. The recent rise in the labor force participation of wives and the uncounted entry of wives into the "underground economy" is in part owing to the pressures of inflation on the household budget.[19] But taking a new job or a second job reduces the time available for increased household work, and traditionally has been the rationale for the use of the more expensive "convenience" foods — a familiar conflict for working women.

When the need for extra income to buy higher-priced necessities cannot be satisfied by labor force work, the consumption manager may be obliged to apply for some form of welfare — another form of work, considering the time, energy, and regulation it entails. Even a simple program, such as food stamps, imposes days of work on the recipient, in registration and documentation of need (although replacing the food commodity distribution scheme, which entailed further hours of work to use the commodities palatably).

All the methods mentioned so far are ways of *coping* with inflation; they mean more housework. When pressure on the consumer budget intensifies, or when particular items shoot up in price, consumers shift from coping to resistance. Resistance has taken the form, historically, of boycotts, public protests, and riots. While the Boston Tea Party is highly publicized as it climaxed the anti-English tax movement, the subsequent riots over price increases during the American Revolution have received much less attention. Rapidly rising prices and low incomes in 1777 led to starvation, riots, vandalism, and other resistance. Items that were price-controlled were rationed tightly by shopkeepers and there was greater interest in receiving wages in "eatables."[20] Later, in 1837, rising prices provoked food riots, notably the New York flour riots. Civil War price inflation stimulated riots in Mobile, Savannah, Richmond, and other cities.[21] Rising prices of kosher meat led immigrant Jewish women in New York in 1902 to boycott their butchers and to march through the city streets burning the overpriced meat.[22] Less spectacular than the riots, but still quite popular, are food boycotts, especially those in recent years against meat and coffee, as shoppers decided their price increases were unjustified. Boycotts indirectly impose more household work, since using substitutes for the boycotted items may require new nutritional learning and new culinary skills. The meat boycotts underscored this problem, as consumer advisers introduced the boycotters to the intricacies of complementary amino acids and protein calculus, demystifying the vegetarian diet.

Beyond coping with inflation by budgeting more closely and shopping more exhaustively, beyond spending more time preparing cheaper foodstuffs, and beyond food riots and boycotts, the inflation-pressed consumption worker may resort to illegal means of stretching the budget. Although the *whole* shopping arena is riddled with fraud, from misleading packaging to unsafe products, ". . . climaxing the ordeal (is) the checkout counter, where investigations have shown a large proportion of retail dishonesty occurs by expert manipulation of the cash register . . . ."[23] Industry sources have tried to estimate how much consumer fraud costs them: $1 billion dollars per year in fraudulently cashed checks, $100 million per year in fraudulently redeemed coupons, and a high estimated cost of shoplifting, passed on to the consumer as price hikes, to a tune of $150 tax per family per year. Although retailers spend an estimated $2 billion per year on "store security,"[24] outright theft may not be the most difficult consumer fraud they face. An interesting study of middle-income housewives in the southeastern United States tried to gauge their responses to various fraudulent consumer activities. In their rather exhaustive list of possibilities, they inquired about the following:

A new, higher price sticker has been placed on a product. A customer is able to peel back the sticker and notices that the older price is lower. The customer completely peels off the new sticker and pays the lower price for the product.[25]

Whereas most respondents usually scored active frauds (shoplifting, etc.) as more grave than passive frauds (for instance, allowing cashiers to make mistakes in consumer's favor), this fraud, certainly active, had the highest percentage of approval and a (relatively) low percentage who thought it was definitely wrong.[26] Furthermore, an overwhelming majority indicated that their friends committed this crime (82.2 percent). When asked what management should do about this crime, the highest percentage of all "nothing" responses were given, and no respondents at all said "notify the authorities."[27] The most reasonable explanation of wide shopper acceptance and participation in the fraud of "peeling price tags" must be their perception that stores are unjustly raising prices and that self-reduction of price increases is justified. It is a crime peculiar to an inflationary period, when prices are rising so fast that stores do not wait for their inventories to sell at the former prices but mark-up everything in stock.

Even from this rather cursory look at the impact of inflation on housework, two major themes must emerge. The first is a reaffirmation of the large quantity and critical importance of the *work* in housework. Housework is no longer pure production (like spinning flax), but consumption management which takes a lot of time and effort and is crucial for the maintenance of living standards, particularly in inflationary times. Furthermore, it should be clear that inflation is a major weapon in business's attack on wage and unwaged workers in modern society.

Notes

1. Dr. Andrews, describing the housewife as "the one who controls spending . . . largely responsible for the quality of life secured by the family income" called housewives the "directors of the family's consumption," and elaborated on the central importance of her work. See "The Home Woman as Buyer and Controller of Consumption," *Annals of the American Academy of Political and Social Science* 143 (May 1929): 41. In this paper, I use the term *consumption manager* to refer to the work of planning, budgeting, shopping, and preparing the household's consumption needs. I do not use the term *housewife* here, although consumption management is largely women's work, because I intend to focus on the real work in consumption, rather than the role of housewife, which includes many other responsibilities.

2. One of the few analyses of this consumption work from a radical perspective (rather than the more typical home economics perspective) is Weinbaum and Bridges, "The Other Side of the Paycheck: Monopoly Capital and the Structure of Consumption," *Monthly Review* 28 (July–August 1976): 88–103.

3. See the evidence compiled by K. Walker, in "Homemaking Still Takes Time," *J. Home Economics* 61 (October 1969): 622, or the conclusions of J. Vanek in "Time Spent in Housework," *Scientific American*, November 1974, pp. 116–20. The jump in time spent in "marketing and record-keeping" is especially obvious between the 1952 sample and the 1967–68 sample, when fulltime urban homemakers *double* their time spent on this consumption work.

4. This argument is advanced most convincingly by Ann Oakley in *Housewife* (Harmondsworth, 1976); H. Gavron in *The Captive Housewife* (Harmondsworth, 1978).

5. This idea that housework expands to fill the time available is well refuted by Vanek's argument on occupational status/day of week workload comparisons of housewives' work time. See Vanek, "Time Spent in Housework," p. 120.

6. See A. Shama, "Management and Consumers in an Era of Stagflation," *Journal of Marketing*, July 1978, p. 49.

7. *Ibid.*, p. 51.

8. *Ibid.*

9. See "Grocery Coupons are Seen Threatened by Growth of Fraudulent Redemption," *Wall Street Journal*, 12 April 1976, p. 30.

10. See A. Andreassen, *The Disadvantaged Consumer* (New York, 1975), pp. 47–49.

11. See Gordon Bloom, "The Future of the Retail Food Industry: Another View," *Journal of Retailing* 54 (Winter 1978), p. 5.

12. Their sales volume increased by 20 percent in 1977 alone (see Bloom's figures).

13. *Ibid.*, p. 6.

14. Herbert Hoover, *Ladies Home Journal*, August 1917, p. 25.

15. Rogers and Green, "Changes in Consumer Food Expenditure Patterns," *Journal of Marketing*, April 1978, p. 15.

16. These trends outlined in "Food: A Consumer Swing Back to Basics," *Business Week*, 14 January 1980, pp. 62–65. They seem to contradict Vanek's hopeful findings that "the opportunity to eat out has been equalized." (*Technology and Culture*, July 1978, p. 365). Of course, since all humans eat, and since some of the same companies own the fast food eateries, the convenience food industries, and the basic food industries, this simply means they readjust their pricing strategies.

17. Shama, p. 51.

18. U.S. Department of Agriculture, Bureau of Human Nutrition and Home Economics, "Time and Money Costs of Meals Using Home and Prekitchen-Prepared Foods," 29 October, 1953 conference statement.

19. See, for example, G. L. Bach, *The New Inflation* (Providence, R.I., 1973), p. 14, for entry into the regular labor force, and recent work by P. Gutmann and E. Feige on the "underground economy."

20. For more detail, see R. Morris, *Government and Labor in Early America* (New York, 1965), especially pp. 127–209.

21. For documentation, see H. Gutman, *Work, Culture and Society in Industrializing America* (New York, 1977), pp. 59–63.

22. Extracts from *New York Times*, coverage in Baxandall, Gordon and Reverby, *America's Working Women* (New York, 1977), pp. 184–86. Likewise the Depression of the 1930s stimulated food riots and food stealing by the unemployed, although this was not due to rising food prices.

23. "Rip-offs — New American Way of Life," *U.S. News and World Report*, 31 May 1976, p. 29.

24. Wilkes, "Fraudulent Behavior by Consumers," *Journal of Marketing*, October 1978, p. 67, for these data.

25. *Ibid.*, p. 68.

26. *Ibid.*, p. 71. For comparison, 98.6 percent thought returning goods after using them was definitely wrong; 58 percent thought price tag peeling was definitely wrong.

27. *Ibid.*, pp. 72, 73.

The Effect of Inflation on the Elderly

DONALD C. SNYDER
BRADLEY R. SCHILLER[1]

Inflation is currently public enemy number one, and its impact on the United States economy and the well-being of its citizens is widely discussed. Among those most adversely affected by inflation are the nation's elderly population. The elderly have little ability to increase their nominal income flows when the pace of inflation quickens. Nor do they have as much discretion to alter their expenditure patterns in response to price increases. Food, energy, and medical care costs command a disproportionate share of elderly people's expenditures. When those prices rise rapidly — as they have in recent years — inflation imposes great hardship on most senior citizens.

This paper intends to describe the impact of inflation on older households. As suggested, inflation affects both the real value of income and the cost of specific expenditures. Hence, we look at both sides of the older person's household budget. In so doing, we identify the extent to which older persons can adjust their income and expenditure patterns to offset inflation's impact. This response potential is the crucial element: the limited ability of older persons to alter income and consumption patterns in response to higher prices is what makes senior citizens so vulnerable to inflation.

A. INCOME DYNAMICS

Income sources of the elderly are distinct from those of younger persons. Most older persons are fully or partially retired. Hence, their ability to maintain real (inflation-adjusted) incomes when prices are rising depends more on nonwork receipts than on higher wages or more employment. However, wage and salary increases are not irrelevant to the older population: one out of three aged households contains an employed worker. Hence, older persons are sensitive to both employment and nonwork sources of income. For any given family, the specific mix of labor and nonlabor income receipts determines its vulnerability to inflation. For most, but certainly not all older families, this mix is largely composed of nonwork sources.

(1) WAGES AND SALARIES

Wages tend to rise faster than prices over the long run. Hence, individuals who continue working stand a greater chance of maintaining real income during an inflationary period. Only one-third of aged households participate in the labor market, however, and participation declines rapidly with age. In addition, many older workers are employed part time. Finally, older workers may not experience average rates of wage growth and so may not benefit from general patterns of wage adjustments to inflation. Hence, wages and salaries, although potentially the best form of inflation protection, are an incomplete inflation hedge for many older households and of no relevance to most.

Three barriers to employment face older workers, limiting their ability to recoup inflation losses by increased work effort. First, poor health restricts their ability to work. Second, even if able to perform work, older workers find it difficult to locate employment opportunities, due to a combination of skill obsolescence, age discrimination, and geographic immobility.[2] Third, Social Security limits the incentives for working. An older worker who earns more than $5000 loses fifty cents in retirement benefits for every additional dollar of earnings. This implicit tax on earnings greatly limits the ability of older workers to beat inflation by working more.

(2) ASSET INCOME

Another potential source of income for the aged is embodied in the assets they have acquired, including their savings accounts, homes, and other property. Asset values do not necessarily rise during inflationary periods, however, and some are not easily converted into income flows.

Long-term savings accounts and bonds tend to be particularly vulnerable to inflation. The real value of both principal and interest payments declines as prices rise. One recent estimate by Professor Edward Kane indicates that during the last ten years the elderly have lost $20 billion in real interest income from savings accounts alone.[3] These losses occur because the government refused to let these interest rates rise.[4] Other losses result from the fixed-income nature of many assets held by elderly households, as well as capital losses when bonds must be sold. The income losses from fixed-income securities, such as bonds and savings accounts, can be altered little. However, passbook savings will become more inflation-proofed as interest-rate ceilings are gradually raised, as they have been recently.

One asset which the elderly have not been able to exploit is their homes. Equity in a house represents a potential source of income that can be used to compensate for other income losses during inflation. Moreover, house values generally rise during inflationary periods. Nearly two-thirds of the elderly have equity in a house. This value is usually available for consumption expenditures only if the house is sold, however. The introduction of Reverse Annuity Mortgages (RAMs) changes this all-or-nothing dilemma by allowing homeowners to borrow against their equity and to receive (supplemental) payments on an annual basis for life.[5] By this means, some elderly households can adjust their income flows to replace fixed income lost due to inflation (e.g., from private pensions). Many older families, however, are reluctant to mortgage their most important possession.

Older households that do not own homes or own low-valued housing (50 percent of them owned homes valued at less than $25,000 in 1975) or have very little equity cannot transform their house into an income flow by borrowing through a RAM-like instrument. These households must adjust the other side of the income-expenditure equation — by reducing discretionary or noncommitted expenditures, for example.

(3) TRANSFER PAYMENTS

Forty percent of the income received by the aged population comes from public transfer payments, of which Social Security is by far the largest. Hence, the well-being of the aged during inflationary periods depends first and foremost on the speed with which transfer payments are adjusted to inflation.

Most transfer payments are adjusted for inflation, but the adjustment is less complete than most people realize. The Social Security Administration (SSA) has indexed benefits automatically since 1975, with the increase in benefits occurring in July following measurement of the previous year's prices. There are two points of crucial importance: first, SSA measures the rate of inflation with the all-consumer price index. Since this index is based on the expenditure patterns of the "average" consumer, it may not accurately reflect the price experience of older persons. Second, cost of living adjustments are made with a considerable lag, well after income erosion has actually been experienced. As a result of this lag, significant losses are still incurred by the elderly.[6]

If we take the case of a worker who retired in June 1975 and hence has enjoyed the inflation protection offered by the Social Security system through June 1978, the following exercise is instructive.[7] The average benefit received by workers retiring in June 1975 was $215 a month. This benefit was increased three times during the period June 1975–June 1978, and reached $257.97. A a result of the (automatic) annual adjustments, the *cumulative* amount of benefits paid over the three years amounted to $8498.

A more complete inflation adjustment would respond to price changes each month, rather than annually (and with a lag). Indeed, had Social Security benefits been increased in this way, cumulative benefits paid June 1975–June 1978 would have been $8720. Hence, current (automatic) adjustment procedures imply a nominal income loss to this worker of $222 in a three-year period.

If the initial benefit amount of $215 was immediately and correctly adjusted each month for inflation losses, the retiree would have gotten exactly what he was entitled to — a real benefit of $215 a month for 36 months totaling $8720.21 in current dollars. What he gets under the lagged SSA approach is benefits totaling $8498.01 over the period. This cumulative difference between a mechanism that is very close to inflation-proofing and the one SSA uses results in an indirect loss of more than a month's benefits over the period 1975–1978. In the limit, if a 12 percent erosion in purchasing power occurs in 1980, it will be June 1981 before Social Security benefit checks are increased. Beneficiaries may lose as much as two months' benefits due to lagged adjustments in the period June 1978–June 1980.

(4) PRIVATE PENSIONS

Private pension systems are rarely indexed automatically. One recent study has found that only 4 percent of the pension plans have an automatic indexing provision.[8] A study by Thompson indicates that even though some firms make ad hoc adjustments in years of good profitability, the average private pension recipient has seen the real value of his pension fall significantly during the period 1970–79.[9] One union, the UAW, declared that its top priority in bargaining with auto firms last year was pension adjustments for all retirees.[10]

Pension benefits paid to retirees from the public sector are also not regularly adjusted for inflation, federal government pensions being the exception. State and local government employees may be covered by a pension plan that is integrated with Social Security or they may be covered by a public pension only — with no FICA taxes paid. The retirement incomes of the latter individuals would not be protected by the automatic adjustment features of Social Security and they have to rely on the governmental unit sponsoring the plan (and its tax posture) to adjust pensions for inflation.

(5) PUBLIC ASSISTANCE

Public assistance payments provide only 2 percent of the total income of the aged population. Such payments, however, are critical to the low-income households that depend on them. Such payments are particularly important to minority aged, as Table 1 attests. Their greater reliance on public transfers is a mixed blessing, however. Greater reliance on public transfers may imply better protection against inflation losses, even though Black incomes are less than white incomes, but only if government adjusts those transfers in a timely manner and in proportion to price changes.

Public assistance programs for the aged (particularly Supplemental Security Income) contain almost guaranteed, but not automatic, infla-

Table 1. Source of Income of Social Security Beneficiaries 1971

Percent of households with	Blacks	Whites
Earnings	35	29
Income other than earnings:		
Government	3	5
Private pension	8	19
Public assistance	27	6
Income from assets	13	53
Other	10	13

Source: Socioeconomic Characteristics of the Elderly, table 16, p. 19.

tion adjustment as they are periodically adjusted by Congress to account for inflation. Congress, however, also uses these opportunities to amend the programs as well, and individual states may not raise benefits as fast as inflation, adversely affecting minority elderly who depend on public transfers more than whites. More generous eligibility rules or increased coverage may expand the number of recipients, however, thereby helping to alleviate the effects of inflation.

The general tenor of the foregoing descriptions connotes an image of older persons suffering hardships from inflation, yet we are aware that not all older persons are quite so vulnerable to inflation. Among those who are employed, many are at the highest skill levels or are self-employed. The income of both groups is likely to be positively affected by inflation, at least as long as unemployment does not change.[11]

Not all effects of inflation lower the flow of income from wealth, either. Owners of real property stand to gain from inflation, for example.[12] Housing prices have increased more rapidly than the CPI in many areas, causing the major asset of the elderly to increase in value. In contrast to fixed-income assets — such as bonds and savings accounts — real property often grows in value during inflation. Antiques, art, jewelry, and precious metals have all risen in value more rapidly than the price level during the last decade.[13]

Such asset growth does not directly alter the income flow received by the elderly, however. Without taking some explicit action to convert the greater value of these assets into income received, consumption levels cannot be maintained. Since housing represents the major asset of the elderly, the ability to "convert" mortgages to provide an income flow — through RAMs, for example — offers an important mechanism through which retirees may combat losses from inflation.

Much of the current concern of inflation's effects on the elderly focuses on those who are already retired, out of the labor force, and existing on a mix of fixed pension and asset income and on inflation-adjusted public transfers. This group has little ability to adjust its income patterns. Even those who are older, but not yet retired, have very limited ability to alter their retirement income, except by delaying retirement. Advance financial planning can (help) protect younger families' savings for retirement, however. Investing in real assets, for example, may bring a return above the rate of price increase, thus allowing younger households to "get ahead" of inflation while working. But after retirement the battle against erosion of income by inflation begins, no matter what precautions were taken during the working years.

B. EXPENDITURE DYNAMICS

To the extent that older persons have distinctive expenditure patterns, inflation may disproportionaly reduce their purchasing power. Many elderly report that "coping with the high cost of living" is their most important day-to-day problem.[14] In recent years, rapid increases in medical, housing, and food costs have particularly squeezed the incomes of older persons. Younger persons, who tend to spend lower proportions of their income on these goods and more on discretionary puchases, have been less penalized by inflation.

(1) BUDGET SHARES

Unfortunately, the elderly do not have many expenditures that could be fairly termed *discretionary*. As we see in Table 2, over 55 percent of an aged household's income was spent for food and housing in 1973, less than 50 percent for younger families. Medical care consumed another 10 cents out of every older person's average dollar. Because of such expenditures, less than half of the elderly reported any expenditures on pleasure trips — trips represent the *sine qua non* of retirement for many retirees.

(2) MEASURING PRICE CHANGES

The index used to measure inflation is based on the "average" United States consumer and his or her expenditures in 1973 — the Consumer Price Index (CPI). Older persons are not "average" consumers, however. As noted, they spend their budgets on different goods and in different amounts on similar goods. Second, no index based on a 1973 market basket is representative of the United States today or in the future. Rapidly rising food, housing, health, and energy prices, all of which the elderly purchased in budget shares well in excess of those of the average consumer in 1973, have undoubtedly realigned expenditure patterns to a significant extent.

Considerable research has been conducted on the correct price index to use for policy analysis of inflation's effects. The Laspeyres index used by BLS (the CPI) is used to measure price changes across groups

Table 2. Relative Importance of Expenditures for Selected Groups of Goods and Services

| | 1960–61[a] | | 1973[b] | |
	Wage and Clerical Workers	Retirees	All Consumer Units	Units with Head 65 +
Food				
At home	20.1	22.6	17.0	21.2
Away from home	5.1	3.8	2.2	1.5
Housing				
Shelter	13.2	16.8	16.2	15.8
Fuel	6.0	6.6	5.3	7.4
Furnishings and operation	9.1	10.5	9.0	9.5
Apparel	10.7	6.8	8.3	6.4
Transportation	14.7	11.0	20.3	14.9
Medical care	6.2	10.2	6.1	10.2
Reading, recreation	5.6	3.9	10.2	8.1
Miscellaneous	9.3	7.8	5.4	5.0

Note: Expenditures as a percentage of total consumption outlays.

[a] Norwood, *Cost-Of-Living Escalation of Pensions. A Monthly Labor Review*, Reprint, U.S. Dept. of Labor Bureau of Labor Statistics, June 1972, p. 21.

[b] Calculated from expenditures data, pp. 44–53, 1972–1973 Survey of Consumer Expenditures.

by adjusting the weights used to create the price index. The problem with this approach is that the considerable changes in budget shares that accompany relative price changes are not captured in year-to-year comparisons. For some purposes, price change effects should be estimated for current budgets.

Not all groups have the same budgets, introducing a further complication. When an index is created for a particular subgroup, e.g., the elderly, King reports significant disparities in budgets are present even when controlled for income.[15]

Lamale was the first to report finding differential rates of price increase between average and elderly consumers.[16] Investigating the period 1950–60, she found that prices had increased 5.2 percent faster for older persons than was measured by the all-items CPI. Waldman investigated three periods: September 1954–January 1967; January 1959–January 1967; January 1965–January 1967.[17] He reported finding prices rising between 7 and 9 percent faster for older persons in all three periods. Since his was the first work in the post-Medicare period, he reduced the importance of the medical care weight by 40 percent and after doing so found the difference reduced to 3 percent to 6 percent.

Hollister and Palmer, who studied the price experience of the elderly poor, and Torda, who focused on the elderly, also made this 40 percent adjustment in the medical care weight. Torda initially found a 2 percent faster rate of price increase for the elderly over the period January 1967–July 1972, but after making the adjustment for medical care found no difference in the rate of price increase.[18]

Hollister and Palmer report on price indexes constructed at two levels of disaggregation.[19] One index was constructed using 12-item groups and was compared to the CPI over the period 1947–67. They found prices rising 6.9 percent faster for the elderly poor prior to the Medicare adjustment and 2.1 percent after it. With a more highly disaggregated index, however, prices were found to rise more slowly for both the poor and the elderly poor than was measured by the CPI. From 1953 to 1967, prices rose 10.1 percent more slowly after disaggregation.

Although Mirer did not study the price experiences of the elderly per se, his work is an update of Hollister and Palmer's work on a poor person's index.[20] He found that although prices might have been rising for poor persons at a slower than average rate in the late 60s, the early 70s indicated a dramatic reversal. From August 1971 to June 1974, his index showed prices rose 11.2 percent faster for poor persons (and presumably elderly poor persons, as well) than was measured by the CPI.

The Bureau of Labor Statistics has also studied this subject. An August 1973 study compared the price experiences of the employed and the retired over the 1960–72 period.[21] They found that, over this time, prices rose about 3.8 percent faster for retired persons than for the general population.

A study by Micheal has shown that there is considerable variation in the impact of inflation within homogenous households, however.[22] He finds that the within-group dispersion of inflation effects is greater than between-group variations. The presence of sizable within-group dispersion reported by King and Micheal implies that use of a separate price index for older persons may not make treatment of all elderly more equitable.

It remains true, however, that the most straightforward way to appraise the differential impact of inflation on the average elderly household is to use a separate price index.[23] Such an index requires current information on the share of the budget devoted to each category of expenditures in light of the rapid increases in prices of different goods which have occurred since 1973. For example, appraisal of the impact of recent energy price increases requires some knowledge of what share ot the budget energy costs were absorbing prior to these increases. In 1973, energy absorbed roughly 7 percent of the average older person's budget. Although turning down the thermostat is one way of avoiding higher energy prices, many elderly people begin to experience physical pain below temperatures of 70. Hence, we would expect them to exhibit far less price sensitivity — i.e., their demand for heat is price inelastic — than would be the case with the younger population. Over the past seven years, then, it seems likely that the elderly have increased the share of their budgets going to heating costs and that further energy price increases will affect them much more severely than the average consumer.

Further, the cost of heating varies with the type of fuel used. Table 3 shows that older homeowners who heat with fuel oil number 2 will have increased the share of income spent on heating by more than the average for all older homeowners during 1978–80. Establishment of the nature of these consumer spending shifts and their magnitude — the proper weights for a retiree's CPI in light of price changes since 1973 — is critical before we can judge how inflation's impact differs across old and young households and across older households.

Table 3. Percent Increases in Energy Costs

	77–78	73–78	78–80*
Natural Gas	11.2	108.1	20
Fuel Oil #2	7.7	82.5	100
Electricity	7.2	66.5	15
Other	7.7	40.4	—
CPI	8.3	47.1	27

* estimated.

(3) ESTIMATING EXPENDITURE IMPACTS

In the section on income dynamics during inflation we saw that increases in nonwage retirement income are generally less than price increases. This loss of (real) purchasing power during retirement is worsened by a pattern of price changes that heavily increase the cost of budget items the elderly consume in greater proportions than all other households. Food, housing, and medical care costs have risen much faster than average prices. These items constitute over 80 percent of expenditures of low-income retirees and over 70 percent of high-income retirees in 1975, but only 56 percent of the expenditures of all units were made on these items in 1973 (Table 4).

The budget shares devoted to these categories by retirees have changed significantly since 1967. Comparing retirees' budgets in 1967

Table 4. Household Budget Shares, 1960–77

Expenditures	1960–61[a] Clerical (1)	1960–61[a] Retirees (2)	61–62[b] All Units (3)	1967[c] Retirees Low (4)	1967[c] Retirees Middle (5)	1967[c] Retirees High (6)	1972–73[d] All Units (7)	1972–73[d] 65+ (8)	1973[e] All Units (9)	1973[e] 65+ (10)	1975[f] Retired Couples Low (11)	1975[f] Retired Couples Middle (12)	1975[f] Retired Couples High (13)	1977[g] Retirees Low (14)	1977[g] Retirees Middle (15)	1977[g] Retirees High (16)
Food	25.2	26.4	28.2	29.5	27.2	21.3	21.0	24.3	19.2	22.7	33.1	31.4	27.0	34.0	32.0	27.0
At home	20.1	22.6	23.1				16.4	20.8	17.0	21.2	30.7	28.2	23.1			
Away	5.1	3.8	5.1				4.6	3.5	2.2	1.5	2.4	3.2	3.9			
Housing	28.3	33.9	32.6	35.2	34.4	34.2	30.2	32.9	30.5	32.7	35.0	36.0	37.7	37.0	38.0	39.0
Shelter	13.2	16.8					16.5	16.8	16.2	15.8	26.2	23.0	22.5			
Fuel	6.0	6.6					5.1	7.2	5.3	7.4						
Furnishings	9.1	10.5					8.6	8.9	9.0	9.5	8.8	13.0	15.2			
Apparel	10.7	6.8	8.8	*	*	*	8.1	6.1	8.3	6.4	4.6	5.5	5.8	*	*	*

Transportation	14.7	11.0	11.8	7.2	9.9	11.3	19.8	14.6	20.3	14.9	6.8	9.5	11.9	6.0	9.0	12.0
Medical	6.2	10.2	5.9	11.0	9.7	5.0	5.9	9.5	6.1	10.2	12.8	9.1	6.3	13.0	10.0	7.0
Reading, Rec.	5.6	3.9	5.5	4.3	4.0	11.7	8.0	7.1	10.2	8.1	0.2	0.4	1.1	.2	.4	1.0
Personal			2.3	8.1	9.3	9.0	1.3	1.7			3.0	4.4	6.4	7.0	9.0	11.0
Miscellaneous	9.3	7.8	5.1	4.7	5.5	7.5	0.9	0.8	5.4	5.0	4.4	3.7	3.8	2.8	1.6	3.0

a&e Thomas Borzilleri, "The Need for a Separate Price Index for Older Persons," *Gerontologist*, April 1978.

b *Monthly Labor Review*, 1962 Statistical Supplement.

c George S. Tolly and Richard Burkhauser, "Economics of the Elderly" (mimeo).

d Consumer Expenditure Survey Series: Interview Survey, 1972–73.

f U.S. Department of Labor News, 19 August 1976.

g Estimates by the authors.

* Clothing and Personal Care combined.

(Columns 4–6) with the retired couples' budgets in 1975 (Columns 11–13) we can see some of the effects of inflation on expenditures. For instance, low-income retirees spent 76 percent of income on food, housing, and medical care in 1967 (compared to 81 percent in 1975). Middle- and high-income retirees spent 71 and 61 percent, respectively, on these items. By 1975, they were spending 77 and 71 percent, respectively, on these items.

Between 1967 and 1975, the proportion of the household budget spent on food by middle-income retirees increased from 27.2 to 31.4 percent. Low-income households saw an increase of nearly 4 percent; high-income households showed the largest increase, nearly 6 percent. In the category of food away from home, a discretionary expense not separately recorded for retirees in 1967, average expenditure appears slightly lower in 1975 than in 1961 (and 1973 for all households age 65 and over).

Since the 1975 survey does not separate shelter, fuel, and furnishings expenses, only total housing expenditures can be compared. For the middle group, the budget share rose from 34.4 to 36.0 percent in the period 1967–75. In this case, low-income groups exhibit the same (35.0) portion; high income retirees were 3.5 points higher (37.7). This may occur because higher-income groups own larger houses, and hence, have greater heating costs.

Transportation expenses of low- and middle-income retirees dipped slightly between 1967 and 1975, but rose for high-income retirees. Since the price of transportation (i.e., gasoline) rose during this same period, we may conclude that this is a discretionary expense which has been cut back by retirees facing inflation.

In order to accommodate these greater expenditures, retirees have lowered their consumption of discretionary items. Reading and recreation expenditures are negligible by 1975; in 1967, nearly 1 in 20 dollars was spent in this fashion. High-income retirees reduced these expenditures by 10 percent. This sizable decline partly offset an increase in personal expenses, though low-income retirees reduced their expenditures on these items as well. Middle- and high-income retirees also cut miscellaneous expenses, by half for the latter group.

This overview of shifts in the share of retirees' budgets allocated to separate items provides the reader with evidence that retirees have been hurt more than others by inflation during period 1967–75. Further, we saw that the impact of inflation is not even across income classes of retirees. A quantitative estimate of differential rates of price change across retired and nonretired households and across income classes of retirees can be seen in Table 5.

During the period 1967–75, the all-items CPI increased by 61.2 percent. Using the budget shares in 1975 and item-specific CPI's, we

Table 5. Cost-of-Living Differences between All Items CPI
and Retirees CPI

	1967	1975	1977*	Percent Change 1975–77	1977†	Percent Change 1975–77
All Items	100	161.2	181.5	12.6	181.5	12.6
Low-income Retirees	100	166.31	187.83	12.9	188.6	13.4
Middle-income Retirees	100	165.31	186.5	12.8	187.55	13.5
High-income Retirees	100	163.84	184.84	12.8	185.51	13.2

*Calculated using the 1975 retired couples budget.
†Calculated using the (estimated) 1977 retirees budget.
Source: Author's calculations.

estimate a retirees' CPI for the three income classes. The retirees' CPI
increased by 64–66 percent, indicating that retirees' cost-of-living increased more than that of all other household units. This relative
change is even more dramatic for 1975–77. Using the 1975 budget
shares, we calculate that price increases were in the range of 1.6–2.4
percent greater for retirees. This may seem small, but if such a differential is projected over a 20-year period of retirement, the cost-of-living
for retirees could increase by 35–50 percent! Even this projection
seems low, however, if we consider that budget shares devoted to food,
housing, and medical care rose even higher. Using the estimated 1977
budget shares (Columns 14–16 in Table 4), we calculate that prices rose
at an alarming 4.8, 7.1, and 6.3 percent faster for high-, middle-, and
low-income retirees in 1975–77, respectively. Continued inflation during 1978–80 can only have worsened the plight of retirees.

The admittedly rough estimates of higher inflation rates faced by the
elderly consumer we have made are consistent with the estimates
generated by Borzilleri (1979) and others. An important additional
dimension of our estimates, and what distinguishes our results from
others, is the demonstration that differences in low- and high-income
retirees' inflation rates are present. We also suggest that further disparities would be uncovered if more detailed budget data were available
(and if income losses were incorporated). We also show that estimates
of relative rates of inflation are affected by the budget shares used in the
computation. It is clear that in order to learn more about inflation's
effects greater budget detail across various groups of elderly households is required.

C. SUMMARY

The impact of inflation on any household depends on the sources of
household income, the patterns of household expenditure, and the

response of both to general inflation. The major conclusions to be drawn from this discussion are (1) older persons tend to have unique patterns of income and expenditure; (2) those patterns allow less discretion in adjusting to inflation; (3) recent inflation have disproportionately hurt older persons.

Because the elderly poor depend most heavily on public transfers (both Social Security and public assistance), their incomes though low, may be best "inflation-proofed." The expenditures of low-income elderly tend to be concentrated on goods whose prices have risen fastest, however. In contrast, higher-income retirees have more discretionary expenditures and more assets. Hence, they may be better able to make adjustments in both income and expenditure patterns during inflation.

Notes

1. The authors are indebted to Thomas Borzilleri of the American Association of Retired Persons for providing data and comments.
2. These forces tend to compel many older workers to retire involuntarily when they cannot find suitable employment; see Bradley R. Schiller, *The Economics of Poverty and Discrimination*, 3d ed. (Englewood Cliffs, N.J., 1980), chap. 6.
3. E. J. Kane, *Hearings*, Statement, U.S. Senate Committee on Banking, Housing, and Urban Affairs, Federal Reserve's First Monetary Policy Report for 1979, 20, 23 February 1979, pp. 154–60.
4. Though Regulation Q Ceilings will gradually be increased after 1981. See "Dateline Washington . . . ," *Consumer's Research Magazine* 63 (May 1980): 4.
5. R. E. Carlson, "Retirement Strategies-Income from Home Ownership," presented at the Gerontological Society meetings, 29 November 1979 (Mimeo).
6. B. R. Bergmann, "Inflation's Impact on the Less Affluent," University of Maryland, 1979, estimates these losses (Mimeo).
7. A fuller discussion of this issue is contained in T. C. Borzilleri's prepared statement, *Hearing*, Subcommittee on Human Services, Select Committee on Aging, U.S. House of Representatives, 25 September 1978, pp. 49–52.
8. B. R. Schiller and D. C. Snyder, *Older Workers and Private Pensions*, final report submitted to HEW, Administration on Aging, 1979.
9. G. B. Thompson, "Impact of Inflation of Private Pensions of Retirees, 1970–74: Findings From the Retirement History Study," *Social Security Bulletin* 41 (November 1978): 19.
10. G. Darst, "UAW Tells Fringe Demands: GM Calls Them Unbelievable," *Washington Post*, 24 July 1979, see A, p.1.
11. If the demand for output falls, often the case following prolonged periods of inflation, older workers may be released and business profits fall, contracting the income of workers and proprietors. These contractions are not even, however. See "Inflation's Winners," *The Baltimore News American*, 22 April 1980, Col. 1, p. A1.

12. *Wall Street Journal*, 25 July, 1979, p. 1.

13. "Collecting For Profits," *Wall Street Journal*, 13 March 1978, p. 34.

14. *Developments in Aging (Part 1)*, Special Committeee on Aging, U.S. Senate, 1979, p. 31.

15. J. King, "The Consumer Price Index," *Technical Paper* No. 5, The Measure of Poverty Reports, U.S. HEW.

16. H. H. Lamale, "The Impact of Rising Prices on Younger and Older Consumers," *Bureau of Labor Statistics Report No. 238–2*, December 1963.

17. S. Waldman, "OASDI Benefits, Prices, and Wages: 1966 Experience," *Social Security Bulletin* 30 (1967): 9–36.

18. T. S. Torda, "The Impact of Inflation on the Elderly," *Federal Reserve Bank of Cleveland Economic Review*, October-November, 1972.

19. R. G. Hollister and J. L. Palmer, "The Impact of Inflation on the Poor," University of Wisconsin Institute of Research on Poverty, Madison, 1969.

20. T. W. Mirer, "The Distributive Impact on Purchasing Power of Inflation during Price Controls," *Quarterly Review of Economics and Business* 15 (1975): 93–96. See also F. Abott and J. W. Leasure, "Income Level and Inflation in the United States: 1947–1977," (Mimeo. University of Kentucky and San Diego State University).

21. U.S. Department of Labor, Bureau of Labor Statistics, Office of Prices and Living Conditions. Press release, "Revision of the Consumer Price Index: Definition of Consumer Units to be Covered in the Revised Index," 30 August 1973.

22. R. T. Micheal, "Variation Across Households in the Rate of Inflation," *Journal of Money, Credit and Banking* 11 (February 1979): 32–36.

23. In his remarks before this conference ("Costs and Benefits of Antiinflation policies"), Professor James Tobin disparaged such studies. His reference point is macroeconomic policy, however, and is apparently not concerned with distributional impacts. Therefore his remarks should not be interpreted as direct criticism of this or the related studies cited.

Contributors

Walter F. Abbott, Associate Professor of Sociology, University of Kentucky, Lexington, Kentucky.

Peter S. Albin, Professor of Economics, John Jay College, CUNY Graduate Faculty, New York.

Nicholas W. Balabkins, Professor of Economics, Lehigh University, Bethlehem, Pennsylvania.

Paul Beckerman, Assistant Professor of Economics, Boston University and University of Illinois, Champaign-Urbana, Illinois.

Bettina Berch, Assistant Professor of Economics, Barnard College, New York.

Ljuben Berov, Professor, Doctor of Economic Sciences, Higher Institute of Economics, Sofia, Bulgaria.

Roslyn Wallach Bologh, Associate Professor of Sociology, St. John's University, New York.

Patricia F. Bowers, Professor of Economics, Brooklyn College, New York.

Menachem Brenner, Senior Lecturer of Finance, School of Business Administration, Hebrew University, Jerusalem, Israel.

Y. S. Brenner, Professor of Economics, University of Utrecht, Utrecht, The Netherlands.

Robert Cherry, Assistant Professor of Economics, Brooklyn College, New York.

Thomas Childers, Associate Professor of History, University of Pennsylvania, Philadelphia, Pennsylvania.

David Colander, Associate Professor of Economics, University of Miami, Coral Gables, Florida.

William G. Dewald, Professor of Economics and Editor of *Journal of Money, Credit and Banking*, Ohio State University, Columbus, Ohio.

Allen Douglas, Scholar in Residence in History, University of Virginia, Charlottesville, Virginia.

Gerald D. Feldman, Professor of History, University of California at Berkeley, California.

Dennis O. Flynn, Assistant Professor of Economics, University of the Pacific, Stockton, California.

Dan Galai, Senior Lecturer in Finance, School of Business Administration, Hebrew University, Jerusalem, Israel.

Walter W. Haines, Professor of Economics, New York University, New York.

Yogesh C. Halan, Senior Lecturer, The Rajdhani College of the University of Delhi, India.

Edwin Harwood, Domestic Studies Fellow, Hoover Institution, Stanford, California.

Carl L. Holtfrerich, Professor of Economic and Social History, Der Johann Wolfgang Goethe-Universitat, Frankfurt, West Germany.

Janos Horvath, The John W. Arbuckle Professor of Economics Research Scholar, Holcomb Research Institute, Butler University, Indianapolis, Indiana.

Mugur Isarescu, Senior Researcher at the Institute of World Economy, Bucharest, Romania.

Paul Jonas, Professor of Economics, University of New Mexico, Albuquerque, New Mexico.

George Katona, Professor of Psychology and Professor of Economics, University of Michigan.

Hugo M. Kaufmann, Associate Professor of Economics, Queens College CUNY, Queens, New York.

Zbigniew Landau, Professor of Economic History, Central School of Planning and Statistics, Warsaw, Poland.

William J. Leasure, Professor of Economics, San Diego State University, San Diego, California.

Wilhelmina A. Leigh, Analyst, Congressional Budget Office, and formerly Senior Research Associate in the Research Department of the National Urban League, Inc.

Cynthia B. Lloyd, Population Affairs Officer, Population Division, United Nations.

Bernard Malamud, Professor of Economics, University of Nevada, Las Vegas, Nevada.

Edward Marcus, Professor of Economics, Brooklyn College, CUNY, New York.

Mildred Rendl Marcus, Professor of Economics, Borough of Manhattan Community College, CUNY, New York.

Hyman P. Minsky, Professor of Economics, Washington University, St. Louis, Missouri.

Beth T. Niemi, Associate Professor of Economics, Newark College of Arts and Sciences, Rutgers University, New Jersey.

Paul Ormerod, Senior Economist, Economist Intelligence Unit, London; formerly at the National Institute of Economics and Social Research, London.

György Ránki, Professor of History, Vice Director Hungarian Academy of Sciences, Institute of History, Budapest, Hungary.

Hyman Sardy, Professor of Economics, Brooklyn College, New York.

Bradley R. Schiller, Professor of Public Administration and Economics, The American University, Washington, D.C.

Richard T. Selden, Carter Glass Professor of Economics, University of Virginia, Charlottesville, Virginia.

David J. Smyth, Professor of Economics, Editor, *Journal of Macroeconomics*, Wayne State University, Detroit, Michigan.

Donald C. Snyder, Assistant Professor, Howard University, Washington, D.C.

Miklos Szabo-Pelsóczi, Senior Economic Advisor, Bache Stuart Halsey Shields, Inc., New York.

Wolfgang Teckenberg, Professor, Institute of Sociology, University of Kiel, West Germany.

Alice Teichova, Professor of Economic History, University of East Anglia, Norwich, United Kingdom.

James Tobin, Professor of Economics, Yale University, New Haven, Connecticut.

Ronald L. Tracy, Assistant Professor of Economics, Southern Illinois University, Carbondale, Illinois.

Paul B. Trescott, Professor of Economics, Southern Illinois University, Carbondale, Illinois.

Eddy van Cauwenberghe, Master of Research at the Belgian National Foundation of Science; Professor at the UFSAL, Brussels, Belgium; Lecturer at the Ku-Leuven, Belgium.

Herman Van der Wee, Professor of Economics and Economic History, Director of the Postgraduate Workshop in Quantitative Economic History, University of Leuven, Belgium.

Arthur J. Vidich, Professor of Sociology and Anthropology, Graduate Faculty, New School for Social Research, New York.

Steven B. Webb, Assistant Professor of Economics, University of Michigan.

David J. Webber, Assistant Professor of Political Science, West Virginia University, Morgantown, West Virginia.

Thomas F. Wilson, Associate Professor of Economics, Butler University, Indianapolis, Indiana.

Peter-Christian Witt, Professor of Social and Economic History, University of Cassell, West Germany.

Sherrin M. Wyntjes, Chair, Liberal Arts Division, Mount Ida Junior College, Newton Centre, Maine.

BROOKLYN COLLEGE STUDIES ON SOCIETY IN CHANGE
Distributed by Columbia University Press (except No. 5)
Editor-in-Chief: Béla K. Király

No. 1

Tolerance and Movements of Religious Dissent in Eastern Europe. Edited by B. K. Király, 1975. Second Printing, 1977.

No. 2

The Habsburg Empire in World War I. Edited in R. A. Kann, B. K. Király, P. S. Fichtner, 1976. Second Printing, 1978.

No. 3

The Mutual Effects of the Islamic and Judeo-Christian Worlds: The East European Pattern. Edited by A. Ascher, T. Halasi-Kun, B. K. Király, 1979.

No. 4

Before Watergate: Problems of Corruption in American Society. Edited by A. S. Eisenstadt, A. Hoogenboom, H. L. Trefousse, 1978.

No. 5

East Central European Perceptions of Early America. Edited by B. K. Király and G. Barany. Lisse, The Netherlands: Peter de Ridder Press, 1977. Distributed by Humanities Press, Atlantic Highlands, NJ.

No. 6

The Hungarian Revolution of 1956 in Retrospect. Edited by B. K. Király and P. Jónás, 1978. Second Printing, 1980.

No. 7

Brooklyn U.S.A.: Fourth Largest City in America. Edited by R. S. Miller, 1979.

No. 8

János Decsy. *Prime Minister Gyula Andrássy's Influence on Habsburg Foreign Policy During the Franco-German War of 1870–1871,* 1979.

No. 9

Robert F. Horowitz. *The Great Impeacher: A Political Biography of M. Ashley,* 1979.

* * *

Nos. 10–19

Subseries: *War and Society in East Central Europe* (See Nos. 30–40 also)

No. 23
Jason Berger. *A New Deal for the World: Eleanor Roosevelt and American Foreign Policy*, 1981.

No. 24
The Legacy of Jewish Migration: 1881 and Its Impact. Edited by D. Berger, 1982.

No. 25
Pierre Oberling. *The Road to Bellapais: Cypriot Exodus to Northern Cyprus*, 1982.

No. 26
New Hungarian Peasants: An East Central European Pattern of Collectivization. Edited by Marida Hollós and Béla Maday.

No. 27
Germans in America: Aspects of German-American Relations in the 19th Century. Edited by E. Allen McCormick.

* * *

Nos. 30–40
Subseries: *War and Society in East Central Europe* (Continued) (See Nos. 10–19 also)

No. 30 — Vol. XI
The First War Between Socialist States: The Hungarian Revolution of 1956 and Its Impact. Edited by Béla K. Király, Barbara Lotze, Nándor Dreisziger. Forthcoming.

No. 31 — Vol. XII
István I. Mocsy. *Effects of World War I: The Uprooted: Hungarian Refugees and Their Impact on Hungarian Domestic Politics: 1918–1921*

No. 32 — Vol. XIII
Ivo Banac. *Effects of World War I: The Class War after the Great War: The Rise of Communist Parties in the East Central European "Red Wave": 1918–1921*.

No. 33 — Vol. XIV
The Crucial Decade: East Central European Society and National Defense: 1859–1870. Edited by Béla K. Király.

No. 34 — Vol. XV
The Political Dimensions of War in Romanian History. Edited by Ilie Ceausescu.

No. 35 — Vol. XVI
East Central European Classics of Military Thought: Rákóczi and Kosciuszko. Edited by B. K. Király, E. Halicz and J. Decsy.